THE
NOBLE
REVOLT

THE
NOBLE
REVOLT

The Overthrow of Charles I

JOHN ADAMSON

Weidenfeld & Nicolson
LONDON

First published in Great Britain in 2007
by Weidenfeld & Nicolson

1 3 5 7 9 10 8 6 4 2

© 2007 John Adamson

A CIP catalogue record for this book
is available from the British Library.

ISBN 978 0 297 84262 0

Typeset by Input Data Services Ltd, Frome

Printed in Great Britain by Butler and Tanner Ltd,
Frome and London

Weidenfeld & Nicolson

The Orion Publishing Group Ltd
Orion House
5 Upper Saint Martin's Lane
London, WC2H 9EA

www.orionbooks.co.uk

G. D. C. R. S.
QUI FIERI
FECIT

CONTENTS

LIST OF ILLUSTRATIONS

Sir Anthony van Dyck, *Robert Rich, 2nd Earl of Warwick*. Oil on canvas, *c.* 1635. Metropolitan Museum of Art, New York, Jules Bache Collection, 1949, inv. no. 49.7.26.

Leez Priory, Essex. (Photograph © Lavenham Photographic Studio.)

Samuel Cooper, *John Pym*. Miniature, *c.* 1630. The Adminstrative Trustees of the Chequers Trust.

Robert Peake, *Henry, Prince of Wales, hunting with the 3rd Earl of Essex*. Oil on panel, *c.* 1605-10. The Royal Collection © 2007, Her Majesty Queen Elizabeth II.

George Glover, *Robert Devereux, 3rd Earl of Essex*. Engraving, 1642. (Photograph: Weidenfeld and Nicolson Archive.)

Pieter Meulener, *An Artillery Emplacement*. Oil on canvas, *c.* 1645. The Royal Armouries, I 330.

Claude de Jongh, *The Thames at Westminster Stairs*. Oil on panel, *c.* 1630. Yale Center for British Art, Paul Mellon Collection. (Photograph: Bridgeman Art Library.)

Anglo-Dutch School, *View of Old Palace Yard and Westminster Hall*. Oil on canvas, *c.* 1670. House of Lords Collection.

Wenzel Hollar, *Rioting in Old Palace Yard, May 1641*. Detail. Engraving, *c.* 1641. Private Collection.

Unknown artist, *Robert Greville, 2nd Baron Brooke*. Woodcut, *c.* 1641. National Portrait Gallery, London.

Robert Walker, *Sir Arthur Hesilrige*. Oil on canvas, 1640. National Portrait Gallery, London.

Sir Anthony van Dyck, *Thomas Wentworth, 1st Earl of Strafford, Lord Lieutenant of Ireland*. Oil on canvas, *c.* 1639-40. Trustees of the Rt. Hon. Olive, Countess Fitzwilliam's Chattels Settlement, and Lady Juliet de Chair. (Photograph: Bridgeman Art Library.)

(Between pp. 330 and 331)

Pieter Nason, *Oliver St John*. Oil on canvas, 1651. National Portrait Gallery, London.

Sir Anthony van Dyck, *Francis Russell, 4th Earl of Bedford*. Oil on canvas, *c.* 1635. Woburn Abbey, Bedfordshire. His Grace the Duke of Bedford and the Trustees of the Bedford Estates.

Adriaen Hanneman, *Edward Hyde, later 1st Earl of Clarendon*. Oil on canvas, *c.* 1651. Private collection. (Photograph: Weiss Gallery, London.)

Adam de Colone, *William Fiennes, 1st Viscount and 8th Baron Saye and Sele*. Oil on canvas, *c.* 1625. Broughton Castle, Oxfordshire, on loan to the Collection of the Lord Saye and Sele.

Sir Anthony van Dyck, *George, Lord Digby, later 2nd Earl of Bristol, with William, Lord Russell, later 5th Earl and 1st Duke of Bedford*. Oil on canvas, *c.* 1637. Althorp, Northamptonshire, Collection of the Earl Spencer.

Unknown artist, after Sir Anthony van Dyck, *George, Lord Goring and Mountjoy Blount, 1st Earl of Newport*. Oil on canvas, *c.* 1635-40. National Portrait Gallery, London.

William Dobson, *Colonel William Ashburnham*. Oil on canvas, *c.* 1640. Private collection. (Photograph: the Weiss Gallery, London.)

Unknown artist, after Sir Anthony van Dyck, *Sir John Suckling*. Oil on canvas, *c.* 1640. National Portrait Gallery, London.

Remigius van Leemput, *Queen Henriette Marie*. Oil on canvas, *c.* 1637. Private Collection. (Photograph: the Weiss Gallery, London.)

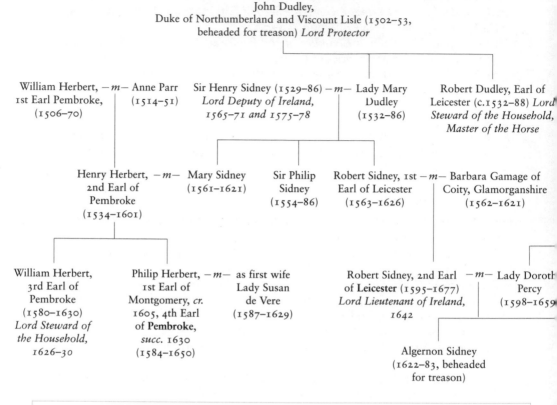

John Dudley,
Duke of Northumberland and Viscount Lisle (1502–53,
beheaded for treason) *Lord Protector*

William Herbert, — *m* — Anne Parr
1st Earl Pembroke, (1514–51)
(1506–70)

Sir Henry Sidney (1529–86) — *m* — Lady Mary
Lord Deputy of Ireland, Dudley
1565–71 and 1575–78 (1532–86)

Robert Dudley, Earl of
Leicester (c.1532–88) *Lord
Steward of the Household,
Master of the Horse*

Henry Herbert, — *m* — Mary Sidney
2nd Earl of (1561–1621)
Pembroke
(1534–1601)

Sir Philip
Sidney
(1554–86)

Robert Sidney, 1st — *m* — Barbara Gamage of
Earl of Leicester Coity, Glamorganshire
(1563–1626) (1562–1621)

William Herbert,
3rd Earl of
Pembroke
(1580–1630)
*Lord Steward of
the Household,
1626–30*

Philip Herbert, — *m* — as first wife
1st Earl of Lady Susan
Montgomery, *cr.* de Vere
1605, 4th Earl (1587–1629)
of **Pembroke**,
succ. 1630
(1584–1650)

Robert Sidney, 2nd Earl — *m* — Lady Doroth
of **Leicester** (1595–1677) Percy
Lord Lieutenant of Ireland, (1598–1659
1642

Algernon Sidney
(1622–83, beheaded
for treason)

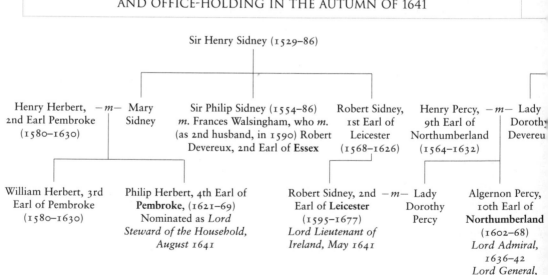

Sir Henry Sidney (1529–86)

Henry Herbert, — *m* — Mary
2nd Earl Pembroke Sidney
(1580–1630)

Sir Philip Sidney (1554–86)
m. Frances Walsingham, who *m.*
(as 2nd husband, in 1590) Robert
Devereux, 2nd Earl of **Essex**

Robert Sidney,
1st Earl of
Leicester
(1568–1626)

Henry Percy, — *m* — Lady
9th Earl of Doroth
Northumberland Devereu
(1564–1632)

William Herbert, 3rd
Earl of Pembroke
(1580–1630)

Philip Herbert, 4th Earl of
Pembroke, (1621–69)
Nominated as *Lord
Steward of the Household,
August 1641*

Robert Sidney, 2nd — *m* — Lady
Earl of **Leicester** Dorothy
(1595–1677) Percy
*Lord Lieutenant of
Ireland, May 1641*

Algernon Percy,
10th Earl of
Northumberland
(1602–68)
*Lord Admiral,
1636–42
Lord General,
1640–41*

Note: figures who appear in the narrative are highlighted in bold.

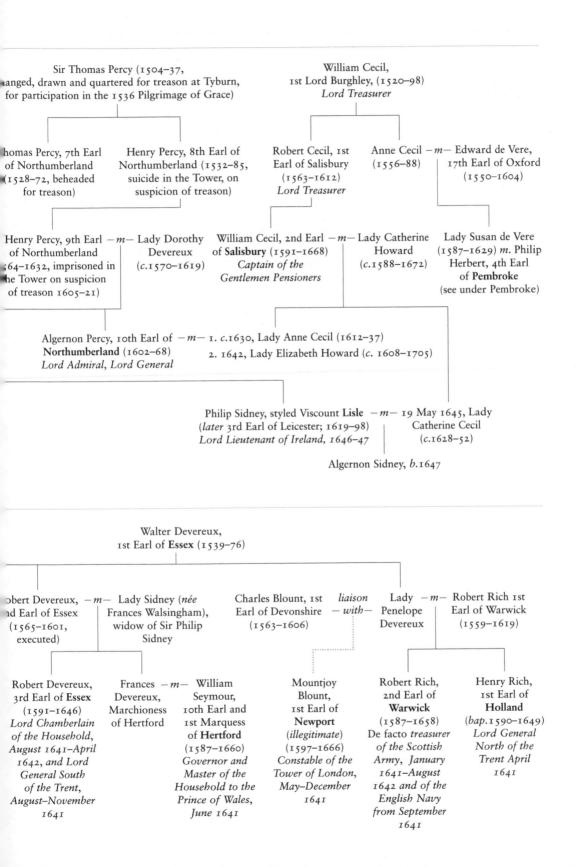

Sir Thomas Percy (1504–37,
hanged, drawn and quartered for treason at Tyburn,
for participation in the 1536 Pilgrimage of Grace)

William Cecil,
1st Lord Burghley, (1520–98)
Lord Treasurer

Thomas Percy, 7th Earl
of Northumberland
(1528–72, beheaded
for treason)

Henry Percy, 8th Earl of
Northumberland (1532–85,
suicide in the Tower, on
suspicion of treason)

Robert Cecil, 1st
Earl of Salisbury
(1563–1612)
Lord Treasurer

Anne Cecil —*m*— Edward de Vere,
(1556–88) | 17th Earl of Oxford
(1550–1604)

Henry Percy, 9th Earl —*m*— Lady Dorothy
of Northumberland | Devereux
(1564–1632, imprisoned in | (*c*.1570–1619)
the Tower on suspicion
of treason 1605–21)

William Cecil, 2nd Earl —*m*— Lady Catherine
of **Salisbury** (1591–1668) | Howard
Captain of the | (*c*.1588–1672)
Gentlemen Pensioners

Lady Susan de Vere
(1587–1629) *m*. Philip
Herbert, 4th Earl
of **Pembroke**
(see under Pembroke)

Algernon Percy, 10th Earl of —*m*— 1. *c*.1630, Lady Anne Cecil (1612–37)
Northumberland (1602–68) | 2. 1642, Lady Elizabeth Howard (*c*. 1608–1705)
Lord Admiral, Lord General

Philip Sidney, styled Viscount **Lisle** —*m*— 19 May 1645, Lady
(*later* 3rd Earl of Leicester; 1619–98) | Catherine Cecil
Lord Lieutenant of Ireland, 1646–47 | (*c*.1628–52)

Algernon Sidney, *b*.1647

Walter Devereux,
1st Earl of **Essex** (1539–76)

Robert Devereux, —*m*— Lady Sidney (*née*
2nd Earl of Essex | Frances Walsingham),
(1565–1601, | widow of Sir Philip
executed) | Sidney

Charles Blount, 1st *liaison* Lady —*m*— Robert Rich 1st
Earl of Devonshire —*with*— Penelope | Earl of Warwick
(1563–1606) | Devereux | (1559–1619)

Robert Devereux,
3rd Earl of **Essex**
(1591–1646)
*Lord Chamberlain
of the Household,
August 1641–April
1642, and Lord
General South
of the Trent,
August–November
1641*

Frances —*m*— William
Devereux, | Seymour,
Marchioness | 10th Earl and
of Hertford | 1st Marquess
| of **Hertford**
| (1587–1660)
| *Governor and
Master of the
Household to the
Prince of Wales,
June 1641*

Mountjoy
Blount,
1st Earl of
Newport
(*illegitimate*)
(1597–1666)
*Constable of the
Tower of London,
May–December
1641*

Robert Rich,
2nd Earl of
Warwick
(1587–1658)
*De facto treasurer
of the Scottish
Army, January
1641–August
1642 and of the
English Navy
from September
1641*

Henry Rich,
1st Earl of
Holland
(*bap*.1590–1649)
*Lord General
North of the
Trent April
1641*

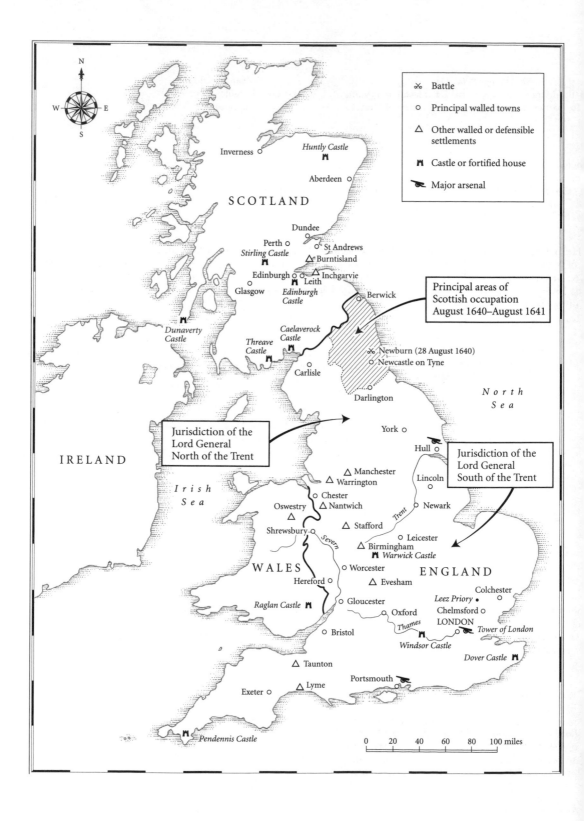

N

W — E

S

Battle
Principal walled towns
Other walled or defensible settlements
Castle or fortified house
Major arsenal

Inverness

Huntly Castle

Aberdeen

SCOTLAND

Dundee

Perth
Stirling Castle
St Andrews
Burntisland
Edinburgh
Leith
Inchgarvie
Glasgow
Edinburgh Castle

Berwick

Dunaverty Castle

Caelaverock Castle
Threave Castle

Carlisle

Newburn (28 August 1640)
Newcastle on Tyne

Darlington

North Sea

Principal areas of Scottish occupation August 1640–August 1641

York

Hull

Jurisdiction of the Lord General North of the Trent

Lincoln

IRELAND

Irish Sea

Manchester
Warrington
Chester
Oswestry
Nantwich
Shrewsbury
Stafford

Newark

Trent

Jurisdiction of the Lord General South of the Trent

Leicester
Birmingham
Warwick Castle

Severn

WALES

Worcester
Hereford
Evesham

ENGLAND

Leez Priory
Colchester

Raglan Castle
Gloucester
Oxford
Chelmsford
LONDON
Thames
Tower of London

Bristol
Windsor Castle

Dover Castle

Taunton

Lyme
Portsmouth

Exeter

Pendennis Castle

0   20   40   60   80   100 miles

Ireland
Counties and Principal Places

ULSTER

Coleraine
Letterkenny
LONDONDERRY
ANTRIM
DONEGAL
Carrickfergus
TYRONE
Belfast
Omagh
Newtonards
Dungannon
FERMANAGH
Armagh
DOWN
Sligo
Enniskillen
ARMAGH
Newry
Clones
SLIGO
LEITRIM
Cavan
MAYO
CAVAN
Dundalk
LOUTH
CONNAUGHT
ROSCOMMON
LONGFORD
Drogheda
Roscommon
Athboy
MEATH
WESTMEATH
GALWAY
Athlone
DUBLIN
Maynooth
Galway
Dublin
KING'S COUNTY
Loughrea
KILDARE
Atlantic Ocean
LEINSTER
Maryborough
WICKLOW
QUEEN'S COUNTY
CLARE
Carlow
Wicklow
Ennis
CARLOW
Kilkenny
Kilrush
Limerick
KILKENNY
WEXFORD
LIMERICK
TIPPERARY
Old Ross
Irish Sea
Clonmel
Wexford
MUNSTER
WATERFORD
Waterford
KERRY
Lismore
CORK
Dungarvan
Cork
Youghal

0 20 40 60 80 miles

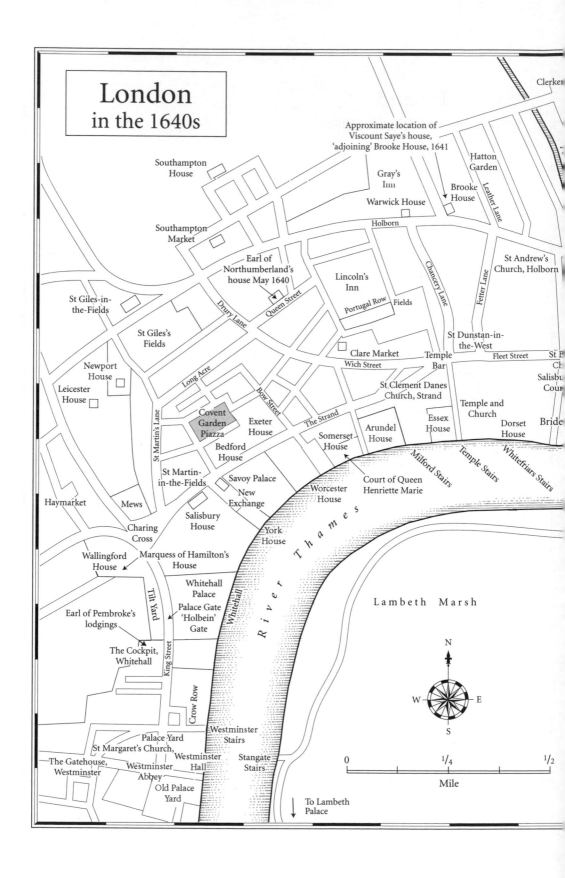

London
in the 1640s

Approximate location of
Viscount Saye's house,
'adjoining' Brooke House, 1641

Southampton
House

Gray's
Iɪɪɪ

Hatton
Garden

Brooke
House

Leather Lane

Warwick House

Southampton
Market

Holborn

St Andrew's
Church, Holborn

Earl of
Northumberland's
house May 1640

Lincoln's
Inn

Chancery Lane

Fetter Lane

St Giles-in-
the-Fields

Drury Lane

Queen Street

Portugal Row   Fields

St Dunstan-in-
the-West

St Giles's
Fields

Clare Market

Temple
Bar

Fleet Street

St B
Ch

Newport
House

Long Acre

Wich Street

St Clement Danes
Church, Strand

Salisbu
Cour

Leicester
House

Bow Street

St Martin's Lane

Covent
Garden
Piazza

Exeter
House

The Strand

Somerset
House

Arundel
House

Essex
House

Temple and
Church

Dorset
House

Bride

Bedford
House

Haymarket

Mews

St Martin-
in-the-Fields

Savoy Palace

New
Exchange

Worcester
House

Court of Queen
Henriette Marie

Milford Stairs

Temple Stairs

Whitefriars Stairs

Salisbury
House

York
House

River Thames

Charing
Cross

Wallingford
House

Marquess of Hamilton's
House

Whitehall
Palace

Palace Gate
'Holbein'
Gate

Whitehall

Lambeth   Marsh

Earl of Pembroke's
lodgings

Tilt Yard

The Cockpit,
Whitehall

King Street

Crow Row

N

Palace Yard

St Margaret's Church,

Westminster
Stairs

Westminster
Hall

Stangate
Stairs

W   E

The Gatehouse,
Westminster

Westminster
Abbey

S

Old Palace
Yard

To Lambeth
Palace

0   1/4   1/2

Mile

Clerke

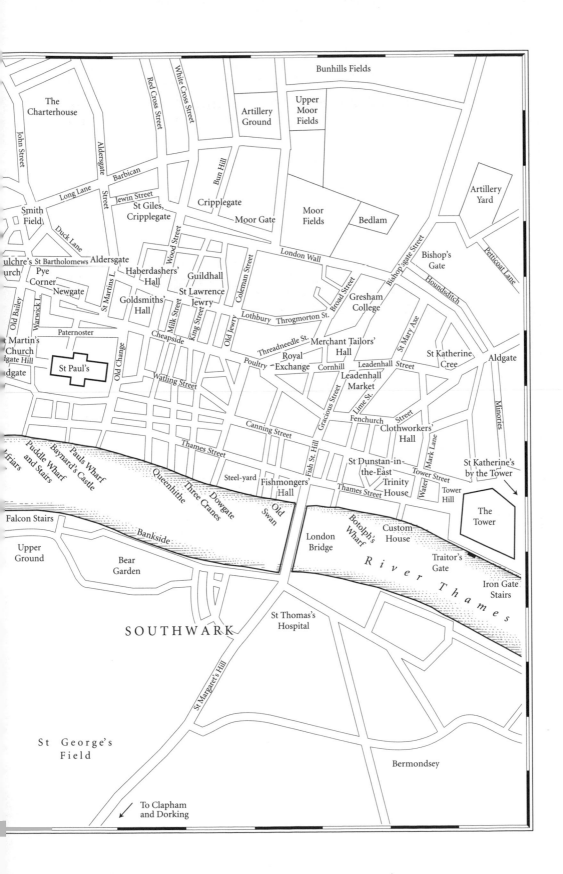

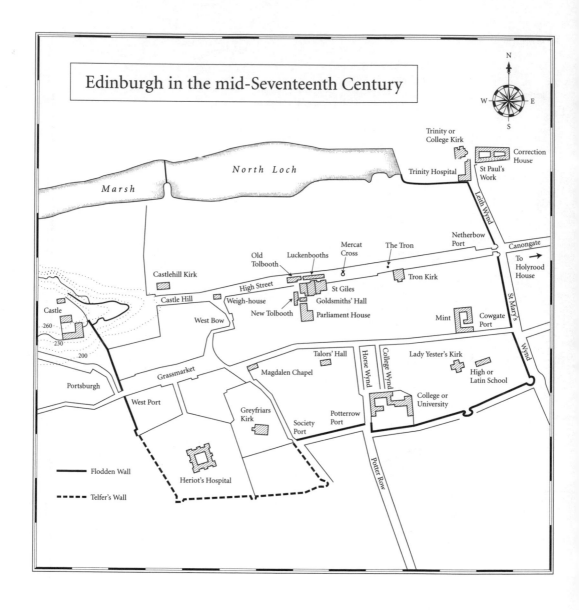

Edinburgh in the mid-Seventeenth Century

N
W · E
S

North Loch

Marsh

Trinity or
College Kirk

Correction
House

St Paul's
Work

Trinity Hospital

Leith Wynd

Netherbow
Port

Canongate

To
Holyrood
House

St Mary's

Castlehill Kirk

Old
Tolbooth

Luckenbooths

Mercat
Cross

The Tron

Tron Kirk

High Street

Castle Hill

St Giles

Weigh-house

Goldsmiths' Hall

New Tolbooth

Parliament House

Castle

260
230
200

West Bow

Mint

Cowgate
Port

Wynd

Talors' Hall

Horse Wynd

College Wynd

Lady Yester's Kirk

High or
Latin School

Grassmarket

Magdalen Chapel

Portsburgh

West Port

Greyfriars
Kirk

Society
Port

Potterrow
Port

College or
University

Flodden Wall

Telfer's Wall

Heriot's Hospital

Potter Row

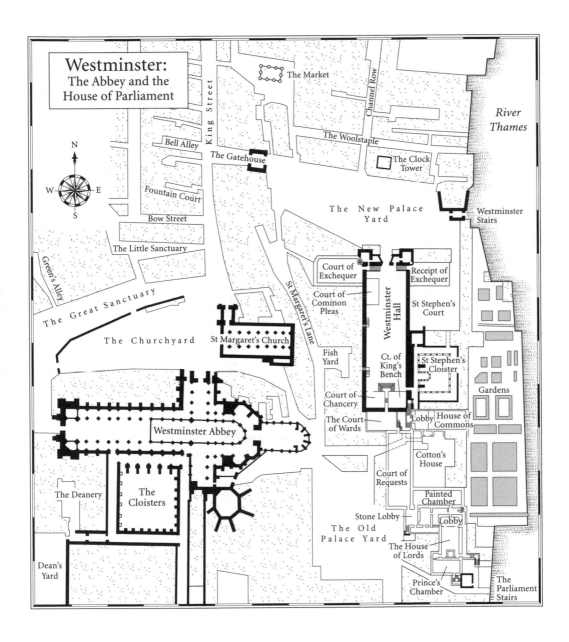

Westminster:
The Abbey and the
House of Parliament

The Market

Channel Row

River
Thames

King Street

The Woolstaple

Bell Alley

The Gatehouse

The Clock
Tower

N

Fountain Court

W   E

S

The New Palace
Yard

Bow Street

Westminster
Stairs

The Little Sanctuary

Court of
Exchequer

Receipt of
Exchequer

St Margaret's Lane

Green's Alley

Court of
Common
Pleas

Westminster Hall

St Stephen's
Court

The Great Sanctuary

St Margaret's Church

The Churchyard

Fish
Yard

Ct. of
King's
Bench

St Stephen's
Cloister

Gardens

Court of
Chancery

Westminster Abbey

The Court
of Wards

Lobby   House of
Commons

Cotton's
House

The Deanery

The
Cloisters

Court of
Requests

Painted
Chamber

Stone Lobby

Lobby

Dean's
Yard

The Old
Palace Yard

The House
of Lords

Prince's
Chamber

The
Parliament
Stairs

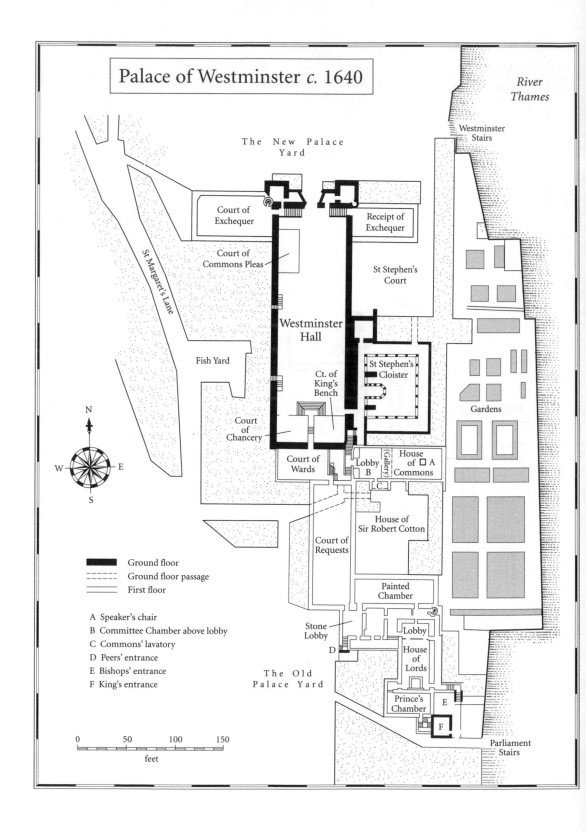

Palace of Westminster *c.* 1640

River Thames

The New Palace Yard

Court of Exchequer

Receipt of Exchequer

Court of Commons Pleas

St Stephen's Court

Westminster Stairs

St Margaret's Lane

Fish Yard

Westminster Hall

Ct. of King's Bench

St Stephen's Cloister

Gardens

Court of Chancery

N
W — E
S

Court of Wards

Lobby
B

(Gallery)

House of A Commons
C

House of Sir Robert Cotton

Court of Requests

Painted Chamber

Ground floor
Ground floor passage
First floor

Stone Lobby

Lobby

A Speaker's chair
B Committee Chamber above lobby
C Commons' lavatory
D Peers' entrance
E Bishops' entrance
F King's entrance

D

House of Lords

The Old Palace Yard

Prince's Chamber

E

F

Parliament Stairs

0   50   100   150
feet

ACKNOWLEDGEMENTS

Writers on the great crisis, political and religious, which afflicted mid seventeenth-century Britain and Ireland cannot but be aware of their good fortune in being the inheritors, however unworthily, of one the finest bodies of scholarship in the whole canon of historical writing in English. From Samuel Rawson Gardiner and the great masters of the late nineteenth century through to the twentieth-century historian grandees (R. H. Tawney, Lawrence Stone, Hugh Trevor-Roper, Christopher Hill, and Conrad Russell), the question why civil war erupted in England and in its neighbour kingdoms in the 1640s has fascinated some of the most acute practitioners of the historian's craft. That we who come after them may have any new insights to offer owes much to the vision, imagination and sheer industry of these writers who, in earlier generations, have made this subject their own.

But I have an equal awareness of just how much this book owes to historians who are very much alive. At various points in this project, I have benefited from the advice and conversation of Phil Baker, Tim Blanning, Chris Clark, David Cressy, Richard Cust, Barbara Donagan, Kenneth Fincham, Alan Ford, John Guy, Clive Holmes, D. E. Kennedy, Sean Kelsey, Peter Lake, Anthony Milton, John Morrill, Jane Ohlmeyer, Jason Peacey, John Scally, Brendan Simms, Kevin Sharpe, Johann Sommerville, Charles Spencer, David Starkey, Geoffrey Smith, Elliot Vernon, Andy Wood, and Blair Worden. Particular thanks are due to those who have had the patience and the stamina to read part or all of the typescript: Andrew Murison, Ian Gentles, Jake Leeper, Allan Macinnes, Michael Prodger, John Scally, and Malcolm Smuts. David Scott actually read the entire book in more than one recension, and was a vigilant and incisive critic, running a figurative red pencil through anything that was indulgent or irrelevant, and sharing generously of his vast knowledge of the manuscript sources for the period. Likewise, Christopher Thompson took on the task of reading, commenting and checking the whole typescript, and improving it immeasurably in the process. The references to the two of them in the endnotes, frequent as they are, are but a meagre acknowledgement of all the assistance they have provided. With so much help and support, this book ought to be perfect; that it is not is something for which I take full responsibility.

One colleague to whom this book also owes much, Conrad Russell, is sadly no longer alive to receive its author's thanks. Not since S. R. Gardiner at the end of the nineteenth century has any British scholar contributed as much as he to the understanding of the politics of the reign of Charles I. And although this book comes to conclusions that are very different from his own, and from which he would almost certainly have strongly dissented, it would be churlish in the extreme not to acknowledge the debt which I owe him, both personal and intellectual. He would have relished the argument, and it is a source of regret that he is not here to share in it.

Private owners of manuscripts have generously allowed access to their collections, and for permission to quote from their archives I am grateful to the Marquess of Anglesey, the Duke of Argyll, the Marquess of Bute, the Duke of Buccleuch, Viscount De L'Isle and Dudley, the Earl of Dunfermline, the Duke of Hamilton, the Marquess of Lothian, Susan Viscountess Hereford, the Duke of Northumberland, Lord Montagu of Beaulieu, Lord Sackville, the Marquess of Salisbury and Sir Lionel Tollemache, Bt., and the Archbishop of Westminster.

Working with Weidenfeld and Nicolson – Anna Hervé, who began the editorial work on this book, and Bea Hemming, who saw it so smoothly to its completion – has been one of the pleasures of the project. Any author is fortunate to have Ion Trewin as his editor; and, throughout it all, he has been an unfailing source of enthusiasm, patience, and sensible advice. Thanks are also due to Tom Graves for his work in sourcing the black-and-white images in the text and the colour plates. One of the greatest contributions, however, was made by Miranda Long, the paragon of a Fellows' Secretary at Peterhouse, whose efficiency, professionalism, and hawk-eye for infelicities of expression have earned her the gratitude and admiration of all of us who are lucky enough to have dealings with her.

Particular thanks are also due to the numerous friends who have offered their support, practical and moral, in the course of completing this book: Eric and Lindsay Avebury, Geoffrey and Ann Blainey, Niall Ferguson, Miriam Gross, Michael and Caroline Keeley, my agent Peter Robinson, Maiko Rothermere, George and Annabelle Weidenfeld; and, not least, my dear mother, whose tact in not asking the question which all authors dread – 'Is it finished yet?' – will long be remembered with gratitude.

One obligation more is recorded in the dedication.

PROLOGUE

WHITEHALL, TUESDAY, 5 MAY 1640

I thought wee had as good cause to celebrate the 5 of May [1640] as the 5 of November [the anniversary of the Gunpowder Plot]. [For Strafford's] designes in Ireland, in levying an armie ther, was to the utter subversion of this realme and the Lawes therof.

Sir Simonds D'Ewes, diary note, 17 April 1641[1]

The meeting's unconventional hour was itself an intimation of crisis. North-umberland rose shortly before dawn. The Privy Council was summoned to meet at six that morning;[2] and the journey to Whitehall, by coach from his town house in Queen Street, at the eastern end of London's fashionable new suburb of Covent Garden, would take some twenty minutes.[3] He dressed with the habitual fastidiousness of a courtier; but the last two items were always the same: a small gold-and-enamel medal, on which St George drove a lance into a writhing, mortally wounded dragon, suspended from the neck by a ribbon of sky-blue silk;[4] and finally his riding cloak, a light, wholly impractical mantle, its left side blazing with a star-shaped aureole of silver rays, some twelve inches in diameter, embroidered in silk and metal thread.[5]

At Whitehall, these semaphores of status were easily read. The insignia of the Garter, worn daily at the king's express command, proclaimed its wearer's fellowship with the nobility's inner élite, his possession of both social rank and royal favour – the two preconditions of major power in the England of Charles I.[6] To Algernon Percy, 10th Earl of Northumberland, however, these marks of princely esteem signified something more than simply personal accomplishment. They witnessed to a revolution in the fortunes of a dynasty, which, ever since the days of Hotspur, had been blighted by treason and revolt. For most of the previous century, his forebears had been almost continuously, and often violently, ostracized from the court. All three of his immediate predecessors in the earldom had either been imprisoned or beheaded for treason. His great-grandfather, Sir Thomas Percy, had died an even grislier death: half-strangled, disembowelled alive, and his body quar-tered at Tyburn in 1537 as a traitor against Henry VIII. Even his father,

Henry Percy, the 9th Earl of Northumberland – the first in a century not to die a violent death – had spent sixteen years incarcerated in the Tower as a suspected traitor, accused of complicity in the Gunpowder Plot.[7]*

With Earl Henry's death in 1632, however, the wheel of courtly fortune suddenly turned. The long decades of political exclusion gave way to a new era, as bright with opportunity as the preceding half-century had been dark with the threat of the scaffold.[8] Even before Earl Henry's death, Charles I had thought highly of the heir to the earldom of Northumberland. Aged twenty-nine at the time of his succession, Algernon Percy combined intelligence, energy and courtly charm with a pedigree that traced his descent, proudly if improbably, back to the Emperor Charlemagne.[9] To a king anxious to restore his standing with the 'old nobility' after the scandals of the late 1610s and 1620s – when the reigning favourite, the Duke of Buckingham, had put even earldoms up for sale[10] – Northumberland had seemed an almost ideal candidate for preferment. From the outset, the king had showered the new Earl of Northumberland with 'such a quick succession of bounties and favours', noted one contemporary, 'as had rarely befallen any man who had not been attended with the envy of a [court] favourite'.[11] Royal regard brought him membership of the Privy Council; the office of Lord Admiral and, with it, command of the largest English fleet created since the days of Henry VIII.[12] Such were the powers delegated to him in the summer of 1639, while the king was campaigning on the Scottish border, that he was openly referred to as the 'Lord Protector'.[13] The most recent intimation of royal favour had come in February 1640, with his appointment to the post of Captain General – commander-in-chief – of the king's army. At thirty-eight, Northumberland was master of all England's military forces, both land and sea.[14]

Diligence and ability only partly explained this rapid accumulation of preferments. It appealed to Charles I's sense of decorousness (and flattered his vanity) to be attended at court by such grandees of 'ancient lineage' and to have them occupying the great offices of state. Northumberland, for his part, relished the new-found trappings of power. Admission to the Order of the Garter in 1635 had set the seal on his dynasty's rehabilitation, and he had marked it with one of the costliest and most ostentatious public celebrations witnessed in London in living memory: £5,000 – for many peers an entire year's income – had been spent in a single, profligately triumphant day.[15]

This 'princely splendour' marked his daily appearances in the capital and at court. Even the relatively short journey to Whitehall required him to be accompanied by an entourage commensurate with his rank.[16] His footmen, coachmen, and postillions were richly attired in liveries of blue silk, embroidered at the chest in silver wire, with the Garter surrounding a crescent, the earl's heraldic badge. Nor were these inconsequential details. 'Magnificence'

---

* Both his paternal great-uncle and his grandfather, respectively the 7th and 8th Earls of Northumberland, suffered for joining the 1569 Rebellion of the Northern Earls against Elizabeth; the one had been beheaded, the other committed suicide in the Tower.

in early modern England was a tool of politics; not merely a public affirmation of power, but a component of power itself; and nowhere more so than in the competitive world of the court.[17] Political calculation lay behind these outward manifestations of 'greatness'; and, as one contemporary noted, the Lord Admiral and commander-in-chief was punctilious in presenting himself, 'in all his deportment, a very great man'.[18]

The circumstances of that Tuesday, 5 May 1640, cast an ominous shadow over this courtly pomp. England was embarking on the second year of a war to suppress a major rebellion in Scotland, and, within a matter of months, Northumberland knew that he would be expected, as the newly appointed Lord General, to lead an English army into the field.[19] The overriding problem he faced was one of finance. The Exchequer was nearly empty. The Crown's credit was exhausted. Only a Parliament, Northumberland believed, could authorize the necessary taxation required to make the war viable, even though it was unlikely to provide the whole of the cost, estimated at £1 million.[20] Only a Parliament, too, could provide a sense of national unity, which, no less than guns and money, was essential for a successful campaign. He and the king had wrangled over this question six months earlier, in the autumn of 1639, and Northumberland's counsel had eventually prevailed.[21] To almost universal rejoicing, a new Parliament had assembled on 13 April 1640, the first to meet in over a decade. Now, however, only three weeks into its debates, its continued existence was in doubt. If its premature dissolution were to be averted, he would have to confront the king once more.

Concerns about the Parliament's chances of survival had troubled Northumberland even before it had met. The elections had not gone well. 'Such as have dependance upon the court are in divers places refused,' he reported to his brother-in-law, the Earl of Leicester, 'and the most refrectorie persons chosen.' In consequence, he had 'cause to feare that this parlament will not sitt long'.[22] Many of the king's policies during the previous eleven years of 'Personal Rule' had been highly controversial – in the law, the Church, and his choice of counsellors at court. No taxation would be granted, the Commons had threatened within days of their meeting, until these 'grievances of the nation' were first redressed. Parliament would only fund Charles's new Scottish war in return for domestic reform.[23]

To Northumberland, that bargain, however distasteful, was the king's only option. The pretended alternative – that the war could be paid for out of revenues raised on the king's 'prerogative' (which included a power, in cases of emergency, to expropriate his subjects' goods without parliamentary assent)[24] – was unlikely to bring in more than a fraction of the projected costs, and would provoke yet further discontents.[25] Charles had already gone to war once without a Parliament, to fight the previous year's campaign against the Scots: a costly fiasco, which had emptied the Exchequer and ended in stalemate in July 1639, with barely a shot being fired.[26] Incredible though it appeared to Northumberland, this was the reckless course Charles proposed to repeat; and few, if any, in the Council would have the audacity to oppose him.[27]

How the king would approach the problem was hardly in doubt. The arguments Northumberland knew all too well. From the king's perspective, waging war with an empty Exchequer was an obvious gamble. But its risks were preferable to the certain humiliation that would follow from an enforced compromise with Parliament. Were the two Houses given their way, the whole structure of government and royal finance, so painstakingly established during the last decade of 'Personal Rule', looked almost certain to be dismantled; and the king's counsellors would be questioned in ways the monarch regarded as incompatible with the 'honour' of the Crown.[28]

Northumberland already knew what was signified by the pre-dawn summons to court, and that the Council meeting ahead would prove fractious.[29] The crisis they had to confront had intensified steadily over the last three weeks, but in other respects had been building for years, even decades. Its consequences – for the three Stuart kingdoms and, not least, for himself – looked likely to be immense. If rumour of the king's intentions proved true, that day would determine perhaps the greatest realignment in royal policy – in diplomacy, law, and, potentially, even in religion – since the advent of Protestantism sent its shock-waves through Western Europe, a century ago. But whatever was decided, the Lord General knew that the king's ongoing favour, the foundation of his preferments and prominence at court, would be sorely tested, possibly even destroyed, by the advice he intended to offer that day.

Still in darkness, Northumberland's coach, with its retinue of liveried postillions and footmen, left Queen Street for Whitehall. He had his counter-arguments prepared. If they failed before the Privy Council, he was the general who would have to fight the forthcoming war, starved of arms and money; his own the honour that would suffer the ignominy of near-certain defeat.

*

Already in its fourth year, the Scottish revolt posed the most serious threat to the stability of the English state since the days of the Spanish Armada, half a century before. England and Scotland had been united under a single crown only since 1603, when Charles's father, James VI of Scotland, had brought the Stuart dynasty south to accept the throne left vacant by the death of Elizabeth, the last of the Tudors.[30] After centuries of warfare and political strife between the two kingdoms, that 'union of the crowns' had been understandably slow to produce any substantive integration – legal, political, or religious – between the two kingdoms.[31] From his own accession in 1625, Charles had gone far beyond his father's tentative efforts to unify his realms and embarked on what became an ambitious attempt to re-form the British Isles as an Anglo-centric 'empire': a unity in which the two kingdoms of the Celtic fringe, Scotland and Ireland, were to be subordinated – and in part assimilated – to the religion and government of England, the richest and most powerful of the Stuart kingdoms.[32] Scotland's revolt posed a fundamental challenge to that grand, but often inconsistent, design and to the authority of what Charles called his 'Imperiall Crown'.[33] It menaced the religious unity of all three kingdoms, for, by abolishing bishops (the chief instruments of royal control of the Church in each of the three Stuart realms) and repudiating the authority of Whitehall, the Covenanters seemed likely to ensure that royal power, already reduced in Scotland to little more than a cipher, would be permanently curbed.[34] Their revolt, moreover, gave encouragement to dissidents in other parts of Charles's realms. Unless it were rapidly checked, its cost to the English Exchequer threatened the entire system of prerogative government, built up so assiduously during the previous eleven years of non-parliamentary rule.[35]

Within the Scottish nobility, grievances against Charles's style of absentee rule had been accumulating almost since 1625. Policies adopted by the king at his accession provocatively called into doubt the legal basis of lordship and property tenure; and, when it came to the allocation of high office, there was widespread resentment at the king's intrusion of bishops and social 'parvenus' into places traditionally occupied by the great territorial magnates within the nobility.[36] Far more widespread resentment, however, was created from 1633 by the king's attempts to recast the Scottish Church – with its long-standing traditions of Presbyterianism, local autonomy, and extempore prayer – as a copy of the English, with its tradition of rule by bishops (inherited from before the Reformation), centralized control, and uniform 'common prayer'. Religion was frequently the tinderbox of rebellion in a world where almost all men and women believed in the reality of Heaven and Hell, and where the promulgation of doctrinal error was believed capable of leading whole nations to eternal damnation. To the Scots, who prided themselves on the 'purity' of the Reformation they had embraced eighty years earlier, at the hands of the Calvinist John Knox,[37] the king's attempt in 1637 to impose a new 'popish' Scottish Prayer Book,[38] even more ceremonious than the English, seemed both to imperil true religion and to epitomize a more sinister English strategy against Scotland: what the Scottish cleric, Robert Baillie, called a design to see 'our poor country made an English province'.[39] When first used in St Giles' Kirk in Edinburgh in July that year, the new liturgy provided the occasion for carefully planned public protests.[40]

Religious zeal and a sense of affronted Scottish nationhood galvanized these initial protests against the Prayer Book into a nationwide revolt. The Scottish nobility moved quickly to fill the vacuum created by the collapse of royal power.[41] By February 1638, the leaders of the rebellion had entered into a National Covenant, an oath to purge the Scottish Kirk of bishops and all other 'novations ... [which] tend to the re-establishing of the popish religion and tyranny',[42] and established a new noble-dominated government in Edinburgh, determined to reduce Charles's authority as ruler of Scotland to little more than that of a puppet king. In effect, from early in 1638, 'Covenanter' Scotland had become a semi-autonomous aristocratic republic, looking to Sweden for moral and military support,[43] and Charles was under no illusions as to its implications.[44] 'So long as this Covenant is in force,' he wrote in June 1638, 'I have no more Power in Scotland than as a Duke of Venice.'[45]

Salvaging his rule in Scotland – and, with it, the restoration of the recently abolished bishops to their place in the Scottish Church – became Charles's all-consuming passion, a matter, not merely of re-establishing his government, but of vindicating his own, and England's, honour.[46] This last consideration struck a chord that resonated well beyond the confines of the Whitehall court. Even many of those who had scant enthusiasm for the king's religious policies, and were indifferent as to how the Scots chose to govern their Church, could regard the Covenanter rebellion as an affront to English authority and honour that cried out for immediate redress. English noblemen who had counselled against Charles's policies in Scotland faced an invidious choice. As one English officer was to summarize the dilemma, to negotiate with the Covenanters would be 'deare in the dishonourable'; but if there were to be war, '[the] purse and vaines of the nobility must bleede, [including] those who most apposed his Majestie – or [we must] see a publique ruine [in England]'.[47]

These ancient antipathies had helped to provide a measure of unity, both at court and in the country at large, when Charles first rallied an English army against the Scots in 1639. When negotiations, conducted throughout 1637 and 1638, failed to return the Covenanters to their obedience, there was sporadic support as well as criticism for the king's decision to reimpose his rule on Scotland by force. True, there were murmurs of dissent. Some counties proved laggardly in producing their allotted contributions of men and materiel. In April 1639, two dissident peers, Viscount Saye and Lord Brooke, both long-standing opponents of Charles's régime, achieved national notoriety by obeying the king's summons of the nobility to York, but refusing a newly devised military oath whereby they would have been bound to support the king to 'the utmost of my power and hazard of my life' – an undertaking they flatly refused to give.[48] In spite of all, however, by the summer of 1639 the king had succeeded in deploying an army of around 18,000 men on the Scottish border;[49] and, in his role as Lord Admiral, Northumberland had worked loyally in support of the war effort, co-ordinating a naval blockade of Edinburgh that was intended to cripple Scottish maritime trade.[50]

This 1639 mobilization against Scotland – the first 'Bishops' War' – had been a formidable accomplishment. Reluctant to allow his régime's opponents their most effective platform, a new Parliament, Charles had insisted that the war should be fought without the two Houses meeting, the first time since 1323 that any English king had attempted to mount a major military campaign without first seeking parliamentary financial and moral support.[51]

Charles had good reason to avoid the re-summoning of Parliament. In an age when the legislature convened only as often, and for as long, as the king determined, its sessions over the previous three decades had been intermittent, often acrimonious, and almost invariably short. Parliament had met only once between 1610 and 1621 (and that, in 1614, in a brief and ill-tempered session); and though Parliaments had been summoned five times in the 1620s, primarily to meet the costs of the Stuarts' ill-starred wars with France and Spain, relations between the king and his two Houses had become increasingly fractious throughout the decade.[52]

How extensively, and by whom, the various aspects of government should be funded – in particular the prime function of government, the defence of the realm – had been a recurrent point of contention throughout the reign. Since the early fourteenth century there had been a time-honoured assumption that, when need arose, Parliament would grant the monarch the right to collect taxation – for a limited period and up to a roughly predetermined final sum – in return for the remedying of grievances which 'the Parliament-men', his Lords and Commons, brought to his attention in the course of the session.[53] By 1629, when Parliament had met for the last time before the military crisis of 1640, many of Charles's Councillors had concluded that this old compact – taxation in return for the redress of grievances – had long outlived its usefulness.[54] 'Redress of grievances', many of Charles's closest advisers had come to believe, meant, in practice, an increasingly strident series of demands that the king should relinquish the very sources of revenue on which he had come to depend: the 'prerogative revenues' – from customs duties to charges imposed to meet the costs of levying soldiers. In return, Parliament offered short-term grants of tax revenue (or 'subsidies'). Yet, unlike Parliament's ad hoc and time-limited grants of taxation, Charles's prerogative revenues – particularly the lucrative customs revenues, which funded almost half of all royal spending – provided a continuous and steadily rising income, year on year. From the king's perspective, the problem with what Parliament was prepared to concede was simple: the value of the taxation on offer (and which was guaranteed, at most, for only four or five years into the future) never came near to compensating the monarch for the prerogative-based (and non-time-limited) revenues he was being asked to give up.[55]

By 1629, Charles had come to believe that only a deliberate conspiracy to undermine his government could explain the manifest unreasonableness of Parliament's demands.[56] For it seemed that the two Houses had been hijacked by a small but vociferous minority – most active in the Commons, but also represented in the Lords – intent on using the power of the purse to compel changes in royal policy in areas where Charles insisted they had no business to interfere: in dictating how he should conduct his wars; in trying to remove his ministers against his will (most notoriously in 1626, when Parliament had initiated impeachment proceedings against the then Lord Admiral and royal favourite, the Duke of Buckingham); and in attempting to meddle in the affairs of the Church. By 1629, only four years into his reign, Charles's patience with Parliaments had been exhausted. To achieve his ambitious plans for 'order and decency' within his realms, the king would need to re-found his government – and the royal finances – on a basis that emancipated him from further reliance on the legislature. As in contemporary France and the Spanish Kingdoms, revenues based on the king's prerogative powers seemed to be the way of the future, not the medieval system of funding through parliamentary grant.[57]

If government itself was in a state of flux, so too was the realm of political ideas. English intellectual life, for all the insular uniqueness of its Common Law tradition, partook of a larger cosmopolitan Humanist culture in which

theories of political authority were in ferment, and in which the extent of
royal power and the limits of subjects' rights were hotly contested.[58] Europe's
periodic political crises of the century after the Reformation – the French
Wars of Religion, the Dutch Provinces' revolt against Spanish Habsburg rule,
the early years of the Thirty Years War – each spawned a rich polemical and
theoretical literature that helped shape the character and content of political
debate in England. Europe's religious schisms of the mid sixteenth century,
which had made theological controversy the staple reading of the educated,
and the increasingly large proportion of gentry that spent time at the Inns
of Court, combined to make the mid-seventeenth-century nobility and gentry
perhaps the most theologically and legally literate in English history. Yet
religion and the Common Law were by no means the only source of moral
and intellectual authority. The Renaissance re-engagement with Classical
culture in general, and Roman history in particular, provided a rich but
ambivalent inheritance, in which republican and monarchical forms of rule
each had their defenders and detractors.[59]

Aided by the massive expansion in the reading and circulation of books
and pamphlets in the century after 1540, received theories of the subject's
rights and duties were being qualified, and sometimes subverted, by novel
ideas and theories: that kings exercised their powers only 'by contract' with
their subjects, for example, and that this contract was one that subjects
were at liberty to revoke; or that rebellion, even tyrannicide, in certain
circumstances could be justified. The polemicists who came to the defence
of the first two Stuart Kings responded, in their turn, with a complex range
of defences of monarchical power.[60] Two, however, had come to achieve a
particular prominence in the late 1620s: the principle that the monarch,
having received his powers directly from God, was answerable only to Him
(and not to his subjects) for their exercise; and, second, the doctrine that for
'reason of state', the interests of the whole kingdom, the king could dispense
with received law and constitutions – and that the ruler alone could judge
what these best interests actually were.

For almost a decade, until the late 1630s, this change to prerogative
finance – justified partly by reference law and partly by 'reason of state'[61] –
had seemed a realizable goal. By 1630, Charles had extricated himself from
his foreign conflicts, and begun to bring a measure of order to the perpetually
straitened royal Exchequer.[62] Lacking any substantial income from land
(Queen Elizabeth's sales of the royal demesne to fund her wars against Spain
in the 1580s and 1590s had ended that),[63] Charles worked effectively, often
ingeniously, to find alternative sources of revenue. In defiance of the Parliament-men who had denounced such practices as illegal, he revived the
imposition of long-defunct feudal dues, collected customs duties (in particular,
Tonnage and Poundage) on his own authority, and introduced new levies
(taxation in all but name) to meet the cost of defending the realm. By far
the most successful of these was Ship Money, a de facto tax, imposed from
the mid 1630s, to meet the costs of the navy.[64] Despite a celebrated challenge
to its legality, launched by John Hampden in 1637, Ship Money brought in
a regular income of between £150,000 and £200,000 a year until 1638 (after

which yields declined steeply)[65] – all of it paid directly into the Treasury of the Navy.[66] Northumberland was Ship Money's direct and arguably principal beneficiary. It provided him with extensive powers of patronage, and went to meet the costs of his large and improving fleet.[67]

However, the most ambitious experiment in prerogative government during the 1630s was to be found, not in England, but in Ireland. Governed from 1633 by its energetic Lord Deputy, Thomas, Viscount Wentworth (created Earl of Strafford and Lord-Lieutenant of the kingdom in 1640), Ireland became something of a testing ground for the extension of monarchical power. Perhaps the most intellectually gifted of all Charles's ministers, Wentworth was energetic, clear-sighted, and ruthless in the attainment of his goals. Despite a public rhetoric of legality and consensus, he treated the Irish Parliament, which met in 1634, as little more than a source of tax-gathering for the royal Exchequer; exploited flaws in the legal titles of the native Irish to expropriate to the Crown vast swathes of land; and used the prerogative jurisdiction of the Court of Castle Chamber to intimidate and silence his critics.[68] Power, in Wentworth's view, depended not on consent but on military force – that 'Pillar of your Authority', as he put it to the king, which was 'of absolute Necessity'.[69] And the most disquieting aspect of Wentworth's government of Ireland, as viewed from the other side of the Irish Sea, was not only its apparent success, but also the prospect that these policies, having been tried and proven, would be extended in time to England and Scotland as well.

This entire fiscal and governmental system, in both England and Ireland, was directly threatened by the Scottish revolt. Were the king to go to Parliament to fund the rebellion's suppression, any grant of taxation was likely to be hedged around with unacceptable conditions. The king's ministers and policies would be publicly traduced and questioned; and ignorant laymen would presume to challenge the doctrine and practices that the Supreme Governor had approved for the English Church. In 1639, therefore, the king's refusal to seek parliamentary aid in the first Scottish War surprised few. Had he succeeded in crushing the Covenanter revolt at this first attempt, there was the strong likelihood that his 'Personal Rule' might well have been immune to any further internal military threat.[70]

Yet Charles's Scottish war of 1639 ended in an inconclusive stalemate. The army that the king had successfully raised without the aid of Parliament was marched to the Scottish border, but never engaged. For two days that June, it confronted the Covenanter force ranged against it on the north bank of the Tweed, the river that marked the boundary between the two British kingdoms. Deterred, however, by exaggerated reports of the Covenanters' reserves, Charles's nerve failed him. He declined to risk a battle with an army which, he believed, was outnumbered by the Scots.[71] When the Covenanter leadership offered to treat, their offer was quickly accepted. Apart from a single reconnaissance mission, this 'Bishops' War' of 1639 had ended without a shot being fired. The subsequent Pacification of Berwick enabled Charles to regain custody of his Scottish fortresses (including Edinburgh Castle), and met his demand for the dissolution of the Covenanters' interim government, the series of committees known as the Tables. In return, however, he was forced to concede the calling of a Scottish Parliament and a General Assembly of the Scottish Church – thereby providing his critics with the public forum (and the sources of institutional authority) they needed to mount a concerted assault against the Scottish dimension of his Personal Rule.[72]

Eleven months on, however, in May 1640, it was now clear to the Covenanters that the king's concessions had never been more than a feint. Charles had negotiated merely to buy time, not to conclude a lasting peace; and in February 1640 he had declared what most had long suspected: that he intended to rescind the current Pacification and renew the Scottish war.[73] Northumberland's appointment as Captain-General, made that same month, was calculated to win support for the new campaign. Algernon Percy commanded extensive local influence in the northern counties, on which the costs of the war and the presence of troops would fall most heavily. More important, he was wholly untainted by any association with the 'popish' party at court. He had long been an advocate of English involvement on the Protestant side in the Thirty Years War, and his presence in command of the war effort served to counter Scottish claims that this second 'Bishops' War' was being driven on by a Catholic conspiracy at Whitehall.[74]

In 1640, however, the king not only planned to mobilize an English army; he hoped to deploy it in conjunction with a second Irish force, raised and commanded by Lord Deputy Wentworth, newly promoted to the earldom of Strafford. Come the summer, his two loyal kingdoms would combine to crush the insubordination of the third. With such overwhelming force at his disposal, victory seemed within his grasp.

For all the king's belligerent determination, however, one question remained unresolved: how was the new campaign to be paid for? From the outset, it seemed clear that last year's extraordinary series of loans and prerogative exactions could not be repeated. In 1639, the English gentry had rallied, for the most part effectively, to Charles's summons to raise an army, only to see their efforts wasted by pusillanimous generals in the field. They were unlikely to respond to a call to arms a second time.

With all other avenues seemingly foreclosed, a Parliament appeared the only remaining alternative. On the positive side, there were reasons for believing it might prove more tractable than at its last meeting in 1629. Many of the troublemakers in the 1620s House of Commons were now dead or in their dotage. A new generation of Parliament-men might well look more favourably on Charles's policies than had their forebears in the ill-tempered session of 1629. But within the Privy Council, even the most sanguine advocates of a Parliament doubted whether it would produce taxation on anywhere near the scale necessary to meet the new war's projected cost. Adequate funding would not be available, Northumberland confided to his brother-in-law, 'unless the [1640] Parliament be more liberall in their supplies of the Kinge than they have ever beene since my time' – experience that went back to the Parliament of 1626, which he had attended in his early twenties.[75] Of one thing, however, Northumberland was convinced. A new campaign was wholly unfeasible unless Parliament agreed to provide 'supply' (principally, direct taxation), a course that would almost certainly involve the king in some irksome bargaining over the redress of grievances. Indeed, the central danger with this strategy was that, in seeking parliamentary funding for the war, the king risked opening the floodgates to a tide of pent-up criticism of his Personal Rule.

To broaden his room to manoeuvre, Charles agreed to the summoning of not one Parliament, but two. The Irish Parliament was convoked to meet in Dublin in March 1640, three weeks before the opening of the English Parliament in Westminster. There, the Earl of Strafford, recently promoted from Lord Deputy to the higher office of Lord Lieutenant of Ireland, brimmed with optimism.* He promised the king that he could gain parliamentary approval for a new army for use against Scotland – and the funds needed to pay it. And he proved as good as his word. The Irish Parliament voted some £180,000 (with promises of more to come, should it be required) for Charles's war effort, and undertook to raise an army of 9,000 men, which would be ready by the end of May that year.[76] The Irish contingent alone would supply roughly a third of the troops Charles had estimated were needed for his Scottish war, and the grant of taxation (together with promised further sums of roughly around £90,000) would yield somewhere between a quarter and a third of the campaign's projected budget.[77] Strafford's Irish Parliament did not solve all Charles's financial problems, but – together with loans and prerogative exactions – it made some form of military offensive against Scotland viable, whether or not his English Parliament proved compliant. Royal credit might be stretched to defaulting point, but Charles was now confident that negotiation with his forthcoming English Parliament was merely a desirable option, no longer an unavoidable necessity. If the two Houses at Westminster failed to cooperate, the king could afford himself the indulgence of refusing to be coerced. As the French ambassador put it, Charles intended to hold a 'Parlement à sa mode'.[78]

The urgency of the king's requirements was clearly spelt out at the opening of Parliament in a speech to both Houses by the senior law officer, the Lord Keeper, Sir John Finch.[79] Prominent Covenanter nobles, Finch claimed, had already made a treasonable approach to the French king, Louis XIII, in a bid to reconstruct the 'auld alliance' between France and Scotland.[80] The gravity of the military crisis permitted of no delay. Pre-empting criticism of Charles's policies during the 1630s, Finch insisted that any debate on the kingdom's grievances would have to wait until the question of subsidies – how much taxation the Commons would yield to fund the war effort – had first been resolved.

Charles's critics, however, were in no mood to be cowed, particularly those who could count on the support, and if necessary protection, of powerful

---

* Beyond its honorific significance, Strafford's promotion entitled him to reside in England and appoint a Lord Deputy of his own to rule Ireland in his absence. For Strafford's detractors, the prospect of the earl becoming a major presence at the Whitehall court was perhaps the most disquieting aspect of his elevation.

aristocratic grandees. The authors of the four speeches that were probably the most influential (and, subsequently, widely publicized) of the Parliament's opening days – Harbottell Grimston, Sir Francis Seymour, Sir Benjamin Rudyard and John Pym – were all men with powerful patrician defenders:* the Earl of Warwick of Grimston,[81] the Earl of Hertford of Seymour (the earl's younger brother), the Earl of Pembroke of Rudyard,[82] and the Earls of Bedford and Warwick of Pym, who served both men as confidant and man-of-affairs.[83] And while it was not only the well-connected who were bold, it seems no coincidence that all these men's protectors were, in varying degrees, like-minded critics of Charles's régime. Moreover, they were all powerful enemies of the Earl of Strafford, now widely regarded as the most belligerent member of the Privy Council – notwithstanding that men such as Bedford and, still more, Pembroke were also familiar figures at the Whitehall Court. (Indeed, Pembroke was Charles's Lord Chamberlain, the royal Household's senior official.)[84]

Grimston's speech gives some sense of the force and directness of their assault. The internal dangers posed to the body politic by the 'pestilentiall humors' of Charles's régime, Grimston argued, greatly exceeded any external threat offered by the Scots.[85] The subversive corollary of this hardly needed to be spelt out: there should be no grant of subsidies, he implied, until those malign 'Humours' had been purged and their 'authors and causes' brought to account.[86] This was a heavy hint, to put it no stronger, that there should be impeachments, and that, as in the 1620s, errant ministers should be sent for trial before the Lords. Grimston's critique was amplified the following day by John Pym, whose widely reported speech, lasting over two hours, catalogued in detail the encroachments on the subjects' liberties that had been perpetrated during the last decade. Illegal prerogative exactions threatened the subject's property, Pym argued, just as much as popish innovations in religion imperilled the health of the Church.[87]

To Northumberland, the Parliament's new irascibility carried with it a powerful sense of déjà vu. Writing on 17 April, the day of Pym's speech, he was reminded of the bitter debates of the 1620s, observing that 'the lower House fell into almost as great a heat as ever you saw ... in my Lord of Buckingham's time [1626-28], and I perceive our House [of Lords is] apt to take fire at the least sparkle'.[88] In this atmosphere of heat and combustibility, the Privy Council's hopes of gaining subsidies without substantial compromise over the kingdom's 'grievances' dwindled by the day. By 23 April 1640, only ten days after the Parliament had opened, and with no grant of taxation in sight, Northumberland was already predicting the Parliament's imminent

---

* This is not to imply that, simply because a particular peer conferred his patronage or protection on a member of the Commons, this created some servile relationship of dependency, still less that the peers were the 'string-pullers' of business in the lower House. Where cooperation between members of the two Houses can be discerned, it almost invariably depended on shared political and religious principles, and a desire to see the achievement of common goals; not on some sense of 'obligation' arising from favours conferred. These relations are explored in detail in Chapter 5.

demise.[89] The disaster unfolding at Westminster brought a sense of unreality to the king's preparations for war. As Lord General, Northumberland was besieged by pushy courtiers, recommending clients and protégés for well-paid positions in the army;* yet there seemed little prospect that the army which they were clamouring to join would ever take the field. 'To what purpose is it', Northumberland asked, 'to talke of, or take care of, these matters when we are all breaking to peeces here in our parliament, and know not how we shall be able to paye the army for one month?'[90]

By the first week of May 1640, Charles had become convinced that his régime was being undermined by an English Fifth Column, intent on exploiting the Scottish crisis in order to advance its own political ends.[91] Doubts about the allegiance of some of the lords were current even before the Parliament had met – hence his refusal, later reluctantly rescinded, to issue writs of summons to Saye, Mandeville, and Brooke.[92] All three were known to be in sympathy, perhaps in treasonous communication, with the leaders of the Covenanter rebellion,[93] and were members of a wider network of godly critics, whose hostility to the king's policies – both religious and secular – had been obvious from within a few years of Charles's accession.[94]

Yet Viscounts Mandeville and Saye were relatively small fry. Richer, better connected, and more dangerous by far were the more senior members of this Puritan 'knot', men whose status and influence made them commensurately difficult for the régime to bring to heel. Two, in particular, were pre-eminent. The first was Francis Russell, 4th Earl of Bedford, the most urbane and courtly of the dissidents, whose extensive network of friends in the king's Household did not preclude him from employing (and granting legal protection to) several of Charles's most abrasive parliamentary critics, notably Oliver St John and John Pym.[95] Far more assertive in manner and tone, was Robert Rich, 2nd Earl of Warwick, the landed magnate, anti-Spanish privateer, and 'great patron and Mecænas [sic] to the pious and religious Ministry',[96] who had been in the forefront of resistance to Charles's efforts to raise compulsory loans during the 1620s.[97] Both Warwick and Bedford, in their very different ways, were known to be the patrons and employers of some of the Commons-men, who, from Charles's perspective, had done most to obstruct the granting of parliamentary supply.[98] And, as Charles well knew, these major grandees were linked to many of the other leading dissidents – in particular to Lords Saye and Brooke – through a myriad of mutually reinforcing connections: through patronage of godly ministers, shared opposition to Ship Money and other prerogative exactions, and through business ventures that aspired to join Puritanism and profit.[99]

By far the most important recruit to the ranks of the dissidents, however, was Robert Devereux, 3rd Earl of Essex. The Lieutenant-General of the

---

* 'I pray God', Northumberland wrote to Viscount Conway on 26 April, 'the rest of the officers preferred by my Lord Cottington [the Chancellor of the Exchequer] prove better then my Quarter maister: his Lordship hath lately recommended to me a rare chirurgion [surgeon], but I heare he is accused of running away with a horse the last summer, whilst the King was in the army.'

Horse in the previous year's war against the Scots, Essex had temporarily experienced the status that went with royal favour in 1639, and been tipped for membership of the Garter, only to be dismissed peremptorily by the king at the end of the campaign. The humiliation of dismissal added to a long catalogue of insults he had suffered at the Stuart court, going back to the early years of James's reign.[100] Yet he was a dangerous man for the king to have alienated, for, as the heir of the 'rebel earl' of 1601 (who had post-humously acquired almost martyr status), and having spent much of his adult life campaigning against the Habsburgs on the Continent, Essex was one of the most popular men in the country – a man, in the words of one con-temporary, 'generally beloved'.[101] Essex had been aligned with this group of aristocratic critics for some twenty years,[102] but his final breach with the court constituted a major coup for the king's critics at Westminster. His very first recorded action in the new Parliament was to raise the case of Dr Roger Maynwaring, a royal chaplain who had argued in print the 'absolutist' case that kings were above the law, and unaccountable to their subjects for their actions. Though impeached and condemned by the last Parliament, in 1628, Maynwaring had later been pardoned and promoted to the bishops' benches by the king – a case which Essex raised as a matter of urgency, in the words of one eyewitness, 'concerning to us all'.[103]

For any Privy Councillor who feared a conspiracy between dissident Commons-men and these godly grandees, the first weeks of the Parliament had seemed to provide evidence of collusion in abundance. Of course, not all the obstruction to the war was emanating from this bicameral group, suspected of being in sympathy with the Scottish rebels. The grievances of the Commons were sufficiently numerous by the spring of 1640 that they did not need lordly prompting in order to find an advocate. But not all such opposition was so innocent or so spontaneous. By the beginning of May, the congruencies between the strategies pursued by the dissidents in the Lords and their 'allies-men' in the Commons were sufficiently frequent for the Privy Council's suspicions to be raised.[104]

But whether spontaneous or concerted, by the first week of May, this insistence on the redress of grievances had effectively brought the Parliament to a standstill. For Northumberland and Strafford – the commanders, respect-ively, of Charles's English and Irish armies – the Westminster Parliament's failure to produce *any* offer of supply threatened the feasibility of the entire military venture.[105] Caught between the king's unrealistic belief that the war could still be funded without Parliament, on the one side, and, on the other, the hostile obstructiveness of the two Houses, Strafford and Northumberland made a desperate attempt to broker a compromise. When the Privy Council met on Sunday, 3 May, to review the week's calamitous proceedings, Strafford and Northumberland persuaded the king to make one final offer. He would agree to give up Ship Money (worth between £150,000 to £200,000 a year) if the Commons would agree to offer twelve subsidies, which could be expected to bring in somewhere around £650,000, at most – still substantially less than the £1 million that the summer's campaign was expected to cost,[106] but almost certainly enough, when combined with subventions from Ireland

and the remaining prerogative sources of revenue, to provide a chance of fighting the war to a successful conclusion.[107] Financially, this offer was a massive concession on the king's part, with major implications for the long-term solvency of the Crown.[108] Still anxious to reach some form of compromise with the Parliament, however, the Council gave its approval, and Sir Henry Vane, the more articulate of the king's two Secretaries of State, was deputed to put the case to the Commons when it reconvened the following morning.[109]

That debate of Monday, 4 May, decided the future of the Parliament. Northumberland and Strafford seem to have mobilized the Commons-men who were part of what contemporaries termed their 'interest' – their friends, employees, and other dependants – to speak forcefully in favour of the proposal. As Lord Admiral, Northumberland was the officer of state who would be most directly affected by the abolition of Ship Money; support from his Commons allies was the clearest signal that could be given as to the authenticity of the offer, and that the Lord Admiral, whatever his private misgivings, was publicly behind it.[110]

Yet, in the cramped and overcrowded Commons chamber – the medieval Chapel of St Stephen, adjacent to Westminster Hall – debate soon degenerated into an ill-tempered fracas. Despite some 'eight or nine houres more debating'[111] it early became apparent that the abandonment of Ship Money would not, on its own, suffice to win a grant of supply. Yet there was little agreement among the Commons-men as to what their minimum terms should be. John Hampden, the hero of the unsuccessful legal challenge to Ship Money in 1637, won wide support for a motion that Ship Money be declared illegal before a penny of new taxation were granted. But others wanted monopolies struck down; others 'innovations' in religion; still others, abuses by the prerogative courts. Debate meandered on until nightfall, ever more unfocused as to purpose, but with an increasing asperity of tone. The House adjourned at 6 p.m., resolving to reconvene for further debate at eight the following morning.[112]

If this day's debate proved inconclusive in the Commons, it nevertheless elicited a decisive response from Whitehall. To Charles, it seemed the only purpose being served by the Parliament was to provide his enemies – men who were 'perverting [Parliament] to their own unworthy ends' – with a platform from which to traduce his government.[113] That evening, the king decided to bring the Parliament to an end. He considered carefully the text of the speech he was to deliver the following morning, the draft of which was prepared by his Scottish favourite, the Marquess of Hamilton.[114] Precedent, however, dictated that the Parliament's dissolution should first be referred to the Privy Council, if only to rubber-stamp his decision.

The Council's messengers were despatched that night to command the Councillors' presence at Whitehall at six the following morning, Tuesday, 5 May.[115]

*

Shortly before sunrise, Northumberland's coach reached its destination. Swinging through the Whitehall gate, it entered the Great Court, the large cobbled quadrangle beyond, the heart of the palace from which England was ruled. What caught the eye, however, was the gabled wing that jutted into the court, midway along its southern range. Despite the early hour, the first-floor windows glowed with candlelight. Figures could be discerned moving in the large tapestry-hung room within: the Privy Council Chamber, which Elizabeth I had added to the warren of rooms and galleries – the monarch's private lodgings – that constituted the Great Court's southern side. There, the decision on the Parliament's future, and, with it, the feasibility of Northumberland's unwanted war, would shortly be made.

The Lord Admiral alighted and made his way to Privy Gallery on the palace's first floor. The chances of averting a dissolution were slim. Even before the Council's offer to relinquish Ship Money had been spurned by the Commons, Charles had been impatient to see the Parliament dissolved. Twice already in the course of the session the king had been persuaded to stay his hand.[116] But after the previous day's display of the Commons' disaffection, there was little prospect that he would allow the two Houses another chance.

When the Council meeting began, there was one important absentee, the Earl of Strafford; but the Lord-Lieutenant of Ireland was known to be ill (currently being treated for gout and 'the stone'), and despite his failure to appear, the king began the meeting punctually.[117] Taking command of proceedings from the outset, Charles presented the Council with a fait accompli: he would go to the House of Lords that morning to announce an immediate dissolution. The Commons' Speaker, John Glanvill, he informed them, had already been instructed not to take the chair that day – thereby preventing the House from conducting any business,[118] and avoiding the possibility of the chaotic scenes that had accompanied the dissolution of the last Parliament, in 1629, when the government's critics had forcibly held down the Commons' Speaker in his chair, to prevent the session's proceedings being brought to an end by his rising.

Initially, at least, Charles seems to have been reluctant to hear his Councillors' opinions. What changed the meeting's atmosphere decisively was the belated arrival of the Earl of Strafford, gaunt from illness and apparently alarmed at the news of the Parliament's impending dissolution. He had been one of the Councillors who had advised its calling, and, while Strafford was becoming adept at gauging the king's mood and realigning his advice to match its direction, he seems to have been reluctant to acquiesce in the dissolution without at least some discussion. Whether this was a genuine attempt to postpone the dissolution, or a ploy to force opponents of the king's will to declare their hands, is impossible to determine.[119] But it appears to have been at Strafford's instigation that the whole question of the Parliament's future was reopened, and that the king sought individual Privy Councillors' opinions before finalizing his decision. Protocol demanded that Councillors speak in reverse order of precedence, with the most junior – the two Secretaries of State (almost the only Councillors not to be peers) – speaking first. The junior Secretary of State, Sir Henry Vane, gave the verdict that the king expected to hear: there was no hope that the Commons 'would give one penny'.[120] The other Secretary of State, Sir Francis Windebank, concurred.[121] As opinions were taken around the table, only two Councillors had the temerity to oppose the Parliament's immediate dissolution. Northumberland's first cousin, Henry Rich, Earl of Holland, who had served as Lieutenant-General in the previous year's campaign, expressed his doubts; but the one Councillor to offer his opinion forcefully 'against the breking of the Parlement' was Northumberland himself.[122] No verbatim account of Northumberland's speech survives, but his major argument against abandoning the Parliament emerges forcefully in his correspondence at the time (though some of this passion may well have been moderated in his discourse before the king). He was not uncritical of the Commons, who, he believed, might have 'gained their desires' if they had acted less intemperately.[123] But to 'break the Parliament', Northumberland believed, was quite simply to doom the planned summer campaign. An under-financed war was likely to prove a fiasco; and it was his own and the king's honour, as much as the English nation's, that would be compromised in the event of an English defeat. If Northumberland gave his opinion at the Council with one-tenth the exasperation that emerges in his letters, his dissenting speech must have had an electrifying effect. Indeed, it was later reported that the Lord Admiral's boldness before the king was 'not well taken', and that, at court, his having spoken against the dissolution 'will mutch rest ine the King's thoughts [against him]'.[124] Northumberland's intervention seems to have been taken by Charles as an act of disloyalty, one that he would neither forgive nor forget.[125]

Yet it did not deflect the king from his chosen course. With his decision ratified by the Privy Council, Charles departed by barge almost immediately for the Palace of Westminster, barely half a mile away. By mid morning, the king was seated on the throne in the Painted Chamber, explaining his motives for the sudden dissolution:[126]

> I will not lay this fault on the whole House of Commons – I will not judge so uncharitably of those whom, for the most part, I take to be loyall and well-affected subjects, but it hath been the malicious cunning of some few seditiously affected men that hath been the cause of this misunderstanding.[127]

The Parliament, in other words, had been deliberately sabotaged, and in the days that followed, one of the king's chief priorities was to confirm his suspicions as to the identities of these 'few seditiously affected men'.

Whatever the truth of this charge, the failure of the Parliament left Charles's government more vulnerable than any since the Spanish Wars of the 1590s, and more unpopular, perhaps, than any since Richard III.[128] Not a penny had been granted in tax revenues; not a single statute passed. To defeat the Scots, Charles had nothing but an ill-paid and mutinous army, his uncertain credit, and the almost maniacal optimism of Strafford – 'the only parsone ... hopefull of the King's afairs' – on which to rely.[129]

No sooner had the king returned from Westminster after the dissolution than Northumberland convened a meeting of the Committee of War, the Privy Council's eight-man military steering committee, in an effort to make his colleagues confront the consequences of that morning's decision. The Lord General now presented his colleagues with some highly unpalatable options: that they should 'doe nothinge, or to lett them [the Scots] alone', an option that would have been unthinkable within the Council even the day before; or they could attempt the alternative, an option Northumberland seems to have posed with heavy irony: to 'go on with a vigorous warr'.[130]

Various opinions were offered, but the decisive intervention, not least because it offered the counsel Charles craved to hear, was that of Strafford. Broken in body by gout and the regular lettings of blood its treatment entailed, Strafford nevertheless remained indomitable in spirit, and convinced that he would now be the pivotal figure in any campaign. His own Irish forces would be more critical than ever, and the allure of his becoming the saviour of Charles's régime – and the thought of the rewards and influence that would follow – seems to have swept aside any doubts as to practicalities. His speech survives only in a series of rough jottings taken by Sir Henry Vane in the course of the meeting; but the forcefulness of his argument, addressed directly to the king, is still detectable amid the telegraphic abruptness of Vane's hastily scribbled notes:

> Goe vigorously on ... noe defensive warr. Losse of honor and reputacon. The quiett of England will hold out longe ... Goe on with a vigorous warr, as you first designed, loose[d] and absolved from all rules of government, beinge reduced to extreame necessitie, everything is to be done as power will admit – and that you are to do.
>   They [the Parliament] refusinge, you are acquitted towards God and man. You have an army in Ireland, you may imploy here to reduce this kingdome. [I am] confident as anythinge under Heaven Scotland shall not hold out five monthes. One sumer well imployed will doe it.[131]

The force of Strafford's rhetoric – its appeals to honour, its boldness and emotional élan – carried all before it. And it certainly carried the king. From that afternoon, Charles's government committed itself to waging an 'offensive war' against Scotland, one that took the fighting across the border and into the lands of the enemy. Strafford, uniquely among Charles's counsellors, was able to offer the king the conviction that there was a way out of the maze in which he found himself trapped. Strafford had hoped to make the Parliament work; but, now that it had failed – notwithstanding the generosity of the king's offer over Ship Money – he was equally determined to seek other courses. It was the optimistic counsel that Charles had wanted to hear, and ensured that Strafford, not Northumberland, was to be principal strategist of the forthcoming summer campaign.

As to the cost of this campaign – moral, financial or political – Strafford was no longer counting. Strafford belonged to a group at court whose view of politics little room for the veneration of the Common Law or the traditional institutions of English public life. His was a bleak but internally coherent creed in which the monarch's duty to impose peace and order in his realms took precedence over all institutional rights and the subject's 'liberties'; the ruler's duty was to maintain and augment his power, constrained in its exercise only by his care for the good of the realm – a good of which he alone, as a Christian prince, was judge.[132] Parliaments existed, in the first instance, to provide for the financial needs of the monarch; where they defaulted, as had the most recent, their failure emancipated the king to seek revenues by whatever means he could. Charles, Strafford insisted, was now 'loose[d] and absolved from all rules of government'; free to do 'everything ... as power might admit'.[133] The conventional rule of law had given way to the dictates of 'reason of State'.[134]

Yet the most immediate and controversial consequence of Strafford's advice was the decision to forge a military entente with England's traditional enemy: Catholic Spain. Here, too, financial necessity provided the spur. If, as was planned, an army was to be put in the field by June, there was no time to levy exactions in England, even by such arbitrary means as a forced loan. Money had to be borrowed almost immediately, and on a massive scale; and to provide it Strafford turned to King Philip IV of Spain.[135] Strafford had long been associated with the pro-Spanish faction at the English court, and it was little wonder that his advice to the Council of War on 5 May was enthusiastically backed by his fellow Hispanophiles, Archbishop Laud and Lord Cottington, the Chancellor of the Exchequer and a former ambassador to Madrid – both of whom had long been advocates of precisely such a Spanish alliance.[136]

For Northumberland, as for many in the political nation, those decisions of 5 May 1640 constituted a moment of ominous transition. 'Known ways' of counsel and government were being cast aside for expedients which, if successful, threatened to destroy the institution of Parliament and turn the English king into a pensioner of Spain. Whether Strafford's gamble would pay off remained to be seen; but the fact that the king was prepared to countenance so desperate a course revealed a ruthlessness – and a reck-lessness – that many of his Councillors found profoundly disquieting.

Between Northumberland and the king – the great restorer of the House of Percy – the events of 5 May created a gulf that was only to widen in the months ahead. Ever unable to distinguish dissent from disloyalty, Charles henceforth nursed an 'unsatisfactione to the Earl of Northumberland', and an equal coolness towards his friends, 'beleeving them all to be of the same opinions'. Charles's French-born consort, Queen Henriette Marie, went even further, speaking 'lowdly against of [sic] Northumberland' for his opposition to the dissolution.[137] Too grand to be dismissed, the earl retained his posts as Lord Admiral and Lord General, unable to 'beleeve that wise men would ever have brought us into such a straight as now we are in',[138] but thereafter sidelined by the king, humiliatingly, when it came to the formulation of tactics or policy. Strafford supplanted him as commander-in-chief in all but name. In the aftermath of the deliberations of 5 May, the new war became Strafford's war; and Charles trusted him, apparently abso-lutely, to deliver victory.

Yet the king and his inner circle of advisers remained convinced that there were traitors in their midst: those 'few seditiously affected men' whose 'malicious cunning' had been responsible for the Parliament's failure.[139] Windebank, the king's spymaster and the senior of the two Secretaries of State, believed he knew who they were. Before Strafford turned his attention to the rebellious Scots, there was an enemy to confront much closer to home.

The raids began the next day.

I

TREASON IN PARADISE

SUMMER 1640

Then [Jeremiah Burroughes, a suspended minister who was acting as the Earl of Warwick's household chaplain] fell again upon the point of the people's power, [and argued] that they did originallie choose there kinges, and prescribe them conditiones and limited their power by lawes. Then I [John Michaelson, the Rector of Chelmsford] told him this wes not true of the kinges of England and Scotland, who were never elected b[y] the people ... Still he urged the people's power ... [and] [t]hen he began to decline to speake anie more of the King of England, and propound cases of Elective Princes, as of the King of Poland and Duke of Venice, and especiallie of a people going to the West Indies, and choosing amongst themselves a king with limitations. 'Whence has he a power', [Burroughes asked], 'if not from the people?'

John Michaelson, Rector of Chelmsford, describing a conversation with Jeremiah Burroughes in the Earl of Warwick's garden at Leez on 5 August 1638[1]

Sir William Becher appeared at the great gate of Warwick House in Holborn on Wednesday, 6 May, acting on a warrant from the Privy Council to 'seize the person' and search the property of its patrician and troublesome owner.[2] It was an unwelcome assignment. Almost sixty, and a former secretary and protégé of the Duke of Buckingham, Becher had spent a lifetime of diligent courtly service, successfully avoiding controversy, growing steadily richer, and rising – despite suspicions that he was a covert Roman Catholic – to his current modest eminence as a Clerk of the Privy Council. Now, approaching the end of a blameless career, he seemed about to acquire an entirely invidious notoriety.[3] Warwick enjoyed widespread popularity in the capital, and to be the agent of his arrest risked not only the hatred of an increasingly menacing London crowd,[4] but also the future censure of Parliament – if and when it should ever reconvene.[5] It was testimony to the seriousness of the current case, and the status of his prime suspect, that Becher had been instructed to deliver the warrant in person. Of all the 'seditiously-affected men' whom the Council held responsible for the recent Parliament's failure, Warwick was by far the most senior in rank and experience, and the obvious candidate as the dissidents' ringleader.[6]

The search was meticulous. Warwick's study was scoured for incriminating correspondence and other evidence of contacts with the Scots. And in a final, humiliating gesture, Becher compelled the earl to turn out his pockets for inspection, carefully noting their contents and removing a series of suspicious items for further investigation.[7] Further raids were carried out that same day: at Brooke House, also in Holborn, a few yards to the east, where Lord Brooke was also subjected to the indignity of having his pockets searched;[8] and at Viscount Saye's rented lodgings, apparently also in Holborn,[9] where an extensive cache of suspicious-looking papers was also bundled up for perusal by the Council.[10] The key troublemakers in the Commons, known to be associated with this aristocratic cartel – Pym, Hampden, and Sir Walter Erle[11] – were also searched and questioned.[12] The target list was carefully chosen; for, despite their wide disparities in social rank, all six men were part of a recognizable pro-Scottish parliamentary interest (what one Commons-man was later to call 'the precise partie', which contrived matters 'by the[ir] correspondents in both howses'),[13] and shared friendships and common concerns – over the state of the law and the subject's liberties, and the subversion of the English Church by a 'popish' clique – which stretched back well into the 1620s.[14]

In London, word of the searches and the suspicions that provoked them caused a sensation. To Edward Rossingham, the professional newsletter writer, the searches were the major story of the moment, and he correctly supposed that

> this search was made to discover what Scotch papers or remonstrances were in their hands [and] to see whether any correspondences were held between the Covenanters and any of the members in Parliament.[15]

The tale of the noblemen's fate grew in the telling. By the time the news had reached the Leicestershire market town of Lutterworth, once the home of John Wycliffe, all three peers were assumed to be languishing behind bars. One sympathizer, outraged at the reports of their fate, was moved to exclaim that 'The best men of the kingdom – Saye, Brooke, and Warwick – are imprisoned by the King'.[16] This statement later proved to have been incorrect; but it is nevertheless revealing as an indication as to who were regarded, in the aftermath of the May dissolution, as the heroes of the hour.

In fact, what emerged when the peers were forced to turn out their pockets to Sir William Becher was enough to suggest disaffection, but still far short of treason. Warwick was discovered to have records relating to the case of Roger Maynwaring, the Laudian divine who had been impeached and condemned in the 1628 Parliament for preaching that kings were above the law:[17] all of which seem to have been related to moves, championed by Warwick's cousin, Essex, to have Maynwaring's subsequent pardon by the king either censured or overturned.[18] Lord Brooke had a manuscript treatise opposing the Church's established liturgy by the New England Puritan, John Cotton.[19] But the closest the Privy Council came to finding clear-cut evidence of collusion between these peers and the Scots was a document in the pockets of Viscount Saye: a copy of a letter from the Covenanter grandee, the Earl of Rothes, to the king's own Lord Chamberlain, the Earl of Pembroke, justifying the taking of the Covenant – a revelation that can only have enhanced the king's growing suspicion that Pembroke, a veteran of the court and a former favourite of James I's, was now in league with his enemies.[20]

Yet in ordering these raids, the two Secretaries of State, Windebank and Vane, were not acting upon mere surmise. Conclusive evidence of collusion between the English dissidents and the Covenanters seems to have been obtained almost immediately after the Parliament's dissolution. By 5 May, information had been received[21] (later drawn up as a formal deposition) that various Commons dissidents had been holding meetings with 'som or all of the Scotts Comissioners' then in London, including one 'Mr Bartlett'.[22] These Covenanter sympathizers in the Parliament had been planning a dramatic demonstration of their support for the Scots, set for Thursday, 7 May. One of their number, 'conceived [to be] Mr Pimm', was intending to use the Thursday session to table a Covenanter declaration in the House of Commons,[23] and to propose a petition from the Parliament to the king, urging him to a 'reconciliation with ... his subjects of Scotland'.[24] But these plans had to be hurriedly revised. With the souring of the atmosphere in the Commons on Monday, 4 May and the growing fear of a dissolution, the dissidents met that same evening and brought forward their plans to the following morning, Tuesday, 5 May. The Scots' declaration was to have provided the opportunity to debate, and probably to censure, the king's planned campaign against the Covenanters.[25] Nathaniel Fiennes, Viscount Saye's second son, was reportedly ready to move that any money raised through Parliament should be debarred from use against 'their brethren of Scotland'.[26] Had this motion (or one like it) passed the Commons, it would have been tantamount to a declaration of solidarity with the Scots against the king.[27] The entire moral basis of Charles's war would have been destroyed.[28]

The king's primary motive for ordering the Parliament's dissolution appears to have been his belief that the Commons were refusing to fund his war. However, there is strong circumstantial evidence to suggest that the timing of the decision, and the extreme haste with which it was carried through, was prompted by the discovery of the Commons dissidents' negotiations with 'Mr Bartlett' that Monday evening:[29] hence the order to the Commons Speaker, that same night, to prevent the House from sitting the following day; hence, too, the summons to Northumberland and his fellow Privy Councillors to be at Whitehall at 6 a.m. that same morning.[30]* In ordering the dissolution, it is possible that the king believed that he had averted a plan to sabotage his war with Scotland only by a matter of hours.[31] But of the reality of these contacts, between 'som of the howse of Comons'[32] and the Covenanters' representatives in London, the Council had little doubt.

---

* A report by the godly gentleman, Brampton Gurdon, suggests that the Speaker was summoned by the king very early on the Tuesday morning, and taken in the royal barge to the House of Lords, to prevent him taking the chair in the Commons.

'Mr Bartlett' was quickly discovered to be Robert Barclay,[33] the Provost of Irvine, the former tutor and confidant of the Earl of Argyll, the most powerful of the Covenanter nobility. Indeed, Barclay appears to have been operating as Argyll's personal emissary to the dissidents in England, having arrived in London on 12 February 1640, as part of a four-man commission that also included Lord Loudoun, the Earl of Dunfermline, and Sir William Douglas of Cavers.[34] Moreover, within forty-eight hours of the dissolution, the Council had intercepted a letter from another of the Scots Commissioners in London, sent on Tuesday, 5 May, the Parliament's final day, announcing that the Commons 'are *this day* about to petition his Majestie to hearken to a rec-onciliation with you, his subjects of Scotland'.[35] The first question the Privy Council had ready to ask Robert Barclay was: 'Have not some of the House of Comons had frequent conference with you during the tyme of this ... Parliament[?]'.[36] The interrogatories put to Warwick, Saye, and Brooke do not survive, but almost certainly shared the same preoccupation.

Yet Warwick and his fellow suspects were not imprisoned. Perhaps because they had anticipated the likelihood of searches at the end of the parliamentary session, the Council found plenty that suggested disaffection, but nothing that established treason. The suspected pro-Scots Fifth Col-umnists were allowed to go free – not that this stopped Archbishop Laud boasting that 'he had matter Enough [to secure a conviction] against the Lord Say'.[37]

Charles, too, seems to have been confident of his suspects' guilt, and to have regarded their offence in highly personalized terms. For the king, the Scottish campaign of 1640 was a war of self-affirmation against those who doubted his judgement within the court, and of eventual revenge against his enemies outside it. Military victory against the Covenanters, an outcome that he still believed lay within his grasp, would be the prelude to a settling of scores with the English 'traitors'[38] who had worked to undermine him. What he needed was documentation. From the moment that the raids on the houses of Warwick, Saye, and Brooke failed to produce conclusive proof of treason, Charles's spymaster – the crypto-Catholic Sir Francis Windebank – worked assiduously to assemble evidence of the collusion between this network of English dissidents and the rebellious Scots. Known Covenanter sympathizers were placed under surveillance. Suspect correspondence was intercepted and opened by the Council clerks. Gradually, painstakingly, the details of the conspiracy were pieced together.

By the beginning of September 1640, Charles and his immediate entourage had begun to form a detailed picture of the identity and whereabouts of the ringleaders of what, to the king, was clearly a treasonous plot.[39] Then, just as the second Anglo-Scottish war in as many years reached its moment of climacteric, Windebank knew that three of his most wanted suspects – the Earl of Warwick, John Pym, and a dissident cleric, Calybute Downinge, who had just preached publicly in London in justification of a noble-led revolt – were all to be found at an Essex country house, situated a little beyond the end of the Chelmsford Road.[40] By then, however, the moment when the king could have moved against them had already passed.

The spiritual and intellectual odyssey that brought these three men to this pass had begun much earlier, and it is this road to Leez that we must briefly retrace.

I. 'PARADISE'

In the summer of 1640, Leez Priory was a large mid-Tudor house of warm red brick, lying in the gently undulating country of northern Essex, some seven miles due north of Chelmsford. First impressions were then, and remain, deceptive. The two squat towers which flank the gatehouse and the low-slung crenellated ranges to either side give the impression of a prosperous manor house – little more. Only on entering the first, outer, courtyard does the visitor gain an impression of the monumentality of its inner core. Dominating the range to the right was a massive, second, 'great' gatehouse, rising in three lofty storeys – an octagonal battlemented tower at each of its four corners – which provided the entrance to the residential inner quadrangle beyond. The house's private apartments and rooms of state, on the first floor of the eastern and western sides of this court, were large, high-ceilinged and brightly lit, with large six-light mullioned windows looking inwards, on to the court and its central fountain, and outwards, on to the formal gardens adjoining the house, and the parkland beyond. The roofline, like that of Hampton Court, its near-contemporary, bristled festively with stone-capped gables, slender pinnacles, soaring chimney stacks of elaborately worked Tudor brick, and a tall ogee-domed lantern, which provided light and ventilation to the amply proportioned hall. Although most of the house was demolished in 1753, the inner gate tower – as large as the near-contemporary 'Holbein Gate' at Whitehall – still witnesses not only to the scale and magnificence of the original Tudor and early-Stuart house, but also to the power and affluence of its owners: the Riches, Earls of Warwick.[41] With its extensive formal gardens, fountains, and brave Parkes',[42]* Leez was a house on a palatial scale, and as one admiring visitor – the Northamptonshire Puritan, Richard Knightley of Fawsley – quipped, with appropriately godly humour, its owner needed to be sure of his own salvation, otherwise leaving 'such a Paradise ... [would be a] dismal exchange'.[43]

Yet Leez, the rural idyll, was also a monument to an earlier age of religious revolution: Henry VIII's dissolution of the monasteries and the spoliation of the late medieval Church.[44] Its builder – Warwick's great-grandfather, Sir Richard Rich – had been one of the most influential figures in this first phase of reformation, presiding over the dissolution of the lesser monasteries in the 1530s, taking a leading part in the downfall of Bishop John Fisher and

---

* The formal approach to Leez was from the south, via a causeway, over a mile and a half in length, which ran through the great deer park – some five miles in perimeter and enclosing 648 acres. Deer parks were one of the manifestations of aristocratic status in Tudor and Stuart England; and Warwick's was on an imposing scale.

Sir Thomas More, and serving as Speaker of the House of Commons in the final session of the Reformation Parliament, in 1536.[45] Leez Priory, confiscated from the Augustinian Friars by Henry VIII and granted to Sir Robert Rich that same year, was the first of a series of rewards for his service in the destruction of 'popish superstition' that culminated, under the ultra-Protestant Edward VI, with promotion to the peerage, as the 1st Baron Rich, and the office of Lord Chancellor. His grandson, the 3rd Lord Rich, an equally zealous Protestant, purchased an earldom in 1618 in order to maintain his status in James I's much expanded peerage (in which relative parvenus had been advanced to earldoms, thus outranking barons of pre-Stuart creation such as himself), taking the title of 'Earl of Warwick'.[46] And at Leez, the ruins of the great Priory Church, immediately beside the main house, stood as a daily reminder to the 1st Lord Rich's great-grandson – Robert Rich, 4th Baron Rich and 2nd Earl of Warwick – of how directly his worldly prosperity was founded on the destruction of Popery.[47]

Insofar as the network of resistance to Charles I in the summer of 1640 can be said to have had a topographical and moral centre, Leez and its owner were probably where it was to be found. Of course, those who shared Warwick's desire to undo the legal and ecclesiastical innovations of the 1630s included some powerful men – among them, as we have seen, the Earls of Bedford and Essex, Viscount Saye, and, from the younger generation, Viscount Mandeville and Lord Brooke. But while some (like the Earl of Bedford) could surpass Warwick in wealth and lineage, and others (like Saye and Brooke) matched his intellectual acuity and commitment to the cause of reform, none possessed that amalgam of qualities that set Warwick apart: his intelligence and energy, his burning sense of the iniquity of Charles's régime, and, not least, what the Venetian ambassador, Anzolo Correr, termed his 'courage for the greatest enterprises'.[48]

Born in 1587, Warwick's entire youth had been spent in the shadow of Elizabeth's wars with Catholic Spain. The Essex in which he grew up was in the front line of the repeated invasion scares of the 1580s and 1590s; and, like most men of his generation, his image of Popery was formed by the 'black legend' of Philip II's Spain, an evil distillation – in the words of Edmund Calamy, who served as one of Warwick's household chaplains – of 'heresie, Idolatry and tyranny'.[49] Moreover, his mother's family, the Devereux, Earls of Essex, were at the forefront of campaigns against the Spanish 'Antichrist' in the last decades of Elizabeth's reign. Warwick's uncle, the 2nd Earl of Essex, was the self-appointed champion of the strongly Protestant 'military men' at court, and his circle stressed the concept of noble 'virtue' – a public duty to act for the good of the nation as a whole – that found its most dramatic, and perhaps quixotic, expression in Essex's abortive *coup d'état* of 1601: his failed attempt to topple the 'basely born evil counsellors' who had monopolized power, to the exclusion of nobles of 'ancient lineage' such as himself, during Elizabeth's final years.[50] Warwick's values and world-view seem to have remained fixed, almost unchangingly, in the verities of his youth, when England's sea dogs had humbled Spain's armadas, and the trenchant anti-Popery of the English Church had found its complement in the militant Protestantism of royal foreign policy.[51] During the 1620s he invested heavily in 'privateering' ventures – piracy in all but name – against Spanish shipping in the Caribbean, and put money into colonial ventures in the Americas (in Bermuda in 1615, Virginia in 1617–19, and tried to secure control over Barbados, Trinidad and Tobago in the late 1630s). In these, Protestant piety and the profit motive harmoniously combined.[52] In the process, he built up an unrivalled network of contacts with fellow shipowners and colonial investors in London's merchant community – connections that were to be highly useful in the political struggles that awaited him in the early 1640s.[53]

Like many of his fellow-godly, Warwick cultivated an interior life of reflection and prayer, was 'exact' in what his chaplain called 'his closet [or private chapel] duties', and assembled a series of 'religious collections, written with his own hand for the good of his soul' – apparently anthologies of his spiritual reading and reflections – compiled as a means of tracking his progress in his spiritual life.[54] For Warwick and his co-religionists, the experiences of the political world were inseparable from the workings of Providence: that universal and often inscrutable ordering of events and circumstances by which God realized his purposes for the world.[55] Politics, it followed, was almost invariably viewed refracted through the prism of religion. Its transcendent reality was endowed with a commanding, prescriptive force: the ability to determine, at times with absolute clarity, which of various competing options would lead to salvation, and which formed the road to Hell.[56] Within months of the new reign, however, Warwick was at the forefront of a group of English peers (with Saye, again, as his principal ally) who sensed that Charles I and the circle of divines who enjoyed his favour posed a fundamental threat to this Elizabethan and Jacobean inheritance.[57]* To this close quartet of Puritan critics – Warwick and Mandeville, Saye and Brooke – what was at stake was something far more important than the outward forms of worship.[58] It was nothing less than the preservation of Christian truth: the pristine doctrine handed down from the time of the Apostles, defiled for centuries by popish superstition, and only recently reclaimed in its 'purity' by the heroic figures of the Reformation.[59]

The 1630s witnessed a campaign for ecclesiastical change on a variety of fronts, promoted by the bishops with enthusiastic royal support: in the

---

*In February 1626, less than a year into the new reign, Warwick and Saye had tried to enlist the royal favourite, the Duke of Buckingham, to prise the young king away from both the theology and ceremonialism of his new ecclesiastical entourage, the most dangerous of whom appeared to be the king's chaplain, Matthew Wren, and the Bishop of St David's, William Laud, already tipped for major preferment. The resulting York House Conference, two days of theological debate at Buckingham's residence in February 1626, was a decisive moment in the fortunes of both the duke and the Church under Charles I. The duke, anxious not to do anything that would risk his position of favour with the new king, came out decisively in favour of the 'new churchmanship' of Laud and Wren – Charles's preferred position. Warwick and Saye, in consequence, emerged as leading opponents not only of the duke (whom they attempted to impeach in Parliament later that year), but of the entire thrust of Charles's policies for the English Church.

physical arrangement of churches, where the communion table was ordered to be placed at the east end, and surrounded by rails 'altar-wise', in a manner that inevitably recalled Roman Catholic usage; in the conduct of services, where there was a new emphasis on ceremonialism, often at the expense of preaching; in doctrine, in the repudiation of the Calvinism that had been the dominant theology of the Jacobean Church; and in the social position of the ministry, where there was a concerted attempt to improve both the wealth and prestige of the clergy. Although these developments had a variety of origins, in some cases stretching back to Elizabeth's reign, the 'godly' during the 1630s tended to see them all as connected by a single, darkly conspiratorial thread: an attempt to turn back the clock to a pre-Reformation world of doctrinal error and prelatical power.[60] To the godly, many of these initiatives were overtly 'popish'. And to those who had been brought up on the robustly anti-Catholic divinity of James's reign, Rome was not merely an errant Church; it was nothing less than the Antichrist itself, a demonic power in league with the secular tyrannies of Europe, intent on destroying England's true, Protestant religion.[61] Charles, it followed, was either the agent or the dupe of this popish conspiracy. The impact of his policies and those of his archbishop – for which 'Laudianism' is a convenient, if imperfect, shorthand – polarized opinion within the Church. While some rejoiced that the 'ancient glory' of the Church had at last been recovered,[62] many of the self-styled godly despaired that the 'light of the Gospel' was about to be extinguished in England for ever. To men of Warwick's stamp the experience of 1630s England was evidence of diabolical and supernatural forces at work: the agency of Antichrist – or, in Saye's preferred phrase, 'these Mysteries of iniquities' abroad in the world.[63]

Throughout the late 1620s and the 1630s, Leez in Essex and Warwick House in London became the focal points for discreet but sustained resistance to the policies of Charles's régime. Calvinist divines who fell foul of the ecclesiastical authorities – such as Edmund Calamy,[64]* Jeremiah Burroughes,[65] John Gauden,[66] and Obadiah Sedgwicke, all of whom were to come to national prominence in the decade ahead – found employment in Warwick's 'family', safe in the knowledge that their protector's rank and Whitehall connections would generally secure them against persecution by the Court of High Commission.[67] Godly laymen were also drawn to Warwick's houses:[68] for the quality of preaching in his household chapels,

---

* In 1636, Warwick had presented Calamy to the living of Rochford in Essex – the location of the earl's second major country house in the county, Rochford Hall – to protect him from persecution by the Laudian, Bishop Matthew Wren. There Calamy hoped, 'under the Wings of such a Patron, and a quieter Bishop, to have more repose'. But while Calamy enjoyed his freedom from meddling bishops, he found Rochford had 'one of the most unhealthful airs in England', and he prevailed on Warwick to find him a position in London, at St Mary Aldermanbury, in 1639. Their friendship remained strong, however, and as Calamy himself later remarked, 'his Patron did not loose him, but follow'd him to London'. Ever after, he blamed the unhealthful air of Rochford for his recurrent bouts of 'Dizziness in his Head'.

and for what one contemporary called his 'bountiful and Prince-like' hospitality.[69] Some flavour of the subversive opinions to be found in this household emerges in the deposition (part of which is cited at the head of this chapter) made in the summer of 1638 by John Michaelson, the conformist 'Parson of Chelmsford',[70] who visited Leez on 5 August and attended a service in its chapel conducted by Jeremiah Burroughes, who was then acting as household chaplain.[71] What first struck him was the omission – in what was otherwise a *Prayer Book* service – of any prayers for the king or the local bishop. However, it was the conversation he had subsequently in the Leez garden that caused him particular alarm, as Burroughes defended the Scottish Covenant, denied that the king held power 'immediatlie from God', and insisted that all monarchs ruled by contract with their people. 'What', asked Burroughes, 'if the Supreme magistrate [the king] refuse or neglect that which he ought to doe and is necessarie to be done? May not the people give power to some other, to supplie his neglect and defect?' And he went on to discourse on the virtues of elective monarchy, as practised in Poland and in the Republic of Venice, with an enthusiasm that had his interlocutor rushing to report such dangerous opinions to the ecclesiastical authorities.[72]

It cannot be assumed, of course, that Warwick would have endorsed every aspect of Burroughes' political theory; but, as Burroughes himself later recalled, 'my Lord knew all the businesse' and, despite the controversy that the churchman's opinions provoked, Warwick continued to support the embattled divine, seeking his ministrations when he was ill, and evidently granting him legal protection as a 'peer's household servant' (which offered a partial safeguard against arrest).[73] Indeed, Burroughes' place in Warwick's household and the lengths to which his master went to protect him suggest that his views on the contractual and popular foundations of sovereignty, and likewise on the legitimacy of the Covenanter revolt, were broadly representative of Warwick's own.

With varying shades of emphasis, Warwick's circle – those who came to join him in resistance to the Crown in 1640 – shared his general political and religious views. Perhaps his nearest kindred spirit was his son-in-law Edward Montagu, Viscount Mandeville – the heir to the 1st Earl of Manchester – who had married his daughter, Lady Anne Rich, in 1626.[74] Often on strained terms with his Privy Councillor parent, Mandeville found an alternative father-figure in Warwick (who referred to him affectionately as 'good son'), and seems to have used Warwick House as his London base in preference to his father's house in Channel Row, near the Palace of Westminster. Over the years, Mandeville developed friendships with other members of his father-in-law's extended 'family', including Warwick's courtier younger brother, Henry Rich, Earl of Holland, and their charismatic Devereux first cousin, the Earl of Essex, and his political ally, Lord Brooke – both of whom were to assume major roles in the political crisis of 1640–41.

In the context of national politics, these 'Warwick House peers' were never an extensive network – perhaps, at their centre, no more than half a dozen,

or some five per cent of the nobility as a whole.* Moreover, as later events
were to prove, there were important shades of difference, both political and
religious, between them. What gave them a powerful measure of unity in
1640, however, was a broadly shared sense of the nature of 'true religion'
and the 'subject's liberties', and a record of concerted action in defence of
these ideals that stretched back, in the case of most of them, to the earliest
years of the reign.[75]

Despite the intensity of their hostility towards many of Charles's policies,
these were men who realized, during the 1630s, that this was a régime with
which they had no alternative but to deal, and they were probably cleverer
at disguising their true opinions from their contemporaries than seems apparent with the benefit of hindsight. Until the very late 1630s, there was no
breach between the 'court' and what were later called the 'country lords'.
Warwick participated in major court celebrations, taking up the entitlements
of his rank, participating in a masque for Queen Henriette Marie in 1632,[76]
riding (as one of 'the ancient Nobility of England') from London to Windsor
for an investiture of Knights of the Garter in 1634,[77]† and exchanging New
Year gifts with the king until as late as 1638.[78] Warwick was a far more
dangerous and two-faced critic of the régime than Charles realized;[79] in
consequence, he was allowed to retain his post as Lord Lieutenant of Essex,
treading a fine line between public dutifulness and private insubordination.

Bit-parts in court festivities and the often thankless task of local administration were, however, no substitute for the influence and standing that
came with appointment to major public office. And it was here that those
who incurred the king's disfavour paid most heavily, not merely in rewards
denied but also in that still more valuable currency: aristocratic honour.[80] In
a society in which the 'ancient nobility'[81] had a tradition of considering itself
as the *consiliarii nati* – the king's 'counsellors born' – the withholding of
such preferments tended to be regarded not simply as ill fortune, but as a
denial of what, by inheritance and the proper customs of the realm, was
their rightful due. Calybute Downinge, one of the divines who was to find
a refuge at Leez in 1640, was in no doubt about what ought to have been
the ideal: a world in which 'the [e]state of the Nobility, especially taken for
the Council ... were the eyes and ears of the King in public providence and
intelligence ... the watch-towers of the state [upon whom the king] should

---

* They can be identified as Warwick himself; his son-in-law Mandeville; his fellow New-
World investor, Lord Brooke; his cousin, Essex; and, at a slight distance, his courtier
brother, the Earl of Holland, and Holland's own son-in-law, Lord Paget. The Earl of
Bedford, though he employed many of the same figures as did Warwick, notably John
Pym and Oliver St John, seems to have been on far better terms with the régime than the
Earl of Warwick, and lacked the militant 'godliness' that characterized Warwick himself
and most of those in his immediate circle. The contrasts and tensions between their two
households is explored in greater detail in Chapter 3.
† Perhaps significantly, Warwick accompanied a Scot, the 7th Earl of Morton, the Lord
Treasurer of Scotland (1630–36), when the latter was invested as a Knight of the Garter
in May 1634. He was joined in the celebrations by his cousin, the Earl of Essex, and
half-brother, the Earl of Newport.

heap and bestow ... the greatest and highest honours in the state'.[82] Of
course, the golden age that Downinge evoked – when kings heeded the advice
of their great lords and rewarded them accordingly – was largely fictitious;
but in early Stuart England the ideal nevertheless retained a powerful prescriptive force, if only as a critique of the very different practices pursued
by James and Charles.[83]

Perhaps unsurprisingly, a consistent characteristic of almost all the members
of the nobility associated with the resistance to Charles I – and all twelve of
the peers involved in petitioning for a new Parliament in the summer of
1640 – is that they had been consistently debarred from the Privy Council,
from the principal chivalric orders (in particular, the Garter), and from the
major offices of state.

The sense of *dis*honour involved in the exclusion from office was
inevitably intensified, during the 1610s and 1620s, as the perquisites of royal
favour seemed to be dispensed disproportionately by a succession of 'lowly
born' favourites: the parvenu Earl of Somerset and James Hay (later 1st Earl
of Carlisle) in the early years of James's reign, and then Buckingham, the
most egregious of them all, during the 1620s.[84] During the 1630s Archbishop
Laud, though never a 'favourite' in the conventional sense of the term,
nevertheless closely conformed to the parvenu stereotype, as a man of humble
origins who had achieved high office, acquired lordly ways, and become a
far more influential power-broker than most of the secular nobles on the
Privy Council.[85] Resentment of what was perceived as the ousting of the
'ancient nobility' from its proper place in the king's counsels provided one
of several points of common interest on which godly aristocratic critics of
the régime could ally themselves with those whose religion was of a far more
conventional hue. Neither Essex nor Bedford, for instance, was as zealously
'godly' as Warwick, Brooke or Viscount Saye; yet, on a number of issues,
the concerns of the régime's less-than-wholly-Puritan critics overlapped with
those of the aristocratic 'godly': resentment at exclusion from office, the
growing influence of the 'prelatical' bishops within secular affairs, and at the
subversion of the 'subject's liberties' more generally – all of which they tended
to ascribe, with age-old patrician disdain, to the malign consequences of the
king's preference for the counsels of courtier arrivistes over those of his noble
grandees.

Measuring the exact depth of these 'secular' resentments felt by men such
as Warwick and Essex is inevitably a highly subjective task; but we perhaps
get some insight into the attitudes prevailing in Warwick's household in a
tract written by its steward in the 1630s and 1640s, Arthur Wilson. Although
directed principally against James's favourite, the Earl of Somerset (who had
blighted Essex's early career), it is also illustrative of what Wilson – and his
noble patrons – regarded as a larger malaise:

> There was no demand but [Somerset] had it, no fruit but he obtained
> it; whether it were Crowne lands, lands forfeited or confiscated, nothing
> [was] so deare but the King bestowed [it] upon him, whereby his revenues
> were enlarged, and his glory so resplendent, that he drowned the dignity

of the best of the Nobilitie, and eminencie of such as were much more excellent.

These themes were still sufficiently current for this treatise to be printed in 1643, with the pointed subtitle: *The Condition of the State of England.*[86]

II. RESISTANCE DENIED

If such, by the late 1630s, was the condition of England, as viewed from Warwick House and beyond, what avenues lay open to dissident noblemen to do something about it? The history books on which they had been brought up were full of tales of Simon de Montfort, Warwick the Kingmaker, and other heroic aristocratic opponents of despotic monarchs past. In practice, however, in 1630s England the possibilities for any nobleman resisting, still less forcibly changing, any major aspect of the monarch's policies were highly circumscribed. Of course, grandees of Warwick's rank and influence could be difficult and obstructive within their localities (as Warwick had been, for example, over the collection of Ship Money in Essex).[87] They could also influence the formulation of opinion in England's already extensive 'public sphere' – the large and growing audience for political commentary in news, treatises, and works of literature, both in manuscript and in print – through the patronage of like-minded authors, clerics, and pamphleteers.[88] Influence within the pulpit was one area where this group appears to have made a concerted effort to counteract the prevailing churchmanship of the Laudian divines, both by funding 'lecturers' (usually, unbeneficed clergy) and providing them with hospitality and protection within their households.[89] Warwick's house at Leez, for example, was described by one royalist critic as 'the common Randevouz of all Schysmaticall Preachers'.[90] There was no shortage of ways in which dissident grandees could make trouble for the régime; what they could no longer do was to make war.[91]

Here, as in religion, the world had changed markedly in the course of Warwick's lifetime. The dissident nobleman's traditional form of protest *in extremis* – the armed revolt – had ceased to be a viable option in England as early as the reign of James I.[92] True, it was only seventy years since Elizabeth's régime had been seriously threatened by the 1569 Rising of the Northern Earls.[93] But in the forty years since 1600, English society had been comparatively demilitarized, though members of the nobility retained what might be termed a 'military ethos', a belief that service in war was the highest and most honourable calling of the nobleman, which bore only a passing relation, by the 1630s, to their actual experience of battle.[94] Noble arsenals – which, sixty years earlier, had the capacity to arm and equip tens, if not hundreds, of men – now tended to have smaller stocks of weaponry (even if claims that they had been reduced to no more than a few rusting swords and pikes seem to have been exaggerated).[95] England's most recent aristocratic revolt, led by Warwick's uncle, the 2nd Earl of Essex, in 1601, had been little more than an instance of chivalric grandstanding. Almost wholly confined to

London, it had never come close to posing a serious military threat to the régime.[96] Stuart noblemen seemed to have learnt their lesson. Warwick, who was aged around fourteen[97] when his uncle had been beheaded, had seen the grisly consequences of an unsuccessful revolt. As a military option the age of baronial rebellion was dead – though the ghosts of the medieval past nevertheless continued to exercise a powerful influence on the imaginations of seventeenth-century noblemen.[98] To be effective, any future insurrection would need to call upon military resources that went beyond those at the disposal of any one group of dissident peers; and during the 1630s, that contingency was extremely remote indeed – at least until the Covenanters' military successes during the course of 1639. This, in turn, made the prospect of a Parliament all the more important, as almost the one remaining means by which the course of royal policy might be corrected and errant ministers brought to book – provided, of course, that the king could be prevented from dismissing it before its reforming work was done.

The evils consequent upon the 'long intermission' of Parliaments were resented in many places in England during the 1630s, but arguably nowhere more passionately than in the household of the Earl of Warwick.[99] And while most bore their resentment in deferential silence, Warwick eventually decided to make a public stand. In January 1637, he confronted the king in person and, in presenting the case for a Parliament, advocated a wholesale reorientation of royal policy. In one of the most extraordinary altercations witnessed at court during the entire reign, Warwick stood before the king to denounce the illegality of Ship Money, to urge him 'to make war against the [Habsburg] House of Austria' for the recovery of the Palatinate, and to promise that if Charles 'meant to maintain the dominion of the sea by force' – that is, to declare war on Spain[100]* – then

> he, Warwick, ventured to promise for all [the nation], and to stake his head, that Parliament would readily consent to supply him with all that he might desire to ask of it ... [There was] no point which he did not touch on and no consideration which he did not advance in order to induce the king to summon Parliament.[101]

Perhaps what is most striking about Warwick's intervention is the extent to which he presumed to speak for the broader political nation – in effect, offering to act as the 'undertaker' for the next Parliament: the nobleman of pre-eminent standing and influence who could broker the necessary deals

---

* Something of Warwick's boldness in attempting to manage a de facto foreign policy, almost independent of the Crown, emerges in a holograph letter from Warwick to Cardinal Richelieu, sent around March 1636, in which Warwick offered himself and his private fleet to Louis XIII, for service in a naval war against Spain. The idea resurfaced, in the spring and summer of 1637, in a scheme, canvassed within the Privy Council, for Charles I to lend fourteen royal ships to a fleet commanded by the Elector Palatine, intended to prey on Spanish shipping. Warwick was involved in this proposal, too, via the Providence Island Company, which promised to contribute to the venture.

over the redress of grievances in order to see that the Crown was provided with supply. The assumption of this role does not seem to have been a matter of chance (or bluff). In urging the summons of a Parliament, noted the Venetian ambassador, Anzolo Correr, Warwick was speaking 'practically [as] the chief' of his 'followers'.[102] And when the king, 'smiling and composed', politely refused Warwick's request, a number of the 'leading men of the realm' were reported to have met secretly and decided 'to draw up a paper which many will sign, to be handed to his Majesty in the name of all, with an open request for the convocation of Parliament'. The identity of these 'leading men' of the realm involved in this petition is unknown, but the clear implication of Correr's despatch is that their initiative was made in response to the royal rebuff to Warwick's plea.[103] If so, the most likely subscribers would have been Warwick's inner circle – Essex, Mandeville, Saye, and Brooke – and their powerful if slightly more distanced ally, the Earl of Bedford.[104] For the moment, nothing further was heard of this 'paper for the convocation of Parliament' – perhaps because its supporters regarded the petition's rejection by the king as an almost foregone conclusion. Yet the possibility of a petition was not forgotten within Warwick's circle, and, as we shall see, the proposal was to re-emerge, first in 1638 (when it was again stillborn),[105] and again, in a far more assertive form, during the summer of 1640, with Warwick once again cast in a central, organizing role.[106]

So long as the king could evade the summoning of the legislature, however, there was only one forum remaining in which royal policy might be openly called into question: the courts of law; and it was here that the members of the Warwick House group seem to have turned, as a last resort, after the king's rejection of Warwick's call for a Parliament at the beginning of 1637. Their calculation appears to have been a straightforward one. If prerogative exactions such as Ship Money could be declared illegal by the judges, Charles would have had little alternative – come the next military crisis – but to convoke the Lords and Commons, however reluctantly, in order to fund the defence of the realm.

Paradoxically, the failure of the Saye–Hampden legal challenge – and, still more, what it revealed about the state of the contemporary judiciary – only served to intensify opposition to the levy and obstruction towards the régime.[107] The undermining of the judiciary's independence had been going on in a variety of subtle ways since the Stuarts' accession, not least by rewarding compliant judges with peerages and high office at the end of their time on the bench.[108] Hampden's case, however, had seemed a moment of fundamental redefinition. With the majority of the judges succumbing to government pressure to find in favour of the Crown, their compliance appeared to mark the moment when the 'lions under the throne' had been transformed into the lapdogs of the royal prerogative; and the judiciary's submissiveness looked likely to become even greater as the older judges died off and were replaced by biddable Caroline appointees.[109]

If these developments caused widespread anger and dismay, none felt their implications more acutely than did Warwick and his fellow 'godly'. For the ongoing debasement of the law looked likely to foreclose almost their last option for reversing the debasement of true religion: the summons of a Parliament. By upholding the legality of Charles's expedients for raising money on the royal prerogative in Hampden's case, the judges effectively freed the king from most of the financial constraints that might otherwise have impelled him to call a Parliament.[110]* In doing so, they therefore deprived the godly of the one forum in which they might have hoped to call Laud and his fellow 'popishly affected' prelates to account. Only by means of a Parliament, and the fiscal and legal pressures it could bring to bear, might they hope to rescue what remained of the 'true religion' within the English Church. These interconnections between legal, ecclesiastical, and even financial concerns, should caution us, in our search for motives, against trying to compartmentalize any one of these concerns too rigidly, and, still more, against attempting to regard 'religious' and 'constitutional' concerns as somehow alternative modes of explanation. In the eyes of the Warwick House group, as to many of the 'godly', the threats of Popery, prerogative finance, and the suborning of the law were so closely interrelated in Caroline England that it is almost meaningless to consider any one in isolation from the others.[111]

*

By early 1638, then, the last avenues for challenging royal policy by legal means seemed to have been foreclosed. Faced with the apparent impossibility of internal reform, their response was not to rise in rebellion but to make a dignified retreat. The time had come to leave the familiar world of the shires and to create, in a place almost unimaginably remote, the 'godly commonwealth' that had hitherto eluded them in England.[112] Warwick, Saye, and Brooke had been the leading figures in the foundation, in 1630, of the Providence Island Company.[113] This business venture originated as a project to colonize a small island in the West Indies (with modern-day Colombia to the south and Nicaragua to the west) and attracted a series of Puritan notables as co-investors – among them John Pym (the lawyer who worked almost exclusively as a man-of-business for Warwick and Bedford), the Yorkshire gentleman Henry Darley (a close friend of Lord Brooke, who served twice as the company's deputy governor), and Warwick's secretary William Jessop.[114] By 1635 (and perhaps earlier), Saye and Brooke had begun to consider the feasibility of emigrating to their colony in Connecticut.[115] In early 1638, however, these tentative plans seem to have altered to a firm resolve, with a much larger group, now including Warwick and Darley,

---

* These concerns about the implications of 'prerogative finance' for the future of Parliaments can be traced back within this group at least to the mid 1620s. At the time of the Forced Loan of 1626, for example, John Holles, 1st Earl of Clare, wrote to Viscount Saye, lamenting that 'we gallopp all to the overthrow of Parliament, and consequently to that of the state ... : I speake to a good patriott, and therefore more freely, [for] the way [of raising money] by privy seales [i.e. forced loans] and [compulsory] benevolences is so easy, and that of Parlaments so conditionall and uncertayn, as nothing is more in thought then their abrogation [as] a diminution of monarcall power'.

coming around to the view that only in the New World could they ever realize the 'godly commonwealth' that Charles's benighted rule made impossible in England.[116]

And yet something, apparently at the last moment, induced them to abandon their plans for retreat, and resolve instead to fight a new series of battles at home. What brought about this change of heart is unknown; however, the timing of the postponement – coming shortly after they received news of the Scottish rebellion and the signing of the Scottish National Covenant – is highly suggestive.[117] Events in Scotland in early 1638 heartened the godly throughout England, and it is unlikely that Warwick, Saye and Brooke were untouched by the hopes to which the Covenanter revolt had given rise. Even so, that these three noblemen *ever* seriously contemplated emigration perhaps reveals something of the depths of their despair at the state of 1630s England.[118] A seventeenth-century nobleman's rank, authority and sense of self-image were intimately tied to place and locality: to his family seat, the church that contained the tombs of his ancestors, the network of local patronage and neighbourliness that were the expression of his status and power. For Warwick and his friends to abandon all this was, in a sense, to renounce most of the trappings that defined their identity and position in the world. Only the bleakest expectations of England's future could have made that renunciation, and the perils that awaited them in the New World, seem a preferable, even attractive, alternative to 'the current state of England'.[119]

If these plans reveal a measure of desperation, they also attest to a willingness to take grave, if calculated, risks. On this point, at least, Charles and Windebank had guessed correctly. The dissident English peers *had* discerned an opportunity in the Covenanter revolt: the possibility of an internal challenge to Charles's régime, which, however fraught with danger, offered a nobler course of action than withdrawal to either the jungles of Providence or the forests of New England.

III. COVENANTERS AND COLLUSION

In fact, by the time Sir William Becher raided Warwick's study in May 1640, in the hunt for evidence of collusion with the Scots, contacts between the leading English dissidents and the Covenanter leadership in Edinburgh already went back at least half a decade. A number of godly gentlemen in London – including Warwick's man-of-affairs, Sir Nathaniel Rich, and Sir Philip Stapilton – were in contact with their 'brethren' in Scotland in the mid 1630s.[120] However, the key figure in these early links was Sir John Clotworthy, an adoptive Ulsterman and investor in the Londonderry plantation who had fallen foul of Lord Deputy Wentworth (the future Earl of Strafford). The brother-in-law of Warwick's part-time man-of-business, John Pym, Clotworthy seems to have been in touch with this godly circle at least since 1635.[121] In June 1638 he travelled to England to supplicate the king on behalf of the Londonderry tenants against the policies of the Lord Deputy, routing his journey via Edinburgh, where he met with one of the senior figures in the Covenanter revolt, Archibald Jhonston of Wariston, on 11 June.[122] On reaching London he provided Jhonston with a series of partly coded despatches on Charles's plans to suppress the Scottish revolt, and, after making contact with the aristocratic dissidents in England, sent encouraging reports to Edinburgh of their new-found optimism – a confidence directly prompted by the Scottish revolt.[123] Clotworthy reported their plan to form a group in England to petition for the summons of a Parliament – which, as we know from the Venetian archives, had first come together at the time of Warwick's confrontation with the king the previous year.[124] Clotworthy also explained to Wariston why nothing had come of it then: though others approved of the idea in principle, only two peers – 'you may guess who they are' – had then been prepared to make a public stand. And although the two are unnamed in the letter, the most probable candidates are the familiar duo of Warwick and his Holborn neighbour, Lord Brooke.[125] Yet, events in Scotland had given them new heart, and the lords who had planned to emigrate to the New World – a group which, as we have seen, comprised Warwick, Saye, and Brooke, and the Yorkshire gentleman Henry Darley – had now suspended their 'foreign designs' until they had seen the outcome of the resistance in Scotland. Two prominent lords (again, possibly Warwick and Brooke), Clotworthy reported, might even opt to find their 'America in Scotland'.[126]

Unsurprisingly, we only have the occasional fragments surviving of what was a much larger (and doubtless highly incriminating) correspondence. But, it is clear that these initial contacts, set up by Clotworthy, soon developed into direct exchanges between the Edinburgh leadership and the leading dissident peers. By February 1639, Sir Thomas Hope of Craighall was noting in his diary that Viscount Saye and Lord Brooke were the chief 'intelligencers [or providers of information] to the Scots'. Hope, moreover, was in a position to know. Like Jhonston of Wariston, he had been a draftsmen of the National Covenant of 1638 and, as Lord Advocate of Scotland, one of the central figures in the Edinburgh administration ever since.[127]

Ironically, the Scots seem to have turned to Warwick and his allies initially, not because they believed they had identified a group of would-be rebels, but because they believed that they had located a potential source of moderating influence at the Whitehall court – with Holland and Mandeville (Warwick's brother and son-in-law, respectively) regarded as the likeliest brokers on their behalf.[128] The Covenanters' first attempt to exploit this influence came in the summer of 1639, when Charles's attempts to put down their 'rebellion' had ended in stalemate, and both sides had drawn back from engaging their forces, opting instead, for a negotiated peace.[129] The Scots needed allies who would be ready and willing to plead their cause, and, by June, were actively canvassing for support in England.

In that month, a letter was drawn up by the Covenanter leadership for circulation among potential allies within the English peerage (the list for which may well have been provided by their 'intelligencers', Saye and Brooke), inviting 'the Englisch Nobilitie' to take control of the impending negotiations.[130] Probably drafted by John Campbell, Lord Loudoun – the kinsman and chief ally of the Earl of Argyll[131] – the letter asked the Scots' allies among the 'Englisch Nobilitie'

> that it may be insisted [upon] by your lordships that, if it is possible, by a meeting in some convenient place of some prime and well affected men to the reformed religion and our common peace, matters may be accomodat[ed] in a fair and peaceable way.[132]

Insofar as men such as Mandeville and Warwick were regarded as politically useful,[133] it seems to have been in providing the Covenanters with the entrée to the Earl of Holland, the Groom of the Stool and Lieutenant-General in the 1639 campaign, who was the major advocate within the Privy Council of a negotiated settlement with the Scots.[134] 'God forgive them [within the Privy Council]', Holland had written to Mandeville in July 1639, 'that thus doe advise our master [the king] to spoyll and distroye this honourable and happy accommondasion' with the Covenanters.[135]*

Nor was Holland the only senior courtier who had been drawn into the Covenanters' orbit. By February, the pro-Scottish peers were also in contact with Thomas, Viscount Savile – like Holland, one of the king's Gentlemen of the Bedchamber – and he appears to have been instrumental in setting up a further conduit of communication between the Covenanter leadership in Edinburgh and their patrician, London-based 'friends'. Having evidently cleared the proposed arrangements with Lord Brooke, Savile met in London with the Scottish merchant and Covenanter supporter, James Stewart of Kirkfield, to persuade him to allow Gualter Frost, one of Brooke's household servants, to pose as the Scottish merchant's servant in his journeys up and down the Edinburgh road. Savile prevailed, and over the following months – including, it would seem, the period of the Parliament of April–May 1640 (what later came to be known as the 'Short Parliament') – Frost carried letters to and from the Covenanter leadership, allegedly hidden in a hollow cane.[136]

Even so, none of these contacts seems to have had any overtly seditious, still less treasonous, intent. A memorandum drawn up in Edinburgh on 30 April 1640 by Jhonston of Wariston – a week before the Short Parliament's dissolution – makes it clear that the desires of the Covenanters in relation to their English parliamentary 'friends' were limited to using them as lobbyists in favour of a negotiated settlement to the Scottish crisis. Their 'friends' were

---

* There may well have been an international dimension to Holland's impatience with those who obstructed a settlement with the Covenanters. For the group at court that hoped the king would eventually adopt a far more interventionist role in the contemporary conflicts within the Holy Roman Empire – a group that included Northumberland and Leicester, as well as Holland – it must have been profoundly frustrating that the king was squandering his kingdom's limited military resources on an internal British quarrel, between fellow Protestants, when he was doing nothing to check the Catholic menace on the European mainland.

to press for the release of Lord Loudoun (the Covenanter Commissioner to London whom Charles had imprisoned in the Tower), and to persuade their fellow Parliament-men that the Scots had no hostile intentions towards England.[137] That was all.

Likewise, a letter from Jhonston of Wariston, also written on 30 April and addressed to a 'particular friend in the parliament [possibly Warwick]', took a similar line. It exhorted their English allies to prevent either England or Scotland going the way of Ireland and becoming a conquered nation. But, once again, the emphasis was on 'fair terms for intercession with our prince' and the avoidance of war, not on any concerted attempt to undermine the régime.[138] As this was essentially the Earl of Holland's line within the Privy Council, such collusion as there was between the Warwick House peers and the Scots during the Short Parliament seems to have had been directed towards strengthening the anti-war party at court.[139]

Insofar as the expectations of Warwick and his allies at the end of the Short Parliament can be divined, two outcomes seem to have been regarded as most likely. First, that the king's now chronic shortage of funds would render the aggressive war policy of the Council's (mostly Hispanophile) hawks untenable. And second, that this would shift the balance of power at court towards the conciliar 'doves': towards Holland, the prime advocate (as we have seen) of a negotiated peace; and towards Northumberland, the chief proponent of abandoning the war effort once it had become clear that parliamentary supply would not be available for its funding.[140]* Either way, by intensifying the financial pressures on the régime, and making a successful campaign against the Scots ever less likely, the peremptory dissolution can only have been welcome news to Essex, Bedford and the dissidents at Warwick House. St John's reportedly upbeat reaction to the Parliament's failure offers a clue to the dissidents' reactions more generally: 'All was well', he allegedly declared, within an hour of the dissolution, for 'it must be worse before it could better'.[141]

Yet not even St John could have anticipated how much worse, and how promptly, it became. At court, the winners by the Parliament's failure were the Council's hawks. Instead of opting for compromise, Charles chose a course which, though it had been rumoured darkly as an option during the last days of the session, few seem to have believed was a serious possibility:

---

* Within days of Northumberland's appointment as the army's commander-in-chief, in February 1640, he had taken the extraordinary step of writing to Mandeville – then one of the most notorious of the Covenanter sympathizers – *apologizing* for his failure to appoint Mandeville to a command in the forthcoming campaign. 'If my new imployment were not against *our brethren in Scotland,*' Northumberland wrote, 'I should hope that your Lordship would accept of some commaund in the army. But this Generallship will, I feare, utterly ruine my reputation, and make me [to] be thought almost as greate a reprobate as any Bish[op]. But I shall not much consider that so long as I may still continu[e] happie in your good opion, which no man doth more esteeme.' Few moments witness more clearly to the fragility of the Personal Rule by 1640 than the sight of Charles's Lord General writing to a known ally of the king's enemies, and doing so to denounce the very war that he was about to fight.

a total repudiation of the 'Protestant Cause' and the forging of an alliance with the most iniquitous of all the papist 'tyrants'. To fund his war against Scotland, Charles, it seemed, was about to become the pensioner of King Philip IV of Spain.

*

Some 'popish plots' were flights of fevered Protestant fancy. This one, for a change, was real, and it received active encouragement from the Earl of Strafford. Within a week of the Parliament's dissolution, the Lord Lieutenant had turned – with Charles's clear approval – to the Spanish ambassadors in London, the Marqués de Velada and the Marqués Virgilio Malvezzi, to broker both military and financial aid for the king's impecunious régime. The extent of Strafford's concessions emerges clearly in Velada's correspondence, surviving in the Brussels Archives Générales du Royaume. Strafford offered two key concessions: a military alliance between England and Spain against the Dutch, and permission for Velada to recruit 3,000 men in Ireland for service in the armies of Spain.[142] It was also probably relevant that the English navy – if given sufficient inducement to intervene – could help to secure Spanish supply routes to Habsburg-held Flanders, against the depredations of the Protestant Dutch.[143] In return, Spain offered a loan of £300,000: enough, with the subsidies already promised by the Irish Parliament, to fund the forthcoming Scottish campaign. Of course, there had been earlier moves towards a rapprochement with Spain, but these had almost invariably been justified as a means of obtaining Spanish mediation in favour of the Elector Palatine. This new alliance, in contrast, was without any extenuating benefits for the wider Protestant cause.[144] Its purpose was quite straightforwardly financial. Papist gold would be used to fund a war, on Charles's side, against his Scottish Protestant subjects, and, on the Spanish side, against Protestant rebels in the Netherlands.[145]

Despite Strafford's efforts at secrecy, most, if not all, the details of the treaty were known at Westminster in May 1640, within weeks of the Parliament's dissolution. The Venetian ambassador, Giustinian, reported that the 'Puritans and others' were claiming that Spain had bribed Charles to 'break' the Parliament;[146] and these claims seem to have been made credible by the tactless boasting of the Spanish ambassadors themselves that they had money available for use against the Covenanters.[147]

The existence of this treaty was to have a series of far-reaching consequences, and nowhere more clearly than in the factional balance at court. In foreign policy terms, the English court had been polarized for more than two decades along lines that roughly paralleled the combatants in the Thirty Years War. On one side was a Hispanophile party, which saw the interests of European Protestantism as being best served through the pursuit of a rapprochement with Habsburg Spain – a policy that conveniently avoided any need for the summons of a Parliament. On the other was a rival group, closely identified with Northumberland and Holland, which broadly supported Richelieu's France, since it was aligned with the Protestant, anti-Habsburg interest in the German states.[148] This Francophile faction was regarded as pro-parliamentary, since the English naval and military intervention on the Continent that it argued for could not be financed except with parliamentary funds. Unsurprisingly, the dramatic reorientation of royal policy towards Spain in the days following the May dissolution made the Hispanophiles more dominant than ever, with three Privy Councillors – Strafford, Laud, and Charles's Scottish-born favourite, the Marquess of Hamilton (a trio that was, in Northumberland's phrase, 'as much Spanish as Olivares') – consolidating a virtual monopoly over the formulation of royal policy.[149]* Indeed, his expectation of the Spanish loan seems to have been the basis for Strafford's almost manic (and otherwise inexplicable) optimism about the viability of Charles's war effort, throughout the period between May and July. On the other hand, those who wanted to avoid the war (such as Northumberland), and who were already under suspicion for their opposition to the Parliament's hasty dissolution, found themselves ostracized by Charles more than ever before.[150]

Beyond Giustinian's claims that the Puritans were blaming the Spanish for Parliament's dissolution, we have no contemporary record of the reaction among the Warwick House peers to the news of the Spanish treaty. But it can be readily surmised. The fact of the treaty negotiations spoke for itself. Charles – or so it appeared to most of the zealous 'godly', if not necessarily to all Protestants – was prepared to enter a league with the 'Popish Antichrist'.[151] And, of course, in entering into a treaty with Spain against the Protestant Dutch, he and Strafford were signalling England's final abandonment of the Elector Palatine (then a prisoner of the French)† and the wider German Protestant cause. The likely impact on Warwick, who, three years earlier, had berated the king for *not* coming to the aid of the Dutch and the forces of the Elector Palatine, is not difficult to imagine.

Against this background, Archbishop Laud, Strafford's major ally over the Spanish Treaty, embarked on the imposition of a new series of Canons (the doctrinal and ceremonial formularies for the English Church produced during the recent Convocation), further strengthening the impression that there was a popish conspiracy to subvert the kingdom's 'true religion'. Controversially, these included provisions upholding Charles's divine right in the face of Scottish resistance, and enjoining an oath upon all clergy, requiring them to disavow any attempt to alter 'the government of this church' by bishops – a measure that was clearly designed to flush out any Covenanter sympathizers within the ministry.[152] Once again, it seemed that Laud was exploiting the structures of the Church – and its roughly 9,000 pulpits the length and breadth of the country – to affirm a highly tendentious reading of the extensiveness of the king's prerogative powers.

The plausibility of these threats in the eyes of the godly – the twin perils

---

* The Conde-Duque (or Count-Duke) de Olivares was the chief minister of the Spanish king, Philip IV.
† Charles Louis, Prince-Elector of the Palatinate, had been arrested, on Cardinal Richelieu's orders, while travelling through France in October 1639; he was not released until August 1640, partly in response to diplomatic pressure from England.

of tyranny and Popery – in the weeks following the dissolution of the Parliament needs to be stressed, for in hindsight it is all too easy to assume that, once Charles had committed himself to another war without the backing of Parliament, the downfall of his régime was somehow fore-ordained.[153] That was not how it appeared in May and June of 1640. Were the king to acquire his Spanish subsidies – as 'the Puritans' in the Short Parliament believed he was likely to do – the suppression of the Scottish revolt might yet be feasible. And, if that were done, Stuart government would most likely enter a new and altogether far more authoritarian phase. Strafford, insistent that the king was now 'loosed and absolved' from the rules of government, would be the dominant figure in the royal counsels. And Laud's 'popish influence', his power further enhanced by the new Canons, looked set to be even more pernicious within the Church. Of course, by midsummer, the arrival of Spanish aid was beginning to look extremely unlikely. But here, too, the lateness of this realization is worthy of emphasis. It was only after news of a revolt against Philip IV in Catalonia reached England in early August that the likelihood of Spanish gold arriving in time to be of use was thrown seriously into doubt.[154] Until then, it seemed that Strafford's policy of a new war against the Covenanters might yet end in victory for the king.

*

Of course, in the preparation for this campaign, there was much that went wrong. 'The whole kingdome', Northumberland confessed to his sister, the Countess of Leicester, in July 1640, 'conspires ... in preventing our intended journie into Scotland'.[155] Of the several conspiracies that threatened Charles's régime in the summer of 1640, this was certainly the most broadly based, and revealed in the slowness with which Deputy-Lieutenants responded to royal commands to levy troops; the obstructiveness of muster masters; the blind eyes that were turned by local magistrates to militiamen who either absconded or failed to appear. To be effective, English government depended in large measure on the broad consent of the governing class, and by the high summer of 1640 it was clear that in many parts of the country this consent was being obviously withheld.[156]

Yet, for all Northumberland's midsummer gloom, the ineffectiveness of the régime's call to arms should not be overstated. It is testimony to the resilience of Charles's government that, within some eight weeks of North-umberland's remark, it succeeded in putting a large, if relatively poorly equipped, army into the field – estimated, by one observer, to be 32,000 strong – notwithstanding the parlousness of the royal finances and the with-holding of parliamentary funds.[157] Even to Viscount Saye, no well-wisher to Charles's cause, the royal army of 1640 seemed 'much stronger than [the Scots'] and better armed';[158] and while this, too, is probably an overstatement, what nevertheless seems clear is that the response to the mobilization, though dilatory and often resentful, was far more successful than naysayers such as Northumberland had earlier predicted. Despite serious rioting in London and Southwark in the aftermath of the Parliament's dissolution in May,

England in the summer of 1640 was not yet on the point of anarchy, nor its government on the brink of collapse.[159]

The perils that confronted it were daunting nevertheless.[160] In 1640 it was no longer the case that Charles could ensure the survival of his régime by simply avoiding an outright military defeat, as he had done the previous year. He could not allow the existence of a 'rebel' government in Scotland, acting almost wholly independently of Whitehall, to continue indefinitely without fatally undermining his prestige – the 'honour', without which seventeenth-century kingship was unsustainable – in his other two kingdoms.[161] The king either had to go on to the offensive and impose his rule in Scotland by force, as Strafford advised; or he needed to come to some face-saving settlement with the Covenanters, which removed the need for war by satisfying at least part of their demands. The first of these options, the military route, was fraught with hazard, as everyone except the king and Strafford seemed prepared to concede; even if the king avoided defeat in open battle (as he had done successfully in 1639), any extended stalemate on the Scottish border was likely to place demands on the northern English counties and his own near-bankrupt Exchequer that neither was likely to be able to meet.

However, the second possibility, a negotiated settlement, remained a viable option for far longer than, in hindsight, it is often assumed. Neither side had ruled out a compromise that avoided war, and throughout May and June, the Marquess of Hamilton, the king's former viceroy in Edinburgh, and Lord Loudoun, the senior Covenanter representative in London, worked towards an Anglo-Scottish peace that might yet avert a clash of arms.[162] Indeed, at least until late July, there was the possibility that the mobilization in England might actually aid this eventual outcome, by strengthening Hamilton's hand. Nor was Charles wholly opposed to this route. In public, of course, he remained insistent that he would never dispense with episcopacy in Scotland. In reality, as the Earl of Holland (who was in a position to know) noted as early as 1639, the king was likely to concede their abolition (as he eventually was to do in 1641), provided the overall settlement preserved his remaining powers in Scotland more or less intact. Of course, any negotiated settlement with the Scots was likely to create almost as many problems as it solved, for, if Scotland's Covenanter majority could throw off the bishops imposed on the Scottish Church by James I and return to a Presbyterian Kirk, might not Ireland's Roman Catholics, the majority of the population, demand the same freedom of worship for themselves?[163] Such collateral dangers were clearly inherent in the Anglo-Scottish negotiations of late spring and early summer 1640. But they were not an insuperable obstacle to an eventual deal, if only because, from Charles's perspective, with the Scottish problem settled once and for all, there was every likelihood that any Catholic insurrection in Ireland could be relatively easily contained.[164]

Developments in Scotland also increased the probability, in the early summer of 1640, that negotiation might yet prevail over outright war. Divisions had begun to emerge within the Covenanter leadership in Edinburgh over the wisdom of a renewed war against England. A substantial body of opinion within the Committee of Estates (the Covenanters' Edinburgh-based

executive) regarded any large-scale incursion across the Anglo-Scottish border
as entailing unacceptable risks. In an 'offensive strategy', many more things
could go wrong, and an unsuccessful campaign against Charles I had the
potential to jeopardize all that had been achieved in Scotland since the
beginning of the Covenanter revolt. Moreover, beyond these differences of
opinion over practicalities, there were ideological divisions about what the
National Covenant actually meant and what it was that its subscribers had
sworn to defend.[165] With some of the more radical Covenanter nobles, particularly those associated with the Earl of Argyll, rumoured to be talking of
deposing the king, suspicions were beginning to be voiced that such men
regarded the Covenant as little more than an opportunity for realizing their
private ambitions.[166]

These divisions boded well for the avoidance of an Anglo-Scottish war.
And if the king could achieve that outcome, then another meeting of the
Westminster Parliament, the one body that *could* seriously challenge his
existing style of rule, might yet be deferred. Indeed, it might not be necessary
to convene it for many years to come.[167]

*

What thwarted these expectations, and in so doing drastically shortened the
odds on the survival of Charles's régime, was a shift in the balance of opinion
within the Edinburgh Committee of Estates: gradually, and in many ways
unexpectedly, during June and July, this altered in favour of an all-out invasion
of England. By early August the advocates of a conservative, defensive strategy
had been definitively overruled. Scotland was about to embark on an offensive
war.

The belief, in the event mistaken, that financial constraints would prevent
Charles from mobilizing an effective army doubtless provides part of the
explanation for why the Covenanter leadership came to believe that this
strategy was worth the risk. Offers of military support from Sweden for the
new Covenanter régime also helped tip the balance in favour of an offensive
war.[168] But the most powerful inducement to action seems to have been that
Charles's government looked vulnerable as never before. Military weakness,
however, was only one component of that vulnerability. In contrast to their
experience in 1639, the Covenanter leadership in 1640 found the prospect
of an invasion actively encouraged, indeed directly requested, by a potentially
powerful group of English allies. In support of a Scottish invasion, these
English 'friends' (as they were discreetly termed by the Covenanter leaders)[169]
offered to destabilize the régime from within: to provide a clear public voice –
and, if necessary, military leadership – for the forces of internal dissent.

It would seem, then, that it was something close to desperation, not a
sense of predestined victory, which impelled Warwick, Saye and their allies
to reconsider their relations with the Covenanters.[170] Neither Warwick nor
any of his allies had the arms and militarized tenantry required in order to
emulate the Scots and mount a military revolt of their own. Of course,
this did not mean that they were wholly bereft of military resources. Lord
Lieutenants of the counties commanded their county militia forces, the

Trained Bands, and there were to be a number of points in 1640 when, as we will see, the Privy Council believed that these were more likely to support the dissident noblemen who were their commanders than be obedient to the orders of Whitehall.[171] Yet, if this provided a potential means for a noble-led mobilization (a potential that was eventually to be realized in the summer of 1642), in 1640 there were still too few Lords Lieutenant among the dissidents' allies to make this a viable strategy.

What the dissident English peers could do, however, was to bring the Scottish revolt into England. If the Covenanters could be persuaded, not just to defend their borders, as in 1639, but also to advance their army deep into the North of England, Warwick and his allies might then be in a position to compel the king to summon a new Parliament. There was but one awkward detail. To invite a foreign army into England was treason, and so defined by the Treason Act of Edward III. By the late spring of 1640, however, Warwick and a small group of fellow 'godly' noblemen had decided that was a risk worth taking. Whatever their ultimate motive, at some point around this time Warwick and his principal allies – Mandeville, Saye, Brooke, Pym and Henry Darley – ceased to be mere apologists and intermediaries for the Covenanters. By late June they had begun to make detailed plans for a Scottish invasion of the North of England.[172]

iv. TREASON

Although the earliest references to a common strategy come from the Covenanter leadership in Edinburgh, it is apparent that these were made in response to 'promises' from the English peers, made earlier via Loudoun, offering friendship and support.[173] Loudoun – conveniently close to hand as Charles's prisoner in the Tower, where he remained until 27 June 1640[174] – once again provided the point of contact between the Warwick House group and the Covenanter leadership in Edinburgh. The instigators of these contacts in May are unnamed, but their identities are clearly established in the papers exchanged between the two sides in late June, which list Warwick, Mandeville, and Essex, together with Warwick's long-standing friends and business partners Saye and Brooke, and the Earl of Bedford. Only one of the seven, Viscount Savile, appears not to have been an intimate of the worlds of Leez and Warwick House.[175]

In Edinburgh, the Covenanter leadership's first response to these requests for joint action was to demand some form of public commitment from the dissident English nobles that would irrevocably tie their fortunes to the Covenanters' own. Jhonston of Wariston came up with two possibilities. Writing to Loudoun on 23 June 1640, he suggested that the disaffected English peers should be moved to join in a defensive league 'as that in 1585' – a reference to Lord Burghley's Bond and Act of Association of that year to defend England in the event of a Spanish-backed, pro-Catholic coup.[176] The alternative, Jhonston suggested, would be for the English peers to send one of their number to join in leading the Scottish army of invasion on its march into England – an open act of rebellion from which there could be no turning back. The Scots also wanted a cast-iron assurance that their English 'friends' would make a public declaration in their favour, 'after our Entry [into England,] according to their [earlier] Resolutions and Promises'. Loudoun, still in London, was to obtain that assurance not later than Friday, 10 July, a deadline that gave the English peers just under a fortnight in which to consider, and despatch, their response.[177]

Some time around the end of June,[178] therefore, Warwick and his six fellow conspirators – his cousin, the Earl of Essex, his son-in-law, Viscount Mandeville, together with Bedford, Saye, Savile and Brooke – put their names to a letter assuring the Scots of their willingness to act in concert with them, and to share the obvious risks.[179] This was directed through Lord Loudoun, the kinsman and client of the Earl of Argyll, for wider circulation;[180] and, though it is impossible to corroborate, the early-eighteenth-century lawyer and antiquary, Roger Acherley (who had access to documentary sources since lost), offered a plausible list of recipients: namely Argyll, Jhonston of Wariston, and Argyll's ally and protégé, the Earl of Rothes (who was soon dealing with Bedford and Warwick on a daily basis as one of the Scottish Commissioners to London).[181]

Their ultimate aim, the seven dissident peers protested, was 'all one': 'a free Parliament to try all Offenders, and to settle Religion and Liberty, and to make our abus'd King more great in Goodness than they [his evil counsellors] have made him unhappy in Ill'.[182] But the English peers drew back from the Scots' requests that they should give a solemn undertaking (by 'Covenant'), even before their invasion, to join the Scots army (as the Covenanter leadership had evidently demanded) with 'Horse and Foot, and Men, and Money, and Credit', pointing out that it was 'absolute Treason by our Law of England to be of Council for the bringing in of any foreign Force'. Warwick and his confederates also stopped short of promising to join the Scots at the head of their army, as Jhonston of Wariston had suggested in his letter of 23 June. Maintaining the legal and moral high ground was essential to the success of their cause, dissident English peers insisted; they therefore had to avoid any unequivocal gesture of solidarity that would enable Charles to accuse them of treason – and in so doing hand a major propaganda advantage to their own and the Scots' common enemies.[183]

But Warwick and his allies emphasized that their Covenanter friends would not be disappointed by the alternative tactics they had in mind: 'we are resolv'd to do more, and more effectually, for obtaining [your] and our honest Ends than either [you] can expect or desire, but it consists in so many Particulars as it cannot well all now be recited'.[184] The exact meaning of this phrase may well have been explained to the Covenanter leadership by the letter's courier. However, a clue to what the dissident peers had in mind is contained in a question they posed towards the end of their letter: 'may not a Prince be as easily won to do his Subjects Right by a just Expostulation of his Nobility and Subjects in an opportune Season as well as in an unlawful Convention?'[184] Warwick and his friends seem to have been drawn back to the option, first discussed (and eventually shelved) in January 1637, of a public petition to the king, demanding the summons of a Parliament.[186]

If Savile's own account is to be trusted, he carried the dissident peers' letter from London as far as Yorkshire, during the first week of July, before forwarding it to Lord Loudoun (whom he had met in London the previous week and who had only just returned to Edinburgh). He enclosed it in a covering letter of his own. In this missive, the authenticity of which seems beyond doubt,[187] Savile amplified and explained a number of the points in the seven peers' letter, providing detailed intelligence on the weakness of the garrison at Carlisle, the king's first line of defence against any invasion directed down England's western seaboard, and assuring the Scots that there were numerous Fifth Columnists in the king's army. In particular, Savile mentioned 'a Regiment of Foot [which] … will turn to you [the Covenanters]' – a plausible claim, as one of the regimental commanders was Sir John Meyrick, a devoted friend and member of the household of the Earl of Essex (himself a signatory of the letter of invitation to the Scots). Meyrick had accompanied Essex on campaign against the Spanish in Flanders in 1620, and actually lived in Essex House.[188]*

The key undertaking to the Scots, however, was that

> their Persons [i.e. Warwick and his six fellow signatories] are mutually engag'd, one to another, upon the first Assurance of your Entry into the Kingdom, to unite themselves into a considerable Body, and to draw up a Remonstrance to be presented to the King, wherein they will comprize yours and their own just Grievances, and require a mutual Redress.[188]

Yet, this 'Remonstrance', as Savile termed it, planned in the summer of 1640, would be different in one crucial respect from other addresses to the king: it would not be merely a petition of grace (*requesting* action of the king), but a petition of right (a formal declaration of pre-existing legal entitlements, albeit couched in the outwardly deferential form of a petition).

On this score, the dissident peers were evidently the beneficiaries of the antiquarian researches of the petition's reported draftsman, Oliver St John, the friend of Warwick, in-house lawyer to Bedford, and counsel for Saye and Hampden in the Ship Money case of 1637.[190] St John had discovered that

---

* Meyrick, who was born around 1600, was descended from a family that had been intimately involved in the affairs of the Devereux dynasty for at least two generations. His uncle, Sir Gelly Meyrick, had been the steward of the 2nd Earl of Essex's Welsh lands and had been executed for his part in the 'Essex Rebellion' of 1601. Sir John was in Swedish service in the early 1630s, and later resumed his friendship with the 3rd Earl of Essex. He was returned to the Parliament of April 1640 as a knight of the shire for Staffordshire as a result of Essex's patronage, and the long-standing relationship continued in 1642 when Essex appointed him his deputy (with the rank of Sergeant-Major-General) as commander-in-chief of the parliamentarian army. Meyrick named his son, Essex Meyrick, in his patron's honour. If there was any officer in the king's army in 1640 whom Essex could rely upon to side with the dissident peers and their Scottish allies, it was this man.

the Oxford Parliament of 1258 – the Parliament that enacted the 'Provisions of Oxford' imposing a permanent baronial council on Henry III – had also 'erected the twelve peers' authority': a power vested in twelve noblemen to summon a Parliament in their own name where the king failed to do so.[191]

For Warwick, Bedford and their allies, these powers had an obvious relevance to their predicament in the summer of 1640. If these thirteenth-century baronial powers could be effectively revived, they would provide them with an alternative to the 'illegal Convention [i.e. a Parliament]' that the Scots had suggested in their approaches in June. Provided Warwick, Bedford and their initial core of supporters could bring their number to twelve, the precedent of 1258 would enable them to present the king with an ultimatum: either he called a new Parliament (which was the peers' declared objective in their correspondence with the Scots) or, should he refuse, they could go beyond the Scots' original suggestion and summon a Parliament of their own.[192]* Where the Scots were indispensable to the plan was that, if the king initially refused the petition from the Twelve Peers, demanding the summons of a Parliament, the Scots could provide the military leverage required to make him comply. There was even the option, now backed by the precedent of 1258, that if he still proved obdurate, the Twelve Peers might issue the summons themselves.[193]

This appears to have been the undertaking on the part of the Scots' English 'friends' that shifted opinion decisively in favour of invasion within the Edinburgh Committee of Estates. Indeed, by mid July 1640 the 'friends' were pressing for the invasion to take place at the earliest possible opportunity. At least part of this information was successfully intercepted by Secretary Windebank. At the end of July, the governor of the border town of Berwick, Sir John Conyers, obtained a letter sent from an unnamed Covenanter to his fellow Scot, Sir James Douglas, explaining that the Scots were making rapid progress in their preparations, 'because their party in England sends daily intelligence to their General [Alexander Leslie] to hasten his coming'.[194] Scottish troops were later reported to have stated 'universally, with one voyce, that they were sent for, to invade ... by their Friends in england, and some say the Lords in the sowth sent for them'. This was allegedly put even more robustly by General Leslie's secretary, who swore: 'The Devil take my Soule ... if our good Friends in the South did not send for us and promise us assistance'.[195] Such evidence, of course, needs to be treated with caution, for it was a standard line of the extensive propaganda campaign that preceded and accompanied the Covenanters' invasion of 1640 that they had come as godly 'friends' rather than as ancient enemies.[196] Even so, the readiness with which these Covenanter troops identified 'the Lords in the sowth' as the source of the invitation to invade attests to the currency of the belief within

---

* It is noteworthy in this regard that, within less than a year of this discovery, the right of twelve peers to summon a Parliament on their own authority had been given statutory force by the Triennial Act of February 1641.

the Scottish army, and tends to corroborate the evidence for collusion between the two sides which is available elsewhere.

Nor should these Scots protestations of 'friendship' and common purpose with their English allies be dismissed as mere propaganda, aimed as masking the 'nationalist' agenda that was supposedly inherent in the broader Covenanter cause. The political culture of the Scottish élite in the mid seventeenth century was characterized by a strongly cosmopolitan outlook, and the motives for intervening to effect reform in England, at least within the circle of the Earl of Argyll, the most influential of the Covenanter advocates of intervention,[197] sprang not from some simple proto-nationalist desire to 'Scotticize' the southern kingdom, but from a belief in the possibility of creating a new, exemplary civic society within the two British 'Common-wealths' (as Argyll was to term them):[198] unified by a Calvinist Protestantism, treating the two realms as equals (and hence rejecting Charles I's perceived 'subordination' of Scotland to the dictates of Whitehall), and intent on the moral transformation of all the peoples of the Stuart kingdoms, under a powerful, godly, aristocratic leadership.[199] As we will see, the aspiration towards British 'Union' was to acquire an almost mystical significance in the politics of 1641.

This was a vision of the transformation of the British kingdoms[200] that Warwick and his allies could – and in the event did – embrace.[201] In seeking to bring it about, their desire for Leslie to 'hasten his coming' had a clear strategic objective. By the end of May, the postponement of the royal army's general rendezvous, formerly planned for 10 June, to mid August, was common knowledge.[202] If the Covenanters' offensive could be launched well before Northumberland's army was mobilized and deployed in the North, they could secure an advantage that would make possible a swift (and, ideally, unopposed) advance deep into the North of England. Newcastle, the strategically vital port on England's north-east coast, was their prime objective, not least because it controlled the coal supply to London and the South. Once Newcastle was taken, Warwick and his fellow conspirators expected the Scots to wait, again avoiding, if possible, a set-piece battle with the king. If that much could be achieved, then, as Viscount Saye was to put it, 'their staying in Newcastle would give their friends [the dissident peers] opportunity to ... obtain their desire much better – sooner, and with more safety to them[selves] – than if by showing forwardness to shed English blood, [the Scots] should have incensed [the people against them]'.[203] Public opinion in England was fickle. Warwick and his allies seem to have realized that whatever measure of sympathy existed for the pro-Covenanter cause at the start of the campaign was unlikely to survive if there were a military engagement involving heavy English casualties. Hence, the 'daily intelligence' from the English rebels, intercepted by Conyers on 30 July, urging the Covenanter general to make haste.

These encouragements appear to have produced results. On 3 August, four days after Conyers had intercepted the incriminating letter, the Committee of Estates decided unanimously that the planned invasion of England should take place immediately. Revealingly, in their letter to the king's Scottish Secretary, the Earl of Lanark, giving notice of the forthcoming invasion, the

Committee of Estates declared that their purpose in crossing the border was not to wage war but to present the king with 'petitions'.

v. INVASION

The first Scottish forces, cavalry units commanded by the Covenanter Earl of Montrose, crossed the border into Northumberland at Cornhill-on-Tweed on Monday, 17 August 1640. The formidable commander of the Scottish army, Alexander Leslie – a veteran of Gustavus Adolphus's campaigns who had fought at the battle of Lützen – followed three days later with the bulk of the army. The baggage train included 5,000 cattle and 10,000 sheep, evidence of the Scots' concern not to alienate the English by living off the country as they advanced.[204] The declaration issued by the Scots on their entry into England stated that they had no hostile intentions towards the English people, but were acting to defend their religion and liberties from the government of Charles I.[205] Blame for any ill consequences that followed, they insisted, lay with king; it was he, 'misled by the crafty and cruel faction of our Adversaries, who began this war, not we'.[206]

Initially, the Scots encountered no opposition. Despite numerous warnings of an impending invasion, the sheer speed of the Covenanter advance took Charles's military leadership almost completely unawares. Any effective English response was prevented, not only by the delays in the royal army's recruitment and supply, but also by Northumberland's sudden withdrawal from active command, allegedly on the grounds of illness, just as the Covenanter army was poised to strike. While Northumberland's illness appears to have been genuine (malaria has been suggested as the cause),[207] its timing was nevertheless highly fortuitous, particularly when viewed in the light of his earlier correspondence with Mandeville, privately expressing his distaste for the war. There was no doubt as to who would fill his place. Charles immediately turned to Strafford, naming him as Lieutenant-General – nominally Northumberland's subordinate, but for all practical purposes the army's commander-in-chief. To improve the army's morale and to take an active part in military decisions, the king decided to go to the front in person, leaving London for York on 20 August with such haste that he had 'noe provisions' for such an extended journey.[208] Strafford, despite being scarcely less debilitated from illness than Northumberland, took steps to secure the capital, before he left for the front, by placing control of the Tower of London in the hands of Lord Cottington, one of the Privy Council's leading Hispanophiles and crypto-Catholics.[209]

But it was far too late. The Covenanter army had advanced deep into the North long before the king's ill-provisioned party ever reached York. Only now did the full, catastrophic implications of Strafford's Spanish alliance begin to appear. While Swedish supplies reached the Covenanters, evading an incompetently maintained royal naval blockade of Scotland's east coast, the gold that had been promised to Strafford by Velada and Malvezzi failed to arrive. The revolt against Philip IV's rule in Catalonia, which had broken out on 7 June, had compelled a reappraisal of Spain's earlier undertakings to England. The funds and materiel which Philip had once earmarked for assisting Charles against the Covenanters were now required for the suppression of rebels of his own.[210] The £300,000 that Strafford had counted on to pay for Charles's second Scottish war would now never arrive.[211]

In the absence of Spanish assistance, the result of Charles's August campaign was the fiasco that Northumberland had foreseen. Viscount Conway, the senior military commander *in situ* when the Scots advanced, had less than half the 22,000 troops that he had been promised to defend the North. Faced with the impossibility of defending the border, he was forced to withdraw to the line of the Tyne, the river that marked the boundary between Northumberland and County Durham. In consequence, Leslie's Covenanter army marched through Northumberland unopposed. On 27 August Leslie's forces reached the Tyne at Newburn, a ford across the river a few miles from Newcastle. Here, on the most unpropitious of ground, Conway attempted to halt the Scots' advance.

Newburn's topography provided the Scots with a massive advantage. A higher north bank, where Leslie deployed the Scottish artillery, dominates the ford. Flat, low ground stretches away from the south bank on the other side. Here, on 28 August, with only a small fraction of the king's total forces available for deployment in the field, the battle was fought to its predictable conclusion. The unopposed play of the Scottish cannon caused havoc among Conway's infantry, most of whom turned and ran. His cavalry bravely tried to engage with the Scots as they crossed the river; but, outnumbered and outgunned, they too were forced to retreat. The English defeat turned into a rout.

*

The English dead at the battle of Newburn numbered twenty-six cavalrymen and three hundred infantry. By the standards of the contemporary German wars, the entire engagement was little more than a minor skirmish. Yet the consequences of this one small battle were wholly disproportionate to the tally of the dead. In the immediate term it rendered Newcastle, which could not be defended from its southern side, an easy prey for the Scots. Conway foresaw the inevitable and withdrew his garrison on 30 August, abandoning the city to the Covenanters without a fight. This was arguably the key event of the war. In taking Newcastle, the Covenanters had secured control of the London coal trade; and with winter approaching, they were therefore in a position to cut off the capital's major source of fuel. Moreover, with Newcastle in their hands, the Covenanter army was free to move south to occupy County Durham, which was now undefended in the wake of Conway's retreat.[212] In the short term, at least, further military resistance to the Scots by Charles's forces appeared to be an impossibility. As Strafford summed up the situation disconsolately to Sir George Radcliffe on 1 September, 'the country from Berwick to York [was] in the power of the Scots, an universal affright in all'.[213]

The political implications of Newburn were even more immense. It spelt defeat for Charles's attempt to Anglicize Scotland by force: to impose his imperial vision of 'nearer conformity' with England on a resistant population. More important, Newburn revealed what some court insiders, such as Northumberland, had been beginning to realize since the start of the year: that the Scots had become an effective force – an interloping fourth estate – in the politics of Stuart England. The greatest beneficiaries of the victory, however, were Warwick and his immediate allies: that small, noble-led coalition which had been instrumental, either wholly or in part, in persuading the Covenanter army to invade. With Newburn, Warwick and his allies acquired the power-base that was the *sine qua non* of an effective opposition, and in so doing massively enhanced their capacity to influence the future course of Charles's régime. No longer was the king the 'sole effective source' of power within England.[214] For the first time since the rebellion against Richard III in 1485, there were rival parties, each with large-scale military resources on which to call, on foot on English soil.

2

THE FIRST REVOLT

SEPTEMBER–NOVEMBER 1640

> The king [had no] cause to fear the power of the Scots, would the
> nobility and power of England have ingaged with him; but he quickly
> saw what he might expect (and what the Scots knew well enough, and
> did prudently, to wait for) by that Petition, which the noble men sent
> from London to him, and which was seconded by the desires of the citie
> and whole kingdom: . . . it was the very hinge upon which all our affairs,
> for the good of both kingdoms, at that time turned about.
>
> Viscount Saye and Sele, writing in 1646[1]

On Tuesday, 1 September 1640, the street in front of Whitehall Palace
reverberated to the sounds of war. Carpenters and stonemasons were making
adjustments to the 'gun platform' in the corner where the Banqueting House
abutted the palace's Privy Gallery range. Detachments of soldiers were hauling
artillery pieces called 'drakes' into position here and by the palace gate. Still
others were taking up position at the palace's approaches and around the
Great Court within. The royal residence was being turned into a 'garrison'
for the first time in its century-long history.[2] Further down-river, at the Tower,
the scene was similar. New platforms were being constructed for the mounting
of ordnance, and, to the noise of picks and shovels, new earthwork defences
were being constructed to screen the fortress's ancient walls from the power
of modern artillery.[3] In the City, chains were being erected across the major
streets to impede the movement of any rioters or attackers,[4] and the Lord
Mayor and Aldermen were urged to have forces, drawn from the City's
militia, 'for their own defence, whensoever they shall have warning'.[5]

Yet these precautions were only indirectly the result of the previous week's
invasion, and the Privy Council, which ordered them, had no expectations
that the Scottish army would ever present itself outside London's dilapidated
medieval walls. These were measures to defeat an imminent English, not a
Scottish, rebellion; against an internal, not an external, enemy. Of course,
the Council had been jittery about the capital's security ever since the disorders
which had followed the 'breaking of the Parliament' and Maytide riots that
had seen a full-scale assault on Lambeth Palace.[6] These, however, had been

essentially plebeian disturbances, mostly 'prentices and seamen',[7] and lacking 'links to the gentry or parliamentary élite'.[8] This new threat, however, was of an entirely different order. For the first time since the Essex Rebellion of 1601, the Privy Council confronted the possibility of a large-scale insurrection within London itself – and, with it, the danger that a metropolitan revolt might light the touchpaper for risings elsewhere. The Council prepared for the worst. As early as Wednesday, 26 August, it was pondering whether Windsor Castle might 'be not a place of more safety than Hampton Court' as a place of retreat.[9] By the following Sunday it had decided that it was. Whitehall was abandoned for Hampton Court, with the option of a further remove to the fortress at Windsor, a few miles up-river, if and when the insurrection actually occurred. For the skeleton staff of Councillors left in the capital to carry on the king's government, the days that followed were some of the tensest in the entire reign. On 5 September, Secretary Windebank confided his fears to the king's ambassador in Madrid: 'I hope in God we shall overcome this danger, which I believe the greatest that had threatened this state ever since the [Norman] Conquest'.[10]

Fey, slippery, and self-important, Windebank had a taste for melodrama in moments of political crisis.[11] But for once his anxieties were fully shared by the rest of his Council colleagues.[12] There were two prime causes of this nervousness. One was the generally fractious state of London, where the Council suspected there was widespread sympathy for the Covenanter cause, partly connived at by the City magistracy.[13] The second, and the more dangerous, was the recent appearance within the capital of most of the leading aristocratic critics of the Personal Rule – the Earls of Warwick, Essex, and Bedford as well as Lords Saye and Brooke, and Hampden and Pym. Windebank informed the king that 'these have had their meetings, and the Lords [of the Council of War], as they have reason in this distraction of your Majesty's affairs, do much apprehend it for some dangerous practice, or [to hold] intelligence with the Rebels of Scotland'.[14]

There had been a series of meetings at Warwick House in the months since the dissolution of the Parliament in May 1640, notionally to transact business of the Providence Island Company; but, given those involved, it seems unlikely that these discussions were confined exclusively to colonial ventures in the Caribbean. The list of those gathering at Warwick House reveals a familiar group of activists: Warwick, Saye, Mandeville and Pym on 7 May (immediately after all four men had been searched by the Privy Council's agents); Mandeville and Pym a week later (14 May); and Mandeville, Saye, Brooke, and Pym (16 May).[15] There is then a pause until mid-June, by which time there seems to have been agreement between the two sides on a plan for a Scottish invasion of England by way of a pre-emptive strike, before the king's army could be properly mobilized. Just as the contacts with the Scots were renewed at the end of June, this 'Warwick House circle' was again convening with unusual regularity: Warwick and Pym met on 19 June; Warwick, Saye, and Pym on the 20th; Warwick, Mandeville and Pym, on the 25th, and the same trio again the following day, by which time they were likely to have received Jhonston of Wariston's letter of 23 June.[16]

Perhaps the conversation of which one would most wish to have a transcript, however, is that which took place between Warwick and Pym – again at Warwick House – on Tuesday, 25 August, by which time both men certainly knew that the Scots army had crossed the Tweed and entered England (on 17 August). Presumably by this time, too, Pym, Warwick and the leading dissident peers were putting the final touches to their 'Remonstrance', already promised to the Scots in the event of their crossing into England, and which was to be signed by Warwick, Mandeville, Brooke, and nine other noblemen three days later.[17] Indeed, it was this 'Remonstrance', news of which reached the Privy Council in the last days of August, that caused the Board its greatest concern. If extensively backed within the City, this had the potential to destroy the entire moral basis for the king's current military campaign – the pretence, already strained to near-breaking point, that Englishmen were at one with their monarch in their determination to repel the Covenanter invasion.

*

On Sunday, 30 August Windebank informed the king, then with the army in Yorkshire, of the latest developments in the capital. With a courtier's practised obsequiousness, he asked for royal instructions while simultaneously suggesting to his master what those instructions should be:

> If those discontented Lords should have an intention to join in a petition to your Majesty, as it is doubted [i.e. suspected] they will, I do humbly beseech your Majesty to consider what you will have done to prevent or divert it. If they could be handsomely dispersed, it might be of singular advantage to your Majesty's service.[18]

Windebank's notes of the Committee of War's meeting the following day provide some clue as to what he regarded as the source of concern. In these jottings, two observations are juxtaposed. In the main text is a memorandum: 'To give accompt to His Majesty of the Lords being in Towne and of the dangerous consequence of it'; and, in the margin: 'The City mustering'.[19] Each of these apparently unremarkable occurrences was ultimately linked to the Scottish invasion, and the background to both needs to be examined if we are to understand how close England came to civil war in the late summer of 1640.

I. MANIFESTOS

The peers who gathered in London in the last week of August that year – and whose presence Windebank found of such 'dangerous consequence' – had one simple purpose. News of the Covenanter army's invasion of England would have reached Warwick, Bedford and the other peers in league with the invaders probably not later than Sunday, 23 August; and in the course of the following week they moved urgently to honour their pre-invasion promises to the Scots.[20] As Lord Savile, one of the leading conspirators in

Yorkshire, had earlier explained to Lord Loudoun, once they had 'the first Assurance of your Entry into this Kingdom, [they were resolved] to unite themselves into a considerable Body and to draw up a Remonstrance to be presented to the King, wherein they will comprize [the Covenanters'] and their own Just Grievances, and require a mutual Redress'.[21] This was precisely what Warwick, Bedford, and their allies now did. By the end of that week in which they received news of the Scots army's 'entry', the Remonstrance – what Bedford and Warwick termed 'a just Expostulation in an opportune Season' – had taken its final form, couched in the ancient form of a Petition of Twelve Peers, demanding the summons of a Parliament.

The idea of public petitioning by the nobility had come a long way since the time of Warwick's confrontation with the king in January 1637, when only two peers had been prepared to offer their public endorsement to such a course. By the last week of August 1640, support for a petition demanding a Parliament had reached the legally and symbolically critical number of twelve – the number required to invoke the precedent of 1258, permitting the noblemen subscribers to summon a Parliament on their own authority.[22] Accordingly, on Friday, 28 August, buoyed by the news of their Scottish allies' success, Warwick and Bedford met with other fellow dissidents in London – at Bedford House, at the western end of the Strand – to approve a final version of the Petition of the Twelve for submission to the king.[23] Windebank's spies provided him with a list of at least some of those present. Apart from Warwick and the meeting's host, the Privy Council's 'intelligencers' noted the presence of the Earl of Essex, Viscount Saye and Lord Brooke – who seem to have constituted the Petitioners' inner core. These were joined by Hampden, Pym and Bedford's eldest son (although, not being peers, none of these actually signed the Petition).[24] But there were others, unnamed by Windebank's informants, for whom there is evidence to suggest that they were probably also present at the Bedford House meeting of 28 August. The Earls of Hertford, Bolingbroke and Mulgrave are all recorded as having been in London for a meeting of the dissident peers around this time. And it can safely be assumed that Viscount Mandeville and Lord Howard of Escrick (the two peers chosen to courier the final version of the Petition to the king) were also present in town during this same week.

Once it had been signed by the Twelve, Mandeville and Howard of Escrick set out for the journey northwards, arriving at York, the King's headquarters, by 3 September.[25] In the meantime, the Petitioners remaining in London maintained a deliberate silence. No copy of their manifesto was published in the capital, and even the news of its imminent presentation to the king was kept secret.

Contemporaries made major claims for the historical significance of this Petition. To Viscount Saye, one of the original Twelve, its emergence was the pivotal moment of the entire crisis of 1640: 'the very hinge upon which all our affairs, for the good of *both* kingdoms, at that time turned about'[26] – though it may be objected, given his own involvement (and predisposition to vanity), that this was a predictable exaggeration. Saye's assessment, however, is also supported by others, including men of a very different

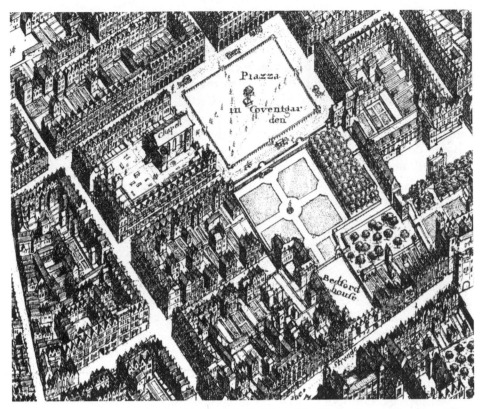

Bedford House: the setting for the signing of the Petition of the Twelve Peers. A large, rambling, late-Tudor mansion, Bedford House and its extensive formal garden were set on the north side of the Strand – the main east–west route connecting Westminster and London. To the north, during the 1630s, the 4th Earl of Bedford had created an entirely new residential *faubourg* to plans by Inigo Jones, with a gigantic open 'piazza' (the modern-day Covent Garden Market) at its centre, modelled on the Parisian Place Royale of 1612 (later renamed the Place des Vosges). The new development's chapel (modern-day St Paul's Covent Garden) is clearly visible to the left of the image.

political stamp from his own. Peter Heylyn, Laud's devoted chaplain and protégé, later argued, for instance, that it 'threat[e]ned greater danger to the King and Church, than either the arms of the Scots, or the Tumults in Southwark [the anti-Laudian riots of May that year]'.[27] And this sense of the 'dangerous consequence' of the Petition emerges clearly in Secretary Windebank's manuscript notes recording the contemporaneous response of the Privy Council.[28] The seventeenth-century historian of the conflict, Gilbert Burnet, records a story (which cannot be dismissed out of hand) that Strafford regarded the Petition as so 'favourable to the Enemy' that he obtained a private resolution from the Council of War that Lord Howard of Escrick (who delivered the Petition of the Twelve) and Lord Wharton (one of the additional signatories to the Petition[29] and a suspected organizer of the Yorkshire dissidents) 'should be Shot at the Head of the Army, as Movers of Sedition', an outcome that was only averted when more temperate counsels prevailed. It was pointed out to Strafford that to attempt an execution would be to risk a 'Mutiny and, probably, Revolt' by the army.[30] Whatever the truth of this last claim, the extensiveness with which the Peers' Petition was regarded as 'dangerous' by contemporaries prompts an obvious question: how could a mere petition, a document cast in the forms of outward deference, constitute a more hazardous threat than the Covenanter army, still less be the turning point – the 'very hinge' – of 1640?

Part of the answer seems to be that their Petition was intended from the outset to be something far more assertive than its innocuous title might imply. Always destined for eventual publication, the Petition seems to have been conceived, not as a supplication to the king, but as a defiant political manifesto, the rallying point for a prospective party. From the Petition's first appearance on the streets of London, its signatories made no secret of the fact that they intended to act: if the king declined to hear their plea, then 'they protest[ed] that they will summon it themselves [presumably on the precedent of 1258], to the end that they might save their country still greater troubles'.[31]

The petition offered a comprehensive indictment of Charles's government over the previous decade – what one Privy Councillor, on eventually seeing it, described as a 'heap of complaints'.[32] The whole kingdom, the Petitioners claimed, had 'become full of fear and discontents' as a result of the current war; and they went on to itemize the 'great distempers and dangers now threatening the Church and State'. The catalogue of misrule was a familiar one: innovations in religion; the 'increase of popery'; Ship Money; commercial abuses, such as monopolies; and 'the great grief of your subjects by the long intermission of Parliaments' and the premature dissolution of such as had met. Only a new Parliament, the peers declared, could cure the kingdom's ills and bring their 'authors and counsellors' to a 'legal trial and condign punishment'. The malefactors were not named, but the nature of the complaints clearly entailed the initiation of impeachment proceedings against Strafford at the very least, and almost certainly against Laud as well. The challenge to the king was fundamental. Charles, who was notoriously prone to regarding attacks on his counsellors as slights against his own kingship and 'honour', was being asked to give up his most loyal servants to 'condign punishment' – the severity of which was unspecified, but, given the gravity of the charges, there was a strong presumption that this meant death.[33] Still more controversially, the king was being asked to abandon his war against the Scots in what he regarded as mid campaign – despite all that such an abandonment would entail: the humiliation of defeat; the renewed charge that revenue had been squandered, as in 1639, to zero gain; and the almost certain end to the years of Personal Rule.

These were not requests to which Charles was expected to accede voluntarily. Quite apart from the king's known aversion to Parliaments, it was almost inconceivable that he would ever willingly submit his principal Councillors to parliamentary trial and punishment. If the king *were* ever to agree to such demands, it would only be because he had succumbed to the threat of insuperable force; and it was this menace – the precise source of which remained uncertain – that so frightened Windebank in the last days of August. Even before the Petition was published, the reports of its existence seemed to be linked directly to the threat of an imminent insurrection in London, possibly a noble-led *coup d'état* to be launched during the forthcoming muster of the City's militia forces, planned for early September.[34] Hence, the garrisoning and strengthening of Whitehall and the Tower, and the Privy Council's withdrawal to Hampton Court.[35] Comparison between the Council's reaction to this new threat and its earlier response to the Maytide riots, which followed the Parliament's dissolution, is instructive. Confronted then with the violence of a 'rude rabble', the Council had stood its ground.[36] Now, assailed by this new challenge, a threat from within the governing order itself, it chose to run.

Windebank's suspicions that the dissident peers were currently involved in plans to stage some form of military coup against the government seem to have been well founded. Seasoned campaigners like Warwick and Bedford knew Charles I well enough to realize that the king was unlikely to respond to persuasion alone. Military force thus formed a central element of their plans; and, while their Covenanter allies were obviously expected to lead the initial assault on Charles's forces, the Petitioners also laid plans in the late summer of 1640 for the creation of an English army which, if necessary, would act in conjunction with the Covenanter Scots.[37] This, the boldest element in the Petitioners' strategy, can be documented in the letters which Bedford and the Petitioners' supporters exchanged with the Covenanter leadership during the week immediately following the Scots' victory at Newburn. The core of this English rebel army – so Bedford and his Petitioner allies assured the Scottish leadership – was to come from dissident elements within the king's army, augmented by other disaffected officers from the county militias: '9 regiments commanders have given ther words,' wrote Bedford and others around 5 September, and '9 coronells of the trained bands hes declared [that] they will join with [us] upon [our] declaration'.[38] By combining disaffected elements from the king's own army with dissident elements in the county Trained Bands, they planned to create a force which, they had agreed, would have the name 'the armys for the comounwealth': this would be an English rebel army that could be used, as a last resort, to 'rescue' the king from his evil counsellors in the name of the commonwealth.[39] As we will see, this was not the last time that the word 'commonwealth' would be appropriated to designate a political interest, and a potential source of legitimacy, that was wholly distinct from the person of the king.[40]

These claims are difficult to verify, but entirely within the bounds of plausibility. Northumberland had already noted the 'mutinous' temper of the king's own army,[41] and the defection of nine regiments (on the assumption that the rank-and-file were likely to follow their commanding officers) would have reduced the king's army – estimated by Bedford and his allies to be some 24,000 men and 1,700 horse – by roughly a third. The Petitioners' further claim, in their correspondence with the Scots during the week after Newburn, that they had the support of an additional nine regiments of the Trained Bands (the county militia forces) is equally believable, though impossible to prove. The king was deeply distrustful of the elements of the

Yorkshire Trained Bands and their officers, and the Council was so doubtful of the allegiance of the Essex Trained Bands (most of whose officers were appointed by Warwick as the county's joint-Lord Lieutenant) that it ordered all of the county's forces dismissed, notwithstanding the pressing danger posed by the Scots.[42]

Charles's distrust of the Yorkshire Trained Bands appears to have been largely justified. Recent research on Yorkshire's response to the crisis of 1640 has identified an influential clique within the county's godly gentry who were acting in collusion with the Petitioner Peers, led by Henry Darley of Buttercrambe, the former Deputy Governor of the Providence Island Company, and a close friend of both Warwick and Brooke. It was Darley who, in 1638, had resolved to accompany Warwick, Saye, and Brooke on their planned journey to the New World. During 1640, and in the intervening years, he had been intimately involved in the contacts between the Scots and the Warwick–Bedford group.[43] 'A heady, insolent Puritan',[44] Darley, by August 1640, was working to obstruct the king's war effort in Yorkshire in concert with a series of other godly 'countrymen', who included his own brother-in-law, John Alured, Sir Matthew Boynton (whose son, Francis, had married Saye's daughter three years earlier),[45] and Philip, Lord Wharton (one of the lords who added his name to the Petition after the original Twelve).[46]

By rallying county opinion on what seemed blamelessly localist issues – in particular, the disproportionately large burden that fell on Yorkshire as a result of the current campaign – they succeeded in paralysing the royal war effort during the critical weeks in late August, when the outcome of the conflict hung in the balance. Charles had been counting on using Yorkshire's Trained Bands, some 13,000 strong, in a bid to turn back the Scottish advance. In the event, the delaying tactics of Darley and his friends ensured that by the time the Yorkshire Trained Bands came to be mobilized, the Scots had already marched through Northumberland and taken Newcastle unopposed. Nor was this the Yorkshire dissidents' only success. In early September, by which time Northumberland and County Durham had fallen to the Scots, the Petitioners' Yorkshire allies were again causing difficulties, this time obstructing the king's efforts to raise funds for a counterattack.[47] Little wonder that Strafford, the field commander of the king's army, exasperated beyond endurance by these spoiling tactics, ordered Darley's imprisonment in York Castle on 20 September on a charge of treasonous collusion with the Scots. Darley was in custody, pending trial, by the 30th.[48]

The existence of these plans to create what amounted to an English rebel army points to the crossing of a major legal and psychological threshold on the part of the Petitioner Peers. By the last days of August 1640, they were already preparing for the contingency that their English forces loyal to the 'commonwealth' might be used in battle (either alone or, more likely, in conjunction with the Scots) against the forces faithful to the king. Of course, the prime objective behind the creation of these Armies for the Commonwealth seems to have been to overawe Charles to the point of capitulation: to make clear the pointlessness of further military resistance; not to push the issue to an actual battle. The war that the Petitioners would have preferred was one

of menace and intimidation, a war of wills and minds, in which victory –
Charles's acquiescence to the summons of a Parliament – would be achieved
by deploying the threat of force, not its reality.[49] Yet, as Warwick and Bedford
almost certainly knew, the prime rule of war is the Law of Unintended
Consequences. At the time Bedford and his friends were working for the
creation of these Armies for the Commonwealth, they had no means of
knowing whether or not they would need to use them, and they seem not to
have flinched from the possibility that, however briefly and in however noble
a cause, Englishmen might have to shed their compatriots' blood.[50]

It is hardly surprising, then, that in these anxious days following the
Scottish invasion (the last week of August and the first days of September),
Bedford, Warwick and their allies pondered the future with an acute sense
of their own vulnerability. They were almost certainly unaware how much
of their treasonous correspondence with the Scots had been intercepted by
Windebank's spies, nor – if Windebank *was* in possession of evidence against
them – whether they would suffer Darley's fate: imprisonment, pending
trial for treason, and the likelihood, beyond that (unless their strategy was
successful), of the gallows or the block. The public reaction to the Scottish
invasion posed another potential threat. Once the Petition (with its implied
solidarity with the Scots) was in the public domain, the 'popularity' they
currently enjoyed might be quickly dissipated, particularly if there were
further English casualties in the course of the Scots' southwards advance.
(Indeed, this consideration probably motivated the dissident peers' proposal
to the Scots, back in June or early July, that the Scots should send an army
to London even before the king's army had been fully mobilized.) The lords'
popularity was the principal deterrent to the Privy Council from moving
against them. If that were lost, the knock at the door by the Council's agents
was likely to follow – if not immediately, then when the temper of the London
crowd had cooled.

With the possibility of arrest ever present, the dissident lords planned
accordingly. Turning once again to their Scottish allies, in the first days of
September they urged them to have a crack force of 'selected troops in
perpetuall readines, which must be ready to march for our securities upon
an[y] furder warning'.[51] Given that the writers of this letter were all based
in the capital, this request seems to have envisaged the despatch of a highly
mobile Scottish force (by definition, cavalry or dragoons) as far south as
London. How viable, or effective, this would have been, given the distances
involved, must be an open question; but it closely resembles a request to
Lord Loudoun, made by Savile in early July on behalf of the dissident peers,
in which he conveyed his fellow conspirators' 'recommendation' that,

> ...upon your [the Covenanter army's] Entry, you should march with all
> possible Speed to London, where the Lords and [the] City will be ready to
> receive you and join with you.[52]

By September, that advance of the entire Scottish army towards London no
longer appeared practicable; but the Petitioners clearly hoped for some more

limited link-up with Scottish forces, should the circumstances require it, and
the fact that Warwick and his allies were preparing what appears to have
been a potential escape route to Scottish-held territory probably reveals
something of their own sense of the risks they were taking and their uncertainty of ultimate success. All would depend on how the kingdom – and
London, in particular – responded to their declaration of solidarity with the
Scottish 'rebels'. Would Englishmen react by rallying behind their call for
the abandonment of the war and the settling of differences in a Parliament –
or by maintaining, as one critic was to put it, 'that all these Lords that
subscribed the petition were Traytors and Covenanters and ... deserved to
be hanged'?[53]

ii. THE 'FRIGHTED' COUNCIL

The disaffected grandees who gathered at Bedford House, however, were not
the only noblemen uncertain of their personal safety. During the fortnight
that followed the Scottish invasion, the anxieties of the Privy Council, evident
in the last days of August, grew steadily closer to panic. Without the commanding presence of Strafford, and lacking clear instructions from the king
(who was still with the army at York), the Council was paralysed by internal
disagreement over tactics and, in consequence, by indecision.[54] Distanced
from what was happening in London, Charles was repeatedly exasperated
by what he regarded as its pusillanimousness. But the Board's diffidence is
understandable. To have arrested the dissidents – particularly those, like
Essex and Warwick, who enjoyed substantial popularity – risked provoking
riots on a scale even larger and more menacing than those that followed the
premature dissolution of Parliament in May. To do nothing, however, was
equally fraught with risk, particularly given the suspiciously large number and
uncertain intentions of the dissident peers who were gathering in London.[55]

Compounding the problem was the Council's lack of information as to
how far the conspiracy – and conspiracy, by now, they were convinced it
was – had spread. Even Privy Councillors were under suspicion. One of
Windebank's first responses to news of the Scottish invasion was to obtain
authorization from the Committee of War to intercept all correspondence
addressed to the Earl of Northumberland, the Lord Admiral and (still,
nominally) Lord General. (With the true thoroughness of the bureaucrat,
Windebank wrote a minute to authorize himself: 'The Lord Admiralle's
pacquetts and lettres [are] to be opened by me.')[56] As we will see, Windebank's
suspicions that the Lord Admiral might prove sympathetic to the dissident
peers were to be amply justified.

To reduce the danger posed by the confluence of dissident noblemen in
the capital, the Council requested *all* peers in London to return to their
localities to attend to their duties as Lord Lieutenants.[57] Indeed, in response to
the initial shock of the Covenanter invasion, on 26 August, it even considered
advising the king to appoint some of the suspected peers to membership of
the Privy Council itself (with Essex, Hertford, and Bedford, once again, as

the most likely appointees).[58] Incorporating some of the dissident peers into the Privy Council was worth doing, Windebank noted in his minutes of the Council's meeting of 1 September, 'if it be but to engage them'.[59] This idea – in effect, a proposal to buy off the king's opponents through promotion – was to recur throughout the crisis, and while, in this instance, it met with the stone wall of royal disapproval, it nevertheless reveals something of what the Council regarded as the dissidents' ultimate objectives: Bedford, Warwick and their allies were after a place in government, a voice in the 'counsels of the realm'. A well-timed preferment or two – so the Council's argument ran – might yet detach them from their Scottish allies.

The most dangerous figures, in the Privy Council's view, were the generals of the 1639 war against the Scots whom the king had failed to re-employ in the current campaign: Arundel and Essex. Both men had suffered slights at the hands of the régime, and had a history of intermittent opposition going back to the days of Buckingham. Imperious, and notoriously independent-minded, Arundel was particularly well placed to legitimize a planned uprising by virtue of his post as Earl Marshal, one of the 'medieval' great offices of state. This office, by tradition, empowered him to raise forces in defence of the 'common weal' in circumstances in which the king was deemed to be incapacitated or to have fallen into the clutches of 'evil men'. With his wounded *amour propre,* high sense of the rights of the 'ancient nobility',* and record of opposition to the king (he had joined with Warwick and Saye, for example, in attacking Buckingham in the 1620s), Arundel seemed a plausible recruit – at least in the eyes of his fellow Councillors – to the ranks of the dissident lords.[60] This assessment seems to have been shared by the dissidents themselves, for there is at least circumstantial evidence that he had been the object of approaches from Bedford on behalf of the Petitioners as a whole.[61]

To win Arundel over, the Council prevailed on the king to reappoint him as one of his Lieutenants-General – this time with responsibility for all forces south of the Trent. It was a clever device, intended to turn a possible poacher into a gamekeeper by restoring to him his former military rank and making him responsible for the security of London (which fell within his bailiwick south of the Trent).[62] Arundel was presented with his new commission on 26 August, and promptly ended his post-1639 sulk, taking immediate measures to garrison Whitehall Palace and strengthen the Tower against any possible attack.[63]

---

* Arundel chose to emphasize his own 'ancient lineage' by scorning the fashions of the Caroline court, with its taste for rich clothes and carefully cut hair and beards, and dressing in the manner of a Tudor grandee, in simple clothes, with his beard untrimmed, and with only the badge of the Order of the Garter as an outward indication of his rank. His portrait by Rubens (now in the National Gallery), which depicts him with a heavy fur collar, in the manner of a Tudor nobleman, is a deliberate study in archaism, an implicit reproof to the ostentation of the parvenu Stuart nobility. After Buckingham's death in 1628, Arundel had been brought progressively back into royal favour; but he nevertheless remained a figure of substantial independence and unpredictability.

The Council's major cause for concern, however, was the Earl of Essex –
the other of the two Lieutenants-General of 1639 who had suffered the
humiliation of dismissal. Unlike Arundel (of whom Edward Hyde remarked
that the only thing military about him was 'his presence and his looks'),[64]
Essex was an experienced and capable commander, whose exploits on the
Continent as a volunteer, fighting the Spanish and Austrian Habsburgs, had
made him a hero of the Protestant cause. Arundel apart, of all the peers
suspected of being in collusion with the Scots, Essex was the only one with
the military experience and personal popularity to make him a viable rebel
general. To Windebank and the Privy Council's Committee of War, winning
over Essex was therefore essential if the threat of an insurrection in London
were to be neutralized.

The Secretary of State, deputed by the Committee of War to put the case
to the king, set out the arguments in a letter written on Monday, 31 August:

> If this Lord were taken off, the knot would be much weakened, if not
> dissolved. And besides that, it will be of great importance to sever him
> from that ill-affected company [of Warwick, Saye, and the other dissident
> peers].* He is a popular man, and it will give extraordinary satisfaction to
> all sorts of people to see him in employment again. This is the humble
> opinion of the Committee, which they have commanded me to represent
> to your Majesty.[65]

Within twenty-four hours, word was out of Essex's imminent appointment.
After the 'very Close [i.e. secret]' Council meeting at Hampton Court on 30
August, one London-based commentator reported that 'it is thought my Lord
of Essex, *being generally beloved,* will be recommended to be General of the
Horse in the north'.[66] In the meantime, the work on the new gun emplacements went ahead at Whitehall and the Tower, in expectation of the revolt,
which, the Council feared, Essex might actually lead.

In this case, however, the Council had recognized the potential problem
far too late.

While Windebank waited nervously for the king's response to his proposal,
Essex and 'that ill-affected company' were involving themselves ever more
deeply in the plans for military resistance against Charles I. They were
working to suborn elements of the king's army, and to provide intelligence
of the king's military weakness to their Scottish allies. So far as Essex was
concerned, the die had already been cast. By the time Windebank sealed his
letter to the king, imploring the earl's preferment, Essex and his fellow

---

* Edward Hyde reached a similar conclusion, arguing that 'it was a great pity that the
Earl of Essex was not again taken in [to military office, after the failure of the Short
Parliament], which had infallibly preserved him from swerving from his duty ... But he
was of a rough, proud nature, and did not think his last summer's service so well requited
that he was earnestly to solicit for another office, though there was no doubt but that he
would have accepted it, if it had been offered'. Only this last claim, that Essex would
have accepted military office in the 1640 campaign, seems seriously open to doubt.

Petitioners already knew that the war was going their way: that the Scottish army had advanced as far as County Durham; that Newcastle had fallen; and that Yorkshire – partly as a result of Darley's efforts – had mostly failed to respond to Charles's call to arms.[67] If their 'Armies for the Commonwealth' would need to be called into being, the moment was rapidly approaching. Public opinion needed to be carefully prepared. To court it, the peers turned to the largest and most influential constituency in the kingdom, the seat of Charles's government: London.

III. THE ARTILLERY YARD

England's capital, in 1640, was one of the largest and fastest growing cities in Europe. With a population, including its suburbs, of around 400,000 it was roughly twenty times the size of its nearest English rivals, Norwich and Bristol, which numbered 29,000 and 20,000 inhabitants respectively.[68] This concentration of wealth, population and economic power also made London the principal political audience of the realm. Within this sprawling, densely packed urban space – the city and suburbs could be walked across, from end to end, in a matter of a few hours – information circulated quickly and, through an already sophisticated metropolitan network of news distribution, exercised a disproportionate influence over the shaping of opinion. From a military perspective, too, the capital was exceptional as potentially the king-dom's single major source of troops.[69] With a militia force of more than 6,000 men, and a relatively well-trained officer corps, its manpower ought to have made a sizeable contribution to the king's war effort in 1640. Instead, the Privy Council so distrusted the allegiance of the City forces that, despite the king's urgent need for men and materiel, none of these forces was called upon for service in the current campaign. Indeed, the Council was adamant that, this year, the City's forces should not even be allowed to assemble for their autumn muster (a usual fixture of late August or early September). As Windebank explained to the king on 31 August, the members of the Privy Council were:

> exceedingly jealous [i.e. suspicious] of suffering any considerable forces, more than necessarily must, to be drawn together at this present, unless the City were in a better temper, and your Majesty's affairs in the North in a more prosperous condition.[70]

If Essex and the other 'ill-affected' lords were to attempt to rally opinion (or even soldiers) within the capital, the musters would have provided them with their obvious opportunity.

There was one muster, however, which the Council could not prevent: that of the privately run Artillery Company, a five-hundred-strong, merchant and gentry-dominated association for military instruction and the 'exercise of arms', which had grounds in Spitalfields and Moorfields, just outside the city walls. Warwick and the other leading dissidents appear to have chosen the

Artillery Company's annual muster in Moorfields on Tuesday, 1 September (the day after Windebank had moved to prevent the larger City militia musters) as the occasion of their first public appeal for support.[71] The event had much to recommend it for these purposes. With its combination of serious military training and elements of pageantry and display, it was often attended by a large audience, including members of the metropolitan nobility and gentry.[72] Most of the membership can be presumed to have taken part, and though we lack reliable statistics for the number present as observers, an overall figure of at least a thousand would seem to be a conservative estimate.[73]

Here, at least, Warwick and the other 'ill-affected lords' could count upon a sympathetic audience. While later royalist claims that it was a seminary of sedition are doubtless exaggerated,[74] the Artillery Company was nevertheless disproportionately infiltrated by politically engaged Puritans, among them Warwick's friend and business associate, Maurice Thompson;[75] the prominent City Puritan, Praise-God Barbon (after whom the nominated 'Barbone's Parliament' of 1653 was to be named);[76] the godly diarist, Thomas Juxon;[77] Richard Overton, possibly the future Leveller;[78] and John Venn, who was shortly to come to prominence as a radical Puritan in the City government and a highly influential figure in the organizing of popular support for the reformist cause within London.[79] Whatever the truth of the claim that, at the Artillery Company, a subversive creed 'was instill'd into [its members] that the blessed Reformation intended could not be effected but by the sword',[80] there is no doubt that the annual muster of 1640 did much to reinforce that reputation.

Later claims that opponents of Charles's regime had deliberately targeted the company as a potential power-base within the City apparently have some justification. At least from the late 1630s, three peers in particular – Warwick, his cousin, Essex, and Lord Brooke – seem to have taken a keen interest in the company's affairs.[81]* Warwick's friend and former chaplain at Leez, Obadiah Sedgwicke, joined the Company in October 1638 (his name being entered in the admission book in letters of gold);[82] and, the following year, one of Essex's closest friends in the military, Philip Skippon, also entered the company's service. Essex and Skippon had served together as officers under Sir Horace Vere in the campaigns against the Spanish in the Netherlands during the early 1620s, and had been together at the surrender of Breda to

---

* As one Royalist claimed in 1643, 'at last, when it was instill'd into them that the blessed Reformation intended could not be effected but by the sword, these places [offices in the Artillery Company] were instantly filled with few or none but men of that [Puritan] Faction. We were wont, you know, to make very merry at their Training, [as] some of them in two yeares' practice could not be brought to discharge a Musket without winking; We did little imagine then that they were ever likely to grow formidable to the State, or advance to that strength, as to be able to give the King Battle; but after a while they began to affect, yea, and Compasse the chief Offices of command, so that when any prime Commanders dyed, new men were elected, wholy devoted to that Faction; and it became a Generall Emulation amongst them who should buy the most, and the best Armes'.

the Spanish in June 1625, where Skippon had been wounded.[83] The traumas of war had forged a close and lasting bond between the two men, an affection that is attested to by Essex's will, written in the summer of 1642, in which he bequeathed to his friend of almost twenty years' standing one of his most valuable possessions: his armour.[84] Indeed, Essex seems to have used his brief moment of influence at court, as Lieutenant-General North of the Trent in 1639, to secure a royal recommendation for Skippon as the Captain-Leader (or commanding officer) of the company.[85] Skippon was to appear as the commanding officer at the 1640 muster.

At least one of the dissident peers – and one actively involved in keeping up contacts with the Scots – was even more closely interested in the company's affairs. Lord Brooke, who was still in his early thirties, was reported to have taken part in the company's training and exercises,[86] and was joined there by a prominent member of his household – the Warwickshire gentleman, William Bridges of Alcester – who is listed in the company accounts as 'Lord Brooke's'.[87] With a membership such as this, it was hardly surprising that the company's muster of 1640 was regarded by the Privy Council with considerable disquiet.

As befitted a military unit with a reputation for godliness, the key element in this annual muster – other than the formal military manoeuvres – was a rousing sermon, preached by a visiting cleric, and usually on the glories of the 'Christian soldier'. In this regard, the closeness of the company's connections with the Essex–Warwick circle during the late 1630s is also striking. In 1638 the preacher had been Obadiah Sedgwicke, a choice that had been all the more significant because Sedgwicke – having been forced out of his London parish the previous year for non-conformity by the Laudian Bishop of London, William Juxon – was *persona non grata* with the ecclesiastical authorities; so much so, in fact, that at the time of his sermon to the Artillery Company he had been constrained to seek the Earl of Warwick's protection and was then living at Leez.[88]*

For the preacher at the muster of Tuesday, 1 September 1640, the Artillery Company once again turned to one of Warwick's controversial clerical protégés: this time, to Calybute Downinge, a Cambridge Doctor of Laws who had been the 'pastor' of the Essex parish of Hackney since 1637. Warwick had been married in the church, and the parish's major grandee was Lord Brooke, who had kept a pew there at least since 1634.[89] At a time when the Privy Council was already nervous about a possible assertion of authority by the dissident noblemen in London, the choice of Downinge provided cause for still further misgivings. Downinge had achieved notoriety in 1632 for a treatise on *The State Ecclesiasticall*, dedicated to the Earl of Salisbury, in which he had emerged as a trenchant defender of the nobility as 'the watch-

---

* In 1639, the year his sermon to the Artillery Company was published, Warwick appointed Sedgwicke to one of the richest livings in his gift, the vicarage of Coggeshall in Essex, worth £110 per annum. Sedgwicke remained there until 1644 or 1645, when he resigned to become the minister at Warwick's London parish church, St Andrew's Holborn.

towers of the state' and the proper source of the king's counsels.[90] By 1640, Downinge had moved to the protection of the Earl of Warwick,[91] and it is a measure of how closely the Artillery Company leadership was in sympathy with Warwick and Brooke's political objectives that, this year, the company's pulpit was shamelessly commandeered as a sounding board for the dissident peers. Of course, any assessment of Downinge's sermon is hampered by the evidential problem of the relationship between the spoken and the printed word, and to judge from contemporary reports of Downinge's sermon, the vehemence and directness of his pulpit oratory may well have been toned down for the version that eventually appeared in print.[92] Yet even the published text contains ample evidence to justify the contemporary claim that his sermon 'positively affirmed, that for defence of Religion and Reformation of the Church, it was lawfull to take up armes against the King';[93] and in the absence of contemporary notes of the sermon as delivered, it is this printed version that concerns us here.[94]

Not only did Downinge justify the previous week's Scottish invasion; he went far further than any other contemporary polemicist, presenting the case for the timeliness and legality of a noble-led rebellion against the 'evil counsellors' of Charles I. These, Downinge claimed, had ensnared and deluded an otherwise virtuous king, with the result that England was at the point where its very survival as an authentically Protestant state was now in jeopardy. His chosen text – Deuteronomy xxv, 17: 'Remember what Amalack did unto thee by the way when you were come out of Egypt' – invited an obvious comparison between the experience of the ancient Israelites and that of the present-day people of England. Under Moses, Israel had escaped the bondage of Egypt (just as England had been rescued from the tyranny of Rome by the early Reformers); but, no sooner had the Chosen People escaped Egyptian bondage – so the biblical story ran – than they had been attacked by a new enemy, the Amalekite tribe, intent on destroying them before they reached the Promised Land. The contemporary analogies were clearly delineated in Downinge's text: the new Amalekites were the 'Enemies of the Peace of the Church and State', the agents of Popery and Jesuitical conspiracy, who were intent on destroying Protestant England now that it had escaped from its own 'Egyptian bondage' (the centuries when it had been in communion with papal Rome).[95] In the course of his sermon Downinge extends his definition of these latter-day Amalekites to include not only the 'enemies of religion' but also the king's 'evil counsellors' – in this case, identified as the supporters of the current war. Before this Artillery Company audience, they hardly needed naming: Strafford and Laud were his obvious targets.

From diagnosing the ills of the kingdom (and their parallels with the experience of biblical Israel), Downinge moved on to prescribe remedies. Reformation of the king's counsels, he insisted, was the urgent necessity of the moment. Given that the king's current counsellors were 'dareing and driving in destructive ways',

we have reason, and it is religio[us], safe, and therefore seasonable, to change our temper and [the] constitutions of our counsels – and [to do] that before dangers and difficulties grow too great, and the worke prove an impossible pull.[96]

Downinge concluded bluntly that in this 'there is ... all the justifiable causes of a legall warre'.[97] In part, this argument was intended as a defence of the Covenanter invasion of England: this was a lawful, pre-emptive strike against Charles's government 'by way of prevention'.[98] But Downinge was equally concerned to stress that these arguments, justifying (indeed, sanctifying) the Covenanter war effort, applied equally to England's own predicament. Englishmen had a corresponding moral obligation to take action before it was too late.

His programme for action is advanced with startling directness. His first remedy was to propose a petition to the king for 'execution' against evil counsellors – one of the central demands of the Petition of the Twelve, which, though signed three days earlier, had not yet been published in London. Indeed, Downinge lays the groundwork for the publication of the Petition of the Twelve Peers with such thoroughness that, if the printed text is anything like an accurate record of what was delivered, this alone provides evidence of extensive advance consultation, possibly via Warwick or Brooke, between the preacher and the Petitioner Peers.[99] From here, the preacher sweeps on to the conclusion which religion and logic prescribed: 'extraordinary times', he declares, '... allow extraordinary undertakings'.[100] Military resistance was now justified against the king's government, even if it were strictly against the 'Laws of the Land', because the 'Laws of Nations' provided that the safety of the people was the supreme law.[101] And to substantiate this, he invoked the celebrated contemporary Dutch jurist, Hugo Grotius, as his authority: 'in such a case... Grotius is clear, that *in gravissimo et certissimo discrimine, lex de non resistendo non obligat* [i.e., in a most grave and undoubted crisis, the law concerning non-resistance does not apply]'.[102]

This takes Downinge to the subversive hub of his argument: who could legitimately issue this call to military resistance? Ideally, he concedes, it would require parliamentary approval; but where the representative body was 'hindered from assembling by the common Enemy', there was an alternative.[103] To the question who had the right to lead the commonwealth in this moment of crisis, Downinge gives a response so seditious in its implications that he felt constrained, in the printed text, to render it in the decent obscurity of Latin: 'it can be commanded by a Councillor Born [the traditional phrase for a nobleman of ancient lineage], by right of his nobility, and not by virtue of [any] office': '*Consiliarii nati ratione nobilitatis licet non ratione officii Ordinari*'.[104] Far beyond the justification of the Covenanter rebellion, Downinge was advancing the case for the legality of an English war – an English *civil* war – not as some contingent possibility in the future, but as the urgent moral imperative of the moment.

*

Within London, the sermon caused a sensation. In the controversy that followed, Warwick clearly declared himself as Downinge's protector – and revealed himself, too, as perhaps the most militant of all the Petitioner Peers. One royalist contemporary, Sir John Berkenhead, describes what followed:

> [Downinge], having thus Kindled the fire in the City, for feare of being questioned (for as yet it was not lawfull to Preach Treason), retired privately to the Earle of Warwick's house in Essex [Leez], the common Randevouz of all Schysmaticall Preachers, this Sermon in every place administring matter of discourse.
>
> People censured it as they stood affected, which gave occasion to the Ringleaders of this faction to enter upon a serious examination and study of this case of Conscience; ... [and] because, without admitting this doctrine, all their former endeavours would vanish into smoak, they stood doubtfull no longer, ... [and] shaking hands in this poynt of Rebellion, ... subscribed to D[r] Downing's doctrine, as an Evangelicall truth.[105]

Dating from 1643, this account needs to be treated with considerable caution. Analysis of the Artillery Company's membership reveals it to be rather less homogeneously 'puritan' than its detractors pretended (among its more prominent members were Sir Paul Pindar, the Crown financier,[106] and Sir Nicholas Crisp, a successful slave trader and future royalist officer, who was the arch-enemy of the godly Maurice Thompson).[107] Similarly, it is impossible to verify the claim, made in 1643, that Downinge and Stephen Marshall (another Essex-based ally of the Earl of Warwick and future chaplain to the Earl of Essex) had 'whispered this doctrine long before in their Conventicles'.[108] As we have seen, the plans to create forces 'for the Commonwealth', ready to stage or at least threaten some form of insurrection, clearly predate the delivery of Downinge's sermon on 1 September by at least some months. Indeed, it was *because* the ringleaders were already agreed on preparing for military resistance to the king that Downinge seems to have been invited to preach in such inflammatory terms in the first place – not the sermon that made up the ringleaders' minds.[109] What Downinge's homily did achieve, however, was to place a coherent justification of a noble-led revolt against the king's evil counsellors firmly in the public domain. Almost every aspect of what was later to be termed 'Parliamentarianism' was anticipated within its pages.

*

At Whitehall and Hampton Court, where Downinge's sermon of 1 September was also 'administering matter [for] discourse', the effect of the Artillery Company muster was to strike terror into the embattled Privy Councillors. The imminence of a possible aristocratic revolt prompted a straightforwardly 'aristocratic' solution: now, more than ever, they renewed their pleas to the king to disengage Essex – the revolt's likely leader – from the other dissidents, by offering him a major preferment. That same day, Windebank conferred with Arundel, now the commander responsible for London's security, and, without waiting to return to his own house in Drury Lane, dispatched from Arundel House yet another letter to the king, urging an approach to Essex –

the second such letter in as many days – as a matter of the highest urgency. His anxiety is almost palpable in the texture of his prose:

> It is of *extraordinary* consequence to your Majesty's present affairs; and therefore I must humbly *beseech* your Majesty to take it to heart, and to call that Earl to you with a letter *written with your own hand,* and in an obliging way.[110]

To add even more persuasive force to his plea, he obtained a letter from the queen to the same effect, reiterating Windebank's own advice that the king should 'write to that Earl himselfe'.[111]

That night, Tuesday the 1st, insubordination seemed rife in the capital. In celebration of their success at Newburn, Scots (and, presumably, Covenanter-sympathizers) in London and Westminster 'made feasts ... in triumph for that newes'. More disturbing (because evidently set in train by locals), there was 'much ringing' of church bells in London during the night, as citizens rejoiced at the king's defeat.[112]

By Wednesday – twenty-four hours after the Artillery Company sermon – the Committee of War was in a state of abject panic and making contingency plans for what should happen in the event of London's fall to the rebels. The talk was no longer of a withdrawal to Windsor Castle. Some of the members of the Committee of War were advising that Portsmouth, the major royal fortress on the South Coast, should be prepared immediately with arms and victuals – 'it being a place, as they conceive, of greatest safety for a retreat for your Majesty and your royal Consort and Children, in case of extremity'. Portsmouth would become the seat of the court, and, if necessary, the government and royal family could then escape from there by sea to Wales, where the king could raise forces for a counter-attack.[113] Windebank reported all this to the king merely as 'advice'. But he was being less than frank. In fact, the Council's assessment was far more pessimistic than Windebank dared reveal in his letters to the king; and, without waiting for Charles's response, the Committee of War had already begun transferring gunpowder from the Tower of London to Portsmouth, provisioning it as a last redoubt in the event of a total collapse of royal authority in Southern England.[114]

Though it has scarcely been mentioned by historians writing after the seventeenth century, both the threat of this insurrection and the Privy Council's understanding of its likely perpetrators exercised a powerful influence on the Caroline régime's response to the broader political and military crisis of September 1640. Even without having seen the dissident noblemen's petition, Councillors like Laud and Cottington were sufficiently familiar with the objectives of Warwick and his friends to have a fairly accurate sense of what they were seeking to achieve: a complete dismantlement of the structures of the Personal Rule – legal, fiscal, and religious – through a new Parliament, and the creation, in its place, of a new noble-dominated régime in which the reformist peers would take their place. What was new and so profoundly dangerous about the current crisis was that, for the first time, these dissident noblemen were publicly asserting the rights of the ancient nobility – the *consiliarii nati* - as the authority by which military force could be used to attain this.

This appeal to noble rights and privileges on the part of the 'Rebels', in turn, suggested to the Council a possible solution. What if the king outflanked the dissident peers by summoning to his Council not just some of the 'Country lords' (as had been mooted on 26 August), but *all* the English peerage – just over a hundred noblemen? How could Charles be seen to be guided by 'evil counsellors' if he were surrounded by the entire nobility, and publicly seeking its counsel? It was a desperate measure, because – as most of the London-based Councillors were coming to believe – the summoning of a Parliament, however irksome, was now unavoidable, given the dissident peers' apparent preparedness to use force. To deny them the summons of a new Parliament was to risk provoking a full-scale rebellion in the South of England.

Once again, Windebank put the options to the king in the starkest of terms:

> The question is: whether your Majesty will not rather give the glory of redress of grievances, and of a Parliament, to *your own Lords* [who were to be summoned to York], or rather to yourself by their common advice, than to the Rebels, if your power and force be inferior to theirs.[115]

iv. CIVIL WAR?

Windebank was not being frightened by mere shadows. The threat from Warwick, Bedford and their allies – the 'greatest that had threatened this state ever since the Conquest'[116] – was real and imminent. Like Windebank, they also realized that it was the superiority of 'power and force', the compelling logic of soldiers, armies, and guns, that would decide which party emerged victorious from the current confrontation. On the Petitioners' side, perhaps the clearest evidence of this realization emerges in the letter, already noted, that Bedford and seven other Petitioners sent to the Covenanters around 5 September, in which they informed them of the nine regiments in the royal army, and equal number of Trained Bands, whose commanders had agreed to form the 'Armies for the Commonwealth'. The most striking aspect of the Petitioners' advice to the Scots, however, is its belligerence. They actually wanted the war to go on in order to maintain the military pressure against the king, notwithstanding the risk that this entailed of further English casualties. Their counsel to the Covenanter leadership, then based at Newcastle, was therefore to *reject* any overtures the king might make suggesting a treaty, lest he use these negotiations to sow divisions between the Covenanters and their English 'friends'. Victory was in sight, the Petitioners assured their Scottish allies, 'if your army can subsist bot 14 days at Newcastle'.[117] What gave cause for this optimism, Bedford and his friends insisted, was the overall weakness of the king's resources and the contrasting strength of the English forces that were now prepared to back the Petitioners' revolt.[118]

Of course, these military preparations were aimed, paradoxically, at the avoidance of further war – towards the creation of a military context in which any rational king would have no alternative but to yield to their demands: for a new English Parliament, and for the immediate abandonment of the war. No one, however, could be sure how Charles would react – particularly given that his chief adviser in the field was the Earl of Strafford, who stood to lose his career, and possibly his life, if the asked-for Parliament ever actually met. The possibility of further fighting – either between the Scots and the royal army, or between the English 'Commonwealth' forces and those loyal to the king – was therefore clearly implicit in the circumstances which the Petitioners had created, and might well become unavoidable if the king were to persist in refusing the peers' demands. In that case, wrote Bedford and his allies, '[we] may (as [we] are bound) endevour to [do] that [which] is expedient for the peers of Ingland to doe in regard of [our] great entresse [i.e. interest] therin'. And the 'expedient' course that these peers were contemplating clearly involved a willingness to use military force – both their own and the Scots' – to defeat the 'evil counsellors' who were resisting their just demands.[119] Moreover, that willingness appears to have been fully developed as early as the Petitioners' contacts with the Scots in June and July.

Military force, however, was only one aspect of their strategy. The Petitioners were equally alive to the weight of public (or at least gentry) opinion. Combined with the military threat, this had a formidable power to intimidate both the king and his Privy Council, not least by demonstrating the massive blow to royal authority that would follow from London's falling to the Petitioner Lords, and a consequent withdrawal of the royal administration to Portsmouth. Thus, during the first week of September, the Petitioners' efforts to create their vestigial Armies for the Commonwealth proceeded in tandem with their plans to court public opinion within the capital. Downinge's sermon and the controversy it provoked had made a start, by alerting the City that some form of intervention by the dissident lords would shortly be forthcoming. What remained to be seen was how the City would respond once the Petition of the Twelve – the 'Remonstrance' they had promised the Scots once news of their entry into England had been confirmed – was finally in the public domain.

The timing of the Petition's publication was thus a matter of acute sensitivity. To elicit a positive response within the City, it was important not only that the Scots had already been victorious, but that they had also achieved their success with only minimal loss of English life. Only, therefore, when news of Newburn became widely known in London after 1 September did the Petitioners feel sufficiently confident to proceed with the publication of their manifesto.[120] Even then, Bedford and the other peers in London seem to have waited to consult Warwick, who had decamped to Leez by the middle of that week. John Pym, the West Country lawyer who had long served both Bedford and Warwick, acted as the Petitioners' messenger, and journeyed to

Leez on or shortly before Thursday, 3 September to seek Warwick's view. Before departing, however, he left a manuscript copy of the Petition of the Twelve at Warwick House with William Jessop, the earl's secretary (who also doubled as secretary of the Providence Island Company),[121] who was to make manuscript copies, ready for distribution, if and when the go-ahead for publication was granted.

That same night, 3 September, Pym, now safely arrived at Leez, sent an urgent letter back to Warwick House in Holborn, London, announcing to the earl's secretary that

> it was now resolved that the Copyes which I intreated you to write shalbe published, and I pray you to deliuer to his bearer 3 or 4 Copyes to be brought hither [i.e. back to Leez] to morrow night. [Send] to Sr John Clotworthy, the like nomber, and to Mr [Peter] Sterry as many, and to any others as you please and your time[?] will allowe.[122]

Sir John Clotworthy, as we have seen, had been the point of contact between the English godly dissidents and the Covenanters since the mid-1630s – a man for whom Warwick would shortly arrange a parliamentary seat;[123] and his involvement, together with that of Peter Sterry, chaplain to another of the Petitioner Peers, Lord Brooke[124] – located only a few doors away at Brooke House, also in Holborn[125] – points to a relatively sophisticated series of preparations in advance of the Petition's publication. Jessop received Pym's letter at Warwick House by Friday, 4 September, and promptly went into action. The Earl of Manchester, Viscount Mandeville's estranged father, obtained a copy of the Petition of the Twelve on Sunday, 6 September,[126] and by Monday, copies of the Petition were reported to be 'frequent [i.e. numerous] in town'.[127]

By the time of Warwick's return to London, planned for Saturday, 5 September,[128] the would-be 'rebels' were in bullish mood. Word had reached them that the presentation of the Petition to the king had had an electrifying effect on the royal court at York. 'The petitioun mutch started them,' Bedford and his allies wrote to the Scots – so much so, they believed, that if the Scots had made an offer of a treaty, it 'had been quickly imbraced'.[129] This may well have been an overly optimistic reading of the king's readiness to hoist the white flag, but it helps explain the boldness of the Petitioners' next move. On Sunday, 6 September, Bedford and Hertford (Essex's brother-in-law), on behalf of the rest, approached Arundel, as Earl Marshal and commander of the king's forces in London, apparently in a bid to induce him to join their campaign for the summons of a Parliament. Arundel's reaction is undocumented; but the end result of the encounter was the appearance of Bedford and Hertford before the Privy Council's Committee of War the following day,[130] where the two peers made the same startling proposal to members of the Privy Council.

Aware that the Privy Councillors had obtained copies of the newly published Petition of the Twelve, Bedford and Hertford offered them an ultimatum. Either the Councillors went over to the side of the Petitioners and added the Board's support to their demands for a Parliament and the abandonment of the war; or, should they refuse, the Petitioners would 'wash their hands from the mischiefs that will happen if the Lords [of the Council] do not join with them'.[131] The element of menace in the remark was unmistakable. Unless the king yielded, some kind of bloodshed, possibly civil war, was imminent.

Stunned by the effrontery of Bedford's proposal, the Committee of War was reduced to prevarication. Unable to respond positively without incurring the anger of the king, but equally anxious not to offer the Petitioners any provocation, it deputed Windebank and the three Council members most concerned with the security of London – Arundel, Cottington (the Constable of the Tower), and Sir John Finch (the senior law officer)[132] – to withdraw and confer privately with the rebel emissaries. Arundel assured Bedford and Hertford that their conversation would be merely an off-the-record discussion 'as friends'. But the questioning quickly turned to the investigation of the extent of the Petitioners' collusion with the Scots. Windebank noted suspiciously that Hertford and Bedford would not refer to the Scots as 'rebels', but only as 'the Scotch army'. Hertford denied any complicity in the Scottish invasion, but Bedford's shifty and equivocating replies fooled no one. Asked if he knew of any covenant that was to be sworn in England like the 1638 National Covenant (the foundation of the rebellion in Scotland), Bedford pretended not to know of any – but 'more faintly' than Hertford had done.[133] And when, after the group returned to the Council Chamber, it emerged that Arundel had revealed to his Privy Council colleagues what had been said during their private discussion 'as friends', Bedford lost his temper and angrily complained of the breach of trust. The mood of the meeting soured rapidly. When Bedford and Hertford protested that they sought only the good of the kingdom, they received a sarcastic riposte from Arundel: 'they had very ill luck in the manner of expressing [their good intentions], seeing they seemed in their complaints rather to join with the Rebels'.[134]

For the Councillors, the interrogation of Bedford and Hertford was the climax of an intensely unsettling seven days. They had been left in no doubt that Bedford and Hertford *were* in support of, and probably in contact with, the Scots; but the Councillors seem to have feared that any punitive measure against them, or against the other Petitioner Lords, was likely to produce disorders on the streets of London on a scale even greater than those that had followed the Parliament's dissolution in May. The Council's control over the capital was already precarious. On Sunday, 6 September, the day the Petition of the Twelve had been published, placards had gone up around London 'inviting the Apprentices to rise, and to meete for the reformation of Religion' – a rising, Windebank believed, which had only been foiled by the Lord Mayor's timely ordering of all apprentices to remain indoors, and by the doubling of the City watches.[135] Whether or not those two events were connected, the Council could be excused for thinking that they were.

Yet Hertford and Bedford were released by a Council apparently convinced of their guilt, but too nervous to take action against them. Windebank's briefing paper on that Council meeting, when it arrived at York, prompted a furious rejoinder from the king: 'I see ye ar all so frighted ye can resolve on nothing'.[136]

*

How far were the Council's fears of an aristocratic rebellion actually justified in the first week of September 1640? Until recently, that question has been almost unaskable, for in the old Whig and Marxist narratives of the causes of the Civil War, the nobility was always peripheral – a decaying and largely powerless element of the *ancien régime* that was about to be swept away by the rising tide of bourgeois radicalism (personified by Hampden and Pym).[137] True, many of the key documents that establish the extent of the noblemen's military preparations in 1640 were not available before the 1990s. However, even in the anti-Whig 'Revisionist' accounts of the 1980s and 1990s, which have generally accorded greater attention to the political role of the nobility, the possibility of serious conflict *within* England (whether noble-led or otherwise) has tended to go unconsidered because it sits so uncomfortably with the Revisionists' broader assumptions about the nature of English society in the decade before the end of Charles's Personal Rule. Even in 1640, it is argued, England remained an essentially unified society, and it would require a full year of disruptive and polarizing meddling by the Scots before the nation's internal divisions reached the point where civil war became a possibility. As late as January 1642, so the argument runs, it would need another six months before each of England's 'county communities' would be ready for war.[138]

Yet one can question whether these were the only circumstances in which an English 'civil war' was possible. Such a conflict did not actually require that rival forces, ideologically opposed, be armed and arrayed in every county of England. At its most minimal, all that a civil war needed were two rival parties of fellow Englishmen, each with recourse to a substantial force of armed men, and each with the willingness to resort to violence in order to achieve their political ends. In these very specific terms, England does appear to have been poised for, or perilously close to, a civil war in the late summer of 1640. That Charles's government expected some form of insurrection that September is beyond doubt. What now seems clear – thanks to the manuscript discoveries since 1990, and not least to the advances made by social historians of the period[139] – is that at the time when the Privy Council was making its contingency plans for the 'retreat' of the royal family to Portsmouth, it was responding to real and well-founded fears.[140]

v. CONTESTS

What followed over the fortnight after the publication of the Twelve Peers' Petition was nothing less than a contest for the leadership of the political nation. As the Twelve appealed for – and found – further support within the nobility, and sought to mobilize a party within London and the localities, the king attempted to outflank them by making his own appeal for the nobility's allegiance. In effect, he adopted the advice which Windebank had sent on 3 September, in the immediate aftermath of the Artillery Company sermon, that, 'to save the Monarchy', he should summon a 'Great Council of Peers', an assembly of all the English nobility, thereby trumping the claims of the Twelve to speak in the name of the noble estate.[141] If the nobility would respond as Windebank had predicted, the king (who had been desperately short of funds throughout the summer) would acquire the financial means to fight the war to a successful conclusion – and could possibly even avoid the need to summon a Parliament at all.[142] Already on Saturday, 5 September (the day when copies of the Petition of the Twelve began circulating in London), the king announced that the Great Council would meet at York in just under three weeks' time: on Thursday, 24 September.[143]*

Yet the debate over whether to summon the peers to York had split the Privy Council. Although the record of how Councillors cast their votes has not survived, the division is likely to have followed a familiar fault line, with the Hispanophile party centred on Archbishop Laud, the Marquess of Hamilton, and Lord Cottington supporting the Great Council option – indeed, almost any option that avoided the summons of a Parliament – and a rival party, associated with Holland and Northumberland, insistent that only a meeting of *both* Houses would serve to unify the nation and solve the Crown's fiscal crisis. To the king, the question seems to have been nothing less than a test of allegiance. Unusually, Charles asked Windebank to provide him with a list of all the Councillors who had spoken in favour of a Parliament. On 7 September, the Secretary, as Privy Council sneak, duly provided his master with the list he had requested, 'so your M[ajesty] will find how they were'. 'So I doe,' was the king's ominous note in the margin of Windebank's despatch. From that moment, in the king's eyes, the pro-parliamentary Councillors were marked men.[144] Indeed, he seems to have treated any public request for the meeting of a Parliament as a coded endorsement of the demands of the 'rebels'.[145] He placed his faith in the Great Council. This, he hoped, would provide him with the funds – or at least the credit (by acting as underwriters of new loans) – to resume his offensive against the Scots. And in the meantime, any suggestion of negotiation with the Twelve was emphatically rebuffed.

As Charles struggled to continue his war, the Petitioners redoubled their efforts to force him into abandoning it. Part of their strategy was to instigate the presentation of further petitions, each supportive of their own, from the Covenanter leadership in Newcastle, their allies in Yorkshire and in other

---

* Like so much that was novel in early Stuart political culture, this expedient was another instance of Caroline 'gothic': the revival of a medieval institution which had not met since the death of Elizabeth I. So remote was the memory of its last meeting that the Earl of Leicester's man of affairs (mistakenly) described it as 'such a Counsell as hath not been called since K. Edward the first['s] time' – the late thirteenth century; though, regarded as a body summoned to support the king financially in war, the Great Council's prior history justifies this statement rather more than it may at first appear.

English counties,[146] and – most important of all – from their constituency in London. When, for example, Windebank provided Sir Henry Vane, the other of the two Secretaries of State, with a detailed account of the interrogations of Hertford and Bedford on 7 September, Vane could not help noticing that the Covenanter leadership's response to the announcement of a Great Council had been 'the same that Bedford hath declared unto the lords [of the Privy Council]'.[147] Similarly, when the gentry of Yorkshire presented a petition to the king on 12 September, Vane observed that this document, too, 'conclud[ed], as the 12 peeres did: for a parlement'.[148] The royal chaplain, Dr John Pocklington, sniffed collusion: 'it may bee you will imagine of some correspondency betwixt the Petitioners on both sides [i.e. the Scots and the English],' he wrote from York on 14 September.[149]

'Some correspondency' was an understatement. In the light of what we now know about the detailed exchanges of advice and information between the Covenanter leadership and the Petitioner Peers, these 'correspondencies' – the similarities of phrasing and objectives between their respective addresses to the king – do not appear to have been a matter of chance. Each instance served to remind Charles and his York-based court that the Scots and the 'Lords of the South' constituted a unified axis of opposition. As the Venetian ambassador observed, they showed 'ever more clearly the secret communication between the two, the English being informed of their coming, and approving of their stay'.[150]

Evidence of the southern lords' success in winning 'hearts and minds' was also coming in from other quarters. Most disconcerting of all for the Privy Council were the persistent reports during those middle weeks of September that new signatories (possibly as many as twenty additional noblemen) were coming forward to add their names to the original Petition of the Twelve, and that the original signatories were actively canvassing for more.[151] Analysis of the surviving copies of the Peers' Petition reveals that over fourteen variant versions were produced in the weeks after 28 August 1640, as differing copies were circulated, acquired new signatures, were re-copied, and passed on to other noblemen for further signatures and re-copying. Twenty-three peers can be identified as having signed – or just under a quarter of the entire English nobility of 1640 (excluding the lords spiritual, the bishops).[152] A large proportion of the eleven 'new signatories' came from the extended families of the leading conspirators – among them Saye's son-in-law, the Earl of Lincoln;[153] Lord Paget, who was married to Warwick's niece;[154] and the Earl of Bristol, whose son and heir, Lord Digby, was married to the daughter of the Earl of Bedford.[155]* In Warwickshire, Lord Brooke seems to have won the support of his neighbour, Lord Dunsmore, at a meeting held on 16 September at the Swan in Warwick (although Dunsmore's name does not

---

* The alliance between the Russells and the Digbies is commemorated in Van Dyck's double portrait of Lord Digby and Lord Russell (the Earl of Bedford's eldest son), painted around 1635, of which Sir Oliver Millar has written 'there was no more sumptuous or successful composition in Van Dyck's years in London'.

appear on any of the surviving copies).[156] At York, the resident Secretary of State, Sir Henry Vane, noted this trend with alarm, observing that 'diverse of the nobilitie are come to London, and the[i]r purpose [is] to stay, to see what wilbee the Issue of these businesses'.[157]

The Petitioners' quest for support, however, was not confined to members of the political élite. Circulating in London by 10 September,[158] and almost identical in its demands to the Petition of the Twelve, was a second petition in favour of a new Parliament and the abandonment of the war. Like the original Petition of the Twelve, this too seems to have been promoted extensively through the dissident peers' godly allies within the Artillery Company. Here, once again, Warwick's political and mercantile network figures prominently. The major named promoters of this City Petition were the Artilleryman Maurice Thompson – an affluent London shipowner and Warwick's long-standing business partner[159] – and John Venn, the London silk trader, who, like Warwick, was an investor in projects for 'godly' colonization in New England.[160] More to the point, Venn was one of the most influential figures in the Artillery Company: he had stood for election as its Captain-Leader in 1631 (when he had been thwarted by a future Royalist), been successful in his bid to become its Serjeant-Major in 1636, and in September 1640 was serving as its Deputy President.[161] Within just over a fortnight, this Thompson–Venn petition was reported to have attracted the signatures of four aldermen and some 10,000 citizens. And when Thompson set out for York to deliver the petition on Wednesday, 16 September,[162] he was accompanied by a 'Mr Alford', most likely another of his Artillery Company comrades-in-arms, John Alford, who had served in John Venn's own detachment of troops during an Artillery Company pageant of 1638.[163] The London merchant Richard Shute was the third member of the delegation, a man who was 'probably Thompson's commercial factor' and closely involved with the City's godly network.[164]

Indeed, the 500-strong membership of the Artillery Company may well have provided the organizational infrastructure by which the petition was so quickly circulated and signed. Almost every one of the officers in the City's Trained Bands (its citizen militia) belonged to the company by 1642, and even if this proportion was smaller in 1640, the Artillerymen would have nevertheless been in an ideal position to collect signatures from their own regiments and return them to the Artillery Company's management in readiness for their forwarding to the king at York.[165]

If it is reasonable to identify, albeit tentatively, the influence of a Warwick 'interest' at work in the promotion of the City Petition, this is perhaps even more strongly evident in yet another declaration of support for the objectives of the Twelve, this time from London's godly clergy. The three clergymen reported to be most closely involved were Warwick's long-standing friend, Edmund Calamy (in whose London church he worshipped and who was eventually to preach the earl's funeral sermon);[166] the preacher of the Artillery Company sermon, Dr Calybute Downinge (only recently returned from Leez);[167] and Bedford's client,[168] Cornelius Burges, a puritan cleric who had served the Russells devotedly for over two decades.[169] Here, too, the Privy Council appears to have suspected the connection between the Petitioner Lords and this latest bout of troublemaking, and even took steps to prove it. On 18 September, it issued warrants for searches to take place at the houses of Calybute Downinge and Cornelius Burges ('a very black man of a midling stature [who] is said [to have] bene in Scotland'), in the hope of finding incriminating papers.[170] This did nothing to deter them. When the London clergy's petition was despatched to the king at York a few days later, its two bearers were none other than the selfsame Drs Burges and Downinge – the latter in open defiance of a Privy Council's warrant for his arrest.[171]

*

By the middle of September, it was becoming apparent to all but the most optimistic of the royal counsellors that the king's continuing refusal to summon a Parliament was likely to result in a catastrophic collapse of royal authority. With support for the Petitioner Lords growing almost daily, the king's inner group of Councillors was beginning to fear that many of the nobility would simply boycott Charles's planned Great Council in York. 'Fewe of the other nobilitie will bee heare [in York] att the day appointed for mettinge,' warned Secretary Vane on 14 September; and, if that were the case, 'itt is considerable [i.e. worth considering] whether itt should bee helde or not'.[172] So serious had the threat of a boycott become by 16 September (the day that Maurice Thompson left London with the City petition),[173] that, back in London, the Earl of Arundel proposed a motion that the Council should write to the king, 'that presently He declare the calling of a Parliament: that he may have the honor of it himselfe'.[174]

Arundel's remark in relation to Parliament – 'that [the king] may have the honor of it himselfe' – suggests that the Privy Council was now taking seriously, if it had not already done so, the Petitioners' threat to summon a Parliament on their own authority.[175] Whether or not the Petitioners actually would go this far, it was becoming clear to Charles's advisers that the belief that most of the nobility would accept a Great Council as a substitute for a Parliament was almost certainly misplaced. If and when the Great Council did convene on 24 September, there was now a serious risk that the majority of those attending would declare themselves in favour of the course already demanded by Warwick, Bedford and the other Petitioner Peers.

This visible faltering of royal authority in England coincided with yet another blow to the fortunes of the royal cause: the arrival in London of the news of the near-extinction of the king's authority in Scotland. During the last weeks of the summer, the few remaining bastions of Charles's military power north of the border gradually capitulated to the Covenanters. Dumbarton Castle surrendered on 29 August; Edinburgh Castle, his last foothold in the Scottish capital, on 15 September; and a few days later the royalist Earl of Nithsdale's Caerlaverock Castle, on the Solway Firth, was handed over to the Covenanters. This marked the effective end of the first of the various civil wars that were to afflict the Stuart kingdoms in the 1640s, a contest between Royalists and 'rebels' in which the latter had triumphed. News that the Covenanters now were victorious through most of the length and breadth of Scotland reached York on 22 September – two days before the opening of the Great Council – and can only have deepened Charles's sense of impending doom.[176]

Against this background, Warwick, Bedford and the other Petitioner grandees staged their boldest gesture of defiance to date. Most of the Petitioner Peers had been expected to stay away from the Great Council, if only because, after Darley's imprisonment on 20 September on charges of treason, they had cause to fear that Strafford had the same fate in store for them. Instead, with brazen effrontery, almost all the Petition's subscribers – now numbering well over twenty[177] – appeared in York en masse.[178] The theatricality of the moment was self-conscious. Rossingham reported on the eve of the Great Council that 'all the subscrybing Lords of the Petition' had staged a dramatic entry into York, arriving 'together', in a highly public display of solidarity. As what must have been a long and impressive cavalcade of coaches and outriders entered the city, the dissident lords sent out an uncompromising message to the king: they had resolved, they insisted, 'not to recede from one tyt[t]le of the petition'.[179] Nothing less than a Parliament, an end to the war, and justice upon 'evil counsellors' – in effect, the king's complete abandonment of his key policies and current ministers – would provide satisfaction.[180]

The sheer daring, almost showmanship, of the Petitioner Peers' entry into York prompts the question why they were prepared to take such an obvious risk of appearing in person at York, the king's military headquarters, all the more so if Strafford's reported response to the bearers of the Petition – that the two peers should be shot at the head of the army – is credible.[181] One possible explanation for their apparent confidence may have been their trust in the disaffected senior officers in the king's army – the nine regimental commanders who had allegedly undertaken to 'joyne with [the Petitioner] lords upon ther declaratioun'.[182] An even greater source of reassurance, however, may have been provided by the presence in York of the Earl of Essex, their fellow conspirator and arguably the most popular military officer in England in the summer of 1640. Only a few days after Essex's arrival in York with the other Petitioners, Rossingham reported that 'the whole army doe offer to be lead on by the Earle of Essex, who hath the hearts of the Soldiers'. So long as these claims as to Essex's popularity remained even partly true, the arrest of the Petitioners was scarcely a practical proposition.[183]

By the eve of the Great Council, however, Charles did not need the prospect of a mutiny within his army to bring home to him the extreme precariousness of his own position. In the days immediately preceding the first meeting of the Great Council, Windebank's intelligence reports suggested that the number of peers who now supported the invitation to the Scots to invade stood at thirty-seven.[184] Given that the total number of lords present in York was just over seventy,[185] this looked likely to yield the Petitioners a clear majority in the forthcoming assembly – and, with it, almost total control of its business. Charles had gambled on the Great Council as a means of avoiding the summons of Parliament, and lost. The numbers were simply against him.

At some point on Wednesday, 23 September, the day before the Council's opening session, Charles's resolve to block the summons of a Parliament by any means at his disposal finally cracked. The Parliament that he had fought so long to evade – the Parliament that looked certain to destroy much of what he had striven to create over the last decade – was now unavoidable. And if he failed to issue the writs of summons, it was highly likely that the 'Lords of the South' would issue them, on their own authority, in his stead.

*

The Great Council of Peers – an institution, it seemed, 'so old, that it had not been practiced in some hundreds of years'[186] – met for its first session in the hall of the Deanery at York on Thursday, 24 September. The king delivered the inaugural speech. Almost his opening words were a pious protestation: 'I desire nothing more then to bee rightly understood of my people, and to that end I have *of myself* resolved to call a Parliament.'

At those words 'of myself', Warwick, who was listening in the Hall, could have been excused for savouring the irony of that royal boast. To his friends in Essex he sent a simple message: 'The Game was well begun'.[187]

vi. CAPITULATION

The Great Council remained in session for just a month, but its deliberations were to define the terms of reference for English – and, indeed, British – politics for much of the following year. The opening day's debate confirmed the king's worst fears. Far from bankrolling the resumption of an offensive campaign to drive out the Scottish 'invaders', as Charles had hoped, the Great Council sided with the Petitioners by ordering the abandonment of the war. On the motion of Bedford's friend, the Earl of Bristol (one of the additional signatories to the Petition of the Twelve),[188] it was decided to open negotiations for a treaty between England and Scotland. To the bitter resentment of many senior officers, the king would be denied the opportunity of avenging the 'dishonour' of Newburn.

Bristol's insistence that these English negotiators should be 'some lords [whom the Scots] could not except against' was an invitation to the Great Council to appoint known pro-Scots as commissioners for the treaty. Moreover, the proposal comes straight from the list of the Petitioners' objectives, as reported by Nathaniel Fiennes to the Scots three weeks earlier, in which they planned that 'the[re] might be ane comittie apoynted of the uninterested [i.e. disinterested] lords of England, to treat with some of yours, to heir your just compla[i]nts and desyrs, and to seek the peace of both nations'.[189] The resulting commission, composed of some sixteen English peers, effectively conceded management of the forthcoming treaty to the Petitioner Lords.

They took eleven of the sixteen available places,* with a further (twelfth) place going to Warwick's close ally, his brother, the Earl of Holland (who had actively supported the Scots in the 1639 negotiations).[190] Lord Dunsmore, a cantankerous and quarrelsome nonentity, seems to have owed his appointment entirely to his timely appearance the previous week at the Swan in Warwick, where Lord Brooke was gathering signatures for a county-based version of the Petition of the Twelve.[191] Once again, the Lord Brooke–Earl of Warwick axis constituted a powerful interest within the commission; indeed, Warwick and his extended family alone comprised more than a quarter of its entire membership.† 'It has not escaped notice', Ambassador Guistinian noted at the time, 'that these persons so chosen have all declared themselves in the past as biased towards the Scottish cause, and equally zealous for the calling of a Parliament ... [including] some of the most seditious.'[192] 'Most' of the English negotiators, noted the Scottish clergyman, Henry Guthrie, 'had sign'd the Petition'. And on the other side, the Scottish delegation included two of the prime contacts with whom the Petitioners had negotiated the terms of the Covenanter invasion: John Campbell, Lord Loudoun, and Archibald Jhonston of Wariston.[193]

The establishment of the treaty commission was arguably the first and most significant of a series of usurpations of royal authority that were to occur during the following year. In continuous existence for the duration of the Anglo-Scottish negotiations (which were to last until the late summer of 1641), the commission enhanced the Petitioners' standing in three major respects. Firstly, it transformed the legal standing of their correspondence with the Scots: what had hitherto been furtive and illicit could now be transacted entirely legally. Indeed, more than that: because the power to conclude treaties was in theory one of the king's prerogative powers, the Petitioners, *qua* treaty commissioners, were in theory acting in the king's name – and having appropriated the king's authority, they were perfectly prepared to use it to conclude the treaty which they, rather than the king, wished to see established.

Secondly, control of the Anglo-Scottish Treaty effectively empowered the Petitioners to define England's future relations with Scotland. This included deciding upon the political structures that would be acceptable to both parties: a brief that could be extended to the rewriting of key aspects of the

---

* The Petitioners who were appointed negotiators with the Scots were: Bedford, Hertford, Essex, Warwick, Mandeville, Howard of Escrick, and Brooke (all members of the original Twelve Petitioners), and Bristol, Savile, Paget and Wharton (who had added their signatures to the Petition later). The only non-Petitioners to find places on the treaty commission were the Earl of Holland (Warwick's brother), the Earl of Salisbury (the father-in-law of Warwick's cousin, Northumberland), Lord Poulett, and Lord Dunsmore.

† Apart from Warwick himself, the other members of the extended Rich family were his brother, the Earl of Holland; his first cousin, the Earl of Essex; his son-in-law, Viscount Mandeville; and his nephew by marriage, Lord Paget (who was married to Holland's daughter); and the Earl of Hertford, who was married to another of Warwick's first cousins, the sister of the Earl of Essex.

'constitutions' of both kingdoms. And thirdly, in their new guise as 'Lords Commissioners', the Petitioners gained a large measure of influence over how long the Scottish army would remain in England. As this would not leave until the treaty negotiations were concluded, the Petitioners acquired the ability to spin out the negotiations until such time as their own safety – the legal arrangements that would prevent Charles from prosecuting them in the future for their past treasons – had first been assured.

These were extraordinarily broad powers. They would normally have been exercised by Privy Councillors, whereas, in fact, the sixteen-man treaty commission contained only two such established officers (the Earls of Holland and Salisbury – and these two of dubious loyalty to the king).[194] But the fact that they had attained control of what would otherwise have been the Privy Council's business – indeed, arguably what would otherwise have been the most important item on the Council's entire agenda – massively enhanced both the status and political influence of the Bedford–Warwick coalition. From that moment onwards, the 'Lords Commissioners' (as the treaty nego-tiators were termed) became, de facto, an alternative Privy Council – one whose impeccably Protestant credentials were in sharp contrast to the 'real' Privy Council, which continued to be dominated (in popular perception) by the 'popishly affected' and by social parvenus.

Perhaps what is most striking about these arrangements established in the opening days of the Great Council is that almost none of them were to be altered by the assembly of the new Parliament on 3 November. True, the two Houses would eventually play a part in the ratification of the treaty, and would exercise a measure of control via the Commons' power of the purse. The negotiations could continue only so long as the lower House was prepared to foot the bill for the Scots' occupation of northern England. But the actual detail of any proposals remained tightly within the control of the Petitioner-negotiators in general, and the Warwick House group in particular. Which 'evil counsellors' were to be prosecuted? How might the king's powers be limited so as to avoid future Anglo-Scottish wars? To what extent would the Scots attempt to recast the English Church in the mould they had created for the Scottish Kirk?[195] Each of these questions had the potential to be highly contentious. Proposing answers to them, and drafting the precise terms in which they would be put to Parliament, now fell neatly into the hands of Charles's aristocratic opponents, and would remain there for the best part of the following year.

Among the first people to realize the implications of this bouleversement was Warwick's sister-in-law, Isabel Rich, the wife of the Earl of Holland (who, like Warwick, was one of the treaty commissioners): 'I belive the Parliament will be very sharpe, and the lords pourfull,' she predicted on 4 October, just as the treaty negotiations began in the Yorkshire city of Ripon.[196] By deciding that the Anglo-Scottish Treaty was to be conducted so one-sidedly to the advantage of the Warwick–Bedford coalition, the Great Council of Peers at York defined the context within which British politics were to be played out long after the Great Council's own formal sessions ended on 28 October.

Above all, control of the treaty negotiations gave the Bedford–Warwick group the capacity to cripple the king financially. Charles was already profoundly troubled, as the Earl of Traquair (one of the Scots on the English Privy Council) demurely put it, 'with emptines of his Cofers'.[197] However, by committing the king to pay for the upkeep of the Scottish army in England until the treaty was finally concluded, Warwick's group was able to ensure that near-bankruptcy remained the state of the English Crown throughout the opening months of the new Parliament. Under the interim agreement, settled at Ripon in mid October, Charles was committed to paying the Scottish army maintenance of £850 per day for at least the next two months – with the option of further extensions of the arrangement for as long as the Scots' army remained in England. These were massive sums – £25,000 per month – and, with his Exchequer currently empty, the king would now have no alternative but to make heavy concessions with his Parliament if he were to have any possibility of raising them.

The Earl of Northumberland, still recuperating from the malaria-like illness that had stricken him in August, quickly realized the consequences that this would have for the king's relations with the forthcoming Parliament. 'I do beleeve', he wrote on 22 October,

> that untill we have setled those points that were in agitation the last
> Parlament – w[hi]ch was matters of religion, proprietie of goods, and libertie
> of persons, and peradventure some others – we shall hardly bring the [new]
> Parlament to any resolution that may free us from this army of rebels.[198]

Until that reform programme was completed, the Covenanter army was here to stay; and so long as that was so, it was the Lords Commissioners of the Treaty, not the Lords of the Privy Council, who were the major source of political authority in England. Warwick and his friends had finally won their entrée to the world of power.

*

Any lingering hopes that the king may have had of using Parliament to undo the irksome decisions of the Great Council were finally destroyed by the results of the October elections. These were an almost unmitigated disaster for the 'royal interest'. Up and down the country, as the electorate chose almost five hundred new representatives for the House of Commons,* candidates associated with the court found themselves either dissuaded from standing (lest they suffer the 'dishonour' of defeat), or, where they pushed the contest to an actual vote, rebuffed outright at the polls. Anti-court sentiment was most evident in the elections of the knights of the shire, where

---

* In November 1640, the total number of seats in the Commons was 493, a figure that was increased to 507 by May 1641 as seven boroughs (each returning two Commonsmen) had their rights to representation 'restored' by a vote of the whole House.

most of the county's freeholders were entitled to a voice in the decision.*
But even in the borough constituencies, where the number of electors was
generally far smaller and where court influence could be brought to bear
more efficiently, there was a widespread rejection of candidates identified as
supporters of Charles's Personal Rule.[199]

Even so, the king was far from being entirely powerless. Militarily, he
continued to enjoy the allegiance of probably well over half the army at
York, and in Ireland he retained the army (some 9,000 strong) that Strafford
had successfully raised and intended for deployment in the 1640 campaign.[200]
Nor was the nation wholly united in favour of the Petitioners, with their
programme of thoroughgoing political reform. Even in London, where
support for the dissident peers was probably strongest, there remained a
powerful 'king's party', particularly among the aldermen, committed to maintaining the ecclesiastical status quo of the 1630s, and deeply suspicious of
the series of puritan clerics who came in the Petitioner Lords' entourage.[201]
The closeness of the Petitioner Peers' relations with the Scots was also far
from being universally popular, not so much because the Petitioners were
thought likely to follow the Covenanters in demanding the abolition of
bishops, but because, through their de facto military alliance with the Covenanters, they seemed at least partially responsible for a major national
humiliation: a defeat in war. Each of these considerations had the potential
to become, in time, a major political asset for the Crown.

Nowhere was that dishonour felt more keenly than among the loyalist
regiments of Charles's army. One serving officer, Sir Richard Dyott, expressed
what was to become a recurrent indictment of the Petitioner Lords in the
months ahead: that, by bringing the war to a halt when they did, they had
cheated the king of a possible victory. 'Many do wonder', he wrote only four
days after Mandeville had presented the Petition of the Twelve,

> that at such a season, when the Scots had gott such Footing in the Land,
> and the King had bin at soe immense a charge in raising, furnishing, and
> paying soe great an Army, [that] such a petition should be offered, whereby
> this intended accon [i.e. a full-scale battle with the Scots] should be retarded,
> discountenanced, and indeed overthrown.[202]

From this perspective, the 'overthrow' of Charles's war effort in 1640 owed
far more to the interventions of the dissident nobility than to any damage
the Scottish army had inflicted on the English, or were ever likely to inflict,
on the battlefield.

On this question, there are persuasive grounds for thinking that Dyott was
right; for in any balanced explanation of why the Scots were victorious in
1640, their success at the 'skirmish at Newburn' is only part of the explana-

---

* In theory, all adult male residents of each county, owning freehold land capable of
producing an income of 40s. a year, were entitled to give their voices at the election of
their county's two knights of the shire.

tion.[203] Indeed, the Scots' victory left the king's main force, centred on York, wholly unscathed; and this force, far from disintegrating in the aftermath of the encounter on banks of the Tyne, actually grew in size and strength – to the point where Secretary Vane (who had earlier been highly sceptical of the war) could conclude that the mobilization had in the end proved a resounding success. 'Braver bodies of men and better clad have I not seen anywhere,' he wrote of the infantry on 16 September; 'for the horse, they are such as no man that sees them... but will judge them able to stand and encounter with any whatsoever.'[204] How this force might have fared if pitted in battle against Leslie's Covenanters must remain uncertain. The significant point, however, is that many contemporaries believed that the Scots' 'victory' in 1640 did not, in the end, turn upon their superior military prowess (which, ultimately, went untested), but on the political effectiveness of their English allies – their fellow 'rebels' – in making Charles's 'gallant army' politically undeployable.[205]

Several elements had contributed to this conclusion: the obstructionism organized by Darley and the Petitioners' allies in Yorkshire; the suborning of regimental commanders; the king's growing doubts as to the army's political reliability (though how well-founded these were is difficult to gauge); and, above all, by the way in which the Petition of the Twelve, with its insistence on a bloodless, parliamentary resolution to the conflict, caught the imagination of a substantial part of the nation. Viscount Saye, himself one of the Petitioners, concluded that 'without this petition, and the known sence of the City and kingdom concurring therewith, [the Scottish army] had been no more than the fly upon the wheel'.[206] This is an obvious exaggeration, but one, nevertheless, which contains a kernel of truth.

The attribution of responsibility for England's defeat in the war of 1640 profoundly divided the English political nation. Dyott was prepared to concede that the motives of men such as Warwick and Bedford might be 'honorable';[207] but not all contemporaries were so charitable. As reports of the extent of the Petitioners' collusion with the Scots began to circulate during the autumn, it was not long before denunciations of Warwick and his allies were being openly voiced: 'that all these Lords that subscribed the petition were Traytors and Covenanters and ... deserved to be hanged' – a theme that was to be voiced far more loudly and frequently in the two years ahead.[208] This division seems to have been particularly clearly marked within the king's army at York. Even if Bedford's claim was accurate that nine colonels would have declared in favour of the Petitioners,[209] that still left more than half the northern army loyal to the king; and within that section of the military, there seems to have been a profound sense of resentment against the 'Lords that subscribed the petition'.

The king's mindfulness of the Petitioners' treason was to exercise a power-fully destabilizing effect on politics in the months and years ahead. Procuring the invasion of a foreign army (as the Scots were assumed to be in English law) was an instance of 'levying war against the Crown' and therefore treason 'since King Edward IIId's Days'.[210] In late September, Windebank, who already had one eye on prosecuting the Petitioners for treason, once again reassured the monarch that it would be relatively easy to discover the identities of all those who had held intelligence with the 'rebels' and had invited them into England. Charles read this dispatch particularly attentively. Opposite these words he made a brief but menacing marginal note: 'It shall not be forgotten'.[211]

In the quest for any post-war settlement – the task that now fell, first and foremost, to the Lords Commissioners for the Treaty – the fact that the king neither could, nor would, forget massively raised the stakes on both sides. For Warwick, Bedford and their allies the knowledge that the king was aware of their treasonous activities meant that providing for their future security – ensuring their indemnity from future prosecution, both legally and practically – became a major concern. From this point onwards the inner group of Petitioner Peers – Warwick, Bedford, Essex, Mandeville, Saye, Brooke, and Howard – could not sleep easy until the king's powers were reduced to the point where royal vengeance against them was both a legal and a practical impossibility.[212] 'There is no buckler safe enough to fear, nor for the ill-deserver. Therefore they will never be secure,' observed Thomas Webb, the Duke of Lennox's secretary, speaking of the Covenanter leadership in 1640;[213] but his remark applied just as surely to their English co-conspirators in 1640. Danger also arose from what their Scottish allies might reveal. On the eve of the opening of the Great Council an informant of Matthew Wren, the Bishop of Ely and Dean of the Chapel Royal, had reported from York that

> a great Scott sayd that if the English that sent for them and promised assistance to them should fayle them, they would quickly ma[k]e peace with the King, as well as they could, and send him a Roll of those English traytors that sent for them to invade.[214]

If Wren, one of the king's closest confidants, knew (or at least believed) this much, there seems little doubt his royal master did as well.

Within a few weeks of the new Parliament's opening, the king had instructed Sir John Borough, the antiquarian who had already produced the idea of reviving the institution of the Great Council of Peers, to embark on a new line of research. Ominously for the Petitioners, Borough was asked to investigate precedents 'concerning Attainders' – the expedient, much favoured by the Tudors, of using an act of Parliament to condemn and execute troublesome noblemen by simply legislating that they had been guilty of treason. No judicial trial, or even evidence, was necessary. Delivered 'for his Majestie's Especiall service', these attainder precedents were in Charles's hands by December, and were ideally applicable to cases where complicity in treason was widely assumed, but evidence was sparse.[215] For Charles, the day of reckoning with 'those ... traytors' could not come soon enough.

3

OPENING RITES

NOVEMBER 1640

The uttermost of the Scotts' demands are yet vailed from us – and certainly by design of sum even amongst ourselves [the English Treaty Commissioners], so as the minds and opinions of the subjects are infinitly distracted ... for, if they were once made patent, every man's judgment would be satisfied, and soe unity and concurrence in counsels, by God's grace, might follow, which is the only meanes under his goodness to preserve and save ourselves and children by.

Earl of Strafford to Sir George Radcliffe,
Wentworth Woodhouse, 5 November 1640[1]

Charles returned to Whitehall Palace at 4 p.m. on Friday, 30 October, only four days before he was due to open the new Parliament. It was a subdued, almost furtive, homecoming.[2] No trumpets heralded his approach. No City delegation met the royal party on its arrival at Moorgate, the traditional point of entry for returning kings.[3] The monarch's return to Whitehall was barely noticed. Of course, the ignominy of military defeat is a partial explanation for the stealth of this royal entrance. But it also probably reflects the king's judgement on the state of the capital itself. Convinced by Windebank's despatches of recent weeks that the city had been on the brink of insurrection, Charles seems to have looked upon his return to London almost as a foray into enemy territory – a constituency that he had already lost.[4]

The mutinous state of the citizenry was clearly registered in the altered outward face of his palace. When the king had left it, in the blazing sunshine of late August, it had still been the kingdom's seat of power. What he glimpsed now through the gathering dusk, as his coach rolled towards the Palace Gate, was a place literally embattled. Artillery pieces, hastily mounted in September, covered Whitehall's landward approaches. The gun platform in the angle between the Banqueting House and the Privy Gallery range stood armed and ready to rake the open street with fire. The officers and mounted men – the 'cavalleros' or 'cavaliers' as they were coming to be called[5] – of the royal bodyguard, recently called out in force, attended

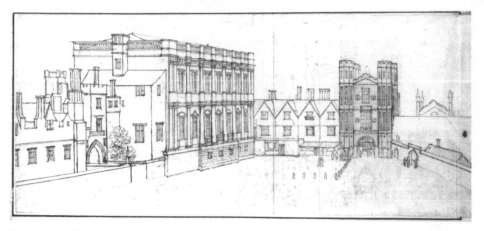

The outward face of the Whitehall court, around 1640, depicting (from left to right): the Palace Gate (Whitehall's main landward entrance); Inigo Jones's Banqueting House (used, from 1622, as the palace's principal Presence Chamber); the western end of the old Tudor Privy Gallery range (the four gables in the centre), which contained the king's private apartments; and the Holbein Gate, which sat athwart King Street (modern-day Whitehall), the major public thoroughfare that ran southwards towards the old Palace of Westminster. The view reveals how vulnerable Whitehall Palace was to landward attack, with crowds being able to congregate in King Street under the very windows of the Banqueting House Presence Chamber.

in the Great Court beyond. This 'strengthening' of the essentially indefensible royal residence was a makeshift and inadequate affair. What it registered, however, and highly effectively, was the state of the government's current relations with the metropolis. King and capital regarded each other with the deepest of suspicion.

Charles had good reason to fear the rebelliousness of the kingdom's principal city. Seditious 'libels' – printed or handwritten single sheets, either pasted up at street corners, or circulated in samizdat copies, denouncing the king's current ministers and sometimes calling for violence against them – had been appearing throughout the city since the spring.[6] And October had seen a recrudescence of the anti-Laudian rioting that had been largely contained since the attack on Lambeth Palace in May. Only a matter of days before the king's return, a London mob had entered 'St Paul's Church' (the recently restored and re-edified cathedral that was one of Charles's great showpiece projects of the 1630s), and attacked its stone altar: the communion table, fixed and railed against the eastern wall of the church.[7] The location and railing of communion tables in this east-end position (the site, before the Reformation, of the altar used for the celebration of the Mass) had been one of the régime's most controversial policies of the 1630s. In the eyes of the policy's critics, railed altars came to symbolize not merely a dubious theology (potentially suggesting that the Church of England's communion service was a 'sacrifice', like the Roman Catholic Mass), but also the régime's supposed indifference to the rule of law, as there was no authority for the policy in either statute law or the

Church's Canons.[8]* Throughout the country, during the year ahead, altars and their rails would often serve as the flashpoints for local disturbances, but the St Paul's riot of October 1640 was the more shocking because it struck at the 'mother church' of the realm. In the course of the riot, service books had been torn to shreds, and a number of the clergy regarded as the 'archbishop's agents' had been forced to flee to avoid being lynched by the angry mob.[9]

Yet even when confronted with this brazen affront to public order and the religious policies of the last decade, the Privy Council remained in a state of paralysis. The riot caused 'grave annoyance' at Whitehall, but nothing effective was done to apprehend the St Paul's rioters, notwithstanding Laud's demands for resolute action, lest this provoke risings that were yet 'more serious'.[10] His warning proved well founded. Only a week later, there was further rioting in the immediate environs of St Paul's. After the Sunday sermon on 1 November, a 'great many rude people' broke into the offices of the Court of High Commission – the highest ecclesiastical court, and the jurisdiction that had enforced many of the controversial 'innovations' of the 1630s – and tore many of the records 'in peeces'.[11] By the time the Convocation met at St Paul's to hear a sermon on Wednesday, 4 November (an audience that included many of the bishops and clergy who had been prominent in enforcing the policies of the previous decade), it was necessary to provide them with an armed guard, both 'horse and foote', to protect them from attack.[12]

This was the London of Charles's return. Whitehall, literally and metaphorically, was on the defensive, an island of safety within a disaffected and tumultuous city. And these physical and psychological realities affected the king's attitudes towards the new Parliament, and the traditional ceremonies that marked its opening, from the outset.

1. ENEMY TERRITORY

By the afternoon of the king's return, preparations for the state opening of Parliament, set for Tuesday, 3 November, were already well advanced. The officer responsible for the ceremonial, the Lord Chamberlain, the Earl of Pembroke, had issued orders for the railing of the processional route as early as 10 October. From Whitehall to the west door of Westminster Abbey, barriers had been erected on both sides of the street to keep back the expected crowds.[13] Bishop Skinner of Bristol, the prominent Laudian who had been chosen to preach before the two Houses at the Abbey, had been given a month's notice to prepare his sermon.[14] The peers and judges had similarly

---

* The intellectual and political implications of the policy were to be criticized at length in *The Altar Dispute,* a work written in mid 1641 by Viscount Saye's nephew, Henry Parker (soon to become the leading polemicist working on behalf of the Petitioner Peers), of which Saye was also the dedicatee.

been warned to furnish themselves with their Parliament robes (and the scarcely less magnificent equipage needed for their horses) for the traditional cavalcade from Whitehall to Westminster: the equestrian procession in which the king, crowned and robed in a mantle of purple velvet and ermine, and accompanied by the judiciary and the entire nobility, rode through the streets of Westminster in a public affirmation of the unity of the nation's political élite.[15]

The ironies of such symbolism, at least in the context of November 1640, do not appear to have been lost on the king. Hence, despite the advanced state of preparations for the state opening (already a month in the planning), Charles issued orders for the cancellation of the equestrian procession, the central public element of the state opening, shortly before he reached London.[16] For whatever reason – concern for his safety, anger at the peers who had failed him so recently at the Great Council at York, fears that he would be exposed to the taunts of 'the vulgar' as he rode through the public streets – Charles resolved to make his arrival at the new Parliament almost as surreptitious as his entry into the capital. Instead of a public procession, he would travel 'in a more private way then ordinary,' by barge, to the Parliament Stairs, wholly unseen by the London crowd.[17] From this landing stage, there would be a much scaled-down procession – on foot and confined within the precincts of the old Palace of Westminster, well out of sight (and earshot) of potentially jeering crowds.

The cancellation of these public ceremonies, as contemporaries noted, sent out a powerfully negative signal. It was as though this were a Parliament that had been forced upon the king, and that he was not prepared 'to own'.[18] Of course, the element of coercion in the Parliament's calling was all too evident; but, as the Venetian ambassador noted, in cancelling the Parliament-day procession, Charles had simply played into the hands of his opponents: it showed 'to his people, more clearly than ever, that he consented to the [Parliament's] summons merely from compulsion by the enemy, and not of his own freewill'.[19] His behaviour gave the impression of a man 'terrified by [the] apprehension of personal danger,'[20] not a sovereign in control.

As often when he considered himself under siege, Charles's instinctive response was to dig in: to defend his honour by standing fast to the policies – and the ministers – that had already failed. The preparedness to compromise, evinced (however unwillingly) during the opening days of the Great Council at York, was now gone. He had returned to London convinced of Strafford's counsel that the war against the Scots was not yet definitively lost, and that the well-affected members of the new Parliament might yet provide him with the means to resume the offensive. If his army at York, which had still not been tried against the Scots, were actually committed to a full-scale battle, the 'skirmish' at Newburn might yet be avenged. And once the Scots were defeated, he could savour the moment of reckoning with the English Fifth-Columnists – with Warwick, Bedford and the other Petitioner Lords – who had encouraged and abetted the Scots' invasion. Securing parliamentary funding for the resumption of the Scottish War was therefore the first element in a larger programme of royal revenge.

The state opening also provided the king with his first opportunity to attempt to sow dissension within ranks of the Petitioner Peers. He began with the Earl of Essex, the most 'generally beloved' – and therefore the most dangerous – of the Twelve.[21] Perhaps responding at last to Windebank's repeated advice that, if Essex could be detached from the others, the conspiratorial 'knot would be much weakened, if not dissolved',[22] he assigned Essex one of the most prestigious roles in the now much-curtailed procession. Essex was to carry the cap of maintenance (one of the chief symbols of the monarch's sovereignty, next only to the crown itself), walking immediately in front of the king – a place of honour, which, pointedly, had been Strafford's at the state opening in the previous April. But this was a gesture intended to divide his enemies, not to conciliate them.[23]

Shortly before 1 p.m. on Tuesday, 3 November, the royal barge rowed away from the Privy Stairs at Whitehall, bound for Westminster, bearing an angry and impenitent king.

*

The king's new-found assertiveness – his refusal to contemplate compromise with his enemies, domestic or foreign – pervaded most of the state opening's public oratory. If it were not already apparent in the sermon preached to the two Houses by Bishop Skinner, a man adept at sugaring the defence of royal authority with a superficial rhetoric of moderation, it was abundantly obvious in the king's own speech from the throne in the House of Lords.[24] Bluntly referring to the Scots as 'Rebels', Charles declared his determination to resume the war at the earliest opportunity and appealed to Parliament to fund a new military offensive to 'Chas[e] [them] out'. Both Houses were moved to consider the 'calamities' that would be suffered by the inhabitants of the North as a result of the Scottish occupation for so long as the treaty negotiations, begun by the Great Council at York, were allowed to continue. The implication was clear: the current negotiations – for the moment firmly in the hands of Warwick and the other Petitioner Peers – should be abandoned, and the attack on the Scots resumed forthwith. Even Charles's one apparently emollient remark – his entreaty to the assembled Parliament-men to 'lay aside all Suspition one of another' – was subtly barbed, with its clear suggestion that at least some of the Lords and Commons *were* currently the legitimate objects of mistrust.[25] In substance, the king had little altered his demands since his famously uncompromising address at the opening of the 'Short Parliament' in April. It was a familiar quid pro quo. Only once the Scots were defeated – and his subjects had opened their purses to see his armies properly paid – would there be time to consider the redress of grievances. Parliament's grant of money must come first.

As custom required, the king's sentiments were amplified in the speech by the Lord Keeper, Lord Finch, which immediately followed. This was not the moment, however, to lecture the two Houses for failing to appreciate the king's exemplary virtues: 'you had need [only] wipe the Glass, and wipe your eyes', Finch upbraided his audience, 'and then you shall truly behold him [as] a King of Exemplary Piety, of Rare Endowments and Abilities of

Nature'.[26] And the ill-judged tone of Finch's speech merely reinforced the impression, at least as perceived by Charles's critics, that the court was functioning in some parallel world, disengaged from the realities of defeat. Northumberland's sister, the politically astute Countess of Carlisle (who seems to have been present at the state opening), was not alone in regarding Finch's oration as 'the worse speetch, to my thinking, that ever wase mayd'.[27]

Yet it would be a mistake to see the Parliament as wholly unsympathetic to the king's objectives, still less as broadly united behind the reformist, pro-Scottish interest represented by Warwick, Bedford and Pym. For them and their fellow Petitioner Lords, it had been a major disappointment that the Council of Peers at York had refused to sanction the disbandment of the king's army so long as the Scots were in the field. It must have been more disconcerting still that the Parliament's opening speeches were received with 'the universal acclamations of all those present'; and while some claimed that this enthusiasm was wholly feigned, there were others in the king's audience – like the Commons-man Sir William Widdrington, to whom the Scots were 'invading rebels' – who were clearly in sympathy with the king's belligerently anti-Scottish message.[28] At least part of that 'universal acclamation' for the king's robustly anti-Covenanter stance may well have been entirely sincere.

To dismiss the assertiveness of the king's speech as merely another instance of royal gaucherie would seem to be equally misplaced.[29] For on the eve of the state opening, Charles had come to a decision that helps explain much of the forcefulness of his rhetoric the following day. He had commanded Strafford, the most determined advocate of resuming the offensive against the Scots, to leave the army in the North and return at once to Westminster. As Charles knew full well, this act, once made public, would be regarded as tantamount to a declaration of war against the Petitioners – against Warwick, Bedford, Essex and their friends – for whom Strafford was the ultimate *bête noire*: the advocate of an authoritarian monarchy founded on military power;[30] the prime 'evil counsellor' whom they were determined to bring down.[31]

Strafford, for his part, had already telegraphed to the Petitioners his own uncompromising view of what he expected the new Parliament's role to be. An exchange in September 1640 between Strafford and Harbottell Grimston, Warwick's long-standing ally, is here revealing. Grimston had journeyed to York to present the king with the Essex gentry's petition, backing up the Petition of the Twelve, and at some point during his stay had come face to face with the Lord-Lieutenant. In what seems to have been a deliberate attempt to telegraph a warning to Warwick and the other Petitioner Lords, Strafford had taken Grimston 'aside in the gallerie [of the king's lodgings at York], and told him *how necessarie a compliance was with the Kinge*'.[32] And compliance with the king, to Strafford, meant one thing: resuming the war against the Scots and prosecuting it to the defeat of the Covenanter 'rebels'.

*

Still in Yorkshire with the army at the time of the state opening, Strafford fully realized how provocative his recall would seem to his enemies, yet was undaunted by the forthcoming confrontation. 'I am hastened up [to London],' he wrote from Wentworth Woodhouse, his Yorkshire seat, on the eve of his departure, as it was 'of absolute necessity to be ther, and therfore noe delay [was] to be used'.[33] On Friday, 6 November, within twenty-four hours of receiving the king's entreaty, and three days after the new Parliament's inauguration, Strafford set out from Wentworth Woodhouse for London, troubled still by 'the stone', but otherwise much recovered in health.[34]

He reached Huntingdon, sixty miles north of London, on Sunday, 8 November, in optimistic mood. The first attack against himself, Strafford believed, was likely to come from the Irish Parliament, and, having been briefed as to the substance of its accusations, he was confident that they could be straightforwardly rebutted. The charges were 'better th[a]n I expected', Strafford informed his legal adviser and man-of-affairs, Sir George Radcliffe, 'ther proofes being very scant'.[35] By Sunday afternoon, with London only a day's ride away, Strafford was in combative mood: 'God's hand is with us', he assured Radcliffe. 'All will be well, and every hower gives more hope th[a]n [the] other.'[36]

ii. DIVIDED COUNSELS

At Westminster, the Petitioner leadership was proceeding cautiously and methodically in preparing its case against the Earl of Strafford. Pym was reported to have been gathering evidence for the earl's impeachment as early as 'the begininge [of] Michelmas terme [29 September 1640]' – that is, within a few days of his learning that a new Parliament had been called.[37] And Warwick's concern to have the adoptive Ulsterman, Sir John Clotworthy, elected for his pocket borough of Maldon in Essex was probably likewise motivated by the hope that Clotworthy's Irish connections would prove useful in managing the Dublin end of the accusations and evidence against the Lord Lieutenant.[38] Indeed, it may well have been that they were intending to wait for charges to be formally levelled against Strafford by the Irish Parliament, before following up with their own assault.[39] This caution was amply justified. Even with the régime as wounded as it was in the autumn of 1640, attempting the impeachment of the king's most powerful minister was an inherently hazardous activity; and, once the Parliament had settled down to business at the end of the first week of November, the precariousness of the Petitioner Lords and their allies was quickly exposed.

The first practical test of the Petitioners' ability to make good an attack on Strafford came on Friday, 6 November – the day when Strafford set out from Wentworth Woodhouse. Bitter controversy erupted in the House over a technical, but highly consequential, matter of procedure. Friday the 6th was the Commons' first business day, and hence, by custom, largely taken up with the appointment of the Commons' Grand Committees: the standing Committees of the Whole House that were to meet regularly throughout the parliamentary session. At first, all this went ahead without any notable dissent. When, however, towards the end of the day, it was proposed that a

'Committee for Irish Affairs' should be established, the suggestion sparked a highly acrimonious debate.

Anodyne as its title might sound, this Committee for Irish Affairs was clearly the body likely to control any Commons investigation into Strafford's conduct as viceroy of Ireland since his appointment in 1633.[40] More particularly, it was self-evidently the committee to which the Irish Parliament's accusations against Strafford – already known to be in preparation – would eventually be referred. Successful impeachments depended on careful bicameral cooperation: between the formal accusers (who had to come from the Commons) and those peers who were prepared to drive forward the prosecution within the House of Lords (the 'court' before which the charges were heard). Even had Pym not been used to meeting with Warwick, Saye, Mandeville, and Brooke monthly, and sometimes daily, over the previous six months, Strafford's impeachment would have provided him with a compelling motive for seeing that those contacts were kept up assiduously over the weeks ahead.

Conversely, for these 'Warwick House peers', it was vital that all of these Strafford-related committees in the Commons were strongly influenced, and ideally controlled, by their political allies. Hence, when the issue of creating a Committee for Irish Affairs was first mooted in the Commons on 6 November, a mixture of the Petitioners' placemen and men-of-business dominated the anti-Straffordian side of the debate.

Pym and Grimston, two of the most vehement critics of royal policy in the ill-fated Short Parliament, achieved the key advance of the day, persuading the Commons to accept the principle that the English Parliament had an 'imperial' jurisdiction over Ireland (notwithstanding that Ireland had a Parliament of its own). The Westminster Parliament could therefore summon subjects of the Crown of Ireland to appear before its committees as witnesses as though they were native Englishmen, and regard charges against Strafford emanating from the Irish Parliament as justiciable before itself.[41] This was to have massive constitutional implications for the future,[42] leading to the claim in May 1641 that the English Parliament 'is the supream Judicature in the said Realme [of Ireland]'.[43] For the present, however, its major consequence was to confer a decisive procedural advantage on the anti-Straffordians, since it enabled the Commons and its committees to consider crimes committed in Ireland – including charges brought by the Dublin Parliament – as though they had occurred in England.

But the Petitioners' allies wanted something more. To ensure that their own influence was deployed to maximum effect, a proposal emerged from the Petitioner group – probably from Pym, Grimston or Clotworthy, all of whom were active in the debate – that this Committee should not be a Committee of the Whole House (at which every member of the Commons had the right to attend and speak) but, instead, a small 'select committee' that could meet in private, well away from the Commons' chamber, and beyond the scrutiny of most of its members.[44] Strafford's prosecution, in other words, was to be managed by a small 'junto' or cabal, not by the Commons as a whole. Yet this proposal encountered fierce, and possibly unexpected, resistance. The prospect that 'Irish Affairs' in general – and Strafford's prosecution in particular – should fall into such overtly partisan hands provoked a strong reaction. A number of Commons-men, including Sir Edward Bayntun and the die-hard Straffordian, Sir Richard Lee,[45] pushed for the question to be referred to a Committee of the Whole House, an outcome that threatened to stop any prosecution in its tracks. As this expedient would require that *every* witness against Strafford, and there were potentially hundreds, should be questioned before the entire House of Commons, it looked likely to reduce any prosecution to a snail's pace, as well as bringing most other parliamentary business to a standstill.

Some indication of the partisanship that this question aroused is provided by the fact that it was forced to a division: a relatively rare procedure in a House that still valued maintaining at least the carapace of consensus, and which required the 'voices' on either side to be counted by four tellers, two from either side.* In the division, the Straffordian, Sir Richard Lee, was joined by the idiosyncratic serial adulterer, Sir Edward Bayntun,[46] in counting the votes in favour of making the Irish Affairs Committee a 'Committee of the Whole House' (with all the delays that this would entail). On the other side, it was the anti-Straffordians – Clotworthy, again, and Sir Henry Mildmay – who counted the votes in favour of hiving off the investigations to a select committee.[47]

Had the Parliament been even close to being united in its support for the Petitioner cause, this was a question that Clotworthy, Grimston, Mildmay and Pym might have been expected to win without a division. Instead, the result was a crushing, if still relatively narrow, defeat. By a margin of just thirteen votes in a House of over three hundred – 165 votes to 152 – the Commons decided in favour of transferring the matter to the large and unwieldy setting of a Committee of the Whole House.[48] The Petitioner Peers and their Commons allies had just sustained their first tactical defeat.

If this first disputed vote of the parliamentary session was not yet a *party* division, it was at least one that was highly partisan, with one of the great

---

* Settling matters by division, at this stage in the life of the Parliament, was a highly unusual procedure. In the vast majority of votes in the House of Commons, the question was decided by simple acclamation: the Speaker decided which of the two sides had the more 'voices'. On rare occasions, however, where there was uncertainty over numbers and neither side was prepared to give way, a division would be called. The side advocating change would leave the chamber and be counted by two 'tellers' as they entered the Commons' lobby, while those opposing the departure from the status quo remained in their seats, to be counted by two tellers of their own. In a culture in which to lose publicly was to lose face, and which consequently strove to preserve at least the illusion that decisions were arrived at consensually, the calling of a division almost invariably signalled that the question involved had been highly controversial. For such factiousness to be manifest on a Parliament's first business day – when courtesy was still at a premium and tempers had not yet had time to fray – points both to a question of more than usual contentiousness and a very narrow margin between the opposing sides.

political questions of the moment – the fate of the king's senior minister, and
the propriety of his actions during the Personal Rule – obviously at stake.
Revealingly, every one of the Commons-men noted as intervening in this
debate was firmly associated with Warwick House: John Pym and Harbottell
Grimston most obviously; but also the two Commons-men who acted as
tellers for the anti-Straffordian side in the division. Both tellers sat for the
same constituency, Warwick's pocket borough of Maldon in Essex: Sir John
Clotworthy, a carpetbagger who was Warwick's nominee, and Sir Henry
Mildmay, who was married to Warwick's stepdaughter, and was to profit
handsomely from Warwick's rise in the months ahead.[49] This does not seem
to be a random conjunction of Strafford's enemies. Even so, the prominence
of this 'interest' with links to Warwick's godly circle should not be read as
implying some servile 'patron-client' relation, but attests instead to a concerted political interest, united in a common purpose – the reform of the
Church and what they were coming increasingly to speak of as 'the commonwealth'[50] – and willing to collaborate in order to see its attainment.
Such patronage as Warwick conferred on these fellow 'godly' men was,
first and foremost, the outward expression of that inward religious and
ideological bond, not a favour that made the recipient beholden to a lordly
puppeteer.[51]

Enough is going on here to caution us against assuming, as historians have
repeatedly done hitherto, that the House of Commons was united in its
hostility to the Crown and its ministers from the outset; and that only
gradually, in the course of 1641 and in reaction to an increasingly overbearing
'puritan leadership', did divisions emerge. Indeed, perhaps the most striking
aspect of the new Parliament's first formal division in November 1640 is
how closely it foreshadows, at least in numerical terms, the split that was to
emerge twelve months later, when the Commons divided on whether to
approve the 'Grand Remonstrance': the great catalogue (which Pym, Clotworthy, and Grimston were also to be involved in preparing) that itemized
the iniquities of the Personal Rule. A year away, in November 1641, the
balance of the two sides would be strikingly similar: 159 votes for, and 148
against[52] – or within twenty of the numbers on either side in the Commons'
very first working day.[53]

The reformist leadership – the cluster of Parliament-men allied to Warwick,
Pym, Clotworthy, and the Petitioner Peers – seems to have learnt from that
Commons' division of 6 November 1640, and in its immediate aftermath
trod with extreme caution in all matters relating to the Earl of Strafford.
Astonishingly, Pym's wide-ranging speech on the ills of the commonwealth,
delivered in the Commons on 7 November and reported to have lasted some
two hours, failed to make a single reference to Strafford by name.[54]
Over the following week, as the Commons' chamber resounded to denunciations of 1630s abuses, there was not a word about impeaching the 'great
incendiary'.[55]

This first rebuff to the Petitioner leadership seems to have confirmed the
king in his view that a resolute policy of confrontation with his régime's
enemies, early in the Parliament, might yet carry the day.[56]

III. THE RETURN OF THE 'GREAT INCENDIARY'

Well before Strafford left Huntingdon, on the final leg of his journey to London, he was preparing himself to confront the Scots' English accomplices: the Petitioner Lords, by whom his campaign against the 'rebels' had been, in Sir Richard Dyott's phrase, 'retarded, discountenanced, and indeed overthrown'.[57] He had already made clear his view that the lords who delivered the Petition of the Twelve should be 'Shot at the Head of the Army, as Movers of Sedition';[58] and though his later correspondence does not mention the Petitioners by name, there is little doubt that his references to his own likely accusers allude to Warwick and the Petitioner Peers. The depth of their guilt (for their collusion with the Scots) was their principal motive, Strafford believed, for what he expected would be a forthcoming assault on himself. 'It is not to be believed how great the[ir] malice is,' he had written to Sir George Radcliffe, his friend and future executor,[59] on the eve of his journey to London,

> and how intent they are about it. Little less care there is taken [by them] to ruin me than to save ther owne souls.[60] Nay, for themselves, I wishe ther attention to the latter [saving their souls] were equal to that [which] they lend me in the former; and certainly they will racke [i.e. rake] heaven and hell, as they say, to doe me mischief.[61]

This view – that the attack on himself was being planned by his enemies as a means of deflecting attention away from their own guilt – appears to have suggested to him his strongest line of defence: a well-timed pre-emptive strike, to be mounted almost as soon as he was back in London; to denounce their treasonous collusion with the Covenanters, before they had an opportunity to turn their fire on him.

Within a short time of the state opening, reports were already beginning to circulate at Westminster that the Lord Lieutenant intended to 'preferr an accusation of high Treason against divers members of *both* houses of parliament'.[62] Strafford's friend, Archbishop Laud, who was in a position to know, noted that it was thought, '(upon good Grounds) that the Earl of Strafford had got Knowledge of the Treason of some Men, and that he was preparing to accuse them'.[63]

That such a strategy might have succeeded was not entirely fanciful. Once the extent of the Petitioners' treasonous collusion with the Scots was out in the open, there was a strong possibility that their current prestige and authority would be fatally undermined. Despite (and, in some cases, doubtless because of) the past year's barrage of pro-Covenanter propaganda, a deep-seated anti-Scottishness remained the defining characteristic of many Parliament-men; and, if even half those who had applauded the king's plans to 'Chase out' the Scots had been sincere, there might well be a constituency large enough in Parliament to act upon the charge that the Petitioner Lords and their allies were 'Traytors [that] deserved to be hanged'.[64]

*

Strafford – still in command of the English *and* Irish armies, forces numbering, in total, over 30,000 men – reached London on the evening of Monday, 9 November.[65] The king's response to his arrival could not have been more emphatic. He received Strafford warmly, 'with great expressions of favour and renewed assurances of protection', and appears to have given his endorsement to Strafford's plan to pre-empt the attack on himself with the denunciation of his own prospective accusers.[66] Within twenty-four hours, Charles and Strafford had resolved on a double strike against their enemies: first, a reassertion of royal authority within the City of London through the strengthening of the garrison and fortifications at the Tower; and, second, an immediate pre-emptive strike to arrest the leading Petitioner conspirators and indict them for treason.[67] The two initiatives appear to have been connected, for the Tower – commanded since August by Lord Cottington, Strafford's friend and personal nominee as Constable – was almost certainly the intended place for the conspirators' detention. In the plan to arrest the English Fifth-Columnists, the Tower's strengthened fortifications and additional gun-emplacements were to serve as a deterrent to the mutinous City, once the 'traitors' had been detained pending trial, against any attempt to release them by force.

Strafford's arrival in London was also marked by a sudden flurry of military activity in and around the capital.[68] 'Since his comming to Towne',[69] new guns were mounted at the Tower, and a series of 'basketts with ladders' – so-called 'gabions', wicker baskets filled with earth or stones – had been set in place 'to defend the gunners'.[70] Further pieces of ordnance had been 'tried' (i.e. tested) at Deptford, where part of the navy lay at anchor – apparently creating a fear that these men-o'-war would be used to bombard the City (a tactic that had been threatened against the Edinburgh port of Leith the previous year).[71] The garrison at the Tower was reported to have resumed 'training'.[72]

Against this background, reports of Strafford's plan to initiate treason prosecutions of his own quickly reached their presumed victims.[73] The same six Parliament-men who had been suspected of collusion with the Scots by the Privy Council at the end of the 'Short Parliament' – Warwick, Saye and Brooke from the Lords; and Pym, Hampden, and Sir Walter Erle from the Commons – were likely to have figured again on Strafford's new list, perhaps now with the addition of the names of Bedford, Essex, and Sir John Clotworthy.[74] But the actual extent of Strafford's planned prosecutions was of secondary importance. Once it was known that Strafford was intending to bring prosecutions, *all* of those who had colluded with the Scots must have regarded themselves as potential targets.[75]

From that moment, those whom Windebank termed 'the knot' of the conspiracy – Warwick, Essex and Brooke, Pym and Clotworthy – knew they were in grave danger. They had no reason to doubt the seriousness of Strafford's intention to act. Apart from his request to have Lords Howard of Escrick and Wharton tried for sedition, Strafford had already arrested one of the Petitioners' closest confidants, Henry Darley – the intermediary in the transmission of their invitation to the Scots to invade – and imprisoned him in York Castle, awaiting trial for treason;[76] and neither Warwick nor any of his colleagues had any way of knowing whether Darley had talked.[77]

To sharpen these anxieties, reports were coming in throughout Tuesday, 10 November (the day after Strafford's return) of a sudden flurry of military activity at the Tower.[78] In what may have been a deliberate 'leak', one of Strafford's servants – 'one Fereby' – quoted his master as saying that 'hee hoped the Citty would bee subdued in a short time'.[79] Nor was this the only report of moves being made against the reformists within the capital. A lawyer in the Bishop of London's Consistory Court – was alleged to have said that 'the Cittie [forces] should shortly be about the Citizens' eares'[80] – a rumour that was the more plausible for the strong support the king still enjoyed with London's conservative aldermanic élite.

As rumours proliferated, plans were being made at court for the king to travel to the Tower the following day, 11 November.[81] Though this was nominally to view the garrison 'training' before it was disbanded, this explanation is scarcely credible,[82] particularly when taken in conjunction with the mounting of heavy ordnance at the Tower in the previous forty-eight hours (that is, since Strafford's return to London). Given that Charles and Strafford were still intent on laying charges against the Petitioner leadership, it is more likely that the king was assuring himself of the garrison's loyalty as a preliminary to his own withdrawal to this, the only defensible royal residence in the capital. In the event of the rioting that was almost certain to follow any attempt to arrest the Petitioner 'traitors', the Tower was likely to be decisive to his efforts to retain control of the capital.

Already by Tuesday, 10 November, the eve of the royal 'visit' to the Tower, the broad outlines of these plans appear to have come to the knowledge of the Warwick House peers.[83] That same day, they took what action they could to prevent accusations being laid against themselves. In the Lords, steps were taken to forestall any attempt to gather evidence against them by declaring that the raids (in May) on the studies of Warwick, Saye, and Brooke had been a breach of parliamentary privilege – a vote with which the Commons hurriedly concurred.[84]

The Warwick House leadership then responded as Strafford perhaps expected. Panicked by the prospect of an attempt to establish their treasonous complicity with the Scots, this inner group of the Petitioners prepared to take the offensive, attacking their likely accuser in order 'to save ther owne souls'.[85] As Laud observed, this 'fear' that treason charges were impending against themselves, 'both hastned and heated their proceedings against [Strafford]'.[86]

At the end of the Parliament's first week, the question was which of the two rival sets of accusers would have the audacity – and the evidence ready – to make the first strike.

*

To Warwick, Bedford and the other Petitioner grandees, the 'legal trial and condign punishment'[87] of Charles's evil counsellors had been one of the prime

reasons for their insistence on a new meeting of Parliament. Yet the beginning
of that judicial process was much less tidy than this high-minded purpose
might suggest. The Warwick House group appears to have been wrong-
footed by Strafford's return to London on 9 November. Despite Pym's preparations during October for an impeachment, the Petitioners' attack on the
Lord Lieutenant seemed to have emerged as a defensive measure, hurriedly
contrived – what the Earl of Northumberland was to call 'the hastie and
violent proceedings ... against my Lord Liftenant'.[88] Over the night of
Tuesday–Wednesday, 10–11 November, measures were taken to cobble
together a case that would substantiate an impeachment charge against the
Lord Lieutenant,[89] and, no less importantly, to justify a motion that he should
be 'sequestered' from the House of Lords. Acceptance of this latter proposal
was vital; for, unless Strafford were deprived of the right to sit in the Lords
that same day, he would remain at liberty to present charges against whom-
soever he wished, and to make his accusations under the protection of
parliamentary privilege.[90] Once 'sequestered' and deprived of his right to sit,
however, the earl was effectively silenced, for no counter-accusations could
be entertained from one who was himself under investigation for treason.

Inflicting this double blow against Strafford – both the preliminary accusation and his immediate removal from the Lords – in turn required meticulous
coordination between the Petitioners' allies in the two Houses. If Strafford
were to be muzzled by being 'sequestered' immediately, the peers had to
receive the Commons' charges and agree to the accused's committal that
same day: Wednesday, 11 November. Timing was of the essence.[91]

Even so, Strafford's would-be accusers can have had only uncertain hopes
of success when they arrived at the 'Parliament-House' (as it was known to
contemporaries) that Wednesday morning. After the previous week's division,
there was the serious possibility that any impeachment proposal would be
referred to the Committee for Irish Affairs (in other words, to the whole
House of Commons, meeting without the Speaker), where deliberation on
the issue looked likely to be endlessly delayed. This, above all, was the
outcome that Warwick, Pym and Clotworthy had to avoid. Somehow, they
had to convince a sceptical House of Commons that Strafford posed a threat
to the Parliament so acute – and so pressing – that decisive action against
the accused was imperative that same day.

Not for the last time, it was Charles I who unwittingly came to his enemies'
aid.

iv. ACCUSATION

On the morning of Wednesday, 11 November – as Charles readied himself
for the short trip down-river to the Tower and Strafford made his way to
Westminster to take his seat in the House of Lords – rumours that some
form of coup was imminent were already rife in the City. The Commons
convened that morning to hear reports of the sinister activities of Papists
and priests, the familiar villains of 'popish plotting', relayed by Clotworthy

and the radical London puritan, Isaac Penington.[92] The most alarming revelations, however, came from Matthew Cradock, one of Warwick's prime contacts in the City's godly merchant community,[93]* who alerted the Commons to the new artillery emplacements being erected at the Tower, the trials of ordnance in the nearby naval dockyards, and that 'Souldiers at the Tower [were] still training and mounting gunns *this day* – and [that] many other gunns were [already] mounted'.[94]

All these developments, Cradock left his audience in little doubt, were interconnected: not only with some plan of Strafford's to 'subdue' the City, but also with the king's reported intention to remove himself to the Tower that same day.[95] The explanation offered by the otherwise widely respected Privy Councillor, Sir Thomas Rowe, that the king was at the Tower merely to review Lord Cottington's garrison, met with a derisive riposte from Penington. Why, then, were 'the baskets [fortified gun-emplacements] and Granadoes [small explosive shells thrown or rolled towards attackers]' still being set up, if the king's visit were 'onely a Triumph'? (The sneer implicit in Penington's reference to the defeated king holding a 'triumph' would have been lost on no one.)[96]

The Commons were sufficiently shaken by these revelations to order that strangers should be cleared from the lobby and that 'the outward door upon the Stairs Head† [was] to be kept locked'.[97] How many of these interventions from Clotworthy, Penington, and Cradock had been prearranged with the Warwick House leadership in advance is unknowable; but the fact that all three alarm-mongers were supporters of the Petitioner cause, and that two out of three had close associations with Warwick, at least suggests this as a strong possibility.[98]

As the Commons took these precautions, only a few hundred yards away, at the southern end of the palace, Strafford took his seat in the House of Lords. There, as one unnamed peer recalled, 'he received expressions of

---

* In March 1628, the Earl of Warwick had been granted land in Massachusetts by the Crown that established the New England Company, 'the unincorporated predecessor of the Massachusetts Bay Company', whose membership included a number of Warwick's godly friends in the City and among the East Anglian gentry. 'Warwick's protégé, the minister, Hugh Peter[s], ... played a critical role in helping to forge this alliance', and when the New England Company came to appoint its first governor, it was Matthew Cradock who was chosen. Cradock had become well acquainted with Warwick during the late 1620s and early 1630s, as it was he, as governor, who 'appears to have taken primary responsibility for mediating between the colonizing aristocrats [of whom Warwick, Saye, and Brooke were pre-eminent], who were especially needed to defend the project against royal repression, and the company's small-trader, small-gentry leadership'. When a new charter was granted to Cradock's company in 1629, formally setting up the Massachusetts Bay Company, one of Cradock's co-investors, John Humphrey, remarked, 'We are all much bound to the Lord Saye for his cordial advice and true affections. As also my Lord of Warwick. Sir Nathaniel Rich [Warwick's cousin and principal man-of-affairs until 1636] deserves very much acknowledgement for his wise handling ...'
† This was the door (the old west door of St Stephen's Chapel) that gave entry to the Commons' lobby. The stairs led down to St Stephen's Cloister, at ground-floor level, which adjoined Westminster Hall; see map p. xx.

honour and observance [deference] answerable to the dignity of his place [and] the esteeme and credit which he had with his Majestie as the cheifest Minister of the State'.[99] Yet the expected attack on the 'traitors' in both Houses did not come. A moment when, arguably, decisive action against the conspirators might still have been viable was allowed to slip away. S. R. Gardiner's explanation, first advanced in the 1880s, ascribed this omission to a failure of will on the king's part, not Strafford's – a theory that meshed well with Gardiner's view of Charles's larger deficiencies of 'character'.[100] But it is likely that both the king and Strafford had sound practical reasons for delaying the presentation of any charges against the Warwick House grandees. Arresting members in Parliament-time was always a highly controversial activity (a lesson that had been learnt from the fracas that followed the arrests of the Earl of Arundel, Sir Dudley Digges and Sir John Eliot during the Parliament of 1626),[101] and the desire to delay the planned arrests of 1640 is readily explicable by the need to ensure that the evidence against the accused was in order, and (perhaps as important) that the recently implemented improvements to the defences at the Tower – the traditional place of remand for accused traitors – had been properly completed.

For whatever reason, however, the accusations against the Petitioner 'traitors' in both Houses were deferred. (In fact, it was to be more than a year before Charles felt confident enough to move against these 'traitors' – and by then the opportunity had irrevocably passed.) As the business of that Wednesday, 11 November extended late into the afternoon, Strafford (who, as commander of the army, had an abundance of other pressing matters awaiting him) returned to Whitehall Palace, presumably to hear the king's reactions to what he had seen earlier that morning at the Tower.[102]

In the now locked Commons, debate on the crisis created by Cradock's warning of an imminent *coup d'état* continued amid confusion as to the king's intentions in going to the Tower, and uncertainty as to whether or not the military measures to 'subdue' the City had already been set in train. What followed, the dramatic moment of Strafford's accusation, has entered historical myth as one of the great set-piece moments of the 'English Revolution'. A supremely confident Pym, ever the 'master of timing'[103] – so the argument runs – spoke for the nation in accusing the earl of high treason; and an acquiescent House of Commons promptly followed his authoritative lead. In the view of S. R. Gardiner, the great Victorian whose *History* has been the foundation of most narratives of the period, this was a moment of epiphany: the hour when Pym 'saw that his time was come'.[104] He 'rose and moved that the doors should be locked', wrote Gardiner, and there followed the 'dramatic opening of the accusations against Strafford'.[105] And an overwhelmingly united House 'agreed with Pym'.[106]

This supposed unity, revealed by the Commons' willingness to follow Pym's lead in the Strafford impeachment, is an essential foundation of Gardiner's broader – and massively influential – thesis: that Pym was the dominant figure in either House of Parliament. The widespread support for Pym's leadership in the Strafford impeachment, Gardiner supposed, was symptomatic of a broader unanimity within the two Houses so long as reform was confined to 'constitutional issues'. Parliament only became divided, so the argument runs – and divided to the point of resorting to arms – when Pym and his friends pushed their programme for reform beyond secular concerns and towards the question of religion.[107] Ergo, it was religion, not 'constitutional' issues, that was the true cause of the 'Puritan Revolution'.[108]

We will return to the question of the validity of this dichotomy between 'religious' and 'constitutional' motives later;[109] what concerns us here is the pervasive influence of Gardiner's canonical narrative about the role of Pym. Throughout most of the twentieth century, this version of events has been repeated, with ever growing authority, from text to text.[110] By the time we reach the 1990s, the Parliament's initial unity is so complete and Pym's mastery of the Commons so absolute that Strafford's impeachment is almost casually achieved, within a matter of hours of the Lord Lieutenant's arrival in London. The impeachment, wrote the leading late-twentieth-century authority on the causes of the Civil War, was 'formally moved by Pym on 11 November, the day Strafford arrived in town from Yorkshire, [and] he was immediately sent to the Tower'.[111]

In fact, as we have seen, Strafford did not arrive 'in town' on the day of his impeachment, but two days earlier. Indeed, the provocative action he had taken in the period since his arrival was almost certainly one of the key precipitants of the accusation against him. Nor was he 'immediately' sent to the Tower; that did not happen for over a fortnight after his arrival in London – on 24 November.[112] If these two points are demonstrably wrong, what then of the third claim: that Strafford's impeachment was 'formally moved by Pym' – an assertion ultimately derived (like so much else) from Gardiner, who assumed that 'our only knowledge of the debate comes from Bodvile's Diary [the parliamentary journal of the Welshman, John Bodvile]'?[113]

Since Gardiner's day, five further parliamentary diaries have come to light to illuminate this critical debate. From these, a very different picture begins to emerge of the circumstances of Strafford's accusation.[114] True, Pym did make a speech – but about an 'Irish Preist' and the 'carelesnes' of Secretary Windebank; and though this intervention against Windebank was a necessary element of the Petitioners' broader strategy, his speech was not, however, a speech about the Earl of Strafford.[115] Pym's approach was logical, if nowhere near as heroic as Gardiner assumed. If anyone had the wherewithal to prove the Petitioners' treasonous collusion with the Scots, it was Windebank. Destroying his credibility as a potential accuser was therefore of vital concern to all members of the Bedford–Warwick interest; and to do this, Pym produced the claim that Windebank was guilty of misprision (the culpable concealment) of treason – a capital offence.

The plot, Pym claimed, which Windebank had been informed of, but ignored, involved an Irish chaplain in the household of Queen Marie des Médicis (then living in exile at St James's), Father William O'Connor.*

---

* Queen Marie des Médicis (the widow of Henri IV and mother of Queen Henriette Marie); members of her above-stairs household would have enjoyed the entrée to most

O'Connor, so the story ran, was planning an English version of the St Bartholomew's Day Massacre, in which London Papists were to rise and 'cutt the Protestants' throats'; and, while he hoped for royal support for his murderous scheme, O'Connor had reportedly claimed that he would kill the king should this approval be withheld.[116] Outlandish as these accusations may seem in hindsight, they probably had considerable force in the context of the moment; and Pym's choice of this particular charge against Windebank is all the more intriguing in that the source for the story – Mistress Anne Hussey, a respectable Irish woman who had converted from 'Popery' to a zealous Protestantism – was believed by Windebank to 'hav[e] some relation to the Earle of Warwick'. Indeed, Windebank's own observations on the case can be read as suggesting that Warwick had put Hussey up to making her charge against him in the first place.[117] And by a happy coincidence, it was St John and Grimston who now stepped forward to corroborate Pym's claim and to 'aggravate' (or make more heinous) this charge that Windebank had concealed a real threat to kill the king.[118]

As a strategy for discrediting Windebank as a potential accuser, all this seems to have been highly effective. But nothing in Pym's speech touched even indirectly on the Earl of Strafford. The great speech which Gardiner read as Pym's moment of epiphany – his realization that 'his time was come'[119] – was not actually delivered by Pym at all, but by Sir John Clotworthy.[120] Yet not even Clotworthy mounted a direct attack on the Lord Lieutenant, choosing as his target, instead, Strafford's legal adviser and chief confidant, Sir George Radcliffe.[121]

In attacking Radcliffe, however, Clotworthy made one oblique, but profoundly damaging, revelation about the Earl of Strafford: that Radcliffe had admitted that Strafford's Irish army had been intended, not only for use against the Scots, but also for the suppression of any opposition the king might encounter domestically; it existed so that Charles might 'have what he pleaseth in England'.[122] What the Commons was expected to make of these revelations was clear enough: as Radcliffe could be assumed to be his master's voice, these plans to use the Irish army to quell dissent in England had been Strafford's, and had threatened the imposition of a martial tyranny.[123]* This, if proven, was a sensational charge; yet the evidence to substantiate it was pure hearsay, and what remains striking about Clotworthy's speech, as reported, is its avoidance of any direct accusation against the Lord Lieutenant.

This was a very roundabout way of launching an impeachment, and Clotworthy's speech looks less like a display of anti-Straffordian confidence than a very tentative attempt to test the waters. Levelling accusations against Sir George Radcliffe, a Straffordian deputy relatively unknown in England, while

---

parts of Whitehall Palace; so the plot, as retailed to the Commons, had considerable plausibility.
* Pym was later to observe, with donnish humour, that 'the Spirit [i.e. the breath – from the Latin *spiritus*] of my lord of Strafford could move in Sir George Radcliffe, whensoever it was spoken'.

subtly implicating his master, provided a means of gauging the Commons' likely reaction were Strafford himself to be attacked. Only after Clotworthy's revelation had registered did Pym come forward with a related proposal of his own that: 'itt may bee orderde the lord lieutenant should declare himself wh[e]ther hee had advised the Irish armie to be brought in[to England]'.[124] Yet the significant thing about this motion was that the Commons simply failed to take it up.[125]

Instead of moving towards an attack on Strafford, debate meandered back and forth among a series of apparently unrelated accusations against Secretary Windebank. Pym, meanwhile, doubtless alarmed at the Commons' failure to respond to his motion, and fearful that the peers 'might rise [i.e. adjourn]' before he and his friends had an opportunity to have a formal charge against Strafford approved, asked leave to visit the House of Lords. Once there, he assured the Commons' Speaker, he 'did not doubt [that he could] intimate to some [of the peers] that they might sitt'.[126] Pym was evidently becoming desperate;[127] if the Lords adjourned before the vote to 'sequester' Strafford was accepted by the Commons and sent on to the upper House, the impeachment would have to be postponed to another day and Strafford, forewarned, would be forearmed.[128]

As Pym implored his friends in the Lords (unnamed in the sources, but almost certain to have included Warwick, Bedford, and Brooke) to keep the upper House in session, debate back in the Commons returned, yet again, to the baiting of Secretary Windebank.[129] Here, too, the only circumstantial detail that implicated the Lord-Lieutenant, even potentially, was that in May 1640 Windebank had claimed that the Short Parliament's troublemakers were 'traitours' and had 'spoken [these words] in Leicester Howse' – that is, Strafford's London residence, which he had been renting at the time from the Earl of Leicester.[130]

Only towards the end of a wide-ranging and rather unfocused debate about threats posed from a variety of quarters, including the resumption of work to reinforce the Tower in the two days since Strafford's return, did the Commons appoint a small select committee to 'prepare matter for a conference' – a formal meeting of representatives of the two Houses – that was to be requested with the House of Lords.[131] This six-man committee was heavily loaded with Strafford's enemies, all of them from the Bedford–Warwick group: Pym, St John, and Clotworthy – who had been actively involved in the drafting and publication of the Petition of the Twelve – together with Bedford's son-in-law, Lord Digby; and two of the 'patriot' heroes of the 1629 parliamentary session, William Strode and Denzel Holles, who were both closely involved in Pym's and Bedford's political world.[132]

According to the fair copy of the House of Commons' *Journal* (the official record, compiled, some days after the events to which they relate, from rough notes taken at the time), this committee then retired to the Committee Chamber to prepare the agenda for 'a conference to be prayed with the [House of] Lords, and the charge [against] the Earl of Strafford'.[133] However there are reasons for supposing that this second phrase is a later interpolation (added by the Commons' Clerk, Henry Elsynge, in the light of what the committee actually did), and that the committee's brief, as originally defined, made no mention of preparing charges against Strafford. The one eyewitness to record the committee's original terms of reference merely noted that it was 'to collect such matters as might cause jealousies of alteration of the Church and State';[134] and the suspicion that the committee's original instructions made no mention of the preparation of a charge against Strafford would seem to be corroborated by the fact that Denzell Holles (Strafford's brother-in-law) initially agreed to serve – something that would have been inconceivable had the committee's mandate actually extended to indicting his brother-in-law on a potentially capital charge.*[135]

What seems to have happened is that as soon as the committee withdrew, the Warwick–Pym group deliberately ignored their much more general Commons-approved instructions. Effectively hijacking the committee, they redirected it towards the highly specific task of preparing a 'charge', though not yet formal impeachment articles, against the Earl of Strafford. In doing so, they were taking a major risk: in effect, seizing the opportunity to create, de facto, the select committee for Irish Affairs to investigate Strafford that they had tried, and failed, to set up on 6 November. That they were prepared to act so boldly, probably without prior authorization from the House, can perhaps be explained by the gravity of the threat that they regarded as looming over themselves. They had to take action against Strafford urgently – before he had the opportunity to move against themselves.[136] Rather than risk a motion explicitly authorizing the preparation of an impeachment charge being defeated, they seem to have opted for presenting the House with a fait accompli.

By the time the committee returned to the Commons' chamber, they had the grounds of a general charge against Strafford already agreed on.[137] Pym did not 'move the motion', but acted as the reporter of the long catalogue of reasons why there were grounds for 'jealousies' that there was a plot afoot to force an alteration 'in Church and State' (as was the committee's original brief). This included the king's visit to the Tower that morning; the discovering of a stockpile of arms in the house of a Berkshire Papist; and, not least, the words attributed to Sir George Radcliffe, that Strafford had intended to use the Irish army in England.[138] In so far as these amounted to a case against Strafford, however, they concerned his recent and current actions: that he was even now counselling the king to renew the war against the Scots; that he had plotted 'to breake the treatie' which the Petitioner Peers (as Treaty Commissioners) were currently conducting with the Scots; and that he had been responsible for the 'continuing preparation [for] fortifying the Tower' since his arrival in London,[139] portended a plot 'to subdue the Cittie'.

> [M]y Lord Lieutenant, [Pym continued], hath done things conformable to
> such a plot. Hee hath sent Warrants for imposition [the forcible levying of

---

* Indeed, the very next day, when it had become clear that this select committee *had* turned itself into a vehicle for attacking his brother-in-law, Holles was given permission to withdraw 'at his own request'.

money] on paine of death, and certainly, if hee had power, hee would doe it ... [140]

All this gave plausibility to the charge, still no more than hearsay, that he had intended to use the Irish army – and, most likely, was still so minded – in order 'to subdue England'.[141]

In the altered circumstances of what was believed to be an impending coup, there was no question of a division. The committee's report, for all its brazen opportunism, caught the mood of a majority within what was now a thoroughly alarmed and frightened House. Even so, the committee-men encountered opposition. At least one Commons-man, Viscount Falkland,* protested that it was premature to bring in an accusation until its truth had first been established.[142] But Pym dismissed these legal scruples (which threatened to squander the crucial advantage of surprise), warning of the likely consequences of delay. As recalled by Falkland's close friend, Edward Hyde, Pym argued

> that such a delay might probably blast all their hopes, and put it out of their power to proceed farther than they had done already; [and] that the earl's power and credit with the King ... was so great that ... he would undoubtedly procure the Parliament to be dissolved rather than undergo the justice of it; or take some other desperate course to preserve himself, though with the hazard of the kingdom's ruin.[143]

If Hyde's recollection is not necessarily a verbatim record of Pym's words, it is nevertheless almost certainly a shrewd guess as to what he and the other members of the Warwick–Bedford coalition believed the consequences of any delay would be.

In the light of Cradock's evidence that Strafford was already embarked on a 'desperate course' to intimidate the City, a majority of those in the locked Commons chamber came around to accepting that only by presenting the Lords with a charge of high treason against the Lord Lieutenant immediately could they provide for the Parliament's security. There was no time to draw up formal written articles, but they agreed to request that Strafford be 'sequestered' – placed under arrest and prevented from taking his seat – for 'two or three daies', until such time as detailed impeachment charges and proofs could be brought in.[144] Yet there was no question of sending Strafford

---

* Falkland was one of a number of members who were eligible for election to the House of Commons, despite being holders of peerages, because their Scottish or Irish titles did not entitle them to sit in the English House of Lords. The other 'Lords' – such as Lord Digby or Viscount Lisle – who sat in the Commons were the eldest sons of earls, who (like all peers' sons) were permitted to stand for election to the lower House as their titles were merely honorific 'courtesy titles'. The one exception to this was a small group of the eldest sons of earls, who, on receiving a writ of summons from the king, had been advanced to the House of Lords during their fathers' lifetimes – such as Viscount Mandeville, the eldest son of the 1st Earl of Manchester.

'immediately' to the Tower.[145] Here, too, Pym and his fellow committee-men moved tentatively, not daring to risk alienating moderate opinion by appearing to prejudge Strafford's guilt before detailed impeachment articles and evidence had been presented.

Not until late afternoon was Pym deputed to make the short trip – for the second time that day – through the ancient palace to the House of Lords. Thanks to his earlier warning to his friends among the peers, the Lords had remained in session throughout the afternoon, in the expectation that some form of impeachment was imminent. Accompanied by most of the Commons-men,[146] Pym appeared at the bar of the House to deliver the accusation of high treason against the Lord Lieutenant of Ireland, and to desire that he might be 'sequestered from Parliament', pending the presentation of 'particular accusations and articles against him'.[147]

Strafford was absent from the Lord's chamber when the Commons' delegation arrived, but news that measures were being taken against him reached him at Whitehall in the course of the afternoon. Determined to confront his accusers, he immediately departed for Westminster. By the time he arrived, however, the Commons' delegation had already been received, and Pym was waiting in the peers' lobby while the Lords considered their response. It is perhaps an index of how seriously the peers had taken the reports of an imminent coup that a majority in the House was sympathetic to the Commons' request for the earl's immediate 'sequestration', notwithstanding that they had not yet received any detailed charges – still less evidence – of his treason.

By the time Strafford re-entered the Lords' chamber, the debate on his fate was still in progress. As he approached his place on the earls' benches, he was assailed with shouts of 'Withdraw, withdraw!'[148] Forced to retire from the chamber while the peers completed the consideration of the Commons' message, Strafford lost the last moment when he might have had an opportunity to level counter-accusations against his accusers.

When bidden to return, he was forced to kneel at the bar as a 'delinquent' to hear the decision of the House: that he was to be deprived of his right to sit, and assigned to the custody of James Maxwell, the Gentleman Usher of the Black Rod – the officer responsible for the enforcement of the Lords' decrees – until such time as he had vindicated himself against the charges that would be laid against him.[149] Strafford surrendered his sword and was escorted to his place of confinement, the house of the Gentleman Usher.[150] The suddenness of his fall sent shock-waves through Westminster that reverberated far beyond. One contemporary memoirist – possibly the Petitioners' fellow-traveller, the Earl of Bristol – caught the irony of the moment: 'Thus he whose greatnes in the morneing owned a power over two Kingdomes, [by] the Evening straiten[ed] his person betwixt two Walls'.[151]

v. THE HOSTAGE

The implications of these 'hastie and violent proceedings'[152] were so momentous – for Strafford, for Parliament and, no less, for the king – that it is easy to overlook how uncertain of success, at the beginning of the day, the Warwick–Pym group's strategy actually was. Whatever the cause of Strafford's delay in levelling charges against the dissidents (whether it were Charles's failure of nerve, the need to complete the strengthening of the Tower's defences, or the anticipation of some more ambitious plan to 'subdue' the City), the combination of Strafford's dilatoriness and his enemies' speed handed a major advantage to the reformist caucus at Westminster. For in the battle of accusation and counter-accusation over who had committed treason in the summer of 1640 – whether it had been Strafford by advocating the use of the Irish army against the English 'rebels', or Warwick and his fellow conspirators in soliciting a Scots invasion – the advantage was always going to lie with whichever party was first to attack.

For Charles, Strafford's impeachment and committal constituted a blow perhaps only second to his defeat at Newburn. Not only was Strafford, once in custody, effectively silenced as a potential accuser, he was also neutralized as a military commander. So long as the impeachment proceedings were in progress, the king was debarred from returning him to command the English army in the North; and, without Strafford in command, the king's hopes of expelling the Covenanter occupation by force were brought to naught. The one personality within his inner entourage whom his enemies seem genuinely to have feared was immobilized – though, as yet, far from being destroyed.

With Strafford under restraint, the king had no alternative but to abandon – at least for the present – any hopes of using the Tower (and its garrison) as a base from which to quell the popular disturbances that most likely would have followed had the planned arrests of Saye and other 'traitors' been actually attempted.[153] Within forty-eight hours of Strafford's arrest, the king had been forced, in response to parliamentary pressure, to dismiss Lord Cottington as Constable of the Tower, to stand down most of the garrison, and to dismount the artillery pieces that been recently set up (either to intimidate the City or as part of some more ambitious plan to quell the insubordination of the capital).[154] The confrontation of 11 November also spelt the end of Windebank's career at court. As the figure who had issued the warrants for searching Warwick, Saye, and Brooke, and as the one who probably knew most about their contacts with the Scots, Windebank assumed that he would be the next target in their sights. He wisely fled to Paris, slipping out of his house in Drury Lane in the early hours of Thursday 3 December – the same day that his questioning before the Commons' committees was due to begin.[155]

We should be wary, however, of construing the reformers' first tactical success as evidence that they and their programme commanded universal approbation. The very tentativeness with which they advanced Strafford's prosecution – both initially on 11 November, and subsequently – would caution otherwise.[156] From the beginning of the Parliament one can detect in the Commons something that, if not yet a 'king's party', was at least a substantial body of opinion – whose membership in the Commons seems to have commanded somewhere between 100 and 150 votes – which, for a variety of reasons (anti-Puritan, anti-Scots), was less than enthusiastic about replacing the current set of 'evil counsellors' with a coalition of the self-styled 'godly'. Tracing this group within a Parliament of some 120 peers and 500 Commons-men, in which only a relatively small proportion of members are recorded as making speeches, is inevitably a highly speculative activity. Yet it surfaces intermittently in the early months of the Parliament – as, for instance, at the reading of the final version of the impeachment articles against Strafford, on 30 January 1641, when D'Ewes was appalled to find that more than a third of the Commons' members refused to affirm their assent.[157] Many of these Commons-men seem to have preferred absenteeism to futile dissent, and stayed away for much of the spring and summer of 1641, when the reformists seemed to be sweeping all before them.[158] By the autumn, however, when this 'anti-oppositionist' group had acquired a measure of leadership (and, in consequence, found its parliamentary voice),[159] those 100 to 150 Commons-men were to become a powerful and, in the eyes of the godly 'Junto', a highly obstructive force.

The element of self-interest – indeed, of self-defence – in the anti-Straffordian movement emerges clearly when we consider the identities and past actions of the men who set the prosecution in train. Men from the Warwick–Bedford group – particularly, Clotworthy, Grimston, St John, Strode, and Pym – dominated those hasty, at times almost desperate, proceedings; and there is a strong suspicion that the initial contributions from the City radicals, Penington and Cradock, which did so much to raise the temperature in the Commons before Clotworthy rose to suggest that the Irish army had been intended for use against England, were also coordinated beforehand. Indeed, this aristocratic coalition's control of the Strafford prosecution was strengthened still further the following day, 12 November, with the expansion of the Commons committee charged with preparing the impeachment. Hampden, Erle, and Grimston joined Pym, Strode, St John, Lord Digby, and Clotworthy,[160] while Holles (who had been nominated on 11 November) withdrew, now that the committee's earlier, more generalized, brief had been refocused on the single task of bringing his brother-in-law, Strafford, to justice. For Warwick, Bedford and Saye, this list of Strafford's prosecutors could hardly have been bettered. Of the (now eight-man) membership of the committee in charge of the prosecution, all but one of the committeemen were intimately bound up in the social and political worlds of Bedford, Warwick, and the other leading Petitioner Peers.[161]*

---

* This 'Close Committee' – so called because it met in private – was arguably the most powerful of all the Commons' bodies during the Parliament's first year. Every one of its members was closely linked with the leading Petitioner Peers: Lord Digby (Bedford's son-in-law), Oliver St John (Bedford's and Warwick's legal counsel and one of the draftsmen of the Petition of the Twelve), John Pym (man-of-affairs to Bedford and Warwick), John Hampden (friend and co-investor with Saye and Warwick), Sir John Clotworthy (Warwick's nominee at Maldon, involved in the publication of the Petition of the Twelve), Harbottell Grimston (the beneficiary of Warwick's electoral patronage and a strong ally of the earl in Essex), Sir Walter Erle (a long-standing friend and client of Saye's), and William Strode (Erle's brother-in-law, a friend of Pym and Bedford, and the likely recipient of the Earl of Essex's electoral patronage). Relations between them are discussed in greater detail in Chapter 5.

Of course, the way ahead was fraught with perils. Strafford, though prevented from joining the king's army in the field, nevertheless continued to issue commands from his place of imprisonment, a practice that was to cause renewed alarm at Bedford House and Warwick House in the weeks ahead.[162] He, at least, was determined that the army remained in fighting form; and – despite its defeat at Newburn – the possibility that it might resume the offensive, either to prevent a Scottish advance on London (in the event of another peremptory dissolution) or to enforce a return to the king's Personal Rule, was to loom over English politics well into the summer of 1641.[163]

Even so, Strafford's arrest initiated a new, far more confident phase in the Petitioners' dealings with the Parliament. Few public gestures witnessed to the precipitousness of Strafford's fall than the sight of the once great Lord Lieutenant of Ireland, kneeling at the bar of the House of Lords 'as a delinquent', and surrendering his sword to the Gentleman Usher of the Black Rod.[164] Strafford's departure from the House of Lords as Maxwell's prisoner caused a sensation – 'all [men] gazing, no man capping [removing his hat] to him, before whom that morning the greatest of England would have stood dis-covered [bareheaded]'.[165]

For the moment, at least, the shadow of an immediate dissolution – imposed on the Parliament at gunpoint by Strafford – had receded, if not entirely disappeared. There was a sense that the massive task of 'reforming the commonwealth', tentatively begun over the previous week, now had some reasonable chance of achieving completion.

None captured this new-found sense of optimism in the reformist camp better than Sir John Wray, the affluent Lincolnshire knight, in a speech delivered to the Commons on the day after Strafford's arrest. 'I discern that out of all question, some great work is here to be done,' Wray declared, 'some thing extraordinary is here to be decreed – or else God and the King, beyond all our expectations, at the last breath [i.e. the eleventh hour], would never so soone have cemented us again, to meet in this great Councell [of Parliament].'[166] For the first time since Parliament had met, back in April, for that brief and abortive session, the 'great work' of reform – the noble enterprise for which Warwick and Bedford, Clotworthy and Pym, had risked their lives and fortunes – was no longer in Strafford's large and intimidating shadow. Parliament could set about the redress of grievances, the righting of wrongs, and attending to the vast tide of petitions that was flowing into both Houses.

And in their bargaining with the court, on the pace and extent of reform, the Petitioner coalition had suddenly acquired that most useful of assets to negotiation: a hostage.

4

THE AUDIT OF MISRULE

NOVEMBER–DECEMBER 1640

When a man layes his eares to the severall Committees [in Parliament], and heares what a world of evill is discovered in each Committee; what filthinesse, and lewdnesse of filthinesse in this and that Priest, in this and that Officer; how can a man but break forth and say – or rather sob: Good Lord, what a lamentable condition was this poore Land in?

William Bridge, preaching before the House of Commons, 6 April 1641[1]

On Saturday afternoon, 28 November, almost exactly a month after the king's furtive, uncelebrated return to the capital, London finally witnessed the splendours of the royal entry it had hitherto been denied. Reports of the procession's imminent arrival had been circulating since early that morning, and, doubtless encouraged by the weather – 'the sun sh[ining] most gloriously upon them, without any cloud'[2] – large numbers of citizens had ridden out, some as far as Egham, twenty miles to the west of the City, to meet its approach. Church bells tolled joyously along the processional route, and at stages there were impromptu 'feastings', as well-wishers provided food and drink to refresh the huge retinue as it made its stately advance towards the capital.[3] To maintain order, the London Marshal was despatched with a troop of horse to escort the procession during its final miles, from the Mews* into the City.[4]

Progress was slow. By the time the great cavalcade had reached Charing Cross, immediately to the north of Whitehall Palace, it was travelling at barely 'one mile an houre', and dusk was beginning to fall.[5] With at least two thousand mounted men and 'innumerable followers on foote',[6] the great concourse of people was so large 'that they were neare three houres in passing from Charing Crosse to ... the Citie, having Torches caryed to light them when it grew darke'.[7] Here, too, 'they rang the bels for joy'.[8] The crowd's

---

* These were the stables that served Whitehall Palace, situated immediately to the south. Parts of these stables survived until the 1820s, when they were demolished to create Trafalgar Square.

acclamations resembled 'a kinde of *Hosanna*'.[9] And delighted citizens strew the 'wayes where they rode with hearbs and flowers, and running to their Gardens, brought Rosemary and Bayes thence' – a gesture in which royal and martyrological symbols converged.[10] Not since the coronation procession of 1625 had the capital witnessed a cavalcade of such size, nor perhaps such spontaneous public rejoicing.[11]

Yet the focal point of this November procession was not King Charles. Instead, it honoured two of the most celebrated victims of the prerogative courts during the 1630s: the voluble Lincoln's Inn lawyer, William Prynne, and his still more famous fellow-sufferer, the godly Rector of St Matthew's Friday Street, Henry Burton. Their ordeal was well known. Together with the Colchester physician, Dr John Bastwick, Burton and Prynne had been prosecuted in Star Chamber in 1637 for publishing attacks on the Laudian bishops,[12] and their punishment – the imposition of crippling fines, the cutting off of part of their ears,[13] and 'perpetual imprisonment' in remote parts of the kingdom – had seemed so savagely disproportionate to their offence that it had outraged both puritan and non-puritan opinion alike.[14]

The fate of the godly minister, Henry Burton, the central figure in the celebrations of November 1640, had attracted particular sympathy. As acting Clerk of the Closet (or private chapel) to King James's heir, Henry Prince of Wales, Burton had once been an ecclesiastical high-flier at court: an orthodox, Calvinist divine who flourished in royal favour. After Prince Henry's death in 1612, Burton fulfilled the same role in the household of the young Prince Charles, and had seemed assured of major preferment once his master succeeded to the throne.

His fate was emblematic of the fortunes of Calvinism in the English Church more generally post-1625. Instead of promoting him, shortly after his accession King Charles dismissed Burton for writing a letter bitterly critical of his favoured bishop, William Laud. In the years that followed, Burton had become an increasingly vitriolic opponent, first of the new Laudian bishops' theology, and finally of episcopacy itself.[15] To the godly, Burton's fall in 1637 dramatized how completely the Calvinist courtier-divines of James's reign had been marginalized and pilloried – in Burton's case, literally – by the new cohort of 'popishly affected' prelates. His release from imprisonment on the island of Guernsey in November 1640, and his subsequent triumphant return therefore had a powerful symbolic force.[16] As Burton himself later recalled, there was something about the moment – accentuated by the seemingly providential brightness of the weather ('never was there a day in Somer more cleare')[17] – that seemed to inaugurate a new era of optimism and hope:

> a sweet and glorious day, or time, which the Sun of righteousnesse, arising over *England,* with healing under his wings, was now about to procure for us, after once that black cloud, which hanged over the Land, was by degrees chased away.[18]

The bright day of England's freedom had, it seemed, finally dawned.

1. 'A WORLD OF EVILL DISCOVERED'

To many of the godly, the exhilaration of those cold, clear winter days –
when prisoners were being freed and the entire apparatus of their 'persecution'
was tottering and set to fall – was something beyond their fondest imaginings.
'If the Lord turn away our captivity, we shall be like them that dream',
wrote Lady Harley, the wife of the Herefordshire Puritan, Sir Robert, in the
optimism of the new Parliament's first weeks.[19] Yet, week by week, the news
reaching her household at Brampton Bryan and countless other households
in England, told how, steadily, that dream was being turned into reality. By
the eve of Burton's ceremonious entry into the City, James Oxinden, a young
Suffolk man in town, could report back to his brother that, although '[t]here
was much talke of breakinge up of the Parlament' – by another premature
dissolution – 'that is leaft [i.e. ceased], thanks bee to God, and they goe on
verie cheerfully and curragiously'.[20]

   As the numbers who joined in the celebration of Burton's return perhaps
suggest, that sense of optimism at the beginning of the new Parliament's 'great
work' was not the exclusive preserve of the godly.[21] The new Parliament's
opening precipitated an avalanche of accusation and recrimination, and over
the following weeks petitions flooded in from almost every county in England,
cataloguing instances of arbitrary rule, financial exactions 'unlawfully'
imposed, 'innovations' in the life of the Church, and plots to introduce 'Popery'.

   The very first of these county petitions – from Hertfordshire, presented on 7
November, by Arthur Capell[22] – was characteristic of many. A
bulging portmanteau of complaint, the Hertfordshire petition urged the
Commons to take action against matters that ranged from 'Innovation in Religion' to the corruption of legal officials, the illegality of Ship Money, and, for
good measure, added a further list of 'Grievances', enumerated at the end:

   1. Not having Parliaments [since 1629] and [the] breaking upp [of] the
       last.
   2. [The] Cannons [of the Church] lately made.
   3. The unsufficient and unmeete [i.e unworthy] Ministrie.
   4. The great abuse of ordinances [apparently meaning ecclesiastical
       regulations].
   5. [The prohibition on] Sermons in the afternoone.
   6. The oath *Ex officio*.[23]
   7. Unduely raising of Militarie charges.
   8. The pressing [forcible conscription] of men [for military service].
   9. The Pattentee of Saltpeter [a key ingredient of gunpowder, in search
       for which the owners of the monopoly had the right to dig on land
       without the owner's approval].
   [10.] The ignorance of the Traine band [the county militia] in the
       discipline . . .

*

It finished by reiterating one of the key demands of the Petition of the Twelve Peers: that the 'fomenters of the calamities of this Kingdome' should be identified 'that they may bee punished'.[24]

In different order and with different emphasis, these grievances of the Hertfordshire gentry were replicated countless times over in the weeks ahead. 'Petitions did crowde in from several counties and places', noted the Commons diarist, Geoffrey Palmer;[25] and while the existence of a concerted campaign cannot be proven, their content, number, and the promptitude with which they were presented suggest that many of these petitions were reworkings (or simply re-presentations) of the county petitions that had been organized back in September to support the Petitioner Peers' campaign for the summoning of a new Parliament.[26] When the London petition was presented on 9 November by Alderman Penington, for example, one Commons-man noted that most of its provisions 'were in the King's petition' – that is, the one set in train in the fortnight after the Artillery Company muster – to which a series of more recent grievances had been added (including, notably, the new danger posed by 'Souldiers at the Tower').[27]

Almost every aspect of the religious policies pursued by the king and Archbishop Laud came in for censure. The most widely noticed cases, inevitably, involved godly critics of the régime who had suffered, often cruelly, for their opposition at the hands of the prerogative courts of Star Chamber or High Commission. None had quite the iconic significance of Henry Burton's fate – the sober, mainstream Calvinist under James, radicalized by his experience of the Church under Charles and Laud; but there was no shortage of lurid cases to exemplify the archbishop's supposedly 'tyrannous' ways towards his critics. Among the earliest were two raised by the as yet little-known East Anglian farmer, Oliver Cromwell: a close friend and cousin of Oliver St John, through whom he appears to have been on the fringes of the Earl of Warwick's godly circle.[28] Years later, an eyewitness could recall the emotionalism of Cromwell's intervention, delivered 'out of the Gallery, [in which he] dropt teares down with his words',[29] pleading for the release of the puritan minister and physician, Alexander Leighton,[30] who had been imprisoned since 1630. Almost as shocking, however, was the case Cromwell raised of the puritan layman, John Lilburne, sentenced in 1638 in Star Chamber to a 'Whipping of 200 stripes, from Westminster to the Fleete [Prison]' and imprisoned indefinitely for circulating seditious books.[31] Orders for the victims' release quickly followed.[32]

It was the less dramatic, but more pervasive, effects of Laud's ascendancy that figured most prominently in parliamentary debates. Reports from the universities, where the new theology and ceremonialism encouraged by Laud had often been enthusiastically received, provided hours of scandalous revelations.[33] And reports of 'popishly inclined' or scandalous ministers in the parishes came in almost daily. In many parts of the country, of course, aspects of the religious policies pursued during the 1630s – the railing in of altars, the adornment of churches with images, such ceremonial practices as the receiving of communion kneeling at the rail – had found favour with substantial sections of the laity.[34] But for parishioners who had opposed the ecclesiastical innovations of the 1630s – like those of All Hallows, Barking, who had been denounced by their Laudian minister as 'black toads, spotted toads, and venomous toads, like Jack Straw and Watt Tyler' – the time for settling scores had come.[35] The complaints against William Grant, the vicar that Laud had recently arranged to have appointed to the parish of Isleworth, Middlesex, were characteristic of many.[36]*

Appointed in July 1640 in order to oust a 'Puritan', Laud's protégé had a series of views and habits that riled the sensibilities of his more godly parishioners: he believed the area railed in around the altar to be 'holy ground' on which the laity could not tread; desired to install a painted 'image' of St Paul; encouraged bowing towards the altar; and regarded Foxe's *Book of Martyrs* – a near-sacred text to the Elizabethan Church – as a 'book of lyes'. He had also trodden on his parishioners' toes by indicating a clear preference for solo organ music over the singing of the 'unlearned', and scandalized others by playing cards 'untill two or three of the clocke in the morning'.[37] Such partisan accusations arguably reveal as much about their authors' expectations of the new Parliament as they do about the habits of the card-playing Master Grant. But the parish broils of Isleworth reveal in microcosm a clash of rival cultures, theologies, and personalities that seems to have been replicated, with varying degrees of intensity, during 1640 and 1641 in many of the kingdom's 9,000 parishes.[38]

Nor were the régime's critics drawn solely from the ranks of the 'godly'. Men who were later to join the ranks of the 'king's party' – among them Arthur Capell, Sir Francis Seymour, and the lawyers Edward Bagshaw and Edward Hyde – were equally vocal in denouncing the 'abuses', secular and ecclesiastical, of the years of Personal Rule. In secular affairs, speeches came back, time and again, to the way in which the royal prerogative – the powers the king claimed as sovereign, independently of any parliamentary statute – had been extended beyond their proper bounds: to invade the subject's rights of property (as through Ship Money), or to infringe his liberties (as through the 'arbitrary' proceedings of the prerogative court of Star Chamber). Likewise, in relation to the Church, those opening weeks revealed a perhaps surprising degree of consensus. At least among those who chose (or dared) to make speeches, there was broad agreement that many of the ceremonial and doctrinal 'innovations' implemented during the years of Laud's

---

* The case offers an oblique, but nevertheless revealing, sidelight on the court politics of July 1640 – the month before the Scottish invasion – when Strafford, Laud, and Cottington were riding high in the king's esteem and Northumberland was more than ever out of favour. In what seems to have been a deliberate snub to Northumberland, Laud intervened to dismiss William Jemmet, one of Northumberland's household chaplains, who had officiated in Isleworth as parish lecturer and acting vicar for the previous fourteen years. Laud's candidate could hardly have been more provocative: a ceremonialist who had been chaplain to the Bishop of Gloucester, Godfrey Goodman, one of the most 'popish' of all the bishops. On assuming possession of the living, after the 'Faste-day in July last [i.e. after 8 July 1640]', Grant (Laud's candidate) professed that he had no personal objection to Northumberland's chaplain, but that he was taking over the parish 'that he might root out the Puritans there'.

dominance (with the support, and often at the insistence, of the king)[39] had been imposed unlawfully, and they had moved the English Church dangerously close to the Church of Rome.[40]

When it came to the nomination of one of the Commons' most important committees – the Committee of Twenty-Four, established on 10 November 1640 to investigate 'the estate of the kingdom' – its membership included not only a comprehensive list of the Petitioner Peers' accomplices and principal allies, but a strong showing (over a third of the total) by men who were later to be Royalists.[41]* Marked differences of opinion would eventually emerge among these men when it came to prescribing remedies; but during those early months of the sessions there was a broad (if possibly illusory) consensus in the diagnosis of the commonwealth's ills.

On the major cause of these maladies, historical tradition gave them a convenient, and superficially plausible, diagnosis on which most in Parliament – 'the great Phisitian of the commonwealth' – could agree.[42] As Sir Francis Seymour, a veteran of the Parliaments of the 1620s, put it in one of the very first speeches to the Parliament on grievances, the king and his subjects were 'poore by ill counsell'.[43] Indeed, over the months that followed, to cast blame on 'evil counsellors' was to provide a catch-all explanation for the nation's woes. Three groups of counsellors were most frequently blamed: Strafford and his allies on the Privy Council as authors of the disastrous Scottish war; Laud and his clerical supporters for the growth of 'popery and superstition' within the Church; and the judges – particularly those who declared in Charles's favour in the great Ship Money trial of 1637 – for the erosion of the subject's liberties. The 'judges have overthrowne the Lawe and Bishops Religion', Harbottell Grimston complained on 7 November, adding ominously: 'and we hope wee shall have the like punishment against them as against Trisilian and other predecessours'.[44]

Yet the rhetoric of 'evil counsel' was less bland – and, potentially, far less exculpatory of the king – than it might at first appear. Grimston's historical analogy introduced, albeit with the obliqueness that the subject required, the most controversial of all the elements in the new calculus of blame: the responsibility of the monarch himself. For, as would have been familiar to the lawyers in his audience, 'Trisilian' – Sir Robert Tresilian – had been the Chief Justice who had advised the tyrannical Richard II that he could ignore the constraints imposed upon him by his nobles during the Parliament of 1386 – advice for which the Lords Appellant, the leaders of the baronial resistance to the king, later had Tresilian convicted of treason and executed.[45] As we will see, the tyrant-king Richard II and the crisis of 1386–88 were to

---

* Supporters of the Petitioner Peers: Oliver St John, John Pym, Harbottell Grimston, Sir Walter Erle, Sir John Clotworthy, John Hampden, John Crewe, George Perd, Sir Thomas Barrington; Sir Robert Harley should probably also be counted in this group. Other future Parliamentarians: Sir Thomas Widdrington, John Selden, Sir Peter Heyman, William Pierrepont, Sir Benjamin Rudyard. Royalists: Lord Digby, Sir Francis Seymour, Sir John Culpeper, Sir Miles Fleetwood, Edward Kirton (steward to the Earl of Hertford), Sir John Strangways, Edward Bagshaw, Arthur Capell, Henry Belasyse.

recur frequently as points of comparison for the crisis of 1640–42.[46]

Grimston's allusion subtly posed a question that was to be asked countless times over the next two years, most frequently in relation to Richard II, but also with reference to other 'tyrannical' rulers (from the Roman emperor, Tiberius, to the equally despotic and ill-counselled Edward II): if Charles's current 'evil counsellors' were the modern-day equivalents of Chief Justice Tresilian, was not Charles himself, by implication, also the modern-day incarnation of Richard II? How closely could the parallel be drawn? This was a question – and a point of historical reference – that was to have particular relevance to Grimston's friends among the Petitioner Peers over the next two years; and one that was to be answered with emphatic clarity in the spring of 1642.[47]

ii. REMEDIES

The first question of November 1640, however, was what was to be done? At least one thing seemed clear to the Petitioner Lords and their allies: the answer did not lie in the passing of a vast new body of legislation. This in itself marks a striking break with the past. If the practice of the previous 'parliamentary decade', the 1620s, had been any guide, these committees ought to have set about making new laws as the means of remedying the nation's ills. The 1624 Parliament, for example (perhaps the most productive of the 1620s Parliaments), dealt with a substantial legislative programme of thirty-eight private and thirty-five public Acts of Parliament, all within the space of a session that lasted, in total, no more than fifteen weeks.[48] In comparison to this, the legislative achievements of the 1640 Parliament's first six months – from the beginning of November 1640 to the end of May 1641 (by which time it had comfortably broken the record for the longest parliamentary session ever held) – is, at least in quantity, astonishingly small. Only eight public acts, almost all extremely brief, reached the statute book. Three of these dealt with 'constitutional matters'.[49] But of the remaining five, not one dealt with reform.[50]

Even on subjects where there was broad agreement as to the desirability for reform – such as the abolition of the prerogative courts of Star Chamber and High Commission – legislation was not introduced until late March 1641, five months into the session; and it was not to be until June that year that the bill was eventually ready to be sent up to the House of Lords.[51] Action to deal with Ship Money, one of the key grievances that had wrecked the previous parliamentary session, went forward at an even statelier pace.[52] Oliver St John chaired the committee investigating the subject from December 1640, but it was not until 12 June the following year that a bill was finally brought in to declare the levy illegal and overturn the judges' 1638 ruling against Hampden.[53] When it came to religious reform, the pace of legislative change was even slower still,[54] and often lagged far behind what was going on in the parishes, where enthusiasts for 'further reformation' were frequently taking the law into their own hands.[55]

Commons proceedings were, of course, notoriously slow and difficult to manage; 'you remember well enough', one Commons-man later recalled, 'that our long debates – which sometimes held from morning till night, and then almost from night till morning agen – looked little better then great brawles'.[56] But these difficulties were not insuperable where groups of members decided to coordinate tactics and guide debate;[57] and even allowing for the time taken up by Strafford's impeachment, the relative rarity of proposals for *legislation* remains striking.

The main priority of the parliamentary leadership became, instead of new laws, the public exposure of the former régime's indifference to the old. During the first six months of its existence, the new Parliament embarked on a massive information-gathering exercise: a vast audit of misrule, assembling petitions, reports and depositions from all over the country as to 'abuses' perpetrated during the previous decade. In both Houses, the investigation of this 'world of evill' was turned into a highly specialized business. In the Commons, beside the traditional Grand Committees (or Committees of the Whole House),[58] the first weeks of the Parliament saw ad hoc investigative committees proliferating by the dozen. By Christmas 1640, almost every aspect of government during the previous decade had been assigned its own dedicated series of inquisitors: to consider the cases of Leighton and Lilburne; monopolists and 'projectors';[59] legal records in King's Bench;[60] papists serving in the king's army;[61] decisions of the courts affecting 'illegal taxes' and the subject's rights of property;[62] abuses in the prerogative courts of Star Chamber and High Commission;[63] and dozens more besides. So numerous had the Commons' committees become by the end of the year – barely eight weeks into the session – that a new committee to investigate committees was established to provide some order to the current chaos. By the time it gave its opinion on 12 January 1641, sixty-five committees were nominally in existence, of which almost a third (twenty-one in total) appear to have been dropped entirely, without the Commons waiting to hear them report.[64]

The investigation of religious 'abuses' perhaps provides the clearest example. Under the tutelage of Hampden, Pym, and the other members of the reformist 'Junto', investigations into the state of the Church were quickly transferred from the floor of the Commons to a select committee where business could be tightly controlled by themselves and their co-religionists.[65] Established in December, with a membership including (as well as Pym and Hampden) most of Warwick's godly mafia,[66] this body – soon dubbed 'the Committee for Scandalous Ministers' – had power to consider almost every aspect, at parish level, of the kingdom's religious life. But their key concern was to find 'where there are persecuting, innovating, or scandalous ministers' and to consider how they might be put out and replaced.

Moreover, they set about actively touting for business. Not content to rely on cases referred from fellow Parliament-men, its organizers advertised publicly, inviting submissions from every parish in England. Copies of the relevant order were printed and distributed, assuring readers that it was *expected* by Parliament that all ingenious [i.e. ingenuous] persons in every County of the Kingdome will be very active to improve the present opportunity, by giving true information of all the Parishes in their severall Counties ... [in particular, where] there are persecuting, innovating, or scandalous Ministers ... The Committee desires informations from all parties, if it be possible, within this moneth ...[67]

In a revealing touch, the godly network involved in seeing that this message reached the parishes accorded the contract for its printing to a fellow Puritan, Henry Overton, one of the few printers who had undergone military training with another godly network, the Artillery Company.[68]

This appeal to 'all parties', regardless of social status, to come forward with information defines one of the most striking aspects of the reformist Junto's tactics during the Parliament's first session. It actively fostered political interaction between Westminster, with its committees and commissions, and the 'public sphere' beyond: not just the metropolitan audience for politics in London, but also that much larger pamphlet-buying, newsbook-reading audience of the politically aware throughout the kingdom. Parliament-sponsored interventions, such as the December pamphlet urging the submission of petitions and 'informations', almost certainly helped to foster that process of politicization country-wide.

But eliciting petitions was only the start. Through the process of questioning, evidence-gathering, and hearing of parties that these petitions initiated, the Commons' and (perhaps still more) the Lords' committees entered into a dialogue with literally hundreds of groups and individuals, each of which had an 'outrage' to denounce, a score to settle, a 'vice' to expose in the committee chambers of Westminster. They descended on Westminster in their hundreds, almost overwhelming the harassed committee-men who had invited their participation. By mid February 1641, the Commons had to recruit a series of marshals to 'regulate and prevent such disorders as are committed by disorderly multitudes that press in [to the committee-rooms]'.[69] The dialogue with the nation was threatening to become a Tower of Babel.

For those on the receiving end of these inquisitions, the experience was often traumatic, sometimes ruinous, and almost invariably humiliating. Neither the Commons nor its committees had the power to deprive a minister of his living. But merely by launching an investigation against a minister accused of promoting 'superstitious innovations', these committees could initiate a process of vexation which, for its victims, could be as crippling financially as a formal sentence of deprivation. Compelling a minister to come to London for hearings; forcing him to engage legal counsel; subjecting him to the expense of accommodation in the capital while he waited around, often for weeks or months, until such time as his case was heard (and keeping him under threat of censure for contempt if he departed without the Commons' leave): all these measures were capable of disrupting the lives and lightening the purses of ministers under accusation, whether or not their cases actually proceeded to a final conclusion. Accusations came cheaply, and the task of establishing innocence seems to have lain firmly with the accused. 'To the

Lawyer must the Divine go, if he will preach without feare of being made a scandalous Minister', one London cleric bitterly complained; 'I have known 20 shillings [in] Fees given to a lawyer to plead at the Committee for Religion in the behalfe of some Doctrines ... for which the Preacher never got twenty pence'.[70]

Gauging just how many petitions were received by the Committee for Scandalous Ministers – or by any of its equally nosy siblings – is almost impossible; the great fire of 1834 which consumed most of the medieval Palace of Westminster destroyed almost all the Commons' archives, including most of the petitions submitted in response to the December advertisement seeking information on scandalous ministers.[71] However, estimates by contemporaries suggest a tally, in the six months of evidence-gathering to June 1641, of around 900 petitions relating to religious grievances alone.[72] 'The grievous Effects' of Laud's rule, Pym claimed when he came to deliver the impeachment articles against him, were 'most manifest to the Commons House, *there being divers hundred complaints there depending* in the House against scandalous Ministers – and yet (I believe) the hundred part of them is not yet brought in.'[73]

Of course, Pym was prone at times to exaggeration,[74] and this claim – with its implication that he was expecting more petitions against 'scandalous Ministers' than actually there were clergy in the whole of England – needs to be regarded with some scepticism.[75] But the precise number is, in some respects, beside the point. Already by early in 1641, the conviction that a very high proportion of the country's parishes were in revolt against the 'innovations' of the Laudian bishops – a 'fact' evidenced by the profusion of local petitions – had become part of the reformists' self-defined mythology. For the men who challenged Charles's authority in the summer of 1640, the sheer bulk, or alleged bulk, of this documentation had a political usefulness that far surpassed its relevance to the framing of new laws. It provided validation for their claim that they were acting *representatively,* in the name of the 'commonwealth', in seeking justice against the 'Incendiaries' of the 1630s. Those 'hundreds of petitions' were the Commonwealthsmen's moral mandate for further reformation in both Church and state. 'When a man layes his eares to the severall Committees', observed William Bridge in a sermon to the Commons early in 1641, 'and heares what a world of evill is discovered in each ... – what filthinesse, and lewdnesse of filthinesse in this and that Priest, in this and that Officer; how can a man but break forth and say – or rather sob: Good Lord, what a lamentable condition was this poore Land in?'[76]

III. USURPATIONS: THE PETITIONER PEERS AND THE LAW

If revealing the lamentable condition of the land had become, in the Commons, a highly partisan business, an almost exactly parallel process went on in the House of Lords. The crucial difference, however, was that where the Commons' committees were largely concerned with investigation of past 'abuses', the House of Lords possessed the judicial powers to do something about them. Here, too, the reformist 'Junto' worked through committees, and used the receiving of petitions – and the encouragement of their submission – to build up a darkly malevolent view of government during the 1630s. For Warwick, Bedford and the reformist peers, the crucially important power base which they needed to capture at the beginning of the Parliament was, perhaps unsurprisingly, the Committee for Petitions. For this had not only the power to review, but also to prescribe legal remedies; and over the months ahead it was to become one of the most powerful bodies at Westminster: the blandness of its moniker offers little clue as to how subversive, from the king's perspective, its operations were going to be.

Named on 6 November 1640, just three days after the state opening, the choice of its members reflects the prestige enjoyed by the Bedford–Warwick coalition at the start of the Parliament, and, perhaps too, the expectation that these one-time dissidents were now destined for higher things. But however it was achieved, the comprehensiveness with which the reformists came to dominate the new committee remains astonishing.[77]* The committee had thirty-six members. Of these fully half – eighteen lords – had actually signed the Petition of the Twelve,[78] and a further eight peers were broadly supportive of the reformist cause: all but one of them were future Parliamentarians.[79] This gave the Bedford–Warwick coalition a combined tally of twenty-six of the thirty-six lay peers' places on the committee; and while an additional eight bishops were also nominally members, one of these (Wren of Ely) was shortly to be debarred from attending by impeachment, and the remaining seven bishops appear to have been a fitful and powerless presence at its meetings. Even were all of its potential opponents present, the Bedford–Warwick grouping constituted an unassailable majority on the new Committee for Petitions which met near the House of Lords, in the imposing medieval surroundings of the Painted Chamber.

What marked out this body from any other committee at Westminster was the extent of its power. Like the Commons' committees, this Lords' Committee for Petitions dealt with grievances and complaints in their hundreds. But this body claimed the authority to function as a court of law and to grant its petitioners legal redress. Exploiting the power vacuum created by the near-collapse of royal authority over the previous two months, Bedford, Warwick, and their allies steadily reasserted – and, in time. massively extended – the powers of judicature that the House of Lords had exercised, in living memory, only since 1621. Here, too, the peers who set out to check the power of the king were the beneficiaries of the early-seventeenth-century vogue for antiquarian scholarship, and the exploitation of medieval precedents to reassert the nobility's judicial powers, which had not been exercised

---

* This pattern was replicated on almost all of the other committees appointed by the House of Lords during the first five months of the Parliament. One survey has noted that of the thirty-nine committees appointed during this period, thirty-one of them – eighty per cent overall – were controlled by the Petitioner Peers and their allies.

since the days of those 'discords betweene the Houses of Yorke and Lancaster', back in the mid fifteenth century.[80]

Impeachment was obviously the most eye-catching of this recently reburnished arsenal of legal weaponry. But the Parliaments of the 1620s also saw the reassertion, albeit on a limited scale, of the Lords' early-medieval power to act as a de facto court of appeal from the other courts of law: King's Bench, Common Pleas, Exchequer and Chancery. The procedure was relatively simple. Dissatisfied litigants could petition the House of Lords for a writ of error whereby the proceedings and judgements of these inferior courts were reviewed by the peers – which, in practice, meant the members of the Committee for Petitions, advised by the law officers – who were empowered to 'correct' the determinations of the judges at first instance.[81] In November 1640, this claim – that the nobility had the collective right to sit as the kingdom's highest judges – revived an appellate jurisdiction that had not been exercised (except briefly between 1621 and 1629) for 'almost three hundred years'.[82] Even during the 1620s, the actual number of cases dealt with by the peers was relatively slight: an average of between thirty and forty per parliamentary session.[83]

With what seems to have been the active encouragement of the committee's members, the trickle of cases that had been seen between 1621 and 1629 now suddenly became a flood. Within a matter of weeks of the Committee for Petitions' establishment, requests for legal remedies averaged around one hundred per month between December 1640 and February 1641 – when the committee, overwhelmed by this tidal wave, made a half-hearted effort to prevent further submissions until the initial inundation had been cleared.[84] But the stream continued unabated. By May of 1641, just over six months into the session, the committee had received some 400 petitions.

Most of these have survived. While the Commons' archive has been largely destroyed, the archive of the Lords' Committee for Petitions is substantially intact, and permits far more precise analysis not only of the volume, but also of the type of cases brought to the Lords' attention. Few collections of papers better attest to the way in which the reformists – in effect, the Petitioner Peers and their allies – were perceived to have won control of the House of Lords than these petitions. Where cases related to the years of Personal Rule (and there were at least 241 of them), '*all* of them' involved petitioners who 'had fallen foul of the king's government at some point ... : by standing out against the Laudian innovations in the Church, or by refusing to pay or collect Ship Money, ... by challenging the king's right to make law by proclamation and [to] regulate trade by patent, or simply by acting to protect their rights of private property and personal liberty'.[85] If the peers needed any reminding of the inefficacy of statute alone, as a means of binding kings, it was provided, week by week, in rich and sometimes lurid detail by these hearings in the Painted Chamber. The biggest single class of cases (more than a third of the total) dealt with instances of arbitrary imprisonment and other contraventions of the 1628 Petition of Right.[86]

In contrast, relatively few cases dealt with matters arising from ecclesiastical disputes: merely forty-one cases in all; though this is partly explained by the notoriously vague and, at times, self-contradictory nature of the Canons, rubrics, and other regulations that governed the English Church (ambiguities which the 'innovators' of the 1630s had exploited to the maximum). For those wishing to harass members of the Laudian clergy, rather than seek a judicial determination against them, the Commons' religious committees probably offered an equally effective, and cheaper, recourse than formal litigation before the Lords.

However, the significance of the Lords' Committee for Petitions went far beyond the actual volume of its case-load. The key development, evident from the beginning of the session, was the way in which the committee ('dominated by noted critics of the Crown and would-be reformers – Essex, Bedford, Bristol, Warwick, Saye, Mandeville, and Brooke'),[87] successfully asserted its jurisdiction not just over the four courts of common law and equity (King's Bench, Common Pleas, Chancery and Exchequer), but also over the prerogative courts of Star Chamber and High Commission. Even formal determinations of the Privy Council were held to be subject to the Committee for Petitions' jurisdiction. Indeed, one of the most striking developments in the course of 1641 was the way in which, as the authority of the Privy Council declined, this aristocratic Committee for Petitions usurped many of its former functions. Subjects who, before November 1640, might have sought redress or mediation before the Privy Council turned, in their hundreds, to this new source of 'justice' in the Painted Chamber.

The effect of all this, combined with the Petitioner Peers' dominance of the Committee for Petitions, was to allow Warwick, Bedford and their allies to act in many areas of England's public life as though they were already its lawfully constituted government. The Painted Chamber at Westminster became their 'council chamber'. From there, Warwick, Bedford, Essex, Brooke, and Saye could already shape public policy through the medium of the law – by ruling definitively against the Laudian altar policy, dismissing Justices of the Peace, reversing excommunications, quashing the convictions of those who had opposed the king's government, ordering reparations from royal servants who had been the agents of 'arbitrary rule' – and doing all this without any other qualification beyond their status as *consiliarii nati*: born counsellors of the realm. Among the first to feel the benefits of their newly won authority was Henry Darley, Warwick's and Brooke's Providence Island Company colleague who had been imprisoned by Strafford on the suspicion (completely justified) that he had been negotiating with the invading Scots. Now, as the controlling interest on the Committee for Petitions, Warwick and his friends were in a position to see to his immediate release.[88]

Yet, as the Petitioner Lords can only have been acutely aware, their possession of this newly won judicial supremacy was highly precarious, and wholly dependent for its exercise on the frequency with which Parliaments actually met. In the event of another long intermission between Parliaments, there would be nothing to stop Charles and his judges from returning to what – in the eyes of Warwick, Bedford and their Petitioner allies – were the illegalities of the 1630s: imprisonment without trial; invasion of the subject's rights of property; the imposition of religious change without the authority of statute. This predicament suggested its own remedy. If the Lords' new-found supremacy over the 'inferior' courts of law was to mean anything beyond the present crisis, the Parliament needed to become a regular feature of the kingdom's legal system – not an intermittent assembly, convoked purely at the convenience of the king. As we will see, the Commonwealthsmen's efforts to meet this concern would shortly involve them in an ambitious plan to remove the arrangements for the Parliament's future meetings from the king's hands altogether.[89]

*

As the Christmas of 1640 approached, the 'usurpations' that had been carried off by Bedford, Warwick and the other Petitioner Peers had already made major inroads into areas of government that had hitherto been the responsibility of the king and his Privy Council. The process had been incremental. Their Scottish allies and the Great Council of Peers at York had sanctioned their first 'usurpation', by preventing the Privy Council from conducting the treaty negotiations with the Scots and ceding almost all the sixteen places as Lords Commissioners for the treaty to Bedford, Warwick, and the other Petitioner Peers.[90] But the second major coup was provided by the Lords' Committee for Petitions. As the committee's controlling 'interest', Warwick, Bedford and their friends acquired the means to usurp the Privy Council's role as a forum for arbitration, and, perhaps still more importantly, to assert – in the name of the House of Lords – an appellate jurisdiction over almost every other judicial body in England. The judges may still have been the king's judges; but from 6 November 1640, they became answerable, ultimately, to this same formidably powerful group of peers: the very same group that was managing the Scottish treaty and which, in September, had brought the kingdom to the brink of civil war.

Already by December 1640, then, the Bedford–Warwick coalition had brought off two major incursions into what had traditionally been the monarch's – and his Privy Council's – territory. These were substantial achievements and, for the foreseeable future, secure ones, for Charles was powerless to dissolve the Parliament while the Scots army remained in the north of England. And as the authority of the king's discredited Privy Council at Whitehall steadily diminished, the success of the Bedford–Warwick coalition in gaining de facto control of these key elements of government made the case for its formal admission by the king as a new, 'virtuous' Privy Council seem more unanswerable by the day.[91]

However, the new Parliament's opening months also witnessed another successful incursion by the Warwick–Bedford group into terrain that had hitherto been almost exclusively a court preserve: the staging of civic ceremonial. Indeed, it was probably in this sphere that the triumph of the new 'Commonwealthsmen' registered most clearly, in their usurpation of the court's traditional language of power: pageantry and ceremonial – a 'public space' from which the king – with his reluctance to stage a formal entry into the capital and his cancellation of the state-opening procession – had seemed to withdraw.

iv. PAGEANTS OF POWER

The earliest indication of the Petitioner Peers' willingness to invade this courtly preserve came early in the session, on 16 November 1640. It concerned the most prominent of all the churchmen to fall foul of Charles and Laud during the 1630s: John Williams, the suspended Bishop of Lincoln and Dean of Westminster, who had been imprisoned in the Tower, again at the orders of Star Chamber, since 1637.

Among the Commonwealthsmen of 1640, Williams enjoyed an almost heroic status for his resistance to the king's Personal Rule. One of the Jacobean survivors on the bishops' bench (he had been appointed to the See of Lincoln in 1621),[92] Williams had opposed both Ship Money[93] and one of the defining policies of Laud's years at Canterbury: the insistence that communion tables in parish churches should be railed and placed, 'altar-wise', against the east wall: in exactly the same place where stone altars had stood before the Reformation.[94] His resistance enhanced his reputation as a 'favourer of Puritans' and won him the plaudits of the godly. The Earl of Essex (who had consulted him in 1630 over his divorce) and Viscount Mandeville (whose house at Kimbolton, Huntingdonshire, was only a few miles from Williams's seat at Buckden) were both friends and visitors to his house, where the walls were reported to be adorned with the provocative quotation from Tacitus: 'PRINCIPES MORTALES, RE[S]PUBLICA AETERNA' – 'Princes are mortal, but the commonwealth endures forever'.[95] In July 1637, Charles and Laud moved against him.[96] Condemned in Star Chamber on trumped-up charges of perjury, he was suspended from all his ecclesiastical offices, and imprisoned in the Tower.[97]

On 16 November, just five days after the arrest of Strafford, Williams's friends moved for another of the Lords' powerful standing committees, the Committee for Privileges, to review the case[98] – knowing full well that this committee, established only ten days earlier, was absolutely controlled by the Petitioner Peers. Of the seventeen lay peers who considered Williams's case, fifteen were either Petitioner Lords (ten in all, including Bedford, Warwick, Essex, Saye, and Brooke)[99] or their supporters.[100] With this partisan body reviewing his case, the result was a foregone conclusion: the Lords ordered that Williams was to be released to attend in the House of Lords that same afternoon.[101]

However, it was not the fact but the manner of Williams's release that caused a sensation. 'Most of the upper and lower house[s] [of Parliament]' met the newly-freed bishop at the Tower, and then conducted him, in procession, through the City streets to Westminster, 'as it were, in triumph'.[102] And as any courtier would have recognized, this route from the Tower to Westminster traced a well-established processional way: Tower Wharf was the regular place of greeting for new ambassadors coming to court, whence they would be attended through the streets to Westminster.[103]

That so large a proportion of the Parliament should convene at the same time and place entirely spontaneously, in the absence of any order from either House, is to strain credulity. The scale of the parliamentary involvement in this coach procession argues for a substantial degree of prior planning and coordination, with the Petitioner Lords turning the event into what might be termed an impromptu pageant of liberation. Nor did they go unrewarded for their pains. When later safely installed in the House, Bishop Williams gratefully acknowledged the nation's debt owed to the Petitioner Peers, moving a motion 'that [the Twelve Peers'] names should be entered upon record in [the Lords'] journal book ... as an acknowledgement of the service they had done the kingdom'.[104]

*

The partisan triumphalism of Williams's great coach procession on 16 November suggests that we should perhaps look again at the far more extravagant public celebrations – extending from Saturday, 28 to Sunday, 29 November – attending the release and return of that other iconic clergyman, Henry Burton, twelve days later. In fact, for all its appearance of spontaneity, almost every aspect of Burton's return to London – from the presentation of the petition requesting his release to the service of thanksgiving in his honour – was either set in train by, or closely involved, the 'Commonwealthsmen' (with Warwick, Brooke, Pym, and Hampden all in varying degrees involved).

Arrangements for Burton's return had actually begun on 7 November (just over a week before Williams's triumphal procession), when Pym, loyally seconded by Hampden, had presented a petition for Burton's and Bastwick's release.[105] Once Burton had reached the capital, however, it was the godly nobility who formed the most prominent part of his triumphal procession. Just as they had done for Bishop Williams a fortnight earlier, the reformist peers turned out to honour Burton with substantial pomp. Their coaches – clearly distinguished by their owners' entitlement to have 'six horses a peece' – formed the most conspicuous part of the massive carriage procession – 100 strong, and involving several hundred horses – that accompanied Burton on his journey through the city streets.[106]* To contemporaries, the symbolism was obvious. Other than ambassadorial processions to court, the only entry parades into the City that were usually joined by noblemen in their coaches were formal entries by the monarch;[107] and it is hard to avoid the conclusion that the ostentatious pageantry of Burton's torch-lit 'royal entry' was planned, at least to some degree, as a taunt to a king whose own return to the City, almost exactly four weeks earlier, had been such a conspicuous non-event.

The culmination of these public celebrations, however, came the following day, when, in Burton's presence, a solemn service was held to 'give thanks

---

* One of the instances of Archbishop Laud's *folie de grandeur* alleged against him at his trial was that he had presumed to have his coach drawn by six horses, a practice deemed a presumption to marks of status beyond his station.

for [his] safe returne'.[108] Here, too, the pair of Holborn neighbours, Warwick and Brooke, had been active. Warwick appears to have provided the church – his own place of Sunday worship, St Mary Aldermanbury, near Guildhall, where his long-standing protégé, Edmund Calamy, was rector[109]* – while Lord Brooke provided the preacher of the thanksgiving sermon, Simeon Ashe – his own household chaplain.[110]

It would be an exaggeration, of course, to see Burton's entry into London as a purely staged affair. At least part of this vast crowd that accompanied him was made up of Burton's friends and neighbours, and his 'old Parishioners' from St Matthew's Friday Street.[111] At the same time, the complex logistical exercise of getting together 100 coaches and somewhere between 200 and 600 coach horses in processional formation in London's cramped and narrow streets was something that required extensive prior planning and coordination. Indeed, it is this complex fusion of spontaneity and choreography, parody and solemnity, the demotic and the aristocratic, which marks out the two political processions of November 1640 as great moments of political theatre. In these very public displays of the 'triumph' of the new order, reformist grandees consciously took politics, and themselves, to the London streets: both responding to, and helping to create, an appetite for political involvement and engagement that extended well beyond the traditional ruling élites.

Nor were these isolated instances. Over the months ahead, there were to be a series of moments when the reformist grandees sought to co-opt traditional modes of celebration – processions, bonfires, and bell-ringings – to mark significant milestones along the road to reform: the release of political 'martyrs'; the passing of major items of legislation;[112] and the trials of the commonwealth's 'enemies'.[113] And they had their effect. In the days immediately after the Burton procession, for example, one conformist cleric claimed that 'a Divine in his habit could not walke the streets of London without being reproached in every corner by the name of "Baal's Priest", "Popish Priest", "Caesar's friend", and the like scoffings'.[114] Politics had taken to the streets.

*

The 'great work' of reform had begun. Warwick, Bedford and the other 'Commonwealthsmen' had secured control of all the Lords' major committees; and in the Commons, their allies enjoyed a dominance that was almost as absolute. Yet Parliament, in its traditional role as a maker of statutes, was paradoxically almost irrelevant to their plans. Indeed, the legislative initiatives that they were to pursue with any seriousness over the next year could be counted on the fingers of one hand. New laws were not, of themselves, to be the remedy for the kingdom's ills.

---

* Warwick, for whom the church of St Andrew's Holborn would have been far more convenient to his London house, changed his allegiances to St Mary's Aldermanbury in September 1639, shortly after he had used his influence to see his protégé (and former guest at Leez), Edmund Calamy, installed as rector. Warwick chose a pew in the east end of the church's 'Little Gallery'.

This caution, or perhaps cynicism, is readily explicable. Men of Warwick's and Pym's generation had tried once before to bind the monarch to rule within the law: by passing the Petition of Right (in effect, a declaratory statute), reaffirming the laws, going back to Magna Carta, that were the foundations of the subject's liberties.[115] But if the experience of the previous decade had taught Parliament-men anything, it was the sheer redundancy of statute as a means for fettering kings. So long as Charles chose to appeal to 'reason of state', he had the law of 'necessity' to override the authority of statute.[116]

This was a lesson that Bedford and Warwick – and, perhaps still more, their professional lawyers, St John and Pym – had taken to heart. Durable reform of the commonwealth could not be built on the words of statute alone. It required a fundamental redefinition of the limits, and perhaps even the origins, of royal power. To attain that, the Petitioner grandees sought something far more ambitious than even the dominance of Parliament and its committees. They needed to take over the running of the royal government itself.

5

BEDFORD'S COMMONWEALTH

NOVEMBER 1640–JANUARY 1641

It was also thought fit [by the Essex rebels of 1601] that, because they would be Commonwealths-men, and foresee that the businesse and service of the publique State should not stand still, they should have ... at hand certaine other persons to be offered to supplie the offices and places of such her Majesties Counsellors and servants as they should demand to be removed and displaced.

Francis Bacon, *A Declaration of the Practises and Treasons [of] Robert, Late Earl of Essex* (1601)'

Government, in seventeenth-century England, was not the business of Parliaments, but of councils and courts. It followed, therefore, that the reform of government – the essential preliminary to healing the 'ills of the commonwealth' – had to start with a purge of the so-called 'great officers' of Church and state; the men, almost all of them noblemen, who had exercised power in the king's name during the years of Personal Rule. Charles, of course, was almost certain to resist. Prone to regarding attacks on his ministers as indirect attacks on himself,[2] he had notoriously chosen to dissolve the 1626 Parliament – notwithstanding that he thereby forfeited the tax revenues it might otherwise have granted – rather than allow it to proceed with the impeachment of his most powerful minister, the Lord Admiral, the Duke of Buckingham. Not the least of his reasons for avoiding the summons of a Parliament during the 1630s was that it would almost certainly have involved the public criticism, and possible impeachment, of the men whose service he most esteemed.

In November 1640, with a depleted Exchequer, two armies to pay, and the threat that any default towards the Covenanter army would bring it marching south towards London, Charles no longer enjoyed the luxury of a peremptory dissolution as a means of saving his servants from Parliament's wrath. The impeachment of Strafford on 11 November was clearly only the start of the Commonwealthsmen's plans. This time, however, the king seemed to have no alternative but to acquiesce. 'The King is in such a straight', the Earl of Northumberland wrote on 13 November 1640, two days after

Strafford's committal, 'that I do not know how he will possiblie avoide (without indangering the losse of the whole kingdome) the giving way to the remove of divers persons, as well as other things, that will be demaunded by the Parlament.'³ A week later he was commenting on the unanimity of the two Houses in their resolution to effect 'a reformation of all things', and again expecting a purge at court:

> I do verily beleeve we shall see many persons questioned [who], within these [last] 6 months, thought themselves in greate securitie; and such are the King's necessities that he will not be able either to defend those men, or to helpe himselfe, be [the Parliament's] proceedings never so distastefull to him.⁴

'The King's necessities' – his financial crisis, deepening by the day – would, it seemed, dictate the logic of change. Within a matter of weeks, many of the kingdom's most powerful and lucrative offices would be vacant – among them, the Lord Lieutenancy of Ireland, at least one of the two Secretaryships of State, and the Lord Treasurership of England (potentially, the most lucrative of all public offices), currently occupied by the Bishop of London, William Juxon,⁵ a figure who was unlikely to survive long in the prevalent climate of anticlericalism. For well-regarded noblemen, a bonanza loomed. By 19 November, Northumberland was sufficiently confident of the impending purge to provide his brother-in-law, the Earl of Leicester, a man of unimpeachably Protestant credentials, with a list of the posts that were likely to fall vacant; Leicester simply had to let him know which one he 'doth most affect'.⁶ The major beneficiaries of the new appointments, however, were believed likely to come from outside the existing ranks of the court: from the Petitioner Peers, with the Earl of Bedford the figure most likely to take the plum office, the Lord Treasurership of England.⁷

Not for the last time, however, Charles confounded predictions, and proved doggedly resistant to the logic of his 'necessities'. By early December, Strafford and Laud were in custody (though not, as yet, convicted of any offence), and the prudent Windebank had fled. But there was still no sign that the king would willingly accede to any change in his counsels, nor even to the dismissal of the officers who were currently under threat of impeachment. If endangering 'the losse of the whole kingdome' was the only alternative to dealing with his parliamentary critics, that, it seemed, was a risk which Charles seemed prepared to take.

Throughout the first two months of the Parliament, the king responded neither to blandishment nor threat. Rumours of Bedford's appointment as Lord Treasurer flickered among the Westminster gossip-mongers towards the end of November, and had come to be regarded as a near-certainty by early December. Revealing as this was, perhaps, of the Parliament's wishful thinking, to the insiders within the Whitehall corral the report seemed without foundation. Replying to a friend who had heard the news, the Countess of Carlisle brusquely punctured this balloon of speculation: 'what you hear conserning my Lord of Bedford['s appointment to office] is sartunly the news of the towne,' she wrote on 3 December; but 'nothing of it [is] aithere true or possible with out sutch a change as I dayr not thinke of'.[8]

For all the noise and bustle at Westminster, and the talk of reform in the pulpits, as the Christmas of 1640 approached, the Parliament had had little to show for its first eight weeks of deliberations. With the exception of Strafford and his loyal lieutenant, Sir George Radcliffe, most of those against whom impeachment proceedings had been initiated by the end of the year were free on bail. From 23 December, even Archbishop Laud, then in the relatively congenial custody of the Lords' Gentleman Usher, was at liberty to 'take the air' at Whitehall or any of the king's other houses, provided he went in the company of his custodian.[9] The 'popish' Bishop Wren, the Dean of the Chapel Royal, was still presiding at services in Whitehall six months after impeachment accusations had been levelled against him.[10]

No progress had been made towards remedying the insolvency of the crown, or even towards providing a secure basis for paying the English and Scottish armies, for which Parliament was now responsible. By the end of December, not a penny in new taxation had actually been approved by the Commons, and the only funds made available towards paying the forces in the North had been £100,000 advanced by private lenders on the security of anticipated revenues – fully half of it from Bedford's friend and adviser, the customs farmer, John Harrison.[11] Yet neither Bedford nor any of his Petitioner allies was one step closer to achieving public office. Only a few days after the Countess of Carlisle had dismissed the reports of Bedford's promotion to the Lord Treasurership, the hoped-for appointee himself fell ill, rendering any immediate reconciliation between the Junto and the court still more unlikely.[12]

I. IMPASSE

If there was one overriding reason for this lack of progress, it was the continuing belligerence of the king. To the bafflement of contemporaries, so long as there was the remotest chance of his resuming the war effort against the Scots (and exacting vengeance on the 'traitors' who had sabotaged it during the summer), Charles held back from making any significant concessions.[13] With the Bedford–Warwick Junto controlling the treaty negotiations with the Scots, Charles seems to have been planning to disown the treaty at the earliest opportunity and to renew his war against the Covenanters and their English allies. The evidence for this is circumstantial – chiefly the initiatives that were taken to prepare the army for a future engagement – but nevertheless compelling. Far from preparing to disband his forces, Charles managed to maintain his army at York throughout the autumn at roughly what it had been in early September: around 17,500 men.[14] Only three days after his arrest, Strafford issued a 'Spetiall Command' to the Lieutenant-General of the Artillery to provide powder and match for fifteen regiments, the bulk of the army still regarded as loyal to the king:

sufficient to provide for the army's 'Exersiseinge' up until early January 1641.[15] Signals from the Scots suggested that they, too, were preparing for a resumption of the war. 'From all parts', it was reported from Yorkshire on 23 December, 'the Scots rayther strenthenes them selves [than disband]'; and a provocative example of this was the garrisoning of Darlington (the major town in the south of County Durham) by a Covenanter garrison some 600 strong.[16]

Such manoeuvrings can, of course, be interpreted merely as attempts by both sides to strengthen their hands in the contemporaneous treaty negotiations in London. On the king's side, however, these military preparations do not appear to have been mere feints. In December, plans were prepared by Sir John Conyers, the field commander of the army at York, to defend the line of the Tees (the river that formed the border between English-controlled Yorkshire and Scottish-controlled County Durham), and to resume the offensive with a two-pronged attack on the Scots. In Conyers' plan, a seaborne diversionary assault was to be mounted, either on the Edinburgh port of Leith or the garrison at Berwick (near the Scottish border), with the objective of dividing the Scots' forces; meanwhile the main English army was to advance northwards from York.[17]

Whether or not such a plan would have been practical, these ongoing military preparations suggest that there remained a faction within the king's government committed to a further military confrontation with the Scots, notwithstanding that any renewal of hostilities was likely to escalate into (at very least) a limited civil war in England. For so long as the king aimed, however quixotically, at re-establishing his authority through success in battle, he had little interest in humouring the 'traitors' – Warwick, Bedford and the other Petitioners – who had fatally compromised his autumn campaign. Accordingly, throughout November and December, Sir John Borough continued his work supplying the king with legal precedents relating to acts of attainder, in readiness for the happy day when Parliament recovered its traditional hostility to the Scots, and the Bedford–Warwick 'Junto' could be brought to account for its treasons.[18] Unsurprisingly, reports that Charles might still order a dissolution – knowing full well that this would trigger a Scottish advance southwards and, despite the onset of winter, a full-scale pitched battle between the English and Scottish armies in the North – remained current well into November.[19] Whether or not Charles actually contemplated this option is unknown; but the signals emanating from fortress Whitehall during November and December suggested that the king was still inclined towards confrontation rather than compromise. The settlement he seemed to have in mind did not involve the Petitioners' incorporation into the Privy Council, but rather the display of their decapitated heads on London Bridge.

All this compels a thorough reassessment of what has been termed the 'projected settlement of 1641': the discussions that supposedly took place between the Bedford House group and the court between November 1640 and the following March about an accommodation in which offices would be traded by the king in return for parliamentary financial support.[20] This, it has been suggested, was a relatively irenic episode, a moment when an impoverished king had no alternative but to put aside thoughts of war and to do business with his parliamentary critics, and when a plausible *via media* might have been reached. It was the negotiations' breakdown in the spring of 1641, so the argument runs, which propelled English politics into a far more unstable and confrontational phase.[21]

Yet, apart from some possible desultory contacts between Bedford House and individual courtiers,[22] there is no evidence of there having been any 'negotiations' in the opening months of the Parliament; and though arguments from silence have their own hazards, Charles I's court was sufficiently porous an institution, and this news (were it to have existed) sufficiently weighty, that something was almost bound to have seeped into the gossip of the day. Moreover, although Charles's prestige had suffered greatly as a result of the Covenanter invasion, it is all too easy to exaggerate the weakness of the king's position. Despite his difficulties in maintaining pay to the army, the monarch was still in receipt of the all-important customs revenues (his largest single source of revenue), and it was this small but steady trickle of funds that seems to have enabled him, throughout the autumn, to keep his government from insolvency.[23] Of course, by December, the soldiers' pay was weeks in arrears (the loans of £100,000 approved on 13 November notwithstanding).[24] But, as Charles seems to have calculated, with the two Houses now in session, the army was far more likely to blame the Parliament, rather than himself, for the failure to provide it with funds. Indeed, it may well have been suspicions of the king's intentions as to the use of the army that made the Junto leaders in Parliament so hesitant about providing adequately for its pay.[25] Little wonder, then, that on 3 December it was reported that 'the King makes himself merie' at the rumours that Bedford was to be appointed as Lord Treasurer.[26]

This royal merrymaking at Bedford's expense was to be short-lived. Two days later, the king and queen were struck by a private tragedy that further helps explain the king's indifference to any approaches that may have come from Bedford House. On 5 December, the four-year-old Princess Anne, the couple's fifth child, died at Richmond Palace.[27] Even in an age habituated to high levels of mortality among the young, the death of a child remained a profoundly traumatic event.[28] For Charles, who doted on his children and who had never before experienced such a loss, the impact of the bereavement can only be imagined.

The king's quixotic hopes and private griefs were not the only obstacles in the way of the Junto's admission to office. When it came to the choice of the kingdom's 'great counsellors', all the precedents were stacked in Charles's favour. Under the prevailing conventions, the king alone chose his ministers and he alone determined the term for which they served. No Parliament in living memory had ever presumed to dictate to a king whom he should appoint as his counsellors; and although, since 1621, Parliament had begun to assert the power to *demote* ministers – through the revival of its medieval powers of impeachment – no Parliament had succeeded in actually removing a minister by this means except where the monarch had chosen to offer his cooperation.[29] Thus where the Parliament of 1624 had James I's reluctant acquiescence for its attack on his unpopular Lord Treasurer, the Earl of Middlesex, and was therefore unable to prevent an impeachment trial to remove him from office, the 1626 Parliament's attempt to impeach the Duke of Buckingham had failed because Charles I stood by his servant, preferring to dispense with the Parliament than to see the public disgrace of his servant. Judging from past experience, the prospects during November and December 1640 of forcing the formal removal from office of either Strafford or Laud looked questionable – a point that the immense slowness of the impeachment proceedings against both men only served to underscore.

*

For Warwick, Bedford, and the other leaders of the Petitioner Junto, the challenge of breaking this impasse, without recourse to war, posed an almost insurmountable problem. True, the Petitioners' alliance with the Covenanters gave them a formidable military power base, but one that, paradoxically, they could not risk deploying against their fellow Englishmen without inciting an anti-Scottish reaction that was certain fatally to compromise their 'popularity' – for the moment, the key constituent of their authority. If further pressure were to be brought to bear on the king, then, the Junto leaders needed an alternative to the threats of military brinkmanship and organized resistance within London that they had employed so effectively during the summer. They found it in the precariousness of the king's finances. If they could cut off the sources of revenue that were keeping the Crown solvent (if only just), Charles might yet be coerced into opening negotiations. That, in turn, meant building a bicameral party or 'interest' that was capable of dominating the wayward and unruly legislature, and persuading it to follow an agenda largely defined at Bedford House and Warwick's residence in Holborn.

The consolidation of a body of support for the Petitioners in the two Houses was an incremental process, and we should be wary of regarding its apparent dominance during the first six months of the Parliament as evidence of unanimous or even near-unanimous support. In early November 1640, there was at least one attempt to have the Petition of the Twelve Peers formally read (and presumably approved) by the Commons, which had ended in failure. 'Another Mo[ti]on' was made by Sir John Clotworthy (possibly acting on behalf of Warwick House) on 18 November, prompted by reports that one William Freestone had been defaming the Petitioners in the most virulent terms, claiming that 'all these Lords that subscribed the petition [of the Twelve Peers] were Traytors and Covenanters' and deserving of capital punishment.[30] This time, Clotworthy sought to have the Petition enrolled in the House's Journal, its legal record, together with a declaration that it 'was lawfull, and thankes should bee entered in the name of the whole body of the Kingdome'.[31] Yet the Commons' response was much more muted than either Clotworthy or his nobleman allies would have wished. The Commons agreed to a resolution that the Petitioner Lords 'have done nothing, but what was legal, just, and expedient for the good of the king and kingdom'.[32] But they stopped short of enrolling the Petition, and a second motion (whose proposer is unnamed, but probably was also Clotworthy) that some members should go to give the Petitioner Lords the Commons' thanks failed to find a seconder; it merely 'fell of[f], without anie order upon it'.[33] This was far from an enthusiastic endorsement of the Petitioners' actions, and, like the early division on the Committee for Irish Affairs (with its implications for the management of Strafford's prosecution), points to a sizeable group in the Commons that had misgivings – to put it no stronger – about the conduct of the Petitioner Peers and their adherents.[34] Against this background, the Petitioners and their allies depended as much, perhaps, on the disorganized and mostly leaderless state of its potential opponents as on any managerial skills of their own. And these practical realities counsel us, despite the relative rarity of contested votes, against reading the reformists' frequent successes in the Parliament's early months as stemming from some bland 'unanimity' among either Commons or Lords.[35]

However grudgingly the admission was made, by December 1640 there was widespread recognition that what was variously called a 'ruling party', a 'governing party', or a 'Junto' – the terms seem to be used almost inter-changeably – had emerged in the Parliament, and that this was necessarily a bicameral grouping of Lords and Commons-men.[36] Importantly, however, the word 'ruling party', used in a political context in Stuart England, did not imply a group of members who constituted a majority; rather it most frequently referred to a small group of individuals who, by coordinating initiatives and inducing supporters to act in concert, could exercise a disproportionate influence over their otherwise independent-spirited and unmanaged colleagues. Although contemporaneous references to this party as a 'Junto' or 'Junta'[37] are numerous, perhaps the most perceptive analysis of its workings was penned several years later, by Edward Hyde, who, in 1640, was an ambitious barrister aged thirty-one and a man closely familiar with the men and the political world he describes. Hyde – who also spoke of 'the governing party' in Parliament[38] – identified six men as the 'great contrivers and designers' of the proceedings during the opening months of the Parliament, and in the prosecution of Strafford in particular: the Earl of Bedford, Viscounts Saye and Mandeville, and the Commons-men Oliver St John, Hampden, and Pym. These six, Hyde claimed,

> were of the most intimate and entire trust with each other, and made the engine which moved all the rest; yet it was visible that Nathaniel Fynes [Fiennes], the second son of the Lord Say, and Sir Harry Vane [junior], eldest son to the Secretary [of State, Sir Henry Vane, senior], were received by them with full confidence and without reserve.[39]

When it came to influence within the respective Houses, he named 'the Earls of Essex, Bedford, Warwick, [and] the Lords Say and Kimbolton [i.e. Viscount Mandeville]' as the 'governing voices', supported by Lords Brooke, Wharton and Paget, among others. In the Commons, it was Pym, Hampden, St John, Holles, and Fiennes, 'stoutly seconded upon all occasions by Mr

[William] Strode', Strode's brother-in-law Sir Walter Erle, young Sir Henry Vane (Northumberland's Treasurer at the Navy Office), and the York-shireman, Sir John Hotham, an inveterate enemy of the Earl of Strafford.[40]

What is most striking about these lists, though Hyde fails to point out the connection, is that every one of the peers was one of the signatories of the Petition of the Twelve and privy to the contacts with the Scots in the summer of 1640. Most of the Commons-men had either been involved in the Petition's drafting and promotion (as with St John, Pym, Fiennes and Hampden), or were close kin of the Petitioner Peers who constituted this Junto (Sir Arthur Hesilrige, Brooke's brother-in-law, and Bedford's son-in-law, Lord Digby).[41]

The relations between these men had their obvious inequalities: of age and experience, as with the near-sexagenarian Viscount Saye and the youthful Lord Digby;[42] and between the stupendously wealthy Bedford, with his income of over £15,000, and his employee, Pym, who scraped by on perhaps as little as £200 a year.[43] Nor was this Junto entirely homogeneous in its attitudes towards the ways in which the commonwealth should be reformed. In a perceptive aside, Hyde (who was to collaborate with Bedford in the course of Strafford's prosecution), noted that 'neither the Earl of Essex, Warwick, nor Brooke himself, no, nor Mr [Denzell] Holles or [William] Strode' was fully part of the most influential group, centred on Bedford and Saye in the Lords and Pym, Hampden and Fiennes in the Commons.[44] As rapidly became apparent once negotiations began on the Junto's admission to office, early in 1641, 'Warwick House' and 'Bedford House' represented rival foci of influence within the Junto, and while that rivalry was for the most part amicable, there remained subtle but important differences of emphasis between the two groupings: in their attitudes towards the Scots, the future role of the court, the severity with which errant ministers should be punished, and, perhaps most important of all, in their assessment of how far the king was worthy of trust.

What bound them together – peer and commoner, rich and relatively poor – was a sense of the providential nature of the opportunity that lay before them: to reset the tottering Church and commonwealth on new and sure foundations; to establish a political order for the future that would be proofed against the follies and vagaries of kings. Such differences as there were within this Junto – disparities of age, wealth, and rank – were therefore blurred, and usually transcended, by bonds of mutual trust, affection, and, perhaps not least, by the common experience of exposure during the summer of 1640 to potentially mortal risk. All but a handful of them had been intimately involved, as we have seen, in the Petition of the Twelve and the treasonous collusion with the Scots;[45] and it seems to have been this com-bination of common purpose and common danger that inspired what Hyde, speaking of the Junto's inner core, termed 'the most intimate and entire trust [they shared] with each other'.[46] Other Commons-men spoke of parliamentary business being 'contrived by the *correspondents* in both howses';[47] of Bed-ford's group as moving their fellow Parliament-men;[48] while the royalist minister, Robert Chestlin, later wrote of 'Lord Say, Mr Pym, Hampden, Stroud [William Strode], and other Parliament drivers' during this period as the men who 'swayed all'.[49] These 'engaged men' – motivated, committed, acutely aware of the possibly fatal consequences of failure – exercised a sway over parliamentary proceedings in both Houses that was wholly disproportionate to their actual numbers.

*

Yet Parliament was only one forum in which those who aspired to power required standing and influence. As all Parliament-men realized, once their current deliberations were ended (and in December 1640 not even the most pessimistic imagined they would last longer than a year), the court would once again become the focal point of political authority: the hub of the political life of the realm.[50] It would therefore be the changes to the personnel of the court – the Privy Councillors and the great officers of state – that would determine for the future, far more effectively than any legislation, how Charles's kingdoms would be governed. And in this world, lineage and rank remained the normal prerequisites for the 'great offices' such as the Lord Treasurership or Lord Admiralship, if not for more junior posts (which nevertheless carried Privy Councillor rank) such as those of Secretary of State or Chancellor of the Exchequer.* Dealing effectively with the court also, inevitably, entailed dealing with the king – a king, moreover, who regarded the Petitioner Junto with profound mistrust. It was unsurprising, therefore, that the Earl of Bedford – arguably the most courtly of all the Petitioner Lords – came to be regarded as the most plausible builder of bridges between the Junto's Council-in-waiting and Charles's increasingly isolated court; nor that, in December, his imminent appointment as Lord Treasurer came to be the 'news of the towne'.[51]

Ironically, Bedford was probably the figure in 'town' most sceptical of such reports. More than most Parliament-men, he appears to have realized that so long as Charles had an army in the field, the gates of Whitehall would remain firmly shut to the Petitioners. Opening them would require a radical transformation of the financial – and, through the financial, the political – structures of the English state. Almost uniquely among the Petitioners, Bedford combined the social and intellectual credentials to render him acceptable as a potential great officer at court with the political acumen and ruthlessness that made him – in conjunction with his fellow 'contrivers' in the two Houses – perhaps the most effective manager of Parliament since Lord Burghley in Elizabeth's reign.[52] It was a formidable combination, and needed to be. For as Bedford and his fellow members of the emergent Junto gradually came to realize, Charles's hostility towards the admission of 'traitors' to the greatest offices of the kingdom was unlikely to be overcome except by further threats and coercion. To hold the power of the purse was

---

* The almost universal acceptance of this principle is one of the most striking features of early Stuart political culture. Later, in August 1641, when the Commons began to assert the right to nominate those who should be appointed to these 'great offices', not one of the Commons' nominees came from their own House; all were peers.

to hold the keys to Whitehall. Bedford, moreover, had a plan by which that power might be acquired.

II. FETTERS OF GOLD

Energetic, urbane, and with a courtier's eye for fashion, Francis Russell, 4th Earl of Bedford, comprehensively confounds the traditional stereotype of the austere puritan grandee. The once conventional assumption that he was an outsider, 'more familiar with Warwick House than with Whitehall',[53] bears little relation to his actual position in the social and economic life of the metropolis – and in the life of Charles I's court. In June 1630, for example, Bedford was assigned a central (and highly honorific) role in the celebrations in the Whitehall Chapel for the christening of the king's newborn heir, Prince Charles. In the opening procession Bedford carried the baptismal font – a 'great gylded covered bason' – and took his part in a ritual that was conspicuous for its sacramentalism and liturgical splendour, presided over by Laud himself.[54] This patron of the godly clergy could accommodate himself, without any outward indication of dissent, to the 'Laudian' churchmanship of the Whitehall Chapel Royal.

Nor was this moment unique. Bedford was regularly assigned roles of honour in royal household ceremonial during the 1630s – as, for example, in 1635, when Charles nominated him to escort the Swedish ambassador to his ceremony of leave-taking in the Presence Chamber at Whitehall.[55] Only after the escalation of the Scottish crisis in 1637 does Bedford seem to have become more distanced from Whitehall's social world;[56] and, even then, he remained (like his friends, Essex and Hertford) sufficiently *persona grata* to attend the Garter Feasts of 1638 and 1640.[57]

Such social and religious amphibiousness was the hallmark of Bedford's political style. Born in 1593 and seven years Charles's senior, he seems to have been respected as much for his intelligence and learning,[58] as for his 'ancient lineage' and massive wealth, most of it derived from ex-monastic lands acquired by the Russells in the reign of Henry VIII.[59] In manner, dress and deportment, Bedford was unashamedly a man of the court. He kept his beard and moustache neatly trimmed in the same manner as the king's. He had a penchant for black silk suits, a style of dress ultimately derived from Spanish court usage,* and in vogue in English courtly circles since the 1620s.[60] These habits of style and appearance therefore had nothing to do with declaring his 'Puritanism';[61] rather, they gave expression to his membership of a pan-European aristocratic élite, his standing as a man of cosmopolitan culture, refinement and fashion.[62]

He counted a number of prominent courtiers (albeit drawn exclusively

---

* It was a taste Bedford shared, to judge from their van Dyck portraits, with such younger men of the court as Lord Digby, his son-in-law, and Charles's cousin, the 4th Duke of Lennox (from 1641, 1st Duke of Richmond), both of whom were twenty-eight in 1640.

from the Privy Council's anti-Spanish faction) among his friends, and perhaps none more so than the court's most senior officer: Philip Herbert, 4th Earl of Pembroke, the Lord Chamberlain of the Household. So highly was Bedford regarded by Pembroke that when relations between Pembroke and his wife deteriorated in 1634 and they began bickering about their household finances, Pembroke turned to Bedford and the 1st Earl of Manchester (Mandeville's father) to arbitrate their dispute.[63] By the late 1630s, the Countess of Pembroke was reliant on Bedford's influence with her husband to obtain the smallest of favours.[64] It was such friendships – and the potential for influence that went with it – that made Bedford such an asset to the Petitioners, and his position among them unassailable, in the crisis of 1640–41.

Yet the earl's courtly insouciance concealed an inner steeliness: a passion for business, projects, and litigation – activities that created abundant work for his in-house lawyers, Oliver St John and John Pym. During the 1630s he had embarked on two of the most ambitious 'improvement' schemes ever undertaken in Caroline England: a massive project of land reclamation through the drainage of the fens between Bedfordshire and East Anglia – the area which bears his name as 'the Bedford Level';[65] and a scheme to create an entirely novel form of urban space in London: a new piazza, lined with arcaded houses – based on the Paris Place Royale (later the Place des Vosges) – in Covent Garden, immediately to the north of Bedford House. These projects partly explain Bedford's need to maintain at least working relations with the court;[66] for it was thence that he drew many of his major investors, and, not least, his architect for Covent Garden, Inigo Jones, the Surveyor of the King's Works.[67] Those who worked for him – like Pym, St John, and Robert Scawen (Pym's great-nephew) all of whom served Bedford for over a decade* – came to recognize in their master a figure of formidable vigour and capacity for work; but there was also a streak of ruthlessness and a readiness to take risks that was generally concealed behind the carapace of courtly charm.[68]

Yet there was one more great 'project' that gradually came to preoccupy Bedford in the course of the 1630s, one that drew him ever more closely into the social world of the Earl of Warwick – with whom he shared the services of John Pym – and the wider network of godly noblemen and gentry for whom Warwick was 'head'.[69] This was the project to refashion the England of Charles I as a godly 'commonwealth', a world in which the monarch's powers would be subordinate to statute and the common law, and where an essentially Jacobean Calvinist divinity would once again define

---

* Scawen was less tolerant of Bedford's vagaries than his great-uncle, and by February 1636 was on the verge of leaving Bedford's employment. In an incident that captures Pym's role as Bedford's troubleshooter, Scawen later recalled that 'Mr Pyme came to [me] from the said Earle' and tried to persuade him to continue in Bedford's service, telling '[me] from him [the Earl of Bedford] that the said Earle was very willing to have [me] continewe [as] his servant' (Alnwick Castle, Northumberland MS, Box Y. III. 2 (4) 7, fos. 33–4). But Scawen had had enough, and by 1639 had entered Northumberland's service, a career that was to bring him a Commons seat, and, by the mid 1640s, a major role in the management of the New Model Army.

the mainstream doctrine of the English Church. Bedford's support for Hampden's challenge to the legality of Ship Money in 1637 had been clearly signalled by the participation of St John – Bedford's cousin and closest confidant – as Hampden's counsel (a role he would not have assumed without Bedford's approval). But he was also at one with the Warwick House circle, if less militantly, in their hostility to the ecclesiastical innovations of the 1630s. The new Arminian divinity and sacramentalism promoted by Charles and his bishops, Bedford believed, was 'the little thief put into the window of the church to unlock the door [to Popery]'.[70] And – like his friend and rival, Warwick – Bedford regarded Charles's diplomatic rapprochement with Spain as an abandonment of England's providential role as an 'elect nation', chosen by God to be the defender of Protestant truth and therefore the mortal enemy of Habsburg Spain.[71]

Bedford's efforts to remedy these ills were informed by a range of historical and theological reference, which, even in an age already exceptional for the learning of its political élite, few of his contemporaries could match.[72] Bedford's commonplace books reveal a highly practical concern with the qualities that made for good and bad kingship, and the relationship between the royal finances and political power. His voluminous notes attest to careful consideration of a variety of alternative constitutional systems – from Classical Greece and Rome to the contemporary Venetian and Dutch Republics – that extend well beyond the supposedly insular boundaries of the 'Common-Law mind'.[73]

At one level, Bedford's objectives were profoundly traditional: the wholesale refashioning of the king's counsels through a series of dismissals from, and promotions to, the great offices of state – the demand that had been a set-piece of almost every aristocratic reform movement from the days of Simon de Montfort to the Essex Revolt of 1601.[74] Hyde was half right when he wrote of Bedford that he had no wish to effect 'a subversion of the government', and that 'it quickly appeared that he only intended to make himself and his friends great at Court, not at all to lessen the Court itself'.[75] But if Bedford was content to retain the outward appearances of courtly government, there was a dimension to his plans that was far more subversive than Hyde's assessment allows. In fact, Bedford's plans for financial reform so emasculated the Crown that they amounted to a radical redefinition of balance of power between the king, on the one side, and the great officers and Parliament, on the other.[76]

From Bedford's surviving working papers and the political initiatives he promoted during the winter of 1640–41, something approaching a coherent series of preoccupations begins to emerge. Central to this project was a plan to dismantle all claims by the Crown to raise revenues on the authority of the royal prerogative (the assertion of which had justified Charles's collection of his most lucrative sources of income during the 1630s, from Ship Money to the customs). Instead, Bedford proposed to re-found England's public finances on a new series of Parliament-controlled sources of funds. By using the 'High Court of Parliament' to invalidate the king's prerogative claims to such revenues as Ship Money and the customs, Bedford hoped to be able to threaten the Crown with insolvency in order to extract one central concession: a public admission of the illegality of revenue-raising expedients founded on the prerogative that would forever after render the monarch dependent on Parliament for his principal sources of revenue. This, in turn, would provide the financial leverage with which he and his allies could at last prise open the doors of the Privy Council.[77]

*

The key elements of this strategy were revealed early in the Parliament by St John and Pym – Bedford's most trusted household men.[78] On 27 November 1640, St John launched into an impassioned attack on Ship Money, the most egregious of all the 1630s expedients for raising money on the royal prerogative, arguing that there was 'noe use of Parliaments' if the legality of Ship Money were allowed to stand.[79] Not only did this receive broad support; it served as an incitement to other members, including the garrulous Sir Simonds D'Ewes, to denounce the collection of Tonnage and Poundage – the most lucrative of the customs revenues – as equally illegal and 'without authoritie of Parliament'.[80]

The acceptance of this principle – the illegality of *all* prerogative revenue-raising – was Bedford's starting point in his dealings with the king. But it also enabled Pym, who was shortly to be tipped to play Chancellor of the Exchequer to Bedford's Lord Treasurer[81], to offer the king a highly attractive proposal. 'They would make the King the richest King in Christendome,' Pym declared, on the basis of a re-grant to the king of the customs revenues, which, since the Commons were insistent that these could not be collected without parliamentary consent, were now in the two Houses' gift. As a practical gesture towards this, he moved that Charles should henceforth have Tonnage and Poundage* 'graunted by Acte of Parliament'.[82] The offer contained a typically Bedfordian double bind: yes, Charles could have his revenue; but by accepting that Tonnage and Poundage would in future be granted by act of Parliament, the king would be implicitly conceding that his collection of it without parliamentary authority since his accession in 1625 had been illegal all along.[83] This was an expedient that had an immediate appeal to the Commons, which reacted so positively that Pym was ordered to have a new Tonnage and Poundage bill ready for consideration within the week.[84]

Given that the Parliament had been in session for less than four weeks, this was pushing matters faster than the Bedford House men necessarily

---

* Tonnage was a subsidy (or duty) imposed on imported wine at a specified rate per tun (or cask). Poundage was a duty, usually set at 12 pence in the pound, on all goods imported into and exported out of the kingdom. It had its origins in a 1347 grant of a rate on wine and other commodities, and from the reign of Richard III, the right to collect Tonnage and Poundage had been granted to the monarch by Parliament in the first year of the new reign. On Charles's accession in 1625, however, the new king failed to receive a parliamentary grant, but went on to collect the duty notwithstanding – and, to many of the Crown's critics, illegally.

wanted, and at this point St John intervened to move that the Commons 'might not *in the beginning of the Parliament* grant Tonnage and Poundage'.[85] St John, it seems, wanted some form of 'linkage' (as presumably did Pym): only after they had seen what concessions Charles had on offer would this first part of his revenue settlement be agreed;[86] and 'soe', noted D'Ewes, 'the motion died and came to nothing'.[87]

In the context of the Junto's attempts to place pressure on the king, however, the outcome of this exchange on 27 November could hardly have been more opportune. The two leading members of Bedford's 'family' (as the earl's extended household was termed) had not only proved that they *could* undertake to provide Charles with the revenues he craved, but just as effectively obstruct their provision. The choice was the king's; from 27 November he was under notice that his collection of Ship Money *and* the customs revenues were both likely to be declared illegal.[88]

What gave Bedford and his allies their potential leverage over the king was that they were prepared to offer him a bargain: they would restore Charles his customs revenues (and hence his financial solvency) by re-granting them on the authority of Parliament, but on three principal conditions. The first of these was the call for reform of the king's counsels: Charles should purge his Privy Council and admit the Petitioner Lords in the place of the ousted 'evil counsellors'. But there were two others of almost equal import-ance: that Charles should acquiesce (through the current Anglo-Scottish treaty) to Scotland's transformation into what amounted to a bishop-less, aristocratic republic; and second, that he should accept further reform of the English Church, including a curtailing of the powers of the bishops – if not their abolition outright.

On 14 December, the double act of St John and Pym – again apparently acting as the spokesmen for Bedford House – offered the king a quid pro quo in return for reform of the royal revenues. St John 'moved [the Commons] to consider of the King's revenue and to make reparation [to the king] for Monopolies, shipp-monie and other things [that were to be] taken away'.[89] Pym was even more gracious. Supporting St John, he asked that Sir Henry Vane, senior – the Treasurer of the King's Household and one of the few Privy Councillors to be a member of the Commons – 'might bee intreated to lett the king know the affections of this house towards him, and to desire leave of [the king] to looke into the revenues of his crowne and his expences'.[90] Like Pembroke and Northumberland, Vane had already pinned his colours to the reformists' mast,[91] and it is hardly surprising that he took up Pym's proposal with alacrity: 'his Majestie would bee verie ioyfull', Vane enthused, 'to heare of our care of his revenue and our desire to make him able to subsist like a King'.[92]

But this, like the St John–Pym exchange a fortnight earlier, appears to have been no more than a tableau staged in order that Bedford's supporters within the Privy Council – the likes of Pembroke, Northumberland, and Vane himself – could go to the king with evidence that some form of rapprochement with the reformists was a viable, even advantageous, proposition. And the tactic seems to have worked. On 17 December, Pym duly welcomed a 'gracious message', relayed by Vane from the king, giving the Commons leave to discuss his revenues.[93]

Such princely courtesies, however, must have been uttered through gritted teeth, for the king continued obdurate in his refusal to yield to any reforms of his counsels. Any moves towards reform in this direction – in particular the impeachments of Strafford and Laud – had been made in spite of, not because of, the king. It was at this moment, therefore, that the Petitioner Lords – exploiting their dual role as Treaty Commissioners with the Scots – returned to the attack on 'evil counsellors', preparations for which had advanced little in the intervening weeks. At a conference with the Commons that same day, 17 December, three Petitioner Lords – Viscount Mandeville, Lord Paget, and the Earl of Bristol[94] – presented Pym with the Scots' treason charges against the 'chief incendiaries', Strafford and Laud. The timing of the exchange may perhaps have been fortuitous, but to the world at large it seemed to imply an obvious linkage between favourable consideration of the king's revenues on the part of Parliament and a purge of 'evil counsellors' on the part of the king. Pym could hardly have spelt out the connection more clearly the following day when, at the conclusion of his report of the conference, 'hee wished that [the Commons] would consider of speedie supplie [i.e. the passage of a finance bill] and of having the Archbishop of Canterburie sequestered from the King'.[95] The implication was clear: Charles could not have the one without the other. The impoverishment of the Crown would continue and intensify until such point as the king yielded over the purging of 'evil counsellors'.

Yet throughout November and December, Charles remained inflexible,[96] and by Christmas 1640 the Junto's frustrations at the lack of progress were beginning to tell. Strafford was in the Tower and Laud was in the custody of Black Rod (he was not sent to the Tower until the end of February);[97] but neither had been dismissed from office, and the great cleansing of the court's Augean Stables still looked as unattainable as ever.

Then, in the last week of December, the Petitioners and their Commons allies went on to the offensive with a ferocity that seems to have taken the king wholly unawares. Why the Junto's patience snapped at this particular moment is unclear. It is possible that they had finally had enough of the king's contemptuous prevarication. A more plausible explanation, perhaps, is that Bedford and the other 'Parliament drivers' had received notification of the plans then being devised by Sir John Conyers, the king's field commander at York, for a renewal of the war against the Scots – notice of which would have reached London around 22 or 23 December.[98] It also seems likely that, as many Parliament-men returned to the country to keep Christmas (while many of the godly ignored the feast as a relic of Popery), the Junto took advantage of the relatively thin attendances at Westminster either side of Christmas to push through contentious parliamentary business.[99] They moved quickly and effectively. Over a space of roughly a week, the Junto and its supporters – the 'Commonwealths men' as they were dubbed by the Scottish Commissioners[100] – took the first legislative steps towards England's transformation from a personal monarchy into a monarchical republic, a 'commonwealth'[101] presided over by a king in strings.

III. THE MEANS OF COMPULSION

The last week of December 1640 witnessed the most ambitious attack on the prerogative powers of a reigning monarch since the 1380s, when the Lords Appellant had banded together to limit the powers of the 'tyrannical' Richard II. What distinguished the onslaught of December 1640, however, was that it was not merely a series of stop-gap measures, designed to deal with the temporary problem of an aberrant king, but an assault on monarchy itself: an attempt at a constitutional revolution that would redefine permanently the place of kingship within the English polity.

Of all these novel initiatives to emasculate the powers of the king, none was of greater consequence than the proposal to strip him of the prerogative power to decide when, and how frequently, Parliament should meet.[102] First proposed on 24 December by the Petitioners' ally, William Strode, as a bill 'for annual Parliaments', the legislation was given its second reading immediately after Christmas and referred to a committee that was wholly controlled by the Petitioner 'interest' in the Commons.[103] The bill's key provision was to make the process of calling a Parliament independent of the king's personal will. The legislature was to meet 'everie yeare *whether the King sends out his writt [of summons] or not*'.[104] And to ensure that this was done, the power to issue writs for a new Parliament was vested, *in extremis*, in the Lord Keeper (the senior law officer), or, where he failed to act, in 'twelve peers'. This last stipulation in itself provides a strong hint as to whence this proposal emerged, for the new bill for annual (later altered to triennial) Parliaments gave explicit statutory authority to the claim, first made by the Petitioners' ultimatum to the king back in September, that, if the king rejected their demand for a Parliament, 'they [would] summon it themselves', on their own authority as twelve peers.[105]

Curbing the king's power over Parliament was also combined with measures to limit his access to cash. Here, too, the assault began on 24 December. At the suggestion of Sir Walter Erle – Strode's brother-in-law and a man closely involved in the counsels of the Junto – the Commons agreed that it was the 'English Lord Commissioners' for the treaty with the Scots who should administer the disbursement of the first sums (some £30,000), which were to be raised for the relief of the war-ravaged counties in the North.[106] But as the Treaty Commissioners were, in effect, the Petitioner Lords under another name, the effect of this vote was to place this £30,000 under the immediate control of the Bedford–Warwick coalition.[107] Though this initial sum was relatively small, this was a change of massive significance, initiating a series of novel financial arrangements which, over the next ten months, were to make Warwick House into one of the principal financial offices of the realm.[108]

As efforts were made to extend the Petitioners' control of the state's

finances, moves were made in parallel to deprive the king of such funds as
he continued to receive. On 29 December, Pym moved that the Customers –
the officials who contracted with the Crown to collect the various duties –
should 'forbeare to pay *anie thing* [to the king]' until authorization for
collecting the customs 'weere setled by Parliament'.[109] In the thinly attended
chamber, Pym's subversive proposal – which would have the effect of depriving the king of his principal remaining source of income – was accepted
without division. By the end of the morning's debate, the king had been
prevented from claiming the customs revenues; the one exception was the
small sum allowed for the maintenance of 'the Kings houshold' (and even
this was probably not a courtesy to Charles, but to Bedford's ally, Secretary
Vane, who was also Treasurer of the Household).[110] Over the following
fortnight, they left the Customers in no doubt that they were henceforth
answerable to Parliament for the disbursement of funds.[111]

The crippling implications of all this for the king's revenues were immediately apparent. As the Venetian ambassador, Giustinian, reported a few
days later, the Parliament-men

> have taken from the king the use the revenues of the customs, which are
> the best and most accessible [source of] revenue which he possesses, so that
> the customs officers themselves declare that if these revenues are not
> returned to his Majesty, or if he is not provided by Parliament in some
> other way, it will be impossible for him in the future to support the
> household expenses of his own court.[112]

If the ban were to continue, the king would very soon lack the financial
resources even to pay his own immediate Household servants.

However, depriving the king of his 'best and most accessible' source of
revenue was only the start. From 23 December the Commons at last took
steps to provide for the payment of the English and Scottish armies by passing
a bill to approve the collection of four 'subsidies' – the regular form of
parliamentary taxation, based on income from land, and reckoned to raise
around £60,000 per subsidy. The new bill was therefore expected to bring
in around £240,000 in total.[113] Usually, these monies would have been paid
into the Exchequer, where their disbursement would have been controlled
by the king through his Lord Treasurer (Bishop Juxon) and the Exchequer
officials. On this occasion, however, the Parliament created what amounted
to a parallel public treasury; the funds raised on the subsidy bill were to be
paid in to its own commissioners, named within the subsidy bill, rather than
to any of the Exchequer officials, thereby preventing the king from getting
his hands on a penny of the yield.[114]

This, in itself, was a major step towards the creation of a financial administration for the 'commonwealth', independent of court and Crown. What
followed from it, logically enough, was that having created an independent
treasury, Parliament should also create its own independent Treasurer-at-
War. This, too, formed part of the 'revolution in government' initiated in
that eventful final week of December 1640 and progressively implemented

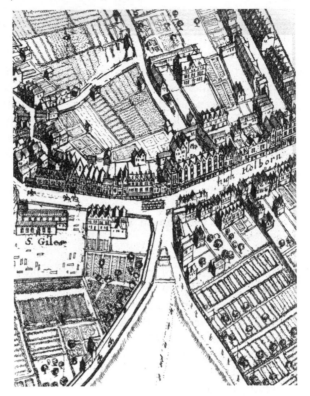

The 'other Exchequer': Warwick House on the north side of Holborn (shown here with a coach and horses outside its extensive street frontage), became the principal treasury for the payment of the Covenanter forces in England, with some £300,000 being paid out by the Earl of Warwick in the course of 1641, from the treasury here, in his capacity as de facto paymaster of the Scottish army.

over the following three months. The key question was: who would dispense, or control the allocation of, the quarter of a million pounds that was expected to be brought in by these four subsidies?

Once again, Warwick, Bedford, and the other Petitioner Peers, in their role as Treaty Commissioners, seized the initiative. At the prompting of the peers' Scottish allies, Parliament agreed that the subsidy money be physically concentrated in, and dispersed from, the house of just one of the Treaty Commissioners – from Warwick House in Holborn[115] – and the hundreds of thousands of pounds that were to pass through his doors in the months ahead were riches the like of which the impecunious king could only dream; and the well-stocked treasury at Warwick House in Holborn stood in mocking contrast to the near-empty coffers of the king's Exchequer of Receipt, beside Westminster Hall.[116]

These gestures could not have sent a clearer signal to the court: if Charles continued to refuse the Bedford–Warwick group access to the major offices of state, this Junto was capable of bankrupting both king and court. Charles was faced with a stark choice: keep his own Lord Treasurer (Bishop Juxon) and have an empty Exchequer, or assist in the purging of his Privy Council and enjoy a full one. The options were mutually exclusive.

To the consternation of the Privy Council, the proposal to divest the king of his prerogative to summon Parliament also met with an enthusiastic response in the upper House. Even before the Commons' bill for triennial Parliaments had been formally transmitted to them, the Lords were reported to have conducted a debate in which they 'not only agree[d] in this principle [that Parliament should henceforth meet triennially], but propose to set up a new public office [a council or board], which, when Parliament was not sitting, would be especially charged to ensure that its decrees were carried out'.[117] The model seems to have been the Covenanters' Committee of Estates, a nobleman-dominated executive that constituted the government of Scotland when Parliament was not in session.[118] The extremely well briefed Venetian envoy, Giovanni Giustinian, shrewdly summarized the massive shift in fiscal and constitutional power that the proposals under discussion would entail:

> If this innovation is introduced, it will hand over the reins of government completely to Parliament, and nothing will be left to the king but mere show and a simulacrum of reality, stripped of credit and destitute of all authority.[119]

The convergence of these various hostile initiatives seems hardly coincidental. This was the bicameral Junto returning to the tactics it had so successfully employed against the king's régime during the crisis of September: a mixture of blackmail, brinkmanship, and coercion. As a demonstration of the power that the Petitioner Junto could exert through Parliament it was formidable; and while it would be an exaggeration to regard this group as the sole arbiters of parliamentary influence, they clearly constituted the core of what Northumberland had started calling 'the ruling party in the Parliament'.[120]

*

If Parliament was providing Bedford, Warwick, and Pym with a battering-ram with which to assail the gates of Whitehall, there were also sympathetic Privy Councillors at court who were doing their best to ease the bolts from inside. Such were the pressures being exerted against the Crown by 'the ruling party in Parliament' during those last days of December that they compelled a major alteration in the alignment of factions at court. Even in the still unpurged Privy Council, a small but powerful group was coalescing, intent on forcing the king to acknowledge – and deal with – the reality of the Junto's power. From a variety of motives, each member of this pro-reformist court faction discerned some measure of personal advantage to be gained from ending the current impasse between the reformists and the court.

Of these, perhaps the most adventitious was James Hamilton, Marquess of Hamilton, Charles's Scottish-born favourite and Master of the Horse. Having been an unashamed ally of Strafford and Laud in the late 1630s, and a central figure in the campaign to suppress the Covenanter revolt, Hamilton had perhaps the most cravenly self-interested motives for ingratiating himself with Bedford House, the more moderate and conciliatory wing of the Junto.[121] In December 1640 he faced the near-certainty of censure in both the English and Scottish Parliaments as an 'incendiary' for his part in the anti-Covenanter policies of 1637–40.[122] In what appears to have been a shameless bid for self-preservation, he agreed to use his influence with the king in favour of Bedford and his allies. They, in return, were to spare him the fate of his two erstwhile collaborators, Strafford and Laud.[123]

However, courtiers' motives for aligning themselves with the 'ruling party in Parliament' were not always so craven. The leading lights in the Privy Council's anti-Spanish faction – Northumberland, Holland, and Pembroke – also added their support during the autumn to a rapprochement between the court and the Bedfordian Junto Lords. Unlike Hamilton, who could still trade on Charles's affection, these three were all to some extent already *persona non grata* with the king: Northumberland for his opposition to the dissolution of the Short Parliament in May; Holland for his alleged pro-Scottish sympathies; and the third of the group – the irascible Earl of Pembroke – for his long-standing and undisguised enmity towards Archbishop Laud. Having already incurred the king's disfavour, each seems to have discerned an opportunity for strengthening (and recouping) his own position by seeking an alliance with the new men of influence in Parliament.

In the context of December 1640, however, this troika – now with Hamilton as their fellow traveller – had a deeper reason for making common cause with the Bedford House wing of the Junto. While there was little love lost between Northumberland and Hamilton (whose close personal rapport with the king Northumberland deeply resented), this grouping was an old and dependable court configuration: essentially, the leaders of the pro-French, pro-Elector Palatine party of the early 1630s, which had long and vainly championed the cause of an English intervention in the Thirty Years War.[124] Northumberland, Pembroke and Holland were fervently committed to the realignment of English foreign policy, away from the Anglo-Spanish entente that had been engineered by Strafford and Laud, and towards an offensive, anti-Spanish, anti-Habsburg pact. Nor was there a more propitious time to effect this. The spectacular failure of Strafford's Spanish alliance of May 1640 – the source, for Charles, of such extravagant hopes, and such cruel disappointment – had left even the king sympathetic, for the first time in a decade, to contemplating a strategic realignment away from Spain and towards the Habsburgs' *bête noire*, the Dutch Republic.

And to exploit this opportunity, the Stadhouder of Holland, Prince Frederik Hendrik of Orange-Nassau, chose the winter of 1640–1 to propose a marriage alliance between his fourteen-year-old son and heir, Prince Willem, and Charles's nine-year-old daughter, Princess Mary. By a happy coincidence, the three Dutch ambassadors, sent to negotiate the marriage treaty, landed at Dover on 27 December – at exactly the moment when the Junto, impatient with the lack of progress with reform at court, were intensifying their assault on the king's prerogative powers.

The arrival of the Dutch delegation produced the first tangible evidence of the thaw in relations between the king's Household and Bedford House. The three ambassadors reached Westminster on 1 January 1641. That evening, as the diplomats were entertained in their new lodgings, in the company of a large number of the court nobility, they received a formal message of welcome from the king. The king's choice of his messenger on such occasions was almost invariably a gesture of royal favour towards the courtier thus honoured. What was striking about his selection on this occasion was that he nominated the senior member of the eight-man Commons team that was in charge of preparing Strafford's impeachment: Lord Digby,[125] Bedford's son-in-law and favourite (who had once professed himself more devoted to Bedford than any 'naturall childe of your owne'), and a man intimately involved in the counsels of the Petitioner Peers.[126]

Charles's decision to seek a rapprochement with the Junto was therefore the product of two convergent forces. Parliament provided a source of external pressure. But from within the court, the Junto's new-found allies – Vane, Northumberland, Hamilton, Pembroke, and Holland – were able to use the prospect of an anti-Habsburg alliance as a means of enlisting the support of Queen Henriette Marie in favour of the admission to office of Bedford and the other leading Petitioner Peers. Bedford's godly Protestant 'commonwealth' had found an unlikely patroness in Charles's Catholic queen. The irony was not lost on contemporaries. Sir John Coke, the son of a retired Secretary of State and a man familiar with the ways of the court, mused on the astonishing démarche: 'if these men come in [to office] by the Queen's side,* there is art enough somewhere'.[127]

Over the following fortnight, the king offered a series of concessions, which together seemed to mark a wholesale repudiation of the policies of the Personal Rule. By the early weeks of January 1641, for the very first time, the Junto members' treasonous gamble for power seemed, at last, to be on the brink of success.

IV. MR ST JOHN'S PROFESSION: THE REFORM OF THE LAW

The ferocious parliamentary onslaught of late December brought results. Serious negotiations between Bedford House and the king appear to have been initiated early in the New Year, and by the week beginning Sunday, 17 January were already well advanced. 'I understand *the king* is brought into a dislike of those counsels that he hath formerly followed', wrote Sir John Temple on 21 January, reporting the sudden *bouleversement* at court, 'and therefore resolves to steere another course.' He went on, discreetly putting the courtiers' names in cipher (rendered here in italics): '*Hamilton* [the king's favourite and Master of the Horse] and [Henry] *Jermyn* [a favourite of the queen and her Master of the Horse]', he believed, had 'deeply contributed to this change', opening up the likelihood that several of the leading members of the Bedford–Warwick Junto would be admitted to high office.[128] Indeed,

---

* This seems to be a reference to the layout of contemporary royal houses, which were generally divided into two 'sides' (King's Side and Queen's Side), each of which was divided into a duplicate sequence of chambers (Guard Chamber, Presence Chamber, and Privy Chamber), which finally met at interconnecting private apartments around their respective Bedchambers. It was therefore physically possible to get to the king by 'the Queen's Side', though any suitor for the monarch's favour would usually have made his approach via the King's Side.

Northumberland's sister, the Countess of Carlisle, had already got wind of this development a week earlier. 'I now beleeve', she wrote to the Countess of Leicester, 'that we shall have great change of oficers': that Bedford would be Lord Treasurer and that the queen and Northumberland would collaborate to secure either the Lord Lieutenancy of Ireland or the post of Secretary of State for the Earl of Leicester.[129]

The starting point of the Junto's 'reformed commonwealth' was the king's public acceptance of the principle that the royal prerogative was bounded by the common law and that it was his High Court of Parliament that was its ultimate interpreter. That, in turn, required the king to renounce a central axiom of the last half century of monarchical theory – from Fleming's pronouncements in *Bate's Case* in 1606, through to the sermons of Maynwaring and Sibthorpe in the 1620s, to Finch's advice in *Hampden's Case* of 1637 and, most recently, Strafford's counsel of May 1640 that the king was 'loose[d] and obsolved from all rules of government': namely, that the king's prerogative powers, being immediately from God, stood above, and therefore unconstrained by, the common law.

To Bedford and his allies, this was the precept that had been the pernicious centre of the Personal Rule. Therefore, it was this doctrine – and the judges who had so subserviently upheld it – that Charles must now publicly renounce; for while it stood, it constituted a potentially lethal threat to the Junto's plans to re-found the kingdom's finances – and with this, the relation between Crown and people – on the principle of the parliamentary grant. To Bedford, precisely how this renunciation was to be finessed in theoretical terms seems to have been a matter of secondary importance. Actions spoke far more bindingly than any written formulation; in particular, it would be what the king did in relation to the judges and the senior officers of the law that would provide the clearest indication of his bona fides. Would he acquiesce in the punishment of those who had exalted the prerogative in *Hampden's Case*, and promote the upholders of the common law? Or would he cling tenaciously, as he was still clinging to Strafford, to those in the legal profession who had been the most public sources of 'evil counsel' during the 1630s?

The attack on the judges, apparently directed from Bedford House, took shape over a month between mid December and mid January 1641. Although Pym played a part, it was Oliver St John – Bedford's household legal counsel – who emerged as the judiciary's major persecutor, and the lawyer in charge of preparing the necessary articles of impeachment.[130] Complaints had been made against the Ship Money judges at the end of December;[131] but the figure who was to act as a lightning conductor for the hostility against them all was Finch. His sins were numerous; but the most egregious was that, as Chief Justice of Common Pleas in 1637, he had been the *éminence grise* who had suborned his fellow judges to find in the king's favour in the Ship Money case – *Rex* versus *Hampden*. St John, who had first moved for Finch's impeachment in mid December[132] (just as Northumberland and Hamilton were beginning to align themselves with the Junto), returned to the attack in mid January (just as Bedford's imminent elevation as the king's chief minister was coming to be regarded at court as a matter of certainty).[133]

A commanding presence and formidable intellect, St John emerged during these weeks as the authoritative spokesman for the Petitioners' reading of the laws of England – the interpretation that Charles I was bound to accept as the non-negotiable precondition of any settlement with Bedford House. To appreciate St John's place in these counsels, however, we need briefly to examine his career and, in particular, his relationship with his employer and 'cousin', Francis Russell, Earl of Bedford.

Oliver St John was much more to Bedford than a jobbing lawyer, retained to offer professional advice. Born in 1598, St John had been brought up as the scion of a well-connected but impecunious junior branch of the nobility, the Lords St John of Bletso. He entered the puritan bastion of Queens' College, Cambridge, in 1615, where he was tutored by the young John Preston, a rising star of the ecclesiastical firmament. From Preston, he seems to have imbibed that zealous but essentially conformist, episcopalian Calvinism which then defined the mainstream of the Jacobean Church – the form of piety that Laud and his acolytes would later strive to marginalize as 'puritan'.

However propitious his standing may have been among 'the godly Elect', St John's worldly prospects were meagre. A younger son with no likelihood of inheriting land, he trained as a barrister at Lincoln's Inn during the 1620s. By the end of the decade, as he entered his early thirties, however, almost all St John's legal work was coming from a single source: his cousin, five years his senior, Francis Russell, whose patrimony (and hence his need for lawyers) had been massively increased on his succession to the earldom of Bedford in 1627.

From the outset, the relationship between the two men was more like that of brothers than of master and employee.[134] Its closeness is clearly attested at the time of the negotiations for St John's marriage in 1630 to Joan Altham, the grand-daughter of the formidable matriarch of the Barringtons, Joan, Lady Barrington. One of the great Essex puritan families, the Barringtons were part of an extensive godly network in the county that looked for political leadership to the Earl of Warwick, and regarded themselves as only marginally inferior, in rank and status, to the nobility. Indeed, it was Warwick's cousin and man-of-affairs, Sir Nathaniel Rich, who first suggested the match between St John and his future bride.[135] St John found himself out of his league. Despite having a decent landed estate and a lucrative income from the law, he failed to satisfy his prospective in-laws' expectations.[136] Only a generous financial subvention from Bedford, who settled an estate on St John as though he were his own son, sufficed to turn him into a landed gentleman[137] and overcome the Barringtons' objections to the marriage.[138] So generous was the settlement to St John that his prospective in-laws feared it might be contested by Bedford's own children in the courts, such was the diminution of their own inheritance entailed in the earl's generosity towards St John.[139]*

---

* We get a glimpse of Bedford's solicitousness towards his 'cosen' in the letter he wrote to Lady Barrington when, now confident of St John's new-found status as a country squire, she had become a firm supporter of the match: 'Madam,' wrote Bedford, 'my cosen St John telleth me that hee had reseved favors from you [in] heapes, which I shall

Indeed, the affinity between the two men may have been considerably closer than has usually been supposed, for St John's lineage was not what it seemed.[140] His father, Oliver senior,[141] had been brought up in the household of Thomas St John (a younger son of the first Lord St John of Bletso, who died in 1582), and had taken his putative father's surname. But he was in fact a bastard son, 'base born',[142] and his biological father was reputedly the second Earl of Bedford (1527–85).[143] If, as seems likely, this report is true, the 'cousinage' between Oliver St John and his employer, the fourth Earl of Bedford, was close indeed: they both shared the same paternal grandfather.[144] This, in turn, would help explain the fourth earl's otherwise almost outlandishly generous settlement of Russell lands on Oliver in 1630. But for the bastardy of Oliver's father, it may well have been this line of the Russells (now forced to masquerade as St Johns) that would have inherited the Bedford earldom on the demise of the childless 3rd Earl of Bedford in 1627 – the title which, instead, passed to the third earl's cousin, Francis Russell, the 4th Earl of Bedford, and the benefactor of Oliver St John, the barrister of Lincoln's Inn.[145]

Whatever the truth of this, the relationship between Bedford and his cousin was exceptionally close. In both politics and religion, the one was almost the alter ego of the other; and just as Bedford seems rarely to have acted without St John's advice, St John's interventions in public life seem to have been calculated, almost invariably, to further the interests and policies of his titled cousin and the wider political interest represented by Bedford House. It was a relationship that was eventually to founder spectacularly;[146] but in the early months of 1641, it was still strong and secure.

*

It is against this background, then, that we need to view St John's place within the inner counsels of the Junto – that 'engine which moved all the rest'[147] – and in particular, the cause he made his own during December–January: the condemnation of Ship Money and the impeachment of its principal judicial upholder, Lord Keeper Finch. St John delivered the most trenchant (and widely noticed) of numerous speeches on these themes on 14 January 1641, just as the recent thaw in relations between Bedford House and Whitehall was beginning to produce the first signs of movement towards a settlement. Presented as a progress report to the Lords on the Commons' investigation into the legality of Ship Money, the speech was turned by St John into a comprehensive manifesto of the Bedford House circle's demands for legal reform: for the necessity to subordinate the royal prerogative to the Common Law to the need to ensure the independence of the judiciary; and the requirement that those judges who had perverted the law should now be purged.[148] Above all, his speech prepared the way for the formal impeachment

---

desier your Ladyship toe beleve that I vallew them at noe less then if you had bestowed soe [many] kiendneses ... uppon me, which I am confident his love and service toe you and yors shall in sume mesuer aunsewer'.

of Finch, the prime 'subverter' of the law, St John claimed, during the years of Personal Rule.[149] And to buttress his case for Finch's punishment as a traitor, St John 'insisted long' on the case of the judges in the reign of Richard II, who had been proceeded against 'as Traitors for giving ther opinions against the libertie of the subject'.[150]

At first sight, this looks like yet another straightforward clash between the parliamentary reformists on the one side, and the coterie around the king – unyielding and uncompromising as ever – on the other. However, there is reason to suppose that rather more is going on here than at first appears. Paradoxically, within a week of the delivery of this speech, Bedford was promoting St John to the king, through the mediation of the Marquess of Hamilton, as a prospective Solicitor-General – an unlikely course of action if St John's speech had been intended to be hostile to Charles himself. Secondly, in attacking Lord Keeper Finch, St John was choosing a target for impeachment who was already safely out of harm's way.[151] For at the time of St John's speech, Finch was already on his way to a relatively comfortable exile in The Hague in one of the king's ships – a privileged mode of escape that could not have been allowed him without the connivance of the Lord Admiral, Northumberland, one of Bedford's chief allies at court.[152] Pembroke may also have been involved, as one of Finch's first acts on reaching The Hague was to write a letter expressing his 'true gratitude' to the Lord Chamberlain.[153]

In fact, St John's appearance as Finch's denouncer seems to have been as much a 'court appointment' as Digby's role as the conveyor of the king's greeting to the Dutch ambassadors a fortnight earlier. True, St John's speech of 14 January was a powerful indictment of the pusillanimous judges of the 1630s.[154] But, by placing the blame for the iniquities of the past so squarely on the absentee Finch, the effect of his oration was to provide an almost complete exculpation for King Charles. Despite the ominous allusions to Richard II, the references to the current monarch were as the innocent dupe of 'evil counsel'. Of course, whether St John believed Charles to be such an ingénue is highly doubtful; in the context of the Bedford negotiations, however, St John's extensively publicized performance begins to look like a carefully prearranged piece of Whitehall theatre.[155]*

And Charles, with his own keen sense of the theatrical, made his response perfectly on cue. The very next day he announced that the judges would no longer hold office 'at the pleasure of the Crown' (which left the judiciary dismissible at will); instead, for the future, they would enjoy what amounted to security of tenure, being removable only on grounds of serious malfeasance.[156] Nor was this the only initiative Charles took to restore confidence in the workings of the law and the judicial system.[157] In a further gesture

---

* Indeed, one of the court masque's most familiar dramatic stratagems was the speech denouncing the sources of discord and corruption within the commonwealth (as part of the 'antimasque', or prelude to the masque proper), as the preparative to an almost equally formulaic *mise-en-scène*: the moment when the king enters as the banisher of vice and the restorer of concord within the realm.

that suggests cooperation between the court and Bedford House over legal reform, Charles seems to have agreed that any existing proclamations that conflicted with the Common Law would be abrogated, and henceforth he would issue only 'such as shall stand with the former Laws or Statutes of the Kingdome'.[158]

More important, Charles finally agreed to a series of appointments and promotions that signalled a transformation of the upper echelons of the judiciary. Here, too, Hamilton – who attended the king daily as a Gentleman of the Bedchamber, and accompanied him in his coach as Master of the Horse[159] – appears to have acted as the immediate source of persuasion, promoting a series of names that were Bedford's and Northumberland's nominees.[160] The deliberations on these new appointments appear to have started around Thursday, 14 January (the date of St John's speech), but by early the following Tuesday evening (19 January) the new list was almost complete.[161] Its effect was to alter the character of the judicial bench decisively in favour of the newly emergent Bedford–Northumberland–Hamilton axis at court.

This new list constitutes the first substantive concession by the king to the reformists' demands. The most senior office to change was that of Lord Keeper, the head of the Court of Chancery. With Finch now impeached, the king conferred the place on Sir Edward Littleton, who appears to have been Hamilton's nominee.[162] When Littleton had been inaugurated as Chief Justice of Common Pleas in 1640, he had named Hamilton as his 'patron' (who helped pay for the creation-ceremony feast, and may well have helped secure his nomination);[163] and from the moment of his appointment as Lord Keeper, noted Hyde, 'they who most opposed the King [his term for the Bedford–Northumberland coalition] ... did exceedingly apply themselves to him, and were with equal kindness received by him'.[164] Littleton, it seemed, had aligned himself squarely with the Bedford House Junto.

Equally satisfactory to the Bedford–Northumberland coalition was the appointment of Littleton's successor as the new Lord Chief Justice of Common Pleas: Sir John Bankes. Currently the Attorney-General,[165] Bankes was a close friend of Northumberland and, though without judicial experience, now leapfrogged all the current puisne judges to the Chief Justiceship, and was to deputize for the new Lord Keeper during Littleton's lengthy illness during the spring.[166] Bankes's promoters are not in doubt: at his inauguration into his new office, he publicly named as his 'patrons' the Earls of Northumberland and Bedford.[167]

Moreover, as evidence of Charles's commitment to the principle that judges should hold office 'on good behaviour', not at his own pleasure, the king actually reinstated Sir Robert Heath, one of the judicial 'martyrs' of recent years, who, having fallen foul of the king – allegedly as a result of his reputation as a Puritan – had been dismissed from the bench in 1634.[168] That Heath had come into the orbit of St John, with whom he was writing joint legal opinions by early 1640, can have done his chances of preferment no harm.[169]

What set the seal on the 'reformist' character of these appointments, however, was St John's own nomination as the new Solicitor-General.[170] Far from being punished for his attack on Finch, which had initiated this round of legal musical chairs, St John now became one of the senior law officers of the Crown. St John was later to give the credit for his promotion to the Marquess of Hamilton;[171] but in placing Bedford's trusted man-of-affairs at the centre of the court's legal affairs, the marquess was publicly aligning himself with the rising Bedford 'interest' at court, and it was Bedford whom Hyde (probably correctly) identified as the prime mover in the promotion.[172]

Almost as significant was the nomination of another of the Junto supporters' placemen, Sir John Temple, the Earl of Leicester's man of affairs, as Master of the Rolls for Ireland – one of the most senior places in the Irish Chancery, and a stepping stone to likely further judicial preferment in England.[173] The appointment was all the more significant in that Temple's patron, Leicester, was the Northumberland–Bedford group's preferred candidate to replace Strafford as Lord Lieutenant of Ireland.[174]

For the Petitioner Junto, the king's concessions over the recent appointments – and, equally important, on the judges' security of tenure – were the first intimations that Charles would, at last, consent to thoroughgoing reform of the 'commonwealth'. In agreeing to the fall of Lord Keeper Finch, Charles was giving the Junto its first evil counsellor's scalp. And in St John's appointment as Solicitor-General, he had offered what appeared to be unambiguous testimony of his intention to embrace, literally as well as metaphorically, the counsels of Bedford House.[175]

v. THE LIMITS OF COMPROMISE

The implications of these developments were not lost on the Whitehall court. There was to be a sea change in the composition of the Privy Council and among the occupants of the great offices of state. And by the penultimate week of January (Sunday 17 to Saturday 23), courtiers were reporting excitedly the names of those who were to be swept away, and those who were expected to rise, on the incoming reformist tide.

Apart from the judges, *all* the new secular office holders were to be drawn from the ranks of the Petitioner Lords or their dependants. Sir John Temple, Leicester's *homme d'affaires* at court, provided a summary of the proposed appointments. 'My Lord of Bedford shall now presently [i.e. immediately] be Lord Treasurer', he wrote on 21 January, 'and [the current Lord Treasurer, Bishop Juxon, shall be moved to be] Archbishop of York. Mr Pimme shall certainly Chancellour of the Exchequer, and my Lord Say Master of the [Court of] Wardes.'[176] A few days later a fuller list was available, naming – in addition to Bedford, Saye, St John, and Pym – 'the good Earle of Essex' as Lord Deputy of Ireland; Bristol as Lord Privy Seal (the officer who controlled much of the king's personal patronage); and his son, Lord Digby (Bedford's son-in-law), as Secretary of State in place of the absconded Windebank.[177]

Here, then, were the outlines of an entirely new administration, a reformed

Privy Council built around the ranks of the leading Petitioner Peers. Once 'our Junta' was settled, wrote Sir John Temple, the influence of the old court power-brokers – like Henry Jermyn, the queen's favourite – looked certain to wane.[178] That these preferments remained on hold does not appear to have been only a matter of reluctance on the king's part to confirm the appointments. It was Bedford's reluctance to accept, rather than Charles's unwillingness to offer, which appears to have maintained the impasse. Among the Petitioners, there seems to have been a mutual agreement that none of them would accept office in the reformed Privy Council unless 'some other accommodations [i.e. appointments to office] were provided for some of the rest of their chief companions'.[179] It was a wise proviso. Without this, it is hard to imagine the Petitioners' unity would have lasted for long. For individuals among them to have accepted offices *seriatim* would have been to fall straight into the trap Windebank and the king had devised, back in September, when they had tried to disengage Essex from the ranks of the other Petitioner Peers: to divide the reformist lords between a class of 'ins' and 'outs', with all the jealousies that were likely to arise between the promoted and those left out in the cold.[180]

However, there was one further precondition that Bedford insisted upon with regard to his own acceptance of public office. He 'was resolved', noted Hyde (who was privy to at least part of these negotiations), 'that he would not enter into the Treasury till the revenue was in some degree settled';[181] and, as we know from Bedford's working papers, this involved the king's renunciation of any claim to raise public finance on the royal prerogative, and his acceptance of a permanent dependency on parliamentary grants.

Here, too, Bedford secured a major advance – again probably backed by Hamilton and Northumberland. Within twenty-four hours of Temple's announcement (on Thursday, 21 January) that the king had resolved 'to steere another course',[182] Charles had conceded Bedford's central demand: that he would relinquish all sources of revenue that Parliament deemed illegal – a category which already included Ship Money as well as the customs revenues (except where expressly granted by Parliament), and was likely to include every single one of the 1630s prerogative exactions. This, it seemed, was a momentous concession.

On Charles's part, this was partly making a virtue out of necessity, since there seemed little prospect for the foreseeable future that any of these revenues might be collected on the authority of the prerogative alone. But that the king was now prepared publicly to acknowledge as much fulfilled one of the central preconditions of any Junto-brokered settlement: henceforth, the king was required to accept his place as the pensioner of Parliament.

*

These financial constraints ultimately had a political rationale. If Bedford and his friends were ever to be secure in office, they had to be certain that future meetings of Parliament did not depend randomly on the fiscal exigencies of the king. Indeed, after fifteen years of Charles's rule, they had sufficient experience of the king's financial ingenuity to know that monetary pressures alone could not be relied upon to ensure the regular convening of Parliaments. This prompted Bedford and his allies to return to the bill to define the frequency of Parliament's meetings by law – the proposal that had launched the Junto's onslaught against the powers of the Crown on 24 December. By the week beginning Sunday, 17 January – just as the Bedford negotiations are reported to have entered a highly promising phase – this legislation, now definitively recast as a bill for triennial (rather than annual) Parliaments, suddenly acquired a critical urgency. If any of the Petitioners were to accept places on the 'reformed' Privy Council, Charles's assent to the Triennial Bill was an absolute *sine qua non*. Without this consent, any of the projected 'new counsellors' would be vulnerable to dismissal by Charles the moment the current Parliament had ceased to sit.

Once again, it was Bedford's 'family' who took the lead in bringing the Triennial Bill to completion, just when it was needed to provide the insurance policy for their future security in office. Between Tuesday, 19 and Saturday, 23 January – the week that saw St John's promotion to Solicitor-General and the proposed reallocation of ministerial portfolios among the Petitioners – the new law briskly assumed its final form. Bedford's son-in-law, Lord Digby, spoke first to commend the Commons committee's report on the bill on Tuesday the 19th; and his contribution was followed by a powerful speech from Pym.[183] Passed unopposed on Wednesday the 20th, the new Triennial Bill was immediately sent to the Lords – with Digby again 'owning' the bill by acting as its courier, physically carrying up the parchment document to the House of Lords.[184] The Lords thus began their consideration of the bill at exactly the moment when agreement was reported to have been reached between the king and the Bedfordians on a comprehensive reallocation of the great offices of state.[185]

The Triennial Bill, together with the new arrangements for the king's finances, which made him fiscally dependent on Parliament, gave the erstwhile 'rebels' of 1640 their all-important guarantee. What appears to have been their one remaining reservation against accepting membership of the Council would fall the moment Charles gave the bill the royal assent.

On the question of ecclesiastical reform, potentially the most explosive of subjects, there were also the first signs that the matter might yet be defused. On Friday, 15 January the Privy Council debated whether the king should make a public declaration that he intended all matters ecclesiastical – including Church government – to be 'reduced to their former state, as it was in the times of Q. Eliz[abeth], which is esteemed the best times'.[186] This, too, brought results. In the course of the following week, the king acquiesced, undertaking to reform the Church to 'the best state and condition' that it had enjoyed 'during Queene Elizabeths raigne'.[187] This phrase was fraught with ambiguity; but it seems to have been taken to mean, at very least, an abandonment of the sacramental theology and ceremonialism of the 1630s, and the ousting of all clergy from positions of secular power (from the heights of the Privy Council to the lowly county bench). As such, it was an encouraging start. Moreover, in a sign that Charles was prepared to embrace yet further ecclesiastical reform, on Thursday, 21 January the king summoned

Archbishop Ussher – the Irish prelate and long standing enemy of Laud who, six months earlier, had been resident at Warwick House[188] – to discuss 'the business of episcopacy'. Also summoned to attend these discussions were two prominent Cambridge divines whose Jacobean Calvinism, like Ussher's, accorded well with the Junto's theological tastes: Dr Ralph Brownrigg, who was married to Pym's niece; and Dr Richard Holdsworth, the Master of Emmanuel College, the university's notorious hotbed of Puritanism.[189]

Discussions along these lines – which clearly assumed the retention of at least some role for bishops – might not have been far-reaching enough to satisfy the Scots, nor even, perhaps, the more religiously zealous members of Bedford's own constituency. But that the talks were taking place at all was an indication that the king was prepared, for the first time, to entertain some form of compromise. And as the broader Junto was showing no signs of seeking the abolition of bishops 'Root and Branch',[190] the remaining distance between the two parties seemed bridgeable. The 'godly commonwealth' was within sight.

By Friday, 22 January, then – the end of the week that had seen the judiciary purged, new law officers appointed, and general agreement as to the reapportionment of the conciliar offices – there were the makings not only of a new government, but also of a new foreign policy, a purged and reformed judiciary, the abandonment of the prerogative revenues, and a religious settlement that promised a return to the pristine virtues of Elizabeth's day.

*

Over this increasingly sunny political landscape there loomed but one awkward and niggardly cloud: the impeachment of the 'grand delinquent', the Earl of Strafford. Yet here, too, the outlook seemed propitious. During that same week of frenetic change, Queen Henriette Marie, who had already done much to reconcile the king to dealing with Bedford House, applied her powers of persuasion to the removal of even this, potentially the most intractable of problems. On 19 January, the day that the new judicial appointments had been finalized and St John named as Solicitor-General, a breathless Will Davenant (the courtier, impresario, and poet) reported the news:

> It is not many howers since it is declard at Courte [that Strafford] must trust to his owne innocence now, and to the mercy of the Houses after judgement; so that his friends beginne to forsake their hopes, and mourne allredy.

Davenant also believed that other 'dilinquents' – presumably meaning Laud, Finch, and the other impeached judges – would also be abandoned by the king; for 'it is not doubted at Court (though the newes be not old) that the Queen hath, upon her knees, diverted the King from all whispers that tend to displease either house [of Parliament]'.[191] Strafford, it seemed, was as good as abandoned, and the purge of the other offenders was only a matter of time.

With respect to Finch and Laud, both of whom Charles seems to have regarded as expendable, Davenant's information was probably correct. But in one respect, at least, his report is an example of court gossip running ahead of itself. As viewed by the king, the punishment of his most trusted servants – men who had served him devotedly for much of his reign – was more than a matter of politics; it trenched deeply on his honour and self-esteem. For a king to be seen to allow loyal servants to go to the scaffold, while 'traitors' such as Bedford and Essex prospered, was a prospect that affronted every fibre of Charles's being. He had a dread of being seen to act under compunction; and having surrendered so much – over the judges, the 'illegal' royal revenues, the Church, even, in principle, the admission of the Petitioners to major civil office – there was one remaining royal prerogative power, as yet uncontested by the Junto, that he could still use to defeat the judicial process against Strafford: his power to pardon. It was on this issue, therefore, as progress was being made rapidly towards a settlement on the other heads, that Charles decided to make a stand.

Saving the Lord Lieutenant became, in Charles's mind, the test of honour that would be definitive not only of his kingship, but of his own moral worth. By now, he knew that he was probably powerless to prevent Strafford's impeachment from going forward to trial. But there remained, for both of them, the possibility of his being issued with a pardon, so long as that power remained one of the prerogative rights of the crown.

The opportunity to assert this right had presented itself, almost fortuitously, two days earlier. At the end of the week the Recorder of London, Thomas Gardiner (the magistrate who tried criminal cases within the City), had presented the king with the list of felons found guilty at the recent Wednesday sessions. He besought the king to exercise his prerogative of mercy as he thought appropriate.[192] But among the condemned was the Catholic priest, John Goodman, a convert from Anglicanism, who had been found guilty on a currently little-used provision of the Elizabethan treason laws, merely for being a Catholic priest in England.[193] Unless reprieved, he would shortly suffer the grisly punishment of hanging, drawing (evisceration alive) and quartering. Who first alerted Charles to the possibility of pardoning Goodman is uncertain. Henriette Marie and the papal agent in London, Count Carlo Rossetti, may well have entered their pleas for leniency; but the obvious candidate is probably Recorder Gardiner himself. As Gardiner was one of Strafford's defence counsel in his impeachment trial, he may well have had a particular motive for encouraging the monarch to assert his prerogative of mercy.[194] But whoever offered the advice, the final decision to issue Goodman with a royal pardon was Charles's alone, and put into effect late on Friday, 22 January.[195]

This reprieve sent a powerful message to the reformists. As Baillie noted, the pardon was 'taken by all to have been done of purpose, for a preparative to save the life of the Lieutenant [of Ireland, Strafford] and [the Archbishop of] Canterburie'.[196] And by having forced a reluctant Secretary Vane to be the means of the reprieve's procurement, Charles guaranteed that news of his action would be transmitted almost instantaneously to the Bedford–Warwick Junto and its parliamentary supporters.[197]

Charles had made a stand. The following afternoon – Saturday – he would address the two Houses in the Banqueting House, and he instructed Vane to convey his summons.[198] Beneath Rubens's celestial apotheosis of kingship, Charles would reveal how wholeheartedly he had reinvented himself as a monarch bounded by the earthly law. Of course, he would mention various 'Rocks' that lay in the way of an accommodation. However, the largest and most intractable of these was to go unmentioned. It had already been declared when the king affixed his signature to the priest's reprieve. Charles's power to pardon convicted felons – to save Strafford's life and, with it, his kingly honour – was now the stumbling block in the way of further progress towards Bedford's 'commonwealth'. And, little though Charles probably realized it, in this he had finally lighted upon a 'Rock' that could split the Junto in two.

6

TERMS OF ENDEARMENT

JANUARY–FEBRUARY 1641

> Theopomus, kinge of the Mollosians, by cutting some part of the king's power, he augmented the kingdome, in continuance of tyme. Inasmuch that, in a certaine manner, he made it not lesser, but greater; as it is reported that he answered his wife, when she did chide [him], and demanded if it were not a great shame for him to leave the kingdome lesse [in his own power] then he had received it from his father: no (said he), because I leave it them in such plight [i.e. good condition], as it shall last the longer.
>
> Entry in the Earl of Bedford's Commonplace Book[1]

If Charles remained committed, inwardly, to eventual revenge, he was never-theless sufficiently deft as a politician to recognize, at least sometimes, the virtues of temporary retreat. His encouraging offers to the Bedfordians had thus far been largely private transactions, making little impact beyond the relatively closed world of the court. On Saturday, 23 January 1641, however, the king chose to reveal his change of heart to the political nation. His speech initiated an extended period of self-reinvention, the beginning of a gradual metamorphosis, which persuaded at least some of the public, from his being a despotic autocrat to being the upholder of England's 'known ways' and ancient laws.[2] The king's own attitude to that process of reinvention was always ambivalent, and at times implicitly hostile. But for a relatively extended period, from that Saturday in January until early May 1641, Charles kept up an outward show of having renounced his former high-handed ways that persuaded many of those who dealt with him that he was, if not wholly sincere in his conversion, then at least resigned to its unavoidability. By the end of that Saturday, the erstwhile sponsor of 'Popish innovations' in the Church had declared himself the defender of its Elizabethan – and unim-peachably Protestant – inheritance.

To contemporaries, the king's choice of venue immediately suggested that there was to be something exceptional about the promised royal oration. Normally, when kings chose to address their Parliaments, they did so either in the Painted Chamber at Westminster or from the throne in the House of

Lords, with the Commons, or those of them who could find room, crammed into the highly constricted space below the bar of the House. Charles's choice of the Banqueting House as the alternative, however, did more than merely solve this problem of accommodation. It afforded the king a setting of dazzling splendour and theatricality.

Completed in 1622 and modelled on the imperial basilicas of antiquity, Inigo Jones's massive Banqueting House – a double cube 110 feet in length by 55 wide – was not so much a dining or masquing hall, but the Presence Chamber (or throne room) of Whitehall Palace: its principal ceremonial space. Almost every one of its surfaces was adorned with the images glorifying monarchy, from its tapestry-covered walls, coruscating with gold and silver thread, to its vast, Venetian coffered ceiling, enriched with Rubens's great allegorical canvasses eulogizing the greatness of Charles's father, James VI and I.[3] In 1641, the Rubens paintings had been *in situ* for barely five years, and the building itself had no equal in scale or opulence anywhere in England. For many Parliament-men, up from the shires and unfamiliar with the world of the court, the gilded setting in which they found themselves must have evoked a sense of awe and wonderment. Here, a king who had spent the previous week offering to trade away much of the substance of his power, could at least appear surrounded by its illusion.

Yet even before Charles took the stage, Sir Henry Vane, senior, the king's increasingly alienated Secretary of State, had decided that this was a *mise-en-scène* that he was determined to subvert.

*

On Saturday morning, 23 January, the Secretary entered the Commons after the House had convened, and as a Privy Councillor took his seat, as convention dictated, on the right side of the Speaker's chair.[4]* As bidden by the king, Vane dutifully conveyed his master's summons: both Houses were to attend him that afternoon 'at 2 of the clocke, in the banqueting howse'.[5] But this was not the only news he brought from Whitehall. Still resentful at the pardon of Father Goodman the previous evening – and still more, it seems, by its implications for the exoneration of Strafford – Vane did not keep the 'scandal' to himself for long. Reports of the king's action in reprieving the condemned priest spread quickly around Westminster, and had been raised by Alderman Penington, the most zealously 'godly' of the City's four Commons-men, earlier that morning.[6] Once in the Commons' chamber, Vane provided not only confirmation of the reality of Goodman's escape from the gallows, but, anxious to stress that his own part in the reprieve, as Secretary, had been entirely involuntary, he also made it absolutely clear that the orders for the pardon had come directly from the king.[7] For Vane, the Goodman

---

* The seventeenth-century seating of the Privy Councillors immediately to the right of the Speaker's chair – that is, on the left side of the House as one looks at the chair – survives into modern parliamentary usage as the location of the 'government benches', with the ministers of the Crown seated at the front, nearest the Speaker's chair.

case was a critical moment of transition in his own transformation from royal servant to prospective rebel. Royal leniency towards popish priests was always guaranteed to rile the sensibilities of the godly. In making public the circumstances and consequences of Goodman's reprieve – sabotaging, in the process, any prospect that the Parliament would give a sympathetic hearing to the king's speech that afternoon – Vane was publicly siding for the first time with the Junto against the king. In Parliament, his revelation acted as a match to tinder, and the emergency conference held that same morning with the Lords blazed with anger at the implications of Goodman's reprieve.[8]

Much has been made of this moment by historians, both as evidence of an increasingly hysterical anti-Popery, and to suggest that this hysteria created an irreconcilable divide between the parliamentary godly and a king who happened to be married to a Catholic queen.[9] Just how 'irreconcilable' was this divide will be considered later. True, there were many Parliament-men who regarded any gesture of royal indulgence towards Catholics with profound suspicion. In the immediate context of January 1641, however, it was not the religious dimension of Charles's actions that attracted the most vehement censure. What struck contemporaries – but which has been almost wholly ignored by interpreters of the Civil War as a 'war of religion' – was the pardon's implications for the exercise of royal power, implications that extended far beyond the fate of a single 'scurvie priest'.[10]

Pressure to consult the Lords in seeking to reverse the royal pardon came almost exclusively from the Junto's men in the Commons: Strafford's current and future prosecutors (Hampden, St John, Erle, and Glynne) constituted almost half the committee appointed to arrange and manage the conference with the upper House.[11] Before the peers, it was one of the least 'godly' Commons-men – the Earl of Pembroke's protégé, John Glynne (like his dyspeptic patron, a man with a reputation for swearing and profanity) – who presented the case against allowing Goodman's reprieve to stand.[12] As D'Ewes reported this speech, Glynne played up the broader danger posed by Catholic priests at large within the capital. But it was that the king should dare to issue this pardon 'in Parliament time' that was his prime objection.[13] An anonymous newswriter recorded Glynne's central objection more fully:

> If the Parliament did suffer the King to use the perrerogative in this, whiles the Parliament was actually sitting, hee did not see to what purpose they should labour to prove guilty and condemne the Lo. Lieutenant of Ireland, the Archbishop, the Judges, and other delinquents ...

If the king could undo a judicial condemnation for treason at the stroke of a pen, would he not also pardon Strafford, and revert to despotic, 1630s-style business-as-usual, once the present Parliament had been dissolved? If this prerogative of mercy were allowed to stand in the Goodman case, the various impeachments against the 'evil counsellors' of the 1630s were merely a time-consuming charade.[14] It was Strafford's treason, therefore, not Goodman's Catholicism, which dictated that the priest must die.[15]*

1. ROYAL RENUNCIATIONS

Vane's intervention on the morning of Saturday, 23 January, succeeded in creating an atmosphere of suspicion and mistrust within Charles's intended audience. Not even this, however, sufficed to subvert the overwhelmingly positive impression eventually created by the king's oratory later that afternoon. Often an ungainly combination of haughtiness and diffidence in his public performances, Charles on this occasion combined confidence with a shrewdly judged rhetoric of moderation. Shortly after 3 p.m., having allowed a full extra hour for members to return from 'dinner' (the early afternoon meal), and speaking 'verie loud', to overcome the building's difficult acoustics, Charles courteously explained the reason for their summons. His intention, he declared at the outset, was merely 'to hasten, not to interrupt', their deliberations – a remark that offered a subtle dig at the Parliament's now widely criticized lack of progress in implementing substantive reform.[16]

What followed defined a new royal *via media*: a monarchy under the law – indeed, in fiscal matters, firmly subordinate to Parliament – but prepared to stand firm against extreme and unwarrantable change. 'There are some men', he warned in a coded reference to the Junto's more radical members, 'that, more maliciously than ignorantly, will put no diference between Reformation and Alteration of Government.' The king's pleas that money should be provided for the payment of the two armies in the North (English *and* Scots), and for the navy, played to his advantage by emphasising that financial responsibility for these forces was now Parliament's concern, not his (a stance which, over the months ahead, was to enable him to play to his own advantage the army's growing resentment at Parliament's failure to provide for its pay).[17]

Despite these occasional glints of steel, the most pronounced feature of the speech was its rhetoric of conciliation. In a startling self-reinvention, Charles sided firmly with the cause of 'Reformation' – the first of a series of moments during the next eighteen months in which he was to try to steal his opponents' ideological clothes. Indeed, after the hostile stand-off of the previous ten weeks, the king's new-found readiness to offer concessions was

---

* That it was the political rather than the religious aspects of the Goodman case that made it so explosive is illustrated in a revealing exchange between the godly Viscount Saye and Lord Brudenell, a Catholic peer who dared to defend the priest. The two peers had clashed acrimoniously in the House of Lords, with Saye pressing for Goodman's execution, while Brudenell remonstrated at the injustice of 'have[ing] a Roman Catholike Preist executed meerly for being a Preist'. Saye later met with Brudenell and 'commended his zeale, and assured him he disliked not his reply', implying a measure of sympathy for his argument. But, as with Glynne, it was the political implications of the Goodman reprieve that, for Saye, provided the imperative for his execution.

nothing short of astonishing. In relation to the law, he affirmed his intention that all 'Courts of Justice may be reformed', a task on which he had already begun with the previous week's judicial appointments. On the question of the Church, potentially the most prickly of issues, he offered balm, undertaking to return it to the practices of 'the best and purest times, as they were in the time of Queen Elizabeth' – a line that was to become a recurrent theme in the king's public rhetoric as a declaration of his willingness to abandon the doctrinal and liturgical innovations of the 1630s.[18]

Charles's most substantive concession, however, was made in relation to his revenues. It amounted to a complete re-foundation of the finances of the English Crown: 'Whatsoever part of my revenue shall be found Illegal, or heavy to my Subjects, I shall be willing to lay it down, trusting in their Affections'.[19] In one simple sentence, the king had relinquished Ship Money, impositions, forest fines: the entire repertoire of prerogative finance. In practice, henceforth, the solvency of the Crown would be dependent on Parliament. Its political significance was momentous. This was the *sine qua non* of Bedford's financial and political settlement: the symbolic and practical manifestation of the king's resolve, in future, to put aside 'arbitrary courses' and to rely solely on his subject's 'affections'. In practical terms, the balance of power between the three estates of king, Lords and Commons had just shifted decisively in favour of the latter two.

However, this offer to return to a 'politics of affection' – a world in which cooperation, rather than coercion, characterized the relationship between subject and sovereign – came with conditions. Charles appealed over the heads of the Junto, with whom he had been negotiating thus far, to the broader constituency of Parliament-men – men whose instincts naturally disposed them to agree with the king's stricture that the virtuous task of 'reformation' should not be perverted to a mischievous hankering after 'alteration' in government. In insisting that there were clear limits beyond which he would not be drawn, Charles shrewdly cast himself as a moderate, defending the traditional order against malevolent and wanton change. Bishops, predictably, were the first: there was to be no question of removing their entitlement to sit in Parliament (where their votes might yet be crucial in preventing Strafford's condemnation); still less of abolishing them 'Root-and-Branch'. Even here, however, the king allowed the possibility of further reform. 'If some of them have over-stretched their Power and encroached too much upon the Temporality [the secular sphere]', then the king was content that these secular encroachments should be curbed. Bishops, in other words, must be retained, but could be reformed; and this concession left the door sufficiently ajar to allow space for Archbishop Ussher's proposals for a 'modified episcopacy' – the solution that seems to have been Bedford's, and even the more radical Warwick's, preferred option.

The king's only other major point of insistence – his hostility to the Triennial Bill – similarly revealed scope for further negotiation. His objections were clearly stated. The bill impugned his 'honour' in that it allowed his power of calling Parliament to be assumed by third parties ('Sheriffs, and Constables, and I know not whom'). As such, the king's objection struck at the heart of the bill: the Junto's insistence that if the king failed to issue writs for a new Parliament every three years, it could be summoned by twelve peers, acting without the monarch's approval. Even here, however, Charles's stance allowed room for manoeuvre. He conceded that he was prepared to agree to the 'substance' of the bill, and this, in turn, opened up the possibility of further horse-trading with the Parliament's managers.[20]

Perhaps most tellingly of all, Charles seemed to be having second thoughts about Goodman's reprieve, promising to send an explanation of the 'reasons' for his action to the House of Lords two days later – an action that itself indicated the matter was not definitively closed.[21] In the event, the king was to spend much of the next week engaged in negotiation on this point, eventually agreeing to remit Goodman's punishment to the two Houses, on the apparent understanding that the priest would be imprisoned but not killed.[22] Given that Goodman's fate was widely regarded as predictive of Strafford's likely end, agreement on this question opened up the possibility of a similar compromise at the end of the Lord Lieutenant's trial.

What is striking about the king's speech of 23 January, however, is the extent to which it offered the possibility of agreement on most of the points still in contention between himself and the Junto leadership. Of course, fervent Root-and-Branchers – the advocates of the bishops' abolition – departed the Banqueting House unsatisfied; D'Ewes wrote melodramatically that the speech 'filled most of us with sadd apprehensions of future evills, in case his Majestie should be irremooveablie fixed to uphold the Bishops in ther wealth, pride and Tyrannie'.[23] To many in that Banqueting House audience, however, Charles's willingness to renounce his prerogative revenues – the very foundations of his government during the Personal Rule – afforded prima facie evidence of his new-found receptiveness to the 'Commonwealthsmen': Bedford, and the group around the Petitioner Peers. The royal counsels were clearly changing. To underline the point, Charles dropped a heavy hint that there were new appointments in the offing: 'those Ministers I have, *or shall have,* about me', he declared, would be the means 'for the effecting of these my good Intentions'.[24] Further progress was possible, Charles was implying; but only on condition that Bedford and the Junto ceased parroting the Scots' demands for Root-and-Branch abolition of bishops and for the execution of the Earl of Strafford. And after the sulky obstructionism of the last three months, this, at least, was a viable bargain.

There is an underlying tactical coherence to what Charles was, and was not, prepared to concede. The three issues on which he signalled his readiness to move (the financing of government, limited 'further reformation' to the Church, and the Triennial Bill) corresponded closely to the Northumberland–Bedford group's reformist concerns. Conversely, the matters on which he declared himself intransigent, abolition of bishops 'Root-and-Branch', and the execution of Strafford, were objectives that Bedford's key allies at court – Northumberland, Pembroke, Arundel, and Hamilton – frankly opposed. Bedford (himself no enthusiast for Root-and-Branch) had no alternative but to follow suit if he were to have any hopes of retaining his leverage at court, even if this risked alienating his erstwhile Covenanter allies.[25]*

Charles had set out a viable plan for a settlement in his speech on 23 January. It remained to be seen whether the Junto leadership would abate their hostility towards the Church, as the price of their admission to a reformed Whitehall court.

*

Charles did not have to wait long for a response. The first signal that the courtier reformists would endorse his opposition to Root-and-Branch came the very next day – 24 January – in the Chapel Royal of Whitehall Palace. As Lord Chamberlain, Pembroke was responsible for appointing the Sunday preachers before the king;[26] and, while his support for the Junto was now widely known, his choice of preacher for that Sunday was daring, if not overtly provocative. Come the sermon, courtiers would have been astonished to find the most celebrated anti-Laudian of the entire 1630s, John Williams, Bishop of Lincoln – until eight weeks ago a prisoner in the Tower[27] – mounting the steps to the pulpit. A one-time Lord Keeper to James I who had fallen foul of Buckingham and Laud, Williams belonged – like his friends Essex and Pembroke – to that generation of Jacobean 'patriots' whose political and religious values had been so comprehensively spurned by the men who had come to power in the years since Charles's accession.[28]

Ambitious, plausible, and opportunistic, Williams had powerful friends in the Junto leadership,[29]† and stood to gain handsomely from their eventual dominance at court.[30] In turn, he sided shamelessly with his new benefactors, proposing, as we have seen, the motion in the House of Lords that the Petition of the Twelve Peers should be recorded in the House's Journal, with a grateful affirmation of 'the great Good it had wrought both to the king,

---

* Charles may well have relished the difficulties this posed the Scots' English accomplices. Even so, the effect of his demand was never to pose the Junto leadership with a simple, mutually exclusive choice: either a deal with the king, on condition that they renounced Root-and-Branch; or one with the Scots, in which the bishops' abolition was a *sine qua non*. Certainly, Lord Loudoun and the other Scots Commissioners were to press strongly over the next six weeks that their 'Commonwealthsmen' friends should endorse their demand for the abolition of bishops, insisting that 'we cannot conceive ... how our peace shall be firme and durable ... if Episopacie shall be retained in England'. Yet, throughout this period and well into May 1641, Warwick, Bedford and the other Treaty Commissioners were to remain steadfastly non-committal, in their formal responses to the Scots, on the question of the bishops' abolition; and while this introduced an element of tension into their relations with their Covenanter 'brethren', it never pushed them to breaking-point. The fate of these initiatives is discussed in detail, below, Chapter 11.

† Until his imprisonment in 1637, Williams's household at Buckden, Huntingdonshire, had been something of an informal college for the children of the court grandees who were out of sympathy with the direction of the Caroline régime. The sons of the Earls of Pembroke, Salisbury, and Leicester all spent time in his household during the 1630s.

the Kingdom and Religion'.[31] Williams's Chapel Royal sermon of 24 January sent out a clear signal that his new-found allies had no intention of trespassing on to ground that the king regarded as sacrosanct. In an unambiguous rebuff to the Scots, Williams condemned the 'Geneva Discipline' – the Presbyterianism practised by the Scots – as a form of Church government 'fit only for Tradesmen and Beggars'.[32] Coming from such a staunch ally of the Junto – indeed a man who owed his release from the Tower to its actions, and who was shortly to defend Saye in public against the charge that he was a 'separatist'[33] – Williams's pulpit oratory seems to have been calculated to allay fears that the reformists harboured plans for radical ecclesiastical change.

Leicester, monitoring changes in England from Paris, had learnt of Williams's sudden cosying up to the Junto within the week, and wrote to Viscount Mandeville to warn him about their latest recruit: 'I pray, take heed of your neighbour of Bugden' – Bishop Williams, whose house at Buckden, Huntingdonshire, was near Mandeville's at Kimbolton, in the same county; 'I doubt not but you know him well, yet I could tell you some things of him which, I believe, you have not yet heard, and I am sure you would not like.'[34] Events were to prove Leicester's warning amply justified. For the moment, however, as Mandeville and his allies strove to demonstrate their own pro-episcopalian credentials at court, a well-disposed English bishop was a timely and useful political asset.

By January 1641, however, the Junto moderates had more pressing reasons for distancing themselves from Scottish Presbyterianism than its fitness 'only for Tradesmen and Beggars'. The usefulness of their alliance with the Covenanters more generally was increasingly being called into question by the cost of the Scottish presence in England. Hitherto, the financial pressures to come to an agreement had been almost exclusively on one side – exerted by the Junto, through the Parliament, against the king. By the end of January, however, there was a countervailing financial constraint at work against the Junto, and one that could only intensify – and work increasingly to Charles's advantage – over time. The magnitude of that problem had only become widely apparent in the week leading up to the Banqueting House speech, when Parliament was confronted for the first time with the stark reality of the cost of the Scots' invasion: already the gargantuan sum of £514,000, and rising every day that the Covenanters remained in occupation of the North of England.[35] Debate over whether to meet this prodigious cost – and, if so, how – had already proved highly contentious in the Commons. When the matter had been discussed on 21 January, Sir Benjamin Rudyard – a prominent member of the Pembroke clientele and a man the Junto could ill afford to alienate – pointed out that £514,000 (the equivalent of about half the king's total pre-1640 annual revenue) was 'more than ever we gave the King' at one time; 'a Portentous Apparition', which 'shews it self in a very dry time ... [and] which, to my seeming,' urged Rudyard, 'will be an utter draining of the People'.[36] Gervase Holles (Denzell's cousin) concurred, denouncing the Scots' demands for payment as 'dishonourable for this Nation to suffer', and warning that 'I fear we have nourished in our bosom those that will sting us to Death'.[37] The 'liberated' were coming to resent the cost of their liberation.

Resentment of the Covenanters' fiscal demands did not end at the Scottish Commissioners' door. Having so publicly identified themselves with their Scottish 'brethren' during the crisis of the previous autumn, Bedford, Pym and their friends could hardly be surprised that they, too, were starting to be blamed for the invasion's prodigious expense. Now, for the first time, Bedford and the other Petitioner Peers confronted the unnerving prospect that the Covenanter force, once the indispensable guarantor of their security, was fast becoming a political as well as a financial liability. And the burden imposed on the northern counties by the Scots was compounded by the disruptive presence of the king's army, forced to take free quarter (the requisitioning of accommodation and supplies in return for promissory notes of questionable, if any, value) and prone to regular breaches of discipline. For Bedford and his allies at court, the pressure to achieve a settlement that enabled the king's army to be paid off and the Scots to be sent home was intensifying by the day.

11. WHAT PRICE THE BRETHREN?

How best to deal with this problem elicited a variety of responses within the Junto. Bedford's reaction inevitably reflected the anti-Covenanter prejudices of his new-found allies at court: Hamilton, Pembroke, and Northumberland. Maintaining their support, Bedford now seems to have believed, was of greater immediate utility than gratifying the religious ambitions of the Scots – all the more so because the imminent anti-Habsburg alliance with the Dutch (for which the Junto needed the continuing support of Northumberland and his friends at court) now promised to do even more for the 'Protestant Cause' than any treaty with the Covenanter Scots.[38]*

But perhaps the strongest inducement for the Junto leaders to distance themselves from the Root-and-Branch reforms demanded by the Scots was the prize represented by the Triennial Bill, and the king's hint that he would agree to its 'substance' in return for Parliament disowning the campaign for the bishops' abolition. Precise details of the Junto's communications with the king and his inner entourage during this period have not survived. What seems probable, however, is that in the week after Charles's Banqueting House speech the Junto leaders agreed to offer the king something close to a quid pro quo. Bedford and Warwick agreed to drop their support for the Scots' demands for Root-and-Branch, in return for Charles's relinquishing of

---

* On 14 January, the French diplomat in London, Jean de Montreuil, had identified the chief negotiators of this Anglo-Dutch treaty as Hamilton, Arundel, Northumberland, Holland, and Secretary Vane – at this point, all supporters of the Bedfordian reforms – and Bishop Juxon, the Lord Treasurer, who was shortly to resign his office in order to create a vacancy for one of the 'new Councillors'.

his prerogative to determine when, and for how long, Parliaments should meet.[39]

Nor was this the only point relating to 'further reformation of the Church' where the Junto leadership was prepared to temper the rigour of the Scots' ecclesiastical demands in order to effect a political settlement. Even the prospects of Archbishop Laud, regarded by the Covenanters as the 'great Incendiary' and contriver of the 'Bishops' Wars', suddenly improved as the Junto leadership moved, disregarding the likely protests of the Scots,[40] to meet the offer of compromise from the king with substantial concessions of their own. Already on 21 January, the very day that Sir John Temple reported the interim agreement on Bedford's appointment to the Lord Treasurership and the other major preferments to office,[41] Laud had been sent word that his principal opponents in the Lords were now prepared to mitigate any punishment against him. He recorded in his diary for 21 January:

> A Parliament [man] of good note, and interessed [with] divers Lords, sent me word, [that] by reason of my patient [and m]oderate carriage since my [commmit]ment, four Earls of great [power][42]* in the Upper House [of] the Lords were not [now] so sharp against me [as at] first. And that now they [were] resolved only to se[quester] me from the King's Coun[cil, and] to put me from my [Arch]bishopric.[43]

It seems hardly coincidental that this message reached Laud only the day after the Triennial Bill had completed its passage through the Commons and been conveyed to the Lords by Lord Digby,[44] and – in yet another conciliatory gesture to the court – the Commons finally set a date for considering 'the bill for the queen's jointure', a Junto-driven proposal to confirm the gift of extensive estates by the king to Queen Henriette Marie, in such a way that the grant could not be revoked by the king's successors.[45]

In the meantime, the Triennial Bill, the cornerstone of the Bedfordians' plans for a reformed and godly commonwealth, made steady progress. Once that was completed and approved, the Parliament's regularity of meeting (and its newly won control of the royal purse strings) would guarantee that the king would never again be able to construct a government – or pursue policies – that went against the will of the political nation. And if securing this meant parting company with the Scots over Root-and-Branch, this was a concession worth making. As we will see,

---

* The identities of these four earls is a matter for speculation, but the four most likely, perhaps, are Bedford, Pembroke, Hertford, and Northumberland. Warwick's position at this point is difficult to assess; in some respects he was the most virulently anti-Laudian peer of them all (he was to be responsible, on 26 February, for moving Laud from the relatively comfortable confinement of Black Rod's house in Westminster to a bleak cell in the Tower). But as he was also backing the Triennial Bill strongly, it is just possible that he, too, was among the 'Earls of great power' who were in favour of moderating Laud's eventual punishment.

Bedford (though, revealingly, not Warwick) was prepared to go further, undertaking to delay the beginning of formal proceedings against Strafford, and eventually working to ensure a compromise whereby his life could be saved.[46]

The Junto's vacillations over the question of the bishops is all the more striking because, until this point, its members had been in the forefront of the campaigns to rally opinion in favour of episcopal reform. Hostility to Laudian 'prelacy' was sufficiently widespread to have a life of its own, irrespective of any promptings from the oppositionist peers. Nevertheless, the leading puritan grandees, Warwick, Saye, and Brooke, appear to have been active in the campaigns to give voice and direction to this hostility, both in the radical London Petition, presented on 11 December 1640, which called for the abolition of bishops' Root-and-Branch; and a second, more moderate manifesto – a 'Remonstrance', signed by between 700 and 800 parochial clergy, which censured the bishops while stopping short of demanding outright abolition.[47] Brought to completion in January 1641 against the far more optimistic background of Charles's negotiations with Bedford House, this ministers' Remonstrance was organized through Warwick's 'spiritual adviser' and client, Edmund Calamy. As Calamy later admitted, it was in his house that 'the *Remonstrance* [was] framed against the prelates: here were *all* [the] meetings'.[48] Such was the extent of Calamy's involvement that there is little doubt that he was acting with at very least his patron's consent. Significantly, the other leading figures involved in its promotion – Cornelius Burges, Calybute Downinge, and Stephen Marshall – were all ministers enjoying the protection of members of the Bedford–Warwick coalition.[49]

Like the London Root-and-Branch Petition of December 1640, the Remonstrance was not merely a vehicle of protest but also defined a detailed agenda for practical reform. In over eighty 'heads', the Remonstrance itemized what one writer has termed 'a standard of the reform demanded ... in the name of the moderate majority alike of clergy and laity'.[50] Its fine print ranged from major objections to the bishops' 'sole power of ordination and jurisdiction' and their slavish support for 'the prerogatives of the king', through to relatively minor matters such as their 'scandalous' behaviour in 'drinking healths' and proposing toasts.[51] The crucial distinction between this Remonstrance and the earlier London Root-and-Branch Petition is that this document called for the reform of the episcopal order, not its eradication. As such, its demands were broadly compatible with Archbishop Ussher's proposals for 'modified episcopacy'. Still more important, it might just be acceptable to the king.

With a timing that does not appear to be coincidental, this Calamy-organized Remonstrance was presented to the Commons on Saturday, 23 January – at the end of the week that had seen St John's appointment as Solicitor-General and interim agreement between the king and Bedford House over a far more extensive reassignment of offices. Moreover, it was tabled by the godly Herefordshire knight, Sir Robert Harley, an independent supporter of the Junto (in the sense that he was no one's 'client'), yet one who –

like Calamy – was also on close terms with the Earl of Warwick.[52]*

The presentation of the ministers' Remonstrance, combined with Charles's emphatic rejection of Root-and-Branch in his speech later that day, endowed the question of the retention or abolition of bishops with a sudden urgency. Unless it were resolved, it would be the 'Rock' – as Charles warned on 23 January – obstructing the path to further agreement. Bishops immediately became the principal topic of the moment. In a single morning, on 25 January – the first sitting of the Parliament after the king's Banqueting House speech – petitions 'tending to the abolishing of Bishopps' were presented from Hertfordshire, Buckinghamshire, Bedfordshire, Sussex, Surrey, Cheshire, Warwickshire, Gloucestershire, Suffolk, Norfolk, and Cambridgeshire – at least one of which (from Suffolk) claimed to have over 4,400 signatures.[53]

As 'Pym's party' has traditionally been characterized, this ought to have been the moment when the Junto-men – 'the Scottish [and hence, pro-abolitionist] party' in the Parliament – put their weight behind Root-and-Branch.[54] In fact, what is striking about their behaviour is the lengths to which the Commons-men associated with Bedford House (notably Pym, St John, and Digby) – and even Warwick's key allies in the Commons (Grimston and Clotworthy in particular) – went to obstruct, and even discredit, the consideration of Root-and-Branch. Their tactics differed; but their objective was strikingly consistent: to oppose any measure that tended to the outright abolition of bishops within the English Church. It was a strange reversal, as, during the last months of 1640 – when Charles had been adamantly refusing all attempts to open negotiations – the Junto leaders, and certainly their clerical clientele, seem to have been active in mobilizing petitions, both in London and the counties, calling for the episcopate's wholesale abolition of bishops.

The fortunes of the Calamy-organized Remonstrance – the less radical alternative to the London Root-and-Branch Petition – provide a case in point. Pym had already declared his opposition to the abolition of bishops in December 1640, when the London Petition had been laid before the

---

* Something of Warwick's relationship with Harley in the conduct of the Commons' business emerges in a letter he wrote to him barely a week after the presentation of this Remonstrance. Seeking to defend the interests of Thomas Withering, who enjoyed the lucrative office of 'Postmaster of England for Foreign Parts' and who had been temporarily suspended from office, Warwick wrote to inform Harley that his case 'is appointed for the first Cawse [or case to be considered by the Commons] this day, in the afternoone [3 February 1641]. My requeste therefore is That you wilbe pleased to be there, and doe him what lawfull favour you can. So I reste your assured frend, Warwicke.' A similar letter from Warwick to Harley, a year later, requested 'that you would favour mee by being there [in the Commons] at their first sitting of your house, and call upon Mr Glyn[ne] to make his report'. Such letters should not, however, be read as implying that the Lords were regularly engaged in pulling the strings of the lower House. Cooperation from members of the Commons was requested by peers as a favour, not a matter of right, and was part of a system in which Commons-men could equally seek to influence business in the upper House. Shared political goals, not simple 'clientage', underpinned the frequent collaborations between these bicameral 'interests'.

Commons.[55] His response to the ministers' Remonstrance, despite its more moderate tone, was scarcely more welcoming. When first discussed on 1 February 1641 (after a deferral from January 23), Pym *opposed* allowing the Commons as a whole to debate the subject, moving, instead, that it might be palmed off to 'a spetiall committee'.[56] Digby went even further and, having misunderstood a conversation with Cornelius Burges and Calybute Downinge earlier that morning (two of the Remonstrance's organizers), attempted to discredit the document by suggesting that 'divers Ministers ... did now disavow the Remonstrance'.[57] Oliver St John, arguably the Commons-man closest to Bedford, followed suit when the question was revived on 2 February. Once again, a proposal was made that the ministers' Remonstrance should be considered by the whole House of Commons. But this was countered – as D'Ewes noted, with a hint that his recently acquired office may have had something to do with his intervention – by 'Mr St John, newly created the king's sollicitour'.

Like Pym, St John wanted the anti-episcopal Remonstrance referred to (and, it seems, forgotten by) an existing select committee. And St John's choice of committee is highly significant: not the Committee of Religion (which would have involved the whole House), but the so-called 'Committee of Twenty-Four' (also known as the Committee on the State of the Kingdom), the general committee on the nation's grievances that had been appointed on 10 November: a body that included a string of fiercely pro-episcopal Commons-men and whose highest-ranking member was none other than Bedford's son-in-law, Lord Digby.[58] Once the Remonstrance was there, the chances that the committee would submit any recommendation to the full House of Commons 'tending to the abolishing of Bishopps' were practically zero.

On this occasion, however, the whole matter of the ministers' Remonstrance was deferred to the following morning;[59] and, when the following morning came, quietly allowed to drop. By 3 February, the whole matter of episcopal reform – which had suddenly burst into life in response to the king's rejection of Root-and-Branch on 23 January – had gone exceedingly quiet. But St John had not forgotten the expedient of disposing of unwanted episcopal controversies in the bishop-friendly hands of the Committee of Twenty-Four; and, as we shall see, this expedient was to be revived at the culmination of another, far more famous, debate on the bishops' fate, barely a week away.

III. THE FORTUNES OF THE LORD LIEUTENANT

Nor was the abolition of bishops the only matter of principle on which Bedford and his friends were distancing themselves from their erstwhile Scottish 'brethren'. Strafford, the 'great incendiary' whom the Scots were insistent on bringing to the scaffold, was also suddenly being looked upon in a new, and far kindlier, light. Bedford was far too accomplished a courtier not to notice that the promise of leniency towards Strafford provided him with his most valuable bargaining counter in the negotiations with the king.

Hence, the severity of the Junto's threats against Strafford – and, correspondingly, the generosity of its offers of leniency – generally tracked the fortunes of the negotiations between the court and Bedford House.

The stop–go pace of Strafford's prosecution is itself revealing. After the Junto's first pre-emptive strike in November, preparations for his trial proceeded with conspicuous lack of vigour. Only at the end of December, frustrated by the king's intransigence, did the Junto reactivate the prosecution – and extend the attack to Strafford's lieutenant, Sir George Radcliffe – as part of a series of measures intended to bludgeon the king back to the negotiating table. However, once the negotiations over the reform of the law and the new appointments to the Privy Council began to make progress during early January 1641, Strafford's impeachment was once again placed on a back burner, though the fact that it might at any time be brought to the boil provided the Junto with a useful element of potential menace in their dealings with the king. By the time the detailed impeachment articles were presented to the Lords by Pym on 30 January,[60] the political (and judicial) environment at Westminster had been transformed. A Bedford–Northumberland alliance seemed about to dominate the court. St John had already been appointed the king's Solicitor-General, and was set to have a major role in the trial (if, in the end, a trial there should be). And the newly appointed Lord Keeper Littleton, the presiding officer of the House of Lords, was doing all he could to ingratiate himself with '[those] who most opposed the King'.[61]

For Strafford, this rapprochement between the Junto and the court might have been expected to bode ill; in fact, it appears to have worked strongly to his advantage. True, the impeachment process had now formally begun and this was both an obvious source of pressure on the king, and a useful sop to Edinburgh at a time when relations between Bedford House and the Scottish Commissioners were increasingly strained. This much accomplished, however, the Junto's immediate response, after the presentation of the impeachment articles, was again to press for delay. The 'reformation of the king's counsels' was going far too well at the beginning of February to jeopardize it by victimizing Strafford, the one minister with whose fate the king saw his own 'honour' as intimately entwined. Outside the Tower, there were hostile crowds baying for Strafford's blood.[62] Within the Commons, however, there were signs that members' interest in the Lord Lieutenant's prosecution was beginning to wane; on 30 January, as the detailed impeachment articles were read one by one, D'Ewes was shocked to find that more than a third of the House remained silent, refusing to endorse the articles as they were put forward for approval by acclamation.[63]

Perhaps the most striking feature of these detailed charges, with their accompanying 'proofs', is their omission of any firm evidence on what was to be the most serious charge against him: that Strafford had advised the use of the Irish army to quell political dissent in England, at the meeting of the Privy Council's Council of War, immediately after the dissolution of May 1640. Evidence for Strafford's proposal existed, in the form of manuscript notes taken by Secretary Vane, a copy of which had been taken by Vane's son, Sir Henry junior.[64] Yet, given that these notes had been circulated within the Junto to at least Bedford, Pym and Clotworthy (and perhaps to others), and been known since the previous autumn, it raises the puzzling question why the Junto leadership chose not to disclose this evidence to the Commons, to include it in the dossier of 'proofs' sent to the Lords on 30 January. Was this 'silver bullet' – the evidence most likely to convict Strafford of treason – being deliberately kept back so as to ensure the Lord Lieutenant escaped a capital sentence? Or was it being held in reserve, in the event that the king proved uncooperative – or double-crossing – so that it could be used as and when it was needed?

By early February, the horse-trading between Whitehall and Bedford House was beginning to yield results. On 2 February,[65] Bedford, Saye, and Pym were observed to have had an audience of the queen,[66] who was reported to have been acting as an intermediary between members of the Junto and the king over both the Triennial Bill and a possible compromise over Strafford. The results of this meeting appear to have come to fruition the very next day. Strafford was the immediate beneficiary. A broad range of Junto Peers – from Saye, the aspirant courtier (one of those closest to Bedford and Pembroke), through to Brooke, Paget, and Mandeville (who seem to have been closer to Warwick and the Scots) – stood up in the Lords to argue that Strafford should be given an extended period to present his answer to the accusations against him. To the chagrin of the Scots, this intervention 'so swayed [the Lords] that [Strafford] was allowed 15 days for bringing in his answer in writing'.[67] But if this signal to the court was conciliatory, it also carried an implied condition: Charles's recent concessions – on the law, the Dutch alliance, appointments to office, and the enforcement of laws against Catholics – had created the circumstances within which he could win the deferral of Strafford's impeachment. Further postponements, however, would necessarily depend on further reform.[68]

The Junto Peers' concession over Strafford also provided the conditions in which Charles, without loss of honour, could rescind his pardon of Strafford's surrogate, the hapless Father Goodman. Probably forewarned by the queen of their intended favour towards Strafford, the king had his response prepared. For the past fortnight, the question of Goodman's reprieve had been the prime 'topic of conversation' at Westminster. As Count Carlo Rossetti, the papal emissary to the court, observed on 29 January, 'the question whether [Goodman] shall live or die has turned into a question whether the supreme authority lies with the king or Parliament'. No sooner had the Lords granted their two-week deferral of Strafford's trial, however, than Charles offered the Parliament a harmonious resolution.[69] Once again summoning the Lords and Commons to the Banqueting House, the king promised a comprehensive series of measures against papists: a proclamation to banish all priests and Jesuits from the kingdom within the month; the dismissal from the court of the papal emissary, Rossetti; and 'special care' to prevent English Catholics from attending mass in the queen's or ambassadorial household chapels. However, his key concession – an implicit gesture of trust in the Junto's future treatment of Strafford – was to rescind his reprieve of Father Goodman, remitting his punishment to Parliament, but warning of the 'ill consequence that may ensue' should the Parliament decide on his execution.[70] Once again, the Junto's policy of carefully rationed acts of compromise had produced a major tactical victory.

By the first days of February, Leicester was looking forward enthusiastically to the consequences of these 'great changes in England', and writing to Mandeville to wish that he, too, would find preferment in the imminent reapportionment of office. 'I wish with all my heart that you may have that part which the voice of the people gives unto you ... And though I expect little other, yet I hope for this benefit that, by your mediation, I may hereafter be better paid [as an ambassador] by our new Lord Treasurer [Bedford] than I have been; for the modern bishops [Bishop Juxon being the current Lord Treasurer] have not much favoured me'.[71] With a prominent position within the Junto, Mandeville looked set to become a major broker of influence in the new Bedford-dominated court.

In this altered environment, even Strafford could regard the completed impeachment articles against him with something approaching a sense of confidence. On 3 February – the day he was awarded the two-week deferment and Charles rescinded Goodman's reprieve – Strafford expressed his relief in a letter to the Earl of Ormond: 'I thank God I see nothing capital in their charge, nor any thing which I am not able to answer as becomes an honest man'.[72] His optimism was no mere chimera. By the time Strafford would be required to submit his answer to the impeachment – on 18 February – the Triennial Bill (currently before the Lords) would have completed its progress through Parliament, and have been presented for the royal assent. Were that forthcoming, the Bedford group's principal precondition for entering the Privy Council would have been met, and the political firmament looked likely to be totally transformed.

iv. BURYING ROOT-AND-BRANCH

Apart from Strafford, there remained only two major obstacles in the way of the Junto Lords' formal admission to the Privy Council – the event that would be the public acknowledgement that the king had definitively renounced the despotic 'evil counsels' of the years of Personal Rule. On the Junto's side it remained the Triennial Bill; without that, they could have no security in office, as there would always be the fear, once the current Parliament was sent home, that the king would ignore or dismiss his new Councillors, and set out, once again, to construct an 'arbitrary', non-parliamentary system of rule. On the king's side, it remained his fear of how far the Junto, seemingly so beholden to the Scots, would attempt to oblige them by rooting out bishops from the government of the English Church.

In fact, the catalyst for the long-deferred debate on the London Root-and-Branch Petition looks to have been the completion of the Lords' consideration of the Triennial Bill, and their return of the amended text to the Commons on Saturday, 6 February. This was entrusted to a committee that was virtually a roll-call of the Junto's principal supporters in the Commons – including

Bedford's son (Lord Russell), his son-in-law (Lord Digby), his household counsel (St John), and principal man-of-affairs (Pym).[73] However, until the question of Root-and-Branch were disposed of once and for all, further progress with the Triennial Bill was pointless, as Charles had already intimated that nothing would be done on that score so long as he believed the episcopate to be under threat. Accordingly, the issue of episcopacy became the all-consuming subject of the Commons' very next sitting day.

Here, too, the context of the debate had been subtly changed by the Junto's improving relations, brokered by Bishop Williams of Lincoln, with the more acceptable members of the episcopal bench. Until this point, much of the hostility against the bishops' right to vote in Parliament had derived from the expectation that, in the forthcoming impeachment trials, they would use this right to vote en bloc in favour of acquittals. On 3 February, the *dies mirabilis* when Strafford had been granted his two weeks' grace, Williams had defused this potentially explosive issue by announcing openly in the House of Lords that he had reached an agreement with his episcopal confrères: 'that he would not speak in this Cause, nor any of his Brethren of the Bench'.[74] By neutralizing the bishops for the duration of Strafford's trial, he had at a stroke removed the principal short-term motive for attacking the episcopate's parliamentary role.

Revealingly, when the debate on Root-and-Branch began on Monday, 8 February, it was not initiated by the bishops' enemies, but by their friends – by two courtiers who were supporters of the Junto's settlement plans: Pembroke's client, Sir Benjamin Rudyard, the Surveyor of the Court of Wards;[75]* and Bedford's son-in-law, Lord Digby, the Commons-man who had earlier carried the Triennial Bill up to the House of Lords.[76] 'Reformation, not alteration' was the predominant theme from the outset. Opening the debate, Rudyard outlined an argument that sat squarely on the middle ground delineated by the king in his Banqueting House speech of 23 January. On the one side, he attacked 'prelacy' – the powerful, authoritarian episcopal order created by Laud, with its preference for 'specious, pompous, sumptuous Religion' and desire for 'Temporal Greatness'. On the other, he warned against the whole-sale abolition of bishops, lest a Parliament that was against 'innovation' should bring in 'the greatest Innovation that ever was in England'. This was an only thinly veiled reproof of the Root-and-Branchers: those who wanted 'a Popular Democratical Government of the Church' – that is to say Scottish-style Presbyterianism.[77] In its place, Rudyard advocated what appears to have been the Junto's preferred option: an episcopate of carefully limited powers 'according to the usage of Ancient Churches, in the best times, that by a well-temper'd [i.e. well-tuned] Government, they may not have power hereafter to

* Rudyard (1572–1658) sat for Pembroke's pocket borough of Wilton, Wiltshire, where the earl had his country seat and had been elected to 'six previous Parliaments under the Herbert patronage'. As Surveyor of the Court of Wards, he had good reason for wishing to be on good terms with the Junto leadership: Saye, who was mooted for appointment as Master of the Court of Wards from late January (and eventually appointed in May), was to be his immediate superior.

corrupt the Church [and] to undo the Kingdom'[78] – or in other words the 'primitive episcopacy' that was being advanced, under the Junto's aegis, by Archbishop Ussher.[79]

Digby, following Rudyard, seconded him with what, initially, seems to have been the Bedford–Warwick 'party line': that bishops might be retained, 'yet [he] desired a Reformation, and that ther power and Revenues might bee shortened'.[80] But Digby's 'bold and waspish' tongue got the better of him,[81] and he argued that the London Root-and-Branch Petition should be rejected outright, rather than receiving at least the courtesy of scrutiny in committee.

Two other advocates of reform followed: Viscount Falkland, who seems not to have been involved in the Junto (though selectively supportive of its programme for reform), and Harbottel Grimston, who was. Both supported the Rudyard–Digby *via media* that bishops should be reformed, but nevertheless retained. These speakers were men of very different spirituality and religious outlook, yet their congruency of argument on the question of episcopacy – like their congruency of support for the Triennial Bill – is striking; so much so that Baillie seems to have been justified in referring to these opening speakers as a 'prepared companie'.[82]

These four speeches inaugurated a marathon debate that extended into the late afternoon, and was carried over to the following morning. In the historiography of the causes of the English Civil War, few parliamentary confrontations enjoy such an iconic status as this 'Root-and-Branch debate' of 7 and 8 February. From the 1880s to the 1990s, this has been regarded as the decisive moment when Parliament split between proto-royalist and proto-parliamentarian factions. To S. R. Gardiner, in the 1880s, it was 'the first day on which two parties stood opposed to one another ... on a great principle of action'; when 'the future leaders of the Parliamentary party were all for the committal of the [London Root-and-Branch] petition', while their opponents were the future Royalists.[83]

To show how the battle lines in this debate prefigured the future Royalist–Parliamentarian divide, historians (both Victorian and modern) have used a simple test. The motion that formed the subject of the debate was procedural: whether the London Root-and-Branch Petition (of 11 December) and the ministers' Remonstrance (of 23 January) should be referred to a Commons' committee. To be in favour of committing either (or both) of these petitions – so the argument runs – indicates support for the abolition of bishops, and hence marks out the speaker as a future Parliamentarian. To be against committing the petitions, on the other hand, indicates support for bishops, and, by and large, that the speaker is a future Royalist.[84] Thus a leading historian of the 1990s, Conrad Russell, after a detailed examination of the same debate, could affirm Gardiner's conclusion of a century earlier: 'As far as we can tell, there seems to have been a clear party line-up, in which the pro-Scots and future Parliamentarians were on one side, and the anti-Scots [and] future Royalists on the other'.[85] Here, then, we have the seeds of the Civil War – indeed, of the Civil War as a straightforward 'war of religion'.

Yet, while there is a strong case to be made that the two sides in February

1641 correlate closely with the speakers' known allegiances after 1642, the issues at stake in this debate and the attitudes of its participants were more complex than this simple correlation might suggest. Several future Parliamentarians, for example, who (by the Gardiner–Russell logic) ought to have been *in favour* of Root-and-Branch, were in fact against allowing the petitions to be considered in committee (a group that included John Selden and Sir Neville Poole). Conversely, a number of prominent future Royalists, who should have *opposed* allowing either of the petitions to be considered, were actually in favour of committing either the London Petition or the Remonstrance – or, in some cases, both.

Careful examination of the debate reveals even greater problems with the 'party line-up' theory – in particular its contention that being in favour of committing the Root-and-Branch Petition correlates with support for the bishops' outright abolition. The issues involved are somewhat technical, but must be confronted if the true significance of the debate is to emerge. The central problem lies in the assumption, which has been made since the days of Gardiner, that supporting the petition's committal – its formal consideration by a Commons' committee – is a reliable indicator of support for Root-and-Branch abolition of the English bishops. Yet, even where Commons-men (including future Parliamentarians) argued that the Root-and-Branch Petition *should* be committed, it does not follow from this that they were indicating their agreement with the Petitioners' demands for an end to episcopacy. Almost the whole of the very lengthy London Root-and-Branch Petition was devoted to itemizing liturgical and doctrinal innovations that needed reform;[86] hence it was perfectly possible for Commons-men to be in favour of considering the petition's checklist of things requiring attention, without necessarily agreeing with its abolitionist conclusions.

Harbottell Grimston provides a case in point. Few in the Commons were godlier (or, for that matter, more closely associated with Warwick, the Scots' leading ally within the Junto) than he. True, Grimston – the future Parliamentarian – was all for having both petitions considered further in committee (hence, for the 'party line-up theory', so far, so good). Yet, although Grimston favoured giving a *hearing* to both the Root-and-Branch Petition and the ministers' Remonstrance, this does not indicate that he favoured the bishops' abolition. In fact, Grimston 'spake that Bishops might onlie bee reformed', admitting that the structures of episcopacy 'may need repair' – including the removal of the bishops' right to sit in Parliament and their hated ecclesiastical courts – but otherwise opposing abolition Root-and-Branch.[87] He, like many of the godly, wanted 'not ... Subversion' of the episcopal order, but 'Reformation'.[88] In fact, many of those who, like Grimston, were generally sympathetic to the Covenanters' demands, warned the Scottish Commissioners in February that the moment was not yet right for an outright assault on episcopacy in England, a pragmatic argument that the Commissioners (who are often depicted as inflexibly doctrinaire) accepted with surprisingly good grace.[89]

Pym's line throughout January and February seems to have been very similar. Although he is not recorded as having spoken in the debates of 8 and 9 February, he had stated his position clearly when the London Root-and-Branch Petition had been first presented to the Commons, back in December: that 'it was not the intention of the House to abolish either Episcopacy or the Book of Common Prayer, but to reform both, [in points] wherein offence was given to the people'.[90]

If the case of Grimston – the future Parliamentarian – warns us that support for the commitment of the London Petition and the ministers' Remonstrance cannot be read as evidence of support for wholesale abolition, the case of Viscount Falkland – the future Royalist – gives the lie to the traditional claim that Falkland's stance defines the position of future Royalists.[91] Indeed, though Falkland spoke in favour of retaining the office of bishop, he was so strongly in favour of the proposal that 'they might bee reformed' that he urged the House to *take up* the ministers' Remonstrance – with its extensive catalogue of episcopal abuses.[92] Consideration of this document, Falkland argued, ought to provide the House with a list of what could be reformed in relation to the bishops without abolishing their office; however, if – after this investigation – it seemed that bishops were completely irreformable, then, he added with a rhetorical flourish, it would be unnecessary to commit the London Petition, but 'let us grant it' forthwith, and abolish bishops without further ado.[93]* Clearly, Falkland never thought that matters would reach such a pass. But he believed that there was merit in committing the ministers' Remonstrance, as a starting point for purging abuses. Other future Royalists went even further, wanting to use the far more radical London Root-and-Branch Petition to kick-start episcopal reform. Sir Ralph Hopton – soon to emerge as Royalist commander in the West Country – 'disliked the [London Root-and-Branch] petition', but nevertheless 'wished it might bee referred to a Committee'.[94] So, too, did Sir William Carnaby (a supporter of Strafford), and the lawyers Edward Bagshaw and William Chadwell.[95]

It is because figures as diverse as Grimston, Falkland and Hopton could all agree that committing these petitions was perfectly compatible with both the reform and the retention of bishops that the argument that this debate represents a clear divide between 'pro-Scots' on one side and 'anti-Scots' on the other must be regarded with some scepticism.[96] Almost all of the speakers – including most of those who were members of, or supportive of, the Junto – stopped far short of calling for the outright abolition of bishops. Indeed, the irony of what is often referred to as the 'Root-and-Branch debate' is that, for all practical purposes, Root-and-Branch – that is, complete abolition of episcopacy – was never seriously on offer. Of the two petitions against bishops that were under discussion, it was not the London Root-and-Branch Petition but Calamy's 'ministers' Remonstrance' – with its extensive list of desired reforms premised on the assumption that bishops were to

---

* One can begin to understand why Laud's chaplain, Peter Heylyn, noted in his diary on hearing of Falkland's death in 1643: 'this day died Lord Falkland, in whom the Church lost no great friend'.

be retained – that seems to have attracted the broadest support.[97]

Amid this chorus of reformist moderation, however, there was one sharply discordant voice – one that emanated, anomalously, from within the inner counsels of the Junto. In a long and closely argued speech, Nathaniel Fiennes, one of the Junto's occasional loose cannons,[98] boomed uncompromisingly in favour of the bishops' outright abolition.[99] But his assertiveness misfired. Even D'Ewes, no friend to the bishops, thought that in calling into question the 'function and office of Bishops', Fiennes had fallen on the subject 'unseasonablie'.[100]

But such unequivocal support for Root-and-Branch seems to have been an exception in a debate that otherwise had a very different tone.[101] By the end of the first day of debate, Secretary Vane – now firmly in support of the Junto – was able to summarize the emerging sense of the House. Far from the matter proving divisive, Vane argued, the debate had shown that 'wee all tended to one end, that was reformation [of the bishops, rather than abolition], onlie wee differed in the way'.[102]

Equally telling is the failure of Pym, Hampden, and St John to make any major contribution towards the debate. All three were already minor celebrities, and had any one of them argued for the outright abolition of bishops, his speech would almost certainly have been noticed by the diarists, and would most likely have found its way into print. Yet their contributions seem to have been minimal, not going beyond endorsing the resolution to refer the petitions to a committee – a position which, as we have seen, was completely compatible with that already taken up by their friends, Rudyard, Grimston, and Falkland. There is no evidence to sustain the claim that Pym 'seems to have argued for the abolition of episcopacy'.[103] As Hyde affirmed, when it came to the abolition of bishops, 'Mr Pimm was not of that mind'.[104]

The final outcome of the debate was a triumph for Bedford House. The Commons returned to the solution which St John had advocated when the ministers' Remonstrance had come up for discussion a week earlier, on 2 February: that the matter of episcopal reform should be entrusted to the Committee of Twenty-Four,[105] with the brief to consider the contents of all the anti-episcopal petitions – the London Root-and-Branch Petition, the ministers' Remonstrance, and the various county representations.

This choice of the Committee of Twenty-Four as the body to draw up recommendations is one of the most significant features of the entire debate. Its effect was to refer the whole question of the future government of the Church to a body that was not only filled with the Junto's supporters, but also dominated by pro-reformist episcopalians. Unsurprisingly, the more zealous reformers (what Baillie referred to as 'our partie' in the Commons) successfully moved to reinforce the 'godly side' by the naming of six additional members (including Fiennes and Sir Henry Vane junior) – most of them advocates of thoroughgoing ecclesiastical reform.[106]* Even this, however, was

---

* Of the six, Nathaniel Fiennes and Sir Henry Vane junior were supporters of Root-and-Branch (Baillie referred to them as 'our firm friends'); Sir Thomas Rowe, Denzell Holles,

a pyrrhic victory, because the committee's terms of reference specifically excluded any power to question the continuance of bishops – 'the House reserving to itself the main point, of episcopacy'.[107]

If we need anything to remind us that this debate cannot be reduced to a simple battle between 'pro-Scots' and 'anti-Scots', it is the sight of Sir William Carnaby – a supporter of Strafford and future Royalist – acting as one of the tellers *in favour* of adding religious zealots such as Fiennes and the younger Vane to the Junto's otherwise nicely pro-episcopal Committee of Twenty-Four. On the other hand, opposing the addition of Fiennes and Vane (and what Baillie referred to as 'our partie') was Sir John Clotworthy – ironically, one of the architects of the Petitioners' 1640 alliance with the Covenanters, and arguably the most pro-Scottish man in the Commons.[108] Far from polarizing the Parliament along religiously partisan lines, the Root-and-Branch debate successfully resolved, for the foreseeable future, a major point of contention.[109]

Paradoxically, the Root-and-Branch debate was the Junto's peace offering to the king, the quid pro quo for his acceptance of the Triennial Bill – the Parliament's most important piece of legislation to date, and the presentation of which to the king was barely a week away. However, the connection between the two initiatives is not merely a matter of congruity of timing. Almost all the Commons personnel involved in promoting compromise – the reform-but-retain option in relation to the bishops – not only belonged to the Junto or were clients of Junto peers, but were also concurrently involved in the committee negotiating the Triennial Bill with the House of Lords. The congruity is perhaps most clearly marked in the case of Lord Digby, one of the two speakers in favour of the retain-but-reform option that initiated the entire debate, who was not only a member of the Triennial Bill committee, but had already identified himself publicly with the legislation by carrying it up to the House of Lords.[110] Of the Junto members who also sat on the Triennial Bill committee, all but Fiennes came out against Root-and-Branch and in favour of the reform-but-retain *via media;* besides Digby, this group certainly includes Secretary Vane, Grimston, and Erle (who spoke 'moderatelie'), and probably Pym, Hampden, and Sir Thomas Barrington.[111]

Analysis of the debate in these terms also resolves what is otherwise the most glaring anomaly of all: Sir John Clotworthy, – Warwick's placeman, siding *against* the Root-and-Branchers and in favour of the Junto-backed middle way. His actions are wholly incomprehensible if this debate is seen in terms of opposing pro-and anti-Scottish 'parties' (or proto-Parliamentarians against Royalists).[112] Viewed in terms of the politics of settlement, Clotworthy's behaviour is entirely consistent with a concern that, with the Triennial Bill shortly to go to the king, this was no time to rock the boat.[113] In fact, the prominence of Warwick's clientele in *opposing* Root-and-Branch

---

and Geoffrey Palmer appear to have been advocates of reforming clerical abuses, while stopping short of supporting the bishops' abolition; while Robert Holborne, the sixth of the new additions, was a staunch defender of the episcopal status quo.

suggests that, on this issue at least, the puritan grandee and his allies were at one with the Bedfordians. He recognized the need to guarantee the retention of the episcopacy if further progress were to be made with secular reform. Privately, the Covenanters' 'best friends' were frank in justifying their pragmatism to the Scottish Commissioners. To press ahead with Root-and-Branch, they warned them, 'would make a division in [the] Lower House and would lose at least 100 [members] who were set to oppose the earl of Strafford and now are in a fair way for the public weal'.[114]

Concern for the 'public weal' and, in particular, for the fate of the Triennial Bill seems to have been the motive of Oliver St John — the Commons-man who straddled both the Warwick and Bedfordian 'interests' – for choosing the Committee of Twenty-Four as the body to consider future episcopal reform. Not only was this a venue where he and his fellow Bedford–Warwick men could see that any radical proposals were firmly scotched; most of the Twenty-Four were also committee men for the Triennial Bill, actively engaged in considering the Lords' amendments to the legislation during that same week. In this company, Bedford and Warwick could rest assured that nothing would happen to the bishops that would in any way undermine this central pillar of their commonwealth-to-be.[115]

Equally strikingly, the Junto carefully avoided making religion an issue in Strafford's impeachment – to the disgust of some of their own supporters, like young Sir John Coke: 'that nothing concerning religion, after so great a clamour, should be so much as objected [against] the Earl of Strafford', wrote Coke, 'sticks somewhat with me'.[116]

The Scots took time to appreciate how comprehensively their aspirations to 'nearer union in religion' had been bartered away.[117] A deluded Robert Baillie – possibly deliberately misinformed by his Junto friends – imagined that 'our partie' had put up a stout defence of Root-and-Branch. The reality was that, at the end of the debate, the bishops' abolition looked more unlikely than ever. If the Commons' anti-episcopalians, even with a Scottish army at their backs, could not do better than this, then at least for the foreseeable future, far-reaching change to the government of the English Church was no longer a serious prospect. As Hyde noted, 'the House was then *so far from being possessed with that spirit* [of hostility to the bishops]' that all they did was to allow the Root-and-Branch Petition 'to remain in the hands of the clerk of the House, with the direction that no copy of it should be given [out]'.[118] A London petition in favour of episcopacy was apparently abandoned because its sponsors concluded that, after the recent debates, 'the function of bishops was like to stand'.[119] The way was now open for a settlement based on the Ussher–Williams proposals for 'primitive episcopacy': an episcopal order modelled on the presumed practices of the early Church.[120]

More importantly for Bedford and his friends, this is how the outcome of the debate was interpreted at court. From there, two days later, Leicester's *homme d'affaires*, William Hawkins, reported how completely the question had now been laid to rest: 'the matter [of the bishops] *hath been* held doubtfull; but now those that would down with the [bishops'] function seeme to be the lesser number, yet all are for a round [i.e. general] reformation and limitation'.[121] That much was not in doubt. But with the question of bishops' votes in Parliament no longer a political priority (now that the bench had renounced its right to vote in Strafford's trial), Bedford, and even Warwick, could live with that. And unless there was a renewed attempt at abolition – a contingency that became more unlikely by the day – so too could the king.[122] The 'Rock' which Charles had warned might shipwreck the settlement had been safely circumnavigated. The shores of the godly commonwealth now looked tantalizingly close.

7

THE REWARDS OF SEDITION

FEBRUARY–MARCH 1641

> To six members of the higher nobility [the Earls of Bedford, Essex, and Hertford, Lord Savile, and Viscounts Mandeville and Saye], principal leaders of the revolts last year and his most obstinate persecutors, the king has distributed the highest offices of the Crown and given them the places of counsellors of state [Privy Councillors] ... without a care for the evil example of using honours as rewards for sedition.
>
> Giovanni Giustinian, Venetian ambassador in London, 27 February 1641[1]

On Wednesday morning, 10 February 1641, small groups of men, hatted and cloaked against the winter cold, assembled as usual at Temple Stairs to await the boats – small and often leaky wooden skiffs – that would row them the short distance to Westminster. Parliament-men, lodging cheaply at the nearby Inns of Court, mingled with lawyers, anxious litigants and obsequious clerks on the long wooden jetty that extended out over the shallows – the broad, reeking flats of mud exposed at every low tide – and carried the boatmen's passengers out to where the water was deep enough for the skiffs to dock. Among the Commons-men the conversations were far more animated than usual for the early hour. The unexpectedly harmonious resolution to the previous day's debate on Root-and-Branch had given rise to a cautious optimism; and there were rumours, possibly spread among the Thames boatmen, the city's habitual purveyors of gossip, that the king himself was intending to visit the 'Parliament House' later in the day.

Such optimism – the belief, consciously fostered by the king, that he had resolved to trust 'in [his people's] Affections'[2] – seemed to be corroborated by Charles's almost every action in the days following the 'burying' of Root-and-Branch. The ensuing week witnessed a diplomatic and a constitutional revolution, both peaceably attained, that seemed to inaugurate an entirely new political order: a 'commonwealth' in which not only the threat, but even the possibility, of regal tyranny might yet be permanently removed.

The first of these 'revolutions' – the diplomatic – came within twenty-four hours of the king learning the outcome of the debate on Root-and-Branch, and was arguably its direct and immediate consequence. For those, like Essex, Warwick, and Saye, whose memories went back to the early 1620s, it was a reprise of the happy moment in 1624, when the young Prince Charles, freshly returned from Madrid, had declared himself the enemy of Spain, and advocated an offensive alliance against the Habsburgs.

The boatmen's rumours proved correct. That same Wednesday morning, 10 February, Charles travelled from Whitehall to Westminster to make the decisive announcement to the peers. The treaty with the Dutch – the offensive league against Spain that Northumberland, Hamilton, and Vane had been negotiating since early January – was on the verge of completion, and was to be sealed with a marriage alliance between Charles's daughter, Mary, and the eldest son of the Stadhouder, the Prince of Orange. The Dutch ambassadors, however, had been insistent that nothing would be concluded unless Charles first came to an agreement with his English Parliament. The successful resolution of the Root-and-Branch debate on the 9th now placed that agreement in sight, and it was this which permitted the king's triumphant appearance in the House of Lords the following day, to pose as a champion of the 'Protestant Cause'.

I. TWO REVOLUTIONS

Speaking from the throne, Charles revealed that he was 'in purpose of a Match with his Eldest Daughter to the Son of the Prince of Orange'. Skilfully exploiting the moment to further his own reinvention as a godly Protestant prince, he professed his motive to be the 'use which may redound from [this treaty] for the Regaining of the Palatinate to his Sister [the widowed Queen Elizabeth of Bohemia], and his Nephews'.[3] The restoration of the Palatinate to the exiled Elector – *the* great foreign policy objective of the 1620s – was once again the priority of Stuart diplomacy. This was the 'Blessed Revolution' for which the godly had so long prayed, and the most striking evidence to date of the king's abandonment of Straffordian counsels. It was only ten months since the king, on Strafford's advice, had been looking to Philip IV to bankroll his campaign against Scotland and his suppression of English internal dissent.

This repudiation of his 'old counsels' was underlined by an unprecedented display by the king of his willingness to embrace anew the counsels of Parliament. Hitherto, the Stuart monarchs had brusquely rejected any attempts by the two Houses to offer advice on royal marriages. Now, in what appeared to be a further renunciation of his prerogative powers, Charles publicly sought the peers' (even if not the Commons') advice. He pointed out that the treaty was nearly concluded, 'yet he would in no way Ratify it', he insisted, 'till he had the Counsell and Approbation of [the] House [of Lords]'.[4] It was, as the Venetian ambassador observed, 'a step never taken by any of his predecessors'.[5]

Rapid progress with an anti-Habsburg alliance; interim agreement on the composition of the disposal of offices within the reformed Privy Council; an

emergent consensus on reform of the Church along the lines advocated by
Archbishop Ussher: all these developments fed the Junto's growing optimism
about the feasibility of a comprehensive settlement – and, paradoxically,
served to buoy Strafford's confidence that his own case might be equally
amicably resolved. 'You would not beleeve he hade ever binne happier', the
Countess of Carlisle observed of Strafford, early in February.[6] And nothing
witnessed more clearly to the Junto leadership's expectations than their new-
found willingness to provide the king with funds. In place of the surly
obstructionism of the winter, the Junto men in the Commons were suddenly
full of loyal concern for 'the business of his Majesty's revenue' – and this,
too, followed the successful sidelining of Root-and-Branch.[7]

By 10 February, then, the omens for a definitive agreement were looking
auspicious. Many of the elements of the settlement – a new, vigorously
Protestant foreign policy; a purge of the judiciary; interim agreement on a
scheme for the replacement of old, 'evil counsellors' by the virtuous and new;
the basis of a new settlement of the royal revenues – were either already in
place, or shortly poised to be. Only the Triennial Bill – the keystone of the
Junto's godly commonwealth – required completion. And even this looked
as though it would slot into place after the successful resolution of Root-
and-Branch. Merely a few minor amendments remained to be negotiated
between the two Houses, and Hampden brought these to a successful conclusion over the following days. By the Monday of the following week, 15
February, the Triennial Bill – the prize for which the Junto had abandoned
radical reform of the episcopate – was ready for the royal assent.[8]

Only one discordant element intruded itself into the otherwise harmonious
chorus of amity: the army which had been raised in Ireland by Strafford in
early 1640, and which was still under arms and potentially available for use.
These forces, moreover, were far from negligible. Currently estimated at some
8,000 strong, of which all but 1,000 were Catholics, this army cost some
£300,000 a year to maintain and seemed to have no practical use – unless,
of course, it was intended for deployment in mainland Britain (its intended
destination in the previous year).

Even here, however, there seems to have been a divergence of opinion
within the Junto leadership as to the ease with which this problem could be
resolved. When the subject was raised by the Commons as a matter of
concern – on 13 February, just as the settlement negotiations appeared to be
moving towards a happy conclusion – the two most prominent members of
the Bedford House interest, Pym and St John, were notably silent, perhaps
unwilling to make a fuss over a question that might yet be resolved out of
Parliament by other means. Instead, it was Sir Robert Harley, Sir Walter
Erle, and Sir John Clotworthy who made the running, urging the Lords to
join the Commons in demanding the Irish army's immediate disbandment.
Clotworthy, in particular, took a militantly anti-Straffordian line, employing
rhetoric that was sharply at variance with the spirit of 'accommodation'
evident earlier in the week. 'This [Irish] Army', he declared before the Lords,
'is to force [upon us] a Tyrannicall Government', for Strafford's commission as
general gave him a 'boundless power', leaving all to his discretion, including, it

was said, 'to stay [i.e. to check] tumults in England'.[9] Nor was this simply a matter of dangers past. So long as Strafford was Lord Lieutenant of Ireland, the existence of the Irish army remained a current and potentially potent menace.

Clotworthy's alarmist rhetoric was the first premonitory rumble of a storm to come. During the opening months of the Parliament, he can be read almost as a weathervane for the direction in which Warwick, his parliamentary patron, was also tending. And if Warwick believed, like Clotworthy, that Strafford was still bent on establishing a 'Tyrannical Government' – and that, with the Irish army, he had the means to do so – the prospects that any of the Warwick House group (in particular, Warwick himself, Essex, Mandeville and Brooke) would agree to serve in the king's government looked extremely bleak.

For Bedford, however, this was a problem for the future. Too much was going well for him to be deflected by the alarm-mongering of Warwick House.[10] Instead, he and his allies pressed on with the completion and presentation to the king of the Triennial Bill, the *sine qua non* of their new 'monarchical republic'.[11] Bedford's son-in-law, Digby, had had the honour of carrying the bill to the Lords when it had first passed the Commons on 20 January.[12] Now, on Monday, 15 February, with the Lords' amendments finally dealt with, it was the son of another of Bedford's West Country friends, William Strode – the Commons-man who had first introduced the bill – who had the distinction of carrying the completed bill back to the upper House, to be forwarded for the royal assent.[13] That afternoon, Bedford himself formed part of a delegation of five peers which travelled to Whitehall to present the king with the proposed new statute.[14]

*

Dusk was falling as the procession of the peers' coaches entered Whitehall's Great Court, bearing the proposed new statute 'engrossed' on a parchment roll. Even in this half-light, however, the coats of arms clearly visible on the coach doors, testified to Bedford's skill in constructing an alliance between the Petitioner Peers of August 1640 and the pro-reformist elements – the 'Protestant Lords' – within the existing Privy Council. Bearing the Triennial Bill to court on behalf of the Petitioners were Bedford himself and the Earl of Hertford. Representing the Council's reformist faction were the Earl of Arundel (the Earl Marshal) and the Earl of Pembroke (the Lord Chamberlain). Last came the Earl of Holland, who straddled both groups as brother to the Earl of Warwick and Groom of the Stool to the king.[15]

That three of the most senior figures in the royal Household should side so publicly with Bedford and the reformers, and in a matter that trenched so directly on the monarch's powers, sent its own clear message to the court. Further royal opposition to the Triennial Bill – so the presence of the five peers declared – would leave the king estranged not only from the Parliament, but also from some of the most powerful members of his own entourage. Above all, that the Lord Chamberlain, Pembroke, was prepared to side so overtly with Bedford indicated to the rest of the court which 'party' he thought would eventually prevail. It also helps explain his earlier invitation to Bishop Williams to preach in the Chapel Royal, and the prominence of leading members of his clientele – Rudyard, Glynne, and Hyde in particular – in furthering the Junto's parliamentary programme during January and February, and on into the period of Strafford's trial.

The five peers were able to offer Charles three inducements towards acceptance of the Triennial Bill, the legislation that would so severely limit his future powers. The most obvious – and most public – of these was the Commons' offer of four subsidies (with a likely yield of some £240,000), which was conveyed to the king by Secretary Vane that same afternoon.[16] But as these funds were to be administered by treasurers appointed by Parliament, and over the disbursement of which the king would have no control, the Commons' use of the traditional rhetoric that these subsidies were a gesture of loyal affection, a 'free gift' from the subject to the Crown, rang distinctly hollow. Only the reassurance that Root-and-Branch had now been consigned to oblivion and, it seems, the promise of further leniency towards Strafford appear to have carried any weight as concessions from Parliament, at least as viewed by the king.[17]

Nevertheless, the Whitehall audience was fraught and acrimonious. It could hardly be otherwise with a king who had made his right to disregard the counsels of Parliament into one of the central axioms of his rule. 'Remember', he had warned in 1626, 'that Parliaments are altogether in my power for the calling, sitting and continuance of them. Therefore as I find the fruits either good or evil, they are to continue or not to be.'[18]

Confronted by the actual text of the present Triennial Bill, with its clauses empowering twelve peers to summon a Parliament in the event of his refusal – in effect, legitimizing retrospectively the Petitioners' threatened course of action during the previous September[19] – Charles's first reaction was to renege on his earlier promise to accept 'the substance' of the bill. Only now, it seems, does he appear to have grasped how comprehensively he was to be rendered irrelevant to Parliament's future 'calling, sitting, and continuance'. Realizing, as Giustinian reported, that the bill's effect 'would be to ruin his authority entirely, [the king] became very angry', and at first bridled at the peers' request for the royal assent.[20]

This squall of rage in a monarch who otherwise prided himself on his stoic control of his 'passions' is itself highly revealing.[21] For all his public affirmations of his willingness to embrace reform, Charles knew he was being frog-marched towards the abatement of his powers; and the frustration and humiliation this induced were to corrode any sense, on his part, that these were agreements that he was obliged to observe. He was only induced to accept the Triennial Bill under coercion, the threat of 'the most extreme designs' against him should his assent be withheld.[22] It reportedly took the blandishments of Queen Henriette Marie to reconcile the king to accepting what it was no longer in his power to refuse.[23] After what was doubtless a troubled night, by the following morning Charles had agreed to allow the bill to pass. Perhaps not since King John had yielded to his barons at Runnymede had any English king conceded so large a diminution in his powers as sovereign.

*

Despite the reluctance of the king's assent, the Junto's moment of victory – played out in the House of Lords later that Tuesday morning, 16 February – was staged as a tableau of reconciliation. Escorted to the bar of the House by Secretary Vane and Denzell Holles (soon to be spoken of as Vane's fellow Secretary of State), the Speaker presented the king with the recently passed four subsidies as the Commons' 'free gift'.[24]* And the king, appearing crowned and robed in his ermine-lined surcoat and mantle of dark blue velvet, responded with a speech from the throne calculated to burnish his newly minted image as a reasonable and a conciliatory prince.[25]

Possibly drafted for him by Edward Nicholas, the Privy Council clerk and former Buckingham protégé on whom Charles was increasingly dependent for backroom counsel and advice, the speech represented the king's assent to the Triennial Act as an instance of singular royal bounty. Referring back to the two 'Rocks' that had earlier lain in the way of a settlement – the Triennial Bill and the threat to the bishops – Charles openly acknowledged the quid pro quo that had moved him to his latest concession. 'The first of those rocks' – the Triennial Bill – he had now removed 'himselfe', by 'yeilding upp to [Parliament] one of the fairest flowres in his garlande'.[26] He therefore hoped that Parliament would not 'presse [him] too hard' upon the second – the reform (but at least no longer the abolition) of the bishops.

Charles also sounded a note of warning. The Parliament

> had proceeded to the disjointing almost of all parts of his government. But hee hoped wee did onlie in that, as a skillful workeman doth with a watch which is out of order. He takes it in peices and cleanseth it, and then setts it againe together, without diminishing one pinne of it. For if that alone bee wanting, it will not goe right.[27]

This caution apart, the overall effect of the king's speech was wholly positive, and 'their Lordships ... [expressed themselves] full of joy for his Majesty's gracious answer'.[28] Once again, Charles had skilfully exploited the public moment to further his reinvention as a constitutional king, hinting that, should Parliament not press him too far, further concessions would be forthcoming.

In private, however, the king could barely contain his rage at the 'disjointing' of his government.[29] The impact of the new legislation was profound. As the Solicitor-General, Sir Edward Herbert, declared, the bill 'tooke from

---

* Not even Charles can have failed to notice the irony of Holles's ceremonial role. In 1629, Holles had tried to prevent the Parliament's dissolution by forcibly holding the Speaker in his chair, and had been imprisoned by the king for his pains; now he was acting to conduct the Speaker to his place, in a ritual that would end with Charles's public renunciation of many of his parliamentary powers.

the King one of the supreame prerogatives of his crowne, which was to call Parliaments'.[30] That now looked lost beyond recovery.

Taken together with his renunciation of his prerogative revenues on 23 January, his assent to the Triennial Bill rendered Charles for ever the dependant of his Parliament. Except for the Dutch Stadhouder or the Doge of Venice, no other European ruler was so deeply, nor so permanently, beholden to his legislature. Moreover, the new law altered in perpetuity the balance of power between the sovereign trinity of king, Lords and Commons – to the point where England moved closer to being (as, de facto, Covenanter Scotland already was) a republic in all but name. Significantly, the word 'commonwealth' – a term that was being increasingly, and at times pointedly, used as an alternative to the word 'kingdom' – enjoyed an ambivalent status in English parlance. It could be used relatively neutrally to mean the 'common good' or 'common interest' of the kingdom (*commune bonum* in Latin) – and was used in this way even by Charles himself. Yet it also had a more exact meaning as a synonym for a 'republic', as in the Venetian 'Commonwealth'.[31] Indeed, Venice figures recurrently in Charles's thoughts as the archetypal monarchical commonwealth in which the 'monarch' is nothing more than a puppet prince.

In the Triennial Act, the English had gone yet further than the Covenanter Scots, who, until that point, had come closest to reducing the king's power to that of 'a Duke of Venice'.[32] Yet, after the passage of the English Triennial Act, it was not long before the Earl of Argyll, the Junto's formidable ally in Edinburgh,[33] was commending 'our Brethren of England ... whose prudent example' should be 'our pattern for doing the like here in this Kingdome'.[34]

This, too, was the assessment of London's resident Venetian, Giovanni Giustinian – a man who could recognize a doge in the making when he saw one. 'At present', he wrote on 19 February, 'nothing is left to [Charles I] but the mere titles and bare appearances of a king, and he does not know how to conceal the inner anguish [*l'interne passioni*] that understandably afflicts him.'[35] This assessment of Charles's powerlessness is probably overstated; nevertheless, given the value he attached to his prerogative powers (for the exercise of which he regarded himself as answerable only to God), it may not have been far from how the king himself viewed his predicament. His 'inner anguish' was real. And in the weeks ahead it was to combine explosively with an already long-nurtured desire for revenge against the 'traitorous' Junto Lords.

The public euphoria that greeted the news of the Triennial Act can only have added to the king's sense of captivity and frustration. The night of Tuesday, 16 February witnessed popular celebrations in the capital on a scale not seen, perhaps, since Charles's and Buckingham's return from Madrid in 1624. The king, it seemed, had renounced for ever the era of non-parliamentary rule, and the people responded with 'outward expressions of ... thankfullness and Joy'.[36] Church bells rang festively 'through the whole city'.[37] In the London parish of St Bartholomew Exchange, for example, the churchwardens paid two shillings and sixpence to the ringers 'for joy of the triennial parliament'.[38] And when news reached Norwich, one of the three largest cities of the kingdom, on 18 February, its church bells also rang to celebrate 'the public triumph' at Westminster – a pattern of festivity that was probably repeated across the kingdom.[39]

As the bells tolled in rejoicing, the crowds in London gathered at street corners and in open yards to enjoy the warmth of the 'very many bonfires' that blazed in celebration.[40] These public bonfires were a relatively rare (and expensive) form of public jubilee. They were staged, argued John Stow of such late-sixteenth-century festivities, to mark the return of 'good amity amongst neighbours, that, being before at controversy, were there, by the labour of others, reconciled and made, [from] bitter enemies, loving friends'.[41] If bonfires retained any part of this significance in 1640s London, these rituals of 'good amity' probably had an obvious attraction in the increasingly polarized and fractious circumstances of February 1641.

Yet the Triennial Act celebrations were not purely spontaneous 'popular' festivities. In London, at least, they were held at the specific request of the Lords,[42] and it is perhaps not difficult to guess who the proposers of that motion had been. The bonfires and bells of that Tuesday evening were part of a recurrent pattern of aristocratic engagement with, and co-option of, the forms of popular culture – street processions (as with the entry of Burton, Bastwick, and Prynne and on Bishop Williams's release from the Tower), bonfires and bell-ringing, and, as we will see, the spectacle provided by public executions – all of which served, almost certainly deliberately, to take 'politics' to the people, fostering an awareness of the battles being fought for the 'commonwealth' that extended far beyond the metropolitan world of Westminster.[43] Moreover, this co-option of popular culture seems to be of a piece with the reformists' own awareness of the extent to which 'popularity' was an essential element of their own political authority. When, in the midst of the Triennial Bill debates, Leicester wrote of Viscount Mandeville's aspirations to public office 'that you may have that part which the voice of the people gives to you', he was acknowledging a power inherent in the *vox populi* that was both a mainstay of the aristocratic Junto's current success and one of the prime reasons why the king found their ascendancy so abhorrent.[44]

The night of 16 February was yet another incremental stage in the politicization of the capital. In the Privy Lodgings at Whitehall, Charles was spared the sight of the bonfires. But not even the oak shutters and heavy curtains of the king's bedchamber could muffle the ringing of an entire city's bells, and their irksome peals of 'joy'.

II. THE JUNTO DIVIDED

The bonfires at Charing Cross that night would have been clearly visible from the Long Gallery at Bedford House, a few dozen yards away in the Strand. For Bedford, however, the 'triumph' of the Triennial Act must have been tinged with an element of apprehension. That it had been brought successfully to the statute book was in large part the consequence of his coalition's unanimity and internal discipline in opposing Root-and-Branch.

Further progress – towards admission of the Junto Lords to membership of the Privy Council, and the redistribution of the offices of state – now depended on that unanimity being maintained in relation to the trial of Strafford. And on this matter, the constituent elements of the Junto were sharply divided.

Bedford was confronted with a choice. At one extreme were Warwick and Brooke – closely allied with the Scots – insistent that Strafford should be brought to trial immediately and eventually punished with a capital sentence. At the other were Hamilton, Northumberland, and Pembroke – his own key allies at court – pressing for a deferral of the trial, and an eventual compromise that saved Strafford's life, not least, perhaps, because this was the only way of calming an irascible and humiliated king. The choice for Bedford was between his old allies and his new. And, not for the last time, the supposed leader of the 'Scottish party' at Westminster decided that the future of the English commonwealth would be best secured by distancing himself from, if not wholly abandoning, his Scottish 'brethren'.

Bedford did not have the luxury of lingering long over his decision, for, on the morning of 17 February, with the embers from the previous night's bonfires not yet cold, the House of Lords was forced to come to a decision that had an obvious bearing on the timing of Strafford's trial. The matter at issue was whether or not the Lord Lieutenant should be granted a further postponement in order to prepare his defence. Partly at Bedford's prompting, Strafford had already been granted fifteen days, on 3 February, to prepare written answers to the charges against him; and he was clearly playing for further time. On the 13th, he had requested a postponement in order to obtain documents from Ireland, a request that the Lords had declined because it opened up the possibility (as Strafford, and perhaps Bedford, intended) of an indefinite delay.[45] On the morning after the passing of the Triennial Act, therefore, Strafford entered a new plea for time in which to prepare his written responses, probably expecting that the king's massive concession of the previous day would have inclined the Junto peers to regard his new request with indulgence.

Whatever Strafford's expectations, however, the striking aspect of the Lords' response was that a clearly defined 'Bedfordian' group within the Junto – Saye, Bristol, Savile, and Bedford himself – was almost cravenly forward in its willingness to gratify the Lord-Lieutenant's request. Charles's acquiescence to the Triennial Act was clearly being rewarded with indulgence towards his favourite minister. Indeed, to the courtier and army officer, Daniel O'Neill,[46] this conciliatory tone suggested something more than simply another postponement of Strafford's trial. The indications from the 'whole debate [in the Lords]' were such as to suggest 'that clearly he [Strafford] *will escape that house*'.[47] This is an ambiguous phrase; but one of three possible options – an acquittal, an abandonment of the trial, or the Bedfordians' consent to the granting of a royal pardon – appears to have been in prospect.

Not all members of the Junto, however, were persuaded of the wisdom of Bedford's policy of indulging Strafford's requests for the trial's deferment. During the debate on the postponement that day, the Junto Lords were clearly divided. While Bedford and Saye supported Strafford's request for a further delay, an equally well defined anti-Straffordian group within the Junto, loosely associated with Warwick House – Warwick himself, his brother Holland, his son-in-law Mandeville, and his cousin Essex – opposed the granting of any further favours to Strafford.[48] In the event, Bedford's side carried the day in the Lords, and Strafford was granted a further postponement.

Yet, for Bedford, this was an ambiguous victory. The extension granted Strafford was only seven days,[49] although (as Daniel O'Neill seems to have assumed), this could be further extended. Still more disconcerting for Bedford was the discovery that, on this question, Pym and St John were siding with Warwick House.[50] Pym was pressing for an immediate trial;[51] and St John, in particular, was insistent that *all* the concessions thus far granted Strafford – further time, permission to consult his lawyers, liberty to put his answers in writing – had in fact been 'contrarie to all use and against law'.[52] The trial, the Commons insisted, should proceed forthwith. The Junto grandees were at loggerheads, and the very public dissent highlights the independence of judgement and manoeuvre enjoyed by the Junto's Commons-men when they disagreed with friends and even patrons in the upper House.

At the root of Warwick's and St John's impatience seems to have been Clotworthy's insistent warnings about the intended – and, so long as Strafford was in command, likely current – purpose of the Irish army. The problem, Clotworthy argued, was urgent. The likely future, come the campaigning season of 1641, was suggested by what Strafford and the king *had* planned to do with the Irish army in their 1640 campaign – if only they had had the chance. As Clotworthy had revealed to the Commons as early as 29 January, the Irish invasion force (composed of predominantly Catholic troops) had been intended to rendezvous with another Catholic-led force, raised in the Marches of Wales by Henry Somerset, 5th Earl of Worcester.[53] A Catholic with vast estates and prodigious wealth, Worcester constituted a 'popish threat' that, for once, was not the mere product of puritan paranoia. Based in his medieval fortress, Raglan Castle, he enjoyed an almost feudal dominance of South Wales, and he had both the local prestige and the financial resources to raise a substantial private army.[54] The belief that Worcester might well prove the saviour of Charles's 'personal monarchy' had already figured in Windebank's contingency plans of September 1640 for the withdrawal of the royal family from London and its rendezvous with Worcester's forces in Wales.[55]*

The central point of Clotworthy's revelations of January and February 1641, however, was that, as neither Strafford's nor Worcester's commission had been recalled, the 1640 plan for a joint Irish–Welsh counter-attack against the English 'rebels' could be reactivated at any point. The possibility of this conjunction constituted a profoundly menacing and current Catholic threat.

---

* Charles continued to regard Worcester as the potential saviour of his monarchy as late as 1645. It was to Worcester's Raglan Castle that Charles fled after the catastrophe of Naseby in June that year, in the hope that Worcester might yet raise another army in the Royalist cause.

Hence, in the second week of February, as Clotworthy alerted the Lords to the continuing danger posed by the Irish army, Worcester was being inter-rogated over the 'large commission granted him [by the king] the last summer for commanding the forces in Wales'.[56] Pym seems to have taken his cue from Clotworthy. Bringing Strafford to trial immediately, he urged the Lords on 16 February, was imperative because the Lord Lieutenant was 'the head *also of the Popish partie in England*'.[57] Worcester and his extensive papist clientele, Pym claimed, were an extension of the Straffordian, Irish-army threat.

As Clotworthy's sleuthing gradually uncovered Strafford's invasion plans of the previous year, what shocked the Commons was not only how narrowly England had avoided a full-scale war in the previous summer, but that the major foreign force raised for that invasion remained poised and ready for use in the months ahead. Given the current internal stability of Ireland, it seemed that the king's only possible reason for its retention – at vast cost, and at a time when the king was otherwise virtually penniless – was an intended counter-attack in the spring or summer of 1641, as soon as weather conditions permitted. As Sir John Temple warned the Earl of Leicester on 4 March, the army in Ireland 'remaines ther entire, consisting of 8,000 foote, most of them Papists, but very expert soldiers', and if the Lord Lieutenancy were not soon transferred to a person of 'great abilities, wee shall sodainely fall into some ill condition there'.[58] It was to remove the danger of that sudden 'ill condition' – as Temple demurely put it – that Pym, Clotworthy and the Warwick group were so insistent on hastening the trial: convicting and punishing Strafford was the most effective means of ensuring he never again had the opportunity to make good his designs of the previous summer.

Yet the division between the Bedfordians and the Warwick House group was not, in fact, about whether or not the Irish army constituted a danger – on that, all elements of the Junto coalition appear to have been agreed. Rather it was about which of two sharply contrasted strategies for disposing of the problem the Parliament should pursue.

Bedford's behaviour ultimately seems to have been determined by his very different evaluation of both the opportunities created by the king's actions to date and the strength of the Junto's own position. While he appears to have realized the necessity of disbanding the Irish army no less than Warwick, Bedford also seems to have believed that the most effective way of achieving this was by working *through* the court and his new-found courtier allies. By offering concessions to Strafford (and hence minimizing the king's loss of face), Bedford believed, Charles could yet be persuaded to disband his Irish forces and to place the Lieutenancy in politically acceptable hands.

Warwick's tactics, in contrast, appear to have been premised on a far more sceptical reading of the king's capacity to respond to 'virtuous counsel'. Coercion, not courtliness, Warwick consistently maintained, was the only means by which Charles would be induced to dismiss Strafford and disband the Irish army. Hence, while Bedford successfully urged delaying the Lord Lieutenant's trial, Warwick and his allies (including, most influentially, the Scots)[59] supported the demands of the Commons' majority, strongly encouraged by Clotworthy, that Strafford should not only be brought to trial, but to the scaffold. Until that were accomplished, England remained on the brink of new wars – or, in Warwick's phrase, '*civil* wars' – as long as the king had the means to recoup his position by force.

This division was formalized on 19 February when six 'principal leaders of the last year's revolts' – Bedford, Essex, Hertford, Saye, Mandeville, and Savile – together with Digby's father, the Earl of Bristol,[60] were all summoned to attend the Council meeting held at Whitehall that day. For the Junto Peers, as a group, this was an important moment in terms of the symbolism of power, the point when the role they had exercised de facto as a Privy Council-in-waiting was formalized by their formal admission to the 'Council Board'. From that moment they, too, became 'courtiers', not merely attending White-hall for Council meetings, but also taking their places in the regular cycle of courtly ceremonies – from the weekly public processions to the Chapel Royal, to the reception of foreign ambassadors – that continued to take place, despite the cash-starved state of the Exchequer.[61]

This move has been interpreted blandly 'as an earnest of good faith in the negotiations between [this] group and the king' and as an intimation of royal 'favour'.[62] Yet this misreads both Charles's attitudes and intentions. Having been forced to the demeaning concessions inherent in the Triennial Act, the king's thoughts towards Bedford and his friends were far from charitable, still less inclined to a show of princely favour. Indeed, when Hamilton had first proposed the appointments, they had been 'bitterly rejected by the king'.[63] Contemporaries at court, however, offered a more plausible explanation: that the promotions to the Privy Council were intimately connected with the politics of the Strafford trial. On the one hand it was a reward to the Junto Peers who had supported the trial's postponement (Bedford, Hertford, Saye, Savile, and, it seems, Bristol). On the other it was a ploy to buy off two peers who, though currently in the Warwick camp (Essex and Mandeville), had long been thought potentially biddable. What finally appears to have rendered these promotions acceptable to the king was their capacity for exacerbating the incipient schism within the Junto by failing to promote some of its most influential members. Warwick and Brooke – the leaders of the campaign to try Strafford immediately – were punished for their militancy by forfeiting the chance of preferment.[64] That Brooke was passed over is perhaps unsurprising, given his relative youth. But the omission of Warwick – the de facto head of the Treaty Commissioners, a Lord Lieutenant, and a political grandee with a long record of military service to the Crown – was clearly intended by the king as a public humiliation, its sting made all the more acute by his son-in-law's promotion above him.[65] Nor was Warwick alone in nursing his resentment; the promotions 'hath discontented many of those', Temple reported on 25 February, 'that thinke thay had just cause to expect the same [advancement]'.[66]

If these promotions played on pre-existing divisions within the Junto coalition, they also created a series of new and far more insidious tensions. For those who had received promotion, the proximity of power – and the promise of office – offered a variety of inducements to equivocation. Over

the following months, the clear-eyed certitudes of opposition – the reassuringly binary world of 'enemies' and 'friends' – were gradually compromised
by the deal-making and alliance-making that was the essence of politics at
court. There were exceptions. Essex – for whom the promotion was a case
of too little, too late – remained a sea-green incorruptible, openly contemptuous of 'new courtiers' (like Saye, who placed private interest above
'the commonwealt'), and inflexible in his hostility to Strafford.[67] For Hertford
and Bristol, however, the two Junto grandees who identified perhaps most
strongly with their new surroundings, membership of the court and the
opportunities this afforded for access to the king also helped retune their
susceptibility to Charles's considerable, if only selectively deployed, personal
charm. Admission to the king's counsels had turned the head of many an
oppositionist before (Strafford himself being the most notorious example);
and Hertford and Bristol, in particular, appear to have identified strongly
with a sense of honour-bound 'duty', created by their new positions as
Privy Councillors. They, with Bedford and Saye, all recalibrated their former
hostility with at least one eye to their future preferment to office.

Yet it would be simplistic to regard this as merely a sycophantic quest for
royal favour. Rather, it derived from a realistic assessment on the part of the
Bedfordians that the king's mulish stubbornness was far more likely to be
moved by the carrot than by the stick. So long as Charles regarded *any*
attack on Strafford as an attack on himself and his 'honour', a policy of
leniency towards Strafford – and hence of damage limitation in relation to
the king's *amour propre* – was more likely to produce a disbandment of the
Irish army than the confrontational methods preferred by Warwick and the
Scots.

Predictably, then, this divergence over tactics also conditioned the two
groups' contrasting attitudes towards the Covenanters. The 'new Councillors', Baillie noted with disgust, 'were found to plead for some delay to
Strafford's [impeachment] processe, and to looke upon the Scottish affaires
not altogether so pleasantly as they [were] wont'.[68] As Bedford and most of
the 'new Councillors' continued to distance themselves from the Covenanters
(a process that had already been evident in the debates on Root-and-Branch),
so Warwick and Holland now realigned themselves more strongly than ever
with 'the brethren', looking to the Scottish Commissioners to join the parliamentary chorus demanding Strafford's speedy despatch.

These disagreements over tactics were intensified by rivalries over personnel. Warwick and Bedford represented not only contrasting styles of
political leadership within the Junto – the populist and confrontational versus
the courtly and conciliatory. They were also competitors for the Straffordian
inheritance. Both groups were running what amounted to rival tickets for
the series of lucrative offices that would fall vacant once the old 'evil counsellors' had been culled.

On one side was the Bedford–Northumberland axis, backing the Earl of
Leicester (Northumberland's brother-in-law) as the new Lord Lieutenant of
Ireland, and Lord Digby (Bedford's son-in-law) as the new Secretary of State.[69]
Through a deal brokered under duress by the queen's handsome, thirty-six-

year-old favourite, Henry Jermyn – her Master of the Horse and the Vice-Chamberlain of her Household[70] – Northumberland had even succeeded in obtaining Strafford's approval for Leicester's appointment.[71] Shortly before 11 February, Jermyn had persuaded Strafford to write a letter to the king 'to lett him know his willingnesse to resigne [as Lord Lieutenant of Ireland], so the Earl of Leicester might succeede him'. The offer, which Jermyn arranged to have delivered via the queen, thereby released Charles from any private obligation of honour that required he insist on Strafford's continuance in office.[72]

By mid February, however, a rival Warwick House interest was staking its claim to both these offices. Warwick's brother, Holland, was its preferred candidate to replace Strafford in Ireland; while the Secretaryship of State was a contest between rival sons-in-law, with Mandeville, Warwick's son-in-law, as the alternative to Bedford's son-in-law, Digby.[73] And, if the Earl of Holland won the Lord Lieutenancy, other prominent members of Warwick's clientele also stood to rise on Holland's coat-tails. Holland was reported to have promised a major preferment in Ireland (apparently Lieutenant-General of the Irish army) to Clotworthy, in order 'to engage him and the rest [Warwick's other placemen in the Commons]'.[74] By 25 February – little more than a week after Bedford's admission to the Council – Clotworthy had organized a petition to the king, urging Holland's appointment as viceroy of Ireland.[75] Clotworthy was an active and effective ally. His contemporaneous efforts to highlight the danger posed by the Irish army, as long as Strafford remained in charge, neatly dovetailed with his petitioning campaign to secure Holland's appointment as the earl's successor.[76]

These three highly combustible elements – divisions within the Junto Peers promoted and excluded from conciliar office, competition over who should succeed to the Lord Lieutenancy, and disagreements over parliamentary tactics – combined explosively on 24 February in an attempt by Bedford's Junto opponents to enlist metropolitan opinion in favour of summary justice against Strafford. The moment was carefully chosen. This was the day when Strafford was due to appear in the House of Lords to present his formal written responses to the treason charges. It was a critical point in the pre-trial procedures, the first time when the Parliament – and the public at large – would get a sense of the relative strengths of the defence and prosecution cases.

In a provocative bid to influence the judicial process, the Scots' Treaty Commissioners in London presented a brief but closely argued paper to their English opposite numbers – in effect, to Warwick and Holland as the leading pro-Scottish peers among the Commissioners – demanding Strafford's speedy trial and execution.[77] Censuring Bedford without actually naming him, the Scots argued that it 'were impiety to spare, much more to plead for, guilty Agag [the King of the Amalekites, the Israelites' mortal enemies, and the antetype for Strafford]' whom 'God in his justice hath destinate to destruction'.[78] Divine vengeance called out for the Lord Lieutenant's blood. And it called on 'your Lordships' – Warwick, Holland and the anti-Straffordian Treaty Commissioners – to see the trial promptly begun.

Such an attempt to influence the English Parliament's judicial processes would have been controversial under any circumstances. This intervention proved doubly scandalous when, within twenty-four hours, the document had been printed as a handbill, a single sheet to be passed from hand to hand and pasted up in public places around the city, in an obvious attempt to rally anti-Straffordian opinion within London. Of course, gossip and hearsay about the Strafford trial had been current in the capital and beyond for weeks. The provocative aspect of the Scots' appeal was that, in courting metropolitan public opinion (what the king would have censured as 'seeking popularity'),[79] they had endowed the trial process with an entirely new dimension.[80]

Hitherto, the deliberations over Strafford's fate had been one of the *arcana imperii* – the hidden affairs of state – conducted within the 'High Court of Parliament'. As yet, none of the numerous Commons speeches against Strafford appears to have found its way into print; and, apart from the original accusation against him in November, the detailed impeachment articles, tabled in January, had been kept under wraps in the House of Lords.[81] The Scots' decision to court opinion *outside* the Parliament broke this political embargo.[82] Scandalously, they had appealed to the world beyond the confines of Westminster's political élite. And Charles, ever suspicious of any attempt to exploit 'popularity',[83] was reported to have 'runne starke mad' after reading a manuscript copy of the declaration.[84]

Yet the Scots did not break this embargo alone. Their appeal for a prompt conclusion to Strafford's trial coincided exactly with Clotworthy's petition for the Earl of Holland's appointment as Strafford's successor in Ireland. And it was Holland who personally 'put in hand' the arrangements for the Scots' paper's printing and distribution – an act that is almost inconceivable without his having the support and approval of his brother and fellow Treaty Commissioner, Warwick.[85] Rather than being seen as an exclusively 'Scottish' intervention, therefore, the Covenanters' published declaration of 24 February is probably more accurately viewed as a collaborative initiative on the part of the Scottish Commissioners and the Warwick House peers, and closely connected with their contemporaneous campaign to see Holland appointed to a vacancy which the trial itself was intended to create.[86]

This attempt to take the trial into the 'public sphere' marks a critically important moment of transition. From this point, metropolitan opinion – and eventually, its physical manifestation, the London crowd – was to become a participant, and a highly partisan one, in the judicial process. Nor was this a matter of chance. Ever since the king had issued his reprieve of Father Goodman, those who wanted Strafford punished had confronted the obvious loophole in the impeachment process: that, whatever the final verdict against the accused, the king retained, and would doubtless try to use, his prerogative of pardon. To Warwick and the other hardline anti-Straffordians, the Lord Lieutenant not only needed to be found guilty by his peers; he had to be condemned in a context of such universal *public* execration that, for the king, the grant of a prerogative pardon was no longer a feasible option. Metropolitan opinion would clearly be essential to the creation of that context of execration, and hence also in closing the one loophole through which Strafford might otherwise escape. From 24 February, a series of further 'leaks' followed, each designed both to shape metropolitan opinion and to satisfy a ready appetite for news. By 1 March, for example, the detailed impeachment articles against Strafford (unpublished since their completion at the end of January)[87] were suddenly printed in an unauthorized edition, despite the best efforts of the House of Lords.[88] And later that month, for the first time, the series of parliamentary speeches that had been delivered against Strafford since the beginning of the Parliament finally started to become available, though still probably under the counter and with the names of their printers suppressed. Tracing the promoters of these samizdat publications is inevitably difficult; but at least some can be identified – like the declaration of 24 February, which first broke the news embargo – as emanating from the Warwick–Brooke households and their immediate allies.[89] What was clear, however, was that the engagement of 'the public' as participants in the Strafford trial had begun.

III. STRAFFORD'S TRIAL: PROBLEMS AND PROSPECTS

If the controversy over whether to hasten or further delay Strafford's trial had the capacity to tear the reformist coalition apart, something of the Junto's internal cohesion – perhaps, even, its instinct for survival – is suggested by its leaders' response to this outbreak of internal dissent. Bedford's reaction to the threat of schism, in particular, displays the tact and persuasiveness that made him, if not the most radical, then, arguably the most effective, of the reformist peers. While Warwick, passed over for conciliar preferment, sulked like Achilles in his tent, Bedford and his allies worked to meet the old campaigner (and his Scottish allies) at least halfway.[90]

Unable any longer to offer the Scots Strafford's scalp (if all went according to Bedford's plans), the Bedfordians took steps to present them with the next best thing: the head of Archbishop Laud. On 22 February, Pym moved in the Commons that the committee to prepare Laud's impeachment articles (dormant since December) should reconvene that same afternoon.[91] After months of delay, this initiative suddenly produced 'a long reporte' on the archbishop's treasons; and with suspicious promptitude, a comprehensive series of impeachment articles against Laud was ready two days later[92] – at the very moment when the Scottish Commissioners were publishing their declaration calling for justice against the 'two Incendiaries'.[93]

For the Bedford House group, this was a shrewd change of tack. Laud's prosecution was a cause around which both wings of the Junto could unite; and no sooner had Pym delivered the impeachment articles against the archbishop on 26 February than the 'Earl [of] Warwick moved to have him presently sent to prison and to be sequestred from all Eccl[esiast]icall Power'.[94] Moreover, redirecting the Parliament's vengeance against Laud looked likely to provide the Bedford House group with a sacrificial offering that would gratify the Scots, but without necessarily alienating the king. Indeed, for a king who had recently declared himself an enemy of 'innovation' and a restorer of 'Elizabethan purity' in the Church, the old archbishop was an embarrassment. Laud suddenly became expendable; and, in striking contrast to the king's devotion to his secular councillor, his abandonment of his highest-ranking prelate was heartless, cynical, and complete. By the first week of March, Laud himself realized that he had been cast adrift, and resigned himself to imminent martyrdom.

This successful change of tack – the refocusing of parliamentary censure on Laud, rather than Strafford – goes part of the way towards explaining why, by early March, the Commons' calls for an immediate trial of Strafford had been all but stilled. Gradually, during the last days of February and the first days of March, a majority of Junto members in both Houses came round to the Bedfordian position. Pym appears to have been among the first to change his mind. Despite repeated attempts by the Junto's reformist allies in the City – led by the godly firebrand Alderman Isaac Penington – to force the start of the trial by threatening to withhold City loans if it were further delayed, Pym resisted the City's attempts to use these as a means of hastening proceedings.[95] Even Warwick eventually followed.[96] By the beginning of March, the strident importuning for an immediate trial had suddenly ceased. Bedford's counsels of procrastination had prevailed. Not until 22 March – almost a month later – did the trial proper begin in Westminster Hall.

It is tempting to explain this delay – as, cynically, did some contemporaries – as yet further evidence of Bedford's willingness to trade indulgence to the Lord Lieutenant in return for the promise of courtly advancement.[97] Yet this would be to ignore the entry of an entirely new element into the various sides' calculations in the last week of February: Strafford's expected bravura as a master of legal rhetoric and argument.

*

Whatever hopes had been raised within the Junto by the 'triumph' of the Triennial Act, they were profoundly unsettled by the events of Wednesday, 24 February: the first occasion on which the Lords heard Strafford's detailed refutation of the impeachment articles against him. One by one, Strafford went through all twenty-eight of the articles, responding with a mixture of polished legal learning and devastating wit.[98] The lucidity and erudition of the rebuttal made it apparent that, if and when the formal impeachment began, Strafford would be a formidable defendant.

No less disconcerting, however, was the deportment of the king, who attended the Lords' sitting in person, admiring Strafford's performance from the throne. In a series of ostentatious gestures – removing his hat deferentially to Strafford when he appeared in the chamber, and publicly averring 'He had done him no wrong for ought he knew, and that [Strafford] had spoken all Truth, so far as concerned him'[99] – Charles declared himself convinced of the Lord Lieutenant's innocence.[100]

From that moment, if not before, it was evident that Strafford's removal from office could be achieved only by one of two means: either by *persuading* the king, if necessary with a measure of parliamentary coercion (the option preferred by Bedford and his allies at court); or by destroying the Lord Lieutenant at law, by prosecuting him through to condemnation and creating an environment in which the king had no alternative but to consent to his execution (the outcome desired by Warwick and the Scots). The dilemma for both these anti-Straffordian parties was that neither course of action was a viable option except in the presence of a watertight prosecution case. And from the moment the final impeachment articles were first made public, on 30 January, this case looked leaky at almost every seam. Sir John Temple, one of Strafford's enemies, found that the charges against the Lord Lieutenant were not 'so heavy as was expected'. Certainly, he admitted, they contained instances of his 'high injustice'; 'but for treason, I doe not conceive that above one or two Articles in it can pretende to make him guilty, and those – they say – are but slenderly proved.'[101] This was a view many others came to share.

After Strafford's rebuttal of the charges before the Lords on 24 February, it was more evident than ever that the specifically treasonous part of the case against him might yet prove too 'slender' to secure a conviction.[102] This had an obvious impact on the Junto's room for manoeuvre. Pym's denunciations of Strafford as a 'traitor against the kingdom and commonwealth' had been highly effective as a *rhetorical* strategy; but it was far from clear that the claim would stand up in a court of law. Treason had traditionally been defined as an offence against the king's person or sovereign authority; it was highly doubtful, therefore, whether the novel doctrine of 'treason against the commonwealth' would suffice to ensure a conviction in law'[103] – particularly in the face of a king who was prepared to declare in public that the prisoner 'had done him no wrong'. Charles was well aware of this legal point, and, even before Strafford had presented his rebuttal on 24 February, he reminded the Lords that 'What Treasons are, *or shall be'*, had been defined in 'the 25th [year] of Ed. 3' – Edward III's great Treason Statute of 1352.[104] Little of the current prosecution case came within its ambit.

The Junto's problems in law were compounded by problems with evidence.[105] The strongest charge against Strafford – that he had advocated the use of the Irish army to quell English internal dissent – rested on the testimony of only one witness, Sir Henry Vane senior, the Secretary of State, whereas two witnesses were required in law to substantiate a charge of treason. Vane may have been the Junto's only witness on this point, but at least he looked authoritative and his testimony was compelling. After Strafford's performance in the Lords on 24 February, however, even this source was left looking severely tainted. Levelling his own counter-accusations against his accuser, Strafford argued that Vane himself had been the culprit primarily responsible for the dissolution of the Parliament in May 1640. Vane, argued Strafford, was guilty of two acts of deception. To the Commons, he had deliberately misrepresented the scale of the king's demands for subsidies (insisting on twelve when Charles would have accepted eight), thereby deterring them from making a counter-offer. To the king, Vane had then conveyed the false impression that the Commons were unwilling to negotiate, and thus 'advised [him] to break [the Parliament]'. Strafford's charges against Vane seemed both grave and credible. Reporting this development to Leicester, Temple believed that Strafford's allegations 'will light very heavily upon Mr Treasurer [Vane was Treasurer of the Household as well as Secretary of State], and that he will be brought within the compasse of litle less then treason'.[106] The Junto's star witness now looked like finding himself accused and in the dock.[107]

With their principal witness severely compromised and their case questionable in law, the Junto was forced to reassess its tactics. On 4 March, it was reported that the parliamentary leaders were now doubtful 'whether to proceed on in the way thay are now in' – that is, they were considering abandoning the trial entirely. So flimsy was their case in law that an alternative procedure had briefly been considered: condemning Strafford by bill of attainder – a procedure, not used since Tudor times, whereby the crimes of the accused were simply declared to be treason by act of Parliament.[108] But this was rejected on the telling ground that, because Charles would have to be a party to any act of Parliament, 'it can not be done without the King's consent'.[109] At least with the trial, Strafford could be condemned by the Lords alone, with or without the king's consent. Even the execution would not require the king's consent, merely that he be constrained by parliamentary and popular opinion from issuing a pardon.

Although we cannot be certain, it seems that it was this sudden realization, in early March, of just how precarious their case was against Strafford that reforged the unity between the Bedfordians and their rivals at Warwick House. Once again, the Bedfordians – who had recently been striving to distance themselves from the Scots – were thrown back on their erstwhile Covenanter allies, less as a means of coercing the king than as an insurance policy in the event of Strafford's acquittal. From this point there was an urgent, almost panicked, tone to the Junto's requests for the funding of the Scottish army of occupation. Accordingly, on 6 March, when Warwick issued an emergency appeal for £25,000 to pay the Scottish army (and accompanied it with the threat that the Scots would advance southwards if their army went unpaid), it was the courtier, Sir Henry Vane, a man firmly in the Bedford–Northumberland camp, who backed Warwick most forcefully. If Warwick's demand were neglected, Vane argued, it 'might, within 48 houres, prove the destruction of the kingdome'. For once, the Commons responded with alacrity to Vane's request. Warwick was to be paid £25,000 for the relief 'of the northern counties' – that is, to pay the Scottish army so that it did not need to take free quarter – and he was given complete discretion as to how the money was disbursed.[110]* A week earlier, and Vane would have

---

* This vote also has implications for our reading of Edward Hyde's political behaviour at this time. Hyde, who was actively involved in the impeachment proceedings against Strafford, later claimed (in his *History of the Rebellion*) that his involvement in the various money bills before Parliament at this time was in order to advance the interests of the king; and it is true that, during February 1641, he had an important role as chairman of the Committee of the Whole House that discussed the granting of two subsidies 'for the maintenance of the king's army and supply of the northern parts': *CJ*, II, 88, 89, 91. But

been an improbable Commons spokesman for Warwick and the Scots; with
the outcome of the judicial process against Strafford so uncertain, however,
all sections of the Junto coalition were pulling together – and taking a
renewed interest in maintaining the Covenanters' support.

This new-found sense of the trial's uncertainty of outcome not only
accounts for the further, nearly month-long, delay after Strafford's performance on 24 February; at least in the short term, it settled the argument
within the Junto decisively in favour of Bedford's preferred tactic of persuasion and conciliation: of deferring the trial still further in the hope that
Charles could be brought round, voluntarily, to accepting Strafford's resignation and the disbandment of the Irish army. Bedford's logic, insofar as
it can be recovered, was at least plausible. Strafford's dismissal, if freely
granted, would have a powerful symbolic force: an attestation that the king
truly had renounced the 'evil counsels' of the 1630s and embraced new,
parliamentary ways. Moreover, as Strafford would no longer be his servant,
the king ought no longer to be debarred by scruples of 'honour' from giving
his personal support to the trial. Might not Charles, who had already been
induced to relinquish so much, be persuaded in time to make this final act
of renunciation? After the king's numerous, if usually last-minute, lurches in
the direction of reform in the weeks since early January, the hope that he
would clear this final hurdle was not yet entirely fanciful.

IV. THE IMMINENCE OF WAR

For much of the period that followed, from late February to the opening of
the trial on Monday, 22 March, the Junto marked time, waiting for the king's
response. Perhaps the clearest insight into the thinking current within the
Bedford–Warwick group during this crucial period is provided in an extended
essay by Calybute Downinge, the cleric who had already appeared as a public
apologist for the Petitioner Lords, and who in 1641 continued to enjoy
Warwick's protection.[111] Written some time between the admission of the
seven Junto Peers to the Privy Council (19 February) and the final decision
to press ahead with the trial (taken in mid March),[112] Downinge's essay
captures this critical moment when the aristocratic reform movement was
teetering uncertainly between optimism and pessimism; between a hopeful
future – in which, in Downinge's phrase, the king might yet see a 'universall

as Warwick had first call on any monies raised by virtue of these subsidies, and the king
had no control over funds paid to his army through the Treasurer-at-War, Hyde's activities
benefited the Junto, not the king, and it was with the former that he was clearly identified
at this time, despite his later attempts, in the *History* (written when he had become a
loyal servant of the Crown), to cover the tracks of his reformist past. Revealingly, when
there was an attempt to unseat him on 3 March 1641, by having his election at New
Sarum declared invalid, the opposition to Hyde was led by the future Royalist George Fane,
and 'Mr Ashburnham' (most likely, his fellow Wiltshire burgess, William Ashburnham, the
Army Plotter, but possibly William's royalist brother, John): *CJ*, II, 95.

reformation' – and a nightmare in which England finally succumbed to the 'destructive distempers' of civil war.[113] Which of these possible futures came to pass depended, Downinge argued, on whether or not Charles abandoned Strafford and agreed that he should be sent for trial. Downinge's treatise therefore offered a carefully argued rationale as to why it was in the king's, no less than the kingdoms', interests that Strafford should go to the scaffold. The work's cumbrous title – *A Discoursive Conjecture upon the Reasons that produce a Desired Event of the Present Troubles of Great Britain, different from those of Lower Germany* – belies the topicality of his argument and the urgent directness of his prose.[114]

To Downinge, the multiple Stuart kingdoms in February–March 1641 stood in the same position as the Spanish Netherlands (the modern Low Countries) had done in the 1560s: at the beginning of the 'Dutch revolt'. In this extended comparison, the Scottish Stuarts, by implication, parallel the Spanish Habsburgs, with England under Charles I standing as the analogue for the Low Countries under Philip II; Laud and Strafford, too, had their antetypes in Philip II's 'evil counsellors': Cardinal Granvelle, whose campaign to impose doctrinal orthodoxy caused the Low Countries to revolt; and in the ruthless Duque de Alva – the antetype for Strafford – who was sent in by Philip to put down the noble-led opposition.[115] The parallel offered a series of cautionary lessons for contemporary England. Alva (Strafford) had dealt with this earlier generation of Petitioner Peers by 'cut[ting] off [the] chiefe of the Nobilitie's heads, who set their hands to the complaint against ill Counsellors and petitioned for composing all' – a reference which may well reflect the current anxieties of Downinge's own Petitioner patrons.[116] And Alva, too – like Strafford – had counselled the sending of a foreign army to put down internal dissent '(which counsell was Treason …)'.[117]

Yet despite all, Downinge concluded, there were grounds for hope. Charles had the option of learning from Philip's mistakes, and there were indications that Britain might therefore escape the civil wars that laid waste the Low Countries, and resulted in the creation of the Dutch Republic. The king's 'deserting [of] many of his Ministers' – an apparent reference to Finch, Laud, the Ship Money judges – gave cause for optimism that he might yet abandon Strafford.[118] There were pressing reasons why he should do so. Addressing the king's notorious prickliness in relation to his honour, Downinge argued that the king could cast Strafford aside without shame, for 'a moderate Prince … may *with honour,* safety, transcendent justice, and great content, bequeath notorious suspected ill Counsellors to a publique triall'.[119] Apparently speaking for the Junto, Downinge insisted that there was no intention that *all* the ministerial impeachments begun thus far should result in capital sentences or the execution of 'multitudes of men'.[120] Such carnage, Downinge assures the king, is 'not what *we* aim at' – the adoption of the form 'we' at this point is surely significant – 'either as justifiable or plausible'.

> But *what we propose* stands thus, and we may make it good to the whole world: that it is most honourable, just, and safe for a supreme Potentate [the king], … in exigents of State, to give up notorious and manifest

Ministers of ill Counsels, [and leave them] to his own extraordinary supreme
Councell [Parliament] ...

Nor need Parliament be slavish in its adherence to precedent. Parliament not
only had the power to act according to precedent, Downinge argues, *'but
also occasionally to create them'*, when 'reason of State' required. Parliament
need not be 'foiled in their deliberations by over-punctuall, pædantique,
literall interpretations' of the law.[121] His admission of the weakness of the
Junto's case against Strafford could hardly be clearer.[122]

The crux of Downinge's argument, however, is his revelation of the likely
consequences if Charles refused to cooperate with the trial. If the king agreed
to Strafford's impeachment, there was still the possibility that the three
kingdoms' constitutions could be re-founded on a 'universall love of his
Majestie's Royall person' – what Downinge expands on as 'the present
concurring of all the three States to serve him upon *new endearing obligations*'.[123] The alternative – not as some distant prospect, but as an immediate
consequence should Charles refuse to part with Strafford – was civil war.[124]*

That disaster, narrowly averted once, in the summer of 1640, was unlikely
to be avoided a second time. 'Those civill cruell wars' in the Netherlands
were 'an example of caution' against a danger that was still not yet passed.[125]
And the king's agreement to the trial is the only way 'to prevent it'[126] – a
view that was already, or shortly became, Warwick's settled belief as to why
Strafford must fall.[127]

This, in turn, tells us much about the Junto leadership's perception of the
king. That Downinge regarded civil war as already a possibility was a tacit
acknowledgement of the strength of the king's position. Yet it is also strikingly
at variance with most recent accounts of the political crisis of 1640–2. These
have suggested that it was not until mid 1642 that the nation was sufficiently
'polarized' to be capable of civil war. Nor would this point of polarization
have been reached except for the reformists' zeal for radical religious change –
a zeal allegedly first glimpsed in the Root-and-Branch debates of February
1641, and which was to intensify, to the exclusion of any possibility of a
settlement between the king and his opponents, into the winter of 1641–42.
Only in response to the reformists' attacks on the traditional Church of
England (and bishops in particular) – so the argument runs – did the king
eventually acquire widespread support in the nation at large. And only then
did civil war become a serious possibility.[128]

That is not how it seemed to Downinge and perhaps, too, to his Junto
patrons as they contemplated the possibility of Strafford's acquittal in that
same critical month of March 1641. True, religious divisions had not yet
polarized the nation; indeed, if anything, there was a broad consensus emer-

---

* Downinge hopes that the 'ROSES and LILLIES [the heraldic emblems of England]
may not grow, or rather be blasted, in his People's blood' – until 'lately' the catastrophe
to which the kingdom had seemed to be heading in 1640. The reference is to the closeness
to which England approached civil war in the summer of 1640.

ging, at least at Westminster, in favour of a reformed episcopate and a purge
of liturgical 'innovations'. Yet, even without the polarization of the nation
at large, a military conflict was already possible. In the spring of 1641, there
were more men under arms in England, Scotland, and Ireland, than at any
point for over a century: over 20,000 English, 25,000 Scots, and some 9,000
Irish. Charles already possessed a 'military party', and one that was far larger
in March 1641 than that which he was to enjoy at the beginning of the
conflict in 1642. His possession of an army in Ireland, another in the North
of England, and his potential for raising a third force under Worcester in the
Marches of Wales, gave him the wherewithal to wage a war almost irrespective of his 'popularity', or lack of it, in the country as a whole. Even
without parliamentary funding, he probably had the capacity at least to fight
a single-season campaign (just as he was to do again, without parliamentary
funding, in 1642).[129] And if the Scots stood by their 'Fifth Columnist' allies
and fought against the king's forces on English soil, Charles would have been
able to play the patriotic card, and might well have turned his campaign
against 'the rebels' into a popular crusade to drive the foreign invaders out
of England. Either way, some form of civil war looked almost inevitable.

These potentialities, in turn, made the prospect of Strafford's acquittal so
menacing to the Junto – an outcome to the trial that seemed possible even
before it started, and was to seem even more likely once it had begun. If
the prosecution failed, the Lord Lieutenant's political rehabilitation seemed
assured; and so, too, was the resumption of the war of 1640: a campaign
to drive the Scots out of England and to turn on their English abetters. By
refusing to dismiss Strafford from his Lord-Lieutenancy – and still more, by
keeping the Irish army 'entire' – Charles seemed to be signalling that he
intended to have use for both in the event of Strafford's acquittal.

These possibilities are unlikely to have gone unnoticed by the king. Charles's
continuing commitment to Strafford has usually been explained as a mixture
of regal stubbornness and a defensive concern for the 'dishonour' that would
ensue if he were seen to disavow his most loyal servant.[130] In February and
March, however, there was a more practical reason for the king's refusal to
dismiss his Lord Lieutenant of Ireland. With Strafford's acquittal a serious
possibility, and his Irish forces still intact, the king could once again look
forward to the prospect – as he had done at the beginning of the Parliament –
of resuming his war against the Covenanters, and destroying their English
'friends'.

Moreover, in the spring of 1641, new military possibilities appeared to be
opening up for the king.[131] His army in the North remained surprisingly
stable, both in numbers and *esprit de corps*, and was now disposed to blame
Parliament, not the king, for its failure to be paid since December. There
seemed little likelihood, now, that dissident pro-Junto regiments would join
with the Covenanters to create the 'armies for the commonwealth'.[132] And
while there was a general belief that the king's forces would not fight until
they had received part of their arrears, 'yett our men say that, after thay are
payd', they would not withdraw from the North so long as there was a single
Scot between the Trent and the Scottish border. 'Some of our commaunders

that come thence', Temple reported on 4 March, 'say thay are in very good state now, and much superior to the Scotish forces.'[133]

v. ARMY PLOTS

Some of those 'commaunders', in town in March 1641, were not slow in suggesting how this superiority might be turned to the king's advantage. A number of senior officers – among them Henry Wilmot, William Ashburnham, Hugh Pollard, and the Captain of the King's Bodyguard, Henry Percy[134] (all of them also members of the Commons) – recognized that the army's increasing dissatisfaction with Parliament might be manipulated in Charles's favour. The provocation that moved them to action appears to have been the Commons' decision, on 6 March, to prioritize the payment of the Scottish army over the English, and to assign £25,000 (formerly earmarked for the pay of the English forces) to the Earl of Warwick as de facto paymaster of the Scottish army.[135] Percy and his fellow officers channelled their indignation into a coherent political programme. Apparently mimicking the tactics of the Twelve Peers the previous autumn, they, too, resolved on the preparation of a 'petition' to be signed by the officers of the northern army and presented to the Earl of Northumberland, as the army's Lord General. In fact, like the Peers' Petition, this officers' petition was actually intended as a public manifesto demanding specific actions, backed with the tacit threat of military force in the event of non-compliance. The signatories promised to stand by the king if Parliament attempted to compel him to disband the Irish army before the withdrawal of the Scots; if attempts were made to remove bishops from the House of Lords; or if his revenues were not returned to his hands. It was a statement of bellicose intent. Circulated within the army during mid March – almost certainly with Charles's approval – the officers' petition publicly affirmed that the army in the North was a 'king's party' in waiting.[136] Indeed, in a bid to prise Essex away from his Junto friends, Wilmot and Ashburnham proposed offering him the post of Lord General, and, without disclosing the conspirators' motives, privately sounded out Essex as to whether he would accept.[137]

Other officers went further. By the time Henry Percy conferred with the king about this petition, shortly before 20 March,[138] a second 'army plot' was already in progress, organized from within the queen's Household, and with an even more belligerent series of objectives. Ironically, its originator was Henry Jermyn, the queen's Master of the Horse, and a figure who hitherto had been working to ingratiate himself with Bedford and the Junto leadership, in the hope of preserving his existing position at court. In January 1641, one court observer had feared that 'the Junta [the Bedford–Warwick group], once being settled, . . . will find a way to cutt [him] short' – meaning that he feared at least Jermyn's dismissal, and probably impeachment, if the 'Junta' ever gained control of the king's government.[139] Hence, in February, sensing himself to be 'in great danger' from the reformists, he had vociferously backed their appointment to the Privy Council.[140] By March, however, with the Junto's stock declining as the likelihood of Strafford's acquittal rose, Jermyn looked elsewhere for his salvation, and began working to create a militant and highly interventionist 'king's party' within the northern army.

Like the army petitioners, Jermyn had his own allies within the army's officer corps who made much of the soldiers' resentments – in particular, their outrage at the Junto's siphoning off of £25,000 of its pay, via Warwick's private treasury.[141] Two officers in particular, Colonel George Goring and Sir John Suckling, became his principal accomplices, and he also succeeded in drawing in Henry Percy, from the ranks of the army petitioners, who attempted to rally support for the new plan from a deeply sceptical Wilmot and Ashburnham. The Jermyn–Suckling plan, however, went far beyond the army petitioners' scheme: it went, in Percy's own phrase, 'moore highe and sharpe [than the other], not having limits, either of honour or [of] law'.[142] Central to its success would be the alteration of the army's high command so as to enable the king to resume an 'offensive war' against both the Scots and his internal opponents. Two key posts had to be changed. The Lord General, Northumberland, who had shown himself far too close to Bedford and members of the Junto, was to be replaced by a loyal friend of Strafford's, the Earl of Newcastle.[143]* And Northumberland's protégé, Sir John Conyers, the current Lieutenant-General of Horse, was to be ousted to make way for Colonel Goring, a man who was be trusted to act (perhaps mistakenly) in the service of the king.[144] Goring, moreover, was Governor of Portsmouth, the heavily fortified port, which, since September 1640, had been regarded as a strategically vital point of 'retreat' for the king and his family 'in case of extremity'.[145]

By mid March 1641, Jermyn, Goring, and Suckling were planning for just such extremities. If the king and Parliament came to another impasse – if, say, Strafford were acquitted and the Parliament refused to sanction his release, or condemned and the king insisted on using his prerogative of pardon – the army's new commanders, Newcastle and Goring, were to bring the king's forces south, towards (if not actually to) London, to support the king, overawe the Parliament, and secure Strafford's release.[146]

How much of this had reached the ears of the Junto during March is unknown. But neither Bedford nor Warwick needed precise knowledge of the two army plots to realize that the failure of Strafford's impeachment was likely to result in some form of civil 'confusion': almost certainly an abandonment of the Anglo-Scottish treaty, and a reactivation of Strafford's earlier plan to put down the 'rebellions' in Scotland and England by force. If Parliament divided in response to that acquittal, as Temple was already hinting that it would – between Junto supporters on the one side, and a pro-Straffordian king's party on the other – Downinge's bleak predictions of

---

* Here, too, the 'king's party' appears to have been aping the tactics of the Junto. These requests to the king to change the General and Lieutenant-General of the English army look like a riposte to the Junto-backed petition to the king, presented on 25 February, requesting the replacement of the current General and Lieutenant-General of the Irish army with Holland and Clotworthy.

'Civill War' looked likely to be fulfilled. Little wonder that the Junto leadership moved so slowly, throughout late February and March, in bringing Strafford to trial, and why – if Downinge's treatise is any guide – they were so desperate to persuade the king to give his backing to the judicial process.

Bedford and his Junto colleagues can hardly have been surprised at Charles's reluctance to respond to their promises of future 'endearment'. Ever since September 1640, the Junto leadership had been using the threat of military force, either direct or implied, to 'Venetianize' the English state: to place a regularly meeting 'Great Council' of Parliament at the centre of English political life, to strip the king of his power to control its summons, and to achieve an ever tighter grip on the royal finances. Having established the ground rules of politics as intimidation and coercion, the Junto cannot have been surprised that Charles seized the opportunity to retaliate in kind the moment the apparent improvement in his (and Strafford's) fortunes permitted him to do so. The prospect of Strafford's trial had always been intended by the Junto leaders to intimidate, even to humiliate, the king. By continuing to refuse their demands for Strafford's dismissal, Charles called the Junto leadership's bluff, deliberately making himself – as Strafford's employer and defender – a vicarious defendant in the trial.

By mid March, the Junto leadership's bluff had been called so comprehensively that they had no alternative but to proceed with the trial, a contest they approached with apprehension, and in which victory was far from assured.[147] Their one insurance policy was the extension of the Scottish treaty by a further month, to 16 April, thereby ensuring the Covenanter army remained in England at least for what was expected to be the trial's duration.[148] Proceeding with the impeachment did not mean, of course, that the Junto leadership had given up all hopes of achieving further reforms through bargaining with the king. But the terms of that bargain had now changed, and they knew that the king was likely to prove even less biddable than he had been hitherto. Indeed, whatever Charles's actual intentions, all the signals emanating from the court suggested that, were Strafford either exonerated or otherwise freed, the king intended to go on the offensive, come the summer of 1641, against both the Covenanters and the English 'traitors' of 1640. These intimations of belligerence were intensified, from early April, as the king deliberately allowed news of the various army plots to leak into the public domain. With either the explicit or tacit assent of the king, Goring divulged the plan for the English army's advance towards London to Warwick's half-brother, the Earl of Newport, the Master of the Ordnance; and Newport – as Goring surely intended – immediately asked him to repeat his disclosure to Bedford, Mandeville and Saye.[149]*

---

* In making these disclosures to Bedford, Saye, and Mandeville, Goring posed as a 'Commonwealthsman', evidently using the partisan language of 'commonwealth' current in Junto circles. Indeed, to establish his credentials he went so far as to make 'a protestation unto the lords of his fidelitie to the Commonwealth, and of his readiness to runne all hazards for it'. This is a use of the term 'commonwealth' that seems to presuppose its superiority to, or possibly even the exclusion of, the person of the king.

Disagreements remained within the Junto over Strafford's eventual fate. Warwick, Essex, and a small group of fellow hardliners seem to have been immovable in their conviction that Strafford was too dangerous to be allowed to live.[150] Against this, Bedford, Pembroke and Saye (backed by Pym) argued that further concessions might yet be attained – not least, their own appointment to office – by sparing Strafford's life. In practice, however, the two positions complemented each other so neatly that the antithesis seems to have been almost deliberate. It was, after all, the extremism of the Warwick House 'Strafford-must-die' position[151] that created the political space for Bedford and his friends to portray themselves, as they had done successfully hitherto, as agents of moderation: to interpose themselves between the king and the Parliament as brokers of a deal: Strafford's life in return for Charles's renunciation of the means of fighting a new war. Almost throughout the trial, the actions of the two wings of the Junto complemented each other so conveniently that it appears, at times, that we are watching a 'hard cop-soft cop' double act.[152]

For the Junto leaders – and in particular for the Petitioner Lords who had first called for Strafford's 'condign punishment' back in August 1640[153] – these appeals to 'the public' were motivated by something more than merely the need to intimidate the king. In proceeding to the trial, Bedford, Warwick and their fellow 'Commonwealths men' knew they were taking a massive risk. If the reports proved accurate that Strafford had 'made such a partie [in the House of Lords] that it will be caried [in his favour] by votes',[154] the outcome of the trial might yet, as Downinge was already predicting, reduce England to a state of 'Civill War'.[155] Of course, Bedfordian moderation might yet prevail. But contingencies had to be allowed for. And in shamelessly courting 'popularity' throughout the trial, the Junto was staking its claim, in the event of conflict, for the allegiance of the English people.

8

THE THEATRE OF JUDGEMENT: THE TRIAL OF THE EARL OF STRAFFORD

MARCH–APRIL 1641

God hath propounded and layed open in this corrupt age, a Theatre of his Judgements, that everie man might be warned thereby.

Thomas Beard, *The Theatre of God's Judgements, Revised and Augmented* (1631)[1]

Well before dawn on the morning of Monday, 22 March 1641, the opening day of the impeachment trial, Strafford was woken and told to prepare himself for the journey, by barge, to Westminster. He dressed entirely in black. With what seems to have been studied melodrama, he chose a 'mo[u]rning suite and long cloke', the familiar apparel of those taking part in a funeral cortège ('funeral blacks', as they were known). The once haughty viceroy – whose very 'Physiognomy, posture of person, [and] proud carriage' proclaimed his 'insolencies ... and tyrannies'[2] – would go before his judges in the garb of grief and penitence. His George, the medal that signified his membership of the Garter, he wore suspended from a discreet gold chain, rather than the usual ribbon of sky-blue silk.[3] Even his hair, deliberately left uncombed and tousled – what one observer described as 'far from what hee was wont to doe heretofore' – conformed to the established conventions of public sorrow and mourning.[4]

Strafford descended the stone staircase leading to the Tower's heavily fortified watergate, later known as Traitors' Gate. Torches lit the gate's cavernous stone-vaulted interior, open towards the river and partially flooded to allow boats to moor within the fortress's walls. Damp and smoky, the half-lit gatehouse and the open space beyond bristled with soldiers, the metalwork of their muskets glinting in the torchlight. Strafford embarked, accompanied by his Scottish-born gaoler, Sir William Balfour, the Lieutenant of the Tower, and a guard of soldiers. As the oarsmen rowed out into the river beyond, they were 'girded [about] with barges in which

The Traitors' Gate: built by Edward I in the 1270s, this water-gate provided the principal secure river entrance to the Tower of London. It was from here that Strafford's barge and its small flotilla of guard-boats departed for its almost daily journeys, during the trial, to and from Westminster Hall.

were many muskettiers'[5] – six barges in all, with fifty oarsmen between them, and a hundred soldiers from the Tower garrison, each armed with a 'partizan', a long-handled spear, ideally suited to repelling any river-borne attack.[6] The heavy-laden convoy then turned westward for the journey up-river, passing the long series of wharves that serviced the City, already beginning to stir into activity; on past the great arc of river-front palaces which lined the Thames's northern bank between the Inns of Court and Whitehall; on until they reached the medieval bulk of the Palace of Westminster, ponderous and disorderly in the dawn half-light. They dis-embarked at the long wooden jetty known as the Parliament Stairs around 6 a.m. From there, escorted by a hundred-strong guard from the Westminster Trained Bands, Strafford was taken to a room adjacent to Westminster Hall, to await the convening of the court.[7]

As the prisoner's choice of a 'mourning suit' suggests, Strafford's trial had a histrionic, play-like element from its opening day. Set for hearing in Westminster Hall, the largest secular covered space in England, it was expected to attract an audience of well over a thousand on each day of the proceedings, and both sides – accusers and accused – realized that this stage provided an unparalleled opportunity to shape the perceptions and attitudes, not only of the court, but also of a sophisticated metropolitan audience, intent on witnessing the proceedings in person, and a still larger audience beyond, hungry for news of the trial and its protagonist's performance. As a piece of judicial spectacle, the trial was on a scale unlike any in living memory; 'never was there or anywhere else', one of the prosecutors noted, 'seen a more solemn and majestic tribunal'.[8] And in the weeks ahead con-temporary commentators would slip easily into the language of the theatre to describe how Strafford – 'this great Personage, now upon the Stage'[9] –

'act[ed] his part'[10] in this very public drama. To the barrister and Commons-man, Bulstrode Whitelocke (himself one of the trial managers), the setting for the trial was, quite simply, 'the theatre'.[11]

Of course, such theatricality was not unique to Strafford's trial; it was central to the functioning and moral purpose of almost all criminal trials in early Stuart England.[12] Far more complex an event than simply an enquiry into innocence or guilt, a trial provided a stage for the affirmation of the community's civic, religious and ethical values; a venue in which the public deportment of those accused – their displays of contrition, of deference towards the court, the apparent sincerity and frankness of their defence, and, above all, their willingness to endorse the social nostrums they were accused of having infringed – all affected the court's decisions as to innocence or culpability, and the leniency or severity of any punishment.[13] For Strafford, the stage he was about to tread afforded opportunities, as well as risks; not least, the chance to confound the public's expectations of himself, and to explode the legend of 'Black Tom Tyrant' that had been carefully created by the Junto leadership over the previous five months.

His accusers had little confidence in their own position. Indeed, Strafford's furtive arrival, under such a large and heavily armed escort, was one of the many signals that indicate the Junto's nervousness on that opening day, a state of anxiety that was to intensify as the trial progressed. Some form of armed escape attempt, an interception of Strafford's barge as he was in transit between the Tower and Westminster, remained a constant threat. Even the loyalty of the London population was open to doubt. Throughout the City and suburbs, detachments of the Trained Bands were set 'to keepe men in order' – a measure that suggests the possibility of clashes between pro- and anti-Straffordian parties.[14] In and around Westminster Hall there was a heavy military presence. Even before the revelations about plotting in the army began to emerge in April,[15] the threat of disorder, or some form of insurrection, formed part of the context of the trial from the outset.

Yet if at one level the trial was addressed to the 'public', at another it was clearly directed towards an audience at the Whitehall court. Despite the atmosphere of incipient violence, the trial continued to be regarded, at least by the Bedford House group, as a form of negotiation – an extension of the process of bartering between Charles and his aristocratic opponents whereby, as Whitelocke later recalled, 'Strafford's enemies should become his friends, and the king's desires be promoted', if Charles would only 'prefer some of the grandees to offices at court'.[16] The beginning of the trial was not, therefore, a sign that the negotiations had irretrievably broken down. Instead, it offered a route by which the Junto could pursue those negotiations by other means. Their objectives remained the same: their own and the commonwealth's security, first and foremost;[17] and, once attained, their appointment to public office. Hence, throughout the trial, Bedford and Saye – working closely with some, if not all, of the prosecution team in the Commons – remained prepared to offer Charles a compromise. With their security to be achieved through the king's disbanding of the Irish

The Tower of London in the 1640s: despite its antiquity (its central keep was built by William the Conqueror in the 1070s), the Tower remained of contemporary strategic importance during the 1640s, not only because it was England's principal military arsenal, but also because, as a last resort, its cannons could be trained on the City.

army and his dismissal of Strafford as Lord Lieutenant,[18] they were prepared to effect a trade, the terms of which appear to have been that Strafford would be condemned and debarred from public office, but saved from the scaffold, in return for the appointment of the Junto grandees to the great offices of state, their Commons allies to ancillary posts in the royal bureaucracy, and the reduction of the king, in the radically changed post-Triennial Act world, to a figurehead prince.[19]*

This was a plausible bargain – and, as we will see, one towards which Bedford made substantial progress. On the one side, it permitted Charles to salvage at least a measure of honour by being seen to have saved his most powerful ex-minister from the scaffold. In advancing this course, Bedford encountered trenchant opposition from his rival Junto 'grandees', Warwick, Essex, and Brooke;[20] but otherwise few within the Junto seem to have been inflexibly committed to the pursuit of Strafford's death. Bedford appears to have persuaded most of his Junto colleagues that once Strafford had been disgraced, stripped of his offices, and confined to rustic obscurity, either in prison or, more likely, under house arrest, he would no longer pose a serious danger to 'the commonwealth' or themselves. If Charles were prepared to renounce Strafford's policies with such clarity that any future attempt to rehabilitate him would leave his own 'honour' tarnished irreparably, there

---

* One of the fears articulated by Oliver St John, a central figure in Strafford's prosecution, was that if Strafford went unchecked, he would visit 'punishment upon his impeachers, so that the triennial Parliament will be of no such force as is expected'. The Triennial Act was fundamental to the Junto's expectations of the future, and their efforts to reduce the monarchy to an office with merely doge-like powers.

was still the possibility that the 'great incendiary's' life might be saved. The severity of Strafford's eventual punishment was thus intimately linked to the question of the genuineness or otherwise of Charles's disavowal of authoritarian rule.

If this was the conciliatory element of the Junto's tactics during the trial, it also had a harsher, indeed draconian, complement. The king had to be persuaded that, were his cooperation to be withheld, the implications would be correspondingly bleak. If the king refused to dismiss Strafford from his offices and ban him permanently from court, he was to be left in little doubt as to the potential consequences. Once the prosecution had finished delivering their case against Strafford, opinion in Westminster and beyond needed to be so hostile to the 'arch-delinquent', and the popular clamour for his execution so strong, that his death would be almost unavoidable – unless the Junto, in return for Charles's cooperation on other fronts, interposed to stop it. This, in turn, determined the vituperativeness of the prosecution's case and the very public nature of his prosecution. Since the Lord Lieutenant had to be blackguarded to the point where 'the public' opposed any possibility of mercy, his prosecution was planned from the outset as an exercise in the courting of 'popularity',[21] a quest for the moral outrage and political concurrence of the English political nation. To a degree hitherto unparalleled, the managers of the trial deliberately fostered (and did their best to satisfy) an appetite for news that made Strafford's crimes the talk of every market place and alehouse in the kingdom.[22]

For two main reasons, this was a bold and extremely high-risk strategy. As almost every charge against Strafford entailed an implicit condemnation of Charles's policies during the Personal Rule, the king was already the trial's unnamed, but obvious, co-defendant.[23] From the outset, Charles's honour was intimately involved in the outcome of the trial, and this imported a highly volatile element into the entire legal process. There was a danger that the king's instinctive response to the threat to his honour would be to reach for his sword – the accepted reaction of any gentleman of rank when slighted.[24]

The second major danger lay in the highly public nature of the trial itself, as staged in Westminster Hall. With the impeachment proceedings accessible to so large an audience, able to witness the legal arguments at first hand, the court-room duel between Strafford and his accusers inevitably took on a gladiatorial aspect; and, as with any such combat, there were unforeseeable risks and contingencies that rendered the outcome open to doubt. The Junto leaders seem to have taken a calculated risk: that the weaknesses in their legal argument would be more than counterbalanced by the popular hostility towards Strafford and his policies, once the true extent of his plans to introduce an authoritarian, 'absolutist' monarchy into England and Ireland had been revealed. By proving the earl's treasons against the 'commonwealth' not merely before the court, but also at the bar of public opinion, the Junto's lawyers aimed to create a momentum that swept aside what Downinge had termed the 'over-punctuall, pædantique, literall interpretations' of the law that might otherwise prove a bar to Strafford's conviction.[25]

Legal and evidential quibbles apart, this strategy had one grave and, at least at the outset, seemingly unnoticed flaw. In making the trial so public and theatrical an event, the Junto leadership was not only providing itself with a platform from which to denounce the villainies of the past; they were also affording Strafford (and, through him, the king) a stage on which they might yet turn the spotlight onto the Junto's own penchant for 'arbitrary courses': its readiness to play fast and loose with the law in order to secure a conviction; and the self-interested vindictiveness against the accused that was driving the prosecution. The Junto's choice of Westminster Hall as the trial's venue might yet redound against it. And in dressing as a penitent, in a suit of 'mo[u]rning',[26] for his first public appearance, Strafford struck his first blow against the Junto's characterization of him as 'Black Tom, tyrant'.

At eight o'clock on Monday 22 March, the members of the House of Lords, some seventy in all, filed into Westminster Hall, two by two, and the trial began.[27]

I. BODY POLITICS: THE STAGING OF THE TRIAL

For all its subsequent familiarity as a means by which errant ministers might be brought to account, impeachment in 1641 was a relatively novel and unfamiliar procedure. Although often used during the Middle Ages, it had fallen into desuetude in the mid fifteenth century, and not been revived until 1621, the best part of two centuries later. For precedents, lawyers were forced to go back to the days of the Wars of the Roses,[28] and ever since the revival of formal impeachments in the 1620s, aspects of its procedures had remained in a state of flux. But at least certain features had already become relatively fixed. Accusations were delivered in the name of the Commons, whose members provided the prosecution counsel, while the House of Lords – in this case, minus the bishops (who withdrew rather than involve themselves in a 'cause of blood') – acted as the sole arbiters of fact and law. The judges, who sat in the House as legal assistants,[29] could be called on for advice; but the accused's guilt or innocence was for the peers alone to decide.[30] The usual setting for impeachment trials had been the Lords itself, the far more intimate chamber at the southern end of the Palace of Westminster. This allowed space for a limited number of Commons-men, who bribed or pushed their way to a place, to watch the proceedings from beyond the bar of the House; but for few others.

The decision to transfer the impeachment trial to Westminster Hall, made after a series of conferences between the two Houses, therefore constituted a major break with recent precedent.[31] Strafford's impeachment continued to be technically a trial before the House of Lords, despite its physical relocation to Westminster Hall, which was converted into a duplicate 'House of Lords' for the occasion.

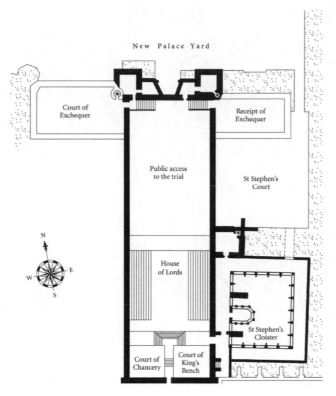

Westminster Hall at the time of the Earl of Strafford's impeachment, March–April 1641. The entire northern end of the Hall was opened as viewing space for the public, enabling thousands, during the course of the trial, to have first-hand access to the proceedings.

Part of the physical arrangements for this relocation exactly replicated those to be found in the peers' usual meeting place. Hence, for Strafford's trial, a long rectangular space was marked out at the Hall's southern end, on an axis with the line of the building, roughly the same size as the regular House of Lords. Within this space, a series of spatial hierarchies were clearly articulated. As usual, the 'state' – the king's throne, set on a dais, surmounted with a canopy and cloth of estate – stood at the far end: the physical representation of the 'king-in-Parliament' as the nation's sovereign power.[32] To either side, the earls and other senior ranks of the peerage sat in two long rows to the right and left, with the viscounts and barons seated on forms between them. For trials, all peers were required to wear their Parliament robes of crimson wool trimmed with ermine, and sat hatted as a sign of their status, while all others appeared bareheaded before them. Among them sat the judges, robed, but unhatted, in symbolic deference to the peers. Finally, recording the proceedings were the humble (and also hatless) clerks, obliged to take their notes from a kneeling position, in acknowledgement of the 'great ones' around them.[33]

The bar of the House, a rail running across the lower end opposite the throne, defined the threshold of the transposed Lords' chamber. Here, a small

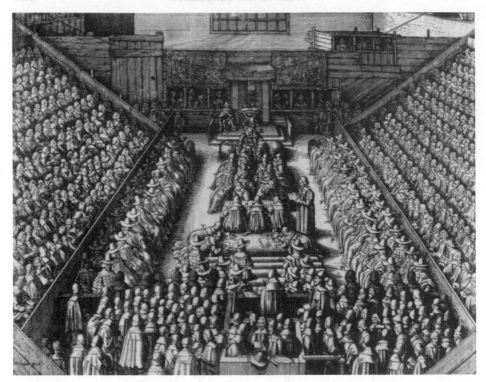

The king-less theatre of judgement: the setting was constructed under the supervision of Inigo Jones. Wenzel Hollar's contemporary engraving of Strafford's impeachment trial in Westminster Hall. King Charles was forbidden to use the throne throughout the trial, and forced to watch proceedings from one of the lattice-covered boxes immediately behind 'the state': the dais, chair, and canopy that together symbolized the king's 'other' body: his abstract, politic capacity as sovereign.

dock had been constructed, apparently panelled on all four sides – 'a little place like a pue', wrote one eyewitness[34] – where the accused was expected to stand throughout the proceedings, again, exactly replicating the arrangements that had prevailed at trials in the Lords' usual place of meeting.[35] All this occupied only a little more than half of Westminster Hall's gargantuan, hammer-beamed interior, some 240 feet in length and sixty-seven in breadth.[36]

Within the Hall, however, were a number of visually striking – and, politically, highly significant – departures from the practice that had prevailed in any previous impeachment trial. Between the bar (marking the threshold of the House of Lords) and the Hall's great door (at the northern end of the building) stretched an open space that could accommodate well over 1,000 people. For the first time in living memory, it was decided to make a state trial accessible to a relatively large section of the population, both native Londoners and many from out of town, drawn to the capital by the prospect of the impending show. Their presence ensured that what happened in the trial was relayed to an even larger national audience, in hundreds of private letters,[37] hastily copied manuscript news-sheets, and, later, in printed accounts.[38]

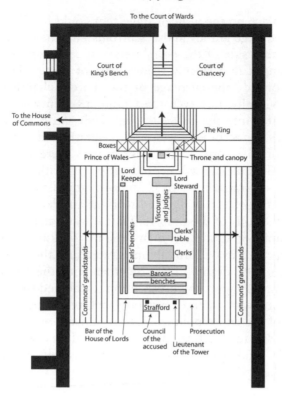

To the Court of Wards

Court of
King's Bench

Court of
Chancery

To the House
of Commons

The King

Boxes

Prince of Wales

Throne and canopy

Lord
Keeper

Lord
Steward

Viscounts
and judges

Earls' benches

Clerks'
table

Clerks

Barons'
benches

Commons' grandstands

Commons' grandstands

Strafford

Bar of the
House of Lords

Council
of the
accused

Prosecution

Lieutenant
of the Tower

Detail: The southern end of Westminster Hall during the trial of the Earl of Strafford, revealing how the seating arrangements of the House of Lords were replicated in the Westminster Hall, with the Commons flanking them in grandstands ('scaffolds') to either side.

This opening up of the *arcana imperii* – the 'hidden mysteries of power' – to so large an audience was unprecedented, perhaps the first exercise in broadcasting the proceedings of Parliament. Involving an audience of such massive size in parliamentary proceedings otherwise usually conducted out of the public gaze also had a powerful symbolic force – all the more so because, as became evident from the outset, much of the prosecution's case hinged on redefining the law of treason to encompass, not merely direct or indirect harms to the king, but also treasons committed against 'the common weal of the realm'.

This point was still further emphasized by the formal inclusion of the House of Commons – again, a complete novelty – as a visually prominent part of the tableau that greeted the 'audience' on entering Westminster Hall. The Commons' traditional role in impeachment trials had, in practice, been very limited. True, they drew up and approved the impeachment articles, and were responsible for presenting the evidence against the accused. But once the trial was under way, the only Commons-men formally 'in court' (actually before the House of Lords) were the small group of lawyers, deputed to act as prosecuting counsel, who addressed the peers – the judges in such trials – from the outward side of the bar.

The novel arrangements for the Strafford trial assigned the entire House of Commons a place on the judicial stage that could hardly have been more conspicuous. Two large grandstands ('scaffolds') for the Commons-men were juxtaposed to either side of the peers' benches, each capable of seating just under 300, arranged in a steeply rising series of tiers.[39] These grandstands technically lay outside the curtilage of the 'Lords' chamber' within Westminster Hall.[40] Visually, however, the Commons-men were otherwise completely incorporated into the *mise-en-scène*. They sat, bareheaded,[41] together as two blocs, with 'noe other [persons] ... intermixed with the members', on either side of the Lords.[42] The higher tiers were occupied by 'many hundreds more of gentlemen who could get places with them'.[43] Only a low wooden parapet separated the two Commons' grandstands from the formal House of Lords area that they flanked to right and left.[44]

Viewed from the body of Westminster Hall, it was a striking visual montage. These serried ranks of Commons-men (literally looking over the shoulders of the peers) appeared to be formally integrated into the 'judicial space' that was the setting of the drama. This, together with the Commons lawyers' procedural role in managing the prosecution, combined to create the impression that Strafford was on trial, not only before his peers, but before the representatives of the entire political nation. Indeed, one of the options that the House of Lords had investigated before the trial was 'Whether the Comons may be Judges';[45] and, while this possibility was rejected, in practice, the dispositions at the end of the Hall suggested a much more inclusive judicial body.

However, if the Lords were willing to accommodate the Commons within this scene of the Great Council arrayed in judgement, the trial managers were equally at pains to exclude the king. In a decision pregnant with symbolic meaning, Charles was formally debarred from appearing 'publicklie' at the trial: that is, forbidden from taking his seat on the throne which – complete with dais, canopy, and cloth of estate – nevertheless remained the focal point of the entire tableau.[46] This decision was reported to have been made by the Lords 'the night beefore the triall'. But as there had been no meeting of the House of Lords that evening (being a Sunday), these 'lords [who] did meete to consult' must have been an informal committee – most likely, the great officers responsible for the trial (Arundel, as Lord Steward of England, and Pembroke, as Lord Chamberlain of the Household), and some of the principal Junto peers.[47] The likeliest source of the prohibition, however, was Viscount Saye. In a move that seems to have been calculated to influence the conduct of the forthcoming proceedings, Saye chose on 18 March, only four days before the trial began, to protest against the king's presence in the Lords' chamber on 24 February, when Strafford had submitted his written rejoinders to the impeachment charges. Expounding a principle that had obvious relevance to the proceedings in Westminster Hall, Saye argued that the king's sovereign authority – the power of his abstract 'politic body' – was actually vested in the two Houses for so long as they remained in session. For the king to be present in his 'physical body', therefore violated this premise – a belief that led him to the extreme, if logical, corollary that the House of Lords 'was not a House while the King was there'.[48]

This highly subversive precept – that the king could not take his seat 'publicklie' in his own House of Lords – was rigorously enforced when the trial began four days later.[49] On arriving at Westminster Hall for the trial's opening session, Charles discovered that he had been reduced to watching the proceedings from one of the series of 'lattise'-covered boxes – like those in a seventeenth-century theatre – that had been erected near the throne, at the far end of the hall, rendering him almost invisible.[50] Indignant at this humiliation, the king's first action at the opening session on 22 March was to tear down his box's lattice screen so that he could be viewed.[51]

Yet his angry intervention only served to reinforce the symbolic point that the trial managers had intended to make by their insistence on an empty throne. All who visited Westminster Hall could see that Charles had been entirely marginalized from the business of the 'High Court of Parliament'. Officers of the court made their obeisances, not to the royal box where the king was actually present (*'incognito*, though conspicuous enough,' as Hyde put it),[52]* but instead to 'the state' with its manifestly vacant throne.[53]

The effect of this scene was not lost on contemporaries. Strafford, noted one observer, seemed to 'hold dispute against the whole Kingdome'.[54] Never before had the representatives of the whole kingdom, the entire body of Lords and Commons, together with the judges (probably somewhere between 500 and 600 persons on any day of the trial) been held up to public view in this visually striking way. Viewed en masse, individuals disappeared, merging in the serried ranks of heads and hats – as they do in Wenzel Hollar's engraving which records the astonishing scene.[55] Here was Leviathan: the state as the abstract composite of the many; a representative image of the 'commonwealth', in which the king has become a constitutional non-person, represented by an empty chair.[56]

Such symbols and gestures had a didactic power, adapting familiar visual tropes to delineate new political realities. It was a medieval commonplace, almost universally accepted in early Stuart England, that the king had 'two bodies': one sovereign: abstract and undying; the other human: physical and mortal.[57] However, the 'body language' of Strafford's trial articulated the division between these two capacities more sharply and demonstratively than had ever been done before – at least during the reign of an adult king. The vacant throne that the king was forbidden to occupy provided an allegory of England's post-Triennial Act constitution: power within the traditional sovereign trinity of 'king, Lords, and Commons' had been reapportioned in such a way as to marginalize the first person of the trinity from the real representatives and custodians of the 'commonwealth', the Lords and Commons.

Here, the 'Venetianization' of English government – the attrition of royal authority of which Charles repeatedly complained[58] – was represented as an accomplished fact. Moreover, in abstracting the king's sovereign authority

---

* Sir Simonds D'Ewes describes the royal box as a 'private gallerie, where he used to stay behinde the chaire of estate, on the right side of it'.

so completely from his physical person, the Junto was articulating a political principle that was perhaps working already as a powerful solvent of personal allegiance to the king. Symbols, of course, need to be read with caution. But it is not entirely fanciful to see, in the staging of Strafford's trial, the doctrine which, barely a year later, would make it intellectually possible for many of these same Parliament-men to make the otherwise nonsensical claim that they could be loyal to the king in his 'politic capacity', while simultaneously taking up arms against his person.

II. THE 'SOLEMN AND MAJESTIC TRIBUNAL'

If the trial's external arrangements strove hard to convey an image of Strafford arraigned before the totality of the realm, the actual conduct of proceedings was vested in a rather more select managerial band. No issue required more careful collaboration between peers and Commons-men than an impeachment – where the lower House prosecuted, and the upper judged. The distinctive feature of Strafford's impeachment trial – and the subsequent parliamentary bill of attainder against him – is that it was effectively controlled by a small bicameral group, the core of which was provided by the Conspirators of 1640: the men whom Strafford himself had intended to accuse of high treason had they not succeeded in pre-empting him back in November.[59] In the Lords, the principal figures involved in the attack on Strafford were the Earls of Warwick, Essex, and Bedford, Viscounts Saye and Mandeville, and Lords Paget and Brooke, with the equivocal support of the Earl of Bristol.[60] But Bedford also seems to have secured limited, if highly influential, support among the pre-November 1640 Privy Councillors. Two figures stand out: Arundel and Pembroke – not coincidentally, the same two 'old Councillors' who had accompanied him, a month earlier, to deliver the Triennial Bill to Whitehall. Both men were to have a major influence on the conduct of the trial: Arundel,[61] as the officer chosen by the Lords to preside over the court as Lord Steward of England, because he enjoyed extensive control of procedure;[62] and Pembroke, as Lord Chamberlain and the officer responsible for the Palace of Westminster, because he had overall responsibility for the trial's staging. And with Pembroke came two of his most influential lawyer protégés: John Glynne and Edward Hyde – both of them members of the Commons' committee charged with managing the proceedings.[63]

The majority of the Commons trial managers, however, came from the ranks of the Junto; indeed, the most prominent members of the prosecuting team were, almost without exception, the Commons-men most closely tied to Bedford, Pembroke, Warwick, and Saye – with Pym, Glynne, and John Maynard managing the English side of the prosecution,[64] while the Irish dimension was handled by Clotworthy[65] and Sir Walter Erle.[66] The tensions within the Junto between the Bedfordians and the 'Warwick House interest' had not gone away – and, as we shall see, were to resurface spectacularly at a critical moment in the trial. For the moment, however, they were subordinated to the common objective of using the trial as a means of exerting leverage against the king. Strafford's claim that his impeachment 'is followed by Faction and Correspondence [the coordination of like-minded groups]' and that there was 'a strong Conspiracy against me' was little less than the truth.[67]

Although this was a potentially powerful team, the central point of vulnerability in the case they were trying to establish remained its dependence on the novel assertion that treasons could be committed against the 'commonwealth', as well as the person of the king. The essence of the case against Strafford, contained in the first of the twenty-eight detailed impeachment articles, was therefore that he had attempted to subvert the known laws and endeavoured to set up an 'arbitrary government', in England as well as Ireland.[68]

Central to the prosecution's case was the contentious claim, clearly articulated in Article 3 of the impeachment charges, that the 'Realm of Ireland having been, time out of mind, annexed to the Imperial Crown of this His Majesties Realm of England', it was therefore 'governed by the same Laws'.[69] This had two major implications. First, it meant that the English Parliament's jurisdiction extended as much over Ireland as it did over any part of England – an assertion that was met with growing alarm by the Catholic members of the Irish Parliament, present in London to give evidence against Strafford before and during the trial.[70] And second, it meant that Strafford's attitudes towards the law while viceroy in Ireland could be used as evidence of his disregard for the laws of England. The Lord Lieutenant's high-handed policies in Ireland, the prosecution implied, had merely been a dry run for the tyrannical courses he would have unleashed on England – had not the present Parliament providentially intervened.

Nevertheless, substantiating these claims – and, still more, making them fit within the existing law of treason – remained highly problematical. The most sensational, and potentially damning, charge against Strafford remained the accusation that he had counselled the king to use the Irish army in the summer of 1640 to suppress internal dissent in England. However, none of the charges against him constituted a knockout blow. The prosecution was therefore forced to rely on the contention that they *cumulatively* substantiated the defendant's treason:[71] his intention to create a regal despotism in all three Stuart kingdoms. Hence the bewilderingly lengthy list of Strafford's 'oppressions' that made up most of the twenty-eight articles against him. These ranged from Strafford's embezzlement of the king's Irish revenues, to his deployment of soldiers to enforce the rulings of the Irish Privy Council – a charge that the Commons insisted amounted to 'levying war' against the kingdom, and therefore against the king, thus bringing Strafford's action within the Treason Statute of 1352. But the very multiplicity of the charges revealed the prosecution's central problem: the lack of a single heinous act – other than the charge relating to the Irish army (which was itself bedevilled by evidential problems) – that would secure the Lord Lieutenant's guilt.

*

Strafford was not slow to notice these chinks in his opponents' legal armour. Confronted, on the trial's first day, by the intimidating – and now king-less – majesty of the court, Strafford initially appeared cowed and overwhelmed by the ordeal before him. He looked 'gas[t]lie and grim', observed Maurice Wynn, '[and] much dejected'. Yet, as the impeachment articles were read out, and Strafford realized how little the prosecution case had advanced beyond what he had already answered at the preliminary hearing on 24 February, his spirits rose. 'Hee was seen after to smile', and when the first day of the trial concluded at 2 p.m., 'went away cherefull'.[72]

This outward confidence and good humour, a façade seemingly maintained with immense emotional and physical effort, had defined Strafford's public performances from the moment the treason accusations had first been made.[73] Although granted the favour of legal counsel to assist with the preparation of his case, a privilege usually denied to those accused of treason,[74] Strafford's command of law and factual detail was nevertheless formidable. Ignoring his physical infirmities (he had been suffering acutely from the stone since the previous spring),[75] he brought the full force of his intelligence and his devastating powers of sarcasm to bear against his accusers. He mastered his brief and had a command of detail and a quickness of repartee that repeatedly confounded his slower-witted opponents. To cite but two examples; his retort to the charge that using soldiers to enforce decisions of the Irish Council amounted to 'levying war against the king' (a long-established treason) is characteristic of his style: 'These be wonderful wars if we have no more wars than such as three or four men are able to raise. By the grace of God, we shall not sleep very unquietly.'[76]

Similarly, Strafford relentlessly mocked the Junto's tendentious attempts to construct an 'accumulative' treason charge out of individual instances,[77] none of which would amount to treason on its own: 'When a thousand misdemeanours will not make one felony, shall twenty-eight misdemeanours [the number of impeachment articles against him] heighten it to a treason?'[78]

In a culture that admired 'finenesse of wit'[79] and verbal dexterity, the bravura of Strafford's responses and his politely confident deportment in the dock won him many admirers.[80] English Lord Lieutenants of Ireland had a tradition of brusque treatment of the Irish that went back to the days of Elizabeth; and at least some of the audience in Westminster Hall were frankly unconvinced by the prosecution's claim that Strafford's high-handedness against the Irish was evidence of a broader conspiracy eventually to apply the same tactics in England. Maurice Wynn's reaction after listening to the trial's first week was probably not atypical. He had heard and reported to his brother the prosecution's claim that at the York assizes in August 1633, Strafford had claimed that 'the king's litle finger should bee hevier to the subject then the lawes of the land'.[81] But that did not stop Wynn forming an overwhelmingly positive impression of the Lord Lieutenant. 'If Stradford [sic] be condemned,' he wrote to his brother, Owen, 'I beeleeve the king will loose the ablest Subject of his 3 kingdoms, ... and if the best cownsellor in this kingdom were but to act his part, hee would fall far short of him.'[82]

Others not necessarily well-disposed towards Strafford reached similar conclusions. Sir John Temple slipped naturally (and revealingly) into the same theatrical metaphors to describe Strafford's performance during the trial's opening week: 'his Lordship ... continewes still to act his part gallantly and to say as much as is possible for any man living in defence of his cause. All sides give his Lordship greate testimony of his greate abilities'.[83] These were not the reviews of 'Black Tom Tyrant' that Bedford and Pym had been expecting, particularly from a commentator, like Temple, otherwise broadly sympathetic to the Junto's case.

By the end of the trial's second week, it was already apparent that Strafford was not only stealing the limelight; there was a real danger that he would steal the show.[84]* Such was Strafford's effectiveness in parrying the individual charges that after two weeks of witnesses and legal argument, the Junto's line of attack was appearing dangerously exposed. The sheer ineptitude of many of the prosecution witnesses did not help. None was more disastrous than Sir Thomas Leyton, an inveterate enemy of Strafford's in his native Yorkshire,[85] who was called to testify that the notorious remark attributed to the accused – that the 'little finger of the king is heavier than ... the law' – had been made in his hearing during the York assizes of 1633. When questioned in court, however, the prosecution witness turned out to be almost totally deaf. Such was his 'infirmity in hearing', Strafford mercilessly pointed out to the court, 'that he must now be whoopt to at the Barr [of the House], before he can hear'.[86]

Taken in isolation, these moments were of little account. Cumulatively, however, and in combination with Strafford's self-conscious humility of dress, 'graceful' deportment, and general good temper, they began to have a powerful effect.[87] The dehumanized, demonic image of Strafford that had been built up so carefully by Pym, Clotworthy and others over the previous four months of pre-trial debate suddenly seemed to dissolve when set beside the reality of the self-evidently reasonable figure – 'his behaviour exceeding graceful, and his speech full of weight, reason, and pleasingness' – on public view in Westminster Hall.[88] As the Venetian ambassador put it, Strafford was 'endeavouring by his subtle arguments to change the universal hatred against him into sympathy'.[89] And, in this, he was aided by the histrionic and hectoring tone of his prosecutors; 'they so banked and worried his lordship', observed one eyewitness, 'as it begets pity in many of the auditors'.[90]

III. FROM SOLEMNITY TO FARCE

By Friday, 2 April, the end of the trial's second week, it was glaringly apparent to the Junto leadership that the proceedings thus far were failing as an

---

* Behind the scenes, the king was also doing what he could to placate Strafford's most intemperate critics; on 30 March, just as the trial was entering its second week, Charles, in a timely act of generosity, presented Lord Brooke – like Essex and Warwick, an advocate of a capital sentence against the earl – with the gift of a horse. But its recipient was unmoved.

exercise in public persuasion.[91] More worryingly still, they were also failing completely in their primary political purpose: as a means of exerting pressure on the king. An entire chain of events depended on the trial forcing Charles to disband the Irish army, and to dismiss Strafford as its commander-in-chief. Until this were done, the Junto could not risk the sending home of the Scottish army. And until the Scottish army left England, there could be no question of a unilateral disbandment of the English forces still in the field. This, in turn, posed the Junto with a serious financial dilemma. So long as both these armies (English and Scottish) remained on foot, the English Parliament – and the English taxpayer – continued to be liable for the crippling cost of their ongoing pay.

Yet Charles had little incentive to part with either the Lord Lieutenant or his Irish army, so long as the trial was going Strafford's way. Under these circumstances, even if the Lords did find Strafford culpable of treason, there looked likely to be sufficient doubt as to his guilt to create the leeway in which the king could realistically consider the issuing of a royal pardon. On Friday, 2 April, Giustinian reported a hope, 'which seems to be growing', that Strafford 'will be saved'.[92] The prospect of the Lord Lieutenant's political rehabilitation loomed.

*

As the Junto leadership contemplated the opening of the trial's third week, from Monday, 5 April, they desperately needed a new line of attack, one capable, not merely of scoring points against the accused, but of wounding him beyond hope of recovery. To do so, they shifted the pro-secution's focus from Strafford's misdeeds as Lord Lieutenant of Ireland (the 'cumulative' case for treason) to what, from the beginning of the impeachment process, had always been the most damning charge of all: the claim that Strafford had counselled the king to use an Irish army to suppress dissent in England.

Maynard and Glynne, who had carried the prosecution case during most of the first two weeks, now gave way to two new prosecutors: the Middle Temple barrister, Bulstrode Whitelocke, who had acted as counsel to Hampden (his 'countryman and kinsman') in the great Ship Money case of 1637;[93] and the Commons' self-appointed expert on the Irish army, Sir Walter Erle, a gruff ex-soldier in his mid-fifties and 'a close ally of Lord Saye'.[94]

Both Whitelocke and Erle had familial as well ideological reasons for ensuring that Strafford was never able to exact what St John termed 'pun-ishment upon his impeachers': those involved in the 'great treason' of 1640.[95] Whitelocke led, focusing on Strafford's advice to the king at the time of the dissolution of the Short Parliament in May 1640. Not only had Strafford been the instigator of the 1640 war with Scotland, claimed Whitelocke, he had also raised the new Irish Catholic army with the deliberate intention of using this 'for the ruin and destruction of the kingdom of England ... and [the] altering and subverting [of its] fundamental laws and established government'.[96] This was the crux of the Junto's broader case against Strafford. Not only was he a figure who *had* constituted a danger in the past, he was also a *current* danger. So long as the Irish army continued to exist and Strafford remained in post as its commander, then 'ruin and destruction' continued to threaten England, and only the disbandment of the one and the dismissal of the other would avert the threat. If the Junto could substantiate the charge that Strafford had counselled the king that he was 'loosed and absolved from law' and that he intended to deploy the Irish army in England, then a guilty verdict against Strafford looked assured.

To sustain it, Whitelocke produced the one witness they had who was prepared to testify that he had heard Strafford utter the incriminating words: Sir Henry Vane senior, one of the Privy Councillors actually present at the meeting of the Committee of War on 5 May 1640. Confronted with the vast throng in Westminster Hall, however, Vane's recollections of that event proved defective. Perhaps mindful of how the king (who was present) would regard any betrayer of Strafford, Vane initially fought shy of denouncing the accused.[97] Only when questioned a third time did he 'recall' Strafford's supposedly incriminating words:

> My Earl of Strafford did say in a discourse [at the meeting of Privy Councillors], 'Your Majesty, ... you have an army in Ireland, which you may employ here to reduce this Kingdom', or some such words to this effect.[98]

The ambiguity in Vane's report of Strafford's words – whether '*this* Kingdom' referred to England (as the prosecution insisted) or to Scotland (as Strafford maintained) – was immediately seized on by two members of the court, the Earl of Clare and Lord Savile, and turned to Strafford's advantage. When followed up, later that day, with a contribution from another Junto moderate, the Earl of Bristol – who found his own memory of his conversations with Strafford suddenly unreliable and reminded the Lords that, in any case, the testimony of a single witness could not work 'to the prejudice of a Man, charged with High Treason'[99] – something close to a pattern begins to emerge in these contributions. Given that Savile and Bristol (certainly) and Clare (possibly)[100] were now allied with the Bedfordian wing of the Junto, this looks strongly like an attempt to blunt what had hitherto seemed the sharpest weapon in the prosecution's arsenal:[101] they all cast doubt on the charge with which, from the outset, the prosecution seems to have hoped to deliver the *coup de grâce*.[102] Vane's equivocating response to the questions of Clare and Savile – 'far be it from him ... to Interpret them'[103] – weakened still further his credibility as a witness, a credibility already severely strained because his testimony was directly confuted by a written submission from Northumberland who had been present at the same meeting.[104] Moreover, to sustain a charge of treason (as Bristol had reminded them), two witnesses were needed as to the fact; in this case, the prosecution only had one – and a shifty and unpersuasive one at that.[105] This session of Monday, 5 April ought to have been the turning point of the trial. Instead, the combination of Vane's vacillating testimony and Whitelocke's repeated trouncings in his exchanges with the accused produced a growing belief at Westminster that the prosecution evidence was simply not strong enough to sustain the treason charge. Once again, Strafford appeared to have worsted his opponents.

By Wednesday, 7 April, halfway through the trial's third week, the prosecution case against Strafford was obviously faltering. Yet too much was at
stake to allow Strafford to escape conviction on Article 23, the charge that
he had intended to use the Irish army against England, the most important –
but, as yet, the most ill-proven – of all the impeachment articles. In what
seems to have been a panic move after the inconclusive session of Wednesday,
7 April, Whitelocke was replaced as the prosecution's 'leader' by Erle. Given
Erle's almost total absence of legal training,[106] this was a risky choice. But any
doubts as to his forensic skills were probably outweighed by his experience as
a speaker in the Commons and his almost monomaniacal concern with the
Irish threat.[107] For the Junto grandees, it was a chance worth taking.

*

On Thursday, 8 April, before an audience of well over 1,000, Erle rose to
offer what he regarded as irrefutable evidence that Strafford's Irish army had
indeed been intended for use in a major military offensive in England. He
had made what he claimed was a damning discovery. Strafford's formal
commission as Lord General in 1640, passed under the Great Seal, included
an explicit clause empowering him to suppress revolts in England. Such a
clause, he contended, would have been entirely superfluous if – as Strafford
asserted – the Irish army had actually been intended for use against the
Scottish Covenanters, not against Charles's opponents in England. The revelation stunned his audience in Westminster. This, surely, had delivered the
Junto's *coup de grâce* against Strafford, and Erle briefly savoured his moment
of triumph.

But Strafford parried the blow – and to crushing effect. The supposedly
incriminating clause in his commission, Strafford retorted, was nothing more
than a standard formula in most generals' commissions of appointment. In
fact, he went on, it had been copied directly from the commission granted
to the blameless Earl of Northumberland, the Junto's favourite in the Privy
Council and a figure beyond reproach, when he had been appointed Lord
General in February 1640.[108] Strafford's retort was annihilating. The prosecution's most substantial piece of evidence had dissolved in its hands. Erle
had no idea how to respond. Humiliated before both Houses of Parliament
and the still larger audience in the body of the hall, Erle stood tongue-tied,
lost for words.

In an attempt at damage limitation, Pym tried to break the embarrassing
silence and came to his colleague's rescue. Erle, Pym suggested, had been
simply acting 'uppon a mistake'. But this statement of the obvious merely
triggered an explosion of derisive guffaws from the Hall. Further legal argument was only able to resume after 'the Lords had done laughing, and the
Company [in the Hall had] left off their jeering att the Knight [Sir Walter
Erle]'.[109] Ridicule had always been the most lethal rhetorical weapon of the
seventeenth-century courtier, and Strafford was able to inflict it with a duel-
list's deadly skill.[110] What was so damaging to Strafford's opponents was
that these outbreaks of merriment were further destroying the atmosphere

of menace and urgency – the belief that a wholesale subversion of England's laws had been averted only just in time – that the prosecution needed to sustain if its case were to succeed. With every ripple of laughter, the charges against Strafford were looking ever more overblown and absurd.

After Pym's counter-productive intervention, John Glynne again took over the task of prosecution. In a desperate bid to silence Strafford, Glynne moved that if Strafford had anything more to say, 'hee should now speake'; after which he would be heard no more. The prosecution would then spend the remaining days of the trial summing up 'the whole charge together' – the entire case against Strafford – and 'did expect [that the prosecution would] have the last worde'.[111] The manoeuvre was clearly intended to wrong-foot Strafford, forcing him to make his concluding speech on the spot, without either notes or time for preparation. But the manifest unfairness of this gambit affronted the Lords, and they granted Strafford's request – over bleatings from Maynard and Glynne that it was 'against all former precedents' – to have leave to defer his reply to the morrow so as to prepare his case.[112]

The following day, Friday, 9 April, there were no hearings in Westminster Hall – notionally in consideration of Strafford's 'indisposition' – and the Junto took advantage of what must have been a welcome respite to reconsider its tactics. Their key objective was now to minimize Strafford's opportunities for speaking by bringing the trial to a 'peremptory end'. The Lord Lieutenant was to be allowed only one further opportunity to refute the charges against him; after that, the trial would be concluded with a lengthy summation by the prosecution, to which Strafford would have no right of reply. Two prominent Bedfordians, Lord Russell and John Pym, set the arrangements in train in the Commons, persuading their colleagues to endorse a request to the Lords that, from tomorrow (Saturday), they would bring the trial to a close. Strafford was to be given a chance to reply to the evidence presented thus far, but, after that, was to have no opportunity to introduce anything new relating to matters of fact. All that would then remain would be for the Commons prosecutors to give their final 'replication' – their last rebuttal and summing up – and the Lords could forthwith proceed to judgement: to all of which the peers acquiesced.[113]

*

If Bedford and the Junto leaders needed any reminder of how the prosecution's failures in the trial were affecting their standing in Parliament, it was provided during that same Friday recess. An ill-tempered debate had raged in the Commons throughout the day, concluding only at '7 at night', on whether or not the current truce with the Scots (which expired on 16 April) should be extended. Renewing the 'cessation of arms' would have the effect of authorizing the Scots' continued presence in England, and renewing the English Parliament's liability for its upkeep. And while a familiar cast of Clotworthy, Holles, and Pym pressed the case for the truce's continuance, this time there was a powerful body of opinion in the Commons that voiced its resentment at the ongoing financial burden which the Scots' presence entailed. Opponents of the truce argued that it would be 'dishonourable' that such a proposal should receive parliamentary sanction.[114] Anti-Scottish or anti-Junto sentiment (the two were closely related) was reaching what, for Pym and his allies in the Commons, were alarming proportions. Indeed, by the time the question of the renewal of the truce was pressed to a division, the Junto interest could only manage a majority of thirty-nine votes in a House of almost 300.[115] Holles and another member of Warwick's extensive 'family', Sir Edward Hungerford (who was married to his stepdaughter),[116] counted the votes in favour of the renewal of the cessation, while two future Royalists opposed.

This registered a sea change in the Commons' attitude towards the Scots and their political allies. In theory, if the cessation had not been renewed, the current treaty would have been suspended and English and Scottish forces would have returned to a state of war in the North of England.[117] While the Junto's majority of thirty-nine had averted that dire contingency, the fact that so large a proportion of the Commons was prepared even to allow such a possibility points up how precarious the Junto's control of the lower House had become. Commons-men were suggesting openly that the Scots should be 'declared enemies' if they dared to come south of the Tyne, the river which marked the boundary between the counties of Northumberland and Durham.[118] Here was a groundswell of anti-Scottish resentment from which the king might one day be able to create a party. Yet the Junto was in no position to hasten the treaty to its conclusion in order to pacify this anti-Scottish caucus. Lord Loudoun and the other Scottish Commissioners would not hear of completing the treaty and withdrawing their army until the Strafford trial was concluded. Even those who were favourably disposed towards the Junto were acutely aware that the cost of 'sojourning the Scots'[119] in the meantime was producing a steady attrition of their support.

By the end of that week, the management of the trial was in crisis. A majority of the Lords was reportedly unpersuaded by the arguments presented as to Strafford's guilt on the charge of treason.[120] Yet unless there were a speedy and successful conclusion to the trial, the Junto's own position might rapidly become irrecoverable. The crux of their accusation remained Article 23 – that Strafford had proposed the use of the Irish army in England – and unless that were proven, their treason case against Strafford, whatever else he might be convicted of, was as good as lost. This dilemma seems to have forced the Bedfordians to a reluctant change of tack.

There was one expedient, however, that might retrieve the prosecution. Sir Henry Vane senior may have been an unimpressive witness under cross-examination. But the trial managers still had one sure-fire remedy for the vagaries of the Secretary's imperfect powers of recall. As early as September 1640,[121] Pym (and, shortly thereafter, Bedford as well) knew that Vane had kept verbatim notes of the Privy Councillors' discussions on 5 May that year – the fateful meeting at which Strafford was supposed to have counselled the use of the Irish army. And these, they believed, established Strafford's guilt beyond reasonable doubt.[122] Yet, while Bedford and Pym had obtained a copy of this vital evidence, months before the trial, they were clearly reluctant to allow its use in open court. Quite why they were so diffident remains unclear. But one possible explanation is that the notes also incriminated other members of the Privy Council (Cottington was one) whom Bedford, for tactical reasons of his own, was trying to protect.[123] Another is the adverse consequences that publication of the notes would have for Vane (a Bedfordian ally) in his already strained relations with the king – even if Vane denied being the source of the 'leak'.[124]* Whatever the reasons, however, this was a document that Bedford and Pym were deeply reluctant to place in the public domain. Only now, with the trial teetering on the brink of collapse, and anti-Scottish sentiment reaching danger levels in the Commons, did they take the decision to present it in open court when the trial resumed on the morrow.[125]

That morning, Saturday, 10 April, the court reassembled in Westminster Hall at 8 a.m. – the scarlet-robed peers filling the benches of the House of Lords, the dark-suited Commons-men occupying the grandstands to either side – awaiting a resumption of the prosecution case on Article 23. Once again, there was a change of leading counsel. After Erle's humiliation on Thursday, the task of substantiating the charges relating to the use of the Irish army in England was returned to the far more experienced hands of John Glynne.[126] Glynne's continuing willingness to serve at this sensitive point in the trial sent its own powerful message to the peers, intimating that the Lord Chamberlain, still a powerful figure at Whitehall, remained firmly committed to Strafford's prosecution.[127]

At first, the disclosure of the new evidence proceeded according to plan. To the surprise of many in the Hall, Glynne announced that he had new testimony to offer, hitherto undisclosed to the court and on which he intended to summon new witnesses. Despite the advanced stage of the trial, he sought the court's leave to present it.

Once again, Strafford parried the prosecution's last-minute attempt to introduce new evidence with a counter-proposal of his own. Perhaps sensing a shift of opinion in his favour, he responded to Glynne's intervention by claiming that if the prosecution were to present new evidence as to fact, then he, too, 'deseered the like favour', and hoped to present further argument on four of the impeachment articles.[128]

This confronted Arundel, the court's Lord Steward, with an almost impossible choice. Equity demanded that both parties be heard as to fact. On the other hand, it was obvious that any positive response to Strafford's request would potentially drag out the trial for days, possibly weeks, to come and constitute a breach of the Lords' prior commitment to the Commons that Strafford should not be given any further opportunity 'for saying any more to the matter of fact'.[129] Arundel had no alternative but to order an adjourn-

---

* Vane senior's oral testimony before the court on 5 April had already done him much damage in his relations with his master, even without the revelation of the existence of these notes. Sir John Temple wrote on 8 April 1641 that 'certainly it hath much lessned him in the King's and Queene's good opinion'.

ment for the Lords to withdraw and debate in camera how best to proceed.

When the peers returned to their places after a lengthy delay, Arundel announced that the Lords had ruled in Strafford's favour, prompting immediate protests from the representatives of the Commons, and a request that the order might be reconsidered.[130] Once again the Lords retired to their own chamber, accompanied by the judges, returning after half an hour with their definitive ruling on how the trial would proceed. Arundel delivered their decision. Ignoring their undertaking to the Commons made only the previous day, the peers upheld an earlier order of the court that, if new material were presented by the prosecution, the prisoner should have the 'like libertie'.[131] In consequence, Strafford, too, was at liberty to introduce more 'matter of fact', once Glynne had made his submission.[132]

But the significance of the ruling went far beyond its implication that the trial would now extend into a fourth week. To many in the Commons this ruling appears to have revealed the existence of a pro-Straffordian majority among the Lords; for if a majority in Strafford's favour existed on this vital procedural question, the prospect of Strafford's acquittal had suddenly become far more than a distant possibility.

The ruling provoked outrage. The stately tableau of 'the Lords and Commons assembled in judgement' dissolved into pandemonium. Convinced that the pro-Straffordians in the Lords were deliberately stringing out proceedings, some of the Commons-men, high up in the grandstands, started heckling their scarlet-robed colleagues below. Maurice Wynn, who was watching in the Hall, described the extraordinary scene that followed.

> Heering this answere [from the Lords], [the Commons] were soe verie outragious – the king and queene beeing within the view – they all cried allowed [to their counsel, who were appearing before the Lords] 'withdraw, withdraw[!]'.[133] Upon that, they [the Commons] rose in a tumult and with greate discontent.[134]

One observer noted that it was the 'precise part', apparently his term for the Junto-supporters in the Commons, that was responsible for the calls for the Lords to withdraw.[135] In the mayhem, some of those in the body of Westminster Hall misheard the cries of 'Withdraw!' and believed that the Commons were shouting 'Draw, draw!' Seventeenth-century gentlemen wore weapons in public as a matter of course, and this cry, noted Wynn, 'made many prepare their swords, in redynes to draw, thinking that they should all fall by the ears'.[136] Sword hilts were grasped in expectation of an imminent mêlée.

Confronted with impending chaos in Westminster Hall, the Earl of Southampton – a moderate reformist and cousin of the Earl of Essex – called on the peers to adjourn to their own chamber.[137] He was quickly joined by others.[138] Over the rising tumult, Arundel pronounced the order for the Lords to adjourn. Glynne's moment to present his startling new evidence had passed. Vane's notes went undisclosed. And as the peers departed the Hall unceremoniously, the Commons-men 'rose in great confusion'.[139] Both

Houses, reported one eyewitness, 'went in little better then a tumultuarie manner from the Hall'.[140]

Amid scenes of near-bedlam, the court broke up without any order for its resumption.[141] The stately theatre of judgement had degenerated into farce. Strafford beamed, so delighted at the outcome 'that he could not hide his joy'.[142] And in his box behind the throne, but still clearly 'within the view',[143] the king was seen to be laughing.[144]

9

STRAFFORD: HUBRIS

APRIL 1641

> For Majesty in an eclipse, like the Sunne, drawes eyes that would not so
> much have looked towards it, if it had shined out and appeared like it
> selfe.
>
> Sir John Suckling [writing in the spring of 1641][1]

Strafford had '[held] dispute against the whole Kingdome', and to many, it
seemed, he had got the better of the argument.[2] The collapse of the prosecution
on Saturday, 10 April 1641 was the culmination of a series of procedural
tussles with the earl over the previous three weeks, which had left his accusers
dazed and reeling. Time and again, the miscalculated theatricality of the
trial's setting had played to Strafford's advantage. The public censure of 'evil
counsel', the integrated *mise-en-scène* of Lords and Commons, the continuously empty throne: all these seem to have been intended by the Junto to
inaugurate a new, post-Triennial Act political order – to mark the 'beginning
of the People's Happiness'[3] – in a solemn, extremely public, renunciation of
the years of Personal Rule. Strafford was being made to stand as proxy for
the entire attempt to establish an authoritarian monarchy, founded on the
'subversion of the law', during the last decade. Instead, this stately tableau
had dissolved into confusion. What had been planned to affirm the nation's
unity, the 'whole Kingdome'[4] united against the architect of an attempted
despotism, had ended in an undignified parade of faction and division. Having
staked so much on the trial's success, the chaos in Westminster Hall on 10
April was, for the Junto, little short of catastrophic.

The key problem lay in the likely consequences of the prosecution's collapse.
After the débâcle in Westminster Hall, there was now little likelihood that
Strafford would be convicted of high treason. True, he might yet be found guilty
of lesser offences – 'misdemeanours' at most – and debarred by the Lords from
office. But, after a prosecution that had seemed both hectoring and incompetent,
even this much was uncertain; and a half-hearted condemnation by the Lords
would almost certainly leave the king at liberty to pardon his former servant,
and reinstate him to his offices as soon as the current Parliament was dissolved.[5]

For the advocates of reform, developments in the world beyond Westminster rendered the trial's derailment all the more dangerous. Their enemies, who had been on the defensive since the autumn, now seemed to be growing in number and confidence. Part of the problem was military. Strafford's Irish army remained a source of anxiety. More worrying still, however, were the English forces in the North, in which anti-parliamentarian restiveness was reportedly growing by the day. The other side of the problem was political. The Commons' growing reluctance to pay for the Covenanter army in England threatened to destroy the Junto's key line of defence. If, as seemed possible, this resentment grew to the point where the Commons declined *any* further payments to the Scots, the Junto looked likely to be deprived of the very forces they had been counting on to act as a counterweight – should hostilities be renewed – against any attempt by the king's English and Irish armies to reimpose his 'Personal Rule' by force.

That breach with the Scots looked perilously close. As the controversy of 9 April over the renewal of the ceasefire with the Covenanters had revealed, the faltering state of Strafford's prosecution had emboldened a pro-king, anti-Junto party in the Commons to make a stand against providing the Scots' forces with further pay.[6] If the size of recent Commons' votes was anything to go on, this anti-Scottish caucus needed only a few dozen more votes in order to block the renewal of the current ceasefire. This marked a significant shift in the allegiances of the House. For the first time since the Parliament's opening, it looked as though a substantial part of the Commons was coming round to the king's position, announced so controversially at the Parliament's opening: that the presence of a Covenanter army of occupation in England was a 'dishonour' to the nation, and that the war against the Scots should be renewed.

For the reformists, what loomed was the stuff of nightmares: the likelihood of a diplomatic rupture between the English Parliament and the Scots; a king with armies at his disposal in both England and Ireland; and with Strafford's acquittal on charges of treason now in prospect, the likelihood that the Lord Lieutenant of Ireland would soon be free to command them. And if that crisis were still in the future, there was a more immediate conundrum facing Bedford and Pym as a result of the trial's collapse. Unanimity within the Junto coalition had only been maintained hitherto on the basis that the impeachment trial would result in Strafford's conviction. With that outcome in doubt, Warwick and his friends were losing patience with Bedford's courtly ways. A challenge to the very idea of continuing the trial now appeared imminent – and, with it, a threat to subvert the entire edifice of Bedford's projected settlement with the king.

I. IMPEACHMENT OR ATTAINDER?

Even before the fiasco of that Saturday morning, 10 April, there had been murmurs of discontent within the reformist bloc. The inept management of the trial was one focus of concern; but there was a broader anxiety about whether the trial was capable of effecting its strategic objective: to render Strafford 'harmless to the commonwealth' for the future. This was a proposal to abandon the trial completely and to adopt a simpler, but far more con- troversial, expedient: to use an act of Parliament – an act of attainder – simply to legislate that Strafford was guilty of treason, and was to be punished with death. Such a possibility had first surfaced in the Commons on 19 November 1640, when Oliver St John had requested access to the records relating to acts of attainder kept under lock and key in the Court of King's Bench. Despite opposition from the then Solicitor-General, Sir Edward Herbert, and possibly also from Pym,[7] a committee had been established, headed by St John, empowered to search these records 'as they shall think fit';[8] but nothing further seems to have been done. It is tempting to discern St John's hand in a similar proposal, a month later, from the Scottish Treaty Commissioners to their English opposite numbers, that the Parliament should simply 'declare [the Incendiaries'] censure', rather than going through the complex procedures of a trial; but this had been dismissed by the English Commissioners as unworkable, not least because it met with the implacable hostility of the king.[9] Nevertheless, the possibility of using an attainder bill against Strafford resurfaced on 26 February 1641, forty-eight hours after the Lord Lieutenant had impressed enough of the Lords with his rejoinder to the impeachment charges (delivered on the 24th) for it to be doubtful whether the prosecution case was strong enough to secure a conviction on a charge of treason. Here, too, the proposer was a prominent Bedfordian, Lord Digby, who feared these weaknesses were so extensive that 'hee did thinke wee could nott attaine unto our purpose by any other way then by Bill [of attainder]'.[10]

On 26 February, Digby's attainder proposal had failed to find a seconder.[11] Six weeks later, however, with the trial so evidently faltering, there was a minority in both Houses willing to see the attainder option reconsidered. After the day of high comedy in Westminster Hall on Thursday, 8 April, when Erle's 'proofs' of Strafford's planned Irish invasion had dissolved into farce, some Commons-men had again begun to speak privately 'of not pre- ssing the Lordes to passe sentence [in Westminster Hall], but to draw up a bill to attaint his Lordship [Strafford] of treason'.[12] After the further débâcle on Saturday the 10th, it seemed unlikely that the attainder option would be much longer confined to whispers.

For the Bedfordians, such talk was fraught with dangers – but not without potential opportunities as well. An act of attainder usually stipulated in the body of the bill that the traitor should suffer death, a penalty that the king could neither alter nor mitigate in giving his royal assent. This did not, as has sometimes been stated, 'deprive the king of the power of commuting Strafford's sentence'[13] – because, as Charles would have known from the research on attainders he had commissioned from Sir John Borough,[14] the king still had a prerogative power to delay the execution indefinitely and to have the attainder reversed in another Parliament. Only *force majeure* – some external, extra-legal pressure – could prevent him.[15]

The problem with the attainder bill, so far as the king was concerned, was twofold. First, it required him to become involved personally in the business of Strafford's condemnation to death – as the Covenanter, Robert Baillie, put it, it forced him 'either to be our agent ... or else doe the world knows not what'.[16] That was something which, for reasons of conscience, the king emphatically refused to do.[17] And second, given his inflexibility on this point, an attainder opened up the prospect, were the bill ever passed, of an all-out confrontation between his own authority and that of the Parliament – one which, in the current political environment, he seemed almost certain to lose, and with fatal consequences for Strafford.

But by taking away the king's 'charitie',[18] his power to pardon, the attainder bill also posed a major problem for the Bedfordians. Unless the Bedfordians could deliver the king a settlement that kept his hand free to save Strafford's life – which meant continuing to proceed against him by impeachment, or amending the attainder bill to substitute some other punishment than death – all deals in relation to the reformation of the king's counsels (and their own advancement to office) were off.

On the other hand, for the Bedfordians (and the Junto more generally), a trial that failed to convict Strafford on *any* major charge was equally dangerous, as it would rob them of the one really big stick with which they hoped to intimidate the king into offering them concessions. To this extent, the attainder option, so long as it was not developed too far, was probably regarded by the Bedfordians as a useful background threat, but one with which they could not associate themselves *publicly* without incurring Charles's ire and placing in jeopardy the negotiations over appointments.[19]

This was the tightrope that Pym had to walk when the Commons returned to their chamber on Saturday, 10 April after the chaotic morning in Westminster Hall. For Pym and his allies, silencing this nascent 'attainder party' depended on revitalizing the prosecution in Westminster Hall and persuading the Commons that, in spite of all, he and his fellow prosecutors were still capable of securing Strafford's conviction on a charge of treason. Unless that were done, the field would be open to those who were ready to try more aggressive courses.

Pym and his key ally, John Glynne, had but one card to play: the dramatic new evidence relating to Strafford's plans to use the Irish army against England, material that the trial managers had planned to offer in court that morning, but been prevented from so doing by the Lords' sudden decision to adjourn.[20] After insisting that the Commons' doors were locked, always an indicator that something momentous was about to be revealed, Glynne rose to reveal the notes Sir Henry Vane senior had made of the Privy Council's Committee of War on 5 May 1640, where the use of force to suppress internal dissent in England had apparently been discussed.[21] This was evidence that Bedford, Pym, and Clotworthy had first obtained back in the September of the previous year.[22] Only now, however, with the prosecution struggling to reassert its credibility, were they prepared to divulge the notes and their contents,[23] and relate the story of how they had acquired them. Glynne told the tale: how Secretary Vane had kept detailed notes of the Privy Councillors' advice to the king on 5 May 1640, where Strafford had first proposed the use of the Irish army;[24] how the original version of these notes had since been destroyed, but before their destruction, a copy had been made by Vane's son, Sir Henry junior, the Treasurer of the Navy;[25] and how, finally, Vane junior, realizing the notes' significance,[26] had presented his transcription to Pym and Clotworthy, out of 'Dutie and', as he put it, '[as] a *sonne of [the] Commonwealth*'.[27]

As recorded by Vane senior, Strafford's advice to the king seemed to contain two particularly incriminating phrases: first, that because the Commons had refused to provide the king with supply in time of war, he was 'loose and absolved from all rules of government' – which seemed a clear invitation to the king to act as a tyrant.[28] And, second, they contained an offer from Strafford that appeared to have the potential to make this tyranny a reality: 'You have an army in Ireland, [Strafford advised the king, which] you may imploy *here* to reduce *this kingdome*'.[29]

Of course, the charge that Strafford had intended to use the Irish army to this purpose was nothing new. The significance of the newly disclosed notes – and what made them potentially so damning to Strafford – was that they could be construed to remove any doubt that the intended destination of the Irish invasion force was not Scotland (as Strafford had consistently maintained) but 'this kingdome': England.[30] There remained the now familiar evidential problem that Vane's notes constituted the testimony of a single witness, whereas, at law, two were required to substantiate a charge of treason;[31] but the disclosure of the new evidence seems to have made a suitably shocking impression on the Commons.[32] The House ordered that checks should be made on the notes' authenticity;[33] but, otherwise, the revelation appears to have achieved its intended purpose. This looked like the evidence that was needed to re-energize the prosecution, and, with the House apparently content that the trial should continue as usual, members turned to other business.[34] An attainder bill no longer looked to be necessary. The Bedfordians could rest content: the trial would go on, and with it the negotiations to save Strafford's life on which their hopes of office depended. Towards the end of the day, many of the members gradually drifted away, doubtless looking forward to their Sunday reprieve from parliamentary business.

It was then that the attainder supporters staged an ambush. Reconstructing exactly how and when they seized their opportunity from the surviving eyewitness accounts is problematic, but the sequence of events seems broadly clear. Still dissatisfied with further reliance on the impeachment trial (either as a process for securing Strafford's conviction, or as a means of guaranteeing his eventual execution), a small but resolute group of Commons-men – their identity, as we will see, is a matter of contention – were determined to abandon the trial and to proceed, instead, by bill of attainder.[35] As often with controversial measures, they waited until the House was thinly attended, and then made their move. Sir Philip Stapilton, who had come up against Strafford in his native Yorkshire, spoke first,[36] proposing 'to goe *by a bill of attainder* as beeinge the shortest and the best way'.[37] Then, either in response to Stapilton or later in the same debate, a relatively obscure Leicestershire knight, Sir Arthur Hesilrige, happened to have a fully drafted bill for Strafford's attainder, which 'he drew out of his pocquet'.[38] His bill was immediately seized on – or so the conventional account runs – by a House dominated by 'country members',[39] rustic souls, suspicious of would-be courtiers like Bedford and Pym, who willingly gave the attainder bill its first reading.

This moment – indeed, this account – occupies an emblematic place in the lore about the coming of the English Civil War. The attainder, perhaps more than any other source of antagonism, was to drive king and Parliament apart during the spring of 1641. Yet its origins, it has usually been argued, were casual, almost accidental, and nothing to do with the world of the puritan grandees. Rather, it was a backbench initiative, a reaction by 'country members of all sorts against the would-be new court'.[40]

Attractive though the idea is that 'country members' were walking around with fully drafted bills of attainder in their pockets, this account does not stand up to detailed scrutiny. In fact, neither Stapilton nor Hesilrige can be regarded as an ordinary 'country member'. In different ways, both men seem to have been close to the most anti-Straffordian of the Junto grandees.[41] Stapilton, who first proposed proceeding by attainder, is the more difficult of the two to pin down; by the spring of 1641 he had become a friend and loyal lieutenant of the Earl of Essex – whose personal bodyguard he was to command from 1642, and one of the handful of peers who were insistent from the outset, contra Bedford, that Strafford should die – though how far this Stapilton–Essex friendship went back, if at all, into the 1630s is difficult to date.[42] With Hesilrige, however, we are on firmer ground, for his connections with the Junto's militantly anti-Straffordian wing – in particular, with Warwick and Brooke – extended over a decade.[43]* His closest links, however, were with Lord Brooke, his brother-in-law; indeed, in 1641, Hesilrige and his wife were living in part of Brooke House – a stone's throw from Warwick House – and dining together regularly.[44] Warwick and Brooke were at the centre of Hesilrige's life and concerns – familial, political, and financial – and it seems very doubtful (to put it no stronger) that in introducing so controversial a piece of legislation, Hesilrige did not act in conjunction with the men who were already known to be Strafford's most forceful opponents in the Lords, and who were also so closely tied to his own domestic and political milieu.[45] This suspicion becomes even stronger when one realizes

---

* Hesilrige's first marriage provided him with the entrée to this 'godly' world: his spouse had been the daughter of Thomas Elmes, a protégé of Warwick's friend, Richard Knightley, and also of Pym. But it was his second marriage, shortly after his first wife's early death, which connected him far more closely to this puritan clique. He married the sister of Lord Brooke, 'the head of a circle of "Puritan Opposition" in the West Midlands' and, since 1632, had been a patentee of the most uncompromisingly puritan of the Caroline plantations in New England: Fort Saybrook, a project to erect a 'godly commonwealth' in Connecticut, named in honour, respectively, of Viscount Saye and Lord Brooke. Hesilrige's own daughter by his first marriage was married to the colony's current governor, George Fenwick, who also acted as agent for the 'Warwick patentees' in New England.

that Warwick, Essex, and Brooke were shortly to emerge as vociferous champions of Hesilrige's bill once it was sent to the upper House.[46] Nor, as we
shall see, was this the only occasion when Hesilrige acted as the cat's-paw
for the Junto.[47] Writing on 12 April, one Commons-man noted that 'the
precise partie', meaning the godly Junto, were 'still most prevalent in the
higher house [the Lords] too, and it was *so contrived by the correspondents
in both howses*' that affairs were managed to the achievement of their
common ends.[48]

But, however, it was managed, Hesilrige's remedy to the 'Strafford problem'
was grimly uncompromising. His bill laid down that the earl should suffer
the traditional horrors of a traitor's death: hanging (to induce partial
unconsciousness), 'drawing' (castration and evisceration alive), and quartering (dismemberment so that the four parts of his corpse could be publicly
displayed).[49]

The sudden emergence of this pro-attainder lobby on 10 April – centred
on Hesilrige and Stapilton in the Commons, and Warwick, Essex, and Brooke
in the Lords – reopened an earlier divide within the reformist Junto between
the conciliationist Bedfordians and a more radical group of reformers centred
on Warwick House, a fissure that had been temporarily papered over during
the lead-up to, and opening stages of, the trial. Newly widened by the
trial's near-collapse, this divide manifested itself again as a disagreement over
strategic objectives and, as well, the means of attaining them. Should Strafford
be hounded from office and disgraced, but saved from a capital sentence, in
the interests of retaining some form of working relationship with the king:
the Bedfordians' preferred *modus operandi*; or was Strafford so dangerous
to the state, as Warwick's circle maintained, that it was imperative, even at
the risk of a complete breakdown of relations with the monarch, to pursue
the Lord Lieutenant to the death? Underlying this disagreement lay a deeper
point of contention: whether the foundations of the new post-Triennial Act
commonwealth were to be built, as Bedford and Pym had maintained, on a
mixture of conciliation and discreet coercion, saving whatever could be
salvaged of the 'king's honour'; or, as the Warwick House group would have
it, on a far greater degree of force, irrespective of its cost in terms of the
king's slighted *amour propre*. Warwick was looking to something much
stronger than purse-strings to bind the king, indeed, the logical corollary of
this position – a commonwealth grounded on force – was the Parliament's
assumption of control, independent of the king, over the means of its military
defence, an idea that had first emerged during the summer of 1640 in the
plans for the creation of the 'Armies for the Commonwealth'. As we will
see, this call for an independent, Parliament-controlled military force was to
re-emerge, with Warwick's closet ally Essex as its advocate, within days of
the attainder's first reading.[50] This was the great dilemma of the age: in the
language of contemporaries, whether government was best grounded on
'love' or 'force'– the binary polarities whose gravitational pull was gradually
drawing the two wings of the reformist Junto apart.[51] To Stapilton and
Hesilrige, and to the aristocratic cartel that was allied to them, 'love' and
conciliation had been tried and failed. And having proved futile, their failure

was threatening the survival of the entire reformist cause. The moment for compulsion and violence – the public, judicial violence of the gallows – had now come.

*

Yet, in a deeply divided House of Commons, where Strafford had a growing body of admirers, it was far from clear that Hesilrige's attainder bill would make any progress beyond its opportunistically timed first reading.[52] Opponents of the measure prevented it receiving a second reading that day (albeit 'with much adoe'),[53] and by the time the House next convened, on Monday, 12 April, the number of members present – and in consequence, it seems, the overall mood – had changed decisively. Perhaps predictably, a number of the Commons-men allied to the Bedfordian side of the Junto worked to delay the attainder, if not to kill it off entirely.[54] A motion from the pro-attainder lobby to give the bill a second reading was postponed 'to the next sitting of the House' (words which, in practice, very often meant consigning the measure to oblivion);[55] and in a complementary move, Glynne, Pym, and Hampden managed to persuade the House to refocus its attention on the trial, with a view to restarting it as soon as possible.[56]

With a series of dextrous procedural manoeuvres, the Bedfordians gradually undid the damage caused by Saturday's unseemly public confrontation between the two Houses. First to be addressed was the Lords' ruling that, if the prosecution introduced new witnesses, Strafford should have the right to do likewise – the action that had provoked the Commons' walkout. Pym proposed a solution. Desperate to mend fences, both within the Commons and with the Lords, he persuaded his colleagues to communicate Vane's notes to the peers; but not, now, as evidence relating to Strafford's trial, but on the pretext that they were relevant to two quite separate impeachments, those of Archbishop Laud and Lord Cottington, both of whom had also advanced 'absolutist' arguments in the course of the meeting recorded in Vane's notes.[57] It was a deft resolution. Pym thus managed to avoid the time-consuming debates about the authenticity and admissibility of Vane's evidence, which would have arisen had the notes been read in Westminster Hall, while at the same time ensuring that the Lords were nevertheless made fully aware of how damning the new material against Strafford actually was. The Bedfordians regained the initiative, with Hampden and Strode – the proposer of the Triennial Act and Pym's ally in the campaign against the attainder – taking the messages to the Lords whereby these arrangements were jointly agreed.[58]

The trial was once again on track, and Tuesday, 13 April was settled on for its resumption.[59] With the attainder bill deferred, if only briefly, there was an opportunity to revive the impeachment trial and bring it to a conclusion in which Strafford was condemned and disbarred from office, but which left Charles with the freedom (which the attainder would have denied him) to issue a pardon that would save his servant's life and fortune. Bedford's central objective looked attainable once again.

*

Tuesday, 13 April was to be a decisive moment in the fortunes of the Bedford settlement. Strafford was called in to Westminster Hall to make his defence, but bound, in accordance with Pym's new compromise with the Lords, 'not to produce anie new matter [of fact]'.[60] His comprehensive riposte to the charges against him lasted the best part of two and a half hours, from around 9 to 11.30 in the morning.[61] Apparently well aware of the use that the prosecution had been making of Vane's notes, Strafford focused his rebuttal on Article 23, making much of the fact that Vane's testimony that the Irish army was intended for use in England had been flatly contradicted, in the course of earlier cross-examination, by two other Privy Councillors who had also been present at the 5 May meeting. Both Northumberland and Hamilton, Strafford reminded the court, had declared 'the saied Irish army was originallie and wholly intended *for Scotland*'.[62] Not coincidentally, perhaps, the two Privy Councillors who were prepared to stand as witnesses in Strafford's defence were also, as we have seen, the two key backers at court of the Bedfordian settlement.

It is from this point, too, that the Bedfordians began to manifest a new-found protectiveness towards the king, going out of their way to distance Charles from any complicity in Strafford's plans. Responding to Strafford's claim that the Irish army had been designed for use in Scotland, rather than England, Glynne now conceded that 'perhaps *the King* indeed intended it soe; but *his* [Strafford's] designes were for England'.[63] Indeed, Glynne went further, insisting (in a line that seems to have been intended specifically to ingratiate himself with the king, listening in the nearby royal box), that

> wee are all as jealous of the King's prerogative as the Earl of Strafford, ... and wee assure ourselves that our impeaching of him of high treason shall stand with that prerogative and your Lordshipps' justice.[64]

Pym followed suit,[65] arguing loyally that 'the [king] is husband to his people, the head to his subjects', and exonerating him of any evil intent by placing all blame on the evil counsels of Strafford. It was he, not Charles, who sought to 'dissolve the bond of protection' between paternal monarch and filial subject.[66] The 'politics of love' had not yet had their day.

While Pym appeared to be learning the manners of the courtier, his performance as a prosecution counsel was much less accomplished. Perhaps because he realized that the continued viability of the impeachment would depend on the success of the trial that day, perhaps because he was simply under-prepared, his speech proved to be at least as ill-judged and accident-prone as Erle's disastrous effort the previous Thursday. Pym's metaphors were inept to the point of bathos ('[Strafford's] offences are a seminarie of crimes as the earth [is] of vegetables').[67] His argument rambled without ever scoring an effective point. At one crucial moment, his memory failing, he completely lost the thread of his argument. Alone, with both Houses of Parliament before him, and a capacity audience at his back, he was lost for words. 'It was a sport', wrote one pro-Straffordian observer, 'to see how Master Pym in his Speech was fearfully out, and constreined to pull out his papers and reade with a great deale of confusion and disorder before hee could recollect himselfe; which failing of his Memory was no small advantage to the [Lord] Lieuetenant.'⁶⁸ Even Robert Baillie, who was on Pym's side, believed that God must have intervened 'to humble the man'.⁶⁹

If the Junto's hardliners – Stapilton and Hesilrige, Warwick and Essex – had so far looked as though they would be disappointed in their plan to have Strafford attainted, the 'humbling' of Master Pym proved to be their salvation. By the time the Commons resumed the following day, Wednesday, 14 April, members' lack of confidence in the trial's management had reached the point where a majority was now prepared to give further consideration to the attainder. After an ill-tempered debate, in which D'Ewes was 'amazed' at the number of Commons-men who were ready to speak in Strafford's favour, the attainder bill narrowly received its second reading – the point at which the House decided to consider it in detail.⁷⁰

From this moment, these two rival modes of procedure were in open contention: the impeachment trial, with its near-certainty of saving Strafford's life; the attainder, with its seemingly immutable demand for a sentence of death. Battle was joined over relatively technical points of Commons usage. Opponents of the attainder managed to ensure that the bill was referred to the Committee of the Whole House – an expedient that allowed all members to speak in the debate on the billy's committee stage, thereby guaranteeing that it would make only the slowest of progress.⁷¹ Nevertheless, after a faltering start, the attainder was now coming to be regarded as a viable alternative strategy. Just one more slip-up in the management of the impeachment looked likely to turn the attainder into the Commons' preferred mode of settling the score with Strafford. Former allies found themselves on opposing sides. St John, who had consistently pressed for speed in the despatch of the trial, was now 'absolutelie against' hearing anything further in Westminster Hall, 'if wee intended to proceed by bill of Attainder'.⁷²

Faced with this dissent from within its own ranks, the Bedfordians managed, nevertheless, to keep the impeachment option open. On Thursday, 15 April Pym and Strode were 'the cheife movers' of a proposal that the Commons should be present in Westminster Hall on the next day of the trial, to hear Strafford's counsel argue points of law.⁷³ On Friday the 16th Pym seconded Hampden in arguing that the Commons would 'much dishonour' themselves if they abandoned the impeachment.⁷⁴ And after a conference between the two Houses in which Viscount Saye and the Earl of Pembroke (both backers of the Bedford settlement) assured the Commons that they would strictly confine Strafford's counsel to matters of law,⁷⁵ the counsels of Pym and Strode eventually prevailed. The Commons agreed to be present on the following day to hear legal argument in Strafford's defence.⁷⁶

There were further auguries in Strafford's favour. At the end of that week the Commons were still unable to agree on whether Strafford's actions amounted to treason – the *sine qua non* of any attainder.⁷⁷ The furthest they would go was to decide 'it is sufficiently proved that Thomas Earl of Strafford had endeavoured to subvert the ancient and fundamental laws of these realms of England and Ireland, and to introduce an arbitrary and tyrannical government, *against law*';[78] yet what sort of crime this amounted to – treason, felony, or misdemeanour – was left unspecified. The Commons themselves could not agree and, after Strafford's counsel was heard on Saturday, 17 April, the issue was muddier still.[79] An attempt by St John to resolve the matter once and for all – by having the House agree that, if Strafford could be proved to have counselled the king to 'bring [the Irish army] hither', he was guilty of treason – was abandoned at St John's own request, presumably after failing to attract sufficient support to be carried.[80] Doubtless to the delight of the Bedfordians, the consideration of the attainder bill had to be deferred to yet another day. What Stapilton had claimed, when first proposing the attainder, would be the 'shortest and the best way'[81] had turned out, instead, to be 'full of delay and dispute'.[82] The proposal to kill Strafford by statute looked likely to founder long before it came to be ever sent up to the House of Lords.

Yet, almost from the start of the new week, the attainder bill suddenly became the talk of Westminster. Much of Monday and Tuesday was taken up with debate on the proposal, not as mere filibuster, but in pursuit of a revised text that satisfied majority opinion within the Commons. Progress was rapid. As early as Monday, the House had formally resolved that Strafford's 'endeavour ... to subvert the ancient and fundamental laws of the realms of England and Ireland, and to introduce an arbitrary and tyrannical government ... is high treason'.[83] By the end of Wednesday morning, 21 April, agreement had been reached on a series of 'additions and amendments', and that same afternoon the completed attainder bill passed the House of Commons by a majority of almost four to one. Something more than mere frustration with the current procedures had transformed the attainder party from an embattled minority, at the end of the previous week, unable to achieve consensus even on whether Strafford was guilty of treason, into an overwhelming majority, ready to send him to the scaffold – and all within a matter of three or four days. How is this sudden eclipse of Pym and the Bedfordian *via media* to be explained?

ii. THE ARMY AND ITS DISCONTENTS

This unexpected lurch of support in favour of Strafford's death owes less to the persuasiveness of the attainder's advocates than to the provocations of an impatient and interventionist king. Alarmed by the ongoing, but actually inconclusive, debates on the attainder of his favoured servant, Charles decided to issue what amounted to a military threat to the Parliament. Possibly as a preparatory step to a new mobilization or, at very least, as a gesture designed to give this impression, the king instructed Holland, the new Lord General, to issue orders over the weekend of 17–18 April that all officers should return to their regiments forthwith. When the Commons reassembled on Monday, 19 April, the army's Commissary-General, Henry Wilmot – himself one of the leading 'Army Plotters' – announced openly that he and all the other army officers who were members of the House 'had received command[s] to go down to their charges in the army *very suddenly*'.[84] As no funds had yet been provided by Parliament for the army's disbandment (and the king would not allow this while the Scottish army remained in England), there seemed no chance that the order for officers to return to their regiments was for the purpose of seeing its break-up. And even if the motive for the orders was entirely innocent, the announcement of a general rendezvous of officers appeared to confirm the rumours already current at Westminster that, rather than see Strafford convicted, Charles would take some form of military action to break the power of his persecutors. If the exact way in which he intended to use the army remained at this point vague, that uncertainty merely served to compound the effectiveness of the threat.[85]

Reports reaching Westminster of the temper of the army in the North made these suspicions seem eminently plausible. An English army, which, in the September of 1640, had been reported ready to hail Essex as its commander-in-chief, had come round by the end of April to regard the king as its natural defender. More alarming still, it was showing an ever-growing 'affection' for the Earl of Strafford, and a marked zeal to see him released.[86] Perhaps the strongest 'affection' for the imprisoned Lord Lieutenant, however, came from the two regiments (formerly Yorkshire militia forces) that held the front line against the Scots. These were commanded by two staunch Straffordians, Sir Thomas Danbie (who owed his knighthood to Strafford),[87] and the ultra-loyal Sir William Pennyman (a man who had 'confessed himself to honour the Lord Lieutenant so far as to die for him'),[88] whose regiment defended the English-held southern bank of the River Tees against a Scottish advance on York.[89] Were Strafford to return to the North as the army's Lieutenant-General (a rank he still held), it looked possible, perhaps even, likely that he would be welcomed back with open arms. In that event, a further rendezvous between this army and Strafford's Irish forces would probably have been a matter of time.[90]*

For this change in the army's temper, the Junto had only itself to blame. Ever since Warwick had been made de facto paymaster of the forces in the North in early March 1641,[91] the English army's conviction that Parliament was more concerned with funding the Junto's Scottish allies than with providing for its own arrears had provided a fertile ground for the growth of anti-parliamentarian sentiment.[92] Parliament's total failure to address the question of the army's pay had left the forces in the North resentful and

---

* These suspicions appeared to be corroborated in late April when it was discovered that Strafford's secretary, Guilford Slingsby, had kept a ship manned and ready to sail at Tilbury for the past eight weeks, apparently 'prepared to convey away the Earle of Strafford' to a rendezvous with the army in the North. From that moment, Strafford was secured as a 'close prisoner', under strict watch. The size of the vessel in question obviously aroused suspicions, as it was clearly large enough to be seagoing, and able to undertake a lengthy journey (hence the point of her being well victualled) in coastal waters. This seemed to provide further corroboration of a plot to take Strafford northwards (presumably by sea to Hull) to join the king's army in the North, though whether this was Slingsby's actual destination is impossible to prove.

disillusioned. 'Money or Mutiny!' was reported to be the soldiers' slogan by the spring of 1641. 'From the Parliament and the Devill, good Lord delyver us', was the infantryman's new prayer.[93] By mid April, the Earl of Holland was warning that Parliament's failure to provide for the army's pay was likely to produce a wholesale breakdown of discipline. The mutinous state of the Berwick garrison, just south of the Scottish border, was of particular concern;[94] and as a desperate stop-gap measure, 'some of the Lords' – most likely Beford and his fellow Junto peers – offered to club together to provide 'speedilie' just under £4,000 from their own pockets to forestall an all-out revolt.[95] Once again, the Exchequer and the usual arrangements for such payments through the king's Treasurer-at-War were entirely circumvented. This money 'was agreed to be paid in this afternoon at Bedford House', from whence it was to be disbursed directly to the Berwick garrison.[96]

It is hardly surprising that Charles discerned an opportunity in the army's discontents. Egged on by a group of radicalized officers (among them Henry Wilmot, William Ashburnham, and Henry Percy), he had been courting the loyalty of the officer corps since the end of March. He made little attempt to cover his tracks; indeed, he seems to have wanted the Junto leaders to know of, and feel pressured by, the army's new-found sympathy for his cause. Colonel George Goring's revelation to the Earl of Newport in early April, and later to Bedford and Saye, of a conspiracy to bring the army southwards towards London had been the first of these attempts at intimidation.[97]* Hitherto, however, this threat had been generalized and indistinct. Wilmot's announcement on Monday, 19 April that all officers had been ordered back to their field commands changed all that. The possibility of an intervention by the army suddenly seemed pressing and real.[98]

It is difficult to explain why the king chose this moment – just when the Commons was so seriously divided over the attainder that the bill looked like becoming irretrievably bogged down – to take such a provocative step. One possible explanation, however, is suggested by the arrival at court only twenty-four hours earlier of the news that Prince Willem of Orange-Nassau, the intended husband of Charles's daughter, Princess Mary, had arrived in England, along with his extensive train.[99] This was reported to be carrying a substantial sum in gold (one report put it at 1,200,000 'ducats' – Dutch guilders – or £120,000),[100] apparently intended as a gift or loan to the king, made in connection with the forthcoming marriage. The Dutch ambassadors, clearly embarrassed at being held responsible for funding a possible military coup, later denied that any such sum had been intended as a subsidy to the king's army.[101] But the contingency that the king received a substantial sum in specie cannot be discounted. Expenditure on military supplies in the days

---

* Goring seems to have been chosen for this role because he had a foot in both camps. He remained loyal to the king; but he was also close to the Earl of Newport – with whom he twice sat to Van Dyck for a double portrait during the late 1630s – and to whom he divulged the details of the plot. The relationship between Goring and Newport was also underpinned by family connections, as Newport's wife, Anne (née Boteler), was the aunt of Goring's brother-in-law, George Porter (Porter having married Goring's sister).

that followed suggests that these reports had some foundation. By the last week of April, Charles had somehow found the money to pay for materiel supplies, including some 480 barrels of powder, 1,800 picks and 4,000 shovels, 'to bee sent into the North to the English armie'.[102] Some 1,500 barrels of powder were later reported as en route for Portsmouth.[103] Whether this Dutch 'dowry' existed or not, the rumours of its arrival were so widely credited at the time that the report that Charles had suddenly acquired the financial wherewithal to mount at least a limited military campaign was being taken as fact.[104] 'The Dutch-men have offered mony to the King for a new service of warre', it was allegedly claimed in the Commons: '[S]hortly with us the Hollander will bee no lesse odious then the Spanyard'.[105]

Nor were these the only potential threats. Writing on Tuesday, 20 April (the day after Wilmot's revelation of the order summoning officers to their commands), Archibald Jhonston of Wariston noted that there were widespread suspicions 'of the French ... coming over'. The queen was believed to be planning to seize control of Portsmouth, the obvious bridgehead for any foreign landing. In advising his countrymen, Jhonston of Wariston thought the signals were unambiguous: 'expect war rather [than] peace'.[106]

These rising expectations of a new war – directed either against the Covenanter army of occupation in the North, or perhaps against their 'Commonwealthsmen' allies in the South – transformed the 'Strafford question' almost overnight. From this moment, the debate on Strafford's fate ceased to be primarily a question of how far he was guilty of crimes past and became, instead, a matter of how far he was likely to be the author of further villanies to come. Executing Strafford came to be seen as a means of depriving the king of the one general who, if ever allowed to rejoin the army, possessed both the ruthlessness and the requisite popularity within the rank-and-file to lead it against the Parliament. 'Every day [the army's] affection to the Lord Strafford's deliverance and safety doth appear more evidently,' wrote one of Lord Fairfax's informants from Yorkshire;[107] and, as one pamphleteer warned, Strafford had 'power, under his Majesty, to raise armes'.[108]

Ironically, had Charles let the impeachment proceedings take their course – and, even now, Bedford and Pym were struggling to make this possible – there is a strong probability that Strafford would have been acquitted, at least on the charge of treason. The king's public threat to use force, however, refocused the Parliament on the likelihood of Strafford's imminent re-employment and the king's continuing willingness to resort to war. The attainder bill – which, at its introduction, had seemed such an arbitrary course of action – was increasingly coming to be viewed as no harsher a remedy than the gravity of the crisis required.

III. DISSOLUTION

The morning that brought news of the general rendezvous of officers, Monday, 19 April, was also the moment when the Commons suddenly resolved their doubts about the extent of Strafford's guilt. Pre-empting any formal judgement by the Lords in the impeachment trial, they declared that Strafford's 'endeavour' to subvert the laws and introduce 'an arbitrary and tyrannical government' in England and Ireland 'is high treason'.[109] The shift in mood was palpable; when the vote was taken, supporters of the attainder outnumbered its oppoents by three to one.[110] Nothing now seemed to stand in the way of the Commons giving the attainder bill its final reading.

Even at this late stage, however, Pym tried to throw obstacles in its way, calling into question the latest resolution, and demanding a debate among the House's professional lawyers ('those of the long roabe') as to whether an endeavour to subvert the laws 'weere Treason or not'.[111] It was, nevertheless, a losing battle. By Wednesday morning, 21 April, the evidence that Charles was about to engage in some form of military resistance was becoming compelling. At Hamilton's suggestion, Jhonston of Wariston had an audience of the king that morning, and read much into the king's demeanour and body language. He found him conspiratorial and shifty, concluding that 'his mind seems to be on some project here shortly to break out'.[112] 'It is thought there is some present plot [about] to break forth here,' he reported later that same day. Clues to what this 'project' might be were provided to Jhonston by the king's own canvassing of a number of possible options. The most alarming of these was a plan to adjourn the two Houses for ten days, 'on [the] pretext of the festival days [for the celebration of his daughter's forthcoming wedding to Prince Willem of Orange-Nassau]'.[113] This, Jhonston believed, was merely a ruse, and would be followed, as soon as the members had adjourned, by the declaration of a formal dissolution.[114] To old Commons hands, it must have looked as if the monarch was reverting to the tactics he had employed in 1626, when he had dissolved the then Parliament in order to block a planned Commons' attack on another favoured servant, the Duke of Buckingham.[115] In 1641, the attractions of this same course were self-evident. The impeachment proceedings against Strafford and the attainder bill would be both voided by the act of dissolution; and the king would then be free to release Strafford as and when he determined, and to return him to his military commands.

News of the impending dissolution spread rapidly in the course of Wednesday, 21 April, with Jhonston of Wariston and his friends at Warwick House its likeliest sources. The dissolution threat fatally undermined Pym's efforts to oppose the attainder bill and keep the impeachment trial on track. For to bring the trial to a conclusion would still take days, if not weeks; and with the Parliament now living under the shadow of a dissolution, perhaps only hours away, the majority in favour of passing the attainder became overwhelming. If nothing else were achieved, passing the bill would place on the formal parliamentary record the depth of the Commons' abhorrence of Strafford's 'tyranny'. When the House reassembled after the dinner recess that same day, the third reading of the attainder bill was the first item raised.[116]

The sense of crisis created by this threat of imminent dissolution drove the attainder on. That afternoon, as the Commons completed their final debate on the attainder, the Junto's allies in the City began collecting a crowd that would later go to Westminster as a 'human shield', to prevent any commission of dissolution from being read.[117] Wariston reported that the Junto leadership had received promises from its City allies that they would send 5,000 men 'to guard the Parliament ... on apprehension of [a] dissolution'.[118] In fact, towards dusk,[119] a crowd at least as large as had been promised, and possibly much larger (D'Ewes estimated its size at 10,000), accompanied '3 Captaines of the cittie' – three officers in the City militia – to the Palace of Westminster, to present a petition calling for Strafford's death.[120] Revealingly, the central concern of these petitioners was not vengeance on Strafford for crimes past, but the 'feare that some dangerous matters *are in hatching* to hinder the birth of the endeavours of the Parliament for the publike good'.[121]

Well before that crowd, thousands strong, had descended on Westminster,[122]* it was clear that the Bedfordians' advocacy of conciliation had become untenable. A new logic held sway in the Commons. With the threatened dissolution of Parliament so clearly motivated by the king's desire to save his favoured servant, and perhaps to use him to impose a new phase of military-backed despotic rule, Charles had succeeded in creating a direct linkage in the minds of many Parliament-men between ensuring the earl's execution and providing for the survival of Parliament itself. The only alternatives seemed to be Strafford's death or the extinction of Parliaments. Ironically, it was the king's actions that silenced the Junto's advocates of compromise. With the Parliament's very continuance believed to be in jeopardy, and large numbers of citizens gathering in the hope of preventing the threatened dissolution, the afternoon of Wednesday, 21 April was an inauspicious moment to be seen as a defender of Strafford's life. Only one of the Bedfordians – Bedford's son-in-law, Digby – was prepared to break ranks and offer a public word of opposition to the attainder bill. It was an unwelcome contribution. When he sat down, Digby was rounded on by a series of his Bedfordian colleagues – including Pym, Strode, and Glynne (all of them, hitherto, opponents of the attainder) – who 'fullie confuted' his speech.

Propelled onwards by the threats and intimidation of the previous seventy-two hours, the attainder acquired an unstoppable momentum. When the

---

* To what extent were Warwick, Essex and the other militant anti-Straffordians involved in this formidable display of 'popular power'? We have one clue, which, if inconclusive, is at least strongly suggestive. The principal spokesman for this vast concourse of Londoners was Captain John Venn, the sixty-three-year-old London silk merchant and Merchant Taylor, whose title of 'captain' did not derive from any commission granted by the king, but from the Artillery Company, whose Captain-Serjeant-Major he had been elected in 1636. Since then, Venn had become one of the company's most influential senior officers – he was shortly to become the company's Deputy President – and he also enjoyed an extensive influence among the City godly. All that was needed, it was later claimed, was for 'Captain Ven [to] send his summons by his Wife to assemble the Zelots of the City'; and while this is an obvious oversimplification, his prominence in the Artillery Company and commitment to godly reform make it highly likely that in this instance he was working with the reformist group around Warwick, Essex, and Brooke – the chief supporters of the attainder in the Lords.

final vote was taken, by division, those in favour of Strafford's execution outnumbered the pro-Straffordians by almost four to one: 204 in favour; a mere 59 against.[123] A relatively united House of Commons[124] had decided that Strafford must die. And to affirm its new-found unanimity, Pym, one of the most belated of all the converts to the attainder cause, was chosen to carry the bill, now formally engrossed on parchment, up to the Lords.[125] Almost the entire House of Commons left their places to accompany him to its delivery;[126] and the sight of this phalanx of men, some two hundred-strong, shortly after 6 p.m., crowding into the lower end of the House of Lords, and spilling into the lobbies beyond, made an intimidating impression on Strafford's remaining friends. They 'looked sadly' on the attainder bill, some of them beginning 'to doubt the worst'. Saye, for whom the passing of the attainder bill threatened the overthrow of all he had worked for with Bedford since the parliament had begun, did not wait to witness its delivery. Suddenly overcome with a timely illness, slipped away from the Lords' chamber before 3 p.m., and immediately took to his bed.[127]

*

Yet there was more going on beneath this panic-driven consensus, perhaps, than meets the eye. Less than half the Commons' membership actually voted in the division; and while not all the absentees can be assumed to be pro-Straffordian, it is likely that the real number of Commons-men who opposed the attainder was a far larger group than the fifty-nine who bravely cast their votes against it on 21 April. Many of those who opposed the bill, recalled Sir Philip Warwick, 'withdrew themselves from the House' well before the final division.[128] Even of the 204 who voted in favour of the attainder, doubtless some only gave their 'yeas' because they confidently expected the bill to be derailed, or at least its provisions mitigated, once it was revised by the Lords.[129] And of those who stayed, peer pressure, heavily exerted by the pro-attainder lobby, seems to have dragooned a number of uncertain members into voting 'yea'. Arthur Capell, one of the two Hertfordshire knights of the shire, later attributed his acquiescence to 'a base Fear ... of a prevailing party'.[130] There were doubtless others.

But while the 'prevailing party' carried the day, the pro-Straffordian minority was not merely a rump of defiantly hardline 'king's-party' men. The opposition between the Warwick House and Bedfordian wings of the Junto remained in evidence right to the final vote. It is perhaps most clearly marked on the pro-attainder side, where the tellers who counted the votes for the anti-Straffordian majority were two of Warwick's closest friends and supporters: Sir Thomas Barrington, and Barrington's brother-in-law, Sir Gilbert Gerard.[131] More puzzling is the behaviour of the Bedfordians, who still desperately needed to foil the attainder bill if they were to retain any credit in their negotiations with the king, and yet who appear to have joined the 'prevailing party' in seeking Strafford's death.

On closer examination, however, a far more complex picture emerges. To start with, Digby's much criticized speech[132] offers one hint that the Bedfordian option of compromise was not yet entirely dead. His speech has come down to posterity almost as an apologia for Strafford, a defiant appeal against 'committing murder with the sword of justice',[133] and the moment when Digby reveals himself in his true colours as a 'Royalist' *avant la lettre*. In fact, both Digby's rhetoric and his specific proposals for action were far more measured in tone, and hostile to Strafford in their implication, than the received reading of his speech allows:[134] Digby it was, after all, who had first suggested the expedient of proceeding by attainder, in the event of the trial evidence not sustaining a treason charge.[135]

Appealing to the lawyers in the House, Digby had made great play of the prosecution's difficulties in establishing a valid case for treason within the existing law. Nevertheless, his conclusions were far from allowing Strafford to escape scot-free. Digby argued emphatically *for* Strafford's punishment: the Lord Lieutenant was still 'that grand apostate of the common wealth, whoe cannot have his pardon in this life, till he come to another' – a line that seems to announce Digby's hostility to any suggestion that Strafford might receive a royal pardon.[136] Obviously the fallen minister ought to be punished, Digby conceded, and a bill should be introduced to 'secure the State from my Lord of Strafford' for the future[137] (presumably by his permanent debarment from office). But he maintained that Strafford's life should be saved, as the evidence against him was ambiguous and to kill him was likely to create yet further divisions.[138]

So Digby was not revealing himself as a 'Straffordian', still less as an uncritical king's-party man, in declaring himself against the attainder. Instead, he was articulating what had been the standard Bedfordian line from the outset, and which was still being supported by the moderate reformists – notably Bedford, Hertford, and Saye.[139] Nor was Digby the only Junto supporter to shift uneasily when confronted with the likelihood of the attainder's imminent success. Hampden, a likely beneficiary of any Bedford-brokered settlement, conspicuously abstained from offering his support, going out at the beginning of the final vote on the attainder bill and staying outside the chamber until the vote was over.[140] So did Sir Henry Mildmay, a man usually in the Warwick–Barrington stable, who reportedly 'hid ... [in] th'Privy', rather than be seen to vote against the Lord Lieutenant.[141] Other prominent reformists who voted against the bill included Northumberland's secretary, Robert Scawen,[142] Edward Kirton, a placeman of Hertford's, and John Selden.[143]

If these instances hardly amount to a phalanx of Bedfordian opposition to the attainder, they nevertheless appear to be something more than merely chance anomalies. They highlight the way in which the Strafford question was not so much a division between proto-Parliamentarians and proto-Royalists, but a contest *within* the reformist faction, decided in favour of the Warwick House group and the other anti-Straffordian militants only by the panic induced by that morning's dissolution scare.

One reason why the Bedfordians seem to have offered no more than token resistance to the attainder is that, for them, there remained a second line of defence: the House of Lords; and there remained a long process of negotiation between the two Houses before Strafford's punishment was finally agreed.[144]

This, in turn, created other, subtler means of sabotaging the bill than the blunderbuss of Digby's moralistic tirade.

Predictably, among the most dextrous players of this game – and therefore the most difficult to read – is John Pym. At first sight, Pym looks like a convert, albeit a last-minute one, to the attainder cause.[145] Certainly, the fact that he was chosen to carry the bill to the upper House indicates, at very least, that – at the third reading – he had voted in its favour. Yet there is reason to believe that Pym was playing a longer game than this apparent 'change of side' might suggest. Far from abandoning the objective of saving Strafford's life, he was looking to secure his position in the future negotiations over the Lords' amendments to the bill in the hope of achieving precisely this objective. Procedural technicalities matter here. Had he voted against the bill, he would have disbarred himself from the committees that would eventually negotiate these amendments with the Lords – a consideration that may well have acted as a powerful, if purely tactical, motive for voting in favour of the attainder.[146]

Pym certainly appears to have been uncomfortable with his role as the bill's delivery boy, and performed badly in front of the peers. Once again, the technicalities of parliamentary procedure are relevant. Pym assured the Lords that the Commons would 'offer satisfaction' if the peers had any doubts as to points of law; but when taxed by the Lords as to *where* this satisfaction would be given, he equivocated. His response to being put on the spot is highly revealing. Despite clear instructions from the Commons that any legal argument would be presented at a conference, Pym was evasive as to what the status of this next meeting would be. The location mattered. If it were to be at a 'conference' (one of the procedures involved in the passage of *legislation*), it indicated that the Commons had turned their backs on the impeachment trial and would now only deal with the attainder: saving Strafford, in other words, was no longer up for discussion, only the terms of his death. On the other hand, if the legal arguments were to be heard in Westminster Hall, as they had been hitherto, it signalled – notwithstanding the presentation of the attainder bill – that the trial remained as a still viable alternative, and, with it, the prospect that the earl's life might yet be saved.

With life or death in the balance, the Lords understandably pressed Pym to clarify which of the two possible venues was intended. Still Pym fudged his answer. Then, almost inaudibly, he eventually admitted that there was to be a *conference* – the news which, had it been heard, would have signalled to the Lords that the Commons regarded the trial as at an end. But Pym mumbled 'in soe low a voice', noted D'Ewes, 'as I beleeve [he went unheard]'.[147]* The remark that the Lords did hear, however, was that

---

* The reason for Pym's reluctance to say the words 'in a conference' is unclear, but the likeliest explanation would seem to be that he was still hoping, even at this late stage, to keep the impeachment trial on track, in which case the appropriate setting for the presentation of legal argument to the Lords would have been Westminster Hall, not a conference between the two Houses. And in the event, partly thanks to Pym's management of the subsequent negotiations with the peers, this was the venue eventually chosen for

Strafford was still to 'come to his triall', clearly giving the impression that the impeachment proceedings in Westminster Hall were to continue, despite the act of attainder – just as Bedford and the majority of the Lords hoped that it would.[148]

These deliberate equivocations did not go unnoticed by Pym's colleagues. When quizzed the following day in the Commons about exactly what he had told the Lords, he claimed feebly that he had 'forgotten' to tell them exactly where the next round of legal argument would be.[149] The message which, in the heat of the moment and with a dissolution expected at any minute, Pym had actually been charged to give – that the trial was as good as over, and the Commons would now only deal with Strafford by bill of attainder – never got through.

*

There was method in Pym's mumbling. Once the panic over the threatened dissolution of 21 April had subsided, much of the momentum that had carried the attainder bill to its final Commons reading abated as well. By conveniently 'forgetting' what the next stage in the Strafford prosecution was going to be, Pym left all options open; and, in the generally calmer atmosphere that prevailed in the Commons immediately after the attainder bill had gone to the Lords, Pym and a series of fellow opponents of Strafford's execution managed to reassert control over the negotiations with the peers as to what should happen next.

By the following afternoon, Thursday, 22 April, when the Commons had their first conference with the Lords to discuss the attainder, Pym and Strode were once again in charge of the discussions, joined for this meeting by two prominent *pro*-Straffordians: Sir Thomas Widdrington (whose reputation as a client of Strafford's had almost prevented his election to the Parliament)[150] and Denzell Holles (Strafford's brother-in-law) – both of them determined to save the Lord Lieutenant from the scaffold.[151] When, two days later, we find Bedford's son, Lord Russell – of all people – being sent up to the Lords to arrange a conference to discuss the London petition demanding 'speidie justice' against Strafford,[152] it is evident that the management of Hesilrige's bill had been largely commandeered by its erstwhile opponents. Brazenly, they were refashioning the legislation to serve what had been their prime objective all along: an outcome in which Strafford was declared guilty of *some* crimes, but nevertheless saved from the scaffold.[153] In a masterly display of parliamentary tactics, Pym and his pro-Straffordian colleagues had jumped on the attainder bandwagon, only to steer it safely away from the executioner's block. The bill's initial advocates, Hesilrige and the Warwick group hardliners, had been comprehensively outflanked.[154]*

---

the peers' 'satisfaction in matter of law'.
* The idea of a non-lethal, Bedfordian-managed attainder bill is perhaps not quite as strange as, at first sight, it may seem. In fact, the earliest mention of a proposal to draw up an attainder bill against Strafford came, as we have seen, from Lord Digby, Bedford's 'son', on 26 February, immediately after Strafford's performance in the House of Lords

In that enterprise, Pym and the Bedfordians could also count on a large number of willing accomplices in the Lords. An upper House that had been unconvinced of Strafford's culpability on the basis of the arguments presented in Westminster Hall so far ('without question they will acquit him', wrote one Commons-man on 17 April)[155] was unlikely to be persuaded to cut off Strafford's head by the arbitrary instrument of statute.[156] Perhaps inevitably, the hitherto latent antagonism between Warwick's anti-Straffordian hardliners and Bedford's would-be placemen came to the surface when the attainder bill was first introduced into the upper House on 24 April. When Essex, Warwick's most influential ally, tried to have the attainder bill read in the Lords that day, he was firmly rebuffed by two erstwhile Petitioner Peers (both of them supporters of the Bedfordian compromise), Bristol and Savile, who succeeded in having the attainder shelved.[157] It seems hardly coincidental that this is the same pair, both tipped for preferments at court, who had intervened during the impeachment trial, in ways helpful to Strafford, when the all-important Article 23 (the charge concerning the Irish army) had been considered in Westminster Hall on 5 April.[158] Now, three weeks later, Savile went so far as to denounce the attainder bill as a breach of the Lords' privileges, on the grounds that the impeachment proceedings in Westminster Hall had not yet come to an end. And when Savile was answered by the Earl of Stamford – a supporter of the attainder and Leicestershire neighbour of Hesilrige's – the ensuing verbal altercation grew so heated that it almost resulted in a duel.[159]

Such moments of melodrama attest to the Warwick group's weakness in the upper House, not its strength. Despite the panics of the previous days, the threatened dissolution had failed to materialize, leaving the scaremongers looking as though they had been crying wolf. And with Pym and his allies now firmly in control of the Commons' side of the attainder discussions by 24 April, all looked in place for a compromise that would eventually satisfy a majority in the Lords and, less certainly, the Commons as well. Indeed, over the previous forty-eight hours, Pym had even managed to inject some semblance of life into the faltering impeachment proceedings in Westminster Hall. After consultations between the two Houses on 22 April, a compromise had been reached in which the Lords reluctantly agreed to take the attainder bill into consideration (eventually giving it its second reading on 27 April).[160] In return, the Commons accepted what amounted to a resumption of the public hearings in Westminster Hall, on the under-standing that the arguments they would offer were intended to establish only 'the justice and legality' of the attainder bill.[161] In other words the Lords, if

forty-eight hours earlier, where he had rebutted the Commons' charges against him, and had thrown into doubt the possibility of gaining a conviction in the impeachment trial. 'Lord Digby saide: That hee conceived the best and only way of attaining our inds in doing Justice upon my Lord Strafford was to doe it by Bill, rather then by Judgment [of the House of Lords], because muche scruple might remaine with the Lords and others of the quality of the offences, [as to whether they could be considered] to bee Treasons'.

convinced by what they heard, would condemn and sentence Strafford, not by a formal judgement of their House convened as a court, but instead by passing the bill of attainder, suitably amended so as to stop short of depriving him of his life.

In terms of likely outcomes, that compromise amounted to a resumption of the impeachment trial in all but name. Once again, the Bedfordians appeared to be in control.

iv. THE FOUNDATIONS OF GOVERNMENT: THE DILEMMAS OF 'LOVE' AND 'FORCE'

If the Bedfordians' success is undeniable, their motives are perhaps more difficult to explain. Why did Bedford and Pym stand out so conspicuously against the killing of the Lord Lieutenant? Indeed, their stance is all the more puzzling in that so many of their more radical allies – Warwick and Essex, Barrington and Stapilton, and almost all the Covenanter Scots (convinced that he was a man '[whom] God in his justice hath destinate to destruction')[162] – were determined that Strafford should die. Contemporary cynics, of course, had their ready answer: the Bedfordians had been seduced by the promise of office and preferment, and self-interest had extinguished their reformist zeal. Yet the riposte to this charge later offered by one of Viscount Saye's defenders – 'if hopes or promises of promotion ... would have altered him from a Patriot to a Courtier, he had been one long ago' – has some force, and can also be offered, perhaps even more appropriately, in the cases of Bedford or Pym.[163] They scorned those betrayers of the Patriot Cause – men like the parvenu Earl of Strafford, who, as plain Thomas Wentworth, had been Pym's erstwhile ally in championing the subject's liberties during the Parliaments of the 1620s – and who seemed to have been bought off by the lure of courtly preferment.

Their position in 1641 was clear. The Bedfordians repudiated the argument of the militant anti-Straffordians that to allow Strafford to live would be to leave 'the triennial Parliament ... of no such force as is expected', and the commonwealth prey to another 'lamentable storme'.[164] Underlying that repudiation was a sharply divergent assessment of the risks posed, on the one hand by allowing Strafford to live, and, on the other, by hounding him to a traitor's death. This was not a division between hardliners and appeasers, selfless Patriots and would-be 'courtiers'. As Bedford had repeatedly demonstrated, he was not averse to coercing the king, and the parliamentary and financial constraints that he had helped set in place with the Triennial Act would eventually leave the king both economically and militarily powerless. But Bedford and those around him also seem to have realized that they had no alternative but to reach a *modus vivendi* with the man, Charles Stuart. There were certain non-negotiable issues – of which the saving of Strafford's life was the pre-eminent – where any attempt to coerce the king against his conscience was likely to risk provoking him to an impetuous and possibly violent response, far more dangerous in its potential outcome than anything that might follow from permitting Strafford to live. Nor were the Bedfordians indifferent to Charles's threats to use violence to break the Parliament – the numerous 'army plots', rumours of which had been reaching them steadily since late March. Nevertheless, they seem to have recognized in Charles's threats and sabre-rattling an element of bluff, and appear to have adopted a tactic of meeting their monarch halfway as the best way of ensuring that this bluff was never called.

Moreover, there was a compelling reason why the Bedfordian argument so frequently prevailed. For by the time the attainder bill went to the Lords, Bedford could point out that this strategy – trading limited clemency towards Strafford in exchange for the reform of public office-holding – was beginning to be met with tangible success. Dating the crucial breakthrough is difficult; but the surviving evidence points to around the end of the second week of April, just when the attainder bill began its final stages in the Commons, as the moment when Bedford finally succeeded in extracting a compromise agreement with the king: that if the 'violent prosecution' against Strafford (the demands for his death) were laid aside, Charles would allow his fallen minister to be 'rendered so secure that there need remain no fears of that man's ever appearing again in [public] business'. In return, Bedford, Saye, and the other advocates of compromise would garner the rewards of office: the change in personnel at Whitehall on which, they insisted, the future security of the 'godly commonwealth' depended.[165] As Edward Hyde observed, 'they who treated for the promotions at court were solicitous to finish [the Strafford case]', because Charles would confirm nothing in relation to the offices of state until he knew that Strafford's life was safe. 'And the Earl of Bedford, who had, in truth, more authority with the violent men than any body else, laboured heartily to bring it to pass.'[166]

Yet securing control of preferment, for Bedford, was always a means to an end, a device for establishing a Patriot-dominated government, never an end in itself. And in his pursuit of this objective, the attainder bill's parliamentary debut on 10 April seems, paradoxically, to have been an unforeseen boon, bringing home to the king how dependent he was on Bedford and the other Junto moderates to mitigate Parliament's severity. The realization induced him to offer a series of promotions to members of the Junto both Bedfordian and militant.

Essex and Holland – both anti-Straffordian hardliners, firmly in the Warwick camp – were the first to be targeted. In Essex's case, the offer appears not to have gone beyond the stage of discussion, almost certainly because Essex remained emphatic that Strafford's life should not be spared. But these talks were nevertheless sufficiently advanced by 10 April for the usually well-informed papal emissary, Rossetti, to report confidently that Essex was to be appointed as Lord Lieutenant of Ireland[167] in Strafford's stead – the office that had been earmarked for Essex under the reallocation of places Bedford had reportedly agreed with the king back in January.[168]

In Holland, Warwick's brother, the king found a more receptive and biddable audience. Approaches to him must also have been made around 10 April; for, only four days after Rossetti had reported Essex's imminent preferment to the Lord Lieutenancy, Holland was offered – and actually accepted – another highly prestigious military command: as Lord General north of the Trent, in place of Northumberland. (Northumberland happily relinquished an office that he had never wanted and which he had been trying to rid himself of for several months.)[169]

The timing of these offers is highly suggestive, as they coincided closely with the introduction of the attainder bill on 10 April, and with Pym's successful move to have it postponed on 12 April for long enough to have the impeachment trial resumed. The Venetian ambassador, Giovanni Giustinian, discerned a clear link between Holland's preferment and the politics of the trial: 'although [Holland] is a leader of the Puritans and an enemy of the [Lord] Lieutenant [Strafford], it is hoped that ambition and the profit of this office may lead him to revise his opinions'.[170] Perhaps so; but it is hard to avoid the conclusion that Charles was using Holland's promotion as a means of reassuring Bedford and the Junto moderates that he had no intentions of using the northern army, whatever they may have heard to the contrary, against either the Parliament or the Junto's Scottish allies. Accordingly, Holland's first public act, immediately after his appointment, was to quash rumours that the English army in Yorkshire and County Durham had any offensive intent. His role, he announced to the House of Lords, was limited: 'rather to disband [the army] with honour and safety then [with] a fight'.[171] And on 24 April, Bedford House was appointed to become the treasury for the emergency monies loaned by various peers to pay the most hard-up of the English forces in the North.[172] These were moves that had both practical and symbolic significance. With Warwick's brother now in command of the army, and Bedford seeing to its (still meagre) provision of funds, surely the Parliament's fears of 'plotting' should be diminished, if not entirely stilled?[173]

These conciliatory gestures on the part of the king were, however, merely a start. During the following fortnight, even as the Warwick House group pushed the attainder forward to its third reading, Charles renewed his promises of high office to Bedford and his closest supporters. These were nevertheless conditional: the formal letters patent of appointment were to be held over until after the Strafford case had been brought to an honourable and non-fatal conclusion.[174] Bedford himself was to be the main beneficiary. As early as February 1641, Leicester had been writing of Bedford – confidently, if a little prematurely – as our 'new Lord Treasurer'.[175] By around mid-April, however, Bedford was evidently so assured of his own preferment to high office that he told John Harrison, a Commons-man and one of the customs farmers (and hence a major figure in the organization of the royal finances), 'that he [Bedford] was to have the white staff of the lord high Tre[asure]r of England', and was already seeking Harrison's 'advice and assistance in sundry affaires relating to th[at] great office'.[176] Apparently certain of his imminent promotion, Bedford was also looking to the interests of Saye and Pym, arguably his most effective allies in his campaign to forestall Strafford's execution. Saye was to receive the Mastership of the Court of Wards – another firm offer, the patent for which passed the Great Seal in early May.[177]

And at the Treasury, Bedford naturally wanted Pym, his *homme d'affaires* of so many years, as his Chancellor of the Exchequer (an office usually regarded as being in the Lord Treasurer's gift).[178]

Bedford's effectiveness in exploiting the various crises of April 1641 in order to advance the Junto's hold on public office gives the lie to the traditional claim that 'the Bedford settlement' was dead as early as mid March, the moment when Charles first began to toy with the idea of threatening his opponents with military force.[179] Bedford seems to have recognized that using the threat of military coercion was a game that two could play, and, having played it himself against the king during the autumn of 1640 so successfully, he does not appear to have taken undue umbrage when, from March 1641, Charles indulged in a little sabre-rattling of his own.

Instead, throughout the debates on the attainder bill – from its introduction on 10 April to the last public hearing in Westminster Hall on the 29th – Bedford made steady progress towards the promotion of his allies to positions of power. His reaction to Cottington's refusal to resign as Chancellor of the Exchequer and Master of the Wards is revealing. Bedford gave Cottington a simple choice: he could either wait to be hounded from office by impeachment; or, alternatively, Bedford would undertake to prevent this, 'upon condition that [Cottington] should ... surrender all his Offices of Chancellor and under-Treasurer of the Exchequer [and] Master of the Wardes'.[180] Blackmailed out of office, Cottington resigned before the month was out.

Politically, too, Bedford's 'hearty labours' were bringing important results. Towards the end of the third week of April, Charles finally gave up the struggle to prevent *any* censure falling on his Lord Lieutenant of Ireland and conceded the principle that Strafford could, after all, be punished by Parliament, provided this stopped short of taking away his life. Here, too, paradoxically, the Commons' passing of the attainder bill on Wednesday, 21 April seems to have played to Bedford's advantage, finally convincing the king of the need to meet his moderate opponents at least halfway, lest more radical counsels prevail. By Friday, 23 April, St George's Day, the king had come round to accepting that any final judgement on Strafford would, at very least, result in his exile from the court and his permanent disbarment from public office. For Charles, it was a massive concession.

The king broke the news of his change of heart in a letter to Strafford that same day:

> The Misfortune that is falen upon you by the strange Mistaking and Conjunctur of thease Tymes [is] such that I must lay by the Thought of imploying you heereafter in my Affaires[.] Yet I cannot satisfie myself in Honnor or conscience without asseuring you (now in the midst of your Trobles), that, upon the Word of a King, you shall not suffer in Lyfe, Honnor, or Fortune. This is but Justice, and therefore a verie meane Rewarde from a Maister ... yet it is as much as I conceave the present Tymes will permit.[181]

If Charles truly had reconciled himself to Strafford's permanent banishment from court, then his letter suggests that Bedford's belief in the viability of compromise was not entirely misplaced. The king's tone is both resigned and realistic: Strafford's dismissal and debarment from future office was the best deal 'the present Tymes will permit'. And while it is impossible to know what messages the king may have sent verbally, via the courier, for once, it seems, there is at least the possibility that Charles was acting in good faith.

A similar sense of realism characterizes Strafford's response to what now seemed to be a settled deal. On Saturday, 24 April, probably on receipt of the king's letter of the previous day, he wrote to the Marquess of Hamilton, the power-broker at court who had played such an important role in the Bedfordians' rise, expressing his gratitude that compromise had finally prevailed. All he asked was the liberty to attend to his domestic affairs, divested of any public role, with as few marks of infamy as his friends could procure. Strafford was optimistic:

> It is told me that the Lords are inclinable to preserve my life and family, for which – ther generouse compassions – the greate god of mercy will reward them. And surely, should I die upon this evidence, I had much rather be the sufferer then the Judge.[182]

These developments, in turn, provide the background to that same week's parliamentary proceedings. They render explicable the otherwise bizarre sight, on Thursday, 22 April, of Strafford's brother-in-law and such stalwart pro-Straffordians as Sir Thomas Widdrington joining Pym in the discussions on the future of the attainder bill;[183] and Bedford's son urging the 'expediting' of the same bill on the 24th, presumably confident that any final vote on the attainder in the Lords would produce the desired life-preserving result.[184] Here the medieval precedents were relevant, for during the great age of attainder, during the fifteenth-century 'Wars of the Roses', attainders for treason had more often been used to take away lands than to take away life; and though these, too (like the Strafford attainder), had stipulated the dire penalties of treason, those punishments were only selectively enforced and the vast majority were subsequently reversed.* Precedents also existed for Strafford to be attainted and imprisoned (as the Earl of Surrey had been in 1489), or attainted and exiled.

Such non-lethal possibilities for the outcome of the attainder bill – actively supported by Bedford[185] – account for Pym's successful bid to revive the public hearings before the Lords in Westminster Hall, as though the impeachment trial were still continuing; and the two Houses' decision to have a day of argument on points of law, scheduled for Thursday, 29 April, before the Lords were to give their final verdict. With the prosecution lawyers having proved so ineffectual over the previous six weeks, few could have imagined

---

* Of the 120 attainders passed during the reign of Edward IV, for example, eighty-six had been reversed. During Richard III's reign the reversal rate was even higher, at ninety-nine out of one hundred.

that this additional day of legal wrangling would play any other way than to Strafford's advantage.

*

As that Thursday approached, both the king and Bedford redoubled their efforts to consolidate their own caucus of support. Tracking Bedford's contacts with the king after the attainder bill went to the Lords, on Saturday, 24 April, is extremely difficult given the destruction of large portions of what must have been his archive; but there are some circumstantial clues. Perhaps the strongest is that on Monday the 26th, Bedford was able to give Edward Hyde, whom he met on the upper bowling green at Piccadilly, a detailed account of the king's attitude towards the attainder bill and the terms of the compromise the king was proposing, which would involve Strafford's disbarment from office and either banishment or imprisonment for life.[186] This suggests a recent meeting (or at least an exchange of messages) between the two, probably on Sunday, 25 April, the day when Bedford, in his capacity as a Privy Councillor, would have attended on the king in the course of the regular Sunday procession from the Privy Lodgings to the Whitehall Chapel Royal.

What seems clear is that, by this point, Charles was adamant that his conscience would not allow him to sign an attainder bill that condemned Strafford to death for treasons of which he believed he was innocent, and that to avoid being required by Parliament to do so, he was prepared to make extensive concessions to Bedford. He was ready to reward friends and to buy off expected opposition. This is partly conjecture, but perhaps the only way of explaining the cornucopia of preferments that, poured in the Junto's direction in the three days between that Sunday (the 25th) and the final hearing in Westminster Hall, on the following Thursday (the 29th).

Perhaps the most astonishing of these concessions, and one which must have required all of Bedford's courtly powers of persuasion, was the belated appointment – also on Sunday, 25 April – of the Earl of Warwick, the Petitioner grandee so conspicuously passed over in the conciliar appointments back in February, to membership of the Privy Council.[187] For Charles, this must have been particularly irksome, as Warwick was prominent among those arguing strongly for Strafford's execution.[188]

Yet the blandishments continued. The next day, Monday, the Earl of Hertford, another Petitioner Peer and an influential supporter of the compromise scheme, received a verbal promise from the king that he would be raised to a marquessate, the second-highest rank in the peerage.[189] On Tuesday the campaign to oust Cottington from his offices reached its culmination, and a combination of Bedford's blackmail and Charles's entreaties had their effect.[190]* Cottington submitted his resignation as Master of the Wards and

---

* On Monday, 26 April Pym (the intended recipient of Cottington's office as Chancellor of the Exchequer) was reported to have 'been with the King twice of late' (presumably over the previous few days), meetings which were construed to relate to his imminent preferment.

Chancellor of the Exchequer that same day – exactly forty-eight hours before what was expected to be the final session of the Strafford prosecution in Westminster Hall[191] – leaving the two offices vacant for, respectively, Saye and Pym.[192]

But perhaps the best documented, and most revealing of Bedford's initiatives was the approach which he made to Essex, also at the beginning of that week, confident that 'he should not despair of [his compromise], if he could persuade the Earl of Essex to comply'.[193] Using Hertford and Hyde as his intermediaries – a fact which itself may indicate the strained relations between the two principals – Bedford urged Essex to give his support to some form of punishment for Strafford that stopped short of a capital sentence. Fines, imprisonments, permanent debarment from office – the range of punishments that often accompanied fifteenth-century attainders: would not these suffice?

Essex's response gives some measure of the depth of the gulf that separated the Bedfordian assessment of Charles's trustworthiness from the far bleaker view of his more radical opponents. Quoting the proverb, 'Stone-dead hath no fellow', Essex explained why: because

> if [Strafford] were judged guilty in a *praemunire* [the offence of infringing the king's authority] ... or fined in any other way, and sentenced to be imprisoned during his life, the king would presently grant him his pardon and his estate, release all fines, and would likewise give him his liberty, as soon as he had a mind to receive his service – which would be as soon as the Parliament should be ended.[194]

That prospect threatened the entire edifice of reform, so painstakingly constructed since November 1640. Confronted with the likelihood of Strafford's return to royal 'service', Warwick and Essex seem to have regarded Bedford's belief that financial constraints would be sufficient to curb the king as, at best, naive; at worst, potentially suicidal.

Nor were they alone in such thinking. Perhaps the most articulate expression of what can be described as the 'Warwick House' case against Strafford appeared as a polemical tract, composed just before the impeachment trial collapsed at the end of the first week of April, and was overtaken by the bill of attainder.[195] Published as *A Declaration shewing the Necessity of the Earle of Straffords Suffering*, its anonymous author warned of the vengeance that Strafford was likely to wreak if, after all, he were to escape punishment. The Lord Lieutenant was like a savage animal – a '*homo hominibus lupus* [a man who had become a wolf to his fellow man]' or 'the Mastive [mastiff] worried [i.e. strangled or bated], [which] returns with others to kill'; and his wrath, were he ever allowed to give vent to it, would be the more terrible for the indignities he had suffered thus far.[196] Given the opportunity, Strafford would bring 'punishment upon his impeachers, so that the trienniall Parliament will bee of no such force as is expected', and the 'Common wealth' would revert to its earlier baleful state.

The experience of Richard II's reign, argued the anonymous author of the

Declaration, provided a cautionary tale. In his unhappy reign, another would-be 'break[er] of the Parliament' – appropriately, the Duke of Ireland – had turned on the aristocratic proponents of reform, the Lords Appellant, and attempted to provoke a civil war.[197]*

Strafford was likely to do the same, for

> the madde Bull, wounded and let loose, doth more mischiefe: so, if the Earle shall get out of the net, he will be more savage then before, like the Duke of Ireland, who persecuted the Patriots of the Common wealth.[198]

Strafford was clearly a man who would never be content until he had exacted vengeance; even his haughty bearing and pallid colour 'sheweth revenge'.[199] To allow him to escape was to endanger nothing less than 'the cause of God'; Parliament would 'never have the like opportunity'.[200]

To those like Warwick and Essex, who broadly shared the sentiments of the author of *Declaration shewing the Necessity of the Earle of Straffords Suffering*, Bedford's fastidiousness about the monarch's 'honour' was a luxury that 'the commonwealt' (as Essex termed it) simply could not afford.[201] The crisis of the moment required radical solutions. In fact, there is evidence that Essex, who had long experience of the Dutch system of government, may have already arrived at an essentially republican view of the monarch's role within the constitution. As he reportedly insisted to Hyde, the king had no right to a 'negative voice' in any legislation: he was 'obliged in conscience', Essex declared, 'to conform himself and his own understanding to the advice and conscience of his Parliament'.[202] In the English commonwealth, as in the other 'commonwealths', the Dutch and the Venetian, the monarch was to be no more than a Stadhouder or doge: a figurehead cipher prince.

These were conclusions that still affronted most of Essex's fellow members of the nobility (and which in time he would recant himself), as well as large sections of opinion in the House of Commons (probably a clear majority, particularly if the large number of absentees are counted as well).[203] A political nation habituated, through a thousand sermons and treatises, to regarding 'love' and affection as the proper relation between kings and their subjects

---

* Robert de Vere (1362–92), 9th Earl of Oxford, had been the favourite and chief counsellor of the young Richard II, by whom he was showered with honours and favour. In 1385, the king created him Marquess of Dublin and granted him the lordship of Ireland, with quasi-regal powers, promoting him the following year to the title of Duke of Ireland. Although accused of treason in 1387 by the Lords Appellant – the Earls of Gloucester, Arundel, Derby, Nottingham, and Warwick – he continued to be protected by the king, and raised an army of 6,000 men against the Lords Appellant. Outmanoeuvred by the Appellants, however, he fled into exile in the Low Countries, and the earls used the subsequent 1388 Parliament, nicknamed the 'Merciless', to effect a wholesale purge of Richard II's 'evil counsellors'. De Vere's conduct in Ireland, and Richard II's attempts to protect him after he was accused of treason, suggested obvious parallels to the polemicists of the early 1640s, not only between Robert de Vere and Strafford, but also between Richard II and Charles I. It was a favourite topos of Oliver St John's, who had referred to it on 11 November 1640 when Strafford was first formally accused in Parliament.

Courtier and rebel: Algernon Percy, Earl of Northumberland – the Lord High
Admiral of England and, in 1640, the reluctant Lord General in the campaign
against the Scots. Of all the king's ministers to throw in his lot with the reformers,
Edward Hyde observed, Northumberland 'may well be reckoned the chief, in respect
of the antiquity and splendour of his family, his great fortune and estate, and the
general reputation he had amongst the greatest men'.

Leez, near Chelmsford, the Earl of Warwick's seat in Essex, from where Pym sent word of the decision to publish the Petition of the Twelve Peers in September 1640. The house was conceived on a palatial scale, and, though much of it was demolished in 1753, the great gate-tower still gives some impression of the splendour of its heyday in the 1630s and 1640s.

John Pym: one of the most influential Junto Leaders in the Commons and long-standing friend, counsellor, and man-of-business to both Bedford and Warwick.

posite page: A man of 'courage for the greatest enter-
ses': Robert Rich, Earl of Warwick, the Covenanter Scots'
 ally in England, and perhaps the most powerful and
:ermined of all Charles's domestic enemies. Significantly,
 rwick chose to wear the famous 'orange tawny' livery colour
 the Devereux, Earls of Essex, his mother's family – later to be
 pted as the parliamentarian colour during the Civil War.

Blighted ambitions: Robert Devereux, Earl of Essex –
viewed by the Privy Council as the most dangerous of the
Petitioner Peers – had not always been a court outsider.
Depicted here in his mid-teens *(above, left)*, Essex had
been one of the closest friends of the heir to the throne,
Henry, Prince of Wales *(above, right)* – a friendship which
briefly augured a career, come the next reign, as the new
king's favourite. By 1613, however, when Essex was just
twenty-two, his world had collapsed. The prince was
dead; his own loveless marriage had ended in divorce and
public humiliation; and his looks had been permanently
disfigured by smallpox. Thwarted at court, he turned to a
military career abroad, fighting for the 'Godly Cause' as a
volunteer against the Catholic Habsburgs. His exploits
won him a reputation as a Protestant hero, and by 1641,
at the age of fifty, he was probably the most popular man
in England. Inexpensive printed portraits (such as this,
left) were widely circulated.

A gun emplacement, with its 'gabions' – wicker baskets, filled with stones, to protect the gunners. The mounting of such gabions on the Tower's defences in November 1640, helped convince many Parliament-men that Strafford was about to launch a pre-emptive strike against his prospective accusers.

The 'Parliament House': the sprawling, mostly medieval, Palace of Westminster. In this contemporary view, the massive bulk of Westminster Hall, the venue for Strafford's trial, looms in the centre. Immediately to its left is the Commons' meeting place: the tall and slender Chapel of St Stephen, completed in *c.* 1300, and modelled on the Sainte Chapelle in Paris.

Left: Old Palace Yard was the setting for the anti-Straffordian protests of May 1641, and again for the demonstrations against the king's-party bishops in November and December that year. The turrets of St Stephen's Chapel (the House of Commons) are visible on the skyline to the right in this painting of 1670, while the arched portal on the lower right was the principal entrance to the House of Lords. Although violent disorders of the kind depicted in Wenzel Hollar's vignette (*opposite page, below*) were probably rare, an element of menace was rarely absent from these gatherings. At court, there was a widespread belief that such 'tumults' had been set in train by the Junto.

Strafford's assailants: the Leicestershire grandee, Sir Arthur Hesilrige (*below, right*), the Commons-man who produced – out 'of his pocquet' – the fully drafted bill to attaint the Earl of Strafford after the impeachment trial had collapsed on 10 April 1641. In London, Hesilrige lived at Brooke House in Holborn, renting an apartment from his brother-in-law, Robert Greville, Lord Brooke (*below, left*) – his close friend, and fellow campaigner (with Warwick and Essex, among others) for Strafford's death.

The quarry: Thomas Wentworth, Earl of Strafford. Imperious, ambitious, and formidably astute, Strafford was the one man who, the Junto feared, had the acumen and force of character to create a successful authoritarian monarchy within the three Stuart kingdoms. Having embarked on a campaign to see him executed, his persecutors were justly terrified of his revenge, should he escape the block: 'the madde Bull, wounded and let loose, doth more mischiefe', warned Oliver St John, 'so, if the Earle shall get out of the net, [he will] be more savage then before'.

had an almost instinctive aversion to concluding that *this* king, their own king, was uniquely unworthy of trust.[204] Paradoxically, it was Bedford's and Pym's appeal to that trust – and their apparent confidence that the post-Triennial Act financial constraints would be sufficient to deter Charles from attempting his fallen minister's rehabilitation – that remained their strongest suit in their efforts to save Strafford's life.

Of course, they still faced formidable opposition, perhaps more from outside Parliament than within. In the City, a petitioning campaign was reported to be in progress, demanding Strafford's execution – an initiative in which the Warwick House group was probably implicated.[205] Strafford's own partisans were also a problem. A report on Wednesday, 28 April that his secretary, Guilford Slingsby, was hatching an escape bid prompted a flurry of counter-measures, including a House of Lords order for strengthening the guard at the Tower.[206] And Charles's own interventions, even when well intentioned, tended to be counter-productive. In a speech to the two Houses that same Wednesday afternoon, in the Banqueting House, the king agreed to the 'disarming' of Catholics (a concession which, *inter alia,* was set to take the Earl of Worcester's arsenal out of commission); but whatever he gained in good opinion from this concession was cancelled out by his continuing delay in the disbandment of the Irish army, at which 'many' in his audience 'weere much greived'.[207] Members' humour was not improved when, as they were leaving to return to Westminster, they were caught in a torrential spring downpour. Within minutes, they were soaked to the skin.[208]

The inclemencies of the weather apart, however, by Wednesday, 28 April – the eve of St John's speech – Bedford's circle had reason for cautious optimism. Many of the political indicators seemed set fair for a settlement that both saved Strafford's life and confirmed Bedford's pre-eminence as Lord Treasurer and principal counsellor of the realm. The attainder bill would either be heavily amended to exclude a capital sentence (if the peers opted for condemning Strafford by statute), or set aside altogether and replaced with a formal judgement by the peers, finding Strafford guilty of offences short of treason (if the peers chose to bring the impeachment to its formal conclusion). As Sir John Temple summarized the position on the eve of the final session, the Lords 'too morrow are to heare the conclusion of the evidence against [Strafford] brought in by Mr St Johns, and [are] so to proceede to judgement, which, I believe, will not be for the taking away of his life'.[209] The generally well-informed contemporary chronicler of Strafford's trial, known only by his initials 'S. R.', reached the same conclusion, arguing that 'it is very likely the Lord Strafford might have passed free by the voices of the Lords', and that it was 'both possible and probable that [the king] might have gained the [peers'] Declaration . . . for him'.[210] Protests against such leniency were to be expected, of course, from the anti-Straffordian militants in the Commons, and perhaps from Warwick and Essex as well. But all that was necessary for Charles to save his former servant, it seemed, was for him to sit still, rely on the House of Lords, and to allow his 'new Privy Councillors' to fulfil their promises and guide the proceedings to their carefully planned and non-lethal end.[211]

*

For Bedford, after two long decades spent frustratingly on the fringes of power, the fulfilment of his life's ambitions seemed merely a matter of days away. Planning was already under way for sweeping reforms of the Exchequer under his new management, including, as one memorandum advised, the need to re-establish a 'dependencie ... betweene your lordship and the lord deputy [of Ireland] and the other officers of that kingdome' – a subordination of the Irish viceroy to the English Lord Treasurer that had been allowed to lapse during the days of Strafford's rule.[212]

Only the recurrence of Bedford's earlier illness clouded a prospect that was otherwise so full of promise.[213] Influenza-like symptoms – 'a feverish disposition' and an 'oppression of choller in the stomacke' – had been troubling him from around the middle of that week. But his physician, Dr Thomas Cademan, assured him that it was 'but a simple boyling of [the] blood, which he had often formerly had', and the doctor treated it straightforwardly with emetics and purges.[214] Otherwise, Bedford – and, not least, Strafford and the king[215] – were optimistic.

What Bedford's physician called 'this yeare that has beene fertile of wonders'[216] seemed about to bring forth yet another: the great business of the Earl of Strafford was about to reach an unexpectedly happy resolution.

10

STRAFFORD: NEMESIS

APRIL–MAY 1641

As the faces of all Britane shew their hearts and inclinations, so ... they
would appeare fearefull of the future, were not the representative body
of the State carefull to cure the present malady, purge the distempered
humours and save the much-gangrend body by cutting some rotten and
putrifide members off, which infect, infest, and invade the republique.

A Discourse Shewing in what State the Three Kingdomes are in at this Present
([late April–early May] 1641)[1]

Strafford was visibly 'merry' when he was brought to the bar on Thursday,
29 April for the final day of argument in Westminster Hall.[2] Gone now was
the dejected figure in funereal black that had appeared at the trial's opening.
This was the assured Strafford of old: masterful, confident and apparently
relishing another opportunity to lambast his accident-prone accusers. An
equally good-humoured king took his place in his box to the right of the
throne,[3] partly visible to the crowd in the body of the hall.[4] The trading with
the Bedfordians had brought results, and the Lords, as Strafford had explained
to Hamilton a few days earlier, were now 'inclinable to preserve my life and
family'.[5] That Thursday's session was expected to be the last public hearing
before the Lords proceeded to a vote, and Charles must have been reassured
that it was Oliver St John, his own Solicitor-General and the very first of the
Bedfordian circle to have received preferment, who had been chosen to make
the case.[6]

What the Lord Treasurer-elect needed from the king's Solicitor-General
was a speech that established Strafford's treason, persuaded the Lords that
he should be attainted, but left the peers at liberty to mitigate his punishment.
That was a compromise that both the king and Bedford had accepted,[7] which
had already, in the last four days, produced Warwick's appointment to the
Privy Council, the removal of the hated Cottington as Master of the Wards
and Chancellor of the Exchequer, and the promise of further promotions to
high office from within the Junto. There seemed to be every reason to suppose
that St John – whose own rise to Solicitor-General was the result of that

earlier phase of Bedfordian wheeler-dealing – would use his speech to bring this settlement to its successful conclusion.

St John had been heard relatively little in Westminster Hall hitherto, and although he had been supportive of the attainder, and shown some impatience with the trial's numerous postponements, his earlier contributions to the debate had given relatively few clues as to the arguments he was likely to deploy. Of course, St John was expected to argue strongly for Strafford's guilt and that the Lords' should therefore condemn him.[8] But, prima facie, there was nothing in either of these objectives that was inconsistent with Bedford's plans for an outcome that left Strafford attainted of treason, but which confined his punishment to disbarment from office, and imprisonment or exile. Indeed, if St John *failed* to persuade the Lords both of Strafford's guilt and the need for his punishment, the entire foundation of Bedford's negotiating position with the king would have collapsed.

However, in one critical respect, the king and Strafford – and, it seems, Bedford as well – were labouring under a delusion. Privately, St John had been convinced, at least since early April, that the only way of securing the post-Triennial Act constitution was by Strafford's death. Unbeknownst to Bedford, the anonymous author of the *Declaration shewing the Necessity of the Earle of Straffords Suffering*, published some three weeks earlier – one of the most vicious of all anti-Straffordian tracts, with its denunciation of 'the man who was a wolf among men', 'the madde Bull wounded and let loose', the 'Mastive [that] returns with others to kill'[9] – had been St John himself.

1. 'THIS STRANGE CONCLUSION'

St John rose to speak shortly after nine in the morning, delivering his speech from his place in the front row of the right-hand 'scaffold' reserved for members of the Commons.[10]* Glynne and Maynard flanked him to either side, ready to read relevant extracts from such statutes and law books as St John required to substantiate his case.[11] Except for these interventions, the task of persuading the Lords of Strafford's guilt was his alone. The daunting circumstances of the Hall, which had been the undoing of many an earlier prosecution counsel – the massive crowd, the Parliament-men assembled in their hundreds, the cavernous space that his voice somehow had to fill – left St John unfazed. He had prepared his speech with meticulous care, bringing to his argument a combination of rhetorical flair and a mastery of medieval

---

* Hitherto, the prosecution counsel had delivered their speeches at the bar of the House, and with their backs to the 'audience' in the body of the Hall. This occasion was different. Because the two Houses were technically meeting as committees rather than with the Lords constituted as a court, St John did not go to the bar but remained standing in his place in the Commons' grandstand. This was a minor detail, but one which meant that, unlike all previous speakers in the trial, St John spoke from a position that was both elevated and facing down the Hall, both circumstances that made him far more visible (and probably more audible) than any counsel who had spoken before him.

history and legal precedent that few of his legal colleagues in the Commons could match. For weeks, the prosecution's speech-making had rarely risen above the mediocre, and had occasionally descended into farce. From St John's opening lines, however, it was apparent that this speech was to be qualitatively different in tone and substance.[12]

In a virtuoso display of forensic oratory lasting almost three hours, St John rehearsed the case for Strafford's guilt. His central concern was the problem that had confounded all the prosecution counsel hitherto: how could Strafford's 'crimes' be made to come within the existing law of treason? To resolve this question, St John returned to first principles. Strafford's most pernicious crime, he argued, had been to subvert the law, and this, even on its own, could be demonstrated to be an act of treason. Referring to the theory of the King's Two Bodies, which had been so central to the visual symbolism of the trial from the outset, St John gave a radical new gloss to the words 'levying warre against the King'; for 'it is plaine', he argued, 'that [this phrase] is not meant against the *meere person*' of the king. 'To subvert [the] lawes'[14] – and the laws, by implication, constituted the king's other 'person', his abstract, politic body – was akin to levying war against the king in his most important capacity: his abstract capacity as sovereign. Moreover, this abstract body, St John repeatedly implied, should be identified with Parliament, the 'great bodie politicke' of the realm.[14] All of this followed naturally from St John's arguments in his defence of Hampden in the great Ship Money case of 1637, when, in a novel interpretation of the 'King's Two Bodies' principle, he had argued that 'those powers which derived from a responsibility to preserve the state could be exercised only through Parliament'.[15] Once again, the king was being reduced to a cipher, a 'meere person', in a monarchical republic in which the two Houses were already de facto sovereign.

Much of the effectiveness of St John's oration lay in the way in which this radical, even revolutionary, theory of the state was dressed up in the profoundly conservative rhetoric of social control. Above all, he both flattered, and played on the anxieties of, the House of Lords – the constituency that would now decide Strafford's fate. Insisting to this hierarchy-conscious audience that Strafford's treason threatened to bring in a pernicious egalitarianism ('My lords, take away law, and their is noe pearidge [peerage], but every swaine is equall'),[16] he effectively discounted the notion that impeachment and attainder were mutually exclusive and rival modes of proceeding. Far from it: St John argued that the peers' final verdict on the attainder bill, rather than being an abandonment of the trial in Westminster Hall, was actually the most effective means of bringing the impeachment process to a legally safe conclusion. Without the attainder bill, however, there were inevitable doubts as to whether Strafford's crimes came within the existing law of treason. Proceeding by statute, however, would avoid any such ambiguities; and to clinch this point, he cited the dictum of one of Richard II's judges: that he 'could not Judge [a particular offence] treason in Westminster hall [i.e. in the courts of law], but [he] could in parliament'.[17]

So far, all this was perfectly compatible with the Bedfordians' agreed compromise. They, too, wanted Strafford convicted – if necessary, through an act of attainder – but with the Lords left free to mitigate the final punishment.

But, then, as he was nearing his peroration, the tone of his speech suddenly changed. St John – the king's Solicitor-General, the apparently reliable Bedfordian placeman – stunned his audience by abandoning the measured language of legality and reason, adopting, instead, a far more direct and, in its passion, unlawyerly style. Speaking now, not of law and precedent, but of wolves and foxes, beasts and predators – references that must have appealed directly to the experience of an audience of countrymen and landowners – St John argued emphatically that Strafford must be killed, for the good of the commonwealth.

Recalling the language he had already deployed in the argument for the *Necessity of the Earle of Straffords Suffering,* St John provided his audience with what was to be the most arresting and long-remembered section of his speech. Strafford, St John maintained, was like a marauding animal, a predator that endangered the life of the entire body politic. 'It was never accounted either cruelty or foul play', he insisted, 'to knock foxes and wolves on the head as they can be found, because they be beasts of prey.'[18] For the safety of the realm, nothing short of Strafford's execution would suffice.

Intellectually, this was an argument for 'reason of state', the belief that the preservation of the commonwealth legitimates the contravention of standard moral and legal codes (a principle to which Strafford, with equal ruthlessness and from his very different perspective, also adhered).[19] Politically, it marked St John's abandonment of the Bedfordian quest for consensus and his declaration of solidarity with the hardline anti-Straffordians – with Warwick, Essex, and Hesilrige – and their grim precept that 'stone-dead hath no fellow'.

*

Both the king and Strafford were dumbfounded by what they had heard. Georg Weckherlin, the Privy Council secretary, who was among the throng listening in Westminster Hall, described the unexpected and electrifying impact of St John's oratory:

> Then the whole scene seemed changed. And I am tolde that the king himself as well as the Earle (who tooke notes with their owne hands) gave over writing as soone as St Johns proved that the house of Commons sitting in Parliament had absolute power to pronounce what was treason, though the same were not found or layd downe so by Statuts or Lawes.[20]

This was not an assertion of unicameral Commons' sovereignty, but rather the claim, which St John's anonymous treatise had advanced earlier, that the lower House had the right 'to declare the facts of the Lord Strafford['s] treason'.* The viciousness of St John's rhetoric left the king aghast. Henriette

---

* St John had earlier used an almost identical argument as the peroration to his *Declaration shewing the Necessity of the Earle of Straffords Suffering*: that in the reign of Henry VI, 'the Judges [held] they had no power to judge of any Act of the house of Commons, but were subject to them, and what the house of Commons should set downe was Law; by which it appears plainly that they have power to declare the facts of the Lord Strafford

Marie, who had been closely involved in attempts to win over Charles's opponents, did not even wait for the Solicitor-General to finish. 'Seeing this strange conclusion', she abruptly left Westminster Hall and returned to Whitehall.[21] Strafford, however, pretended to be unimpressed. At the end of the speech, he responded contemptuously: 'What? Is this all hee can say?'[22]

When St John eventually sat down, his performance was acclaimed as the formidable act of theatre that it undoubtedly was: the entire Hall erupted in 'great applause'.[23] From that moment, it was evident that the acuity of St John's argument, and the warmth of its reception, had drastically narrowed Strafford's chances of escaping the axe. D'Ewes's report of the emergent consensus was probably not wide of the mark: St John's 'learned Argument gave high satisfaction to all men generally'.[24] Even moderates like the Earl of Bath, a future 'king's-party' man, wrote later that day that St John 'did excellently acquitte himself'.[25]

St John's speech of 29 April 1641 is one of that handful of political speeches from the 1640s which can genuinely be said to have changed the course of events. It powerfully influenced a centre group of peers (of whom Bath was probably one), overnight reducing what had been a clear pro-Straffordian majority to a minority, and decisively strengthening the pro-attainder vote. Before St John's speech, one contemporary had estimated, the rival parties in the Lords stood at around thirty in favour of the attainder and fifty against. After 29 April, 'many of the 50 [anti-attainder] Lords are come about, and therefore it is generally conceived the Earl will loose his head'. The explanation was straightforward: 'St John did make such an exelent argument [that it] satisfied the opposites'.[26]

Not all St John's audience seem to have regarded his performance so admiringly. To the king, this 'strange conclusion' to the trial can only have seemed a betrayal. After all his concessions of the last two weeks – Holland's promotion as Lord General, the renewed promise of the Treasurership to Bedford, the ousting of Cottington to make way for Pym and Saye, even, most galling of all, Warwick's appointment to the Privy Council – it must have seemed almost a calculated affront. Bedford's man, it seemed, had double-crossed them all; and whether or not he regarded Bedford as party to St John's assault, the harm had been done – and, ironically, by the very first of the Junto-men whom he had rewarded with preferment. An anti-Junto libel, distributed shortly afterwards, spoke of St John and Vane, who provided the most damning evidence against Strafford, as 'both Judases': men who had sold their lord.[27] Something of the king's bitterness at this betrayal, still rankling over a year later, emerges in a proclamation in which the Junto-men were reminded that

[they] themselves know what overtures have bin made by them, and with

---

treason, which I humbly submit to the high Court of Parliament' (*Necessity*, sigg. B2r-B2[1]). There are moments when *The Necessity* reads almost as a dry run for St John's speech of 29 April.

what importunity for Offices and Preferments, what great services should have bin done for Us and other undertakings [which] were [made] (*even to have saved the life of the Earle of Strafford*), if We would [have] confer[red] such Offices upon them.[28]

Whatever Bedford's personal intentions, there was now little prospect of his being able to deliver the parliamentary compromise that would honour his undertaking to save Strafford's life. The lethal persuasiveness of St John's oratory had driven a stake through the heart of his plans for a settlement.

Bedford's own reaction to St John's speech is unrecorded. But, coming from a man whom he had promoted, almost as a son, for the best part of two decades, it is difficult to see how he could have regarded St John's vehemence against Strafford as anything other than a personal betrayal.[29] Why, then, did St John turn on the Lord-Lieutenant so ferociously, knowing full well, presumably, what its implications would be for his patrician cousin's attempts to broker a wider settlement? Unlike many others at Westminster, it was not the king's preparations for war over the previous week that had panicked him into demanding Strafford's death. For St John's belief in the Lord-Lieutenant's dangerousness, both to his 'impeachers' (as he termed them) and to the reformed commonwealth, seems to have been fully fixed well before the revelations of the previous week.[30] Of course, St John had argued in public strongly against Strafford before; yet, except for his anonymously published pamphlet, nothing he had said hitherto had been so directly insistent on Strafford's death. His speech of 29 April and its disastrous consequences for Bedford's plans illustrate dramatically how even the strongest bonds of aristocratic patronage and friendship had their breaking point. If, as seems to have been the case, St John had become convinced that executing Strafford was the surest way of forestalling the king's march to war, this would almost certainly have triumphed over even the closest ties of kinship and worldly obligation. There are also hints that, religiously, he had drawn closer in the late 1630s to the more 'zealous' of his friends, a circle that not only included Warwick, but also his own fervently godly cousin, Oliver Cromwell.[31] With it came a certain chilliness of demeanour. Contemporaries noted an almost ancient Roman austerity about St John's high-mindedness, a rigid adherence to principle and conscience that won respect, if seldom affection.

It is also possible, however, to discern another less elevated aspect to St John's breach with his former patron. By 1641, something had clearly changed in the relationship between the earl and the man who had once been 'my Lord of Bedford's only favorite',[32] and who had risen to high legal office on his coat-tails. The young man whom Sir Thomas Barrington had commended in 1629 for his 'sweetness' of nature,[33] had become in early middle age a man of 'dark and clouded countenance'; a moody autodidact, who, for all his intellectual brilliance, lacked a 'pleasing deportment'.[34] By 1641, his professional relations with Bedford may also have been under strain. For all the earl's generosity and his undoubted affection for his protégé, Bedford could, too, be a capricious and patronizing employer, whose bullying ways had recently driven another of his *hommes d'affaires*, Robert Scawen, to an acrimonious parting of ways.[35] In St John's case, the state of the evidence does not permit clear-cut conclusions; but, if Bedford's treatment of Scawen is any guide to his relations with St John – the scion of the Russells' bastard line – St John's position of subordination towards his rich and querulous cousin must have been particularly hard to bear.

Much of this is inevitably speculation. What is certain, however, is that his speech of 29 April marked a decisive moment of severance from his erstwhile patron.[36] From that moment, the two men – very publicly – were on opposing political sides.[37] And it now looked as though it would be Bedford's adversaries within the Junto who, with St John's decisive help, would eventually prevail.

II. COUNTER-ATTACK

The disarray among the Bedfordians was compounded by another, more prosaic and entirely contingent cause. Just at the moment when all Bedford's political wizardry was required to dispel the gathering storm, the earl's 'simple boyling of [the] blood' suddenly took a more ominous turn.[38] Around Friday, 30 April, the day after St John's speech, Bedford's daughter, Lady Brooke, noticed 'some red spots' in 'divers parts of his skin' – a possible symptom of smallpox, one of the most terrifying of all diseases in Stuart England, threatening death or, at best, permanent disfigurement to its victim. Summoned once again, Bedford's physician, Dr Thomas Cademan, assured his patient that there was nothing to worry about; that smallpox was most unlikely; and that the malady would be cured in due course by rest.[39] Nevertheless, as a precaution, Bedford instructed all members of his family to leave the house until the seriousness of his ailment was ascertained.[40] From that moment, he was effectively incommunicado, isolated in Bedford House; and, though at this stage his symptoms were still not regarded as life-threatening, it is tempting to suggest that their onset may have been hastened by the shock of his breach with St John the previous day.[41]

Bedford's as-yet-undiagnosed malady robbed those who advocated for some form of mitigated punishment for Strafford of their most effective spokesman; and in Bedford's absence it fell to Viscount Saye, his key ally and nominee for the Court of Wards, to try to convince the king that the Bedfordian compromise remained a salvageable option.

Saye was hardly an effective substitute. Not yet the parliamentary power-broker that he would later become, his standing, at this point, seems to have been heavily compromised by his almost craven ambition for office; and, as Hyde later recalled, he had 'neither [Bedford's] credit with the King, nor his authority with his confederates'.[42] Starting from this unpromising base, Saye nevertheless tried one last gambit. To counteract the effect of St John's speech, he advised Charles to appear in person before the Lords (who had yet to vote on the attainder bill), not merely to make an appeal on Strafford's behalf, but also to rebut St John's principal charge: that Strafford had counselled him to subvert the established law.[43] Perhaps unsettled by the ferocity and persuasiveness of St John's speech, the king was more than ever undecided as to how to respond to this latest challenge to his authority and 'honour'. Veering, as he was to do again, between two mutually contradictory approaches – between frightening his Parliament into submission or conciliating it – Charles eventually took Saye's advice to address the Parliament, and the diplomatic approach seemed to have prevailed. Indeed, in a tactful display of deference to the legislature, Charles consented to go to Westminster, rather than (as would have been more usual) summoning the two Houses to attend him at Whitehall, in order to address the Parliament.[44]

Hence, on Saturday morning, 1 May – two days after St John's speech in Westminster Hall – the king took his place on the throne in the House of Lords. Black Rod was despatched to summon the Commons to attend him in the upper House.[45]*

Inducing the king to go to Westminster was one thing; controlling what he said was quite another. In the presence of the assembled Houses, Charles became nervous and defensive – and, as so often before when he had felt cornered, he disastrously miscalculated the tone of his remarks.[46] Desperately, he reaffirmed his commitment to the Bedfordian compromise, offering that Strafford should be permanently debarred from office, even deploying the topical language of 'commonwealth' to make his point: 'I thinke my lord of Strafford is not fitt here after to serve me, nor in the commonwealth, in any place of trust: hoe, not soe much as to be a [village] high constable'. Moreover, in what seems to have been a deliberate contradiction of St John's key charges in Westminster Hall, he denied ever having intended to use the Irish army against England or having considered the alteration of the laws.[47]

Had the king left matters there, his concession might well have undone some of the damage caused by St John's speech. Instead, however, he went on to the offensive, hedging this one substantive concession with imperious royal demands for the respect of his 'conscience'. It was the sort of language that many of those who had heard such provocative language in the Parliaments of the 1620s hoped never to hear again. 'My lords,' Charles declared,

> I hope you know what a tender thing the conscience is: yet I must declare unto you [that] to satisfy my people I would doe great matters; but in this [being a matter] of conscience, neither [any] feare nor respecte whatsoever shall ever make me goe against it.

Once again, the king left no doubt that, if he were presented with a bill of attainder that found Strafford guilty of high treason, it would be vetoed.[48] His most provocative words, however, he kept for last. Despite having conceded, in principle, that he was willing to disband the Irish army,[49] he insisted that all military forces currently on foot should be disbanded together: 'I

---

* So jittery were the Commons about the threat of a dissolution that when they glimpsed Black Rod enter the chamber, 'some feared it had been to dissolve [the Parliament]'.

desire *and require* your assistance', was the king's haughty phrase, 'for the disbanding of *all* the Armyes'.[50] Strafford's army in Ireland, he implied, would never be cashiered until the Scots had also departed from the North of England.[51] To a Parliament that had already heard, over a period of many months, a long string of mostly spurious excuses for the king's failure to disband the Irish army, this looked like yet another attempt at stalling. And although Charles publicly denied that he had ever 'any intencion of bringing over the Irish army into England',[52] it seemed (perhaps unfairly) that his only possible motive for continuing to delay the disbandment was because he intended, at some point soon, to do precisely this. His earlier pleas of poverty seem to have failed to convince.

None of Charles's public utterances to date had shocked his audience so deeply as this. Quite apart from the threat implicit in the continuing existence of the Irish army, the speech amounted to a pre-emptive statement that there were certain topics (the punishment of counsellors adjudged to be 'evil' by the Lords and Commons) on which the royal conscience was sovereign, and where he would refuse to accept the advice of his 'Great Council', the Parliament. This opened up the possibility of the king declaring a series of constitutional no-go areas, where conscience forbade him to accept the counsels of his Parliament. More importantly in the context of May 1641, however, it carried the implicit imputation that Parliament's collective judgement (such as might be contained in an attainder bill passed by both Houses) might be so flawed, either by mistakes as to fact or by malice, that the king would be justified in rejecting it. In other words, 'conscience' – and the superiority of the king's conscience over the collective conscience of his Parliament – had become a new moral justification for Charles's refusal to accept his relegation to the status of a purely figurehead king.[53]

At this distance, it is difficult to judge whether it was the king's direct threat to veto the attainder if it were passed by the Lords with a provision for capital punishment, or the threat implicit in his slowness to disband the Irish army that weighed more heavily on his audience. But eyewitnesses were agreed that the main effect of the speech was to provoke a mixture of shock, bafflement and anger – emotions that were to intensify sharply in the days ahead. 'Wee heard what astonisht us all', wrote D'Ewes; so much so that 'wee refused to proceed in anie business.' The Commons, on returning to their chamber, sat in stunned silence until some members spoke briefly of 'our calamitie.[54] Pym, who still seems to have been working loyally to keep the Bedfordian compromise in play, moved for an adjournment, 'lest they should break out into some rash distemper'.[55]

What made Charles's words seem such a 'calamitie' was not that they suggested he was prepared to risk a confrontation between Crown and Parliament – and so risk a civil war – in order to save Strafford, but rather the reverse: that the most likely motive for his wanting to save Strafford – his leading general and the advocate of the ruthless suppression of internal dissent – was precisely *in order* to fight a civil war.[56] For D'Ewes, the patient chronicler of these momentous days, this was literally the stuff of nightmares. 'I dreamt', he confided to his wife, 'of nothing but horror and desolation [that was to occur] within one fortnight', and 'the consideration of yourself and my innocent children drew teares from me.'[57] Among moderate Commons-men, there was already an expectation that some form of conflagration might actually be necessary if the impasse between king and Parliament were to be cleared. 'We shall be cured by a confusion', declared the Kentish Parliament-man, Sir Edward Dering; by 2 May, the day after the king's speech, Dering was looking forward to this 'confusion' almost optimistically, confident that 'if the French play not the devills with us, the confusion will be *short and safe*'.[58]

Over the following twelve months this belief in the curative power of 'confusion' – the idea that a 'short and safe' armed clash between the two sides might be an effective way of cutting the Gordian knot – was to become a highly influential idea, first at Westminster, and later in the country at large. It seemed alluringly simple; and there was the recent precedent of the Covenanter Scots – who had gained virtually all their political objectives through the single 'confusion' of their own, the 'skirmish' at Newburn – as evidence of how effective such a solution could be. On Saturday, 1 May, after hearing the king's 'calamitous' speech, many at Westminster seem to have concluded that, like it or not, that matter had already been taken out of their hands. Some form of military confrontation seemed to have become the king's preferred course of action.

*

Whether or not Charles had actually decided on the resort to force before he addressed the two Houses on Saturday, 1 May, there is little doubt that it had become his settled resolve by later that same day. At some point between the afternoon and evening of that Saturday, the king's patience finally snapped. Since Thursday, it had become increasingly apparent that Bedford and his diminishing band of allies no longer had the capacity, perhaps not even the will, to deliver their promised quid pro quo.[59] The king was decided. Having exhausted all legal and parliamentary options for securing Strafford's release, the time had come for 'other courses'. Many elements in the king's plans are obscure, but at least his principal objectives seem clear: the release of Strafford, through a combination of stealth and force, from the Tower; the 'breaking' of the Parliament; and finally, the advance of part of his army in the North southwards to quell any resistance to the dissolution.[60] That day, evidently in response to a royal fiat issued only slightly earlier, the Ordnance Office provided the king with a detailed listing of his holdings of gunpowder: 160 lasts* in the Tower, and more than half as much again at Portsmouth, whose fortress was also to figure prominently in the planning for the imminent coup.[61]

Talk of a forcible dissolution, of course, had long been current in the lobbies and alehouses of Westminster. Charles himself had been dropping

---

* A last was 24 barrels, each containing 100 lbs of gunpowder; the holdings in the Tower alone constituted 3,800 barrels as of 1 May 1641.

intermittent hints that he might have recourse to the army ever since Goring had revealed the existence of a plot to four of the leading Junto peers (Newport, Bedford, Mandeville and Saye) back in early April.[62] Only now, however, did the king give his approval to the implementation of a specific scheme. The prime objective was the seizure of the Tower of London, with the intention of securing Strafford's person (and allowing his escape).

Who counselled the king to adopt this bold and risky strategy is unknown. One suspect would appear to be the beleaguered Lord Cottington, the arch-Hispanophile and friend of Strafford, who had been hounded from office in the course of that same week. Moreover, Cottington had been involved, as Constable of the Tower, in the earlier failed attempt, in November 1640, to use the fortress as the springboard for an anti-parliamentarian coup; it looks very much as if this second venture was a rerun of that earlier scheme.[63] The likeliest source for the plan, however, was a group around the queen that included her Master of the Horse, Henry Jermyn, and her well-born favourite, Henry Percy (Northumberland's younger brother and presumptive heir). In collusion with at least some of the disgruntled army officers who had been fomenting anti-parliamentarian sentiment in the ranks since March, these conspirators were intent on following up the coup's initial success in London, by bringing the army southwards – with the objective, it seems, of enforcing a dissolution of Parliament.[64]

The first stage of the plot was simple. A small group of soldiers would be introduced into the Tower under the guise of reinforcing its garrison. This would then take control of the fortress, secure Strafford (and ensure his escape), and use their control of the stronghold as a means of cowing 'rebellious London' into submission. The soldiers for this mission were to be provided by a small force of mercenaries raised by Sir John Suckling, the thirty-two-year-old son of a middle-ranking courtier who had been Comptroller of the Household during the 1620s.[65] Suckling had a licence from the king to recruit a troop of horse and three infantry regiments (a force that, when fully mustered, would have numbered some 3,000 men), on the pretext that they were destined for service with the Portuguese king, João IV.[66]* By late April, Suckling had enlisted around 100 recruits, and this band, though small, was certainly large enough to secure the Tower and effect Strafford's release.

Soldier and poet, gambler and card-sharp (he was reputed to have invented the game of cribbage), and distinguished by a well-coiffed mane of reddish-blond locks, Suckling was almost the parody of the rakish cavalier 'gallant'.[67] His skills were various. Like so many of his generation, he had served as a volunteer in the Netherlands, campaigning against the Spanish in the 1620s; served on a mission to Gustavus Adolphus of Sweden in 1631; and written

---

* The Portuguese revolt against Spanish rule was only a matter of months old: the Portuguese nobleman, João, Duke of Bragança, having been proclaimed king as João IV on 1 December 1640. Suckling's claim to be raising mercenaries for a forthcoming anti-Spanish campaign was therefore superficially plausible – at least until this was confuted by the Portuguese ambassador, who denied any knowledge of Suckling's mission.

a play, *Aglaura,* with echoes of *Hamlet,* that was performed before the king and queen in April 1638.[68]* This, at least, finally succeeded in impressing the king, and in November that year Suckling was appointed a Gentleman of the Privy Chamber Extraordinary, a position that afforded less intimate access to the king than membership of the more prestigious Bedchamber, but still placed him as a member of the king's inner entourage. One of the first to volunteer for the anti-Covenanter war of 1639, Suckling fought at the battle of Newburn,[69] and it was probably on this campaign, too, that he was brought into contact with the two key 'Straffordian commanders' in the North, Sir Thomas Danbie and Sir William Pennyman – whose regiments were Strafford's likely destination in the event of a successful escape. More to the point, Suckling connected all three of the major constituencies among the plotters: he knew the officers of the northern army, was a close friend of Jermyn, and had more than a passing acquaintance with the Earl of Newcastle, the Governor (or guardian-*cum*-mentor) of the Prince of Wales and friend of Strafford's, who was to have rendezvoused with the army, on its march southwards to London, with a force of a thousand horse.[70]

Yet Suckling was no uncritical defender of Charles's *ancien régime.* Ironically, he firmly believed in the need for reform and doubted the wisdom of Charles's attempts to save unpopular ministers such as Strafford.[71] What prompted him to resort to violence in the spring of 1641 was not hostility towards reform per se, but against the personal ambitions of the would-be reformers. These, he believed, were traitors whose consciousness of their own guilt forced them to impose ever more swingeing constraints on royal power. Writing to Jermyn, shortly after the attack on Strafford had begun, Suckling wrote of the Junto leaders that

> they will not bee content (while they feare, and have the upper hand) to fetter onely royaltie, but perchance (as timorous Spirritts use) will not thinke themselves safe whiles that is att all [i.e. while monarchy exists at all] – and possibly this may bee the present state of things [in England].[72]

For Suckling, as perhaps for Jermyn, the recourse to force was not intended to halt the implementation of necessary reforms, but rather to reassert the king's dominance of the political process to the point where he – and not the 'cowardly' Junto – could garner people's 'love' in gratitude for the redress of grievances.[73] If Suckling's motives are in any way representative of his fellow plotters, they were actuated more by concerns with honour (particularly with affronts to the king's) and the unfitness of the current Junto

---

* His portrait by Van Dyck, painted around 1638 and now in the Frick Collection, New York, depicts him in exotic, quasi-Oriental costume in the manner of Inigo Jones's masque designs. He is holding a copy of Shakespeare's First or Second Folio, open at a page from *Hamlet* – perhaps the 'earliest pictorial reference to Shakespeare and his works'.

to exercise power than with any consideration of either religion or political theory.

Suckling's and Jermyn's efforts had probably made the recourse to force a viable, if hazardous, option not much later than the middle of April. And perhaps the most revealing aspect of the entire scheme is how early Charles appears to have given it his blessing – if only as a fall-back position, in the event of his agreement with Bedford going unfulfilled. Soldiers were being recruited, apparently to take the Tower, from around 24 April – two days after the attainder bill had been delivered to the Lords – and around the same time the queen's plate (which could be melted down to pay soldiers) was reportedly packed up for conveyance to Portsmouth.[74] Even as Charles had been accepting Warwick into the Privy Council, and forcing Cottington to resign to make way for Saye and Pym, he had been at least toying with the possibility of a future recourse to arms.

Yet the king's decision to act upon it as the means of Strafford's deliverance seems to have been taken impulsively, with very little time between the issuing of the king's commands on the Saturday, 1 May, and the plot's actual execution the following day. No later than that Saturday, one of Suckling's officers, Captain William Billingsley, was summoned to the Privy Lodgings at Whitehall.[75] Billingsley's appearance at this point links the 'courtly' dimension of the plans devised by Suckling and Jermyn, and Strafford's own immediate entourage; for Billingsley, described at the time as a former page to Strafford,[76] had actually served as a man-of-affairs to the Lord Lieutenant since at least the mid 1630s, acting with the (now impeached) Sir George Radcliffe as Strafford's agent for the purchase of extensive landholdings in County Kildare, worth over £13,000.[77] Billingsley was Strafford's man; and while it is unclear whether he saw the king in person, or one of the House-hold officers, what is clear is that he received orders, which he *believed* to have come from the king, for the rallying of 100 men, with the objective of seizing control of the Tower. The plan was to be set in train on Sunday, 2 May.[78]

The plan was probably workable, at least as a short-term holding operation, until such time as reinforcements arrived from the army in the North. More-over, gaining entry to the fortress was not expected to pose a problem, as the Lieutenant of the Tower, Sir William Balfour, had been sent a 'command' (what appears to have been a verbal instruction)[79] ordering him to admit Billingsley's force.[80] Overall numbers were small enough to be manageable (and to be mobilized without attracting undue attention), yet large enough to overcome any opposition that might be offered by the Yeomen Warders, should they try to prevent Strafford's release.

The timing of the attempt could scarcely have been more opportune, for that Sunday, 2 May, had earlier been chosen for a royal wedding: the nuptials of Charles's nine-year-old daughter, Mary, to the fifteen-year-old Prince Willem, the heir to Prince Frederik Hendrik of Orange-Nassau, the senior prince within the Dutch Republic.[81] For reasons of economy, there was to be no nuptial masque, but the royal wedding remained a major court festivity, and was to include an impressive cavalcade, with around sixteen noblemen's coaches, drawn by six horses apiece, appointed to conduct the young prince from his lodgings in Arundel House, at the eastern end of the Strand,* to Whitehall.[82] Indeed, it seems likely that Charles was intending to use the wedding celebrations, which would last from eleven in the morning until after ten at night, as a cover for the Suckling–Billingsley mission to the Tower. With many members of both Houses at Whitehall for the wedding ceremonies,[83] and with the streets between the City and Westminster likely to be congested with coach traffic until late at night, the day of the wedding offered a propitious moment to strike.

Warwick, perhaps because he had been appointed to the Privy Council only a matter of days before, was among the noblemen nominated to attend the young Prince Willem, though it is tempting to speculate that Charles's real motive for honouring his old enemy in this way was to keep him harmlessly occupied, and oblivious to what was going on elsewhere in the capital, throughout the period when it was planned that Suckling would be seizing the Tower.

*

Come Sunday, the two events – the Whitehall marriage and the Tower Plot – progressed in almost surreal counterpoint throughout the day. As the young Prince Willem's coach procession made its way down the Strand towards the Palace,[84] Suckling was gathering his armed posse a mile away, at the White Horse Tavern on the corner of Bread Street, not far to the east of St Paul's.[85] From late morning, the marriage took its decorous course: the cavalcade to Whitehall, the ceremony within the cramped confines of the king's Closet, the dinner and diplomatic courtesies that occupied most of the afternoon and early evening.[86] The palace, as expected, was thronged with spectators, including the Commons-man John Moore, who found the Presence Chamber and Guard Chamber (the court's principal semi-public rooms) filled with 'an innumerable number of people'.[87]

Suckling's plans, on the other hand, unfolded less smoothly. By the afternoon, he and Billingsley had only assembled some sixty men, less than two-thirds of the number expected; and though these were well presented in buff coats (the battledress of the period) and armed with swords and pistols, they were well short of the hundred-strong force stipulated in the king's command. Expecting the imminent arrival of the remainder of his recruits, Suckling kept his party together at the White Horse Tavern, ready to move as soon as these forces arrived. Still he waited, well into Sunday night. Only much later, when the expected reinforcements had failed to materialize, did he take the decision to postpone his move on the Tower yet again, ordering his men to regroup the following evening, Monday, 3 May.[88]

These delays proved to be the plot's undoing. Even with the substantial

---

* Arundel House was one of the largest aristocratic palaces in London, with a large garden fronting on to the Thames. The site is close to the modern-day Temple underground station.

distraction of a royal wedding, the concentration of sixty armed and buff-coated men in a central London tavern, only a couple of streets away from the City's Guildhall, did not escape notice for long. Any lingering possibility of surprise disappeared when the existence of Suckling's force, and its likely destination, were brought to the attention of the radical City alderman Isaac Penington.[89] News of a threat to the Tower spread rapidly in the City throughout the afternoon. Pym was reportedly among those first alerted;[90] and it is likely that Warwick was warned at some point not long after.[91] Warwick had failed to take part in the Whitehall wedding, excusing himself later in the day on the grounds that he had been 'constantly [concerned] with affairs of state and Parliament' – a highly unusual explanation given that, it being the Sabbath, there was no formal parliamentary business that day.[92]

Yet, there was no shortage of 'affairs of state' to preoccupy Warwick throughout that Sunday. Either spontaneously or, more likely, in response to an initiative taken by Penington and the Junto leadership, steps were taken to defend the Tower against any advance by Suckling's men. By nightfall, around 1,000 people had gathered on Tower Hill to forestall any coup, and to monitor movements in and out of the fortress.[93]

*

As anxious Londoners held vigil outside the Tower that evening, on the other side of the capital, at Whitehall, the rituals of dynastic marriage were reaching their festive culmination: the semi-public bedding of the new bride and groom. At 10 p.m., as custom dictated, the king and the Dutch ambassadors filed into the newly-weds' bedchamber, to witness, as the Master of Ceremonies delicately put it, 'as much of the consommation of that marriage as so young years ... would afford'.[94] The irony of the moment could not have been more complete. The Dutch marriage, which had been the Junto's diplomatic triumph – crowning, through a dynastic union, England's reorientation away from Spain and towards the 'Protestant Cause' – was being used by the king as a diversion to cover the escape of the kingdom's leading Hispanophile, the Privy Councillor who had tried to turn the king into a pensioner of Habsburg Spain.

While, at Whitehall, the Prince and new Princess of Orange fumbled their way to an imperfect consummation, on Tower Hill, the presence of a large and hostile crowd around the approaches to the fortress spelt the end of Suckling's plans for a coup.[95] This defence of the capital's ancient fortress seems to have been motivated by something larger than simply the need to prevent Suckling's band of soldiers-of-fortune from gaining entry to the Tower. What would have happened next, had Suckling's plot succeeded, was believed to be in little doubt: Strafford's release; his escape, possibly to Yorkshire; perhaps even his return to the command of an army, of which he remained formally in post as its Lieutenant-General – an army now reportedly so hostile to Parliament that it was likely to do his bidding. His release, so narrowly prevented, appeared to be the first move in what was intended to be a new 'confusion' – a swift but violent resolution to the current political impasse, by force of arms. And in all this, the circumstantial case for the king's complicity seemed overwhelming.

One observer, who was probably closely involved in that improvised defence of the Tower, had no doubts as to what the king's actions portended. Explaining to Prince Willem of Orange why 'affairs of state' had prevented his attendance at Whitehall that day, the Earl of Warwick was blunt: 'we see civil wars, from which, I hope, God will deliver us'.[96]

III. THE 'GREAT DELIVERANCE'

By Monday morning, news of Suckling's botched Sunday-evening coup – and the nation's providential deliverance from 'civil wars' – was the talking point of the capital. As peers and Commons-men arrived at Westminster, they found the public areas of the palace already teeming with London citizens, once again out in force. The crowd's motives were probably multifarious: to vent their anger; to forestall any attempt to dissolve the Parliament; to be first to hear the breaking news. But their various fears and concerns now had a single focus: Strafford seemed the linchpin of the king's design to raise a new war. In a hastily drafted petition from a number of citizens to the House of Lords,[97]* they expressed their concerns for the security of the Tower and their belief that Strafford was intending to 'make his escape'.[98] The full significance of this last phrase hardly needed spelling out. It was this possibility that linked Suckling's attempt to seize control of the Tower to the 'civil wars' Warwick had discerned in the offing that same day.

Whatever Warwick's role had been in the defence of the Tower that Sunday, this was the moment when he emerges as the key figure in Parliament's response to the crisis. The presentation of the City petition to the Lords on Monday provided Warwick's faction with its cue for a sweeping series of counter-measures that enabled it to take control of the capital. The prominence of Warwick and the members of his immediate circle in these initiatives is striking. In the Commons, Sir John Clotworthy – Warwick's trusty lieutenant – moved for the apprehension of Suckling and two of his officers;[99]

---

* This London crowd was no mob of revolutionary *sans-culottes*. One apprentice who was part of their number referred to them as led by '40 grave cittyzens, men of renowne, and, after them, about 10,000 others – some, nay most of them, of very good fashion'. Even so, there was sporadic violence. A minister who denounced the crowd as 'none ... but a company of crop[-]eard puritans' was assaulted; his assailants 'kicked him like a football'. But the crowd that morning was otherwise orderly; there to protect, not to intimidate, the members of the two Houses. None of the London citizens who appeared that morning is named in the Lords' Journal (its formal record of proceedings). But a stray note by a clerk gives us an important clue that links the events of that day back to the members of Downinge's auditory for the Artillery Company sermon the previous autumn. On the back of the Lords' order that between six and ten of the 'multitude' were to be called in to address the Lords, a clerk has scribbled: 'Cap. Venn' – the Deputy President of the Artillery Company – 'spake for the rest'.

while in the upper House, the peers ordered the Earl of Newport – Warwick's illegitimate half-brother[100] – to take charge of the Tower on grounds that, as Master of the Ordnance (responsible for the kingdom's arms and munitions), he should secure the fortress's arsenal. Newport was instructed to inform the king of, but not seek his approval for, his new role.[101]

Warwick's faction also took command of the investigation into the plot and its ramifications. That same Monday, a six-man delegation, dominated by members of Warwick's parliamentary 'interest' (among them, the Earl of Stamford and Lords Brooke, Paget, and Wharton),* was hurriedly despatched to the Tower to interrogate Balfour about what he knew of the conspiracy, and to ensure that none of Billingsley's men was admitted.[102] Meanwhile, Warwick's two closest allies – his brother, Holland, and cousin, Essex – were sent to Whitehall, with Hamilton, nominally to inform the king of the Londoners' concerns and hear his response, but in reality to subject the monarch to what amounted to an interrogation as to the extent of his complicity in the Tower Plot. The king's answers to these questions left little doubt as to his guilt. Asked whether Suckling and Billingsley were acting on his royal authority, the king had little alternative – now that the plot had been interrupted – but to admit that he had given the Lieutenant of the Tower, Sir William Balfour, verbal instructions ('upon some discourse' between them) to admit Billingsley and 100 of his men. His motive, Charles feebly insisted, was to guard 'the municion[s]' at the Tower.[103] The reply convinced no one.

*

The Lords adjourned between noon and four to await its various delegations to report back.[104] In the interim, the size and temper of the crowd in Old Palace Yard (the landward entrance to the House of Lords) had changed. By the afternoon, it seems to have been smaller, but far more vociferous and threatening in tone.[105] With Suckling's abortive coup having established more firmly than ever the link between Strafford and the threat of a new war, the clamour for his execution now became deafening. Most peers who left the palace during the adjournment avoided the crowds by departing by boat from the Parliament Stairs; but the few who left by coach – among them the Earl of Holland on his way to Whitehall – encountered a noisy throng urging the Lords to pass the attainder bill with shouts of 'Justice!' and 'Execution!'[106]† Some went still further. Bishop Warner recorded in his diary

---

* Paget and Wharton had both been actively involved in the work of the five-man committee, chaired by Warwick, that had been appointed in January to scrutinize the charges against Strafford and decide which of them 'require[d] witnesses to be sworne': BL, Harl. MS 457 (Minutes of the Anglo-Scottish Treaty, 1640–41), fo. 51v.
† The Earl of Bristol, one of the handful of Petitioner Peers whose support for Strafford was so complete that he was widely regarded as having gone over to the king's party, was threatened as his coach left the Palace Yard, one of the protestors shouting into his coach window: 'For you, my Lord Bristowe [Bristol], we know you are an Apostate from the cause of Christ, and our mortall Enemie: wee doe not therefore crave justice *from* you, but shall (God willing) crave justice *upon* you and your false sonne, the Lord Digby'.

that 'some had said, If they had not Justice to morrow [the day scheduled by the Lords for consideration of the attainder bill], they would either take [that is, lynch] the K. or my L. Strafford.' This was reckless language, spoken in the heat of the moment; but it is nevertheless noteworthy as possibly the first publicly voiced proposal, during the 1640s, for regicide as a solution to the political crisis.[107]

The Lords reassembled at four. Once again courting the London public, they took the decision to send one of the well-known reformists to mollify the crowd. The Earl of Pembroke was chosen, partly perhaps because he was High Steward of Westminster,[108] and therefore naturally concerned with the borough's good order, but also because, as a former Bedfordian who had recently come out in support of Strafford's execution, he was willing to tell the crowd what it wanted to hear. Appearing in state in Old Palace Yard, Pembroke reassured the citizens that they would 'see Justice [done] very shortly'[109] – an act of 'courting popularity' that won him the undying hatred of the king[110] and which was bitterly lampooned in the royalist press.[111]*

In Bedford's absence, the proposal to amend the attainder bill, to provide for Strafford's banishment as an alternative to execution, no longer found an advocate. On hearing Hamilton's report of his interview with the king, the peers immediately despatched a second delegation to Whitehall consisting of five 'virtuous' Privy Councillors – Warwick (a Privy Councillor only since the previous Wednesday), together with Saye, Bristol, Pembroke, and Bath – to insist that the king countermand his orders authorizing Billingsley's entry to the Tower.[112] This was no mere 'request' to the king; its sole purpose seems to have been to force Charles into providing documentary proof, by issue of the countermand, that he *had* earlier given orders authorizing the Suckling–Billingsley venture.

In fact, the Lords had already decided to act on the principle that Essex had earlier enunciated to Hyde: that the king was to be treated as a cipher, obliged to confirm whatever the Parliament decided was for the good of the commonwealth. Even before Warwick had set off on his mission to Whitehall, the House of Lords had already opted to act unilaterally and place control of the Tower in the hands of two of Warwick's closest allies. Without consulting either the Commons or the king, the Lords ordered the Earl of Essex and Lord Brooke – after Warwick, the leading supporters of Strafford's attainder – to join Newport in taking command of the Tower. This triumvirate – Newport, Essex, and Brooke – was then instructed to install their own guard, 500 strong, drawn from the Tower Hamlets Trained Bands.[113]

---

* Thomas Herbert's *Vox Secunda Populi*, published in June 1641, excoriated Pembroke's role:

> The Commons' hearts, when Justice they did crave,
> He [the Earl of Pembroke] pawnd his Honour: Justice they should have.
> Which to the Commons did give such content,
> As that their prayers quicke to heaven they sent.
> That more such Peeres in England he would send,
> So should all Taxes cease, and Schismes end.

VOX SECUNDA POPULI.
OR,
The Commons gratitude to the moft
Honorable P H I L I P , Earle of Pembroke
and Mongomery , for the great affection which
hee alwaies bore unto them.

By *Tho. Herbert*.

My reward is from above.

Printed in the yeare 1641.

The Earl of Pembroke satirized as one of the 'Nobles ... who have striv'd t'usurpe our great Jove's [i.e. King's Charles's] throne', in a pro-royalist pamphlet of June 1641. The king never forgave Pembroke, the Lord Chamberlain (or administrative head) of his Household, for publicly encouraging the anti-Straffordian crowds of May 1641. Two months later, the monarch was to wreak his revenge by dismissing Pembroke from office and requiring that he surrender his emblems of office, in particular the large ceremonial wand, depicted conspicuously in this woodcut.

The raising of this new garrison for the Tower – the size of half a regiment – marked the crossing of an important political, perhaps even psychological, threshold. For the first time, the Lords were deploying military forces on their own authority, without reference to either Crown or Commons; putting into practice Downinge's dictum, first enunciated to the Artillery Company barely ten months earlier, that 'Councillors Born' could act 'by right of [their] nobility, and not by virtue of [any] office'.[114] Slowly, piecemeal, in response to the unfolding exigencies of the crisis, the Junto radicals were constructing what amounted to an alternative political theory of the commonwealth's constitutions. They politely retained a rhetoric of the 'three estates' – in which sovereignty was held to inhere in king, Lords, and Commons; but, as we will see, their political practice so marginalized the office of king from the exercise of real power that the power structures of this new 'commonwealth' were hardly distinguishable from that of an aristocratic republic.

*

While the Lords, unilaterally, took control of major aspects of the kingdom's government, Pym admonished the Commons to consider the gravity of the plot which had just been foiled. Gone, now, was any attempt to revive the option of saving Strafford's life. 'Truly, Sir', he declared to the Speaker, 'I am perswaded that their was some great designe in hande by the papist to subverte and overthrow this kingdome.' And while he still pretended that the king himself was innocent of involvement in the conspiracy to bring in the Irish army, 'yet he had councell given him that he was loose from all rules of government' – a clear attempt to hold Strafford morally responsible for Charles's readiness to be involved in the attempt on the Tower.[115] The reformist lawyer, Edward Bagshaw (a future Royalist), spelt out the conclusion that, even now, Pym was loath to make explicit: that 'the kingdom cannot be saff[e] while [Strafford] lives'.[116]

The threat posed by Strafford was, in Pym's view, part and parcel of the 'great designe ... by the papist to ... overthrow this kingdome'; but it is important, if we are to understand the broader resonances of the Junto's rhetoric of anti-Popery, to be clear precisely how the two are linked. This was something far broader than merely a theological hostility to the errors of Rome, or to the presence of Catholics at the English court. 'The Papist', in Pym's vocabulary, was a historic enemy, almost invariably associated with Habsburg Spain: authoritarian in politics, committed to the extirpation of Protestantism, and intent on establishing its rule – or the rule of a compliant surrogate – on the British kingdoms by force. Post-Reformation English history was a history of providential deliverances from this malevolent 'great design': the Armada in 1588; the Gunpowder Treason in 1605; and, most recently, 'the Fifth of May', the day in 1640 when Strafford had counselled Charles I to use forces, funded by Spain, to put down all internal dissent – the date which D'Ewes thought there was 'as good cause to celebrate ... as the 5th of November'.[117] The memory of the Fifth of May and what was feared would have followed if the 'plot' had succeeded – the suppression of Parliament, the triumph of 'Laudianism', and the establishment of monarchical despotism – was coming to be regarded as the latest in the great, providential sequence of near misses, in which England survived miraculously unscathed. 'Popery' and despotism, in this context, became one and the same. To be an 'agent of Popery', or even 'Popish', was rapidly becoming a shorthand for being an abetter of Straffordian, authoritarian monarchy, irrespective of the agent's actual confessional allegiance. Hence, Strafford could be regarded as pursuing popish designs, notwithstanding that his personal piety seems to have been solidly Protestant. Indeed, by the spring of 1641 it was becoming possible to denounce as 'popish' or 'tending to popery' anything that challenged the post-Triennial Act political order, on the seemingly rational grounds that, if this new order failed, the likely alternative was the triumph of Strafford's policy of May 1640: a king 'loose[d] from all rules of government' and the satrap of Catholic Spain.[118]

'Popery' was thus a portmanteau term, carrying within it a congeries of ideas – despotic monarchy, hostility towards Parliaments, indifference to the rule of law – as well as, but sometimes quite separate from, its associations with religious doctrine.[119] The fact that complex ideological divisions could be rendered as a form of rhetorical shorthand in the slogans of religious polemic tells us much about the centrality of religious controversy to seventeenth-century political discourse. But it simultaneously warns us against trying to explain contemporary political conflict as rooted in theological differences, pure and simple, or, still less, as an incipient 'war of religion'.[120] Polar-opposite values as to politics, law, and the dispositions of constitutional power almost invariably lurked as well behind the dualities of 'Popish' and 'Protestant'.

If the failure of the Tower Plot fitted Pym's model of the Papists' 'great design', it also provided the opportunity for the Junto to make its first explicit appeal, beyond the already highly politicized world of London and Westminster, for the allegiance of the nation. The form of this appeal was to be an instance of neo-Elizabethanism, an oath or 'bond of association' along the lines of the Elizabethan expedient of 1585; it was intended to provide a legal basis by which Protestants 'well-affected' to the commonwealth could raise armies, in the event of a 'popish conspiracy' to overthrow the state, even without the sanction of the monarch. As such, the expedient had had an obvious attraction to members of the reformist Junto, right from the start of their resistance in the late summer of 1640, because it provided a basis for justifying military resistance to Charles's 'evil counsellors'. As early as June 1640, Jhonston of Wariston was recommending to his English 'friends' that they should enter into an oath of association along the lines of the Elizabethan Bond of Association of 1585, as the basis for concerted military resistance to the Crown in the event of Charles's refusal to summon a Parliament.[121] Once the Parliament met, the 'oath of association' idea resurfaced, this time as a means of justifying resistance to the Crown in the event of the king dissolving the Parliament before the 'grievances of the commonwealth' had been remedied. In February 1641, for example, it re-emerged as a contingency plan in the event of Strafford's acquittal and reinstatement to his military commands. Had that happened, it was reported, 'the lower house and that partie of the Lordes which will be against [Strafford]' planned to enter into a defensive oath or 'protestation', apparently as a basis for armed resistance to any Strafford-led campaign to suppress the Lords and Commons.[122]

After the discovery of the Tower Plot on Sunday, 2 May, and with the renewed threat of an immediate dissolution, an emergency meeting of 'the Grandees', reported to have taken place that same day,[123] decided that the time had finally come to implement this 'oath of association'.[124] This oath (or 'Protestation', as it came to be known) was intended to provide the legal authority for a provisional government, composed of anti-Straffordians in both Houses, and the moral authority for resistance in the event of Charles dissolving Parliament. It was a remedy designed for desperate times. As

William Strode, one of Pym's closest allies, explained in his speech in favour of the Protestation, 'the kinge understandeth not what treason is', and 'if care be not taken, we shall be disperst through the kingdom' – a clear reference to the threatened dissolution. The remedy, he suggested, was that Parliament-men 'may all sweare [an oath] to *be true* to our king and to *defend* our church and commonwealth' (the discrimination in his choice of verbs is perhaps highly significant).[125] Strode's proposal was backed by a chorus of members associated with the Warwick House group: Sir Thomas Barrington, Sir Philip Stapilton, Sir Gilbert Gerard, and Sir John Clotworthy – a *Who's Who* of the militant anti-Straffordians* – joined on this occasion by Barrington's usually taciturn first cousin, Oliver Cromwell.[126]

Drafted by a twelve-man committee, which was dominated by Junto men from both the Bedfordian and Warwick–House groups,[127] the new oath embodied the distinction that Strode had made at the outset: Parliament-men undertook 'to *defend* church and commonwealth', while their undertakings towards the king were far less affirmative; indeed, the only direct reference to the monarch is almost incidental, a passing reference that the defence of the 'Protestant religion' was a duty owed to the king's 'royal person, honour, and estate'.[128]

To pre-empt the imminent dissolution, it was claimed, the Protestation had to be drafted, debated, passed, and sworn by members, all in a single day. As Sir Gilbert Gerard warned in the course of debate, if the king's 'evil counsellors' knew what was afoot, 'they would endeavour to dissolve us' almost at once; it was therefore imperative that the oath be approved and sworn 'befor we goe hence'.[129] By seven in the evening, most, if not all, of the Commons-men present had taken the oath, many apparently doing so in the expectation that that Monday might well prove to be the Parliament's final day.

By dusk the capital was in the grip of something approaching hysteria. The prevailing sense of alarm was again compounded by the very uncertainty of the threat. Ever since Sunday, the City had been rife with rumour: that the Irish army was poised to intervene in England; that the army in the North would declare itself for Strafford and fight the Scots; that Papists were planning an insurrection; even that French troops were mobilizing in readiness to come to Charles's aid. As night fell, another large crowd converged on Tower Hill to 'watch' and deter any further attempt to effect Strafford's release.[130] The foiling of the king's plans the previous day seemed narrowly to have prevented a far larger concatenation of evils, all with the same final objective: the destruction of Parliament and the introduction of an 'arbitrary government', with a liberated Strafford at its helm.

By this point, however, the Tower was firmly in the Junto's hands. Already, the new 500-strong garrison, drawn from the Tower Hamlets Trained Bands,

---

* Stapilton had first proposed the attainder as a solution; Barrington and Gerard had acted as tellers in its favour in the division on its third (and final) reading in the Commons; and Clotworthy had been the original source of the claim that Strafford had intended to use the Irish army to suppress dissent in England.

had begun to take up residence; and the Lieutenant of the Tower was now taking his orders from the Junto triumvirate of Newport, Essex, and Brooke.[131] Essex may have gone still further in his efforts to secure the Tower. Later in that week, the king reportedly intercepted a letter in Essex's own handwriting, addressed to General Alexander Leslie, the Covenanter commander in the North, asking the Scottish commander to send fifty of his officers to London.[132] This rings absolutely true. One of Essex's key concerns at this time, conveyed to the Commons as recently as 22 April, was that, in the event of an armed conflict, 'wee had men enough, but commanders and leaders of experience [wee] would want'.[133] If Essex's appeal to Leslie to supply him with fifty officers looks like a clear attempt to remedy this deficiency, it also reveals just how close he believed his allies were to having to fight a civil war. 'Wee knew not how soone wee might be provoked to defend our selves', he had earlier warned the Commons.[134] After the events of 2 and 3 May, Essex seems to have taken the first steps tentative towards the creation of a parliamentarian army.[135]

For Charles and Cottington, the failure of the Tower Plot and the Parliament's counter-measures taken on 3 May constituted a decisive tactical defeat. From this point, with Essex and the Junto leaders in effective command of the Tower, not even a parliamentary dissolution would suffice to bring the process against Strafford to an end. The likely consequences of such a step were now clearly foreseeable: the Lords and Commons who had sworn the Protestation would almost certainly raise forces of their own, as their oath implicitly obliged them to; Strafford would remain the Junto's prisoner, under threat of summary execution; and any attempt to bring the army southwards to retake the Tower was almost certain to result in civil war, with only the most distant hope of securing Strafford's release. For the king, the moment when a coup might have worked had passed. Even a dissolution – hitherto the ultimate sanction against a refractory Parliament – was now a hollow threat.

*

The psychological and moral impact of Charles's attempt to seize the Tower has been relatively little acknowledged by historians.[136] To contemporaries, however, it seemed that England had just escaped a catastrophe comparable with the Armada or the Gunpowder Plot: a moment when the entire system of known law and government had been threatened with destruction, and escaped by the skin of its teeth. The Earl of Stamford made the point most explicitly when Parliament reassembled on Tuesday morning, 4 May, proposing a motion that the House

> give God Thanks for our great Deliverance, which is greater th[a]n that from the Gunpowder-Treason. For by this time, had not this plot been discovered, the powder had been about our Ears here in the Parliament house, and we had all been made slaves.[137]

From Stamford, a loyal ally of Warwick's, such a view is perhaps unsurprising. Yet his view was also supported by three of the bishops (Rochester, Bristol, and Carlisle); and if the king's behaviour appeared to have brought England to the brink of enslavement in the view of three loyal Caroline bishops, it is not hard to understand why the Junto, which had so much more to fear from a royalist coup, reacted with such alarm: why Essex was attempting to recruit Scottish officers to provide the infrastructure of a parliamentarian army, or why his allies in the Commons would press the Lords, that same day, to swear the Protestation 'to defend church and commonwealth'.

Above all, the Tower Plot and its likely outcome seem to have brought home to hitherto wavering peers the sheer dangerousness of the Earl of Strafford. An anti-Straffordian party that had already been powerfully strengthened by St John's speech on the previous Thursday now became unassailable. From the moment of the plot's discovery, there seemed little doubt that the king and senior figures at court were involved in its commission. The discovery later in the week that most of the leading suspects wanted for interrogation had fled – including Henry Jermyn, the Master of the Horse to the queen – seemed to provide silent confirmation of the plotters' guilt.[138]

With the commonwealth secure, Warwick and Essex exploited the moment to complete the destruction of Strafford. Warwick entered the Lords' chamber that morning in triumph, brandishing a vast transcript of the proceedings at Strafford's trial – 'written and bound up in many Quires of Paper' – as though to emphasize the sheer weight of the evidence against him.[139] 'Yet', he said, 'there were seven Quires [groups of pages sewn together]' more yet to come.[140] Essex, Mandeville, and Saye then attempted to use the new Protestation as a means of disenfranchising potential Straffordians; all who refused the new oath were to be denied the right to vote on the attainder bill.[141]* But the precaution was hardly necessary. In the prevailing atmosphere, Strafford's fate seemed no longer in doubt.

Warwick's desire to indulge in a moment of theatrical swagger is, perhaps, understandable. Ever since the opening of the Parliament, he had been the focal point for the Junto hardliners, insistent that only Strafford's death would secure the kingdom from a return to 'despotism', and 'the Patriots of the Commonwealth' from his future revenge.[142] In early January 1641, even as Bedford was beginning his negotiations with the king over appointments to office, Warwick had personally taken responsibility for a key aspect of the prosecution, chairing the committee that decided on which charges 'require[d] witnesses to be sworn'.[143]† His pursuit of severity against Strafford had

---

* The Lords' response to this proposal provides further evidence of how the peers regarded the real nature of the threat they faced as being political and military, rather than religious. What they finally agreed was that those who refused to take the Protestation 'only in Point of [religious] Doctrine' – that is, Roman Catholic peers – *could* vote on the attainder; only those who rejected the Protestation on other – non-religious, political – grounds were to be denied their vote in relation to the Strafford case.

† This committee was appointed by the English and Scottish Treaty Commissioners on 11 January and consisted of Warwick, Lord Paget (his niece's husband), and three other Petitioner Peers, Lords Wharton, Savile, and Howard of Escrick (perhaps significantly, all from Yorkshire, Strafford's home county).

been consistent: from his resistance to Bedford's efforts, in February, to postpone the trial,[144] through to his support for the attainder bill, in April, once the impeachment trial had run into the sand. Now, with the wisdom of his counsel vindicated by the recent Tower Plot, Warwick and Essex personally conducted the interrogations of the plot's key witnesses, expanding their investigations to include anti-parliamentarian conspiracy within the army more generally,[145] and exploiting the subsequent revelations to keep the Parliament's fears at fever pitch.[146]

With Strafford safely in the custody of Newport, Essex, and Brooke, Warwick's faction turned their attentions to the larger question of securing the commonwealth. Here, too, Warwick's actions were founded on principles that went well beyond Bedford's plans for limited reform. Where Bedford had envisaged that the future security of the commonwealth would be founded on parliamentary control of the royal finances, Warwick's prime concern was with military power: with prising from the king at least de facto control of the kingdom's navy and armies, and vesting this in a godly, aristocratic cartel – hence it seems his personal involvement in administering the payments to the Scottish army;[147] his concern with control of the militia, and, ultimately, in 1642, his assumption of direct control of the English navy. Ironically, Warwick's understanding of what was needed to secure the English commonwealth bore a striking resemblance to Strafford's. Both delineated a state that was founded, not on 'love', but on military control. However, where Strafford's version regarded the purpose of military power as service to an authoritarian monarchy, a monarchy sanctified by divinely derived authority and unanswerable to the political nation,[148] Warwick's served what would be, in practice, a republican oligarchy, deriving its power from Parliament, and, in practice, answerable for its stewardship to the representatives of the people. Their understandings of what the English polity should be could not have been further apart; but the similarities between the two men's thinking as to what made a government secure are such that it is possible, perhaps, to discern in Warwick's very personal vehemence against Strafford something of the 'wrath of Caliban', an anger at the likeness he glimpsed of himself, discerned in the mirror of Straffordian 'tyranny'.

Anger, however, had more general applications, and in the aftermath of the Tower Plot the Warwick House group[149] worked effectively to assume practical control of the kingdom's defences. Warwick's son-in-law, Mandeville, with Clotworthy and Stapilton, for example, were despatched by the Lords to Portsmouth, the largest and most modern fortress in the country, to take command of the garrison and to forestall its use as a bridgehead in the event of a possible French invasion.[150] Likewise Warwick took the initiative in urging the Commons to pass an emergency act for the press-ganging of mariners for the fleet.[151] And at a conference with the Commons on 7 May, he explained that Northumberland, as Lord Admiral, had been instructed to see that the navy's ships were in the hands of 'religious officers and commanders' – that is, reliable opponents of any further royal coup.[152]

Traceable from this moment, too, is a hardening of the Junto's attitude towards the choice of royal counsellors. Hitherto, Bedford's plans for the reform of public office holding had been founded on persuasion (admittedly reinforced by financial inducements and, if necessary, penalties), but without challenging the king's prerogative right to choose his own 'great officers'. From 4 May, however, there was a strong case to be made that reliance on Charles for a 'voluntary' change in his counsels had failed. In most respects, this was a natural progression from the bill of attainder, arguably the most forceful expedient thus far adopted to compel Charles to change his coun-sellors against his will. Unsurprisingly, therefore, those who refocused the Parliament's attention on the need to purge the king's 'evil counsellors' were the same group of Junto militants that had been behind the attainder. To test the waters, Sir Arthur Hesilrige (the Commons-man who introduced the attainder bill) moved on 4 May that the Lords should be asked to join the Commons in petitioning the king 'for the putting away of evill counsellors and placing others in ther place'.[153] This was 'well allowed',[154] and while Hesilrige's words are ambiguous as to whether the Junto militants were already thinking that Parliament should have a role in the *choice* of the king's senior officers[155] – a profoundly radical suggestion in the context of seventeenth-century England – the subsequent actions of Hesilrige's allies soon removed any doubt.

The test case was Strafford's replacement as Lord Lieutenant of Yorkshire, an office that the army plots had spotlighted in high relief. For the Yorkshire Trained Bands, which came under the Lord Lieutenant's jurisdiction, con-tained several regiments where personal loyalty to Strafford was strong, and which were therefore likely to take a major role in any pro-royalist coup. When the king nominated the unscrupulous Lord Savile, the erstwhile Peti-tioner Peer who had turned his coat and become a loyal lackey of the court, the Junto militants saw an opportunity to put the principle embodied in Hesilrige's motion into practice.[156]

As a result, the two Rich brothers (Warwick and Holland), with four other Junto peers (Pembroke, Saye, Hertford, and Hamilton), were instructed by the Lords to 'move' the king to abandon any thought of naming Savile, and to appoint Essex instead.[157] The choice of verb is here significant, as the usual phrase would have been 'to petition' or 'to recommend' a matter to the king. 'To move' was a far less deferential term, meaning 'to prompt' or 'impel',[158] and Warwick and his fellow delegates left Charles in little doubt that, should he refuse, the Lords would probably appoint Essex not-withstanding, acting on their own authority. The king had little alternative but to comply. As Giustinian noted accurately, his capitulation over Essex's appointment marked another crucial stage in the erosion of royal authority: 'the Parliament will not even let the king enjoy the use of his [power of] appointment, which is his sole prerogative'.[159] The precedent that it set had massive implications; for the Lord Lieutenants of the shires were those who controlled and appointed the officers of each county's militia forces. And if the Commons could nominate a nobleman to be the Lord Lieutenant of one of England's counties, by implication they could nominate other noblemen to them all. It was a precedent that Hesilrige – the initiator of the debate on Parliament's role in the appointment of the king's counsellors – and his Junto friends would remember six months on, when they proceeded to do precisely this.[160]

Of course, this assertiveness on the part of the Lords, both in their willingness to browbeat the king and their readiness to exercise power, has not gone unnoticed. As one historian of the period has noted, 'the Lords, with the assistance of many of the great officers [of state], were acting as the ultimate repository of supreme authority' within the realm.[161] Yet, while this is doubtless true, what was happening in practice was something even more subversive of regal power than this might suggest. For the beneficiaries of this process were not simply the peers in general; the major consequence of the crisis in royal authority during April and May 1641 was the concentration of the key offices of military power in England in an astonishingly narrow political and kinship clique, a group that was coterminous with the Earl of Warwick and his immediate relations: his brother, Holland, as Lord General; his half-brother, Newport, as the newly-appointed Constable of the Tower; his son-in-law, Mandeville, in charge of Portsmouth, the largest fortress in the country; his first cousin, Essex, as Lord Lieutenant of Yorkshire, commander of the Yorkshire Trained Bands; and another first cousin, Northumberland, as Lord High Admiral of England (the only office which had not been acquired a direct consequence of the current crisis). Of these, only Northumberland, the figure in command at the Admiralty, had been closely identified with the Bedfordian wing of the Junto, and, even here, Warwick was already tending to intrude on Northumberland's turf: speaking on his behalf, suggesting initiatives, and acting as though he were himself one of the Admirals of England.[162] Not even during the eighteenth century were England's key military offices in the hands of so narrow a cousinly cartel.

In the longer term, however, perhaps the most important limitation on the king's prerogatives to flow from the failure of the Tower Plot was the removal of his power to dissolve the current Parliament, as and when he determined. In the short term, this power had already been neutralized, as we have seen, by the Junto's successful bid to commandeer control of the Tower on 3 May. During the remainder of that week, however, the Junto leaders moved to formalize, *de jure*, what they had already achieved in practice. On 6 May a new bill was introduced to provide for the present Parliament's continuance until such time as it should be dissolved with its own consent.[163] In the prevailing environment of fear and suspicion, the legislation was rushed through all its stages in both the Commons and the Lords in a matter of days.[164]

This gradual chipping away of once undisputed prerogatives forms part of a larger declension of royal power. It was the logical corollary of the physical and symbolic 'marginalization' of the king that had been so conspicuous an aspect of the staging of Strafford's trial. Men at Westminster were now thinking and talking about options, which, even twelve months ago, would have seemed fanciful or even seditious. That same week an unnamed viscount (possibly Viscount Savile) claimed that on Wednesday, 5 May – the day the Lords were briefed on the plot to bring the army southwards to London – 'the Parliamentarians' had threatened the king with deposition, warning him that the eleven-year-old Prince of Wales might be crowned in his place.[165]*

*

Strafford, too, recognized that the failure of the Tower Plot had brought about a fundamental alteration in the dispositions of political power. At some point between Monday the 3rd and Wednesday the 5th, he wrote to Charles, releasing him of his earlier promise to protect him 'in life and fortune', and urging him, with heroic abnegation, to pass the attainder 'for [the] prevention of evils which may happen by your refusal'. 'To a willing man', he assured the king,

> there is no injury done, and as, by God's grace, I forgive all the world with calmness and meekness of infinite contentment to my dislodging soul, so, Sir, to you, I can give the life of this world with all the cheerfulness imaginable ...[166]

Such self-sacrifice has its obvious nobility and poignancy; yet we should be wary of taking such words at their face value. This was a letter that was probably written with the expectation that it would receive far wider circulation than within the immediate entourage of the king; and Strafford would have been aware that Father Goodman had written to Charles in similar terms at the point when both Houses were also baying for his blood. The effect of Goodman's self-sacrificing offer, as Strafford well knew, had been to move Parliament to relinquish its demands for his execution.[167]

In fact, far from resigning himself to execution, Strafford was working actively to save his neck. He still believed that some version of the Bedfordian compromise – his permanent disbarment from office, rather than execution – was viable, and later that week drafted a memorandum to the king urging him to pursue it.[168] His letter absolving Charles of his undertaking to protect him needs to be read in the light of these other initiatives and political calculations. Indeed, on Saturday, 8 May, the day the attainder bill was sent to the king, Strafford offered his gaoler, Sir William Balfour, £22,000 'to favour his escape'.[169] For all its elevated rhetoric of self-denial, Strafford's letter to Charles was a document of carefully crafted persuasive power, not a suicide note.

The letter also hints, none too subtly, that Strafford held the king to blame for his current predicament. Of course, Strafford was most likely complicit in the Tower Plot, something that Billingsley's involvement and his own

---

* The report is impossible to confirm; but it is certainly plausible and, if true, would help explain the king's exceptional efforts over the following six months to ingratiate himself with the three most credible pretenders to the throne, should he be deposed: his nephew, Elector Charles Louis, Prince of the Palatinate; the Earl of Hertford, the descendant of Henry VII (whom Charles promoted as Marquess of Hertford in June); and his Stuart cousin, the Duke of Lennox (created Duke of Richmond in August).

attempt to bribe Balfour would tend to confirm. Where Strafford was perhaps justified, however, in holding Charles to account, was in the ineptitude of the Tower Plot's execution – in particular, the decision to entrust so sensitive a mission to Suckling's unreliable hands. Had the conspiracy been promptly and assertively implemented, it might well have succeeded. Instead, at precisely the moment when the Junto was internally divided, and its association with the Scots was sapping its support at Westminster, the attempted coup had unified and re-energized his enemies. And in seeming to confirm the reality of the much larger plot (in the words of the preamble to the Protestation) 'to introduce the exercise of an arbitrary and tyrannical government', Charles had put paid to any hope that the Bedfordian compromise might be saved.[170]

*

By the time the peers turned to the final consideration of the attainder bill against Strafford, between the Wednesday and Friday of that same week (5–7 May), the prevailing atmosphere of crisis had taken its toll on the hitherto pro-Straffordian majority in the House of Lords. After the revelations of the last few days, the Warwick–Essex party was powerfully reinforced,[171] and it secured a major tactical victory when the Lords agreed that, in deciding Strafford's guilt, they would weigh his actions not only by statute and Common Law, but also by the Parliament's power to create new treasons by legislative action – the controversial claim advanced by St John in his attack on Strafford.[172] Strafford's condemnation was further facilitated by the Junto's success in pushing through a motion allowing the peers to abandon the usual rules of evidence: that 'in the discussing [of] the matter of fact in this whole cause, the rule shall only be the persuasion of every man's conscience'. This enabled the Lords to vote that the most serious of the charges against him – what had been Article 23 of the impeachment, that Strafford had planned to use the Irish army against England – was duly proven, notwithstanding the absence of any corroboration for Sir Henry Vane's testimony.

Even so, there remained a sizeable element in the upper House opposed to Strafford's death by statute. The three days of debate produced no less than ten procedural divisions, the narrowest, on Friday, 7 May, by twenty-six votes to nineteen. Around thirty peers (or slightly more than a third of the House's regular membership) sought to avoid associating themselves with either side. From a regular attendance of over eighty the previous week, numbers went down to forty-five by Friday, a decline that seems to have owed less to the 'tumults' of Monday and Tuesday than to the fear of earning the king's displeasure. Yet the final division produced a vote against the earl of fifty-one votes to nine – a margin so large, in a House whose maximum attendance rarely exceeded eighty, that the absentees probably made no difference to the final outcome.[173] In the aftermath of the Tower Plot, belief in Strafford's culpability extended well beyond the Junto's usual constituency of support. Strafford was condemned to death, and the peers' decision was immediately communicated to the Commons.[174]

To concentrate the king's mind, a delegation from the two Houses was despatched to Whitehall the following day to present him with the two great bills that now awaited the royal assent: the bill for Strafford's attainder and execution, and the bill forbidding the Parliament's dissolution except with its own consent. The Commons' very last business before rising was to act upon a suggestion made by Warwick,[175] and to order their newly appointed Close Committee – Junto-men to a man[176]* – to devise proposals for the country's security, and 'to consider what proposition they shall think fit to be made for giving power to command *and to compel obedience*, for the necessary defence of the kingdom'.[177] The ostensible danger was of a French invasion; but the clear implication of these terms of reference was that the 'power to command and compel obedience' was to come from some source other than the king. The timing of this resolution – on the same day that the two Houses had agreed on Essex's appointment to command in Yorkshire, and immediately before the members departed for Whitehall – sent an obvious signal to the court. In the event of Charles refusing his consent to either of the bills before him, the Junto leadership was ready to prepare for war.[178]

iv. RETRIBUTION

By the time the parliamentary delegates set out for the Banqueting House at 4 p.m.,[179] a large and menacing crowd, estimated by one diplomat at 12,000 strong, was present to accompany them on their short journey from Westminster, up King Street, to Whitehall. There it maintained a noisy but orderly presence in the open street to the north of the Holbein Gate.[180] As shouts of 'Justice! Justice!' were heard through the windows of the Banqueting House, Sir John Bankes, acting as Lord Keeper, 'moved the King' to assent to both bills, 'in respect of the distractions and dangers of the present time'.[181] As so often when cornered, Charles played for a delay. 'Looking verie sadlie', he promised that he would give his response at 10 a.m. on Monday morning, a deferral that so displeased the crowd outside that it was feared the palace might be stormed at once.[182] But there was no immediate assault. Instead, the crowd – sullen, intimidating, unpredictable – settled down to a hostile vigil, maintaining its presence outside the Palace Gate throughout the night and the following day, Sunday.

The twenty-four hours following the receipt of the attainder bill were probably the most anguished of Charles's entire life. Outside the gates of Whitehall, the capital was essentially in the control of the Junto militants – with Warwick, Essex and the Close Committee effectively masters of the political process. Within the court, it was believed that this newly dominant

---

* The Close Committee, first named on 5 May, had six members: Denzell Holles, John Pym, John Hampden, and William Strode (all originally on the Bedford–Northumberland side of the Junto), and Nathaniel Fiennes and Sir John Clotworthy (both of whom were closer to the Scots and the Warwick House group). Sir Philip Stapilton (who also belonged to this latter group) was named to the committee two days later.

parliamentary leadership was fully prepared to carry out its threat of force against the king, in the event of his refusing to pass the two pending bills. Military support from adjacent counties (the Trained Bands), it was alleged, had been summoned to the capital in case reinforcements were needed for the London Trained Bands.[183]

None felt that threat more acutely than Queen Henriette Marie. Fearing for her security, she had already decided on the Saturday morning to flee to Portsmouth, and was only dissuaded by the French diplomat, Jean de Montreuil, on the grounds that she was sure to be apprehended en route and exposed to still greater danger, were she to become the Junto's captive.[184] Whitehall was besieged.

*

Scarcely half a mile from the braying crowd outside the Palace Gate, another tragedy was reaching a quieter, but no less agonized, conclusion at Bedford House. For most of the last week, Bedford had been reassured that his persistent fever – his 'simple boyling of blood' – would soon pass. That Saturday night, however, his symptoms suddenly worsened, and though, even now, his physician doubted whether the disease afflicting him was actually smallpox, it was evident that, whatever the malady was, it would now prove fatal. Alone, except for his physician and the few terrified servants who braved the risk of contagion to tend him, Bedford mustered his remaining strength to tend to his pious devotions. He lingered in fitful consciousness throughout the night. But at ten on Sunday morning, 9 May, Bedford died.[185]

*

At Whitehall that Sunday morning, the king was racked with a private agony of his own. Concerned to 'inform his conscience', he summoned five of his bishops to attend him: Juxon of London, Morton of Durham, Williams of Lincoln, Potter of Carlisle, and Archbishop Ussher. All but Juxon were figures of irreproachably Calvinist opinions, a circumstance that points to the king's ongoing concern to dissociate himself from the Laudian past and any taint of being 'popishly affected'. Of the five bishops, all but Ussher appeared at Whitehall, and, although the tenor of their advice is disputed,[186] at least one, Bishop Williams, seems to have counselled him that he should sign the attainder bill.[187] Similar advice was probably received from the majority of the Privy Councillors, whom the king consulted in the afternoon. Charles's nephew, the Elector Palatine, who was at Whitehall during the deliberations and advised his uncle to sign the attainder bill, recorded that the king was in tears at the Council table.[188] If Strafford's fate still remained unresolved, at least one firm decision was taken. In a belated attempt to allay the Parliament's suspicions, Charles agreed to disband the Irish army, apparently persuaded by the practical consideration that, since it had gone so long unpaid, it was now so ill-disciplined that its military usefulness was highly questionable.[189]

Still Charles vacillated over his response to the act of attainder. Only after the Council meeting was concluded could he receive Archbishop Ussher,

whose preaching in Covent Garden had prevented him from responding to
the initial royal summons.[190] Ussher's advice is also disputed, but it would
seem that he complicated matters further by agreeing that the king *could*
save Strafford, 'if other reason of State', of which the bishops would not
presume to judge, 'did not hinder him'. Something of the king's moral anguish
is suggested by the fact that he summoned the bishops for a second meeting
later that night.[191] It is also suggested by the state of the actual parchment
bill, which he had before him that night; this contains, unusually, a number
of large blobs of candle grease, and 'it is tempting to speculate on the
circumstances in which they may have come to be there'.[192]

Outside, the capital remained on the brink of mob violence. During Sunday,
a 'new turbulence' was reported among the London populace in response to
a rumour that French troops had landed at Portsmouth, and that Charles
was therefore refusing to sign the attainder bill.[193] Near the Tower, there was
a riot involving a thousand 'marriners' that resulted in the destruction of
two or three houses,[194] and compelled an officer in the force guarding the
Tower – a 'Captain Geare', a 'City Captain' (an officer in one of London's
citizen militia) – to open fire on the rioters, killing three of them.[195] This is
one of the very few clues we have as to who actually composed this guard
on the Tower during the crisis of early May, and it is perhaps significant that
this was Captain William Geere, 'one of the worthy Captaines of the City',[196]
who trained weekly, as one of the officers in the Artillery Company, under
the command of John Venn,[197] whose prominence in mobilizing crowds of
reformist-minded Londoners has already been noted.[198]

Some time during that same noisy Sunday night, a spoof playbill appeared
near the Palace Gate announcing that 'On the morrow next [Monday] there
was to be acted in the House of Peers a famous Tragi-Comedy called *A King
and No King*'[199] – a reference to the Beaumont and Fletcher play of the same
title, first produced some twenty years earlier, in which the 'King of Iberia's'
right to rule is revealed to be flawed, and the Crown passed instead to the
rightful heir.[200] Again, the implied reference seems to have been to Charles's
imminent deposition.

Physically and emotionally exhausted, at some point in the course of that
night, Charles finally accepted that further resistance was impossible. He
appointed commissioners to go to the House of Lords the following morning
to act on his behalf in giving the royal assent to the two bills – Strafford's
attainder and the bill for the perpetuation of the Parliament – thereby avoiding
the humiliation of having to approve the bills in public and in person.[201]
Even though spared this indignity, the moment cannot have been anything
other than one of abject defeat. In the words of one contemporary historian,
'[at] the same instant, with the same Pen and Ink, the King lost his Prerogative
and Strafford's life'.[202] A sense of guilt at having betrayed Strafford was to
haunt him for the rest of his life.

*

To break the news to Strafford, Charles deputed the earl's kinsman, the Earl
of Cleveland. But Cleveland evidently recoiled from the task, and it was left

to one of the Privy Council clerks, Dudley Carleton, a minor court functionary, to make the journey to the Tower late that Sunday night. Strafford's
response to the message can only be guessed at. The oft-repeated story that,
on hearing the terrible news, he put his hand on his heart and exclaimed
bitterly, 'Put not your trust in princes, nor in the sons of men, for in them
there is no salvation', emerges for the first time only in the 1650s and needs
to be regarded with scepticism.[203] Yet, however fanciful this may be in point
of detail, a conviction on Strafford's part that he had been ill served by the
king who had earlier promised him solemnly that he should 'not suffer in
life or fortune' would only be understandable – indeed, only human. Right
to the last, Strafford seems to have believed that some form of compromise –
at worst, his disablement from all public employment – would be belatedly
accepted by the Lords.[204]

Indeed, there was one rational ground for believing that the attainder act
might even now be circumvented. This was the important technical detail
that, the act having set no date for the execution, it was at the king's discretion
as to when it should actually take place. In theory, no execution could be
effected until such time as the king signed a warrant to the Lord Keeper (the
actual 'death warrant') instructing him to issue the necessary writs under the
Great Seal ordering the Constable of the Tower to deliver the prisoner, and
the Sheriff of London to carry out the execution.[205] In theory, too, there was
nothing to stop the king from deferring the issuing of that warrant to the
Lord Keeper indefinitely, to allow the political climate to turn. And although
the king, by commission, gave his formal royal assent to the attainder on
Monday, 10 May, he still failed to provide the necessary warrant that would
stipulate a date for Strafford's execution.

Fixing that date became the cause for the very final skirmish in the campaign
against Strafford that had been waged by the Junto peers since the Petition
of the Twelve in August the previous year. Anticipating that the king would
seek to vitiate the attainder by simply declining to issue of the necessary
writs, the House of Lords usurped the king's role in the judicial process and
ordered, on its own authority, that the execution was to take place on
Wednesday, 12 May.[206] Work on the scaffold, and the grandstands that would
accommodate the massive crowds expected for the occasion, seems to have
begun immediately.

Charles reacted with two mutually contradictory responses. On the one
hand, he continued to seek to prevent, or at least delay, Strafford's death,
merely by not granting the warrant necessary to set the bureaucratic wheels
of execution in motion. Here, too, then, were the makings of another potential
showdown between the king and the anti-Straffordian peers. And the Junto
responded in kind. The newly appointed Constable of the Tower, the Earl
of Newport, the officer who would otherwise have required a writ under the
Great Seal to deliver his prisoner for execution, declaring openly that, if
necessary, he would send Strafford for execution on his own authority,
without waiting for authorization from the king. As late as Tuesday – the
eve of the execution day, as stipulated by the peers – the king still held out
against signing the requisite death warrant. Instead, in a further bid to nullify

the attainder, he sent the Prince of Wales to deliver a message asking that Strafford be allowed to 'fulfil the natural course of his life in a close imprisonment', an outcome that could have been achieved even without a formal reversal of the attainder act:[207] it simply required that the king should continue to neglect to issue the paperwork required for an execution.

Yet, even as he pleaded for the punishment stipulated in the attainder act not to be put into effect, Charles was forced to acknowledge that, for all practical purposes, the Lords were in control of when and where Strafford would die. Implicitly recognizing as a fait accompli their usurpation of a prerogative once indisputably his own, he pleaded with them that, 'if he must die, it were charity to reprieve him till Saturday [15 May]'.[208] In the meantime, however, he still failed to produce the necessary death warrant.

To concentrate the king's mind, the Lords sent a deputation of twelve peers – the size of the delegation can scarcely have been coincidental – to Whitehall with the barely veiled warning that they could not answer for his own safety or that of the royal family, were the execution to be further delayed.[209] Confronted by these twelve peers (including Warwick, Essex, Holland, Saye, and Wharton), Charles finally capitulated. Exactly as he had done when confronted, back in September 1640, with the Twelve Peers' threat to summon a Parliament on their own authority, he was faced with exercising his prerogative powers against his will (and saving face), or seeing others usurp his authority (and facing public humiliation). The only variable in the outcome was the 'dishonour' entailed; the outcome itself was not in question.

Later that day, Tuesday, 11 May, he reluctantly issued the formal orders – as Arundel had put it in the crisis of September 1640, 'that he may have the honor of it himselfe'[210] – rather than endure the indignity of seeing Strafford killed on a warrant issued by the House of Lords. The Chancery order-book notes that the warrant was 'p[er] ipsum Regem' – from the king himself: writs were to be issued under the Great Seal to Newport to deliver the prisoner, and to the Sheriff of London to see that the beheading was carried out. Strafford was to die the following morning – whatever more the king did, or failed to do.[211]

*

The legal process against Strafford had been, throughout, an act of judicial theatre, acted out before the largest audience that could be accommodated in London. The requirement that the moment of retribution should also be a public ritual dictated the venue and manner of Strafford's death. The earl's request to the king that he might be beheaded privately, within the Tower, was overruled by the Junto leadership.[212] They needed Strafford's execution, like his trial, to be a moment of redefinition: a public repudiation of an old, despotic form of government, which also marked the inauguration of a new régime of virtuous counsel. And this was now firmly founded – thanks to the act removing the king's power of dissolution – on the authority of a Parliament that was secured against premature dismissal. Throughout Monday and Tuesday, carpenters had toiled on Tower Hill to erect the series

'The beginning of the people's happiness'? Strafford's execution on Tower Hill, 12 May 1641. Parliament's eight official witnesses to the execution – the Earls of Warwick, Essex, and Pembroke and Viscount Saye, and four Commons-men whose identities are unknown – are probably among the group that are crowded on to the actual scaffold.

of temporary wooden stands to accommodate the large crowds expected for the execution. The noise was almost certainly audible within the fortress, where Strafford spent the two days settling his affairs, and seeking the spiritual consolations of Archbishop Ussher, Laud's ministrations having been forbidden him by the Lieutenant of the Tower.[213]

On the morning of the execution, Wednesday, 12 May, crowds started gathering on Tower Hill from 2 a.m., anxious to secure an unobstructed view of the scaffold. By daybreak, the entire hill to the north-west of the Tower was covered with spectators. Wenzel Hollar's engraving of the scene, which was probably based on a drawing from life, reveals around seventeen wooden stands, each holding somewhere between 100 and 200 onlookers, most of whom would have paid for their places. Many thousands more filled the open ground around the scaffold;[214] Giustinian estimated the crowd to be 200,000 strong – doubtless an exaggeration, but testimony nevertheless to the immensity of the throng. After the tensions of recent weeks, the atmosphere at the execution was one of 'universal rejoicing'.[215] The raucous spirit of carnival had entered the crowd.

As the crowd on the hill grew ever larger and more rumbustious, Strafford endured an anguished and inexplicably lengthy wait. Five times during the course of that long morning, he was reported to have sent messages to Sir William Balfour, the Lieutenant of the Tower, requesting that he might suffer his ordeal without further delay.[216] Why the execution was so long deferred is unclear, though one possible explanation is that Balfour was awaiting the arrival of the formal delegation of parliamentary witnesses, caught up in the near-immobile coach traffic in the approaches to Tower Hill. For whatever reason, however, it was not until after 11 a.m. that Balfour called at the prisoner's lodgings to escort him to the scaffold.[217] Nervous of the crowd's temper and fearing for Strafford's safety, he urged him to travel the short distance between the Tower gate and the scaffold by coach.

But Strafford was insistent. 'Master Lieutenant', he replied stoically, 'I dare looke death in the face, and I hope the People too. Have you a care that I doe not escape, and I care not how I die, whether by the Executioner or by the madnesse and fury of the People ... it is all one to me.'[218]

Balfour acceded to Strafford's request to walk to the scaffold, but took the precaution of providing an extensive military escort, including a company of the Sheriff of London's men with halberds, Yeomen Warders, and, it seems, a detachment of the newly installed garrison. Attended by the gentleman usher of his own household, and supported spiritually by Archbishop Ussher, Strafford reached the scaffold without interference from the crowd, and mounted the stairs. It was a congested space. There were comforting presences among the throng: his brothers, Sir William and Sir George Wentworth; his cousin, the Earl of Cleveland; his chaplains[219] and members of his household, there to make their farewells and support him in the final moment.

Other faces were doubtless less welcome. There, for the last time, Strafford confronted the men who had been his nemesis. Both Houses had sent formal representatives to observe the execution. Either actually present on the scaffold, or watching from one of the nearby viewing stands (the closest of which was only a few feet away), were four of his most powerful opponents: Pembroke and Saye, Warwick and Essex – the two wings, respectively, of the Junto; the one that had sought to save his life, at least until the failed coup of 3 May; the other that had worked so assiduously and effectively to destroy it.[220] Yet even here, the Warwick House men predominated, with Warwick's half-brother, Newport, and his eldest son, Lord Rich, both forming part of the small group that attended Strafford from 'before his coming out of the Tower'.[221] They were joined by four unnamed observers from the Commons.[222]

Under the gaze of these official witnesses, the established rituals of aristocratic executions were then played out. Strafford's speech from the scaffold, a familiar element in the theatre of almost all public executions,[223] fulfilled the conventional expectations of the genre: he expressed his submission to the judgement that had been passed upon him; offered forgiveness to 'all the world'; and affirmed his loyalty to the king.[224] Yet one passage struck a discordant note, a note of warning to those who had destroyed him. Picking up one of the Junto's oft-repeated themes, that his punishment should inaugurate a new era in the life of the English commonwealth, Strafford admonished his audience:

[I] wish every Man would lay his Hand on his Heart, and consider seriously whether the beginning of the People's Happiness should be written in Letters of Blood.

Strafford's next sentence may well have been addressed directly at Warwick and the other members of the parliamentary delegation standing close by:

I fear that *they* are in a wrong way, [and] I desire Almighty God that no one drop of my Blood rise up in Judgment against them.[225]

As he ended his speech he urged the crowd to be silent and join him in prayer: 'that God blesse this Kingdome, and Jesus have mercy on my Soule'.[226] Strafford then turned to face the party of friends and official witnesses which had stood behind him throughout his speech. Offering a gesture of reconciliation, '[he] Saluted all the noble men' – among them, it seems, Warwick, Essex, Pembroke, and Saye – 'and tooke a solemne leave of all considerable persons on the scaffold, giving them his hand'.[227]

For the impatient, heckling crowd, tightly crammed into the natural amphitheatre formed by the slope of Tower Hill, and for the many hundreds more that had purchased places in the grandstands – the long row of rickety structures that had been hastily thrown up along the Tower's western moat – the scene that followed must have seemed to last an eternity. Discerning what was happening on the scaffold was near-impossible given the obscuring presence of so many halberdiers, witnesses, chaplains, and guards. For almost half an hour, as he knelt to pray with one of his chaplains, Strafford seemed to disappear entirely from view.

The crowd waited. The party on the scaffold seemed motionless. Overladen, one of the grandstands near the fortress's Beauchamp Tower collapsed, hurling spectators and planking into a bone-breaking pile of bodies and debris.[228] Then, at last, there was movement on the scaffold.

Those who had paid for their grandstand view were not disappointed. The Sheriff of London ensured that the beheading took place on the eastern side of the scaffold, that nearest the grandstands and affording them an almost uninterrupted view. There were no more words. Strafford could be seen to summon the executioner; offered him his forgiveness; then removed his doublet and put on a white woollen cap, to keep the hair clear of his neck. He knelt down. Prostrating himself on a 'cushion', placed on the scaffold floor, he took the measure of the low wooden block, one side of which had been cut away to fit his neck, and lay face down. After a few final moments in prayer, he stretched out his hands, the prearranged signal to the headsman to strike. It took only a single blow.[229]

*

Then came the sight which the crowd had waited patiently since dawn to see. The headsman picked up the severed head by the hair and raised his trophy to public view. As custom at executions required, he shouted 'God save the king!'. But his words went unheard, drowned by the jubilant roar from Tower Hill.[230]

I I

THE ELEPHANT AND
THE DROMEDARY

MAY–AUGUST 1641

Before their Lord, the Lyon, they appeird,
And what they were to me, as Lawrence [the Fox] leird [learnt],
I shall rehearse ane part of everie kinde,
As farre as now occurs to my mynde: ...
The Lynx, the Tyger full of tyranie,
The Elephant and ... the Dromodarie.

Robert Henryson, Schoolmaster of Dunfermline,
The Morall Fables of Esope, the Phrygian (Edinburgh, 1621)[1]

The first shot of what appeared to be a military assault on the Parliament rang out on Wednesday, 19 May 1641, exactly a week after Strafford's execution. The firing seemed to come from a window on the south side of the Commons' chamber, the old Chapel of St Stephen, where a wooden staircase led up to the gallery running along the building's west end. At this 'sudden cracke' – taken by all to be the report of musket fire – the lower end of the House of Commons dissolved into pandemonium. Members in the gallery ran for the adjacent Committee Chamber,* swords drawn, in expectation of the second wave of the attack. As a cloud of dust, apparently from the ricocheting bullet, floated down from the gallery, 'all the gentlemen under the gallery, in an amaze[ment], leaped downe and fell one upon another', desperate to escape what they took to be the line of fire. Inevitably, there were casualties. In the mêlée, Sir Edward Rodney, a cousin of the Earl of Hertford, lost his balance and collapsed. So, too, did Sir Francis Popham, a Somerset man approaching seventy and 'a very aged, corpulent man', who fell heavily in his efforts to escape. Even the relatively athletic Thomas Erle – Sir Walter's son and a man barely in his twenties – broke his shin in the scramble to get out.[2]

---

* The Commons' Committee Chamber was on the same level as the gallery, and was situated immediately above the Commons' lobby, in the two westernmost bays of the old Chapel of St Stephen; see Maps.

In the adjoining Westminster Hall – filled with its usual weekday scrum of petitioners, litigants, and lawyers – the chaos quickly spread. Sir John Wray, a Commons-man who had been in the Hall when the panic began, encountered his exiting colleagues and came to the obvious conclusion, that 'ther had been some treason against [the House]'. He promptly joined the fleeing throng.[3] Others, who were not Parliament-men, proved to be of more heroic mettle. Sir Robert Mansell, an old sea dog in his seventies, who had served with the Earl of Essex's father in the celebrated Cadiz raid of 1596, was not one to be daunted by traitors. Attempting to halt the Gadarene rush, he brandished his sword dramatically and exhorted the frightened Commons to 'stand and fight like true Englishmen'. But his stirring words went unheeded. Onwards rushed the members, sweating and breathless; not halting till they reached the security of Old Palace Yard.

Disgusted, the doughty Elizabethan resolved to give battle alone. Mansell was last seen 'advanc[ing] out of the Hall towards the howse of Commons, with his sword drawn'.[4]

1. STRAFFORDIAN CONSEQUENCES: WHITEHALL

Old Sir Robert Mansell lived to fight another day. In fact, there had been no shot; no bullets; no treason against the House. The 'sudden crack' which had started the panicked rush for the doors was no more than the breaking of a few laths, the narrow wooden slats that carried the wall plaster near the gallery stairs. When a member, who had dropped a piece of paper into the interstice between the wall and the wooden gallery, leant over to retrieve it, the old slats had broken under his weight, producing the gunlike crack and dislodging the cloud of ancient lime and plaster that so resembled musket smoke.[5]

All too late, the nature of the false alarm was realized. When the members reassembled in the chamber, dusty, bruised, and shamefaced, they were admonished by Denzell Holles, one of the Junto supporters who would have been a prime target for any real attack, for causing such a disorder 'upon such a frivolous mistake'. Reports of their conduct, he feared, 'would bee a great scandal to the honour and dignitie of this howse'.[6]

Yet the unwitting comedy of this panic 'upon such a frivolous mistake' witnesses graphically to the edginess of Parliament-men in the weeks following Strafford's death. Ever since 2 May, when the Tower Plot had been first discovered, the threat that the commonwealth would be undone by violence – from mercenaries in London, mutiny in the northern army, or a French invasion through Portsmouth, no one knew which – had kept the Parliament almost continuously on edge. A sense that the nation was on the brink of armed conflict, albeit against an adversary not yet clearly defined, was one of the legacies of the crisis of early May. Robert Chestlin, the Rector of St Matthew's Friday Street in 1641, recalled how 'the Puritan Faction, with continuall Alarums, ... drummed [a fear of tyranny] into the people's eares, even to a phrensey of ridiculous feares and jealousies'.[7] And there is no doubt that these 'Alarums' rang louder in the capital than they did outside.[8] The problem for the king, however, was that – after the disclosure of the conspiracy to free Strafford at the beginning of May – it seemed that the 'Cavaliers' would try any expedient, no matter how desperate, in order to break the power of the Junto. Almost all alarms had come to seem inherently plausible.

In the course of the year ahead that anxiety waxed and waned, but never really went away. The Commons order of 5 May, for all members 'to consider in what state and condition their counties, cities and boroughs are in respect of arms and ammunition', doubtless helped foster this sense of imminent attack;[9] and while it is easy to dismiss such initiatives as cynical manipulation of the public mood on the part of the Junto leaders, a quick survey of their own expenditure on arms and ammunition during this period suggests that there was nothing feigned about their concerns. In the first half of May, for example, Lord Brooke – granted, a man who had more to fear from any royalist coup than most – suddenly purchased enough small arms and ammunition to equip every member of his London household, as well as a blunderbuss and a manual on the use of artillery.[10]* In the summer, too, he began repairing the walls of the great medieval fortress that was his country seat, Warwick Castle.[11] It was not enough to fight a war, but sufficient to suggest that Brooke was deeply apprehensive about the possibility of civil unrest.[12]

Throughout the late spring and early summer, Brooke and his immediate allies – his brother-in-law, Sir Arthur Hesilrige, and his near neighbours at Warwick House – worked assiduously to keep that danger at the forefront of the Parliament's concerns. Although investigation into the conspiracy against Parliament had been entrusted in early May to a large bicameral committee (ten Lords – nine of them Petitioner Peers – and twenty Commoners), in practice, it was a much smaller group, broadly overlapping with the Warwick House circle, that took the depositions and managed the subsequent reporting back to Parliament. Warwick and Essex supervised the interrogations of many of the key witnesses in person;[13] and the timing of their subsequent revelations could therefore be manipulated, as and when required, to raise the political temperature at Westminster.[14]

Yet however adventitiously the Junto leaders timed their revelations, and sometimes sensationalized their disclosures, their conviction that there *had* been a serious plot against the Parliament seems to have been both sincere and rationally founded. As the evidence was pieced together over May and June, it appeared that there had been, in effect, three interrelated plots to use force against Parliament, all promoted by members of the king's immediate

---

* The accounts for Lord Brooke's privy purse expenditure in London in early May 1641 reveal the acquisition of twelve new sword belts, three pistols with French locks, six new carbines with belts and cartridges, and sixteen pounds of bullets and shot, as well as the blunderbuss and manual on gunnery.

entourage, with varying degrees of royal sanction: the first, attributed as much to the queen as to the king, to seize the Tower and 'releas[e] the late Lieutenant of Ireland' (the Suckling–Billingsley Plot); a second, to secure the fortress at Portsmouth as a bolt-hole for the king and queen, and as a bridgehead for a French invasion; and the third, the plan to bring the army to London, rendezvousing on its journey southwards at Nottingham with the Earl of Newcastle, who was to provide a further 1,000-strong contingent of cavalry and command the advance on London.[15] Sceptics rightly questioned the 'bias' of the interrogators, who appear to have exaggerated the plotters' cohesiveness, turning what appear to have been several separate anti-parliamentarian initiatives into a single grand design, and wildly overstating the likelihood of any intervention by the French. But the reality of *some* form of plot, in which the king and queen were both implicated, was broadly accepted. So, too, was the Junto's reading of its ultimate objective: as the Venetian ambassador summarized it, 'of crushing the *liberty* of the country completely, in the end'.[16] After those revelations, the relations between the king and those who believed in his complicity could never be the same again.

The Strafford crisis thus produced a series of clearly defined winners and losers. Among the winners was the reformist coalition generally; as John Maynard remarked of Strafford's condemnation, 'Nowe we have done our worke; if we could not have effected this, wee could have done nothing'.[17] Within that coalition, however, it was the Warwick 'interest' that emerged with its political credit and influence most obviously enhanced. Hitherto, 'neither the Earl of Essex, Warwick, nor Brooke himself, no, nor Mr Holles or Strode' was fully integrated into the Bedfordian group that had dominated policy and parliamentary tactics during the opening months of the Parliament.[18]

Early May 1641 marks the moment when there was a decisive shift in the locus of power within this reformist coalition. Viewed in hindsight, Bedford's strategy of accommodation seemed culpably naive; and the earl's death merely facilitated a shift in power within the reformist Junto that would probably have happened anyway: away from the Bedfordians, with their hankering after 'mixed monarchy' and ultimate reliance on the king's good faith for the reformation of the kingdom's counsels, and towards the Essex–Warwick group and their key allies – Holland and Brooke in the Lords, Barrington, Holles, and Hesilrige in the Commons – and their distinctively republican insistence that Charles should be left, as one diplomat summarized it, with 'the mere title of king ... stripped of all authority'.[19]

Once again, the 'Junto' had direction and coherence; but, this time, it was on Warwick's and Essex's terms. And while they worked harmoniously with the former Bedfordians, they seem to have maintained a certain *froideur* towards erstwhile friends, like Viscount Saye, who had allowed their judgement to be clouded by self-interest. Essex's irritation with Saye emerges in a letter he wrote to Hamilton, in which he paraphrased Shakespeare's *Henry IV*, Part I: 'Wee may say well, as Hotspur sayd, ower members loue the commonwealt well; but thear owne barns better.'²⁰* Warwick's steward, Arthur Wilson, also noted how Saye's former 'averse[ness] to the Court ways' mollified as a result of his preferment in 1641, and it

> appeared afterwards, when the harshness of the [anti-courtly] humour was a little allayed by the sweet Refreshments of Court favours, that those stern Comportments, supposed natural, might be mitigated; and that indomitable Spirits – by gentle usage – may be tamed and brought to obedience.²¹

There were the beginnings, here, of an antipathy that was to grow, during the 1640s, into one of the most rancorous political rivalries – Saye *versus* Essex and Warwick – of the decade.²² Pym, too, seems to have kept a lower parliamentary profile for much of the summer. Having opposed the Warwick House group over the attainder, he was conspicuously omitted from a number of important committees during this period, including, for example, the body set up to oversee future payments to the Scots (which, by contrast, was stacked with Warwick's friends and relations).²³

The real loser, however, was the king, whom the Army Plots of May 1641 had exposed as, at best, a dissembler; at worst, a tyrant in the making. Had he prevailed, the likely outcome was nothing so mild as a return to the authoritarian rule of the 1630s, such as it was, but something far more draconian: a 'Straffordian' autocracy, reliant for its solvency, more than likely, on Spanish subsidies (as Strafford had sought in May 1640) or subventions from such Catholic magnates as the Earl of Worcester. Little wonder that the 'arbitrary rule' which threatened in 1641 was so often equated with 'Popery' – or, in Pym's stock phrase, with the Papists' 'great designe'.²⁴

By placing the question of trust in the king's person so directly at the centre of political debate, the crisis of May – and its aftershocks – confronted the political élite with a starkly polarized and highly unwelcome choice: either following Warwick and Hesilrige towards the consolidation of a 'Venetianized commonwealth', with a doge-like king; or clinging tenaciously to the wreckage of 'mixed monarchy' and its essential precondition, the ability to trust the king with discretionary power, in the hope that something closer to England's traditional pre-1640 constitutions might yet be salvaged. By the time that choice was put to the nation at large, in the summer of 1642, both sides had gone to considerable lengths to narrow the apparent gulf between those two options. For the leading members of the political élite, however, May–June 1641 was in many cases the moment when the future battle lines

---

* Essex quotes from Hotspur's soliloquy (*Henry IV*, Part I, Act II, Scene 3), in which he reads a letter from an erstwhile conspirator who had now gone cold on joining his rebellion: '"But for mine own part, my lord, [Hotspur reads aloud from the letter], I could be well contented to be there, in respect of the love I bear your house." He could be contented: why is he not, then? In respect of the love he bears our house: he shows in this, he loves his own barn better than he loves our house [the House of Percy].' That Essex seems to have been thinking of Saye in these terms is highly suggestive, as also, perhaps, is his adaptation of the Shakespeare quotation to include 'the commonwealth'.

were drawn; when the hitherto latent, and therefore manageable, tensions, within both the pre-1640 court and the reformist coalition, became irreconcilable, and a new political landscape came to be defined.

At court, May 1641 was the point of no return in their relations with the king for a series of courtier grandees, all of whom had occupied major positions in the pre-1640 government of the realm. Of course, the Earl of Holland, Charles's Groom of the Stool, had been firmly in Warwick's camp, and supportive of stringent controls on the king's powers well before the crisis of May 1641. The most important new converts to the principle of a Venetian monarchy republic appear to have been Pembroke and Northumberland, respectively Lord Chamberlain of the King's Household and the Lord High Admiral of England. Hitherto, both had been supportive of Bedford's plans to reform, rather than completely subvert, the existing court system; supportive, too, of a compromise settlement that saved Strafford's life (at least until the revelation of Strafford's complicity in the Tower Plot);[25] and keen to distance themselves from both the quasi-republican militancy and the pro-Scottishness of the Warwick House group.

In response to the crisis of May, however, both these courtier grandees identified themselves firmly – and, in the king's eyes, unforgivably – with the régime's harshest critics. Northumberland left little doubt that, in the event of war, he would direct the fleet to side with the Parliament; and proved his loyalty to 'the public' still further, in June, when he revealed to Parliament a private letter from his own brother, Henry Percy, confessing not only Percy's own complicity in the Army Plots, but also incriminating a number of his courtier accomplices.[26] Pembroke's actions in May alienated him from the king just as completely; from the moment the Tower Plot was discovered, Pembroke was backing Strafford's attainder, and siding so publicly with Warwick's 'Commonwealthsmen' – as they were dubbed by the Scottish Commissioners[27] – that he was pilloried in the press as one of those 'Nobles ... who have striv'd t'usurpe our great Jove's throne'.[28]

Even more striking, perhaps, is the alienation of the king's one-time favourite, the Marquess of Hamilton – the Master of the Horse and a senior member of the king's Bedchamber staff – who also seems to have been radicalized, if more ambiguously, by the events of May 1641. Thereafter, he aligned himself publicly with Warwick and Essex, and acted as a linkman between the Warwick House peers and the key advocate of a monarchical republic in Scotland, the Earl of Argyll.[29]

With the possible exception of Holland, none of these was in any sense a natural bedfellow for Warwick and the more radical reformers. As Privy Councillors during the 1630s, all of them had gone along, albeit with varying degrees of enthusiasm, with the implementation of the very policies that the reformers were now denouncing as tyrannous.[30] From May 1641, however, all four threw in their lot with those who 'loved the commonwealth', aiming to effect draconian curbs on the monarch's powers. To many, perhaps, the fact that the king had been abandoned by men of such seniority – the commanders of army and navy and the principal officers of his court, and who knew him so well – was the clearest indication of the truth of the charges being made against him.[31]*

But if Charles's perceived extremism was driving courtier grandees into the arms of Warwick and the pro-Scots hardliners, there was also a steady traffic in the opposite direction. The extremism of Warwick and his 'Commonwealthsmen' – their insistence on Strafford's death, their provocations to the king, and finally their usurpation of royal authority during the weeks following the Tower Plot – alienated many moderate reformers, including a number of the original Petitioner Peers. As many of these refugees from the reformist camp were rewarded by preferments by the king, it is difficult to discern whether the lure of office or a horror of the new commonwealth's republican implications was the stronger motive for their change of heart. The scale and quality of the exodus during May and June is nevertheless striking: the Earls of Bristol and Hertford, and Lord Savile from the ranks of the Petitioner Peers; Lord Digby, formerly one of Strafford's prosecutors;[32] and from around this time, Edward Hyde (another anti-Straffordian) and Viscount Falkland, both men, until this point, firmly in the vanguard of reform.

It would be an oversimplification to say that, post-Strafford's execution, Westminster politics had become straightforwardly bipolar, not least because there remained figures – like the slippery and personally ambitious Viscount Saye – who continued to make efforts to colonize the old Bedfordian middle ground: hoping to achieve a reconciliation of the two extremes by having the king appoint godly reformists to the major offices of state. Yet, for the Warwick–St John group, the folly of achieving a 'reformation of counsel' without also ensuring that 'the commonwealth' had control of the kingdom's military power had been one of the timely lessons of the Tower Plot. If that did not render Westminster politics simply bipolar, it certainly left it far more sharply polarized than ever before, with a clear division now on offer between the cipher monarchy advocated by the Warwick House group and an embryonic (and ideologically heterogeneous) 'king's party', united on retaining a measure of real personal authority for the man Charles Stuart, even if they were divided among themselves as to just how much. These seem not to have been simply factional alignments, but, at least within the political élite, the preliminary taking of sides in the expectation of a potential civil war, albeit one that most wished to avert.

For both sides, then, the post-Straffordian world was preoccupied with the construction of military alliances. As the lesson of the military campaigns of 1639 and 1640 was clearly that Scotland, the most extensively militarized of the three Stuart kingdoms, had the capacity – if sufficiently backed by English domestic dissent – to bring down a government in Whitehall, both rival parties in England sought to forge alliances with rival sections of the Scottish nobility

---

* As Edward Hyde noted, Northumberland 'had the most esteemed and unblemished reputation, in court and country, of any person of his rank throughout the kingdom'. Therefore when he helped disclose his brother's part in the Army Plot, thereby 'disserving the King ... [many] concluded that he had some notable temptation in conscience, and that the Court was much worse than it was believed to be'.

in order to influence the future dispositions of Covenanter military power. That Warwick should turn to the Covenanter nobility to guarantee the future of the English commonwealth was hardly surprising: their support had been decisive to the Petitioner Peers' revolt in 1640, and he had acted as the Covenanters' stalwart ally in the treaty negotiations ever since.

The truly startling sight to emerge from the crisis of May 1641, however, was of the king attempting to create a Covenanter party of his own, arguably the most paradoxical of all the consequences of Strafford's death. Out-manoeuvred and deprived of his chosen commander-in-chief in England, Charles turned, to the bafflement of many of his supporters in England, to the Covenanter Scots – the 'rebels' he had set out to crush in 1639 and 1640 – as the potential source of his salvation. Their support had been decisive to the reformist Junto's success thus far. If he could sever that link between the two sets of 'rebels', in Edinburgh and London, then there was a high probability that he would be able to isolate his English opponents and, given time, reconstruct his authority within England, if necessary by force.

The initiative that inaugurated this new and profoundly unstable phase in British politics was taken by the king on Wednesday, 12 May, a matter of hours after the axe had fallen on Strafford's neck. No sooner had Charles received the news of the beheading, shortly after noon that day, than he summoned the Scots' Treaty Commissioners for an audience at Whitehall. They hardly expected it to be a congenial encounter. Yet the king's deportment on the afternoon of the execution astonished them all. Instead of his being 'melancholie and harse [harsh]', wrote William Drummond, one of the Scottish Commissioners and an eyewitness, they found him 'in a very gud temper', and optimistic about bringing the treaty to a rapid conclusion.

This sudden display of regal charm had two clearly defined objectives. His immediate and pressing concern was to see the treaty completed so that the Covenanter army could be sent home and disbanded, thereby depriving the reformist Junto of what had been hitherto its major military prop.[33] Beyond this, however, Charles had a larger ambition: the creation of a régime in Scotland that would actively oppose any further such military excursions into England. Edward Nicholas, the Clerk of the Privy Council and informal adviser to the king, later summarized its objective in a memorandum to his master: 'if your Majesty shall settle there [in Scotland] such a peace and quytenes as may conteyn at home the Scotts, in good obedience, [the Covenanter army] shalbe no sooner returned [from England] ... but ... those that have depended upon them [in England] will ... fall flat'.[34] 'Containment' of the Scots, in other words, was the key to a royalist revival in England.

What made this policy of 'conteyn[ing the Scots] at home' an achievable objective in 1641 was that the Covenanter élite was far less united by the spring of 1641 than it had been the previous summer, when it launched its invasion of England. In the interim, an aristocratic faction had emerged in Scotland that was highly critical of the decision to invade England, and increasingly unfriendly towards the authors of the invasion, centred on the Earl of Argyll, Scotland's most powerful territorial magnate, and the dominant figure within the kingdom's quasi-republican government. In the Covenanters' divisions – in particular, the first stirrings of an anti-Argyll reaction – Charles gradually came to discern his chance.[35]

11. CRUSHING THE ELEPHANT

Stooped, saturnine, and lugubrious, Archibald Campbell, 8th Earl of Argyll, was in many respects an unlikely leader of the Covenanter revolt. Born around 1607, the scion of one of Scotland's oldest and richest noble houses, his childhood had been dominated by his father's (the seventh earl's) increasing fascination with 'Popery', culminating in 1618, when he had been received as a Roman Catholic and abandoned Scotland to enter the service of the Spanish Habsburgs. Left in control of the vast Campbell inheritance by his absent father, the young Lord Lorne (as he was styled until his father's death in 1638) was brought up in an austere Knoxian Calvinism by his tutor Robert Barclay (subsequently one of the Scottish Commissioners in London and a loyal confidant of his former pupil). On attaining his majority, Argyll set about asserting his feudal rights over his estates and extending the Campbells' regional empire in the largely Gaelic-speaking Western Highlands. Such extensive territorial power could not be ignored by the king, who acknowledged his influence with appointment to the Scottish Privy Council in 1628 and as Hereditary Master of the King's Household the following year. Yet he was profoundly out of sympathy with the king's plans for Scotland during the 1630s, hated the king's religious policies, despised the Scottish bishops, and feared they were excluding the nobility from civil power – a series of prejudices that were to create a firm bond with the English Petitioner Peers in 1640.[36]

Habitually cautious, Argyll took time to commit himself publicly to the Covenanter revolt. When he did so, however, late in 1638, around the time he succeeded to the earldom, his status and territorial influence guaranteed that he was regarded as 'the outstanding noble leader of the covenanting movement'.[37] After the Scottish Parliament convened in July 1640, without royal authority, Argyll and his militant allies used the session to make the institution independent of royal control and to impose drastic limitations on the king's powers.[38] There was also evidently discussion of appointing Argyll 'dictator', on the Roman model: a commander endowed, for a limited period, with almost unlimited powers.[39] This was not pursued; but Argyll's increasingly regal status seemed confirmed, in June 1640, when the Committee of Estates was inaugurated to act as the Covenanter régime's executive body. Even though 'all saw that he was the *major potestas* [the greater power]',[40] Argyll did not become a member of the Committee of Estates, but stood apart 'in an almost kingly way, above the estates of the realm'.[41] During the summer of 1640 he campaigned in the Highlands at the head of an army of around 4,000 men, suppressing royalist resistance to the new Covenanter régime and, in the words of one critic, 'playing *rex*' – assuming the role of king.[42] Reports that he had discussed, in the abstract, the views of theorists who argued that kings could be deposed – indeed, according to one witness, had gone further and spoken of deposing King Charles[43] – provided ammunition to the growing number of Argyll's enemies within the Covenanter movement, suspicious that Argyll was intent on making himself Scotland's ruler and determined to exploit the Covenanter alliance with the dissident peers in England to further this end.

Organized opposition to Argyll's seemingly unlimited self-aggrandizement first crystallized in August 1640, around the twenty-nine-year-old Covenanter general James Graham, 5th Earl of Montrose: the temperamental, as well as political, antithesis of Argyll; flamboyant where he was morose; extrovert and impulsive where his rival was dour and circumspect. Together with some eighteen or nineteen like-minded Scottish noblemen, Montrose entered into a secret association – what became known as the Cumbernauld Band ('band' being Scots for 'oath') – to defend king and country, and to resist 'the particular and indirect practiking of a few':* a vague phrase, but one that could be read, as Montrose surely intended it, as a reference to the machinations of Argyll and his party.[44] As a formal undertaking, the Cumbernauld Band had little effect. Its existence had been divulged to the Committee of Estates by November 1640, and after a campaign of denunciation within the committee and from leading pro-Argyll clergy,[45] twelve of the original signatories, including Montrose, were persuaded by the Committee of Estates to sign a recantation; the original Band was burned.

Despite this public disavowal, however, the sense of grievance that the Band had expressed remained undimmed, and intensified over the winter of 1640–41, as the treaty negotiations in London came to be dominated by the Argyllian interest – in particular, John Campbell, Lord Loudoun, the most effective of the London negotiators, and Argyll's agent and relation. In Edinburgh, towards the end of December 1640,[46] Montrose brought together a small, close-knit group of kinsmen and friends, who later came to be known simply as 'the Plotters' – his brother-in-law, Lord Napier, the nearest thing the conspirators had to a political theorist; his nephew, Sir George Stirling of Keir; and Stirling's own brother-in-law, Sir Archibald Stewart of Blackhall.[47] These agreed that Scotland's ancient tradition of mixed monarchy was being imperilled by an aristocratic oligarchy – Argyll's party – intent on the creation of a de facto republic: in Lord Napier's words, 'the tyranny of subjects, the most insatiable and insupportable tyranny of the world'.[48]

Around the same time, Montrose and his fellow plotters decided to establish their own direct line of communication with the Whitehall court. And in Lieutenant-Colonel Walter Stewart, an officer in the Covenanter army who was also, usefully, a cousin of the Earl of Traquair,[49] Montrose believed he had found his man. Inviting Stewart to his lodgings in Edinburgh's Canongate, shortly after Christmas 1640, the earl impressed on him that there was now a group of noblemen who would take the king's side 'against those who

---

* The Cumbernauld Band was signed by the 6th Earl Marischal, and the Earls of Montrose, Wigton, Kinghorn, Home, Atholl, Mar, Perth, Galloway, and Seaforth, and ten other nobles and eldest sons of peers, including Lord Almond, the Lieutenant-General of the Covenanter army.

wo[u]ld oppose his Ma[jes]tie', and persuaded the Lieutenant-Colonel to accept the role of their emissary to Whitehall.[50] There, Stewart was to persuade the Duke of Lennox and the Earl of Traquair, the king's two senior advisers on Scotland, then at court, of Montrose's 'affectione and [the] affectiones of *others of his mynd,* and to see if the Duke [of Lennox] will joyne with them'. Montrose did not name names, but Stewart immediately understood that the 'others of his mynd' were 'those that had subscribed the Band' – the anti-Argyllian oath of August 1640.[51]

The decisive moment, Montrose realized, would come when the London Treaty, at last finished and approved by the English Parliament, would be sent north for approval by a new session of the Parliament in Edinburgh, some time in the summer of 1641. Only a powerful personal intervention by the king, Montrose believed, could prevent Argyll from using the Edinburgh Parliament to tighten his grip on power in Scotland and effect a clean sweep of the major offices of state. To impose this royal curb on Argyll's ambition, Montrose and his allies proposed an audacious, almost improbable, gambit: they would advise Charles that he come north for the next parliamentary session, scheduled for 25 May, and appear in Edinburgh in person. The plan could hardly have been more far-fetched. Since his accession to the English and Scottish thrones in 1625, Charles had visited Edinburgh only once, in 1633 for his coronation as King of Scots. And though the king had himself proposed a visit to Edinburgh in 1639, immediately after the treaty that ended his first military adventure against the Covenanters,[52] the idea that he would leave Whitehall in the midst of a political crisis in England, with a Parliament in session, was scarcely credible. That he would do so on the advice of a 'rebel' Covenanter general who had taken part in the 1640 invasion of England seemed more improbable still.[53] Undaunted, at some point in late February or early March 1641, Montrose dispatched Stewart as his emissary to the Whitehall court, providing him with coded written instructions as to his *modus operandi* and ultimate goals.[54] Stewart's pretext for seeking an audience with the king was that Montrose had decided to seek service under the Elector Palatine, who was then at court, and was using Stewart to make the necessary arrangements.[55]

Stewart's initial task was to win support for the strategy within the king's London-based Scottish entourage. Some were discounted from the outset. The Marquess of Hamilton, whom the plotters rightly suspected of being in league with Argyll's allies at Westminster, was to be kept in the dark, as was anyone else thought likely to divulge the scheme to 'the Marquesse'.[56] Instead, Montrose pinned his hopes on two highly placed confidants of the king. The first was the absentee Scottish magnate, the Duke of Lennox,[57]* Charles's

---

* In fact, although James Stuart, 4th Duke of Lennox, was the premier Scottish peer, he had been born at Whitehall in 1612, and had spent much of the intervening period in England. A Gentleman of the Bedchamber to Charles I since 1625, when he had been aged thirteen, he had been one of the principal financiers of the campaigns against the Covenanters in 1639 and 1640, having loaned the king the staggering sum of £30,000 by July 1641 – enough to keep the entire royal army in pay for the best part of a month.

fresh-faced and deeply loyal cousin, still in his twenties, who attended him daily as a Gentleman of the Bedchamber. The other, still nominally the Lord Treasurer of Scotland, was the Earl of Traquair, the linchpin of Charles's régime in Scotland during the 1630s, but currently a fugitive from Covenanter justice, in exile at Whitehall.[58] Dire consequences were threatened if their cooperation were not forthcoming. 'Assure *D.* [the Duke of Lennox] and *T.* [the Earl of Traquair]', Montrose commanded his emissary, 'that except they take *Genero* [Montrose himself] by the hand, they will be trod upon at home [in Scotland, by Argyll] and made naked.'[59] Through this combination of Traquair's gravitas and Lennox's boyish charm, Montrose hoped to achieve two major objectives: first, to bring home to Charles just 'how necessary it is that [he should] come to the [forthcoming Edinburgh] Parliament';[60] and, second, to persuade the king to distribute Scotland's great public offices among 'those that had subscrybed the band'.[61]

Yet Montrose's support was not unconditional, and the terms he imposed underline the extent to which this approach was the result of a split *within* the Covenanter cause, not a straightforward royalist conspiracy aimed at restoring the pre-war status quo. Hence, Charles had to grant 'religion' – that is, bless the abolition of bishops in Scotland and accept the new Presbyterian status quo[62] – and confirm the laws passed since the Covenanter Revolt. But if these terms were acceptable, Montrose and his allies maintained that they would take the king's part against their common adversary. Thinly veiling the identities of the parties involved in a series of animal code names, Montrose's written 'Instructions' to his emissary were 'to assure *L.* [Lion, i.e. the king], that *R[eligion]* and *L[iberty]* being granted, he will be powerfull to crush the Elephant'.[63] Cryptic as these allusions may seem to modern readers, they were references that would have been familiar to most educated Scots, not least, perhaps, to Charles himself. For the elephant, like the dromedary (which was also to figure in Montrose's correspondence with the court), was one of the proud and over-mighty beasts, forced to submit before the Lion King, as described in one of the most celebrated works of Scottish Renaissance poetry, Robert Henryson's 1570 translation of Aesop's *Fables*. Reissued in an English edition in Edinburgh in 1621, Henryson's Aesop was probably so familiar to this aristocratic readership that its references were not so much a secretive code as a series of courtly in-jokes. 'L.' – for 'Lion' – became the king's code-letter in the correspondence among the conspirators;[64] and to anyone familiar with the context, the identities of the individuals intended could be easily deduced.[65]

In Montrose's political jungle, the crushing of 'the Elephant' – the Earl of Argyll – was the precondition for restoring leonine regal power. Indeed, the possibility of this happy outcome was offered to Whitehall as the prime inducement for Charles's acceptance of Montrose's plan. Lieutenant-Colonel Stewart raised the possibility of Argyll's destruction in his conversations with the Earl of Traquair 'at his first being at Court'. The Plotters grounded their hopes on the treasonous words that Argyll was alleged to have spoken 'anent [concerning] the deposeing of the King'[66] – back in June 1640, when he was reported to have offered three 'reasons Why a King might be deposed', viz., Invasio [invasion of his own people], desertio [abandonment of his kingdom], ambitio [tyrannous ambition].[67]

And all three reasons were potentially applicable to Charles I as King of Scots: a monarch who was seeking to invade Scotland with an English army; had deserted it to live in London as an absentee king; and whose ambition to turn Scotland into 'an English province' was already abundantly proved.[68] If Argyll's uttering of these words could be substantiated, this was evidence enough to cost him his head. And this, Stewart explained to Traquair, was exactly what Montrose proposed to do: he had witnesses – Sir Thomas Stewart and John Stewart the younger of Ladywell – who could attest to Argyll's words.[69]

Traquair immediately identified the opportunity created by the charge against Argyll, but equally quickly realized the massive risk Montrose and his allies were taking in laying a capital charge against the most powerful man in Scotland. 'It was dangerous to have *heard* such words', Traquair warned Lieutenant-Colonel Stewart, adding that 'there was no Way to Keep [the witnesses] from Harm unles[s] he could get the discourse of Mr Jon Stewart in write[ing]'.[70] Argyll would stop at nothing, Traquair implied, to remove anyone who might testify to his having spoken treasonous words.

Montrose's 'Instructions' and Stewart's representations on his behalf once at Whitehall highlight how little religion had to do with the causation of this split within the Scottish élite. Between Montrose and his arch-rival Argyll, questions of divinity or Church government were not a matter of contention. Both men were equally committed to the abolition of the Scottish bishops and supportive of the country's reformed, post-Revolt Presbyterian Church; hence Montrose's strict preconditions to the king.[71] Instead, what separated Montrose and his Bander allies from Argyll (and what was later to place Montrose at the head of the 'king's party' in a Scottish civil war) was an irreconcilable division over the future government of the realm: whether, in Scotland, a 'mixed monarchy' or an aristocratic quasi-republic presided over by a puppet king would eventually prevail – not questions of religious doctrine, practice, or Church government.[72] To this extent, developments in Scotland bear a close, if not exact, resemblance to the split that was to emerge from May 1641 within the reformist alliance at Westminster.

This fracturing of the Covenanters' military leadership – between Argyll's militants, intent on creating an aristocratic republic north of the Tweed, and Montrose's defenders of a limited, but nevertheless real, personal monarchy – presented Charles with an obvious opportunity: provided, of course, he was prepared to accept the 'Root-and-Branch' abolition of bishops in Scotland as a fait accompli.[73] In his northern kingdom, at least, that was a price that Charles – so often misrepresented as inflexibly dogmatic when it came to the subject of bishops – was prepared to pay. If Montrose and his allies prevailed, the king stood to recoup a substantial element of his personal authority in Scotland. Moreover, he looked likely to be able to block any further military interventions by Covenanter armies beyond the Tweed. The implications of this for his English kingdom were profound. If containment could be achieved in Scotland, Argyll's allies in Westminster – principally the Warwick House faction among the English Treaty Commissioners – would not merely 'fall flat'; they would be highly vulnerable, once they were unable to call out their Covenanter mercenaries in their defence, to Charles's future revenge. Warwick's gentleman-soldier friends in the Artillery Company and the Essex Trained Bands[74] would be hard pressed to defend the 'commonwealth' should the king succeed in raising an army.

Given the scale of the concessions the king was being asked by Montrose to make, it is unsurprising that Lennox and Traquair made slow work of persuading the king that his salvation might lie in the hands of a Covenanter 'rebel'.[75] Stewart returned to Scotland in March 1641, having made little progress, and rendezvoused with Montrose at Broxmouth House, near Dunbar.[76]

Throughout March and April, Charles temporized, refusing to commit himself publicly to the Scottish visit – the centrepiece of Montrose's grand design. Hopes that Bedford's diplomacy might deliver a settlement in England probably provide a partial explanation for the king's indecision. However, it seems that Traquair's doubts about the viability of the planned treason prosecution against Argyll may also have acted as a powerful dissuasive in the king's mind against backing Montrose and embarking on the hazardous journey to Scotland. Reading between the lines of the surviving depositions, it looks as though Traquair (and, on Traquair's advice, the king) had refused to support Montrose's plan unless and until testimony of Argyll's treason had first been secured in writing.[77]

Lieutenant-Colonel Stewart therefore returned to Edinburgh at the end of March determined to obtain the written evidence necessary to ensure Argyll's destruction.[78] After meetings with Sir Thomas Stewart in Stirling, and with John Stewart the younger in Edinburgh, he eventually obtained what he wanted: written depositions from both men attesting to Argyll's guilt. With this part of his mission accomplished around mid April, Lieutenant-Colonel Stewart reported to Montrose at Newcastle, where the earl had rejoined the Covenanter army of occupation. Montrose remained keener than ever to bring the king to Edinburgh for the new session of the Scottish Parliament, and was determined that Stewart should go back for a second visit to the Whitehall court.

This time, however, Lieutenant-Colonel Stewart was able to offer written evidence to verify what had hitherto been purely verbal undertakings. For the first time, Montrose no longer relied solely on Stewart to convey his offers verbally, but reaffirmed them in writing with letters to Lennox and Traquair, insisting that his plans remained the same: 'things Wer not altered [from that] which was formerlie determined' he assured them, and 'they [Lennox and Traquair] s[h]ould hold [firm]'.[79] Perhaps still more importantly, Lieutenant-Colonel Stewart embarked on his second journey to Whitehall bearing the written witness depositions against Argyll, which finally seemed to open the way to a viable prosecution for treason.[80]

Even so, Charles remained understandably reluctant to commit himself to the Scottish journey, that essential precondition of Montrose's support. Only on 21 April (perhaps, significantly, the day that the Strafford attainder bill finally passed the Commons)[81] did the king make his first tentative steps towards accepting Montrose's proposal. He informed the Scottish Commissioners in London that he would make such a journey, provided the Edinburgh Parliament would defer its next meeting (set for 25 May) for long enough to allow him to attend. Nevertheless, the king's commitment to this high-risk course remained uncertain – a tentativeness that was doubtless compounded, in the last week of April, by Charles's apparent conviction that Bedford was close to delivering an English settlement that would save Strafford's life.[82]

Strafford's execution appears to have removed any of the king's lingering doubts about the proposed journey to Edinburgh. Confronting failure on almost every English front – his attempts to save Strafford, to achieve a negotiated settlement with the Junto, and, finally, to re-establish his authority by force – the idea of weakening his enemies at Westminster by depriving them of Scottish military support suddenly acquired a compelling attraction.

*

At Whitehall on 12 May 1641, Lord Loudoun and the Scottish Commissioners stood puzzled before the 'gud temper[ed]' king, who had summoned them at such short notice and now greeted them, apparently cordially, barely two hours after Strafford's beheading. Of Montrose's clandestine diplomacy – the development that had brought such equanimity to the royal demeanour – as yet, Loudoun seems to have known nothing. The king's announcement therefore left him thunderstruck. Charles declared that he had 'prorogued' the Scottish Parliament, due to meet in under a fortnight, on 25 May, for another eight weeks – to 13 July. And 'except [that] siknesse or deathe previn[t] it', the king insisted, he would be present at its opening in person.[83]

III. STRAFFORDIAN CONSEQUENCES: THE DILEMMAS OF WARWICK HOUSE

Charles's decision sent a seismic shock through Westminster. Diplomats noted the disapproval that had greeted it, wondering whether 'there may be some alteration';[84] and it took time for Parliament-men to adjust to the idea that England was about to experience a period of absentee rule. One group, however, seem to have had little difficulty comprehending the likely consequences of Charles's planned Scottish journey. On the afternoon of Strafford's execution, Warwick and Essex still lacked detailed knowledge of Montrose's courtly diplomacy, and of the precise role of Traquair and Lennox in bringing about this diplomatic démarche.[85] But for the reformist Junto, even the possibility of a rapprochement between the king and their own Covenanter allies had major implications for the survival of the reformist cause within England. The mere fact of the king's prospective journey was itself prima facie evidence that the king had received some form of underhand commitment from allies within the Covenanter élite in Edinburgh.[86] Lord Brooke consoled himself with another spending spree on guns:[87] six new carbines this time, and a further twelve pounds of bullets.[88]

A royal visit to Edinburgh, on its own, would have been sufficient to set alarm bells ringing loudly at Warwick House. What amplified these danger signals, in the immediate aftermath of Strafford's execution, was that the Junto leadership's own relations with the Covenanter grandees had deteriorated markedly since the heady days of Newburn. More than seven months into the treaty negotiations, there were still major items on the Scots' agenda where their English 'friends' had failed to make any significant progress towards meeting the Scots' demands. Of the three issues that bulked largest in their concerns – the punishment of 'Incendiaries', Strafford and Laud, the pay of the Scottish army, and progress towards 'uniformity' between the Scottish and English Churches – the Junto, after six long months of the parliamentary session, had yielded satisfaction on only the first of these, with the execution of Strafford. Pay for the Scottish army, on the other hand, remained massively in arrears, and the chances of their financial demands ever being fully satisfied looked bleak.[89] As one Commons-man noted at the time, the Parliament's debts by the end of May 1641 would be £200,000 greater than the total value of its expected tax revenues voted to date,[90] and there was little realistic prospect of raising further sums.[91]

Scottish anger at these unrequited financial demands was compounded by their Junto friends' failure to deliver thoroughgoing reform of the English Church. For the Scottish Commissioners, the creation of a 'religious union' between England and Scotland had been one of the central motives of their intervention in support of the 1640 Petitioner Peers.[92] Purging the English Church of bishops – to the Covenanters, those accursed 'relics of popery' – remained one of the Commissioners' agreed objectives, and was set out in a detailed paper presented to Warwick and his fellow Treaty Commissioners in early March 1641.[93] This was something more than simply an altruistic desire that the light of the Gospel should burn more brightly throughout the whole island of Britain. It stemmed from the pragmatic calculation that the bishop-less Presbyterian Church north of the border would never be safe until such time as bishops were also eradicated, 'Root-and-Branch', in England. As one Commons-man summarized the position adopted by Loudoun and the Scottish Commissioners, '[the Scots] cannot conceive how the peace can be durable in Scotland unless episcopacy to abolished in England'.[94]

Yet, in mid May, when the king confirmed his journey into Scotland, Root-and-Branch abolition of bishops in England still seemed an outcome almost impossibly remote. Not that Loudoun and his fellow Commissioners had been backward in demanding it. Their submission on 'Unity in Religion', presented in March 1641 to Warwick, Bedford, and the other Treaty Commissioners on the English side, had made a forceful case for the need to abolish episcopacy in England.[95] Yet the response of their 'friends' had been simply to bury it. None of the Scots' requests for Root-and-Branch reform was reported to Parliament, an act of censorship that is only partly explicable by the constraints on the parliamentary timetable imposed by the Strafford trial. Despite private intimations of encouragement from Warwick's circle, the Junto had been as inactive as any when it came to the promotion of Root-and-Branch reform.[96]

Indeed, after February 1641, when the Commons' debates on the question had all but closed the subject down, the Junto's expectations for Church reform had focused on the committee chaired by Bishop Williams, meeting in Westminster Abbey's Jerusalem Chamber, and its plans for 'modified episcopacy'. By May 1641, these deliberations had achieved an impressively broad consensus, satisfying not only the 'godly' bishops, but also such influential puritan divines as Edmund Calamy (the prime organizer of the ministers' Remonstrance against the Laudian bishops of January 1641 and an intimate of Warwick's circle).[97] 'By mutual Concessions,' wrote Calamy, 'Things [at Bishop Williams's committee] were brought into a very hopeful Posture';[98] and since this emergent consensus was likely to command widespread support, it is hardly surprising that even Warwick's circle was reluctant to further the Scots' controversial demands for Root-and-Branch.[99]

High promises and paltry returns therefore characterized the Junto's record when it came to furthering 'unity' between the Scottish and English Churches, just as they had disappointed the Scots over the question of the Covenanter army's pay. These were not yet the grounds for an outright breach between the Scots and their English allies, but they remained a source of ongoing friction. Moreover, in the light of the king's new-found willingness to grant most of the Covenanters' demands in relation to Scottish domestic reform, the usefulness of their English friends as brokers – in particular, Warwick's group among the Treaty Commissioners – was much reduced, and possibly superseded altogether.

Charles's Scottish journey – and the rapprochement with sections of the Covenanter leadership that so clearly underlay it – dominated British politics from the late spring to the early autumn of 1641. For Warwick and his political allies, however, it sharply heightened their sense of their own vulnerability, and this, in turn, prompted an almost craven desire to ingratiate themselves with the Covenanter élite in general, and with the Earl of Argyll in particular. The task that faced them nevertheless remained daunting. Loudoun, Rothes and the other London-based Covenanter grandees needed to be reassured, and rapidly, that their Westminster 'friends' *could* still deliver their outstanding demands. Satisfaction of their financial needs, of course, was the *sine qua non* for maintenance of the 'brotherly union' between the two kingdoms. But there was also an expectation – particularly strong, it seems, among the Argyllians in London[100] – that Warwick and his friends would now make belated progress towards 'nearer union' in religion as well.

A race was now on, in advance of Charles's journey to Edinburgh, as to which English interest could prove itself the Covenanter régime's most effective benefactor. And with Charles offering the Scots, through their London Commissioners, ever greater concessions – whatever, in Nicholas's phrase, was needed to settle the Scots in such a 'peace and quytenes as may conteyn

[them] at home'[101] – it was by no means clear that this was going to be a race which the Junto would win.

iv. FISCAL REVOLUTIONS

Warwick started by playing to his strengths, since, if there was one area where the Junto could be guaranteed to outpace the king, it was money. Yet the scale of the task remained intimidating, and was compounded by the fact that any payments to the Scottish army had to be matched by equal generosity towards the English, if the Westminster Parliament were not to run the risk of full-scale mutiny. By May 1641, the Scottish army had gone unpaid since mid January.[102] Just over £1 million was required for the two armies, including the huge ex gratia payment to the Scots of £300,000 – the so-called 'Brotherly Assistance' – made as an expression of thanks for the Scots' assistance in toppling the Personal Rule.[103] The four subsidies voted by Parliament (already regarded as imposing a heavy tax burden on the nation), would yield barely a quarter of this, around a quarter of a million pounds. The rest – £773,900, or more than three-quarters of the total – was still owing.[104]

Raising these gargantuan sums was a task that fell to the Junto-men in the Commons, with Warwick's allies, Barrington and Mildmay, taking a major role in the management of the financial legislation, and Sir John Hotham, one of the first backers of the Petition of the Twelve Peers in Yorkshire,[105] presenting the hair-raising report on 17 June that outlined the extent of the Parliament's liabilities.[106] The scale of the problem seemed almost insurmountable. A small proportion of what was owed could be raised from the customs revenues.[107] But by far the greatest amount – an estimated yield of £700,000 – still needed to be raised from direct taxation; £300,000 would come in from the subsidies that Parliament had already voted; but that still left £400,000 to be raised.[108] Hesitant to impose yet further subsidies (which, being property taxes, fell disproportionately on their own kind, the landed gentry), the Commons took up a proposal for a novel revenue-raising expedient. At the prompting of Alderman Penington and Secretary Vane, they introduced a poll tax: a one-off payment to be imposed on all subjects, and graduated according to social rank, from £100 for a duke, down to a minimum of sixpence for every person above the age of sixteen not in receipt of parish poor relief.[109]

Placed in perspective, the amounts that the Parliament was seeking to raise in the summer of 1641 were four times the annual cost to the taxpayer of Ship Money during the 1630s, and more than double the largest tax burden that had ever been imposed by any other Parliament in English history. As taxpayers felt the burden of the new exactions over the autumn and winter of 1641, the Junto leadership was to pay a heavy price in unpopularity, not merely for the unprecedented scale of these levies, but also because it seemed that the English, humiliatingly, were being forced to remunerate the Scots for having come into the country to defeat them.[110]

*

This massive increase in the size of the 'tax state' has rightly been noticed as one of the ways in which the British crisis of the 1640s accelerated the process of 'state building' in seventeenth-century England. The expansion in the size and cost of government laid the foundations of recognizably 'modern' forms of public finance.[111] Yet, if this dimension can be regarded as forward-looking, there was also another aspect to this fiscal revolution, which, far from pointing towards the modern bureaucratic state, seems to hark defiantly backwards to the days when the state's fiscal administration had not yet been clearly differentiated from the private, household administration of great nobles and the king. The point is perhaps made most clearly by looking at what, by established practice, *ought* to have happened to the tax revenues raised in 1641. These would normally have been administered by the officers of the royal Exchequer; or, in the case of military funds, by the king's Treasurer-at-War.[112] Indeed, where the monies raised in 1641 actually were for payment to the king's army (just over £462,000), this arrangement still pertained (though, even here, the Treasurer-at-War, Sir William Uvedale, was careful to distinguish between 'the kinges monnies' and 'parlament monnies', the latter earmarked for army pay, which the king could not touch).[113]

For the sums due to the Scots, however, an entirely different (and hitherto unnoticed) system was devised, wholly bypassing the established financial bureaucracy of the Crown. In what was a highly unorthodox (indeed, potentially corrupt) development, the Earl of Warwick and his household staff became the paymasters of the entire Covenanter army in England. Nor was this a matter of chance. Ever since December 1640, Warwick seems to have been using his position as one of the Lords Commissioners for the Anglo-Scottish treaty to justify his negotiating directly with members of the Commons about the payment of the Covenanter army.[114] In consequence the Commons made a series of resolutions on financial matters, the astonishing upshot of which was to have *all* the monies due to the Covenanter army routed through Warwick House in Holborn.[115]

In practice, this meant that, from early December 1640, Warwick (together with his brother, Holland, and son-in-law, Mandeville) became the masters of a substantial private Exchequer. The process was an incremental one, with votes, in December and January,[116] for relatively substantial sums (tens of thousands of pounds) set aside for payment to 'the Earl of Warwicke' for use in paying off the Scots[117] – or as the Commons put it demurely, 'for the reliefe of the Northerne Counties'.[118]

But it was not long before this improvised household Exchequer was dealing with very much larger sums. In June, for instance, when the Commons came to consider the financial arrangements for the disbandment of the English and Scottish forces, they ordered that £100,000[119] was to be paid to the Scots through Warwick's private treasury.[120] By August 1641, however, the total that had passed through Warwick's hands was the staggering sum (in contemporary values) of almost half a million pounds.[121] By way of comparison, this was only a third smaller than the revenues by *all* financial departments of the English state during the 1630s – Ship Money, customs revenues, the king's landed estate, and feudal dues all included.

In theory, Warwick derived his authority to disburse these funds from the orders of the House of Commons. In practice, however, as all suitors for payment knew in seventeenth-century Europe, whoever controlled the actual cash enjoyed broad discretionary powers: to delay or withhold altogether moneys due to enemies, and to hasten payments to friends.[122] Practical constraints on Warwick's discretionary powers seem to have been almost non-existent; as late as June 1641, there were no agreed accountancy procedures in place, and a Commons committee had to be directed to 'consider of some way that the Earle of Warwicke may have a sufficient discharge' for the vast sums he had received and disbursed.[123]

Creating what amounted to a new financial office, wholly autonomous from the royal Exchequer officials or the king's Treasurer-at-War, has a significance that goes well beyond the discretionary power that it brought to its patrician custodian. For if the Commons' decision to place such a massive proportion of the kingdom's public revenues in the hands of a single peer looks, at one level, like an instance of administrative medievalism, it also appears to have been contrived to serve a highly innovatory and subversive end. It would be overstating the case to describe this process as amounting to the creation of an Exchequer for the service of 'the commonwealth', as distinct from that serving the Crown. In practice, however, that is very much how it seems to have functioned, with the Warwick House treasury handling sums that vastly exceeded the meagre trickle of revenues into the royal Exchequer.[124] Indeed, with the king's financial department languishing almost into irrelevancy, Charles opted in May 1641 to leave the Lord Treasurership vacant,[125] vesting its responsibilities in a commission of five Privy Councillors.[126]*

An arrangement in which the pay of their entire army was managed, not through the financial officers of the state, but through the household of the Earl of Warwick, had obvious symbolic and practical implications for the Scots.[127] Symbolically, it reaffirmed the close personal bond between the Covenanter forces and the leading English Junto peer – indeed, the peer who was arguably the most influential of all the Petitioner Peers who had invited the Scots to invade in the summer of 1640. More practically, however, these financial arrangements presented Argyll's party in Edinburgh with a vested

---

* The problems these arrangements created for the king's cash-strapped Treasurer-at-War, Sir William Uvedale, must have given particular satisfaction to at least one member of the Warwick House circle: the Earl of Essex. Five years earlier, in 1636, Uvedale had cuckolded Essex, impregnating his wife, and causing a major scandal at court when the Countess of Essex, Elizabeth *(née* Paulet, the earl's second wife, married in 1630) gave birth to a boy in November that year. Essex accepted the child (styled Viscount Hereford) as his own, in the absence of any other male child to inherit his earldom; but the baby died a month later, precipitating the final collapse of his marriage. Since then, Uvedale had been conducting a widely reported – and, to Essex, deeply humiliating – affair with his estranged wife.

326 THE NOBLE REVOLT

interest, not merely in the English commonwealth's survival, but also in the fortunes of their allies at Warwick House.

This was where the 'Brotherly Assistance' of £300,000 came into its own. Despite the massive size of this grant, less than a third of the total – an initial down payment of £80,000 (in August)[128] – was to be paid to the Scots in the course of 1641.[129] The rest was to be paid in two further annual instalments of £110,000 each: the first in midsummer (i.e. June) 1642; the second, more than two years away, in midsummer 1643. The staging of these payments ensured that the Covenanter régime's future financial rewards – the equivalent, in Scottish currency, of nearly £2.6 million[130] – were tied to the survival of the new English régime, at least for the foreseeable future. Within England, meanwhile, it ensured that Warwick and his friends had a potential war chest of some £220,000; more than enough to pay another Scottish army of some 20,000 men, should need arise, for the best part of a year.[131]

*

The implications of all this were not lost in Edinburgh. Henry Guthrie, one of the members of the General Assembly of the Kirk, later recalled that Montrose's party was

> mightily dejected ... conceiving that the Parliament of England was not so prodigal as to have granted such a Sum [as the Brotherly Assistance] (where nothing was owing) unless they had thereby obtain'd from the Scots some secret engagement to be on their side, as soon as [the king's party] should begin to stir.[132]

Whether such a 'secret engagement', between Argyll's faction in Edinburgh and the Warwick House group in Westminster, ever existed is impossible to document; but that there was some type of informal understanding between the two parties would certainly seem a strong possibility.

By the time the final arrangements for the Brotherly Assistance were set in place, these financial emollients, applied between May and early August 1641, had gone a long way towards smoothing the Scots' ruffled feathers; and had powerfully reaffirmed the community of interest between Argyll's régime in Scotland and England's 'Venetianized' aristocratic commonwealth: the brave new world of heavy-taxing Parliaments and pauper kings.

Yet if the Scots had been pacified in relation to Mammon, they were still deeply dissatisfied with the shortcomings of their English brethren when it came to God. By failing to introduce more than tinkering reforms to England's episcopal Church, the Junto had betrayed the promises of 'nearer uniformity' in religion which had helped induce the Scots to assist their English allies in the first place. And at least until the great crisis of early May, most of the Junto leaders seem to have been singularly untroubled by the Scots' disappointment.

By resorting to force in May 1641, Charles had reminded the Junto of how dependent their long-term security was on the stability of their 'union' with Argyll's Scotland. And if that realization suddenly concentrated English

Junto minds when it came to meeting the Scots' financial demands, it operated no less powerfully when it came to the consideration of religion. All that the English Parliament had promised the Scots under the Anglo-Scottish Treaty hitherto was a vague undertaking approving of the Scots' desire for 'conformity' (what the Scots had actually sought was *uniformity*'), and agreeing to proceed with 'the reformation of Church government ... in due time'.[133] Unless the Junto leaders could offer the Scots hard evidence that they would substantiate this most minimal of commitments, they risked something more than the disappointment of their Covenanter brethren. There was also a serious possibility, in the forthcoming Scottish Parliament, that Westminster's non-compliance would be used as grounds for delaying, or even rejecting, approval of the treaty – a result that had the potential to wreck the Anglo-Scottish 'union' which Warwick and his allies regarded as the bedrock of their future security.

By May 1641, it was already apparent to the Junto leaders that nothing could now be done, without incurring potentially endless further delays, to redraft this section of the Anglo-Scottish Treaty. But at least the charge of English indifference to 'nearer union' could be countered. With a timely display of reformist zeal at Westminster, in the weeks leading up to the treaty's approval in the Edinburgh Parliament, the English Lords Commissioners for the Treaty might yet persuade their 'brethren' that they were serious about the 'reformation of Church government ... in due time'.[134] That time had come. At Westminster, the next act of Root-and-Branch was about to be played to the Scottish gallery.

v. POLITIC PIETY: THE FORTUNES OF ROOT-AND-BRANCH

The contrast between the Junto's religious position pre- and post-Strafford's execution is perhaps registered most sharply in the sudden reconsideration, on 17 May, of what the English Treaty Commissioners had actually said to the Scots on the subject of 'further reformation'. Back on 15 March, they had given the Scots a polite but unambiguous rejection of their demands for the abolition of bishops, and this without demur from Warwick, Bedford, Saye, or any of the other Petitioner Peers who constituted the Commissioners' controlling majority. This response was perfunctorily reported to representatives of the two Houses on 15 April, and this might well have been the end of the matter.[135] The king's announcement on 12 May of his visit to Edinburgh seems, however, to have prompted a nervous bout of second thoughts in Warwick and his fellow Commissioners about the wisdom of their initial reply. Five days later, through the Committee of Seven (the leading Junto-men in the Commons),* the question of the Scots' religious demands

---

* The seven were Denzell Holles, John Pym, John Hampden, William Strode, Nathaniel Fiennes, Sir John Clotworthy, and Sir Philip Stapilton.

was reopened in the Commons. Denzell Holles* – whom Hyde associated with Warwick, Essex, and Brooke, as one who had been on the fringes of the Junto during the days of Bedford's dominance[136] – now came forward to make explicit the connection between the commonwealth's future security and the urgent need to reconsider the position of the bishops. 'The danger', argued Holles, 'of the papists' designe' – that code word for royalist plotting – 'upon this howse and kingdome was verie great, and ... therefore wee ought speedily to advize of a remedie [on the question of abolishing the bishops].'[137]

What the ensuing debate revealed, above all, was just how little the godly Petitioner Peers, in their role as Treaty Commissioners, had thus far conceded to the Scots on any subject relating to religion. When their reply to the Scots was read out to the Commons, even a moderate like Sir Simonds D'Ewes, hardly a puritan firebrand, concluded that if this were ever approved by the House, '[it] should not onlie slight the Scottish nation and ther affection, but utterlie lay aside, as it weere, the worke of Reforming Religion'.[138] If that was how a moderate English Puritan regarded the English Treaty Commissioners' approach to 'further reformation', it was little wonder that Warwick and his Junto allies appear to have been having grave concerns as to how their meagre concessions would be received in Edinburgh.[139]

With the promotion of 'nearer union' in religion no longer a purely ecclesiastical matter, but the issue most likely to cause the Covenanters to abandon their support for the new régime at Westminster, the Junto set to work to make up for lost time. At the very moment when even Calamy found Bishop Williams's negotiations on the creation of a reformed episcopate in 'a very hopeful Posture', they were suddenly abandoned.[140] Warwick's and Brooke's network of godly clergy, hitherto deeply sceptical about Scottish-style Church government, equally abruptly changed its tune and began singing the praises of Presbyterianism – the Covenanters' model for Church government.[141] Most controversially of all, however, the proposal for the abolition of bishops Root-and-Branch – the Scots' major desideratum – was taken out of the cold storage to which it had been consigned, apparently to general contentment, back in February,[142] and hurriedly warmed back into life.

Like the initiatives to provide financial satisfaction to the Scots, via Warwick House, this proposal came to fruition during the anxious fortnight following the king's announcement that he would attend the forthcoming Scottish Parliament. By 27 May, a short bill was ready for presentation to the Commons for 'the utter abolishing and taking away of all Archbishopps, Bishopps, ... Deanes and Chapters, Archdeacons ... and Canons ... out of the Church of England'.[143] The whole hierarchy was to go, down to its

---

* Holles was the senior member of the Committee of Seven, seniority in the seventeenth-century English Parliament being determined by social rank. Thus Holles, as the younger son of an earl (the 1st Earl of Clare), outranked the various knighted members of the Committee of Seven, such as Stapilton and Hesilrige. This hierarchy also tended to be scrupulously maintained when committee-men were the multiple signatories to orders and warrants.

most minor functionary. Concerned to cover its tracks, the Junto leadership prevailed on the self-important Kentish knight Sir Edward Dering[144] to introduce the bill,[145] a man whose 'levity and vanity' was flattered by the opportunity to grandstand before his peers.[146] Behind the scenes, however, the key figure was once again Sir Arthur Hesilrige: Lord Brooke's brother-in-law, fellow resident of Brooke House, and member of the Committee of Seven. It was 'S[ir] A. H.', Dering later recalled, who 'pressed [the bill] into my hand', having reportedly conferred about its text with the younger Vane and Oliver Cromwell.[147]* These may not have been the only parties Hesilrige consulted. Around this time, the 'Scoch Lords' – Lord Loudoun, and the Earl of Rothes[148] – were entertained at the house he and Lord Brooke shared in Holborn, an evening that cost Brooke just over a shilling in pipe tobacco.[149]

Whichever smoke-filled room produced the Root-and-Branch Bill, it was always inherently unlikely that such a contentious piece of legislation would ever reach the statute book. In a House of Lords of about eighty active peers (including a dozen bishops), Warwick and his allies could manage only around twenty-five votes in favour of expelling bishops from Parliament; when it came to abolishing the office entirely, the number in favour slumped to single figures.[150] Even in the Commons, a majority of the House's membership seems to have been opposed to Root-and-Branch abolition.[151] True, the Dering–Hesilrige bill received its second reading immediately after its introduction on 27 May, but it passed this hurdle only by the relatively narrow margin of 139 votes in favour to 108 against.[152] As Edward Nicholas had shrewdly noted on the eve of the bill's committal in early June, 'it is conceived [the bishops' abolition bill] will never pass to be made a law'.[153]

What the anti-episcopal debates provided during June and July, as the Warwick House peers dealt with Loudoun and the Covenanter Commissioners over the crucial final stages of the Anglo-Scottish Treaty, was a reassuring background hum of pious good intentions. The fact that, for the foreseeable future, the Junto would be unable to realize the destruction of these episcopal 'relics of popery' was beside the point. Where the Root-and-Branch debate succeeded triumphantly was in providing Lord Loudoun, Argyll's proctor among the Scottish Commissioners,[154] with prima facie evidence that their English 'friends' were sincere in their commitment to 'union' and to bringing their Church closer to the perfection of the Covenanter Kirk. No less importantly, for their Edinburgh audience in the lead-up to the new Scottish Parliament, it seemed to vindicate the wisdom of Argyll's decision in 1640 to support the Covenanters' intervention in England's affairs.[155]

Nevertheless, with a majority in Parliament broadly hostile to Root-and-

---

* The introduction of this bill to abolish bishops forms part of a series of major parliamentary initiatives in 1641 in which Hesilrige acted as the instigator on behalf of the wider aristocratic group of reformists, beginning with the launching of Strafford's attainder in April (above, pp. 242–4) and culminating on 7 December 1641 with the introduction of a bill to place the kingdom's military forces under noblemen nominated by Parliament (below, p. 460) – the proposal that ultimately led to the creation of a 'parliamentarian army' under the Earl of Essex.

Branch, husbanding the bill through its committee stage would clearly require even greater managerial finesse. Reference to a select committee of a few dozen members, meeting in private – the usual procedure with most draft legislation – would have denied the Junto the public stage they needed if the debate were to achieve the notice (and notoriety) that was its prime purpose in the eyes of many of its promoters. All depended, therefore, on having the bill referred to a Committee of the Whole House, where its supporters could grandstand in the Commons' chamber, well noticed by their fellow members and the public outside, whether or not the legislation would ever pass into law. Moreover, in a Committee of the Whole, the sheer number of potential speakers guaranteed that consideration of the bill would drag on for weeks, possibly months, to come – and certainly long enough for the Junto's new access of anti-episcopal zeal to register in advance of the treaty's approval in Edinburgh. Sir John Culpeper, an erstwhile reformist disillusioned by the Junto's willingness to play politics with the English Church, struck dangerously close to the bone when he taunted Hampden that he was acting 'in reverence to the Scotch commissioners'.[156]

The problem for the Junto leadership was that, on most ordinary days, the Commons' inbuilt anti-Root-and-Branch majority was likely to prevent any reference of the bill to a Committee of the Whole. Twice in early June – on the 3rd and 7th[157] – a larger the usual turnout of Commons-men had crammed into the Chapel of St Stephen, expecting to vote on the bill's reference to committee, only to find that the Junto management, realizing that the majority present was pro-episcopalian, prevented 'that business from being fallen upon'.[158] A few days later, when the question was again expected to come up for debate, the Commons was 'soe full that many were forced to stand for want of place', and the Junto was again forced to lie low. Realizing that most were 'for the [ad]vantage of Episcopacy, the enimyes therof purposely avoided the question' and moved for other business to intervene.[159]

Much of the behind-the-scenes manoeuvring that produced such sophisticated parliamentary management has, unsurprisingly, left few traces in the surviving archives. In the case of the third of these postponements, however, that of Thursday, 10 June, we have at least a partial record of those who met later that evening to discuss tactics. Among the men present were Hampden, Pym (both members of the Committee of Seven) and Sir Robert Harley, together with the Essex clergyman Stephen Marshall, a long-standing member of the Warwick–Barrington godly network and the divine who was coordinating a contemporaneous campaign, among the godly clergy, to reassure the Scots of their commitment to 'closer union'.[160] Those present opted for the following day, Friday, 11 June, as the moment to initiate the debate before the all-important Committee of the Whole House.

As with the bill's introduction, the Junto leaders were at pains to conceal their efforts at stage-management. Come Friday, none of the members of the Committee of Seven, the Junto's power-base in the Commons, said a word when it came to launching the debate on the bishops' abolition. Instead, it was once again left to an apparently independent Commons-man, Sir Robert Harley, to move it 'first in the Howse [that the proposal should be discussed

afford's nemesis: Oliver St John, Bedford's and Hamilton's erstwhile protégé and appointee as Solicitor-
neral. St John ultimately rejected his patrons' policy of moderation, and the power of his oratory in
stminster Hall on 29 April 1641 was to be decisive in creating a majority in the House of Lords in favour of
afford's execution.

Above: Edward Hyde, the Commons-man whom Bedford employed, unavailingly, to persuade Essex to abandon his insistence on Strafford's death. In January 1642, Charles was to offer Hyde the post of Solicitor-General (which he refused), as part of last-minute attempt to resurrect the 'Bedfordian' circle that had come so close to brokering a settlement during the previous spring.

Strafford's would-be saviours: both the Earl of Bedford (*above, left*) and Viscount Saye (*left*) worked for a compromise whereby Strafford's life could be purchased by the king, but at the cost of allowing a wholesale take-over of government by the reformist peers.

Opposite page: Bedfordian brothers: George, Lord Digby (*left*) – the son and heir of the Earl of Bristol – married Bedford's daughter, Lady Anne Russell, in the mid-1630s, and quickly became one of his father-in-law's favourites. This double portrait with his brother-in-law, William, Lord Russell (*right*) celebrates a dynastic alliance that was to find political expression in Digby's powerful support for Bedford's plans for limited constitutional reform.

above: Charles I's 'Popish' consort: Queen Henriette Marie. Despite her Catholicism, many of the Junto leaders initially regarded her as a potentially useful, if never wholly reliable, ally in their dealings with the king.

opposite page, above: van Dyck's double portrait of George Goring, the Governor of Portsmouth from 1639 (on the right), and his close friend, Mountjoy Blount, Earl of Newport, the Master of the Ordnance and half-brother of the Earl of Warwick (on the left). Wild, glamorous and rakish, Goring enjoyed the qualified confidence of both the king and the Junto leaders, and acted as a conduit of information between both.

opposite page, below left: Colonel William Ashburnham, one of the anti-Junto plotters in the king's army. In a bid to prise Essex away from his Junto friends, Ashburnham sounded out the earl, in the spring of 1641, as to whether he would abandon the reformists in return for his appointment as Lord General.

opposite page, below right: Sir John Suckling, the least competent and most reckless of the Army Plotters, whose conspiracy to gain control of the Tower and release Strafford in May ended in fiasco.

This view of the House of Commons, in the aftermath of the fire which destroyed it in 1834, provides a clear sense of its dimensions and immediate environs. The disproportionately lofty Commons' chamber occupied the former chapel's first three bays (to the left). The remaining two bays (to the right) were filled with the lobby (where Charles's armed escort waited during his attempt to arrest the five members), and, directly above it, on mezzanine floor, the Commons' committee chamber.

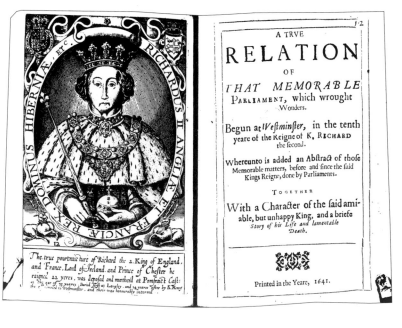

The liberating power of precede the frontispiece portrait of Rich II and title page of Thomas Fannant's account of the Parliament of 1387, when the Lords Appellant demanded that the king remove his unpopular counsellors. Parallels, direct or implied, between Richard II and the crisis of 1380s, and Charles and the events of 1640–41, figu repeatedly in the parliamentary debates of the early 1640s.

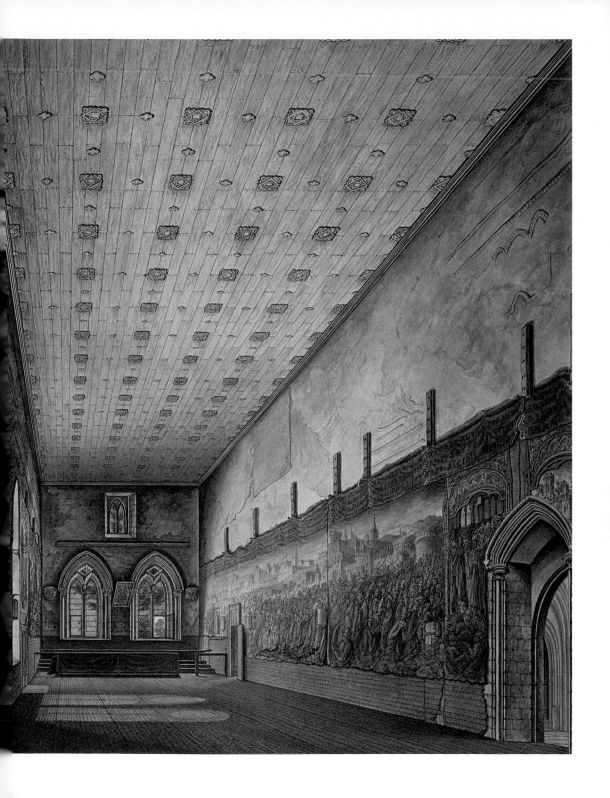

The massive Painted Chamber, in the Palace of Westminster, was the regular venue for 'conferences' between the Lords and Commons, and occasionally for royal speeches to the two Houses. The rich series of wall-paintings which gave the chamber its name – recorded here in 1799 – was completed between 1263 and 1308.

The House of Wittelsbach as an alternative royal dynasty. Charles I's nephew, the Prince-Elector Charles Louis (left), is depicted here with his younger brother, Prince Rupert, the future royalist general. As Europe's premier Protestant exile, and a grandson of James I, Prince Charles Louis was frequently rumoured to be a plausible claimant of the Stuart Crowns in the event of Charles I's deposition.

The medal struck to commemorate the nuptials in 1641 of Charles's daughter, Princess Mary, to Prince Willem of Orange-Nassau. The king seems to have used the marriage celebrations, on Sunday 2 May, as a cover for Suckling's simultaneous attempt to seize control of the Tower.

by a Committee of the Whole]'. But at least some members discerned the puppet-master's hand: 'M[aste]r Hampden', D'Ewes noted indignantly, 'out of his serpentine subtletie, did still putt others to move those businesses that hee contrived'.[161]

Hampden's 'serpentine subtletie' may have affronted D'Ewes; but tactically his initiative was near faultless. By introducing the matter as the last item of business on a Friday, he had found a moment when the Commons was probably more sparsely attended than usual; in the process, he secured a double victory.[162] Not only did the reformist leadership realize its ambition of referring the bishops' abolition bill to the endless talking-shop of the Committee of the Whole House, but, by naming Edward Hyde as the committee's chairman, it effectively silenced one of the bishops' most effective defenders, for committee chairmen were by custom debarred from taking an active part in the debates which they chaired.[163] Speaker Lenthall seems to have colluded in the Junto's management of Commons procedures by refusing to set dates for the resumption of debates in advance, 'because they [the Junto leaders] would make use of the first occasion of an empty house'.[164]

On and on rolled the debate on Root-and-Branch through the summer; sometimes tempestuous, as when godly zealots like the younger Vane spoke of his vision of the New Jerusalem, once bishops were cast down; at other times becalmed in the murky backwaters of scholarly speculation, as members traded pedantries on the customs of the primitive Church.[165] How this debate concluded – and why – we will consider shortly. What it provided, long before it reached its surprising conclusion, however, was apparently abundant evidence of the Junto's desire to pull down the English episcopate in the interests of Anglo-Scottish 'union'. And lest this should all go unnoticed in Edinburgh, Marshall and other ministers were dragooned to write to the General Assembly of the Scottish Kirk (which met concurrently with the Parliament) to express their own new-found enthusiasm for the 'Presbyterian Government'.[166]

*

Such noisy barracking for a radical – and, in many parts of the country, profoundly unpopular – ecclesiastical change inevitably affected the way in which the reformist leadership was regarded in the world beyond Westminster. Just as the price of meeting the Scots' financial demands was a massive and immensely unpopular increase in the scale of direct taxation, so, too, the Junto's addressing of their religious concerns came at equally high cost. In the Commons, the relative harmony that had been recovered in discussions of religion after February – and which, as late as 1 May 1641, had enabled a bill intended to abolish bishops' votes in the House of Lords to pass the Commons 'without one negative [voice]'[167] – was shattered by the series of acrimonious debates on reform of the Church that followed in May and June. In the shires, the Junto's apparent identification with Root-and-Branch helped confirm a conviction, already evident among the reformists' critics even before May 1641, that the advocates of such policies were not only unrepresentative of the political nation, but also, in a sense, un-English: in the words of the Vicar of Chigwell, Essex, reported to the Commons in May, they were nothing but 'a companie of factious men in the Parliament, and ... they had joined with the Scottish rebels'.[168]

Unpalatable as it was to the Junto to have such matters bruited abroad in rustic Essex, as a statement of fact, the charge that a parliamentary faction had 'joined with the Scottish rebels' could hardly be faulted. Throughout the summer, the Junto leaders – Warwick and Essex in the Lords, Hesilrige, Hampden, and Holles in the Commons – repeatedly used the current threats to the commonwealth's security as the justification for a wholly novel emphasis on the need for 'union' with those 'Scottish rebels' who so disgusted Chigwell's royalist vicar. Yet the Junto's declarations of support for their Scottish brethren are not quite what they seem; and as Parliament-men acquired, perforce, a more nuanced understanding of Covenanter factionalism, it gradually became evident that some Scottish brethren were regarded as more brotherly than others. In practice, 'union' meant attaching the Junto's interests to those of Argyll's party in Edinburgh, and the earl's principal representatives in London (Loudoun, Rothes, Wariston, and Henderson). Should Montrose and his Bander allies prevail against Argyll in Edinburgh, one of two consequences would follow. In the event of an attempted royalist counter-attack in England, the best that the Junto would be able to hope for from a Montrose-dominated Scotland was neutrality. Just as likely, however, was a far more dangerous eventuality: that Charles might use an army raised in Scotland to restore his pre-1640 powers and revenues in England. All depended on which faction would prevail.

For four weeks, from the king's announcement of his Scottish journey on 12 May, it was clear that *something* was afoot between the king and Montrose, though its precise nature remained unclear. The presence at court of Montrose's emissary had been noted by the Scottish Commissioners; though here, too, detailed knowledge of whom he was seeing, or what he was discussing, was lacking.

Then, on Saturday, 19 June, the bombshell exploded.

VI. THE TRIALS OF THE DROMEDARY

Of all the emissaries to ply the Great North Road between Edinburgh and London during the 1640s, Lieutenant-Colonel Walter Stewart was perhaps the unluckiest. Discreet as he may have been as Montrose's representative at Whitehall during March and May, his departure for Edinburgh at the end of his second visit had been noted by the Scottish Commissioners at the beginning of June, and they had alerted their masters in Edinburgh to lie in wait for his return.[169] Tantalizingly close to his destination, Stewart had been arrested, and his person and equipage searched. Hidden in the pommel of his saddle were found a series of documents, among them letters, his own instructions from Montrose, and plans for the forthcoming Scottish Parliament. These, taken together with Stewart's testimony under interrogation on 5 June, established beyond doubt that the king's proposed visit to Scotland was part of a larger plot: to destroy Argyll and effect a royalist counter-coup in Edinburgh.[170]

The value of the intercepted cache varied. One item, a letter from the king to Montrose, written in his own elegant italic hand, was harmless enough, merely reiterating the king's intention to attend the Edinburgh Parliament in person, and reassuring Montrose that he would confirm the Presbyterian Church settlement and the establishment of the Scots' 'just liberties'.[171] Far more incriminating, however, was a set of instructions outlining the tactics Stewart was to adopt, once back in Scotland, against the Earl of Argyll. Evidently drafted by the Earl of Traquair,[172] who was still at Whitehall advising the king on Scottish policy,[173] these left no doubt that a plan was afoot to bring down Argyll by reviving the old charge that he had argued treasonously for the king's deposition.

In a further allusion to Argyll as one of the arrogant beasts in Henryson's version of Aesop's *Fables*,* Stewart had been instructed that on returning to Edinburgh

> all meanes [should] be used for trying the Information [i.e. bringing to trial the accusation of treason] against the Dromadary [Argyll], [and for establishing] what further can be found [out] of his carriage.[174]

Traquair and Lennox seem to have been testing Montrose's willingness to move forward with the Argyll prosecution as a trial of his own *bona fides* towards the king.

Montrose had not disappointed. Apparently responding to prompts from London, he had brought his key witness, John Stewart the younger of Ladywell, to Edinburgh in order that he should repeat his claims before the Committee of Estates. There the matter had hung throughout late May and early June, with Stewart of Ladywell imprisoned in Edinburgh Castle pending further investigations, but with little likelihood that it would do Argyll serious harm.[175]† Where the intercepted 'Instructions' turned these expectations on

---

* Even more than the earlier reference to Argyll as 'the Elephant', the literary context of this second Aesopian allusion provides the clue to Argyll's expected fate. For this mention of the dromedary occurs in the course of a speech by the Lion King – the code name for King Charles among Montrose and his fellow plotters – warning the proud beasts how he would punish revolt.

> My Celsitude and hie Majestie, [declaims the Lion,]
> With might and mercie shall bee mingled aye,
> The lowest heart I can full soone up hie,
> And make him Master over you I may:
> The Dromedarie if hee make decay [destruction], . . .
> I can him [make] low, as little as an Mouse.

† Questioned before the Committee of Estates, Stewart of Ladywell had changed his story, claiming that Argyll had spoken merely of the deposition of kings in general, not of deposing King Charles. The Committee of Estates then ordered Stewart of Ladywell's imprisonment until the truth of the charge was determined. His eventual fate is discussed below, p. 347.

their head was in suggesting that the king, with Montrose's willing help, would see this potentially lethal charge revived in the forthcoming Parliament. And there, Argyll would face a far less pliable audience than the usually deferential Committee of Estates. Covenanter had turned on brother Covenanter, and in the judicial mêlée set to ensue, Charles, like the Lion King in Henryson's Aesop, looked set to make the imperious dromedary 'as little as an Mouse'.

*

These revelations had major consequences in both British kingdoms. In Scotland, the forewarning allowed Argyll to go on to the attack. On 11 June 1641, even as copies of the intercepted documents were being forwarded to Loudoun in London, the Committee of Estates ordered the arrests of the leading anti-Argyll plotters – Montrose, Napier, Stirling of Keir, and Sir Archibald Stewart of Blackhall – and their imprisonment in Edinburgh Castle, pending trial in the forthcoming Parliament.[176]

Yet, even with the plotters under lock and key, Argyll remained acutely conscious of his own vulnerability. Assessing the tactics he adopted in response to the crisis is difficult, because much of the evidence is at second hand. But perhaps the clearest indication of his state of mind comes from a letter written by his principal agent in London, Lord Loudoun, explaining Argyll's position to the Earl of Lanark, a wily moderate whose connections extended into most of the Scottish factions, including Montrose's. Far from seeking a showdown with the plotters, Loudoun insisted, Argyll was anxious to avoid a confrontation; and

> although the Erll of Argyll be verie much injured by these malicious calumnies [Montrose's claim that he had spoken of the king's deposition], [yet] I beleeve he will endevore the clearing of his own loyalty and integrity more, nor [seek] revenge against those who have wrongit him.[177]

Given that Lanark could probably be relied upon to convey this message to those it concerned, this looks distinctly like the presentation of an Argyllian olive branch to Montrose – and, perhaps, too, to the king. Certainly, Argyll had good reason to avoid a public split among the Covenanter grandees. Behind Montrose and his accomplices stood a much larger body of anti-Argyllian dissent: the noblemen who had signed the Cumbernauld Band; critics of the intervention in England; and a broader swathe of opinion, beyond the ranks of the Banders, hostile to Argyll's oligarchic ways.[178] To this extent, the mere revelation of the plot acted as a check on Argyll's freedom of manoeuvre; and he approached the forthcoming parliamentary session with grave caution, unsure what its outcome, or the effect of the king's presence, might be.

*

If this latest revelation of courtly plotting had left Argyll unsettled on the defensive, its effect in London was more powerful still. Lord Loudoun, perhaps predictably, was the Edinburgh government's chosen conduit for the release of the news. Armed with copies of the intercepted documents forwarded from the Scottish capital, Loudoun convened a meeting in the Inner Star Chamber, within the Palace of Westminster, on Saturday, 19 June, to brief his English allies. His principal audience were the English Lords Commissioners for Treaty. But there was also a selected group of Commonsmen, most likely the Committee of Seven, but certainly including Sir Arthur Hesilrige,[179] himself one of the Seven and a loyal supporter of the Argyll–Warwick axis.

From the outset, the Warwick House circle appears to have regarded the conspiracy against Argyll as a threat to its own attempt to create a godly, Venetianized régime in England – and with good cause. If Montrose succeeded in toppling the chief Scottish exponent of union between the realms, it would obviously further Charles's plan to disengage the Scots from English affairs altogether – 'conteyn[ing] [them] at home', as Nicholas put it, ' ... in good obedience' – and to isolate his English opponents.[180] Deprived of the ally that had made possible their resistance in 1640, the Junto leaders would be highly vulnerable to a royalist resurgence in England – particularly one that turned to good effect the reformists' rising unpopularity at home.

With their own sense of insecurity sharply intensified by Lord Loudoun's revelations on 19 June 1641, Warwick and Brooke, acting together with their key Commons allies, Hesilrige and Holles, were provoked into a series of measures that moved the English commonwealth both closer to Scotland and more sharply in a republican direction than ever before. This was partly achieved by strengthening the financial bonds between Argyllian Scotland and Warwick House.[181] Hence it was on Tuesday, 22 June – the day that Hesilrige disclosed to a shocked House the extent of the king's complicity with Montrose – that the Commons set in place the elaborate financial arrangements for the Brotherly Assistance. These, as we have seen, placed Warwick and his political allies in charge of payments to the Scots totalling £300,000, well into the summer of 1643.[182]

By far the most important consequence of Heselrige's revelations, however, was a decision by the Commons to empower the Committee of Seven – Warwick and Essex's closest allies[183] – to draw up proposals that would address the problem of the commonwealth's long-term security in the light of the king's efforts to suborn their Covenanter allies: an agenda they could put to the Lords 'that some speedie course might be taken for the prevention of dangers and Treasons for the time to come'.[184] What emerged from these deliberations, two days later, was one of the most radical blueprints for the reform of England's constitutions to be devised in the seventeenth century. The handiwork of the Committee of Seven, though reported to the Commons by Pym,[185] these 'Ten Propositions' (as they came to be known) were a mixture of short-term emergency provisions and grander proposals for sweeping and permanent political change. Among the emergency provisions were measures for disbanding the armies and for delaying the king's journey into Scotland until the disbandment had been safely concluded. Three

of the propositions played on the fear of Papists, demanding that the king's
and queen's Households should be purged of most of their Catholic clergy
and courtiers; any future Papal Nuncios sent into England were to be treated
as outlaws.[186] Other provisions responded directly to the Junto's own acute
sense of insecurity, demanding that all Lord Lieutenants (the officers commanding the militia forces of each county) be 'faithful and trusty' – the first
intimation that Parliament might take action to overhaul the command-
structure of the country's forces, which eventually came to fruition, at the
end of the year, in another of Hesilrige's draft bills.[187]

One of the most radical stipulations, however, was a 'special oath' that
was to be imposed 'by the consent of both Houses' on all military officers
from the Lord Lieutenants down – and imposed, by implication, without
reference to the king, so 'as to secure us in these times of danger'.[188] The
text of this oath does not survive; however, Giustinian, the Venetian ambassador, who received a copy of the Ten Propositions within forty-eight hours
of their presentation to the Commons and who may well have seen a draft
of this oath, claimed that it was 'an oath to this Republic [*questa Rep[ub-
bli]ca*] – the very word is used in the bill, which contains other particulars,
all of which strike the royal prerogative to the heart ...' Whether this oath
contained the word 'Republic' is highly doubtful; far more likely is that
Giustinian was translating the word 'commonwealth'.[189] But in using the
Italian word for a 'Republic' (which had a relatively precise anti-kingly
meaning) in his own dispatch, and insisting on the significance of its usage
in the proposed English oath, Giustinian provides a suggestive gloss on
contemporary linguistic usage.[190] The once relatively neutral language of
'commonwealth' had acquired, in the usage of 1641, a powerfully anti-
monarchical spin;[191] so much so that when the Earl of Essex remarked in
the House of Lords that he had 'never [known] but one Bishop in Parliament
stand up for the *good of the Commonwealth*', it seemed to the Royalist,
Robert Chestlin, that he was using 'the old phrase of Rebellion'.[192]*

A number of clauses in the Ten Propositions give substance to this 'republican' reading of its authors' intentions; but the most important are those
relating to the king's Councillors: the men who were actually charged with
the day-to-day business of governing the realm. Here, the decisive change
was that the king should henceforth be denied the free choice of his ministers.
Existing evil counsellors were to be purged – a familiar cry; more importantly,
in future *no* officers were to be appointed 'for managing the great affairs of
the kingdom' unless they were 'such ... as [the king's] people and Parliament

---

* The 'but one [i.e. only one] Bishop' Essex had known to stand up for the good of the
Commonwealth was almost certainly his old friend, John Williams, Bishop of Lincoln,
who had given him spiritual counsel on his decision to remarry in 1630 and was to be
a major supporter of the Junto until the summer of 1641. Complaint had been made of
Williams himself, in October 1635, that he was 'the only man that dare[s] oppose his
Majesty's Government and [who] writes on his walls, *principes mortales, re[s]publica
aeterna* [Princes are mortal, but the Commonwealth is eternal]', a quotation adapted from
Tacitus, *Annæls*, III, 6.

may have just cause to confide in'.[193] This provision stopped just short of demanding explicitly that Parliament assume the right to nominate the Privy Councillors and great officers of state. But there seems to be little doubt that this is what the Junto leadership had in mind; only a matter of weeks later the two Houses began putting forward the names of particular noblemen to vacant offices and urging the king to appoint accordingly.[194]

Here, then, was a blueprint for a radical re-founding of English government in a way that complemented the no less radical changes in the management of the nation's public finances. Had Charles accepted the Ten Propositions, it would have constituted – in the words of Samuel Rawson Gardiner, the greatest nineteenth-century historian of the period – 'a death-blow to that authority which [Charles] had inherited, and which he believed to have been entrusted to him by God'.[195] Some measure of how far, and how rapidly, the thinking of the Parliament-men – at least of those who still remained at Westminster – had moved since the events of the spring is provided by the fact that these Ten Propositions commanded almost universal consent. They were accepted unanimously in the lower House, and with only trifling amendments from the Lords.

To many at Westminster, the king was revealing disconcertingly recidivist tendencies. His plotting with Montrose against the reformist leadership in Scotland formed part of a pattern with his earlier plotting with Strafford against the Junto in London. And to promote that perception, the Junto leadership put up John Browne, the senior functionary in the House of Lords, to prepare a leaked copy of Montrose's 'Instructions' for anonymous publication. It also included, at the end, a detailed summary of the various plots that Strafford and Newcastle had planned against the English Parliament in the spring.[196] The belief that Charles could not be trusted with executive authority, still less military authority, had gained ground by the summer of 1641 to a degree that would have been unthinkable even six months before.

Yet revealing the king's scheming to the world was not the same as preventing these plots from taking effect: the opportunities presented to Charles by the emergence of a 'king's party' in Scotland had not been removed by the arrest of Montrose and his fellow plotters. The king still had cards in his hand yet to play. By the time the Anglo-Scottish Treaty was ready to be sent to Edinburgh for approval, at the end of June, even the Scottish Commissioners were beginning to reposition themselves in advance of a possible sea change in Covenanter politics. Lord Loudoun, one of the two Commissioners appointed to carry the treaty to Edinburgh, remained staunchly loyal to Argyll. By June, however, his brother Commissioner, the Earl of Dunfermline, was already tacking in the direction of the king, his new-found loyalty being rewarded on 25 June, barely a week before his departure, with the timely grant of a Scottish lordship.[197]

At Westminster, Giustinian reported at the beginning of July, there was a 'general opinion' that the Scots, once satisfied with the concessions which they had demanded (and which Charles had promised to yield), might yet side with the king and 'assist him to regain his original authority in England'. With 'fresh changes, advantageous to his Majesty', a daily possibility, 'it is easy to see that great consequences may result'.[198] Scotland, which had been the undoing of Charles's Personal Rule, looked as though it might also prove the undoing of England's Venetianized commonwealth.

VII. THE EDINBURGH ROAD

Throughout July and early August – hot, plague-ridden months that drove Parliament-men out of London in scores – the threat of those 'great consequences' hung ominously over Westminster as the two Houses tried repeatedly, and ever more desperately, to dissuade the king from undertaking his journey to Edinburgh.[199]

For the nervous men at Warwick House, at least some things went well. The massive sums due to the Scots were successfully raised and punctually paid. By 4 August, it was noted in the Commons Journal, the 'Earl of Warwicke ha[d] paid the Scots £500,000', and was to have a further £52,300 paid to him the following morning in order provide them with the last outstanding instalment of their arrears.[200] One motive for this punctiliousness was the Junto's fears that they would need to call on Scottish military support once more, if – as was widely feared – the king attempted to rally the English army to his cause during his journey northwards.[201]* The danger of 'army plotting' had not yet gone away.

If Warwick and his household already occupied a commanding position in the commonwealth's financial administration, their political dominance during the late spring and summer of 1641 was further consolidated by the appointments the king made, as vacancies arose, to the offices of state – the instrumentalities that ran the government of Stuart England and Ireland. In theory, these remained, at least for the moment, in Charles's free gift. In practice, however, in the current climate his hand was powerfully constrained by the threat of parliamentary censure (first felt in May, when he had been forced to abandon his choice of Lord Savile as Lord Lieutenant of Yorkshire in deference to Parliament's insistence on the Earl of Essex),[202] and by a consciousness of his own unpopularity, particularly within the capital in the aftermath of the foiled May coup.[203]

Crown appointments therefore pandered shamelessly to the need to present a façade of 'good government', with almost all the major offices handed out

---

* These fears prompted an unsuccessful motion in the Lords on 23 July, moved by Saye, Mandeville, Brooke, Wharton, and Paget, that the whole of the English army's cavalry force – the contingent thought most likely to side with the king – should be disbanded *before* the Covenanter forces in the North of England began to withdraw. These anxieties also underlay a resolution of both Houses moved on 16 August, this time successfully, that the Mayor of Hull should 'secur[e] the arms there' (the major royal arsenal in the North) to prevent the king gaining access to them. In the Lords, some peers wanted to save the king's face by including a phrase to the effect that the mayor should keep the arms for the king's service; 'but the L[ords] Say, Wharton, [and] Mandeville would by no means admit this last clause'.

during the period between April and August going to the Petitioner Peers. In April, the northern command of the army went, as we have seen, to Holland. This had been followed in May by the appointment of Saye as Master of the Court of Wards and as one of the five new Treasury Commissioners.[204] At the same time the Lord Lieutenancy of Ireland, vacated by Strafford's death, was claimed by Northumberland for his brother-in-law Robert Sidney, Earl of Leicester – another court 'Puritan', who was broadly sympathetic to the Junto's reformist ambitions.[205]

The pattern continued throughout the summer, apparently encouraged by the queen, who still seems to have imagined that the Crown's major aristocratic critics could be bought off. Old Privy Councillors lost their places to the new cadre of reformist grandees. In June Hertford, one of the original Twelve Peers, was raised to a marquessate and given responsibility – reportedly 'with the approval of Parliament' – for the Prince of Wales, Prince Charles, as his Governor (or guardian) and Master of his Household,[206] thereby pre-empting possible moves by Parliament to remove Hertford's predecessor, the Earl of Newcastle, disgraced through his involvement in the Army Plot.[207] And towards the end of July, the king took advantage of a fracas involving Pembroke, the Lord Chamberlain, in which the earl had struck another peer on the head with his wand of office, to relieve him of his post and confer it on the Earl of Essex.[208] But as one perceptive courtier observed, 'My Lord of Pembrooke did not loose his place for this faulte, but for [the] countenauncing of those tumultuous people' in New Palace Yard during the debate on Strafford's attainder.[209] Revenge against Pembroke (for his public advocacy of Strafford's death) dovetailed neatly with the courting of Essex, widely regarded as the most popular of all the oppositionist peers.[210]* Such was the naked opportunism of the royal offer that Essex temporized before responding, finally accepting, on 2 August, out of what seems to have been a mixture of motives: an honest conviction that he could serve the commonwealth through managing the court, but also a craving for the prestige and public recognition, so long denied him, that accompanied such an influential position.[211]

As the date of the king's departure for Scotland neared, the Junto leaders made their boldest attempt to augment their control of government by proposing the revival of the medieval office of *Custos Regni* (literally, the Guardian of the Kingdom): a great nobleman who would be endowed with kingly powers for the duration of the monarch's absence[212] – a post for which Northumberland was the obvious candidate. Revealing rather more of the Junto's intentions for the new viceroy than perhaps was prudent, St John argued that the *Custos Regni*, when appointed, could do 'all things a king might do, as well in Parliament as out of it'.[213] This, on its own,

---

* Commenting on the appointment, which was almost certainly supported by the queen, Giustinian noted that if Charles succeeded in winning over Essex, 'the principal head of the Puritans', the king 'will have achieved a great gain, since that nobleman [*Cavaliere*] possesses the strongest following in Parliament'.

would have been enough to alarm the king. But the Junto leadership compounded its offence by presuming to nominate to two more of the great offices of state, hitherto regarded as being in the king's sole gift. On 9 August, a group of Commons-men, including Hesilrige, Strode, Holles, and the younger Hotham, united in proposing another 'virtuous Counsellor', the Earl of Salisbury, as Lord Treasurer. Salisbury had been reported to have been 'already voted [into the office] by Comon fame' as early as May that year,[214] for no more obvious reasons other than that he was a 'good Counsellor', Northumberland's father-in-law, and that his father and grandfather had occupied the office before him.[215] When the motion was put to the vote on 9 August, it passed without a single dissent.[216] Likewise Pembroke's loyalty to the Junto was rewarded with nomination, again by Holles, as Lord Steward of Household, on the well-founded assumption that its current incumbent, the Earl of Arundel, was about to resign.[217]*

These proposals have been regarded as affirming the essentially conservative constitutional outlook of most Parliament-men, and to 'illustrate how far the parliamentary leaders' hostility was not to the powers of monarchy', but to the policies and person of Charles I. The proposal to create a *Custos Regni* – so this argument runs – 'was not one to diminish the powers of monarchy: it was to transfer them to a different holder, without incurring the guilt of deposition'.[218] Yet this is to ignore the massive diminution that had already been imposed by the Parliament, at the Junto's prompting, on the powers of the Crown. This was partly a matter of formal legal sanctions, the most important of which were the Triennial Act and the permanent abolition of the Crown's capacity for financial solvency independent of the two Houses – not to mention the Anglo-Scottish Treaty of 1641, which, *inter alia,* removed forever the monarch's ability to wage war within Britain without parliamentary consent.

But the permanent diminution of monarchical power in 1641 had also been brought about by subtler means: by the affirmation, in Strafford's trial and attainder, of the principal that even the greatest of the Crown's ministers were answerable for their conduct to the English Parliament; and through shifts in political language and discourse, whereby the task of protecting the

---

* Evidently caught up in the excitement of the moment, Oliver Cromwell, usually a diffident performer in the Commons of 1641, intervened with a proposal of his own. Revealing both his enthusiasm for the principle that the Parliament should have the nomination of the major court offices and his own relative naivety in the world of high politics, Cromwell proposed that Viscount Saye and the new Earl of Bedford should join the Marquess of Hertford (who had recently taken over the post from the disgraced Earl of Newcastle) as joint-Governors of the Prince of Wales. Yet Cromwell had obviously failed to clear this with any of the leading Junto-men, still less with the peers themselves, and faced the embarrassment of discovering that his motion failed to find a seconder. This appears to have been a straightforward matter of Cromwell's misjudgement of the courtly codes of honour and etiquette. As Sir Henry Mildmay pointed out, as Hertford was a marquess, and outranked both Bedford, an earl, and Saye, a step further down in the peerage as a viscount, '[one] cannot joyne any with the Marques, but [it] wilbe [a] diminucion to his honor'.

interests of the English state or 'Commonwealth' were being abstracted from the person of the king and vested instead in the two Houses of Parliament. Cumulatively, these changes in law and political culture reduced the monarch's personal powers to a point where King Charles *and any future monarch* would be little more than a cipher-king. John Glynne's justification for the Commons' asserting the power to nominate the Lord Treasurer is here revealing, for it was not cast in the form of some *ad hominem* objection to the policies Charles had chosen to pursue,[219] but based on a radical extension of the Parliament's control, at the expense of the Crown, over how and by whom the public finances were spent: it was 'Parliament who give the mony; [therefore they] have Interest in him that is to keepe and dispose it'.[220] None of these constraints on monarchical power, whether proposed or actually formalized, was a purely temporary adjustment to constitutional arrangements; singly and collectively they entailed a fundamental shift, both practical and semantic, in the location of sovereign power. By the late summer of 1641, the diminution in the rights and prerogatives of the Stuart Crown – as King of England and, still more, as King of Scots – was extensive, and intended to be permanent.[221]

Against this background, the series of appointments achieved during the period from May to August – combined with defections to the Junto of such grandees as Northumberland, Pembroke, and Hamilton – amounted to a massive consolidation of the aristocratic reformists' formal control over the government of England and Ireland. At court, three of the four major departments were in their hands – the Bedchamber, controlled by Holland as Groom of the Stool; the Household, ruled by Essex as Lord Chamberlain; the stables and the court out-of-doors, under Hamilton as Master of the Horse – with the fourth department, the supply side under the Lord Steward of the Household, already earmarked for Pembroke. When it came to public finance, Warwick already administered the largest private treasury ever created in England, as paymaster of the Scottish army. Naval and military authority was vested almost exclusively in a Rich–Devereux cartel, with Warwick's first cousin, Northumberland, as Lord Admiral; his brother, Holland, as Lord General for the northern half of England; his half-brother, Newport, in charge of the kingdom's munitions as Master of the Ordnance and Constable of the Tower; and Leicester, Northumberland's brother-in-law, as Ireland's Lord Lieutenant and commander-in-chief. This clean sweep of military appointments was completed, at the end of July, with Essex's appointment as Lord General for all of southern England, a post which made him directly responsible for the security of the capital, and of Parliament in particular.[222] None of this can have been other than deeply distasteful to Charles. Indeed, the sequence of appointments demonstrate how far the king's powers had already been diminished, for all practical purposes, even without the Parliament needing to assert that it had a formal right to nominate the great officers of state.[223]

Charles, it seemed, had simply given up the fight, and the Junto's men – many of them closely associated with Warwick – looked set to complete the takeover of power with the king's grudging consent. Even the more junior Household offices looked as though they would be monopolized by the

Junto's men. At the beginning of August, the king undertook to transfer the Treasurership of the Household from the elder Vane, its current holder, to Sir Henry Mildmay, one of the stalwarts of Warwick's Essex power-base[224] – promising that the paperwork would be completed as soon as he returned from Scotland.[225]

Perhaps the most startling newcomer to the reformed Whitehall court, however, was Dr Calybute Downinge. The cleric who had been forced to take refuge at Leez in September 1640 for having 'Preach[ed] Treason'[226] against the king, was now admitted to preach before the royal Household. On Sunday, 1 August, it was reported that 'Dr Downinge preached before the K. at White-hal a very honest sermon';[227] and while the text of Downinge's sermon does not survive, the mere fact that this public defender of the nobility's right of rebellion had gained entrance to the pulpit in the Chapel Royal was an indicator of how far power, even at court, had passed to the Warwick House 'interest' and the men (like Mildmay) who were its allies in the Commons.

Of the existing great officers of state, Hyde recalled of this period, the king's cousin, the Duke of Lennox, 'was almost the only man of great quality and consideration about the King who did not in the least degree stoop or make love to them [the Junto]'. And even his days as Lord Warden of the Cinque Ports seemed numbered, for the Junto 'had a mind to have his office ... from him that it might be conferred on the Earl of Warwick'.[228]

For Warwick,[229]* however, the source of greatest reassurance at the beginning of August was the recent conduct of Argyll's party in Edinburgh. The news could hardly have been more auspicious, and it arrived on Monday, 2 August, when Lord Loudoun returned to London declaring that the draft of the Anglo-Scottish Treaty – almost a whole year in the making – had been accepted by the Scottish Parliament. The amendments sought by the Scots were nothing more than minor points of detail, notwithstanding the failure of the English Parliament to offer any serious progress towards 'nearer uniformity' in the reform of its Church.[230] The one issue that might have completely derailed the treaty – religion – had, at least for the moment, simply gone away.

If the Scots' acquiescence to the treaty worked massively to the long-term advantage of the Junto, its effect on Westminster politics in the immediate term was deeply and strangely paradoxical. The creation of this secular 'Union' might have been thought to have spurred the Westminster Parliament to bring its long-debated plans for Root-and-Branch to their completion.

---

* Recognition of Warwick's central place in the court life of the reformed commonwealth also came in the course of that same week, on Wednesday, 4 August, when the Venetian ambassador was received by the king at a state audience, the most ceremonious form of diplomatic reception, in the Banqueting House at Whitehall. Those watching in King Street as the coach procession approached the Palace Gate would have been startled to find, in the place of honour, the Earl of Warwick, riding in one of the king's own coaches, with the ambassador at his side, at the head of a lengthy cavalcade that included a series of senior courtiers and the entire diplomatic corps.

After nearly three months of discussion, the bill had at last been completed; indeed, just three days before Loudoun's return, it was reported to be 'neer ... ready to be voted'.[231] Yet, instead of crowning the secular 'Union' embodied in the treaty with the 'nearer conformity' represented by an abolition of the English bishops, the Junto leadership did precisely the reverse. Once they had learnt that the secular Union had been safely approved in Edinburgh, debate on the bill to abolish the English bishops was silenced almost in mid-sentence.[232] The legislation had its swansong in the Commons on Tuesday, 3 August, the day after Loudoun's return[233] – and was then decisively dropped.[234] 'Very litle hopes [were] left', Sir John Temple noted a few days later, 'of passing the bill for the rooting out of Bishopes.'[235] In fact, the news of the treaty's ratification in Edinburgh had killed the discussion stone-dead. Not until the English Parliament was again desperate for Scottish military aid, in the winter of 1642–43, would there be another serious attempt in the Westminster Parliament to topple the hierarchy of the English Church.[236]

Nor was the dropping of Root-and-Branch simply a matter of negligence. Although the decision-making process is impossible to document in detail, at the beginning of August 1641 there seems to have been a deliberate abandonment of the campaign to force radical reform of the episcopate, lest the divisions which this was certain to create weakened the Junto's hard-won grip on power at Westminster. Concern that the Scots would reject a treaty that ignored their demands for a religious, as well as secular, Union had been the prime, if not the only, reason why Root-and-Branch had been advanced so noisily during the summer. Once that concern had proved unfounded (as it did with the news Loudoun brought on his return), the Junto's abandonment of radical reform of the Church was almost instant-aneous. By the first week of August, all that was required to bring the secular Union of the two kingdoms to completion was its formal ratification by statute in the two Parliaments. This followed swiftly. Now bereft of any practical provisions for the creation of religious unity between the kingdoms, the treaty was ratified by the Westminster Parliament without controversy in a matter of days.[237] Ratification by the Scottish Parliament would follow before the month was out.

If all this – for the Junto – was cause for rejoicing, the great imponderable remained the military ambitions of the king. In this regard, his journey to Edinburgh posed an immediate and highly perturbing threat. At the beginning of August the immediate anxiety was that his journey into Scotland was merely a feint, and that his true destination was the as yet undisbanded royal army, quartered around York. With opinion in the army reportedly strongly hostile to the Parliament, there was a plausible fear that Charles would attempt to regroup his forces and seek to 're-establish his former authority, and avenge himself' against his enemies in England.[238] As the king's planned day of departure approached – Monday, 9 August – the Junto prompted both Houses to make frantic last-minute efforts (including a Sabbath-breaking emergency Sunday sitting, which scandalized the Scots)[239] to persuade him, if not to abandon the journey, then at least to defer it for a fortnight, by which time most of the English forces in the North would be safely paid off

and on their way home.[240] In the meantime, the threat of a new 'army plot'
loomed.

*

Charles rebuffed every entreaty to postpone his journey, including a final
appeal from the House of Lords, delivered by Warwick himself. Having been
outwardly chastened and compliant in his dealings with Parliament for most
of the period since Strafford's execution, the king now grew daily more
combative and obdurate as the date of his departure drew near. Apparently
confident that Scotland held the key to the recovery of his power in England,
he suddenly abandoned his policy of appeasing the Junto and made a series
of provocative appointments. On Sunday, 8 August, at the persuading of
Bristol, Charles conferred an English dukedom on the Duke of Lennox –
one of the few members of the Lords who 'crossed [the Junto] boldly in the
House'[241] – thus enabling him to outrank every one of the Junto peers, and
simultaneously rewarding one of the principal backers of his new Scottish
alliance with Montrose.[242] Bristol also got his reward. He was sworn a
Gentleman of the Bedchamber – making him a member of the king's intimate
inner entourage – by the new, and grateful, Duke of Richmond that same
Sunday evening. And in a final twist of the Junto's tail, Bristol's son, Lord
Digby, was named as the new ambassador to Paris.[243] By Monday morning,
9 August, it seemed that the king was ready to smile on 'evil counsellors'
once more.

For Charles, the hour of his departure for Scotland could not come soon
enough, and he was growing increasingly impatient and ill-tempered at Parliament's attempts to enforce a delay.[244] That Monday evening, he gave
orders that he would begin his journey at 4 o'clock the following morning,
notwithstanding that he had still failed to make any arrangements for the
passing of bills in his absence – almost certainly a deliberate omission. Finally
persuaded (probably by the Junto leaders) that he could not depart without
making this provision, Charles reluctantly postponed his departure until later
that morning, so as to pass the required legislation in Parliament; but he was
'soe intent upon his Journey that he went not to bedd all night'.[245]

Sleepless and clearly irritated by the enforced delay, Charles finally appeared
in the House of Lords at 10 a.m. that Tuesday morning, 10 August. The
meeting was a tense and frosty affair. Rejecting outright the Parliament's
requests for the appointment of a *Custos Regni*, the king entrusted the realm
in his absence to an unwieldly twenty-two-man commission of regency, with
closely limited powers. Most provocatively of all, he named the Earl of
Newcastle – Strafford's close friend and the general who, in May, had planned
to lead a military advance against the Parliament – as one of its members.[246]
So high-handed was the king's bearing that his tactlessness seemed both
deliberate and the product of some new-found strength. Northumberland,
the grandee whom the king's lately reacquired stubbornness had cheated of
the role as *Custos Regni*, declared himself 'amased' at the monarch's brusque
deportment: 'surely there is a strange alteration in the present affaires, els
the king would never have given such a farewell to the Parlament'.[247]

It had lasted less than an hour. '[B]efore 11', noted Northumberland's secretary, '[the king] was in the Coach and gone'.[248]

*

To most men at Westminster, that 'strange alteration in the present affaires' presaged yet another attempt by the king to recoup his surrendered powers by the resort to force. Revealingly, the Commons' first action on returning to their chamber after the king's 'farewell' was to make preparations for war – 'to consider of a way of putting the kingdom into a posture of defence' – and to begin consideration of how to 'settle some order of government, both in Church and Commonwealth'.[249] Northumberland shared this sense of foreboding: 'We were never fuller of jealousies then we are at this present', he wrote to Sir Thomas Rowe shortly after the king's departure, 'nor lesse hopefull of avoiding *a confusion*' – that contemporary code word for civil strife.[250]

None seems to have felt this danger more acutely than the leading Junto Lords. Preserving their 'Union' with Argyll's Scotland, they realized, might soon require the shedding of blood. The point emerges most clearly, perhaps, in a letter written by Saye to the Marquess of Hamilton, shortly after the latter's departure for Scotland to support Argyll in his forthcoming trials.[251] 'Honest men', wrote Saye,

> will live and dye togeather in that which shall be for the kinge's best service and the union of both kingdomes agaynst factions in either ... This union we must studdy, and this alone I shall recomende unto you thear, as I shall indeavour it hear.[252]

Already Saye and his friends were writing of fighting for the 'king's service' in ways that seem to differentiate the royal office (his 'politic capacity') from the overtly scheming and fallible man who occupied it; and regarding the preservation of their 'union' with Argyll's like-minded régime in Scotland as a necessary condition of their own survival.

*

Charles left London on 11 August 1641 attended by the auguries of war. His departure marked the close of one chapter in his so far ill-starred attempts to re-establish an 'honourable' role for monarchy in a commonwealth that was revealing itself ever more averse to personal kingship; and the beginning of another, in which he looked for new friends, and new alliances, to replace those that had failed him thus far.

Whether he would succeed in this ambition remained unknowable. What was now almost certain, however, was that the future of England's noble revolt would be decided by what happened over the forthcoming weeks in Edinburgh.

12

UNION TRIUMPHANT: THE TWO COMMONWEALTHS

AUGUST–OCTOBER 1641

[B]y the Almightie's providence [we] are united under one King, one
Nation, and one Island, ... and although wee have beene lately ready
to offend each other, yet – being now united in more tender and hearty
affection, one towards another, then ever wee were – [we] shall hold
and maintain such a good correspondence amongst our selves that shall
not onely bring both Nations to a condition of prosperity at home, but
make us formidable to our enemies abroad.

Lord Loudoun, speaking in the Scottish Parliament, 9 September 1641[1]

Pious and prosperous, Edinburgh in 1641 was a substantial metropolis of
well over 20,000 inhabitants, compact but imposing inside its well-kept city
walls.[2] Dominated to the west by its castle, rearing atop a massive outcrop
of basalt, and to the north by the tower of its medieval Great Kirk, the city
had a sophistication of architecture and intellectual life that belied its modest
size and geographical remoteness. In contrast to London, where Parliament-
men improvised their accommodation in the ancient and ill-heated confines
of the Palace of Westminster, in Edinburgh the Scottish Estates had recently
acquired a new, purpose-built 'Parliament House', completed just two years
earlier, in 1639.[3] In the context of the Covenanter Revolt, its splendours
offered their own oblique commentary on the shift of power, which the
rebellion had initiated, from the king to the country's noble-dominated
Estates. The Parliament's housing, with its French Renaissance-inspired architecture, pristine interiors, and fresh stonework, stood in sharp contrast to
the monarch's dilapidated residence, Holyrood, just beyond the city walls to
the east, where, among the palace's 'extreme defects', reported in June 1641,
were rotten matting, broken windows, and missing slates.[4] Nor was the
impoverished king in a position to make the necessary repairs. Only when
the Marquess of Hamilton and the Committee of Estates guaranteed that
the workmen would be paid, shortly before Charles's arrival in mid August
1641, were minimal repairs undertaken to make the house habitable for the
visiting king and his small entourage.[5]

However, the grandees of the Committee of Estates were concerned with graver matters, in the weeks leading up to the king's arrival, than repairing Holyrood's draughty windows and leaking roofs. Argyll had been particularly active. Forewarned of the conspiracy to have him accused of treason in the forthcoming parliamentary session, he had backed up his offers of reconciliation with his intended accusers with ruthless counter-measures against the key witness who might have made their charges stick.

The delay between the date on which Charles had first promised to be in Edinburgh, in mid July, and his eventual arrival almost a month later enabled Argyll and his allies to achieve a major tactical advantage over the king's most powerful Scottish allies, the party headed by the Earl of Montrose and his Bander friends. Come the planned date for the opening of the Scottish Parliament, 15 July, the Argyllians had disregarded the king's insistence that the Parliament should be prorogued until his own arrival, and settled down immediately to consideration of how Montrose and the other anti-Argyllian plotters should be dealt with.[6] In what may have been a gesture of conciliation towards their opponents, Argyll and his allies deferred the trials of Montrose and the other imprisoned Banders until the king's arrival.[7] But they used the period in the interim to move decisively against John Stewart the younger of Ladywell: the sole eyewitness to Montrose's now notorious charge that Argyll had spoken in favour of the deposition of kings.[8]

Stewart of Ladywell's destruction was brutal and swift. Almost as soon as the Scottish Parliament had convened on 15 July, he was indicted, at Argyll's insistence, with the capital offence of lease making (the treasonous slandering of either the king or a member of his Council), on the basis of the claims he had already made against the earl. The outcome of Stewart's trial was hardly in doubt. Arraigned before the Justiciary Court on 21, 22, and 23 July, presided over by the Auditor-General of the Covenanter army, Alexander Colville of Blair, Stewart was found guilty and condenmed to death. He was publicly executed by 'the Maiden', a Scots precursor of the guillotine, on 28 July in a brutal and very public demonstration of the fate that would await any others who dared to challenge the dominance of the Earl of Argyll.[9]

Nor was this the only signal to Argyll's would-be accusers. In a clear warning to the Whitehall court, the Earl of Traquair (the chief backer, in the king's Scottish courtier entourage, of Montrose's various anti-Argyllian schemes), was declared an 'Incendiary' by the Edinburgh Parliament and sentenced to beheading *in absentia*. In a suitably intimidating piece of political theatre, the punishment was carried out, 'in effigie', the day before the king's arrival in Edinburgh'.[10]

No one seems to have understood the implications of the plotters' failure more clearly than the king. His strategic objective remained the same: Scotland's political disengagement from England; for if that were accomplished, he just might, given time, begin the fight to undo the prerogative-destroying settlement that had been imposed upon him in his southern kingdom. But the king had switched tactics. Plan A, crushing the 'Elephant' and the 'Dromedary', looked to have failed even before it had been attempted. His only alternative was a deeply unpalatable Plan B: capitulation to almost all the

Scots' demands – to whatever was required, in fact, to induce the Covenanters to remove their protective blanket from their friends at Westminster.[11] Even for Charles, it cannot have been a difficult calculation. By August 1641, he was a king in little more than name only in both British kingdoms. If he were ever to recover even part of his powers in England, he must begin in Scotland, paradoxically, by signing away what few that he still retained.[12]

I. EDINBURGH: UNION ATTAINED

Charles's surliness towards his English Parliament on his departure from London was only matched by his graciousness, on arrival in Edinburgh, towards his Scottish one. Even before reaching the border, however, he had clearly signalled to the Covenanter régime his new-found compliancy. On reaching Newcastle, he flattered the Scottish Lord General, Alexander Leslie, with a mixture of courtesy and charm, and was rewarded, in turn, with protestations from Leslie's army of their 'obedience and zeale to his person'.[13] The fact that this army had so decisively vanquished his own at Newburn, twelve months earlier, was tactfully forgotten.

From the moment of his entry into in Edinburgh on 14 August 1641, the king engaged in an almost craven exercise in ingratiation. The watching crowds responded with enthusiasm, in the words of Secretary Vane, who accompanied the king, 'with an incredible joy and acclamation'.[14] How much of that 'acclamation' was actually for Charles himself is more ambiguous. The Elector Palatine, who rode in the king's coach, attracted at least as much applause and attention during their stay in Edinburgh as his royal uncle. And the real cause of celebration in August 1641 seems to have been less the simple fact of the king's presence in the Scottish capital than the capitulation that it was believed to symbolize: his acceptance of the renegotiated 'Union' with England, a league between the two 'commonwealths' on far more generous terms than had been conceded in 1603, and in which his own powers, in both realms, had been massively reduced.[15]

Outward acceptance of the new Union, and of his own subordinate place within it, became the defining feature of the king's conduct after his arrival in Edinburgh. Gone completely was his haughty insistence on maintaining English habits of court and chapel etiquette, practices which had so offended Scottish sensibilities during his coronation visit to Edinburgh in 1633.[16] This time, as Vane reported approvingly, the king was 'pleased to take the prayers and preaching according to the forme of the Scottish Church'.[17] On Sundays he would attend divine service publicly in two of the Edinburgh churches, a pious habit that was reported to '[gain] much on the people'.[18] Of the Covenanter clergy, none was in greater royal favour than Alexander Henderson, the author, back in February, of the declaration from the Scots Commissioners calling for Strafford's death, the very document which had provoked the king to run 'starke mad';[19] now Henderson was given the honour of standing beside the king's chair during sermon time[20] – exactly the mark of status that had been conferred upon Laud during the coronation visit of 1633.

Nor were the king's religious concessions confined to gestures alone. During his first fortnight in Holyrood, Charles, the supposedly inflexible maintainer of the ecclesiastical status quo, agreed to the Covenanters' demands that the office of bishop should be abolished in Scotland entirely, and that all the current Scottish bishops should be excluded – along with thieves and outlaws – from the benefit of the Act of Oblivion and Pacification, which otherwise indemnified both sides for acts committed during the recent civil war.[21]

Charles also went out of his way to present himself as a parliamentary monarch, attending the sessions of the Edinburgh Parliament every morning,[22] and even accepting its appointment of Lord Balmerino as its President – a zealous Covenanter who had been sentenced to death for treason in 1633 – with outward good grace.[23] Yet, for all the apparent bonhomie on both sides, there was no ignoring his hosts' marked lack of deference towards their royal guest. One sermon delivered before the king in St Giles railed against the bishops as the king's evil counsellors with such ferocity that, as one of the king's English entourage observed, a year ago it would have been 'a Star Chamber business'.[24] Public enthusiasm often proved far warmer towards the Elector Palatine than it was towards the king.[25] And while there was no shortage of 'cordiality', Charles found himself being addressed by the Provost of Edinburgh, the host of a dinner to celebrate the Treaty of Union, in the egalitarian manner of 'a plain Dutch host'; what one of his retinue termed 'this Scotch familiar way'.[26]

Against this outwardly amiable background, the formal dismantling of Scotland's personal monarchy and its replacement with something very close to an aristocratic republic – twinned with, and partly modelled on, the régime at Westminster – moved steadily forward. Most of the major constraints on the king's powers were contained in the legislation passed by the 'rebel' Scottish Parliament of 1640 (convoked without royal approval), whose acts the king was bound to ratify under the terms of the Anglo-Scottish Treaty. In extolling the virtues of 'Union' to Parliament shortly after Charles's arrival, Argyll recommended the English example to his fellow Scots. Just as the Triennial Act had been the keystone of the new English commonwealth, so Argyll moved that the 'prudent example' of the English 'may be our pattern forthwith to obtaine his Majestie's Royall assent for doing the like here in this Kingdome'.[27]

This was accomplished on 25 August, when the king finally signed the Anglo-Scottish Treaty, *ipso facto* acknowledging the legality of the original Covenanter revolt and confirming retrospectively all acts – including the Scottish Parliament's 1640 Triennial Act – passed in the interim.[28] But it was not only the king's powers to control Parliament that were destroyed by his assent to the Anglo-Scottish Treaty. His control of his armed forces in both kingdoms was also severely circumscribed. Above all, the new arrangements prevented Charles (or any future king) from using forces raised in one British kingdom to enforce his authority in the other. Any future war against Scotland using English *or Irish* troops would require the assent of the English Parliament (something which, so long as the reformists retained their influence, would never be given), just as any use of Scottish troops would have to be

ratified, likewise, by the Parliament in Edinburgh. At least within the Stuarts'
dynastic realms, the king's ancient prerogative power to decide when and
against whom he should make war had been peremptorily abolished.[29] By
thus binding their shared sovereign's hands, the new settlement, it was
claimed, 'knit the 2 Kingdoms in love and peace for the future'.[30] Indeed,
Argyll seems to have envisaged that the Edinburgh and Westminster Parliaments, now committed to meeting triennially, should henceforth coordinate
their sessions, that 'by the wisdome of the Assemblies of both Kingdomes
... the happie peace and union betwixt both Nations' might be maintained.[31]

*

With the Parliament's future meetings thus guaranteed, the key question
became (as it had already done in England) the matter of deciding on Scotland's government when Parliament was not actually in session. Who should
have the right to nominate the great officers of state, the senior judges (the
Lords of Session), and the members of the Privy Council: the power, in other
words, to decide the composition of the future government? Hitherto, this
had been one of the king's undisputed prerogative powers. To make Scotland's
aristocratic republic almost wholly immune from royal interference, Argyll
needed to wrest this power from the king and to vest it in Parliament, a
body which, for the foreseeable future, he and his allies looked certain to
control.

   In this respect, the solution established in Scotland exactly paralleled the
arrangements that had already been proposed in England by the Junto leadership in the Ten Propositions (of June that year) and acted upon by the
Commons in their nominations, in August, of the Earls of Salisbury and
Pembroke to major public office.[32] Once the control of appointments was
transferred from king to the Edinburgh and Westminster Parliaments (or at
least made subject to their approval) the 'Venetianization' of the two British
constitutions would be complete.

   Possibly encouraged by the Duke of Lennox,* who attended in the Bedchamber throughout his residence in Scotland, Charles made control of the
great offices the issue on which he would challenge Argyll, refusing outright
to yield up his ancient prerogatives of appointment.[33] It was a plausible
gambit. He could be confident that the issue would bring to the surface the
latent animosity, already glimpsed in the plotting of Montrose and the
Banders, against Argyll's ever more powerful oligarchic rule.

   Yet, even here, Charles was forced in the end to accept an almost doge-
like subordination. From the end of August, Argyll went on the attack,
proposing himself as Lord Chancellor, the actual head of government, under
a wholly nominal king. The argument raged back and forth between the

---

* James Stuart, 4th Duke of Lennox, had been created Duke of Richmond in the English
peerage on 8 August 1641, shortly before he accompanied the king on his journey to
Edinburgh. However, he continued to be known by his Scottish title, as Duke of Lennox,
throughout his stay in north of the border.

monarch and the Argyllian party during the first two weeks of September;[34] and met with fierce resistance from the king. But Charles was ultimately forced to hoist the white flag.[35] Despite his initial refusal to sanction any element of parliamentary interference, on 16 September 1641 he conceded that in future Parliament would have a veto over all major appointments (to the Privy Council, the judicial bench, and the great offices of state). In the periods when Parliament was not sitting, provisional appointments would be made with the Privy Council's approval, subject to confirmation or rejection in the next parliamentary session.[36]

In theory, the Scottish Parliament was there merely to 'advise' the king in these matters. In practice, 'there was nothing to stop it simply refusing to approve any nomination by the king unless he nominated the person it wished'.[37] By thus conceding the Edinburgh Parliament de facto power to control the composition of all future governments, Charles finally completed the process of his political emasculation, begun with military defeat at Newburn the previous year.[38]

Argyll's Junto naturally regarded the king's capitulation as providing the signal for a wholesale takeover of all the key governmental offices by his own partisans. Two, in particular, were needed to consolidate their long-term hold on power: the Chancellorship and the Treasurership, the one conferring immense prestige as the highest-ranking of all the Scottish offices of state, and the other offering control of the public finances. It surprised no one that Argyll sought the Chancellorship for himself, and the Treasurership for his Campbell kinsman, Lord Loudoun, who, until his recent return to Scotland, had been Argyll's principal agent (and Warwick's closest ally) among the Scots' delegation in London.[39] The British implications of this strategy were clear. An Argyll–Loudoun duo in the two most senior government posts in Scotland would powerfully consolidate the personal linkages between the two Juntos in Edinburgh and Westminster.

Yet the impending triumph of the Argyllians did not go unchallenged. Conscious of this groundswell of anti-Argyllian opinion, Charles fought a rearguard action, desperate to intrude at least one 'king's-party' man into the higher echelons of Scottish government. However, the king's attempts to promote the Earl of Morton, a former Lord Treasurer from the years of the Personal Rule, as his candidate for the Chancellorship, met with spirited opposition from Argyll.[40] He attacked Morton – his own father-in-law – as decrepit, pusillanimous, and unsuitable for high office, eventually prevailing on Charles to rescind his nomination. On 30 September the king was forced to accept a settlement in which the Argyllian, Lord Loudoun, took the Chancellorship (rather than the Treasurership, as had first been intended), and Argyll himself, having relinquished his own claims on the Chancellorship, resumed his role as Scotland's *alter rex* – its 'alternative king' – spurning any adminstrative office on which to found his power. The 'great dispute'[41] over the Chancellorship was thus resolved definitively in the Argyllians' favour. And when Charles produced a 'king's-party' nominee for the Treasurership – Lord Almond, another anti-Argyllian and signatory of the Cumbernauld Band – Argyll's party were equally effective in blocking this appointment.[42]

Slowly, painfully, the king was realizing that having granted the Parliament a say in the appointment of the kingdom's 'great officers', the legislature's voice spoke far louder and more authoritatively than his own.

This, combined with the Parliament's insistence that anyone who had taken the king's part in the wars of 1639 or 1640 should be debarred from public office, constituted a further affront to the king.[43] Nothing touched the king's already wounded sense of honour more directly than attempts to deprive him of the power to protect those who had served him loyally. And these humiliations eventually began to tell physically on the king. Even the Earl of Wemyss, a former critic of Caroline policy who was now moving towards the 'king's party', was moved by the indignities that were being heaped upon him. 'There was never [a] King so insulted over. It would pity any man's heart to see how he looks, for his is never at quiet amongst them [Argyll's party in Parliament], and glad he is when he sees any man that he thinks loves him.'[44]

Far from Charles's Scottish sojourn providing him with the means to break the power of the English Junto, it had left the Junto's Edinburgh allies – the Argyll–Hamilton faction – more securely in control of the Scottish state than ever. The restrictions the king had been obliged to accept to the royal prerogative 'fulfilled his own prophecy, in the spring of 1638, that the triumph of the Covenanting movement would leave him with no more power than the Doge of Venice'.[45] Moreover, by making still greater concessions in Scotland than he had yet offered in England, the king realized that he had set a precedent that would be seized upon by the Westminster Junto the moment he returned. Charles had lost, in the assessment of Giustinian, 'the most effective means of keeping his subjects obedient to himself' and, in London, the royal surrender was hailed as all that was needed 'to obtain the same advantage [in England] soon'.[46] As early as 24 September, Edward Nicholas, reporting the latest news from London, warned the king that 'there wilbe some attempt to procure the like Act here concerning Officers', once Parliament resumed on 20 October, and that unless the king assented, he would be denied a lifetime grant of Tonnage and Poundage – on which the future financial solvency of the court depended.[47]

Even within the king's own party there now were those who believed that equity alone would demand the king concede control over major ministerial appointments to Parliament. As Thomas Webb, the secretary to the Duke of Richmond and Lennox, put it: 'what is done here [in Scotland] wilbe a rule to us [in England], and I thinck it most just that a nation from whom a king injoyes all those benifitts which ours affords him should receave from him at least as much as another place [Scotland] which yealds him noething but trouble'.[48] An end to royal appointments in both Kingdoms now seemed imminent.

II. LONDON: UNION CONSOLIDATED

Hot, humid, and malodorous, Westminster in the late summer of 1641 was a place uncongenial at best; at worst, seriously injurious to health. An unusually virulent outbreak of plague had sent all but the hardiest of members of both Houses scurrying to their country retreats.[49] Of the Commons' 500 members, barely eighty turned up for business;[50] in the Lords, attendances were down to a couple of dozen. Many of the houses passed by peers and Commons-men on their way to the Parliament House already bore the terrifying 'Red Cross, with a *Lord have mercy upon us*', painted on their doors.[51] And the pestilence seemed to be intensifying by the day.

Yet not even these daily terrors were sufficient to detract from the Junto leaders' delight at the reports coming from Edinburgh. The decisive news that the Scots would formally ratify the Treaty of Union reached London by 28 August, and Mandeville responded immediately with an effusive letter to Hamilton, declaring himself 'very much satisfied with the proceedings of your Parliament'. The Scots' prompt ratification of the Union and their equally speedy withdrawal, without incident, of their army from England, confounded the Junto's anti-Scottish critics and served to prove the 'honesty' of their Covenanter brethren. 'Nowe,' wrote Mandeville, 'many [in London] that could hitherto vent nothinge butt Jealousies and reproaches against the Scoch nation doe much applaude their Cariage towards us, and amongst your selves.'[52]

The new 'Union', it seemed, was on the verge of becoming a constitutional and military reality – no longer focused, as it had been in 1603, on a unity of realms achieved through the sharing of a single sovereign, but on the interdependency of the two Juntos that had come to power in Edinburgh and London, and their shared commitment to the creation of a new political order in both kingdoms, founded on the drastic limitation of monarchical power.

The Westminster sense of relief and jubilation found its clearest expression on Tuesday, 7 September, when, in Essex's words, 'wee ... kept, according to ower agrement in the [Anglo-Scottish] treaty, a general thansgeving for the happy uniting of the 2 nations in soe strict a bond of frendship'.[53] Celebrated in the chapel of Lincoln's Inn and attended by the Lords and Commons remaining in London,[54] this 'thansgeving' was a moment of partisan triumphalism, with two of Warwick's favourite preachers – Stephen Marshall,[55] and his former chaplain, Jeremiah Burroughes[56] – providing the celebratory sermons.[57]* For Essex, St John, and the other Junto-men who had risked so much to create the new post-Triennial Act commonwealth, Marshall's choice of scriptural text – a verse from Psalm 124 – must have had particular resonance: 'Blessed be the Lord, who hath not given us as a prey to their teeth. Our soul is escaped as a bird out of the snare of the fowler; the snare is broken, and we are escaped.'[58]

---

* Marshall was named as the foremost of 'those ministers who gave their voices for my lord of Warwick' and who often preached 'out of their parishes' in the period before the elections for the Parliament of April 1640. By 1641, he seems to have been firmly established in the reformist circle associated with Warwick House. In 1642, he was to become regimental chaplain to the Earl of Essex. Burroughes had enjoyed Warwick's protection at least since 1638, when he served as acting household chaplain at Leez during the absence that year of John Gauden (Warwick's established household chaplain).

The tone of the two sermons was exultant.[59] But Marshall's asserts this sense of joyous release perhaps most empatically:

> This one yeer, this wonderfull yeer, [was a time] wherein God hath done more for us in some kinds, then in fourescore years before: breaking so many yokes, [and] giving such hopes and beginnings of a very Jubilee and Resurrection, both of Church and State. This yeer, wherein we looked to have been a wonder to all the world in our desolations, ... God hath made us a wonder to the world in our preservation – giving us, in one yeer, a Return of the prayers of fourty and fourty years.[60]

This 'Resurrection' of Church and state had a single cause. Marshall regarded the legislation establishing Triennial Parliaments and preventing the current Parliament's dissolution without its own consent as the foundation of the astonishing upheaval in the commonwealth's affairs. Parliament would continue until 'all things be rightly established both in Church and Commonwealth, that the foundations of the Land may be no more out of joynt, [and] that Liberty and Religion henceforth receive no dammage, ... *Quadragesimus primus mirabilis annus* [Forty-One has been a miraculous year]. Oh wonderfull yeer! and so much the more wonderfull that all these things are done for us, ... when *Germany* remains a field of blood'.[61]

Amid the jubilation, however, there was a keen sense of how close England and Scotland had come to sharing Germany's fate. 'You all know our estates, our Liberties, our Religion, and what ever we may cal ours', Marshall reminded his audience, 'were in a manner irrecoverably lost through the malice and practise of wicked Instruments, and a dreadfull cloud hath, these two or three years, been gathering.'[62] These same dark clouds, now on the brink of dispersal, were also visible to Burroughes. For much of the past year, he reminded his audience, 'we looked to have been a wonder to all the world in our desolations'. War – either between the kingdoms or within them – had threatened time and again. Only now, with the establishment of 'Union', was there confidence that the 'doore of hope', opened by the Triennial Act was safe 'from being shut'.[63]

Yet Marshall and Burroughes also used the celebration of Union to urge the Parliament to one outstanding item of business which their Junto patrons intended to complete: the removal of 'Superstitious vanities'[64] and ceremonialist innovations that had become common in English parishes during the decade of Personal Rule. Their sense of the matter's urgency is understandable. Although Parliament had been in session almost continuously by September 1641, the Junto had done nothing substantive as yet to bring the English Church into 'nearer conformity' with the Scottish. Indeed, not a single religious reform had thus far reached the statute book.[65] Some form of dramatic gesture was needed before the Parliament rose for the forthcoming recess.

There had been talk of a new bill for 'abolishing superstition' back in early August.[66] But only now, with attendances in both Houses down to a fraction of their usual levels, did the Junto leadership attempt to bring it to completion. The time could not have been more propitious. With the king away, the bill could be promulgated as a parliamentary 'ordinance' – in effect, a temporary Act of Parliament, which did not require the royal assent[67] – and put into effect immediately. By the time he would be back at Whitehall, the removal of altar rails, the destruction of all crucifixes and 'scandalous pictures' of the persons of the Trinity and the Virgin Mary,[68] and a series of other 'anti-popish' measures, would be a fait accompli in many parishes. Laud's 'beauty of holiness' would have been thoroughly dismantled. And the Junto would have sent the first truly unambiguous signal to Edinburgh that Union in secular matters also meant at least 'closer union' in the Church.

The celebrations of Anglo-Scottish Union on Tuesday, 7 September, there-fore, provided the cue, if belatedly, for the completion of the Parliament's very first item of 'puritan' legislation. In what seem to have been coordinated moves, Pym had managed the final text of the ordinance against innovations in an acrimonious session on Monday the 6th;[69] and, the very next day, Marshall and Burroughes made the case against 'superstitious innovations' from the pulpit.[70]

The central purpose of these measures – in this particular form and at this particular time – against Laudian 'superstition' was to provide Edinburgh with an act of unambiguous religious solidarity from a Parliament which, thus far, had been lagardly in bringing religious reform to the statute book. No sooner had the measure against innovations been proposed, however, than an attempt had been made to subvert it by the courtier, Sir John Culpeper, an Esquire of the Body to the king and fierce opponent of any attempt to Scotticize the English Church. Culpeper made what seemed, super-ficially, an uncontroversial request. He accepted the need to root out 'popish innovations', and merely asked that these reforms should be balanced by an order preventing any public expressions of contempt for the *Book of Common Prayer*.[71] It seemed an inocuous request. Yet, as Culpeper doubtless knew, this was all that was required to compromise the new reformist measures in the eyes of the Scots. For while many, if not all, the members of the Junto had no objection to the use of the *Prayer Book* (Warwick himself seems to have used it in his household chapel), any mention of it threatened to render the order wholly unacceptable to the Scots. Their repudiation of the *Prayer Book,* in its Scottish revision, had been the spark of the initial Covenanter revolt.[72]

For the Warwick House group, then, it was imperative that there should be no mention of the *Prayer Book* anywhere in the proposed new ordinance, and this group's key members rallied accordingly. When it came to resisting Culpeper's proposal, all four of the speakers named in the parliamentary records came from the Warwick–Barrington connection: the Junto's pro-spective appointee as Treasurer of the Household, Sir Henry Mildmay; Sir Thomas Barrington himself; his brother-in-law, Sir William Masham; and their cousin, Oliver Cromwell[73] (the only speaker not to have a commission from the Earl of Warwick as a Deputy-Lieutenant for Essex).[74] By the time the proposed ordinance against 'innovations' resurfaced in its final form on 8 September – the day after the solemn thanksgiving for the Union – the Junto-controlled drafting committee had ensured that any reference to the

Prayer Book, either for or against, had been studiously omitted.[75]

This all boded well for the measure's success. The ordinance was passed that day, and the Commons added a resolution (significantly, not an order)* that, although the legislation only made a start at the great work of Church reform, it should nevertheless be printed and published – as was standard practice with any public act.[76] But there was no question of *ordering* anything to be printed, still less of passing the legislation, without consultation with the Lords. Indeed, as the measure was clearly intended to be implemented as an 'ordinance' of *both* Houses (or temporary Act of Parliament, passed without needing the king's consent), a conference was immediately arranged by the younger Vane to be held in the Painted Chamber.[77] There, St John – one of the drafting committee and a known moderate in religious matters – put the case to the Lords that they should join in this preliminary move to undo the Laudian altar policy, until such time as a fully developed 'Law' (that is, an Act of Parliament) against 'idolatrie and superstition' could be passed.[78]

This was the Commons Junto-men in pro-Covenanter mode, following the Scots' lead in the removal of 'Superstitious vanities', and clearly expecting that Warwick and his pro-Scottish allies would be able to carry the measure in the upper House.

Indeed, although the established account of this moment represents this measure as 'a calculated snub to the Lords',[79] it was clear from St John's remarks to the peers that the Commons were putting it forward for 'their Lordshipps to joine with us that it might become an ordinance of Parliament', which required the peers' assent.[80] To receive the ordinance, the Lords sent Warwick, accompanied by four other more junior peers, who duly met for a formal conference in the nearby Painted Chamber.[81] All went straight-forwardly, with the Commons politely requesting that the Lords join in passing and publishing the ordinance, until Warwick and his colleagues returned to their House and a formal proposal was made that the whole body of the Lords consider the Commons' bill. At this point, an anti-Junto party tried to defer any consideration of the Commons' bill; but this motion was stopped, if only just, by Warwick and his reformist allies. They won the ensuing division, by the dangerously narrow margin of twelve votes to eleven. Once this was done, however, the Lords gave broad support to the ordinance, making only minor amendments to the Commons' draft, all designed to focus the reforms on 'Laudian' innovations since the king's accession.[82]

On all the major points, Warwick and his allies secured agreement with the Commons. The only substantive changes were designed to show an element of sensitivity towards cases where, in some parishes, allegedly innovatory practices (such as the raising of the altar on steps) actually predated the 1620s. Hence, in the revised ordinance, where communion tables had

---

* 'Resolutions' of the Commons were declarations of intent, which could be (and often were) subsequently disregarded by the House; 'orders', by contrast, were formal commands, usually expected to be enforced.

been set altar-wise and surrounded by rails (in supposedly Roman Catholic fashion), both table and rails were to be removed. All chancel steps that had been installed since 1625 in order to elevate the altar (again in supposed emulation of Roman Catholic usage) were also ordered to be demolished. But where stepped communion tables were Jacobean or earlier, things were to be left as they were.[83]

Likewise, Warwick and his allies in the Lords agreed that all crucifixes and images of the persons of the Trinity 'are to be abolished, without limitation of the time since their erection'. But when it came to depictions of the Virgin Mary, only those put up since 1620 – roughly the date when the 'new divinity' began to be influential in the Church – were to be destroyed.[84] Only on the question of bowing at the name of Jesus did the Lords part company with the Commons (and, even here, only slightly). Warwick's conference-managers suggested a compromise whereby, instead of a blanket ban, it was to be left to individual judgement whether to bow or not – it 'not be[ing] enjoined, nor prohibited, to any man'.[85] These points, 'being distinctly read', were accepted as formal resolutions of the House of Lords, and the one outstanding item in the Commons' ordinance not yet fully discussed – a proposed ban on Sabbath sports – was carried over to the following morning.[86]

By the evening of Wednesday, 8 September, then, the Warwick House group seemed to have established the basis for a new ordinance – one that could be promulgated almost immediately, without requiring the king's assent, once the bill's last remaining clauses were dealt with on the morrow. With so many of the Junto's usual supporters (including Saye)[87] already out of London, it had been a near-run thing: the vote of twelve to eleven on whether to consider the bill at all had been uncomfortably close. But after that point, debate had favoured the Junto lords. The most important sections of the bill had been agreed to (and placed on record, section by section, as resolutions of the House), and these were secure; for once amendments had been resolved on and placed on record as the settled will of the House, the convention was that they stood and were not subsequently re-amended, except in response to representations from the Commons. All that remained to be done was for the two Houses to confer on the following day (Thursday, 9 September), the day on which both Houses attended to adjourn for the planned recess, and to discuss the Lords' amendments, incorporate them into the ordinance, and see to its publication. The newly appointed Commissioners sent from Westminster to the Scottish Parliament – whose 'Instructions' were set for consideration that same day[88] – could then arrive in Edinburgh bearing this tangible, if belated, evidence of the sincerity of the Junto's commitment to bringing about 'nearer conformity' between the English and Scottish Churches. All seemed set for a new phase of selective iconoclasm – a second 'stripping of the altars'[89] – to inaugurate the new age of Anglo-Scottish Union.

Then, on the following day, came the ambush.

*

Explaining what went wrong to Hamilton, the Junto's key ally in Edinburgh, Mandeville referred to the débâcle as having been caused by 'a designe that some Lords ventured upon'[90] to thwart the passage of the ordinance against 'idolatry and superstition'. Thin Houses usually worked to the Junto leaders' advantage, because, with their generally more sophisticated approach to parliamentary management, their side could normally be relied upon to constitute a majority of those present. Thursday, 9 September had looked like being yet another such day. With only twenty peers present in the House of Lords[91] (barely a sixth of its total membership), success should have been assured. However, the early departure of several of his usual supporters for the country,[92] had left Warwick and his allies perilously exposed.[93]

By what, to Warwick, must have been a maddeningly narrow margin (eleven votes to nine), the Junto's opponents voted to abandon any further debate on the ordinance against innovations. Instead, they used their majority to dust off an order passed by the House back in January 1641, enjoining that church services should be performed according to the *Book of Common Prayer,* 'as it is appointed by the Acts of Parliament of this Realme'.[94]* Still more confrontationally, the anti-Junto majority ordered that this should be printed and published, without consulting the Commons as to whether they would be prepared to join with them.[95] This was an obvious spoiling tactic: 'a designe', in Mandeville's phrase, to prevent the ordinance against innovations becoming law before the parliamentary recess, and a deliberate snub to the Scots and their Westminster allies.

Almost for the first time since the beginning of the session, back in November 1640, Warwick and his Junto allies found themselves outmanoeuvred. They protested against their colleagues' unilateral action, but, not because it favoured the *Prayer Book*, but because they 'thoughte itt nott fitt to [insist on it usage] att this tyme'.[96] Having celebrated the 'Union' between England and Scotland barely forty-eight hours earlier, and being on the brink of despatching Hampden, Fiennes and a number of their other friends as Commissioners to Edinburgh,[97] it is not hard to see why Warwick should have jibbed at the prospect of a religious declaration, which, so far as the Scots were concerned, was so gratuitously off-message. The Junto had been tripped up, and there was now no possibility that the Lords' assent could be got to the ordinance against innovations before the two Houses rose for the planned recess. Once again it seemed that 'godly reformation' had been postponed.

Yet this was only partially a division about religion. Of course, for Warwick and his pro-reformist friends, the provocative aspect of their opponents' behaviour was their outright refusal to move forward with the ordinance against innovations. But compressed into this single issue was the larger question of attitudes for, and against, the Union; and that, in turn, entailed the even larger question of the Junto's relations with the Scots and its dependency on Argyll's régime in Edinburgh as the long-term guarantor of its power.

---

* The irony cannot have been lost on Warwick: this order had been one of Bedford's sops to the king, earlier in the year, to reassure him that the Petitioner Peers had no plans for radical reformation. It had been pushed through the Lords on 16 January – exactly at the moment when the first list of Junto preferments (including St John's own appointment as Solicitor-General) was being finalized.

Accordingly, the line-up on both sides registered antipathies that can be traced back to the Strafford crisis and forward to the outbreak of armed conflict in 1642. Backing the 'designe' to defeat the Junto were the Earl of Cleveland, who had comforted Strafford on the scaffold; his son Lord Wentworth; the suspected Army Plotter, the Earl of Carnarvon; the Catholic Lord Mowbray; and half a dozen other peers who would later side with the king.[98] Perhaps the only anomalous figure in such company was John Williams, the Bishop of Lincoln, the erstwhile favourite of the reformists, who, perhaps unsurprisingly, was becoming deeply alarmed by the Junto's ever-strengthening ties with the bishop-hating Scots.

Against them, finding this a tactless moment to start insisting on the use of the *Prayer Book* and protesting against their colleagues for their refusal to consider the ordinance against innovations, were the Junto grandees: the same men who had produced the Petition of the Twelve Peers, who had hounded Strafford to his death, and who had been the brokers of the Anglo-Scottish Treaty: Warwick and Newport, Wharton and Mandeville (both of whom Strafford had wanted shot the previous September for delivering petitions against the Scottish War), together with Holles's brother (the Earl of Clare) and the new Earl of Bedford.[99]

Nor was it a defeat that Warwick was prepared to accept lying down.[100] With a matter of hours to go before the two Houses rose for their six-week recess, he moved swiftly to minimize the effects of the defeat. Unless the resolution were to be lost, the only alternative was to issue the failed ordinance as a provisional order of the Commons alone – pending reconsideration by both Houses when they reconvened after the recess – and with a printed explanation of the narrowness of the vote in the upper House. This is the provocative option which the Junto grandees appear to have chosen. Within a short time after the vote had gone against him in the Lords, Warwick was briefing favourably-disposed Commons-men on exactly what had happened,[101] and, probably, on what they needed to do. The godly Sir Simonds D'Ewes recorded in his diary that he had been 'partly informed of [what had happened] this morning' by Warwick;[102] and if Warwick partly informed D'Ewes, it is still more likely that he also briefed St John, Barrington and Pym.

In the Commons, an initiative to save the Ordinance against Innovations and Superstitious Images was promptly forthcoming. D'Ewes, for once, seems to have been as good as his word. Acting on information 'from the Earle of Warwick, I stood up and spake a prettie whiles'. Using an argument that is suspiciously close to that used by Mandeville in his letter to Hamilton, D'Ewes argued that the Lords' order in favour of the *Prayer Book* should be opposed, not because he objected to the proposal itself, but because he 'dislike[d] ... the time of proposing it'. Clearly briefed by Warwick as to what had transpired in the Lords that morning, D'Ewes was able to point out that 'divers of those Noble Lords did dissent and ... [protested against] such proceedings in their howse'.[103] Openly acknowledging the Parliament's paltry record in relation to religious reform, D'Ewes argued that for the Commons to assent to the Lords' order in favour of the *Prayer Book* would be to put 'all his Majestie's Religious Subjects into a dispaire, almost, that wee intend no [re]formation in [the] matter of Religion, contrarie to their hope and expectation, with which wee have all this time fedde them'.[104]

After prolonged debate the Commons finally decided to publish the ordinance for the removal of innovations (now recast as a temporary order of the House of Commons), together with a declaration pointing out that the eleven peers who had blocked the ordinance against innovations were unrepresentative of attitudes in the Lords as a whole. As the Commons pointed out, in justification of their controversial decision to publish the ordinance as an order of their House alone, 'other Lords then present [i.e. Warwick and the Junto peers] did dissent from it, so that it may still be hoped, when both Houses shall meet again' that the propositions for religious reform 'may be brought to perfection'.[105]

Mandeville likewise regarded the matter as unfinished business. Again in his briefing to Hamilton, he looked forward to the moment 'when wee meete againe, [as] wee shall have somethinge to doe', clearly blaming the anti-Junto Lords and their 'designe', not the Commons, for the predicament in which they found themselves.[106] In the interim, the Junto Lords declared their solidarity with the lower House by publishing verbatim the official record of proceedings on 9 September, naming names and listing, respectively for honour or execration, Warwick and the peers who had supported the move against 'innovations', and giving equal prominence to those who had been responsible for its stoppage. Not since the last days of the Strafford crisis, when the names of the Commons-men who had dared to vote against the attainder had been posted in Old Palace Yard, had London's political audience been informed in greater detail of exactly who were, and were not, the commonwealth's enemies.[107]

Few parliamentary injunctions were to have a greater, or more disruptive, impact on the life of England's parishes than this order concerning altars and innovations of 9 September 1641, which was to unleash an outbreak of image-smashing and altar-breaking on a scale probably not seen since the reign of Edward VI.[108] Yet the origin of this order was not a crude battle between a religiously radical Commons and a conservative *Prayer-Book*-defending Lords.[109] This was the reformist Junto, both peers and Commons-men, working together to achieve a shared objective, and not being balked by mere legal conventions when the good of the commonwealth required these should be overridden.[110] Left to their own devices on 9 September, it is highly likely that the handful of Commons-men in the chamber that morning would have simply allowed the ordinance against 'innovations' to lapse, or be carried over as unfinished business until after the recess – just as they had with every other major piece of ecclesiastical reform proposed hitherto. Indeed, the initiative to press ahead with the measure, notwithstanding the eleven votes against it in the Lords, seems to have come from the Lords themselves. Warwick, once again prioritizing 'necessity' over strict legality, appears personally to have encouraged his Commons friends to publish the order, so that, as D'Ewes put it after being 'partly informed' by the earl, the godly would not 'dispaire' that the Parliament had given up on religious reform altogether.[111]

The Earl of Salisbury, a peer sympathetic to political reform but deeply hostile to the Junto's relations with the Scots, was in no doubt as to where blame lay for this sudden grant of licence to the iconoclasts. In an angry satire either composed or copied by himself, and purportedly dated 9 September, Salisbury berated the reformist lords – among them Essex, Warwick, Mandeville, and Brooke – for joining with 'Lord Say the Anababtiste', Pym, Hampden, 'St Johns the sollissitor' and others; for they:

> have conspired together against the King, the crowne and posterity, and have subjected our religion to be merely arbitrary, have prostituted the honour of Ingland, have beggered the nation to inriche the Scottes, have protected the ignorant and the licentious sectaryes and sismatikes to stir up sedition … [against a] religious King, whom God preserve from suche conspiratours.[112]

But as the few dozen members still present at Westminster rose that afternoon for a six-week recess, it was evident that the 'conspiratours' had won. The new treaty, so solemnly proclaimed only two days earlier, had inaugurated a new world, a world in which they and their Scottish confederates were now the undisputed masters. And over the weeks ahead they would reveal – to the terror of many in all three kingdoms – just how thoroughly they intended to remake it.

III. THE EXPRESSIONS OF UNION: WESTERN DESIGNS AND THE PALATINE CAUSE

Within the Westminster Junto this euphoria of success – the belief that the new political dispensation was literally the answer to their prayers – prompted them to plan for the future with a confidence which had been impossible amid the sequence of crises that had preoccupied them hitherto. That summer, a group that included Lord Brooke, John Pym, and Viscount Mandeville had invited the Czech savant Jan Amos Komenský (better known by his Latinized name Comenius) to England to advise them in the preparation of plans for the reform of the kingdom.[113] For a moment that autumn, there seemed the possibility that the moves towards ecumenical 'union' between the English and Scottish Church might eventually form part of a larger, Europe-wide scheme for intra-Protestant reconciliation. Mandeville had been in correspondence with the major advocate of such a reconciliation, John Durye, at least since 1639;[114] and it was to ride this wave of reformist optimism that, in August 1641, Durye published his essay on international Protestant Union, *Concerning the Work of Peace Ecclesiastical* – a treatise that he had written three years earlier, and dedicated to his patron, the 'godly' Privy Councillor, Sir Thomas Rowe.[115]

Now, Durye's star appeared to be in the ascendant. His patron, Rowe,

had long been a friend of the new Lord General, the Earl of Essex,[116] one
of the Junto's most powerful men; and the new government was casting its
eye, not just over the state of Protestantism in Britain and Ireland, but over
its fortunes in the western hemisphere more generally.[117] This was a moment
for projects and grand designs, and Durye's was not the only pre-1640 scheme
for remoulding the world that was dusted off and re-examined in the bright
dawn of the Anglo-Scottish Union.

Protestant ecumenism, however, went hand in hand with Protestant militarism. In fact, one of the principal inspirations for schemes such as Durye's,
with their hopes of reconciliation between Calvinist and Lutheran, Presbyterian and Episcopalian, was the dream of what might be achieved to
advance the Gospel, if only denominational rivalries might somehow be put
aside. To men such as Warwick, Essex, Argyll and Hamilton this also appears
to have been one of the most powerful motives for their support for the
Union within Britain. Many of them had served in the 'German Wars' of the
1620s and 1630s, and had a clear sense of England's – and, still more,
Britain's – potential to attain the position which both James's and Charles's
diplomacy had hitherto denied it: as the unquestioned leader of Protestant
Europe. On the Scottish side, Hamilton had long been a passionate advocate
of British involvement in Germany, and in the early 1630s had served in
person with Gustavus Adolphus, the 'Swedish Lion', against the Habsburgs.
The proposal was equally sure of support from within the Covenanter army,
whose Lord General, Alexander Leslie, and many of its officers had first-
hand experience of Swedish or other Protestant service in Germany during
the preceding decade. As Lord Loudoun, Warwick's great ally in the treaty
negotiations, was to explain the benefits of the Union to the Scottish Parliament in September 1641: 'not onely [would it] bring both Nations to a
condition of prosperity at home, but [it would] make us formidable to our
enemies abroad'.[118] The prospect of using the combined military resources
of the two British 'commonwealths' opened up dazzling new possibilities for
Anglo-Scottish interventions against their common enemies. And in both
commonwealths, the two ruling oligarchies – Argyll's in Edinburgh and the
Warwick–Pym faction at Westminster – looked to the prosecution of a joint
Anglo-Scottish campaign both symbolically, as the tangible expression of the
Union, and practically, as a means of consolidating their control of gov-
ernment and military power at home.

Two great military crusades, both planned for implementation in the spring
of 1642, were to crown the Union's inaugural year. The first was a naval
campaign against Spain (the most powerful of the Elector Palatine's Catholic
enemies), targeted against Spanish possessions in the Caribbean and the West
Indies. Planning for this venture had already reached an advanced state by
August 1641, and was one of the first fruits of the Elector Palatine's close
friendships with Essex and Warwick – respectively, the Lord General and the
paymaster of the navy in the new administration – which went back to the
1620s.[119] Moreover, to ensure that it had a well-informed advocate in the
Commons, Essex arranged a Commons' seat for the Elector Palatine's man-
of-business in London, Sir Richard Cave, and the Elector's man was duly

elected at a bye-election on 12 August at Lichfield (where Essex was lord of the manor).[120] The West Indies scheme moved forward in the Commons a fortnight later, with the presentation of a petition from a group of merchants and others willing to invest, which was immediately referred to a committee stacked with Junto supporters, and 'especially committed' to Culpeper and Pym.[121] This, in turn, provided the cue the following day for Sir Richard Cave's maiden speech, which he used to give further details of the new privateering scheme, and, most importantly, to announce that the king had given it his consent (thereby guaranteeing that the all-important royal charter would be forthcoming). The company had one clearly defined objective: to prey on the Spanish colonies in the West Indies and the shipping that plied between them and the Spanish home ports. Profits from the venture were to go jointly to the shareholders and the Elector Palatine – in order, as Cave explained, 'that by this meanes [the Elector] might make some reparations of his losses upon the King of Spaine's dominions ther'.[122]

What Cave did not disclose was the scheme's authorship, which, like his own recently-acquired seat in Parliament, was attributable to the circle of Essex, Warwick and Pym. In fact, it was almost an exact rerun of a proposal first advanced by Sir Nathaniel Rich (Warwick's cousin and business manager),[123]* John Pym, and Sir Benjamin Rudyard, with Warwick's support, back in 1626.[124] It had been revived by Warwick in 1636 (and taken up by the Privy Council in more developed form in 1637), as a venture in which the Providence Island Company was to contribute to a private fleet under the command of the Elector Palatine, once again directed at attacking Spanish shipping in the Caribbean.[125] And in 1639, Warwick had obtained a royal licence to send a small fleet of his own to the West Indies, to prey on Spanish ports and their maritime trade.[126]

If Essex and Cave saw this venture as a means of furthering the Palatine cause, for their friends in the Providence Island Company (Warwick, Saye, Brooke, and Pym), it was a matter of more immediate concern. They, too, had 'reparations for losses' to seek from the King of Spain. Indeed, so far as they were concerned, the planned 'Western Design' was probably nothing less than a war of revenge; for by the time Cave stood up in Parliament to announce the forthcoming campaign, Warwick and his fellow investors had just learnt that their Providence Island venture had met with catastrophe. On 25 May 1641, barely a fortnight after Strafford's execution, a Spanish fleet of eleven vessels and 1,400 veteran troops under Admiral Francisco Diaz Pimienta had landed on Providence Island and overwhelmed its defences. The entire colony, 390 European inhabitants, had been shipped off to Cadiz,

---

* Speaking of Sir Nathaniel Rich's involvement in the Virginia Company, another colonizing project in which Warwick was closely involved in the 1620s, Rich's biographer notes that 'at all times he acted in the Earl of Warwick's interest, and it is striking how often both men were present at meetings together'. Like the father of the Solicitor-General Oliver St John, Rich's father was also the bastard son of the noble house which he served: in Rich's case, his was the illegitimate son of the 1st Lord Rich, Lord Chancellor under Edward VI, and great-grandfather of the 2nd Earl of Warwick.

and its almost equal number of African slaves had been confiscated by the Spanish.[127] When Sir Richard Cave announced to the Commons that 'divers of the Nobilitie and gentrie would joine in that service', there is little doubt that he had the injured Providence Island Company members principally in mind.[128] Legislation was not required. All the new West Indies company needed was a charter (letters patent under the Great Seal), already promised by the king, and their naval war could begin in the coming spring.

This provided the background to one of the more important of the Junto's 'usurpations' during that autumn: the transference, a week later, of financial control over the navy from the Admiralty to a triumvirate consisting of the Earl of Warwick[129] and two of the Junto's leading financial experts: Pym (the Junto's nominee as Chancellor of the Exchequer) and Warwick's stepson-in-law and Essex neighbour, Sir Henry Mildmay (the Junto's candidate for Treasurer of the King's Household). From 6 September 1641 (the eve of the celebrations of the Union with Scotland), Warwick, Pym and Mildmay jointly assumed responsibility for distributing all the 'monies ordered to be paid monthly for supply of the navy'.[130]

The decision to choose this moment, the inauguration of the new Union between England and Scotland, to vest financial control of the navy in the new triumvirate of Warwick, Pym and Mildmay fits a larger pattern of political administrative change in the months following the death of Strafford: the Junto's progressive removal of financial control over major military – and now, naval – expenditure from officers answerable to the king and its transference to themselves.[131] More importantly, perhaps, the conveyance of financial control over the navy – one of the largest departments of the Stuart state[132] – to Warwick and his two under-treasurers placed another vast portfolio of discretionary power and patronage in the Junto's hands. The first step had been taken in a process that would result, in less than twelve months' time, in Warwick assuming personal command of the navy.

Yet this scheme to let English buccaneers loose to plunder the Spanish West Indies was almost trivial beside the Junto's main project of the late summer of 1641: a joint Anglo-Scottish expedition to restore the Rhine Palatinate to its rightful Protestant owners. For men such as Warwick, Essex, and Saye, this literally God-given moment promised the fulfilment of ambitions that they had cherished since the mid 1620s: that brief episode of godly optimism in 1624 and 1625, when it had looked as if the young Prince Charles would accept their counsel, reverse James I's long-standing policy of appeasement towards Spain, and embark on a war to restore the old Elector Palatine (the current Elector's father) to the territories from which he had been forcibly dispossessed.[133]

There were persuasive reasons why the summer of 1641 was a timely moment for a renewed military initiative in support of the Palatine cause. The first was the 'revolution' of the Wheel of Fortune which had brought the survivors of the Patriot coalition of 1624 (particularly, Essex, Warwick, Holland, and Saye) back to a position of influence at court – though, this time, with an ability not just to advise on but also to direct the course of policy. Indeed, Essex, now the English Lord General, had served intermittently in the 'Palatine Cause' for much of the 1620s and 1630s, greatly enhancing his popularity in the process.[134] And his friendship with the young Elector Palatine, Charles Louis, went back at least to 1636, when the Elector had sought Charles I's permission for Essex to join him in a military initiative against the Habsburgs.[135] In 1641, this combination of amity and admiration was further enhanced, on the Elector's side, by his awareness of Essex's growing power as a parliamentary patron.[136]* Instructions sent by the Elector in early August 1641 to Sir Thomas Rowe, then acting as English ambassador to the Imperial court, register his sense of where influence was likely to lie in the new configurations of power. 'I could wish you would ... informe my Lord of *Essex*† of my businesse', the Elector wrote to Rowe, 'for you know how well he is inclined towards it and the power he hath with *parlament*'.[137] The Elector's agent in London, Sir Richard Cave, confirmed this, noting 'the Lord Chamberlain [Essex] promises to do his part'.[138]

But the road to the Palatinate was not merely paved with good intentions. There were sound diplomatic reasons why, in the autumn of 1641, the omens for a new Protestant campaign seemed propitious. July that year had seen the emergence of a new Protestant alliance between Sweden and the recently-acceded Elector of Brandenburg, Friedrich Wilhelm, aimed against the major Catholic princes of the Empire (principally the Emperor himself, Ferdinand III, and the Duke of Bavaria). During the imperial Diet held at Regensburg, which had first convened in September 1640 and had remained in session throughout 1641, Friedrich Wilhelm of Brandenburg emerged as a powerful champion of the Palatine interest, and a natural ally, should the peace talks of summer 1641 break down, for any British force sent to drive Catholic forces out of the Palatinate.[139] This was where men such as Essex discerned an opportunity. For if, as was widely assumed, these negotiations at Regensburg ended in stalemate, there was now the military wherewithal in Germany and, it seemed, the necessary political will in London and Edinburgh, for a new British intervention on the Continent to have a decisive effect.[140]

Yet the motives of Essex and Warwick were not, perhaps, as altruistic as this might suggest. One calculation, clearly articulated by the Junto's allies in the press, was the self-interested one that the security of the British Protestants was intimately tied to the fortunes of Protestantism on the Continent. The connection was so 'evident to the Westerne world', Downinge argued that autumn, that men 'wonder that we ever made it a question';[141] the time was long since passed when England could appear 'as a negligent neuter, with armes infolded'.[142] John Durye put the point even more trenchantly in the pro-interventionist treatise he published in August 1641, asserting that there was an obligation

---

* It was publicly acknowledged by the Earl of Pembroke in the last week of July 1641, when he held a feast in honour of both Essex and the Prince Elector at Baynard's Castle, his Thames-side residence in the City.
† Italicized words are in code in the original manuscript.

to establish a conjunction of endeavours amongst all Protestants for the preservation of the liberties and rites [i.e. rights] civill, religious and Ecclesiastical, of Protestants in Germany, lest the house of Austria [the Habsburg Monarchy] lay for itself a foundation of an universall Monarchy in their ruines.[143]

And in the later summer of 1641, the obvious 'conjunction of endeavours' for English Protestants to make was with their Covenanter brethren in Scotland.

This, then, was the prime motive for the Elector Palatine's decision to accompany the king to Edinburgh in early August: to win the backing of Argyll and the Scottish Parliament for the planned new German expedition. Here, too, diplomatic developments favoured his mission. Reports from Regensburg during the second half of August predicted, with ever increasing confidence, the imminent collapse of the current Protestant–Catholic truce. Moreover, given the Emperor's patronizing disregard for the king's – or perhaps more accurately, the Junto's – ambassador at Regensburg, Sir Thomas Rowe, there were strong hints from both Edinburgh and Westminster that this was not only an expected outcome, but would also be a welcome one. By 20 August 1641, the Elector's London representative was happily reporting that both England and Scotland were now agreed that 'the Emperor … will not believe that we are in earnest except he first see or hear that the Prince Elector is at the head of a royal army of his Majesty's [English and Scottish] subjects'.[144] In Edinburgh, the Elector Charles Louis had never been more buoyant: 'I think my affairs in a very fair way', he reported on 22 August, 'and my interest in great safety'.[145]

In Edinburgh, Charles was forced to acquiesce.[146] Having capitulated to Argyll and Hamilton over so much already, at the end of August he yielded this one thing more: he issued a public declaration (possibly drafted by Loudoun), expressing his belief that the Regensburg negotiations would probably fail, and that,

in which case, … we will use and imploy all such force and power wherewith God hath inabled us, both by our own armes, and the helpe and assistance of all our allyes and friends …[147]

Although the diplomatic outcome still retained an element of uncertainty, by the first week of September, preparatory steps were already being taken, in both Edinburgh and London, on the assumption that the German war would be renewed. The Scottish Parliament moved first. On 6 September, it issued an absolute prohibition on any soldier leaving Scotland until a 'resolute answer' was received from Regensburg in the Elector's favour.[148] The English Parliament followed suit three days later, with Essex once again active in protecting the Elector's interests.[149] In another public humiliation to the king, the two Houses at Westminster directly countermanded a licence the king had given to the Spanish ambassadors to recruit 4,000 Irish troops for Habsburg service. This ordinance, halting recruitment in Ireland and closing the Irish ports, stated its purpose clearly: 'for the better enabling of his

Majesty to aid and assist his allies abroad'.[150] No troops were to leave either England *or Ireland,* lest they be used to reinforce the anti-Protestant coalition abroad.[151] Nowhere was the effect of this ordinance felt more keenly than among the troops of the recently disbanded Irish army. The Spanish ambassadors, 'by relyance upon the sacred word and letter of a King, [had] imprested money and provided shipping for their transport, and been at above 10,000 Crownes charges [£2,500]' for the recruitment of this 'Regiment of Irish' for service in the Habsburgs' wars.[152] Instead, as a result of the English Parliament once again asserting its 'imperial jurisdiction' over Ireland, this large body of disbanded Irish soldiers suddenly found that its future livelihood had been foreclosed.[153] Inadvertently, the Junto had lit the fuse to a powder keg; and the eventual explosion, when it came, was to shake the new commonwealth to its foundations.

Meanwhile, the new German war moved from likelihood to certainty. News of the collapse of the Regensburg negotiations reached Edinburgh and London, apparently simultaneously, on 8 September 1641. 'The Emperour', Sir Richard Cave reported to the Westminster Parliament that same day, 'would enter into no termes of Pacification with the Prince Elector Palatine', and had excluded the Elector from the articles of amnesty published at Regensburg at the same time.[154]

For the twin régimes in London and Edinburgh, this provided them with their *casus belli.* A new army would have to be raised in England – most likely under the current Lord General, the Earl of Essex – early in 1642. This did not interfere, however, with the disbandment of the old royal army, which, after the plots of the spring, was deeply suspect politically. Throughout August and September 1641, this was steadily disbanded, with Parliament's treaty obligations to the Scots and the need to avoid the 'great charge of the Commonwealth' of maintaining it through the winter[155] being pleaded as the pretexts for its disbandment.[156] In creating its new army for Germany, the Junto could now start with tabula rasa.

The greatest opportunity presented by the forthcoming German campaign, however, was not the prospect of recruiting a politically reliable English army, but of creating an Anglo-Scottish force that would to be a tangible expression of the new Union between the two commonwealths. 'It may be', wrote the Earl of Bristol (desperately trying to reposition himself in the Junto's favour), '[that] God hath reserved this business to unite both nations [England and Scotland] in one common cause and against one common adversary.'[157]

Appropriately, the first public proposal for this Anglo-Scottish force against the common adversary came from Lord Loudoun, himself one of the principal architects of the Union. Speaking in the Scottish Parliament on 9 September, Loudoun stressed the domestic as much as the diplomatic benefits that would flow from the proposed joint venture. The new combined army

> may effect great matters, and may, by unity of Councell, raise both King-
> domes to as great estimation and as great honour in the world as ever; and
> how can they be better designed th[a]n to restore the Electorall Family to

their former inheritance? Can there be a better cause th[a]n the truth of God?[158]

'Unity of Councell' between London and Edinburgh was, as we have seen, the centrepiece of the English Junto's strategy for its own survival; and when Loudoun confidently assured the Scottish Parliament that there was 'no doubt, but [that] our Brethren of England will be as willing and forward as wee' in their support of the joint campaign,[159] he was most likely speaking in the knowledge that Essex had already given the Elector Palatine private assurances to this effect.[160]*

Back at Westminster, Essex's response to the news of the breakdown of negotiations at Regensburg was one of barely concealed delight. Writing to Rowe on the day of Loudoun's speech, he declared that, for his own part, he had always believed the Emperor would refuse to part with any of his conquered Protestant territories, no matter how unjustly acquired. But he was confident of the outcome of the forthcoming conflict: 'I doubt not that our master, with the help of his Parliament, will get that *by force* which is so due the Prince Elector, both by the laws of God and nations'.[161] The great crusade in Germany would be the defining policy of the two British 'Juntos' – or so both Essex and Loudoun believed – well into the foreseeable future.

This, then, was the international context to what was otherwise, literally, a parochial crisis: the royalist lords' ambush – that same morning, 9 September – of the ordinance against popish innovations in parish churches. For the Junto, the prospect of the forthcoming Palatine campaign made the pursuit of 'unity' between England and Scotland, as of that very morning, Thursday, 9 September, more urgent than ever before. This, in turn, is what made the spoiling tactics of the eleven anti-Junto peers – their declaring in favour of the *Prayer Book* and refusal to consider the ordinance against popish innovations – so obstructive, provocative to the Scots, and hostile to the spirit of the Union. It also helps explain why Mandeville found the order in favour of the *Prayer Book* 'nott fitt to doe ... att this tyme';[162] and why Warwick seems immediately to have alerted the Commons, so that they could take remedial action. As ever, it was the Junto's broader strategic and diplomatic objectives that were setting the timetable for ecclesiastical reform.

IV. THE 'PERPETUAL LEAGUE'

In the six weeks that followed the Parliament's adjournment – from 9 September to its reconvening on 22 October – the consolidation of Britain's twin 'monarchical republics' went on apace. In London, 'Recess Committees', respectively of Lords and Commons, convened to deal with the problems

---

* A fortnight later, Loudoun made a second impassioned plea for a military expedition into Germany, once again stressing that, '[as] for our Brethren of England, they questionlesse will shew the like readinesse'.

arising from the disbandment of the king's army. And the more active of the two – the Commons' Recess Committee, chaired by Pym and controlled by members and allies of the Junto – met twice-weekly to begin the implementation of the recent order against altar rails and other innovations.[163] Leaving any sort of committee in existence, empowered to exercise parliamentary authority (however limited) during a recess, was wholly unprecedented, and at least some of the Junto's enemies viewed the development as yet another step on the slippery slope that would lead to a fully fledged republic. 'Those well-affected to his Majesty's service', the Venetian ambassador reported a week into the recess, considered that the new committees contained 'the seed of hurtful consequences in the future: namely that it embodies a secret intention to move towards Holland's forms of government [*alle forme di governo d'Olanda*], for which the people here show far too much inclination.'[164]

Executive power, however, continued to reside – as it always did between meetings of Parliament – with the 'great officers': with a series of Junto magnates who, in the course of the last 'miraculous' year, had come to monopolize almost every major department of state. Essex, as Lord General, controlled all matters military in the South of England; and as Lord Chamberlain, he was also the most powerful figure in the Household. Warwick, with Pym and Mildmay, controlled the financing of the navy, and, with a carefully chosen group of friends, remained in charge of the 'Brotherly Assistance' – in effect, the Junto's vast £300,000 subsidy to the Argyll–Hamilton faction in Edinburgh, to be paid over the next two years.[165] Some sense of where political leadership was coming from during this period emerges from Giustinian's despatch written on the first day of the recess, 10 September, in which he recounted the activities of the party which had 'vigorously opposed the king's interests in Parliament'. The 'principal heads of this party [*li capi principali di questo partito*]', he noted, were 'the Earls of Essex [Lord Chamberlain], Warwick [the 'paymaster' of the Scottish army], and Newport [the Master of the Ordnance and Constable of the Tower], and some others', and they had met together with the Earl of Northumberland (only just returned from his convalescence in Bath) for a series of 'long conferences' in the fortnight between 26 August and 9 September.[166] While Giustinian regretted the subject of their deliberations was unknown, there was general agreement, he reported, that these Junto grandees were planning 'the best means of resisting any attempt which the king might make on his return' from Scotland to end a Parliament that was no longer in his legal power to dissolve – the central point, Giustinian noted, that 'offends the rights of his prerogative'.[167] How Charles would try to break the Parliament was unknown; but that he *would* attempt something on his return seemed certain. It was this danger which made the Warwick group's alliance with Argyll – and its diplomatic embodiment, the Treaty of Union – so necessary to their own future safety and the maintenance of 'the commonwealth' as an almost kingless state.[168]

To an extent that had been almost unimaginable when they had first challenged Charles's authority in August 1640, the aristocratic reformists in

London and Edinburgh had transformed the constitutions of both British realms. In little more than a year, by the end of September 1641, Charles's reduction to a cipher-king had already been institutionalized in Scotland, and in England, the process was already well advanced. The English Triennial Act, and the Parliament's near total control of public finance, had begun it; all that was needed now to complete the process was a new act (or ordinance), *à la* Scotland, formally conferring on Parliament the right to control appointments to the great offices of state, and the 'Hollandizing' of the English state would be near complete. Like Giustinian, Edward Nicholas, the Council's underemployed clerk, noted this slippage of regal power with alarm. Towards the end of September, he reported to the king how the Junto was beginning to make definite plans for the forthcoming session set for 20 October; there had been, he explained:

> divers meetings att Chelsey att the Lord Mandeville's house and elsewhere, by Pym and others, to consult what is best to be donne at the first meeting in Parliament, and I believe they will, in the first place, fall on some plausible thing that may redintegrate them in the people's good opinion, which is their anchor-hold and only interest. And (if I am not much misinformed) that wilbe either [against] Papists, or upon some Act for expunging [i.e. purging] of Officers and Counsellors here, according to the Scottish precedent – or on both together.[169]

By the beginning of October the Junto's confidence, much buoyed by the Argyllians' recent success in Scotland, was starting to get on Nicholas's nerves. 'You see ... to what boldnesse that party [the Junto] is growne', he wrote to the Duke of Richmond's secretary at the beginning of October. 'I assure you [that] if the King deferre his comming [back to London] any longer, I expect that there shalbee orders and ordinances made *sans nombre* to the prejudice of his Majestie's affaires.'[170] He believed not only that the Junto was preparing a legislative programme for the forthcoming parliamentary session, but also that it was intent, following the Scottish example, on imposing a new Lord Treasurer and a series of other senior officers on the king.[171] What is more, if this programme were to be advanced as a set of 'ordinances', it could be passed – and have the force of law – without ever being presented for the royal assent. That, too, looked like a move towards 'Holland's forms of government'.

But perhaps the most striking feature of government in both British 'commonwealths', immediately after the Union of August 1641, is the closeness of policy and aspiration between the Westminster Junto and its brother régime in Edinburgh. Hamilton, in a way, was the critically important point of intersection between the two, living a dual life as, in one guise, an English earl (the Earl of Cambridge), an English Privy Councillor, and a member of the English House of Lords; and, in another, as a Scottish marquess and territorial magnate, a member of the Scottish Privy Council, and a powerful figure in the unicameral Scottish Parliament. From his arrival in Edinburgh in August 1641 until his return to London three months later, Hamilton might almost be regarded as the Junto's ambassador to Argyll[172]* – Scotland's *alter rex* who had been the clear victor in the recent power struggles with the king. Communications with London were largely conducted through Viscount Mandeville, who acted, in effect, both as Hamilton's prime source of news and political advice, and also as a clearing-house for Hamilton's own letters to Essex, Saye, and the various other English Junto grandees.[173]

Likewise, the five resident English Commissioners, sent to Edinburgh in late August, nominally to represent the Parliament, functioned in practice as emissaries of this London Junto.[174] Their partisanship was an open secret at Westminster, and Nicholas's advice to the king on how to regard them was blunt: 'These are, as 'tis said, to be noe better than spies on the proceedings [in] Scotland'.[175] This was not far from the truth. Almost all of them (Howard of Escrick, Nathaniel Fiennes, John Hampden, and Sir Philip Stapilton) had been involved to various degrees either in the original invitation to the Scots to invade in 1640, or in supporting the invasion once it had happened; and when they arrived in Edinburgh, their crucial letters of introduction were all provided by the senior Junto office-holders in London, in particular, Mandeville and Essex.[176] It was hardly surprising, therefore that in Edinburgh, Howard of Escrick, Hampden and Stapilton found that they were regarded 'as if wee were here onely to support a party and faction [namely, that of Hamilton and Argyll], against his Majesty'.[177]

Their presence in the Scottish capital formed yet another bond connecting the two Juntos. As plans went forward during September and early October for strengthening that Union still further,[178] couriers to-ed and fro-ed between Edinburgh, London, and The Hague, carrying news of the great Anglo-Scottish army, currently in the planning, that would be deployed in Germany the following spring. By the end of September, the Elector's mother, the exiled Queen Elizabeth of Bohemia, seems to have begun to think of the new régimes in London and Edinburgh as part of a single state, commenting – in a revealing solecism – how she was 'beholden to both the Parliaments *of England*'.[179] Even Bristol was optimistic. The coming winter, he believed, would provide the moment when 'the Parliaments of both kingdoms' would move from general resolutions to 'the ways and means [of] how that business may be pursued with effect':[180] that meant the enlisting of troops, the appointment of officers, and the exchange of further resident commissioners from each of the kingdoms to provide the 'unity of Councell' necessary for a joint campaign.[181]

*

As the summer turned to autumn, domestic peace appeared to have been firmly established in both British commonwealths. Even from Ireland, the

---

* As with most great alliances of the period, its principals sought to reinforce their political bonds through marital and dynastic connections. From around June 1641, therefore, almost from the moment when Hamilton and Argyll discovered the court plots against them, the two men were in discussion over the marriage of Argyll's son to Hamilton's eldest daughter, negotiations which extended throughout the second half of 1641 and into the spring of 1642.

news reaching London from the Lords Justices (Leicester's deputies as Lord Lieutenant) was that all was quiet and in good order.[182] Something of the optimism this brought to the prevailing mood emerges in a report sent on 2 October to the great Irish magnate, the Earl of Ormond, by one of his informants in London, Thomas Salvin. Writing after a recent journey in which he had traversed, and presumably observed, the country from Yorkshire to London, Salvin noted that

> the general report here [in England] is of nothing more than peace, peace, and a secure uniting of both kingdoms in a perpetual league; and nothing more in agitation now than the settling of the Prince Elector in his country again, for which the Scots hath so freely declared themselves that, for their parts, he shall neither want more money nor officers, which makes all London cry with much joy, 'God, a mercy[ful] Scot'.[183]

The new Union seemed to have achieved the impossible, bringing the two nations together in a great crusading cause that might yet transcend the ongoing parish squabbles over images and altar steps.[184] It even seemed to have the potential to reconcile the English to actually liking the Scots.

Yet the very success with which the two Juntos in London and Edinburgh were consolidating their power created its own equal and opposite reaction. Long before the projected Anglo-Scottish campaign against Spaniards and Bavarians ever came to fruition, the victorious Juntos in Westminster and Edinburgh faced the first of a series of attempts to destroy their Union. Some of these were to come from expected quarters, from 'Papists' and other known enemies. But it was the first that caught them most unprepared and made the deepest impression. Within little more than a fortnight after Salvin's report of the 'secure unity of both kingdoms in a perpetual league', reports reached London of the attempted murder of Argyll and Hamilton, by the king.

13

COUNTER-REVOLUTION
AND REVOLT

JULY–OCTOBER 1641

[I]t was not unknown to your lordship how the puritan faction of England, since by the countenance of the Scottish army they invaded the regall power, have both in their doctrine and practice layd the foundation of the slavery of this countrey [of Ireland].

Lord Gormanston to the Earl of Clanricard, 21 January 1642[1]

'The king was deposed, the Palsgrave [the Prince-Elector Charles Louis] was crowned, and ... the king had given the Catholics of Ireland direction to rebel lest the [Irish Protestants] should assist the Puritans in England': such were the startling rumours circulating to the north of Dublin, in the countryside of County Meath, by October 1641.[2] Of course, distance refracted and distorted the news coming from Westminster. Gossip transformed itself into certainty and, in the retelling, alehouse tittle-tattle quickly assumed the status of gospel truth. Yet, in claiming that the king had been deposed by 'the Puritans in England', the rumour-mongers of County Meath, for all their exaggeration, were not entirely wide of the mark. Various members of the Commons had been reported, in early August, to have gone 'so far as to suggest depriving [Charles] of the crown and giving it to the Prince [of Wales] or the [Prince-Elector] Palatine', and it is not hard to see how, in repetition, this could have been transformed into hard news that the king had actually been deposed.[3] Moreover, 'deposition' could take subtler forms. So diminished were the king's prerogative powers; so beholden, henceforth, was the monarchy to the English and Scottish Parliaments, that observers could be excused for thinking that Charles had in fact been toppled from his throne, whether or not he retained the bare title of king. This impression was inevitably enhanced by the beleaguered monarch's departure for Scotland in early August, leaving his southern kingdom, for the next three months, in the hands of what was widely perceived to be a militantly puritan Junto.[4]

For all three Stuart kingdoms, those months of kingless rule in England were a period of watching for signs: of searching in the actions of the present and recent past for the likely shape of things to come. So complete seemed the transference of power at Westminster that, at sufficient distance, almost any report of radical change appeared potentially plausible. Towards the end of July, for example, it was reported that the leaders in the two Houses were 'upon Counsells [discussions] *in favor* of Roman Catholiques'.[5] Indeed, it is perhaps a measure of how successful the Junto had been at distancing itself from intolerant Puritanism during the first half of 1641, that such reports were even plausible.[6] However, as the summer progressed, the reformist leadership came to present a very different religious face to the world beyond Whitehall. Far from favouring Catholics, its policies seemed to have inaugurated a new and particularly bloody phase of anti-papist persecution at home, and anti-Catholic belligerence abroad. After a decade or more during which 'popish priests' had enjoyed a period of relative toleration, persecution of the Catholic clergy was resumed during the summer, with the full barbaric rigour of the law. In the last week of July 1641, at Tyburn, a Catholic priest suffered the gruesome death accorded to 'papist traitors' – being allowed to hang until he was partially asphyxiated, then mutilated, disembowelled alive and finally hacked into quarters.[7] Perhaps inevitably, this execution, which was widely noticed, was taken as presaging a much more extensive pogrom against Catholics and their clergy. And although this never seems seriously to have been intended, the vehemence of the Parliament's anti-papist rhetoric in the summer and autumn of 1641 was such that Catholics in all three Stuart kingdoms had some grounds for assuming that it was. '[Would] that these Locusts, like the Ægyptians' Spies, might bee rooted out of this Kingdome', one pamphleteer urged Parliament in September, and 'the traitorous Jesuits and Priests, and all their factious crue and adulterous seed of that strumpet, may in good time also be dispatched ... that there future hopes of continuing here may be quite obliterated.'[8] Such were the changes already wrought in England and Scotland by September 1641 that an attempt at the 'obliteration' of Catholicism in the Stuart realms was no longer beyond the bounds of plausibility.[9]

1. IRELAND: THE SEEDS OF REBELLION

Nowhere was that message apprehended with greater menace than in Ireland, where Catholics constituted between eighty and ninety per cent of its roughly million-strong population. The Westminster Junto's belligerent anti-papist rhetoric was rendered all the more disquieting to Catholics in Ireland by the way in which radical constitutional change in England had removed the two buffers that had hitherto stood between them and the 'fury' of Westminster's Puritans: first, the moderating influence of the king and, second, the authority of the Irish Parliament (which remained in session intermittently, though increasingly disregarded by Westminster, for much of 1641). These two processes of attrition had advanced in tandem. As Charles had been compelled to ever greater limitations on his prerogative powers, so the Westminster Parliament had extended the scale of its intrusions into Irish affairs – often encouraged by the class of recent English settlers (the 'New English' – so called to differentiate them from the mostly Catholic 'Old English', descended from Ireland's medieval English invaders). Gradually, over the ten months from November 1640, the English Parliament had set about what amounted to a dismantling of Ireland's status as an independent kingdom under the Stuart Crown, and its subordination to the 'High Court of Parliament' at Westminster. In reality, this seems to have demonstrated more by chance and contingency than by a policy of puritan 'imperialism' towards Ireland. The initial impetus to this process had come, of course, from Strafford's prosecution, for without insisting that its jurisdiction extended to Ireland, the English Parliament (and, more particularly, the Junto leadership) could never have tried Strafford for the offences committed outside England, as Ireland's Lord Deputy and Lord Lieutenant. Yet this was merely the start. In the course of 1641, Ireland came to be treated at Westminster as a mere colonial dependency, one for which the English Parliament could legislate directly, as if the Irish Parliament had simply ceased to exist.[10]

Two actions of the English Parliament, both of them initiated by the Junto on the eve of the September parliamentary recess, served to highlight the practical consequences of Ireland's new subordination. First came the decision of the English House of Lords, in September, to extend its appellate jurisdiction over the whole of Ireland: a massively important step, legally and politically, because it made the Petitions Committee of the English House of Lords, in effect, the supreme court of appeal for all cases arising in Ireland – and this committee, as we have seen, was notoriously controlled by Warwick, Essex, and the other 'godly', reformist peers.[11] By the summer of 1641, this committee had already attracted criticism from the Junto's opponents in the Commons: such a 'vast Jurisdiction of the Lords' house', Sir John Culpeper complained, that 'now, upon every Petition presented to them, [they] did order and judge ther [petitioners'] cause definitively – as if they had the sole Legislative power in them'.[12] Further objections to the English peers' authority were raised by the Irish House of Lords in July and early August.[13] But the English Lords were unrepentant. From September 1641, at the prompting of its own supporters in the Commons, the Junto grandees emphatically reaffirmed their jurisdiction – exercised through the Lords' Committee for Petitions – over Ireland. Pym himself managed the conference at which the Lords were invited to take on further 'Irish causes', and the first new batch of cases he recommended to the Lords included five involving members of the Irish House of Lords.[14] Justice in Ireland now seemed to be at the mercy of England's noblemen 'Puritans'.[15]

As if this measure were not ominous enough, its effect was compounded by the Parliament's ordinance of 9 September 1641, passed simultaneously, prohibiting the transportation of Irish military levies abroad.[16] As we have seen, this directly countermanded the king's licences, issued to the Spanish ambassador, Alonso de Cárdenas, allowing him to recruit Irish troops for service on the Continent.[17] In prohibiting Spanish recruitment of Irish troops, the parliamentary leadership's eyes were firmly on the forthcoming Palatine campaign, and the need to prevent any action that might strengthen the

Habsburg side[18] – so much so, that they seem not to have foreseen the ironic consequence of their action: that they had thereby created a reserve of Catholic military strength in Ireland that could be, and eventually was, used against them.[19] Hence, while Catholic opponents of the Westminster régime might secretly have applauded this outcome, they could not also fail to note the ominous precedent set by the English Parliament's decision to legislate for England *and* Ireland as though they were a single realm, and to do so in direct contravention of the king's declared will. Moreover, in proceeding by ordinance, the English Parliament had demonstrated that it could prescribe laws for Ireland without even consulting the king.[20] With the Westminster Parliament, as viewed from Dublin, widely believed to be under the control of a 'puritan Junto', this was a development which seemed to have potentially limitless scope for harming Irish Catholic interests.

Paradoxically, the new régime at Westminster had proved almost as insensitive to the impact of its policies in relation to Ireland as Charles's government had been during the 1630s in relation to the Scots. Obsessed during the summer of 1641 with maintaining good relations with Argyll and Covenanter Scotland, and with the new possibilities this opened up for military intervention on the Continent, the Junto leaders seem rarely to have considered the reaction that their policies were provoking across the Irish sea. Accurate intelligence also appears to have been lacking, a problem compounded by the death, earlier in the summer, of Sir Walter Devereux, the member of Essex's household who had hitherto managed the correspondence between Essex House and the factors who ran the earl's extensive Irish estates.[21] Even Sir John Clotworthy, the Junto's in-house expert on Ulster politics, seems to have been starved of up-to-date information on what was being plotted within the province.[22] The result was that the scale of the reaction against the 'puritan usurpation' at Westminster – which had first gained momentum in the spring and had accelerated rapidly during the summer – was not fully appreciated by the English parliamentary leadership until it was far too late. By mid October 1641, when alarm bells first started to sound, there was already a series of conspiracies ready to be activated, aimed at repudiating the authority of Westminster.

The course of those plots during 1641 was labyrinthine.[23] But two overriding considerations provided the general context in Ireland in which they matured. The first was the conviction that the Westminster Junto's assault on the king's prerogative powers had removed the one effective constitutional check that might otherwise have restrained the 'Puritans' in the English Parliament. It was therefore to the advantage of Catholic Ireland (the Old English and the Gaelic Irish) to defend royal prerogative power against its would-be usurpers at Westminster. Unless checked, the Junto's militant Protestantism, new-found power, and aggressively 'imperial' view of Ireland's subordinate status in relation to England all augured badly for Irish religious and landed interests. In this context, the defence of the king's prerogative powers – or, by the summer of 1641, the restoration of Charles's *lost* prerogatives – came to be viewed by influential sections of the Catholic population as a strategy for survival.[24] As the Catholic peerage of the Pale were to express the point in a declaration to the nobility and gentry of County Galway, 'we believe [that you], with the same resentment, have observed how much the majesty of our prince, in what concerns the kingdom [of Ireland], has suffered in the essentiall rights of it by the management of the affaires of the state by the parliament of England – as if … they would force upon us a further subordination …'.[25]

The second major factor in the conspiratorial politics of 1641 was the presence of Strafford's army of 8,000 Catholic Irish. Even after Charles, under extreme pressure from the English Parliament, had been forced to order its disbandment in the spring, these demobilized troops provided a potential military resource that stimulated a variety of schemes for resistance to the new Westminster régime. Though most of these plots were stillborn, the presence of this body of 'popish' troops nevertheless helped provide a context in which an armed insurrection in defence of Catholic interests at last seemed militarily feasible.[26]

In fact, three major plots seem to have developed separately in the course of 1641, only merging in a single unified design towards the end of that summer. The first, and possibly earliest, centred on the O'Neills, once the greatest of the Gaelic magnate clans of Ulster, whose fortunes had never recovered from the attainder and exile of the head of the clan, Hugh O'Neill, 2nd Earl of Tyrone, in the aftermath of the Nine Years' War.* Many of the O'Neills had accompanied Tyrone into exile, and eventually pursued careers as soldiers in the service of the Kings of Spain. One of the prominent members of the family remaining in Armagh, Sir Phelim O'Neill, had been keeping up, since the summer of 1640, an encoded correspondence with two of his cousins in Spanish service: Owen Roe O'Neill, Tyrone's nephew and the most prominent and perhaps accomplished of the Irish military commanders abroad; and John O'Neill, Tyrone's son, the commander of a regiment in Spanish service and the claimant of his father's forfeited earldom. These

---

* The Nine Years' War (1594–1603), also known as 'Tyrone's Rebellion', was the major challenge to English rule in Ireland mounted during the reign of the Tudors. At various points, the war was waged over the whole kingdom, but its principal theatre and the heartland of the revolt was Ulster, to the north. Before the wars of the 1590s, Ulster had been the only one of Ireland's four provinces to be almost completely outside English rule. In consequence, it was also the most Gaelic part of the island, dominated by the heads of the Irish clans, the O'Neills and the O'Donnells. After their defeat and surrender in 1603, relatively generous terms were granted the vanquished lords and they were regranted their lands under English law. Indeed, one of the rebel leaders, Rory O'Donnell (the younger brother of the clan chief and fellow rebel, Hugh Roe O'Donnell) was granted a peerage by James I – as 1st Earl of Tyrconnell – on the new king's accession to the English throne. However, after Tyrone, Tyrconnell and the other Gaelic lords left Ireland in 1607 for the Continent, in the hope of raising forces for a second insurrection, the lands of Tyrone and Tyrconnell and their followers were declared forfeit to the Crown. The policy of plantation which followed – granting confiscated lands to British 'under-takers', often absentee proprietors who sent English and Scottish tenants to work their newly acquired Ulster lands – inevitably aroused deep resentment among the expropriated Irish. By the 1630s, the British settler population in Ulster stood at around 20,000.

furtive communications gradually came to provide the basis for the involvement of Irish officers serving on the Continent, as what began as yet another
plot by the O'Neills to regain their lost estates in Ulster merged with more
advanced and politically ambitious plans for a rising in Ireland towards the
end of 1641.[27]

Of these plans to overthrow the current English government in Ireland,
the most important also originated among with the Ulster Irish. Its contrivers
were Rory O'More, an Armagh landowner who had lost out through the
'New English' plantations in Ulster, and Connor Maguire, the heavily
indebted 2nd Lord Maguire, a man who also had close links to the
O'Neills.[28]* The origins of this plot went back to the opportunity first
provided by England's defeat in 1640 at the hands of the Scots. Meeting
with Lord Maguire in February 1641, Rory O'More persuaded him that,
with the English thus weakened, and preoccupied with reaching a settlement
with the Covenanters, there was a moment – unlikely to be repeated – for
military resistance to English rule. Maguire agreed, and over the following
months further support was enlisted. Encouraged by the possibilities afforded
by the soon-to-be-demobilized Irish army ('all Irishmen [that is, Gaelic Irish]
and well armed'), a rising was tentatively planned for early in the winter of
1641, when weather conditions would make it difficult for the English to
ship forces across the Irish Sea to suppress it. In the meantime, however, it
was decided to do nothing until the Irish officers serving in Catholic armies
abroad had first been sounded out.[29]

As these plans progressed in Ulster, the various conspiracies acquired a
third strand in the Spanish Netherlands. Sir Phelim O'Neill's correspondent,
the exiled Irish officer Owen Roe O'Neill, had also spotted the possibilities
afforded by the 8,000 Irish troops, and he sought the assistance of allies at
the Whitehall court to bring these demobilized forces under his own control.
His key contact at Westminster was his kinsman, Daniel O'Neill, an officer
in the king's army (indeed, involved in the English Army Plot of May 1641)
and a man on familiar terms with Queen Henriette Marie. Around mid April,
Owen Roe O'Neill decided to act. He despatched one of his own captains,
Con O'Neill (Daniel's brother), to obtain a licence from the king to raise
men in Ireland out of Strafford's former army. The pretext was to be that
they were to serve as mercenaries in Flanders. In reality, the recruits were
intended to be kept in Ireland, ready to form the nucleus of a future rebel
army.

If Charles or, more likely, the queen became involved in these plots
(something that can neither be definitively confirmed nor entirely ruled out),
this was one possible moment when such involvement may have been
solicited. Daniel O'Neill, the conspirators' main contact at Whitehall, was
an accomplished operator at court and had a sophisticated understanding of

* Connor Maguire's title was more correctly the 2nd Lord Enniskillen, but he was almost
invariably styled 'Lord Maguire' by contemporaries. Lord Maguire's mother, Rose O'Neill,
was the niece of the rebel 2nd Earl of Tyrone.

the objectives, personalities and (from his perspective) pernicious effect of the Westminster Junto.[30]

On the Irish side, the dynastic continuities between the insurrection of the 1590s and that planned for 1641 are striking. The leaders of these plots in 1641 were, for the most part, the Gaelic Irish leaders of the Nine Years' War at one or two generations' remove, with Maguire and almost all the O'Neills having close blood ties with Hugh O'Neill, Earl of Tyrone, the most powerful and effective of the Ulster rebels during that earlier Elizabethan revolt.

But if continuities of lineage were apparent on the Irish side, they were no less marked on the English. Just as the would-be Irish insurrectionists of 1641 were the descendants of the rebels of the 1590s, so their prospective adversaries on the English side in 1641 also shared strong dynastic associations with that earlier phase in the English struggle for mastery in Ireland.[31] News of the Earl of Leicester's appointment as Lord Lieutenant – the development that gave the Junto direct influence over the future government of Ireland – reached Dublin around early June 1641, further heightening fears within Ireland's Catholic communities. For Leicester was the grandson of one of the most ferocious of the Elizabethan viceroys, Sir Henry Sidney, a man famed for his 'scorched-earth' policies towards Catholic dissent. As Lord Maguire noted, Leicester's promotion created apprehensions of 'the suppressing of our religion, ... it being, as was said, very confidently reported that the Scottish army did threaten never to lay down arms until an uniformity of religion were [established] in the three kingdoms and the Catholic religion suppressed'.[32] Fears that there were serious plans afoot at Westminster for the suppression of Irish Catholicism can only have been intensified by the appointment, in August, of the Earl of Essex as Lord General[33] (the son of one Elizabethan viceroy of Ireland) and by the new-found prominence at Westminster of the Earl of Newport (the son of another Elizabethan viceroy), as Master of the Ordnance and Constable of the Tower of London. In August 1641, as the plans for a new Irish insurrection were reaching maturity, control of Ireland's government, along with the mastery of military power in England, had come to be concentrated in the hands of men who were not only reputed to be part of the 'puritan faction' at Westminster, but who were also the heirs to the Elizabethan viceroys who had fought to bring Gaelic Ulster under English subjection in the first place. How widely this registered in Ireland is difficult to assess; but the conduits of information between Whitehall and Dublin operated efficiently, and by the summer of 1641 Ireland's Catholic élites had a clear, if not always particularly nuanced, understanding of how the 'puritan lords' had come to dominate politics at Westminster.

✷

Spurred on by the collapse of royal authority in England, progress with the various Irish conspiracies, from the summer of 1641, was rapid. Through the efforts of the O'Neills, and with the support of the Spanish ambassador, the royal licences for the recruitment of Irish troops, and by early June a number of the Irish colonels in Spanish service had arrived in Ireland to begin enlisting men. How many of these colonels were privy to the O'Neills'

plans for an insurrection remains an open question; Maguire later insisted
that only three – fewer than half those involved – were actually 'privy to the
action'.[34] But in the course of July and early August, contact was made
between the colonels and the Ulster conspirators, through Lord Maguire, in
the course of which their plans for a revolt in the north were extended to
include the seizure of Dublin Castle, the nerve centre of English government
in the kingdom. By the time the Irish Parliament adjourned in August 1641,
Maguire was convinced that its Catholic members had become so alarmed
by developments in England and Scotland that they were ready to undertake
some form of military action. They were resolved, he believed, to keep the
soldiers who had enlisted for Spain in Ireland and 'to arm them *in defence
of the king,* [he] being much injured both [by] England and Scotland then,
as they were informed, and to prevent any attempt against [the Catholic]
religion'.[35]

Inevitably, there were obstacles and changes of plan along the way. Support
for the revolt from the Pale, the area of the original English enclave around
Dublin, proved wavering, calling into doubt the viability of the scheme to
seize Dublin Castle. The foreign colonels also withdrew from the planned
revolt, discouraged, in part, by this failure of support from within the Pale.[36]
But these setbacks were offset by the enthusiasm for the proposed the insurrection within Ulster. In early September, an almost chance meeting between
Lord Maguire and Sir Phelim O'Neill brought together the two remaining
separate skeins of conspiracy: the O'More–Maguire plot in Ulster and the
Continental dimension provided by O'Neills. From the now defunct 'colonels'
plot' one strategic objective was retained, the seizure of Dublin Castle, and
at some point during the following weeks responsibility for its capture was
reassigned to Lord Maguire.

By 5 October 1641, when Lord Maguire and other leaders of the insurrection met at Loghross in Armagh to finalize their plans, the major elements
of their plan of action seem to have been in place. Their aim was for a swift
and, insofar as was possible, bloodless *coup d'état.* To effect this, there were
to be coordinated risings in Ulster, to seize the province's forts and places of
military strength, and in Dublin, to capture the castle and seat of government.
The two Lords Justices – Borlase and Parsons, believed to be in sympathy
with the puritan Junto in England – were to be arrested; and the Irish
Parliament was to be induced to declare for the king and against the Westminster Parliament.[37] Further refinements agreed at Loghross included decisions to imprison the English Protestant colonists, but to avoid killing them
except in cases of absolute necessity; and not to 'meddle with' the Scots
settlers, even though these were some of the greatest expropriators of Irish
land – presumably, in order to avoid causing problems for the king, who
was even then in Edinburgh seeking allies among the Scottish Covenanters.[38]
Saturday, 23 October was chosen as the date for the revolt.

Five days before the appointed day, on Monday, 18 October, Lord Maguire
left for Dublin to make the final preparations for his planned assault.[39]

*

Of course, not all the insurgents' motives can be ascribed to the provocations of the recently installed 'puritan Junto' at Westminster. An extended period of harvest failure and economic dislocation had already created a generation of rootless and underemployed young men in Ulster;[40] and the reported motives of those who were eventually to rise against English rule included grievances that went back decades, even centuries. Pre-eminent was a near-universal resentment against the English policy of 'plantation', under which thousands of the native Irish had been forcibly dispossessed, and their lands conveyed to Protestant English (and, in Ulster, Scottish) colonists.[41] Bitterness at the continued presence of the Protestant 'heresy' in Ireland was even more pervasive. Moreover, over the last thirty years, these antipathies had acquired a sharp new edge as Irish clergy and laymen studied in Catholic universities on the Continent and acquired, at first-hand, something of the confessional confidence and militancy of Counter-Reformation Catholicism.[42]

Yet there was also a prominent strand in the insurgents' justifications of their actions which stressed very much more recent events as their motive for revolt. Here, the critical development – difficult to quantify, but a recurrent theme in the depositions taken from those who had been witnesses to the opening stages of the revolt – was England's sudden transformation from a personal monarchy to a state under usurpation; or, as one of the Ulster insurgents put the point: 'The king [Charles I] was no king, for the [English] Parliament would not suffer him to do anything'.[43] This claim – or the variant that he had already been deposed – was to figure prominently in the apologias for the 1641 revolt.[44] In County Leitrim, for example, the leaders of the insurrection were to justify their actions on the grounds that '[the Parliament] had rebelled in England and crowned a new king, and [the Puritans] intended to take the [old] king prisoner'.[45] Similarly, in County Limerick, the rebel Mayor of Limerick City, Dominic Fanning, would drink the health of King Charles, insisting that resistance to the current English régime was 'for, and in behalf of, his Majesty, [and] alleging further that the English and [the] Protestant[s] were rebels, and they themselves [the insurgents] the true subjects'.[46] In this reading, it was the English grandees who had captured control of government who were in a state of revolt against their king. And after all that had happened in England over the previous twelve months, it was far from being an illogical view.

This widely held – and, in essence, perfectly valid – conviction that the king had ceased to wield any significant influence in English politics was also frequently twinned, in the recorded comments of the insurgents, with a bleak assessment of its implications for Irish Catholicism. 'The Puritan faction of the Parliament of England had set all Christendom on fire', argued one priest in County Monaghan;[47] and now that the 'Puritans' had prevailed in England, so the argument ran, it was only a matter of time before there was another English crusade to wipe out 'Popery' in Ireland, and expropriate yet more Catholic lands for plantation. From this perspective, restoring the king's prerogative – his personal authority as monarch – came to be seen as the one effective antidote to an aggressively Protestant parliamentary 'faction'. Indeed, among the most important figures who were to articulate this view was Sir Phelim O'Neill himself. He justified the insurrection, it was claimed, on the grounds that it was

> *for the preservation of his Majesty's prerogative* and their own religion and liberties against the Puritan faction in England, Scotland and Ireland, who intended (as the said Sir Phelim averred) to enact such laws whereby the inhabitants of Ireland should conform in religion [to Protestantism] ... and otherwise [were] to be deprived of life, liberty, and estates.[48]

This threat to religion, in turn, seems to have motivated a number of the Catholic clergy to become involved in canvassing support for the insurrection. In the weeks leading up to the revolt, in both Ulster and Leinster, Catholic clergy were reported to have encouraged 'a pre-emptive strike' against any attempt to erode Catholicism's already precarious position in Ireland.[49] One of the major inducements to such pre-emptive action were reports – usually wildly exaggerated, but often plausible in themselves – that the Westminster Parliament had already begun a systematic persecution of English Catholics.[50] Lord Gormanston, an Irish Catholic nobleman who had observed the new régime at Westminster at first hand, explained his reasons for supporting the revolt in similar, if more measured, terms. At Westminster, he argued,

> they teach that the laws of England, if they mention Ireland, are without doubt binding here; and the parliament has wholly assumed the management of the affaires of this kingdom as a right of preheminence due to it. And what may be expected from such zealous and fiery professors of an adverse religion, but the ruine and extirpation of ours?[51]

Such fears, of course, had long been a recurrent element in the experience of post-Reformation Ireland and had sustained many an insurrection in the intervening decades. Nevertheless, that they were focused so acutely and corrosively in the autumn of 1641 was in large measure a consequence of the sudden and far-reaching political changes that had taken place in Britain in general, and England in particular, over the previous twelve months.[52] It was not only renegade Ulstermen who believed, by the autumn of that year, that 'the king was no king, for the [English] Parliament would not suffer him to do anything'.[53] That was a view that was coming to be endorsed, during the summer of 1641, by substantial numbers of Charles's subjects in all three of his kingdoms. To this extent, the concerns that emerge most frequently among the leaders of the Irish revolt – the erosion of the king's prerogative, the triumph of Puritanism, the capture of government by an anti-monarchist cabal – formed part of a shared, three-kingdoms reaction against the triumph of the Commonwealthsmen at Westminster.

As Lord Maguire made his way to Dublin on Monday, 18 October, in readiness for the coming Saturday's assault on the castle, the political developments at Westminster, which had acted as precipitants for his own planned rebellion, were provoking almost equally strong reactions on the other side of the Irish Sea.

11. ENGLAND: OLIGARCHY AND PURITANISM

The twin evils of oligarchy (government by 'the few') and Puritanism (zealous, and sometimes doctrinally heterodox, Protestantism) were the dominant themes of England's plague-ridden late summer of 1641.[54] The charge of oligarchy against the Junto was perhaps unavoidable. England, by September 1641, was ruled by one of the most inbred cousinly cartels in its post-Conquest history, and the extent to which this small and highly cohesive patrician clique had monopolized executive power, to the almost total exclusion of the king, was bound to incite jealousies and resentments. Beyond the complaints of the obvious losers by this latest 'revolution' of Fortune's Wheel – the ousted office-holders like Cottington, Newcastle, and Bishop Juxon – there was also widespread muttering against the 'closed shop' that had come to characterize government, as power and decision-making had shifted from the relatively accessible world of the Whitehall court to the 'cabinet councils' and 'private juntos' in the town houses of the reformist grandees. No sooner had the two Houses risen for the recess on 9 September than reports started to trickle back to Westminster from the constituencies of members' complaints 'that everything in the Parliament [had] been guided by the sole judgement of a few individuals, who [have] boldly taken in hand the reins of the government'. Even parliamentary debate, it was alleged, had been muzzled by the managerial guile of the 'few': in Parliament, 'this time, there ha[d] not been that freedom of speech which is traditional and which has always been the rule in the past'.[55]

But if the charge of oligarchy was the almost inevitable concomitant of the Junto lords' success in the acquisition of office, their association with militant Puritanism was in large measure a problem of their own devising – and relatively recent devising at that. For, right from the start of the parliamentary session, most of the leading Junto grandees revealed a highly politique sense of how religious controversy could undermine their popularity, both in Westminster and in the world beyond.[56] To retain that good opinion in matters religious, the Junto grandees had repeatedly drawn back from initiating – and, still more, from following through with – major items of 'further reformation'. Hence, the singular unsuccess of Root-and-Branch abolition of bishops: from the Junto leaders' efforts to defuse the question in February 1641, lest it obstruct the passage of the Triennial Act, through to the cynical abandonment of the legislation in early August, after months of debate, when it ceased to be a necessary precondition of the Scots' ratification of the Treaty of Union. Hence, too, D'Ewes's suggestion, on 9 September 1641, just before the Parliament rose for the recess, that they should issue a declaration explaining why it was that secular reforms and the 'great business of disbanding the Armies did keepe us from looking into religion all this time'.[57]

Few doubted, though some privately questioned, the godly zeal of Junto grandees such as Saye, Warwick and Brooke. But until September 1641, it was difficult for their critics to point to any single provocative action that had posed a threat to the peace of the Church. All that changed rapidly in the aftermath of the failure of the Ordinance against Superstitious Images and Innovations on 9 September, and its subsequent issuing as a temporary order of the Commons alone.[58] This time, far from distancing himself, Warwick appears to have taken a prominent role in encouraging the Commons to act unilaterally. And the contemporaneous publication of the list of the peers who had protested against the ordinance's obstructers placed their names in the public domain[59] – so much so that, by the end of the month, Edward Nicholas was referring to Warwick, Mandeville and their allies under the new soubriquet of 'the partie of the Protesters', a designation that seems to have included their Commons allies as well.[60]

Imprecise in its drafting, ambiguous as to its application, and of dubious validity at law, the resulting September Order against Superstitious Innovations was a recipe for 'parish broils'. Rails around communion tables were to be dismantled; altar steps razed, without consideration of when they had been introduced; and superstitious images were to be pulled down and destroyed. Implementation of the order fell to the Commons Recess Committee,[61] under the chairmanship of Pym, a body which met twice-weekly in the Exchequer Chamber, near Westminster Hall. Yet despite the sense of urgency apparent in the debates of 8 and 9 September, the Junto grandees proceeded, at least initially, with their habitual caution. Printed copies were made of the September Order; but for distribution and publication, the Commons had relied on its own members 'to publish this order in their severall Counties, Cities, and Boroughs'. In practice, this gave Commons-men opposed to the order the discretion to prevent publication by simple inaction. Moreover, as the Commons' clerks had no provision for bulk mailing of the printed order to the House's more than five hundred members, they were reliant on the members themselves taking copies of the order back to their constituencies as they departed for the recess. But as the total number of Commons-men remaining at Westminster on the eve of the recess was only around ninety members[62] (less than twenty per cent of the total membership), this virtually killed any chance that the order would reach more than a small fraction of parishes. Four-fifths of Commons-men had long since left plague-ridden London and were therefore not around to receive their copies of the order.[63]

With regard to the printing of the 'Declaration of the Commons in Parliament', passed on 9 September, explaining why the Commons had acted unilaterally, the story is sorrier still. Despite an order of the Commons, that same day, that 'this declaration shall be *forthwith* printed and published',[64] nothing whatever was done forthwith. In fact, there was a delay of almost three weeks before any effort was made to print this declaration or to distribute the original order nationwide. Not until 28 September did the Commons' Recess Committee actually command the printing of the Declaration of 9 September (the justification for the Commons' action), and begin a concerted campaign to have this and the original 8 September Order against Innovations distributed 'to every Parish in this Kingdom'.[65]

The reasons for this three-week delay – or, for that matter, its sudden ending – are far from clear. One possible explanation is that the Junto grandees were trying to avoid ecclesiastical controversy in the three weeks leading up to London's mayoral election, which was held on 28 September, the same day that the Commons Recess Committee finally gave the order to publish. An alternative, but possibly complementary, explanation is offered by Edward Nicholas in his despatch to the king written the next day. The 'partie of the Protesters', explained Nicholas – his term for Warwick, Mandeville and the other Junto grandees – had been emboldened by the news, just arrived from Edinburgh, that the Hamilton–Argyll faction had forced the king to concede parliamentary involvement in future appointments of Scotland's great officers of state. This party of 'the Protesters' was

> observed to be here, of late, very jocund and cheerefull, and [this] is conceaved to arise from advertisements out of Scotland, from whose acc'ons and successes they intend (as I heare) to take a patterne for their proceedings heere.[66]

Such cheerfulness among the Junto was readily explicable, for by mid September, the king's attempts to raise an effective party in Scotland appeared to be destined to failure. Far from 'crushing' Argyll and Hamilton – the original purpose of his journey to Edinburgh – he had been forced to confirm them in power more securely than ever before.

Even so, the belated decision to publish the 8 September Order throughout the nation can be explained in terms other than a sudden access of over-confidence. By the end of the month, it was clear that in many parishes the smashing of altar steps and superstitious images had begun without waiting for receipt of the order's printed text. Reform-minded ministers and con-gregations had acted on their own initiative, sometimes going much further in their destructive zeal than the framers of the order had intended. The experience of the London parish of St Mary Woolchurch exemplifies the problem. One of the churchwardens, a Mr Herringe, acting without apparent reference to the text of the order, had set about removing 'brasse Inscriptions' on tombs, and defacing statues in which the deceased was 'in the posture of praying' – neither of which had been proscribed in the Commons' Order.[67] Outraged parishioners duly brought their complaint to the Recess Committee, pointing out that 'a very faire windowe and other Emblems of antiquity' had been defaced *'without warrant'*, and the committee responded by giving orders for the offender to be brought before it.[68] Four days later, the over-zealous churchwarden found himself roundly condemned by the Commons' Committee. 'This man's indiscretion', complained one committee-man, 'had brought a great scandal upon the howse of Commons, as if wee meant to deface *all* Antiquities ... yet wee had speciallie provided that noe tombs should be medled withall.'[69]

A much more widely publicized 'indiscretion' was perpetrated – again before the September 8 Order had been generally circulated in print – by the godly Sir Robert Harley, one of the few truly committed iconoclasts in the House of Commons, and, ironically, one of the Commons-men involved in the order's drafting. In a notorious incident at Wigmore, Herefordshire, on 27 September 1641, Harley had ordered a stone cross 'beaten in pieces, even to dust, with a sledge[hammer], and then laid it in the foot-path to be trodden on in the churchyard'. Harley's local standing as patron of the living was such as to silence most opposition, and he went on his destructive way, removing other 'scandalous pictures' in other parts of the West Country.[70] Yet the destruction of Wigmore Cross was an example of how the Recess Committee's reluctance to order a general distribution of the September 8 Order may have encouraged the 'indiscretions' they were apparently anxious to prevent. Had Harley's opponents had the actual text of the order, they could have pointed out that only 'crucifixes' – that is, crosses which had a sculpted figure of the crucified Christ – came within its remit; there was nothing to sanction the destruction of crosses per se.[71] Indeed, when a similarly indiscriminate group of Northamptonshire iconoclasts attacked Isham Cross, pleading an 'order of Parliament' as their authority, their opponents were able to point out that this applied 'only for crucifixes' and the activists, in consequence, faced prosecution for riot.[72]

Against this background of sporadic local activism, often going further than either House of Parliament had permitted, the Commons' Recess Committee's apparent change of heart at the end of September – its very belated decision to attempt a general distribution of the Order against Innovations 'to every Parish in this Kingdom' – seems to have been motivated more by a desire to curb godly zeal (by stipulating clearly what could and could not be removed), than by a wish to encourage a nationwide orgy of image-smashing. By the time printed copies of the new Recess Committee Order of 28 September and the accompanying *Declaration of the Commons*[73] against innovations reached the parishes and were read out in the pulpits (Sunday, 3 October would have been the first time this could have occurred), many of the worst excesses had already been perpetrated.

This reading of the Recess Committee's motives would seem to accord with the committee's own guarded attitude towards the order's enforcement. In fact, other than its order to print and disperse the original Commons' Order and the accompanying Declaration (and doing so very belatedly), there seems to have been no centrally directed campaign of enforcement whatsoever. Unlike the Tudor crusades to level chancels and take down superstitious images, no commissioners were dispatched by the Recess Committee to see that the order was carried out. Nor were any specific sanctions imposed in the event of non-compliance.[74] And though accurate assessment is hampered by the incompleteness of the Recess Committee's records, it would appear from what does survive that almost the only occasions where it became involved in the implementation of the order were instances when disputing parties in the parishes petitioned for arbitration before it.[75] Indeed, the Recess Committee was just as likely to engage in parish peace-making, trying to soothe angry tempers where clergy and congregations had clashed over the application of the new reforms, as it was to beat the drum for 'reform'. On one occasion, 'Master Pym' admonished both parson and parishioners 'to live lovingly together';[76] and churchwardens who went beyond the letter of what the order specifically allowed were liable to censure.[77]

Statesmanlike and responsible as all this may have been, it was wholly unable to prevent the impression being formed that the 'partie of the Protesters' and 'Master Pym' had licensed and encouraged religious anarchy. That association appears to have tainted the Junto's patrician grandees like Warwick, Essex and Mandeville as much as its leading figures in the Commons. Moreover, the parochial controversies of that autumn helped to bring upon them a double charge: that they were undermining royal authority in the state, as well as fostering puritan extremism within the Church (strikingly similar charges, in fact, to those circulating contemporaneously in Ireland against the 'faction' at Westminster).

The very style and typography of the Commons' (and Lords') Recess Committees' published orders provided the Junto's enemies with evidence of the Parliament's supposed usurpation of regal forms. Royal proclamations were usually issued in Gothic black-letter type, with the name of the king's printer prominent at the bottom of the printed sheet by way of authenticating the publication.[78] So it was with the orders and declarations issued during the parliamentary recess. These were issued not by any of the printers usually used by the House of Commons, but by the king's printer, and in Gothic black-letter type as though it were an act of Parliament or a royal proclamation. Indeed, the words 'Imprinted at London by Robert Barker Printer to the King's Most Excellent Majestie', in large letters at the bottom of the page, prompted contemporary wits to speculate on who this particular king might be – given that King Charles would have profoundly disapproved of both the letter and spirit of the new orders.[79]

They found the answer in the Commons' Recess Committee's printed Order of 28 September, distributed throughout the country, and accompanying the belatedly printed *Declaration of the Commons* of 9 September. On this Order of 28 September, the name 'John Pym' – added in his capacity as the Recess Committee's chairman – was juxtaposed conspicuously with the familiar words 'Imprinted ... by [the] Printer to the Kings most Excellent Majestie'.[80] As copies of the royal-looking order went into circulation in the first days of October, derisive references to the Recess Committee's chairman as 'King Pym' began doing the rounds at Westminster. Three days later, Edward Nicholas was repeating the joke to King Charles; and 'King Pym's' mocking soubriquet stuck.[81]

Ridicule the Junto leadership could deal with. However, where the printing of the 8 September Order harmed it most directly was in reinforcing, in the world beyond Westminster, the impression that the 'puritan faction' was responsible for what one contemporary called the 'too foule and irreligious tumults lately committed in the House of God, in too many places of the Kingdome'.[82] Just how many parishes in England were affected by 'irreligious tumults' in the summer of 1641 is a question that has so far defied accurate quantitative assessment.[83] Under the terms of the 8 September Order, the parochial clergy and their churchwardens were supposed to carry out the work of destroying communion rails, levelling raised chancels, and smashing superstitious images, in compliance with the Commons' demands. But who, if anyone, within the parish, would take the initiative to ensure that this was done was an open question; and in practice the matter fell to the regular competitors for influence within any parish – the minister, the parishioners, and (in most cases) the patron of the living – to decide whether the order was to be adopted or ignored. The potential for intra-parish conflict opened up by the new order was theoretically almost limitless, as puritan minorities could plead the authority of the order, if the reforms were opposed by either minister or patron, to act unilaterally in defiance of the parish's traditional social hierarchies.[84] In various parts of the country (though it is impossible to quantify how many), the order seems to have served as a licence to the more zealous godly to take the law into their own hands: to destroy images they regarded as superstitious, attack east-end altars and pull down rails as totems of popery, relics of Laud's 'conspiracy' to re-Catholicize the English Church. In some localities, there were parochial tussles – at times, flaring into outbreaks of violence – between godly iconoclasts and defenders of the status quo.[85] The confusion was compounded by the circulation during early September, at the behest of the vestigial king's party in the Lords, of their own order insisting that divine service should be conducted 'according to the law'.[86] 'Here in the Countrey', Lord Cottington reported from Wiltshire, it had bred 'no litle distraccon – at least, very much disorder; for every man makes use of [the two rival orders] according to their severall Palletts and humours.'[87]

More damaging still, however, for the reformist leadership at Westminster, was the way in which the 8 September Order seemed to associate the Junto's religious policy with a more general trend towards the collapse of order within the Church. Stories of the *Book of Common Prayer* being profaned; violence against ministers; laymen and heretics in the pulpits: all these abounded in the late summer of 1641 and were usually attributed, directly or indirectly, to the influence of the 'puritan faction' in Parliament. How numerous such incidents were in reality is again difficult to quantify, and perhaps beside the point. A 'few well-publicized incidents could produce a frenzy of righteous anxiety';[88] and in the prevailing atmosphere of moral panic, the effect of such stories appears to have been wholly disproportionate to either their likely numerical incidence or their intrinsic truth. One lurid exposé published in London in September claimed to have identified no less than twenty-nine sects – not merely common or garden variety Christian heretics, but also 'Mahometans' and assorted 'Saturnian' and 'Bacchanalian' pagans – active and proselytizing within the capital.[89]

Many of the sects mentioned in this tract were probably no more than figments of its author's febrile imagination. Yet there is little doubt that, by the autumn of 1641, London was the one city of the realm where puritan influence was strongest, and where the local implementation of the 8 September Order was probably the most zealous and widespread. News of the order travelled quickly by word of mouth, and handwritten copies were more readily available than anywhere else in the realm. Hence, as early as 24 September, Giustinian could report that, 'in those parishes where the Puritans prevail, the resolution of the lower House has been gladly adopted'.[90] In fact,

'Puritans' seem to have prevailed only in a minority of London parishes, probably no more than one parish in every four; but here, too, their perceived impact seems to have been out of all proportion to their actual effect.[91]* Indeed, to conservatives such as Thomas Wiseman, the City's Remembrancer, the parliamentary recess seemed to be a period when sectaries had been given a licence to run amok:

> The Brownists [Congregationalists] and other sectaries make such havock in oure churches by pulling downe of ancient monuments, glasse windows, and railes that theire madness is intolerable. I thinke it will be thought blasphemye shortly to name Jesus Christ, for it is already forbidden [by the Commons' 8 September Order] to bow at his name.[92]

Instances of disorder were sufficiently widespread to fulfil stereotypical expectations of what happened when Puritans acquired political power: intolerant religious zeal brought in its train a still worse malaise, the disruption of conventional social relations. An anti-puritan reaction was in the making. 'I am credibly assured', Nicholas advised the king at the beginning of October, 'that the Citty of London growes very weary of the insolent carriage of the Schismaticks.'[93]

These developments had a marked impact not only on the standing of the Junto leaders within the capital, but also on the reception of the broader political changes which they had brought into being: and, above all, the shift in power away from the king to a powerful, but still informally constituted, aristocratic council. For once, it was not just Charles I and his martinet-like archbishop who seemed to be the disrupters of the peace of the English Church.[94] As one of Secretary Vane's correspondents informed him, 'the confidence of the late prevailing party unmask'd them soe fast that their deformity appeared, and their lovers fell off'.[95]

This falling off in support for the 'late prevailing party' was registered perhaps most starkly in the London mayoral election of 28 September, which

---

* The City of London had a total of 110 parishes (including the thirteen that were outside its walls, but nevertheless within the jurisdiction of the City); Westminster ten parishes; and Holborn had the important (and well documented) parish of St Giles in the Fields. A survey of the surviving churchwardens' accounts for these metropolitan parishes (eighty-five sets of accounts survive) suggests that around a third of London parishes experienced some kind of response to the 8 September Order. Of the eighty-five documented parishes, twenty-nine record changes: eighteen note instances of images being defaced or removed; fifteen that communion tables or communion rails had been taken down or removed; four that the chancel had been levelled; another four that inscriptions had been removed or defaced; and two that crosses (probably, but not certainly, crucifixes) had been taken away. Obviously, there are evidential problems, in that it cannot be assumed that all iconoclastic activity would be recorded in the churchwardens' accounts. On the other hand, given that most such interventions required expenditure, however limited, there is a presumption that the surviving accounts are a relatively full record (where accounts survive at all) of what actually occurred. On this tally, therefore the number of London parishes experiencing image-smashing was probably around one in every four.

produced a massive swing against the 'Puritans'. Richard Gurney, a loyal 'king's-party' man, was elected as Lord Mayor notwithstanding strong opposition from the pro-Junto lobby in the City – an outcome that would have been unthinkable even three or four months earlier.[96] As in 1640, the candidate of the 'Puritans' – as the opposing party were dubbed – was Thomas Soame, the President of the Artillery Company. This time, however, his supporters 'were overcome with hisses'.[97]

*

There was more to the Junto's waning popularity, however, than the over-zealous implementation of godly reform. Taxation was one widespread griev-ance. For during the summer and autumn of 1641, England – which had been relatively lightly taxed during the years of Personal Rule – was suddenly confronted by demands for subsidies (the traditional tax on landed income) that was more than double anything that had been imposed before. Blame for another equally resented financial burden – the poll tax, imposed regardless of income, according to social status, to meet the cost of the Covenanter army – was also laid at the Junto's door. 'Parliament', noted Giustinian at the beginning of the recess, 'is losing the great credit which it once enjoyed universally, since it appears that, instead of bringing relief, it has imposed expenses and burdens on the subjects.'[98] Essex, Warwick, and Saye – the peers who (as was now widely rumoured) had invited the Scots into England – formed a natural focus for the taxpayer's hostility, a resentment that could be merged easily with the latest wave of popular anti-Puritanism generated by the Commons' order to root out 'innovations'.[99] The Junto, with its godly agenda and obvious closeness to the Covenanter Scots, was easily depicted as a group of self-interested usurpers: a high-taxing, self-interested, and religiously heterodox clique; and with an approach to government as authoritarian as anything that had been experienced during the days of Caroline 'tyranny'. By October 1641, even the Long Acre prostitutes – the 'sisters of the scabbard', who plied their trade on the outskirts of fashionable Covent Garden – were said to be complaining that the new régime was bad for trade.[100]

That month also saw the appearance in London of a new and altogether more menacing constituency of resentment: several hundred officers and soldiers from the recently disbanded 'northern army', the veterans of the forces Charles had raised in 1640 to suppress the Covenanter revolt. During late September 1641, these 'reformadoes' (as they became known) were a loud and often lawless presence within the capital. To confront the menace they posed, a joint sitting of the Lords' and Commons' Recess Committees on 5 October ordered that all 'Officers and Souldiers of the late disbanded Armie' were to leave the capital forthwith 'upon pain of ... Imprisonment'.[101] Sir John Conyers, the Lieutenant-General of Horse during the war of 1640, was a particular focus of the reformadoes' hostility, but there was equal animus towards 'my Lord General' – the 'puritan' Earl of Holland – who was alleged to have short-changed the cavalry troopers at their disbandment.[102]

On the king's side, Edward Nicholas initially viewed these reformadoes as a liability, simply another potential source of disorder.[103] Yet it was not to be long before less scrupulous minds than his discerned in these resentments the potential for another 'army plot', and one which, because of the presence of the soldiers in London, might work far more effectively than any of its predecessors. In these earlier plots, the fear had been that the king's supporters would 'bring the army south' from Yorkshire, to overawe or forcibly dissolve the Parliament.[104] Ironically, instead of removing the possibility of further plots, the disbandment of the army during August and September had, in fact, partly achieved one of the original plotters' central aims: it had brought to London a force of cavalry troopers and infantrymen sufficiently large, and sufficiently resentful, to cause the Junto serious concern. Essex, another of the reformadoes' *bêtes noires*, was taking no chances. Before Parliament reconvened on 20 October, he used his authority as Lord General South of the Trent to establish a substantial guard on the two Houses to foil any planned attack. Not for the last time in the 1640s, the presence of a large body of recently disbanded and discontented soldiers in the capital seemed to provide the wherewithal for a pro-royalist *coup d'état*.

*

These resentments were soon being openly expressed. In the first week of October, just as the disbanded officers were being ordered out of London, a series of anonymous placards started appearing on street-side walls in London, naming the Junto leaders. These placards, it was reported, 'boldly attack[ed]' those who had taken

> the leading part in the past actions [of the Parliament], accusing them of being the authors of seditious deliberations, traitors to the king, the kingdom, *and the nobility* – and of having conspired with the Scots to the hurt of the people here [in England].[105]

And if there was any ambiguity in this first set of posters as to who were the objects of these attacks, it was dispelled in the series that went up three weeks later, timed to coincide with the resumption of the parliamentary session on 20 October. In these, in which 'divers of the Nobility, and Peers of the realme, were much traduced and scandal[iz]ed';[106] or, as another observer put it, they attacked the 'Puritans and their leaders'.[107] It was the godly peers – the likes of Essex and Warwick, Mandeville and Saye – who were sharing the blame for the godly excesses of the autumn.

Such public denunciations mark an important turning point in the fortunes of the Junto. For the first time since the opening of the Parliament, the traitors against the kingdom were no longer by common consent the 'evil counsellors' of Charles I: the likes of Strafford, Windebank, and Laud. There was now a new set of villains: the aristocratic grandees of 1640, the godly clique that had been behind the Petition of the Twelve Peers, and which had been at the centre of the 'prevailing party' ever since. Moreover, this new critique of the 'prevailing party' had the advantage of tapping into a stream of popular hostility towards Puritanism that ran at least as deep as popular anti-Popery, and carried its own set of stereotypical assumptions: that Puritans were killjoys, hypocrites, exploiters of religion as a mask (or, in one of Charles's favourite phrases, 'a vizard') for their secular ambitions.[108] As memories of Charles's involvement in the Army Plots started to fade, it was becoming possible to portray the high-taxing, Puritan-infiltrated Junto as perhaps an even greater threat to the traditional order than the worst of Charles's supposedly 'evil counsellors'.[109]

These October street-side placards are also, perhaps, the first signs of an attempt to create a 'popular' royalist movement within the capital. By their very nature, they were addressed to a non-élite, demotic, urban audience. And they appear to have had an effect. Libellous, unattributable, and (in documentary terms) evanescent, they formed part of a contraband political culture which attempted to explain the political manoeuvrings of the aristocratic grandees to a mass audience, in starkly simplified, black-and-white terms. As Edward Nicholas had observed, 'the people's good opinion' had hitherto been the Junto's 'anchor-hold and only interest'.[110] And as 20 October approached – the date for the resumption of the parliamentary session – there were clear signs that this anchor was beginning to slip.

III. WHITEHALL: THE BEGINNINGS OF A 'KING'S PARTY'

The first suggestion that there might be organized parliamentary resistance to the Junto comes from the king himself, at the beginning of October, in response to the news that Mandeville, Pym and others had been meeting in Chelsea to make preparations for the forthcoming session. 'It were not amiss', Charles wrote to Edward Nicholas, the Westminster bureaucrat who was coordinating his affairs in London, 'that some of my servaunts met lykewais to countermynd their Plots.' For further directions, Nicholas was instructed to take advice from the queen, a far more combative and, in some respects, more astute political tactician than her husband.[111]

The instruction to 'countermine' the Junto's plots proved to be Edward Nicholas's making. Shrewd, discreet, and formidably industrious, he had spent over a quarter of a century at court in various clerkly capacities, without ever achieving a major preferment at court. In 1641, at the relatively advanced age of forty-eight, he was still merely a Clerk of the Privy Council (a relatively poorly remunerated post which he had held since 1627).[112] But with the two Secretaries of State absent from Whitehall – Windebank having fled to Paris, and Vane reluctantly accompanying the king on his travels – Charles needed a dependable secretary to manage his affairs at court, and keep him abreast of political developments in England. Nicholas seems to have acquired the role almost by default. For once, however, Charles made a fortuitous choice. Always finding it easier to confide in his 'menial servants' than in the proud grandees of the Privy Council, Charles quickly developed a relationship of confidence and trust with Nicholas, coming to depend on him to devise and implement much of his English strategy during his absence in Edinburgh. Certain developments were already running in Charles's favour: the reaction against religious 'anarchy' and the unpopularity of the massively increased tax burden of the previous twelve months not least. But that there came to be an effective 'king's party', ready to obstruct the Junto in the resumed parliamentary session, was in large part attributable to the efforts of Edward Nicholas. His was nothing less than a concerted campaign to rebuild the king's political credit in England.

Learning something from the Junto's own habits of parliamentary management, Nicholas set about the creation of a royalist caucus at Westminster. He was under no illusions as to how difficult it would be to challenge the Junto in the Commons. His overriding priority, therefore, was to regain control of the House of Lords. Once that was achieved, the king could at least block, even if he could not wholly prevent, what Nicholas predicted would be the central item on the Junto's new legislative programme: stripping the king of his prerogative power to name the great officers of state – just as Argyll and Hamilton had recently done in Scotland.[113] To stop this, Nicholas identified two groups: roughly a dozen 'well-affected' lay peers (a number of whom had taken part in the ambush of 9 September, which had prevented the Ordinance against Innovations passing the House of Lords), and an almost equal number of bishops. On 8 October, having cleared his plan with the king, Nicholas mustered all his courtly tact and wrote to the eleven lay peers on his party list.

'My very good Lord', he began,

> I have receaved cammaunds from his Majestie to write to your Lordshipp, in his name, not to fayle to attend the first day of the next meetinge [of the Lords] in Parliament, which wilbe the 20th of this moneth [of October]. I know your Lordshipp's good affeccon to the service of his Majestie and the Publique would prompt you to have bene here att that tyme without any remembrance [reminder], but now that your Lordshipp understands his Majestie's desire and expectacon of your presence then, I am confident you wilbe the more dilliegent not to fayle it.

To ensure secrecy, he added delicately:

> I am likewise commanded to entreate your Lordshipp not to [let it] be knowne that you have received any significaccon of his Majestie's pleasure to this effect, least other lords should take excepcon that they have not had the like.

His target-list included three of the peers who had been forced out of office by the Junto – Newcastle (ex-Governor of the Prince of Wales), Cottington (ex-Chancellor of the Exchequer), and Coventry (ex-Lord Keeper) – as well as a number of former Junto allies, men who had been alienated by the radicalism of its political programme and the scale of its usurpation of regal power, notably Bath, Seymour (Hertford's younger brother), and the eternally devious Bristol.[114]

The key to the plan's success, however, was the participation of the bishops.[115] With the bench of bishops at full strength able to muster twenty-six votes, the episcopate constituted around a fifth of the Lords' total membership; and with attendances in the autumn of 1641 hovering between forty and fifty, even as few as ten or twelve 'well-affected' bishops – combined with an equal number of royalist peers – would be sufficient to block any future legislation that was uncongenial to the king. This was precisely the coalition that Nicholas set about creating. His key ally was one of the little noticed victims of the recent 'reformation of counsel': the Privy Councillor, Bishop of London and former Lord Treasurer of England, William Juxon.[116] Threatened with impeachment at the beginning of the Parliament, Juxon had prudently relinquished the Treasurership, thus escaping the persecution that had attended some of his former patrons. But he remained emphatically a king's man,[117] and, in Nicholas's new campaign, became an informal 'party whip' to the episcopal bench. At Nicholas's suggestion, also on 8 October, Juxon wrote 'to all the bishops which are well-affected', giving them just under a fortnight's notice that their attendance was expected at the resumed parliamentary session.[118]

To ensure that the episcopal bench would be at full strength, Charles moved to fill the five vacancies that had occurred since the Parliament's opening. Consultations with Nicholas and Juxon dragged on through the first half of October, but the new appointees were ready for announcement in time for the resumed session. Politically, the list was a masterstroke, as all the five new bishops were men of impeccably Protestant credentials: clergy, in Nicholas's phrase, 'of whome there is not the least suspic'on of favouring the Popish partie'.[119] (Indeed, one of the newly appointed bishops, Ralph Brownrigg of Salisbury, was married to Pym's niece.)[120] Whether they would follow Juxon's lead remained to be seen. What was certain, however, was that Charles had powerfully strengthened the bishops' collective prestige – in effect, proofing them against the charge of Popery – at precisely the moment he was about to call on them to act as a political caucus.

This mobilization of the 'well-affected' in the House of Lords marks the beginning of the creation of an organized royalist party. For the first time since the political crisis of the summer of 1640, Charles was not merely reacting to events, but trying to shape them. And already thoughts were turning, within the king's camp, to the delectable prospect of revenge. 'I wish that those who have been the cause of these miserable distraccons in his Majestie's dominions may feele the weight of punishment which they deserve', Nicholas wrote to Secretary Vane on 9 October – the day after he had dispatched the letters to 'whip in' a caucus of royalist peers. 'I doubt not but that they will doe [so] in due time.'[121]

What made these prospects for a royalist revival in England all the more promising was that the king believed, by the first days of October 1641, that he was also on the brink of success in Scotland. Around 5 October, he wrote to the queen to assure her that he would be back in London by 29 October, well in time to take command of the resumed parliamentary session – a firm promise which suggests that the king now had a clear sense of when, and therefore presumably how, events in Edinburgh would be brought to a conclusion.[122] Further evidence that Charles had a particular conclusion in mind for his Scottish adventure is provided by his notes on Nicholas's most recent

Above: Archibald Campbell, 8th Earl and (from November 1641) 1st Marquess of Argyll: the most powerful aristocratic magnate north of the Tweed. His dominance of the Covenanter government in Scotland prompted a series of conspiracies against him – most notably the plot in October 1641, framed almost certainly with the king's approbation, to seize, and possibly kill, Argyll and his then ally, Hamilton, at the Palace of Holyrood House.

Left: James Hamilton, 3rd Marquess of Hamilton, the highly Anglicized Scottish grandee who served as Master of the Horse – a post traditionally associated with the royal favourite – to Charles I. Though he was later to side with the king, in 1641 Hamilton became one of the Junto leaders' most powerful allies in their quest to create a permanent union between the English and Scottish commonwealths.

Facing page: the fallen courtier – Philip Herbert, 4th Earl of Pembroke, wearing his riding cloak, emblazoned with the Garter star. As the Lord Chamberlain, he had been the senior officer of the king's Household, and had spent almost four decades in royal service. But his warm support for the Junto leadership and active encouragement of the crowds which gathered in May 1641 to demand Strafford's attainder were punished by Charles with dismissal from office. Parliament moved for his appointment as Lord Steward of the Household, by way of consolation. But the king's decision to appoint his twenty-nine year-old cousin, the Duke of Richmond and Lennox (*right*), instead, closed the door to any possibility of a reconciliation.

Below: English Protestant forces going to war to suppress the Catholic insurrection in Ireland in the autumn of 1641. These soldiers' almost jaunty demeanour was belied by the realities of the Irish war, which was marked by acts of savagery on both sides.

Above, left: Robert Ker, Earl of Roxburgh. A veteran of the Jacobean court, this bellicose and scheming Scottish grandee followed the king back to London in November 1641 after the disastrous royal sojourn in Edinburgh, and was the only nobleman to accompany the king to the Parliament, in January 1642, during the attempt to arrest the five members. Though later condemned as a warmonger, Lord Digby (*above right*), opposed the advocates of a violent coup d'état, making a plausible bid, in the last weeks of 1641, to reconstruct a moderate court party around the Junto leaders who had earlier tried to save the life of the Earl of Strafford: Saye, Hertford, his own father Bristol, and even Pym.

Charles's instructions of January 1642 to the Attorney-General, Sir Edward Herbert, for the impeachment of t 'traitors' of 1640. The cancelled name on the fifth line is Viscount Mandeville's reflecting Charles's last-minute decision – reportedly at Digby's insistence – to accuse him of treason with the five Commons-men (hence the king's change of 'fyve' to 'six' in the first line). Essex, Warwick and Saye were reported to have been included a second round of treason prosecutions, to have followed once the first series of arrests had been completed.

…e stereotype of the debauched Cavalier: this anti-royalist polemic of early 1642 makes a direct connection …ween the 'Cavaliers', who came to prominence as the king's armed entourage in November-December 1641, …d Sir John Suckling's 'Roaring Boyes', the soldiers of fortune recruited in May to attempt the seizure of the …wer and Strafford's release. Cavalier wantonness – in the form of gambling, smoking, drinking, and whoring …as already being set up as the antithesis to parliamentarian 'godliness'.

Hampton Court Palace, with the royal barge in the foreground, painted around 1640. Charles fled here, with the royal family, on 10 January 1642, after the final collapse of royal authority in the capital.

The Earl of Essex as Parliament's protector: a medal struck, *c.* 1642–43 as a badge of political allegiance. In a possible allusion to his claim to the Constableship, a medieval office with Dictator-like powers, Essex bears on of the Swords of State from the coronation regalia. From its appearance, this would seem to be the Curtana, of Sword of Mercy. If so, Charles would immediately have recognized the allusion: at his own coronation in 162 Essex had carried this same symbol of the sovereign's power. The Latin inscription on the medal's obverse read 'For religion, law, the king, [and] Parliament'.

Opposite page: The Stuart kingdoms mobilized for war: a detail of Wenzel Hollar's depiction of the conflicts Britain and Ireland as part of a pan-European struggle against Catholic Habsburg power (represented by the eagle partially superimposed on the map of England).

Sed nulla potentia longa est.

Rex Bellicus: Charles I painted in the black armour that he was to wear at Edgehill, in October 1642, the first great set-piece battle of the English Civil War. Despite his slight physical stature, the king nevertheless cultivated an image of himself as a powerful warrior-prince. In the course of a reign that spanned twenty-four years, he was at war – against the French, the Spanish, or his own rebellious subjects – for all but nine of them.

bulletin, made that same day. Responding to a suggestion from Nicholas about the arrangements for a possible 'royal entry' into London on his return, Charles hinted strongly that there was about to be a sudden resolution in Edinburgh:

> When ye shall see littell Will: Murray, then ye shall know certainlie, not only of my returne, *but also how all will end heer* [in Edinburgh].

A few lines on, commenting on Nicholas's report of the Junto's 'jocund and cheerefull' state as a result of the Argyll–Hamilton faction's successes in Scotland, Charles added:

> I belive, before all be done, that they will not have much great cause of joy.[123]

Perhaps the most significant reference here is to 'littell' Will Morray, and the king's hints, first, that Morray would be leaving (or possibly would *have* to leave) Scotland before him; and, second, that Morray knew – or would know – how 'all will end' in Edinburgh. For the Scottish-born Morray was the most influential of the Grooms of the Bedchamber serving the king. As Charles's former whipping-boy and lifelong companion, there were few men at court who were more intimate with the monarch, or spent so much time in private in his company. The king's references to Morray knowing 'how all will end heer' in Scotland, and his further remark that the tables would be turned on the Junto's Scottish allies 'before all be done', take on a heightened significance in the light of what happened next. For, by the time Charles wrote these lines on 5 October, a campaign to destroy the Argyll–Hamilton party's dominance of Scottish government was fast gaining momentum in Edinburgh. An attack was already in an advanced stage of preparation, and if it were launched and successfully carried through to completion, the king knew he could at last break the Westminster Junto's power-base of support in Scotland. And, if that were achieved, the prospects of turning the attack on to the Junto itself, once the English Parliament reconvened in a fortnight's time, would start to look brighter by the day.

Unbeknownst to the still 'cheerful' Junto leadership at Westminster, events in Scotland were approaching a moment of climacteric that would determine, for the foreseeable future, whether or not the twin aristocratic 'Juntos' in London and Edinburgh were likely to survive. And by the time the courier bearing the king's letter of 5 October reached London, Will Morray not only knew 'how all will end' in Edinburgh; he was working hard to guide events to their decisive, and potentially murderous, conclusion.

IV. SCOTLAND: RESISTANCE CHECKED

So overwhelming had been the Argyll faction's dominance of Scottish politics in the autumn of 1641 and so supine had the king been in acquiescing to its demands that it is easy to forget that Charles's original motives for travelling to Edinburgh, when the journey had first been planned back in May, had been to 'crush' Argyll, not to humour him. Edinburgh had been intended as the setting for a royalist revival. Those plans are worth briefly reprising. Montrose and his allies were to have brought Argyll to account as a traitor for having spoken in favour of the king's deposition. The 'Elephant and the Dromedary' – Argyll and Hamilton – were to have been humbled. And government in Scotland was to have been handed over to Montrose and his Bander allies: the 'king's party' among the Covenanters. This house of cards had collapsed, however, with the public exposure of Montrose's plot in June, and Argyll's ruthless countermeasures against the plotters: the arrest and imprisonment of Montrose; the detention of his fellow conspirators and the prompt trial and execution of John Stewart the younger of Ladywell – the luckless figure who was to have been Montrose's key witness in the planned treason prosecution of Argyll.[124]

Yet the revelation of Montrose's plot had only wounded the anti-Argyllian, anti-oligarchic party within the Scottish nobility, not destroyed it entirely. A number of the key figures in the original plot against Argyll, as it had developed between January and March 1641, remained at liberty; and none more important, perhaps, than the sixty-seven-year-old Robert Ker, 1st Earl of Roxburgh. A wily veteran of the Stuart courts in both London and Edinburgh, Roxburgh had attended Charles's father as a Gentleman of the Bedchamber, had served Charles as Scotland's Lord Privy Seal from 1637, and was a well-known opponent of Argyll and the Covenanter party more generally.[125] He had been drawn into Montrose's plotting against Argyll and Hamilton by the spring of 1641 at the latest. Indeed, it had been at Broxmouth House, Roxburgh's country seat near Dunbar, that Montrose had met with Lieutenant-Colonel Walter Stewart, the plotters' emissary to the Whitehall court, on Stewart's return from his first mission in March 1641.[126] Roxburgh's bibulous, Eton-educated eldest son, Harry, Lord Ker,[127] may also have been drawn into the plot around this time, and, as we will see, was to figure prominently in its later stages.

Exploration of the possibility of reviving the plot – despite the incarceration of Montrose, its prospective ringleader, in Edinburgh Castle – seems to have begun within a short time of the king's arrival in Edinburgh in August.[128] Precisely where the initiative came from is difficult to determine, not least because a number of current and recently demobilized officers from the Covenanter army came to be involved, and whether they were recruited, or volunteered their services, is unclear. But if there was a central figure in the conspiracy, a single point at which its various strands converged, it was Will Morray, one of the few members of the king's Bedchamber staff to have been chosen to accompany his master to Scotland.[129] To term Morray the instigator of this plot would be an overstatement, as, at one level, he seems to have been doing no more than reactivating Montrose's earlier plan to accuse Argyll of treason. And many of his fellow conspirators – Montrose, Roxburgh, and Roxburgh's son, Lord Ker – had been part of this original scheme as it had developed earlier in the year.[130]

At first sight, it may appear anomalous that Morray, a relatively humbly born figure (the son of a Scottish clergyman), who occupied a menial post in the king's entourage (an essentially 'below-stairs' servant),[131] should end up managing a plot that came to encompass senior officers in the Covenanter army as well as some of Scotland's most powerful aristocratic grandees. Yet Morray's role conformed to an established pattern of clandestine 'Renaissance diplomacy', in which monarchs frequently used comparatively low-ranking, but highly trusted, body servants to act as their agents in negotiations – what has been termed 'representation through intimacy'.[132] Morray's combination of trusted intimacy with the king *and* menial status was itself the signifier, to those with whom he dealt, that all he said and did was by way of 'representing' the king; for, as everyone he had dealings with could be relied upon to assume, no one of such rank and position would dare act – particularly in high matters of state – without the prior authorization of his royal master.

It is an open question how much the king, having authorized Morray to act on his behalf to further the plot, actually informed himself of its day-to-day progress. It would have been entirely consistent with Charles's intermittent moral fastidiousness, if, having given Morray a broad hint as to the outcome he desired, he had chosen not to sully his delicate conscience with detailed knowledge of the violence the plotters intended. But that the king was privy to the plot's general objectives and *modus operandi* does not seem seriously in doubt.[133]

Using tactics that were reminiscent of the king's failed *coup d'état* in England, Morray had begun sounding out senior officers in the Covenanter army. Colonel John Cochrane, whose regiment was quartered near Edinburgh at Musselburgh,[134] was brought to Morray by a mutual acquaintance, Mungo Murray, the King's Cupbearer, within twenty-four hours of Charles's arrival in Edinburgh. Here, too, it is unclear whether it was Morray or Cochrane who made the first move; but over the following six weeks, Cochrane became deeply involved in the plot, and, as the commander of one of the Covenanter army's three undisbanded regiments, had a potentially decisive role to play in ensuring the armed forces in and near Edinburgh lent their support to the proposed coup.[135] At least on Cochrane's own evidence, Morray worked quite assiduously to persuade him that Hamilton and Argyll were obstacles to peace in Scotland and had to be removed. On an occasion, for example, when the two met in Holyrood's Privy Gallery (significantly, the passageway immediately adjoining the king's private apartments), Morray confided to Cochrane his view, 'I am affeared this peace shall never be concludit till those two men [Hamilton and Argyll] be sequestrat' – that is, removed from the scene – and immediately started asking Cochrane questions about the reliability of his regiment.[136] Morray must have liked the responses, because, on his own admission, 'in the end of one nicht [night], when [the king] wes gone to bed, [Morray] did tak[e] in the said colonel [Cochrane], who talkit in private with his Majestie'.[137] Covenanter officers were not, in general, bidden to late-night bedside conversations with their monarch; and Morray's admission to this meeting between the king and Colonel Cochrane is perhaps the clearest, if nevertheless circumstantial, indicator of Charles's direct involvement in the conspiracy.[138]

What galvanized the plotters into action, however, appears to have been Argyll's success in capturing control of the process by which appointments were to be made to major public office: the moment, on 16 September, when Charles ceded to the Scottish Parliament the right to veto his nominees as Scotland's judges, Privy Councillors, and great officers of state.[139] This was the very development that was to bring the Junto leadership in Westminster such 'cheer' when the news reached London some ten days later. During the fortnight following the king's concession of 16 September, Argyll mounted a sustained campaign to prevent any king's-party peers – in particular, any Banders or allies of Montrose – from sharing power in the future government of Scotland. A parliamentary proposal to exclude from office all Scots who had either left the kingdom or sided with the king during the Anglo-Scottish wars of 1639 and 1640 looked set to restrict the king's freedom of movement even further, and would have debarred a series of figures who were already, or shortly to be involved in the plot, from further public employment – not least Roxburgh and the Earl of Crawford, an indigent soldier of fortune who had served the king against his countrymen during the recent campaigns.[140] The king's powerlessness before Argyll's parliamentary opposition was dramatically demonstrated when, having proposed the Earl of Morton – a moderate king's-party man – for the politically powerful position of Lord Chancellor of Scotland, he was forced to withdraw his nominee in response to the concerted opposition of Argyll.[141]

As the controversy surrounding the composition of Scotland's future government reached its ill-tempered climax in the last days of September, the original parties to Montrose's plot regrouped, now joined by disgruntled officers such as Cochrane, and reconsidered their plan to bring the Argyll–Hamilton ascendancy to an end. But tactics had changed since the spring, when Montrose had first mooted the possibility of an assault on Hamilton and Argyll. Even from his cell in Edinburgh Castle, Montrose remained more than willing to act as Argyll's accuser, and sent a series of letters to Morray, offering to fulfil this role. But with Montrose imprisoned, and the Argyllians dominant in almost every organ of state, there was no longer any question of relying on purely parliamentary means in order to bring charges of treason. Instead, the plotters had little alternative but to opt for a much more hazardous course: a *coup d'état* involving the overpowering and arrest of their chief enemies, and the use of armed retainers (and, potentially, Cochrane's regiment) to secure control of Edinburgh in the name of the king. Charles himself, as ever, appears to have avoided direct contact with the plotters – other than with Cochrane and Morray himself. But Morray's ever more active involvement during the fortnight leading up to its culmination – from 28 September to 11 October – leaves little doubt that the king himself had at very least given the planned *coup d'état* his blessing.[142]

The first public intimation that an attack was being planned against Hamilton and Argyll slipped out, almost certainly inadvertently, just as the pair were intensifying their efforts to exclude Roxburgh, Crawford (and, it seemed, all other king's-party men) from public office. In what does not seem to be an unconnected development, both Crawford and Roxburgh's son, Lord Ker, were found at supper in Will Morray's chamber in Holyrood House on (or shortly before) 29 September. As Morray entertained Ker and Crawford, the party was joined, apparently unplanned, by Sir James Hamilton, a 'Relation to the Marquesse [of Hamilton]', and Sir James's presence – and still more his kinship with the marquess – was enough to provoke Ker to a bitter denunciation of the marquess's allegedly traitorous ways. 'His chiefe (meaning the L[ord] Marquesse)', Ker declared to Sir James, 'was a Traytor, and had juggled with [i.e. deceived] the King those 2 or 3 yeares.'[143] Not content with defamation, and almost certainly emboldened by drink, Ker issued a challenge to Hamilton to fight a duel, a message that was delivered that same evening by the Earl of Crawford, Ker's 'furious and drunken second'.[144]

It is unclear whether this was purely a drink-induced spat or, in fact, a premature disclosure of the charge the plotters intended to deploy against both Hamilton and Argyll – what one contemporary commentator construed as the 'untimely birth' of the larger plot which was later to come to light.[145] But its effect was a sharp and sudden intensification of the factional hostility between the king's-party lords – in particular, Montrose's allies, Roxburgh, Ker, and Crawford – and the Argyllians. Charles went through the outward motions of attempting to defuse these tensions by persuading Ker to withdraw his challenge and apologize.[146] But Lord Ker sent an unrepentant message to the Argyllians when he arrived at the Parliament House, ostensibly to make his submission for his 'false' denunciation of the Marquess of Hamilton, accompanied by an armed retinue of some six hundred followers.[147]

Ker's appearance at the Parliament House with an armed retinue serves as a reminder of how aristocratic politics in Scotland continued to be influenced by the quasi-feudal practice of retaining 'vassals' and 'liegemen',[148] and hence retained a capacity for armed feuding and violence on a scale that had been unimaginable in England for at least half a century.[149] Moreover, the size of Ker's following, far larger than would have been expected of an earl's son, almost certainly points to its having been augmented by the retinues of other king's-party lords. Exact figures are elusive, but the number of noblemen's armed retainers in and around Edinburgh at the end of September was probably well over 6,000 men: Argyll and Hamilton, alone, were reported to have 5,000 armed retainers in Edinburgh between them.[150] And in a city with an adult male population not much over 10,000, this was a massive, and potentially overwhelming, force.

As the cracks in the old Covenanter alliance became daily wider, a growing number of anti-Argyllian nobles (many, though not all, former signatories of the Cumbernauld Band) came to acquire a thoroughly self-interested motive for restoring an element of personal authority to the king. In Scotland, as in Ireland, defence of the king's prerogative had come to seem the most effective antidote to oligarchy: the best means of preventing an imminent takeover of Scotland's government by Hamilton and Argyll. This realization, in turn, created the circumstances in which, perhaps for the very first time since the Scottish crisis had blown up in 1637, Charles was in a position to win

support in Scotland by asserting his powers, rather than by trading them
away. By late September, there was a faction, reported Thomas Webb, the
Duke of Richmond's secretary, that 'say[s] the king might carry everything,
if he did not undoe himself by yealding'.[151] Personal monarchy, these men had
belatedly discovered, might yet prove the undoing of Scotland's 'aristocratic
republic' dominated by Hamilton and Argyll – a régime all the more obnox-
ious because it appeared to be the partially owned subsidiary of England's
own anti-royalist cabal. Indeed, the presence of the Westminster Junto's
representatives in Edinburgh – Lord Howard of Escrick, John Hampden and
the other English Commissioners – seems to have intensified the growing
reaction against the Argyllians: the English Commissioners were in Edinburgh, it was claimed on 28 September, 'onely to support party and faction
against his Majesty'.[152]

Against this increasingly acrimonious background, Charles once again
clashed publicly with Argyll over the question of which of the two of them
would determine the distribution of Scotland's major pubic offices. On 30
September, in yet another attempt to secure the appointment of a king's-
party man, he nominated Lord Almond for the key post of Lord Treasurer
of Scotland, offering what was intended to be a quid pro quo in which
Argyll's kinsman, Lord Loudoun, was to be granted the senior office of
Lord Chancellor, in return for Almond's acceptance by Argyll. Loudoun's
nomination was accepted by Parliament 'without the least contradiction'.[153]
But Argyll repudiated any suggestion of a compromise with the king, denouncing Almond's fitness for the post of Lord Treasurer, claiming that 'in that
place [he] *might have been* also a head and leader to his old friends, the
[B]anders and malcontents'.[154] Revealingly, Argyll simply took it for granted
that, he having denounced him, the rejection of Almond's nomination by the
Parliament was assured.

*

Loudoun's appointment, which Charles seems almost to have been tricked
into making, had a symbolic as well as practical significance. None epitomized
better than he the intimate links between the Westminster Junto and what
appeared to be the copycat junto emerging in Edinburgh.[155] The Covenanter
leadership's principal contact with the Earl of Warwick and the other English
dissidents at least since early in 1640, Loudoun had spent most of the
preceding year in London as the main Scottish negotiator in the Anglo-
Scottish Treaty (a position that had brought him into almost daily contact
with Warwick, Essex, Mandeville, and Saye in their role as Lords Commissioners for the treaty). Here, too, Argyll notched up another success. The
further negotiations on the remaining matters to be agreed with the king
were delegated to a committee consisting of six members each from the three
Estates of Parliament – the nobles (titular peers), lairds (upper gentry), and
burgesses (or town representatives) – with the Argyllians taking five out of
the six places reserved for the nobility.[156] Moreover, from his appointment
as Lord Chancellor on 30 September 1641, Loudoun took on the role of
chief broker between this committee and the king over the terms of 'a faire

accomodation'. And, in practice, this meant deciding the composition of Scotland's future government (the question of appointments of officers of state), and the punishment of 'Incendiaries' (principally, Montrose and Traqu air, for their scheming against Argyll earlier in the year).[157] Few developments could have been more contrived to try the king's remaining patience. He had come to Scotland to find a way out of the 'labyrinth' in which he had been trapped during the previous ten months by Loudoun and his Junto allies – only to discover that the odious Loudoun was once again master of the negotiations that seemed likely to ensnare him yet again.

The difference, this time, was that Charles at last had a small but organized and militant faction on which he could depend: the Scottish grandees who were reassuring him that he might 'carry everything', if he stood firm against further encroachments on his prerogative powers.[158] Buoyed by the emergence of this anti-Argyllian party in Parliament and determined to avoid a second entrapment, Charles took a far more robust line in the negotiations with Loudoun in the days that followed Ker's confrontation with Hamilton. For the first time since his arrival in Scotland, the king began to show a resolutely combative edge. When the Argyllians in Parliament ensured the rejection of Lord Almond, the royalist nominee as Lord Treasurer, Charles retaliated, on 6 October, by promoting him to an earldom, as 1st Earl of Callendar, thereby giving his failed nominee equal rank with Argyll.[159] Indeed, the entire purpose of Almond's nomination as Lord Treasurer, given that his rejection by the Argyllians was a near cast-iron certainty, may well have been to signal to Montrose and the other king's-party lords that office would be theirs – if, and when, the power of the Argyll–Hamilton diarchy was eventually broken.[160]

Charles's new-found bullishness is still more evident in his responses to the Argyll party's demands over the following week. And, for once, a chance documentary survival – the king's holograph notes of his comments on these negotiations – provides a rare insight into the workings of his mind just at the point that his dealings with the Argyll-dominated 'Committee for faire Accommodation' were about to reach breaking-point. Probably compiled on Friday, 8 October, following discussions with Loudoun and other representatives of the Parliament on Wednesday and Thursday (6 and 7 October), these notes are cast in the form of a set of instructions to Lord Loudoun, titled: 'Notes for my L. Chancelor's [i.e. Loudoun's] memorie, that he may better apply himself to my mynde in the intendit way of accommodation'.[161] Charles's personal animosity towards Loudoun – whom Hyde was to regard as the 'principal manager of the [Scottish] rebellion' – is barely suppressed in the headmasterly tone of these jottings, and their clear instruction that Loudoun had 'better apply himself to *my* mynde'.[162]

The central point of conflict, because it touched so directly upon the king's personal influence over the character of the future government, remained the choice of the great officers, the Privy Councillors and the judges of the Court of Session. Argyll's faction had led the successful campaign for the Scottish Parliament to have the right to veto the king's nominees. But Charles was now insisting that *he* alone should have the right to produce the list of

nominees, and Parliament should not exercise its veto capriciously, or vin-
dictively, against king's-party men – in particular, against the signatories of
the Cumbernauld Band (of whom Lord Almond, the king's recently rejected
nominee as Lord Treasurer, was one). Charles lectured his new Scottish
Chancellor:

> I expect that those that I have, or shall, nominate shall be approved, except
> [if] sufficient cause (whether privatlie or publiclie, I doe not care) be showen
> me – of which nature I nether esteeme the gen[eral] citation [the Scottish
> Parliament's nomination of 'Incendiaries'], nor having been a Bander, to be
> anie [sufficient cause].[163]

Montrose and his king's-party allies, in other words, could not be debarred
from office.

Charles's responses to the Scottish Parliament's other demands were equally
assertive and protective of his remaining prerogative rights. The stipulation,
for example, that his major Scottish castles be demolished he rejected outright.[164] And dismissing the Argyllians' request that Scots should be allowed to
attend in the London-based royal households, the king commented haughtily:

> I suppose that the [Scottish] Par[liament] hes more reason to thanke [me]
> then to importune me.[165]*

Only on the question of the arrangements for future declarations of war did
Charles offer a substantial concession, observing simply that 'I have nothing
to say to this, but that great care must be had ... in the choice of the
commissioners [the delegates of the two Parliaments who were to decide
such questions in the intervals when the two legislatures were not sitting]'.[166]

The change in the king's hitherto conciliatory demeanour could hardly
have been more marked. Gone was the almost craven submissiveness that
had characterized his first six weeks in Edinburgh. Retreat had been replaced
by a policy of confrontation, and a newly confident king entrusted these
'Notes' – his first shot across his opponents' bows – to Will Morray, once again
serving as Charles's factotum, for delivery to Lord Chancellor Loudoun.[167]

But the prickly assertiveness of these 'Notes' addressed to Loudoun registers
more than simply Charles's dwindling stocks of patience. If, as seems highly
probable, Charles was already aware of Will Morray's plans as to 'how all
will end heer', his notes of Friday, 8 October were written in the expectation
that Edinburgh's political firmament was about to be radically reconfigured.
The ascendancy of Hamilton and Argyll – 'the two great guiders of the

---

* Nicholas had heard a rumour that this request was going to be made of the king, and
wrote to the king, as early as 3 October, warning him that it was being said in London
that 'all the great offices and places of councellors here wilbe filled upp with Scotsmen'.
The king's response, written on Saturday, 9 October, was emphatic: 'I asseur you that I
doe not meane to grant it'.

affaires of this state' – appeared to be appoaching its end.[168]

Over the following forty-eight hours, the arrangements, weeks in the planning, to bring about this conclusion, entered their final phase.[169]

*

That same Friday, 8 October, probably within a matter of hours of the king penning his rebarbative 'Notes' to Lord Loudoun, Colonel John Cochrane left Edinburgh for the eight-mile ride to Musselburgh, on the south side of the Firth of Forth. Cochrane, as we have seen, was the officer whom Will Morray had recently brought to the king's Bedchamber for a secretive, late-night discussion. And his purpose in riding out to Musselburgh, where his regiment was quartered, was to sound out the willingness of his officers to join him in the prospective *coup d'état*. Calling together his junior officers, 'he drank liberallie with them and said, if they wald [would] be all of his mynd, he hopit to mak[e] them ane fortune'. How much of the plot Cochrane actually revealed, and how warmly his officers responded, is unclear. But with Lieutenant-Colonel Robert Home, his immediate second-in-command, Cochrane was more candid. He promised his deputy a royal reward: 'that, if [Lieutenant-Colonel Home] wald follow his [Cochrane's] way, he wald mak him ane man to leive [live] well, for he had his Majestie's favor, and Mr [Will] Murray had taken him to the Kinge's bed syde'.[170]

During Saturday and Sunday, 9 and 10 October, the plan for the entrapment of Hamilton and Argyll achieved its final form. The conspirators were ready for action. And on the Sunday evening, when Cochrane, Morray, and the Earl of Crawford met for supper at the Earl of Airth's house in Edinburgh, the decision was taken to spring the trap the following afternoon or evening: Monday, 11 October.[171] Access to the two intended victims was easy, as both Hamilton and Argyll were lodging at Holyrood at the time, in their capacity as members of the king's Scottish court.[172] Will Morray was to deliver a summons to them to appear in the king's Withdrawing Chamber, on the pretext that they had been bidden to an audience; and once they were there, well away from the publicly accessible areas of the palace, Lord Almond (the newly created Earl of Callendar) and a party of soldiers would enter the room by the Privy Stairs. Almond was to 'show them how treacherouslie they had delt with the King and cuntrey', and then to arrest them 'in His Majestie's name'. A force of four hundred soldiers was to be ready in the Privy Garden, immediately outside the Withdrawing Chamber, sufficient to defend Holyrood against any attempt to rescue the 'traitors' until the Earls of Roxburgh and Home arrived with their 'freindis' – their armed retinues – to secure the palace. In the event of a 'tumult', as word of the arrests leaked out, the prisoners were to be spirited through the palace garden, or through Holyrood Churchyard, to one of the king's ships moored at Leith.[173]

What should happen to Hamilton and Argyll, once they were in custody, was a matter of some debate among the conspirators. Lord Almond favoured consigning the pair to a legal trial, and finding them guilty of treason in Parliament. Crawford, preferring more summary forms of justice, proposed murdering them at the earliest opportunity. Others, with a more delicate sense of legal nicety, advocated 'cutting their throats', but only if Hamilton and Argyll attempted to use their armed followings to secure their release, citing, in justification, the 'custome of Germanie'.[174]

This was a well planned and thoroughly practicable coup. Almond's involvement gave the plot's military dimension an element of plausibility; as the Lieutenant-General in the 1640 campaign against England, he continued to command prestige and authority within what remained of the Covenanter army – a potentially vital asset if Colonel Cochrane and the other regimental officers involved were to persuade their troops to support the coup. And the short time between the plot's notification to its participants and its actual execution substantially reduced the risk that news of the conspiracy would come to the notice of its intended victims. Had it succeeded, there were probably sufficient Bander noblemen and their supporters to have formed the basis of an alternative government – one, moreover, that 'would have had no truck' with any future plans for a new Scottish intervention in England.[175] Henceforth, the English Junto grandees would have been on their own.

But not even Almond's standing was sufficient to ensure the discretion of all the officers whose support had been enlisted. At some point over the night of Sunday, 10 October and the early hours of Monday morning, Lieutenant-Colonel John Hurry, one of the officers involved, had second thoughts about his task. Instead, he divulged the plot to the army's Lord General, Alexander Leslie. Leslie, in turn, took Hurry back to repeat his story to Hamilton and Argyll. By Monday, 11 October, news of the plot was the talk of Edinburgh.

Yet, although the element of surprise had been lost, Charles seems still to have hoped that the plot might have been reactivated. Argyll and Hamilton wavered, uncertain how to respond. Only on the following afternoon, Tuesday, 12 October, when the king went in state to the Parliament House accompanied by a retinue some five hundred strong – provided by the same Bander nobles who were now publicly implicated in the conspiracy – did Hamilton and Argyll resolve to flee the capital. Declaring their unwillingness to see slaughter in the streets – the likely consequence if the king's retinue attempted to take the two grandees by force – Argyll, Hamilton, and the Earl of Lanark (Hamilton's brother, who was also named as a possible victim of the plot) withdrew to Kinneil, Hamilton's fortified house near Falkirk, twelve miles to the west of Edinburgh.[176]

Charles's speech before Parliament on the afternoon of Hamilton's and Argyll's flight was one of the great theatrical displays of his career. Desperate to clear himself of any complicity, he spoke, with tears in his eyes, of his regret at this 'incident' – the demure periphrasis by which the coup was henceforth known – and his affection for Hamilton, whose arrest (and possible murder) he had been content to allow only twenty-four hours earlier. This did not persuade many for long. As each of the plotters was cross-examined over the next three weeks, the centrality of Will Morray's role was corroborated by witness after witness, and left little doubt as to Charles's guilt.[177]

Predictably, the failure of the coup worked strongly to Argyll's and Hamilton's advantage, strengthening still further their negotiating position with the king, discrediting Montrose once again, and destroying any lingering hopes Charles may have had of securing the appointment of king's-party peers to high office. After the king's brief and disastrous period of assertiveness in the first fortnight of October, he was forced to resume his earlier habit of 'yealding'. In September, Charles had submitted a list of nominees to the Scottish Privy Council which included numerous king's-party nobles; when this was resubmitted after the failed *coup d'état*, he had been forced to remove almost every one of the king's-party lords (including the Earl of Airth, in whose house the coup-plotters had met) and the Earl of Home (one of the royalist peers who was to have helped secure Holyrood after Argyll's and Hamilton's arrest).[178] Likewise, the new judicial appointments further strengthened the hand of the Argyllians, completing the consolidation of the Scottish 'commonwealth' as a 'Venetianized' polity – with an almost exclusively figurehead king.[179]

Will Morray's fellow Groom of the Bedchamber, Endymion Porter, gave a bleak but accurate assessment of the king's fortunes in the wake of the 'Incident'. Writing on Tuesday, 19 October, exactly a week after the plot had been foiled, he lamented the drastic downturn in the king's fortunes:

> [All] this weeke wee have heard of nothing but watching and warding [by armed guards], and threates of deadlie fudes; but I feare all will end in an agreement to our master's disadvantage, and what will be required by the Parlament at first must be yelded to at laste, and soe putt everie thing into a wors condition then wee fownde it . . . wee can looke for[ward to] nothing but a generall confusion.[180]

Little did Porter realize how soon his prophesy of 'a general confusion' would be fulfilled.

*

Even as Porter was writing these lines, the first reports of the 'discovery of a . . . bloody conspiracie at Edenburg' were reaching the Junto leadership in London.[181] And if the failure of the October *coup d'état* had been decisive in Edinburgh, its impact in England was, if anything, to be greater still. For the Westminster Parliament was to reconvene the next day, at the end of its six-week recess. And for the Junto grandees – Warwick and Essex, Hesilrige and Pym – the reports of the abortive *coup d'état* in Scotland were to provide a life-line, just as the 'confusion' Porter had foretold broke around them: an incipient counter-revolution at home, and a full-scale rebellion abroad.

14

ENGINES OF WAR

OCTOBER–NOVEMBER 1641

This land triumphs in you alone (great Peeres),
Who have absolved us from all our feares . . .
And let the influence of your great power
The Gospell's mortall enemies devoure.

John Bond, *Englands Reioycing for the
Parliaments Returne* (October, 1641)[1]

'The sickness att London . . . is soe rife and soe much disperced', wrote Edward Nicholas in October 1641, 'as it will [be] dangerous for the King and Parliament to reside there this winter.'[2] Summer outbreaks of plague were familiar, almost annual, hazards of life in Stuart London. But the virulence and duration of the current visitation – which, as late as the autumn, still showed no signs of abating – indicated a particularly vehement bout of divine displeasure. God had been angered by the sins of the nation, and had poured out his wrath with a baffling, if habitual, lack of discrimination upon saint and sinner, Protestant and Papist, alike. During September and October, the traditional gathering-points of fashionable London society – the City Exchange, the bowling greens of Piccadilly, the theatres in Blackfriars and Drury Lane – were all but deserted. Indeed, so great had been the exodus from the capital that rented housing in the surrounding countryside was all but unobtainable.[3] In the city, the signs of the pestilence were oppressive and all-surrounding: the crudely painted crosses on doors, the disproportionate number of townsmen in mourning black, the almost incessant digging of graves in the city's churchyards. Those marooned within the metropolis were forced to rely on prayers and nosegays (small bunches of flowers and sweet-smelling herbs) to ward off the infection-bearing 'miasma'.

Yet Nicholas, though accurate in his assessment of the current threat to health, found his expectation of Parliament's relocation or adjournment confounded. As the date of the Westminster Parliament's reconvening, Wednesday, 20 October, drew steadily closer, the Junto discovered that even pestilence could have its political uses. Always preferring the relative manageability of 'thin Houses' to the unpredictability of large and well-attended sessions, the Junto leadership seems almost to have relished the way in which the plague could be relied upon to deter all but the most 'engaged men' from putting in an appearance at Westminster.[4]* Indeed, when proposals were made by the two Recess Committees to adjourn the resumed parliamentary session to the plague-free environs of Salisbury, 'Mr Pym [and] those of his Juncto' remained insistent that the two Houses should reconvene only in Westminster (or possibly London), notwithstanding the threat to health.[5] The 'prime governors', Nicholas informed the Duke of Richmond, 'are of the opinion that a Parliament in England cannot succeede so happily any where as in London or Westminster'. Richmond would easily be able to 'judge the reason of this opinion'.[6]

Those 'prime governors' gradually reconvened in London in the week before the resumption of the session, confident that the precedents provided by the king's concessions in Scotland and the deterrent effects of the plague would leave them masters of the forthcoming parliamentary session.[7] Mandeville, whose Chelsea house remained the nerve-centre of the Junto's activities, was optimistic, despite the régime's dwindling popularity in the country at large. Oblivious to the dangers pending in Ireland or Scotland, he made light of recent criticisms of the reformists, collecting copies of the anti-Junto libels that had started circulating in recent weeks and entertaining 'all companies' by reading choice extracts aloud.[8] The Earls of Holland and Essex, the two Lords General (respectively North and South of the Trent) were sufficiently relaxed to spend a short break at Essex's favourite hunting estate, Chartley, in Warwickshire, returning to London around Tuesday, 19 October.[9]† The mood among the reformist grandees was relaxed. That same day, the last of the summer break, Pym was due to chair the final meeting of the Commons' Recess Committee, with nothing more alarming on its agenda than another handful of petitions, prompted by the September Order against Innovations, and yet another group of disgruntled reformadoes, troublesome but not a real threat, pursuing their arrears of pay.[10]

Then, some time before noon that Tuesday, a messenger arrived in Westminster bearing letters from Hampden and the other Parliamentary Commissioners in Edinburgh. He had ridden hard, covering the four hundred miles, which took most couriers six days, in just four.[11] And the news he brought shattered the confidence of England's jesting grandees.

---

* Once the session began, many Parliament-men commuted in to Westminster from outside the capital, rather than risk the contagion in the metropolis. The result was that by the end of October, the Commons were not meeting until 10 a.m., and the Lords not until 11 a.m., in order to allow members time for their journeys.

† Edward Nicholas informed his friend, Thomas Webb (then in Edinburgh with his master, the Duke of Richmond and Lennox), of Holland's departure for Chartley to stay with the Earl of Essex on 5 October 1641, adding, with heavy sarcasm: 'I hope it is to advise for his Majestie's service, as the nearenes of their places about the King [respectively Groom of the Stool and Lord Chamberlain] obligeth them'.

I. ASSASSINATIONS

News of the attempted *coup d'état* in Edinburgh fell on Westminster like a thunderbolt. At that meeting on Tuesday, 19 October, Pym broke the seals on the newly arrived letters from Edinburgh and began reading. Hitherto, as Fiennes and his colleagues had reported from Scotland, all matters had been 'in a very hopefull way of Accommodation' – meaning, tending to a settlement to the advantage of Argyll and the Junto's Scottish allies. Now, however, 'this plot hath put not onely ours, but all other businesses to a stand, and may be an occasion of many and great troubles in this Kingdome [Scotland]'.[12] Their summary of what had happened was succinct and to the point. There had been a 'design' to seize Argyll, Hamilton, and his brother the Earl of Lanark at Holyrood on the night of Monday, 11 October. Thereupon, all three had left court that same night and taken refuge within the City of Edinburgh. They departed the following day for Hamilton's house 'about 12 miles of[f], [at Kinneil], where they continue still'. The Earl of Crawford and two colonels had been 'restrained', but not yet examined. That was all.[13]

However, a much fuller and more sinister account of the conspiracy was also offered to the Junto leadership in London – what Pym later referred to as 'other certaine intelligence come out of Scotland' – most likely, the account provided by the courier himself.[14]* In this reading of events, what had happened had been far more than a plot to 'seize' Argyll, Hamilton and Lanark.[15] The conspiracy's intended victims were to have been charged with 'high Treason; or else, if they had found that course to bee too long and too dangerous, then to have slaughtered them'. The Earl of Roxburgh (Charles's Lord Privy Seal) and the Earl of Crawford were to have come into Edinburgh the following morning (Tuesday, 12 October) 'with great forces to have seized upon the Cittie and soe to have killed such others as they should have thought necessary for their designe'.[16] What would have followed from this planned 'slaughter' was self-evident. With Hamilton and Argyll imprisoned or (more likely) dead, the king's 'friends' – in particular Roxburgh, Crawford, Almond, and Montrose – would have been supreme in Scotland,[17] and the Junto's ability to rely on its Edinburgh allies, its insurance policy in the event of a royalist insurgency in England, would have been at an end. Thereafter, the best that Warwick and his allies could have hoped for would have been that Montrose's government might stand neutral in the event of a civil war in England. Just as likely, however, would have been a new Scottish intervention, this time led by the likes of Crawford and Montrose, with the intention of destroying England's Venetiatized commonwealth and restoring the king's personal prerogative powers.

As retailed by Pym to the Recess Committee that Tuesday morning, the story could hardly have been more shocking. There had been a conspiracy to

---

* This may well have been Gualter Frost, the same emissary that Lord Brooke and his friends had used in their earlier negotiations with Edinburgh in the summer of 1640, and who was currently seconded to the service of Fiennes and his fellow Commissioners in Edinburgh.

exterminate the entire Argyllian leadership in Edinburgh; not only Argyll himself, but Hamilton and at least four other Scottish grandees besides: the President of the Scottish Parliament, Lord Balmerino; the Lord General of the Covenanter army, Alexander Leslie; the Lord Chancellor, Lord Loudoun; and another Argyllian peer, Lord Lindsay – every one of them firm allies of the London Junto.[18] Moreover, this was to have been the prelude to a bloodbath on the scale of the St Bartholomew's Day massacres in France. Once Hamilton and Argyll had been taken, Pym explained to the Recess Committee,

> the Earles of Craford and Roxborough were ready to come into Eden-burrough the next morning, being Tuesday, the 12th day of October, [and to have] ... killed ... all such other worthie instruments either of the Nobilitie, gentrie, or Commons as stoode for the good of the Church or Common wealth.[19]

How closely this version of events related to what Crawford, Almond and Morray had actually planned is difficult to determine. For all its apparent hyperbole, however, this account may have been closer to the truth than it may at first appear. Given the number of armed 'liegemen' and other partisan followers, on both sides, in Edinburgh in October 1641, any outbreak of violence in or around the capital was likely to have resulted in heavy casualties; and there is at least evidence that the anti-Argyllian plotters were indeed preparing for an armed assault. Lord Lindsay, an Argyll supporter who was one of the plotters' intended victims, later received a copy of an order issued by Lord Almond (the peer who was to have arrested Argyll himself) to 'all his vassals and tenants' in Linlithgowshire, immediately to the north-west of Edinburgh, in which he commanded them, 'upon Monday next [11 October], to have, each man of them, Musquitts ..., a pound of powder, and a dozen of balls' – obviously in readiness for some form of military service on the day of Argyll's planned arrest.[20]

Even for those disposed to give the king the benefit of the doubt, the discovery that Lord Almond had been a central agent in the failed coup – the peer who, only a few days before, had been the king's nominee as Lord Treasurer of Scotland – at the very least called into doubt the king's judgement in the choice of his ministers; at worst, it suggested that the king's promise of the Treasurership to Lord Almond had been linked, either as an encouragement or reward, to his involvement in the plot.

*

The despatch rider's exhausting efforts had not been in vain. By enabling the Junto leaders to be the first to receive news of the Edinburgh *coup d'état*, they were able to ensure that it was their version of events that went first into public circulation. The contrast between the treatment of the news in Edinburgh and in London could hardly have been more marked. Ironically, in Scotland, where the Argyllians had already extracted from the king almost all the political concessions they required (including, crucially, his acquiescence to parliamentary control of all major public appointments),[21] the reformists went to great lengths to play down the plot's significance, lest further public revelations – including the possibility that the king's complicity might be established beyond doubt – should provoke yet further ructions within the Scottish élite. Hence, the Scottish Parliament's insistence that any investigation should be by a private committee, in camera; hence, the decision not to press any charges against Will Morray, despite his obvious complicity in the conspiracy; hence, too, the adoption of the almost ludicrously bland term, 'the Incident', referring to the foiled conspiracy.[22] But in Scotland, Argyll and Hamilton could afford to be magnanimous in victory. They had already reduced Charles to a cipher-king, and had little to gain by exposing either the king's, or his courtiers', guilt; they wanted a puppet monarchy, not a wholly discredited prince.

It was otherwise in England, where the great battle over appointments to government office had yet to be fought, and where, in consequence, every current senior office-holder remained potentially dismissible at the royal whim: Essex as Lord General; Leicester as Lord Lieutenant of Ireland; Saye as Master of the Court of Wards – any or all of them could be ousted from office the moment the king requested that they surrender their commissions or their ceremonial wands of office. Remedying this defect – by insisting that Charles allow the same concession over appointments in England as he had already yielded in Scotland – was already high on the Junto's agenda for the forth-coming parliamentary session.[23] But the news from Edinburgh both redoubled the Junto's commitment to achieving that end, and simultaneously gave them the propaganda advantage they needed in order to press home the attack. As a result, the accounts of the failed coup that went into circulation in London – almost all of it issued through printers with close connections with the Junto leadership[24] – were far more sensationalist than its reportage in Scotland. The English coverage of the 'late and Bloody CONSPIRACIE At Edenburg, in SCOTLAND' played up its intended violence, stressing the extensiveness of the conspirators' hit-list,[25] and hinting far more directly at the king's involvement than anything that was in circulation north of the border.[26]

Reactions to the news in England were commensurately extreme. One newsletter-writer (probably Edward Rossingham) thought the news out of Scotland 'so dangerous that Men dare not write those particulars which [in conversation] they say'.[27] But there are clues nevertheless. Few, perhaps, in England apprehended the new threat more acutely than the two cousins who held joint command of the kingdom's military forces: Holland and Essex. Something of their response to the reported assassination plot emerges in an encounter recorded by Edward Hyde, the aspiring courtier who had once been attached to the Junto's Bedfordian wing, but who had become increasingly alienated by the militancy of the now dominant Warwick House group. On the day after news of the assassination attempt reached London, Hyde came across Essex and Holland and was struck by how both men had been affected by the news. Their judgement on recent events was succinct. Implicitly reproaching Hyde for his closeness to the court (by which they seem to have meant Nicholas's circle and the king's Bedchamber entourage), the two peers said 'sadly' that he might now 'clearly discern [from the letters just received from Edinburgh] the indirect way of the court and how odious all honest men grew to them'.[28] Coming from Essex and Holland – the court's presiding officers as, respectively, the Lord Chamberlain and Groom of the Stool – the word 'court' here seems to be being used as a synonym if not for 'the king', at least for the men in whom he chose to confide.

Nor were Essex and Holland alone in their anxieties. The Junto's supporters, Hyde noticed, 'seemed concerned [for themselves] in the danger that was threatened to [Hamilton's] greatness'.[29] And with good cause: the 'greatness' of Hamilton and Argyll in Scotland, and the military assistance they could provide, remained the English Junto's prime source of long-term security. Anything which threatened Scotland's de facto regents directly imperilled the survival of their own régime. Hyde wrote dismissively of the way in which, in hindsight, the Junto leadership had gone about 'husbanding ... the Scotch fears to the terror of the two Houses'.[30] But at the time, the belief in London that there had been a court-backed plot to assassinate the leaders of the reformist party in Scotland was genuine enough. None, perhaps, registered this more sincerely than Hamilton's English brother-in-law, Lord Feilding, himself a supporter of the reformist cause who had attached himself to the Warwick House circle;[31] he wrote to Hamilton on 22 October (two days after Hyde's encounter with Essex and Holland), assuring him that 'I thinke *myselfe concern'd* in that bloody and wicked designe upon your lordship', and reminding him that he had 'manie faithfull servants in this parlament [at Westminster]'.[32]

The psychological impact at Westminster of the reported assassination plot in Edinburgh can hardly be overestimated. Not since the Strafford crisis, at the beginning of May, had the threat to the reformed constitution seemed so acute. The 'indirect way of the court' – in which the king was believed to have covered his tracks by delegating criminal activity to trusted courtiers – was becoming an ominously familiar *modus operandi*.[33] This was the first time, however, that a court conspiracy – or what was genuinely believed by many to be a court conspiracy – had extended to the murder or imprisonment of a large swathe of the reformist leadership. These latest revelations provided confirmation, if any further were needed, that all the king's conciliatory gestures thus far were merely feints: tactical retreats, masquerading as concessions, from ground that Charles intended to recapture as soon as he had the resources to do so. Unless preventative action were taken in England, it seemed only a matter of time before there was a similar attempt, also doubtless managed by the likes of Will Morray and the king's inner entourage, to unseat the reformist leadership at Westminster – also, doubtless, by violent means.[34]

And it was against this background that on Wednesday, 20 October, the very day after news of the assassination plot reached London, the two Houses of Parliament reconvened at Westminster to continue their 'great work' of reform. This time it was Parliament that was on the defensive, and arriving members 'found themselves guarded by a great body of soldiers in arms'.[35]

II. REMEDIES

For a young scholar with a career to make and ambitions to realize, there were few better ways to achieve public notice – and to ingratiate himself to potential patrons – than by the publication of suitably sycophantic celebratory verse. The versifier who sought to endear himself to the Junto grandees by marking the resumption of the parliamentary session was a godly young Cambridge divine, John Bond, a Dorset-man by origin, with connections to the county's resident puritan patriarch, John White of Dorchester. Like many of his fellow Puritans, Bond expected the newly resumed session to move forward with the work of godly reformation that had begun – albeit rather tentatively – during the Parliament's first ten months. Apostrophizing the Parliament-men, Bond urged them on:[36]

> Proceed, renowned Worthyes, then proceed [again]
> And what in action is, perfect in deed ...
> Behold! Armineans tumble every where
> And now are struck with repercussive feare ...
> Behold! The Priests of *Baal*, Atheists
> And Jesuites, with other Popish Priests ...
> You have deliv'red us from all the hands
> Of these, and more – yea, from the Devill's bands.[37]

The resumed session, Bond implied, would see the 'perfection' of the great work of ecclesiastical reform. It was a sensible enough expectation. The Commons' *Declaration* of 9 September had promised no less. A second attempt was supposed to be made to see an ordinance of both Houses passed against religions innovations.[38] And even Viscount Mandeville (a man in the know, if any were) was sure that the controversy over reform of the Church would ensure 'wee shall have somethinge to doe' when the two Houses next met.[39]

Yet the striking feature of the resumed parliamentary session is how comprehensively it confounded the expectations of the likes of the versifying Master Bond and his godly confrères. Before the recess, D'Ewes had consoled himself that, although Parliament's record on religious reform was such as to suggest 'wee intend no [re]formation in matter of Religion', 'yet it should bee the first thing which wee would sett upon at our next meeting againe'.[40] But the cause of 'further reformation' in the Church was the dog that failed to bark during the resumed parliamentary session. The expected clash between the two Houses simply failed to materialize. Still more strikingly, the House of Commons completely abandoned any attempt to enforce its Order of 8 September against images, raised altars, and other 'superstitious' practices. A proposal, early in the resumed session, to punish those who had infringed the order merely pointed up how large sections of the Commons' members doubted even the 'validitie' of the Order.[41] Nicholas, summarizing the Commons' debate that day, may not have been far from the truth when he wrote that the September Order 'was conceaved by most in that House not to be justifiable by lawe, and therefore not binding'.[42] Thereafter, not even the Junto leaders were prepared to defend the order publicly, and they appear to have relied on that tried-and-trusted parliamentary tactic, postponement, to allow the matter to die quietly without its sponsors losing face.[43] An attempt to revive interest in the matter a fortnight later by the London Puritan, Isaac Penington, was likewise 'laied aside'.[44] Thereafter, one of the Junto's key spokesmen on ecclesiastical reform, Harbottell Grimston, did raise the matter in the course of a debate in mid November; but this was to 'speake *against* the order of the howse made the 8 day of September last past for the taking away of innovations'.[45] Of course, this may have been a purely personal initiative; however, given Warwick's close involvement in the promotion of the original September Order, and Grimston's own close connections with Warwick, both local and ideological, it might also be possible to read this as an attempt on the part of the Junto leadership to distance themselves from the controversies and disorders which the September Order had provoked.[46]

The reality was that the priorities of men such as Warwick and Pym, who had been in the vanguard of the September campaign for religious reform, had once again changed – by the time the news arrived of the attempted coup in Edinburgh, if not earlier. When the entire fabric of the reformed commonwealth seemed to be imperilled, the priority for the Junto leadership was shoring up the secular foundations of their power, not provoking a fresh round of parish (and parliamentary) tremors that would only serve to undermine them.

After the two Houses' return, security – the kingdom's, the Parliament's, their own – became Warwick's and Pym's chief concern. Not since May 1641 had the threat of civil war, or an Anglo-Scottish war that produced an English civil war as its by-product, been so acute; and the Junto leadership responded accordingly. The 'great body of soldiers in arms' encountered by Parliament-men as they arrived on 20 October, were in fact officers and men from the Middlesex and Westminster Trained Bands, set in place by the Commons' Recess Committee the previous day, with instructions 'to observe such further direction as they should receive from the Earl of Essex'.[47]

During the resumed session's opening week, events in Edinburgh provided the new session's central point of reference. For, as retailed by Pym, what had occurred in Scotland was simply one element of a larger, coordinated plot to destroy the reformist governments in both kingdoms. 'There is a great Probability', Lord Keeper Lyttelton explained to the Lords after conferring with Pym,

> that the Actors in [this plot] have correspondency [a network of allies] here, to work the same horrid and malicious attempts, and to effect such mischievous practices in this kingdom, as might produce distempers ... , because this business was spoken of here in England before it brake out there.[48]

Central to both conspiracies was, inevitably, the control of military force. 'The armyes both of Scotland and England [having been] sollicited to be of the king's partie', Pym argued; and far from risking a time-consuming squabble with the peers over the standing of the various orders made in September concerning Church reform, he 'desired that the house of Commons would *unite* themselves to the Lords'.[49] Indeed, the military threat was far too acute to permit the luxury of procedural spats. Accordingly, the very first Commons committee established after the resumption of the session was to consult with the Lords about 'the securing of the kingdom and the Parliament'.[50] The peers responded sympathetically, delegating the matter to Northumberland (as Lord Admiral) and Holland (as Lord General in charge of the area closest to the Scottish border) and four others to confer with the Junto leaders in the Commons as to how to respond to the crisis.[51] War again looked a serious possibility, and on 22 October, the Junto grandees secured approval for an undertaking from both Houses that they would use

> the power and authority of Parliament, and of this kingdom, for suppressing of all such as, by any conspiracy ... shall endeavour to disturb the peace of Scotland, and to infringe the articles and the treaty made betwixt the two kingdoms.[52]

Without declaring it in so many words, this was tantamount to an undertaking to offer the Argyllians military support in the event of any further attempt to overthrow their quasi-republican régime in Scotland.[53] At all cost, the Union between the two commonwealths had to be maintained.

*

The security of the kingdom had been attended to. From this point, only two days into the resumed parliamentary session, the critical question became the security of the Junto leaders themselves: their personal safety, and the durability of their grip on power. And in practice, as Nicholas had long foreseen, this meant stripping the king of his last significant prerogative power: his ability to appoint and dismiss Privy Councillors, officers of state, and all other government functionaries, without reference to Parliament. Of course, this idea had been current within the Junto leadership at least since May 1641 – that decisive moment for the hardening of the reformers' attitudes against the king – when Sir Arthur Hesilrige had moved that Charles should be petitioned to heed Parliament's advice in choosing and dismissing his Privy Councillors.[54] Only now, however, had it become a matter of critical urgency. For England to become – like its sister commonwealth, Scotland – secure in its liberties, the same reforms had to be effected in London as had already been forced upon the king in Edinburgh.[55] Moreover, depriving the king of his power of appointment would immediately remove the key inducement Charles was capable of using to win over converts to his 'partie': the promise that those who 'served him' by overthrowing his enemies would be rewarded with public office.

Of all the Junto's strategies for the reformation of the English state, this was the most ambitious, the most wide-ranging in its implications, and consequently the most controversial – not least among the constituency that had been broadly in favour of political and religious reform hitherto.[56] Even if the extent of the reform were limited to giving Parliament the right to approve, and hence also to veto, officers – thereby leaving the king, as a face-saving device, with the right to come up with the actual nominations – recent experience of the practice in Scotland had shown that, in reality, the king could put up only limited resistance when confronted with powerful parliamentary opposition.[57]

The task of inducing the English Parliament to follow this Scottish precedent was nevertheless fraught with perils. Scotland's experience of monarchy during the previous forty years had been of an almost permanently absentee king; against this background – with a king living four hundred miles from the Scottish capital, rarely visiting it, and with little first-hand familiarity with the Scottish élite – the claim that the Scottish Parliament might have a veto over royal nominees to roles in government was far less an affront to the king's powers of judgement than it was when raised in the context of England. There, the king had a personal familiarity with most members of the nobility (the cadre from which the 'great officers' were traditionally drawn). To suggest that the monarch's choices would henceforth routinely require parliamentary scrutiny – and, where necessary, the imposition of a parliamentary veto – impugned the king's powers of discernment far more directly than it did in Scotland; indeed, it was tantamount to a declaration that, when it came to deciding on the kingdom's governors, King Charles was not a man whom the Parliament could trust.

English attitudes towards legal tradition also militated against a parliamentary 'usurpation' of the king's rights. His power to nominate and, without being answerable to any, to appoint the great officers and the judges was widely held to be a lawful prerogative of the Crown. To the novel assertion that this was territory that Parliament might annex to itself, D'Ewes, an otherwise enthusiastic supporter of the Junto's reforms, retorted dismissively that 'wee [the Parliament-men] had noe such right', and any proposal to claim it trenched on 'the ancient and undoubted rights of the Crowne'.[58] From the outset, therefore, it was obvious to the Junto leadership that wresting control over government appointments from the king in England was going to be a far more complex and politically hazardous process than it had been for Argyll north of the border.

One solution, as so often with the Junto's most radically innovative initiatives, seemed to lie in the liberating power of precedent. Antiquarian scholarship, far from being a quaint byway of legal knowledge, had the potential to unlock hidden authorities: long-forgotten conventions, sanctioned by the authority of the past, which could be replicated in the here-and-now so as to redefine the relative powers of nobles and kings. Just how important this question of parliamentary control over ministerial appointments was to Pym (and to the Junto leadership more generally) emerges from a series of notes which Pym prepared on the subject, drawn from the Parliament Rolls in the Tower of London (then the main repository of the kingdom's public records) in the course of 1641. Dated only to '1641' (that is, to after 25 March, then the beginning of the new calendar year), their exact moment of composition cannot be established precisely; but it would seem that they were compiled possibly at various times after March and before late October that same year, with the most likely period being the recess of 10 September to 19 October, when Pym was in London, and was relatively unencumbered by other administrative duties. Ranging from Saxon times to the reign of Richard II, the precedents he compiled related almost exclusively to the ways in which royal counsellors had been chosen in the past, and how these contained some highly inconvenient lessons for the Stuart kings.[59]

Perhaps the most striking feature of Pym's assemblage of precedents – and a possible clue as to the audience for which they were prepared – is that almost every one of them served to support, or substantially to augment, the powers of the nobility. Some of these related to the still controversial area of the House of Lords' judicial functions, where, Pym helpfully found, precedent confirmed that 'The Peers in Parliament were to Judge of *all* wrongs done by the King to any of his Subjects'.[60] By far the largest (and most useful) body of documentation, however, related to the appointment of the officers of state. Under Edward III in the 1340s, for example, it appeared that the king 'was Petitioned in Parliament that the high officers of the kingdome might (as in former times) be chosen in Parliament' – an observation that is accompanied by a note, apparently a reminder by Pym to himself, to 'Quare [i.e. check] the Parliam[ent] Roll and Petitions' in the Tower in order to be sure.[61] The records for the 'tyrannical' Richard II – who was eventually deposed by Parliament in 1399 – proved even more useful, providing evidence that the Lord Admiral, Lord Treasurer, Lord Chancellor, and even the Chief Justice of King's Bench had each been chosen formerly by Parliament.[62] History's lessons were clear: 'The ancient manner of Choosing and appointing of Officers was by those over whom their Jurisdiction Extended', Pym noted, a principle that suggested that political authority rose 'upwards' from the governed to their governors, not 'downwards' by way of delegated authority from a divinely ordained king. Other historical gleanings in his collection pointed to the same conclusion.[63] 'Baronial precedents' validating parliamentary control of major appointments on the basis of medieval history were not, therefore, a strain of political rhetoric that ran in competition to more 'modern' theories of popular sovereignty and ascending theories of power. At least in the Junto's reminting of them, they were simply different, but complementary, facets of the same coin.

Yet the obstacles that lay in the way of realizing this new political order remained immense: a world simultaneously modernized and medievalized, in which Parliaments would vet the noble grandees who would occupy the loftiest offices of state. Persuading Parliament-men that the usages of Richard II's reign were to be preferred to those of Charles I's was one problem, though in the right circumstances not an insuperable one. A more practical difficulty arose from the fact that by October 1641, the Junto was facing an ever more organized opposition. The 'king's partie' (as Pym was already calling it)[64] was a force to be reckoned with, as the anti-Junto Lords' ambush of the Ordinance against Innovations on 9 September had made clear.[65]

Achieving any long-lasting control over who constituted England's government depended, in the first instance, on foiling, or at least severely weakening, this newly confident king's party. On the resumption of the session on 20 October, therefore, the Junto leadership's initial concern was with tactics: with the removal of two of the major props of that party in the Lords, the bishops and the Catholic peers. Only once that was achieved could they have any confidence that so controversial a measure as depriving the king of his monopoly over appointments might win a majority in the upper House. Indeed, although it used to be claimed that the future role of the English bishops was one of the main 'religious issues' that precipitated the division between Parliamentarians and Royalists, the proposal to remove bishops from the upper House was in fact one of the rare issues, as the Junto leaders well knew, that could be guaranteed to unite the Commons almost unanimously. When legislation to implement this reform had last been proposed, in the spring, it had 'passed [on 1 May 1641] without one negative'.[66] Anticlericalism remained the default setting for the prejudices of the English gentry; and at the start of the resumed session on 20 October, the Junto leaders were determined to exploit that force once more as a means of weakening the upper-House king's party. Only then would they move to the second, and far more important, stage of their plans: the introduction of laws to complete the 'Venetianization' of the English commonwealth by divesting the king of his monopoly over appointments to the great offices of state.

The Junto's attack on the bishops' legislative role was initiated on the second day of the resumed session. No sooner had Pym, St John and the other Junto leaders returned from their first conference with the Lords on the securing of the kingdom after the attempted coup in Scotland, than Sir Gilbert Gerard* produced a bill to disqualify all clergy from exercising any secular offices – debarring bishops, for the future, from sitting and voting in the upper House.[67] The tactics were familiar. As usual, the Junto leadership chose a 'thin house' (only eighty-one Commons-men were in the chamber), and then steamrollered the bill through its first and second readings 'without Debate' that day (Thursday, 21 October). It was passed by the Commons two days later, 'tho' many desired it may be stayd [i.e. delayed]', at least 'till Monday'.[68] Speakers in its favour included most of the Commons' prominent Junto-men: Hesilrige, Clotworthy, St John and Strode[69] – precisely the same group which, with Pym, would lead the attack aimed at stripping the king of his monopoly over the great offices of state.

Tactical concerns over the fate of this, the key issue of the resumed session, motivated a supplementary measure, also intended to rob the king's party of its caucus of episcopal support – and at the earliest opportunity. On 22 October 1641, Denzell Holles – one of Essex's key allies in the Commons – was sent to the Lords to request that the Lords reactivate the impeachment proceedings against the thirteen bishops, accused for their part in approving the 'popish' Canons of 1640.[70] Whether or not the bishops were actually found guilty on this charge appears to have been of only marginal concern. What the Junto leaders wanted to achieve by forcing the issue to a trial was the suspension of the thirteen bishops – half the entire English episcopate – thereby removing them from the ranks of Nicholas's vestigial 'king's party', ideally, with immediate effect. Hence, Essex, Mandeville, and Brooke all insisted that they 'would have it [done] presently' [i.e. immediately].[71] But

---

* Gerard was part of the Providence Island Company connection, and was particularly close to Oliver St John, who had married Lady Gerard's niece. Gerard's own kin included the Barringtons (he had married Mary Barrington in 1614, an alliance which had brought him into the orbit of the Earl of Warwick and the godly Essex gentry), John Hampden, and Oliver Cromwell, besides St John. He was to take a major role in the organization of the Earl of Essex's war effort during the years 1642–45.

they were frustrated to find that the Lords' majority, not unreasonably, demanded that the impeached bishops should be allowed a fortnight before the legal process against them began (and any suspension of their votes would have taken effect).[72] The bishops' defence proved just how effective Nicholas's efforts to 'countermine' the Junto were proving to be. Bath and Bristol, two of the peers Nicholas had specifically targeted as part of his 'king's party', leapt to the bishops' defence, followed by the Catholic Lord Brudenell, a brother-in-law of one of the Gunpowder Plotters of 1605. Essex's demands for the bishops' immediate suspension were defeated;[73] and, for the moment, the impeached bishops kept their seats – and their king-defending votes.[74]

Back in the Commons, Pym explained the entirely tactical motives behind the decision to press ahead with the bishops' impeachment with almost impolitic frankness: it was 'to sequester the 13 Bishopps from giving ther votes [on] th[e] bill which was to take away ther votes in the Lordes' howse'.[75] Only once the bishops had been disenfranchised could the Junto Lords be confident of any success with its remaining reforms.[76]

And one reform now mattered more than all the rest. No sooner had the case been made for the purging of the Lords on 27 October, than the Junto leadership turned, on the following day, to *the* great issue of the resumed session: the assertion of Parliament's right to control the appointments of Privy Councillors, judges, and the occupants of the prestigious offices of court and state. Employing an increasingly familiar (and transparently obvious) ruse, the Junto seems to have used a relatively obscure supporter, Robert Goodwyn, a Sussex man hitherto untarnished by any known factional associations, to raise the issue; thereby providing the cue for one of the Junto grandees – in this case, William Strode – to second the motion with a long and (as D'Ewes guessed) 'premeditated' speech.[77] But the line was the same, and just as extreme, from both men. 'All wee had done this Parliament would come to nothing', argued Goodwyn, 'and wee should never be free from danger', unless steps were taken to purge the king's remaining evil counsellors, and to control future appointments.[78] Strode was even more emphatic, seconding Goodwyn 'with great violence' and with suspiciously similar words. He, too, insisted that

> all wee had done this Parliament was nothing, unles wee had a negative voice [a veto] in the place of the great officers of the King and of his Councellors, by whom his Majestie was ledd captive.[79]

Other unnamed speakers (among them possibly Pym) argued that medieval precedent was on Parliament's side: they were no more than reviving 'an auntient right'. Others threatened that 'untill such things as these' were granted by the king, there could be no question of providing the increasingly impoverished monarch with a revenue-settlement.[80]

Ironically, while the proposals to purge bishops from the Lords and debar the clergy from any secular employments had passed the Commons 'without one negative',[81] the question of who should decide the composition of England's future government – whether Parliament had a veto, or whether such matters belonged to the king alone – sharply polarized even those who had hitherto been broadly united on questions of secular reform. Edward Hyde stated the counter-argument bluntly. This was a reform too far, for 'the great officers of the crowne weere to be appointed by the King, [this] being an hereditary flower of the crowne'. The measures abolishing Star Chamber, High Commission, and Ship Money, he agreed, 'had done verie much for the good of the subject, and hee thought all particulars weere in a good condition if wee could but preserve them as they weere'.[82] Nor was Hyde the only speaker to argue that England's 'mixed monarchy' should be defended against the quasi-republican model being proposed by the Junto. Falkland, Strangways, Edmund Waller and Robert Holborne – all enthusiasts for the Parliament's first phase of secular reform – now stood, as Nicholas informed the king, 'as Champions in the maynten'nce of your Prerogative'. And it was a measure of the king's party's increasingly sophisticated organization that Nicholas not only supplied his master with the list of his Commons champions, but that Charles, in response, commanded Nicholas to inform them that he would do something 'for their encouragem't' at his return.[83]

Whether or not there should be 'further reformation' was indeed the rock on which broke the old, and now creaking, reformist alliance.[84] But the contentious issue was not the further reformation of the Church (any radical elements of that programme had long since been abandoned by the Junto leadership),[85] but the further reformation of the state: taking away from the king the one prerogative power that made what James I had called 'true monarchy' possible, namely, his freedom to choose those who were to serve him in the government of the realm.

By the end of that debate, on Thursday, 28 October, it looked as though the king's party had just notched up its first major parliamentary victory. 'Soe many in the Com'ons House [appeared] against this busines', Nicholas reported with satisfaction, that some thought the matter had been permanently laid to rest.[86] Strode and the other Junto spokesmen had failed to obtain the Commons' approval to a single proposal that would have asserted the Parliament's right to exercise a veto. Instead, the king's party seems to have guided the debate to an entirely innocuous conclusion: the preparation of a 'petition' to the king on the subject of evil counsellors, a course of action that left the king's all-important prerogative of appointment completely untouched.[87]

At the end of the Parliament's first full week since its return, Warwick and his fellow grandees had much to be anxious about. If the Commons could not be induced to assert a right of veto over ministerial appointments in these circumstances – notwithstanding the recent Scottish precedent, despite the evidence suggesting Charles's complicity in the planned assassinations of Hamilton and Argyll, and even with the advantage afforded the Junto by a 'thin House' – then it was highly doubtful that the proposal could ever be successfully revived. And the implications of this for their own continuance in power were bleak: all of them could be ejected from their posts the moment the king's star moved – as it already appeared to be doing – back into the ascendant.

On the other side, Nicholas and the adherents of the king's party were impatient to press home the advantage afforded by this initial success. At the end of that week, all that was needed, they believed, was the galvanizing effect of the king's presence at Westminster to tilt the parliamentary balance decisively back in Charles's favour. If only the king could settle his affairs in Scotland promptly, Nicholas argued in a letter to his master on Monday, 1 November, 'soe as you might be here the next weeke [i.e. 8–14 November], your best servaunts here conceave it would then be in your Majestie's power, by your presence, to bring this Parliament to a reasonable good conclusion'.[88] For the first time since they had assembled, almost exactly twelve months earlier, there now seemed to be a majority in both Houses, at least among those who bothered to attend,* that had lost all stomach for further thoroughgoing reform, whether religious or secular. Hyde's view – that 'all particulars [in the commonwealth] weere in a good condition, if wee could but preserve them as they weere'[89] – was rapidly gaining ground.

But in Scotland, Charles was still too preoccupied with the fallout from 'the Incident', and his courtiers' bungled attempt to topple Argyll, to have any hopes of a speedy return to England.[90] Moreover, just when many Parliament-men were coming to regard as increasingly paranoic the 'prevailing party's' recurrent allegations of plots at court to undo the reforms achieved thus far, events beyond even the Junto's contrivance provided apparently cast-iron proof that the 'commonwealth' was indeed assailed by internal and external foes. On Sunday, 31 October, just three days after the Junto's first attempt to wrest control of appointments to public office from the king had been ignominiously talked down, news reached London of a crisis which threw the question of appointments, particularly military appointments, into high relief.

A major revolt had broken out in Ireland, and the very survival of English rule in that kingdom hung by a thread.

III. THE 'IRISH MASSACRE' AND THE MANAGEMENT OF WAR

The Earl of Warwick's investment in finding a Commons seat for Sir John Clotworthy, the Junto's in-house expert on Irish affairs, had already proved its worth more than once in the course of the present Parliament. With the outbreak of the Irish insurrection, however, Clotworthy and his connections came into their own. For the first news of the Irish insurrection to reach England came not via the 'official channels' of the Lords Justices in Dublin, but from Clotworthy's own man-of-affairs in Ireland, Owen O'Connolly.[91]

---

* The active membership of the Commons in October and early November 1641 hovered between a quarter of its total membership and well under a half; a division on 16 November revealed the presence of 223 Commons-men from a possible maximum of just over 500. Attendance levels in the Lords were proportionally only slightly higher.

Mud-bespattered and exhausted from his long journey, O'Connolly reached London by the early afternoon of Sunday, 31 October and appeared at Leicester House,* the austerely classical London mansion of Robert Sidney, Earl of Leicester, Strafford's successor as Lord Lieutenant of Ireland.[92] O'Connolly related the essential elements of the rebels' strategy: that the revolt had begun in Ulster; was being supported in other parts of the island; and that but for the fortuitous discovery of Lord Maguire's plot to seize Dublin Castle, the capital itself would have fallen into rebel hands.[93] Central to O'Connolly's account of the insurrection, however, was his highly coloured portrayal of the rebels' aims. This was nothing less than an attempted massacre of the entire English and Protestant population of Ireland – 'all', he claimed, were to have been 'cut offe'. If the rebellion were to succeed, the Protestants of Ireland would be annihilated.[94]

As with the reports of the failed coup in Edinburgh a fortnight earlier, the Junto leadership first received, and therefore had the advantage of managing, the news of the Irish insurrection, thereby ensuring that it was O'Connolly's alarmist version of events that went into circulation in England.[95] Perhaps not coincidentally, his account could not have been better suited to reviving the fortunes of his political masters in London.

To Leicester, the news cannot have been a complete surprise. Members of the Privy Council had been meeting intermittently – 'all last Weeke' it was reported on 21 October – to discuss 'Irish affaires' and the threat posed by the great flight of 'Papists ... thither with incredible numbers'.[96] Even so, it had not been what Leicester had expected on taking up the Lord Lieutenancy after the execution of the Earl of Strafford in May, when Ireland had seemed the most obedient of all the realms under Charles's triple crown. Scholarly and bookish by inclination, with a penchant for mathematics, Leicester was ill suited in almost every respect to the task of organizing the suppression of a major Irish revolt – except one; as a man of 'godly' piety and as a first cousin by marriage to all four of the Junto's 'military earls' (the Lord Admiral Northumberland, the Lord Generals Essex and Holland, and Master of the Ordnance Newport), he was a man in whom the 'prevailing party' could trust.[97]

Leicester's first response to the news of the rebellion was to brief the Privy Council, which met at 4 p.m. that same day, Sunday, 31 October, and for the first time in weeks had serious decisions to make. What was obviously required was the urgent despatch of money, arms and troops to Ireland – and that would require parliamentary intervention. Moreover, to bring home the gravity of the crisis to the Commons, the Lords of the Privy Council resolved to take the unprecedented step of going en masse to the Commons' chamber on Monday morning, 1 November, to break the news of the Irish rebellion in person. Hence, shortly after 10 a.m., Commons-men were aston-

---

* Leicester House, built between 1631 and 1635, was one of the first Classical houses in London and stood on the north side of the modern-day Leicester Square; it was demolished in the early 1790s.

Built in the 1630s (on the north side of what is modern-day Leicester Square), Leicester House became one of the centres for the planning of the new campaign of English conquest in Ireland in the autumn of 1641.

ished to see the Lord Keeper and sixteen other Privy Councillor peers – including Leicester, Northumberland, Essex, Warwick, Mandeville, and Saye[98] – appearing in person at the bar of the Commons. As a mark of courtesy, they were immediately provided with chairs by the Speaker, as the clerk read out the series of newly arrived letters and depositions, beginning with O'Connolly's sensational testimony.[99] This highly lurid, and perhaps deliberately exaggerated, version of events rapidly became the received account of the insurrection, with the result that it came to be regarded in England as a crime of singular horror: 'so horrid, black, and flagitious [i.e. atrocious] a rebellion', in Bulstrode Whitelocke's words, 'as cannot be paralleled in the stories of any other nation'.[100] Perhaps not coincidentally, this engendered precisely the sense of urgency which the Junto required in order to justify what happened next.

The new military crisis posed an obvious legal problem. The raising of troops was traditionally a prerogative of the Crown. So, too, was the right to order the release of arms and ammunition from the king's arsenals. Yet it was clear that there could be no effective military response to the current crisis if Leicester were required to obtain warrants for his every action from a king who was still four hundred miles away in Edinburgh, a ten-day round trip on autumn roads; longer still in winter. If this posed a practical dilemma, for the aristocratic leadership determined to deprive Charles of the power to govern, it also provided an almost heaven-sent opportunity. Parliament, it now seemed, would have to provide the necessary authority for the military preparations, in the absence of the king; and that meant its usurping, if only temporarily, the king's prerogative to raise troops and issue arms and ammunition from the royal stores. And however temporary the intrusion on the king's prerogative powers might be, a precedent would have been usefully set.

By necessitating the raising of a new army in England, the Irish rebellion gave an irresistible urgency to the Junto's plans, first hinted at by Hesilrige in May and only recently reaffirmed by Strode, to vest control of the great offices in Parliament. Peers and Commons-men were forced to confront the implications of what might happen if an army were raised while the king still enjoyed an unfettered power to appoint and dismiss its commanders at will. This, the Junto leadership seems to have hoped, would finally impel a reluctant Commons – and, with sufficient pressure, the Lords as well – to reclaim their 'lost' medieval jurisdiction over appointments to major military command.

This process was aided by the way in which the Junto Lords, with their current (though potentially transient) monopoly of military office, took the lead in the preparations for the new war. Delegations were despatched to the City to solicit £50,000 in loans.[101] And at the prompting of Sir William Masham – by happy coincidence, an old ally of the Warwick-Barrington network in Essex – a new bicameral Committee for Irish Affairs (of twenty-six peers and the usual proportion of twice that number of Commons-men) was established to assist with preparations for the forthcoming campaign.[102] By 3 November, the Commons were already considering how best to raise the new expeditionary force that would be sent to Ireland; and within twenty-four hours it had resolved to despatch an army of 6,000 foot and 2,000 horse 'with all convenient speed'.[103]

Simultaneously, the Junto leaders set about fanning the flames of anti-Catholic hysteria, reignited by the news of 'massacres' of Protestants in Ireland. On Tuesday, 2 November, Strode successfully proposed a bill to unleash a new wave of prosecutions of Catholic recusants at the next assizes and quarter sessions.[104] With Queen Henriette Marie widely suspected of involvement in anti-Junto plotting, Essex was despatched, at the behest of the two Houses, to ensure that the Prince of Wales was brought back from Oatlands Palace in Surrey, where he had been in his mother's company, to Richmond Palace, where he was to be in the custody of his Governor, Essex's brother-in-law, the Marquess of Hertford.[105] Further revelations of 'popish' conspiracies followed, heightening the sense of panic at Westminster. On Wednesday, 3 November, Pym held the Commons rapt as he elaborated at length on O'Connolly's account of the plot to seize Dublin Castle.[106] And the following day the two Houses received from their Commissioners in Edinburgh copies of the depositions taken by the Scottish Parliament from the conspirators involved in the 'Incident'. Most shocking of all was the evidence from Will Morray, with its revelations that he had taken at least one of the leading members of the conspiracy to a private *tête-à-tête* with Charles in the royal Bedchamber.[107] This was a critically important development. Morray's depositions were not quite the smoking gun; but they were, nevertheless, the closest the Junto leadership had approached to obtaining irrefutable evidence of the king's own guilt: that he was employing as a trusted Bedchamber servant a man who (in the Junto's own telling of events) had been active in a plot to murder most of the leading figures in the Edinburgh government.[108]

When the two Houses rose on Thursday, 4 November, the pendulum of political fortune had swung back sharply in the Junto's favour. It was only a little more than a week since Strode's motion that Parliament should assume control of appointments to great public offices had been resoundingly defeated in the Commons. Arguments from historical precedent – 'that it had bene soe heretofore' and thus was 'an auntient right' – had proved insufficiently persuasive.[109] But, in the interim, the almost kaleidoscopic sequence of threats and dangers that had come to the Parliament's notice (news of the rebellion in Ireland, further revelations of Catholic plotting in England, and finally the arrival of the evidence against the plotters in Edinburgh) had transformed the context of political debate. The general question of parliamentary control of office-holding now had a precise and immediate focus. With an army about to be raised, did the Parliament want that commanded by men chosen by, and dismissible by, a king who was so dangerously susceptible to 'evil counsellors'? Or should Parliament itself determine which members of the nobility it could trust with the kingdom's military forces? In this new environment, there was now a slim chance that, on the morrow, an argument for parliamentary control of office-holding based on the immediate practicalities of the moment, rather than contentious appeals to precedent, might just carry the day. And that chosen morning could not have been more appropriate for such an initiative: the fifth of November – the anniversary of the Catholic plot to assassinate king, Lords, and Commons, at the state opening of Parliament in 1605; a day traditionally marked by the pealing of church bells in the morning and glow of celebratory bonfires after dusk.[110]

The Junto had already decided to make a major occasion out of the 5 November commemoration. As early as 30 October, Strode (one of the sponsors of the original motion on 27 October that Parliament should assert control over military and ministerial appointments), had successfully moved that the anniversary be marked by a public sermon. The late Earl of Bedford's protégé and favourite preacher, Cornelius Burges, was chosen for the task at the nomination of Arthur Goodwin: a loyal Junto supporter who was Hampden's Buckinghamshire neighbour and Lord Wharton's father-in-law, and was to take a prominent role in the campaign for parliamentary control over appointments to public office.[111] The Temple Church was selected as the venue, after fears that the much closer St Margaret's Church (across the street from Westminster Hall) had been infected with the plague.[112] None, however, could have predicted how powerfully Burges would drive home his message: that the commonwealth could not be safe until the Protestant 'ancient nobility' enjoyed their offices, free from the fear that they might be displaced by a petulant or malevolent king.

*

Burges's sermon for Gunpowder Day 1605 was one of the great essays in topical pulpit oratory produced during the 1640s. Delivered to the House of Commons assembled in the Temple Church that morning of Friday, 5 November, his homily left his audience in little doubt as to the connection between the popish conspiracy of 1605 and the threats confronting the king's virtuous counsellors in 1641.[113] Explicitly taking up the theme of appointments to the great offices of state, Burges argued that Charles's attempts to conciliate Catholic grandees throughout his reign by offering them royal favour had been completely misplaced. For in the case of the court's Papists,

sundry degrees of Dignitie and honour have been (in later times, especially) heaped upon divers of them; yea, they have been admitted very neere to his Majestie's Sacred Person, and trusted with Offices of greatest honor and trust in the State. And yet, neverthelesse, neither any, nor all, of these favours together either do – or can – secure us of them.[114]

Treachery was the natural disposition of Catholics, and the great puzzle was why the king promoted such men, notwithstanding the dangers that they posed. Burges, however, had an answer: a highly topical explanation as to why the king might have allowed this situation to arise: 'indeed', he argued,

> this is one of the greatest misfortunes of a Prince … and a sad symptome of his approaching ruin, 'when God smites him in his wits', as he did [King] Rehoboam [of Judah], 'to follow the counsels of those who were brought up with him', and know how to fit his humour, and to reject the counsels of graver men, who advised nothing but for his prosperity and honour.[115]

As Burges's Bible-reading audience would immediately have recognized, King Rehoboam was an almost perfect antetype for King Charles and the Covenanter revolt: for Rehoboam (Charles) was the reckless son of wise King Solomon (himself often identified with King James), whose harsh rule provoked his subjects in northern Judah to rebel and create an independent government. Burges hardly needed to labour the parallel with Covenanter Scotland.

Nor was this the only topical reference. For Rehoboam's evil counsellor, the servant mentioned in this passage who had been 'brought up with' the king, would have been instantly recognizable to anyone familiar with the Caroline court as Will Morray, the king's childhood friend and former whipping boy, who had risen to become one of the most trusted figures in the Bedchamber.[116] As Burges was almost certainly aware, Morray's deposition retailing his involvement in the assassination plot in Edinburgh[117] had been passed around in the Commons only the previous afternoon.[118]*

In alluding to Will Morray as the key source of Charles's deluded counsels, Burges had touched on the villain of the moment.[119] No sooner had the Commons-men reassembled in St Stephen's Chapel for the morning's business than the House was read a series of depositions, taken before the Scottish Parliament a week earlier and forwarded to London by Fiennes, that established the central role of Morray in the failed *coup d'état* against Hamilton

---

* One of the most striking aspects of Burges's sermon, in the light of later developments, is its suggestion, which his audience were surely expected to apply to King Charles, that God 'smites' kings in their wits – that is, leaves them mentally incapacitated – when they had displeased him. How far Burges conferred with Pym or any other of the Junto leaders in the preparation of his sermon is, of course, unknown; but his assertion that Charles was mentally incapacitated for rule was to become an increasingly prominent justification, over the following twelve months, for his marginalization from the business of government and the Junto's ever more extensive 'usurpation' of his powers.

and Argyll.[120] Meanwhile, other depositions, read to the Commons for the first time that morning, ominously disclosed the depth of support for the plot within the Scottish nobility: Montrose, Roxburgh, Almond, and others were all revealed as willing participants in the conspiracy, and generally with few scruples about shedding blood in order to see it succeed.[121]

With their audience thus prepared, the Junto leaders in the Commons turned to the substantive business of the day: a series of measures to take control of the Irish war out of Charles's hands, and in the process to deprive him of the power to appoint (or dismiss) the great officers of the kingdom. Pym introduced two measures – both of them products of his meetings with the Junto grandees in the bicameral Committee for Irish Affairs during the previous night and first thing that morning.[122] Both were ordinances: legislative instruments that had the same force as a statute, notwithstanding that they would neither receive, nor require, the royal assent. If Parliament was not yet ready to insist that it could actually appoint the great officers, the next best thing would be to persuade it to claim a right to *empower* the existing great officers – again, without reference to (and thereby marginalizing) the king.

In a House that had just heard Burges's persuasive oratory and the first-hand evidence of the coup attempt against Argyll, the king's party were all but silenced. Without serious opposition, the two new ordinances were accepted, thus providing a foundation of parliamentary authority for the new war effort.[123] The first empowered the Earl of Leicester, as Lord Lieutenant of Ireland, to issue commissions to officers for the raising of a new army of 3,500 foot and 600 horse (a slightly smaller force than had been voted two days earlier);[124] while the second authorized the Earl of Newport, as Master of the Ordnance, to deliver arms sufficient to equip them.[125]

These two ordinances set a powerful precedent for the two Houses taking military action on their own. Evidently encouraged by this success, the Junto leadership appears to have decided to make one more attempt at persuading the Parliament to assert the right to determine who should serve as Privy Councillors and occupy the major offices of public trust. Ingeniously, they opted to move the question, not as legislation, but almost surreptitiously, attaching it to the new set of formal Instructions that were due to be sent to Lord Howard of Escrick, Nathaniel Fiennes, and the other Parliamentary Commissioners in Edinburgh, whose task it now was to negotiate with the Argyllians for Scottish support in the forthcoming campaign. The gambit seems to have been of Pym's devising. In a resolution of breathtaking temerity, the Commissioners in Edinburgh were instructed to tell Charles bluntly that, unless he dismissed those counsellors of whom Parliament disapproved, then it was evident that

> the aydes [financial contributions] of his subjects will be employed towards
> their destruction; therefore [they were] humbly to desire a remov[al] of such
> counsellors and [that he] take to him[self] to the councell of Parliament.[126]

The king's-party men had no doubt what this meant. 'By such [a clause]', Hyde concluded, 'wee should, as it weere, prevale [over] the King.'[127] Edward

Nicholas went into a panic, rushing off a letter to Charles in Edinburgh recounting what had happened, and explaining that he had written so 'that your Majestie may see how extreamely necessary it is for you to hasten hither'; he added a final plea that Charles should 'burne this letter which is now sent you'.[128]

Against ferocious opposition, St John tempered the original proposal by arguing that they were merely requesting the right of *approving* Councillors and officers of state, not of naming them.[129] But the effect was little different: if Parliament could veto the king's nominees, it could – in theory – do so repeatedly, until the king was at last forced to present a Parliament-acceptable nominee. This was tantamount to an ultimatum: nothing would be done in England to fund the Irish war, in other words, unless Charles accepted Parliament's right to nominate the great officers – including, of course, the commander of the new army for Ireland. Its implication was that, unless he were to lose his kingdom entirely, Charles would be forced to rely on Scottish military assistance, with all that implied for Scottish influence within the three kingdoms both during the war and, still more, in Ireland after the insurrection was suppressed.[130]

This, perhaps more than any other, was the great issue that divided the Parliament most profoundly in the autumn of 1641. A House of Commons that had been united in barring clergy from any role in secular affairs, in ousting the entire episcopate from the House of Lords, and in impeaching half the bench of bishops for their part in framing the Canons of 1640, now split down the centre when it came to the question of whether Parliament should 'prevale' over the king. Sir John Culpeper, who had been at one with Junto leaders in his desire to root out 'superstitious innovations' from the Church, and been involved in drafting the 'puritan' September 9 Declaration, now sided with Hyde and a series of other king's-party men in defending the monarch's prerogative powers. When the matter came to a vote on 8 November, it produced a division as sharp as any in the Parliament hitherto. The Junto carried the day with 151 votes against what appears to have been the 'king's party' and its adherents – including Hyde, Culpeper, and the Yorkshire Royalist, John Belasyse, an officer who had fought for the king in both the Covenanter Wars.[131]

Even in its revised form, however, the force of the ultimatum to the king was barely diminished. Charles was to be 'supplicated' to 'employ only such counsellors and ministers as should be approved by his Parliament', Pym informed the Lords on 9 November; and if the king rejected this supplication, 'we shall be forced, in discharge of the trust we owe to the State, and to those whom we represent, to resolve upon some such way of defending Ireland from the rebels as may concur to *the defending of ourselves* from such mischievous counsels and designs, as have lately been, and still are, in practice and agitation against us'. Any funds raised by Parliament would be entrusted to 'such persons of honour and fidelity as we have cause to confide in'.[132] Once again, the insistence that duty to 'the State' took precedence over any duty to the person of the king formed the moral and legal basis for the Junto's 'usurpation' of military and executive power.

Though it still faced a battle for ratification in the Lords, the Commons' approval of this ultimatum, however narrowly achieved, marked a decisive victory for the Junto, and a critically important further step towards the 'Venetianizing' of the English state. Here, for the first time, the Junto leadership in the Commons – among the proposal's supporters were Strode, St John, Pym, and Hesilrige – had secured acceptance of a principle which, as it had already done in Scotland, effectively removed the business of government from the king's hands. An entire political system, in which royal favour had been an essential prerequisite of political power, was subverted, if not wholly eradicated, at a single stroke. Moreover, the Commons could exercise the power of the purse as a means of persuading – and, if necessary, forcing – its choices on the obstructive king's party in the House of Lords; yet the principal beneficiaries of this flexing of political muscle by the 'representatives of the people' were the Junto's noblemen grandees, the cadre that currently monopolized almost all court and military offices, but whose tenure still formally depended (as had all public appointments hitherto) on the monarch's, rather than the Parliament's authority.

Having established this principle that the great offices should be answerable to the 'State', rather than simply the king, the Junto leadership in the Commons moved swiftly to test whether an already deeply divided House was ready to take that principle to its logical conclusion: to agree to the appointment *by ordinance* of the most important of all the great officers in time of war, the Lord General commanding land forces in the South of England. On 6 November, apparently acting as the Junto's cat's-paw in proposing this major item of business (just as he had earlier done in moving what subsequently became the Triennial Act),[133] Oliver Cromwell stepped forward to propose that both Houses should consider appointing the Earl of Essex as commander-in-chief South of the Trent. The measure was immediately placed on the agenda for the next conference with the House of Lords.[134]

Few initiatives from this period reveal more clearly the Junto grandees' own fears for their future tenure of office. As an ordinance of appointment, this proposal was entirely redundant, as Essex was already Lord General South of the Trent, appointed in the usual way by a commission under the Great Seal, issued by the king. The whole point of Cromwell's proposal was not to *confer* an office on Essex that he already possessed, but to shift its legal basis from the royal prerogative (under which it was currently held) to the authority of the State:

> that the Earl of Essex may have power *from both Houses* to command the Trained Bands on this side [of the] Trent upon all occasions for the defence of the king; *and that this power may continue till this Parliament shall take further order.*[135]

Thus empowered, Essex (whose area of military responsibility included the security of Westminster and the Parliament) would have been proofed against dismissal by the king for as long as the two Houses determined. Unsurprisingly, the newly effective king's party in the Lords immediately sought to obstruct the measure. Indeed, over the weeks ahead, the Junto's insistence that Essex should be England's principal military commander 'by authority of Parliament' became the basis of an intractable disagreement between the king's party and themselves: for it epitomized the far larger question of whether monarch or legislature should have the ultimate authority to allocate the senior military commands and all other major places of public trust.[136]* The contest for what was to become the Militia Ordinance – the final *casus belli* between the king and the Junto – had begun.

As so often during 1641, the dynamic impelling the Junto leaders towards ever more aggressive usurpations of the king's prerogative powers was the need to protect themselves from the consequences of their 'great treason' the previous year. To this extent, the radicalism of 1641 was self-generating. The more the Junto leaders angered the king by their de facto encroachments on his power, the more they were drawn to impose formal curbs on monarchical authority, thereby provoking Charles's ire still further – and his desire for future vengeance. Giustinian, the Venetian ambassador, shrewdly summarized this process in a contemporaneous despatch. 'All control at present', he wrote,

> rests in the hands of those who, as the authors of the recent radical decisions, are called upon – for their own safety's sake – to continue defiantly in the course that they have begun. Truth to tell, they have transformed this country and brought England to the verge of the most dangerous possibilities.[137]

*

Yet the Venetian exaggerated the extent to which the Junto held power in its hands. When it came to control of appointments to office, there remained major obstacles in the way of their plans for the radical reframing of the English state. One, as we have seen, was the sharply divided state of the Commons themselves.[138] The most effective opposition, however, came from the House of Lords, and with good reason. For, if the Commons' proposals for parliamentary control went through, it would not be the nobles as a whole who benefited, but a single and clearly identifiable clique: the 'prevailing party', dominated by Warwick, Essex, and their extensive network of office-holding kin.

And there the proposals stalled. The proposal 'stops in our House', wrote the Earl of Northumberland on 12 November, 'and I believe will hardly pass with us without some alteration'.[139] Pym's ultimatum and the new 'ordinance' for Essex to be Lord General joined an ever-growing log-jam of Commons-approved legislation which, from the resumption of the parliamentary session in October, fell victim to the obstructionism of the king's party in the Lords.

---

* Debate on this question was to lead, on 7 December 1641, to the introduction of legislation by Sir Arthur Hesilrige for the parliamentary appointment of the Lord General and Lord Admiral of England – the antecedent of the Militia Ordinance of February–March 1642.

When pressed, the oppositionist majority in the upper House simply fobbed off requests for haste from the Commons with the polite but legislation-dooming phrase: that they would send an answer at a later date 'by messengers of their own'.

The problem facing Northumberland and the other Junto grandees was all too obvious. Nicholas's highly effective lobbying of the bishops and the 'well-affected' peers in the weeks before the session was part of the explanation. The other half lay with the Junto grandees themselves, and the chaotic, 'godly' campaign against Laudian innovations that had been set in train on the eve of the parliamentary recess. By raising the threat of oligarchy (and hence a 'closed', mono-factional court) and twinning this with the spectre of puritan-inspired disorders in the Church, the Junto had managed to touch two of the English governing élite's most sensitive nerves. That campaign had already alienated substantial sections of the Commons, but, so long as the atmosphere of political crisis was maintained, the Junto leaders could count on enough support to press ahead with their pro-gramme – if only just. In the Lords, however (where Charles's efforts to win hearts and minds had been concentrated), there sufficient anti-Junto feeling to create a vestigial 'party', strong enough, if combined with the voting power of the pro-court bishops, to block any further attack on the king's prerogative powers.

These developments were also noticed outside Westminster. Soon after the resumption of the parliamentary session in October, the London apprentices were reported to have been preparing a petition 'for the removing of the Popish Lords and Bish[ops] out of the House of Peeres'; yet their motives were not based on some crude religious antipathy, but on a relatively sophisticated understanding of the way Parliament was working – or, from the Junto's perspective, failing to work. The bishops and the lay Catholic peers, observed the newsletter-writer, Edward Rossingham, 'are looked upon as the only impediments, that no Bills can passe for the universal good in Ch[urch] or Comon-wealth'.[140]

Unless that impasse were broken, there was no chance that the Parliament would ever win control of appointments to the great offices, and every likelihood that the king would dismiss most of the current Junto from their posts at the earliest opportunity; every likelihood, too, as Strode had warned, that 'all wee had done this Parliament was nothing'.[141] In November 1641, as the Parliament – already the longest-sitting in English history – passed its first anniversary, the fragility of the reformists' achievement was glaringly apparent. So, too, was the solution. Something had to be done to break the power of the obstructive 'king's party' in the House of Lords.

iv. TELLING TALES TO THE PEOPLE

As the raising of an army for service in Ireland proceeded briskly during November – and the question of its future command acquired ever greater urgency – the Junto grandees adopted two main strategies for dealing with their patrician opponents. The first, addressing the critical question of numbers in the House of Lords, was to renew the attack on the thirteen bishops; the second, likewise intended to weaken the king's party, was to oust all the 'popish peers'. And as though to underline the purpose of the twin assaults,[142] these proceeded in tandem with the campaign to induce the Lords to agree to the Commons' vote: that funding for the Irish war was to be dependent on the king's abandonment of his monopoly over appointments to the major public offices.

The attack on the bishops came first. Matters were brought to a head on Saturday, 13 November, a fortnight into the preparations for the Irish campaign, when the Commons, impatient at the 'dilatory and insufficient' responses from the bishops, established a committee under Oliver St John to begin examining witnesses as the prelude to a fully fledged impeachment trial.[143] Once the trial was under way, it seems to have been assumed the Lords would have no alternative but to suspend the bishops for its duration.

Simultaneously, Essex, Warwick, Saye, and a number of other Junto peers moved against the Catholic members of the upper House, setting up a committee to ensure that the statutes against recusants were enforced to the letter.[144] Aided by the discovery of yet another 'popish plot', centred on the household of the papist Earl of Worcester, the new bout of persecution had an immediate effect on the attendance of the Catholic peers.[145] Within a matter of days, an anxious Nicholas was reporting that 'all the Papists Lordes are alreddy removing out of this Towne upon this order'.[146] Meanwhile, in the Commons, the Junto renewed its demand for the Lords to accept the ultimatum on the great offices, insisting (in a resolution drawn up by Pym and Hampden) that it 'is so important that this House cannot recede from it', and threatening to despatch it for presentation to the king in four days, whether the Lords agreed to join with them or not.[147]

With the king's return from Scotland imminent, insulating Essex and Holland from any attempt to remove them from their military commands was a question of ever greater concern. Hence, on 15 November, Denzell Holles introduced legislation, for which Cromwell had earlier acted as stalking-horse, ordering the mobilization of Southern England's Trained Bands and confirming the Earl of Essex as their commander by parliamentary ordinance alone.[148] A similar ordinance, intended to secure Holland's position as commander in the North, quickly followed.

Yet the obstacle posed by the upper-House king's party remained insuperable. Except for scaring the Catholic lords into flight, the Junto's efforts to weaken the king's party proved largely unavailing. Even before Bristol and the other anti-Junto peers received the king's instruction, sent via Nicholas, that 'You must see to cross this [ultimatum] in the Lords' House, if it be possible',[149] the king's-party peers had succeeded in blocking all attempts to have the ultimatum on the control of offices approved in the upper House.[150] The growing conviction that it would not be long before Charles returned to London further buoyed the spirits of this oppositionist group.

For Essex and Northumberland, no less than for Hesilrige and Pym, what made such setbacks all the more frustrating was just how tantalizingly close they were to securing control of the upper House. With only around half of the nobility still attending Parliament (some fifty to sixty peers),[151] the Junto could count on the support of some twenty to twenty-four lords – at least a dozen fewer than could usually be mobilized in support of the king. Once the bishops were removed, however, their own forces looked certain to overmaster the king's, and the flow of reformist legislation needed to consolidate control of the Irish war in the Junto's hands could resume.

In the meantime, anything that might retard the Junto's arrival at this secure and happy outcome was unceremoniously tossed overboard. As ever, the cause of 'further reformation' in the Church was the first to go; and in a letter to the veteran Privy Councillor, Sir Thomas Rowe, the Earl of Northumberland explained why. The bill for abolishing the bishops' votes had just reached 'our House', he wrote, but 'whether *we* shall get it passed or not is very doubtful, unless some assurance [can] be given that the rooting out of their function [as pastors in the Church] is not intended'.[152]

The slightest hint that the Junto intended to press ahead with Root-and-Branch, and the majority of peers looked certain to relaliate by rejecting the attempt to deprive the king's-party bishops of their votes. From November, the Junto-men worked assiduously to convince sceptics – including some within their own ranks – that their abandonment of 'further reformation' was sincere. Pembroke, revealingly, was one of the doubters. 'If we would put the Bishops out of the Lords House', he later recalled, he had been assured that 'no further attempt should be made upon the Church.' 'I am sure I was promised so, by some who would be thought honest men.'[153] Concern to let these sleeping dogs lie likewise motivated the reformists' tactical decision, a few days later, to avoid any debate of the *Book of Common Prayer*: 'wee saw that the partie for episcopacie was soe strong', noted D'Ewes, 'as we weere willing to lay the [matter] aside without further trouble'.[154] Yet this 'partie for episcopacie' was certainly not coterminous with the king's party; for many of these same Commons-men, who constituted a majority in favour of the bishops, were the same legislators who, only the previous day, had finally passed the legislation shifting the basis of Essex's authority as Lord General South of the Trent from that of a commission from the king to an ordinance of Parliament: the intended antidote for any attempt by Charles to dismiss him.[155]

All this bore a marked similarity to the tactics employed during Strafford's trial, when the Junto had also been concerned to sway a potentially obstructive House of Lords, and had been similarly preoccupied with schemes to prevent the bench of bishops from exercising its bloc vote. As during that crisis, however, the concerns of Essex and Warwick, Pym and Strode were not confined to the pressures that could be exerted *within* Parliament. Their behaviour in November 1641 revealed, as it had done throughout the campaign against Strafford, an acute awareness of the power of the 'public sphere' and, in particular, of the need to win over the large and politically interested metropolitan audience on their doorstep. The courting of public opinion had been a staple of the Junto's political repertoire ever since Calybute

Downinge's sermon to the Artillery Company back in September 1640. Nothing hitherto, however, had been as audacious as the scheme it pushed to the fore during the final weeks of the king's absence: a systematic indictment of all the instances of misgovernment the kingdom had suffered going back over a decade and more.

Encyclopaedic in its comprehensiveness, this 'Remonstrance' – what became known, from the nineteenth century, as the Parliament's '*Grand Remonstrance*' – had been in desultory preparation for the best part of a year.[156] But it was only in November 1641, with the question of the king's power to choose officers having acquired a heightened importance amid the preparations for a new war, that the Junto leadership made a serious attempt to bring it to completion. As Edward Nicholas, acting as ever as the king's informant on Westminster politics, noted with alarm, it was much more than simply an attempt to justify all that Parliament had done since its meeting. Prolix, pedantic, and almost obsessively detailed, the Remonstrance was an anatomizing of the follies, vices and ineptitude (as his critics saw it) of Charles's years in power, so thorough that it amounted to a declaration of his unfitness to rule. It 'relates all the misgovernment and unpleasing things that have bene donne by ill Counsells (as they call it)', Nicholas had informed the king on 8 November, ' ... as, if your Majestie come not instantly away [back to London], I trouble to thinke what wilbe the issue of it'.[157] Particularly sinister, Nicholas believed, was its inclusion of all instances of malfeasance back to the third year of the king's reign: 1627, the year of the Forced Loan and the court-sponsored preaching campaign asserting the divine origins of monarchical power and the sinfulness of any form of resistance. Such thoroughness on the part of the Remonstrance's authors suggested that it was intended to serve a darker purpose than merely vindicating the present Parliament; 'for', as Nicholas pointed out to his royal master, 'surely if there had bene in this nothing but an intenc'on to have justefyed the proceedings of this Parliament, they would not have begun soe high [i.e. early] as 3° [i.e. March 1627–March 1628, the third year of Charles's reign]'.[158] What Nicholas had in mind is uncertain, but he could have been excused for thinking that the form of these detailed indictments, spanning almost the entire reign, looked (as they may well have been intended to look) like possible articles of deposition.

Broader concerns than simple self-justification did indeed lie behind the Remonstrance's thoroughness. From early November 1641, if not earlier in its long gestation, the Junto leaders clearly intended their handiwork for publication. They planned to use its damning account of the king's susceptibility to 'evil counsel' to make an unanswerable case for Parliament's expropriation of Charles's last major prerogative powers. Moreover, by timing the document's completion and publication to coincide with the king's arrival in London, the Junto leadership seems to have planned to use it as a spoiler, a means of damping down pro-royalist sentiment in the capital, just at the moment when it looked set to be revitalized by the king's return. By 18 November, Nicholas was already making plans for the stage-managing of Charles's approach to London, reminding the king that 'you will have opportunity to shew yourself grac'ously to your people as your Majestie passeth, and to speake a few good words to them, which will gaine the aff[ecti]ons (especially of the vulgar), more then any thing that hath bene done for them this Parliament'.[159] Both sides realized that the outcome of this contest for 'popularity' would influence, and possibly determine, which of the two would prevail in the larger contest for power at Westminster.

For the Junto men engaged in the Remonstrance's drafting, that quest for popularity necessitated yet another *politique* abandonment of the cause of religious reform. At a late stage in the Remonstrance's preparation, they abandoned a clause concerning the *Prayer Book*'s 'errors and superstitions',[160] and made no objection when the 'episcopall partie', which probably contained a number of their own supporters, brought in a new clause affirming that the House cast no 'aspersions [n]or scandal upon the Book of Common Prayer'.[161] A clause concerning the confiscation of the bishops' lands was dropped entirely. Still more remarkably, the Junto opted not to defend the Order of 8 September against religious innovations, agreeing that this 'shall be totally omitted'.[162]* John Maynard, a staunch Junto ally and formerly one of Strafford's prosecutors, poured reassuring unction on anxious religious conservatives, commending 'the wisdome [of preserving] the respect [for] what is established', and implying that there were no serious plans for further thoroughgoing reform.[163]

Yet while the Junto leadership surrendered clause after clause dealing with religious reform, they fought tenaciously for the Remonstrance's publication and for the larger cause that would help advance: divesting the king of his power to choose the counsellors of the realm. Pym, who was already behaving as if he were a Privy Councillor-elect, seems to have spoken for the Junto in urging the necessity of making government 'papist-proof' after Charles had allowed a succession of Catholics to infiltrate the very heart of the court. 'It is time', declared Pym,

> to deale plainely with the king and Posterity, and come nearer home yet, since all [these] projects have been rooted in Popery. Shall wee forgett that a Lord Treasurer [the Earl of Portland] dyed a Papist? That a Secretary [of State, Windebanke] was a Papist?[164]

The moment for courtly language was passed. 'It's time to speake playne English', another diarist has Pym say, 'lest posterity shall say that England was lost and noe man durst speak [the] truth.'[165] Again, it was the state – England – whose claims on the subject's loyalty took precedence over any courtesies due the king.

The Remonstrance's opponents were numerous and seemingly well-dril-

---

* When Sir Benjamin Rudyard was pressed about why the few remaining religious clauses had been relegated to the Remonstrance's end, he replied sheepishly that they *had* done 'great thinges in this Parliament. Things of the first magnitude.' But religion was 'Reckoned last because least [had been] donne!'

led.*[166]Almost certainly acting on Charles's own instruction, issued from Edinburgh a week earlier, that 'my servants' in the Commons were 'by all meanes possible [to see] this [Remonstrance] may be stoped',[167] the king's-party men lined up in the Commons on Monday, 22 November to denounce the Junto's plans for the Remonstrance's publication. Sir John Culpeper's speech summarized their central objection; captured in the laconic shorthand of a contemporary diarist, it ran:

> This is a Remonstrance to the people. Remonstrances ought to be to the king for redresse; this may cxasperate. This [is] unseasonable; ... this way encrease[s] the divisions off the kingdome. Wee [are] not sent to please the people.[168]

Repeatedly, the king's-party speakers denounced the Remonstrance's populism, with Sir Edward Dering articulating the point perhaps most forcefully,[169] that 'I did not dream that we should remonstrate *downward*', still less to 'tell tales to the people, and talk of the King as a third person'.[170]

That debate on the Remonstrance produced arguably the greatest set-piece confrontation the Commons had witnessed hitherto. Raging for over fourteen hours, from noon that Monday to around two the following morning, it attracted the attendance of over three hundred Commons-men in its early stages, most of whom seem still to have been there in the small hours of Tuesday for the acrimonious division over whether or not the Remonstrance should pass.[171] For the Junto, the final result was a near-run thing. In a House of over three hundred, they secured a majority in favour of approving it of just eleven votes: 159 for, and 148 against. In fact, the extent of the Junto's support was almost identical to the majority of 151 it had mustered a fortnight earlier, when Pym had proposed making financial support for the campaign in Ireland contingent on the king's acceptance of parliamentary control over the officers of state.[172]

The all-important question of publication, however, remained unresolved. Exhausted and ill-tempered, most Commons-men believed that the House would rise promptly after the vote on the Remonstrance's acceptance, leaving the debate over its printing to another day. What happened next is not entirely clear, as contemporary accounts are contradictory. However, it would appear that the king's party partly redressed their defeat by forcing through a vote by acclamation, banning the Remonstrance's 'printing and publishing'.[173]

---

* Edward Nicholas was able to write to the king shortly before midnight on 22 November, when the debate on the Remonstrance still had at least two hours to run, informing him that 'there are diverse in the Com'ons House that are resolved to stand very stiff for the rejecting [of] that Declarac'on; and, if they prevayle not, then to protest against it'. This is precisely what Hyde and a number of other king's-party speakers (including Sir John Culpeper) did some two hours later, suggesting that Nicholas had (at very least) been informed by these speakers of their intentions in advance, or (which is perhaps more likely) that he had had a hand in planning the anti-Junto response, as the king had requested in his instructions to Nicholas sent from Edinburgh on 13 November.

Members then started to leave the chamber. The pro-Junto party then seems to have tried one last, desperate gambit to have this absolute ban on divulging the text of the Remonstrance in public revoked. In a vote which they won by 124 votes to 101, the Junto supporters succeeded in removing the reference banning 'publishing' from the previous vote.[174] The *printing* of the Remonstrance was still forbidden, in other words, but its publication by other means – manuscript copies – was no longer ruled out.[175] Amid noisy scenes, in which angry Commons-men grasped their sword hilts and demanded the right to enter their 'protestations' against the majority vote, the Remonstrance debate came to its unsatisfactory outcome.

The result was pyrrhic victories for both sides. The Junto had secured a Commons' majority for the Remonstrance; but, denied permission to print, was cheated of the opportunity to exploit its polemical force.[176] On the other side, the king's party had failed in their self-appointed task of 'stopping' the Remonstrance; but in obstructing its printing (if not its publication in manuscript) had succeeded in blocking the Junto's efforts to use the Remonstrance to sway 'the people'.

For the major Junto grandees, however, the limited success they had achieved in the Remonstrance debate offered scant reassurance. All the attempts to refound the authority of the Lords General, Essex and Holland, on ordinances of Parliament (rather than on the king's commissions) had been stymied by the king's party in the Lords. And the Junto's broader, republicanizing objective – the quest for control of military and ministerial appointments – had likewise encountered immovable opposition in the upper House (and less than wholehearted support in the lower). With the Junto's majority in the Commons looking increasingly precarious, it also remained uncertain how long the grandees of Warwick House and Essex House could count on their Commons' allies being in a position to exert pressure on their enemies.[177] As Edward Nicholas later recalled, there was a new-found confidence and assertiveness within the king's party, and they were now 'resolved that they would not longer stand to be baffled by such a Rabble of inconsiderable Persons [Pym's party in the Commons], set on by a juggling Junto'.[178]

*

For the true jugglers of that Junto – among them, it seems Essex and Pym, Warwick and Clotworthy, Hesilrige and Brooke – that was troubling enough. But by the time London's scriveners put their first, freshly minted copies of the Commons' Remonstrance up for sale on Wednesday morning, 24 November, the Junto faced a still more unpredictable threat. The king had reached Theobalds, his large Jacobean palace in Hertfordshire, on the final leg of his return journey from Edinburgh, and was less than a day's ride from the capital.

The auguries for Charles's reunion with the Junto grandees were not good. The king, it seemed, was no longer on communicating terms with his Lord Chamberlain, the Earl of Essex, and in advance of his return to London could not bring himself even to instruct Essex to make the necessary preparations for the royal party's return. Instead, Charles delegated the task to the queen,

THE
PROPHECIE OF
The Earle of Effex, Lord Chamberlain, &c.

Prepare your felfe, brave *Robert Effex Earle*,
In Britaine Great, you are a pretious pearle:
God hath ordain'd you for fome other end;
Then in great Britaine all your daye's to fpend,
Your fathers fame, and good report I heare,
It made all Irifh rebels ftand in feare.
He was of valour and of courage ftout,

A 2   And

The Earl of Essex as saviour of the commonwealth: with the outbreak of the Irish 'rebellion', there was intensive speculation that Essex – the most popular and militarily experienced of all the Junto leaders – would be appointed to command the new English expeditionary force destined for Ireland.

who, in turn, passed the buck to the much put-upon Edward Nicholas. Writing to Nicholas from her palace at Oatlands on 20 November, she instructed him to 'tell [Essex] that the king will be at Theobalds [on] Wednesday [24 November], and shall lie there ...' She continued revealingly:

> The King commanded me to tell this to my Lord of Essex. But you may doe it, for these Lords ship are to[o] great prinses now to receave any direction from mee.[179]

In the aftermath of the Remonstrance debates, the days of the 'great princes' appeared to be numbered. Charles's retinue approached the outskirts of London on the morning of Thursday, 25 November. Within twenty-four hours, Essex had ceased to be southern England's Lord General.[180]

15

THE RETURN OF THE KING

NOVEMBER–DECEMBER 1641

Brave *Charlemaine's* return'd, methinks the sound
Should all our forrain enemies confound,
And our Domestick foes to friends convert,
In every breast create a loyall heart . . .
Those demy [lesser] powers of Parliament which strove,
In our Kings absence, to espresse their love
And care of us his Subjects, now shall finde
A Royall guerdon [guidon]. Those that were inclin'd
To practise mischief, of this Judge shall have
A Regall judgement, and a legall grave.

J. H., *Verses Congratulating the Kings Return*, [December] 1641[1]

1. CAVALCADE: THE RETURN OF THE KING

From shortly after eight on the morning of Thursday, 25 November, the welcoming party began assembling in Moorfields, the open expanse of ground immediately to the north of London's medieval city walls. Some 500 horses and their riders – liverymen of the City, all opulently 'habited in Plush, Satin, Velvet, and Chains of gold' – gradually formed up into an orderly procession, ready to accompany the Lord Mayor and Aldermen out to Hoxton, the village only a few miles distant to the north-east, where they were to greet the returning king.[2] The City was in a state of expectancy. Bell-ringers had been summoned; bonfires built; tapestries hung from balconies and windows along the processional route.[3] Londoners were about to witness one of the most lavish ceremonial entries into the capital since the arrival of the Stuart dynasty in 1603.

Such ostentation, however, had not usually been to Charles's taste. Under his Tudor and Jacobean predecessors, royal entries into London had been staged periodically as great ceremonies of state – part theatre, part religious rite – in which the power and charisma of monarchy were displayed and the bond between the sovereign and his metropolitan subjects symbolically reaffirmed. With Charles's accession, however, royal 'theatre' had tended to move inwards, towards more private, court-based festivities. The old-fashioned royal entry, with its open-air processions, public feasting, and appeal to a largely demotic audience seemed unappealing to a monarch with an instinctive distrust of 'popularity'. It had also come to seem slightly passé.[4]

The proposal to revive the practice had originated, not with the king, but with the City government early in November. Conveying the offer to the king (who was still in Edinburgh), Edward Nicholas anticipated Charles's reluctance to accept, warning his master that 'it will not be convenient to declyne'.[5] His advice prevailed, and in conjunction with the recently elected Lord Mayor, Richard Gurney (a man in his mid sixties in 1641 and who could still remember Gloriana's great staged entries into the City), planning went ahead over the following fortnight.[6] From the perspective of the newly assertive king's party, the case for staging such a ceremony was compelling. For over six months, Charles had been at the periphery of political life: rarely seen, publicly maligned, and impecunious to the point that he had been unable to fund the most ordinary festivities of courtly life.[7] The royal entry provided the opportunity to reverse all that: to place the king, visually as well as metaphorically, at the centre of public affairs; and, with the cost of the event underwritten by the City's aldermanic élite, to re-present the monarch to his subjects, once again surrounded by courtly splendour on a scale, which, ironically, the royal court itself could no longer afford.[8]

From the outset, Nicholas's and Gurney's stage-management of this appeal to the 'affections of the people' seems to have been conceived as a royal riposte to the Grand Remonstrance. The Remonstrance was being debated contemporaneously in the Commons, and, on completion, was widely expected to be printed and published.[9] The very idea of the City spending lavishly on a public and highly partisan declaration of loyalty to the king therefore provoked intense opposition from the Junto's supporters within the London Common Council (the 'representative body' of the citizenry). There, the Artillery Company captain and recently elected Commons-man, John Venn, opposed the provision of *any* entertainment to the king, 'as a thing displeasing to the Parliament'.[10] But the Junto's popularity in the City had waned sharply since the heady days of September 1640, and on 17 November 1641, just as debate on the Grand Remonstrance was entering its final week at Westminster, the Common Council overruled these expressions of dissent and approved the appointment of an organizing committee of six aldermen and twelve Common Councilmen to make the necessary preparations.[11] A delighted Nicholas could report back to the king that all was going ahead, 'notwithstanding ... there have been practices underhand to divert [City government] from their settled purpose'.[12] The Junto-supporters' dismay is understandable. For the scale of Gurney's planned entertainment involved more than the extension of polite courtesies; it entailed a massive outlay of cash from the City's coffers: on liveries, on a Guildhall banquet, and, not least, on a staggeringly large gift to the king of £30,000 in gold pieces (or enough to meet the costs of governing Ireland for well over a year).[13] Beyond this, Gurney was said to have supplemented this public expenditure with some £4,000 of his own.[14]

By the morning of Thursday, 25 November, all was in readiness. With Nicholas's collusion, public demonstrations of support for the royal cause had already greeted the king's progress through Hertfordshire, en route southwards, to give 'a good encouragement and comfort', as Nicholas explained to the king, 'to your well affected people here [in London]' that they were not alone in their 'dutifull affecc'ons'.[15] Likewise, in London itself, little had been left to chance.

But this was to be more than simply an occasion for the citizens to register their 'dutifull affecc'ons'. The November royal entry was to mark, in spectacular style, the reinauguration of Charles's rule over England. After a year of humiliation and retreat, this was to be the moment when the monarch, his Scottish troubles finally settled, could be presented as once again secure in his people's 'affections', and ready to go on the offensive against England's 'disturbers of the peace'.[16]

*

If any demonstration were required of how differently Charles valued his English crown as against his Scottish one, it was provided by the 'settlement' he left behind on his departure from Edinburgh. After the failure of 'the Incident' (the abortive *coup d'état* against Argyll and Hamilton), the king had shifted to a policy of abject surrender to almost all of his opponents' demands, relinquishing, with only the most token of resistance, the very same prerogative powers in Scotland that he was determined to defend in England: in particular, his prerogative of appointment of the great officers of state. From the moment that the Incident had dissolved into farce, Charles had hoisted the white flag over Holyrood House. In theory, he retained the right to nominate the great officers, and the Scottish Parliament merely had the power to approve or reject his nominees. In practice, however, Charles realized that he had little alternative but to submit names that he knew would meet with Argyll's and Hamilton's approval. The royal nominees the Scottish Privy Council provide a case in point. When membership of the Council had first been discussed in September, Charles had still been insistent that many king's-party noblemen should find places on the Board. In his revised list of nominees submitted on 13 November, immediately after the failure of the Incident, however, almost all the king's-party men were removed and replaced by loyal Covenanters – most of them allies of Argyll.[17] The pattern was replicated in almost every other aspect of Scottish public life: in the new appointments to the judicial bench; the arrangements for the Treasury (where Charles was forced to abandon his nomination of the conspirator Lord Almond); and in the series of four standing committees to which the Scottish Parliament delegated various of its powers before its dissolution on 17 November 1641. The most important of these, the Commission anent (i.e. concerning) the Articles, empowered a committee dominated by Argyll and Loudoun to conduct the negotiations with the London Junto on the question of what forces Scotland should send to assist in suppressing the Irish rebels.[18] Once again, Anglo-Scottish relations were in the hands of the Westminster Junto's main allies in Edinburgh.

From the king's perspective, this was not a political settlement, but an abject surrender, with perhaps the most humiliating moment being his scattering of titles, on his departure, to the men who had been the authors of the Covenanter Revolt. Argyll was raised in the peerage from earl to marquess, giving him equal rank with Hamilton (who went unpromoted). Argyll's allies, Lords Loudoun and Lindsay (who held mere baronies), and the victor of Newburn, General Alexander Leslie, were all raised to earldoms,[19] while Jhonston of Wariston – one of the draftsmen of the original National Covenant of 1638, the rallying point of the Scottish revolt – received a knighthood. Loyal servants of the Crown who had risked lives and fortunes in Charles's service were left empty-handed.

If Charles had entered Edinburgh as king, he left it, as he feared he would, as a mere 'Duke of Venice'. That the king was prepared to accept that result – and, not least, the destruction of episcopacy within the Scottish Church – testified not only to the way in which his political credit had collapsed after the failed coup, but also to the very different way in which he regarded his Scottish sovereignty. Its rights and prerogatives had come to seem expendable, in Charles's mind, in a way that was still unthinkable in relation to his English realm. And the bitter recollection of all he had abandoned of the 'flowers of his prerogative' in Edinburgh seems to have redoubled his determination, as he travelled from Theobalds to Hoxton, on the last phase of his return journey to London, to foil the Junto's plans to replicate Argyll's Scottish 'Commonwealth' in his southern kingdom.

*

At Hoxton, before a great tent, set up 'in the first field towards London', Charles began the reinauguration of his rule.[20] Greeted in the coach by the Lord Mayor and aldermen, he listened to speeches of welcome from Gurney (whom he knighted on the spot); from the City's Recorder, Sir Thomas Gardiner; and, responding to the City's handsome gift of gold, set out both a highly revisionist account of the various crises past and a summary of his intentions for the immediate future.[21] The tumults earlier in the year, the king now declared, were obviously the work of 'the meaner sort of people', as the 'better and mayne part of the Citie' clearly remained loyal. Far from being influenced by Popery, he vowed once again to protect 'the true Protestant Religion . . . as it hath been established in my two famous Predecessours' times' – Elizabeth and James. Any threat to the established religious order, he implied, came from Parliament, not the court.[22] And in a pointed reference to the Junto's hints of royal complicity in the plot to murder Hamilton and Argyll, the king was able to claim that the citizens' very presence, there at Hoxton, proved that they had not believed 'all those misreports'.[23] The threat to his opponents was clear. Charles was claiming the City – until the mayoral election of September 1641 the Junto's most effective ally – as his own. For the Earl of Holland, who joined the procession in his capacity as Groom of the Stool, perhaps the most disconcerting sight on the Hoxton field was the presence of a contingent of 'Marsse's warlike sonnes, the Artillery men',[24] a reminder, if any were necessary, that not all the City Artillery Company's

members shared the political radicalism of their godly brethren.[25] With courtesies exchanged and the king (now abandoning his coach) mounted on a
'steed ... with a stately sadle imbroydered with gold and silver [thread]',[26]
the procession formed up for the entry into the City.

As occasions for public theatre, royal entries worked less through the
spoken word than by gesture and symbol; and, in this context, the king was
able to exploit the occasion's opportunities to register multiple (and in some
respects mutually discordant) 'messages'. The loudest of these was a refutation
of the argument that the monarch was in thrall to 'evil counsellors'; for when
it came to the allocation of places in the procession from Hoxton to the
City's Guildhall, Charles assigned some of the most prominent places to a
series of grandees, all associated (with varying degrees of enthusiasm) with
the reformist cause: among them, Lord Lyttelton (the Lord Keeper), and the
Earls of Holland, Manchester, Salisbury and Arundel.[27] Perhaps the most
striking instance of this practice, was the assignment of the major role of
honour in the procession – the privilege of carrying the Sword of State, the
symbol of regality second only to the crown itself[28] – to the Marquess of
Hertford, one of the original Petitioner Peers of 1640 and a well-known
advocate of moderate reform.[29]* But the organizers' real coup, was the
presence of the Marquess of Hamilton, riding immediately behind the
members of the royal family, as courtly convention required, in his capacity
as Master of the Horse.[30] Any grudges over the incident were seemingly
forgotten.

Preceded by a retinue of almost 500 liverymen from the City's companies,[31]
and a small contingent from the House of Lords, riding two by two, the
procession moved slowly from Hoxton to its immediate destination, the
City's Guildhall. Its visual culmination, however, was formed by the king's
immediate entourage, whose disposition clearly reflects the king's success in
surrounding himslef with the known advocates of moderate reform.

The Lord Keeper		The Lord Privy Seal
[Lord **Lyttelton**]		[the Earl of **Manchester**]
	Serjeants-at-Arms	
Footmen	The Prince of Wales	*Footmen*
Garter King-at-Arms [the senior herald]	The Lord Mayor of London [Sir Richard Gurney], carrying the City's sword	A Gentleman Usher
The Lord Great Chamberlain [the Earl of **Lindsey**]	The Marquess of **Hertford**, 'bearing the Sword of State'	The Earl Marshal [the Earl of **Arundel**]
	The King	
	A coach carrying the Queen, the Duke of York, Princess Mary, the Prince-Elector	

---

* The allocation of this role to Hertford is all the more significant because the king's
cousin, the Duke of Richmond and Lennox, had a superior claim on this ceremonial
position, as the senior nobleman present.

The Master of the Horse [the Marquess of **Hamilton**[32]], leading the Horse of State

The Captain of the Gentlemen Pensioners, the Earl of **Salisbury**

The Gentlemen Pensioners, 'with their Pollaxes, all mounted with Pistols at their Saddles'

The Earl of **Holland**, 'Lord Generall beyond the Trent' [and Groom of the Stool]

Viscount Grandison, *'with many other Principall Commanders in the late Northern Expedition'*
[*i.e. the 1640 war against Scotland*][33]

TABLE: Part of the Processional Order for the King's Entry into London, 25 November
1641. The titles of English peers are highlighted in bold.

One suspects that Holland and Hamilton may have taken their places in his cavalcade only reluctantly. But in requiring these Privy Councillors to fulfil the ceremonial duties that attached to their lofty offices, the royal entry utilized their participation to serve a shamelessly propagandist purpose: as a *tableau vivant* of 'good counsel'; seemingly irrefutable evidence that Charles had *not* fallen in with Papists and advocates of 'arbitrary government', but was served by men who would honour and preserve the post-Triennial Act political order.[34] Even Essex fulfilled his duty of attendance as Lord Chamberlain of the Household, though, in what was almost certainly a deliberate insult by the king, he was denied any place in the king's immediate entourage (to which his office would have normally entitled him) and forced to take a much humbler place, earlier in the procession, among the non-office-holding earls.[35]

At the parade's first destination, the London Guildhall,[36]* the seat of the City's government, a new set of preoccupations came into play. Here an extravagant banquet had been provided, not only for the king and the peers who had joined his mounted entourage for the entry into the City, but also for 'divers Honourable Lords and Ladyes' (frustratingly unnamed) who had not taken part in the earlier procession, but now 'presented themselves to his Majestie'.[37] Like the processional entry itself, this banquet was also heavily laden with political symbolism. Taken at the seventeenth-century 'dinner' hour, around 2 p.m., the feast publicly affirmed the principle – which was to become a central plank of Charles's public platform in the year ahead – that the monarch, having conceded so much, was now reunited, both politically and personally, with the 'well-affected' members of the peerage. To drive home this point, the Guildhall banquet was turned by the occasion's organizers (principally Nicholas and Gurney) into another moment of elaborate public theatre: a solemn affirmation of the unity between the monarch and the 'well-affected' nobility.

---

* The procession followed the route prescribed for royal entries since Tudor times. It entered at Moorgate, on the City's northern flank, then followed the old Roman wall eastwards as far as Bishopsgate, where it turned south along Bishopsgate Street as far as Cornhill, part of London's main east-west thoroughfare. There, it turned westwards again, making its stately progress along this major street, which changed its name every few hundred years: Cornhill, Poultry, and finally Cheapside. From this point, the king and the members of the nobility turned up St Lawrence Lane, the narrow street that led into

Within the hall itself, the royal table had been set on a temporary stage raised six feet above the floor, with a canopy and cloth of estate at its centre, exactly duplicating the arrangements in the Presence Chamber at Whitehall.[38] Here Charles and his consort dined in state, served with quasi-liturgical solemnity by servants on bended knee, while the other members of the royal family and the Prince-Elector were placed on either side of the canopy, facing down the hall. But they did not dine alone. In front of the royal 'stage', a wooden platform had been erected, some three feet high, extending almost the full length of the Guildhall. Here, in a public affirmation of their solidarity with their king, dined the peers and their wives, seated at two long tables, running lengthwise down the hall: a table marathon of some 500 dishes, served in ten 'messes' (or series of courses).[39] Yet, for all the extravagance of the occasion, neither the Lord Mayor nor the City fathers joined the dining in the hall: this was an exclusive public act of commensality between the monarch and his nobility. True, their hosts, the members of the City government, formed the applauding audience for the ceremonial in the hall. But nothing was allowed to detract from the prime focus of the day: the representation of the king-in-majesty, surrounded by his 'cousins and counsellors', the nobles of the realm:[40] a natural 'king's party', which looked willing and able to block any further encroachments on the monarch's powers.

This political, indeed partisan, edge to the Guildhall festivities was further sharpened by the extensive list of the uninvited and the absentees. In a pointed snub, there were no guests from the Commons – now, more than ever, the reformist Junto's crucial constituency of support. And the Commons leadership responded to the affront in kind. Instead of joining the welcoming party outside the City walls, the lower House spent that same morning considering how they would present the king with their own very different welcome-home present: their new Remonstrance, cataloguing the scores of instances of the king's malfeasance and misrule.[41] Moreover, there was also an almost equally extensive boycott of the 'royal entry' by the more militant reformist peers. Apart from Hamilton and Holland, almost all the Junto grandees failed to take part in the procession – notably Warwick, Northumberland, Pembroke, Newport, Leicester, Saye, and Wharton.[42] Hence, while offering an outward display of unity and celebration, almost every aspect of the royal entry articulated the language of faction: its purpose was not the reconciliation of past divisions, but a triumphalist assertion of how the balance of power had shifted away from the king's enemies and back in favour of the king. Partisanship was the essence of the day.

A royal entry staged on these terms would have been provocative enough to the Junto leadership, which had recently lost its majority in the Lords, and was looking increasingly vulnerable, even in the Commons. Compounding these affronts, however, was a strong emphasis, throughout the day's public processions, on military force. Indeed, to many observers, this military element in the king's return was *the* predominant theme of the entire

---

the forecourt of the Guildhall, the seat of the City government.

day; in the words of one eyewitness, 'Drums beat, Trumpets sound[ed], Muskets Rattle[d], Cannons Roare[d], [and] Flags [were] display'd'.[43] Unusually, and at Lord Mayor Gurney's express order, the 500-strong mounted escort of City liverymen that preceded the king's entourage was armed 'with Swords';[44] and the Lord Mayor himself set the tone, having prepared himself 'and his followers ... in all their warlik[e] [h]abiliments, as if Mars himself, the God of Battel, had beene their conductor'.[45] The ceremonial bodyguard attending the king, the Band of Gentlemen Pensioners, was also exceptionally well provided with arms, as they had all been instructed to carry pistols, in a significant departure from convention, in addition to their usual gilt poleaxes – presumably in the expectation of, and to deter, possible trouble along the processional route.[46]

For the Junto, however, the truly menacing gesture of the day was the decision (almost certainly the king's) to allow large numbers of the 'reform-adoes', the officers and men from the recently disbanded royal army – the very people the Junto had ordered out of London in October on pain of imprisonment – to form the final section of his escort.[47] Precise numbers are difficult to establish, but in all it looks as if Charles was accompanied by upwards of 1,000 armed men on his progress through the capital. Nor were they there merely for show. So many 'libels' (street-side posters, apparently hostile to the king) had been spread around the capital in the days before the entry that 'disorders' had been expected, and this strong military showing had been the event organizers' riposte.[48]

This military aspect to the king's entry procession was, if anything, still more strikingly evident at the conclusion of the Guildhall banquet, as the monarch and his entourage left for the final part of their journey to Whitehall. As it was already dusk, flaming torches were provided to the king's escort by the City authorities to light the way to Temple Bar, and then onwards down the Strand to Whitehall.[49] Commons-men returning towards the City after the House rose around 6.30 p.m. would have walked straight into an astonishing sight: with the king's arrival at Whitehall Palace, the Tiltyard opposite (the modern-day Horse Guards' Parade Ground) was filled with hundreds of horses and their riders, dramatically illuminated by torches and tapers, and with 'Bon-fiers blazing on high' which turned the early-winter evening as bright as day.[50] On every side there were was 'the generall cry ... "The Lord preserve King Charles"'.[51]

Something about that noisy, bizarrely lit, and deliberately intimidating moment of the king's arrival home seems to have impressed itself on the popular imagination that evening – and no aspect more so than the mounted retinue of the 'officers of the late disbanded army'.[52] Within days, these military supporters of the king (most of them, it seems, drawn from the disbanded veterans of the 1640 campaign) were being referred to by a particular, derisively Italianate name, one that had been current for some time, but only now came to be used as a partisan label: 'cavaliers' – from the Italian word *cavaliere* (the rider of a horse, a *cavallo*) , and hence the term for a swaggering, mounted knight.[53] Politics, it seemed to the defenders of further reform, had just returned to the profoundly unstable state of early

May that same year: the days when Charles had been relying on Suckling's squad of armed men to effect a *coup d'état* and secure Strafford's release. Indeed, 'the Sucklington Faction'[54] seems to have become one of the sou-briquets of these new 'Cavaliers': many of them reformadoes, who, resentful at the meagre financial settlement Parliament had allowed them at their disbandment, had now so publicly sided with the returning king.[55]

For Warwick and the other Junto grandees, the emergence of these reform-adoes – the new 'Cavaliers' – as an informal military contingent was made all the more ominous by the changes in the command structure of the kingdom's armed forces that came into effect that same day, 25 November. With the Parliament having failed, as yet, to refound Essex's Lord Generalship South of the Trent on the authority of parliamentary ordinance, his mandate to command (which had been time-limited to the period of the king's absence) terminated on the afternoon of the king's return to Westminster. The king, of course, was at liberty to continue Essex in office; but his refusal to extend his commission and resumption of the powers of the southern Generalship to himself sent a clear signal that, henceforth, the control of military forces in the capital, and in the South of England more generally, was to be directly under the king's control.[56] Charles's first action, on Essex's surrender of his commission, was to dismiss the guards that the now ex-Lord General had placed around the Parliament.[57] His own mere 'presence', Charles declared ominously in a message of explanation to the two Houses, 'is a sufficient guard to his people'.[58]

The reality, however, was that there was now nothing standing between the Parliament and the ever-growing body of royalist vigilantes – the Cavalier reformadoes – who were shortly to set up a makeshift camp at nearby Whitehall. And the armed forces of southern England were no longer answer-able to Essex, but to the king.

II. NEW COUNSELS

Charles's return to London starkly exposed the vulnerability not only of the Junto régime, but also of all that had been achieved by the reformists since the emergence of the Petitioner Peers as a political force in September 1640. Of course, some reforms had achieved the security of the statute book: the Triennial Act, and the Act preventing the current Parliament's dissolution without its own consent, most conspicuously of all. But if the 1630s had taught Englishmen any political lessons, it was that even provisions entered as statutes (such as the 1628 Petition of Right) could be contravened unless the actual personnel of government – the king's Privy Councillors and the officers of state – could be relied upon to honour both the letter and the spirit of these laws. Ostensibly, Charles had wrought that necessary change to his counsels during the first half of 1641, first with the admission of the Bedfordians and, from May, even the appointment of members of the more militant Warwick House circle to the Privy Council and to the major offices of state (Essex's appointment as Lord Chamberlain being the most prestigious). But the dominance enjoyed by this governing Junto had depended, as its members were acutely aware, on their mastery of the two Houses of Parliament. By November 1641, the Junto leaders' dominance of Westminster looked more questionable by the day, and in retrospect their great tactical error of the summer had been their failure to secure parliamentary control of government appointments. Without this, as Strode continued to warn, 'all wee had done this Parliament was nothing'.[59]

From the moment of the king's return to Whitehall, the question of the Junto grandees' dismissal became the talking point of Westminster. Charles's decision, on 25 November, to allow Essex's command as Lord General to lapse was a sign of things to come.[60] Two days later, he made the first of a series of new appointments to public office that were calculated to weaken still further the Junto's grip on power: Edward Nicholas, the strategist who had been partly instrumental in effecting the upturn in the king's fortunes, was promoted to the Secretaryship of State which had been vacant since Windebank's flight in December 1640.[61] A week later, the king wrought his revenge on the elder Sir Henry Vane, the other of the two Secretaries of State, dismissing him from office and leaving Nicholas in sole charge of the secretariat.[62]

With Charles's new assertiveness went a reversion to his old habits of government. The great officers – to whom he had generally deferred in the six months since Strafford's execution – were once again ignored, and royal policy tended to be formulated within the Bedchamber department, among the king's inner entourage. Richmond appears to have further entrenched his position as the royal favourite, with the Digbys father and son (respectively the Earl of Bristol and Lord Digby) as his chief allies. As William Montagu reported on 27 November, the day of Nicholas's promotion, 'they talk much that the king is often very private with Digby and Bristol and that he looks but overly [i.e. dismissively] upon the good lords'.[63] Supplementing these counsels seems to have been the advice, often far more assertive and belligerent in tone than that of the Bedchamber men, of Queen Henriette Marie. She, possibly more than any, appears to have been insistent that Junto grandees' disloyalty should and, in the changed political environment, *could* be punished.

Indeed, in the aftermath of Vane senior's dismissal on 5 December, it was reported that *all* the major Junto grandees were to be removed from the Privy Council and dismissed from their offices. For the moment, it was the lesser fry who felt the force of the king's displeasure. Northumberland's protégé at the Admiralty, young Sir Harry Vane, for example, lost his post as Treasurer of the Navy – allegedly in belated reprisal for his part in Strafford's destruction.[64] But the list of those who were under discussion for culling was far more extensive, including Essex as Lord Chamberlain, Holland as Lord General North of the Trent, Hertford as Governor of the Prince of Wales, Saye as Master of the Court of Wards, and Northumberland as Lord Admiral.[65] Newport, the Constable of the Tower, was also under a cloud for seditious remarks he had allegedly made while at the house of his half-brother, the Earl of Holland, during the king's absence in Scotland; and from early December, the king was impatient to find the right pretext for effecting Newport's dismissal.[66] 'At the palace', Giustinian reported on 10 December, 'they talk freely of changing many of the leading officers [of state] soon, as well as the servants of the court [i.e. the royal Household], who in the late disturbances have publicly conspired against the intentions and interests of his Majesty.'[67] The future of the Junto grandees – the 'good lords', as William Montagu termed them – was looking more uncertain by the day.[68]

The Junto grandees retaliated by playing the one card remaining to them: their effective control, via their Commons allies, of the king's supply of cash. Hitherto, the Parliament's refusal to authorize more than short-term grants of revenue (in the form of Tonnage and Poundage) had acted as a powerful constraint on the king. Faced with the choice between meeting Parliament's desires or facing bankruptcy, he had almost invariably chosen the path of compromise – and financial solvency. Now, the Junto attempted to repeat the trick. The most recent grant of money to the king was due to expire on 1 December. Hence, on the day of the royal entry, St John had introduced a new, temporary bill, which would have allowed the king to enjoy the customs revenues for a few months longer – just long enough for the Junto, if all went according to plan, to evict the bishops and the Catholic peers from the House of Lords, and to bring in legislation to transfer from the king to Parliament the control of the appointment of at least some of the great offices of state.[69] Using this as the bait, the pro-Junto majority in the Commons tried to link this temporary grant to the question of the appointment of the great offices. They added a petition to the king, to be presented simultaneously with the latest grant of the customs, requesting that the Earl of Pembroke should be made Lord Steward of the Household (making him co-head of the royal court, with the Lord Chamberlain, Essex), and that the Earl of Salisbury should be made Lord Treasurer, an office that had been held by his father and grandfather before him.[70]* If granted, these appointments would have completed the Junto's monopoly of every major office, giving them unquestioned control of the court the military, and the royal finances – with only the secretariat, under Nicholas, as an isolated royalist redoubt.[71]

Six months earlier, Charles might well have buckled and acquiesced. Buoyed by the growing strength of the 'king's party' in Parliament, however, his response was to call the Junto's bluff. He accepted Parliament's latest offer of temporary supply, but he simply ignored the accompanying petition for the appointment of Pembroke and Salisbury to major office. More practically, the king took steps to break free from the financial constraints which, for over a year, had kept him so humiliatingly dependent on parliamentary largesse. On Saturday, 11 December, attending his first Privy Council meeting

---

* His grandfather, Lord Burghley, had held the office from 1572 until his death in 1598; his father, the 1st Earl of Salisbury, held it from 1608 until his death in 1612 The proposal to join Salisbury's nomination as Lord Treasurer to the supply bill came from Robert Goodwin, the Sussex Commons-man who had warned on 28 October that all the Parliament's achievements 'would come to nothing' unless Parliament took control of the king's counsels.

since his return, he informed his Councillors that he was not prepared 'to live [any] longer from hand to mouth' and that he would therefore accept no further temporary grants of Tonnage and Poundage: he would accept a grant for life, as had usually been granted to his predecessors, or he would accept nothing at all. He would not be 'bought out of any more flowers of the crown', the king insisted; and in offering this response, Charles repudiated the fundamental premise of Bedford's planned post-Triennial Act constitution: that by confining the Crown's revenue settlements to three-year grants, the Parliament would be able to use the power of the purse, at each of its three-yearly meetings, to deter the king from embarking on 'arbitrary courses'.

In effect, the king had declared his intention to found his government on a principle of financial autonomy from Parliament – with or without the customs revenues; and that meant repudiating, for the future, to the periodic negotiations, in which Parliament would have traded financial support for influence over policy, that had been one of the axioms of Bedford's plans for a future *modus vivendi* between the legislature and the Crown. More immediately, Charles's response also slammed the door against any negotiation over parliamentary involvement in the appointment of the great officers of state. Retrenchments at court would have to be set in train if the king were to live independently of any parliamentary subvention. But he was now insistent that he would survive, 'though below his kingly dignity, upon his own revenue' – which meant, in practice, his landed estate of some £120,000 per annum – rather than be forced to barter away what remained of his prerogative powers.[72] Parliamentary involvement in the appointment of the great officers of state was no longer even open for discussion.

*

This sudden stiffening of the king's resolve is evident, in personal terms, most clearly in his imperious treatment of the Earl of Pembroke, the failed nominee of both Houses of Parliament for the vacant Lord Stewardship of the Household. Of all the Junto grandees, none thus far had been punished more severely by the king for his espousal of the reformist cause than Philip Herbert, Earl of Pembroke. With his dismissal from the Lord Chamberlainship of the Household in July, Pembroke's courtly world had collapsed, and, with it, the major source of his power as a political patron. For almost forty years, ever since his youthful good looks had first caught the eye of Charles's father, Pembroke had been one of the major grandees of the Stuart court. Now, at fifty-seven – balding, irascible, and suddenly officeless – he was determined to reclaim what Hyde, his former protégé, called 'his full share in pomp and greatness'.[73] As soon as Charles had returned from Scotland, Pembroke had written to him, trying to dispel any imputation of disloyalty and expressing his devotion in the most fulsome of terms.

Charles's response was evidently brusque, dismissing the earl's blandishments out of hand. The old courtier reacted, in turn, with shock and anger. Stung by the tartness of the king's reply, and facing a future of complete powerlessness, Pembroke poured out his resentments to the newly promoted

Secretary Nicholas on 29 November. 'It is amongst my greatest misfortunes (and indeed the chiefe cause of all the rest),' he fulminated,

> that after so many yeares (how unprofitably soeuer to my selfe, not without some fruite to other persons), spent in the Court, I know very few men upon [whose] frendship and integrity I can rely, even in the most ordinary [matters] of humanity and justice.[74]

Pembroke's letter provides an insight into the way in which the contest over the control of England's government – the management of court and Privy Council – had acquired an intensely personal edge in the course of the past twelve months. The king and Pembroke had once been intimates, sharing enthusiasms for Italian art and architecture, and maintaining a friendly rivalry in matters of connoisseurship and acquisition. Now, however, that friendship was dead, and where once had been warmth, perhaps even genuine affection, between the two men, the king now maintained a glacial hauteur. Refusing even to communicate with Pembroke directly (a deliberately insulting breach of courtesy towards a Privy Councillor and fellow Knight of the Garter), Charles sent his response via Secretary Nicholas. The king, Nicholas informed Pembroke, doubted whether 'his lo[rdshi]p's affeccons to him are soe g[rea]t as [you] hath written' – an opinion that was 'invoked by the company [Pembroke] keepes soe close to him, and by *his own and his dependents' accons*'.[75] In the context of the moment, the reference to the actions of 'his dependents' seems not only to have been a direct allusion to the Commonsmen who had petitioned for the earl's appointment as Lord Steward,[76] but also to John Glynne, arguably Pembroke's leading 'dependent' in the lower House, who was at that very moment managing the impeachment of the thirteen bishops – with the clear intention of breaking the power of the 'king's party' in the House of Lords.[77]*

Charles, however, delivered one further blow to Pembroke's battered hopes of rehabilitating his court career. Only the day after a Commons delegation had renewed its suit that the earl should be appointed as Lord Steward, the king ignored the parliamentary supplication and conferred the post on the twenty-nine-year-old Duke of Richmond, a nobleman half Pembroke's age, and the court patron who had brought the Earl of Bristol on to the staff of the Bedchamber. This settling of scores was vintage King Charles: almost artfully vindictive; fully justified, at least in the king's own mind, as a response to personal betrayal (Pembroke's part in Strafford's fall); and executed without consideration or comprehension of the wider implications of his actions for his relations with other leading members of the court nobility. For in humiliating Pembroke so comprehensively, and intimating that there

---

* Another of Pembroke's 'dependents' was almost equally prominent in managing the impeachment proceedings against the bishops: the Shropshire serjeant-at-law, John Wylde, of whom Laud remarked: 'Surely I believe he was of the Earl of Pembroke's counsel, or the Earl of his, they jump so together.'

could be no return to royal favour for the older court grandees who had likewise collaborated during 1641 with the Junto's 'traitors', the king deprived himself of a powerful and potentially reconcilable constituency of support. Men such as Northumberland, Salisbury, Leicester, Holland, and Feilding, who had spent their lives in the service of the Crown, were in many respects reluctant allies of such political radicals as Warwick, Saye, and Brooke, with their quasi-republican, 'Venetianizing' agenda for the reform of the Stuart polity.[78] The humbling of the Earl of Pembroke, however, served as a warning to them all. No amount of dutiful past service to the Crown would assuage the king's anger against those he believed had betrayed him in the various crises of 1640 and 1641. If Hyde's observation that Pembroke now 'gave himself up into the hands of the Lord Saye to dispose of as he thought fit' is doubtless an oversimplification, it is a remark that probably also contains more than a grain of truth.[79]

Charles's new-found confidence after his return to London, and the taste for vengeance which this allowed him to indulge, brusquely reconfigured the political landscape. Until that point, there had been bridges – fragile, true, but still crossable – on which the men such as Northumberland, Pembroke, and Leicester might still have returned to a 'king's party' that was committed to maintaining England's post-Triennial Act constitution, leaving behind the radical 'new Councillors' like Warwick and Essex. Charles himself foreclosed this option. Motivated partly by a high-minded sense of justice, partly, it seems, by puerile pique, the king destroyed these bridges, beginning with this exemplary punishment of the Earl of Pembroke. In the process, he left a large proportion of the pre-1640 Privy Council – including some of his most powerful and longest-serving officers of state – with no place to go, but onwards towards a quasi-republican England in which the king's powers were reduced to a state of irrelevancy: a point where neither Charles's animosity nor his future favour would affect the composition of England's government or ruling 'Junto'. Of course, this involved massive risks. Against a background of rising pro-royalist sentiment in London, and probably in the country at large, it was clearly a gamble as to whether the Junto régime would survive (given that it remained, in theory at least, dismissible whenever the king so chose). For Northumberland and Pembroke, Holland and Leicester (the veterans of the pre-1640 Privy Council), Pembroke's fall confirmed what they probably knew already: that an alliance with the Venetianizing 'new Councillors' was their last available bet. The 'good lords', as William Montagu termed them, would sink or swim together.[80]

16

TREASON AVENGED

DECEMBER 1641–JANUARY 1642

... all things hastened a pace to confusion and calamitie from which I
scearce sawe any possibilitie in humane reason for this poore Church
and Kingdome to bee delivered. My hope only was in the goodnes of
that God, who had severall times dureing this Parliament, already been
seene in the Mount, and delivered us beyonde the expectation of our
selves and of our enemyes from the jawes of destruction.

Sir Simonds D'Ewes, diary entry, 24 December 1641[1]

As November's snow flurries announced the beginning of winter, the first
stories began to emerge of the horrors allegedly being perpetrated by 'the
Bloud-thirsty Rebels' in Ireland.[2] The trade in their telling was profitable,
lurid, and brisk. At stationers' shops throughout London, printers and book-
sellers vied with each other to retail the latest grisly stories, fresh off the
packet-boats from Dublin and Carrickfergus. The supposedly eyewitness
account offered, for example, by James Salmon, a Protestant refugee from
Ireland who arrived in London within a few days of the king's return from
Scotland, is typical of the genre. Published under what was to become a much-
used moniker, *Bloudy Newes from Ireland,* his title-page promised stories of
'the barbarous crueltie [practised] by the Papists', including how, at Armagh
and in other rebel-held towns in Ulster, the city gates were festooned with
'Men's quarters' – the chopped-up carcasses of Protestants.[3] Characteristic of
the style and tone of these works is Salmon's account of the aftermath of
Armagh's fall to the Irish 'rebels': the victors wrought their terrible revenge by

first deflowering many of the women, then cruelly murdering them, and
pulling them about the street by the haire of the head, and dashing their
children's brains out against the posts and stones in the street, and tossing
their children upon their pikes, and so running with them from place to
place, saying that those [children] were the pigs of the English sowes.[4]

Salmon's vignette of Protestant babies being tossed from pike to pike was to become one of the defining atrocities of the rebellion: oft-repeated, gorily depicted in woodcut images, and part of a steadily expanding English-devised mythology of the insurrection. At one level this mythology harked back to Spenser and the Elizabethan mythographers of Ireland's 'barbarism'.[5] At another, it sought to portray this latest Irish 'rebellion' as an act of unique treachery and brutality – and justifying, in its suppression, terror and severity in equally unprecedented measure.[6]

In the context of their first emergence in the 1640s, however, these stories fulfilled a more immediate and specifically English political end. At a time when the nation's political élite was preoccupied by its own domestic broils, the almost daily tales reaching London of Catholic advances and Protestant defeats in Ireland served powerfully to concentrate minds at Westminster on the military crisis, and human suffering, being experienced on the other side of the Irish Sea. Whether explicit or implied, the theme of these pamphlets was always the same: that Ireland was about to be 'lost' and, unless Popery were to be allowed to triumph, the English Parliament had no alternative but to raise an army to suppress the rebellion, and to do so fast.[7]

In England, the necessary task of recruiting new forces (and the universal expectations that control of them would confer immense power on its possessor) served to refocus attention at Westminster on a question that had figured intermittently in English political debate ever since Charles's defeat, in the autumn of 1640, at Newburn. With whom did the control of the armed forces – the state's monopoly of violence – properly reside: with men answerable to, and personally appointed by, the king? Or with commanders owing their commissions, and answering to, the king-in-Parliament? As the raising of an Irish army became *the* issue of the moment in December 1641, this was a question that could be evaded no longer.

Contained within that answer, however, as contemporaries realized all too clearly, lay the resolution of the still larger problem: whether England was, or could any longer afford to be, a personal monarchy; or whether it was more properly a Venetianized, though outwardly kingly commonwealth (a 'quasi-republic', in modern usage)?[8] The practical problem of suppressing the insurrection in Ireland thus confronted Englishmen with the most divisive question of the day: did kings enjoy their powers immediately from God? Or were they merely a cipher for a more secular power: the nation as 'represented' in Parliament,[9] and governed by a Parliament-approved Council of 'virtuous' peers? Nor was this a purely theoretical question. Whichever party gained control of England's military forces – whether intended for use in Ireland or at home – would not only enjoy power to wage a war, but also have the means to determine these outstanding constitutional questions more or less as it desired.

1. IRELAND'S RECONQUEST: CONTEXTS AND CONSEQUENCES

Conveniently for Warwick, Pym, and the other Junto leaders, the Irish insurrection had necessitated that at least some of these questions be answered in the weeks before the king's return to London on 25 November. Moreover, when it came to managing a war in Ireland, they already had certain advantages over the king, quite apart from Charles's temporary absence in the Scottish capital. The allegiance of the relevant office-holders was one. Already in post, as Lord Lieutenant of Ireland and the *ex officio* commander-in-chief of any military campaign, was the Earl of Leicester: Northumberland's brother-in-law, and the cousin by marriage of the entire Devereux-Rich connection. What Leicester lacked in military skill (his experience as a soldier was next to nil), he more than provided in factional loyalty; he was 'so conversant with them [the Junto leaders] that they took him to be of their faction cordially', despite his evident nervousness about the Junto's tendency to cut legal corners.[10] Equally conveniently, the officer responsible for arms and military supplies was the Earl of Newport, the Master of the Ordnance: Warwick's half-brother (as we have noted), and a man even more squarely 'of their faction'.

However, the Junto leaders needed something more than Leicester's general amiability and Newport's control of key supplies if it were to be confident that the creation of a new army for Ireland would buttress their power, not undermine it. And here the measures the Junto had taken in early November, just after they had first learnt of the revolt, came into their own.

Most important of all had been their decision to establish what, in a parliamentary context, was an entirely new type of executive body: a standing committee in which members of *both* Houses sat together as a single, bicameral 'Committee for Irish Affairs'.[11] In one sense, this was no more than a formalization of the loose, informal structures in which aristocratic grandees and influential Commons-men had been meeting together privately to concert policy – the original meaning of the word 'junto' – since the start of the Parliament. At the beginning of November 1641, however, in the immediate aftershock of the rebellion, this new bicameral committee served to streamline political decision-making (obviating the need for time-consuming conferences between the Houses), and to consolidate day-to-day control of the new Irish campaigns, almost exclusively in a single parliamentary faction.* For the

---

* The creation of this bicameral 'standing committee' appears to have been a direct response to the Junto peers' increasing difficulty after October 1641 – caused partly by Nicholas's efforts to mobilize a king's party in the Lords – in controlling business in the upper House. It provided a means of transferring major business relating to the Irish war from a forum which the Junto could not control (the House of Lords) to one that it could (the new Committee for Irish Affairs). Its origin appears (or was made to appear) almost accidental. On 1 November 1641, in response to the Ulster crisis, the House of Lords established a committee of twenty-six to scrutinize letters coming from Ireland; but this committee was narrowly controlled by a coalition of five bishops (including the ultra-'popish' Goodman of Gloucester) and king's-party lords (among them, the Earls of Southampton, Bristol, and Bath, and Lord Seymour). On this (exclusively Lords') committee, the Junto peers could only muster ten of the twenty-six places (namely, Essex, Northumberland, Leicester, Warwick, Newport, Saye, Wharton, Mandeville, Brooke, and Robartes) – and would have been almost powerless to influence policy relating to Ireland. By accident, or (more likely) by design, their salvation came the following day. On 2

Junto's supporters enjoyed an overwhelming majority on this new Committee for Irish Affairs (future Parliamentarians outnumbered future Royalists by a ratio of two to one).[12] Here, Warwick and the other Junto grandees could do business with the likes of Clotworthy and Pym (two of the new committee's most active members) with the same efficiency as they would, had they been meeting (as they had often done before) at Warwick House. As we will see, this factional monopoly at the Committee for Irish Affairs* was to provide the Junto with a lifeline during December when the king's party in the House of Lords – that highly effective coalition of bishops and anti-Junto lay peers – began to hamper almost every aspect of their preparations for the Irish campaign.[13]

Warwick, at least, seemed certain of one thing: that control of the army destined for Ireland was indispensable if the Junto was not only to survive, but to complete England's transition from personal monarchy to godly commonwealth. During November and December 1641, he emerged as the central figure in the planning and control of the new Irish campaign. We have already seen how the Warwick House interest had put forward the earl's son-in-law, Viscount Mandeville, as its preferred candidate for the Lord Lieutenancy around the time of Leicester's appointment (in the spring of 1641). Now, partly through the Irish Affairs Committee, Warwick's long reach was felt in almost every aspect of the preparations for the war. The allocation of commands is a case in point. The initial expeditionary force destined for Ireland was to consist of 3,500 men – three foot regiments in all, with one, inevitably, reserved for the Lord Lieutenant.[14] However, when it came to parcelling out the other two regimental commands,[15] Warwick's placemen and kinsmen secured both the remaining vacancies: Sir John Clotworthy taking one, and Richard Boyle, Viscount Dungarvan* – the son of the Earl of Cork, with whom Warwick had recently concluded a dynastic alliance (in which Cork's daughter married Warwick's son) – receiving the other.[16]

The earl's political tentacles extended to almost every other part of the new war-effort as well. Negotiations with the City for the army's funding, for example, were principally managed by men from Warwick's clientele, Sir Henry Mildmay and Sir Thomas Barrington, with two firm Junto allies (Pembroke's client and future executor, Sir Robert Pye,[17] and the Deputy President of the Artillery Company, John Venn) providing further

---

November, when the Commons requested that a group of peers should be appointed to meet with the lower House's own committee dealing with Irish matters, the peers promptly instructed their committee (named on 1 November) to form the Lords' contingent on the new bicameral Committee for Irish Affairs. Once the two committees met together, however, the effect of the amalgamation was to swamp the narrow royalist majority within the twenty-six-man Lords' contingent with a phalanx of Junto-supporters from the Commons (who constituted at least forty members of the fifty-six-strong Commons' contingent). The amalgamation effectively neutralized the king's-party vote, greatly reducing its influence on Irish policy as a whole.
* The alliance between the Boyles, Earls of Cork, and the Riches, Earls of Warwick, had been consolidated with the marriage of Dungarvan's sister, Mary, to Warwick's younger son, Charles Rich, as recently as 21 July 1641.

assistance.[18]* Warwick himself came up with a proposal for transporting part of the new army to Ireland in his ships.[19] Even the provision of the army with 'coats, stockings, shoes and caps' was a matter that the earl tried to bring within the control of his household. His resourceful secretary, William Jessop – the man who, the previous autumn, had coordinated the publication of the Petition of the Twelve Peers – now came up with a scheme, endorsed by the Commons on 13 December 1641, for the army's supply with clothing.[20] All of this had, as its prime focus, the relief of the 'distressed Protestants in Ireland'. But before these forces under Leicester, Clotworthy, and Dungarvan were finally shipped off to the war-zone, they provided the Junto, for the first time, with what amounted to a legally raised army of its own; one which could be used in the service of the Junto's interests just as surely as, earlier in the year, Charles had planned to use his own army against the Parliament. And as relations between the Junto and the king deteriorated sharply in the last weeks of December, Warwick and his friends were to discover just how useful these forces might be.

Control of the English army in Ireland – from the appointment of its colonels to the supply of its boots – was only part of the Junto leaders' strategy for the future security of their régime. There was another, specifically British, concern: the strengthening of their bonds with Argyll's régime in Edinburgh by making the reconquest of Ireland a joint Anglo-Scottish campaign. Of course, this was partly a matter of military expediency. The Scots had a ready supply of tough and seasoned soldiers and, with the support of Argyll (who was ambitious to see Campbell influence extended in Ulster), the Scottish Privy Council was prepared to offer 10,000 troops – fully half of what was expected to become the expeditionary force's eventual total of 20,000 men.[21] But, like the planned Palatine campaign which it supplanted, the Irish venture was also intended – at least, it seems, by Warwick and Argyll – as a manifestation of the relationship of reciprocity and interdependency between the two commonwealths, which had been established by the Treaty of Union.

The new army for Ireland, then, was to be a highly partisan body: officered, provisioned, clothed, armed, and – if Warwick had his way – transported by,[22] men who owed their allegiance to the reformist Junto and their Edinburgh allies:[23] the party centred on the Marquess of Argyll.[24] The implications of the Irish war-effort in terms of the balance of power in Scotland did not go unnoticed by Argyll's enemies – particularly Montrose and his former Bander allies, who increasingly regarded London as the new frontline in their battle against Argyll and his Scottish 'Commonwealthsmen'. Having once failed to topple Argyll through a *coup d'état* in Edinburgh, Montrose's partisans fixed their hopes, instead, on a *coup d'état* in London; for if the Junto's English Commonwealthsmen could be toppled, and 'personal

---

* Nor was this the only Artillery Company connection. When, on 9 November 1641, a series of military advisers were seconded to the new Committee for Irish Affairs, the Artillery Company's Captain-Leader, Philip Skippon, was prominent among them.

monarchy' re-established in England, the chances of achieving the same result in Scotland would be massively enhanced.[24]

Any thought that the Junto's control of the Irish campaign would go unchallenged, therefore, was quickly confounded in the days immediately following the king's return to London on 25 November 1641. Far from facilitating the preparations for the reconquest of Ireland, Charles's arrival in the capital inaugurated a bitter parliamentary struggle, not merely over questions of military control, but over the very nature and extent of the king's – and the Parliament's – powers over the conduct of war. Not for the last time, the 'Irish question' became a battleground for constitutional ideas, not just for warring Catholic and Protestant parties.

*

Perhaps the most unsettling aspect of this contest, for all concerned, was the uncertainty over what the returned king's ambitions actually were. The signals were contradictory. On the one hand, Charles's first parliamentary speech after his return, on 2 December, projected the monarch as a parliamentary prince, steadfastly promising to maintain the reforms that the two Houses had enacted thus far. 'I am so farre from disliking any thing that I have done hitherto [in granting limitations on royal power]', he declared before the assembled members, 'that, if it were to [be done] againe (in the favour and [to the] good of my people), ... I protest I would do it ...'[25] Of course, the implication of this was that he might legitimately refuse *further* concessions, and do his best – with the help of Councillors like Bristol and Digby – to avoid being asked to make them. But, at least on the surface, Charles's words entailed a commitment to proceeding in a 'parliamentary way' and to respecting the existing constraints upon his regal powers. In doing so, he provided encouragement to moderate king's-party men like Falkland, Culpeper, and Hyde – and perhaps even to Digby, who, in the early winter of 1641, far from being a royalist firebrand, was still trying, as a true heir to the Bedfordian political inheritance, to douse the coals of extremism at Whitehall.[26]

The king's *actions*, on the other hand, in the early weeks of December conveyed a very different message, and their belligerence inevitably spoke louder than his pious words. The ostentatious militarism of his processional entry into the City; his opportunistic espousal of the reformadoes (the unruly 'Cavaliers' who had served in his now disbanded English army); the reports of his involvement in 'the Incident' (the failed attempt to subject Hamilton and Argyll to violent arrest): all suggested that the advocates of force remained a powerful presence within the king's immediate entourage. Indeed, one such – Robert Ker, Earl of Roxburgh – had accompanied him from Scotland, and was currently a conspicuous, even notorious, figure at the Whitehall court. *Persona non grata* with the Argyll faction after his involvement in the Incident – in which he had planned to lead his armed retainers to help secure Edinburgh for the king – Roxburgh had an unfastidious approach to the law and a taste for using armed force.[27]* To the king, however, Roxburgh was a man whom he had known since his youth when the earl had served as a Gentleman of the Bedchamber to his father. Roxburgh was accordingly a devotedly loyal, possibly even avuncular, presence. And though it is impossible to gauge how much time he spent with the king during these December days, it is perhaps revealing that, when the crisis eventually reached its climax, Roxburgh was the one member of the nobility (English or Scottish) who was to appear in public at the king's side.[28]

Charles's return, therefore, introduced to the political world of Westminster a series of rival and intersecting polarities. Most obvious, of course, was the conflict between the king and the Junto over 'further reform': the now familiar attempts by Warwick, Holles, and their allies to work towards a Scottish-style settlement (in secular, if not religious, affairs), in which the king was left with a purely nominal role. Simultaneously, however, a second contest was being played out, within the court, over how far, and by what means, the king should respond to this threat. Its protagonists were, on the one side, those, like Roxburgh, who believed that monarchy could only be saved by a violent breach with Parliaments (whether English or Scottish), and an abandonment of the Bedfordian (and in Scotland, the Argyllian) reforms.

On the other side of this court divide, however, were those, like Bristol and Digby – in many respects, the continuators of the Bedfordian principles of early 1641 – who believed that Charles's only viable future lay in accepting the post-Triennial Act constitution and coming to regard Parliaments as unavoidable partners in the future business of rule.[30] This 'Digby faction' was thus forced to fight its wars on two fronts, simultaneously resisting, at one extreme, the ambitions of the Junto leaders to turn the king into a Venetian doge; and, at the other, the counsels of the men of violence – and their most recent incarnation, Roxburgh – with their insistence that the only way to deal with refractory Parliaments and over-mighty lords was by force.[31] The battle between these rival courtly factions was to become something more than a purely political affair. By the first days of January 1642, they were to become nothing less than a contest for the soul of the king, for the identity of the real King Charles. It was to be the tragedy of January 1642 that not even Charles himself seemed to know which of these two identities – the monarch within or outside the law – was actually his.

---

* It had been at Broxmouth House, Roxburgh's country seat near Dunbar, that Montrose had met with Lieutenant-Colonel Walter Stewart, the plotters' emissary to the Whitehall court, on Stewart's return from his first mission to England in March 1641. In his youth, Roxburgh had begun his career in England by having to flee Scotland to avoid conviction for conspiracy to murder. Something of his insouciant attitude to violence emerges in a letter he wrote in October 1641 to Edward Nicholas, in response to the latter's request for information about 'the Incident' in Scotland, in which Roxburgh had been extensively involved. Roxburgh responded robustly that the Incident 'if yee knew all, . . . is not worthe the blocking of so mutche peaper as to say sutche a thing wes, for be[fore] it wes spokine it wes done and I hope newer [i.e. never] more shall be thought of it'.

*

From Warwick, Pym and the other Junto leaders, the king's subtly defiant speech of Thursday 2 December provoked an equally assertive response. They found their inspiration in an earlier moment of political crisis: back in February 1641, when it had appeared that a king's-party majority in the House of Lords would find Strafford innocent on the central charge of treason. Then, a radical and as yet-untried solution had been discussed behind closed doors. If the majority of the Lords failed to find Strafford guilty – so it was proposed in February – then the Commons majority would join with 'that partie of the Lordes which will be against [Strafford]', and stand together as a single interest.[32] The predicament of early December 1641 was almost identical. With the Junto once again holding a majority in the Commons, but only a minority in the upper House, this radical expedient – a formal bicameral coalition of the 'well-affected' – was not only dusted off, but finally revealed to public view.[33]

Advanced by Pym on 3 December (the morning after the king had addressed the two Houses) and quickly approved by his colleagues, this proposal was nothing less than an ultimatum to the king's party. Unless its campaign of obstruction in the House of Lords were ended, then the defenders of the reform – both Commons *and* Lords – were ready to make a public stand.[34] Reminding the peers that the Commons were 'the representative body of the whole kingdom, and [that] their Lordships [sat] but as particular persons', the lower House warned that unless the king's-party peers passed the outstanding bills,

> then this House together with such of the Lords that are more sensible of the safety of the kingdom may join together and represent the same to his Majesty.[35]

The almost anticlimactic loyalism of those final words – 'and represent the same to his Majesty' – should not lead us to underestimate the radicalism of what is actually being proposed. When it came to the 'safety of the kingdom' (a well-established code-phrase for the control of its military forces), the Junto leaders in both Houses were declaring their readiness to act together[36]* – independently, if necessary, of Parliament's traditional two-House structure – and in defiance of the royalist-controlled House of Lords.[37]

It is a revealing moment. Few statements bring to the fore so clearly the inherent paradox at the centre of the Junto's cause: on the one side, its endorsement of 'representation' as the fundamental source of political authority; on the other, its respect for, and practical dependency on, noble leadership

---

* Moreover, in the recently created bicameral Committee for Irish Affairs, they had a ready-made institutional base from which to do so. As the crisis reached its climax at the end of the month this committee – convened in the London Guildhall as the Commons plus the Junto peers – was to serve precisely this purpose.

as an equally important wellspring of social and cultural legitimacy for the reformist cause.[38] Ironically, the more that Commons Junto-men like St John, Hesilrige and Pym found themselves being outmanoeuvred within Parliament by the king's-party peers, the more they seem to have realized how much they would have to rely on their own patrician allies – the likes of Essex, Warwick, and Northumberland – to confer a semblance of respectability on their resistance to the king in the event of all-out war.

*

In the four weeks that followed this 3 December ultimatum, the Junto leaders' legislative programme – all of it, of necessity, introduced in the Commons – was preoccupied with what amounts to a series of contingency plans, drawn up in preparation for war: war in Ireland most immediately; but the contest for military power in England was no less a central concern. The common (and strongly republican) theme running through each such plan is that the institution of monarchy – not merely the person of the current king – was henceforth to be stripped of all its prerogative powers relating to military affairs. Appointments to the major military commands provided their starting-point, with Sir Arthur Hesilrige introducing a far-reaching new bill, on 7 December, that was to end the derivation of the powers exercised by the Lord General and the Lord Admiral from the king's commission (in other words, from the royal prerogative) and to reground these powers on the delegated authority of Parliament.[39] The names of the peers to be appointed to these two commands were left blank in the draft bill, for insertion later in debate.[40] But there seems little doubt that Essex was Hesilrige's intended nominee as Lord General, with either Northumberland being confirmed, or Warwick newly appointed, as the kingdom's Lord Admiral.[41]* In the event, this bill was laid aside a few days later – perhaps because it left open the possibility of an unhelpful contest between Warwick and Northumberland over the Admiralty – and superseded by another still more comprehensive in scope: the work, as we will see, of Oliver St John.[42]

Nevertheless, Hesilrige's original bill reveals both the radicalism of the Junto's ambitions, and the extent to which the need to raise forces for Ireland had made the question of the military command – and from whence commanders should properly derive their authority – as the pre-eminent issue of the moment. The extent of that radicalism also helps explain why the Junto leadership was losing contact with many Parliament-men who had been its erstwhile supporters. Sir John Culpeper's response to this, the latest in a seemingly endless series of encroachments on the king's prerogative

---

* Ensuring security of tenure for current 'good' Councillors was one of the Junto leaders' priorities during the December crisis, with the prevention of Leicester's dismissal as Lord Lieutenant of Ireland being perhaps their uppermost concern. On 18 December, for example, the Commons resolved to raise with the Lords, at their next conference, 'preventing the inconveniences that may happen by the determination of the king's commission [to the Lord Lieutenant of Ireland], either by the death of the Lord Lieutenant of Ireland, or the Lords Justices [the Lord Lieutenant's administrative deputies]'.

powers, was perhaps typical. '[Hesilrige's bill] tooke away that power from the King which the law had left in him, and placed an *unlimited arbitrarie power* in another' – almost certainly one of the Junto grandees.[43]

Likewise, in the House of Lords, the scale of the Junto's intended destruction of the royal prerogative in military affairs shocked a series of moderate reformists, driving them into the arms of the king's party. The Lord Keeper, Lord Lyttelton, and Mandeville's father, the first Earl of Manchester, provide cases in point. Both had been supportive of the earlier programme of Bedfordian reforms. Now, however, they complained that the Junto's proposals to vest control of the militia in Parliament and its appointees took away from the Crown 'a prerogative of which it had been possessed for three hundred years'.[44] A line had to be drawn.

Throughout December, this line was not only drawn, but also vigorously defended by a strong and well organized king's party in the House of Lords. Their success, and the Commons' failure, was in large part a matter of parliamentary arithmetic. In the Commons, the reformist Junto generally enjoyed a majority, and the supporters of the king's interest were usually on the losing side. In the Lords, the position was almost exactly the reverse. So long as the politically active bishops sided with the king's allies among the lay peers, the consequent majority, though small, was more than sufficient to obstruct any unwelcome legislation coming up from the Junto-controlled lower House. And the line was held. Throughout December, the list of reforms that had been sabotaged – either rejected or indefinitely deferred – by the bishops and the king's-party lords grew longer by the day.

Perhaps inevitably, it was the Junto leaders' attempts at reform in military affairs that aroused the king's party's most vigorous opposition. Of course, by December, Bristol and his king's-party allies could do nothing about the measures empowering Leicester to raise troops for Ireland which had already been passed by ordinance: that much was a fait accompli. But, as the sheer scale of the Irish insurrection came to be realized, and the atrocity stories proliferated, it became clear that a much larger force than the 3,500 men and 600 horse allowed in the November ordinance would be needed to suppress the revolt. The broader contest for power – on the one side, the Junto's insistence on deriving military authority from Parliament, and, on the other, the king's equally strong insistence on maintaining that it derived from this prerogative – served to politicize every aspect of the preparations for the Irish campaign.

The question of the army's recruitment – the *sine qua non* of any new campaign – provoked the most acrimonious exchanges. Two options presented themselves for the raising of troops: either through an appeal for volunteers, which required no legislation (the option favoured by the king and broadly opposed by the Junto); or through 'impressment', enforced conscription, which did (the Junto leaders' clear preference). The practical implications of the respective choices were clear. With London currently full of demobilized officers and men from the king's army of 1640-41, a call for volunteers ran the obvious risk (or, from the king's perspective, had the positive virtue) of swamping the new Irish army with reformadoes and

Cavaliers. The army thus created could be almost guaranteed to be mutinous towards Leicester and his Junto allies, and correspondingly loyal to the king.[45] Unsurprisingly, therefore, Charles himself was insistent that *only* volunteers should serve in the new Irish campaign. The Junto, on the other hand (and hence, too, the Commons), was equally insistent on impressment, thus allowing it to create an entirely new (and factionally reliable) officer corps, and to conscript soldiers untainted by service in the king's army of 1640-41.[46] Neither side, in other words, was able to trust the other with military power.

Predictably, the legislation authorizing impressment of troops for Ireland, which the Junto had propelled through the Commons with relative ease, slowed to a crawl in December once it reached the king's-party-dominated House of Lords. Despite, or perhaps because of, strong backing by Viscount Saye, the bill progressed only as far as its second reading and then lay becalmed.[47] The explanation was not far to seek. In the impressment bill, as sent up from the Commons, the Warwick–Pym group had turned once again to antiquarian scholarship to validate their attempt to impose ever-narrower constraints on the monarch's power. Allegedly founded on an unrepealed statute from the reign of Edward III, the new bill specifically denied what, at least since Tudor times, had been one of the few relatively unquestioned prerogatives of the Crown in matters military: the monarch's power to compel men to military service outside their own counties in cases of national emergency.

Under the new bill, however, this prerogative power was expressly repudiated. No internal insurrection could henceforth be put down with conscripted forces, except where the king had obtained Parliament's authority to raise them in the first place. If passed into law, therefore, the new bill would not only permit the Junto leadership to conscript soldiers for service in Ireland (*or* England – the bill treated the two kingdoms as a single jurisdiction),[48] it would also strip the king of any power to raise an army in England for the purposes of putting down an internal revolt. The impressment bill, in other words, was an attempt to deprive the king of the ability to fight a future civil war.[49]

ii. STALEMATE

For all the Junto's early-December bluster – its threats, explicit and implied, its haughty insistence on the 'representative' nature of government, its attempt to legislate out of existence the king's powers in military affairs – Charles's political fortunes after his return to London were such that he could contemplate all this with a sense of equanimity. So long as the bishops remained in the upper House and voting (for the most part) in fraternal alliance with the other king's-party peers, neither the impressment bill, nor any of the Junto's other proposed reforms, was anything more than a purely notional threat. Granted, the Lords went through the motions of trading amendments with the Commons during December, on several of these reform bills (including the impressment bill).[50] But, with the bishops' support, the king's party was able to stall all these reformist measures indefinitely.[51] In the meantime, the royal prerogative remained the only legal (if not uncontested) basis for raising an army in England; though not even Charles was so tactless as to attempt to actually use this power to raise forces for the Irish campaign without parliamentary consent. Plans to put down the insurrection had reached an impasse.

Proposals during December for Scottish participation in the war-effort proved to be equally controversial, notwithstanding – or again, because of – Argyll's forwardness to provide 10,000 troops. Despite the urgent military need, Charles remained determined to prevent the mobilization of any forces that would be allied to the Junto, unless he could raise an English volunteer army of exactly equal size, to be officered by loyal Cavaliers.[52] In consequence, neither proposal advanced.

Analysing the broader political problem – at least as viewed by Warwick, Pym, and the other leading reformists – was straightforward. With daily attendances in the House of Lords rarely rising above sixty, and the lay peers roughly evenly divided, it was the politically active bishops who created the king's party's small but decisive majority. The solution was equally simple; indeed, the first steps had already been taken to give it effect. Legislation to deprive the clergy of all their temporal employments, including bishops of their right to sit in the Lords, had been introduced as soon as the Parliament had reassembled, back in October.[53] But given the strength of the king's party in the upper House and the bishops' hostility towards further reform, (particularly those which concerned themselves), this item of legislation became yet another casualty of the problem it had been invented to solve. The Bishops' Exclusion Bill joined the growing pile of legislation, discarded or indefinitely deferred, that was gathering dust in the House of Lords. For those who gathered at Warwick House, the problem posed by the upper-House king's party was coming to seem unsolvable by any parliamentary means at their command.

*

If all this was profoundly frustrating for the Junto leaders, it at least provided Bristol and Digby – the architects of this policy of lordly obstruction – with clear evidence that the king could yet achieve his political objectives by legal means. 'Violent courses' of the type that Montrose and Roxburgh had supported in Scotland were not only inherently dangerous, but also, they could argue in the English context, practically redundant. Indeed, by mid-December, Charles's position was potentially stronger than it had been at any point since the spring of 1640. In the City, he had a supportive and apparently effective Lord Mayor. Public opinion was turning against the heavy-taxing, pro-Scottish Junto government that had ruled England in his absence. And in the reformadoes and Cavaliers, he had the beginnings of a military party – and a ready source of volunteers for his own expeditionary force for Ireland.

In relation to Scotland and Ireland, too, the king's position was far from bleak. Despite Argyll's triumph in Scotland, the recent parliamentary session (and, not least, the Incident) had revealed the existence of deep-seated opposition to the Argyllians' 'usurpation' of the monarch's traditional regal rights. Even in rebellious Ireland, there was the not entirely unwelcome sight of an insurrection, not against himself as king, but against an English Parliament; and of the Catholic Irish declaring themselves implacably opposed to further constraints on his own prerogative powers.

However, the greatest cause for optimism for Charles – and particularly for the Digbys – was Parliament itself. For the moment, of course, the House of Commons remained an irksome bastion of Junto control. Yet, even here, as the votes on the November *Remonstrance* had proved, the position of the militant reformists was not unassailable; and in the fortnight after his return, Charles turned to a new scheme – which also bears the imprint of Bristol and Digby – to confront the Junto in the very citadel of its power. On 12 December, Charles issued a proclamation summoning 'all the Members of both Houses of Parliament' to return to Westminster 'at, or before, the twelfth of January next [1642]'.[54] Giustinian reported that it was sent to 210 absent peers and members of the Commons – a third of the Parliament's entire membership – with the court confident in the belief that the majority of these absentees were men who, in Giustinian's words, 'most abhor the [political and religious] changes and who disliked being involved in such troublesome disorders'. Their return looked almost certain to tip the balance of power in the lower House in Charles's favour. And if these expectations were fulfilled, then by 12 January 1642 (the date appointed for the absent members' return) he could look forward, at long last, to a majority in the House of Commons that would be at least as acquiescent as the 'prevailing party' currently supporting him in the House of Lords.[55] From 12 January, it seemed likely, Pym's rhetoric of 'representation' could be turned against him: it would be the king's party that could claim to be truly representative of the people's will, with the Junto's claims to speak on the nation's behalf being exposed as the fraud which Charles had always maintained they were.

The king's 12 December summons to absent members – and, still more, the expectations that it set up – was therefore fundamental to the political calculations of the ensuing weeks. From that point, Charles – and Bristol, his leading Councillor – could expect his political options, already far from unpromising, to be radically and felicitously transformed. A broadly sympathetic Parliament had been one of the great desiderata of Charles's decade and a half as king; and, by mid January 1642, that elusive goal seemed likely to be attained.

For the king, the new possibilities were manifold. None, however, was more urgent or alluring than the opportunity, almost certain to be opened up after 12 January 1642, of bringing his enemies to justice. The summons to the absent members and the king's plans for retribution against his enemies seem to have been complementary aspects of a single strategy. Reporting the news of the imminent prosecutions on 16 December, the French ambassador, the marquis de la Ferté-Imbault, noted that the decision to move against the leading members of both Houses for treason had been taken 'four days ago' –

By the King.

A Proclamation for the attendance of the Members in both Houses in Parliament.

 Is moſt Excellent Majeſtie having ſummoned this preſent Parliament, in His princely care of the good and welfare of His loving Subjects; In the continuance of the ſame care doth with advice of His Privie Councell, by this His Royall Proclamation declare His Royall Will and Pleaſure to be; That all the Members of both Houſes of Parliament do repair to the Parliament at Weſtminſter, at, or before the twelfth of January next, and give their due, and diligent attendance in Parliament: To the end that this Kingdom may fully enjoy the benefit, and happineſſe which His Majeſtie intendeth unto them by Summoning, and continuing of this Parliament: And of this His Majeſties Will and Command they are to take notice by this His Proclamation, and to give a juſt obſervance thereunto, upon ſuch pains, and penalties as by Law, and Juſtice may be inflicted upon them.

Given at His Majeſties Palace of VVhitehall, the twelfth day of December, in the ſeventeenth yeer of His Majeſties Reign.

God ſave the King.

¶ Imprinted at London by Robert Barker, Printer to the Kings moſt Excellent Majeſtie : And by the Aſsignes of John Bill. 1641

Counterattack: Charles I's proclamation, issued on 12 December 1641 and reportedly sent to 210 absentee peers and Commons-men, requiring their presence in Parliament by 12 January 1642. The initiative was expected to produce a royalist majority in the Commons and further to strengthen the king's party's existing dominance of the House of Lords.

that is, on 12 December, the very day of the summons to the Commons' absentees – with the object of 'cutting off the heads [*de faire couper la tête*] of several of the Parliament-men'.[56]

In fact, the connection between the king's proclamation of 12 December and the contemporaneous decision to strike against the Junto leaders appears to have been subtly made in the iconography of the printed proclamation itself. Almost all printed proclamations included, apart from the royal arms at their head, an extremely large capital 'H' (the letter initiating the formulaic phrase 'His most Excellent Majestie ...'). For a proclamation issued only two days earlier, dealing with the use of the Prayer Book in divine service, this initial 'H' had been decorated with an anodyne design of interwoven scrollwork.[57] For the summons to the absent members, however, this 'H' was

The imminent fate of traitors: a detail of the initial capital in the king's proclamation of 12 December 1641, depicting Hercules about to smite the Hydra, the many-headed monster – an image repeatedly used in early-modern Europe as an allegory of royal authority triumphing over rebellion. Charles himself spoke of Parliament as 'that hidra ... [which] I have found ... as well cunning, as malitionus'.

superimposed on a dramatic woodcut image: Hercules about to strike and slay the dragon of a hundred heads. In seventeenth-century Europe, this carried a familiar allegorical message: the monarch was about to strike down the figure of 'Rebellion' (traditionally depicted as a 'many-headed monster'); and this purpose was not only the *raison d'être* of the new proclamation, it was physically embedded in its typography.[58]

Arresting as this image of decapitated parliamentarians doubtless is, we should be wary of taking it literally as a summary of the king's intentions in mid-December 1641. Of course, it is quite possible that Charles wished to see retribution in kind meted out to the men who had called for Strafford's head (which perhaps placed the pairings of Warwick and Essex, and Hesilrige and St John, in greatest danger). But there were strong tactical reasons why, for the moment at least, the king needed to – and did – temper his anger. A call for capital sentences against the 'traitors' of 1640 was almost certain to risk alienating precisely the middle-ground constituency – men like Hertford and Bristol, Culpeper and Hyde – on which he was already depending for advice: precisely the group which, after 12 January 1642, he would need to provide his 'managers' in the two Houses.[59] An element of moderation in dealing with his enemies was therefore tactically necessary if he were to turn his current position of strength in the Lords into a broader dominance, post the return of the absent members, of the Parliament as a whole. And this was a necessity of which the king, as we shall see, was fully aware.[60]

Here, too, the king was able to master his opponents' familiar tricks. As the reformists' carefully targeted prosecutions of early 1641 had already demonstrated, once a parliamentary interest had achieved 'critical mass' – or, in a contemporary phrase, once it had become the 'prevailing party' in the two Houses – its dominance tended to be self-perpetuating. Men who regarded themselves as potential targets for impeachment (as Cottington had during the Junto's period of dominance) were generally disposed to keep their heads down and remain out of sight of their potential accusers.[61] Once the king's party had achieved that position in both Houses, as was expected by early in the New Year of 1642, the Junto grandees were likely to behave in exactly the same way. With only a few deftly aimed prosecutions, therefore, the king could inflict sufficient collateral damage to immobilize the Junto interest at Westminster comprehensively. Indeed, by mid-December, with the Junto's supporters in the Commons increasingly demoralized by the effectiveness of the blocking tactics being used against them in the Lords, there were signs that this collapse of morale had already begun. As Hyde observed, the king's opponents at this time 'did very visibly lose ground in the House of Commons, as the king's friends grew daily stronger in the House of Peers'.[62] And this was a process which, come January, the planned impeachments would doubtless accelerate.

Maintaining this constitutionalist poise – waiting until after Christmas for his summons to absentees to take effect, and remaining wedded to impeachment as the means of dealing with those he regarded as traitors – does not appear to have come easily to the king. This was partly a matter of upbringing and temperament. Charles was a man with an acute, almost hypersensitive, sense of his personal and kingly honour; and in the previous fourteen months this had been so often and so publicly traduced by the Junto leaders that the impulse to strike out violently against them must have been almost irresistible. Thoughts of trying another military *coup d'état*, along the lines of the Tower Plot of May 1641, retained their nefarious allure. Indeed, on the evidence of the papal representative, Rossetti, a man 'thoroughly acquainted with the intrigues of the court', Charles had been contemplating the possibility of a renewed – and this time, he hoped, successful – attempt on the Tower even before the crisis of December 1641.[63] Hence, as the king made plans to proceed against his enemies in a law-abiding, 'parliamentary way', and publicly denied any regrets over his earlier concessions,[64] his internal *alter ego* seems to have continued to hanker after the use of force to strike violently – regally – against his opponents. And if, for any reason, the parliamentary solution should fail, there was always the siren voice of Roxburgh, the veteran conspirator and central figure in the attempted coup against Hamilton and Argyll, ready to lure him towards another attempt to resolve the current impasse through violence.[65]

By the third week of December, the summons to the Commons' absentees and the reports of their own imminent prosecution had left the Junto grandees and their supporters in a state of deep alarm. Cornered between the present effectiveness of the king's party in the Lords and the growing effectiveness – and, post-12 January 1642, near-certain dominance – of the king's party in the Commons, it looked as if the Junto had few peaceable options remaining. The only alternative seemed military resistance, as they had planned in 1640 – though, this time, they confronted the disconcerting prospect that it was Charles who looked likely to be able to claim the parliamentary high ground. Summarizing the position in which 'these leaders of the Puritans' found themselves towards the end of that week (on Friday 17 December – the day after la Ferté had reported the plans to behead the leading Parliament-men), Giustinian noted that 'these open enemies of the royal greatness are fearful for their own safety and may adopt the most desperate expedients with dire consequences for the public peace'.[66] The world had changed. By mid-December, it was probably fair to say that if any one side looked more likely to seek a resolution to the current stalemate by extra-parliamentary means, it was Warwick and his allies, rather than the king.

III. TUMULTS

In Parliament, the Junto leaders were left with little room to manoeuvre. Countermanding the king's proclamation summoning the Commons' absentees was, of course, out of the question.[67] Their one remaining hope was that, with sufficient external pressure, they might yet regain their lost majority in the Lords. If this were attained, it could be expected to give them a short period, probably only until the return of the Commons' absentees in mid-January, when they would have sufficient command of the *two* Houses to advance bills (or, if the king proved refractory, possibly ordinances) on to the statute book. Their plans for the Irish campaign, for the appointment of officers of state, for the reform of the militia: all these, already well advanced through the Commons, might then be saved. The central question was: how was this lost ascendancy to be regained?

The answer – the critical point of weakness in the king's political armature – was scarcely a secret. It was to be read in the gossip-writers' December newsletters; glimpsed on fraying handbills plastered to walls throughout the capital; heard shouted by the braying, pro-Junto crowds that intermittently descended on Old Palace Yard. It was reduced to a simple five-word slogan: 'No bishops, no popish lords'.[68] This was not a generalized demand for Root-and-Branch reform – further evidence, as it has often been mistakenly construed, that quarrels over Church government lay at the root of the political crisis. Instead, the cry of 'No bishops, no popish lords' gave expression to a belief, now prevalent in the City and beyond, that (as D'Ewes noted at the time) 'many good Acts and motions, which had past the vote of this howse [of Commons], weere stopped in the Lords howse by reason of the Bishopps having votes and voices ther'.[69] This was a cry first and foremost of political frustration, not of religious militancy; for it had been the bishops' activities as legislators, not as pastors, that had turned them into the arch-villains of the moment. Such was the antagonism towards the prelates for their role in politics, that, as the newsletter-writer Edward Rossingham observed, they were regarded at this time 'as the only impediments, that no Bills can passe for the universal good in Ch[urch] or Comon-wealth'.[70]

Not that Warwick, Pym and the other Junto leaders had missed any opportunity to try to break the power of the bishops in the House of Lords already. Quite apart from their failed legislative initiatives against the episcopate, the impeachments of thirteen bishops (half the entire order) had been pending before the House of Lords, almost wholly ignored, since August 1641.[71] In the interim, however, only one of those accused – William Laud – had actually been placed in custody. The rest, thanks to the indulgence of their king's-party colleagues, continued free to sit and vote whenever they pleased. And so long as the bishops remained in the House, their votes, taken together with those of the lay king's-party lords, were sufficient to resist any attempt by the Commons or the Junto grandees to dislodge them.

Thwarted and frustrated at Westminster, Warwick and the other Junto leaders turned their attentions – as they had done in moments of crisis before – to the public sphere, to the world of thought and opinion outside Westminster's narrow élite, as a last option in their attempts to break the legislative power of the prelates.

*

Efforts to mobilize opinion in the City had begun even before news of the king's decision to prosecute the Junto leaders had become widely known in mid-December. Of these attempts, perhaps the most ambitious had been the petitioning campaign, organized in the City during the first two weeks of this month, to rally support against the episcopal party in the House of Lords. Reportedly signed by 15,000 citizens and measuring twenty-four yards in length, this gargantuan protest was presented to the Commons on 11 December by the City merchant, John Fowke – himself a future militant Parliamentarian. Its complaint was precisely what the Junto leaders wished to hear: 'Many ... good Lawes had passed this howse [of Commons]', the petitioners pointed out; but these, 'by reason that the Bishopps and Popish Lords had votes in the Peeres' howse, were stopped there [in the House of Lords]'.[72]

In one sense, such protests merely served to emphasize the radical reformists' current powerlessness. Where they succeeded triumphantly, however (and in this Fowke's petition was no exception), was as exercises in consciousness-raising among broad swathes of the London citizenry. Through a variety of means, they successfully brought to a metropolitan (and ever more politically-informed) audience an explanation of why all movement towards further reformation of the commonwealth had so comprehensively stalled. The Commons were happy to encourage more of the same. Though Fowke's petition against the bishops' votes had been formally presented to the Commons on 11 December, the organizers were given leave 'to get more hands [i.e. signatures]', even *after* it had been presented to Parliament – underlining the significance of signature-gathering as an exercise in creating political awareness in the parishes, quite independent of its ostensible purpose, the influencing of opinion at Westminster.[73] Little wonder that, on the one side, the royalist Lord Mayor, Sir Richard Gurney, and the City Recorder (London's senior law officer) tried to suppress all attempts to 'get hands';[74] and that, on the other, the Commons tried to censure the Lord Mayor and Recorder for trying to do so.[75]

Of all the attempts to sway public opinion, however, the most controversial was to be instigated, only four days after the presentation of Fowke's petition, by the Junto leaders themselves. On Wednesday 15 December, Sir John Clotworthy and others renewed their efforts to obtain the printing of the Commons' Remonstrance of the State of the Kingdom: the great catalogue of the misdoings of Charles's reign that had bypassed the Commons, so

narrowly and controversially, in November. Their tactics were char-
acteristically and shamelessly opportunistic. Late that afternoon, Clotworthy
and his allies – including Holles and Erle – kept debate going until it was
'soe darke' that the Clerk of the Commons 'could not see to write' in the
crepuscular gloom.[76] Then, with many of the king's-party supporters long
since departed homewards, they sprang their ambush. Without any of the
notice that would usually have been expected for a major parliamentary
motion, they renewed the proposal – in substance already once rejected by
the Commons, apparently definitively – that the Remonstrance should be
forthwith printed and published.[77] On any other day that December, as the
Junto managers doubtless knew, the balance of the rival interest-groups would
have been such that this motion would almost certainly have failed. Yet
through an act of pure procedural chicanery, as inimical to the spirit of law
as anything perpetrated during Charles's Personal Rule, they carried the day.
The vote for the Remonstrance's printing was won in a near pitch-dark
House of Commons by a margin of 135 votes to 83.[78]

The printed *Remonstrance* did far more, however, than provide a public
inventory of the old régime's past misdeeds. It was a clarion call to the
nation to support the faltering work of secular reformation against those at
Westminster who were trying to obstruct it. Far from being triumphalist in
tone, the *Remonstrance* broadcast to the world the Junto leaders' current
predicament. 'What can we, the Commons, [do] without the conjunction of
the House of Lords[?]', the authors of the *Remonstrance* asked;

> and what conjunction can wee expect there, when the Bishops and Recusant
> Lords are so numerous and prevalent, that they are able to crosse and
> interrupt our best endeavours for reformation, and by that meanes give
> advantage to [the] malignant party to traduce our proceedings?[79]

The nation, it followed, must rally to their support, lest the 'malignant
party' prevail. And it was probably no coincidence that this successful, if
procedurally dubious, move to have the *Remonstrance* printed came little
more than forty-eight hours after the king had begun planning for the Junto
leaders' prosecution.

*

As the first printed copies of the *Remonstrance* began circulating in the week
before Christmas 1641, an increasingly desperate and manifestly vulnerable
Junto leadership cast around for a parliamentary issue on which it might
make a stand. Perhaps inevitably, they alighted on the issue where the obstructionism of the king's-party Lords had caused greatest resentment: their stead-
fast opposition to the St John–Warwick plans for the creation of a Parliament-
controlled (or at least Junto-controlled) army. For so long as that question
remained unresolved, no significant English military aid could reach the
English Protestant settlers in Ireland, who were battling on against the rebels,
apparently abandoned by Westminster. As Edmund Calamy, in full rhetorical
spate, declaimed before the Commons later that week, Ireland was in a

'bleeding condition', the victim of the 'inhumane, barbarous, Can-
niballisticall, and super-superlative out-rages, butcheries, and massacres, that
are there committed by those bloudy Rebels'.[80] Yet still nothing was done to
bring them aid.

On Tuesday, 21 December, by which time the impressment bill and the
Scots' offer of military support had both been pending unresolved in the
upper House for well over a fortnight, the Junto leaders made a further
attempt to break the impasse.[81] Once again, they addressed themselves to an
audience beyond the confines of Westminster. Against a background of rising
fury at the do-nothing policy of the king's-party peers, Denzell Holles was
despatched to the upper House to present it with another warning – this
time, even more fiercely worded than that delivered by Pym three weeks
earlier. Reminding the Lords of the 'miseries' being endured by their Protestant
brethren in Ireland, Holles castigated them for their failure to take up the
Scots' offer of 10,000 troops for service in Ulster and warned them that 'if,
after so many messages concerning this particular, [they] cannot receive the
[peers'] resolution [on this matter]', then the Commons 'must acquit themselves to the world of their endeavours'.[82] The implications of that phrase
were not spelt out.[83] But at a time when the Westminster demonstrations
against the bishops and the 'popish lords' were gaining a sharply menacing
edge, Holles's warning contained more than a hint that the demotic power
of the London crowd might bring about change where the protests of the
Commons and the best efforts of Warwick and his allies in the Lords had
so far failed.

Crowds had been an intermittent, and at times devastatingly effective,
element in the capital's political life at least since the Strafford crisis of the
spring.[84] How far they were actively encouraged, or even orchestrated, by the
Junto leaders is impossible to demonstrate. So widespread were contemporary
suspicions to this effect, however, that they raise a legitimate question whether
there could have been quite so much smoke without fire. Some of the Junto's
enemies – like the Earl of Hertford's steward, Edward Kirton – believed that
they had evidence to prove that demonstrations were at least managed;
Kirton, for instance, claimed he had proof that John Venn, the Artillery
Company's Deputy President, was sending round-robin messages to likely
protesters, notifying them when to appear in Westminster.[85] Nor was Kirton
alone. Digby similarly claimed he could prove that Mandeville had directed
a 'rabble' to turn its fury on Whitehall Palace – though, even here, it was
unclear whether Mandeville and his allies had summoned the crowd into
existence, or whether Mandeville had simply taken advantage of a volatile
and possibly spontaneous situation.[86] By the beginning of January, Charles
himself would be sufficiently confident that the Junto leaders were guilty that
he was ready to prove in court that they had 'actually raised and countenanced
Tumults against the King and Parliament'.[87]

Whatever the truth of these claims, two aspects of these 'Tumults' seem
clear. First, whether they were spontaneous or contrived, their prime targets
were almost invariably those blamed for the legislative impasse at Westminster:
principally the bishops and the Catholic peers (though, in practice, almost all

Catholic noblemen, unlike the bishops, had long since ceased to attend at Westminster). And second, both the frequency of these demonstrations and their propensity towards violence intensified sharply during the second half of December – perhaps not coincidentally, from the moment when news of the forthcoming prosecutions of the Junto leaders, and the proclamation of the summons to the absent members, came to be widely known.

From that point, Pym and Holles, Warwick and Brooke – in fact, all those who were striving to create a commonwealth with a cipher-king – knew that they were working against the clock. Unless the current impasse was ended soon, their 'good lawes',[88] currently being ignored by the peers, looked as though they would be lost; particularly if, as was generally expected, the factional balance at Westminster was about to change decisively in the king's favour, with the return of the absent members early in the New Year. This sharply focused minds. By the time Holles presented the Lords with the Commons' warning of 21 December 1641, the reformists had perhaps only a fortnight – three weeks at most – in which to break the power of the king's-party and its loyal caucus of bishops.

With the two Houses locked in immovable stalemate, it was becoming clear that the struggle for supremacy within Parliament would be determined not inside, but outside the Palace of Westminster: above all, by what happened on London's streets. For those vying for power, violence and coercion had once again become an indispensable element of their political calculus.

*

When it came to the control of the capital, Charles believed that he started with one pre-eminent advantage over his enemies: Sir Richard Gurney, the City's fussy, elderly, but devoutly royalist Lord Mayor. Recognizing the threat posed by the Westminster crowds, which had begun gathering as early as late November, Charles had naturally looked to Gurney – the architect of his triumphal entry on 25 November – to see that these 'riots and unlawfull assemblies' were put down. In early December, in response to a series of incidents around the Parliament House, Gurney had been issued with a commission under the Great Seal, authorizing him to take harsh measures to repress these 'tumults' in London, even before they reached Westminster.[89] For the local implementation of the order, however, the king had looked to the Common Councilmen, the representatives of each ward within the City, who were charged with preventing 'apprentices or servants' from taking part in any unlawful meetings.[90]* After the City government's extravagant display

---

* On Wednesday, 1 December, for example, crowds waited to harangue members of both Houses as they left Westminster, shouting '[N]o bishops, no bishops' and calling them 'the limbes of Antichrist'. And on Friday 3 December, 'many hundred of Citizens and Brownists [Congregationalists]', armed with staves and swords, were intercepted by the Middlesex Trained Bands – raised by the county's royalist Lord Lieutenant, the Earl of Dorset – on suspicion that they 'came against the Parliament-house', presumably to protest against the bishops. Further measures were taken to thwart a similar protest a week later, on Friday, 10 December.

of loyalty on the king's return to the capital, his ability to put down any serious challenge to his authority, at least within London, had seemed assured.

However, by the time the Commons issued their protest against the royalist peers' on 21 December, members of the king's party were much less confident of the City's allegiance. 'All things have not happened so much to [the king's] contentment', wrote one City observer, 'as by [his] magnificent entertainment [at his return] was expected.' Another newsletter-writer, articulating the fears of the king's party more generally, prayed that 'we find not that we have flattered ourselves with an imaginary strength and party in the City'.[91] In London, as in Parliament, the margin of difference between the active forces on either side had turned out to be much narrower than the king had earlier assumed.

This belated realization that he might lose control of London – and that the crowds currently menacing Westminster might turn their attentions (as they had in May) to Whitehall – forced the king to a radical reappraisal of his tactics in the week before Christmas 1641. Faced with a fractious, even potentially rebellious capital and a City government that was more divided and less loyal than he had originally supposed, Charles once again turned his attentions to the Tower of London: the great Norman fortress that seemed to hold the key to the control of his kingdom's most important city. Twice before (in November 1640 and May 1641), the king had tried unsuccessfully to use the Tower as a means, *in extremis,* of ensuring the submissiveness of the capital by force. Whether or not Charles was once again toying with the idea of a *coup d'état* in which the Tower could be used to terrify an insubordinate capital into submission (as Rossetti supposed), one thing is clear: he was acutely aware of its strategic significance and anxious that it should be firmly under his own control. It 'was looked upon', as Hyde put it, 'as a bridle upon the City'.[92] There was also the question of its arsenal. For the Tower remained the greatest military storehouse in the kingdom; the ability to control the distribution of arms and ammunition from its stores would confer a massive advantage on whoever was its possessor in the event of the outbreak of civil disorder.

The king's principal problem, which was brought sharply into focus as the tumults at Westminster intensified during the second half of December, was that the Tower's two key officers – its Constable (or nobleman custodian) and its Lieutenant (its day-to-day superintendent) – were both firmly loyal to the Junto. Warwick's half-brother, the Earl of Newport, still served as Constable, while Sir William Balfour, the Scot who had helped thwart the king's efforts to gain control of the fortress back in May, remained in post as Newport's second-in-command. Their removal was therefore the *sine qua non* of any attempt to wrest control of the fortress from the hands of the Junto. Charles planned accordingly. By Monday, 20 December,[93] just over a week after the decision had been taken to go ahead with the Junto leaders' impeachment, the king completed the arrangements for Balfour's replacement. News of the imminent change was reported to the Commons by a deeply alarmed Sir Walter Erle the following day, Tuesday, 21 December – hardly coincidentally, the same date that a furious Denzell Holles was to remind the king's-party lords of the dire consequences that would follow if they maintained their campaign of obstruction.[94]

At court, Holles's threat provoked a bullish response from the king. From that moment, whatever hesitancy he may have felt about Balfour's dismissal hitherto appears to have been dispelled almost at once. Events in the City, moreover, intensified the conviction within the king's inner entourage that something urgent must be done to regain control of the Tower. For that Tuesday, 21 December, had also seen a series of elections throughout London to choose the City's Common Councillors. The results of these confirmed, all too bleakly, that the court's earlier assumptions about the City's loyalty had indeed been misplaced. Instead of consolidating the power of the pro-royalist Lord Mayor, Sir Richard Gurney, and the king's party more generally, the elections had produced a marked swing in favour of the 'godly' interest – a result that gave a powerful boost to the beleaguered Junto.[95] One eyewitness, the Puritan wood-turner, Nehemiah Wallington (who had himself joined in the 'tumults' at Westminster), observed that those Common Councilmen who were deemed 'not well-affected' to the reformist cause were removed, while those that were 'very wise and sound' (by which Wallington seems to have meant the reformist party) were chosen in their place.[96] The change directly affected the Lord Mayor's, and hence the king's, ability to keep order within the capital at large.[97] In its aftermath, the Tower's potential to serve 'as a bridle upon the City' suddenly acquired an altogether heightened utility.[98] The court acted promptly. Balfour's 'resignation' as Lieutenant of the Tower, a departure that was almost certainly forced by the king, followed swiftly the following day (Wednesday, 22 December).[99]

In choosing a new Lieutenant of the Tower, Charles seems to have tried to satisfy two complementary requirements. On the one hand, he needed a Lieutenant who would be unquestioningly loyal (all the more so if he were to serve as the Junto leaders' gaoler, after, as was now widely expected, they were to be impeached). On the other hand, the king also needed to ingratiate himself with the reformado 'Cavaliers', both with officers and men. In Colonel Thomas Lunsford, one of the disbanded officers who had followed him to London in November, he found a candidate who ably satisfied both con-ditions. Abrasive, arrogant and with a reputation for violence, Lunsford was a soldier whose appointment struck terror into the king's opponents.[100]* More than anything Charles had done thus far, Lunsford's promotion identified him provocatively with the cause of the reformado 'Cavaliers'.[101] Over the following week, contingents of these demobilized officers and men took up residence in and around Whitehall, forming an irregular, vigilante guard, ready to be deployed against any tumultuous 'Citizens and Brownists' that might be mustered by the Junto's City supporters.[102]

---

* Lunsford had been outlawed during the 1630s for the attempted murder of a Sussex neighbour. After fleeing to France, where he took service in the army of Louis XIII, he had returned to England in 1639 to fight in Charles's wars against the Scots. He acquitted himself bravely against the Covenanter army during the battle of Newburn, in August 1640, acquiring, in the process, a particular hold on Charles's affections.

To Warwick, as to his closest Commons allies, St John and Pym, Lunsford's appointment was tantamount to a declaration that the king was intent on the use of force against the Parliament. They reacted to the news by pressing on defiantly with their programme to deprive the king of his remaining powers. The view that the nation was approaching a moment of confrontation with despotic regal power had already been clearly articulated in the two sermons – both by clergy with close ties to Warwick House, Edmund Calamy and Stephen Marshall – preached before the Commons at their 'solemn day of fasting' on Wednesday, 22 December. Stephen Marshall likened their predicament to that of the prophet Daniel before the Persian tyrant Nebuchadnezzar, charged with interpreting a dream 'which, in the true exposition, foretold Nebuchadnezzar's fall'. Marshall asked directly: 'Whether this may bee thought to be our owne case'.[103] Gone was the heady optimism of the late summer. Instead, Marshall began to consider how 'now ... the Lord God beginnes to appear against us, not onely in permitting many unexpected blocks and rubbs [from the king's party and the bishops in the Lords]', but also by having 'drawne out and furbished the sword, and made it begin to drinke blood in the Neighbour Nation [of Ireland], which [sword], when it once begins to drinke, seldome is put up againe, till it be drunke with blood'.[104] The nation's sins were bringing down God's wrath upon them.

Firm news of Lunsford's appointment, rumoured over the previous forty-eight hours, finally reached Parliament the following day, Thursday, 23 December.[105] Its inherent menace, coupled with the unsavoury character of the appointee, triggered a reaction of exasperation and revulsion that does not seem to have been confined exclusively to the ranks of the Junto or the supporters of reform. Once again, the reformist majority in the Commons urged the Lords to join them in petitioning the king for Lunsford's dismissal, only to find the way forward obstructed by the king's party and its tame following of legislator bishops.[106]

When the two Houses met the next day, Friday, 24 December, the Commons gave St John's radical new militia bill its second reading. Control of the kingdom's armed forces was henceforth to be removed completely from the king and vested, instead, in the 'well-affected' nobility: in other words, in Essex, Warwick and those peers who were their supporters – the virtuous minority – in the House of Lords.[107] However, as the two Houses prepared to rise for the two-day Christmas break (Saturday and Sunday, 25 and 26 December), it was the king's party in the Lords which was the principal focus of the reformists' anger. Outraged by the king's-party peers' refusal 'to join with us in so important and necessary a request [as the demand for Lunsford's dismissal]', the Commons responded with yet another declaration denouncing 'the delays and interruptions which we have received in the House of Peers, as we conceive, by the great number of bishops and Papists, notoriously disaffected to the common good'.[108] But no more than any of its previous threats and ultimatums did this denunciation have any immediate procedural effect. Once again, the king's-party peers ensured that this latest dyspeptic outburst from the Commons was completely ignored.[109]

Lunsford's appointment was read – possibly incorrectly, but excusably –

as the clearest signal thus far that, at Whitehall, the advocates of violence had prevailed over the favourers of the constitutional, 'parliamentary way'. D'Ewes's reaction was probably typical of a number of those who supported the reformist cause. Reflecting shortly afterwards on the significance of the Lords' majority's refusal even to petition against Lunsford's appointment, he noted in the words cited at the head of this chapter that 'now all things hastened a pace to confusion and calamitie, from which I scearce sawe any possibilitie in humane reason for this poore Church and Kingdome to bee delivered'.[110]

As Warwick and Pym left the Parliament House that evening, the one hope that they could cling to was that the Earl of Newport, the Constable of the Tower and Lunsford's nominal superior, was still in post, and had been formally asked by the Commons, in a letter sent that day, 'to lodge and reside within the Tower, and take custody ... [of] that place'.[111] Yet even this hope proved delusory. No sooner did the king learn of the Commons' approach than he, too, sent a message to Newport, dismissing him as Constable of the Tower forthwith.[112] At the Tower, Lunsford was master of the fortress. At Whitehall, it seemed, the men of violence once again held sway.[113]

*

Violence threatened begat violence in fact. Although Charles quickly realized he had gone too far in appointing Lunsford, and replaced him with the more respectable, but no less loyal, figure of Sir John Byron, the damage had already been done. The three days which followed Parliament's rising on Christmas Eve – from Saturday (Christmas Day) to Monday (27 December) – witnessed a rapid escalation in the rioting around Whitehall and Westminster.[114] On Saturday, 'king's-party' crowds appeared;[115] but these were almost immediately outnumbered by the groups of pro-Junto supporters, united in denouncing the political obstructiveness of the bishops and the Catholic peers. Then, on Sunday the 26th, the attacks on the king's-party bishops intensified. Westminster Abbey and its Deanery (the residence of Archbishop Williams) were attacked,* and elsewhere in the capital, bishops' houses were assailed by hostile crowds. By Monday morning, Matthew Wren, the ultra-Laudian Bishop of Ely, was so terrified he dared not venture out, even for the relatively short journey from Ely House, near Holborn, to Westminster.[116]

There was good reason for Wren's timidity. When the two Houses reassembled that morning, 27 December, groups of the bishops' supporters and their more numerous opponents were again roaming through Westminster Hall and the Court of Wards, and gathering in noisy posses in Old Palace Yard. In the Hall, one 'puffing and blowing' Cavalier goaded those present with the question, '[W]hich of all you dare to speake against the Bishops?' There was jostling and scuffling between the rival factions; swords were drawn;

---

* John Williams, the former Bishop of Lincoln, had been translated to York as archbishop on 4 December 1641.

and the party of Cavaliers was eventually chased away by a party of pro-reformist apprentices.[117]

If there was an element of larrikinism in these altercations in Westminster Hall, even of traditional Christmastide misrule,[118] the crowd in Old Palace Yard that Monday morning wore an altogether more menacing face. Bishops arriving for the resumed parliamentary session had to endure a hostile mob, and a number were assaulted in their coaches as they passed.[119] One, however, was singled out for particular vituperation: John Williams, Archbishop of York. In his earlier incarnation as Bishop of Lincoln, Williams had once been the darling of the London godly; the stalwart opponent of Laud; the hero whose release from the Tower, only a year before, had been greeted with popular demonstrations and the pealing of church bells.[120] But Williams, the erstwhile Junto ally, had also gone over to the new king's party in the months since Strafford's death; and having turned to defending Charles's remaining prerogatives, had been rewarded in November with promotion to the arch-bishopric of York. Now widely reviled as a turncoat and betrayer of the reformist cause,[121] Williams was jostled by the crowd as he left his coach and he responded pugnaciously, lunging out at one of his abusers. In the ensuing altercation, his Parliament dress of rochet and lawn-sleeves was ripped – a personal humiliation that seems to have coloured his broader response to the crowd violence in the days to come.[122]

In all, twelve bishops – including Archbishop Williams – managed to run the gauntlet of the hostile crowd that Monday morning. But it was an experience that few of them chose to repeat. On the following day, Tuesday, 28 December, only two of their number – William Pierce of Bath and Wells, and the near crypto-papist Godfrey Goodman of Gloucester – managed to slip past the waiting crowds and take their seats.[123] For all practical purposes, the 'bench of bishops' had ceased to exist. Crowd violence had accomplished in twenty-four hours what weeks of Commons' threats and protests had otherwise failed to achieve: the breaking of the king's party in the House of Lords. Charles's front line of defence against further encroachments on his prerogative, so effective during the last three months, had at last been breached.

iv. THE JUNTO RESTORED

This shift in 'critical mass' in the House of Lords on 28 December – the change in the 'prevailing party' from the king's men to the reformist Junto – was registered immediately in the conduct of parliamentary business. Indeed, the day's very first item for discussion set the new, and distinctly godly, tone. The Lords ordered the inauguration of a series of monthly days of fasting and sermon-going[124] – 'days of humiliation' – which, over the months ahead, were to provide a powerfully influential public platform for the Junto's clerical protégés – Marshall and Calamy in particular – in the defence of the reformist cause.[125]

From this first order, the log-jam – so firmly maintained by the king's party

since the autumn – was at last broken. After weeks when almost all matters
'for the good of the commonwealth' had been stalled, the pace of public
business became suddenly brisk. Preparations for the Irish campaign took
priority. For the first time in almost two months, the Junto's majority in the
Lords, precariously re-established by the bishops' exit, enabled the Warwick
House grandees to take the initiative in urging 'speedie supplie' for Ireland.[126]
The House of Lords' relations with the lower House changed suddenly from
obstructiveness to willing cooperation. It was now the turn of such peers as
Digby and Bristol to sit, surly and resentful, as the new 'prevailing party'
forced through policies sharply critical of the king. The Earl of Northumberland was one of those who now revealed himself unambiguously as
siding with the militant opposition to the king's Bedchamber entourage. On
the earl's recommendation, the Lords endorsed a Commons' proposal for a
petition to warn the king that there could never be a 'right understanding'
between the monarch and Parliament, except through 'the present [i.e. imme-
diate] discovery and removal of ill counsellors and false informers'.[127] A
further Parliament-sponsored purge of the court and Privy Council was clearly
in the offing, and the latest victims in the reformists' sights were those who
had been responsible for Newport's dismissal as Constable of the Tower. In
a way that would have been impossible during the months of the king's
party's ascendancy in the Lords, *both* Houses were now united in demanding
that Charles should divulge in person the names of those who had counselled
Newport's removal from office.[128]

Bereft of the bishops, the king's-party leaders – Richmond, Bristol, and
Digby – found themselves confronting the overthrow of their entire strategy:
the blocking of any attempts to impose restrictions on the monarch's prerogatives beyond what Charles had already conceded. If peers such as
Warwick and Essex could maintain the Junto's current dominance of the
Lords even for so short a period as a fortnight, they looked able to force
through – and offer up for the royal assent – most of the Junto's remaining
reformist legislation: the impressment bill (with its controversial clause removing the king's power to raise an army without Parliament's consent); the
militia bill (which merely awaited its third reading in the Commons); and,
above all, the bill to deprive bishops, permanently, of their votes in the
House of Lords.[129] In legislative terms, mastery of the two Houses was what
mattered; for if the king should reject legislation that commanded the two
Houses' assent, the Junto could resort either to pressure from the metropolitan
mob (as it had done during the Strafford crisis in May), or, at least in theory,
to procedure by ordinance, obviating the need for the royal assent altogether.

Beyond the legislative threat posed by the resurgent Junto, Warwick, St
John and its other leaders looked likely to broaden their counter-attack to
target the secular peers who had led the recent campaign to block further
reform. One partnership, in particular, was clearly in the Junto leaders' sights:
the father-and-son duo of the Earl of Bristol and Lord Digby. With the
collapse of their power-base in the Lords, however, they suddenly became
vulnerable as never before. Impeachment of these 'evil counsellors' was once
again the talk of Westminster.

Forewarning of the impending assault had come on Monday, 27 December, the first day of business after the short Christmas break, when one of Charles's veteran critics from the 1620s, Walter Long,[130]* had formally 'named the Earle of Bristow [as an evil counsellor]'. In what was probably intended as the prelude to an impeachment charge, two Commons-men allied with the Warwick–Essex circle, Sir Gilbert Gerard and Sir John Hotham,[131] were despatched to fossick in the House of Lords' Journals for records of improprieties committed by Bristol as long ago as the 1620s.[132] Then, on Tuesday, 28 December – the first day of the Junto's re-established majority in the House of Lords – the attack on Bristol as an 'evil counsellor' began in earnest. In the Commons, one Junto-supporter after another rose to denounce the earl's misdeeds: Hotham arguing that he had persuaded the king to convert to Catholicism during the early 1620s;[133] Stapilton and Hesilrige that he had always opposed the interests of the Prince Elector; and Strode, offering the most damning accusation, that Bristol had tried to 'put the Army in a posture against the parlament'.[134]

A fortnight earlier, Bristol could have safely laughed off such accusations, confident that his fellow king's-party peers would have thrown out such claims had they ever reached the House of Lords. But with the upper House now returned to the control of the Junto grandees, the Commons reformists knew that their allies were once again in position to make such charges stick. Thus Oliver Cromwell, another fellow-traveller with the Warwick–Essex group, urged the Commons to 'desire the Lords to joine with them' in asking for Bristol's removal from the Privy Council. The future Parliamentarian, Sir John Holland, put forward an even more radical proposal, urging that it was 'necessarie to remove *the whole Body of the Counsel*' and to make an entirely new slate of appointments 'as the parlament' should approve or recommend.[135]† Were Holland's proposal to have been taken up, the monarch's role in the choice of the English Privy Council would have become as closely circumscribed as it was already in Scotland – and the 'Venetianization' of England's constitutions would have been powerfully advanced. With so many options on offer, however, the determination of Bristol's fate was deferred. Debate was to be resumed on the morrow, Wednesday, 29 December.[136]

---

* Walter Long of Whaddon, Wiltshire, had opposed granting the king supply in the 1626 Parliament and in 1629 had famously been prosecuted in Star Chamber and imprisoned in the Tower for his attempts to resist the dissolution of the 1629 session; he was not released until the summer of 1633. His election to Parliament to sit for Ludgershall in Wiltshire occurred at a by-election in December 1641 following the 'disabling' (i.e. expulsion) of William Ashburnham, the Army Plotter, on 9 December. This contribution to debate on 27 December 1641 seems to have been his first intervention after having taken his seat.

† The intended implication of this proposal does not seem to have been to cashier the entire existing body of Privy Councillors, but rather to give the Parliament an opportunity to purge 'evil counsellors' and to reappoint those who were 'virtuous' – but, this time, with the security of tenure that would have come from appointment to office on the authority of Parliament, not the personal favour of the king.

*

From Tuesday, 28 December, then, Charles faced a double threat. On the one side, the apparently organized intimidation of the bishops and the consequent weakening of the king's party had already destroyed his control of the House of Lords. On the other, the obviously concerted campaign against Bristol threatened to deprive him of his chief strategist and adviser – the figure who had been largely instrumental in the recovery of his fortunes since October. Beyond the question of Bristol's fate lay the larger question of what the Junto might do, now that it had regained a working majority in the two Houses.

Compounding these vexations was the still lingering hope at court that the king's summons to the absent members might yet produce a strengthening of the king's party, possibly to the point where it could topple the Junto from its position as the 'prevailing party', early in the New Year.[137] The confrontation between king and Parliament was reaching its moment of climacteric. Whether England moved still further towards becoming a de facto republic (or 'commonwealth'), or back towards some form of personal monarchy, looked likely to be determined definitively by what happened within the next few days.

Yet the traditional analysis of this as a two-way conflict – between a reformist Parliament and reactionary king (with Digby cast as the royalist villain) – greatly oversimplifies the complexity of the forces in play. In fact, Charles himself appears to have been profoundly irresolute as to how he should respond to the challenge, post-28 December, of a re-ascendant Junto. His problems were compounded by the highly dysfunctional state of the Whitehall court. Alienated from a Privy Council that contained a large bloc of the Junto grandees, and barely on speaking terms with his Lord Chamberlain, the Earl of Essex, Charles retreated to his private apartments – to the suite of rooms known collectively as the Bedchamber – and to the counsels of his inner entourage. It was here, in the most private part of the palace, that the two major factions fought to win over the king to one of two diametrically opposed courses: the way of force and military confrontation, as advocated by Roxburgh (with, eventually, the active support of the queen); or the parliamentary way, as counselled by Digby – the only influential survivor at court of the old Bedfordian circle.

As so often when faced with the choice between the options of coercion or conciliation – military force or parliamentary negotiation – Charles found the easier alternative to allow the two strategies to run in tandem, thus virtually guaranteeing the failure of both. So it was with his reactions to the Junto's re-established parliamentary ascendancy. The military response to the political *bouleversement* at Westminster (what seems to have been the Scottish faction's preferred option) came promptly. On Tuesday the 28th, the king ordered the construction of a Court of Guard, a temporary barracks, outside Whitehall to accommodate the large body of freelance soldiers who had rallied (or been rallied) to the king's defence even before the Christmastide 'tumults'.[138] This involved a substantial body of men. Within a week, those accommodated in the Court of Guard were numbered at 500 – 'about the Court, [and] ready to be imployed upon any desperate designe'.[139] And while their purpose could be explained as a defensive measure, it was obvious that this number of military personnel also could be quickly and conveniently mobilized offensively: against the Parliament House, less than half a mile away to the south, should the king opt to dissolve the two Houses by force. Whether or not Roxburgh had a role in advocating the creation of this mini-army cannot be documented. But it is perhaps significant that by 4 January, it had been placed under the command of one of Roxburgh's closest allies at court, Sir William Fleming: a fellow Scot, friend and close kinsman of Montrose,[140] and son of the zealously anti-Argyllian Earl of Wigtown.[141]

In the persons of Roxburgh and Fleming, the rancorous feuding of Scottish aristocratic politics obtruded itself brusquely into the political world of White-hall. Both men had been intimately involved in various initiatives aimed at checking Argyll's ascendancy in Edinburgh and halting his (largely successful) efforts to recast Scotland as an aristocratic 'commonwealth'. Both had been involved in the Cumbernauld Band (which Roxburgh had signed and which had been drawn up in Cumbernauld House, the Flemings' family seat); and during 'the Incident', Roxburgh – as we have seen – was to have provided the military force to seize Argyll and Hamilton, had the plotters' plans come to fruition.[142] Having failed to topple Argyll through Scottish means, they now seem to have sought to undermine him from England instead. As it was widely known, nothing would have so weakened Argyll's ascendancy in Scotland – and heartened Montrose and his Bander allies – than a blow struck against the Westminster Junto and its attempt to replicate Argyll's aristocratic 'commonwealth' in England. The creation of the Whitehall Court of Guard on 28 December, soon to be under Fleming's command, thus fulfilled a dual purpose. In an English context, it secured Whitehall against any threat from the London mob. But it also had a Scottish dimension, providing two of Montrose's most loyal partisans with the military means to strike against their English enemies, the Argyll-supporting Junto – if only they could per-suade the king to do so.

At Warwick House, the talk was also of military concerns. Observing the steadily increasing militarization of the court, Warwick and his allies looked once again to the army for Ireland – the small but well equipped force under Leicester, Dungarvan and Clotworthy – as their bulwark against Charles's growing band of reformadoes and Cavaliers. On Wednesday, 29 December, the day after Charles gave orders for the construction of the Whitehall Court of Guard, Warwick made the highly unusual proposal to the House of Lords that six hundred men of the new army should be embarked immediately, and not at Chester or Bristol (the usual ports of departure for Ireland), but in the port of London. By happy coincidence, this would require the concentration of the best part of an entire regiment, all under officers loyal to the Junto grandees, within the immediate environs of the capital. Moreover, Warwick had two ships, one massive vessel of four hundred tons and another smaller ship of two hundred and fifty tons, victualled, armed, and provided

with ammunition, and waiting 'in the river'.[143] Conveniently, Warwick's proposal was referred to the bicameral Committee for Irish Affairs, with its
inbuilt Junto majority and of which he was himself a member, to take matters
further.'[144] But it is unlikely that the king's-party supporters failed to note
the hint of menace in both the timing and implications of Warwick's ostensibly
'helpful' gesture. The four-hundred-ton vessel alone probably gave him access,
during the last week of December, to some twenty to thirty pieces of heavy
ordnance, available within only a few miles of Whitehall.[145]

*

For all this sabre-rattling on both sides of the political divide, there were
still those at court who were working steadfastly to avoid a military confrontation. The boldest, by far, remained Lord Digby. His solution to the
threat posed by the Junto's new-found ascendancy in Parliament was to seek
the complete suspension of parliamentary business – at least, it seems, until
such time as the results of the king's summons to the absent members could
be ascertained. Hence on Tuesday, 28 December, the first day of the Junto's
return to dominance in the two Houses, Digby proposed a motion which,
had it been passed, would have suspended all parliamentary business for the
foreseeable future. Peers were invited to concur with the motion that 'this is
no free Parliament', agreement with which would, *ipso facto,* have invalidated
all current and future proceedings – since the Parliament would have been
deemed to be under duress.[146] With pro-Junto crowds still milling in Old
Place Yard, this was a reasonable claim and a potentially far-reaching one. For
if these December 1641 'tumults' invalidated Parliament's current business, it
could equally well be argued that the tumults during May had also rendered
Parliament's proceedings – Strafford's attainder, for instance, and the act
preventing Parliament's dissolution without its own consent – likewise null
and void.[147]

But Digby had not reckoned on the extent to which the bishops'
enforced absence had already depleted the ranks of his king's-party allies.
When put to a vote, the Junto lords and their supporters defeated his proposal
by four votes: a narrow enough margin of success in a House of fifty-four,
but for Warwick and the reformists, their first substantial success since the
king's party had emerged as an organized political force in October.[148]

Digby's failed attempt to buy time – for the king's party in general and
his father in particular – further intensified the Junto leaders' hostility against
himself and his embattled father. On the following morning, Wednesday, 29
December, the Commons appointed a formal committee to prepare evidence
relating to the 'removal of the Earl of Bristol from the king and [Privy]
Council'; and, at the insistence of Sir Philip Stapilton, a formal investigation
was begun into the 'scandal' alleged to have been done to the Commons by
Digby's claim that the Parliament was no longer free.[149] A formal petition
from the two Houses for Bristol's banishment from the court and Council
became more likely by the hour.

Digby and his allies nevertheless continued to believe that the current
disorders might yet be turned to their own and the king's advantage. If his

proposal, the effect of which would have been to suspend parliamentary business, was defeated only narrowly on Tuesday the 28th, might not a new initiative, this time from the excluded bishops themselves (the real victims of the mob), sway sufficient votes in the upper House to succeed where the first motion had failed? That prize – halting all the Junto's legislative and impeachment plans in their tracks – was too alluring not to risk another play for, and a renewed attempt was planned in the course of the following day, Wednesday, 29 December.

The senior cleric in the House of Lords, Archbishop Williams, acted as the organizer and front-man for the new initiative; however, as Gardiner surmised long ago, Williams was almost certainly acting at Digby's prompting and to advance a strategy that was of Digby's own devising.[150] It took the form of a formal petition to the king and the House of Lords from the excluded bishops, dragooned into collective action by Williams, complaining (as Digby had done before) that Parliament was under duress as a result of the continuing tumults. In particular, because violence had been targeted against the bishops and forced their withdrawal, the House of Lords was no longer properly constituted. All laws, orders or other resolutions of the two Houses passed since 27 December – the apogee of the crowd-intimidation and the moment when the Commons had begun their attack on Bristol – were 'Null, and of none effect'.[151] Williams gained the signatures of eleven of the other excluded bishops – in effect, the mitred wing of the king's party – in the course of Wednesday and presented the completed Protest to the king at Whitehall shortly afterwards.

In abler hands, the Digby–Williams strategy – stopping the Junto from being able to do things by suspending the institution through which it planned to do them – might just have been viable. But in the confusion of the moment neither Digby nor the king seems to have scrutinized carefully the arguments deployed in the bishops' Protest (in particular, their implicit claim that no Parliament could be validly constituted without the presence of the episcopate), or to have thought through how provocative such claims would seem, even to the king's supporters. But Charles's government had long ceased to function with any accustomed degree of order; and in a palace that had recently become a noisy caravanserai for several hundred Cavaliers, and where the king's attention was repeatedly distracted, the bishops' ineptly worded Protest was passed on to the Lord Keeper, Lord Lyttelton, for presentation to the House of Lords on Thursday morning (30 December), without receiving either detailed scrutiny or revision.[152]

Come that Thursday morning, Lyttelton did no more than duty required, having the Protest read as bidden, but making no recorded attempt to defend it. With the case for the defence going by default, the bishops' enemies leapt to offer the prosecution case, seizing on the assertion that laws passed in the bishops' absence were invalid to claim that the Protest was an attempt to question the validity of many of the Parliament's past acts and resolutions. If Hyde is to be believed, some of the 'governing lords' – the Junto peers – could hardly believe their luck, claiming with satisfaction that here 'was [the] *digitus Dei* [the finger of God], to bring that to pass which they could not otherwise have accomplished'.[153] The 'governing lords' rounded on the bishops' ill-judged manifesto and, denouncing it as 'intrenching upon the fundamental privileges *and being* of Parliament', called on the Commons to meet them to discuss their joint response.[154]* Far from securing the Parliament's suspension, the bishops' Protest had merely succeeded in uniting a large majority in both Houses in a sudden access of anticlerical indignation. And, with it, the efforts of the court moderates to proceed legally were foiled once more.

*

At one level, the bishops' Protest was so monumental a political gaffe that the Junto grandees might well be excused for attributing it to timely divine intervention. Having struggled since the resumption of the session to shoot down the king's-party bishops, thus far without success, the Junto leaders in both Houses seemed to have been handed a golden bullet by the bishops themselves. The speed with which the two Houses acted is astonishing. That same day (Thursday, 30 December), accusations of high treason against the twelve signatories were approved by the Commons, and presented to, and acted upon by, the Lords. By late afternoon that same day, ten of the twelve protester bishops had already been incarcerated in the Tower, while the remaining two, deemed less culpable, had been entrusted to the more congenial custody of Black Rod.[155] With the Lords once again strongly influenced, if not yet absolutely controlled, by the Junto grandees, Glynne was able to compliment the peers, in an official message of goodwill, for acting with 'so much speed and so much affection' towards their Commons brethren.[156] In a single day, the Junto alliance in the two Houses had finally achieved what it had been trying to do since early in the session: to remove a bloc of bishops sufficiently large so as to prevent the king's party from again obstructing their programme of secular reform.

However, if the Junto leaders could indulge in a little godly glee at the despatch of so many bishops to the Tower, the prevailing response was nevertheless one of foreboding. There was a suspicion that, having thwarted the king's attempt to suspend the Parliament by peaceable means, they had made it all the more likely that he would attempt the same objective by military force. Debate in the Commons that day attests vividly to the reality of this fear. Not for the first time, the most hysterical reaction came from Pym.[157] After insisting on clearing the lobby, bolting the Commons' doors, and checking that no one was hiding in the first-floor Committee Chamber† – precautions which struck even the panic-prone D'Ewes as verging on the absurd – Pym claimed melodramatically that 'there was a plot for the des-

---

* With nice symmetry, the bearer of this message, which would guarantee the Junto's dominance of the Lords for the foreseeable future, was the Chief Justice of Common Pleas, Sir John Bankes – one of the first beneficiaries of the Bedford group's new-found influence, back in February 1641, when he had been promoted to the Chief Justiceship at the joint instigation of the Earl of Northumberland and his ally, the late Earl of Bedford.
† For these various locations, see map pp. xvi–xvii.

troying of the howse of Commons this day', and urged the Commons to summon 'the Traine[d] Bands for our assistance'.[158] Although Pym had a 'fewe' seconders, this extreme response was comprehensively talked down. Some unnamed members proposed instead that the Commons adjourn to Guildhall, which may indicate that they 'believed they were on the point of facing an armed attack'.[159] But these alarmists, too, were overruled. In fact, the furthest the Commons would go to meet Pym's concerns was to renew their request that the Lords join them in petitioning the king for a guard for the Parliament, to be commanded by the Earl of Essex.[160] Even this struck a majority of the Lords, who had just happily incarcerated a dozen royalist bishops, as an over-reaction. To appoint a guard under Essex was effectively to give the Junto a private army in Westminster, an outcome that was probably more likely to provoke than to deter a confrontation with the newly mobilized forces at Whitehall.[161]

If counsels of moderation prevailed at Westminster, they were also far from silent at Whitehall. Faced with the prospect of Bristol's impeachment and the dissolution of the party in the Lords which the earl had helped to build, Charles resorted to the same tactic he had employed earlier in the year, when dealing with the impeachment of Strafford: he tried to rebuild an alliance with those reformers whom he regarded as biddable. Confronted with the collapse of one 'king's party' (founded on the bishops and the 'popish' lords), he tried to construct another, turning this time – possibly on Digby's advice – to a series of moderate reformists. Ironically, almost all were erstwhile opponents of the Crown who, in the spring of 1641, had nevertheless joined Bedford's campaign to save Strafford from the scaffold. Among the first to whom Charles turned was Viscount Saye, arguably Bedford's closest ally in that ill-starred crusade. On 28 December, the day after Bristol's prosecution had first been mooted in the Commons, the king signed a warrant for the payment of £1,200 to Saye for him 'to disburse in his Majestie's special and private service according to his Majestice's directions already given him therein'.[162] Although the precise purpose of this 'special and private service' remains mysterious, the sheer size and confidential nature of the grant suggests that Charles was offering a timely gesture of confidence, if not an out-and-out bribe, to one of his leading former critics. It was only reasonable to expect that Saye, who had been prepared to save Strafford to oblige the king, would be willing to work at least as hard to save Bristol. Moreover, there is some evidence that Charles's efforts to win over Saye as Bristol's protector brought results. That same day (Tuesday the 28th), as many of the leading Junto men lined up to attack Bristol and to demand his removal from the king's Council,[163] one prominent speaker intervened unexpectedly on his behalf: 'Mr Fines' – Saye's son, Nathaniel – spoke up, urging the Commons 'not to medle with my Lord of Bristooe at this time'.[164]

As Digby's attempts to suspend the Parliament failed, Charles redoubled his efforts to create a new 'interest' around the moderate reformers (the supporters of the post-Triennial Act constitution, but who were prepared to allow the king all or most of his remaining prerogative powers), in order to make the two Houses manageable. After a disastrous forty-eight hours –

which had seen the Commons demand Digby's censure as well as Bristol's (Wednesday the 29th) and the imprisonment of most of the royalist bishops (Thursday the 30th) – Charles strengthened his relations with yet another former court critic turned defender of the prerogative. At 7 p.m. that Thursday evening, the Earl of Southampton was sworn as one of the Gentleman of the Bedchamber, thus joining the favoured courtly élite that constituted the king's inner entourage.[165]

Over the course of Friday, Charles – again possibly urged on by Digby – developed plans for an even more ambitious attempt to bring current and former opponents, regarded as not wholly inimical to the prerogative, into the government. The following day, Saturday, 1 January (if the testimony of Sir Edward Dering is to be trusted), Charles finally tried to make his peace with Pym, offering him the office that had been earmarked for him long ago by Bedford: the Chancellorship of the Exchequer.[166] For more than twenty years, Pym had straddled both Bedford's and Warwick's worlds. Now, he was being made to choose between them and the two sides of the ideological divide they had come to represent: between a post-Triennial Act kingdom, in which a limited monarch was trusted to choose the men with whom he would rule; or a 'commonwealth', in which power, though Parliament-derived, was vested in an aristocratic council, ruling in the name of a cipher-king. Pym does not seem to have taken long to decide.

This rebuff did not deflect the king (or Digby, the policy's likely author) from continuing with this strategy of seeking to build bridges with his erst-while enemies. Within two hours of Pym's refusal of the Chancellorship, Charles had summoned another Commons-man, who also had strong reform-ist credentials – Sir John Culpeper – and persuaded him to accept the office that Pym had just turned down.[167] At the same time, the king successfully offered the post of senior Secretary of State (currently vacant) to another Commons-man who had shown reformist leanings, Viscount Falkland.[168]*

That it was Digby who was behind this strategy as a whole is strongly sug-gested by the testimony of Edward Hyde, who had a long conversation with his friend at this time, also directly concerning preferment to office. In his auto-biography, Hyde describes how Digby summoned him to a secret meeting with the king and queen on the evening of New Year's Day (Saturday, 1 January). There, in a further bid to reward those who, like Culpeper and Falkland, had been defenders of his remaining prerogatives, the king offered Hyde the post of Solicitor-General – undertaking to dismiss the current incumbent, Oliver St John (since May, firmly identified with the radical Junto-men of the Warwick House group), in order to create the necessary vacancy.[169] Hyde declined the Solicitor-Generalship for the time being, thinking that both the timing of the offer was inopportune, and fearing that St John would be far more dangerous out of office than in.[170] Given that accepting the post would have placed him in the eye of the

---

* The office had been left vacant by the dismissal of the elder Sir Henry Vane. Sir Edward Nicholas had been recently appointed to the junior Secretaryship of State, which had long been left vacant by the flight of Secretary Windebank.

forthcoming impeachment storm (it was St John as Solicitor-General, he would remember, who had delivered the final speech against the Earl of Strafford), it is not hard to see why he preferred to continue as an informal adviser to the king.

This series of interviews and appointments is highly revealing as to the king's commitment, at least for the moment, to Digby's strategy of trying to reconstruct the old Bedfordian coalition of early 1641. (Hyde, it will be recalled, had been Bedford's and Hertford's emissary in their efforts to persuade Essex to drop his insistence on Strafford's death.) This was one King Charles: the monarch who acknowledged in his head, if never completely in his heart, the need to act within the law; the man who could see the merit of 'altering somewhat, to suit the times'; the *politique* who could maintain a carapace of charm towards men like Digby, Culpeper, and even Saye, who had all, in their several ways, helped destroy the world he had worked to fashion during the 1630s. Yet there was also simultaneously a far more impulsive, less rational King Charles: acutely protective of his honour; impatient of legal nicety and political complexity; and, in moments of exasperation, prone to the use of violence as a means of cutting his way clear of legal and political entanglements. For most of 1641, these two facets of Charles's personality had co-existed in a state of uneasy and indecisive equilibrium. In the highly volatile political environment of late December 1641, however, the external pressures on Charles to decide which of the two was truer to himself and his kingly role intensified by the day.

If confusion still reigned in the king's mind as to which of these two approaches was to be preferred – the 'parliamentary way' or Roxburgh's preference for peremptory violence – the events of that Christmas week had made it clear that he would soon need to make a final and definitive choice. Still, the king's over-riding strategic objective remained stopping the Junto from carrying through its programme of further reform. But his parliamentary means of doing so were rapidly diminishing. Digby's and Williams's attempts to have the Parliament suspended had ended, respectively, in embarrassment and catastrophe. And with the imprisonment of half the episcopal bench on Thursday the 30th, the king's immediate chances of recovering his control of the upper House had slumped to near zero. By Friday the 31st the Junto's control of the legislative process was once again almost absolute. With the Lords now dominated by Warwick and his reformist allies, their dismantling of what remained of Charles's monarchical powers seemed close to certain. Unless this juggernaut were stopped, England's transformation from a kingly to a republican commonwealth could be complete well before Twelfth Night. After that, it was a matter of indifference whether or not the two hundred and ten absentees from both Houses returned to Westminster or not. The battle would already have been lost.

On Saturday, 1 January 1642, after perhaps the most disastrous week of his reign, Charles was compelled into action to defend what remained of his power. The problem he wrestled with – which the *two* King Charleses wrestled with – was a familiar one: to rely on force, the Roxburgh route; or to trust to law and his people's affections, the ancient 'parliamentary way'? Some to whom Charles had spoken of this dilemma – Rossetti, most revealingly –

had concluded that the king's private preference for force was, long since, clear and ingrained.[171] In this regard, the king's refusal to accede to the Commons' demands, most recently on Friday the 31st, for a military guard of its own under the command of the Earl of Essex (a development which would have made a forcible dissolution a far more difficult, and most likely bloody, undertaking)* tends to suggest that the option of using force remained in reserve.[172]

But if there were counsellors at Whitehall pressing the case for a *coup d'état* of the type that had earlier been planned in Scotland, they were comprehensively overruled. On or shortly after Saturday, 1 January 1642, the king decided that the time had come to confront his parliamentary enemies – but not in a furtive, and potentially murderous, putsch of the type Roxburgh had tried to effect in Scotland. Instead, the confrontation with these 'traitors' was to be public, candid, and peaceable, with a punctilious attention to correct parliamentary rules of procedure.

v. PROSECUTIONS

The arrests which Charles planned over that Saturday and Sunday, the first two days of the New Year, were to seal the king's reputation as a bringer of 'bloodshed and desolation',[173] a tyrant intent on the destruction of Parliament itself. That the events of that day ignited one of the greatest political controversies in England's history is incontrovertible. However, if we are to understand the initial purpose behind the king's actions, it is necessary to peer behind the sulphurous clouds of later controversy, and to view them not only in the context of their planning, but also in the light of other initiatives, undertaken contemporaneously by the king, by which he sought escape from the predicament of the moment: in particular, the olive branches extended successfully to Saye, Falkland, Culpeper and (unsuccessfully) to Pym. Amid the swirls of accusation and counter-accusation, there is one point of hard fact: at some point over that Saturday and Sunday – New Year's Day and 2 January – Charles decided to prosecute six of the Junto leaders on charges of high treason: Holles, Hesilrige, Pym, Hampden, and Strode from the Commons, and Viscount Mandeville from the Lords.

The timing of the king's action is perhaps the clearest clue to its broader purpose. Throughout the previous week – indeed, ever since 28 December, when, with the bishops' withdrawal, the king had lost control of the House of Lords – what might be termed 'the Digby faction' at court had been

---

* As recently as Friday, 31 December, the Commons had commanded Denzell Holles to deliver a message to the king, conveying 'their great apprehensions and just fears of mischievous designs and practices to ruin and destroy them', and therefore demanding 'a guard out of the City of London, commanded by the Earl of Essex'. Viscount Saye also seems to have concurred that the king's likeliest motive for refusing to allow the Parliament a guard of its own was his desire to leave open the option of dissolving the Parliament by force.

looking for alternative means of disabling the Junto from passing the pending legislation that would have completed the emasculation of the monarchy. No longer able to rely on the Lords, and lacking as yet an effective king's party in the Commons, Digby had tried an alternative gambit in a bid to stave off the threatened reforms: suspending Parliament by declaring it 'no longer free' (and hence no longer validly convened).[174] But when both attempts to achieve this (his own and his second attempt through Archbishop Williams's) were thrown out by the now heavily Junto-influenced House of Lords, he and the king had been left in an even worse position than that from which they had started. There was now nothing to stop the Junto Lords from seeing to their completion all the outstanding items on their reformist agenda, starting with the wholesale removal of the bishops from the upper House – an act that would massively (and permanently) enhance the Junto's ability to control parliamentary business.[175]

It seems no coincidence that the decision to impeach five of the Junto leaders in the Commons followed immediately on the failure of Digby's two earlier attempts to make it impossible for the Junto leaders to press ahead with further 'reform'. In effect, the impeachments seem to have been a continuation of the same strategy by alternative means – and here, too, Bedford's former protégé is the common element in all three initiatives. Indeed, if Hyde is to be believed, Digby was the king's sole adviser in the project to accuse Mandeville and the five Commons-men.[176]

Like Digby's earlier two previous initiatives, the prime purpose of the impeachments was not justice, but carefully targeted disruption. It was almost inconceivable that the House of Lords, as constituted at the beginning of 1642 – the House which would have to try the cases against the 'traitors'– would ever have agreed to find Holles, Pym and their co-accused guilty of treason.[177] But while it can be doubted whether these prosecutions, mounted in this particular way, at this particular time, ever had – or were intended to have – a serious chance of bringing these miscreants to the scaffold,[178] Charles and Digby could nevertheless be sure of one thing: the prosecutions were likely to disrupt parliamentary business for days (and almost certainly weeks) to come. Major political impeachments almost invariably had the effect of bringing all other parliamentary business to a standstill. And if the king and Digby could obtain this, they would have achieved the objective that Digby's two earlier attempts to suspend parliamentary business had missed.

The legal processes employed against the accused also suggest that, at least as initially planned by Charles and Digby, the project was far more concerned with obtaining a tactical advantage over the Junto leaders than actually removing their heads. Indeed, it is doubtful whether, at the outset, the king actually seriously intended to secure the accused members in custody. Had he wished to make sure of this, he could have had them arrested in their beds, notwithstanding their standing as Parliament-men – and entirely legally, since 'treason was universally agreed not to be protected by parliamentary privilege'.[179] Instead, the plans agreed in the course of Sunday, 2 January removed any element of surprise by ordering the Attorney-General to deliver

the general impeachment accusation against Mandeville and the five Commoners in public, when the House of Lords reconvened at 1 p.m. on
Monday.[180] What the king wanted above all was the accused traitors' papers,
and he issued warrants that these were to be seized without warning in the
course of Monday. But the officers who were 'sent from his Majesty' to seize
the members' trunks and manuscripts appear to have had no orders to secure
those who were actually accused, even if they encountered the suspected
traitors in the course of their raids.[181]

How the leading Scots at court, Roxburgh and Sir William Fleming, with
their more robust attitudes to the treatment of traitors, regarded this English
delicacy in dealing with matters parliamentary is unclear. What is certain is
that the king (and possibly Digby) immediately sought to involve at least
Fleming in one critically important element in their plans: Fleming was given
the task of leading the raids on the accused traitors' lodgings in the course
of that day. And so it was that Montrose's cousin, an anti-Argyllian Scot –
not an English officer of the law – who was to take the first steps in the
prosecution of Mandeville and the 'five members'.[182]*

While Fleming was to be despatched to seize the traitors' papers, the king
planned his moves against the Parliament with an almost fastidious respect
for the Commons' privileges. A single Serjeant-at-Arms was to go to the
House and 'require of Master Speaker' that the five accused should be handed
over to him for arrest.[183] Whatever the response, it promised to work to the
king's advantage. If the House complied, which even the king probably
regarded as unlikely, the Junto leadership would be severely weakened; in
the event of an outright refusal, Charles would be handed an undeniable
propaganda coup: *prima facie* evidence that, as he had so often insisted, the
chamber was dominated by a narrow and unrepresentative clique, ready to
protect even traitors in its midst.

This propagandist aspect of the venture was underlined by the king's own
appeal to the public: his decision to print the impeachment articles – in a
special edition by Robert Barker, the 'Printer to the King's most Excellent
Majestie', as its title page declared – as soon as they had been delivered to
the Parliament.[184] The contrast with the Strafford impeachment only twelve
months earlier is instructive. Then, the impeachment articles against Strafford
had not appeared in print until late in the trial – and months after they had
first been put to Parliament. In the case of Mandeville and the Commons
'traitors', the king saw to it that the impeachment articles were printed
and published within a day of their presentation.[185] Appropriately, their
propagandist import is evident from the very first charge, which contained
the king's central grievance against the Junto as a whole (in Scotland, it had
been the Montrose party's principal charge against Argyll): that the accused

---

* Mandeville, of course, had been at the centre of the pro-Argyllian alliance of English
Parliament-men, at least since early in 1640. During the autumn, his house in Chelsea
had effectively become the Junto's headquarters for coordinating correspondence with
Argyll and Hamilton while the king had been in Scotland.

had sought to 'deprive the King of his Regall Power, *and to place in Subjects* an Arbitrary and Tyrannical power over the Lives, Liberties, and Estates of His Majestie's liege people'.[186] Part, at least, of this charge was incontrovertible; for depriving the king of large portions of his regal power and placing this in the hands of mere 'subjects' had been an essential element of the Junto's godly enterprise from the outset. To achieve this – the impeachment articles went on – they had 'traitorously invited and encouraged a foreign power [Scotland] to invade his Majesty's kingdom of England', and endeavoured to induce the army raised in 1640 'to side with them in their traiterous designes'.[187] Charles, it seemed, knew all about the Petitioner Peers' attempts to create their 'Armies for the Commonwealth' in August 1640; and this, combined with the conspirators' involvement in inciting tumults in the capital during the Strafford crisis and subsequently, amounted to one of the most clear-cut of all treasons: levying 'War against the King'.[188]

Beyond their usefulness as propaganda, however, the impeachment articles had an obvious utility as weapons of disruption. And nowhere was that disruption likely to be greater than in the House of Lords – where the impeachments looked certain to deflect the peers safely away from the pile of reformist legislation, hitherto long deferred, but now, with the ousting of the bishops and the Junto's influence restored, about to be actively taken up. Instead, the impeachment articles looked set to monopolize the Lords' business for the foreseeable future. There would be charges to consider; witnesses to be examined; judges to be consulted; committees obliged to meet. In fact, it is clear from the king's own handwritten instructions to the Attorney-General, compiled over the weekend of 1 and 2 January, that Charles had given careful consideration to this aspect of the impeachments.[189] The Lords would obviously have to set up an investigative committee to examine witnesses, as they had done with Strafford. But to prevent this being controlled by the leading Junto grandees, Charles insisted that the Attorney-General take pre-emptive measures. Hence, the king wrote,

When the Committie for examination is a naming (which you must press to be close [i.e. confidential] and under tey [tie or oath] of secresie), if eather Essex, Warwick, Holland, Say, Mandeville, Wharton, or Brooke,[190] be named, you must desire that they may be spared [i.e. not appointed to the committee], because you ar to examine them as witnesses for me.[191]

This list, not coincidentally, is the list of the peers who, in the spring of 1641, *opposed* the Bedford–Saye compromise scheme to save Strafford's life, and had been closest to Argyll and the Scots Commissioners in London.[192]

Charles may well have regarded these noblemen as even more guilty than the Commons-men who were actually accused – as did others around him. Hyde, for instance, was critical of the fact that the Junto's real heavyweights were absent from the list of the king's intended victims: 'there should [also] have been a better choice of the persons [accused], there being many of the House [of Lords] of more mischievous inclinations and designs against the king's person and the government'.[193]* Here too, however, the king's tactics were no more than realistic. An all-out assault on the Junto's most powerful aristocratic grandees, at a time when they had just recouped much of their former influence in the upper House, risked outright rejection. Yet, at the last minute, Digby overcame Charles's cautious preference for beginning with the lesser conspirators before moving on to the peers; Digby 'particularly named the Lord Mandeville[194]† ... and undertook to prove that he had bade the rabble, when they were about the Parliament House, that they should go to Whitehall [Palace]' – a reference that probably relates to the crowd which had threatened violence against the king if he had failed to agree to the attainder of the Earl of Strafford in May 1641.[195]

All of this suggests that Charles, far from planning a violent *coup d'état* over those first days of January, was actually steeling himself for another attempt at proceeding in a 'parliamentary way'. The attack on the militant Commonwealthsmen – the Warwick House circle in the Lords (who were named as witnesses) and their key allies in the Commons (the actual accused) – neatly complemented the king's contemporaneous efforts to create the foundations of a new government out of what remained of the Bedfordian circle of early 1641. The process was attested in a variety of ways: not simply in the role of Digby, Bedford's 'son', as perhaps the principal royal counsellor of the period, but also in the king's grant of £1,200 to Saye 'in his Majestie's special and private service' (on 28 December); Fiennes's intervention in the Commons to dissuade the House from 'meddling' with Digby's father, the Earl of Bristol (also on 28 December);[196] the swearing of Southampton to the Bedchamber (30 December); the appointments to office of Culpeper and Falkland; the offer of office to Hyde (1 and 2 January). It would also explain the most paradoxical element of the entire puzzle: how Charles could have offered Pym the Chancellorship of the Exchequer one day, and instructed his Attorney-General to impeach him of treason the next.

----

* Hyde's view of the decision to prosecute Hesilrige and Strode is also interesting given the prominence of both men as the introducers of major items of Junto-promoted legislation: 'Sir Arthur Haslerigge and Strowde were persons of too low an account and esteem, and though their virulence and malice was as conspicuous and transcendent as any men's, yet their reputation and interest to do any mischieve – otherwise than in concurring in it – was so small that they gained credit and authority by being joined with the rest, who had indeed a great influence [namely, the unprosecuted noble grandees, and Mandeville, Holles, Hampden, and Pym]'.
† Back in February 1641, Mandeville had also been Digby's rival to succeed Windebank as Secretary of State, when the competing Warwick–House and Bedford–House groups had proposed different slates for the vacant offices of state (see above, Chapter 7). But it is also possible that the king intended to accuse Essex, Warwick, and the other peers who had plotted against him, at a later date. The instructions to the Attorney-General were explicit that he was to 'reserve the power of making additionalls [i.e. naming other offenders who were to be prosecuted]', once the impeachment investigations had begun.

VI. THE UNRAVELLING

However chaotic was to be its outcome, the opening moves in the impeachment of Viscount Mandeville and the five Commons-men, were conducted
with exquisite good manners. When the Parliament resumed, shortly after 1
p.m. on Monday 3 January, the Attorney-General presented the House of
Lords with impeachment articles against all six accused. He conveyed the
king's request that a select committee be established to examine witnesses
('as formerly hath been done in cases of the like nature') and handed over
to the Lords the responsibility for 'the securing of the persons [accused]' –
their holding in custody.[197] Later in the afternoon, 'about night[fall]',[198] one
of the king's Serjeants-at-Arms, Master Francis, appeared in the Commons.
Politely putting aside his mace of office, in deference to the superior jurisdiction of the House, he mentioned nothing of particular charges but simply
'require[d]' the Speaker to deliver him the accused, informing them that 'I
am commanded to arrest them, in his Majesty's name, of high treason'.[199]
By this point, the Commons had already been alerted to the raids that had
taken place, earlier that same afternoon, on the studies of Pym, Holles,
and the other accused. Predictably, these were condemned as a breach of
parliamentary privilege (the raids that had followed the dissolution of the
Short Parliament had been similarly contemned), but not, significantly, the
impeachments themselves.[200] These the Commons promised to 'take into
serious consideration' and to 'answer in all humility and duty'.[201] A four-
man delegation (of which the newly appointed Privy Councillors, Culpeper
and Falkland, formed half) was despatched to Whitehall to wait on the king,
and to promise that the accused would 'be ready to answer any legal charge
laid against them'. As no single specific charge had yet been presented to the
Commons – the seven impeachment articles, as yet, had only been communicated to the Lords – this was a courteous and not unreasonable
response.[202]

Nevertheless, the accusations, together with the continuing presence of the
'soldiers set near the Parliament House, as at Whitehall', had inevitably
refocused attention on the Parliament's security. That evening, for the first
time, both Houses agreed to request the establishment of a permanent guard
for the Parliament, a military contingent to be commanded by someone
approved by both the king *and* the two Houses.[203] But while the impeachments
had clearly raised the political temperature, neither House had contested the
propriety of the king's actions in laying the charges. Despite the obvious
tensions, all parties were acting in a 'parliamentary way'.

So far as Digby was concerned, the gambit had thus far proved a success.
The Commons' refusal to hand over its members can hardly have come as
a surprise. What mattered, however, was that the Parliament looked as though
it would be diverted with arguments over the impeachments and related
questions of privilege for the foreseeable future. Progress towards 'further
reformation' would be slowed, if not altogether stopped; and in little more
than a week, when the absentee peers and Commons-men returned, the king

would, most likely, be in a position to halt further encroachments on his powers.[204]

Only in two respects did the now Junto-dominated House of Lords offer anything approaching provocation to the king: they ordered the unsealing of the accused Commons-men's studies and papers. And at the prompting of William Strode, himself one of the 'traitors' accused, they agreed to approach the king to request he suppress the College of Capuchin Friars which formed part of the queen's Household at Somerset House.[205]

In the event, the queen's Capuchins were to go on unmolested at Somerset House – practising 'Popery' within barely a mile of Parliament, and keeping as true to the spirit of their founder, St Francis, as their palatial surroundings would permit – well into 1643, long after London was supposedly under the 'puritan' rule.[206] But in the queen's household at Somerset House, the nature of the threat was easily misconstrued. The Parliament's initiative to suppress the Capuchins, combined with an attempt the previous Friday to press ahead with impeachment proceedings against the queen's servant, Daniel O'Neill (for his part in anti-Junto plotting over the summer),[207] were easily, but almost certainly wrongly, read at Somerset House as the beginnings of an anti-Catholic crusade, intended to purge the consort's household and deprive Henriette Marie of her sources of spiritual counsel. For those trying to keep the king's reactions to events consonant with the 'parliamentary way', the timing of this slight against his wife could hardly have been less opportune. News of Parliament's plan to deprive her of most of her household clergy reached Henriette Marie on Monday evening, 3 January. By then, if not well before, the queen had become Roxburgh's ally.

The arguments that took place in the Privy Lodgings that Monday night are lost to the historical record. Perhaps the king remained genuinely ambivalent, as he had for so long, as to which of the contrasted courses that were open to him, law or violence, and whose counsels, Digby's or Roxburgh's, should prevail. But towards the end of the evening there came one development which contemporaries read as providing a highly revealing clue: at 10 p.m. that night, 'between 30 and 40 cannoneers' – experts in heavy gunnery – were introduced into the Tower of London.[208] Nehemiah Wallington described the reaction of near panic that the development produced in the City; such was the fear of an imminent attack that 'the Aldermen and Sheriffs were up that night and the gates looked unto and the chains [to obstruct cavalry] pulled across the streets, with knocking at the doors for men to stand upon their guard'. As the news of the development spread around the capital from early on Tuesday morning (4 January 1642), its most obvious implication was that a *coup d'état* was imminent, and the king was preparing to suppress opposition to it in the City, if necessary by force. Shops, noted Wallington, 'were shut up close, with every man [with] his halberd and weapons in a readiness.'[209]

*

By the time the two Houses assembled later that Tuesday morning there was already a widespread suspicion among Parliament-men that the king had decided on the use of force that same day. The signs were easily read. The increased military activity in and around Whitehall's Court of Guard; the arrival during the night of the cannoneers at the Tower; the king's non-committal reply to the two Houses' request for a guard (he had said his response 'may be [given] today – or tomorrow');[210] news that the king had 'yesternight' sent a message to the amateur militiamen of Lincoln's Inn to 'be ready at an hours warning, if his Majesty should have occasion to use them':[211] all this pointed to the likelihood that an attack, probably on the Parliament House itself, might only be a matter of hours away.

Of course, the king had made such menacing preparations before, without actually moving from threat to action; and the evidence of his behaviour that morning suggests that he remained as doubtful as ever as to whether to abandon Digby's 'parliamentary way', and opt for the use of force, which so appealed to Roxburgh.[212] Uncertain as to the nature of the threat, both Houses reacted with equal indecision. In the Commons, at Pym's motion, the President and Deputy President of the Artillery Company (respectively, Sir Thomas Soame and John Venn, both Commons-men) were despatched to the Guildhall to inform the Lord Mayor, aldermen and Common Council of 'what danger the Parliament was in', but with no specific instructions as to what to do.[213] A practical suggestion from Nathaniel Fiennes that observers might be sent to Whitehall to find out 'by what authority' the armed men were assembling was discussed inconclusively, but not even this modest action had been agreed upon by the time the House rose for a dinner recess that ran from noon to some time before 2 p.m.

Neither could the major court office-holders find out what was going to happen. The Earl of Essex, still attending at Whitehall in his capacity as Lord Chamberlain of the Household, was sufficiently worried by midday to send a warning, evidently based on the preparations he had witnessed that morning, to the five members who had been indicted of treason. But this was guesswork on his part, and he could give 'no direct assurance that the ... design should certainly be put in execution'.[214] The Lords, who did not convene until 1 p.m., met with the Commons in the early afternoon to hear the news of the various military preparations and of the 'scandalous' publication of the impeachment articles – the king's own attempt to bring his treason accusations into the public sphere. But the Lords resolved on 'nothing at this time' before adjourning early, apparently anxious to avoid doing anything that might give Whitehall's advocates of force a pretext for intervention.[215]

In the meantime, the Commons tried to interpret the signals that had been coming from Whitehall over the previous hours. These had not been encouraging. After the dinner break, Fiennes had reported the results of his enquiries among the armed men at Whitehall. The soldiers' instructions, noted D'Ewes, were 'to obey *one Sir William Fleming* in all things that he should enjoin them'.[216] Montrose's man – the officer who had presided over the previous day's raids on the 'traitors' lodgings, was to have a major role in the events that were to follow.[217]

*

At Whitehall, the men under Sir William Fleming's orders still waited in the mid-winter cold. Throughout the day, the king had remained closeted in the Privy Lodgings. Then, suddenly, shortly before 3 p.m., by which time there was barely an hour of daylight remaining, there was a flurry of action. Without warning, the king appeared in the Guard Chamber, on the ground floor of Whitehall's eastern range, a room that gave directly on to the Great Court at the centre of the palace. In a despatch written three days later, Giustinian reported that Charles had called out to those present, 'Follow me, my most loyal liege-men and soldiers', whereupon he set out for the Palace of Westminster, accompanied by the armed posse that had been waiting under Sir William Fleming's command: between four and five hundred armed men, a diverse collection of reformadoes, militiamen from the local Trained Bands, and miscellaneous soldiers of fortune. His decision to act appears to have been impetuous. Indeed, such was the haste of the king's departure that there had been no time to prepare his own coach. Rather than wait, he strode through the Great Court and out via the Palace Gate into the open street, where he commandeered a coach belonging to 'a private individual'.[218] The coachman was instructed to drive the short distance, barely half a mile, to the Parliament House. Accompanying the king were his nephew, the Elector Palatine (thus implicating in his actions the man who might otherwise have been the Junto's leading pretender to the throne), and the sexagenarian Earl of Roxburgh.[219]

What precipitated the king's decision to act is imperfectly documented. Giustinian, who had perhaps the most efficient intelligence network of all the foreign ambassadors, reported that the trigger had been the countermanding (by the Lords on Monday afternoon) of his order to seal the studies and papers of the accused members, and the condemnation (by the Commons that Tuesday morning) of the publication of the impeachment articles by the king's printer as 'a scandalous publication' whose publishers were to be punished.[220] But there also appears to have been intense pressure from the queen, whose marriage treaty had been violated by the two Houses' votes banishing her Capuchins the previous evening.[221] Impatient with Charles's repeated vacillations between violence and compromise, she is reported to have shouted at him: 'Go, you coward, and pull these rogues out by the ears, or never see my face more'.[222] Such words seem too colourful to be entirely true. But the two explanations are not mutually exclusive, and it is entirely plausible that it was Henriette Marie's taunts at his inability to maintain his honour that finally, impulsively, turned what had hitherto been merely a contingency plan into a firm decision in favour of action.

That decision taken, the walk between the Palace Gate and Westminster Hall would normally have taken under twenty minutes. However, despite the king's desire for haste, and the acquisition of a coach (not for speed, but as protection against the ubiquitous winter mud), the armed party moved only slowly towards Westminster Hall. News of its approach outran it. A lookout, Hercules Langres, who had been posted by the French ambassador near to Whitehall, slipped through the advancing troop of soldiers and raced to warn Nathaniel Fiennes of the king's imminent arrival.[223] Hesilrige, Pym and the other accused members soon left their places and went to hide in the nearby Court of King's Bench. Barely had the last of the accused members departed, than the king's noisy party was heard ascending the stairs leading from Westminster Hall to the large lobby outside the Commons' chamber. This quickly filled to capacity with around eighty armed men composed of 'divers officers of the late army in the North and other desperate ruffians [who] pressed in' after the king. Most carried pistols and swords. While the king entered alone, Roxburgh stood at the door between the lobby and the Commons' chamber, keeping it open so that members could see the force lying in wait beyond. Opposite him, and in full view of the members in the chamber, was the reformado captain, David Hyde, in one hand 'holding his sword upright in the scabbard' and in the other 'his pistol ready cocked'.[224]

Charles went to the Speaker's chair. 'Gentlemen', he began, 'I am sorry to have this occasion to come unto you',[225] and politely demanded that the five accused Commons-men be handed over to his custody. Roxburgh and his party of armed men, some with their pistols ready to shoot, left little doubt that, should the House refuse to yield up the accused members, they were there to seize them by force. All they awaited was the signal from the king.

Not long into his speech, however, the king realized that his gamble on the use of force had spectacularly failed. All the accused members had already fled. Looking at the benches to his right and left, and into the raised gallery at the former chapel's far end, he muttered: 'I do not see any of them – [and] I think I should know [i.e. recognize] them'. There was nothing remaining to be done but to withdraw.

As he left the chamber, pandemonium broke out. The cry of 'Privilege! Privilege!' was taken up by the members, and pursued the king as he and his armed entourage descended the staircase into Westminster Hall. Many of the members believed that the huge armed retinue that had accompanied the king had been intended to butcher the Commons-men where they sat. This was almost certainly unfounded; but that Fleming's men had instructions to use force, if necessary, in arresting the accused members seems beyond doubt; and, in the event of their resisting arrest, it is hard to imagine how the ensuing altercation – between Fleming's armed men and a group of Commons-men, most of whom habitually wore swords and knew how to use them – could have ended without injuries, and probably fatalities, on both sides. Parliament inferred the king's intentions from the fact that he had allowed this potentiality to arise. But for the timely warning from the French Ambassador, was believed, the floor of the Commons could have become the site of a massacre.

*

By the evening, London was being partitioned into a series of armed camps. At Whitehall, the 'Cavaliers' readied themselves to defend the palace against attack. In the City, supporters of the Junto, fearing that Parliament was about to be dissolved by force, began mobilizing sections of the City militia to guard the two Houses against a repeat attempt at a *coup d'état*.

When the two Houses reassembled the following day, Wednesday 5 January, they did so in the expectation that the king or his ill-controlled supporters might yet launch an all-out assault on the Parliament. The Commons' doors were locked, and look-outs were posted 'to see what number of people are repairing towards Westminster'.[226]

By arriving at the Parliament House, in the words of the Commons' declaration passed that day, 'with a great multitude of men armed, in a warlike manner, with halberds, swords and pistols',[227] Charles had fatally compromised the 'constitutionalist' strategy that had been agreed on within his entourage during the previous week. The impeachments – which had been intended to underline the king's preference for open, legal ways of procedure – had ended, instead, in reinforcing the conviction that the king was intent on the Parliament's forcible dissolution, possibly even ready to allow deaths to occur in the course of arresting Hesilrige, Hampden, Strode, Erle, and Pym.

Fatally indecisive, Charles does not seem to have known, even in his own mind, which of the two options he truly preferred. As a result, the bungled arrests of Mandeville and the five Commons-men seemed to verify, in retrospect, the succession of stories during the last twelve months that had implicated the monarch, time and again, in plotting violence against his opponents.

This amalgam of fear, outrage and indignation, engendered by the actions of the king and 'Cavaliers', worked powerfully to the Junto leaders' advantage. For the first time, there was now a majority in both Houses willing to endorse the Junto's argument that the Parliament would never be safe until it had a military force under its own command: the 'guard' it had requested, repeatedly, to be commanded – so the Commons still insisted – by the Earl of Essex. Unless that were granted, so the Commons declared on 5 January, they would withdraw to the City's Guildhall, until such time as they had 'a sufficient guard wherein they may confide'.[228] The House then formally adjourned until Tuesday, 11 January, in the knowledge that, by the time it next met, the newly elected Common Councillors would have formally taken their seats (on Monday the 10th), and control of the City militia forces would once again be firmly in pro-reformist hands.

In the interim, however, the bicameral Committee of Irish Affairs came into its own as never before. Here was the institution that literally embodied the union between the Junto leaders in the Commons and the virtuous, Junto-supporting Lords. Moreover, it was already empowered to raise forces in the Parliament's name. By ordering the Irish Affairs Committee to meet during the recess, the Commons provided an institution under whose auspices they could consult formally with the leading reformist peers, without ever having to summon the House of Lords.[229] Indeed, almost the last thing the Commons did before rising on 5 January was to ratify a series of recommendations from the Irish Affairs Committee for the issuing of arms from the Tower. A thousand muskets and 1,500 swords, together with large supplies of powder and match, were to be provided to the regiments under Sir John Clotworthy and Lord Conway – both men who were unfailingly loyal to the Junto grandees (to Warwick and Northumberland respectively).[230] Neither regiment had yet been despatched to Ireland. Should Charles attempt to use military force against the Parliament, as was now widely and genuinely feared, these forces might yet be called upon to form the core of a new 'Army for the Commonwealth'.

*

For five days, both the king and the Junto leaders vied for the support of the City Trained Bands – London's citizen militia, some 10,000-strong – that would determine which of the two sides would control the capital. By 8 January, however, the London Common Council had sided firmly with Essex and the other Junto leaders. The struggle for the mastery of London, which had been inaugurated with the Artillery Company sermon in September 1640, now ended, securely in the Junto's favour, with the appointment by Common Council of the Artillery Company's Captain-Leader (and one of Essex's closest friends in the City), Philip Skippon, as the Serjeant-Major-General – the overall commander – of the London Trained Bands.[231]

If Charles had not lost all his supporters in the capital, this was the moment when his attempt to establish an effective and durable 'royal interest' in London – begun so optimistically with Richard Gurney's election as Lord Mayor in September – finally faltered and died. In the struggle for military power within the City government, the Junto's 'interest', based on its dominance of the Common Council, emerged triumphant. By the evening of Sunday, 9 January, it was clear that the king's motley collection of disbanded cavalrymen would be no match for the City's far more numerous, well armed and relatively well disciplined forces. Fearful that there might be an attempt by his adversaries to arrest the queen, who was now being widely blamed for the botched *coup d'état* of 4 January, Charles took the decision to withdraw from London.

On Monday, 10 January, the king's party left Whitehall by barge for the journey up-river to Hampton Court. Charles insisted that Essex and Holland should accompany him, as the two officers responsible, respectively, for the administration of the court's public and private apartments. Both officers declined, Holland having convinced Essex that, if they left London for Hampton Court, they would be murdered there shortly after their arrival.

It was the final breach. The sixteen oarsmen of the king's barge began the long row to Hampton Court, pulling away from the Privy Stairs, the small almost ice-bound jetty, safely distant from the braying mob on the street side of the palace. With him, the king brought the queen, the royal children, and the Prince-Elector – his relations with the Junto leaders now hopelessly compromised, for the moment, by his participation in the attempted arrests of the five members.

From the cabin at the stern of the barge, Charles caught a glimpse of the gilded weather-vanes of Whitehall Palace before the boat turned westwards, past the Abbey, and under the great east window of St Stephen's Chapel – the Commons' chamber, and the scene of his most recent political débâcle. It would be seven years before Charles saw his palace again.

*

It was dark by the time they moored at Hampton Court, Cardinal Wolsey's vast red-brick extravaganza on the Thames. In the haste to leave Whitehall, however, the household servants had not been able to send on any of the king's linen and furniture in time. The royal party arrived to a bitterly cold and largely unfurnished house. That night, as the country began to divide into two armed camps, all five members of the royal family were forced to share the same bed. It was to be the king's first taste of the privations of civil war.

EPILOGUE

[T]hese men, by a new kind of Metaphysick, have found out a way to
abstract the Person of the King from his Office, to make his Soveraigntie
a kind of Platonick idea hovering in the aire, while they visibly attempt
to assaile and destroy his Person...

James Howell, *The True Informer* ([April] 1643)[1]

'Thinges being now brought to a hight, they cannot consist so, but must
change to the great prejudice of the one or [the] other side':[2] such was the
view from the Whitehall court just forty-eight hours after the king's foiled
attempt to arrest the five members. Sidney Bere, who recorded this bleak
prediction, and like so many others who shared his pessimism, did not have
to wait long to see it fulfilled. From the moment Charles abandoned his
capital on 10 January 1642, it became apparent that the impasse between
the two sides was unlikely to be resolved, except by a test of military strength.
Parliament planned accordingly. Among the first things the Commons did
after resuming its sittings at Westminster was to instruct Oliver St John and
others to draft a declaration – to be printed and circulated, with the approval
of the two Houses, throughout the kingdom – advising the people 'to be in
readiness and [in a] good posture of defence ... to defend their several
counties from invasion by Papists, or other ill-affected persons'.[3]

The shock of the king's attempted coup was compounded, over the following weeks, by the after-tremors caused by the revelations of what this
intervention would have presaged, had all gone to plan. In the days which
followed, evidence gradually came to light, revealing – or so it was claimed –
the full extent of the violence which Fleming's men had been ready to inflict.
'We had all the material passages of this design proved unto us by several
witnesses', recorded Sir Simonds D'Ewes, thoroughly convinced and alarmed
by what he had heard, and 'I was fully ... satisfied that if God had not in
a wonderful manner prevented [bloodshed] by the absence of those ... five
members, we had been all in very great danger of having been destroyed.'[4]
Correspondence intercepted in the days immediately after the attempted coup,
and subsequently read to the Commons at Guildhall, suggested that the
treason accusations against Mandeville and the others had been merely the
start of a wider royalist counter-attack. A second phase of arrests, planned
for when the first set of culprits was either 'in the Tower, or their heads

[struck] from their shoulders',[5] would have netted almost all the remaining leaders of the Junto: Oliver St John, Nathaniel Fiennes, and Sir Walter Erle from the Commons, and, 'in the House of the Lords, ... Essex, Warwick, Say, Brook, and Paget must follow', declared one intercepted letter, 'or else we shall not be quiet'.[6] Mandeville and the five Commons-men impeached on 3 January had merely been the beginning.

From here, the decisions which precipitated the kingdom into war quickly followed. After his withdrawal to Hampton Court, the king and his small entourage removed thence to Windsor (where the king arrived on 13 January 1642), with the great south-coast fortress at Portsmouth, with its well stocked arsenal, as their intended destination. (In effect, he put into practice the contingency plans that had been devised in response to that first revolt, in September 1640, in the event of a collapse of royal authority within the capital.) Having forfeited control of the military stores at the Tower, the king's main concern was to secure Portsmouth's arsenal and that at Hull – the two largest in the kingdom, after the Tower – before they were claimed by his enemies.

In February, in a new Militia Bill, the two Houses demanded that the king sign away permanently his 'power of the sword'. Henceforth, every one of the noblemen who held command over England's county Trained Bands was to be nominated and appointed with the approval of the Parliament.[7] And when the king rejected outright this further attempt to usurp his prerogatives, the two Houses simply enacted it under their own authority, as an ordinance, in defiance of the king's hitherto unquestioned power of veto. With Parliament still needing to press forward with the Irish campaign and now confronting the prospect of military conflict within England, a definitive resolution could no longer be deferred. For the Junto grandees, there was only one on acceptable solution on offer: the public denial of the king's 'negative voice' in matters of legislation, and the assertion by Parliament of the power of appointing the great officers of military command: the Lords Lieutenant and, shortly afterwards, the Generals and the Lord Admiral as well.

From the promulgation of the Militia Ordinance, the 'sad distempers'[8] at Westminster impinged directly on every county in the land. By the summer both sides were raising armies. In the autumn, the actual fighting – the English Civil War – began.

*

Over the last quarter century, historians of the three Stuart kingdoms have presented us with a largely accidental Civil War. Chance, missed opportunities, unforeseen events, and the way in which the interconnectedness of the three Stuart kingdoms multiplied these contingencies: these are the themes which have dominated the writings about origins of that conflict. Much has been made of the basic good order and peacefulness of England in 1640 and 1641. Not until 'May or June 1642', it has been suggested, is it possible to find 'much sign of impending war in the counties'.[9]

All 'England's troubles' might have been avoided, is has been claimed, if only the 'Irish Rebellion had been postponed three weeks', from October to early November 1641; and if this had happened, 'it would not have kept the

... Parliament in being', and there would therefore have been no Parliament to fight a civil war.[10] That there were irreconcilable differences within England has once again been largely ascribed (as it had been by the late Victorians) to the divisive force of religion: the great – and, in some accounts, almost the only – determinant of allegiance. In so far as the war was about ideas or institutions – about who held power in the state, and whence that power was derived – it was one, so the argument runs, in which the two Houses only reluctantly asserted their own claims to sovereignty, and even then in a highly provisional form. True, Parliament did indeed 'usurp' some of Charles I's powers as monarch (his 'politic capacity'), but only temporarily, for as long he was 'held captive by evil counsellors'; but not with any serious intention of questioning the institution of monarchy itself.

During the first six months of 1642, both sides, in the war of words which preceded the actual fighting, stressed that sovereign power lay in a 'mixed monarchy' of three estates – king, Lords, and Commons; indeed, this was a principle on which most Parliamentarians and most Royalists could agree. Even Parliament-men could claim to be fighting 'for the king' – that is, for the monarchy to resume its proper 'politic role' within the legislative trinity – notwithstanding that the king's *person* was temporarily absent, 'seduced [away] by evil counsellors'. Much has been made, in consequence, of the broad consensus about constitutional matters, particularly when it came to the institution of monarchy, which prevailed across the Royalist-Parliamentarian divide. Parliament-men in early 1642 were 'reluctant to pursue radical courses', but their 'distrust [of Charles] finally left them no choice but to claim sovereignty for Parliament'.[11]* The course that led from Charles's Scottish crisis in the late 1630s to the contest for military power in England in 1642 was 'a sequence' of largely contingent events, which at a number of points might have ended in a peaceable victory for the king.[12] And at numerous times in the course of 1641, therefore, Charles came very close to being able to dissolve the Parliament, and resume an only slightly modified monarchical business-as-usual.[13] All of this had massive consequences for the explanations which had dominated for most of the previous hundred years. The determinism of the old Whig- and Marxist-inspired 'grand narratives' – with their insistence respectively on long-term political conflict and long-term social change as the origins of the Civil War – was exploded by the revelation, in the 1990s, of just how 'reluctant' and contingency-dependent the entire conflict turned out to be.

Not that these 'Revisionists' denied the English Civil War *any* long-term causes. Even 'fortuitous' events can have long antecedents, and these, it was

---

*This interpretation, the rise of which can be dated to the 1970s, has come to be known as 'Revisionism', in the sense that it repudiated the determinism of the two major interpretations of the previous century: the 'Whig' determinism inherent in the view that England's history was a long and inevitably victorious march towards the sunny uplands of Gladstonian parliamentary democracy; and, second, the Marxist determinism with which, from the 1920s, this theory came to be overlaid, with its conviction that class conflict was the driving motor of historical change.

suggested, were to be found in two great structural problems afflicting the mid seventeenth-century state, whose origins stretched back to the days of the Tudors, if not earlier.[14] The first was the so-called 'problem of multiple kingdoms': that the Stuarts, being the first dynasty to unite all three kingdoms and Wales under a single Crown, had faced a uniquely difficult task in keeping these very different sets of subjects in order. Dissidents in one kingdom could create mischief by allying with troublemakers in another, and concessions granted in one kingdom tended to promote copycat demands from the others. The second great structural weakness, which compounded this first, was the uneven impact of the Reformation in each of these three realms. Not only did Charles inherit a mostly Catholic Ireland and a predominantly Calvinist Scotland, but even the post-Reformation English Church contained its own divergent and, in the end, mutually hostile traditions.

These two weaknesses in the structure of the Stuart state – the creaking girders of the 'multiple monarchy' and the ever-widening fault lines within the post-Reformation English Church – required high skills of any king if he were to achieve even a competent job of maintenance. Entrusted to an incompetent or over-ambitious monarch, these structural flaws constituted a catastrophe waiting to happen. Charles I's inadequacies as a man and as a king, so this theory runs, are the principal reason that it did.[15]

The English war of 1642, in other words, stemmed from the unhappy conjunction of a weak if dutiful monarch and powerful contingent events, not from any fundamental conflict of ideas about the nature of institutions or about monarchical government itself. This, it has been claimed, is why 'revolutionary propensities in England...were so weak';[16] and why, in England at least, 'we are dealing with...a civil war and not a revolution'.[17] Not until the late 1640s, well after the war had been fought, was the belief in the 'mixed sovereignty' of king, Lords and Commons to be called seriously into question. Thus, Parliament's eve-of-war ultimatum to the king, the Nineteen Propositions of June 1642, reveals 'very little sign of any full-fledged Whig commitment to parliamentary sovereignty', but instead a series of improvised, 'ad hoc' responses to happenstance and the (mostly unforeseen) turns of events. Parliament's arguments and, still more, 'the makeshift and almost ramshackle manner in which they were put together to meet circumstances as they arose, tend to suggest that the body of ideas about how the country should be governed were [sic] not really the central element in the cause for which [the Parliamentarians] fought'.[18] Fundamental change to political institutions, and the ideas that might have motivated and sustained such change, was therefore almost irrelevant to the circumstances of 1642. In consequence, people divided 'on almost entirely non-institutional lines'.[19]

*

From what we have seen of the men and events of 1641, it appears unlikely that this is a statement with which men such as Warwick and Hesilrige, or Argyll and Montrose, or even the ill-starred Lord Maguire, the would-be capturer of Dublin Castle, would have agreed. At almost every turn – in Scotland, from the Covenanter Revolt, in England, from the revolt of the

'Lords of the South' in August 1640, through to the outbreak of fighting in England in the summer of 1642 – the men who set out to challenge the Stuart monarchy reveal themselves passionately concerned with the remaking of political *and* religious institutions throughout the three kingdoms. In both England and Scotland, the institutions which became the focus of their attention – the Privy Council, Parliament, the judiciary, the episcopate, and instrumentalities of military power – varied over time, according to the preoccupations of the moment. But if there was one single institution, one single concern, which emerges as paramount in their actions, perhaps even more emphatically than in their words, it is the institution of monarchy, and the urgent need to define its powers in such a way that the subjects' 'liberties' – above all their right to a regularly heard voice in their own government – could henceforth be assured. And, in practice, this entailed, in both British kingdoms, a prolonged, ruthless, and at times breathtakingly successful campaign against the royal prerogative: those particular powers which the monarch exercised *personally*, and which collectively constituted much of his effective authority as king.

Disputes about the prerogative, of course, were in themselves nothing new. At their legal fringes, some had long been contested – particularly where they involved attempts by the Crown to raise money without parliamentary consent; hence the vehemence of the attacks on Ship Money in both the Short Parliament of April-May 1640, and again, in the new Parliament, over the winter of 1640-41. When it came to this question, there were few Parliament-men, in either House, who were not on the side of 'reformation'.

But the parliamentary attack, from November 1640 – led on two fronts by the Petitioner Peers in the Lords and the St John-Pym-Hesilrige group in the Commons – advanced far beyond these questionable legal fringes, and deep into the hinterland of monarchical power. Almost from the opening of the new Parliament, this 'Junto' assailed prerogative powers which had been almost universally regarded, at least until late 1640, as indisputably the monarch's own: those powers which, in the language of the court, were 'the fairest flowers in his garlande'.[20] Partly, this was achieved through the obvious and well-noticed means of Parliament and statute: as with the nullifying of his power, unchallenged hitherto, of deciding when and for how long any Parliament should meet (the Triennial Act) or by the revocation of his power to determine who held the kingdom's great offices (the implication of the Militia Ordinance), and, with it, the denial of a further prerogative power: the royal veto.

But statute was only one means of plucking flowers from the royal garland. The alternative strategy (which, as we have seen, the Junto deployed frequently) was to create the political circumstances in which that garland could not be worn: circumstances, in other words, in which the king's hitherto unquestioned powers, whatever their legal status, could simply no longer be exercised. In fact, one of the most striking features of the extended political crisis of 1640-42 is just how early, and how brazenly, this reformist coalition set about neutralizing Charles's remaining theoretical powers by creating de facto constraints on their exercise. In this context, perhaps the earliest and the most obvious denial of the king's 'negative voice' (the over-riding in a

legal context of his known will) was Twelve Peers' threat to summon a
Parliament on their own authority in September 1640, should Charles refuse
to do so.[21] Of course, this threat was never put to the test. But when, in mid
September, the Earl of Arundel advised his follow Privy Councillors to write
to the king, urging him to announce the summons of 'a Parliament that he
may have the honor of it *himselfe*', it was already clear that, for all practical
purposes, this was a demand which the king had already lost the power to
refuse.[22]

Yet, as Warwick and Pym well knew, substantive change, a 'reformation'
that would endure, required that the king submit to a legally binding agreement which would effect the permanent renunciation of these powers. And
that, in turn, required statute. Hence the great campaign, in the opening
months of the session, to enact the Triennial Bill: to deprive the king – in
the words of his then Solicitor-General, Sir Edward Herbert – of 'one of
the supreame prerogatives of his crowne, which was to call Parliaments'.[23]
Celebrated throughout the country with bonfires and bell-ringing, the royal
assent to the Triennial Act in February 1641 ushered in what was expected
to be a new era in the relations between subject and Crown, for ever after
making the advisory role of Parliament a regular and indispensable part of
the government of the realm. Not least among its clauses, as we have seen,
were its built-in safeguards against kings (including the current one) who
might in future try to evade its provisions: hence the power given to the
Lord Keeper to call a Parliament, if the monarch would not; and, in the
event of even his default, the provision that enabled any twelve peers to
summon a Parliament on their own authority.

This guarantee of regular Parliaments hobbled the powers of the Crown
in ways that extended far beyond the monarch's now largely mechanical
(and, if necessary, wholly dispensable) role in convoking the legislature. The
massively increased power of the parliamentary purse was one. For once the
king had surrendered his prerogative revenues ('whatsoever part of my
revenue shall be found Illegal or heavy to my Subjects')[24] in January 1641,
all future kings were thenceforth committed to a humbling three-yearly round
of financial negotiations with a Parliament, now equipped with the power,
in the event of royal malfeasance, to render the Crown insolvent.[25] The
administrative side-lining of the Exchequer (the principal royal finance
department) in the course of 1641 and creation of what amounted to public
treasuries in the households of major peers – Bedford's, on a small scale, for
the payment of the English forces in the North, and Warwick's, on a massive
scale, to fund the Covenanter army of occupation: both these related developments showed how Parliament could not only bypass the traditional instrumentalities of royal government, but also create agencies of its own.

The effect of these administrative changes was far greater than may at first
appear. Because in removing or marginalizing the king's administrators from
the process of paying the armed forces, Bedford and Warwick and their
household men – the key figures in the reformation of public finance – were
effectively subverting an essential element of the monarch's control over
matters military. The 'king's shilling' was now the Parliament's shilling (and,

for those in the Scots' army in the North, the Earl of Warwick's shilling), and, like all early-modern administrations, the Junto leadership used its new-found powers of patronage in a manner that was thoroughly partisan. It saw that its loyalists were promptly paid, while those whose allegiance was suspect were left to wait for their arrears. Throughout the period of the Scots' occupation, the Warwick House group's clear prioritizing of the Covenanter army over the English one, when it came to payments, illustrated for all to see just how *practical* power over military affairs, post-November 1640, had already been usurped by Parliament, long before the controversies over the Militia Ordinance in the spring of 1642. Both the 'army plots', of the spring and late summer of 1641, took their rise from grievances over the Junto's deliberate policy of diverting funds towards the Scots army of occupation, while keeping the king's army in the North unable to march, as its officers complained in March, as a result of their long want of pay.[26]

No less than Strafford, the Junto grandees – in particular Essex, Warwick, and Brooke (all of whom were to be acquire senior military commands by 1642) – realized that the control of military force was an essential condition of effective government. Warwick, more than any of his colleagues, revealed himself determined to maintain an iron grip on strategic finance. So it comes as little surprise that, having controlled the payment of the Scottish army until its disbandment at the end of August 1641, Warwick turned his attention, the moment the Scots had withdrawn, to the control of the navy – the one perennial manifestation of the state's military power. On Monday 6 September 1641, a matter of days after he paid off the last Covenanter soldiers on their departure from England, control of the 'distributing of the monies ordered to be monthly paid for the supply of the navy' was placed by both Houses in the hands of the Earl of Warwick and two of his closest Commons allies: his stepson-in-law, Sir Henry Mildmay, and his long-time ally and confidant, John Pym.[27] Warwick and his extended household were in control of the English commonwealth's major item of war-related spending.

Moreover, for all the shock caused by the Militia Ordinance of February 1642 – with its implicit claim that Parliament could raise forces and appoint commanders in defiance of the king – this was a usurpation of the monarch's prerogative which the Junto's noble leadership had been prepared to effect even before the Parliament had convened. The clearest (and unambiguously treasonous) evidence for this resolve comes from the preparations made by Warwick, Bedford and the other leading Petitioner Peers for a joint Anglo-Scottish force – the 'Armies for the Commonwealth', as they were to be called – in September 1640. But the principle that the nobility and the people's representatives could act unilaterally to maintain the safety of the commonwealth was to resurface repeatedly in the various military crises of 1641: in Essex's frantic efforts, in April, to assemble a loyal (again, it seems, Anglo-Scottish) officer corps (because, as he told the Commons, 'Wee knew not how soone wee might be provoked to defend our selves');[28] in the House of Lords unilateral decision, in May, to place control of the Tower under the triumvirate of Newport, Essex, and Brooke; and to install their own garrison 500-strong;[29] in Parliament's repudiation of the king's nominee as Lord

Lieutenant of Yorkshire, and insistence that it should go to its own nominee (again, Essex – inevitably);[30] through to the raising of the new expeditionary force for Ireland, from October, when the two Houses usurped the royal right to allocate regimental commands. Giustinian's shocked observation on the Yorkshire Lord Lieutenancy case could be applied to any one of these, or a dozen other instances that might be cited: that it revealed how the Parliament 'will not even let the king use [a power] ... which is his sole prerogative'.[31]

Essex's appointment as Lord Lieutenant of Yorkshire neatly highlights how the de facto constitutional realities of 1641 frequently ran ahead of the formal legislation that would be needed to assure their continuance *de jure* (the objective which was eventually achieved in 1642 by the Militia Ordinance). This was not for any lack of awareness of how critical was the control of appointments to office (military or civilian). William Strode was probably expressing a conviction heartily endorsed by the other members of the Junto when he argued in October 1641, that 'all wee had done this Parliament was nothing, unles wee' – like the Scots – 'had a negative voice [a veto] in the plac[ing] of the great officers of the King and of his Councellors'.[32] But one of the reasons why Warwick, Pym, and the other Junto leaders seem to have been relatively slow in pushing forward legislation to claim for Parliament the right to appoint the great officers of state was that, from Warwick's admission to the Privy Council in April 1641, it looked as though legislation might actually be superfluous. For just under five months (from then until Charles's departure for Scotland in early August), a seemingly beaten and acquiescent monarch seemed ready to hand over to the Junto leaders, voluntarily, almost all the major levers of power within the commonwealth – the Lieutenancy of Ireland to Leicester, the Lord Generalship North of the Trent to Holland, the Constableship of the Tower to Newport, the posts of Lord Chamberlain and General South of the Trent to Essex, appointment as a Treasury Commissioner and Master of the Wards to Saye, with Warwick functioning as an unofficial Treasurer-at-War. The relative poverty of the monarch (since his renunciation of his prerogative revenues) together with the new administrative structures (in particular, what might be termed the privatization of military finance) looked as though they would be sufficient to ensure that henceforth Parliament, or rather its dominant aristocratic cabal, would decide who would wield real executive power in post-Triennial Act England. This moral, as opposed to legislative, denial of the king's 'negative voice' – that most sacrosanct of prerogatives powers – is implicit in the Junto's actions from the very start of the crisis. Indeed, as early as April 1641, Edward Hyde was shocked to find that Essex was prepared to state it in so many words: 'With some commotion [i.e. passion], as if he were in truth possessed with that opinion himself', Essex averred that the 'king was obliged in conscience to conform himself and his own understanding to the advice and conscience of his Parliament'.[33] King Charles mistook his enemies on many points; but his belief that they were determined to render him no more than a 'Duke of Venice' – a purely figurehead king – was not one of them.

Perhaps the deepest challenge to traditional monarchical authority, at least as it had been exercised in the half century to 1640, was the creation of the Anglo-Scottish Union, ratified by both Parliaments in August 1641. Here, too, Warwick and his allies from among the Petitioner Peers were the masters of the treaty negotiations (from which the king was deliberately excluded), and although the two British Parliaments had a say in the treaty's revision, on the English side, it primarily reflected the concerns and political ambitions of its sixteen noblemen authors (of whom eleven were Lords Petitioner). This was no mere tidying up of constitutional loose ends left over from the earlier Union of the English and Scottish Crowns in 1603. The effect of the Union of 1603 (and, to many English statesmen, its prime justification) had been to extend the dominions and, in many respects, the powers of the London-based 'imperial monarchy'. The prime objective of the Union of 1641 was its almost diametric opposite: to ensure that London-based monarch's permanent constraint.

Nor did its English backers make any secret of the fact. In what can hardly have been an idle choice, they selected Jeremiah Burroughes – Warwick's clerical protégé, who, back in 1638, had scandalized the local rector with his praise for the Venetian and Polish practice of elective monarchy[34] – to explain the Union's monarch-restricting virtues at its solemn inauguration in September 1641. The Union, he declared, was the means by which the post-Triennial Act constitution was to be made permanent and secure. In the recent past, 'God [had] indeed opened a doore of hope' by the Triennial Act, but Parliament-men had been in fear of 'the shutting of it almost every day'. His extended metaphor conveys something of the optimism and exhilaration – indeed, the sheer relief – of the moment: for 'now', Burroughes went on, 'for the helping of our weaknes, God hath put in a barre to this our doore of hope, to keep it from being shut: oh, rejoice we this day in this great mercy of our God'.[35] As all present would have been aware, this 'barre to this … doore of hope' that would prevent it from being shut was the guarantee of access to Scottish military aid which the treaty provided the English Junto, in the event of an external attack or – which was more likely – an internal royalist revolt. And to make doubly sure that aid would be forthcoming, there was the 'Brotherly Assistance', the gargantuan subsidy of £2.6 million (Scots) to be paid to Argyll's Junto in Edinburgh over the next two years – its financial management firmly in the control of Warwick and his friends.[36] If that left Charles looking more than ever like a Venetian doge, the parallel which this Union of the two British kingdoms suggested to at least some contemporaries was that other federal maritime republic, the Dutch.[37] Calybute Downinge had already noted the 'similitude betwixt these Brittish troubles and the beginnings of the stirres and storms of the Belgique [Netherlandish] Provinces',[38] in which their nobles had united against despotic monarchical rule.[39] In September 1641, scarcely a week after the new Union's inauguration, Giustinian was noting that 'Dutch' – that is, republican – 'forms of government' were a constitutional pattern 'for which the people here [in England] show far too much inclination'.[40] His prophecy, made in the aftermath of the Triennial Acts, that Charles would soon be reduced to 'the mere titles and bare appearances of a king' had been amply fulfilled.[41]

*

If this manifests a certain consistency of programme, it is also complemented by a remarkable consistency of personnel. From the first letters of invitation to the Scots in the summer of 1640 through to the Parliament's appointment of the commanders who would go to war against the king's party in the summer of 1642, it is the same small group of noblemen – backed by a remarkably loyal series of allies in the Commons – whose names recur at the centre of political and military power at every major point. The Petitioner Peers of August-September 1640 led the campaign for a new Parliament. They were also at the centre of the plans to create the joint Anglo-Scottish 'Armies for the Commonwealth'. They controlled the Anglo-Scottish treaty negotiations from October 1640-August 1641. And they exercised an unchallenged dominance of the Parliament's key judicial body – the House of Lords' Petitions Committee – the body which in many respects usurped the role of the Privy Council from the very first days of the new session.

In turn, it was this same inner core of the Petitioner Lords (among them Bedford, Warwick, Essex, Hertford, Mandeville and Saye) who virtually monopolized all new appointments to the Privy Council (from February to April 1641), and, again, who secured almost every 'great office of the kingdom' (from May-August 1641), as royal authority in England sunk to its nadir in the wake of the army plots of May 1641. Of course, this grouping of noblemen was fluid at its edges, and there were fellow-travellers who were to detach themselves en route (among them, Newport, Savile, Hertford, and eventually Paget). Nor, as we have seen, was it ever wholly homogeneous. At various times, there were tensions between the radicalism of the Junto's Warwick-Brooke axis (with Essex, Warwick, Brooke and Hesilrige as its central figures) and the more politique approach to political settlement advocated by Bedford, Saye, and their 'old courtier' allies such as Pembroke and Northumberland. And with the grandees often at odds on particular items of policy, there was considerable scope for independence of initiative and action for the Commons members of the Junto, as St John's parting of the ways with Bedford in April 1641 clearly shows. But for all these tensions, the basic stability, durability, and instinct for survival manifested by the Petitioners' major figures – the group which became the ruling Junto of 1641 – remains one of the most salient features of the entire crisis of 1640-42.

Come the moment of reckoning in January 1642, it was this same inner core which Charles set out to destroy: first with the attack on their key allies in the Commons and then, it seems, with a second round of prosecutions aimed at the patrician grandees themselves: not just Mandeville (who had delivered Charles the Petition of the Twelve back in September 1640), but, as the Commons heard in the intercepted correspondence read to them on 11 January 1642, 'Essex, Warwick, Say, Brook, and Paget must follow'.[42] With rare exceptions, all of those marked out for prosecution – including St John and Fiennes, who were also to be included in the second-round of accusations – had been closely involved in the efforts to procure the Covenanter invasion of August 1640.[43] Indeed, the very first charge against these

'Commonwealthsmen', as we have seen, was that they had sought to 'deprive the King of his Regall Power'.[44] And no regal power had been usurped earlier, or more effectively, than the king's sovereign authority to command the armed forces of his realms. As the nation moved ever closer to war in the spring and early summer of 1642, *all* the English Parliament's major forces came under the command of the peers drawn from the tiny initial group of seven noblemen who, in the summer of 1640, had urged on the Covenanters to their invasion of England: Essex as commander of all forces deployed in England, Brooke asgeneral of the army destined for service in Ireland, and Warwick as Lord Admiral of England – the place which his old enemy, the Duke of Buckingham, had occupied with such spectacular incompetence in the 1620s.

Yet it would be a mistake to view this as just another, particularly giddy gyration of the wheel of courtly fortune: the replacement of one set of aristocratic 'ins' by the former 'outs'. Not all the Junto-men of 1642 were fired by the godly zeal that is evident in men such as Warwick or Brooke. But this aristocratic takeover seems to have been motivated by something grander in conception than the mere quest for place and office. They believed that they had seen God open 'a doore of hope', and peered through to the new political and religious world that lay beyond. They would fight to prevent it being 'shut again'.[45]

*

This consciousness that the realization of a reformed and godly commonwealth might require the use of military force was not something that dawned only slowly, still less reluctantly, on the noblemen who came to control England's government in the course of that 'yeare ... of wonders', 1641.[46] Of course, it is true that it was not until 'May or June 1642' that one can find 'much sign of impending war in the [English] counties'.[47] But all that was required for a civil war was two English armies, not a general mobilization of the squirearchy of rural England. And with a combined total of somewhere between 25,000 and 35,000 English and Scottish troops quartered in the North of England for the entire year between the summer of 1640 and August 1641, two armies were not going to be difficult to find. In the view of many, perhaps most, contemporaries, some form of military conflict between English troops loyal to the king and English and Scottish troops loyal to the Petitioners would have been the likely outcome, in September and October 1640, if Charles had not capitulated to the Petitioners' demands for the summons of a Parliament. Indeed, the conviction that such a civil war had been narrowly avoided was one of the reasons for the euphoria that greeted the Parliament's optimistic opening months: hence Sir John Wray's delight in November 1640 that, 'beyond all our expectations, at the last breath [i.e. the eleventh hour]', a nation deeply divided had been reunited.[48] Calybute Downinge's registered a similar point, writing in February 1641, when he hoped that the king's 'Roses and Lillies [the heraldic emblems of England] may not...be blasted in his People's blood'.[49]

Throughout the long months of the Strafford trial, the shadow of civil war varied in size and intensity, but never really went away. Civil war loomed in February–March 1641 when it looked as though Strafford's cause might win enough votes in the House of Lords to secure an acquittal; again in May, in the aftermath of the army plots, and the king's failed attempt to capture the Tower; and once again, in August when the king left London – not, it was feared, for his stated destination of Edinburgh, but to rally the royal army in the North for a belated attack on the Scottish army and any English forces that would rally to it. As Stephen Marshall commented in September 1641, when, briefly, the shadow of war seemed to have lifted, England had 'looked to have been a wonder to all the world in our desolations' for most of the previous twelve months[50] – that is, throughout the year since the publication of the Petition of the Twelve Peers in September 1640.

One principal reason why desolation loomed for most of that year is that many of the senior officers in the king's army in the North, cheated of the chance to prove themselves against the Scots by the early truce called in September 1640, spent much of the following year spoiling for a fight. 'Wee are verie sencible [that] the honor of our Nation was unfortunately foyled in the first part of this action', its officers protested at the end of March 1641, 'but wee hope soe to Mannage what is left that, if the perverse endeavo[u]rs of some doe not crosse us, our future proceedings shall neither deserve the worlde's blame nor reproach. And wee are confident. . .to [return] English Armes [to] theire former height of glory.'[51] Viewed against this background, the army plots of March-May 1641 cease to be crack-pot schemes dreamed up in dark corners of the Whitehall court, but real possibilities in which much of the drive towards a confrontation, not just with the Scots but with the English faction which had consistently 'crosse[d]' them, was coming from within the army itself.[52]

What would have happened had the Tower Plot of 2 May 1641 succeeded, and Strafford been left free to take command of this highly motivated but chronically (and, by the Junto leadership, deliberately) under-funded royal army must be a matter of conjecture.[53] But conjecture was exactly what contemporaries indulged in, and what many regarded as the likely outcome of that contingency was enough to fill even those usually well disposed towards the king with a sense of horror and revulsion. The Earl of Stamford, who was certainly no friend to Charles, may be dismissed as being melodramatic when, on the morrow after the Tower Plot was foiled, he proposed a motion of thanksgiving to God for the two Houses' deliverance: had the coup succeeded, he argued, 'the [gun]powder had been about our Ears here in the Parliament house, and we had all been made slaves'.[54] But that Bishop Skinner of Bristol, the prelate who had preached at the state opening,[55] was prepared to speak in support of Stamford's proposal tells us something of how deeply this fear of a new type of tyranny – of a different order of magnitude to anything that had been apprehended in the 1630s – had suddenly struck home.

'Slaves'[56] was a strong word to use to describe the condition, or even potential condition, of the English people under the rule of Charles I.[57] To the Junto leaders, the task of reapportioning the powers within England's mixed monarchy was nothing less than a matter of securing the nation against 'slavery'. As Viscount Saye was later to describe the concerns behind this process of redefinition, 'we love our selves and the Kingdom too well to dig a pit with our own hands to bury our selves and our posterity in for perpetual slaves'.[58] This was no more than both Houses declared at the time. Condemning the king's counsellors in August 1642, the Parliament accused the leaders of the king's party of intending 'to destroy his Parliament and good people by a civill Warre, and by that means to bring ruine, confusion, and perpetuall slavery upon the surviving part of a then wretched Kingdom'.[59] That was a conclusion which a substantial number of the English peers appear to have reached well over twelve months earlier.

The tragedy of 1641 was that the largely successful subversion of monarchical authority in England and Scotland, which was meant to secure what zealous Protestants like Warwick and Argyll or Pym and Wariston regarded as 'liberty', was widely perceived as auguring another sort of slavery for the million-odd Catholics on the other side of Irish Sea. The letter written by Lord Gormanston, one of the supporters of the insurrection, to the Earl of Clanricard, the great Connacht landed magnate and Essex's Catholic half-brother, articulates this perception clearly: 'the puritan faction of England, since, by the countenance of the Scottish army, they invaded the regall power, have both in their doctrine and practice layd the foundation of the slavery of this countrey'.[60]

This, in turn, brings us to the place of the Irish Rebellion in the politics of the three kingdoms, and to question whether, rather than being an essentially random, chance event in its impact on England and Scotland, it might not have been a logical, and perhaps inevitable, consequence of the English 'puritan faction's' invasion of the regal power.

*

Historians who have failed to find a major conflict about the nature of sovereignty and political institutions in the course of 1641 have perhaps inevitably looked to the Irish Rebellion to provide the *diabolus ex machina* – the malign, but chance, external intervention – that turned a tense but otherwise peaceable England towards an internal contest for the control of military power.[61] It was only the chance outbreak of the Irish Rebellion, that 'bolt from the blue', so the argument runs, that prevented the king from being able to wind up the Parliament during the summer, and enabled his enemies – the Junto leaders – to keep it in session.[62] But for this, England and Scotland might have '[gone] their separate ways in peace';[63] and with the Covenanters disengaged from England, and the English generally disenchanted with their Scottish brethren, their Junto allies at Westminster would have simply 'fall[en] flat'.[64]

Yet, far from distancing themselves from the Scots during the summer of 1641, Warwick and the other leaders of the Westminster Junto were working assiduously to make a reality of the new Union between the English and Scottish 'commonwealths', ratified by both Parliaments in August of that year. The almost unprecedented and unexpected orderliness of the Covenanter army's withdrawal from England in August – probably due, in large measure, to Warwick's success in seeing that its soldiers had been fully and promptly paid – did much to silence the Scots' critics.[65] This, in turn, provided the background for the euphoria which greeted the celebration of the Anglo-Scottish Union in September.[66]

All this pointed, however, not to Scottish disengagement from English affairs, but precisely the opposite. It created a political climate in England in which a new Anglo-Scottish campaign on the Continent was not only militarily feasible but also likely to have been highly popular (at least in its opening phases).[67] To the Juntos in both British capitals, the opportunity provided by the proposed intervention on the Continent proved irresistible, not merely as a godly crusade against the Habsburg ambition for 'universall Monarchy',[68] but also as a practical manifestation of what Loudoun, addressing the Edinburgh Parliament in September 1641, called that 'unity of Councell' between the two realms.[69] As Loudoun well knew, having only just returned from almost a year as a resident commissioner in London, maintaining that 'unity of Councell' during the new Palatine war would require, once again, an exchange of commissioners between the two capitals, and a further strengthening of the bonds between the Argyllians in Edinburgh (of whom Loudoun himself was one) and the Warwick-Essex interest in London (which was taking the lead in advancing the Palatine interest in England).[70]

These plans and expectations give the lie to the assumption that, but for the Irish insurrection, Charles might have achieved a separate settlement in Scotland, which somehow disengaged the Covenanters in general (and the Argyllians in particular) from their involvement in English affairs.[71] Joint military operations on the Continent would have demanded a renewed Scottish diplomatic presence in London, whether or not Ireland had decided to revolt; and perhaps, too, the creation of what Henry Parker termed a 'General Junto, or Councell of Union' – a supra-national executive – that would transact the great affairs of the Union.[72] Above all, the new Palatine campaign would almost certainly have ensured that the Westminster Parliament (which, from May 1641, could not be dissolved except with its own consent) would remain in session. European diplomacy and Anglo-Scottish godly militarism – not to mention the planned privateering war against Spain[73] – dictated that Charles would be stuck with his Westminster Parliament, and its irksome ruling Junto, well into the campaigning season of 1642. In such circumstances, the revisionist contention that the king might somehow have sent the Junto grandees packing and recouped his power in a happily civil-war-free England is not so much a counterfactual but counter fact.[74]

Consideration of the European context of British politics in the summer of 1641 thus confounds the claim that the continuance of the English Parliament into the autumn and winter of 1641 was simply a 'fortuitous'[75] consequence of the 'Irish Rebellion'. It stemmed directly from the Junto's need to make the new Union work militarily, so that it would provide the necessary insurance against the possibility of a Cavalier resurgence in England. The Palatine campaign was driven on by Essex, Loudoun, and Leslie perhaps as much for these considerations of internal domestic security as for their concern for the international 'Protestant Cause'.

This issue also points to the inadequacy of taking a purely 'British' or even 'three-kingdoms' approach as the explanatory context for the Irish insurrection itself.[76] If there was any one single event that shaped the politics of the Stuart kingdoms in the second half of 1641, it was the collapse of the Regensburg negotiations between the Emperor Ferdinand III and the supporters of a restoration in the Palatinate.[77] The announcement from Regensburg, news of which reached London and Edinburgh in the first week of September, that the Emperor would 'enter into no termes of Pacification' with Charles's dispossessed nephew, the Prince-Elector,[78] produced a rapid sequence of British consequences. In London and Edinburgh, it seemed to establish beyond doubt that the proposed Anglo-Scottish expeditionary force in support of the Prince-Elector would now become a reality.[79] This, not the later debate over the militia, was the trigger for the Westminster Parliament's decision to enforce 'military' legislation – ordinances – enacted by the two Houses alone (ignoring, if not yet quite denying, the king's 'negative voice').[80] The ensuing ordinance, halting the recruitment of troops in Ireland for service abroad and closing the Irish ports, had a simple aim: to prevent Irish troops, including 4,000 earlier promised by the king to the Spanish ambassador, from fighting on the Habsburg side in the next phase of the struggle for mastery in Europe. Not only was this the first time Parliament had legislated for Ireland without the king's consent, but its actions also directly countermanded the licence which Charles had earlier issued, on the royal prerogative, to the Spanish ambassador to engage in the recruiting which the ordinance now forbade.[81] Clearly, there was far more to the causation of the Irish insurrection than simply the English Parliament's decision to protect the interests of the Elector Palatine at the cost of denying a livelihood to some 4,000 prospective Irish mercenaries. But if we are looking for the intervention that shifted the hitherto uncertain plans for a rebellion 'into top gear', the two British Parliaments' newfound enthusiasm for a military campaign against Counter-Reformation Catholicism looks by far the likeliest suspect.

The insurrection in Ireland, of course, forced the postponement and eventual abandonment of that Anglo-Scottish Palatine campaign. But just as the Palatine campaign had been planned to promote the practical union between the Edinburgh and Westminster Juntos, so the Irish campaign which superseded it was intended to serve the same purpose. Almost every detail of its military planning (as it took shape between October and December 1641) was contrived to deny the king that defining mark of sovereignty, the control of military force: hence, the appointment of officers by ordinance; the bypassing of the king's Treasury-at-War; and the series of initiatives from Warwick House aimed at bringing everything from the new army's supply of boots to the provision of its shipping within the Junto's (and, most often, Warwick's) immediate control.[82] Charles's opposition to the proposed joint Anglo-Scottish campaign, after his return from Scotland in November 1641, was entirely logical. Here, too, he was being threatened with the creation of political and military structures which, more than any statutory provision, threatened to keep him powerless and irrelevant in the conduct of the new Union's wars.

*

How is this series of political changes, with their profoundly anti-monarchical implications, to be characterized? The question was one that baffled contemporaries, as it has baffled later historians no less. It certainly defied Bishop Morton of Durham, an otherwise astute commentator on men and events, and who had observed the Junto leaders at first-hand in the course of 1641; he found the new régime at Westminster, which emerged from the constitutional upheavals of 1641 and 1642, almost impossible to categorize: '[a] Government which, if Aristotle himself were to sit in Councel at their close Comittees, he should not yet resolve what to cal it'.[83] Others discerned in the steady attrition of regal power a more readily nameable development: that in the course of 1641, the conduct of England's government, and even the language that was used to describe it, had acquired a distinctly republican inflection.

In general, historians of English politics (though not the historians of political ideas) have tended to discount the power of republican ideas and aspirations in the crisis that gave rise to the Civil War.[84] Almost all Parliamentarians regarded the retention of kingship as axiomatic, even during the course of the war; and it was not until the late 1640s that there was serious discussion of a kingless, constitutionally republican alternative. That a fully fledged English Republic emerged in 1649 from the chaos of war was almost as much of an 'accident', in this account, as the war itself. The trajectory of radicalism in the 1640s thus traces a rising arc from a low point in the early 1640s through to its zenith in early 1649, with the execution of King Charles and the abolition of monarchy itself. But as a broad consensus prevailed as to 'mixed monarchy' in the early 1640s, and constitutional issues were not to be found at the core of the crisis of 1641, historians seeking to account for the origins of 'Royalism' have been forced to look, once again, to religious differences as the only plausible alternative explanation for the eruption of violence in 1642.

At one level, of course, this account seems incontrovertible. Even after the outbreak of war in the summer of 1642, most Parliamentarians remained committed not only to retaining kingship as an element of government, but also to retaining Charles as their king. Moreover, this commitment to 'mixed sovereignty' acted as a talisman that deprived authentically republican ideas of their potency; theories of a kingless constitution, in other words, were of little interest to the English, scarcely more to the Scots, and none whatsoever to the Irish. In a legalistic sense, perhaps this is true. But legalism, like the statute book, is only an imperfect guide to the subtler realities of actual experience. For notwithstanding the near-universal endorsement of 'mixed monarchy' and the powerful motives – historical, legal, even sentimental – for retaining the kingly office, contemporaries were well aware that 'mixed monarchy' would come in a variety of forms: it was the nature of the mixture – where the balance lay between the constituent elements of king, Lords, and Commons – that determined whether kingship was an active, or merely decorative, element in the mix. Moreover, this critical 'point of balance' could move over time, not through any specific constitutional enactment or pronouncement, but as a result of shifts in the way politics was actually transacted and by the practical authority which particular men were able to wield. As Laud's protégé, Peter Heylyn, had argued in the early 1630s, hard-and-fast distinctions were difficult to make, precisely because all three forms of government – monarchy, aristocracy, and democracy – 'have a secret Inclination to change the one into the other, and to make a Pythagoricall transmigration (as it were)* into each other's being'.[85] The outward forms of one type of government could remain the same, while the *essence* of another type of rule 'transmigrated' into it, transforming its essential characteristics. A state that was outwardly monarchical could simultaneously be, for all the practical purposes of authority and power, indistinguishable from a state – like Venice, Genoa, or the United Provinces – which was formally a republic.

This takes us into a subtler, more elusive, mode of understanding fundamental political change than the scrutiny of laws or constitutions, but one, nevertheless, with which almost any educated seventeenth-century gentleman was familiar. Its archetypal example was Rome's transformation, in the course of the first century BC from a free republic, in which power resided principally in the Senate, to a de facto monarchy, from the reign of Augustus, in which it was firmly held by the prince. Yet despite the radical change in the essence of the Roman state, Augustus, the first of the new imperial monarchs, left the constitutional forms of the old Republic intact: what had shifted was the balance of practical power, emasculating the Senate and leaving executive authority in the hands of a de facto king.

In Scotland from the late 1630s, and in England from the early 1640s, there were many commentators who believed they were observing this same process in reverse: a 'Pythagoricall transmigration' of aristocratic and even democratic elements which was transforming what had been a monarchy both in name and substance into one which was kingly merely in name alone. As Bishop Morton was to put it, 'one part of this Island' was being 'turned from a Monarchy to Roman Decemvirate [the Republic's Council of Ten], a Venetian Senate, a Low-countrey[s] State [or Assembly], nay to the government-without-a-name, God forbid'.[86] What the reformist peers were trying to do, claimed Sir Edward Walker, the king's wartime secretary, was 'to frame an Aristocratical Monarchy by the Hands of [a] Popular Anarchy'.[87]

However it was characterized, none was more acutely aware of that political 'transmigration' than Charles himself. So long as the Covenant remained in force in Scotland, he had written in June 1638, 'I have no more Power … than as a Duke [Doge] of Venice'.[88] His wife concurred. Explaining her husband's predicament to the Dutch ambassador in January 1642, Henriette Marie insisted that he had no alternative but to defend his powers over the militia because, as his affairs stood at present, he was *worse off* than a Venetian doge.[89] And a Venetian doge presided, not over a kingdom, but a 'commonwealth' (the standard seventeenth-century rendering of the Latin words *res publica*, a republic), and though he enjoyed 'the shew of a kingly

---

* An allusion to the theory of the sixth-century BC mathematician and philosopher, Pythagoras of Samos, that souls or essences could 'transmigrate' from one being to another.

power, representing in all thinges the glory, gravitie and dignity of a king, and ... all decrees, lawes, and publike letters go forth under his name',[90] real power lay elsewhere: with a closed oligarchic aristocracy. As a characterization of the constitutional order which Charles would be required to endorse in the Militia Bill – the formal abandonment of all but a nominal role in the exercise of military power – this was not very wide of the mark.

*

None of this is to gainsay the central importance of religion, either in the personal 'godliness' that characterizes so many of the Junto leaders, or as a force for creating nation-wide opposing parties in the spring and summer of 1642. Both sides exploited those reassuringly simple binary polarities of Puritan and Papist, and eventually Roundhead and Cavalier, to characterize (and in the process caricature) their opponent as a mortal peril to the Church: the king's party to depict the Junto-men as intent on destroying the bishops; the Parliament to cast the king's party as connivers at the introduction of Popery. Yet, as we have seen, the origins of that conflict were more complex that these simple binary polarities of press and pulpit might suggest. Whether civil war broke out in England in 1640 or 1641 (as it might have) or in 1642 (as it did), the conflict could never have been exclusively, or perhaps even primarily, a 'war of religion'; for, as all the leading figures in the conflict well realized, the future state of the Church would ultimately be determined by the preferences of those who commanded the structures of secular power: *cuius regio, eius religio*. And that realization, in all three kingdoms, placed the question of each kingdom's 'constitutions' – above all, questions as to who exercised power, in what form and with what limitations – at the very centre of the conflict: 'the Ecclesiastical work dependeth upon the civill confederation', as John Durye argued in 1641, 'as the soul upon the body'.[91] For those godly noblemen grandees and their allies who set out to re-form the English and Scottish commonwealths from the summer of 1640, zeal for the gospel itself dictated that they must re-order the institutions of secular power. Nothing could be achieved in the ecclesiastical sphere without an equal reformation of 'Magistrates and [royal] Ministers'.[92] As Edmund Calamy, preaching in December 1641, insisted, 'there must be a Court-Reformation, a Country-Reformation ... Church and State-Reformation, a General Reformation'.[93] The striking feature, however, of the godly grandees' political conduct in 1640 and 1641 was how much their prioritizing of 'Court- and State-Reformation', the *sine qua non* of durable political change, led them to a series of shifts and compromises when it came to reform of the Church.

*

Yet, for all the prominence of noblemen in the planning and actual leadership of this extended revolt against Stuart monarchy, this was no mere barons' war. True, the conflict which emerged from the crisis of 1640-42 possessed, in the eyes of contemporaries, what might be termed its 'baronial context': a dimension in which the prominence of titular nobles in leading armies – in England, and still more emphatically in Scotland and Ireland – and their evocation of historical precedent as a means of justifying and 'imagining' their conduct suggested obvious parallels with the medieval past. But, even viewed as a dimension of the political culture, this 'baronial context' was only ever that: one context among a series of contextual references – legal, religious, and Classical humanist – that combined with such volatility in the intellectual life of early-Stuart Britain.

Nor, as we have seen, was it a revolt of the nobility, or even the major part of the nobility, acting alone. In the autumn of 1640, when the Petitioners launched their revolt against Charles's régime, they commanded the support of no more than around thirty to at most forty peers – between a quarter and a third of the lay nobility. Two years later, that number had declined slightly but not significantly changed; and with only a few exceptions, they are the same lists. Throughout the eighteen months preceding the outbreak of actual war, the Junto leaders relied on dextrous – at times, even devious – management of Parliament to preserve the illusion that they and their allies spoke for the nation at large. Indeed, in December 1641, it was the danger that their bluff would be called, and that Charles's summons to the absent members might yet produce a king's-party majority in both Commons and Lords, which seems to have produced the suspiciously timely escalation of the 'tumults' in and around Westminster.

Through all the vicissitudes which followed the Petitioners' bold and potentially treasonous stand in the summer of 1640, there remained, on both sides, a realization that this was not merely a fight about power, but about the very systems under which the peoples of the Stuart kingdoms would live and pray for generations to come. Something of that quality is eloquently caught in one of the earliest military histories of the war, by John Corbet, published even before the conflict was over, in 1645. 'The Action of these times', he wrote,

> transcends the Barons Warres, and those tedious discords betweene the Houses of *Yorke* and *Lancaster,* in as much as it is undertaken upon higher Principles, and carried on to a nobler end, and effects more universall.[94]

One need not share the politics or the piety of either side to discern in the 'Action of th[o]se times' why its protagonists might have believed that that they were contending upon high principles and to noble ends.

Appendix: Variant Listings of the Signatories to the Petition of the Twelve Peers, *August–September 1640*

Note: The twelve original signatories are given in capitals.

	NA, SP 16/465/17[1]	Staffs. RO, Dyott MS D661/11/1/5	Surrey RO, Losely MS 133/50	Cambridge UL, Buxton MS (HMC, Various, II, p.255)	Whitelocke, Memorials[2]	BL, Add 3884...
Bath						
BEDFORD	*	*	*	*	*	*
BOLINGBROKE	*	*	*	*	*	
Bristol					*	
ESSEX	*	*	*	*	*	*
EXETER	*	*	*	*		
HERTFORD	*	*	*	*	*	*
Lincoln				*		
MULGRAVE	*	*	*		*	*
Pembroke						*
RUTLAND	*	*	*	*		
WARWICK	*	*	*	*	*	*
SAYE	*	*	*	*	*	
MANDEVILLE	*	*	*	*	*	
BROOKE	*	*	*	*	*	
HOWARD OF ESCRICK	*	*	*	*	*	
Howard [of Charlton?][5]						
Lovelace						
North						
Paget			*		*	
Savile						
Wharton						
Willoughby of Parham						

MS, fos, v-84 *(partial)*	PA, MP, September 1640	BL, Add. MS 1710, fo. 119	NA, SP 16/4 65 fo. 40v.	BL, Sloane MS 1467, fo. 132r-v	Beinecke Library, Yale, Osborn Files, Pym	BL, Add. MS 35331, fo. 78	Northants. RO, Finch-Hatton MS 2619	Cambridge UL, Add. MS 335, fo. 41 (from back)
					*			
	*	*	*	*	*	*	*	*
	*	*	*	*	*	*	*	*
					*			*
	*	*	*	*	*	*	*	*
	*	*	*	*	*	*	*	*
	*	*	*[3]	*	*	*	*	*
		*	*	*	*	*	*	
	*	*		*	*	*		
	*	*	*	*		*		*
	*	*	*	*	*	*	*	*
	*	*	*	*		*	*	*
	*	*	*	*	*	*	*	*
	*	*	*	*	*	*	*	*
		*	*	*	*	*	*	*
	*	*	*		*	*	*	*
							*	
	*	*	*	*		*		*
	*	*	*	*	*			
	*	*	*	*	*	*	*	*
	*	*	*	*	*	*	*	*
	*	*	*	*	*	*	*	*

LIST OF ABBREVIATIONS

AGR	Archives Générales du Royaume, Brussels
AGS	Archivo General, Simancas
ASV	Archivio di Stato, Venice
Baillie, *Letters*	David Laing (ed.), *The Letters and Journals of Robert Baillie*, 3 vols. (Bannatyne Club, Edinburgh, 1841–42)
Baker, *Serjeants at Law*	John H. Baker, *The Order of Serjeants-at-Law* (Selden Society Publications, Supplementary Series, 5, 1984)
Beinecke Lib., Yale	Beinecke Library, Yale University, New Haven, Connecticut
BL	British Library, London
BN	Bibliothèque nationale de France, Paris
Bodleian Lib.,	Bodleian Library, University of Oxford
Bray, *Evelyn Diary and Correspondence*	William Bray (ed.), *Diary and Correspondence of John Evelyn, FRS, to which is subjoined...Private Correspondence*, 4 vols. (1894–95)
Carte, *Life of Ormond*	Thomas Carte, *Life of the Duke of Ormonde*, 6 vols. (Oxford, 1851)
Carte, *Original Letters*	Thomas Carte (ed.), *Collection of Original Letters, found among the Duke of Ormonde's Papers* (1739)
CJ	*House of Commons Journals*
Clarendon, *Rebellion*	Edward Hyde, Earl of Clarendon, *The History of the Rebellion and Civil Wars in England begun in the Year 1641*, ed. W. Dunn Macray, 8 vols. (Oxford, 1888)
Clarendon State Papers	Thomas Monkhouse and Richard Scrope (eds.), *State Papers collected by Edward Earl of Clarendon, commencing from the Year 1621*, 3 vols. (Oxford, 1767–86)
Coates, *D'Ewes Diary*	Willson H. Coates (ed.), *The Journal of Sir Simonds D'Ewes from the First Recess of the Long Parliament to the Withdrawal of King Charles from London* (New Haven, CT, 1942)
Collins, *Letters and Memorials*	Arthur Collins (ed.), *Letters and Memorials of State*, 2 vols. (1746)
Complete Peerage	G. E. C[ockayne], *et al.*, *The Complete Peerage of England, Scotland, Ireland, Great Britain, and the United Kingdom*, 13 vols. (1910–59)
Cope, *Short Parliament Proceedings*	Ester S. Cope and Willson H. Coates (eds.), *Proceedings of the Short Parliament of 1640* (Camden Society, 4th ser., 19, 1977)
CSPD	*Calendar of State Papers, Domestic*
CSPI	*Calendar of State Papers, Ireland*
CSPV	*Calendar of State Papers, Venetian*
CUL	Cambridge University Library
Disp. Inghil.	Dispacci Inghilterra (Dispatches relating to England)

Diurnall Occurrences	*The Diurnall Occurrences, or Dayly Proceedings of Both Houses* (1641), BL, E 523/1
ep. ded.	epistle dedicatory
Exact Collection	*An Exact Collection of all Remonstrances, Declarations, Votes, Orders, Ordinances* (1643), Wing E153
Gardiner, *History*	Samuel Rawson Gardiner, *History of England from the Accession of James 1 to the Outbreak of the Civil War, 1603–42*, 10 vols. (1887)
Gardiner, *Constitutional Documents*	Samuel Rawson Gardiner, *Constitutional Documents of the Puritan Revolution, 1625–60* (Oxford, 1906)
Guildhall Lib.	Guildhall Library, London
Hardwicke State Papers	Philip Yorke, Earl of Hardwicke (ed.), *Miscellaneous State Papers from 1501 to 1726*, 2 vols. (1778)
Harl.	Harleian Manuscript
HL	Huntington Library, San Marino, California
History of the King's Works	H. M. Colvin (ed.), The History of the King's Works, 6 vols. (1963–82)
HMC	Royal Commission on Historical Manuscripts
HPL	The History of Parliament Trust, London, biographies for *The Commons, 1640–60* (in progress)
Jansson, *Two Diaries*	Maija Jansson (ed.), *Two Diaries of the Long Parliament* (Gloucester, 1984)
Keeler, *Long Parliament*	Mary Frear Keeler, *The Long Parliament, 1640–41: a Biographical Study of its Members* (American Philosophical Society, 36, Philadelphia, 1954)
Knowler, *Strafforde's Letters*	William Knowler (ed.), *The Earl of Strafforde's Letters and Dispatches*, 2 vols. (1739)
Laud, *Works*	W. Scott and J. Bliss (eds.), *The Works of the Most Reverend Father in God, William Laud*, 7 vols. (Oxford, 1847–60)
Lindley and Scott, *Juxon Diary*	Keith Lindley and David Scott (eds.), *The Journal of Thomas Juxon, 1644–47* (Camden Society, 5th ser., 13, Cambridge, 1999)
Lismore Papers	Alexander B. Grosart (ed.), *Selections from the Private and Public ... Correspondence of Sir Richard Boyle, 1st Earl of Cork*, 1st series, 5 vols. (Privately printed, 1887–88)
LJ	*House of Lords Journals*
LMA	London Metropolitan Archives
Loomie, *Ceremonies of Charles I*	A. J. Loomie (ed.), *Ceremonies of Charles I:the Note Books of John Finet, Master of Ceremonies, 1628–41* (New York, 1987)
MP	Main Papers, House of Lords
NA	National Archives, London (formerly the Public Records Office)
NAS	National Archives of Scotland, Edinburgh
NLS	National Library of Scotland, Edinburgh
NLW	National Library of Wales, Cardiff
Nicholas Papers	G. F. Warner (ed.), *The Nicholas Papers: Correspondence of Sir E[dward] Nicholas, Secretary of State*, 4 vols. (Camden Society, new ser., 1892–1920)
Northcote Notebook	A. H. A. Hamilton (ed.), *The Notebook of Sir John Northcote* (1877)
Notestein, *D'Ewes Diary*	Wallace Notestein (ed.), *The Journal of Sir Simonds D'Ewes from the Beginning of the Long Parliament to the Opening of the Trial of the Earl of Strafford* (New Haven, CT, 1923)
NRA	National Register of Archives, England
NRAS	National Register of Archives, Scotland
n. s.	new series
ODNB	Colin Matthew and Brian Harrison (eds.), *Oxford Dictionary of National Biography*, 60 vols. (Oxford, 2003)
PA	Parliamentary Archives, Palace of Westminster, London (formerly the House of Lords Record Office)

Parliamentary or Constitutional History	The Parliamentary of Constitutional History of England from the Earliest Times to the Restoration of Charles II, 24 vols. (1751–67)
Pearl, London	Valerie Pearl, London and the Outbreak of the Puritan Revolution: City Government and National Politics, 1625–41 (Oxford, 1964)
PJ, January–March 1642	Willson H. Coates, Anne Steele Young, and Vernon F. Snow (eds.), The Private Journals of the Long Parliament, 3 January to 5 March 1642 (New Haven and London, 1982)
PL	Public Library
PLP	Maija Jansson (ed.), Proceedings in the Opening Session of the Long Parliament, 3 November 1640–9 September 1641: House of Commons, 7 vols. (Rochester, NY, and Woodbridge, Suffolk, 2000–projected completion in 2007)
Prinsterer, Archives...de la maison d'Orange-Nassau	G. Groen van Prinsterer, Archives ou correspondance inédite de la maison d'Orange-Nassau, 2nd ser., 5 vols. (Utrecht, 1857–61)
RO	Records Office
Rushworth, Historical Collections	John Rushworth (ed.), Historical Collections of Private Passages of State, 7 vols. (1659–1701)
Russell, Causes	Conrad Russell, The Causes of the English Civil War (Oxford, 1990)
Russell, Fall of the British Monarchies	Conrad Russell, The Fall of the British Monarchies, 1637–42 (Oxford, 1991)
Searle, Barrington Letters	Arthur Searle (ed.), Barrington Family Letters, 1628–32 (Camden Society, 4th ser., 28, 1983)
sig., sigg.	signature, signatures
STC	A. W. Pollard and G. R. Redgrave (eds.), A Short-Title Catalogue of Books Printed in England, Scotland, and Ireland and of English Books Printed Abroad, 1475–1640, 2 vols. (Bibliographical Society, 1926)
STC2	William A. Jackson, A. W. Pollard and G. R. Redgrave, et al. (eds.), A Short-Title Catalogue of Books Printed in England, Scotland, and Ireland and of English Books Printed Abroad, 1475–1640, 2nd edn., 2 vols. (Bibliographical Society, 1976–86)
uncat.	uncatalogued
unfol.	unfoliated
VAL	Victoria and Albert Museum, London, National Art Library
Van Dyck Complete Catalogue	Susan J. Barnes, Nora de Poorter, Oliver Millar, and Horst Vey, Van Dyck: a Complete Catalogue of the Paintings (New Haven and London, 2003)
Verney, Notes	John Bruce (ed.), Verney Papers: Notes of Proceedings in the Long Parliament, temp[ore] Charles I (Camden Society, 31, 1845)
Whitelocke, Memorials	Bulstrode Whitelocke, Memorials of the English Affairs from the Beginning of the Reign of King Charles the First, 4 vols. (Oxford, 1853)
Whitelocke, Diary	Ruth Spalding (ed.), The Diary of Bulstrode Whitelocke, 1605–75 (Records of Social and Economic History, n.s., 13, Oxford, 1990)

Note: most of the research on the parliamentary diaries used in this book was completed before the publication of Dr Maija Jansson's edition (listed above as PLP, and currently ongoing), which prints most of the surviving Commons' diaries up to September 1641. The references in the endnotes are therefore to the original manuscripts, and a start has been made on cross-referencing these to the volumes of the Jansson edition so far published. It is planned that, when the publication of these volumes is completed, a later impression of this book will incorporate a comprehensive set of cross-references between the manuscripts currently cited and the finished Jansson text.

NOTES

Unless otherwise noted, all references to the foliation of manuscripts are to the 'recto' side of the folio (e.g. ' fo. 27' is 'folio 27 recto'); where the text is to be found on the 'verso', this is noted in the form, e.g., 'fo. 27v'.

PROLOGUE

1 BL, Harl. MS 163 (D'Ewes diary), fo. 64 (*PLP*, III, 607).

2 William Laud, Archbishop of Canterbury, *The History of the Troubles and Tryal of the Most Reverend Father in God and Blessed Martyr, William Laud, Lord Arch-Bishop of Canterbury wrote by himself during his Imprisonment in the Tower* (1695), p. 78 (Wing L586).

3 During the spring of 1640, Northumberland was staying at a rented house in Queen Street, Westminster. In the summer of 1639, he had been assigned the apartments at Whitehall hitherto used by Sir John Coke, the elderly Secretary of State; but Coke proved slow to clear the rooms of the papers and trunks that occupied at least two of the apartment's rooms, and Northumberland never seems to have used it as a residence; see Michael B. Young, *Servility and Service: the Life and Work of Sir John Coke* (Woodbridge, 1986), p. 260; HMC, *De L'Isle Manuscripts*, VI, 254; Knowler, *Strafforde's Letters*, II, 404: Northumberland to Strafford, 4 April 1640, 'From my House in Queen-street'.

4 In Charles I's reign, there were no non-noble members; for the Caroline revival of the order, see Kevin Sharpe, *The Personal Rule of Charles I* (New Haven and London, 1992), pp. 219–22; John Adamson, 'Chivalry and Political Culture in Caroline England', in Kevin Sharpe and Peter Lake (eds.), *Culture and Politics in Early Stuart England* (1994), pp. 161–97.

5 Charles I had given orders in April 1626, that the Knights of the Garter were to wear the arms of St George on the left side of their 'cloaks, coats, and riding cassocks at all times when they shall not wear their robes, and in all places and assemblies ... that the wearing thereof may be a testimony to the world of the honour they hold'; HMC, *Salisbury Manuscripts*, XXII, 210; for the later addition of the aureole of silver rays, see John Adamson, 'Chivalry and Political Culture, p. 174.

6 For Charles's reinvigoration of the Order during the 1620s and 1630s, see Sharpe, *Personal Rule*, pp. 219–22; Roy Strong, *Van Dyck: Charles I on Horseback* (1972), pp. 61–2; Adamson, 'Chivalry and Political Culture', pp. 174–6.

7 Stephen Clucas, '"Noble Virtue in Extremes": Henry Percy, 9th Earl of Northumberland, Patronage and the Politics of Stoic Consolation', *Renaissance Studies*, 9 (1995), 267–91.

8 On Northumberland's career, see G. R. Batho, 'The Education of a Stuart Nobleman', *British Journal of Educational Studies*, 5 (1957), 131–43; Sharpe, *Personal Rule*, pp. 220, 224, 268, 597–8, 823–4; and G. Drake, 'Annotated Bibliography for the Life of Algernon Percy, 10th Earl of Northumberland', *The Colorado College Studies*, 13 (1975), 5–14.

9 For Northumberland's purported descent from Charlemagne, see Adamson, 'Chivalry and Political Culture', p. 178; Edward Bysshe (ed.), *Nicholai Uptoni de Studio Militari Libri Quatuor* (1654), 'In Nicholaum Uptonum Notae', p. 43.

10 Roger Lockyer, *Buckingham: the Life and Political Career of George Villiers, First Duke of Buckingham, 1592–1628* (1981), p. 328; Richard C. McCoy, 'Old English Honour in an Evil Time: Aristocratic Principle in the 1620s', in R. M. Smuts (ed.), *The Stuart Court and Europe: Essays in Politics and Political Culture* (Cambridge, 1996), pp. 133–55.

11 Clarendon, *Rebellion*, II, 538.

12 For Northumberland's time at the Admiralty, see K. R. Andrews, *Ships, Money and Politics: Seafaring and Naval Enterprise in the Reign of Charles I* (Cambridge, 1991); R. McCaughey, 'The English Navy, Politics and Administration, 1640–49' (unpublished Ph.D. dissertation, New University of Ulster, 1983), Ch. 1. I am grateful to Mr Christopher Thompson for drawing my attention to this dissertation.

13 BL, Add. MS 11045 (Scudamore corr.), fo. 27: E[dward] R[ossingham], newsletter to Viscount Scudamore, 11 June 1639.

14 Northumberland's appointments as Lord General and President of the Council of War were made on the same day, 14 February 1640; *Complete Peerage*, IX, 737; the Signet letter discharging him from the Lord Generalship came on 16 April 1641: NA, SO 3/12 (Signet Office Docket Book), fo. 145.

15 'The Garter is grown a dear Honour', wrote George Garrard to Viscount Wentworth on 19 May 1635, 'few Subjects will be able to follow this Pattern': Knowler, *Strafforde's Letters*, I, 427.

16 For a comparison, see NA, E 192/14, Part I, unfol.: accounts for the Earl of Holland for 10 December 1642. Holland regularly went attended by three footmen, two coachmen, and two postillions.

17 Lawrence Stone, *The Crisis of the Aristocracy, 1558–1641* (Oxford, 1965), pp. 562–6; Maria Hayward, 'Luxury or Magnificence? Dress at the Court of Henry VIII', *Costume*, 30 (1996), 37–46; Jane Fenlon, 'Episodes of Magnificence: the Material Worlds of the Dukes of Ormonde',

in Toby Barnard and Jane Fenlon (eds.), *The Dukes of Ormonde, 1610–1745* (Woodbridge, 2000), pp. 137–59.

18 Clarendon, *Rebellion*, II, 538.

19 M. C. Fissel, *The Bishops' Wars: Charles I's Campaigns against Scotland, 1638–40* (Cambridge, 1994).

20 Centre for Kentish Studies, De L'Isle MS U1475/C85/4: Earl of Northumberland to the Earl of Leicester, 12 December 1639 (not calendared in HMC, *De L'Isle Manuscripts*, VI). For the estimated cost, see Russell, *Fall of the British Monarchies*, pp. 92, 119; see also M. C. Fissel, 'Scottish War and English Money: the Short Parliament of 1640', in M. C. Fissel (ed.), *War and Government in Britain, 1598–1650* (Manchester, 1991), pp. 193–223.

21 Centre for Kentish Studies, De L'Isle MS U1475/C85/4: Earl of Northumberland to the Earl of Leicester, 12 December 1639 (not calendared in HMC, *De L'Isle Manuscripts*, VI); and see Russell, *Causes*, p. 181.

22 Centre for Kentish Studies, De L'Isle MS U1500/C2/41: Earl of Northumberland to the Earl of Leicester, 19 March 1640 (not calendared in HMC, *De L'Isle Manuscripts*, VI).

23 The best narrative of the Short Parliament is Russell, *Fall of the British Monarchies*, pp. 90–123; see also, Peter Donald, *An Uncounselled King: Charles I and the Scottish Troubles, 1637–41* (Cambridge, 1990), pp. 227–36; Esther S. Cope, 'The Short Parliament of 1640 and Convocation', *Journal of Ecclesiastical History*, 25 (1974), 167–84; and her 'The Earl of Bedford's Notes on the Short Parliament of 1640', *Bulletin of the Institute of Historical Research*, 53 (1980), 255–8.

24 For the king's prerogative, see J. P. Sommerville, *Politics and Ideology in England, 1603–40* (1986), pp. 36–9; for its pre-Stuart history, see Margaret McGlynn, *The Royal Prerogative and the Learning of the Inns of Court* (Cambridge, 2003).

25 For the background, see Fissel, 'Scottish War and English Money: the Short Parliament of 1640', pp. 193–223.

26 For the nobility's loans to the king, see NA, SO 3/12 (Signet Office Docket Book),

entries for 1639–40. Northumberland lent Charles £5,000 in December 1639 towards meeting the debts incurred in the Anglo-Scottish war of 1639; but he seems to have lent nothing further in 1640 – an omission that would certainly have been noted by the king; see Fissel, *Bishops' Wars*, p. 125.

27 For Northumberland's assessment of the king's military prospects in 1640, see Centre for Kentish Studies, De L'Isle MS U1500/C2/43, fo. 1: Earl of Northumberland to the Earl of Leicester, 14 May 1640. Northumberland's disaffection towards many of his fellow Privy Councillors, whom he described as 'Incendiaries' (perhaps significantly, a favourite Covenanter term for their enemies) emerges in a letter to the Earl of Leicester in December 1639: Collins, *Letters and Memorials*, II, 263.

28 Charles's concern for his own honour figures, almost obsessively, in his declaration issued in the aftermath of the Parliament's failure: *His Majesties Declaration: to all his Loving Subjects, of the Causes which moved Him to dissolve the Last Parliament* (1640), pp. 2, 4, 13 [*recte* 5], 15, 16, 17, 20, 30, 31, 52 (BL, E 203/1).

29 Centre for Kentish Studies, De L'Isle MS U1500/C2/41: Earl of Northumberland to the Earl of Leicester, 19 March 1640 (not in HMC, *De L'Isle Manuscripts*).

30 Jenny Wormald, 'James VI, James I and the Identity of Britain', in Brendan Bradshaw and John Morrill (eds.), *The British Problem, c. 1534–1707: State Formation in the Atlantic Archipelago* (Basingstoke and London, 1996), pp. 148–71.

31 For a classic statement of these difficulties, see Russell, *Causes*, Ch. 2, 'The Problem of Multiple Kingdoms, c. 1580–1630'.

32 Sharpe, *Personal Rule*, Ch. 13; Allan I. Macinnes, *Charles I and the Making of the Covenanting Movement, 1625–41* (Edinburgh, 1991), pp. 77–97; Donald, *Uncounselled King*, Chs. 1–2. Caroline policy towards Ireland is placed in a longer imperial tradition in Nicholas Canny's massive study of the English and Scottish 'plantations' in Ireland, *Making Ireland British, 1580–1650* (Oxford, 2001). For the resistance in Ireland to attempts to make the Irish and English Churches (in Strafford's phrase) 'become one', see John McCafferty, 'John Bramhall and

the Church of Ireland in the 1630s', in Alan Ford, James McGuire and Kenneth Milne (eds.), *As by Law Established: the Church of Ireland since the Reformation* (Dublin, 1995), pp. 100–11, 246–9; and his '"God bless your free Church of Ireland": Wentworth, Laud, Bramhall and the Irish Convocation of 1634', in Julia F. Merritt (ed.), *The Political World of Thomas Wentworth, Earl of Strafford, 1621–41* (Cambridge, 1996), pp. 187–208. See also, Linda M. Ross, 'The Legacy of John Bramhall as Laud's *Alter Ego*', in Gerard O'Brien (ed.), *Derry and Londonderry: History and Society: Interdisciplinary Essays on the History of an Irish County* (Dublin, 1999), pp. 279–302; David Stevenson, 'The English Devil of Keeping State: Elite Manners and the Downfall of Charles I in Scotland', in Roger A. Mason and Norman MacDougall (eds.), *People and Power in Scotland* (Edinburgh, 1992), pp. 126–44. For a critique of the deficiencies of Caroline policy towards Ireland, see Nicholas Canny, 'The Attempted Anglicization of Ireland in the Seventeenth Century: an Exemplar of "British History"', Merritt, *The Political World of Thomas Wentworth*, pp. 184–5.

33 *His Majesties Declaration: to all his Loving Subjects, of the Causes which moved Him to dissolve the Last Parliament* (1640), p. 1 (BL, E 203/1); for another example of Charles's use of the term, see Macinnes, *Covenanting Movement*, p. 108. See also, Francis Bacon, Viscount St Alban, *The Historie of the Reigne of King Henry the Seventh* (1641), p. 3 (Wing B298). Nathaniel Fiennes argued that all ecclesiastical jurisdiction was also annexed to 'the imperiall Crowne of this Realme': *A Speech of the Honorable Nathanael Fiennes, (second son to the Right Honourable the Lord Say) in Answere to the Third Speech of the Lord George Digby* ([8–9 Feb.] 1641), p. 7 (BL, E 196/32).

34 David Stevenson, *The Covenanters: Scotland and the National Covenant* (Edinburgh, 1988); Macinnes, *Covenanting Movement*.

35 Macinnes, *Covenanting Movement*, Ch. 7; Russell, *Fall of the British Monarchies*, Ch. 2; David Stevenson, *The Scottish Revolution, 1637–44: the Triumph of the Covenanters* (Newton Abbot, 1973).

36 Keith M. Brown, *Noble Society in*

Scotland: Wealth, Family, and Culture from the Reformation to the Revolution (Edinburgh, 2000).

37 Walter R. Foster, *The Church before the Covenants: the Church of Scotland, 1596–1638* (Edinburgh, 1975), pp. 176–98.

38 For the 1637 liturgy as a 'popish booke of Common prayer', see [Alexander Henderson?], *Arguments given in by the Commissioners of Scotland unto the Lords of the Treaty, perswading Conformitie of Church Government, as one Principall Meanes of a Continued Peace betweene the Two Nations* ([May] 1641), p. 7 (BL, E 157/2); and see Russell, *Causes*, pp. 112–17; idem, *Fall of the British Monarchies*, pp. 49–50, 69; for the setting, see Andrew Spicer, '"Laudianism" in Scotland? St Giles' Cathedral, Edinburgh, 1633–39 – a Reappraisal', *Architectural History*, 46 (2003), 95–108.

39 The words are those of Robert Baillie, writing in 1637, quoted in Macinnes, *Covenanting Movement*, p. ii.

40 Macinnes, *Covenanting Movement*, pp. 158–9.

41 Macinnes, *Covenanting Movement*, pp. 166–72; John J. Scally, 'The Political Career of James, 3rd Marquis and 1st Duke of Hamilton (1606–1649) to 1643' (unpublished Ph.D. dissertation, University of Cambridge, 1993).

42 Gardiner, *Constitutional Documents*, p. 132.

43 Alexia Grosjean, 'General Alexander Leslie, the Scottish Covenanters and the Riksråd Debates, 1638–40', in Allan I. Macinnes, Thomas Riis, and Frederik Pedersen (eds.), *Ships, Guns and Bibles in the North Sea and Baltic States, c. 1350–c. 1700* (East Linton, 2000), pp. 115–38.

44 See Macinnes, *Covenanting Movement*, Ch. 8, and in particular pp. 200–4, subtitled 'The Scottish Doge'.

45 NAS, Hamilton Red Book 1, 76: Charles I to the Marquess of Hamilton, 25 June 1638; partly printed Gilbert Burnet, *The Memoires of the Lives and Actions of James and William, Dukes of Hamilton* (1677), p. 60. See also Donald, *Uncounselled King*, pp. 83–4.

46 Russell, *Fall of the British Monarchies*, p.

160; Clarendon, *Rebellion*, I, 159. Even the Scottish National Covenant makes reference to the need to preserve 'the King's honour'; Gardiner, *Constitutional Documents*, p. 132.

47 Longleat House, Wiltshire, Devereux Papers I, fo. 357r–v: Richard Herbert to the Earl of Essex, 18 August 1640.

48 NA, SP 16/418/99: letter of intelligence from Edward Rossingham, 30 April 1639; Knowler, *Strafforde's Letters*, II, 351: George Garrard, the Master of the Charterhouse, to Viscount Wentworth, 20 May 1639; NAS, Hamilton MS GD 406/1/1207: Sir Henry Vane senior to the Marquess of Hamilton, 28 April 1638. For the background, see Gardiner, *History*, IX, 11–12; M. L. Schwarz, 'Viscount Saye and Sele, Lord Brooke, and Aristocratic Protest in the First Bishops' War', *Canadian Journal of History*, 7 (1972), 17–36; Sharpe, *Personal Rule*, pp. 822–3.

49 The circumstances of the 1639 campaign, and its potential for success, are discussed in detail in John Adamson, 'England without Cromwell: What if Charles I had avoided the Civil War?', in Niall Ferguson (ed.), *Virtual History: Alternatives and Counterfactuals* (1997), pp. 95–101; and in Fissel, *Bishops' Wars*, pp. 5–37.

50 BL, Add. MS 11045 (Scudamore corr.), fo. 27: E[dward R[ossingham], newsletter to Viscount Scudamore, 11 June 1639.

51 The mobilization is extensively discussed in Fissel, *Bishops' Wars*.

52 There is an extensive literature on the Parliaments of the 1620s; among the works of particular distinction are Conrad Russell, *Parliaments and English Politics, 1621–29* (Oxford, 1979); Christopher Thompson, *Parliamentary History in the 1620s: In or Out of Perspective?* ([Privately printed], Wivenhoe, 1986); Thomas Cogswell, *The Blessed Revolution: English Politics and the Coming of War, 1621–24* (Cambridge, 1989); idem, 'War and the Liberties of the Subject', in J. H. Hexter (ed.), *Parliament and Liberty from the Reign of Elizabeth to the English Civil War* (Stanford, 1992), pp. 225–51; idem, 'The Politics of Propaganda: Charles I and the People in the 1620s', *Journal of British Studies*, 29 (1990), 187–215; idem, 'A Low Road to Extinction? Supply and Redress of Grievances in the Parliaments of the 1620s', *Historical Journal*, 33 (1990), 283–303;

Richard Cust, *The Forced Loan and English Politics 1626-28* (Oxford, 1987); idem, 'Politics and the Electorate in the 1620s', in Richard Cust and Ann Hughes (eds.), *Conflict in Early Stuart England: Studies in Religion and Politics, 1603-42* (1989), pp. 134-67.

53 G. L. Harriss, 'Medieval Doctrines in the Debates on Supply, 1610-29', in Kevin Sharpe (ed.), *Faction and Parliament: Essays on Early Stuart History* (Oxford, 1978), pp. 73-103; G. L. Harriss, 'The Management of Parliament', in idem (ed.), *Henry V: the Practice of Kingship* (Oxford, 1985), pp. 137-58.

54 Conrad Russell, 'Parliament and the King's Finances', in idem (ed.), *The Origins of the English Civil War* (1973), pp. 91-116; on the 1629 session in particular, see Christopher Thompson, 'The Divided Leadership of the House of Commons in 1629', in Sharpe, *Faction and Parliament*, pp. 245-84.

55 Russell, *Causes*, pp. 179-81.

56 Richard Cust, 'Charles I and a Draft Declaration for the 1628 Parliament', *Historical Research*, 63 (1990), 143-61; and his 'Charles I and Popularity', in Thomas Cogswell, Richard Cust and Peter Lake (eds.), *Politics, Religion and Popularity in Early Stuart Britain: Essays in Honour of Conrad Russell* (Cambridge, 2002), pp. 235-58.

57 Harriss, 'Medieval Doctrines'; Clive Holmes, 'Parliament, Liberty, Taxation, and Property', in Hexter, *Parliament and Liberty from the Reign of Elizabeth to the English Civil War*, pp. 122-54.

58 On the European dimension of English political thought in the early seventeenth century, see Johann P. Sommerville, 'The Ancient Constitution Reassessed: the Common Law, the Court and the Languages of Politics in Early Modern England', in R. M. Smuts (ed.), *The Stuart Court and Europe: Essays in Politics and Political Culture* (Cambridge, 1996), pp. 39-64; idem, 'English and European Political Ideas in the Early Seventeenth Century: Revisionism and the Case of Absolutism', *Journal of British Studies*, 35 (1996), 168-94; idem, *Royalists and Patriots: Politics and Ideology in England 1603-40* (1999).

59 For the republican aspect of this political culture, see Quentin Skinner, 'Classical Liberty and the Coming of the English Civil War', in Martin van Gelderen and Quentin Skinner (eds.), *Republicanism: a Shared European Heritage*, ii, *The Values of Republicanism in Early Modern Europe* (Cambridge, 2002), 9-28.

60 For contrasting approaches to the political thought of the early Stuart period, see Sommerville, *Royalists and Patriots*; and Glenn Burgess, *Absolute Monarchy and the Stuart Constitution* (New Haven and London, 1996).

61 Geoff Baldwin, 'Reason of State and English Parliaments, 1610-42', *History of Political Thought*, 25 (2004), 620-41, at 634-5.

62 L. J. Reeve, *Charles I and the Road to Personal Rule* (Cambridge, 1989); Sharpe, *Personal Rule*, pp. 63-130.

63 R. W. Hoyle, 'Introduction: Aspects of the Crown's Estate, c. 1558-1640', and Madeleine Gray, 'Exchequer Officials and the Market in Crown Property, 1558-1640', both in R. W. Hoyle (ed.), *The Estates of the English Crown, 1558-1640* (Cambridge, 1992), pp. 1-57, 112-36; Robert Ashton, *The Crown and the Money Market, 1603-40* (Oxford, 1960), pp. 132-53.

64 Sharpe, *Personal Rule*, pp. 552-8; Andrew Thrush, 'Naval Finance and the Origins and Development of Ship Money', in Mark C. Fissel, *War and Government in Britain, pp. 133-62.

65 K. R. Andrews, *Ships, Money and Politics: Seafaring and Naval Enterprise in the Reign of Charles I* (Cambridge, 1991), pp. 129-30; S. Peter Salt, 'Sir Simonds D'Ewes and the Levying of Ship Money, 1635-40', *Historical Journal*, 37 (1994), 253-87; Conrad Russell, 'England in 1637', in Margo Todd (ed.), *Reformation to Revolution: Politics and Religion in Early Modern England* (New York, 1995), pp. 116-41; M. D. Gordon, 'The Collection of Ship Money in the Reign of Charles I', *Transactions of the Royal Historical Society*, 3rd ser., 4 (1910), 141-62; although it should be noted that Mrs Gordon's figures underestimate the sums actually received by the Treasury of the Navy. More recent, but regrettably unpublished, research by Dr Alison Gill has shown that Mrs Gordon's figures need extensive revision.

66 Charles made much of the fact that 'all the money Collected had been paid to the Treasurer of the Navie, and by him expended' in his declaration after the dissolution of the Short Parliament; *His Majesties Declaration: to all his Loving Subjects, of the Causes which moved Him to dissolve the Last Parliament* (1640), p. 20 (BL, E 203/1). See also, Philip Warwick, *Memoirs of the Reign of King Charles I* (1701), p. 53.

67 Sharpe, *Personal Rule*, pp. 594–5; Thrush, 'Naval Finance and the Origins of Ship Money', pp. 133–62. As Andrews points out, Ship Money did not bring about a major expansion in the navy, though it improved its strength and efficiency; see his *Ships, Money and Politics*, pp. 151–2.

68 For Strafford's rule in Ireland, see Hugh Kearney, *Strafford in Ireland, 1633–41: a Study in Absolutism* (Cambridge, 1989); Canny, *Making Ireland British*, pp. 275–300.

69 Anthony Milton, 'Thomas Wentworth and the Political Thought of the Personal Rule', in Merritt, *The Political World of Thomas Wentworth*, pp. 133–56, at p. 143.

70 This case is argued in detail in Adamson, 'England without Cromwell'.

71 Richard Cust, *Charles I: a Political Life* (2005), pp. 246–7; Russell, *Fall of the British Monarchies*, p. 63; Sharpe, *Personal Rule*, pp. 808–9.

72 Macinnes, *Covenanting Movement*, pp. 192–7; Adamson, 'England without Cromwell', pp. 98–101.

73 BL, Trumbull MS, Georg Weckherlin to William Trumbull, 17 February 1640.

74 For Northumberland, see R. Malcolm Smuts, 'The Puritan Followers of Henrietta Maria in the 1630s', *English Historical Review*, 93 (1978), 26–45; Caroline Hibbard, *Charles I and the Popish Plot* (Chapel Hill, NC, 1983), pp. 131–2, 227–8; Alnwick Castle, Northumberland MS XIV (Political papers, 1636–39): Propositions from Sir Thomas Rowe for the formation of a West Indies Company to make war on 'the King of Spain' (HMC, *Third Report*, Appendix, p. 74).

75 Centre for Kentish Studies, De L'Isle MS U1475/C85/4: Earl of Northumberland to the Earl of Leicester, 12 December 1639 (not

calendared in HMC, *De L'Isle Manuscripts*, VI).

76 Knowler, *Strafforde's Letters*, II, 391, 394, 396–7; NA, SP 16/449/47: Lord Cromwell to Viscount Conway, 31 March 1640.

77 T. W. Moody, F. X Martin, and F. J. Byrne, *A New History of Ireland*, III, *Early Modern Ireland, 1534–1691* (Oxford, 1978), pp. 271–4; Gardiner, *History*, IX, 95.

78 NA, PRO 31/3/71 (Paris transcripts), p. 154, quoted in Russell, *Fall of the British Monarchies*, p. 93.

79 Ester S. Cope and Willson H. Coates (eds.), *Proceedings of the Short Parliament of 1640* (Camden Society, 4th ser., 19, 1977), pp. 115–21; *LJ*, II, pp. 46–7.

80 Stevenson, *Scottish Revolution*, pp. 137–8; Donald, *Uncounselled King*, pp. 221, 227, 229; Gardiner, *History*, IX, 98–9.

81 The Grimstons had enjoyed Warwick's patronage and protection going back almost thirty years; see Cust, *Forced Loan*, pp. 199, 312. For Warwick's influence with the Bailiffs of Colchester in 1628, to whom he recommended Grimston's father, Sir Harbottle, see Essex RO, Morant MS D/Y, 2/4, p. 85. For Warwick's relations with the Grimstons and his influence in Essex during the October 1640 elections, see Clive Holmes, *The Eastern Association in the English Civil War* (Cambridge, 1974), pp. 21–2, 26. I am grateful to Mr Christopher Thompson for many discussions of the patronage of the Earl of Warwick.

82 Keeler, *Long Parliament*, p. 329: Rudyard had been elected to the six previous Parliaments on the back of Herbert patronage. See also, Vivienne Hodges, 'The Electoral Influence of the Aristocracy, 1604–41' (unpublished Ph.D. dissertation, Columbia University, 1977).

83 Christopher Thompson, 'The Origins of the Politics of the Parliamentary Middle Group, 1625–29', *Transactions of the Royal Historical Society*, 5th ser., 22 (1972), 71–86. For Pym and Bedford, see Conrad Russell, 'The Parliamentary Career of John Pym, 1621–29', in Peter Clark, A. G. R. Smith and Nicholas Tyacke (eds.), *The English Commonwealth 1547–1640: Essays in Politics and Society presented to Joel Hurstfield* (Leicester, 1979), pp. 147–65.

84 The attitudes and connections of these four peers are discussed below, Chs. 1, 2, and 5.

85 Cope, *Short Parliament Proceedings*, p. 135; see also Russell, *Fall of the British Monarchies*, p. 104, where Professor Russell attaches rather less weight than I do to Grimston's remarks.

86 For Grimston's speech of 16 April 1640, see Rushworth, *Historical Collections*, III, 1128; *Parliamentary or Constitutional History*, VIII, 422.

87 Judith D. Maltby (ed.), *The Short Parliament (1640) Diary of Sir Thomas Aston* (Camden Society, 1988), pp. 8–10.

88 NA, SP 16/450/101: Earl of Northumberland to the Earl of Leicester, 17 April 1640.

89 Centre for Kentish Studies, De L'Isle MS U1475/C85/13: Earl of Northumberland to the Earl of Leicester, 23 April 1640 (HMC, *De L'Isle Manuscripts*, VI, 254).

90 NA, SP 16/451, fos. 125–26: Earl of Northumberland to Viscount Conway, 26 April 1640.

91 NA, SP 16/452, fo. 282: interrogatories to be put to Sir William Douglas and Robert Barclay.

92 Russell, *Fall of the British Monarchies*, pp. 99–100.

93 These contacts are discussed above, pp. 36–9.

94 On the hostility of this circle towards the policies of the Crown during the 1620s, see Cust, *Forced Loan*, pp. 157–8, 198–201, 225–6, 229–30, 231–4; Thompson, 'The Origins of the Politics of the Parliamentary Middle Group', pp. 71–86. Antipathies within the House of Lords often registered in sniping over procedure; on the Lords' very first business day, 16 April, for example, when the Hispanophile Privy Councillor, Lord Cottington (a close friend of Laud) had tried to present evidence of treason against the Covenanter Lord Loudoun – a 'rebel' peer with whom Saye was almost certainly in private correspondence – Saye interrupted him on a technicality in mid-report, claiming that since Cottington (who was appearing as a member of the House of Lords for the first time) had not gone through the formal ritual of introduction 'in his Roabes', his attempt to address the House was out of order; see Cope, *Short Parliament Proceedings*, p. 58.

95 Russell, 'Parliamentary Career of John Pym'; Clayton Roberts, 'The Earl of Bedford and the Coming of the English Revolution', *Journal of Modern History*, 49 (1977), 600–16; but note, too, the critique of this argument in Derek Hirst, 'Unanimity in the Commons, Aristocratic Intrigues, and the Origins of the English Civil War', *Journal of Modern History*, 50 (1978), 51–71. On Bedford's architectural interests, see Dianne Duggan, '"London the Ring, Covent Garden the Jewell of that Ring": New Light on Covent Garden', *Architectural History*, 43 (2000), 140–61; Dianne Duggan, 'Woburn Abbey: the First Episode of a Great Country House', *Architectural History*, 46 (2003), 140–61. For his commercial enterprises, see L. E. Harris, 'Sir Cornelius Vermuyden: an Evaluation and an Appreciation', *Transactions of the Newcomen Society*, 27 (1956 for 1949–51), 7–18; and Clayton Roberts, *Schemes and Undertakings: a Study of English Politics in the Seventeenth Century* (Columbus, OH, 1985).

96 For the quotation, Edmund Calamy, *A Patterne for all, especially for Noble and Honourable Persons, to teach them how to die nobly and honourably. Delivered in a Sermon preached at the Solemne Interment of the Corps of the Right Honourable Robert Earle of Warwick* (1658), p. 36 (BL, E 947/1).

97 Cust, *Forced Loan*, pp. 145, 198–201, 229–33, 334; and Clive Holmes, *The Eastern Association in the English Civil War* (Cambridge, 1974), pp. 19–21, 26. For Warwick's support for puritan clergy, see Barbara Donagan, 'The Clerical Patronage of Robert Rich, 2nd Earl of Warwick, 1619–42', *Proceedings of the American Philosophical Society*, 120 (1976), 388–419; for his involvement in naval affairs, see Nelson P. Bard, 'The Earl of Warwick's Voyage of 1627', in N. A. M. Rodger (ed.), *The Naval Miscellany V* (Navy Records Society, 1984), 15–93; and *idem*, '"Might and Would Not": the Earl of Warwick's Privateering Expedition of 1627', *American Neptune*, 55 (1995), 5–18; Wesley F. Craven, 'The Earl of Warwick, a Speculator in Piracy', *Hispanic American Historical Review*, 10 (1930), 457–79; V. A. Rowe, 'Robert, 2nd Earl of Warwick, and the

Payment of Ship Money in Essex',
*Transactions of the Essex Archaeological
Society*, 3rd ser., 1 (1962), 160–3.

98 John Adamson, 'Of Armies and
Architecture: the Employments of Robert
Scawen', in Ian Gentles, John Morrill and
Blair Worden (eds.), *Soldiers, Writers, and
Statesmen of the English Revolution*
(Cambridge, 1998), pp. 38–41; and discussed
above, Ch. 1.

99 These links are developed above, Ch. 1.
For Saye's range of interests, see Bodl. Lib.,
MS Rawlinson d. 892 (Saye Papers). For
Brooke, see Anne Hughes, 'Thomas Dugard
and his Circle in the 1630s – a "Parliamentary-
Puritan" Connexion?', *Historical Journal*, 29
(1986), pp. 771–93.

100 For Essex's career, see John Morrill,
'Robert Devereux, third Earl of Essex',
ODNB; and V. F. Snow, *Essex the Rebel: the
Life of Robert Devereux, the 3rd Earl of
Essex, 1591–1646* (Lincoln, NB, 1970).

101 Beinecke Lib., Yale University, MS
Osborn Shelves fb. 111: George Brown to [?],
1 September 1640 (for the quotation); for
Essex's popularity, see also [Robert Chestlin],
*Persecutio Undecima. The Churches Eleventh
Persecution* ([5 Nov.] 1648), p. 9 (BL, E
470/7).

102 Arthur Wilson, *The History of Great
Britain being the Life and Reign of King James
the First* (1653), p. 162 (Wing W2888);
Cogswell, *Blessed Revolution*, pp. 102–5;
John Morrill, 'Robert Devereux, 3rd Earl of
Essex', *ODNB*; there is a revealing letter to
Essex from the Earl of Warwick [*c.* December
1631] – BL, Add. MS 46188 (Jessop papers),
fos. 184–5 – that suggests a relationship of
considerable intimacy and political unanimity
between writer and recipient.

103 Cope, *Short Parliament Proceedings*, p.
98. The MS account, by Lord Montagu of
Boughton, reads 'concerning us to all', but the
transposition of 'us to' seems a simple error.
Saye also seems to have supported Essex on
this case; ibid., p. 63.

104 NA, SP 16/452/114 and 115; and above,
pp. 23–24.

105 Strafford was 'hopelesse of doing any
good [in the raising of loans] in these broken
and ill disposed times', but was less pessimistic
than Northumberland about the possibility

of mounting a campaign. He remained
confident that he could raise an Irish army;
see his letter to George Radcliffe, 2 May 1640,
printed in Thomas Dunham Whitaker (ed.),
*The Life and Original Correspondence of Sir
George Radcliffe* (1810), p. 199.

106 In 1639, the cost of campaigning against
Scotland had been estimated at £935,000 a
year: NA, SP 16/415/119; and see Gardiner,
History, VIII, 384.

107 Russell, *Fall of the British Monarchies*,
p. 119.

108 This point is well made in Mark
Kishlansky and John Morrill, 'Charles I',
ODNB.

109 *CJ*, II, 19; Cope, *Short Parliament
Proceedings*, p. 193. For the later controversy
about Vane's role in the making of this offer,
see Centre for Kentish Studies, De L'Isle MS
U1475/C114/12: Sir John Temple to the Earl
of Leicester, 25 February 1641 (HMC, *De
L'Isle Manuscripts*, VI, 387); BL, Harl. MS
6424 (Bishop Warner's diary), fo. 35r–v.

110 The debate on the offer was conducted
as a Committee of the Whole House, a
procedure which allowed the appointment of
an ad hoc chairman, in this case William
Lenthall, one of Northumberland's counsel
employed in the Exchequer of Pleas and other
courts, and enabling the Speaker, John
Glanvill, Northumberland's principal
Chancery counsel, to take part in the debate.
Northumberland, of course, was not
Glanvill's only patron; he should, perhaps, be
seen as a client of the larger group of pro-
French, strongly Protestant lords within the
Privy Council, among whom
Northumberland, Holland and Pembroke
were the most prominent. Glanvill had owed
his promotion as a King's Serjeant in 1637 to
the 'Erle d'Holland et divers auters':
Cambridge UL, Add. MS 6863 (Sir Richard
Hutton's Journal), fo. 87v, printed in Baker,
Serjeants at Law, p. 384. For
Northumberland's feeing of Glanvill at this
time, see Centre for Kentish Studies, De L'Isle
MS U1475/A98: Northumberland's
engrossed accounts for 1640–41 (a stray from
the series of account rolls at Alnwick Castle).
Of the six speakers listed by Russell as in
'outright support' of the Council's
compromise proposal, Sir Benjamin Rudyard
was closely associated with Pembroke, the

Lord Chamberlain of the Household; Glanvill with Northumberland and Holland; and the Yorkshire members, Sir William Savill and Sir Henry Slingsby, with Strafford. The only other outright supporters, Edward Hyde and Viscount Falkland (a Scottish title, hence his ability to take a seat in the Commons), may also have been prompted to speak at the instigation of members of the Privy Council, particularly in the light of Pembroke's relations with Hyde. See Russell, *Fall of the British Monarchies*, p. 120, for a discussion of the speakers; for the debate, Maltby, *Aston Diary*, pp. 128–44; Cope, *Short Parliament Proceedings*, pp. 193–7, 208–10. I am grateful to Dr David Scott for a discussion of the allegiance of the Yorkshire Commons-men.

111 *His Majesties Declaration: to all his Loving Subjects, of the Causes which moved Him to dissolve the Last Parliament* (1640), p. 40 (BL, E 203/1).

112 NA, SP 16/452, fo. 93: order of the House of Commons, 4 May 1640 (in John Rushworth's hand); Maltby, *Aston Diary*, pp. 128–44; Cope, *Short Parliament Proceedings*, pp. 193–7, 208–10; Clarendon, *Rebellion*, I, 182. As Conrad Russell observes, 'Aston's diary goes a long way to revive the authority of Clarendon on the Short Parliament', even if Clarendon's sense of the order or individual incidents 'remains hopelessly confused'; Russell, *Fall of the British Monarchies*, p. 119n.

113 *His Majesties Declaration: to all his Loving Subjects, of the Causes which moved Him to dissolve the Last Parliament*, p. 48.

114 NAS, Hamilton MS GD 406/1/1805: draft [4 May 1640], in Hamilton's handwriting, of the king's speech at the dissolution on 5 May 1640; see also, Richard Cust, *Charles I: a Political Life* (2005), p. 257.

115 Laud, *History of the Troubles and Tryal*, p. 78 (for the timing of the meeting of 5 May).

116 Centre for Kentish Studies, De L'Isle MS U1475/C86/6: Henry Percy to the Earl of Leicester, 22 April 1640 (HMC, *De L'Isle Manuscripts*, VI, 251–2). I owe this reference to Professor the Earl Russell.

117 The following account of the Council meeting of 5 May is based on Laud, *Works*, III, 284. The king's later claim that he was 'enforced by the advice of His Privie Councell

to resolve to break up ... the Parliament' seems to have been far from the reality; *His Majesties Declaration: to all his Loving Subjects, of the Causes which moved Him to dissolve the Last Parliament*, p. 41. The Lord Lieutenant of Ireland was living, at Northumberland's arrangement, barely half a mile away, in Leicester House, just west of St Martin's Lane, the house of Northumberland's brother-in-law, the Earl of Leicester, which was conveniently vacant during its owner's absence as ambassador in Paris. For Strafford's residence at Leicester House at this time, see Strafford's letters to George Radcliffe of 2 May and 11 June 1640, printed in Whitaker, *Radcliffe Correspondence*, pp. 199–201. For the friendship between Strafford and Leicester, see Alnwick, Northumberland MS 23/16/6, fo. 3: Earl of Northumberland to Earl of Leicester, 16 January 1640; and Centre for Kentish Studies, De L'Isle MS U1500/C2/41: Earl of Northumberland to the Earl of Leicester, 19 March 1640 (not calendared in HMC, *De L'Isle Manuscripts*, VI).

118 BL, Harleian MS 4931 (Political papers, 1617–41), fo. 49.

119 I am grateful to Dr David Scott for the suggestion that Strafford may well have used the meeting as an occasion to flush out, in the king's presence, the dissolution's opponents.

120 Interrogatories 'upon the Earl of Strafford's Defence', printed Whitaker, *Radcliffe Correspondence*, pp. 233–5: 'Questions upon the Earl of Strafford's Defence', interrogatories nos. 6–9. The Privy Council meetings to which this document relates are not dated, but it is clear from internal evidence that the meeting referred to at this point in the text can only be the dawn meeting of Tuesday, 5 May 1640. For the use Strafford was subsequently to make of Vane's counsel, see Centre for Kentish Studies, De L'Isle MS U1475/C114/12: Sir John Temple to the Earl of Leicester, 25 February 1641 (HMC, *De L'Isle Manuscripts*, VI, 387); and BL, Harl. MS 6424 (Bishop Warner's diary), fos. 35–6.

121 For evidence of Vane and Windebank having spoken against the possibility of the Commons providing funds, see Centre for Kentish Studies, De L'Isle MS U1475/C114/12: Sir John Temple to the Earl of Leicester, 25 February 1641 (HMC, *De

L'Isle Manuscripts, VI, 387); Sharpe, *Personal Rule*, p. 874.

122 Laud, *History of the Troubles*, p. 78. That Northumberland was among the last speakers can be inferred from his rank; he was among the most senior Councillors in the table of precedence, and Councillors spoke in inverse order of seniority. For his 'giving his opinione against the breking of the Parlement', see Centre for Kentish Studies, De L'Isle MS U1475/C87/6: Countess of Carlisle to the Earl of Leicester, 7 May [1640] (HMC, *De L'Isle Manuscripts*, VI, 262).

123 NA, SP 16/452. fo. 112: Earl of Northumberland to Viscount Conway, 5 May 1640.

124 Centre for Kentish Studies, De L'Isle MS U1475/C87/6: Countess of Carlisle to the Earl of Leicester, 7 May [1640] (HMC, *De L'Isle Manuscripts*, VI, 262).

125 Ibid. The Privy Council meeting of 5 May 1640 marked another major milestone along the road to estrangement between the king and Northumberland, a journey which was to lead him into the arms of the king's opponents by early in 1641.

126 *His Majesties Declaration: to all his Loving Subjects*, pp. 1–55. For the venue, see BL, Add. MS 4931 (Political papers, 1617–41), fo. 49: notes of the Short Parliament's proceedings.

127 *LJ*, IX, 81. The theme is developed in the king's declaration justifying the dissolution, *His Majesties Declaration: to all his Loving Subjects* (1640), pp. 51–2 (BL, E 203/1).

128 For the background, see Sharpe, *Personal Rule*, pp. 909–21.

129 Centre for Kentish Studies, De L'Isle MS U1475/C87/6: Countess of Carlisle to the Earl of Leicester, 7 May [1640] (HMC, *De L'Isle Manuscripts*, VI, 262).

130 The notes are printed in HMC, *Third Report*, p. 3; the original is in the PA. Extracts are printed in John Rushworth, *The Tryal of Thomas Earl of Strafford … upon an Impeachment of High Treason* (1680), pp. 51–2. The authenticity of these notes is discussed extensively in Gardiner, *History*, IX, 120–1nn.

131 HMC, *Third Report*, p. 3. I concur with Gardiner's analysis of this text that there is

nothing in Strafford's speech that shows that 'any deliberate purpose of preparing for an Irish occupation of England was ever entertained' – as was later claimed at Strafford's trial for treason in 1641; see Gardiner, *History*, IX, 125. I doubt, however, that the final line in Vane's notes – 'Whether a defensive warr as impossible as an offensive, or whether to lett them alone'– is correctly attributed to Strafford. It contradicts the tenor of his preceding argument, and weakens what appears to have been its rhetorically forceful conclusion provided in the previous line ('[I would] venter all I had. I would carry it or loose it'). Instead, the question whether a defensive war was as 'impossible' as an offensive would appear to be a question raised by Northumberland at the end of Strafford's speech, or by another Councillor of the same opinion, not a remark of Strafford's. Indeed, another contemporary copy of Vane's notes clearly assigns the last lines of what has hitherto been taken to be Strafford's speech (as given in the HMC *Third Report* version) to the 'Lord Admiral' – that is, to the Earl of Northumberland: see BL, Harl. MS 4931 (Political papers, 1617–41), fo. 125. This would seem to confirm the hypothesis outlined above. For another copy, see NA, SP 16/452, fo. 106r-v.

132 Anthony Milton, 'Thomas Wentworth and the Political Thought of the Personal Rule', in Merritt, *The Political World of Thomas Wentworth, Earl of Strafford*, pp. 133–56.

133 HMC, *Third Report*, p. 3; NA, SP 16/452, fo. 106r-v.

134 Geoff Baldwin, 'Reason of State and English Parliaments, 1610–42', *History of Political Thought*, 25 (2004), 620–41; for the Continental context, see Yves Charles Zarka (ed.), *Raison et déraison d'état: theoriciens et theories de la raison d'état aux XVIè et XVIIè siècles* (Paris, 1994).

135 J. H. Elliott, 'The Year of the Three Ambassadors', in Hugh Lloyd-Jones, Valerie Pearl and Blair Worden (eds.), *History and Imagination: Essays in Honour of H. R. Trevor-Roper* (1981), pp. 165–81.

136 Discussed above, Ch 1, pp. 40–1.

137 For the king's hostility to Northumberland, see Centre for Kentish Studies, De L'Isle MS U1475/C87/6: Countess

of Carlisle to the Earl of Leicester, 7 May
[1640]; for both quotations, see
U1475/C129/8: Countess of Carlisle to the
Countess of Leicester, 21 May [1640] (HMC,
De L'Isle Manuscripts, VI, 261, 270).

138 Centre for Kentish Studies, De L'Isle MS
U1500/C2/43: Earl of Northumberland to the
Earl of Leicester, 15 May 1640 (not in HMC,
De L'Isle Manuscripts).

139 *LJ*, IX, 81; *His Majesties Declaration: to
all his Loving subjects*, pp. 51–2 (BL, E 203/1).

1. TREASON IN PARADISE

1 Essex RO, T/B 211/1, no. 39: 'The sum of
that Conference which was betwixt one Mr
Burroughes, a Minister laitlie suspendit in the
Dioces of Norwitch for inconformitie, and
John Michaelson, Parson of Chelmesford, the
5 of August last [1638], at Leeghes parva, in
the garden of the … Earle of Warwicke'. (I
am grateful to Mr Christopher Thompson for
supplying me with his transcription of this
important deposition.) For Burroughes, see
Tom Webster, *Godly Clergy in Early Stuart
England, c. 1620–43* (Cambridge, 1997), pp.
22, 32, 80, 87, 131. As Webster notes,
'Burroughes was not, as is often asserted,
chaplain to the family of the Earl of Warwick'
(ibid., p. 211n.); but Burroughes was reported
to have officiated in that place, in an acting
capacity, during Gauden's (and Warwick's)
absence in 1638, albeit that he did not have
the formal standing of household chaplain.
For John Michaelson, see Hilda Grieve, *The
Sleepers and the Shadows: Chelmsford – a
Town, its People and its Past*, 2 vols.
(Chelmsford, 1988–94), II, 8, 14, 38–9 and
other references.

2 For the search, *CJ*, II, 25; Notestein,
D'Ewes Diary, p. 23; Centre for Kentish
Studies, De L'Isle MS U1475/C132/16:
William Hawkins to the Earl of Leicester, 7
May 1640 (HMC, *De L'Isle Manuscripts*, VI,
260–1). Though the search of Warwick House
is commented upon by Kevin Sharpe, it is
unnoticed in most of the major narratives of
the period, in particular those by S. R.
Gardiner and Conrad Russell; though the
arrests of various of the members of the
Commons are; see Gardiner, *History*, IX, 129;
Russell, *Fall of the British Monarchies*, p. 140;
Kevin Sharpe, *The Personal Rule of Charles
I* (New Haven and London, 1992), p. 877.

3 S. A. Baron, 'Sir William Becher', *ODNB*.
Becher resigned his post as a Clerk of the Privy
Council on 27 January 1641; NA, SP
16/476/84. For his suspected Catholicism, see
G. E. Aylmer, *The King's Servants: the Civil
Service of Charles I, 1625–42* (1961), pp.
232, 366.

4 For the unsettled state of the capital, see
Keith Lindley, *Popular Politics and Religion
in Civil War London* (Aldershot, 1997), pp.
4–35; David Cressy, *England on Edge: Crisis
and Revolution, 1640–42* (Oxford, 2006),
Ch. 5.

5 *CJ*, II, 25, for Becher's subsequent
questioning, after a new Parliament met in
November 1640.

6 This was notwithstanding that both Saye
and Brooke had achieved national notoriety
in 1639, for refusing the oath of allegiance
which Charles had imposed on the peers in
May 1639; see Sharpe, *Personal Rule*, pp.
822–3.

7 For the search of Warwick's pockets, *CJ*, II,
25; the inventory of papers taken from
Warwick's study does not appear to survive,
but that papers were seized seems almost
certain from the (documented) seizures of
papers at the houses of Lord Saye, Hampden,
and St John; see Bodl. Lib., MS Tanner 88*,
fos. 1, 2, and 3 respectively.

8 *CJ*, II, 25.

9 NA, SP 16/479, fo. 130v: Nathaniel
Tomkyns to [Sir John Lambe], 22 April 1641.
Saye's house is described by Tomkyns, himself
a Holborn resident, as 'adjoining Brooke
House, neere us in Holborne', though it is not
clear precisely when Saye acquired this.
Brampton Gurdon's language, however, in a
letter written shortly after 5 May suggests
that Saye was already living near Brooke
House at this time: Brampton Gurdon to John
Winthrop [post-5 May 1640], printed in R.
Winthrop (ed.), *The Winthrop Papers*, 5 vols.
(Boston, MA, 1929–47), IV, 243–4. Dr Valerie
Pearl notes that in 1641 Saye also occupied an
office, near Pym's, not far from Westminster
Hall (see Pearl, *London*, p. 42).

10 Bodl. Lib., MS Tanner 88*; Pym may have
burned some of his papers prior to the raid:
see BL, Add. MS 11045 (Scudamore corr.),
fo. 116.

11 The associations between the godly peers

and Pym and Hampden are discussed extensively, below, Chs. 1–3. I concur with Dr Cust in regarding Erle as 'Saye's adherent', a connection that went back to the 1620s, and was later consolidated by the marriage of Erle's son to Saye's daughter; see Richard Cust, *The Forced Loan and English Politics, 1626–28* (Oxford, 1987), p. 233; Keeler, *Long Parliament*, 'Sir Walter Earle [sic]'. For the searches, see HMC, *De L'Isle Manuscripts*, VI, 260–1: William Hawkins to the Earl of Leicester, 7 May 1640. Three other Commons-men were questioned for further information, but, significantly, there was no attempt to seize their papers. Hotham and Belasyse spent ten days in the Fleet Prison for refusing to answer questions, and John Crewe, the chairman of the Commons' Committee on Religion, was also harassed; see *CSPD 1640*, pp. 130, 154–5, 166; *Privy Council Registers, April–June 1640*, X, 476.

12 Centre for Kentish Studies, De L'Isle MS U1475/C132/16: William Hawkins to the Earl of Leicester, 7 May 1640 (HMC, *De L'Isle Manuscripts*, VI, pp. 260–1).

13 NA, SP 16/479, fo. 56v: Nathaniel Tomkyns to [Sir John Lambe], 12 April 1641.

14 Three other Commons-men came under the scrutiny of the Privy Council. Strafford's personal animus seems to have been behind the arrest and brief imprisonment of two fellow Yorkshireman, Sir John Hotham and Henry Belasyse, both of whom had suggested that Yorkshire – the richest and most populous county in the North – was unlikely to contribute to the king's war-effort, whether or not he abolished Ship Money. And as Belasyse's biographer has noted, there is at least the possibility 'the two were also acting in concert with John Pym and his allies in their efforts to prevent the king obtaining parliamentary backing ... for his campaign against the Covenanters'. A third Commons-man, John Crewe, was questioned and also briefly imprisoned for his role as Chairman of the Commons' Grand Committee on Religion. David Scott, 'Henry Belasyse', HPL. Belasyse had long been in Strafford's bad books, and took a prominent role in organizing petitions expressing the county's grievances in the course of the summer of 1640. Sir Hugh Cholmley was also arrested; see J. T. Cliffe, *The Yorkshire Gentry from*

the Reformation to the Civil War (1969), pp. 317–18.

15 NA, SP 16/453, fo. 36v: [Edward Rossingham newsletter, to Viscount Conway], 12 May 1640.

16 NA, SP 16/458/110 (I owe this reference to Conrad Russell).

17 NA, SP 16/453, fo. 36: [Edward Rossingham newsletter, to Viscount Conway], 12 May 1640; another copy of this newsletter is to be found in BL, Sloane MS 1467 (Newsletters, 1640–41), fo. 104.

18 Ester S. Cope and Willson H. Coates (eds.), *Proceedings of the Short Parliament of 1640* (Camden Society, 4th ser., 19, 1977), 82–3, 98–9, 235, 239, 245, 323; *LJ*, III, 855–6.

19 NA, SP 16/453, fo. 36: [Edward Rossingham newsletter, to Viscount Conway], 12 May 1640. This treatise was first printed in 1642 as John Cotton, *A Modest and Cleare Answer to Mr. Balls Discourse of Set Formes of Prayer* (1642), BL, E 108/42.

20 NA, SP 16/453, fo. 36: [Edward Rossingham newsletter, to Viscount Conway], 12 May 1640.

21 The informant may have been Patrick Younge, the librarian of the Royal Library at St James's Palace and himself a Scot, who was later ordered to be 'examined [as to] what some of the Lower house have sayed to hime about this busynes' of the plan to hijack the parliamentary session of 5 May 1640: see NA, SP 16/452, fo. 280: anonymous deposition [c. 5 May 1640], and the endorsement on the back (for the quotation), referring to 'Mr Patrick Younge'.

22 NA, SP 16/452, fo. 280: anonymous deposition, undated [but c. 5–6 May 1641]. There is a note in a different hand to that of the main deposition to the effect that 'Mr Patrick Younge' (identified in a nineteenth-century pencil note to the manuscript as the Master of the Library at St James's) would be examined as to what some of the Commons-men had said to him about the contact with the Scots; though it is unclear from this whether Younge was the source of the original information or regarded as a possible corroborative witness.

23 NA, SP 16/452, fo. 280. This was probably the *Information from the Estaits of*

the Kingdome of Scotland, to the Kingdome of England ([Edinburgh, for J. Bryson], [Feb.?] 1640), *STC2* 21916.

24 NA, SP 16/452, fo. 131: Archibald Jhonston or Wariston to 'John Smith, Merchant', in Edinburgh, 5 May 1640.

25 NA, SP 16/452, fo. 280; SP 16/452/114 and 115.

26 [William Fiennes, Viscount Saye and Sele], *Vindiciae Veritatis* (1654), p. 43 (BL, E 811/2). For the authorship of this treatise, see John Adamson, 'The *Vindiciae Veritatis* and the Political Creed of Viscount Saye and Sele', *Historical Research*, 60 (1987), 45–63; see also, Brampton Gurdon to John Winthrop [post-5 May 1640, printed in Winthrop, *The Winthrop Papers*, IV, pp. 243-4.

27 BL, Harl. MS 4931 (Political papers, 1617–41), fo. 49: contemporary notes of the Short Parliament. According to these, the king commanded the Speaker of the Commons not to go to the House, 'fearing (perhaps) lest that they should urge him to preferr any petition to the upper house ...'.

28 See also NA, SP 16/453, fo. 36: [Edward Rossingham newsletter, to Viscount Conway], 12 May 1640. Rossingham reported two prevailing views as to what was to happen on 5 May, one being that 'protestations were drawne either against the Scotch war or against the pressing of subject to goe to this wa[rr]'; the other that a protestation was being planned against Ship Money, in which the Speaker was likely to collude with the anti-Ship Money lobby.

29 The circumstantial evidence largely comes from the deposition, NA, SP 16/452, fo. 280, and the subsequent series of interrogatories, drafted for the questioning of two of the Scottish Commissioners (Sir William Douglas and Robert Barclay), ibid., fo. 282. What is unclear is precisely when this information reached the ears of the king; hence one can merely conjecture as to whether it played a role in moving him to dissolve the Parliament.

30 Brampton Gurdon to John Winthrop [post-5 May 1640]: Winthrop, *Winthrop Papers*, IV, 243-4

31 Such thinking would have been natural, perhaps, to a monarch who had experienced the tumultuous end of the 1629 parliamentary

session (an observation I owe to Professor Malcolm Smuts).

32 NA, SP 16/452, fos. 280, 282.

33 NA, SP 16/452, fo. 282.

34 NA, SP 16/446/48, SP 16/448/23; SP 16/450/41; and Donald, *Uncounselled King*, p. 223. For the commissioners, see also *Information from the Estaits of the Kingdome of Scotland*, p. 11 (*STC2* 21916).

35 NA SP 16/452, fo. 131: Archibald Jhonston of Wariston to 'Mr John Smith, Merchant', in Edinburgh, 5 May 1640. This tallies with the information contained in the deposition in SP 16/452, fo. 280.

36 NA, SP 16/452, fo. 282: interrogatories to be put to Sir William Douglas and Robert Barclay. Barclay's denials do not carry conviction, given that Barclay knew that any statement in the affirmative would almost certainly have resulted in the arrest of any he so named; see also Russell, *Fall of the British Monarchies*, p. 122.

37 BL, Harl. MS 6424 (Bishop Warner's diary), fo. 44v.

38 For the conviction that these Fifth Columnists were traitors, see Cambridge UL, MS Mm. 1. 45 (Historical papers), pp. 99, 112: letter of intelligence to Dr Matthew Wren, Dean of the Chapel Royal, from York [c. 24–25 September 1640]. I owe this reference to Mr Christopher Thompson.

39 For Windebank's use of this phrase, see Clarendon, *State Papers*, II, 94–5: Sir Francis Windebank to Charles I, 31 August 1641; HMC, *De L'Isle Manuscripts*, VI, 260–1: William Hawkins to the Earl of Leicester, 7 May 1640. That Warwick's house was also among those searched at the end of the Short Parliament is confirmed by the evidence presented at a conference between the two Houses during the next Parliament, on 10 November 1640: Notestein, *D'Ewes Diary*, p. 23.

40 Lancashire RO, Hulton of Hulton MS, DDHu/46/21: John Pym to William Jessop, from Leez, 3 September [1640]; Calybute Downinge, *A Sermon Preached to the Renowned Company of the Artillery, 1 September 1640* (1641), pp. 30-1 (BL, E). For Downinge's presence at Leez, see [Sir John Birkenhed], *A Letter from Mercurius Civicus*

to Mercurius Rusticus, or, Londons Confession but not Repentance (1643), p. 8 (Wing B6324).

41 Nicholas C. Lamming, *A Brief History of the Buildings and People of Leez Priory* (Hartford End, Essex, 4th edn., 1998), pp. 14, 16.

42 J. M. Hunter, 'Littley Park, Great Waltham – Historical Survey', *Essex Archaeology and History*, 25 (1994), 119–24, esp. 119.

43 Edmund Calamy, *A Patterne for All, especially for Noble and Honourable Persons* ([2 June] 1658), p. 38 (BL, E 947/1). Calamy simply refers to 'Mr. Knightly of Northamptonshire (well known to some here)'; but Richard Knightley of Fawsley seems the only plausible candidate, as he was both one of Warwick's nominees as one of the Saybrook 'Patentees' of 1632 and a member of the Oxfordshire–Northamptonshire godly network, with which Calamy would have been well familiar. For his connections with Saye, Sir Nathaniel Rich, John Crewe, Pym, and Hampden during the 1630s, see Northamptonshire RO, Knightley MS K 37, 38, 40, 42, 107; see also Christopher Thompson, 'The Saybrook Company and the Significance of its Colonizing Venture' (unpublished paper read at the Institute of Historical Research, University of London, on 11 March 1999), p. 8 (I am grateful to Mr Thompson for providing me with a copy of his paper); Cust, *Forced Loan*, p. 233.

44 Eamon Duffy, *The Stripping of the Altars: Traditional Religion in England,* c.1400–c.1580 (New Haven and London, 1992).

45 P. R. N. Carter, 'Richard Rich, first Baron Rich', *ODNB*.

46 Warwick was a county with which he had no territorial connection, and the likeliest reason for his choice of style was that it was a private homage to the title's most recent holder, Ambrose Dudley, Earl of Warwick – the son of the great reforming Duke of Northumberland of Edward VI's reign, and a celebrated champion of 'Puritans' in Elizabeth's reign. For the choice of title, see Brett Usher, 'Robert Rich, first Earl of Warwick', *ODNB*. Half of the twenty-five works dedicated to Ambrose, Earl of Warwick were by puritan divines; see Simon

Adams, 'Ambrose Dudley, Earl of Warwick', *ODNB*.

47 Royal Commission on Historical Monuments, *Essex*, II, 158; I am grateful to Mr Simon Heffer for his assistance during a visit to what remains of the house. The dining hall of the Tudor house was built on the foundations of part of the nave of the medieval priory church.

48 *CSPV 1636–39*, p. 124: Anzolo Correr to the Doge and Senate of Venice, 6/16 January 1637.

49 Calamy, *A Patterne for All, especially for Noble and Honourable Persons*, p. 27 (BL, E 947/1). His was a binary world in which the dualities of heroes and villains, true religion and popish error, Christ and Antichrist, were each clearly, even luridly, defined. Of course, by the time Warwick was in his twenties, these black-and-white certitudes were coming to be blurred in England's 'public discourse', first by James I's peace with Spain, concluded in 1604, and later, from the 1620s, by a gradual lessening in the confidence with which many English divines identified the Antichrist with the Church of Rome. Nicholas Tyacke, *Anti-Calvinists: the Rise of English Arminianism, c. 1590–1640* (Oxford, 1987), Chs. 1–3; Anthony Milton, 'The Church of England, Rome and the True Church: the Demise of a Jacobean Consensus', in Kenneth Fincham, (ed.), *The Early Stuart Church, 1603–42* (Basingstoke, 1993), pp. 187–210; and Anthony Milton, *Catholic and Reformed: Roman and Protestant Churches in English Protestant Thought, 1600–40* (Cambridge, 1994).

50 For the 2nd Earl of Essex and his circle, see Paul E. J. Hammer, *The Polarisation of Elizabethan Politics: the Political Career of Robert Devereux, 2nd Earl of Essex, 1585–97* (Cambridge, 1999); Alzada J. Tipton, '"Lively Patterns ... for Affayres of State": Sir John Hayward's 'The Life and Reigne of King Henrie IIII and the Earl of Essex', *Sixteenth Century Journal*, 33 (2002), 769–94.

51 For Warwick's hostility to Spain, see Thomas Cogswell, *The Blessed Revolution: English Politics and the Coming of War, 1621–24* (Cambridge, 1989), pp. 102–3; *CSPV 1636–39*, p. 124: Anzolo Correr to the

Doge and Senate of Venice, 6/16 January
1637.

52 In 1627, following in an Elizabethan
tradition, he personally commanded a
privateering raid on the Spanish West Indies,
losing heavily financially in the process, but
greatly enhancing his own status as a paladin
of the Protestant cause; see W. F. Craven, 'The
Earl of Warwick, a Speculator in Piracy',
Hispanic-American Historical Review, 10
(1930), 457–79.

53 Robert Brenner, *Merchants and
Revolution: Commercial Change, Political
Conflict, and London's Overseas Traders,
1550–1653* (Cambridge, 1993), pp. 100, 109,
111, 125, 156, 157, 161, 244, 251–3, 265,
269, 273, 276, 291, 302, 354. This theme
will be documented more fully in Mr
Christopher Thompson's forthcoming
biography of the 2nd Earl of Warwick.

54 Barbara Donagan, 'The Clerical
Patronage of Robert Rich, 2nd Earl of
Warwick, 1619–42', *Proceedings of the
American Philosophical Society*, 120 (1976),
388–419; Calamy, *A Patterne for All*, p. 35.

55 Clarendon's claim of Warwick that he was
a hypocrite – 'a man of less virtue could not
be found out' – is itself a familiar topos of
anti-puritan polemic; given the numerous
testimonies to Warwick's personal piety and
religious conviction, Clarendon's assessment
should be regarded with considerable
scepticism; see Clarendon, *Rebellion*, II, 544;
see also Sharpe, *Personal Rule*, pp. 741–2.

56 For an introduction to the religious history
of the period generally, see Diarmaid
MacCulloch, *Reformation: Europe's House
Divided, 1490–1700* (2003). This, of course,
was no more than the prevailing orthodoxy of
the time. What separated men such as
Warwick and Saye from their less zealous
contemporaries, however, was not that they
held views on the nature of religion that were
fundamentally different from those of their
fellows, but the fervour and intensity with
which they embraced those principles and
acted upon their implications in their daily
lives. Peter Lake, 'Calvinism and the English
Church, 1570–1635', in Margo Todd (ed.),
*Reformation to Revolution: Politics and
Religion in Early Modern England* (New
York, 1995), pp. 179–207; Peter Lake, '"A
Charitable Christian Hatred": the Godly and

their Enemies in the 1630s', in Christopher
Durston, Jacqueline Eales (eds.), *The Culture
of English Puritanism, 1560–1700*
(Basingstoke, 1996), pp. 145–83.

57 Roger Lockyer, *Buckingham: the Life and
Political Career of George Villiers, 1st Duke
of Buckingham, 1592–1628* (1981), pp.
306–7; Nicholas Tyacke, *Anti-Calvinists: the
Rise of English Arminianism, c. 1590–1640*
(Oxford, 1987); Barbara Donagan, 'The York
House Conference Revisited: Laymen,
Calvinism and Arminianism', *Historical
Research*, 64 (1991), 312–30. I am grateful to
Professor Peter Lake for a discussion of this
point. For hostility to Buckingham more
generally, see Linda Levy Peck,
'Monopolizing Favour: Structures of Power in
the Early Seventeenth-Century English
Court', in J. H. Elliott and Laurence W. B.
Brockliss, *The World of the Favourite* (New
Haven, CT, 1999), pp. 54–70.

58 Like most men of his generation, including
his friend, Viscount Saye, born in 1582 and
five years his senior, Warwick's sense of what
constituted 'true religion' had been formed by
the prevailing theology and practices of the
late Elizabethan and early Jacobean Church.
Theirs was a fundamentally Calvinist divinity,
with its belief that the 'elect' – those destined
for salvation – were a small minority, chosen
by God for all eternity in an inscrutable and
(to mere mortals) unfathomable act of
goodness. Their churchmanship placed an
emphasis on the pulpit and 'the Word' at the
centre of the parish's spiritual life, rather than
the communion table and the operation of
sacramental grace. And they applauded the
Jacobean episcopate for its uncompromising
anti-Catholicism, its distinction in the pulpit,
and the relatively light hand with which it
wielded its jurisdictional powers. Lake,
'Calvinism and the English Church,
1570–1635'; Tyacke, *Anti-Calvinists*, Chs. 1
and 2. On the changing role of bishops, see
Kenneth Fincham, *Prelate as Pastor: the
Episcopate of James I* (Oxford, 1990).

59 Ann Hughes, 'Thomas Dugard and his
Circle in the 1630s: a "Parliamentary-
Puritan" Connexion?', *Historical Journal*, 29
(1986), 771–93; Lake, 'Calvinism and the
English Church, 1570–1635', in Todd,
*Reformation to Revolution: Politics and
Religion in Early Modern England*, pp.
179–207; Lake, '"A Charitable Christian

Hatred"', pp. 145-83; Jason Peacey, 'Seasonable Treatises: a Godly Project of the 1630s', *English Historical Review*, 113 (1998), 667-79.

60 Peter Lake, 'The Laudian Style: Order, Uniformity and the Pursuit of the Beauty of Holiness in the 1630s', in Fincham, *The Early Stuart Church*, pp. 161-85; Anthony Milton, 'The Creation of Laudianism: a New Approach', in Thomas Cogswell, Richard Cust and Peter Lake (eds.), *Politics, Religion and Popularity in Early Stuart Britain: Essays in Honour of Conrad Russell* (Cambridge, 2002), pp. 162-84; David R. Como, 'Predestination and Political Conflict in Laud's London', *Historical Journal*, 46 (2003), 263-94; Kenneth Fincham, 'The Restoration of Altars in the 1630s', *Historical Journal*, 44 (2001), 919-40; Kenneth Fincham, 'William Laud and the Exercise of Caroline Ecclesiastical Patronage', *Journal of Ecclesiastical History*, 51 (2000), 69-93; Andrew Foster, 'Church policies of the 1630s', in Richard Cust and Ann Hughes (eds.), *Conflict in Early Stuart England: Studies in Religion and Politics, 1603-42* (1989), pp. 193-223.

61 Milton, *Catholic and Reformed*, pp. 93-127, 173-4, 372-3; Peter Lake and Michael Questier, *The Anti-Christ's Lewd Hat: Protestants, Papists and Players in Post-Reformation England* (New Haven, 2002); Peter Lake, 'Antipopery: the Structure of a Prejudice', in Cust and Hughes, *Conflict in Early Stuart England*, pp. 72-106.

62 For an example, see Ian Atherton, 'Viscount Scudamore's "Laudianism": the Religious Practices of the 1st Viscount Scudamore', *Historical Journal*, 34 (1991), 567-96; and his *John, first Viscount Scudamore 1601-71: a Career at Court and in the Country, 1602-43* (Akron, OH, 1995).

63 Saye, *Vindiciae Veritatis*, p. 11.

64 For Warwick's successful application for a pew in St Mary Aldermanbury in September 1639, see Guildhall Lib., MS 3750/2 (Vestry minutes), fo. 43v. He was given the choice of having Calamy's own pew in the chancel, or the more discreet position of one at the east end of the 'Little Gallery', and chose the latter; ibid., fo. 50v. (I owe these last two references to Mr Christopher Thompson.) See also, A. G. Matthews (ed.), *Calamy Revised: being a Revision of Edmund Calamy's Account of the Ministers and Others Ejected and Silenced, 1660-62* (Oxford, 1934), p. 1. For Calamy's ministry in Rochford, see Philip Benton, *The History of Rochford Hundred* (Rochford, Essex, 1867), pp. 861-2.

65 Essex RO, T/B 211/1, no. 39: 'The sum of that Conference which was betwixt one Mr Burroughes, a Minister laitlie suspendit in the Dioces of Norwitch for inconformitie, and John Michaelson, Parson of Chelmesford, the 5 of August last [1638], at Leeghes parva, in the garden of the ... Earle of Warwicke'.

66 Gauden was Warwick's household chaplain at Leez in the late 1630s: Essex RO, T/B 211/1, no. 39.

67 Calamy, *A Patterne for All*, p. 37; for Burroughes and Warwick, see his *A Vindication of Mr Burroughes* (1646), pp. 18-19 (BL, E 345/14), referring back to a conversation in the Earl of Warwick's garden during the Bishops' Wars; on which see Derek Hirst, 'The Place of Principle', *Past & Present*, 92 (1981), 79-99, at p. 98. Burroughes was reported to be 'attend[ing] on the Lo. Mandeville' in April 1637, and it is likely that Mandeville and Warwick were the 'great Lords that [were reported to] countenance him': Bodl. Lib., MS Tanner 68, fos. 7v, 8. Warwick's brother, the Earl of Holland, intervened on Burroughes's behalf in September 1637 'as he was recomended to me by his freinds' – presumably Mandeville and Warwick again: Bodl. Lib., MS Tanner 68, fo. 248: Earl of Holland to Bishop Matthew Wren, 21 September 1637. For Sedgwicke, see Barbara Donagan, 'Obadiah Sedgwick', *ODNB*; and below, Ch. 2.

68 It should be noted that the Earl of Warwick had a second house in the county, Rochford Hall, Essex; but the favoured seat seems to have been Leez; see D. D. Andrews, 'Richard Lord Rich's Mansion at Rochford Hall', *Essex Archaeology and History*, 3rd ser., 34 (2004 [for 2003]), 69-90.

69 Calamy, *A Patterne for All*, p. 37. Many of those who gathered at Leez during the 1630s shared Warwick's anti-Spanish colonizing interests in the New World, notably Lords Saye and Brooke; John Pym and his erstwhile patron (and admirer of Warwick's gardens), Richard Knightley of Fawsley, Northamptonshire; the Buckinghamshire

gentleman and Ship Money resister, John Hampden; and the Providence Island investor Henry Darley. For Darley, see David Scott, 'Henry Darley' (unpublished biography, HPL); for Knightley's visits to Leez, see Calamy, *A Patterne for All*, p. 38.

70 On Michaelson, see *The Autobiography of Sir John Bramston* (1845), p. 95. I owe this reference to Mr Christopher Thompson.

71 Essex RO, T/B 211/1, no. 39: John Gauden, the principal household chaplain, had left to accompany the Earl of Warwick to the Dutch Republic to bring back the body of Warwick's recently deceased son, Henry Rich; during Gauden's absence, the Countess of Warwick had sent down Burroughes, who had apparently been based in Warwick's London household, 'to officiate that cure [i.e. as household chaplain]'.

72 Essex RO, T/B 211/1, no. 39.

73 Jeremiah Burroughes, *A Vindication of Mr Burroughes against Mr Edwards his Foule Aspersions* ([23 July] 1646), p. 20 [*recte* 21]-22 (BL, E 345/14). I infer, albeit tentatively, that Burroughes enjoyed some measure of protection, partly because of his position in the household, and partly from his claim (ibid., p. 20 [*recte* 21]) that he spent around three weeks in London 'going freely up and down the City', despite the controversy that Michaelson's report of his opinion had caused.

74 Lady Anne Rich was present at Leez at the time, though the sources do not record whether her husband, Viscount Mandeville, was also there; Essex RO, T/B 211/1, no. 39.

75 These actions included opposition to Laudian 'innovations' in the Church; involvement in the attack on the dominance of Charles's first court favourite, the Duke of Buckingham (who was ultimately murdered in 1628); and resistance to the Crown's attempts to raise revenues on the royal prerogative, without parliamentary assent. This fund of common experience, reinforced by bonds of friendship and kinship, shared religion and hospitality, seems to have created a powerful sense of mutual trust, without which the actions they undertook in 1640 could scarcely have been sustained.

76 NA, C115/M35/8390. (I owe this reference to Mr Christopher Thompson.)

77 Knowler, *Strafforde's Letters*, I, 242:

George Garrard to Lord Deputy Wentworth, 1 May 1634.

78 BL, Harley Roll T2; cited in Sharpe, *Personal Rule*, p. 742.

79 I owe this observation to a private communication from Mr Christopher Thompson, whose study of Warwick's political career is in an advanced state of preparation.

80 Mervyn James, 'English Politics and the Concept of Honour, 1485-1642', in his *Society, Politics, and Culture: Studies in Early Modern England* (Cambridge, 1986), pp. 308-415; Kristen B. Neuschel, *Word of Honor: Interpreting Noble Culture in Sixteenth-Century France* (Ithaca and London, 1989), p. 16. For a comparative perspective, see José Antonio Maravall, *Poder, honor, y élites en el siglo XVII* (Madrid, 1979), pp. 32-41; V. G. Kiernan, *The Duel in European History: Honour and the Reign of Aristocracy* (Oxford, 1988), pp. 92-115.

81 For the use of this term, see, for example, John Stow (continued by Edmund Howes), *Annales, or a General Chronicle of England* (1631), sig.¶5[2]; Knowler, *Strafforde's Letters*, 242: George Garrard to Lord Deputy Wentworth, 1 May 1634.

82 C[alybute] D[owning], *A Discourse of the State Ecclesiastical of this Kingdome* (Oxford, 1633), p. 46 (wing D1609). At the time of the work's composition, Downinge was household chaplain to Salisbury.

83 This theme is touched on in Caroline Hibbard, 'The Theatre of Dynasty', in R. M. Smuts (ed.), *The Stuart Court and Europe: Essays in Politics and Political Culture* (Cambridge, 1996), pp. 156-76. It is worth noting that in the early decades of Elizabeth's reign, this objection was raised by Catholic and crypto-Catholic noblemen; and it formed an important theme in the criticisms of the court emanating from the 2nd Earl of Essex's circle in the 1590s. (I am grateful to Professor Malcolm Smuts for a correspondence on this point.)

84 Linda Levy Peck, 'Monopolizing Favour: Structures of Power in the Early Seventeenth-Century English Court', in J. H. Elliott and Laurence Brockliss (eds.), *The World of the Favourite* (New Haven and London, 1999), pp. 54-70; for a comparative perspective, see

A. Lloyd Moote, 'Richelieu as Chief Minister: A Comparative Study of the Favourite in Early Seventeenth-Century Politics', in Joseph Bergin and Laurence Brockliss (eds.), *Richelieu and his Age* (Oxford, 1992), pp. 13–43.

85 On Laud, see the outstanding biography by Anthony Milton in the *ODNB*.

86 [Arthur Wilson], *The Five Yeares of King James, or, the Condition of the State of England* (1643), p. 8 (CUL, R.10.16/7). For the identification of Wilson as the putative author, see *Notes and Queries*, 4th ser., II, 489.

87 V. A. Rowe, 'Robert, second Earl of Warwick, and the Payment of Ship Money in Essex', *Transactions of the Essex Archaeological Society*, 3rd ser., I (1964–65), 160–3; Cust, *Forced Loan*, pp. 229–32. For a comparison, see the case of Lord Brooke, in Ann Hughes, *Politics, Society and Civil War in Warwickshire, 1620–60* (Cambridge, 1987), and her 'Thomas Dugard and his Circle in the 1630s – a "Parliamentary-Puritan" Connexion?', *Historical Journal*, 29 (1986), 771–93.

88 Richard Cust, 'News and Politics in Early Seventeenth-Century England', *Past & Present*, 112 (1986), 60–90; Alexandra Halasz, *The Marketplace of Print: Pamphlets and the Public Sphere in Early Modern England* (Cambridge, 1997); David Zaret, *Origins of Democratic Culture: Printing, Petitions, and the Public Sphere in Early-Modern England* (Princeton, NJ, 2000); Peter Lake and Michael Questier, 'Puritans, Papists, and the "Public Sphere" in Early Modern England: the Edmund Campion Affair in Context', *Journal of Modern History*, 72 (2000), 587–627. For a later comparison, see Tony Claydon, 'The Sermon, the "Public Sphere" and the Political Culture of Late Seventeenth-Century England', in Lori Anne Ferrell and Peter McCullough (eds.), *The English Sermon Revised: Religion, Literature and History, 1600–1750* (Manchester and New York, 2001), pp. 208–34; Jason Peacey, 'Seasonable Treatises: a Godly Project of the 1630s', *English Historical Review*, 113 (1998), 667–79; Michael Mendle, 'News and the Pamphlet Culture of Mid Seventeenth-Century England', in Brendan Dooley and Sabrina Alcorn Baron (eds.), *The Politics of Information in Early Modern Europe*

(London and New York, 2001), pp. 57–79; Joad Raymond, 'Irrational, Impractical and Unprofitable: Reading the News in Seventeenth-Century Britain', in Kevin Sharpe and Stephen Zwicker (eds.), *Reading, Society and Politics in Early Modern England* (Cambridge, 2003), pp. 185–212; and Joad Raymond, *Pamphlets and Pamphleteering in Early Modern Britain* (Cambridge, 2003); David Randall, 'Recent Studies in Print Culture: News, Propaganda, and Ephemera', *Huntington Library Quarterly*, 67 (2004), 457–72.

89 E. W. Kirby, 'The Lay Feoffees: a Study in Militant Puritanism', *Journal of Modern History*, 14 (1942), 1–25; Irvonwy Morgan, *Prince Charles's Puritan Chaplain* (1957).

90 [Sir John Berkenhead], *A Letter from Mercurius Civicus to Mercurius Rusticus, or, Londons Confession but not Repentance* (1643), p. 8 (Wing B6324): for an account that would see this remark as justified, see Donagan, 'The Clerical Patronage of the Earl of Warwick'.

91 It was this frustration, perhaps, which deflected their energies into colonial and privateering schemes, many of them in conjunction with London's godly merchant community, as Robert Brenner has shown: Robert L. Brenner, *Merchants and Revolution: Commercial Change, Political Conflict, and London Overseas Traders, 1550–1653* (Cambridge, 1993).

92 On the demilitarization of the early Stuart nobility, the *locus classicus* is Lawrence Stone, *The Crisis of the Aristocracy, 1558–1641* (Oxford, 1965).

93 J. K. Lowers, *Mirrors for Rebels: a Study of Polemical Literature relating to the Northern Rebellion, 1569* (Berkeley, CA, 1953); Anthony Fletcher and Diarmaid MacCulloch, *Tudor Rebellions* (4th edn, Harlow, 1997).

94 John Adamson, 'The Baronial Context of the English Civil War', *Transactions of the Royal Historical Society*, 40 (1990), 101–5.

95 For this older view, see Stone, *Crisis of the Aristocracy*; and for the later critique, see Barbara Donagan, 'The Army, the State and the Soldier in the English Civil War', in Michael Mendle (ed.), *The Putney Debates of 1647: the Army, the Levellers and the English*

State (Cambridge, 2001), pp. 79–102. I am also grateful to Mr Christopher Thompson for information on the substantial size and currency of the 2nd Earl of Warwick's arsenal at Leez, Essex.

96 R. C. McCoy, '"A Dangerous Image": the Earl of Essex and Elizabethan Chivalry', *Journal of Medieval and Renaissance Studies*, 13 (1983), 313–29; Mervyn E. James, *Society, Politics and Culture: Studies in Early Modern England* (Cambridge, 1986).

97 The precise date of Warwick's birth is unknown; I am grateful to Mr Christopher Thompson for this estimate of Warwick's age at the time of the 2nd Earl of Essex's execution.

98 For an example of this interest in medieval military precedent, BL, Sloane MS 3071 (Thomas Gainsford [or Gaynsford], 'The One and Twenty Battles of Yorkes [and] Plantaginet'), fos. 6–87v, which is dedicated to the 2nd Earl of Warwick; another copy exists in Cambridge UL, MS Kk. v. 21, which bears a number of pencil annotations in what appears to be Warwick's handwriting. (I owe my knowledge of this copy to the kindness of Dr Anthony Milton.) The work appears to have been written in a bid to elicit Warwick's patronage, though it is unclear what, if any, patronage Gainsford actually received from the earl. Perhaps the most revealing aspect of the treatise is that Gainsford, who seems to have been adept at turning his literary talents to the interests of potential benefactors, clearly believed that the subject (and sentiments) contained in his treatise would have appealed to Warwick. For Gainsford's rather chequered career, see M. Eccles, 'Thomas Gainsford, "Captain Pamphlet"', *Huntington Library Quarterly*, 45 (1982), 259–70.

99 The 'intermission of Parliaments' was also a major grievance in Scotland, as well; see *An Honourable Speech made . . . by the Earle of Argile [13 September 1641]* ([September] 1641), p. 2 (BL, E 199/17).

100 Archives du Ministère des Affaires étrangères, Paris, Correspondence politique Angleterre, 46, fos. 164–5v: Earl of Warwick to Cardinal Richelieu [March 1636] (I owe this reference to Professor Malcolm Smuts). For the 1637 scheme, see Smuts, 'The Court

and the Emergence of a Royalist Party' (forthcoming).

101 *CSPV 1636–39*, pp. 124–5: Anzolo Correr to the Doge and Senate of Venice, 6/16 January 1637. Some of the concerns for the state of the continental war, current in Warwick's circle in the 1630s, emerge in William Jessop's shorthand copies of the letters sent by Warwick, Mandeville and others concerning the Somers Island Company (responsible for the colonies on Bermuda, Barbados, Antigua, and Nevis), in BL, Add. MS 10615 (Jessop letter-book).

102 *CSPV 1636–39*, pp. 24–5.

103 Ibid. Warwick is not named explicitly in this paragraph of Correr's despatch, but as this reference follows directly after his account of Warwick's own demand for a Parliament, the implication seems to be not only that Warwick was one of the 'leading men of the realm', but also probably the prime instigator of the petition.

104 Bedford's relations with this group are discussed in greater detail in Ch. 5, above.

105 NLS, MS Wodrow Folio 66, fos. 109–10: [Sir John Clotworthy, unsigned holograph letter] to [Archibald Jhonston of Wariston], 11 July 1638.

106 Above, pp. 45–50.

107 Alison Gill, 'Ship Money during the Personal Rule of Charles I: Politics, Ideology and the Law, 1634–40' (unpublished Ph.D. dissertation, University of Sheffield, 1991).

108 Ironically, Viscount Mandeville's father is a case in point.

109 For these themes, see James S. Hart, *The Rule of Law, 1603–60: Crowns, Courts and Judges* (2003). The dissentient minority who found in Hampden's favour were mostly septuagenarians, at the end of their careers, and with little to lose by risking the king's disfavour. In a few more years, as mortality disposed of these remaining troublemakers, the bench looked likely to be composed almost wholly of compliant stooges of the court; see Adamson, 'England without Cromwell', pp. 109–13.

110 P. R. Seddon (ed.), *The Letters of John Holles, 1587–1637*, 3 vols. (Thoroton Society, 1975–86), II, 334: John Holles, 1st

Earl of Clare to Viscount Saye and Sele, 12 September 1626.

111 For a different perspective on this theme, see John Morrill, 'The Religious Context of the English Civil War', *Transactions of the Royal Historical Society*, 5th ser., 34 (1984), 155–78.

112 David Cressy, *Coming Over: Migration and Communication between England and New England in the Seventeenth Century* (Cambridge, 1987); A. Zakai, 'The Gospel of Reformation: the Origins of the Great Puritan Migration', *Journal of Ecclesiastical History*, 37 (1986), 584–602; Karen Ordahl Kupperman, *Providence Island, 1630–41: the Other Puritan Colony* (Cambridge, 1994); and her 'Definitions of Liberty on the Eve of the Civil War: Lord Saye and Sele, Lord Brooke and the American Puritan Colonies', *Historical Journal*, 32 (1989), 17–33; Charles E. Banks, 'Religious "Persecution" as a Factor in Emigration to New England, 1630–40', *Proceedings of the Massachusetts Historical Society*, 63 (1931), 136–54; Norman C. P. Tyack, 'The Humbler Puritans of East Anglia and the New England Movement: Evidence from the Court Records of the 1630s', *New England Historical and Genealogical Register*, 138 (1984), 79–106.

113 For the Providence venture, see Kupperman, *Providence Island, 1630–41*; its significance in relation to resistance to the king is first noted in [Sir John Berkenhead], *A Letter from Mercurius Civicus to Mercurius Rusticus, or, Londons Confession but not Repentance* (1643), p. 3 (Wing B6324): the rebellion was conceived in Banbury (near Saye's seat, Broughton Castle), 'shaped in *Grays-Inne-Lane,* where the undertakers for the Isle of *Providence* did meet and plot it, yet you know it was put out to Nurse to *London*'.

114 NA, CO 124/2, fos. 72, 77v, 98, 115, 120, 122v, 140v, 148v, 152v, 154v. For Darley's relations with Brooke, see John Wallis, *Truth Tried: Or, Animadversions on a Treatise published by . . . Robert Lord Brook* (22 Mar. 1643), sig. A (BL, E93/21), and David Scott, 'Henry Darley' (HPL, unpublished biography).

115 Christopher Thompson, 'The Saybrook Company and the Significance of its Colonizing Venture' (unpublished paper read at the Institute of Historical Research,

University of London, on 11 March 1999), p. 17. I am grateful to Mr Thompson for providing me with a typescript of his paper.

116 NA, CO 124/2, fo. 159. Detailed negotiations were entered into with the existing colonists of Massachusetts as to the constitutional arrangements that should prevail after the peers' arrival; for theirs was a strictly hierarchical vision of New Jerusalem, with the determination of policy in the hands of the hereditary nobility. For Saye's and Brooke's earlier proposals, of *circa* 1636, for the constitution of the Massachusetts Bay Colony, see Thomas Hutchinson, *The History of the Colony and Province of Massachusetts-Bay*, ed. L. S. Mayo, 3 vols. (Cambridge, MA, 1936), I, 410–13; R. C. Winthrop, *Life and Letters of John Winthrop*, 2 vols (Boston, MA, 1864–7), II, 426. It is interesting to speculate on the extent to which these Providence Island Company activists were thinking of the struggle against imperial Spain as a global conflict, with Scotland, Germany, and the Caribbean as different theatres of a single war. (I am grateful to Professor Malcolm Smuts for a correspondence on this point.)

117 The intensification of resistance to Ship Money during the late 1630s may also have been a consideration that was a source of new-found optimism for the dissident peers.

118 On the problems of the emigrants, see Cressy, *Coming Over* .

119 Niall Ferguson, *Empire: How Britain Made the Modern World* (2004 edn.), pp. 60–1.

120 W. K. Tweedie (ed.), *Select Biographies. Edited for the Wodrow Society, chiefly from Manuscripts in the Library of the Faculty of Advocates*, 2 vols. (Edinburgh, 1845–47), I, [150]; see the life of John Livingstone, in which he recalls his stay in London shortly after November 1635, where he 'got acquaintance with my Lord Forbes, Sir Nathaniel Rich, Sir Richard Saltonstal, Sir William Constable, Sir Philip Stapelton, Sir Matthew Boynton, Doctor [William] Gouge, Doctor Stibs [Richard Sibbes, a clerical friend of Saye's], Mr Philip Rye [presumably Philip Nye], Mr Thomas Goodwin . . . and others'. I owe this reference to Mr Christopher Thompson. See also Winthrop, *Winthrop Papers*, III, 187, 190–3, 195–6.

121 Keeler, *Long Parliament*, p. 136n.

122 G. M. Paul (ed.), *Diary of Sir Archibald Johnston of Wariston, 1632–39* (Edinburgh, 1911), p. 351; Donald, *Uncounselled King*, p. 191.

123 For the letters, see NLS, MS Wodrow Folio 66, fos. 92–3: [Sir John Clotworthy, unsigned holograph letter] to [Archibald Jhonston of Wariston], 26 June 1638; and NLS, MS Wodrow Folio 66, fos. 109–10: [Sir John Clotworthy, unsigned holograph letter] to [Archibald Jhonston of Wariston], 11 July 1638, printed in David Dalrymple, *Memorials and Letters relating to the History of Britain in the Reign of Charles the First* (Glasgow, 1766), pp. 39–45, where the author of the letter is not identified.

124 NLS, MS Wodrow Folio 66, fo. 109v: [Sir John Clotworthy, unsigned holograph letter] to [Archibald Jhonston of Wariston], 11 July 1638; *CSPV 1636–39*, pp. 124–5: Anzolo Correr to the Doge and Senate of Venice, 6/16 January 1637.

125 NLS, MS Wodrow Folio 66, fo. 109v: [Sir John Clotworthy, unsigned holograph letter] to [Archibald Jhonston of Wariston], 11 July 1638. Dr Donald suggests that Saye and Brooke are the likeliest candidates. This is plausible, but as much so as the pairing of Warwick and Brooke; and it is noteworthy in this connection that Warwick subsequently found Clotworthy a seat in the Parliament of November 1640: cf. Donald, *Uncounselled King*, pp. 192, 194.

126 NLS, MS Wodrow Folio 66, fos. 109–10: [Sir John Clotworthy, unsigned holograph letter] to [Archibald Jhonston of Wariston], 11 July 1638.

127 Thomas Thomson (ed.), *A Diary of the Public Correspondence of Sir Thomas Hope of Craighall, Bart, 1633–45* (Edinburgh, 1843), pp. 93–4. His testimony suggests that the two peers' protest against Charles's intended war, at York in April 1639, when they refused the oath tendered to all English nobles to support the king in the imminent campaign, was intended as much for Scottish as for domestic consumption. Saye and Brooke seem to have been encouraging Covenanter resistance to the king by publicly signalling the presence of support for their cause within the English nobility. For the protest, see M. L. Schwarz, 'Viscount Saye and Sele, Lord Brooke, and Aristocratic Protest to the First Bishops' War', *Canadian Journal of History*, 7 (1972), 17–36; Hibbard, *Charles I and the Popish Plot*, pp. 117–20.

128 Clotworthy, on the other side, warned Jhonston of Wariston of the risks posed by moderates such as the Earl of Cassilis, and Lords Loudoun and Lindsay, whom he believed had been duped by Hamilton's offers of compromise; Donald, *Uncounselled King*, p. 195. There is an excellent pen portrait of Holland in Sharpe, *Personal Rule*, pp. 164–6. For his role as a patron of godly divines and his interests in the Providence scheme, see Barbara Donagan, 'A Courtier's Progress: Greed and Consistency in the Life of the Earl of Holland', *Historical Journal*, 19 (1976), 317–53.

129 For the best recent account of the military aspects of the 1639 campaign, see Mark C. Fissel, *The Bishops' Wars: Charles I's Campaigns against Scotland, 1638–40* (Cambridge, 1994).

130 NLS, ACC 9769/14/3/46 (Crawford MS): [the Tables?] to 'the Englisch Nobilitie', June 1639. This copy survives in the papers of the 1st Lord Lindsey of Balcarres (1587–1641).

131 For Loudoun, see David Stevenson, 'John Campbell, first Earl of Loudoun', *ODNB*. I am grateful to Professor Allan Macinnes for information on Loudoun's relations with Argyll.

132 NLS, ACC 9769/14/3/46 (Crawford MS): [the Tables?] to 'the Englisch Nobilitie', June 1639.

133 For Mandeville's residence at Warwick House, see Boughton House, Northamptonshire, Montagu MS 6, fo. 93: Viscount Mandeville to the first Lord Montagu of Boughton, 9 March [1639]. Relatives by marriage frequently lived under the same roof in London. Lord Brooke and his brother-in-law, Sir Arthur Hesilrige, lived together at Brooke House, only a few doors away from Warwick House in Holborn.

134 Holland's motives for avoiding a Scottish invasion may not have been wholly disinterested, as any Scottish advance was bound to focus on the strategically vital east-coast port of Newcastle, which controlled the London coal trade. Any disruption of that trade looked likely to affect Holland adversely

financially, as by virtue of letters patent granted by the king in April 1634, he, the Earl of Dorset and Job Harbie had rights to the collection of the customs duties imposed on exported sea-coals: West Yorkshire Archive Service, Leeds, Temple Newsam MS WYL100/PO/6/II/11, and WYL100/PO/6/VI/4–9. (I owe these references to Mr Christopher Thompson.)

135 PA, Willcocks (Manchester) MS 2/1/465: Earl of Holland to Viscount Mandeville, 16 July [1639]: 'If I hadde seen you [in person],' Holland wrote to Mandeville, 'I would have sayd something that I am unwillinge to writ unto paper. Yet I will tell you: if the Lords in Scotland will only stand upon the taking awaye the Episcopall government, they will doe well to declare that in all other thinges they will paye the perfect and sivil dutye of subiects'. Cf. HMC, *Eighth Report* (Manchester MSS), II, 55: Lord Loudoun to Viscount Mandeville, 13 November 1639. The Duke of Manchester's archive has been sold and dispersed, and although I have been able to trace many of the documents to their current locations, this one (MS 468 in the nineteenth-century numeration) has eluded me. It is also noteworthy that another courtier with a reputation for godliness, the Earl of Leicester – the king's ambassador in Paris and the husband of another of Warwick's first cousins – placed his daughter in Mandeville's household in the summer of 1639. His declared motive was that she might learn from 'the conversation and example' of Warwick's daughter, Anne Rich: Mandeville's then wife and, when in London, another of the residents of Warwick House; HMC, *Eighth Report* (Manchester MSS), II, 55: Earl of Leicester to Viscount Mandeville, 28 July 1639. Given the Riches' reputation for Puritanism and opposition to Charles's régime, this seems to have been a deliberate gesture of solidarity, and helps explain why Leicester soon had to defend himself against the charge that he, too, was a Puritan, and disaffected towards the court; Centre for Kentish Studies, De L'Isle MS U1475/C124/2: Earl of Leicester to Charles I, draft [1640] (HMC, *De L'Isle Manuscripts*, VI, 355–8).

136 [J. Denniston] (ed.), *Coltness Collections* (Maitland Club, Edinburgh, 1842), pp. 20–1; Gilbert Burnet, *History of My Own Times*, ed. Osmund Airy, 2 vols. (Oxford, 1897), I,

42. For the story of the cane, see Richard Baker, *Chronicle of the Kings of England* (1670), p. 492; David Stevenson, *The Scottish Revolution, 1637–44* (Newton Abbot, 1973), p. 188. Brooke's household accounts would suggest that the story, at least in general terms, was accurate. The accounts for August 1640, for example, record that Gualter Frost was despatched with the handsome provision of £13 to cover the costs of a journey into Northumberland, a sum that suggests he was under instructions to make an express (and hence expensive) journey, with frequent changes of horse along the way; Warwickshire RO, Warwick Castle MS, CR 1886/CUP.4/21A (Brooke household acc.), 'Gifts', *s.v.*. The entry is undated, but immediately precedes a series of entries (listed in chronological order) from August 1640. For Savile's role at court, see also Loomie, *Ceremonies of Charles I, p. 151*.

137 NLS, MS Wodrow Folio 64, fo. 163: memorandum by Archibald Jhonston of Wariston, 30 April 1640.

138 NLS, MS Wodrow Folio 64, fos. 164–5: Archibald Jhonston of Wariston to [a friend in the English Parliament], 30 April 1640.

139 Ironically, by withholding supply – or at least by deferring it so long that it called into question the viability of a military campaign that year – the Scots and their English friends were probably making the survival, or rather the resumption, of Charles's Personal Rule more likely, not less; because it was through the avoidance of war with Scotland that the security of the Caroline régime seemed most likely to be maintained.

140 PA, Willcocks (Manchester MS) 2/1/471: Earl of Northumberland to [Viscount Mandeville], 4 February 1640 (briefly calendared in HMC, *Eighth Report*, II, 56).

141 Clarendon, *Rebellion*, I, 183. Hyde claimed to be reporting the substance of a conversation he had had with St John on 5 May 1640.

142 AGR, Brussels, Secretairerie d'État et de Guerre (période espagnole) MS 374, fos. 153–6v, 201–3v, 214–18v: Marques de Velada to the Cardinal Infante, Governor of the Spanish Netherlands, 18/28 April, 2/12 May and 8/18 May 1640; Secretairerie d'État et de Guerre (période espagnole) MS 374, fos.

248–51v, 258–63v, 268–71v, 276–9v: the Marques de Velada to Philip IV, 16/26 May, 15/25 May, 13/23 May, 11/21 May 1640; see also, *Clarendon State Papers*, II, 83: Sir Francis Windebank to Sir Arthur Hopton, 11 May 1640.

143 I am grateful to Professor Malcolm Smuts for this observation.

144 Simon Adams, 'Spain or the Netherlands? The Dilemmas of Early Stuart Foreign Policy', in Howard Tomlinson (ed.), *Before the English Civil War: Essays on Early Stuart Politics and Government* (1983), pp. 79–102, esp. pp. 98–101.

145 For his part, Philip IV regarded the 'loan' (in effect, a grant, as there was little likelihood of repayment) as a sound investment. Charles's régime was evidently tottering, and it was of prime importance to Spain to avert its fall; for, as he wrote to his ambassadors in London in June, 'should that country become a republic, I have no doubts that I will lose my province of Flanders' – the Spanish Netherlands. AGS, estado 2575: Philip IV to the Marques Virgilio Malvezzi, 25 June 1640; quoted in A. J. Loomie, 'Alonso de Cárdenas and the Long Parliament, 1640–48', *English Historical Review*, 97 (1982), 289–307, at p. 292.

146 *CSPV 1640–42*, p. 47; BL, Add. MS 279621 (Salvetti correspondence), fo. 53. Salvetti uses the prevailing idiom of 'breaking the Parliament' ('rompere il parlamento').

147 NA, PRO 31/3/72 (Paris archives), fos. 130, 163, 182. For the background, see also Hibbard, *Charles I and the Popish Plot*, pp. 150–2.

148 On these themes, see the subtle analysis by Malcolm Smuts in 'The Court and the Emergence of a Royalist Party' (forthcoming); I am grateful to Professor Smuts for the opportunity to read his important article prior to publication.

149 Collins, *Letters and Memorials*, II, 617: Earl of Northumberland to the Earl Leicester, 14 November 1639. His reference to this clique governing 'absolutely' may be an intentional pun.

150 Charles's reaction is perhaps understandable. The policy line being advocated by Pembroke, Holland, and Northumberland would have resulted in his having to reverse his current strategy, and having to act in ways that would have weakened the authority of the Crown.

151 For Charles's determination to press ahead with the Spanish loan, see BN, MS français 15995 (Montreuil corr.), fos. 89, 91.

152 For the background, see Sharpe, *Personal Rule*, pp. 879–84; J. H. Elliott, 'The Year of the Three Ambassadors', in Lloyd-Jones, Pearl, and Worden, *History and Imagination: Essays in Honour of H. R. Trevor-Roper*, pp. 165–81.

153 As early as 1646, Saye had to reprove those who assumed that the failure of Laud's and Strafford's policies was somehow foreordained. [Viscount Saye and Sele], *Vindiciae Veritatis* (1654), pp. 28–9. Saye notes that if the Scots 'had pressed upon the whole body of the [English] army, which was much stronger than theirs and better armed, they might not onely have lost their victory … but their army, and been constrained to go home without their errand'.

154 News of the revolt of the Catalans, which broke out on 7 June 1640 and which threw Philip IV's plans into confusion, could only have reached England towards the end of the month at the earliest; even so, it was not for more than two months that the extent of the rebellion and its implications for Spain's military undertakings elsewhere became clear. J. H. Elliott, *The Revolt of the Catalans: a Study in the Decline of Spain, 1598–1640* (1984); and see his 'The Year of the Three Ambassadors', pp. 165–81.

155 Centre for Kentish Studies, De L'Isle MS U1475/C127/3: Earl of Northumberland to the Countess of Leicester, 2 July 1640 (HMC, *De L'Isle Manuscripts*, VI, 292).

156 For examples, see Sharpe, *Personal Rule*, pp. 899–901; Russell, *Fall of the British Monarchies*, pp. 130–31; Cressy, *England on Edge*, pp. 73–80.

157 BL, Add. MS 11045 (Scudamore correspondence), fo. 119: [Edward Rossingham's] newsletter, 29 September 1640.

158 [Saye], *Vindiciae Veritatis*, p. 28.

159 On this campaign, see Fissel, *Bishops' Wars*.

160 I am grateful to Dr David Scott for a

discussion of the chances of the régime's survival in the summer of 1640.

161 On the theme of honour, see Richard Cust, *Charles I: a Political Life* (2005), pp. 9, 28–30, 418–19, 438–9, 466–7; and his 'Honour and Politics in Early Stuart England: the Case of Beaumont *v.* Hastings', *Past and Present*, 149 (1995), 57–94; Barbara Donagan, 'The Web of Honour: Soldiers, Christians, and Gentlemen in the English Civil War', *Historical Journal*, 44 (2001), 365–89.

162 Gilbert Burnet, *The Memoires of the Lives and Actions of James and William, Dukes of Hamilton and Castleherald* (1677), p. 171; Donald, *Uncounselled King*, pp. 242–3. Hamilton had been responsible for securing Loudoun's release from the Tower, so that he might return to Scotland as a force for conciliation, in June 1640.

163 On Ireland and the crisis of 1640, see Nicholas Canny, *Making Ireland British, 1580–1650* (Oxford, 2001).

164 On the state of the two nations in the early 1640s, see David Scott, *Politics and War in the Three Stuart Kingdoms, 1637–49* (2003), Ch. 1. There were real structural similarities between the crisis within the Stuart kingdoms occasioned by the Scottish revolt, and that in the Spanish kingdoms, caused by the 1640 revolt of the Catalans. Charles's ambassador in Madrid, Sir Thomas Aston, viewed the Spanish crisis (in hindsight, ironically) as more serious than that facing Charles I, believing that, if the revolt spread from Catalonia to Castile, it might precipitate the fall of the Spanish monarchy; see Smuts, 'The Court and the Emergence of a Royalist Party' (forthcoming), and Elliott, 'The Year of the Three Ambassadors'.

165 David Stevenson, *The Scottish Revolution, 1637–44: the Triumph of the Covenanters* (Newton Abbot, 1973), pp. 197–9, 206–7.

166 NLS, MS Wodrow Folio 65, fos, 60, 85; for the background to these allegations, see Russell, *Fall of the British Monarchies*, pp. 309–11. [Mark Napier] (ed.), *Memorials of Montrose and his Times*, 2 vols. (Edinburgh, 1848–50), I, 254–5; Stevenson, *Scottish Revolution*, pp. 197–9, 206–7; Baillie, *Letters and Journals*, I, 247; Donald, *Uncounselled King*, p. 243.

167 The case for this is set out in detail in John Adamson, 'England without Cromwell: What If Charles I had avoided the Civil War?', in Niall Ferguson (ed.), *Virtual History: Alternatives and Counterfactuals* (1997), pp. 91–124.

168 Alexia Grosjean, *An Unofficial Alliance: Scotland and Sweden, 1569–1654* (Leiden, 2003), and *idem*, 'Sweden and the Covenanters during the Bishops' Wars', in Allan Macinnes, T. Riis and F. Pedersen (eds.) *Shaping Identities: Ships, Guns and Bibles in the North Sea and Baltic States* (Edinburgh, 2000).

169 NLS, MS Wodrow Folio 64, fo. 163: memorandum by Archibald Jhonston of Wariston, 30 April 1640.

170 The detailed evidence for this statement is presented in the second half of this chapter.

171 See below, Ch, 2 for an example of members of the Privy Council suspecting the loyalty of the Earl of Warwick's Essex Trained Bands, see NA, SP 16/464, fo. 219.

172 Buckminster Park, Lincolnshire, Tollemache MS 4103/2: letter of intelligence from a Scottish agent in London to [Lord Maitland?], undated, but on internal evidence from between 5 and 31 May 1640; see also, Peter Donald, 'New Light on the Anglo-Scottish Contacts of 1640', *Historical Research*, 62 (1989), 221–9; and the evidence presented in the following two sections of this chapter.

173 NAS, GD 112/40/3/2/45; Donald, *Uncounselled King*, p. 245; Stevenson, *The Scottish Revolution*, pp. 181–93. For Loudoun's character, see *Complete Peerage*, VIII, p. 159n.

174 For the date of his departure, see Gardiner, *History*, IX, p.168; and HMC, *De L'Isle Manuscripts*, VI, p. 293: William Hawkins to the Earl of Leicester, 2 July 1640. See also, NAS, GD 112/40/2/3/45.

175 [John Oldmixon], *The History of England during the Reigns of the Royal House of Stuart* (1730), p. 143: Bedford, Essex, Warwick, Saye, Mandeville, Savile, and Brooke to [Archibald Jhonston of Wariston], [late June–early July 1640]. For the complex issues surrounding these letters see Donald, *Uncounselled King*, p. 247; Gardiner, *History*, IX, 179–81nn; Stevenson,

Scottish Revolution, p. 207. The matter is more fully discussed below, Note 179.

176 Perhaps significantly, Warwick's acting household chaplain, Jeremiah Burroughes regarded the Scottish National Covenant as having been based on the Elizabethan Bond of Association (which, if the report of his conversation was accurate, he mistakenly believed to have been promulgated in 1580); see Essex RO, T/B 211/1, no. 39: 'The sum of that Conference which was betwixt one Mr Burroughes, a Minister laitlie suspendit in the Dioces of Norwitch for inconformitie, and John Michaelson, Parson of Chelmesford, the 5 of August last [1638], at Leeghes parva, in the garden of the … Earle of Warwicke'. For these Bonds, see also David Cressy, 'Binding the Nation: the Bonds of Association 1584 and 1696', in his *Society and Culture in Early Modern England* (Aldershot and Burlington, VT, 2003), pp. 217–34.

177 [Oldmixon], *History of England*, pp. 141–2: 'Nathaniel Black' [Jhonston of Wariston] to Lord Loudoun, 23 June 1640.

178 [Oldmixon], *History of England*, p. 143: [Lord Savile] to 'the Right Honourable John, etc. The rest is cut out' [i.e. John Campbell, Lord Loudoun], [8 July 1640]. Savile's letter, the authenticity of which is not in dispute, dates his receipt of the letter from Jhonston of Wariston to 27 June, and states that 'two days [i.e. 29–30 June] were spent in London, to let your friends know the State of your Affairs, and to settle a way of giving them certain and speedy Intelligence of your Proceedings'. It would seem that the letter of the seven peers was signed during these days, and that Savile carried it with him as he travelled to Yorkshire, where he arrived on 5 July, before forwarding the seven peers' letter, together with a covering letter of his own, on 8 July.

179 [Oldmixon], *History of England*, pp. 142–3: Bedford, Essex, Warwick, Saye, Mandeville, Savile, and Brooke to [Henry] Darley, [end June–early July 1640]. Gardiner, *History*, IX, 179, follows Oldmixon in dating this letter to 8 July, though I hesitate to trust to Oldmixon's chronology, notwithstanding that I accept, as Gardiner did, the authenticity of this letter. As Gardiner observes, this letter printed by Oldmixon, 'contains no engagement which those lords [who signed it] did not fulfil'. The discovery, in the 1980s, of

further correspondence between the two sides has tended to corroborate the authenticity of this letter, which was obviously more open to doubt when it appeared the unique survival of (what now appears to have been) an extensive correspondence between the dissident peers and the Covenanter leadership; for this latter correspondence, see Donald, 'New Light'; Donald, adopting a slightly more sceptical view than Gardiner, nevertheless regards it as 'certainly possible' that the seven peers signed this letter of late June–early July 1640; see Donald, *Uncounselled King*, p. 247.

Consideration of this letter is further complicated, however, by a story, apparently originating with an anonymous memoir of 1640–41 (now BL, Add. MS 15567, fos. 7–8) and later repeated by the antiquarian, John Nalson, that Lord Savile forged the signatures of six of his fellow dissident peers, on his own initiative, in order to induce the Scots to invade (see John Nalson, *An Impartial Collection of the Great Affairs of State* (1682), II, 427). Several points may be made in relation to this. First, if this 'forged letter' ever existed (as Gardiner, following Add. MS 15567, fos. 7–8, and Nalson assumed it did), it must have been a letter quite distinct from the letter of late June–early July printed by Oldmixon; Savile's supposed forged letter contained undertakings that its putative 'signatories' failed to honour, whereas, as Gardiner himself points out, 'the letter in Oldmixon contains no engagement which those [seven] lords did not fulfil' (Gardiner, *History*, IX, 180n). Oldmixon's identification of the supposed 'forged letter' with the one he himself prints is therefore almost certainly mistaken; they are not one and the same.

But it also seems open to doubt whether the 'forged letter' story is actually true, either in whole or in part. Gardiner regarded the evidence for it as being 'of the highest authority', as it comes from a 'an extract from the memoirs of the Earl of Manchester, who, as Lord Mandeville, was one of those whose signatures was forged' (Gardiner, *History*, IX, p. 180n). This would doubtless be true, were Gardiner's assumption as to the authorship of these memoirs (i.e. that they were by the 2nd Earl of Manchester, an attribution he took unquestioningly from Ranke) actually correct. Unfortunately, there is nothing in these so-called 'Manchester memoirs' (BL, Add. MS 15567) to suggest that they are by the 2nd Earl of Manchester, and much internal evidence that suggests that they are not. The attribution of authorship on the manuscript is in an eighteenth-century hand and seems to have been no more than a librarian's semi-educated guess. True, the author of this MS was clearly familiar with this patrician 'Junto' and on the fringes of the group of dissident peers; but, whoever he may have been, he clearly regarded the activities of the Petitioner Peers of 1640 with some scepticism, a position that seems highly unlikely to have been attributable to the then Viscount Mandeville (the future 2nd Earl of Manchester and the memoir's alleged author). There are several figures who are more plausible as this work's author than the 2nd Earl of Manchester, and perhaps few more so than the Earl of Bristol (a point which might account for why so many of the speeches by Bristol's son, Lord Digby, are transcribed *in extenso* in Add. MS 15567). Manchester, however (and *pace* Professor Perez Zagorin), can almost certainly be ruled out, a conclusion that makes this text a much more questionable source for the inner workings of the Petitioner Peers than Gardiner and Ranke assumed. See also Perez Zagorin, *The Court and the Country: the Beginning of the English Revolution* (1969), p. 207 (which accepts the attribution to Mandeville).

Whoever this memoir is by, however, we are still left with the problem of how to deal with its report that Savile admitted that he had forged the signatures of several of the peers in order to encourage the Scots to invade. Here, there are two explanations that seem the most plausible. The first (following Gardiner), is that there *was* a forged letter, but that it was a different letter from that which Oldmixon printed (in his *History*, pp. 142–3), and it seems not to have survived. The second is that the whole story of Savile's having forged *any* signatures is itself a fabrication, for by the time Savile supposedly made his admission most of the peers involved in collusion with the Scots in 1640 were looking for promotion to high office, and seeking a *modus vivendi* with a defeated and humiliated king. Savile's supposed confession to having forged at least *some* correspondence with the Scots (a story repeated by Gardiner on the questionable testimony of the 'Manchester memoir') provided the Petitioner Peers – who were otherwise inculpated – with a suspiciously convenient mode of exonerating themselves (see Gardiner,

History, IX, 210–11n) from any treasonous contacts with the Scots.

Whichever of these explanations is the correct one in relation to the 'Savile forgery' story, however, it does not materially affect the genuineness of the letter printed by Oldmixon or the likelihood that it came from the seven dissident peers (Oldmixon, *History*, pp. 142–3). About the authenticity of the second, slightly later, letter printed by Oldmixon (Lord Savile to Lord Loudoun, *ibid.*, pp. 143–4), informing the Scots of the state of the military preparations in England, there seems to be little doubt.

180 Gardiner, *History*, IX, 179; [Oldmixon], *History of England*, p. 141.

181 Roger Acherley, *The Britannic Constitution: or, the Fundamental Form of Government in Britain* (1727), p. 390.

182 [Oldmixon], *History of England*, p. 143: Bedford, Essex, Warwick, Saye, Mandeville, Savile, and Brooke to [Henry] Darley, [end June–early July 1640].

183 [Oldmixon], *History of England*, p. 142.

184 [Oldmixon], *History of England*, p. 143: Bedford, Essex, and others to Darley, [end June–early July 1640].

185 [Oldmixon], *History of England*, p. 143.

186 *CSPV 1636–39*, p. 124: Anzolo Correr to the Doge and Senate of Venice, 6/16 January 1637.

187 A number of the detailed points made by Savile in this printed letter of 8 July 1640 are corroborated in the later (and unquestionably authentic) correspondence between the dissident peers and the Covenanter leadership which was discovered (and later printed) by Dr Peter Donald: Savile's promise, for example, that 'some Troops of Horse [in the king's army], the Number whereof is not yet certain, and a Regiment of Foot, besides particular Persons out of every Regiment, will turn to you' ([Oldmixon], *History of England*, p. 144) is taken up by N[athaniel] F[iennes] in a letter to the Covenanter leadership of September 1640, in which he was able to confirm the presence of Fifth Columnists in the ranks of the royal army, and point out that the number of regiments that looked likely to declare for the Petitioner Peers: New College Lib., Edinburgh, MS X15b 3/1, vol. i, fo. 262: Bedford and other

Petitioners to the [Covenanter leadership], *c.* 5 September 1640 (Donald, 'New Light on Anglo-Scottish Contacts', p. 229).

188 Andrew Hopper, 'Sir John Meyrick', *ODNB*. When in London, Sir John Meyrick actually lived with the 3rd Earl of Essex, having a chamber at Essex House in the Strand. It is scarcely credible, given the friendship between the two men, that the third Earl did not take Meyrick into his confidence about the negotiations with the Scots. For evidence of their continuing friendship in the later 1640s, see BL, Add. MS 46189 (Jessop papers), fo. 160; and Longleat House, Wiltshire, Devereux Papers III, fos. 135–8; IV, fo. 264.

189 [Oldmixon], *History of England*, p. 144: Lord Savile to John [Lord Loudoun], [8 July 1640].

190 For St John and Bedford, Alnwick Castle, Northumberland, MS Y. III. 2 (3); during the Long Parliament he became the principal dredger of precedents for this political group: *The Substance of a Conference* (27 October 1641), pp. 3–5. St John's career is discussed extensively above, Ch. 5. It may also be significant that St John is to be found acting for the Sheriff of Essex, Sir Martin Lumley, a Warwick ally, in relation to the county's Ship Money in 1640: BL, Add. MS 25277.

191 BL, Add. MS 25266 (St John's legal notes), fo. 113v.

192 16 Car. I, *cap.* 1, § 2.

193 For the peers' reported willingness to summon a Parliament on their own authority, see above, pp. 56, 80, 82.

194 NA, SP 16/461/57/1: [anonymous letter] to Sir James Douglas, 28 July 1640; NA, SP 16/461/56: Sir John Conyers to Viscount Conway, 30 July 1640.

195 Cambridge UL, MS Mm. 1. 45 (Historical papers), p. 112: letter of intelligence from York to Matthew Wren, Bishop of Ely [*c.* 24–25 September 1640]. I owe this reference to Mr Christopher Thompson.

196 For a discussion of the literature accompanying the 1640 campaign, see Raymond, *Pamphlets and Pamphleteering*. I

am also grateful to Professor Malcolm Smuts for a discussion of this point.

197 Argyll's career is considered below, pp. 314–5.

198 Archibald Campbell, 8th Earl of Argyll, *An Honourable Speech made ... by the Earle of Argile* (September–October 1641), p. 1 (BL, E 199/17).

199 A number of these themes are persuasively developed in Arthur Williamson, 'Scotland and the Rise of Civic Culture, 1550–1650', *History Compass*, 4 (2006), 91–123; and see also his 'Patterns of British Identity: "Britain" and its Rivals in the Sixteenth and Seventeenth Centuries', in Glenn Burgess (ed.), *The New British History: Founding a Modern State 1603–1715* (1999), pp. 138–73; and Colin Kidd, *British Identities before Nationalism: Ethnicity and Nationhood in the Atlantic World, 1600–1800* (Cambridge, 1999). For the ideas of Union current within Argyll's circle, see below, Chs. 11 and 12.

200 Ireland's place, however, was regarded by both the Covenanters and the English godly 'reformists' as inferior to either England or Scotland; most future Parliamentarians in the English Parliament of November 1640 tended to regard it as wholly subordinate to, and incorporated within, the Crown of England – a stance, which, as we will see, helped provoke rebellion in Ireland in 1641; see above, pp. 374-6.

201 For this, see Chs. 11 and 12, above.

202 NA, SP 16/452, fo. 112v: Earl of Northumberland to Viscount Conway, 5 May 1640 (for the date in June); for the postponement, see Centre for Kentish Studies, De L'Isle MS U1475/C85/15: Earl of Northumberland to the Earl of Leicester, 21 May 1641. The rendezvous was postponed, Northumberland reported, 'till the middle of Aug[ust]; a season not so proper for the drawing an army into the field in these Northerne countries, and [if] I be not much deceaved we shall then be as unable to undertake this action as now we are, which must needes bring us into contempt abroad, and into disorders at home'. The news of the postponement was widely known.

203 New College Lib., Edinburgh University,

MS X15 b 3/1, volume I, fo. 263; [Saye], *Vindiciae Veritatis*, p. 29.

204 For the baggage train, see Trevor Royle, *Civil War: the Wars of the Three Kingdoms, 1638–60* (2004), p. 111; for Leslie's experience in Swedish service, see Grosjean, *Unofficial Alliance*.

205 Edinburgh UL, MS Dc. 4. 16 (Register of the Committee of Estates), fo. 1r-v.

206 Rushworth, *Historical Collections*, II, ii, 1223–7; see also Stevenson, *Scottish Revolution*, pp. 205–6.

207 Henry Percy reported it as 'past the worst' on 27 August; Centre for Kentish Studies, De L'Isle MS U1475/C86/15: Henry Percy to the Earl of Leicester (HMC, *De L'Isle Manuscripts*, VI, 319).

208 Centre for Kentish Studies, De L'Isle MS U1475/C86/15: Henry Percy to the Earl of Leicester, 27 August 1640 (HMC, *De L'Isle Manuscripts*, VI, 319).

209 For Strafford's appointment, see Centre for Kentish Studies, De L'Isle MS U1475/132/145: William Hawkins to the Earl of Leicester, 20 August 1640 (HMC, *De L'Isle Manuscripts*, VI, 317). Strafford was so weak in early July that he had to be carried as he ventured to take the air in the garden of Leicester House; he was still reported as 'sicke heere of the stone' on 30 July: HMC, *De L'Isle Manuscripts*, VI, 293, 308.

210 News of the Viceroy of Catalonia's assassination was current in Paris at the end of June: see HMC, *De L'Isle Manuscripts*, VI, 290.

211 The ironies of this extended further, however, than the simple question of the king's expectations of funding and military supplies. For without Strafford's expectation of Spanish gold, there is a strong possibility that Northumberland's counsel against a military campaign that summer would have prevailed, and that Charles would have been forced, either to renew the Pacification of Berwick and accept the Covenanter régime in Scotland for the foreseeable future, or to call another Parliament in order to complete the deal he had refused to conclude in May: the redress of grievances in exchange for parliamentary support for his war against the Scots. Either eventuality would have greatly reduced, and probably completely removed,

the circumstances in which it was feasible for a civil war to break out in England. We are in a highly speculative realm, but viewed in this broader context, it is at least arguable that the revolt of the Catalans is no less important than the revolt of the Covenanters in explaining why civil war in England became a serious probability after the summer of 1640; see Elliott, 'The Year of the Three Ambassadors'. In August, Strafford was hoping to raise the lesser sum of £50,000 – enough to fund the army for about six weeks; see Sharpe, *Personal Rule*, p. 899.

212 Stevenson, *Scottish Revolution*, pp. 208–9; Russell, *Fall of the British Monarchies*, p. 145.

213 Whitaker, *Life of Radcliffe*, p. 203: Strafford to Radcliffe, 1 September 1640.

214 This quotation is derived from Russell, *Fall of the British Monarchies*, p. 145, on whose conclusions this paragraph depends more generally.

2. THE FIRST REVOLT

1 [William Fiennes, 1st Viscount Saye and Sele], *Vindiciae Veritatis* (1654), p. 29 (BL, E 811/2).

2 NA, SP 16/465, fo. 111v: Windebank's notes of the Committee of War, 31 August 1640. The Whitehall gun platform had a field of fire that commanded the palace's most vulnerable point: the open street beside the Banqueting House leading northwards from the Holbein Gate to Charing Cross. For the location of the gun platform, see the map in John Adamson, 'The Tudor and Stuart Courts, 1509–1714', in *idem* (ed.), *The Princely Courts of Europe: Ritual, Politics, and Culture under the Ancien Régime, 1500–1750* (1999), p. 98. The royal bodyguard was also mobilized and ordered to be ready with horses, servants, and arms, to defend the queen and the royal children: NA, SP 16/465, fo. 107: Windebank's draft of the king's letter to the Earl of Salisbury (the Captain of the Gentlemen Pensioners), 31 August 1640. Valerie Pearl, *London and the Outbreak of the Puritan Revolution: City Government and National Politics, 1625–43*, (Oxford, 1961), p. 105.

3 For the Tower, see ASV, Senato, Dispacci Inghil. 42, fo. 118: Giustinian to the Doge

and Senate, 5/15 September 1640 (*CSPV 1640–42*, p. 77); and NA, SP 16/464, fo. 219: Windebank's notes of the Committee of War, 25 August 1640; NA, WO 49/72 (Ordnance Office papers), fos. 49, 50, 52; WO 55/455, pp. 71, 73. Windebank informed the king on 31 August that 'there is care taken by my Lord Cottington [the Constable of the fortress] of strengthening the Tower': Richard Scrope and T. Monkhouse (eds.), *State Papers Collected by Edward, Earl of Clarendon*, 3 vols (Oxford, 1767–86), II, 94–5: Sir Francis Windebank to Charles I, 31 August 1641.

4 NA, SP 16/465, fo. 111v: Windebank's notes of the Committee of War, 31 August 1640.

5 *Clarendon State Papers*, II, 94–5: Sir Francis Windebank to Charles I, 31 August 1641.

6 David Cressy, *England on Edge: Crisis and Revolution, 1640–42* (Oxford, 2006), pp. 110–26; and Keith Lindley, *Popular Politics and Religion in Civil War London* (1997), pp. 4–9.

7 *All the Memorable and Wonder-Striking Parliamentary Mercies . . . [of] 1641 and 1642* (1642), quoted in Cressy, *England on Edge*, p. 126; see also Lindley, *Popular Politics*, pp. 4–8.

8 Cressy, *England on Edge*, p. 125.

9 NA, SP 16/464, fo. 97v: Sir Francis Windebank's notes of Council proceedings, 26 August 1640.

10 Bodl. Lib., MS Clarendon 19, no. 1418: Sir Francis Windebank to the English ambassador in Madrid, 5 September 1640.

11 For Windebank, see Patricia Haskell, 'Sir Francis Windebank and the Personal Rule of Charles I' (unpublished Ph.D. dissertation, University of Southampton, 1978); and Kevin Sharpe, *The Personal Rule of Charles I* (New Haven and London, 1992), pp. 157–61. The best short biography is Brian Quintrell, 'Sir Francis Windebank', *ODNB*.

12 *Clarendon State Papers*, II, 94–5: Sir Francis Windebank to Charles I, 31 August 1641; NA, SP 16/464, fo. 98v: Windebank's notes of Privy Council business, 6 September 1640; SP 16/467/53.

13 For the City's attempts, in June, to petition the king over grievances and for the calling of a Parliament, see Pearl, *London*, pp. 108–9.

14 *Clarendon State Papers*, II, 94–5: Sir Francis Windebank to Charles I, 31 August 1641.

15 NA, CO 124/2 (Providence Island Company minutes), pp. 374–81 (I owe this reference to Mr Christopher Thompson).

16 Ibid. BL, Harl. MS 383, fo. 174 (for Sir John Seton). On the contacts between the Covenanters and their English friends, see also NLS, MS Wodrow Folio 64, fo. 203: 'Instructiones for James Murray'; Baillie, *Letters*, I, 275; Peter Donald, *An Uncounselled King: Charles I and the Scottish Troubles, 1637–41* (Cambridge, 1990), p. 246.

17 NA, CO 124/2 (Providence Island Company minutes), pp. 374–81 (I owe this reference to Mr Christopher Thompson).

18 *Clarendon State Papers*, II, 94–5; compare Windebank's notes of the Council meeting of 30 August, NA, SP 16/465/56.

19 NA, SP 16/465, fo. 111: Windebank's notes of the Committee of War, 31 August 1640.

20 [John Oldmixon], *The History of England during the Reigns of the Royal House of Stuart* (1730), p. 143.

21 [Oldmixon], *History*, p. 144: Lord Savile to [Lord Loudoun], [8 July 1640].

22 Above, p. 48.

23 For the dating of this meeting, see *Clarendon State Papers*, II, 111 Sir Francis Windebank to the king, 7 September 1640.

24 NA, SP 16/464, fo. 98: Windebank's notes of Privy Council proceedings; *Clarendon State Papers*, II, 94–5: Sir Francis Windebank to Charles I, 31 August 1640.

25 New College Lib., Edinburgh, MS X15b 3/1, vol. I, fo. 262: Bedford and other Petitioners to the [Covenanter leadership], c. 5 September 1640; printed in Peter Donald, 'New Light on the Anglo-Scottish Contacts of 1640', *Historical Research*, 62 (1989), 228–9. There is an apparent anomaly in that Mandeville's and Howard of Escrick's names both appear as signatories to this letter of c. 5 September, originating in London, despite the fact that they had already departed at least a couple of days earlier in order to present the

Petition to the king. The most obvious resolution to this is that the letter was forwarded to them in Yorkshire, and that they signed it there before passing it on to the Scots. There was much forwarding and circulation of documents for signature at this time (see Appendix); and where large numbers of signatories are listed as signing petitions or letters it is not necessarily the case that all signatures were affixed at the same time.

26 [Saye], *Vindiciae Veritatis*, p. 29; my emphasis.

27 Peter Heylyn, *Aerius Redivivus or, the History of the Presbyterians* (Oxford, 1670), pp. 437–8. I am grateful to Dr David Scott for this reference.

28 NA, SP 16/465, fo. 111: Windebank's notes of the Council of War, 31 August 1640.

29 For Wharton's addition to the list of signatures see BL, Add. MS 44848 (Historical papers), fos. 283v–84. Copies of the Petition of the Twelve that have Wharton's name among the additional signatories also tend to be 'signed' by Lord North, the Earl of Lincoln, and Lord Savile, and it is tempting to think that a messenger, riding north, gathered these additional signatures *en route*, respectively, in Cambridgeshire, Lincolnshire, and Yorkshire (where Savile and Wharton signed); for the variant lists, see Appendix.

30 Gilbert Burnet, *History of My Own Time*, ed. Osmund Airy, 2 vols. (Oxford, 1897), I, 45–6; this is the source for the account in Roger Acherley, *The Britannic Constitution: or, the Fundamental Form of Government in Britain* (1727), p. 408 (for the two quotations). This story is rendered only slightly less plausible by Acherley's mistaken claim that, in delivering the Petition, Lord Howard of Escrick was accompanied by Lord Wharton (instead of Viscount Mandeville). Wharton seems to have been involved in the separate Yorkshire petition (organized in support of the objectives of the Twelve); for Wharton and his links with Bedford, and the dissident Yorkshire gentry, see G. F. Trevallyn Jones, *Saw-Pit Wharton: the Political Career from 1640 to 1691 of Philip, Fourth Lord Wharton* (Sydney, 1967), pp. 22–4, 25–7, 31–3.

31 ASV, Senato, Dispacci Inghil. 42, fo. 117v: Giustinian to the Doge and Senate, 5/15 September 1640: 'alt[r]imenti gli protestano

di chiamarlo dà se stessi ad oggetto di muovere travagli magg[iori] alla loro Patria' (cf. *CSPV 1640–42*, p. 77). See also, Rusell, *Fall of the British Monarchies*, p. 150, The original dispatch strongly suggests that Giustinian's source for this information was the queen and the Privy Council ('ministers').

32 *Clarendon State Papers*, II, 111: Windebank to Charles I, 7 September 1640.

33 The authoritative text of the petition would appear to be NA, SP 16/465, fo. 33, a copy endorsed in the hand of Edward Nicholas, the Privy Council clerk; for other discussions of its significance, see Gardiner, *History of England*, IX, 199. It is printed in his *Constitutional Documents*, pp. 134–6, although Gardiner has arranged the signatures – supposedly in 'order of precedence' – in the wrong order.

34 NA, SP 16/465, fo. 111r-v: Windebank's notes of the Committee of War, 31 August 1640. Windebank's memorandum that they should seek the king's advice on what was to be done in the event of the peers in London joining in a petition immediately follows on from a discussion of how important it was for the Council to prise Essex away from Saye and Brooke, and of the Council's orders for Whitehall to be garrisoned and provided with artillery. For his anxieties about the forthcoming City muster, see *Clarendon State Papers*, II, 95: WINDEBANK TO CHARLES I, 31 AUGUST 1640.

35 Russell, *Fall of the British Monarchies*, p. 147, seriously underestimates the severity of the threat posed to the régime by the events of late August–early September 1640, both in reality and as it was perceived by contemporaries; and completely overlooks the Privy Council's withdrawal from the capital. The Council, with its extensive intelligence system, was perhaps better able to assess the reality of that threat than a late-twentieth-century historian.

36 Cressy, *England on Edge*, pp. 125–6, and p. 116 (for the quotation).

37 New College Lib., Edinburgh, MS X15b 3/1, vol. I, fo. 262: N[athaniel] F[iennes] to the [Covenanter leadership], *c.* 3 September 1640 (Donald, 'New Light on Anglo-Scottish Contacts', p. 227).

38 New College Lib., Edinburgh, MS X15b

3/1, vol. 1, fo. 262: Bedford and other Petitioners to the [Covenanter leadership], *c.* 5 September 1640 (Donald, 'New Light on Anglo-Scottish Contacts', p. 229). The version of this letter surviving in the New College MSS has been modified by the Scottish copyist so that some of the pronouns that were in the first person in the original have been rendered in the third person in the copy. Hence, as Donald notes (ibid., p. 222), the versions we have here 'are not truly transcriptions, but they are more than paraphrases'. Except where there is any ambiguity about reading, I have reinstated the first-person forms in my quotations for this manuscript, rendering editorial modifications in square brackets.

39 New College Lib., Edinburgh, MS X15b 3/1, vol. 1, fo. 262: N[athaniel] F[iennes] to the [Covenanter leadership], *c.* 3 September 1640 (Donald, 'New Light on Anglo-Scottish Contacts', p. 227).

40 On this theme, see above, pp. 194, 225, 336, and for the word's republican associations, see the remarks of David Wootton, 'Oxbridge Model', in *The Times Literary Supplement*, 23 September 2005. On the later usage of the term, see David Wootton, 'Introduction : the Republican Tradition: from Commonwealth to Common Sense', in *idem* (ed.), *Republicanism, Liberty, and Commercial Society, 1649–1776* (Stanford, CA, 1994), pp. 1–41, 407–15.

41 Centre for Kentish Studies, De L'Isle MS U1475/C85/15: Earl of Northumberland to the Earl of Leicester, 18 June 1640 (HMC, *De L'Isle Manuscripts*, VI, pp. 284–5). On the mutinous state of the armies see also, Cressy, *England on Edge*, pp. 86–90.

42 One of the questions that Arundel, Windebank, and Cottington (the Constable of the Tower) had discussed at a meeting in the Tower on 25 August was 'Why the Essex men are not dismist[?]': NA, SP 16/464, fo. 219. See also, Beinecke Lib., Osborn Shelves Fb 111: George Brown to [?], 1 September 1640; New College Lib., Edinburgh, MS X15b 3/1, vol. 1, fo. 262: Bedford and other Petitioners to the [Covenanter leadership], *c.* 5 September 1640 (Donald, 'New Light on Anglo-Scottish Contacts', p. 229). Warwick was joint Lord Lieutenant with the Laudian 1st Lord Maynard, a diarchy that must have been uncomfortable for both men; see NA, SP 16/465, fo. 145. But there seems little

doubt that Warwick was the dominant figure in the partnership. (I am grateful to Mr Christopher Thompson for his advice on this point.)

43 For the state of the Yorkshire Trained Bands, see David Scott, '"Hannibal at our Gates": Loyalists and Fifth-Columnists during the Bishops' Wars – the Case of Yorkshire', *Historical Research*, 70 (1997), 269–93.

44 Cambridge UL, MS Mm. 1. 45 (Historical papers), pp. 99, 112: letter of intelligence to Dr Matthew Wren, Dean of the Chapel Royal, from York [*c.* 24–25 September 1640].

45 For Boynton's connections with Viscount Saye, see Bodl. Lib., MS Rawlinson d. 892 (Saye estate papers), fos. 72, 82, in addition to the references cited by Scott, 'Loyalists and Fifth-Columnists during the Bishops' Wars'.

46 Scott, 'Loyalists and Fifth-Columnists during the Bishops' Wars', p. 279; Scott, 'Henry Darley' (unpublished biography, HPL). In the late 1620s, Darley had been involved in a clandestine network of godly gentlemen which promoted the writing, printing, and distribution of Puritan treatises, and whose members included two other members of Warwick's network, Sir John Clotworthy and Richard Knightley of Fawsley: Sheffield UL, Hartlib Papers, 50H/23/2/17A-18B (I owe this reference to Dr Jason Peacey). For Wharton's signature to the Petition of the Twelve, see (among other copies) BL, Add. MS 44848, fos. 283v–84; and Northamptonshire RO, Finch-Hatton MS 2619.

47 Scott, 'Loyalists and Fifth-Columnists during the Bishops' Wars', pp. 282–92. 'The [dissident] peers' skill', Dr Scott has concluded, 'in exploiting the parochial grievances of the Yorkshire gentry during the summer of 1640, undoubtedly contributed much to the successful outcome of their design'; ibid., p. 292. For evidence of Wharton, Cholmley, Hotham, and Henry Belasyse, see Trevallyn Jones, *Wharton*, pp. 22–3.

48 *HMC Fourth Report*, p. 30; *LJ*, IV, 100–1;

49 This concern to avoid bloodshed emerges in both Fiennes's letter of *circa* 3 September and the letter from Bedford and his fellow Petitioners, sent a few days later: New College Lib., Edinburgh, MS X15b 3/1, vol. 1, fos.

262–3 (Donald, 'New Light on Anglo-Scottish Contacts', pp. 226–9).

50 Whether all twelve of the Petitioners were aware of the extent of these plans is open to question, but it seems safe to assume that the group privy to them included the eight signatories of the overtly treasonous letter of advice to the Scots sent after the capture of Newcastle (Earls of Bedford, Hertford, Bolingbroke, Exeter, and Lords Saye, Mandeville, Howard of Escrick and Brooke). They also probably included Warwick and Essex, both of whom signed the earlier letter inviting the Scots to invade, and whose popularity and military experience made them obvious commanders for any army 'for the Commonwealth'. This would leave only the Earl of Mulgrave, the Armada veteran, and the Earl of Rutland, the survivor of the Essex Rebellion of 1601, the two most elderly of the Petitioners, the extent of whose involvement in the plans for military resistance is unknown. In the case of the others, however, the daring – indeed, almost the recklessness – that is involved in their plans needs hardly to be stressed.

51 New College Lib., Edinburgh, MS X15b 3/1, vol. I, fo. 262: N[athaniel] F[iennes] to the [Covenanter leadership], c. 3 September 1640 (Donald, 'New Light on Anglo-Scottish Contacts', p. 227); and see also Donald, Uncounselled King, pp. 248–9. Even so, it is hard to see how the most carefully selected of Scottish rescue forces could have assisted the London-based Petitioners had the Privy Council succeeded in arresting them and securing their persons (presumably in the Tower).

52 [Oldmixon], History of England, p. 144: Lord Savile to John [Lord Loudoun], [8 July 1640].

53 BL, Add. MS 11045 (Scudamore correspondence), fo. 144v: [Edward Rossingham's] newsletter, 25 November 1640.

54 Bodl. Lib., MS Clarendon 19, fo. 25: Sir Francis Windebank to Charles I, 7 September 1640 (Clarendon State Papers, II, 110).

55 NA, SP 16/465, fo. 111: Windebank's notes of the Committee of War, 31 August 1640; for the committee's concerns about the City's imminent musters.

56 NA, SP 16/464, fo. 97v: Windebank's notes of business, 26 August 1640.

57 NA, SP 16/465, fo. 111: Windebank's notes of the Committee of War, 31 August 1640; NA, SP 16/465, fo. 52: the Earl of Hertford (at Tottenham) to the Council, 28 August 1640, presenting a series of pretexts as to why he could not go to Somerset to execute his commission of lieutenancy. Bedford was similarly disobedient.

58 NA, SP 16/464, fo. 98v: this proposal had first emerged on 26 August, when the question had been raised before the Privy Councillors 'Whether it will not be fit to call som of the Country nobility to the Boord'.

59 NA, SP 16/466, fo. 7: Windebank's notes, 1 September 1640 (for the quotation); Clarendon State Papers, II, 97–8.

60 Kevin Sharpe, 'The Earl of Arundel, his Circle, and the Opposition to the Duke of Buckingham, 1618–28', in idem (ed.), Faction and Parliament: Essays on Early Stuart History (Oxford, 1978), p. 234. The only modern biography of Arundel is David Howarth, Lord Arundel and his Circle (New Haven and London, 1985).

61 I infer this from the Committee of War's decision to use Arundel, after he had been added to the Committee, as their mediator with Bedford in early September 1640, and from Bedford's angry response when he believed that Arundel had disclosed confidences to the Privy Council – in particular, information about Bedford's own involvement in the Petition of the Twelve – which Bedford had imparted to Arundel 'as a friend'. NA, SP 16/465, fo. 111: Windebank's notes of the Committee of War, 31 August 1640; Clarendon State Papers, II, 111–12: Windebank to Charles I, 9 September 1640. In February 1641, Arundel was one of the principal supporters of the Triennial Bill – the central element of Bedford's scheme for a constitutional settlement – and Arundel accompanied Bedford to Whitehall on 15 February 1641, when the bill was presented to the king for the royal assent; LJ, IV, 162. It is also noteworthy that Arundel's property was protected during the Civil War by Viscount Saye, and the earl himself retained his entitlement to sit in the parliamentarian House of Lords until his death in 1646.

62 NA, SP 16/464, fo. 219: Windebank's

notes of the Committee of War at the Tower, 25 August 1640; SP 16/464, fo. 97v: Windebank's working notes, 26 August 1640.

63 NA, SP 16/464, fo. 219: Windebank's notes of the Committee of War, 25 August 1640; SP 16/465, fo. 111: Windebank's notes of the Committee of War, 31 August 1640.

64 Quoted in *Complete Peerage*, I, 257n.

65 *Clarendon State Papers*, II, 94–5: Sir Francis Windebank to Charles I, 31 August 1640 (for the quotation); see also NA, SP 16/465, fo. 111: Windebank's notes of the Committee of War, 31 August 1640. Windebank adds cryptically: 'Lords Say and Brooke another time'.

66 Beinecke Lib., MS Osborn Shelves Fb 111: George Brown to [?], 1 September 1640; my emphasis.

67 New College Lib., Edinburgh, MS X15b 3/1, vol. 1, fo. 262: N[athaniel] F[iennes] to the [Covenanter leadership], c. 3 September 1640 (Donald, 'New Light on Anglo-Scottish Contacts', p. 227).

68 Pearl, *London*, p. 14; Roger A. P. Finlay, *Population and Metropolis: the Demography of London, 1580–1650* (Cambridge, 1981); Vanessa Harding, 'The Population of Early Modern London: a Review of the Published Evidence', *London Journal*, 15 (1990), 118–28.

69 Pearl, *London*, pp. 104–5.

70 *Clarendon State Papers*, II, 95: Windebank to Charles I, 31 August 1640.

71 For the information that it was probably this 'new' Artillery Ground that was in use in 1640, rather than the old ground (on what is now Spitalfields Market), I am indebted to Mr James Armstrong, Archivist of the Honourable Artillery Company, London. For the size of the company, approved by the Privy Council in 1614, see Pearl, *London*, p. 171.

72 The earliest surviving account of a 'General [Muster] Day' surviving in the company's archives dates from 1658, and describes a tripartite format of military muster at the Artillery Ground, followed by a march to the church where the sermon was to be preached, followed in turn by a dinner in a livery company hall (in the 1658 case, Merchant Taylors'). This format would seem to have been in place as early as 1638 (which

also finished with a dinner in Merchant Taylors' Hall), and can probably be assumed to be the basic arrangement for Artillery Company 'General Days' during the 1640s. See Armoury House, London, Honourable Artillery Company Archives, Court Book A (1657–61), pp. 41–2; compare William Barriff, *Mars his Triumph. Or, the Description of an Exercise performed the xviii of October, 1638, in Merchant-Taylors Hall* (1639), which gives an account of the final element of the 1638 General Day. For another example of the almost theatrical quality which these annual musters had acquired by the 1640s in the City more generally, see *Scotish Dove*, no. 134 (13–20 May 1646), p. [664] (BL, E 337/28); *Moderate Intelligencer*, no. 63 (14–21 May 1646), p. 453 (BL, E 337/32).

73 I am grateful to Mr James Armstrong, the Archivist of the Honourable Artillery Company, for advice on the questions of its annual musters.

74 [Sir John Berkenhead], *A Letter from Mercurius Civicus to Mercurius Rusticus, or, Londons Confession* (Oxford, [25 August] 1643), p. 4 (BL, E 65/32).

75 G. A. Raikes, *The Ancient Vellum Book of the Honourable Artillery Company, being the Roll of Members from 1611–82* (1890), p. 40. For the history of the company see G. Gould Walker, *The Honourable Artillery Company* (1926), and G.A. Raikes, *The History of the Honourable Artillery Company*, 2 vols. (1878). For the 'missing' records for the period before 1657, see Anon., 'The Lost Records', *Journal of the Honourable Artillery Company*, 10 (1932–3), 379.

76 Armoury House, London, Honourable Artillery Company Archives, Quarterage Book 1628–43, unfol., 'Prayse Barebone', *s.v.*, entries for quarterage, from 1633. Raikes, *Vellum Book*, p. 42.

77 Armoury House, London, Honourable Artillery Company Archives, Quarterage Book 1628–43, unfol., 'Thomas Juckson' or 'Juxon', *s.v.* quarterage entries from 1635.

78 Armoury House, London, Honourable Artillery Company Archives, Quarterage Book 1628–43, unfol., 'Richard Overton', *s.v.*, entries from 1632.

79 Raikes, *Vellum Book*, p. 20; Armoury

House, London, Honourable Artillery Company Archives, Quarterage Book 1628–43, unfol., 'John Venn', *s.v.*, entries from 1635

80 [Berkenhead], *A Letter from Mercurius Civicus to Mercurius Rusticus*, p. 4; Robert Ashton, *The City and the Court, 1603–43* (Cambridge, 1979), pp. 174–5. For the question of authorship of *A Letter*, see Pearl, *London*, p. 133; P. W. Thomas, *Sir John Berkenhead, 1617–79: a Royalist Career in Politics and Polemics* (Oxford, 1969), pp. 107–8.

81 [Berkenhead], *A Letter from Mercurius Civicus to Mercurius Rusticus*, p. 9. Quotations in this book are from this edition. Thomason's copy, printed at London in the same month is BL, E 65/32.

82 Raikes, *Vellum Book*, p. 55; his name was entered in letters of gold: 18 October 1638; for the spelling of his name, see his letter to Lady Vere of Tilbury, [undated]: BL, Add. MS 4276 (Letters of divines), fo. 137; for his career, see Barbara Donagan, 'Obadiah Sedgwick [*sic*]', *ODNB*.

83 For their respective careers, see John Morrill, 'Robert Devereux, 3rd Earl of Essex', and Ian Gentles, 'Philip Skippon', in *ODNB*.

84 Essex bequeathed Skippon his armour and gauntlets under the terms of his 1642 will: BL, Add. MS 46189 (Jessop papers), fo. 153; see also, LMA, City Cash Book 1/4, fo. 227v.

85 Ashton, *The City and The Court*, pp. 174–5; Pearl, *London*, p. 173. For Skippon, see also the reference to him in Beinecke Lib., Osborn Shelves Fb 64, folder 15: Walter Strickland to John Pym, 1 November 1642.

86 [Robert Chestlin], *Persecutio Undecima* ([5 Nov.] 1648), p. 56 (BL, E 470/7). Unfortunately, the Company Minutes of the Artillery Company only begin in 1657 (those for earlier periods being currently lost, and possibly destroyed in the Great Fire of 1666). However, there is a sidelight on the internal politics of the company in 1645, at the time of the Self-Denying Ordinance, which would suggest that the presidency of the company was, at times, fiercely contested: LMA, Repertories 57, fo. 94 (second series of foliation).

87 Armoury House, London, Honourable Artillery Company Archives, Quarterage

Book 1628–43, unfol., 'William Bridges', *s.v.*, entries from 1642; for Bridges, see Hughes, *Warwickshire*, p. 301.

88 Donagan, 'Obadiah Sedgwick', *ODNB*; Obadiah Sedgwicke, *Military Discipline for the Christian Souldier Drawne out in a Sermon Preached to the Captaines and Souldiers Exercising Armes in the Artillery Garden, at their Generall Meeting in Saint Andrew's Undershaft, in London, October 18. 1638* (1639) STC 22152. This meeting was also accompanied by a masque-like entertainment presented in the Merchant Taylors' Hall, an account of which was published as [William Barriff], *Mars his Triumph. Or, the Description of an Exercise performed the* XVIII *of October, 1638* (1639), STC 1505. See also, Harold Smith, *The Ecclesiastical History of Essex under the Long Parliament and Commonwealth* (Colchester, n.d. [1936]), p. 310.

89 Calybute Downinge, *A Sermon Preached to the Renowned Company of the Artillery, 1 September, 1640*, (1641), title page (BL, E 157/4). Daniel Lysons, *The Environs of London*, 4 vols. (1795–96), II, 483–4, 491.

90 C[alybute] D[owning], *A Discourse of the State Ecclesiastical of this Kingdome* (Oxford, 1633), p. 46. At the time of the work's composition, Downinge was a household chaplain to Salisbury. On Downinge (1606–44), see Barbara Donagan's biography in the *ODNB*; he matriculated at Emmanuel College, Cambridge in 1623, then migrated to Oriel College, Oxford, where he took his BA in 1626. He returned to Cambridge where, ironically, he entered Peterhouse, an ultra-Laudian bastion, where he proceeded to his MA in 1630 and, in 1637, to the degree of Doctor of Laws. How Downinge came to be appointed as preacher is difficult to establish in the absence of the company's Court Books for this period. But one possible connection is through Mary, Lady Vere of Tilbury, the widow of Lord Vere of Tilbury, whose patronage obtained for Downinge the living of Hackney in 1637. Skippon had served in Lord Vere's regiment on the Continent in the 1630s, and may well have encountered Downinge through the widow of his former commanding officer. For Downinge's will, see NA, PROB 11/192, qu. 15; see also Brian P. Levack, *The Civil Lawyers in England, 1603–41* (Oxford, 1973) p.225

91 [Berkenhead], *A Letter from Mercurius Civicus to Mercurius Rusticus*, p. 8.

92 Downinge, *Sermon Preached to the Company of the Artillery*, pp. 30–1. For the reaction, see [Berkenhead], *A Letter from Mercurius Civicus to Mercurius Rusticus*, p. 8.

93 [Berkenhead], A Letter from Mercurius Civicus to Mercurius Rusticus, p. 8.

94 For the evidential problems relating to the variance between the printed and the 'delivered' versions of seventeenth-century sermons, see Peter E. McCullough, *Sermons at Court: Politics and Religion in Elizabethan and Jacobean Preaching* (Cambridge, 1998).

95 Downinge, *Sermon Preached to the Company of Artillery*, pp. 2–3, 6–7, 11–13.

96 Ibid., p. 2; compare also pp. 28–9.

97 Ibid., p. 10.

98 Ibid., p. 13.

99 Ibid. Addressing the assembled citizen-soldiers – the 'Chief Legionaries of this royall City' – Downinge posed four questions: 'First, see if you have not such condition'd Enemies [as the Amalekites]. Secondly, whether there be not Records and Acts of State [legal precedents that would justify their punishment] entered against them. Thirdly, if there be not reason to petition the execution of them'. The central problem, however, was what should happen if – as seemed likely – such a petition were rejected. This prompted Downinge to pose a fourth question: might 'you be not to be blamed for forgetting [the Amalekites]', he asked, if they failed to resist these evil counsellors now? Compare ibid., p. 33: These latter-day Amalekites, Downinge claimed, were 'in the Commonwealth, but not of it, … fully and fouly against it, knotted into a great party, tied in dependance to the greatest forrein Enemy [Catholic Spain], … [striking] at Church and State … a blow, … [seeing] the anchor of the State is religion, which, if shaken, the State will float [away], and for fundamentall Lawes, they pull them up, that they may pull us down'.

100 Downinge, *Sermon Preached to the Company of Artillery*, p. 25 (*recte*, p. 35).

101 Ibid., pp. 36–7.

102 Ibid., p. 37. The quotation is from Hugo

Grotius, *De iure belli et pacis* (Paris, 1625).

103 Downinge, *Sermon Preached to the Company of Artillery*, pp. 37–8.

104 Ibid., p. 32 [*recte* p. 38].

105 [Berkenhead], *A Letter from Mercurius Civicus to Mercurius Rusticus*, p. 8.

106 Armoury House, London, Honourable Artillery Company Archives, Quarterage Book 1628–43, unfol., 'Sir Paul Pindar', *s.v.*; see also Brenner, *Merchants and Revolution*, pp. 305–6.

107 Armoury House, London, Honourable Artillery Company Archives, Quarterage Book 1628–43, unfol., 'Sir Nicholas Crispe [*sic*]', *s.v.*; see also Brenner, *Merchants and Revolution*, pp. 163–4, for Crisp's interest in the Guinea Company. For the correct spelling of his name, Bodl. Lib., MS Tanner, fo. 672.

108 [Berkenhead], *A Letter from Mercurius Civicus to Mercurius Rusticus*, pp. 8–9. For Marshall's connections with Warwick, see NA, SP 16/449/48, printed in John Nalson, *An Impartiall Collection of the Great Affairs of State*, 2 vols. (1682), I, 269 (*recte* 279); and see Tom Webster, *Stephen Marshall and Finchingfield* (Studies in Essex History, 6, Chelmsford, 1994), p. 17 (I am grateful to Mr Christopher Thompson for drawing my attention to this pamphlet); and Tom Webster, 'Stephen Marshall', *ODNB*.

109 In other respects, however, the account by *Mercurius Civicus* tallies with what can be gleaned from other sources. The claim that Downinge 'retired privately' to Leez under Warwick's protection would accord with what is known of Warwick's movements at this time. The earl, who was in London on 28 August, made a brief visit to his Essex country house in the course of the following week; he is reported as being at Leez on Thursday, 3 September (two days after the Artillery Company muster, though he had probably arrived slightly earlier), and as intending to return to Warwick House in London on Saturday the 5th. The evidence is not conclusive, but it would be at least consistent with Warwick having made a short trip at this time to convey Downinge safely out of the capital and install him in the security of his country retreat. NA, SP 16/464, fos. 97v-98: Windebank's Privy Council notes, 31 August 1640; Lancashire RO, Hulton of Hulton MS,

DDHu/46/21: John Pym to William Jessop, from Leez, 3 September 1640.

110 *Clarendon State Papers*, II, 96: Windebank to Charles I, 1 September 1640, from Arundel House; NA, SP 16/464, fo. 98: Windebank's notes of Council business, 2 September 1640. Compare his memoranda for 1 September, in which he notes 'An Army to be in a redinesse heere to back the King's forces in case of disaster': SP 16/466, fo. 7.

111 NA, SP 16/464, fo. 98: Windebank's notes of business and correspondence, 2 September 1640.

112 Bodl. Lib., MS Radcliffe Trust c. 32, fo. 2: Sir Francis Windebank to Charles I, 2 September 1640 (summarized in *Calendar of the Clarendon State Papers*, v, 722–3); I am grateful to Mr Christopher Thompson for alerting me to this reference, and to Dr David Scott for providing me with a transcription.

113 *Clarendon State Papers*, II, 98: Windebank to Charles I, 3 September 1640.

114 NA, SP 16/464, fo. 98r-v: Windebank's notes of business and correspondence, 2 September 1640.

115 *Clarendon State Papers*, II, 98: Windebank to Charles I, 3 September 1640. Interestingly, by this stage, the Secretary seems no longer to be distinguishing between English and Scottish 'Rebels': the opposing parties were now 'your own Lords' and, by implication, those lords who refused to side with the king and were clearly in league with the Scottish Covenanters.

116 Bodl. Lib., MS Clarendon 19, no. 1418: Sir Francis Windebank to the English ambassador in Madrid, 5 September 1640.

117 They were unable to send 'mony and victuals' from London, as the Scots had evidently requested; but, they wrote, 'we suppose Newcastle, Durham and the countrie about may afford you victuals for more than 14 dayes': Donald, 'New Light on Anglo-Scottish Contacts', pp. 228–9.

118 'All the king's forces', wrote Bedford and his friends, 'ar 24,000 foott and a [further] 1,700 horse – Trained Bands and all – whereof few ar able to feght, and non[e] willing [to do so], and many officers and others [are] full of feares. And the more Traine[d] Bands comes, the more for your advantage. Assure yourself:

9 regiments commanders have given ther words [and] 9 coronells of the Trained Bands hes declared they will joyne with [us] lords upon [our] declaratioun . . .' New College Lib., Edinburgh, MS X15b 3/1, vol. 1, fo. 263: Bedford and other peers to the [Covenanter leadership], *c.* 5 September 1640 (Donald, 'New Light on Anglo-Scottish Contacts', pp. 228–9). The five other named signatories were Hertford, Bolingbroke, Exeter, Mulgrave, and Howard of Escrick. The absence of Warwick's signature from this letter suggests that it may well have been dispatched before his return from Leez. An alternative possibility is that Warwick did sign, but that his name was omitted by the copyist. Mandeville and Howard of Escrick must have been sent the letter in York, where they were around 5 September.

119 New College Lib., Edinburgh, MS X15b 3/1, vol. 1, fo. 262: N[athaniel] F[iennes] to the [Covenanter leadership], *c.* 3 September 1640 (Donald, 'New Light on Anglo-Scottish Contacts', p. 227).

120 By the chance survival of a letter, written by John Pym from Leez on 3 September – Lancashire RO, Hulton of Hulton MS, DDHu/46/21: John Pym to William Jessop – we are able to reconstruct in some detail the sequence of events that led up to the Petition's publication, a process that also provides us with a rare insight into the relationships of power and influence within the Twelve. The initial stages of the process can only be established highly speculatively, but from the timing of the eventual decision to publish it is clear that the Petitioners deferred publication of their Petition-cum-'remonstrance' until after news of the Scottish victory at Newburn had reached London (around Tuesday, 1 September), and until they had had a chance to assess the response to Downinge's call to arms at the Artillery Company muster (held that same day). What appears to have happened then is that Saye, Brooke and the other Petitioners in London took the decision to publish, in principle, within forty-eight hours of the Artillery Company muster – around Wednesday, 2 or Thursday, 3 September. Unwilling, however, to go ahead without first consulting Warwick, who was then at Leez, someone (Brooke?) appears to have despatched Pym to seek the earl's approval – though it must again be stressed that much of this reconstruction is highly

provisional. Jessop was warned in the letter to expect Warwick's arrival back in London on Saturday, 5 September. (I am grateful to Mr Christopher Thompson for a correspondence on Warwick's movements during this period.)

121 For some of Jessop's secretarial duties during the 1630s, and the network of 'godly' investors with whom he worked, see BL, Add. MS 10615 (Jessop letter-book), and its deciphering, BL, Add. MS 63854, at, for example, fos. 147, 151, 246.

122 Lancashire RO, Hulton of Hulton MS, DDHu/46/21: John Pym to William Jessop, from Leez, 3 September 1640 (for quotation). This letter reveals a mostly familiar network. Clotworthy, as we have seen, was the Anglo-Ulsterman who had first discussed the dissident peers' efforts to organize a petition back in 1638, and for whom Warwick was shortly to arrange an English parliamentary seat: Maldon, in Essex, the constituency which the earl himself had represented earlier in the century. Similarly, there is little doubt that 'Mr Sterry', to whom Jessop was to provide copies of the Petition (presumably for distribution), was Peter Sterry, Lord Brooke's domestic chaplain, who resided only a few hundred yards away at Brooke House in Holborn. Once again, however, it is Warwick's residences that appear to have been the decision-making centres of the oppositionist movement, with Leez the venue whence issued the decision to publish, and Warwick House in Holborn providing the secretarial wherewithal to see that this was done. (This apparent cooperation between Warwick House and Brooke House in the arrangements for publishing the peers' 'remonstrance' against evil counsellors is worth noting: as we shall see, when the campaign for justice against the worst of them – Strafford – reached its climax, this same Warwick–Brooke axis would once again come to the fore.) For Clotworthy, see NLS, MS Wodrow Folio 66, fos. 109–10: [Sir John Clotworthy, unsigned holograph letter] to [Archibald Jhonston of Wariston], 11 July 1638; see also CSPV 1636–39, pp. 124–5: Anzolo Correr to the Doge and Senate of Venice, 6/16 January 1637. For Warwick's efforts on Clotworthy's behalf to win a parliamentary seat, see Donald, Uncounselled King, pp. 192, 194. For Sterry, see Blair Worden, 'Toleration and the Cromwellian

Protectorate', in William J. Sheils (ed.), Persecution and Toleration: Papers read at the Twenty-second Summer Meeting and the Twenty-third Winter Meeting of the Ecclesiastical History Society (Oxford, 1984), pp. 199–233, at 208n.

123 Below, note 38 to Ch. 3.

124 Peter Sterry (1613–72), a Fellow of Emmanuel College, Cambridge, from 1637 to 1639, had been strongly influenced in Cambridge by the Platonist, Benjamin Whichcote. He resigned his fellowship to become Brooke's household chaplain in 1639, and in February 1641 was to marry another member of the household, Frances Asheworth. It is likely that Sterry was one source for the Platonism evident in Brooke's own published writings, particularly his A Discourse opening the Nature of that Episcopacie which is exercised in England (1641), BL, E 177/22; see also, Nabil Matar, 'Peter Sterry', ODNB. Brooke's privy purse accounts contain a number of references to Sterry, including one involving moneys paid to 'Mr Dillingham … by my Lord's appointment p[er] [i.e. through] Mr Sterrye, for intelligence': Warwickshire RO, OR 1886/CUP.4/21A (John Halford's Accounts, I), unfol., 'Gifts'.

125 Holborn was a fashionable aristocratic quartier. By December 1642, William Pierrepont – a younger son of the 1st Earl of Kingston, and prominent Parliamentarian – was living in a house in Holborn 'over against [i.e. directly opposite] Warwick House': Bodl. Lib., MS Nalson 11, fo. 229v (I owe this reference to Dr David Scott).

126 NA, SP 16/464, fo. 98v.

127 Clarendon State Papers, II, 112: Windebank to Charles I, 7 September 1640.

128 For the date of Warwick's return, see Lancashire RO, Hulton of Hulton MS, DDHu/46/21: John Pym to William Jessop, from Leez, 3 September 1640.

129 New College Lib., Edinburgh, MS X15b 3/1, vol. I, fo. 263: Bedford and other peers to the [Covenanter leadership], c. 5 September 1640 (Donald, 'New Light on Anglo-Scottish Contacts', p. 228).

130 NA, SP 16/464, fos. 98v.–99: Windebank's notes of Privy Council business, 6 September 1640; see also Clarendon State

Papers, II, 110–12: Windebank to Charles I, 7 September 1640.

131 NA, SP 16/464, fo. 98v: Windebank's notes of the Privy Council, 6 September 1640; SP 16/466/75: Windebank's notes of business, 7 September 1640; printed in John Bruce (ed.), *Notes of the Treaty carried on at Ripon between King Charles and the Covenanters of Scotland, A.D. 1640, taken by Sir J. Borough, Garter King of Arms* (Camden Society, 1869), p. 79.

132 Finch was Lord Keeper of the Great Seal.

133 Bodl. Lib., MS Clarendon 19, fos. 24–5: Sir Francis Windebank to Charles I, 7 September 1640 (*Clarendon State Papers*, II, 110–12). The fact that the question was asked at all can be read as suggesting that the Council's agents had intercepted Jhonston of Wariston's letter to Lord Loudoun (the dissidents' principal contact among the Covenanters), in which he had urged that their English allies, should join in some form of covenant like the Bond of Association of 1584–85; for this letter, see [Oldmixon], *History of England*, pp. 141–2: 'Nathaniel Black' [Jhonston of Wariston] to the Lord Loudoun, 23 June 1640.

134 Bodl. Lib., MS Clarendon 19, fo. 24: Sir Francis Windebank to Charles I, 7 September 1640 (*Clarendon State Papers*, II, 111).

135 Bodl. Lib., MS Clarendon 19, fo. 25: Sir Francis Windebank to Charles I, 7 September 1640 (*Clarendon State Papers*, II, 112).

136 Bodl. Lib., MS Clarendon 19, fo. 25: Sir Francis Windebank to Charles I, 7 September 1640.

137 The classic exposition of this is to be found in Lawrence Stone's *The Crisis of the Aristocracy, 1558–1641* (Oxford, 1965), pp. 746–53; for the influence of this view, see, for example, Brian Manning, *The English People and the English Revolution* (Harmondsworth, 1978), p. 9, where he describes the struggle between the royalist and parliamentarian sides in the Civil War as 'a conflict between the aristocracy or governing élites and independent small producers [sic]'. For a far more sophisticated view, see Roger B. Manning, *Swordsmen: the Martial Ethos in the Three Kingdoms* (Oxford, 2003).

138 Russell, *Fall of the British Monarchies*,

Ch. 3, and see especially Russell's commentary on Strafford's wildly optimistic speech to the Committee of War at the dissolution of the Short Parliament: 'One of the most interesting, and least remarked, passages in this speech is the assertion that "the quiet of England will hold out long" ... The fears which sometimes swept over Windebank or Arundel, though fears to which most Tudor and Stuart gentlemen were subject, seem to have been exaggerated. England, however angry or disgruntled it might be, was not on the edge of revolt. The quiet of England held out another two and a half years'; ibid., p. 126. It is questionable whether Strafford, who had spent only a few months in the country over the previous seven years, is the most reliable guide to the temper of England in 1640. For an important challenge to this new orthodoxy about high politics, largely argued from the perspective of demotic and popular politics, see Cressy, *England on Edge*, especially pp. 9–10, where he points to the 'early dating of the revolution' having been 'swamped by the revisionist tide'.

139 Cressy, *England on Edge*; John Walter, *Understanding Popular Violence in the English Revolution: the Colchester Plunderers* (Cambridge, 1999); idem, 'Popular Iconoclasm and the Politics of the Parish in Eastern England, 1640–42', *Historical Journal*, 47 (2004), 261–90; idem, '"Abolishing Superstition with Sedition?" The Politics of Popular Iconoclasm in England 1640–42', *Past and Present*, 183 (2004), 79–123.

140 For the Petitioners' uncertainties, see New College Lib., Edinburgh, MS X15b 3/1, vol. I, fo. 263: Bedford and other peers to the [Covenanter leadership], c. 5 September 1640 (Donald, 'New Light on Anglo-Scottish Contacts', pp. 228–9), on which these extrapolations of the Petitioners' thinking at this time are based.

141 *Clarendon State Papers*, II, 97: Windebank to Charles I, 3 September 1640. Windebank despatched one of the most experienced of the Privy Council Clerks, Edward Nicholas, to explain the proposal to the king in person; and Nicholas left London with a draft text of a letter from the king to the Earl Marshal (Arundel) 'for calling the Lords – if your Majesty like that way'.

142 The courtier nobility had produced

massive sums in the course of 1640 by way of loans to the king: the Earl of Newcastle (Governor of the Prince of Wales) produced £10,000; the Earl of Salisbury (Captain of the Gentlemen Pensioners), £10,000; the Earl of Pembroke (Lord Chamberlain of the Household), at least £7,000; Lord Cottington (Master of the Court of Wards and Chancellor of the Exchequer), £5,000; and the Duke of Lennox (a Gentleman of the Bedchamber and royal favourite), £30,000, as recently as July 1640. The extent to which Charles's war against the Scots in 1640 – the 'Second Bishops' War' – was a campaign funded in large measure by the nobility has never been properly recognized; see NA, SO 3/12 (Signet Office Docket Book), fos. 78v, 102v, 105, 110. In the case of Pembroke, however, it should not be assumed that contribution to the 'loan' indicated approval of the cause on which the money was to be spent. Given his prominence in the court, Pembroke could hardly have escaped making a substantial contribution unless he were to have risked alienating the king completely and forfeiting his position in the Household.

143 Just as the Petition of the Twelve appears to have been reliant on Oliver St John's antiquarian researches, the revival of the Great Council of Peers seems to have originated in the archival gleanings of Sir John Borough, the Keeper of the Records at the Tower. Borough had helpfully come up with evidence from the reign of Edward III that the king might seek supply in time of war from the nobility, assembled in a Great Council, as an alternative to seeking parliamentary supply. NA, SP 16/476, fo. 75: accounts for the payment of Sir John Borough and William Ryley, for research among the records in the Tower, February 1641; for the precedent of Edward III, *Calendar of State Papers Domestic, 1640–1*, Preface, p. vii. For the quotation concerning Edward I's time, see Centre for Kentish Studies, De L'Isle MS U1475/C132/150: William Hawkins to the Earl of Leicester, 10 September 1640 (HMC, *De L'Isle Manuscripts*, VI, 325); I am grateful to Dr David Scott for drawing this passage to my attention. For the precedents, see Austin Woolrych, *Britain in Revolution* (Oxford, 2004), p. 147; and Bodl. Lib., MS Ashmole 1729 (Historical papers), fos. 39–89v, 97.

144 Bodl. Lib., MS Clarendon 19, fo. 25: Sir Francis Windebank to Charles I, 7 September

1640; NA, SP 16/464, fo. 99: Windebank's notes for 7 September 1640.

145 In mid-September, for example, when Strafford had insisted on removing a request for a Parliament from a petition of Yorkshire grievances to the king, two gentlemen – Sir John Hotham and Sir Hugh Cholmeley – had protested to Charles against the clause's omission. The king's response provides us with some insight into how he regarded the Parliament supporters within the Privy Council. With Hotham and Cholmeley, his normally glacial self-control briefly deserted him and he behaved as the irascible despot of puritan caricature. If Hotham and Cholmeley continued to meddle in such matters, the king snapped, he would have them both hanged. How closely, if at all, Hotham and Cholmeley were involved with the London-based Petitioners remains obscure; yet it is at least noteworthy that Hotham and Essex and the Captain-Leader of the Artillery Company, Philip Skippon, were all former comrades-in-arms: all three were veterans of Sir Horace Vere's company that had campaigned against the Habsburgs in the Netherlands during the early 1620s, and had been present together in Breda in the summer of 1625, when the town was forced to surrender to the Spanish. Jack Binns (ed.), *Memoirs and Memorials of Sir Hugh Cholmley of Whitby, 1600–57* (Yorkshire Archaeological Society Record Series, 153, 1997–98), p. 102 (I owe this reference to Dr David Scott); see also David Scott, 'Sir John Hotham' (HPL); Ian Gentles, 'Philip Skippon', and John Morrill, 'Robert Devereux, 3rd Earl of Essex', *ODNB*.

146 Hertfordshire's Petition was delivered to the king at York by Arthur Capell of Hadham (1604–49), who also seems to have been on the fringes of the Warwick–Mandeville circle. He had been born and brought up in Essex (his father was Sir Henry Capell of Raines Hall), and his mother, Theodosia Montagu (the daughter of the 1st Lord Montagu of Boughton and niece of the 1st Earl of Manchester) was Mandeville's first cousin; he was a 'kinsman and friend' of Sir Thomas Barrington, one of the central figures in Warwick's social network. (The Capells had been electoral allies of the 3rd Lord Rich – the future 2nd Earl of Warwick – since 1604.) Lord Brooke also organized a Warwickshire Petition: BL, Add. MS 23146 (Dugard diary), fo. 90; Ann Hughes, *Politics, Society and Civil*

War in Warwickshire, 1620–60 (Cambridge, 1987), p. 125.

147 NA, SP 16/467, fo. 8v: Sir Henry Vane, senior, to Windebank, 10 September 1640 [from York].

148 NA, SP 16/467, fo. 109r-v: Vane to Windebank, 13 September 1640.

149 'This is certayne', he continued, 'the Scotts' first petition came but a fewe dayes before the Lords Mandevill and Howard brought the petition of the Lords of the South to one and the same effect, and now the Scotts have backt [the Twelve Peers'] petition with another to the like purpose'; NA, SP 16/467, fo. 127r-v: [Dr John Pocklington to Sir John Lambe], 14 September 1640.

150 *CSPV 1640–42*, p. 79: Giustinian to the Doge and Senate, 11/21 September 1640.

151 NA, SP 16/467, fo. 183: the Privy Council to Charles I, 18 September 1640; SP 16/467, fo. 201: Windebank's notes of the Privy Council, 18 September 1640. For a sampling of the copies of the Peers' Petition which record more than twelve signatories: Surrey RO, Guildford Muniment Room, Loseley MS 1131/50 (17 signatories); Northamptonshire RO, Finch-Hatton MS 2619; Cambridge UL, Add. MS 335 (Historical papers, *c.* 1640–50), fo. 41 (foliation from the back); Beinecke Library, Yale University, Osborn Files, Pym; BL, Add. MS 44848 (Historical papers), fos. 283v–84.

152 Above, Appendix.

153 Northamptonshire RO, Finch-Hatton MS 2619: the Noblemen's Petition [28 August 1640], signed by Lincoln; see also the version of the petition in BL, Add. MS 44848, fos. 283v–84, which also lists him among the signatories.

154 For Paget's signature, see the copy of the Petition in BL, Harl. MS 4931 (Political papers, 1617–41), fo. 67r-v; and Surrey History Centre, Loseley MS 133/50. For thirty as the likely number of supporters, see New College Lib., Edinburgh, MS X15b 3/1, vol. I, fo. 263: Bedford and other Petitioners to the [Covenanter leadership], *c.* 5 September 1640 (printed in Donald, 'New Light on Anglo-Scottish Contacts', p. 229).

155 For Bristol's signature to the Petition of the Twelve, see the versions of the document

preserved in Cambridge UL, Add. MS 335 (Historical papers, *c.* 1640–50), fo. 41 (foliation from the back); Beinecke Library, Yale, Osborn Files, Pym. For Sir Oliver Millar's comments on the Digby–Russell double portrait, see *Van Dyck Complete Catalogue*, pp. 503–5 and plate IV.92.

156 BL, Add. MS 23146 (Thomas Dugard's diary), fo. 90; Hughes, *Politics, Society and Civil War in Warwickshire*, p. 125. Although Dugard's diary does not state explicitly that Dunsmore (who was a future Royalist) actually signed the petition, this can probably be inferred both from his presence and from the fact that he was named the following week, at the Great Council of Peers, to the sixteen-man commission to negotiate the treaty with the Scots – a commission that was dominated by Petitioners and their close kin. For the commission, see Nottingham UL, Clifton Papers, Cl C 617: Sir William Savile to Sir Gervase Clifton, York, 25 September 1640.

157 NA, SP 16/467, fo. 8v: Sir Henry Vane, senior, to Windebank, 10 September 1640 [from York].

158 For the date of its circulation, see NA, SP 16/464, fo. 99.

159 Raikes, *Vellum Book*, p. 40.

160 For Venn's biography, see Pearl, *London*, pp. 187–9.

161 Venn acquired the post of Deputy President in 1639, coinciding with the arrival of Philip Skippon as Captain-Leader and the election of Alderman Thomas Soame as President. Raikes, *Vellum Book*, p. 20; Pearl, *London*, pp. 188–9; Matthias Milward, *The Souldiers Triumph and the Preachers Glory. In a sermon Preached to the Captains and Souldiers exercising Arms in the Artillery Garden, at their Generall Meeting in S. Michaels Church Cornhill in London, the 31. of August, 1641* (1641), p. 1 (BL, E 175/7).

162 For the date of Thompson's departure, see NA, SP 16/467, fo. 225: memorandum, 19 September. The bearers of the City petition were reported to have departed on last Wednesday afternoon.

163 NA, SP 16/467, fo. 225: memorandum, 19 September, describing 'Mr Alford' as a linen draper in Cheapside. This would seem to be the John Alford of Cheapside who married at St Mary le Bowe, Cheapside, London, on 4 January 1631: W. Bruce Bannerman (ed.), *The Registers of St Mary le Bowe, Cheapside, All Hallows, Honey Lane, and of St Pancras, Soper Lane, London*, 2 vols. (Harleian Society, XLIV–XLV, 1914–15), II, 326; the original reference is: Guildhall Lib., MS 4996 (St Mary le Bow, Register General, 1538–1631), fo. 93v. (I am grateful to Dr Phil Baker for these last two references.) For John Alford's membership of the Artillery Company, see [William Barriff], *Mars his Triumph. Or, the Description of an Exercise performed the XVIII of October, 1638, in Merchant-Taylors Hall* (1639), p. 9; Armoury House, Honourable Artillery Company Archives, Quarterage Book 1628–43, 'John Alford', *s.v.*, entries from 1638. For the delivery of the City petition, see NA, SP 16/467, fo. 225: memorandum, 19 September 1640; SP 16/467, fo. 266: Sir Henry Vane, senior, to Sir Francis Windebank, from York, 22 September 1640 (printed in *Hardwick, State Papers from 1501 to 1726*, 2 vols (1778), II, p. 184). For Thompson's links with Warwick, see Russell, *Fall of the British Monarchies*, p. 152n. The text of the City petition is Beinecke Lib., Yale University, MS Osborn Shelves b. 297.

164 Brenner, *Merchants and Revolution*, p. 313 (for the quotation). For Shute's politics, see Pearl, *London*, pp. 252–3, 260–1. Once war had broken out in 1642, Shute was to be one of the major proponents of the City's petition of December 1642 – of which Warwick cordially approved – against any accommodation with the king until an absolute victory had first been achieved. Interestingly, the three clergy who joined in the promotion of this petition – Jeremiah Burroughes, Hugh Peters, and John Goodwin – were all protected by either Warwick (Burroughes and Peter) or Saye (Goodwin); cf. Pearl, *London*, pp. 253–4; Barbara Donagan, 'The Clerical Patronage of Robert Rich, 2nd Earl of Warwick, 1619–42', *Proceedings of the American Philosophical Society*, 120 (1976), 388–419; Sean Kelsey, 'Robert Rich, 2nd Earl of Warwick', *ODNB*. For Burroughes and Warwick, see his *A Vindication of Mr Burroughes* (1646), pp. 18–19 (BL, E 345/14), and Essex RO, T/B 211/1, no. 39: 'The sum of that Conference which was betwixt one Mr Burroughes, a Minister laitlie suspendit in the Dioces of

Norwitch for inconformitie, and John Michaelson, Parson of Chelmesford, the 5 of August last [1638], at Leeghes parva, in the garden of the ... Earle of Warwicke'.

165 G. Goold Walker, *The Honourable Artillery Company, 1537–1947* (Aldershot, 1954), p. 50, goes so far as to claim that *all* the officers of the London Trained Bands were members of the company by 1642.

166 In 1640, Calamy wrote the preface to William Fenner's *The Souls Looking-Glasse, lively representing its Estate before God* (1640), a work dedicated to the Earl of Warwick; for Warwick's funeral sermon, see Edmund Calamy, *A Patterne for All, especially for Noble and Honourable Persons* (1658), BL, E 947/1. For his relations with Warwick, see also A. G. Matthews (ed.), *Calamy Revised: being a Revision of Edmund Calamy's* Account *of the Ministers and Others Ejected and Silenced, 1660–62* (Oxford, 1934), pp. xlix–l.

167 NA, SP 16/467, fos. 192, 194, 196: Privy Council warrants, 18 September 1640.

168 I use the term 'protégé' in the relatively strict sense of someone who received the protection of a peer, whether formally a member of the nobleman's household or not. Thus, for example, Calybute Downinge was 'protected' by Warwick and allowed to reside for a time in his country seat, even though (so far as I have been able to establish) he was never formally one of the earl's household chaplains.

169 For Burges and the Russells: see [Cornelius Burges], *Baptismall Regeneration of Elect Infants, professed by the Church of England* (Oxford, 1629), ep. ded. to the [4th] Earl of Bedford, sig. ¶2–¶3, referring to 'how much I stand obliged to your Noble Predecessors, the late [3rd] Earle and Countesse of Bedford, now with God'. See also Burges's reminiscence of the family life of the 3rd Earl of Bedford in his letter to Lord Wharton, 28 August 1648: Bodl. MS Rawlinson Letters 52 (Wharton corr.), fo. 143. It was probably through the Russell connection that he knew Pym, whose one and only nomination of a fast-day preacher fell upon Burges: J. F. Wilson, *Pulpit in Parliament: Puritanism during the English Civil Wars, 1640–48* (Princeton, 1969), p. 106. From his house on London Bridge, he was supposed to have organized his 'Myrmidons' in 1641 to protest against the presence of bishops in Parliament; see Peter Heylin, *Aerius Redivivus* (1670), p. 439; [Sir John Berkenhead], *A Letter from Mercurius Civicus to Mercurius Rusticus, or, Londons Confession* ([Oxford], 25 August 1643), p. 9 (BL, E 65/32).

170 NA, SP 16/467, fo. 201 (for the quotation, from Windebank's Privy Council notes, 18 September 1640); and see also fos. 192, 194 (the Council warrants for the search of Burges's house, 18–19 September) and fo. 196 (for the search of Downinge's house, where he is mistakenly referred to as 'George Downing, Dr in Divinity'. This seems to have been a simple error, both as to Christian name and as to degree, as Downinge was a Doctor of Laws, not of Divinity (though it is an understandable mistake). 196: Privy Council warrants, 18 September 1640.

171 NA, SP 16/467, fo. 225: Privy Council memorandum, 19 September 1640.

172 NA, SP 16/467, fos. 125–6v: Sir Henry Vane, senior, to Sir Francis Windebank, 14 September 1640.

173 NA, SP 16/467, fo. 225: Privy Council memorandum, 19 September 1640.

174 NA, SP 16/467, fo. 157: Windebank's notes of the Privy Council, 16 September 1640.

175 ASV, Senato, Dispacci Inghil. 42, fo. 117r-v: Giustinian to the Doge and Senate, 5/15 September 1640 (*CSPV 1640–42*, p. 77).

176 Baillie, *Letters and Journals*, I, 258; Gardiner, *History*, IX, 207.

177 This tally is based on a comparison of the following copies of the Petition: Beinecke Library, Osborn Files, Pym; Northamptonshire RO, Finch-Hatton MS 2619; Surrey History Centre, Loseley MS; Cambridge UL, Add. MS 335, fo. 41 (from back); BL, Add. MS 44848, fos. 283v–84; NA, SP 16/465, fo. 40v. One cannot date precisely when these signatures were added; however, as the objective of the Petition was satisfied on 24 September, when the king agreed to the summons of a Parliament, that provides the logical *terminus ante quem*. All the 'additional' signatures would appear to have been gathered between the beginning of September and that date. See also Appendix.

178 William Hawkins noted that the Petition 'is said to be subscribed by XXII of them', a figure which tallies almost exactly (twenty-three being my own computation) with the list of those who can be documented to have signed: see Centre for Kentish Studies, De L'Isle MS U1475/C132/150: William Hawkins to the Earl of Leicester, 10 September 1640 (HMC, *De L'Isle Manuscripts*, VI, 325); and Appendix.

179 BL, Add. MS 11045 (Scudamore corr.), fo. 119: [Edward Rossingham's newsletter], 29 September 1640. For Bedford's presence at the opening session of the Great Council on 25 September, see LMA, RO, Historical Papers I/14: newsletter from Sir Kenelm Digby, 25 September 1640.

180 The shock of the Petitioners' appearance at York must have been extensive. The Privy Council had expected that only Hertford and Essex – believed to be the most moderate, and potentially conciliatory, of the dissidents – would make the journey north. The entry of 'all the subcrybing Lords' may also have entailed many more than the original Twelve Peers; by the eve of the Great Council, the number of subscribers and 'adherents' of the Petition had reached around thirty peers: New College Lib., Edinburgh, MS X15b 3/1, vol. I, fo. 263: Bedford and other Petitioners to the [Covenanter leadership], *c.* 5 September 1640 (Donald, 'New Light on Anglo-Scottish Contacts', p. 229).

181 Acherley, *Britannic Constitution*, p. 408.

182 New College Lib., Edinburgh, MS X15b 3/1, vol. I, fo. 263: Bedford and other Petitioners to the [Covenanter leadership], *c.* 5 September 1640 (Donald, 'New Light on Anglo-Scottish Contacts', p. 229).

183 BL, Add. MS 11045 (Scudamore corr.): [Edward Rossingham's newsletter], 29 September 1640.

184 *Clarendon State Papers*, II, 120; NA, SP 16/468/23: Sir Henry Vane to Sir Francis Windebank, 24 September 1640. Russell suggests that 'thirty-seven peers sounds an incredible number for support for the Scottish invasion', and I am inclined to agree. It is most likely an exaggeration, but perhaps not by much; the letter from Bedford and seven other Petitioners of *c.* 5 September 1640 claimed twenty other peers 'adherent', which would produce a total of twenty-eight, and it

is quite possible that this number increased in the course of the month. If so, Windebank's advice to the king may not have been wide of the mark. See Russell, *Fall of the British Monarchies*, p. 153n; Donald, 'New Light on Anglo-Scottish Contacts', p. 229.

185 NA, SP 16/466, fo. 113: the Earl of Lanark's reply, on behalf of the king, to the Scottish Petition, 5 September 1640; for the Great Council, see Russell, *Fall of the British Monarchies*, p. 157n.

186 William Blackstone, *Commentaries on the Laws of England*, 4 vols. (Oxford, 1765–69), I, 221 (for quotation). Among those attending was the Scottish Earl of Traquair, the Secretary of State in the king's Scottish Privy Council: Staffordshire RO, Dyott MS D661/11/1/5: Sir Richard Dyott to [?], 25 September 1640. For Warwick, see [Chestlin], *Persecutio Undecima*, p. 56.

187 NA, SP 16/468, fo. 2: the king's speech at the opening of the Great Council, 24 September 1640; Staffordshire RO, Dyott MS D661/11/1/5: Sir Richard Dyott to [?], 25 September 1640. For Warwick, see [Chestlin], *Persecutio Undecima*, p.56.

188 For Bristol as one of the signatories, see Cambridge UL, Add. MS 335 (Historical papers, *c.* 1640–50), fo. 41 (foliation from the back), and Beinecke Lib., Yale University, Osborn Files, Pym Papers: a copy of the Petition of the Twelve; Whitelocke, *Memorials*, I, 105. Russell's suggestion that Bristol had refused to sign the Petition seems to be mistaken: compare Russell, *Fall of the British Monarchies*, pp. 155n, 158n, and the evidence that led Russell to this (I believe erroneous) conclusion: *Clarendon State Papers*, II, 114.

189 New College Lib., Edinburgh, MS X15b 3/1, vol. I, fo. 262v: N[athaniel] F[iennes] to the [Covenanter leadership], *c.* 3 September 1640 (Donald, 'New Light on Anglo-Scottish Contacts', pp. 227–8).

190 Nottingham UL, Clifton Papers, Cl C 617: Sir William Savile to Sir Gervase Clifton, York, 25 September 1640. Only three members of the commission can be regarded as possibly being anti-Petitioner and anti-Scots: the Earls of Salisbury and Berkshire, and Lord Poulett. For a rather different analysis of the composition of the

commission, see Russell, *Fall of the British Monarchies*, p. 158n.

191 BL, Add. MS 23146 (Thomas Dugard's diary), fo. 90. Dugard, a local schoolmaster in Brooke's pay, wrote out the Petition, and although the diarist does not mention its contents, I concur with Professor Hughes that 'it is difficult to imagine what else it could have been about'; see Hughes, *Warwickshire*, p. 125.

192 ASV, Senato, Dispacci Inghil. 42, fo. 130v: Giustinian to the Doge and Senate, 2/12 October 1640 (*CSPV 1640–42*, pp. 86–7).

193 *Memoirs of Henry Guthry, Late Bishop of Dunkel* (1702), p. 74. For the Scottish Commissioners, see BL, Harl. MS 457 (Minutes of the Anglo-Scottish Treaty), fo. 1.

194 Bristol had been a Privy Councillor in James I's reign (sworn 3 April 1616), but had not sat on the Board at any point in Charles's reign; he was re-sworn on 19 February 1641. *Complete Peerage*, II, 320.

195 On this question, see Baillie, *Letters*, I, 263.

196 Isabel Rich, Countess of Holland to Sir James Thynne (her son-in-law), 4 October [1640]: Longleat House, Wilts, Thynne MS IX (Correspondence 1639–70), fo. 7.

197 Staffordshire RO, Dyott MS D661/11/1/5: Sir Richard Dyott to [?], 25 September 1640.

198 Centre for Kentish Studies, De L'Isle MS U1500/C2/44: Earl of Northumberland to Earl of Leicester, Syon, 22 October 1640 (not calendared in HMC, *De L'Isle Manuscripts*).

199 Yet it would be a mistake to see even these elections, the most polarized in half a century, as a simple contest between 'the court' and 'the country'. By the early 1640s England had one of the most politically aware electorates in Europe, a 'public sphere' in which many voters were politically well-informed to the extent that they could easily distinguish, when it came to assessing candidates and their backers, between those who were allied with 'virtuous' counsellors and those supported by tame lackeys of the Crown. Hence, while the support of a Strafford or a Cottington could be the kiss of death in the elections of October 1640, the endorsements of Privy Councillors with reputations for staunch Protestantism and a

concern for the subject's liberties – men such as Northumberland, Holland or the king's Lord Chamberlain, the Earl of Pembroke – generally continued to be regarded with respect. See Vivienne Hodges, 'The Electoral Influence of the Aristocracy, 1604–40' (unpublished Ph.D. dissertation, Columbia University, 1977); Derek Hirst, *The Representative of the People: Voters and Voting in England under the Early Stuarts* (Cambridge, 1975); John K. Gruenfelder, *Influence in Early Stuart Elections, 1604–40* (Columbus, OH, 1981); R. N. Kershaw, 'The Elections for the Long Parliament, 1640', *English Historical Review*, 38 (1923), 496–508; A. H. Dodd, 'Caernarvonshire Elections to the Long Parliament', *Bulletin of the Board of Celtic Studies*, 12 (1946), 44–8; Gordon C. F. Forster, 'Elections at Scarborough for the Long Parliament, 1640–7', *Transactions of the Scarborough and District Archaeological Society*, 1 (1960), 3–9; Jacqueline Eales, 'The Rise of Ideological Politics in Kent, 1558–1640', in Michael L. Zell (ed.), *Early Modern Kent 1540–1640* (Woodbridge, 2000), pp. 279–313; Jason Peacey, 'Tactical Organization in a Contested Election: Sir Edward Dering and the Spring Election at Kent, 1640', in Chris R. Kyle (ed.), *Parliament, Politics and Elections 1604–48* (Camden Society, 5th ser., 17, Cambridge, 2001), pp. 237–72; Keeler, *Long Parliament*, pp. 8–9; Violet A. Rowe, 'The Influence of the Earls of Pembroke on Parliamentary Elections, 1625–40', *English Historical Review*, 50 (1935), 242–56.

200 As Fiennes noted of the Irish forces, they were 'more than all [the king] hath [in England] and bettir men': Donald, 'New Light', p. 228.

201 For the London elections of September 1640, see Pearl, *London*, pp. 110–12; Brenner, *Merchants and Revolution*, pp. 323–3.

202 Staffordshire RO, Dyott MS D661/11/1/5: Sir Richard Dyott to [?], 7 September 1640.

203 For the use of the phrase, see Staffordshire RO, Dyott MS D661/11/1/5: Sir Richard Dyott to [?], 7 September 1640.

204 *Hardwicke State Papers*, II, 180: Sir Henry Vane to Sir Francis Windebank, 16 September 1640. The review had taken place on 10 September, at York.

205 *Clarendon State Papers*, II, 98: Sir Henry Vane to Sir Francis Windebank, 3 September 1640.

206 [Saye], *Vindiciae Veritatis*, p. 29.

207 Staffordshire RO, Dyott MS D661/11/1/5: Sir Richard Dyott to [?], 7 September 1640. On my own reading of these letters, it is difficult to agree with Professor Russell's conclusion that Dyott regarded the Petitioner Peers as, 'in effect, in collusion with the enemy'; see Conrad Russell, 'Why did Charles I call the Long Parliament?', in his *Unrevolutionary England, 1603–42* (London and Ronceverte, 1990), p. 259.

208 BL, Add. MS 11045 (Scudamore correspondence), fo. 144v: [Edward Rossingham's] newsletter, 25 November 1640.

209 Of the colonels in the king's army, the one most likely to have been in contact with the Petitioners was Sir John Meyrick, a devoted friend of the Earl of Essex's and the nephew of the 2nd Earl of Essex's secretary, Sir Gelly Meyrick, executed for his part in the Essex Rebellion of 1601; *CSPD 1640–41*, p. 570; Paul Hammer, 'Sir Gelly Meyrick', *ODNB*.

210 The dissident peers themselves acknowledged that this was so: [Oldmixon], *History of England*, p. 142: Earls of Essex, Bedford, Warwick, Viscounts Saye and Mandeville and Lords Brooke and Savile, to [Archibald Jhonston of Wariston?], [late June–early July 1640].

211 *Clarendon State Papers*, II, 120.

212 Russell, *Fall of the British Monarchies*, p. 153.

213 *Nicholas Papers*, I, 39.

214 Cambridge UL, MS Mm. 1. 45 (Historical papers), p. 112: letter of intelligence to Dr Matthew Wren, Dean of the Chapel Royal, from York [c. 24–25 September 1640]. The identity of the 'great Scott' is unknown, but from the context, it seems to have been one of the senior Scottish grandees at either Newcastle or Durham; the four senior Scots at Newcastle at the end of September were the Earls of Rothes, Montrose, Cassilis, and Lindsay: Staffordshire RO, D661/11/1/5 (Dyott MS), unfol.: Earls

of Rothes, Montrose and others to Sir William
Carnaby, from Newcastle, 30 September
1640.

215 NA, SP 16/476, fo. 75: accounts for the
payment of Sir John Borough and William
Ryley, for research among the records in the
Tower (February 1641). The payment to
Borough for his work is dated 4 January
(1641), 'for use in this present Parliament';
so, while the exact date of the commission to
Borough to conduct the research cannot be
established precisely, it would seem to have
been no later than early December 1640, and
may well have dated from as early as
September.

3. OPENING RITES

1 Thomas D. Whitaker, *The Life and Original
Correspondence of Sir G[eorge] Radcliffe*
(1810), p. 219.

2 On the theme of the royal entry, see
Malcolm Smuts, 'Public Ceremony and Royal
Charisma: the English Royal Entry in London,
1485–1642', in A. L. Beier, David Cannadine,
J. M. Rosenheim (eds.), *The First Modern
Society: Essays in English History in Honour
of Lawrence Stone* (Cambridge, 1989), pp.
65–93.

3 For the date of the king's return, see Loomie,
Ceremonies of Charles I, p. 292.

4 For Windebank's reports on the mutinous
state of the City, see above, pp. 70–1.
Strafford, on his return to London on 9
November, was reported to have insisted that
the City needed to be 'subdued': see Notestein,
D'Ewes Diary, p. 24.

5 For the usage of this term, see J. H. Bettey
(ed.), *Calendar of the Correspondence of the
Smyth Family of Ashton Court, 1548–1642*
(Bristol Record Society, 35, 1982), p. 145 (my
knowledge of which I owe to Professor David
Cressy); and see David Cressy, *England on
Edge: Crisis and Revolution, 1640–42*
(Oxford, 2006), pp. 107–9.

6 This process is well described in Cressy,
England on Edge, p. 116; and on the
increasing insubordination of the print trade
more generally, see Joad Raymond,
*Pamphlets and Pamphleteering in Early
Modern Britain* (Cambridge, 2003), Chs. 5
and 6.

7 ASV, Senato, Dispacci Inghil. 42, fos.
149v–150: Giustinian to the Doge and Senate,
30 October–9 November 1640 (*CSPV
1640–42*, p. 93). For Charles's project for the
restoration of St Paul's, see Kevin Sharpe, *The
Personal Rule of Charles I* (New Haven and
London, 1982), pp. 322–8.

8 Henry Parker, *The Altar Dispute, or, a
Discourse concerning the Severall
Innovations of the Altar* (1642), p. 78 (BL, E
140/19); Edward Dering approved the tract
for printing on 3 July 1641. On Parker's
relations with Saye, see Michael Mendle,
*Dangerous Positions: Mixed Government, the
Estates of the Realm, and the Making of the
Answer to the XIX Propositions* (University,
AL, 1985), pp. 128–34.

9 ASV, Senato, Dispacci Inghil. 42, fos.
149v–150: Giustinian to the Doge and Senate,
30 October–9 November 1640 (*CSPV
1640–42*, p. 93).

10 Ibid. For Laud's calls for the use of Star
Chamber to prosecute the offenders, see Keith
Lindley, *Popular Politics and Religion in Civil
War London* (1997), p. 11.

11 HMC, *De L'Isle Manuscripts*, VI, 339:
William Hawkins to the Earl of Leicester, 5
November 1640; and for the attack on the
High Commission records, see also HMC,
Cowper Manuscripts, II, 262. For the Court
of High Commission during the 1630s, see
Julian Davies, *The Caroline Captivity of the
Church: Charles I and the Remoulding of
Anglicanism, 1625–41* (Oxford, 1992); and
Cyndia Clegg, 'Censorship and the Courts of
Star Chamber and High Commission in
England to 1640', *Journal of Modern
European History*, 3 (2005), 50–80.

12 HMC, *De L'Isle Manuscripts,* VI, 338–9.

13 NA, LC 5/134 (Lord Chamberlain's order
book), p. 420.

14 NA, LC 5/134 (Lord Chamberlain's order
book), p. 418; Skinner was appointed on 3
October 1640.

15 David Dean, 'Image and Ritual in the
Tudor Parliaments', in Dale E. Hoak (ed.),
Tudor Political Culture (Cambridge, 1995),
pp. 243–71; Elizabeth Read Foster, *The
House of Lords, 1603–49: Structure,
Procedure, and the Nature of its Business*
(Chapel Hill, VC, 1983), pp. 3–5.

16 HMC, *De L'Isle Manuscripts*, VI, 337: William Hawkins to the Earl of Leicester, 29 October 1640. The decision 'not [to go] through the streets' was reported by Hawkins that day; see also: ASV, Senato, Dispacci Inghil. 42, fo. 148v–49: Giustinian to the Doge and Senate, 30 October/9 November 1640, reporting that the king intended to go 'privatamente' (*CSPV 1640–42*, pp. 92–3).

17 For the quotation, HMC, *De L'Isle Manuscripts*, VI, 339. See also, BL, Add. MS 11045 (Scudamore correspondence), fo. 131v: [Edward Rossingham's] newsletter, 3 November 1640; HMC, *Buccleuch Manuscripts*, III, 387; Clarendon, *Rebellion*, I, 200. Foster, *House of Lords*, p. 5. For the opening months of the Parliament, see Sheila Lambert, 'The Opening of the Long Parliament', *Historical Journal*, 27 (1984), 265–87.

18 Edward Hyde noted that this going 'privately' was 'as if it had been to a return of a prorogued or adjourned Parliament': Clarendon, *Rebellion*, I, 220.

19 ASV, Senato, Dispacci Inghil. 42, fos. 148v–9: Giustinian to the Doge and Senate, 30 October/9 November 1640 (*CSPV 1640–42*, p. 92).

20 ASV, Senato, Dispacci Inghil. 42, fo. 156: Giustinian to the Doge and Senate, 13–23 November 1640 (*CSPV 1640–42*, p. 95).

21 Beinecke Lib., MS Osborn Shelves Fb 111: George Brown to [?], 1 September 1640; my emphasis.

22 *Clarendon State Papers*, II, 94–5: Sir Francis Windebank to Charles I, 31 August 1640 (for the quotation); see also NA, SP 16/465, fo. 111: Windebank's notes of the Committee of War, 31 August 1640. Windebank adds cryptically: 'Lords Say and Brooke another time.'

23 Lambert, 'The Opening of the Long Parliament', pp. 265–87.

24 For the identification of the preacher, see *CJ*, II, 20; BL, Add. MS 11045 (Scudamore correspondence), fo. 131v: [Edward Rossingham's] newsletter, 3 November 1640; and Rushworth, *Historical Collections*, Part III, I, 11. Skinner's ability to wrap a relatively hard-line message in what seemed, superficially, a rhetoric of moderation must have commended him to the king; see Peter

Lake, 'Joseph Hall, Robert Skinner and the Rhetoric of Moderation at the Early Stuart Court', in Lori Anne Ferrell and Peter McCullough (eds.), *The English Sermon Revised: Religion, Literature and History, 1600–1750* (Manchester and New York, 2001), pp. 167–85. For Skinner's insistence on such 'Laudian' practices as bowing at the name of Jesus and enforcing kneeling at the reception of communion, see *Articles to be Ministred, Enquired of, and Answered in the Visitation of the Right Reverend Father in God, [Robert Skinner], by Gods Divine Providence, Lord Bishop of Bristol* (1640), STC 10145.3; and Anthony Milton, *Catholic and Reformed: the Roman and Protestant Churches in English Protestant Thought, 1600–40* (Cambridge, 1995), p. 336.

25 Rushworth, *Historical Collections*, Part III, I, 12.

26 Ibid., pp. 12–16; quotation at p. 13; for an alternative version of the speech, see BL, Add. MS 15567 (Anon. memoir), fos. 17–21v. This memoir has been attributed to the 2nd Earl of Manchester by S. R. Gardiner; but there is nothing conclusive within the text that identifies it definitively with the earl (who was then styled Viscount Mandeville). On the other hand the text seems to have been composed by a peer who was one of the sixteen Treaty Commissioners appointed by the Council of Peers at York to negotiate with the Scots; and he seems to be extremely familiar with, though not necessarily one of, the inner group of Petitioner Peers. The Earl of Bristol is, perhaps, the likeliest contender (and in this regard it may be significant, has been noted earlier, that the text incorporates two lengthy speeches by his son, Lord Digby – more than by any other member of the Commons); though, in the absence of further evidence, this identification must be at best provisional.

27 Centre for Kentish Studies, De L'Isle MS U1475/C87/8: Countess of Carlisle to the Countess of Leicester, 4 November 1640 (HMC, *De L'Isle Manuscripts*, VI, 337).

28 ASV, Senato, Dispacci Inghil. 42, fo. 157v: Giustinian to the Doge and Senate, 6/16 November 1640 (*CSPV 1640–42*, p. 94); Giustinian explained the acclamation for the opening speeches as a reflection of the anti-court party's confidence that 'in the king's weakness they will be able to direct all the

deliberations [of the Parliament] according to their own way [*a loro modo*]'. For Sir William Widdrington, see *CJ*, II, 25.

29 Russell, *Fall of the British Monarchies*, pp. 207.

30 Anthony Milton, 'Thomas Wentworth and the Political Thought of the Personal Rule', in Julia F. Merritt, *The Political World of Thomas Wentworth, Earl of Strafford, 1621–41* (Cambridge, 1996), pp. 133–56.

31 Whitaker, *Life of Radcliffe*, pp. 229–30: Sir George Wentworth's narrative of Strafford's fall (undated, but probably dating from the early 1640s). This narrative suggests that Secretary Vane and the Marquess of Hamilton, 'anxious to make their peace with parliamentary leaders', persuaded the king to send for Strafford: in other words, that he walked into a trap. This claim is unsupported by contemporary evidence (which does not, in itself, render it false); but it seems implausible for two reasons: the first, that Hamilton and Vane do not appear to have begun any form of close cooperation with Strafford's likely accusers until January at the earliest (see above, chs. 5 and 6); the second, that Charles is unlikely to have needed any persuading to have wanted to bring Strafford south. The king trusted – indeed, almost depended upon – the figure who had been the prime director of his strategy since May; it was only logical that he should desire Strafford's presence about him after his return to London.

32 Sir John Bramston, *Autobiography* (Camden Society, 32, 1845), pp. 76–7 (emphasis added). Bramston was recalling a conversation he had had with Grimston at Chelmsford shortly after the latter's return from York.

33 Whitaker, *Life of Radcliffe*, p. 220: Earl of Strafford to Sir George Radcliffe, 5 November 1640.

34 For Strafford's recovery, see Whitaker, *Life of Radcliffe*, p. 222: Earl of Strafford to Sir George Radcliffe, 'Sunday, after dinner [i.e. 8 November 1640]'.

35 Ibid.

36 Whitaker, *Life of Radcliffe*, pp. 222–3.

37 BL, Harl. MS 1601 (Anon. diary), fo. 5v, entry for 10 April 1641.

38 For Clotworthy, see above, pp. 36–7; for his election at Maldon on Warwick's interest, see Keeler, *Long Parliament*, 'Sir John Clotworthy', and John H. Timmis, *Thine is the Kingdom: the Trial for Treason of Thomas Wentworth, Earl of Strafford, First Minister to King Charles I and Last Hope of the English Crown* (University, Alabama, 1974), p. 48. Clotworthy was also proposed for the West-Country constituency of Bossiney, on the nomination of 'Lord Ro:' – Lord Robartes of Truro, Warwick's son-in-law and a future Parliamentarian. The intervention raises the intriguing possibility that Lord Robartes was already part of the Petitioner Lords' network at this time, although I have not found a version of the Petition of the Twelve that has his name appended. There is a draft letter from Sir Bevil Grenville to Sir Ralph Sydenham, undated [October?, 1640], relating the confusions that produced the double return at Bossiney: BL, Add. MS 42711, fo. 37v. (I owe this reference to Dr Jason Peacey.) Circumstantial evidence that Robartes may have made these arrangements for Clotworthy's election at Warwick's behest (beyond the fact of their familial relation) would seem to be provided by the fact that Robartes was living at Warwick House, in Holborn, in February 1641 (and had probably been there since the opening of the Parliament): BL, Add. MS 34253 (Civil War correspondence), fo. 2v: Elizabeth Cholwell to Lord Robartes 'at Warwick hows', 4 February 1641. For an example of Warwick reportedly nominating Robartes as his proxy in a matter relating to an appointment of one of the earl's former chaplains to a living, see William Laud, Archbishop of Canterbury, *The History of the Troubles and Tryal of the Most Reverend Father in God and Blessed Martyr, William Laud, Lord Arch-Bishop of Canterbury wrote by himself during his Imprisonment in the Tower* (1695), pp. 194–5 (Wing L586).

39 Perhaps revealingly, this is from whence Strafford himself believed the first attack would come; Whitaker, *Life of Radcliffe*, p. 222: Earl of Strafford to Sir George Radcliffe, 'Sunday, after dinner [i.e. 8 November 1640]'.

40 On Strafford's rule in Ireland, see Hugh Kearney, *Strafford in Ireland 1633–41: a Study in Absolutism* (Cambridge, 1989); Merritt, *The Political World of Thomas Wentworth, Earl of Strafford*; and Nicholas

Canny, *Making Ireland British, 1580–1640* (Oxford, 2001).

41 Notestein, *D'Ewes Diary*, p. 3. D'Ewes's account seems reliable on the point of Pym's and Grimston's advocacy of the English Commons' jurisdiction over Ireland; however, he fails entirely to mention that there had been a division over the question of whether a Committee of the Whole or a Select Committee should be established; cf. *CJ*, II, 21; *PLP*, I, 22.

42 This theme is developed in Nicholas Canny, *Making Ireland British, 1580–1640* (Oxford, 2001).

43 Trinity College Lib., Dublin, MS 1180 (Southwell Papers), fo. 3: copy of the declaration of the two Houses of the Westminster Parliament, 24 May 1641.

44 *CJ*, II, 21. This view would tend to be supported by Pym's remarks in the Commons on 7 November: see Notestein, *D'Ewes Diary*, p. 11 and nn; *PLP*, I, 39–41, 43.

45 *CJ*, II, 21. The Commons' clerk, apparently still unfamiliar with many of the members, noted Sir Richard Lee as 'Sir Richard Luson'. But no such 'Luson' existed, and it seems to be a straightforward mistake for Sir Richard Lee; for Lee's Straffordianism see Keeler, *Long Parliament*, p. 246.

46 For Bayntun and his adulteries, see *CSPW, 1629–31*, pp. 92, 116; Keeler, *Long Parliament*, p. 101. Bayntun was a highly improbable future Parliamentarian.

47 *CJ*, II, 21.

48 Ibid.

49 For Sir Henry Mildmay, see Keeler, *Long Parliament*, p. 274. Mildmay was married to one of the daughters of Susan Halliday (the widow of Alderman William Halliday, who died in 1624). Susan Halliday then married the Earl of Warwick, as his second wife, before 20 January 1626; she lived until January 1646, predeceasing the earl; see *Complete Peerage*, XII, Part 2, p. 411. Warwick was thus Mildmay's stepfather-in-law; and Mildmay (who also signed himself 'Myldemay') referred to the earl with more than merely conventional deference as 'Yor Lord[shi]pps humble servant to be commaunded': see, for example, Mildmay to the Earl of Warwick, 24 January 1642: BL,

Add. MS 34253 (Civil War correspondence), fo. 7. Warwick had exercised electoral patronage in Maldon, Mildmay's borough, since 1624, and by 1628 seems to have controlled all the Essex parliamentary seats. (I am grateful to Mr Christopher Thompson for this last point and for his advice on Mildmay's kin.) For Mildmay's expectation of the post of Treasurer of the Household, as one of the series of offices promised during Warwick's ascendancy in the late summer of 1641, see above, Ch. 11.

50 The implications of this usage of the term 'Commonwealth' are discussed above, Epilogue.

51 It is arguable that it was the crudeness of the 'patron-client' model imposed on the period by some 1970s Revisionist historians that discredited the very notion of the nobility exercising a significant political role in the politics of the early 1640s; see, for example, Paul Christianson, 'The Peers, the People, and Parliamentary Management in the First Six Months of the Long Parliament', *Journal of Modern History*, 49 (1977), 575–99, at 584–6.

52 *CJ*, II, 322. Once again, in November 1641, Sir John Clotworthy was one of the tellers (with Lord Wharton's father-in-law, Arthur Goodwin) on the anti-court side of the division.

53 While it would be rash to assume that the 165 Commons-men who voted in (what amounted to) Strafford's favour on 6 November 1640 included all the 148 who later took the 'king's side' in the vote on the Grand Remonstrance, a substantial degree of overlap between the two groups is not improbable. If *how* the Commons divided on that first working day is uncertain, that fact that it *was* divided – and divided almost straight down the middle – is not. As no lists were kept, or at least none have survived, to indicate the names of those who voted on either side (other than the names of the tellers), it is impossible to gauge how closely the two parties of December 1641 corresponded to the (numerically suspiciously close) division of November 1640.

54 *PLP*, I, 43, 46–7; Bodl. Lib., MS Rawlinson c. 956 (Holland diary), fos. 5–7v; Notestein, *D'Ewes Diary*, pp. 7–11; Rushworth, *Historical Collections*, Part III,

I, 21–4. The speech is discussed in Russell, *Fall of the British Monarchies*, pp. 216–17.

55 *CJ*, II, 23–4.

56 J. P. Cooper, *Land, Men and Beliefs: Studies in Early Modern History* (1983), pp. 198–9.

57 Staffordshire RO, Dyott MS D661/11/1/5: Sir Richard Dyott to [?], 7 September 1640.

58 Gilbert Burnet, *History of My Own Time*, ed. Osmund Airy, 2 vols (Oxford, 1897), I, 45–6; Roger Acherley, *The Britannic Constitution: or, the Fundamental Form of Government in Britain* (1727), p. 408 (for the quotation).

59 Whitaker, *Life of Radcliffe*, p. 292.

60 The printed text reads 'then': Whitaker, *Life of Radcliffe*, p. 218.

61 Ibid.: Earl of Strafford to Sir George Radcliffe, 6 November 1640; for confirmation of this, see BL, Add. MS 15567 (Anon. memoir), fo. 31r-v.

62 BL, Add. MS 15567 (Anon. memoir), fo. 31v (my emphasis). The author of this memoir does not commit himself as to whether the reports were true or not, merely that they were believed to be true at the time. The evidence from Laud (who was close to Strafford), cited in the next note, suggests that they were well founded.

63 Laud, *History of the Troubles*, p. 85.

64 BL, Add. MS 11045 (Scudamore correspondence), fo. 144v: [Edward Rossingham's] newsletter, 25 November 1640. On anti-Scottish prejudice in the Long Parliament in general, see David Scott, 'The "Northern Gentlemen", the Parliamentary Independents, and Anglo-Scottish Relations in the Long Parliament', *Historical Journal*, 42 (1999), 347–75.

65 Baillie, *Letters*, I, 272; see also Timmis, *Thine is the Kingdom*, p. 47, where the date of Strafford's arrival is given as the 10th; and Russell, *Fall of the British Monarchies*, p. 221, where it is given as the 11th.

66 BL, Add. MS 15567 (Anon. memoir), fo. 31v.

67 Discussed above, pp. 101–3.

68 Cambridge UL, MS Kk. VI. 37 (Palmer diary), p. 34 (*PLP*, I, 102).

69 Ibid.

70 Notestein, *D'Ewes Diary*, p. 24; *OED*, 'gabion', *s.v.*

71 For the use of Hamilton's fleet in the Firth of Forth in 1639, see David Stevenson, *The Scottish Revolution, 1637–44: the Triumph of the Covenanters* (Newton Abbot, 1973), p. 143.

72 Notestein, *D'Ewes Diary*, p. 24.

73 Laud, *History of the Troubles*, p. 85; BL, Add. MS 15567 (Anon. memoir), fo. 31v.

74 The anonymous 'Manchester' memoir states that the intended victims were drawn from both Houses of Parliament; BL, Add. MS 15567 (Anon. memoir), fo. 31v.

75 BL, Add. MS 15567 (Anon. memoir), fo. 31v. Even allowing for the court's notorious porousness when it came to news and gossip, the possibility cannot be excluded that the Lord Lieutenant (or the king) deliberately allowed the news to filter out in the hope of precipitating the prime suspects into flight – with the admission of their guilt that this would imply.

76 BL, Add. MS 15567 (Anon. memoir), fo. 7v (for Darley's role as an intermediary). It is unclear whether Darley was formally charged with treason. By the time his brother, Richard Darley, presented a petition to the Commons on 13 November 1640 for his case to be investigated, he had already had two writs of habeas corpus procured on his behalf out of the Court of King's Bench, which had been ignored or refused by the Keeper of York Castle; *CJ*, II, 28.

77 HMC, *Fourth Report*, p. 30; *LJ*, IV, 102; David Scott, 'Henry Darley' (unpublished biography, HPL).

78 I infer this dating from the fact that they were reported by Matthew Cradock first thing on Wednesday morning, 11 November; so the actions described related to information gleaned the previous day; Notestein, *D'Ewes Diary*, p. 24 *PLP*, I, 100.

79 Notestein, *D'Ewes Diary*, pp. 24–5; for the attribution of these words directly to Strafford, see ibid., p. 28. This news was reported to the Commons first thing on

Wednesday morning, 11 November, but must relate to preparation that were already in train on the previous day. Fereby is named in Cambridge UL, MS Kk. VI. 38 (Palmer diary), p. 37 (*PLP*, I, 103).

80 Notestein, *D'Ewes Diary*, p. 24.

81 For the king's visit to the Tower, see Notestein, *D'Ewes Diary*, p. 24; Cambridge UL, MS Kk. VI. 38 (Palmer diary), p. 34. The exact moment at which plans for the Tower visit were decided upon is unknown; but even allowing for the relatively short notice at which such arrangements could be made in early-modern courts, preparations must have been set in train at very least the day before, and possibly earlier. *PLP,* I, 103).

82 The explanation offered by the Privy Councillor, Sir Thomas Rowe: Notestein, *D'Ewes Diary*, p. 24. *PLP*, I, 100.

83 Laud, *History of the Troubles*, p. 85. For the dating of Strafford's meeting with the king, I follow Gardiner: *History*, IX, 231. The anonymous memoir (BL, Add. MS 15567, fo. 31v) states that Strafford's intention to accuse various members of both Houses was intimated 'to some of the house of Comons'. It seems inconceivable, however, that these Commons-men (of whom Pym was likely to have been one) did not pass the information on to the peers who were similarly threatened.

84 *CJ*, II, 25; Notestein, *D'Ewes Diary*, p. 23; Cambridge UL, MS Kk. VI. 38 (Palmer diary), p. 33. (*PLP*, I, 84). Bedford's son-in-law, Lord Digby, made the report of the conference on this matter to the House of Commons; *CJ*, II, 25.

85 Whitaker, *Life of Radcliffe*, p. 218.

86 Laud, *History of the Troubles*, p. 85; compare the anonymous memoir: 'it wrought the effect designed[:] to hasten their intended impeachment of high treason against him'; BL, Add. MS 15567 (Anon. memoir), fo. 31v.

87 'Petition of the Twelve Peers', in Gardiner, *Constitutional Documents*, p. 136.

88 Centre for Kentish Studies, De L'Isle MS U1475/C85/19: Earl of Northumberland to the Earl of Leicester, 13 November 1640 (omitted from HMC, *De L'Isle Manuscripts*).

89 These were presented in the Commons on the following day, 11 November, and later submitted to the Lords; Notestein, *D'Ewes*

Diary, p. 28; a summary of these was compiled by the younger Sir John Coke (HMC, *Cowper Manuscripts*, II, 262–3), including 'Instances of proof'. But it is a measure of how rough-and-ready this indictment actually was that the accusation was not submitted to the Lords in written form; and that many of the 'instances of proof' mentioned on 11 November were subsequently dropped.

90 For the belief that Strafford was about to accuse 'the Lord Saye and some others', see Clarendon, *Rebellion*, I, 227. Hyde's uncertainty as to whether this was actually true can, I believe, be dispelled by the evidence in Rushworth, *Strafforde's Trial*, p. 2.

91 Clarendon, *Rebellion*, I, 225–6. I am grateful to Mr Christopher Thompson for a discussion of the significance of this passage.

92 *CJ*, II, 26.

93 The footnote to the text is based on Robert Brenner, *Merchants and Revolution: Commercial Change, Political Conflict, and London's Overseas Traders, 1550–1653* (Cambridge, 1993), pp. 137–40, 276, whence the quotations in the footnote.

94 Notestein, *D'Ewes Diary*, p. 24 (emphasis added).

95 Ibid.; Cambridge UL, MS Kk. VI. 38 (Palmer diary), fo. 34.

96 Notestein, *D'Ewes Diary*, p. 24 (PLP, I, 97).

97 *CJ*, II, 26; for a short biography of Cradock, see Pearl, *London*, pp. 185–7. Gardiner's claim that it was Pym 'who rose and moved that the doors should be locked' is one of the many instances where Gardiner makes Pym the author of actions in the absence of any direct evidence to justify the attribution; Gardiner, *History*, IX, 233. If true, however, the speculation (and it is no more than that) would suggest that this was a more self-interested initiative than his fellow Commons-men may have realized.

98 For Clotworthy and Pym, who certainly were involved in the Warwick House plans for an attack on Strafford, the practical import of the locking of the Commons' outward door may have been that it prevented the admission of any 'messengers' from the House of Lords – the couriers who, if and when Strafford

made his expected accusation of treason against various members of the lower House, would have conveyed the peers' request for those accused to be committed to the Serjeant at-Arms. For the Lords' messengers, see Elizabeth Read Foster, *The House of Lords, 1603–49: Structure, Procedure, and the Nature of its Business* (Chapel Hill, NC 1983), pp. 12, 31, 65, 71–2, 130–31.

99 BL, Add. MS 15567 (Anon. memoir), fo. 31v.

100 Gardiner, *History*, IX, 233: 'The only reasonable supposition is that, when the moment for execution [of the plan to accuse the Petitioner leaders] came, Charles drew back, as he had so often drawn back before'. In Gardiner's favour, this was very close to what Charles had done the previous year (1639), when, on the eve of engaging the Covenanter army in battle, he had decided to postpone the moment of confrontation with his enemies, hoping to do so from a position of greater strength in the near future. For the king's (arguably profoundly mistaken) decision to postpone the confrontation with the Covenanters in 1639, see John Adamson, 'England without Cromwell: What if Charles I had avoided the Civil War?', in Niall Ferguson (ed.), *Virtual History: Alternatives and Counterfactuals* (1997), pp. 99–100.

101 Kevin Sharpe, 'The Earl of Arundel, his Circle and the Opposition to the Duke of Buckingham, 1618–28', in Kevin Sharpe (ed.), *Faction and Parliament: Essays on Early Stuart History* (Oxford, 1978), pp. 209–44.

102 BL, Add. MS 15567 (Anon. memoir), fo. 32.

103 C. V. Wedgwood, *Thomas Wentworth, First Earl of Strafford: a Revaluation* (1961), p. 314; compare Timmis, *Thine is the Kingdom*, p. 48: 'John Pym was a master of timing' a skill which he repeatedly demonstrated during the next three years.

104 Gardiner, *History*, IX, p. 233.

105 *Ibid*. The last quotation is Notestein's description of this moment in Gardiner's narrative: see Notestein, *D'Ewes Diary*, p. 25, n. 15.

106 Gardiner, *History*, IX, 235.

107 For Gardiner's methods and broader influence, see John Adamson, 'Eminent

Victorians: S. R. Gardiner and the Liberal as Hero', *Historical Journal*, 33 (1990), 641–57; and see also Blair Worden, *Roundhead Reputations: the English Civil War and the Passions of Posterity* (2001).

108 For a more recent restatement of this Gardinerian view, see John Morrill, 'The Religious Context of the English Civil War', *Transactions of the Royal Historical Society*, 5th ser., 34 (1984), 155–78.

109 See above, Epilogue.

110 Compare Timmis, for a characteristic statement of Pym's primacy: 'John Pym was the principal architect of the constitutional revolution of the next eighteen months in England, and therefore one of the most significant single figures, and one of the most remarkable intellects, in the constitutional history of England'; Timmis, *Thine is the Kingdom*, p. 43.

111 Russell, *Fall of the British Monarchies*, p. 221. Not one of these three statements is correct: the impeachment was never 'formally moved' by Pym (merely reported from a select committee); Strafford did not return from Yorkshire on 11 November, but two days earlier, on the 9th (Baillie, *Letters*, I, 272); and he was not immediately sent to the Tower, but committed to the custody of the Gentleman Usher of the Black Rod (*LJ*, IV, 88) – indeed, the Commons' original request to the Lords was merely that the earl should 'stand committed *for two or three daies* untill witnesses and proofe came in' (Notestein, *D'Ewes Diary*, p. 29). See also Paul Christianson, 'The Peers, the People, and Parliamentary Management in the First Six Months of the Long Parliament', *Journal of Modern History*, 49 (1977), 575–99, at p. 584.

112 HMC, *Twelfth Report*, II, 262; Wedgwood, *Strafford*, p. 321.

113 Gardiner, *History*, IX, 233n–234n.

114 Cambridge UL, MS Kk. VI. 38 (Palmer diary); Minnesota UL, MS 137 (Peyton diary); Bodl. Lib., MS Rawlinson c. 956 (Holland diary); and PLP, I, 93–112.

115 As Wallace Notestein pointed out as early as 1923, Bodvile 'erred' in attributing this speech, which was by Pym, to Sir Francis Seymour, just as 'Clotworthy, not Pym, made

the following': Notestein, *D'Ewes Diary*, p. 25n.

116 Notestein, *D'Ewes Diary*, p. 25; Minnesota UL, MS 137 (Peyton diary), p. 10; John Nalson, *An Impartiall Collection of the Great Affairs of State*, 2 vols (1682), I, 523.

117 Bodl. Lib., MS Clarendon 19, fos. 30, 48, 51; *Clarendon State Papers*, II, 116; *CSPD, 1640*, pp. 602–3; and see Caroline Hibbard, *Charles I and the Popish Plot* (Chapel Hill, NC, 1983), p. 183.

118 Minnesota UL, MS 137 (Peyton diary), p. 11 (Notestein, *D'Ewes Diary*, p. 27n); *PLP*, I, 105. Among those who also pressed home this charge was Edward Kirton, a household officer of the Earl of Hertford, another of the Petitioner Peers; Keeler, *Long Parliament*, p. 242, n. 55.

119 Gardiner, *History*, IX, 233–4.

120 Gardiner's misattribution was the result of his reliance on a mistaken reference in Bodvile's notoriously error-prone parliamentary diary: Notestein, *D'Ewes Diary*, p. 25, n. 15; compare Cambridge UL, MS Kk. VI. 38 (Palmer diary), p. 34.

121 For Clotworthy's experience of Strafford's government of Ireland, see Jane Ohlmeyer, 'Strafford, the "Londonderry Business" and the "New British History"', in Merritt, *Political World of Thomas Wentworth*, pp. 209–29, esp. pp. 216–8.

122 Notestein, *D'Ewes Diary*, pp. 25–6 (emphasis added); Cambridge UL, MS Kk. VI. 38 (Palmer diary), p. 34.

123 John Rushworth, *The Tryal of Thomas Earl of Strafford* (1700), p. 112; quoted in Fiona Pogson, 'Sir George Radcliffe', *ODNB*. For Radcliffe's relations with Strafford, see also Julia Merritt, 'Power and Communication: Thomas Wentworth and Government at a Distance during the Personal Rule, 1629–35', in her *The Political World of Thomas Wentworth, Earl of Strafford,*, pp. 109–32.

124 Cambridge UL, MS Kk. VI. 38 (Palmer diary), p. 34 (*PLP*, I, 103).

125 This can be inferred from the *Commons Journal* of the day, where any successful motion would usually have been recorded; see *CJ*, II, 26–7.

126 Cambridge UL, MS Kk. VI. 38 (Palmer diary), p. 36 (*PLP*, I, 103).

127 As Hyde observed, if the Lords had not been 'kept from rising...[it] would very much have broken their measures'; Clarendon, *Rebellion*, I, 225.

128 See Clarendon, *Rebellion*, I, 225–6.

129 Here, too, the Petitioners probably had self-interested motives for their selection of victim. Given that Windebank had been spying on the régime's critics for more than a year, and would have been a key figure in any Strafford-led prosecution of these 'traitors', this too looks like an attempt by Warwick House to pre-empt a potential accuser. Windebank was charged with being negligent in failing to investigate evidence of preparations for an armed rising by Catholics in England (the alleged 'popish plot' that was to bulk ever larger in the months ahead); and, even more seriously, he was reported to have declared that all those who had conspired to deny the king supply during the last Parliament (in April and May that year) were 'traitours'. Notestein, *D'Ewes Diary*, pp. 26–7. The attack on Windebank was initiated by Thomas Coke, the son of Windebank's court rival, the former Secretary of State, Sir John Coke. He seems to have had his own (possibly familial) reasons for bringing down the Secretary, unconnected with the concerns of the Junto; even so, the timing of the attack, which was backed up immediately by two other speakers, played into the hands of the Junto leadership to such an extent that it strains credulity to suggest that it was coincidental; *PLP*, I, 102.

130 For the mention of Leicester House, Notestein, *D'Ewes Diary*, p. 27; for Strafford's residence at Leicester House, see *Radcliffe Correspondence*, pp. 200–1. From that point, Windebank was effectively under notice: if he made any move against the Petitioners, he, too, could expect formal impeachment proceedings against him. Even before formal charges were laid against him, Northumberland regarded Windebank's Secretaryship, as well as Strafford's Lieutenancy in Ireland, as soon-to-be-vacant offices; HMC, *De L'Isle Manuscripts*, VI, 339–40: Countess of Carlisle to the Countess of Leicester, 10 November [1640].

131 Notestein's critique of Gardiner on this

point is highly persuasive: 'Gardiner has given the impression that this accusation was the result of debate in the House, but the evidence from [the diaries of] Palmer and Peyton shows that he was wrong on many small points that lead to that conclusion'; Notestein, *D'Ewes Diary*, p. 30, n. 50. Significantly, the *Commons Journal* makes no mention of any order for impeachment articles to be prepared or brought in; and the one reference (which, like all Journal entries, was compiled after the day's proceedings) to the establishment of the select committee describes what the committee subsequently did, not what it was established to do: 'This select committee retired into the Committee Chamber to prepare matter for a conference to be prayed with the Lords, and the charge against the Earl of Strafford'; *CJ*, II, 26. It is impossible to be sure, but the last phrase looks suspiciously like a clerk's interpolation when the Journal was compiled some time after the event.

132 *CJ*, II, 26; Whitelocke, *Memorials*, I, 113–14. For Strode and Pym, see Cornwall RO, MS WW642, for Strode as a signatory to the marriage settlement of Pym's daughter, *c.* 15 January 1641. Strode and Holles were near contemporaries, both having been born in 1599. As Hyde noted, Holles's relation to Strafford 'did not otherwise interrupt the friendship he had with those most violent of [Strafford's] prosecutors'; and in all other matters 'he was in the most secret councils with those who most governed' – namely, the circle around Bedford (and, one might add, the Earl of Warwick). Clarendon, *Rebellion*, I, 250 (for the quotation); for Hyde's identification of 'those who most governed', see ibid., I, 241–9, where he names the leading figures as Bedford, Saye, and Mandeville, from the Lords, and Pym, St John, and Hampden, from the Commons – the group that I associate with Bedford House. The Devonian, William Strode, was a generation younger than Bedford, who was a friend and 'honest broker' to the family more generally, and had been close to William's father, Sir William Strode of Newnham, Devon (*d.* 1637). There is a revealing moment in January 1638, when William Strode's brother, Sir Richard, sought and gained Bedford's mediation (presumably in relation to the settlement of their father's estate), acknowledging, in a letter to Bedford of 31 January 1638, that 'it did this day please your Lordship, out of your

great respecte to my decessed father, to pittie the case of his disagreeinge sonnes'; BL, Harl. MS 7001 (Historical papers), fo. 137: Sir Richard Strode to the Earl of Bedford, [31 January] 1638. For Bedford's holograph notes on his reply, see ibid., fo. 138v. Strode was also linked to the Petitioner circle through his friend, Pym (for whom Strode was to act as a pallbearer), and, perhaps as strongly, through his brother-in-law, Sir Walter Erle; see also C. H. Firth (revised L. J. Reeve), 'William Strode', *ODNB*. There is also the possibility that Strode owed one or other of his double returns for the November 1640 Parliament (he was elected at Tamworth and at Beeralston, Devon), to the Earl of Essex and Lord Robartes (a suggestion I owe to Mr Christopher Thompson).

133 *CJ*, II, 26; PLP, I, 94.

134 Minnesota UL, MS 137 (Peyton diary), p. 12 (PLP, I, 106).

135 *CJ*, II, 26.

136 The newly created committee not only had to persuade the Commons to accept impeachment articles against the earl; they had to deliver them to the Lords and ensure that they deprived Strafford of his right to sit – all that very same day. Hence, Pym sought (and was granted) permission to go to intimate what was being planned to some of the Lords 'privately' – almost certainly the group around Warwick and Bedford – to ensure that they remained in session until the impeachment proceedings were delivered that same day. Bodl. Lib., MS Rawlinson c. 956 (Holland diary), fo. 23v (PLP, I, 108).

137 For the timing, see BL, Add. MS 15567 (Anon. memoir), fo. 31v: Pym went to the House of Lords at some time between 4 and 5 p.m.

138 Minnesota UL, MS 137 (Peyton diary), p. 12; Notestein, *D'Ewes Diary*, pp. 28–9; PLP, I, 106.

139 Notestein, *D'Ewes Diary*, p. 28; for the last quotation, see Minnesota UL, MS 137 (Peyton diary), p. 12.

140 Notestein, *D'Ewes Diary*, p. 28 (for quotations); PLP, I, 99).

141 Notestein, *D'Ewes Diary*, p. 28.

142 Notestein, *D'Ewes Diary*, p. 29, n. 46.

143 Clarendon, *Rebellion*, I, 225–6. I am grateful to Mr Christopher Thompson for a discussion of the significance of this passage.

144 Notestein, *D'Ewes Diary*, p. 29.

145 Russell, *Fall of the British Monarchies*, p. 221.

146 Clarendon, *Rebellion*, I, 226. Hyde gives the time of the Strafford's decision go to the House as 'about three of the clock' (ibid.), which would roughly tally with a time of around 4 p.m. for the actual presentation of the charges against him (see ibid., p. 228).

147 *CJ*, II, 26.

148 *LJ*, IV, 88–9; Timmis, *Thine is the Kingdom*, p. 50.

149 *LJ*, IV, 89.

150 The most vivid account of Strafford's committal remains C. V. Wedgwood, *Thomas Wentworth: First Earl of Strafford, 1593–1641 – a Revaluation* (1961), pp. 315–7. Certain colourful details, however – such as the moment when Strafford, on his way out of the Lords' chamber, passes 'Lord Cork, his hat pulled firmly upon his brows, [who] stared at him in unconcealed triumph' – seem to be pure invention; the Earl of Cork was not a member of the English House of Lords; ibid., p. 317.

151 BL, Add. MS 15567 (Anon. memoir), fo. 31v.

152 Centre for Kentish Studies, De L'Isle MS U1475/C85/19: Earl of Northumberland to the Earl of Leicester, 13 November 1640 (omitted from HMC, *De L'Isle Manuscripts*).

153 The dissolution of the pro-Spanish party in the wake of Strafford's arrest is discussed in Hibbard, *Popish Plot*, pp. 176–7.

154 ASV, Senato, Dispacci Inghil. 42, fo. 157v: Giustinian to the Doge and Senate, 13/23 November 1640 (*CSPV 1640–42*, p. 96). Giustinian's name is sometimes rendered in supposedly authentic Italian form as 'Giustiniani' by authors evidently intent on removing the Anglicizations imposed by the nineteenth-century editors of the *Calendar of State Papers, Venetian*; but 'Giustinian' is the standard form of the name in Venetian, and the form that the ambassador used in his signature (see ASV, Senato, Dispacci Inghil. 42 and 43, *passim*).

155 Brian Quintrell, 'Sir Francis Windebank', *DNB*; for Windebank's career during the 1630s, see P. Haskell, 'Sir Francis Windebank and the Personal Rule of Charles I', (Unpublished Ph.D. dissertation, University of Southampton, 1978).

156 On the delay in bringing detailed charges against Strafford, see also HMC, *Buccleuch Manuscripts*, III, 390.

157 *CJ*, II, 76; Notestein, *D'Ewes Diary*, pp. 303–4.

158 These absences are discussed above, Chs 12 and 13; and see V. F. Snow, 'Attendance Trends and Absenteeism in the Long Parliament', *Huntington Library Quarterly*, 18 (1954–55), 301–6.

159 Partly through the activities of Edward Nicholas: see above, Chs. 12–13.

160 For these three appointments, see *CJ*, II, 27.

161 Moreover, once the impeachment proceedings reached the upper House, it was this same Bedford–Warwick connection that came to the fore as Strafford's most vociferous accusers. See above, Chs. 8–10.

162 Staffordshire RO, Dartmouth MS D(W)1778/I/i/11. The regiments are those of the 'Lord Marquis [Hamilton]'; the Lord General [Northumberland]; the Earl of Newport; the Serjeant-Major-General; Colonel Goring; Lord Grandison; Colonel Aston; Lord Barrymore; Colonel Wentworth; Colonel [Sir John] Meyrick; Colonel Colepeper; Sir Charles Vavasour; Colonel Vavasour; Colonel Lunsford, and Colonel Ogle.

163 Ibid., and see Ch. 5.

164 BL, Add. MS 15567 (Anon. memoir), fo. 32v.

165 Quoted in Wedgwood, *Strafford*, p. 317; citing *LJ*, IV, 88–9; BL, Add. MS 15567 (Anon. memoir), fo. 32; Baillie, *Letters*, I, 272–3; *Lismore Papers*, V, 164.

166 Sir John Wray, *Eight Occasionall Speeches, made in the House of Commons this Parliament* ([mid] 1641), p. 1 (BL, E 196/10).

4. THE AUDIT OF MISRULE

1 William Bridge, *Babylons Downfall: a Sermon lately preached at Westminster before Sundry of the House of Commons [6 April 1641]* (1641), p. 12 (BL, E 163/3).

2 Bodl. Lib., MS Rawlinson d. 141 (Diary of an anonymous Maidstone man), p. 9.

3 This description of the procession is based on Bodl. Lib., MS Rawlinson d. 141 (Diary of an anonymous Maidstone man), p. 9; [William Prynne], *A New Discovery of the Prelates Tyranny, in their Late Prosecution of Mr William Pryn* (1641), pp. 114–5 (BL, E 162/1–2); Henry Burton, *A Narration of the Life of Mr Henry Burton* (1643), pp. 40–3 (BL, E 94/10).

4 [Prynne], *A New Discovery of the Prelates Tyranny*, pp. 114–5.

5 Bodl. Lib., MS Rawlinson d. 141 (Diary of an anonymous Maidstone man), p. 9; [Prynne], *A New Discovery of the Prelates Tyranny*, pp. 114–5.

6 Ibid.; May, *History of the Parliament*, p. 80. The element of exaggeration would appear to be small: the figure of 100 coaches in the procession is confirmed by the report in William Hawkins's letter to the Earl of Leicester of 3 December 1640: HMC, *De L'Isle Manuscripts*, VI, 346.

7 [Prynne], *A New Discovery of the Prelates Tyranny*, p. 115.

8 Bodl. Lib., MS Rawlinson d. 141 (Diary of an anonymous Maidstone man), p. 9.

9 [James Howell], *The True Informer, who in the Following Discours or Colloquy, discovereth unto the World the Chiefe Causes of the Sad Distempers in Great Brittany and Ireland* ([12 April] 1643), p. 17 (BL, E 96/10).

10 [Prynne], *A New Discovery of the Prelates Tyranny*, pp. 114–5.

11 Malcolm Smuts, 'Public Ceremony and Royal Charisma: the English Royal Entry in London, 1485–1642', in A. L. Beier, David Cannadine, J. M. Rosenheim (eds.), *The First Modern Society: Essays in English History in Honour of Lawrence Stone* (Cambridge, 1989), pp. 65–93; and for points of comparison, see William Leahy, *Elizabethan Triumphal Processions* (Aldershot, 2004).

12 The key works objected to were Prynne's,

A Looking-Glasse for Lordly Prelates (1636), STC 1493:04; Henry Burton, *A Divine Tragedie lately Acted, or a Collection of Sundry Memorable Examples of Gods Judgements upon Sabbath-Breakers* (1636), STC 1214:13; and John Bastwick, Πραχεις των Επισκοπων sive apologeticus ad praesules Anglicanos criminum ecclesiasticorum in Curia Celsae Commissionis ([Leiden?], 1636), STC (2nd edn) 1576; and his *The Letany of John Bastvvick, Doctor of Phisicke* ([Leiden], 1637), BL, E 203/5.

13 Bodl. Lib., Bankes Papers 18/21: examination of John Lilburne, 17 May 1638; for the widely circulated account of their sufferings, see Bodl. Lib., MS Tanner 299, fo. 146; [William Prynne], *A Briefe Relation of Certain Speciall and Most Material Passages* (1637), p. 30.

14 NA, C 115/N8/8806: 6 July 1637; quoted in Kevin Sharpe, *The Personal Rule of Charles I* (New Haven and London, 1992), p. 763; see also Laud's concerns, in Knowler, *Strafforde's Letters*, II, 99: Archbishop Laud to Viscount Wentworth, 28 August 1637.

15 For Burton's escalating radicalism, see his *The Christians Bulwarke, against Satans Battery. Or, the Doctrine of Iustification* (1632), STC 1196:23; *Grounds of Christian Religion laid downe briefly and plainely by way of Question and Answer* (1635), STC2 4144; *For God, and the King. The Summe of Two Sermons preached on the Fifth of November Last in St. Matthewes Friday-streete. 1636* ([Amsterdam], 1636), STC2 4142.

16 For its impact on contemporaries, see [Howell], *The True Informer*, p. 17; [Robert Chestlin], *Persecutio Undecima. The Churches Eleventh Persecution* ([5 Nov.] 1648), p. 21 (BL, E 470/7).

17 Burton, *Narration*, p. 41; for contemporary confirmation of this point, see Bodl. Lib., MS Rawlinson d. 141 ('Maidstone diary'), p. 9.

18 Burton, *Narration*, p. 41.

19 Quoted in Anthony Fletcher, *The Outbreak of the English Civil War* (1981), p. 2.

20 Dorothy Gardiner (ed.), *The Oxinden Letters, 1607–42: being the Correspondence of Henry Oxinden of Barham and his Circle*

(1933), p. 187: James Oxinden to his brother, Henry, 27 November 1640.

21 Sir John Wray, *Eight Occasionall Speeches, made in the House of Commons this Parliament* ([mid]1641), p. 1 (BL, E 196/10), for the quotation.

22 *CJ*, II, 22.

23 The Council and ecclesiastical courts used the oath *ex officio* in both criminal and civil proceedings. Defendants were first required to take the oath and were then presented with a series of questions based on the prior examination of witnesses and informants. The defendant was not told the charges against him, and he was required to answer all questions. Contradictory answers were then used against the defendant in an effort to force a confession of guilt.

24 Notestein, *D'Ewes Diary*, p. 5; also reported in Minnesota UL, MS 137 (Peyton diary), p. 3 (PLP, I, 42).

25 Cambridge UL, MS Kk. VI. p. 38 (Palmer diary), p. 23 (PLP, I, 66–7).

26 For Capell and Mandeville, see Keeler, *Long Parliament*, 'Arthur Capel [*sic*]'; for the Capell family's relations with Warwick, see and Christopher Thompson, 'The Essex Election of 1604', *Essex Journal*, 14 (1979), 2, and n. 8; idem, *Parliamentary Selection and the Essex Election of 1604* (Privately printed, Wivenhoe, 1995), pp. 1–2, 6–9. Arthur Capell also seems to have been involved in the Barrington network; see BL, Egerton MS 2646 (Barrington letters), fo. 140: Arthur Capell to Sir Thomas Barrington, 30 December 1640.

27 Notestein, *D'Ewes Diary*, p. 16. The Commons-man doing the noting at this point is John Bodvile, the knight of the shire for Anglesey.

28 For Cromwell's relations with St John, see his letter to Mrs St John (possibly St John's second wife), 13 October 1638, printed in W. C. Abbott (ed.), *The Writings and Speeches of Oliver Cromwell*, 4 vols. (Oxford, 1988), I, 96–7; and see Northamptonshire RO, L(C)854. Among those in Warwick's circle whom Cromwell knew well, were Sir William Masham, in whose household one of Cromwell's sons appears to have been living in the late 1630s (for which see Abbott, *Letters and Speeches*, I, 96–7); and Sir Gilbert

Gerard, in the settlement of whose estates Cromwell was involved in 1640: see Centre for Buckinghamshire Studies, D-X 1/72. The possibility of Cromwell's connection, through St John, with Warwick's circle is considered in John Morrill, 'The Making of Oliver Cromwell', in John Morrill (ed.), *Oliver Cromwell and the English Revolution* (1990), pp. 34–5, 42–5.

29 G[iles] S[trangways?], *A Letter from an Ejected member of the House of Commons to Sir Jo[hn] Evelyn* (16 Aug. 1648), p. 6 (BL, E 463/18).

30 *CJ*, II, 24.

31 Ibid.

32 As the Commons lacked formal powers to countermand the sentences of any court, these orders were usually couched in the form of instructions to their gaolers to release the offenders so that they could be questioned by the House concerning the circumstances of their trial. In theory, the sentences still stood, unless subsequently overturned by the House of Lords. In practice, however, given the near-total collapse of the authority of the Privy Council and the prerogative courts, these notionally 'temporary' orders for the offenders' release were as good as absolute.

33 Peterhouse, Cambridge, topped the table for the most shocking disclosures. See Notestein, *D'Ewes Diary*, p. 58, for the case of a minister, John Norton, whose son, then a student at Catherine Hall, various Fellows of Peterhouse had attempted to 'seduce … to popery', alleging that the Master, Dr John Cosin, would make him a Fellow if he were prepared to accept their views and 'come hither'; see also *CJ*, II, 35.

34 Peter Lake, 'The Laudian Style: Order, Uniformity and the Pursuit of the Beauty of Holiness in the 1630s', in Kenneth Fincham (ed.), *The Early Stuart Church, 1603–42* (Basingstoke, 1993), pp. 161–85; Andrew Foster, 'Archbishop Richard Neile Revisited', Peter Lake and Michael Questier (eds.), *Conformity and Orthodoxy in the English Church, c. 1560–1660* (Woodbridge, 2000), pp. 159–78; Anthony Milton, '"That Sacred Oratory": Religion and the Chapel Royal during the Personal Rule of Charles I', in Andrew Ashbee (ed.), *William Lawes (1602–45): Essays on his Life, Times and Work* (Aldershot, 1998), pp. 69–96.

35 *CJ*, II, 35; further information relating to the case is to be found in Cambridge University Lib., MS Mm. 1. p. 45 (Baker collection), p. 34.

36 *The Petition of the Inhabitants of Isleworth in the Countie of Middlesex against William Grant, Minister of the Said Parish* (1641), pp. 1–3, quotation at pp. 2–3 (Wing P1802). The 'fast' referred to in this petition is that held on 8 July 1640 in order to seek deliverance from the plague: *A Forme of Common Prayer; to be Used upon the Eighth of July: on which Day a Fast is appointed by His Majesties Proclamation, for the Averting of the Plague* (1640), STC2 1655.

37 *Petition of the Inhabitants of Isleworth*, pp. 4, 5. The singing of the 'unlearned' almost certainly referred to their habit of singing psalms to a simple chant, a practice that had figured prominently in the Church's pre-Laudian practice, and which was much esteemed by Puritans.

38 On this theme, see John Walter, 'Anti-Popery and the Stour Valley Riots of 1642', in David Chadd, (ed.), *History of Religious Dissent in East Anglia, III* (Norwich, 1996), pp. 121–40; John Walter, 'Popular Iconoclasm and the Politics of the Parish in Eastern England, 1640–42', *Historical Journal*, 47 (2004), 261–90; idem, '"Abolishing Superstition with Sedition"? The Politics of Popular Iconoclasm in England 1640–42', *Past and Present*, 183 (2004), 79–123. On parish politics more generally, see Keith Wrightson, 'The Politics of the Parish in Early Modern England', in Paul Griffiths, Adam Fox, and Steve Hindle (eds.), *The Experience of Authority in Early Modern England* (Basingstoke, 1996), pp. 10–46; and Dan Beaver, 'Parish Communities, Civil War, and Religious Conflict in England', in R. Po-Chia Hsia, *A Companion to the Reformation World* (Malden, MA, 2003), pp. 311–31.

39 Richard Cust, *Charles I: a Political Life* (2005), pp. 133–47.

40 Something of this unanimity emerged, paradoxically, in the so-called Root-and-Branch debate of February 1641, discussed above, Ch. 6.

41 *CJ*, II, 25.

42 Notestein, *D'Ewes Diary*, p. 7. The metaphor of Parliament as physician to the sick nation was so commonplace it became a subject of satire: see the manuscript verses, George Thomason's handwriting, [Anon.], *A satyre upon the state of things this Parliament* ([Nov. 1640]), BL, E 205/3.

43 Notestein, *D'Ewes Diary*, p. 7.

44 Ibid., p. 6.

45 John Leland, 'Sir Robert Tresilian', *ODNB*; see also Minnesota UL, MS 137(Peyton diary), p. 3 (PLP, I, 42–3).

46 *LJ*, V, 76–7. For Richard II, see also Bodl. Lib., MS Rawlinson d. 924 (Miscellanea), fo. 139v: 'The Earle of Strafford Characterized' [1641]; John Browne, *The Kings Articles and the Parliaments Honour. Declaring how the Archbishop of Yorke, the Duke of Ireland, the Earle of Suffolke, and some False Knights and Justices, have seduced his Majestie by Wicked Counsell to make Suddain Warre against the Parliament* (1 Aug. 1642), pp. 3–4 (BL, E 108/32); *A Declaration or, Remonstrance of the Office of a Prince, and his Counsellors* ([3 August] 1642), p. 5 (BL, E 108/38); and John Adamson, 'The Baronial Context of the English Civil War', *Transactions of the Royal Historical Society*, 40 (1990), 93–120, at p. 100n.

47 *LJ*, V, 76–7 (where the Lords cite the Parliament Roll for 11 Richard II in justification for their declaring those who assist the king in his war against Parliament traitors). The relevant extracts from this Roll were published by John Browne, the Clerk of the Parliaments (and of the House of Lords), as *The Kings Articles and the Parliaments Honour*, pp. 3–8; see also a 'Well-wisher to the Common-wealth', *The Life and Death of King Richard the Second who was Deposed of his Crown* ([12 July] 1642), pp. 2–8 (BL, E 155/15); and *LJ*, IV, 144.

48 Statistics from Sheila Lambert, 'The Opening of the Long Parliament', *Historical Journal*, 27 (1984), 265–87, at p. 273; see also her 'Procedure in the House of Commons in the Early Stuart Period', *English Historical Review*, 95 (1980), 776–9. The impeachment in 1624 was of Lionel Cranfield, 1st Earl of Middlesex, James's Lord Treasurer. It should be noted that the decline in the use of legislation, or at least in the Parliament's ability to bring new bills to completion, seems to have begun in the late 1620s; see David Rabaut, 'Secular Legislation in the English

Parliament 1604–28', (unpublished Ph.D. dissertation, Temple University, 1987).

49 These were the Triennial Act, Strafford's Act of Attainder, and the Act preventing the Parliament's dissolution without its own consent.

50 Lambert, 'Opening of the Long Parliament', p. 273. Three concerned taxation; another with press-ganging seamen for the navy; and the fifth, passed at the behest of the Commons' lawyers, prescribed the length of the Michaelmas legal term.

51 *CJ*, II, 211, 216, 224, 225. I am indebted to Miss Lambert (see note 50) for much of the material in this paragraph.

52 Even this did not reach the statute book until 7 August 1641.

53 *CJ*, II, 173; Gardiner, *Constitutional Documents*, pp. 189–92.

54 The major religious reforms are discussed above, in Chs. 6 and 11.

55 David Cressy, *England on Edge: Crisis and Revolution* (Oxford, 2006), pp. 167–210.

56 S[trangways?], *A Letter from an Ejected Member of the House of Commons p. 5.*

57 For examples, see pp. 138, 369.

58 *CJ*, II, 21. Monday afternoons were assigned to abuses in religion; Wednesday afternoons to general grievances; Thursday afternoons to 'Irish Affairs' (which, in practice, meant Strafford's government of the kingdom); and Friday afternoons to pursuing malfeasance in the 'Courts of Justice'.

59 CJ, II, p.30.

60 CJ, II, p.31.

61 CJ, II, p.34.

62 CJ, II, p.38.

63 CJ, II, p.44.

64 Lambert, 'Opening of the Long Parliament', p. 274.

65 *CJ*, II, 54.

66 Ibid.: among them, Sir Arthur Hesilrige (Lord Brooke's brother-in-law), Sir Gilbert Gerard, Sir William Masham, John Pym, Sir Thomas Barrington, Matthew Cradock, and Sir Thomas Cheeke (Warwick's brother-in-law). Other prominent Puritans included Sir

Robert Harley, John Rous (Pym's half-brother), Arthur Goodwin (Lord Wharton's father-in-law), Sir Oliver Luke, Zouche Tate, John Crewe (who had close connections with Viscount Mandeville), and Oliver Cromwell. It is perhaps a reflection of Cromwell's relative obscurity at this time that he is listed, in the printed account of the committee's membership, as 'M[r]. Cornewell'. The committee was technically 'a Sub-committee made by the grand Committee for Religion [i.e. the full House of Commons convened as a committee without the Speaker]'; see *An Order made to a Select Committee: Chosen by the Whole House of Commons to receive Petitions touching Ministers* ([Dec.] 1640), sigg. A2 (for Cromwell), a3 (for quotation); (BL, E 206/6).

67 *An Order made to a Select Committee … to receive Petitions touching Ministers*, sigg. a3[v]-a3[r].

68 Ibid., title page: 'printed by I. D. for Henry Overton, … to be sold at his Shop entring into Popes-head Alley out of Lumbard streete'. For Henry Overton's membership of the Artillery Company, see Armoury House, London, Honourable Artillery Company Archives, Quarterage Book 1628–43, unfol., 'Henry Overton', *s.v.*, entries from 1633. A Richard Overton had joined the Artillery Company the previous year, who may have been related. For the problems of the Overtons' biographies, see B. J. Gibbons, 'Richard Overton', *ODNB*.

69 *CJ*, II, 88; and see Clarendon, *Rebellion*, I, 269.

70 [Chestlin], *Persecutio Undecima*, p. 35.

71 Patrick Cormack, 'The Great Fire of Westminster, 1834', *The Historian* [London], 4 (1984), pp. 3–6; for the subsequent development of the palace, see R. J. B. Walker, 'The Palace of Westminster after the Fire of 1834', *Walpole Society*, 44 (1974 for 1972–4), 94–122.

72 The estimate is D'Ewes's; see William A. Shaw, *A History of the English Church during the Civil Wars and under the Commonwealth, 1640–60*, 2 vols. (1900), I, 14; for its acceptance, Cressy, *England on Edge*, p. 177.

73 John Pym [attrib.], *The Speech or Declaration of John Pymm, Esq. to the Lords of the Upper House, upon the Delivery of the*

Articles of the Commons Assembled in Parliament, against William Laud, Archbishop of Canterbury ([early] 1641), p. 28, emphasis added (BL, E 196/33–34).

74 To judge from the Journals of the two Houses (the official record of their proceedings), the number of cases where either House took formal measures to censure 'scandalous' Laudian clergy (other than through the impeachments of Laud and other errant bishops) was, in fact, extremely small: a grand total of only fifty-five from the opening of the Parliament to the beginning of 1642 (or an average of roughly two cases per month in both Lords and Commons). Once again, however, these bald statistics give only a fragmentary picture of the measures that were actually being taken, many (possibly most) of the cases brought to the attention of the Committee for Religion and its offshoots would never have been raised on the floor of either House, and therefore went unrecorded in the Journals; see Shaw, *English Church during the Civil Wars*, ii, 295–8.

75 Assuming 'divers hundred' to be, at least, 200; and this, as he claimed, was merely one 'hundred part' the total, the minimum number of expected complaints would have stood at 20,000. In 1641, there were roughly 9,000 parishes in England.

76 William Bridge, *Babylons Downfall: a Sermon lately preached at Westminster before Sundry of the House of Commons [6 April 1641]* (1641), p. 12 (BL, E 163/3).

77 For the peers, see J. B. Crummett, 'The Lay Peers in Parliament, 1640–44' (Unpublished Ph.D. dissertation, University of Manchester, 1970); and James S. Hart, *Justice upon Petition: the House of Lords and the Reformation of Justice, 1621–75* (1991), p. 99, n.11.

78 *LJ*, iv, 84. The eighteen signatories of the Petition of the Twelve were (in the order they are named in the Journal) the Earls of Rutland, Bath, Bedford, Hertford, Essex, Lincoln, Exeter, Warwick, Bristol, and Bolingbroke; Viscount Saye, and Lords Wharton, Paget, Kimbolton (i.e. Viscount Mandeville), Brooke, Lovelace, Howard of Escrick, and Savile. The 'Lord Howard' has to be Lord Howard of Escrick as his namesake, Lord Howard of Charlton, was not introduced to the House until 24 November.

79 Ibid. Those on the Committee of Petitions who were broadly supportive of reform were the Earls of Salisbury, Holland, Berkshire, and Stamford; and Lords Montagu of Boughton, Grey of Warke, Robartes, and Herbert of Cherbury. Only the Earl of Berkshire was to be a future Royalist, and a distinctly lukewarm one at that.

80 John Corbet, *An Historicall Relation of the Military Government of Gloucester, from the Beginning of the Civill Warre betweene King and Parliament, to the Removall of Colonell Massie from that Government* (1645), sig. A2[v] (BL, E 306/8).

81 The pioneering study of this subject is Hart, *Justice upon Petition*; reviewed by John Adamson in the *Cambridge Law Journal*, 51 (1991), 547–50; and see Hart's earlier article, 'The House of Lords and the Appellate Jurisdiction in Equity, 1640–43'. *Parliamentary History*, 2 (1983), 49–60.

82 Hart, *Justice upon Petition*, p. 2.

83 The total for the decade was around 200 cases overall; ibid., Ch. 1.

84 Ibid., pp. 66–7.

85 Ibid., p. 69 (for quotation).

86 Ibid., Table 2.1.

87 Ibid., p. 65 (for the quotation); Professor Hart may have added that every one of the figures he names was one of the original signatories of the Petition of the Twelve.

88 For Darley and Providence Island Company, see NA, CO 124/2, fos. 72, 77v, 98, 115, 120, 122v, 140v, 148v, 152v, 154v; for his relations with Brooke, see John Wallis, *Truth Tried: Or, Animadversions on a Treatise published by … Robert Lord Brook* ([22 March] 1643), sig. A (BL, E 93/21); David Scott, 'Henry Darley' (HPL, unpublished biography). The order for his release was made on the advice of the 'Lords Committees' [i.e. for Petitions]; *LJ*, iv, 10. His case is discussed in Hart, *Justice upon Petition*, p. 97.

89 This measure was to become the Triennial Act, passed on 15 February 1641; 16 Charles I, cap. 1. For the text, see Gardiner, *Constitutional Documents*, pp. 144–55; the provisions for the summons of a Parliament by twelve peers are stipulated at p. 148.

90 Discussed above, Ch. 2.

91 Discussed above, Ch. 5.

92 On Williams's administration of his diocese, see Helena Hajzyk, 'The Church in Lincolnshire, c. 1595–c. 1640' (Unpublished Ph.D. dissertation, University of Cambridge, 1980), pp. 120–48, especially, pp. 129–32.

93 Hajzyk, 'Church in Lincolnshire', p. 132; Tacitus, *Annals*, III, 6.

94 For the background to Williams's trial and imprisonment, see Gardiner, *History*, VIII, 251–4.

95 Lambeth Palace Lib., MS 1030, fo. 62: letter of intelligence from Sir J[ohn] M[onson?], 20 October 1635.

96 Sharpe, *Personal Rule*, p. 338. The *casus belli* between them was Williams's anonymous publication of a treatise, *The Holy Table: Name and Thing* (1637), STC 25724, which had attacked the altar policy advanced by Peter Heylyn, Laud's own chaplain, in *A Coale from the Altar* (1636), STC 13270.

97 *LJ*, IV, 92.

98 Ibid. Technically, they were to consider the conditions which the king had attached to Williams's writ of summons to the Parliament, which included a warning that the king would re-imprison him at the end of the session if he had not been minded, before that time, to restore him to favour. The condition could be read as an attempt by the king to offer Williams his liberty in return for backing the Crown subserviently during the forthcoming session.

99 The full list is the Earls of Bedford, Hertford, Essex, Lincoln, Warwick, Bristol, Viscount Saye, and Lords Wharton, Brooke, and Savile; *LJ*, IV, 84. The total is eleven if one also includes Bath as a signatory (as listed in the Beinecke Library copy of the Petition of the Twelve: Osborn Files, Pym).

100 The supporters were the Earls of Manchester (Mandeville's father), Bath, and Lords Montagu of Boughton (Mandeville's cousin), Grey of Warke, and Robartes (Warwick's son-in-law); *LJ*, IV, 84.

101 Ibid. p. 92.

102 Dorothy Gardiner (ed.), *The Oxinden Letters, 1607–42* (1933), p. 187: James Oxinden to his brother, Henry, 27 November

1640; for the quotation, see HMC, *De L'Isle Manuscripts*, VI, 342: William Hawkins to the Earl of Leicester, 19 November 1640.

103 For the reception of ambassadors at Tower Wharf, see Loomie, *Ceremonies of Charles*, pp. 57, 63.

104 [Saye], *Vindiciae Veritatis*, p. 29 (for the quotation); for Williams as the motion's proposer, see BL, Harl. MS 6424 (Bishop Warner's diary), fo. 52.

105 Notestein, *D'Ewes Diary*, p. 4.

106 [Prynne], *A New Discovery of the Prelates Tyranny*, pp. 114–5; May, *History of the Parliament*, p. 80. Shortly before his fall, Burton had addressed an appeal to the 'true-hearted Nobility' of the Privy Council, urging that its members stand up to the Laudians' malign influence in the Church: see Henry Burton, *An Apology of an Appeale also an Epistle to the True-hearted Nobility* ([Amsterdam], 1636), pp. 27–8 (STC2 4135).

107 See, for example, the description of the king's entry into Oxford in 1643: *Mercurius Aulicus*, 28th week (9–16 July 1643), p. 370 (BL, E 62/3).

108 New College, Oxford, MS 9502 (Robert Woodford's diary), 28–29 November 1640 (HMC, *Ninth Report*, Appendix, II, 499). Prynne also appears to have been in the congregation.

109 Guildhall Lib., MS 3750/2 (St Mary Aldermanbury Vestry minutes), fos. 43v, 50v (I owe these references to Mr Christopher Thompson).

110 Ashe is mentioned in Brooke's privy purse accounts in various capacities, including, in the autumn of 1640, paying a messenger who had carried a letter to Lord Brooke 'into the country' (presumably when the latter was in Warwick): Warwickshire RO, OR 1886/CUP.4/21A (John Halford's Accounts, I), unfol., 'Necessaries'; for Brooke's relations with Ashe, see also Ann Hughes, 'Simeon Ashe', *ODNB*. For the spelling of his name, see his signature, along with that of Edmund Calamy, in Trinity College Library, Dublin, MS 840 (Depositions and Miscellanea), fo. 39v: petition to the Commons in support of Dr Henry Jones, undated [1642]. Calamy's weekday lecture at St Mary Aldermanbury had an extensive aristocratic following, 'there being seldom so

few as twenty coaches outside his church':
Daniel Neal (revised by Joshua Toulmin), *The
History of the Puritans*, 5 vols. (Bath,
1793–97), IV, 424.

111 Burton, *Narrative*, p. 40.

112 For the bonfires that marked the passing
of the Triennial Act, in February 1641, see
BL, Harl. MS 6424 (Bishop Warner's diary),
fo. 22; New College, Oxford, MS 9502
(Robert Woodford's diary), 16 February 1641
(HMC, *Ninth Report*, II, 499).

113 For the preparations for Strafford's trial,
proceeding at the time of the return of Prynne
and Burton on 28 November, see *CJ*, II, 37–9.
For Laud and Strafford as the principal
culprits: Baillie, *Letters*, I, 274.

114 [Chestlin], *Persecutio Undecima*, p. 21.
Chestlin was probably the object of particular
hostility, given that he had succeeded to
Burton's own parish of St Matthew's Friday
Street. In turn, the reformist leadership appear
to have played on the strong emotions
unleashed by the celebration of Burton's
triumph over suffering to advance their
programme of 'reformation'. On 3 December,
just four days after the service of thanksgiving
for Burton's return, the Commons established
a committee of enquiry into 'the several
abuses' committed in the Court of High
Commission and the Court of Star Chamber.
As ever, with Pym, Hampden, Erle, Grimston
and Bedford's eldest son, Lord Russell, all
involved in the investigations, the leading
Junto-men and their allies formed a
prominent and probably controlling interest
on the committee; *CJ*, II, 44.

115 For the text, Gardiner, *Constitutional
Documents*, pp. 66–70; L. J. Reeve, 'The
Legal Status of the Petition of Right',
Historical Journal, 29 (1986), 257–77; John
Guy, 'The Origins of the Petition of Right
Reconsidered', *Historical Journal*, 25 (1982),
289–312.

116 Geoff Baldwin, 'Reason of State and
English Parliaments, 1610–42', *History of
Political Thought*, 25 (2004), 620–41.

5. BEDFORD'S COMMONWEALTH

1 Francis Bacon, *A Declaration of the
Practises and Treasons attempted and
committed by Robert, Late Earl of Essex*
(1601), sig. E3 (STC 1133).

2 This theme is well developed in Richard
Cust, *Charles I: a Political Life* (2005).

3 Centre for Kentish Studies, De L'Isle MS
U1475/C85/17: Earl of Northumberland to
the Earl of Leicester, 13 November 1640
(HMC, *De L'Isle Manuscripts*, VI, 284–5).

4 Centre for Kentish Studies, De L'Isle MS
U1475/C85/20: Earl of Northumberland to
the Earl of Leicester, 19 November 1640
(HMC, *De L'Isle Manuscripts*, VI, 343).

5 For the controversies surrounding Juxon's
appointment, see Brian Quintrell, 'The
Church Triumphant? The Emergence of a
Spiritual Lord Treasurer, 1635–36', in Julia F.
Merritt (ed.), *The Political World of Thomas
Wentworth, Earl of Strafford, 1621–41*
(Cambridge, 1996), pp. 81–108.

6 Centre for Kentish Studies, De L'Isle MS
U1475/C85/20: Earl of Northumberland to
the Earl of Leicester, 19 November 1640
(HMC, *De L'Isle Manuscripts*, VI, p. 343).
For a similar period, following the eclipse of
the Spanish faction at court in 1624, see
Thomas Cogswell, *The Blessed Revolution:
English Politics and the Coming of War,
1621–24* (Cambridge, 1989), pp. 271–3.

7 HMC, *De L'Isle Manuscripts*, VI, 346:
Countess of Carlisle to the Countess of
Leicester, 3 December [1640]. She and
Northumberland had just come from 'a
consultatione' on the advancement of
Leicester's appointment.

8 Ibid.

9 *LJ*, IV, 116.

10 BL, Harl. MS 6424 (Bishop Warner's
diary), fo. 57v; BL, Harl. MS 477 (Moore
diary), fo. 132.

11 *CJ*, II, 30, 36; HMC, *Cowper
Manuscripts*, II, 265; BL, Stowe MS 326
(Misc. papers), fos. 75–7 (for Bedford and
Harrison), and above, ch. 9.

12 BL, Harl. MS 457 (Minutes of the Anglo-
Scottish Treaty), fos. 25–50; Bedford was
listed as 'sick' in the minutes of the treaty
negotiations with the Scots from 9 December,
and did not resume his place until 7 January.
During December 1640, Northumberland,
too, was struck down with a recurrence of the
ailment that had incapacitated him during the
summer, thereby immobilizing, temporarily,
one of Bedford's principal allies at court; NA,

SP 16/476, fos. 6–7: Sir John Conyers to Viscount Conway, 1 January 1641. *Northcote Notebook*, p. 105, also reports Northumberland as 'being sick', on 23 December.

13 HMC, *Cowper Manuscripts*, II, 266: Lord Newburgh to Sir John Coke, senior, 7 December 1640.

14 NA, SP 16/476, fos. 209v–210: table of musters of the sixteen regiments at York, [January 1641]. The muster of 7 September put the army at 17,747; that of 28 November at 17,553. As late as the end of January 1641, the York-based army remained at 17,420 men.

15 Staffordshire RO, Dartmouth MS D(W)1778/I/i/11. The regiments are those of the 'Lord Marquis [Hamilton]'; the Lord General [Northumberland]; the Earl of Newport; the Serjeant-Major-General; Colonel Goring; Lord Grandison; Colonel Aston; Lord Barrymore; Colonel Wentworth; Colonel [John] Meyrick; Colonel Colepeper; Sir Charles Vavasour; Colonel Vavasour; Colonel Lunsford, and Colonel Ogle.

16 NA, SP 16/473, fo. 190: Sir Jacob Asteley to Viscount Conway, from Ripon, 23 December 1640.

17 NA, SP 16/473, fo. 154: Sir John Conyers to Viscount Conway, 18 December 1641. Holy Island, on the Northumberland coast, was also mooted by Conyers as a possible location for a seaborne assault. As the army was never put to the test, it is impossible to know whether it would have obeyed, or whether pro-Covenanter elements within the king's forces would have mutinied and gone over to the side of the Scots (the contingency for which the Petitioners had planned back in September). New College Lib., Edinburgh, MS X15b 3/1, vol. I, fo. 262: N[athaniel] F[iennes] to the [Covenanter leadership], c. 3 September 1640 (Peter Donald, 'New Light on Anglo-Scottish Contacts of 1640', *Historical Research*, 61 (1989); 227).

18 NA, SP 16/476, fo. 75: accounts for the payment of Sir John Borough and William Ryley, for research among the records in the Tower, [Feb. 1641].

19 Dorothy Kempe Gardiner (ed.), *The Oxinden Letters, 1607–42: being the Correspondence of Henry Oxinden of Barham and his Circle* (1933), p. 37.

20 Russell, *Fall of the British Monarchies*, p. 237 (for the negotiations as 'a court scheme'), pp. 237–43 (for the proposals and negotiations between September and December 1640).

21 Brian Manning, 'The Aristocracy and the Downfall of Charles I', in idem (ed.), *Politics, Religion and the English Civil War* (1973), pp. 36–80, at pp. 54–7; Roberts, 'The Earl of Bedford and the Coming of the English Revolution', *Journal of Modern History*, 49 (1977), 600–16; Russell, *Fall of the British Monarchies*, pp. 267–73.

22 The parliamentary records for this period reveal Arundel, Pembroke, Hamilton, Holland, and the elder Vane as working, in varying degrees of cooperation, with the Petitioners Lords; *LJ*, IV, 89,106,130, 132.

23 NA, SP 16/476/94: notes of the musters of the sixteen regiments at York, 28 January 1641.

24 *CJ*, II, 28.

25 When they eventually did so, in January, it was with the stipulation that none of the money should be paid through the usual Exchequer channels.

26 Centre for Kentish Studies, De L'Isle MS U1475/C129/10: Countess of Carlisle to the Countess of Leicester, 3 December [1640] (HMC, *De L'Isle Manuscripts*, VI, 346); De L'Isle MS U1475/C85/22: Earl of Northumberland to the Earl of Leicester, 3 December 1640 (not calendared in HMC, *De L'Isle Manuscripts*); printed in Collins *Letters and Memorials*, II, 364.

27 NA, LC 5/134 (Lord Chamberlain's Order Book), p. 424.

28 Ralph Houlbrooke, 'Death in Childhood: the Practice of the "Good Death" in James Janeway's *A Token for Children*', in Anthony Fletcher and Stephen Hussey (eds.), *Childhood in Question: Children, Parents and the State* (Manchester, 1999), pp. 37–56.

29 C. G. C. Tite, *Impeachment and Parliamentary Judicature in Early Stuart England* (1974).

30 BL, Add. MS 11045 (Scudamore correspondence), fo. 144r–v: [Edward Rossingham's] newsletter, 25 November

1640. Rossingham refers to the peers' defamer as 'Mr Preston' but the Journal makes it clear that it was 'Mr William Frieston [Freestone]', who was the source of the report; *CJ*, II, 30; see also Notestein, *D'Ewes Diary*, p. 42.

31 Notestein, *D'Ewes Diary*, p. 42. D'Ewes seems to have confused Clotworthy's proposal with the actual text of the order (*CJ*, II, 30), the terms of which were much more limited.

32 *CJ*, II, 30 (18 November 1640); Notestein, *D'Ewes Diary*, p. 42.

33 BL, Add. MS 11045 (Scudamore correspondence), fo. 144v.

34 For the very different and far more enthusiastic response by the Lords, when a similar motion was moved by Bishop Williams of Lincoln on 8 March 1641, see BL, Harl. MS 6424 (Bishop Warner's diary), fo. 52. Saye alludes to the moment in his rambling and anonymously published account of the politics of the 1640s, [William Fiennes, Viscount Saye and Sele], *Vindiciae Veritatis. Or an Answer to a Discourse intituled, Truth it's Manifest* (1654), p. 29 (BL, E 811/2).

35 *CJ*, II, 21.

36 Collins, *Letters and Memorials*, II, p. 366: Earl of Northumberland to the Earl of Leicester, 31 December 1640; Clarendon, *Rebellion*, I, 284; Centre for Kentish Studies, De L'Isle MS U1475/C114/7: Sir John Temple to the Earl of Leicester, 21 January 1641 (HMC, *De L'Isle Manuscripts*, VI, 367). For later references back to what seem to have been the usages of 1641, see [Robert Chestlin], *Persecutio Undecima. The Churches Eleventh Persecution* ([5 Nov.] 1648), p. 53 (BL, E 470/7).

37 Centre for Kentish Studies, De L'Isle MS U1475/C114/7: Sir John Temple to the Earl of Leicester, 21 January 1641 (HMC, *De L'Isle Manuscripts*, VI, 367). Temple had a cipher for the term that he used in his correspondence with Leicester.

38 Clarendon, *Rebellion*, I, 284.

39 Clarendon, *Rebellion*, I, 247.

40 Clarendon, *Rebellion*, I, 263n.

41 Notestein, *D'Ewes Diary*, p. 41. Even Strode (the tenth of Hyde's 'contrivers') may have been closer to the Petitioner leadership than the surviving evidence suggests; it was he who, on 18 November, was responsible for moving that the Twelve Peers should be formally thanked by the Commons 'for their Petition to the King for a Parliament'.

42 Ronald Hutton, 'George Digby, 2nd Earl of Brisol', *ODNB*.

43 Conrad Russell, 'The Parliamentary Career of John Pym, 1621–29', in Peter Clark, A. G. R. Smith, Nicholas Tyacke (eds.), *The English Commonwealth 1547–1640: Essays in Politics and Society presented to Joel Hurstfield* (Leicester, 1979), pp. 147–65, 248–53.

44 Clarendon, *Rebellion*, I, 263n. Hyde also includes Mandeville in this Bedfordian managerial group, though I believe that most of the surviving evidence locates him rather closer to Warwick than Bedford in the period up to May 1641, and even closer to Warwick thereafter. See above, pp. 146, 178, for Mandeville taking an essentially anti-Bedfordian line over the Strafford impeachment.

45 See above, Chs. 1 and 2.

46 Clarendon, *Rebellion*, I, 247.

47 NA, SP 16/479, fo. 56v: Nathaniel Tomkyns to [Sir John Lambe], 12 April 1641 (emphasis added).

48 Clarendon, *Rebellion*, I, 247.

49 [Chestlin], *Persecutio Undecima*, p. 53.

50 On the pre-1640 court, see especially, Kevin Sharpe, 'The Image of Virtue: the Court and Household of Charles I, 1625–42', in David Starkey (ed.), *The English Court: from the Wars of the Roses to the Civil War* (1987), pp. 226–60; and, for the place of the court in early-modern political culture more generally, John Adamson, 'The Making of the *Ancien-Régime* Court, 1500–1700', in idem (ed.), *The Princely Courts of Europe: Ritual, Politics and Religion under the Ancien Régime, 1500–1750* (1999), pp. 7–41.

51 HMC, *De L'Isle Manuscripts*, VI, 346: Countess of Carlisle to the Countess of Leicester, 3 December [1640].

52 For Lord Burghley, M. A. R. Graves, 'Thomas Norton the Parliament Man: an Elizabethan MP, 1559–81', *Historical Journal*,

23 (1980), 17–35; idem, *Elizabethan Parliaments, 1559–1601* (1987); and his 'Elizabethan Men of Business Reconsidered', *Parergon*, 14 (1996), 111–27.

53 Clayton Roberts, 'The Earl of Bedford and the Coming of the English Revolution', *Journal of Modern History*, 49 (1977), 600–16, quotation at p. 603. For a subtler view of Bedford's relation to the court, see Russell, *Fall of the British Monarchies*, pp. 3–4.

54 Loomie, *Ceremonies of Charles I*, pp. 88–9. For Bedford and Burges, see Nicholas Tyacke, *Anti-Calvinists: the Rise of English Arminianism*, c. 1590–1640 (Oxford, 1987), pp. 78–9.

55 Loomie, *Ceremonies of Charles I*, p. 180. The 'Presence Chamber' at this period was usually the Whitehall Banqueting House.

56 The court's Master of Ceremonies records Bedford's last participation in any of the major court ceremonies as taking place in 1637; Loomie, *Ceremonies of Charles I*, p. 220.

57 NA, LC 5/134 (Lord Chamberlain's Order Book), pp. 256. 439, 218, 265; quoted in Russell, *Fall of the British Monarchies*, p. 4n.

58 Woburn Abbey, Bedford MSS (Fourth Earl) III, XII, XXVI: 4th Earl of Bedford's Commonplace Books.

59 For his wealth, Roberts, 'The Earl of Bedford', p. 608.

60 For Bedford's portrait, see *Complete Catalogue Van Dyck Complete Catalogue*, plate IV. 18; for Charles's dress during the 1620s, see Patricia Wardle, 'John Shepley (1575–1631), Embroiderer to the High and Mighty Prince Charles, Prince of Wales', *Textile History*, 32 (2001), 133–55.

61 See, e.g. Roberts, 'The Earl of Bedford', p. 608: he was 'Puritan in his personal life ... In dress he was plain, in countenance severe, in glance direct, as Van Dyke's [*sic*] portrait of him reveals.'

62 *Van Dyck Complete Catalogue*, p. 441 (plate IV. 18); AND SEE THE COLOUR PLATES TO THIS BOOK. An early *cartellino* painted on the lower right-hand corner of this painting, now at Woburn Abbey, describes Bedford as 'Anno 1636, Aetatis suae 48 [In the year

1636, at the age of forty-eight]'. One of these figures is wrong, as Bedford was born in 1593 and thus did not reach the age of forty-eight until 1641, the year of his death. It is possible that the painting was commissioned to celebrate his imminent admission to high office, just as his friend, Sir Edward Littleton, had recently done on his appointment as Chief Justice of Common Pleas, a portrait executed at some point in the twelve months up to January 1641: *Van Dyck Complete Catalogue*, p. 553 and plate IV. 159.

63 Sheffield City Library, Elmhirst MS EM 1352/3: declaration signed by the Earl and Countess of Pembroke, 12 May 1634.

64 BL, Harl. MS 7001 (Misc. letters), fo. 143: Anne, Countess of Pembroke to the Earl of Bedford, 14 January 1639. She needed to come up to London from the country and requested Bedford to obtain her husband's permission that she might stay for up to a fortnight in either the Cockpit (Pembroke's extensive lodgings in Whitehall) or at Baynard's Castle, in the City.

65 NA, SO 3/12 (Signet Office Docket Book), fo. 113: grant to Bedford and his fellow 'participants' of some 40,000 acres in the Great Level, August 1640. There is also an interesting letter concerning this project from Bedford to Sir Miles Sandys, 20 September 1633: Bedfordshire RO, Bagshawe MS X171/5. For the background, see S. Wells, *The History of the Drainage of the Great Level of the Fens, called Bedford Level*, 2 vols. (1830); L. E. Harris, *Vermuyden and the Fens: a Study of Sir Cornelius Vermuyden and the Great Level* (1953).

66 For some of these difficulties, see NA, C115/M36/8445 (a reference I owe to Mr Christopher Thompson). In 1626, the 1st Earl of Clare had been disappointed to find that 'even' Bedford (then styled Lord Russell), who he had expected to refuse the Forced Loan, had agreed to pay his contribution: *Holles Letters*, II, 339.

67 Alnwick Castle, Northumberland MS Box Y. III; John Adamson, 'Of Armies and Architecture: the Employments of Robert Scawen', in Ian Gentles, John Morrill and Blair Worden (eds.), *Soldiers, Writers, and Statesmen of the English Revolution* (Cambridge, 1998), p. 39. Some hints as to Bedford's working relations with St John are

to be found in Northamptonshire RO, Finch Hatton MS 2817. (I owe this reference to Mr Christopher Thompson.)

68 Alnwick Castle, Northumberland MS, Box Y. III. 2 (4) 7, fos. 33–4: Scawen's case papers in a Chancery suit against the Earl of Bedford, 1637.

69 Barbara Donagan, 'The Clerical Patronage of Robert Rich, second Earl of Warwick, 1619–42', *Proceedings of the American Philosophical Society*, 120 (1976), 388–419. For Pym and Warwick, see BL, Add. MS 46190 (Jessop corr.), fo. 4: indemnification of Pym for having stood bound for Warwick's debts, 18 February 1634; Lancashire RO, Hulton of Hulton MS, DDHu/46/21: John Pym to William Jessop, from Leez, 3 September 1640.

70 Bedford, quoted in J. P. Sommerville, *Royalists and Patriots: Politics and Ideology in England, 1603–40* (2nd edn, 1999), p. 211.

71 For the Tudor origins of this sense of England's 'election', see James McDermott, *England and the Spanish Armada: the Necessary Quarrel* (New Haven, 2005), pp. 109–14.

72 Woburn Abbey, Bedfordshire, Bedford MS, Fourth Earl Addenda; for a case study of a contemporary, Sir William Drake, with similarly wide-ranging interests, see Kevin Sharpe, *Reading Revolutions: the Politics of Reading in Early Modern England* (New Haven and London, 2000), Ch. 2.

73 James W. Tubbs, *The Common Law Mind: Medieval and Early Modern Conceptions* (Baltimore, MD, 2000).

74 R. F. Treharne and E. B. Fryde (eds.), *Simon de Montfort and Baronial Reform: Thirteenth-Century Essays* (1986); for the Essex Rebels of 1601, see Bacon, *A Declaration of the Practises and Treasons Attempted and Committed by Robert, Late Earl of Essex*, sig. E3.

75 Clarendon, *Rebellion*, I, 241.

76 In this respect, Bedford's financial plans complemented the political theorizing of Saye and Brooke, who likewise saw the solution to England's political crisis in terms of a reapportionment of power between the three 'co-ordinate' estates of the realm to the disadvantage of the king, and in favour of the two Houses; see John Adamson, 'The *Vindiciae Veritatis* and the Political Creed of Viscount Saye and Sele', *Historical Research*, 60 (1987), 45–63.

77 This paragraph is heavily indebted to Russell, *Fall of the British Monarchies*, pp. 252–8.

78 Centre for Kentish Studies, De L'Isle MS U1475/C85/22: Earl of Northumberland to the Earl of Leicester, 3 December 1640 (not in HMC, *De L'Isle Manuscripts*).

79 Notestein, *D'Ewes Diary*, p. 74.

80 Ibid., p. 75.

81 Centre for Kentish Studies, De L'Isle MS U1475/C114/7: Sir John Temple to the Earl of Leicester, 21 January 1641 (HMC, *De L'Isle Manuscripts*, VI, 367).

82 NA, PRO 30/53/9/11 ('Diurnal Occurences'), fos. 11–12; *Northcote Notebook*, p. 12. I owe these two references to Professor the Earl Russell.

83 Michael J. Braddick, *Nerves of State: Taxation and the Financing of the English State, 1558–1714* (Manchester, 1996), Ch. 3, and esp. pp. 52–5.

84 Notestein, *D'Ewes Diary*, p. 75.

85 Notestein, *D'Ewes Diary*, pp. 75–6 (emphasis added).

86 The suggestion that this is an instance of 'linkage' is Professor Russell's; though my own reading of D'Ewes's diary would suggest that it was St John, rather than Pym, who seems to have advanced it. Notestein, *D'Ewes Diary*, pp. 75–6; Russell, *Fall of the British Monarchies*, p. 242.

87 Notestein, *D'Ewes Diary*, p. 76.

88 The severity of this threat to the royal revenues emerges most clearly if we turn briefly to Charles's balance sheet. Roughly three-quarters of the king's income during the 1630s had been derived from sources which had been claimed on the basis of the royal prerogative (including the two largest, the customs revenue and Ship Money). To put this in round figures: Charles I stood to lose around £650,000 of the income of roughly £836,000 per annum he had enjoyed during the relatively prosperous days of the mid 1630s. What remained of the king's 'legal' income (mostly derived from land) was

wholly insufficient to fund either the royal households or the costs of government. Braddick, *Nerves of State*, Ch. 3 (for the contribution of the customs).

89 Notestein, *D'Ewes Diary*, p. 146; see also the account of St John's speech in *Northcote Notebook*, pp. 59-60.

90 Minnesota UL, MS 137 (Peyton diary), fo. 147 (*PLP*, I, 596). In Peyton's account, the reference is to 'a noble person nere the Chayre': the seats nearest the Speaker's chair being reserved, by custom, for Privy Councillors who were members of the House. It was Vane who responded to Pym's motion; Notestein, *D'Ewes Diary*, p. 146.

91 For Vane's allegiances at this time, see above, pp. 165-7; Thomas D. Whitaker, *The Life and Original Correspondence of Sir G[eorge] Radcliffe* (1810), pp. 228-9. Pym had not chosen this Privy Councillor at random. For only three months earlier, in August – the very moment when Bedford was under suspicion for colluding with the imminent Covenanter invasion – it was Secretary Vane who had acted as Bedford's intermediary with the king in securing the freehold of some 40,000 acres of land in the Great Level; NA, SO 3/12 (Signet Office Docket Book), fo. 113. It is also noteworthy that, on 30 December, Vane (listed in the journal as 'Mr Treasurer') was the very first Commons-man named to the committee which revised the bill that eventually became the Triennial Act: *CJ*, II, 60. That Vane had sided with the Petitioners is also strongly suggested by his letter to Edward Nicholas, written that same day, reproving Nicholas for working against what can only be Bedford and his circle: 'ingage not your selfe that way,' Vane warned, 'but take heed you turne them not against you'. NA, SP 16/473, fo. 208: Sir Henry Vane senior to Edward Nicholas, 30 December 1640. Nicholas wrote a hostile reply to Bedford's proposal for the reform of the Court of Wards, which dates from either late 1640 or early 1641: NA, SP 16/487/35. It is possible that Vane was referring to Nicholas's drafting of this document, or perhaps his evident hostility to Bedford's plans more generally. For Nicholas's reply to Bedford, see also Russell, *Fall of the British Monarchies*, pp 253-4.

92 Notestein, *D'Ewes Diary*, p. 146.

93 Ibid., p. 164; Rushworth, *Historical Collections*, Part III, I, 119.

94 For Paget as a Petitioner, see Surrey, History Centre, Loseley MS 133/50; Bulstrode Whitelocke, *Memorials of the English Affairs*, 4 vols. (Oxford, 1853), I, 105.

95 Notestein, *D'Ewes Diary*, p. 169. Pym was immediately seconded by Harbottell Grimston – yet another instance of co-operation between what might be termed 'the Bedford House and Warwick House networks' in the Commons. In the event, it was not until 26 February 1641 that the Lords ordered that Laud should be incarcerated, and then it was on the Earl of Warwick's motion: BL, Harl. MS 6424 (Bishop Warner's diary), fo. 42v.

96 NA, SP 16/473, fo. 154: Sir John Conyers to Viscount Conway, 18 December 1641. Holy Island, on the Northumberland coast, was also mooted by Conyers as a possible location for a seaborne assault.

97 BL, Harl. MS 6424 (Bishop Warner's diary), fo. 42v.

98 It is perhaps no coincidence that it was during this week of exchanges on the king's finances that Conyers formulated his plans for a renewal of the war against the Covenanters: NA, SP 16/473/74: Sir John Conyers to Viscount Conway, 18 December 1641.

99 Both Houses were adjourned between 25 and 28 December, inclusive: *CJ*, II, 58-9.

100 For the usage, see Allan I. Macinnes, *Charles I and the Covenanting Movement, 1625-41* (Edinburgh, 1991), p. 199.

101 This usage is discussed in detail, above, chapters 11 and 17; for some trenchant observations on the republican significance of the word 'commonwealth' in seventeenth-century English usage, see David Wootton, 'Oxbridge Model', *Times Literary Supplement*, 23 September 2005, p. 9.

102 Notestein, *D'Ewes Diary*, p. 188 (first reading); *CJ*, II, 60, for the second reading and committal of the bill 'for the yearly holding of Parliaments'.

103 The Petitioners' supporters, who constituted well over half this committee, included (in the order they are named in the journal) Sir Henry Vane senior, William

Strode, Denzell Holles, John Pym, John Hampden, Sir John Culpeper, Sir Gilbert Gerard, Sir Thomas Barrington, Sir Francis Seymour, Bulstrode Whitelocke, John Glynne, Sir Gilbert Pickering, Sir Walter Erle, Lord Digby, Sir Henry Cholmley, Oliver Cromwell, John Maynard, Sir Philip Stapilton, Sir Henry Mildmay, Edward Hyde (probably), Harbottell Grimeston, Lord Fairfax, Lord Russell, Nathaniel Fiennes; *CJ*, II, 60.

104 Notestein, *D'Ewes Diary*, p. 196; for the background, see Pauline Croft, 'Annual Parliaments and the Long Parliament', *Bulletin of the Institute of Historical Research*, 59 (1986), 155–71; eadem, 'The Debate on Annual Parliaments in the Early Seventeenth Century', *Parliaments, Estates and Representation*, 16 (1996), 163–74.

105 ASV, Senato, Dispacci Inghil. 42, fo. 117: Giustinian to the Doge and Senate, 5/15 September 1640 (*CSPV 1640–42*, p. 77).

106 Notestein, *D'Ewes Diary*, pp. 184, 188 (23–24 December 1640).

107 The quorum required to authorize disbursements – three peers – could be found among the Treaty Commissioners who were members of Warwick's family alone. *CJ*, II, 58 (for the order); Notestein, *D'Ewes Diary*, p. 188 (for the quorum). Any three of Warwick, Holland (his brother), Mandeville (his son-in-law) or Paget (who was married to his niece), were entitled to authorize disbursements. The Treaty Commissioners' audit committee, established on 21 December, comprised the Earls of Warwick and Holland (brothers), Viscount Mandeville (Warwick's son-in-law), Lord Paget (Holland's son-in-law), together with the Earl of Berkshire, and Lords Wharton and Poulett: BL, Harl. MS 457 (Minutes of the Anglo-Scottish Treaty, 1640–41), fo. 36. A month later the quorum of this committee was conveniently reduced to three, making it possible for a far smaller group – in practice, than just Warwick, Holland, and Mandeville – to deal directly with the Commons on the arrangements for the Scottish army's supply; BL, Harl. MS 457 (Minutes of the Anglo-Scottish Treaty, 1640–41), entry for 19 January 1641. As Warwick's accounts reveal, the trio of Holland, Mandeville, and Warwick himself had already been the active quorum even before the order of 19 January; see NA, SP 46/80 (State Papers, supplementary), fo. 171:

receipts signed by the Scottish Commissioners for sums received on 28 December 1640 and 9 January 1641 from Warwick, Holland, and Mandeville. (I am grateful to Mr Christopher Thompson for his loaning me his transcription of these important accounts.)

108 These are discussed in detail in Ch. 11, above.

109 Notestein, *D'Ewes Diary*, p. 192 (emphasis added).

110 *CJ*, II, p. 59; Notestein, *D'Ewes Diary*, pp. 193–4; although this order was later revoked, when the customers pointed out that it would prevent them from honouring existing debts, the Commons nevertheless condemned the customers' taking of Tonnage and Poundage 'and other unlawfull impositions not granted by Parliament'; *CJ*, II, 60; Notestein, *D'Ewes Diary*, pp. 200–1.

111 *CJ*, II, 66, 67.

112 ASV, Senato, Dispacci Inghil. 42, fos. 185v–6: Giustinian to the Doge and Senate, 1–11 January 1641 (*CSPV 1640–42*, p. 112).

113 Notestein, *D'Ewes Diary*, pp. 185, 191; *CJ*, II, 57 59 (where it is called 'An act for the relief of the king's [army]').

114 ASV, Senato, Dispacci Inghil. 42, fo. 185v: Giustinian to the Doge and Senate, 1/11 January 1641 (*CSPV 1640–42*, p. 112).

115 NA, SP 46/80 (State Papers, supplementary), fos. 171, 180, 181v, 182, 184r–v: accounts of monies disbursed to the Scots by the Earl of Warwick, December 1640–August 1641; SP 16/483, fos. 90v–91r: Earl of Warwick's accounts for the sums received by him over the period 28 December 1640–13 August 1641; *Diurnall Occurrences* (1641), p. 46 (BL, E 523/1). (I owe this last reference to Dr David Scott.) The Earl of Warwick was appointed by the Scottish Treaty Commissioners to receive the £25,000 allowed them by Parliament.

116 Even where some of the Parliament-raised subsidy money was routed through royal officials such as the Treasurer-at-War, the officers in question seem to have been scrupulous in regarding all Parliament-raised funds as out of bounds to the king. In December, Charles twice asked the Treasurer-at-War, Sir William Uvedale, to repay him a 'loan' of £5,000 which the king had earlier

made to the Treasury-at-War. Uvedale replied firmly that he could give the king no hope of this, 'for out of the parlament monnies it canot come': NA, SP 16/473, fos. 172–3v: Sir William Uvedale to his deputy, Matthew Brodley, 22 December 1640.

117 ASV, Senato, Dispacci Inghil. 42, fo. 190: Giustinian to the Doge and Senate, 7/17 January 1641. This is mistranslated in the published calendar (*CSPV 1640–42*, p. 114), as referring to a single person (a 'new magistrate, who …'); however, the Venetian 'un nuovo Magistratto, il quale …' refers to the office in the abstract – *magistrato* seeming to mean, in this context, a 'council' or 'board', charged with specific responsibilities.

118 The idea was to be more fully developed in a treatise by Saye's nephew, Henry Parker, in a work printed at the charge of Sir John Danvers: H[enry] P[arker], *The Generall Junto, or the Councell of Union* (1642), pp. 29–30 (Wing P402); see also NAS, Hamilton MS GD 406/1/1700.

119 ASV, Senato, Dispacci Inghil. 42, fo. 190v.

120 Collins, *Letters and Memorials*, II, 366: Earl of Northumberland to the Earl of Leicester, 31 December 1640.

121 BL, Add. MS 15567 (Anon. memoir), fos. 30–1. Hamilton nevertheless continued to enjoy a measure of royal favour, a fact that made his 'conversion' doubly useful to the Petitioner Junto.

122 See NAS, Hamilton MS GD 406/1/1437: Henry Jermyn to the Marquess of Hamilton, 4 October [1640]. Jermyn wrote to Hamilton assuring him that his own recollection of their discussions concerning Scotland was that the marquess had advised that his 'contrimen should be rather reduced to thir due and just obedience then [i.e. than] destroyed, which is reason enough to perswade the world that, if counsels of moderation could have prevailed, you would not willingly have advised those of violence'.

123 For further light on Hamilton's activities in early 1641, see the forthcoming biography by Dr John Scally. Hamilton's post-Restoration biographer, Bishop Burnet, glosses over his subject's activities in this regard with an anodyne formula 'the Marquess … did not slacken his endeavours

to bring things to a final Settlement'; Gilbert Burnet, *Lives of James and William, Dukes of Hamilton and Castleherald* (1677), p. 181.

124 For the background see R. Malcolm Smuts, *Court Culture and the Origins of a Royalist Tradition in Early Stuart England* (Philadelphia, 1987). For Northumberland's antipathy towards Hamilton, see Centre for Kentish Studies, De L'Isle MS U1475/C85/22: Earl of Northumberland to the Earl of Leicester, 3 December 1640 (not in HMC, *De L'Isle Manuscripts*).

125 Loomie, *Ceremonies of Charles I*, p. 297. The three ambassadors – Jan Wolfert, Lord of Brederode, Francis Aerssens, Lord of Sommelsdijk, and Jan van der Kerkhoven, Lord of Heenvliet – were lodged at the house of Sir Abraham Williams in Westminster; ibid., pp. 295–6.

126 BL, Harl. MS 7001 (Historical papers), fo. 124: Lord Digby to the Earl of Bedford, 21 August 1637. For his appointment to the eight-man committee to prosecute the Earl of Strafford, see *CJ*, II, 26–7. Charles's motives for supporting the Dutch alliance seem, as ever, to have been at least partly prompted by his ongoing quest for the military resources to crush the Parliament; in February 1641 the papal envoy, Count Rossetti, reported that the king hoped to procure a mercenary force from the United Provinces, and to use it to dissolve the Parliament and release Strafford from the Tower – though, as Rossetti was profoundly hostile to the Dutch alliance, this testimony cannot be taken at face value; see Hibbard, *Charles I and the Popish Plot*, pp. 176–7.

127 HMC, *Twelfth Report*, II, 272).

128 Centre for Kentish Studies, De L'Isle MS U1475/C114/7: Sir John Temple to the Earl of Leicester, 21 January 1641 (HMC, *De L'Isle Manuscripts*, VI, 367).

129 Centre for Kentish Studies, De L'Isle MS U1475/C129/12: [Countess of Carlisle] to the Countess of Leicester, 14 January [1641] (printed in HMC, *De L'Isle Manuscripts*, VI, 361).

130 Notestein, *D'Ewes Diary*, pp. 168–9 (for Pym), 172, 253 (for St John). A revised version of St John's speech was printed after his appointment as Solicitor-General: *The Speech or Declaration of Mr. St.-Iohn, His*

Majesties Solicitor Generall … as it is Revised and Allowed ([late February–early March] 1641), BL, E 196/1. Comparison of the printed text with D'Ewes's diary account of the speech suggests that the published version was considerably toned down (as befitted a publication by someone who was now a royal official), particularly in respect to the attack on the judges.

131 Besides Finch, these were Sir John Bramston, Chief Justice of King's Bench; Sir Humphrey Davenport, Chief Baron of the Exchequer; and two puisne judges, Sir Robert Berkeley and Sir Francis Crawley, and two Barons of the Exchequer, Sir Richard Weston and Sir John Trevor; see *CJ*, II, 56; Rushworth, *Historical Collections*, Part III, I, 130. For the case, see W. R. Prest (ed.), *The Diary of Sir Richard Hutton, 1614–39* (1991), pp. 110–11.

132 Notestein, *D'Ewes Diary*, p. 172.

133 The Countess of Carlisle's letter announcing Bedford's imminent appointment as Lord Treasurer was written on the very day – 14 January – of St John's speech to the Commons formally moving Finch's impeachment: Centre for Kentish Studies, De L'Isle MS U1475/C129/12: [Countess of Carlisle] to the Countess of Leicester, 14 January [1641] (HMC, *De L'Isle Manuscripts*, VI, 361); Notestein, *D'Ewes Diary*, pp. 253–4; *CJ*, II, p. 68.

134 St John soon found himself moving in the godly but acutely status-conscious world of the Russells and their close-knit network of fellow puritan patricians: the Riches (Earls of Warwick) among the nobility; the Barringtons, Gerards, and the Cromwells among the knightage and gentry, to most of whom St John – like Bedford himself – was linked in varying degrees of cousinage. For St John's connections with these families, see the genealogical tables in Searle, *Barrington Letters*, pp. 25–7.

135 Searle, *Barrington Letters*, pp. 116, 119. I am grateful to Mr Christopher Thompson for this information.

136 St John's income was estimated at some £300 a year in land, and approximately double that from the law: Searle, *Barrington Letters*, pp. 116, 119 and n. 114. But the actual figure may have been considerably smaller.

137 Searle, *Barrington Letters*, p. 125: Lady Elizabeth Masham to Lady [Joan] Barrington, 26 January 1630. Lady Masham urged 'how inconvenient it may be for hir [the future Mrs St John's] posterity to injoye that which, by right, belongs to my lord [of Bedford]'s one children, yet I know not what discomfort she may reseave from his [i.e. Bedford's] children after him [i.e. after the fourth earls' death]'. Bedford also seems to have been responsible for enlisting the Earl of Warwick and Warwick's man of affairs, Sir Nathaniel Rich, to help smooth out any remaining points of conflict over the marriage settlement; Searle, *Barrington Letters*, pp. 119, 127, 229.

138 Ibid., pp. 118–19. The mother of St John's intended bride wrote on 30 December 1629 that she heard 'very worthyly of the man, but it semes his estate is very small, not above 200*li.* a year'; see also the objections of Lady [Elizabeth] Masham, ibid., p. 120.

139 BL, Egerton MS 2645 (Barrington corr.), fo. 186: Earl of Bedford to Lady [Joan] Barrington, 7 May 1630, from Bedford House; printed in Searle, *Barrington Letters*, p. 149.

140 For St John's genealogy, see Cordelia Donovan Smith, 'Oliver St John: Servant to the King, to his Parliament, and to his Commonwealth' (unpublished Ph. D. dissertation, State University of New Jersey, 1975), pp. 12–13.

141 His father, Oliver St John senior, purported to be the grandson of yet another Oliver St John, the first Lord St John of Bletso (d. 1582), through the latter's younger son, Thomas.

142 Searle, *Barrington Letters*, p. 119. Hyde also has a waspish reference to St John as 'being a gentleman of an honourable extraction (if he had been legitimate)'; Clarendon, *Rebellion*, I, 280–1.

143 Craig Muldrew, 'Oliver St John: the "Dark Lanthorn" of the Commonwealth', *The Queens' College Record* ([Cambridge], 2002).

144 *Complete Peerage*, II, 75–7. Francis Russell, 2nd Earl of Bedford, married Margaret St John, daughter of Sir John St John, and thus became the cousin of the Oliver St John, 1st Lord St John of Bletso.

145 Muldrew, 'Oliver St John'.

146 See above, pp. 269–75.

147 Clarendon, *Rebellion*, I, 247.

148 One of the best discussions of this theme remains J. S. Cockburn, *A History of English Assizes, 1558–1714* (Cambridge, 1972).

149 For the impeachment articles, Notestein, *D'Ewes Diary*, pp. 253–5; for St John's speech, see St John, *The Speech or Declaration of Mr. St.-Iohn*, pp. 1–38.

150 Notestein, *D'Ewes Diary*, p. 255.

151 In almost every respect, Finch's impeachment closely resembles the court-backed prosecutions of the early 1620s – the fall of Sir Giles Mompesson, the monopolist, in 1621 is a case in point – when the Crown willingly sacrificed an unpopular (and absentee) official to parliamentary censure, and privately colluded in the prosecution. Elizabeth Read Foster, *The House of Lords, 1603–49: Structured, Procedurer and the Nature of its Business* (Chapel Hill, NC, 1983), pp. 153–5; Cogswell, *Blessed Revolution*, pp. 59, 141. Like Finch after him, Mompesson had made for the safety of the Low Countries (in his case Brussels, in the Spanish Netherlands) to sit out the parliamentary storm.

152 For Finch's flight, see Clarendon, *Rebellion*, I, 234–6; Whitelocke, *Memorials*, I, 115; HMC, *Cowper Manuscripts*, II, 270. For the use of the king's ship, see Lieuwe van Aitzema, *Saken van staet en oorlogh, in, ende omtrent de Vereenigde Nederlanden, beginnende met het jaer 1621*, 6 vols ('s-Gravenhage, 1669–72), II, 740.

153 *A Letter Sent to the Right Honourable the Lord Chamberlaine, from John Lord Finch, late Lord Keeper of the Great Seale of England, from the Hage* (1641), single sheet (BL, 669 f. 4/3). On internal evidence, the letter appears to be genuine.

154 This develops an argument St John had first made on 27 November 1640, when he had argued that Ship Money itself was not the grievance, but that 'the opinion off the Judges in the exchequer chamber is the grievance ... *Bonum publicum* is the argument and soe large as it takes away all property'; Notestein, *D'Ewes Diary*, p. 543.

155 Hugh Craig, 'Jonson, the Antimasque and the "Rules of Flattery"', in David

Bevington and Peter Holbrook (eds.), *The Politics of the Stuart Court Masque* (Cambridge, 1998), pp. 176–96; and see Sharpe, *Criticism and Compliment: the Politics of Literature in the England of Charles I* (Cambridge, 1987).

156 Gardiner, *History*, IX, 263. The Latin phrase, to be incorporated in the new patents of appointment, was *quam diu se bene gesserint* ('as long as they should behave themselves well').

157 Perhaps significantly, it was Viscount Falkland and Edward Hyde – two Commons-men with close connections to the court, and who were to emerge in due course as Royalists – who presented the formal impeachment articles against Finch to the House of Lords; Notestein, *D'Ewes Diary*, p. 255.

158 NA, SP 16/476, fo. 237: draft declaration by the king and Privy Council [January 1641]. For royal proclamations, see Esther S. Cope, 'Sir Edward Coke and Proclamations, 1610', *American Journal of Legal History*, 15 (1971), 215–21; Sommerville, *Royalists and Patriots*, pp. 168–70; Glenn Burgess, *Absolute Monarchy and the Stuart Constitution* (New Haven, 1996), pp. 201–2.

159 Nottingham UL, Portland Literary MS Pw V92 (Charles II's 'Orders for the Government of Our Bedchamber and Privy Lodgings in the same form as they were established in the Reignes of Our Royall Father and Grandfather of ever blessed [memory]'), fos. 3v–4v.

160 For the evidence on which this statement is based, see the following two paragraphs. Northumberland appears to have shared Bedford's belief in the supremacy of the common law over the prerogative, see George Drake, '10th Earl of Northumberland', *ODNB*.

161 Centre for Kentish Studies, De L'Isle MS U1475/C132/171: William Hawkins to the Earl of Leicester, 21 January 1641 (HMC, *De L'Isle Manuscripts*, VI, 366). This names Sir Thomas Gardiner (the current Recorder of London) as Solicitor-General, with St John to move to the Recorder's post vacated by Gardiner. This suggests either that Hawkins was misinformed, or that there was still some discussion going on as to the final allocation of places. The dropping of Gardiner's name,

if he ever were seriously in contention, was another minor victory for the Junto.

162 Littleton was raised to the peerage as Baron Lyttelton of Mounslow on 18 February 1641; *Complete Peerage*, VIII, 316. Hyde later claimed that he had been made a baron on the recommendation of Strafford, Clarendon, *Rebellion*, I, 289; II, 111. For his sympathies with the Bedford House group, see ibid., pp. 110–11.

163 Baker, *Serjeants-at-Law*, pp. 93 (for quotation), 440 (for Littleton's list of patrons). His other patrons were Laud and Strafford.

164 Clarendon, *Rebellion*, I, 235, 279; II, 111. This was in spite of the fact that Littleton had been Solicitor-General during *R. v. Hampden* (1637).

165 The vacancy arose by virtue of the promotion of Littleton, the current Chief Justice of Common Pleas, to the Lord Keepership.

166 For Bankes as Littleton's deputy during the latter's illness, see BL, Harl. MS 163 (D'Ewes diary), fos. 121, 154.

167 NA, CP 45/314 (Common Pleas remembrance roll), mem. 3; printed in Baker, *Serjeants-at-Law*, p. 440. Bankes's third patron was named as Prince Charles, but as he was ten at the time, his political involvement in the appointment may probably be discounted. For Bankes's friendship with Northumberland see, George Bankes, *The Story of Corfe Castle* (1853).

168 Sharpe, *Personal Rule*, p. 660. T. G. Barnes, 'Cropping the Heath: the Fall of a Chief Justice', *Historical Research*, 64 (1991), 331–43. The humility with which Heath took his demotion seems to have won him numerous admirers; see Prest, *Diary of Sir Richard Hutton*, p. 110. Nevertheless, Heath's appointment is in some respects puzzling, not least because, earlier in his legal career, he had taken a 'maximalist' view of the royal prerogative; see John Reeve, 'Sir Robert Heath's Advice to Charles I in 1629', *Bulletin of the Institute of Historical Research*, 59 (1986), 221–2; Sharpe, *Personal Rule*, p. 660. How far, if at all, Bedford supported Heath's restoration to the bench is unclear; but it may be significant that Heath was involved in the earl's schemes to create the Bedford Level, and Heath's well-known Puritanism accorded

well with Bedford's plans to create a new and 'godly' Privy Council; see Woburn Abbey, Bedford MS, Fourth Earl Addenda 27, fo. 12: indenture of 16 July 1631. Heath also appears as one of the debtors of the 3rd Earl of Bedford, for £300 (owed jointly with 'Mr Mason') in 1620; filed in Bedford MS, Fourth Earl Addenda 13/IV.

169 Northamptonshire RO, Finch Hatton MS 3500: a joint opinion by Sir Robert Heath and Oliver St John on the election of a burgess for Higham, for the Short Parliament of 1640.

170 The first notice we have of the list is on 21 January, but it seems likely that it was already in existence (with St John's name approved) as early as Tuesday, 19 January, when Littleton received the Great Seal: HMC, *De L'Isle Manuscripts*, VI, 366; HMC, *Cowper Manuscripts*, II, .272.

171 HMC, *De L'Isle Manuscripts*, VI, pp. 366–7; NAS, Hamilton MS GD 406/1/1657: Oliver St John to the Marquess of Hamilton, 2 June 1642. Hyde, on the other hand, gave the credit to Bedford; Clarendon, *Rebellion*, I, 280.

172 It is tempting to speculate whether Hamilton, like Lady Barrington a decade earlier, also received a letter from Bedford assuring him that any 'favors' done to St John would be esteemed 'noe less then if you had bestowed soe much … uppon me'. BL, Egerton MS 2645 (Barrington corr.), fo. 186: Earl of Bedford to Lady [Joan] Barrington, 7 May 1630, from Bedford House (Searle, *Barrington Letters*, p. 149). Nor was this Hamilton's only attempt to align himself publicly with Bedford House; within six weeks of these appointments, the marquess was reported to be negotiating to marry Bedford's daughter. NAS, GD 112/40/2: Archibald Campbell to the [Laird of?] Glenorchy, 9 March 1641; quoted in Roberts, 'Earl of Bedford', p. 603n.

173 Centre for Kentish Studies, De L'Isle MS U1475/C114/8: Sir John Temple to the Earl of Leicester, 27 January 1641 (HMC, *De L'Isle Manuscripts*, VI, 369–70).

174 See above, p. 153.

175 Centre for Kentish Studies, De L'Isle MS U1475/C132/171: William Hawkins to the Earl of Leicester, 21 January 1641 (HMC, *De L'Isle Manuscripts*, VI, 365–6). St John's patent of appointment passed the Great Seal at the end of the following week, on Friday, 29 January. Roberts ('Earl of Bedford', p. 603) states that St John was 'named' that day; but the nomination had been made over a week earlier.

176 Centre for Kentish Studies, De L'Isle MS U1475/C114/7: Sir John Temple to the Earl of Leicester, 21 January 1641 (HMC, *De L'Isle Manuscripts*, VI, p. 367).

177 NA, SP 16/476, fo. 212: the list is an enclosure in Sir John Conyers' letter to Viscount Conway of 29 January 1641, sent from York. The list must have been sent to Conyers not later than 25 January. Centre for Kentish Studies, De L'Isle MS U1475/C114/7: Sir John Temple to the Earl of Leicester, 21 January 1641 (HMC, *De L'Isle Manuscripts*, VI, 367). For the role of the early Stuart Lord Privy Seal, see Linda Levy Peck, *Northampton: Patronage and Politics at the Court of James I* (1982); and Anon., '[Calendar of Privy Seals, 8–11 Charles I]', in *Report of the Deputy Keeper of the Public Records*, 48, Appendix ([c. 1887]), pp. 451–560.

178 Centre for Kentish Studies, De L'Isle MS U1475/C114/7: Sir John Temple to the Earl of Leicester, 21 January 1641 (HMC, *De L'Isle Manuscripts*, VI, 367).

179 Clarendon, *Rebellion*, I, 281.

180 In December 1640, for example, an attempt had been made at court to propose the Petitioner Earl of Hertford as a rival for the Treasurership to the Parliament-backed Earl of Bedford; if this were a ploy to divide the Petitioners, it seems to have been thwarted by Hertford's deferring to Bedford's superior claim, and by the agreement that none should accept office before *all* the Petitioners who sought office had received an acceptable offer; Collins, *Letters and Memorials*, II, 366: Earl of Northumberland to the Earl of Leicester, 31 December 1640.

181 Clarendon, *Rebellion*, I, 281. Hyde also claims that both Bedford and Pym were working to settle the customs revenues (in the form of a grant of Tonnage and Poundage) on the king for life. This may well have been discussed at some point, but (Clarendon apart) the evidence is far stronger for the conclusion that the two men advocated three-yearly grants. The apparently divergent

accounts may perhaps be reconciled if one assumes that Bedford was already working on the assumption (as seems highly probable) that the Triennial Act would be passed, in which case he would not need the discipline of three-yearly grants of the customs to compel the king to summon regular Parliaments. Under the circumstances that would prevail post-Triennial Act, it was perhaps possible for Bedford and Pym to contemplate a life grant of Tonnage and Poundage to the king – for it would have been potentially revocable by act of Parliament, at three-yearly intervals, if the king failed to honour his part of the settlement terms.

182 Centre for Kentish Studies, De L'Isle MS U1475/C114/7: Sir John Temple to the Earl of Leicester, 21 January 1641 (HMC, *De L'Isle Manuscripts*, VI, 367).

183 Notestein, *D'Ewes Diary*, pp. 263–4 (for Digby); Minnesota UL, MS 137 (Peyton diary), fos. 69–70.

184 Notestein, *D'Ewes Diary*, p. 265; *PLP*, II, 228–9.

185 Centre for Kentish Studies, De L'Isle MS U1475/C114/7: Sir John Temple to the Earl of Leicester, 21 January 1641 (HMC, *De L'Isle Manuscripts*, VI, 367). The same day, the French ambassador also reported that Bedford, Essex, and Pym might receive office, though adding that this was still 'fort incertain': NA, PRO 31/3/72 (Paris transcripts), p. 406.

186 NA, SP 16/476/19 (Nicholas's Privy Council notes), 15 January 1641; on this topic, see also the king's interventions in the meeting of Monday, 25 January. This was of a piece with the assurances Charles had given when he had dissolved the Short Parliament in May 1640: see Esther S. Cope and Willson H. Coates (eds.), *Proceedings of the Short Parliament of 1640* (Camden Society, 4th ser., 19, 1977), pp. 198, 210.

187 These concessions were to be announced in a speech by the king delivered on Saturday, 23 January (from whence these quotations are taken); but they must have been settled upon in the course of that week, and not later than the Friday evening, the 22nd; Notestein, *D'Ewes Diary*, p. 280 (for D'Ewes's account of the speech), and see also the versions in *LJ*, IV, 142 and Nalson, *Impartial Collection*, I, 735–6; *PLP*, II, 264–5.

188 Edward Berwick (ed.), *The Rawdon Papers, consisting of Letters on Various Subjects … to and from Dr John Bramhall, Primate of Ireland* (1819), pp. 78–9: Sir George Wentworth to Dr John Bramhall, [day] June 1640; Hugh Trevor-Roper, 'James Ussher, Archbishop of Armagh', in his *Catholics, Anglicans and Puritans* (1989), pp. 120–65.

189 For the meeting, see Centre for Kentish Studies, De L'Isle MS U1475/C114/7: Sir John Temple to the Earl of Leicester, 21 January 1641 (HMC, *De L'Isle Manuscripts*, VI, 367); for Brownrigg, see NA, WARDS 9/163 (Court of Wards Order Book), fo. 62; and Russell, *Fall of the British Monarchies*, pp. 109–10. Holdsworth was also a friend of the godly peer and future Parliamentarian, Lord North, see Dudley North, 3rd Lord North, *A Forest Promiscuous of Several Seasons Productions* (1659), Part III, p. 217.

190 The complex question of Root-and-Branch is discussed extensively above, pp. 329–31, 342–3.

191 Staffordshire RO, Dartmouth MS D(W)1778/I/i/12: Will Davenant to William Legge, 19 January 1641.

192 For the circumstances, Rushworth, *Historical Collections*, Part III, I, 156; John E. Jeaffreson and William Le Hardy (ed.), *Middlesex County Records*, 4 vols. (1886–92), III, 73; Hibbard, *Charles I and the Popish Plot*, p. 182.

193 Hibbard, *Charles I and the Papish Plot*, pp. 182–3. Goodman was chaplain to the exiled anti-Richelieu grandee, the Marquis de la Vieuville.

194 For Gardiner's appointment as Strafford's counsel, on 27 November 1640, see *LJ*, IV, 100.

195 Notestein, *D'Ewes Diary*, p. 278; BL, Add. MS 72433 (Georg Weckherlin's diary), fo. 84.

196 Baillie, *Letters*, I, 295 (for quotation); Westminster Cathedral Archives, MS A. xxx. 1: anon. newsletter, *c.* 29 January 1641. This MS letter contains a detailed account of the Commons' debate of 23 January.

197 For its discussion in the two Houses the following morning, see Notestein, *D'Ewes Diary*, pp. 277–9; Westminster Cathedral Archives, MS A. xxx. 1: anon. newsletter, *c.* 29 January 1641.

198 Notestein, *D'Ewes Diary*, pp. 279–81.

6. TERMS OF ENDEARMENT

1 Woburn Abbey, Bedford MS, Fourth Earl Addenda 44 (Political and Philosophical Commonplace Book), pp. 49–50.

2 This point is discussed in C Russell, *Causes* pp. 156–7.

3 Simon Thurley, *Whitehall Palace: an Architectural History of the Royal Apartments, 1240–1698* (New Haven and London, 1999); Per Palme, *Triumph of Peace: a Study of the Whitehall Banqueting House* (Stockholm and London, 1957); Maria Varshavskaya and Xenia Yegorova, *Peter Paul Rubens: the Pride of Life* (Bournemouth and St Petersburg, 1995), pp. 120–7; John Harris and Gordon Higgott, *Inigo Jones: Complete Architectural Drawings* (New York, 1989), pp. 108–17.

4 For the location of Vane's seat, see Notestein, *D'Ewes Diary*, p. 278.

5 Ibid. p. 277.

6 Ibid. Pennington linked the question to other instances of indulgence towards criminal or fugitive figures: the Queen of Bohemia's reported hospitality towards Lord Keeper Finch at The Hague, and the Earl of Leicester's (as ambassador in Paris) towards Secretary Windebank. In the latter case, Leicester was actually deeply embarrassed by Windebank's reception at the embassy in Paris, which he had been unable to prevent, and from which he distanced himself at the earliest possible opportunity.

7 Ibid. pp. 278–9.

8 Ibid.

9 Russell, *Fall of the British Monarchies*, pp. 258–62. Once again, Russell's interpretation takes its cue from the Scot, Robert Baillie, whose reports of Parliament's business are often misinformed and almost myopically concerned with religion. For more balanced, and eyewitness, accounts of the debate of 23 January, see Westminster Cathedral Archives, A. xxx. 1: anon. letter, *c.* 29 January 1641; and Notestein, *D'Ewes Diary*, pp. 278–9.

10 For the quotation, see Westminster

Cathedral Archives, A. xxx. 1: anon. letter, *c.* 29 January 1641.

11 *CJ*, II, 72. The committee to prepare the heads for the conference with the Lords comprised nine members, of whom seven can be closely identified with the Petitioner Peers: Hampden, St John, Sir John Hotham, Sir Walter Erle, John Glynne, Sir Thomas Barrington, and Sir Gilbert Gerard. Only Sir Peter Heyman and Sir John Culpeper seem to have come from outside this circle.

12 *CJ*, II, 72. Russell lists Glynne among the 'politically godly', a category that makes the existence of a 'Puritan Revolution' an assertion that is self-fulfilling. Russell, *Fall of the British Monarchies*, pp. 258-62, also regards Charles's action as 'the deliberate raising of a test case', but sees the question at issue as being, not Strafford, but the king's 'concern that life should not be made impossible' for Catholics (ibid., p. 258).

13 Notestein, *D'Ewes Diary*, p. 279.

14 Westminster Cathedral Archives, A. xxx. 1. The author of this speech is unnamed in this newsletter, but as Glynne was the Commons' spokesman at the conference with the Lords, it seems safe to conclude that this is a fuller account of Glynne's argument, recorded by D'Ewes, that the king had issued the pardon 'in Parliament time'; Notestein, *D'Ewes Diary*, p. 279.

15 Westminster Cathedral Archives, A. xxx. 1.

16 Notestein, *D'Ewes Diary*, p. 279; Rushworth, *Historical Collections*, Part III, I, 154-5 (where the king's speech is misdated to 25 January).

17 Rushworth, *Historical Collections* Part III, I, 154; see also the version in Nalson, *Impartial Collection*, I, 736-7.

18 For the king's repetition of this undertaking in the form of a solemn oath, sworn in the presence of Archbishop Ussher in 1643, see *The Kingdomes Weekly Intelligencer*, no. 28 (25 July-1 Aug. 1643), pp. 217-18 (BL, E 63/1); and BL, Add. 18980 (Rupert correspondence), fo. 110: Prince Maurice to the corporation of Barnstaple, 27 August 1643.

19 Rushworth, *Historical Collections*, Part III, I, 155.

20 Ibid.

21 Notestein, *D'Ewes Diary*, p. 280; *LJ*, IV, 142-3.

22 For the king's final concession on this point, delivered on 3 February, see Rushworth, *Historical Collections*, Part III, I, 166; ASV, Senato, Dispacci Inghil. 42, fos. 209v-10: Giustinian to the Doge and Senate, 5/15 February 1641 (*CSPV 1640-42*, pp. 122-3).

23 Notestein, *D'Ewes Diary*, p. 281.

24 Rushworth, *Historical Collections*, Part III, I, p. 155 (my emphasis) this differs slightly from the wording in *LJ*, IV, 142 (*PLP*, II, 265).

25 *Pace* Russell, *Fall of the British Monarchies*. For the references to the footnote, see [Alexander Henderson?], *Arguments given in by the Commissioners of Scotland unto the Lords of the Treaty, perswading Conformitie of Church Government, as one Principall Meanes of a Continued Peace betweene the Two Nations* ([May] 1641), p. 8 (BL, E 157/2), for the quotations in the footnote. This paper seems to date from early March 1641, being written to accompany the discussion among the English and Scottish Treaty Commissioners during the first fortnight of that month; see BL, Add. MS 70003 (Harley Papers), fos. 64-73v: 'The desiers of the Scottish Commissioners concerninge Unity of Religion 1640 [i.e. 1641]', 10 March 1641. For the English Treaty Commissioners' reply, see BL, Harl. MS 163 (D'Ewes diary), fo. 192.

26 On the growing influence of the Lord Chamberlain in governing preaching at court, see Peter E. McCullough, *Sermons at Court: Politics and Religion in Elizabethan and Jacobean Preaching* (Cambridge, 1998), pp. 64-76.

27 For Williams's release, see Dorothy Gardiner (ed.), *The Oxinden Letters, 1607-42* (1933), p. 187: James Oxinden to his brother, Henry, 27 November 1640; and HMC, *De L'Isle Manuscripts*, VI, 342: William Hawkins to the Earl of Leicester, 19 November 1640.

28 For Williams's admiration of Saye, see BL, Harl. MS 6424 (Bishop Warner's diary), fo. 45. Williams was one of a group of reformists which included Lord Brooke, Pym, and probably Viscount Mandeville, who invited

the Bohemian philosopher and polymath, Jan Amos Kosmensky (better known by his Latinized name, Comenius) to visit England in the summer of 1641; R. F. Young, *Comenius in England* (Oxford, 1932), pp. 38–9, 42–4.

29 For the education of noblemen's sons at Buckden, see Helena Hajzyk, 'The Church in Lincolnshire, c. 1595–c. 1640' (Unpublished Ph.D. dissertation, University of Cambridge, 1980), p. 129; for Leicester, see HMC, *Eighth Report*, Appendix (Duke of Manchester's MSS), II, 57–8: Earl of Leicester to [Viscount Mandeville], Paris, 5/15 February 1641 (for the footnote quotation). Williams had other connections among the Junto leadership. Essex had turned to Williams in 1630, when he had sought advice on whether or not he might remarry after divorce; see John Morrill, 'Robert Devereux, third Earl of Essex', *ODNB*. And despite Williams's defence of Saye against the charge of being a sectary, in the House of Lords in 1641, it is noteworthy that Saye had been among those most insistent on the removal of Williams as Lord Keeper in 1625; see John Hacket, *Scrinia Reserata: a Memorial offer'd to the Great Deservings of John Williams, D.D.*, 2 vols. (1693), II, 17–18.

30 William Hawkins described him in December as 'now among all the Byshops ... the most vigorous man' and likely to be restored to all his former offices and benefices: Centre for Kentish Studies, De L'Isle MS U1475/C132/168: William Hawkins to the Earl of Leicester, 31 December 1641 (HMC, *De L'Isle Manuscripts*, VI, 355).

31 BL, Harl. MS 6424 (Bishop Warner's diary), fo. 52; and see above, p. 129.

32 BL, Mam. MS 6424 (Bishop Warner's diary), fo. 9v. Williams also made reference to King Conarus and 'his Dyet [or assembly]' – the tale of the supposed twenty-fourth King of Scotland, who 'was cast into Prison by the Parliament' because he had transacted the major affairs of the kingdom 'by private advice, without the judiciall Ordinance of Parliament' – which may have been an oblique criticism of the king, or possibly as a criticism of the presumption of the Scottish Parliament. Bishop Warner's summary of the reference is too oblique for its meaning to be clear: 'The Bishop of Lincoln preaching before the King at Whitehall had this passage, That Conarus his Dyet [i.e. Parliament] (which Conarus

joyned with Lessius) ...'. For the story of Conarus, see Samuel Rutherford, *Lex, Rex: the Law and the Prince: a Dispute for the Just Prerogative of King and People* (1644), p. 450 (BL, E 11/5). The reference to Lessius, which is complicated by the obscure syntax, may be reference to the celebrated Flemish Jesuit theologian, Leonard Leys (1554–1623), whose surname was Latinized as Lessius. If so, how Lessius's writings were invoked is unclear.

33 Williams defended Saye in March 1641 against Laud's charge that he was a separatist: '[the] Bishop of Lincoln said, His Grace [Laud] would not have called the L. Say Separatist, had he known him so well as he. For the L. Say hath joined with him in his Chappel in all the Prayers and Service of the Church, but his Grace (saith he) abounds in passion and rashness'; BL, Harl. MS 6424 (Bishop Warner's diary), fo. 45.

34 HMC, *Eighth Report*, Appendix (Duke of Manchester's MSS), II, 57–8: Earl of Leicester to [Viscount Mandeville], Paris, 5/15 February 1641.

35 Notestein, *D'Ewes Diary*, pp. 268, 272–5; Rushworth, *Historical Collections*, Part III, I, 167 (for the sum).

36 Rudyard's speech is printed in Ibid. p. 167–8, but misassigned to 4 February; for the correct dating, see Notestein, *D'Ewes Diary*, p. 268n.

37 Rushworth, *Historical Collections*, Part III, I, p. 168; for the dating of this to January, rather than 4 February (as in Rushworth), see Notestein, *D'Ewes Diary*, p. 268n, where the speech by Sir Benjamin Rudyard to which this was a reply is dated to 21 January. Little wonder that St John, speaking for the Junto, tried to draw that sting – and bring an increasingly anti-Scottish debate to a peremptory close – by referring the whole question back to the 'Lordes Commissioners againe [i.e. to Warwick and the other Treaty Commissioners], to see to how low a quantum they could draw it'; Notestein, *D'Ewes Diary*, p. 273.

38 *CSPV 1640–42*, p. 116n.

39 The evidence for this statement is presented in the final section of this chapter.

40 *From the Commissioners of Scotland, 24 February, 1640[-41]* (24 Feb. 1641), single

sheet (BL, 669 f. 3/4); see also [Henderson?], *Arguments given in by the Commissioners of Scotland unto the Lords of the Treaty, perswading Conformitie of Church Government.*

41 Centre for Kentish Studies, De L'Isle MS U1475/C114/7: Sir John Temple to the Earl of Leicester, 21 January 1641 (HMC, *De L'Isle Manuscripts*, VI, 368).

42 For Warwick's motion in the Lords for Laud's remove to the Tower of London and his sequestration from all ecclesiastical powers, see BL, Harl. MS 6424 (Bishop Warner's diary), fo. 42v.

43 William Laud, 'Diary', entry for 21 January 1641, in Laud, *Works*, III, pp. 239-40.

44 *CJ*, II, 70; Notestein, *D'Ewes Diary*, p. 265

45 Ibid. The bill was eventually passed as a gesture of thanks towards Henriette Marie for her assistance in persuading the king to accept a series of reformist statutes. It received its second reading immediately after the king accepted the Triennial Bill; see *CJ*, II, 87.

46 See pp. 178-196.

47 *CJ*, II, 72; Notestein, *D'Ewes Diary*, p. 277.

48 Edmund Calamy, *A Just and Necessary Apology* (1646), p. 9 (BL, E 319/25); emphasis added.

49 For their involvement, see Notestein, *D'Ewes Diary*, pp. 313-14; Elliot Vernon, 'A Few Engaged Men: London, the covenant, and the politics of settlement 1640-47', in John Adamson (ed.) *The Civil Wars: Revolution and Revolt in the Three Stuart Kingdoms* (2007). John White, the celebrated patriarch of Dorchester also appears to have been involved; Notestein, *D'Ewes Diary*, p. 313. To the delight of the Scots, whom the Remonstrance was partly intended to reassure, the document offered a resounding condemnation of the bishops, accusing them of being the authors of the English Church's corruption 'in doctrine, discipline, lyfe, and all'; Baillie, *Letters*, I, 292 (a reference I owe to Dr Elliot Vernon). A partial reconstruction of the contents of the Remonstrance is attempted in William A. Shaw, *A History of the English Church during the Civil Wars and* *Under the Commonwealth, 1640-60*, 2 vols (1900), I, p. 24-6.

50 Shaw, *English Church during the Civil Wars*, I, 24-6.

51 For the contents of this Petition and Remonstrance, see Ibid.

52 BL, Add. MS 70001 (Harley Papers), fos. 59, 232: Earl of Warwick to Sir Robert Harley, 3 February 1641 and 26 March 1642 (for the footnote quotations). I agree with Dr Eales that, while Harley broadly shared Warwick's political objectives, he 'did not have any obvious patronage links with these [Junto] peers and cannot be regarded simply as a client of any individual member of the House of Lords'; Jacqueline Eales, *Puritans and Roundheads: the Harleys of Brampton Bryan and the Outbreak of the English Civil War* (Cambridge, 1990), p. 102.

53 Notestein, *D'Ewes Diary*, pp. 282-3.

54 Russell, *Fall of the British Monarchies*, pp. 180-2, 184-5, 190-4.

55 Edward Bagshaw, *A Just Vindication of the Questioned Part of the Reading of Edward Bagshaw, Esq.* (1660), pp. 3-4 (BL, E 1019/6).

56 Notestein, *D'Ewes Diary*, p. 309. The alternative proposal to Pym's special committee was that the Remonstrance be referred to the Grand Committee for Religion (i.e. to the whole House, convened as a committee).

57 Melbourne Hall, Derbyshire, Coke MS 11, 272: Sir John Coke junior to Sir John Coke senior, 2 February 1641; printed in Notestein, *D'Ewes Diary*, p. 315. Digby's impetuous intervention redounded against him when Burges and Downinge later affirmed their broad support for the Remonstrance's reformist agenda. But that both Pym and Digby should have gone to such lengths to prevent a general debate on the question of episcopal reform is telling. Digby's attempts to discredit the Remonstrance seem to have less to do with any deep-seated commitment to the old episcopal order than with a desire that the Bedford interest should be seen to accept the king's implied quid pro quo of 23 January: that the royal assent might be granted to the 'substance' of the Triennial Bill if moves to abolish bishops were abandoned.

58 Notestein, *D'Ewes Diary*, p. 314. Again,

the Committee of the Whole was the Grand Committee for Religion; St John wanted the matter referred to the Committee on the State of the Kingdom, appointed on 10 November – otherwise known as the 'Committee of Twenty-Four' – which was dominated by Junto-men, including Digby, St John himself, Pym, and Hampden; and which also included the pro-episcopalians Sir John Culpeper, Sir Francis Seymour, John Selden, Sir John Strangways, Henry Belasyse (a man with strong Catholic connections) and Sir Benjamin Rudyard. Reference to the Committee of Twenty-Four, in other words, was almost certain not to produce a recommendation in favour of Root-and-Branch, as St John must certainly have known when he made his motion. For the committee's membership, see *CJ*, II, 25; for Henry Belasyse, see his biography by David Scott, HPL.

59 Notestein, *D'Ewes Diary*, p. 315. What looks like a concerted Bedford House campaign to prevent a full-scale debate on Root-and-Branch succeeded when, either fortuitously or by design, Speaker Lenthall suddenly announced that he had needed to leave for a 'grand day' dinner in Lincoln's Inn, and that any vote on whether to commit the Remonstrance would now have to be postponed to another day. On the question of whether D'Ewes actually delivered the speeches he ascribes to himself in his diary, see John Morrill, 'Getting over D'Ewes', *Parliamentary History*, 15 (1996), 221–30.

60 *CJ*, II, 76.

61 Clarendon, *Rebellion*, II, 211. This was in spite of the fact that Littleton had been Solicitor-General during *R. v. Hampden* (1637).

62 PA, MP 30 January 1641: William Raylton to [the Lord Keeper] (HMC, *Fourth Report*, p. 45).

63 *CJ*, II, 76; Notestein, *D'Ewes Diary*, pp. 303–4.

64 A copy of these notes, taken by Vane at the Council of War on 5 May 1641, is in the PA, and printed in HMC, *Third Report*, p. 3; see also BL, Harl. MS 164 (D'Ewes diary), fos. 162v, 167v. Their authenticity was established beyond reasonable doubt by Gardiner (*History*, IX, 120–1, n. 4) and Russell (*Fall of the British Monarchies*, p. 287). Gardiner suggests that Pym had

acquired his copy of the notes from the younger Vane during the autumn of 1640; Gardiner, *History*, IX, 229. Significantly, the existence of this crucial evidence was not disclosed to the Commons until 10 April, by which point the trial was on the point of collapse: BL, Harl. MS 164 (D'Ewes diary), fo. 162; and below, pp. 241–2.

65 It is perhaps not coincidental, therefore, that this was also the day that St John chose to try to bury the minister's Remonstrance with Digby's Committee of Twenty-Four. See above, p. 176.

66 Melbourne Hall, Derbyshire, Coke MS p. 176: Sir John Coke junior to Sir John Coke senior, 2 February 1641 (calendared in HMC, *Twelfth Report*, II, 272).

67 BL, Harl. MS 6424 (Bishop Warner's diary), fo. 13.

68 What we do not know is just how conciliatory the Junto grandees were prepared to be. Among the various options that are likely to have been discussed are a trial that stopped short of a capital sentence; or possibly the postponement of that trial until after the Scottish treaty had been completed and the Covenanter army sent home, the departure of which would have removed the principal source of demands for Strafford's head. Quite apart from these considerations, the Junto leaders had an obvious interest in dragging out the judicial process as long as possible; next to their control of the royal purse, it was their most effective means of exerting influence over the king – a means of influence that would obviously cease with the completion of the trial. But whatever disagreements there were within the Junto over Strafford's eventual fate, there seems to have been general agreement that the pre-trial judicial process – the consideration of charges, questioning of witnesses and collecting of evidence – should proceed at a stately pace.

69 As Count Carlo Rossetti wrote to Cardinal Barberini on 29 January/8 February 1641, 'The question whether Goodman shall live or die has turned into a question whether the supreme authority lies with the king or Parliament. There is no other topic of conversation at present'; quoted in A. O. Meyer, 'Charles I and Rome', *American Historical Review*, 19 (1914), 13–26, at p. 24.

70 Rushworth, *Historical Collections*, Part III, I, 165–6.

71 HMC, *Eighth Report*, Appendix (Duke of Manchester's MSS), II, 57–8: Earl of Leicester to [Viscount Mandeville], Paris, 5–15 February 1641.

72 Carte, *Life of Ormond* V, 245: Earl of Strafford to the Earl of Ormond, 3 February 1641.

73 *CJ*, II, 80 (for the reference to the committee); ibid., p. 60 (for the composition of the Triennial Bill committee). The committee included, beside Vane (who, revealingly, was its first-named member), Lord Russell, Lord Digby, Strode, Pym, Holles, Hampden, St John, Harbottell Grimston, Sir Henry Mildmay, Sir Gilbert Gerard, and Sir Thomas Barrington, Erle, Sir Gilbert Pickering, Glynne, Whitelocke, Cromwell, Sir William Brereton, Sir Philip Stapilton, Edward Hyde, Sir Francis Seymour, Lord Fairfax, and Nathaniel Fiennes. Of these, only Fiennes and (probably) Cromwell took an unequivocally pro-Root-and-Branch stance in the debate on episcopacy of 8–9 February.

74 BL, Harl. MS 6424 (Bishop Warner's diary), fo. 13.

75 Keeler, *Long Parliament*, p. 329.

76 Notestein, *D'Ewes Diary*, p. 335.

77 Rushworth, *Historical Collections*, Part III, I, 183. Even before the debate began, Giustinian reported that the bishops were unlikely to face abolition, and that 'it is thought that they will only be reduced in numbers, their revenues cut down and diverted to more useful employments, and the privilege of sitting in Parliament taken away'; ASV, Senato, Dispacci Inghil. 42, fos. 208v–9: Giustinian to the Doge and Senate, 5/15 February 1641 (*CSPV 1640–42*, p. 122).

78 Rudyard's speech is mentioned as opening the debate in Notestein, *D'Ewes Diary*, p. 335; the text is printed in Rushworth, *Historical Collections*, Part III, I,

183–479 For Warwick's support for Ussher, see Hugh Trevor-Roper, 'James Ussher, Archbishop of Armagh', in his Catholics, Anglicans, and Puritans: Seventeenth-Century Essays (1987), pp. 148–9; for what may be a manuscript text of this, see Cambridge UL, Add, MS 44/6, fos. 1–2. For

Calamy's involvement in these discussions in the Jerusalem Chamber of Westminster Abbey, see A. G. Matthews (ed.), *Calamy Revised: being a Revision of Edmund Calamy's Account of the Ministers and Others Ejected and Silenced, 1660–62* (Oxford, 1934), pp. xlix–l.

80 Notestein, *D'Ewes Diary*, p. 335; BL, Harl. MS 164 (D'Ewes diary), fo. 113.

81 The phrase is John Vicars's; see his *Jehovah-Jireh God in the Mount, or, Englands Parliamentarie-Chronicle* (1644), quoted in Notestein, *D'Ewes Diary*, p. 335n.

82 Baillie, *Letters*, I, 302. The slightly hysterical tone of Baillie's letter recounting the episcopacy debate of 8–9 February 1641 appears a reflection of his concern that, from the Covenanter point of view, it had gone so badly.

83 Gardiner, *History*, IX, 281.

84 Russell, *Fall of the British Monarchies*, p. 195. Anthony Fletcher, *The Outbreak of the English Civil War* (1981), pp. 98–9, is more cautious, noting that the debate of 8 February was 'so incoherent' that Gardiner's claims about its predictive qualities 'will not stand up'.

85 Russell, *Fall of the British Monarchies*, p. 195.

86 For the probable contents of the ministers' Remonstrance, see Shaw, *English Church during the Civil Wars*, I, 24–6; for the London Root-and-Branch Petition, see Gardiner, *Constitutional Documents*, pp. 137–44.

87 Grimston's speech: quotations, respectively, from Notestein, *D'Ewes Diary*, p. 336, and Rushworth, *Historical Collections*, Part III, I, 187.

88 Ibid.

89 NLS, MS Wodrow Folio 22 (Dispatches from London), unfol.: Scottish Commissioners in London to the members of the Committee of Estates in Newcastle, despatches of late February 1641. On the Junto's overriding concern to avoid divisions within the English Parliament, at least until the Strafford prosecution was completed, see Baillie, *Letters*, I, 314.

90 Edward Bagshaw, *A Just Vindication of the Questioned Part of the Reading of Edward*

Bagshaw, Esq. (1660), pp. 3–4 (BL, E 1019/6). Although this account was not published until 1660, its author had been an eye-witness of the 'Root-and-Branch' debate of 8–9 February 1641.

91 Gardiner, *History*, IX, 281: 'Almost every member of note in the House, and very many who were of no note at all, rose to express an opinion on one side or the other. Pym and Hampden, St John and Holles, the future leaders of the Parliamentary party, were all for the committal of the petition ... Hyde and Culpepper [*sic*], Selden, Hopton, and Waller, the Royalists of the days of the Grand Remonstrance, followed Digby and Falkland ... their parting gave the colour to English political life which has distinguished it ever since ...'.

92 For Falkland's speech see Notestein, *D'Ewes Diary*, pp. 335–6; 'William Drake's Parliamentary Notebook', in Jansson, *Two Diaries*, p. 2; *the fullest text is Rushworth, Historical Collections*, Part III, I, 184–6. This gives the lie to Gardiner's implicit claim that Falkland was against committal.

93 Rushworth, *Historical Collections*, Part III, I, 186 (for the quotation in the text); Peter Heylyn, *Memorial of Bishop Waynflete*, ed. J. R. Bloxam (1851), p. xxiv (for the quotation in the footnote). On cool response to Falkland's death see Robert Wilcher, *The Writing of Royalism, 1628–60* (Cambridge, 2001), pp. 193–4. I owe these last two references to Dr Anthony Milton.

94 Notestein, *D'Ewes Diary*, p. 337.

95 Ibid. pp. 336–8. Chadwell's motion came towards the end of the debate, when it seemed committal was going to carry the day, hence his proposal 'that if it were committed, hee desired it might bee referred to a Committee of the whole Howse'; ibid., p. 338. For Carnaby, see *CJ*, II, 81.

96 See, for example, Russell, *Fall of the British Monarchies*, p. 195. The truly controversial option – almost guaranteed to produce political fireworks – was the proposal to refer the question of bishops' abolition to a Committee of the Whole House. In practice, this was the full House of Commons, meeting in their usual chamber; but, freed from the usual rule that members spoke only once in a debate, discussions in a Committee of the Whole had the potential to go on almost

indefinitely, and with far greater acrimony, as members' ability to reply to counter-arguments was so much more extensive. This was the preferred option of Sir Henry Mildmay, one of the most extreme Puritans in the Warwick circle, who only a fortnight earlier had advocated a nationwide campaign of iconoclasm in order that 'Images and Idols might bee taken away' (Notestein, *D'Ewes Diary*, pp. 270 (for quotation), 337). But it was also the preferred course advocated by two future Royalists: the barristers, William Chadwell and Richard King, both of whom were associated with the reformist group in the Commons. Once again, the assumption that there is a simple correlation between Commons-men's attitudes to the London Root-and-Branch Petition and their future allegiance proves unfounded.

97 It is noteworthy that Selden, one of the Commons-men who upheld episcopacy most trenchantly, argued that the reason for rejecting the London Petition was 'because wee have matter enough in the ministers' Remonstrance' – i.e., he accepted that the Remonstrance was to be taken into consideration in committee; Notestein, *D'Ewes Diary*, p. 337.

98 For the passion of Fiennes's reformist convictions, see Edward Hyde, *The Life of Edward Hyde, Earl of Clarendon, written by Himself*, 2 vols. (Oxford, 1857), pp. 74–5. For his occasional 'unreliability', I am grateful for a discussion with the late Professor Conrad Russell. Fiennes's first-hand experience of the bishopless Scottish Kirk, during his stay in Scotland in 1639, may also have influenced his attitudes.

99 'To speak plain English,' Fiennes insisted, 'These Bishops, Deans and Chapters, do little good themselves ... and if they were felled, a great deal of Timber might be cut out of them for the use of the Church and Kingdom at this time.' More puzzling is why – if our assumptions hitherto about Fiennes's centrality to the reformists' counsels are correct – he should have jeopardized the Junto's relations with the king by appearing so stridently off-message; and this, moreover, at a moment when so many of his godly friends were striving to dispel the king's fears that they intended the eradication of the bishops. One possible explanation is that Fiennes's speech was a personal credo, a

public statement of radical beliefs, passionately held, that he could no longer keep to himself. Yet, without impugning the sincerity of Fiennes's motives, it is also possible to read his support for Root-and-Branch – otherwise, from the perspective of Bedford and Pym, so untimely – as an attempt by Fiennes to retain the favour of the Scottish Commissioners, with whom he was one of the Junto's chief points of contact. Whether or not Fiennes was deliberately playing to the Scottish gallery, his support for Root-and-Branch enabled the Junto leadership to claim that they had at least made a stand, however unsuccessful, in favour of abolishing episcopacy. Indeed, when it came to recounting the debate to the Scottish Commissioners, their English 'friends' (Warwick and Fiennes are the most likely suspects) seem to have deliberately misinformed the Scots as to what had occurred, exaggerating the extent of the support that had been revealed for Root-and-Branch, and even telling Baillie that the question had been referred to the Committee of Religion (a committee of the entire House of Commons), when in fact it had been consigned to the far from sympathetic clutches of the Committee of Twenty-Four; see Baillie, *Letters*, I, 302. Baillie was under the impression that 'our partie carried it, that it should be referred to the Committee of Religion [*sic*]'. For Fiennes's speech, see Notestein, *D'Ewes Diary*, p. 336. It would seem that it was this speech that subsequently appeared in print as Nathaniel Fiennes, *A Speech of the Honorable Nathanael Fiennes (Second Son to the Right Honourable the Lord Say) in Answere to the Third Speech of the Lord George Digby. Concerning Bishops and the City of Londons Petition, both which were made the 9th of Feb. 1640* ([March?] 1641), *passim* (BL, E 196/32). Despite its putative date (the 9th), this looks to have been the speech delivered by Fiennes on 8 February. It is printed in Rushworth, *Historical Collections*, Part III, I, 172–83 (to which subsequent references will be made).

100 Notestein, *D'Ewes Diary*, p. 336.

101 The one possible exception to this was the contribution of Alderman Isaac Penington, who was involved in collecting signatures in favour of the London Root-and-Branch Petition; however, as reported by D'Ewes, even he stopped short of calling for outright abolition in his remarks on 9 February to the House of Commons; Notestein, *D'Ewes Diary*, p. 339.

102 BL, Harl. MS 164 (D'Ewes diary), fo. 113 (printed in Notestein, *D'Ewes Diary*, p. 337). Although there was no likelihood that the Root-and-Branch Petitioners' request would be granted, there was a clear majority in favour of at least *considering* their grievances in committee, if only because the Petition contained such a comprehensive catalogue of the ecclesiastical 'innovations' and 'abuses' that required further reform. This can be inferred from Sir Francis Seymour's reference to the 'Committee, to *which wee intended* to referre the London petition' – implying that it was already accepted that this would be the outcome of the eventual vote; Notestein, *D'Ewes Diary*, p. 341.

103 Russell, *Fall of the British Monarchies*, p. 194. The only notice of the content of Pym's speech is a rather laconic and obviously incomplete entry in Sir William Drake's diary; in full, this reads: 'Mr Pym moved that some consideration might be taken of the present state of the King's expense and to settle things in that way. He moved that could in [*illegible*] be disposed to the most necessary and material uses in the first place'; Jansson, *Two Diaries* p. 3. It is therefore difficult to see how Professor Russell gets from here to concluding that Pym 'seems to have argued for the abolition of episcopacy'. It looks far more likely to have been an argument in favour of the confiscation of dean and chapter lands, a scheme which Bedford had contemporaneously under consideration; see Woburn Abbey, Bedford MS, Fourth Earl Miscellaneous Papers, 'The Proiect upon the Clergie and Colledges'. Deans and chapters were, of course, among the elements of the hierarchy attacked in the London Root-and-Branch Petition.

104 Clarendon, *Rebellion*, I, 309.

105 Notestein, *D'Ewes Diary*, p. 314 (for 2 February); *CJ*, II, 81 (for 9 February).

106 *CJ*, II, 81. That Geoffrey Palmer should be regarded on the pro-reformist side is suggested by his (admittedly rather oblique) remarks, recorded by Drake, in which he advocated extending the committee's brief to

allow it to 'touch upon episcopacy'; Jansson, *Two Diaries*, p. 3.

107 Notestein, *D'Ewes Diary*, p. 342; *CJ*, II, p. 81.

108 Ibid.; Baillie, *Letters*, I, 302. Baillie's account of the Root-and-Branch debate appears to have been deeply misinformed; he even mistakes that committee to which Root-and-Branch was eventually referred, mistaking the Committee of Twenty-Four for the 'Committee of Religion'.

109 For a strongly differing view, see Russell, *Fall of the British Monarchies*, p. 195: 'What was clear at the end of this debate was that the avoidance of adversary politics could not survive much discussion of this issue, or of the general demand for "further reformation" which lay behind it'.

110 *CJ*, II, 70.

111 Ibid. (for their membership of the Triennial Bill committee); Notestein, *D'Ewes Diary*, p. 337 (for Erle); for the opinions of the other speakers, see above pp. 180–2. This linkage between the Triennial Bill and Root-and-Branch is, if anything, even more marked during the second day of the debate. Of the seven speakers recorded that day by D'Ewes, every one of them was a supporter of the Triennial Bill – and six out of seven of them were actually members of the bill's revising committee: Sir John Strangways, Oliver Cromwell, John Pym, Denzell Holles, Sir Francis Seymour, Sir John Culpeper, and Lord Falkland; all except Falkland were on the Triennial Bill committee: *CJ*, II, 60, 80. Of course the degree of unanimity between them should not be overstated. At very least, their contributions reveal a tactical disagreement, if not over whether bishops were to be retained, then over how many of their existing privileges were to remain.

112 Russell, *Fall of the British Monarchies*, p. 195.

113 Of the other members of the Warwick interest, Harbottell Grimston's insistence that bishops should be reformed but not abolished seems also to have a *politique* element.

114 Reference misplaced; but see also NLS, MS 33.4.6 (Dispatches from London), fo. 133r-v: Scottish Commissioners in London to General Leslie, February 1641.

115 For the Committee of Twenty-Four, see *CJ*, II, 25. Of its twenty-four members, probably only Sir Robert Harley was a convinced Root-and-Brancher.

116 HMC, *Cowper Manuscripts*, II, 280: Sir John Coke to his father, Sir John Coke senior, 24 April 1641.

117 BL, Add. MS 70001 (Harley papers), fos. 64–73v: 'The desiers of the Scottish Commissioners concerninge Unity in Religion, 1640[/1]', provides their considered response, noted as having been sent on 10 March 1641. This MS was prepared for the English Treaty Commissioners; and it is perhaps suggestive of Harley's closeness to the Warwick House group – whose members constituted the most pro-Scots faction among the Treaty Commissioners – that the document survives in Harley's papers.

118 Clarendon, *Rebellion*, I, 270–1 (my emphasis); Notestein, *D'Ewes Diary*, pp. 336–8.

119 Fletcher, *Outbreak*, p. 107.

120 For Williams's House of Lords committee, which considered these proposals, see A. G. Matthews (ed.), *Calamy Revised: being a Revision of Edmund Calamy's Account of the Ministers and Others ejected and silenced, 1660–62* (Oxford, 1934), p. 1.

121 Centre for Kentish Studies, De L'Isle MS U1475/C132/174: William Hawkins to the Earl of Leicester, 11 February 1641 (HMC, *De L'Isle Manuscripts*, VI, 378).

122 *Privy Council Registers*, XII, entries for 24 January 1641. Charles had stated that he 'cannot in his conscience give way that episcopacy shalbe abolished either in the function or for their voice in P[ar]liament'; quoted in Russell, *Fall of the British Monarchies*, p. 245.

7. THE REWARDS OF SEDITION

1 ASV, Senato, Dispacci Inghil. 42, fo. 225: Giustinian to the Doge and Senate, 27 February/8 March 1641 (*CSPV 1640–42*, p. 128). It is perhaps significant that Giustinian mentions *six* promotions to the Privy Council, rather than the seven that were actually made; presumably, he regarded Bristol as innocent of involvement in the 'revolts' of the previous summer.

2 Rushworth, *Historical Collections*, Part III, I, 155.

3 BL, Harl. MS 6424 (Bishop Warner's diary), fos. 16v–17 (for quotations); see also Rushworth, *Historical Collections*, III, I, 188. For the earlier stages of the negotiations, see Loomie, *Ceremonies of Charles I*, p. 297; and BL, Add. MS 72433 (Weckherlin diary), fo. 83v, where the dates of the Dutch ambassadors' audiences are itemized.

4 BL, Harl. MS 6424 (Bishop Warner's diary), fos. 16v–17.

5 ASV, Senato, Dispacci Inghil. 42, fos. 213–5: Giustinian to the Doge and Senate, 12/22 February 1641 (*CSPV 1640–42*, pp. 124–5).

6 Centre for Kentish Studies, De L'Isle MS U1475/C129/13: Countess of Carlisle to the Countess of Leicester, undated [February 1641] (HMC, *De L'Isle Manuscripts*, VI, 374).

7 Minnesota UL, MS 137 (Peyton diary), fo. 82; Notestein, *D'Ewes Diary*, p. 343; *CJ*, II, 82; and see above pp. 185–6.

8 *CJ*, II, p. 85; Notestein, *D'Ewes Diary*, pp. 359–60, 361–5.

9 BL, Harl. MS 6424 (Bishop Warner's diary), fo. 19v, where Warner refers to him mistakenly as 'Sir Thomas Clotworth'. The speech is mentioned in Notestein, *D'Ewes Diary*, p. 360.

10 For the increasing stridency of Warwick and his immediate circle during February and March, see above, pp. 206–9,213.

11 *CJ*, II, p. 86; Notestein, *D'Ewes Diary*, p. 361. Clotworthy and Erle had earlier raised the matter of the need to disband the Irish army on 4 January: *CJ*, II, 62.

12 *CJ*, II, 70; Notestein, *D'Ewes Diary*, p. 265.

13 Notestein, *D'Ewes Diary*, p. 361; *CJ*, II, 85. For the friendship between the Strodes and Bedford, which went back to the time of William's father, see BL, Harl. MS 7001 (Misc. corr.), fo. 137: Sir Richard Strode (William's brother) to the Earl of Bedford, [31 January] 1638.

14 *LJ*, IV, 162.

15 *LJ*, IV, 162. Like his conduct at Strafford's

trial, this support for the Triennial Act would suggest that Arundel had become a supporter of the Bedford–Saye group within the Junto. On 24 February, Arundel ('the Lord Marshall') sided with Mandeville, Saye, Paget, and Brooke, in demanding that the bishops have no part in the proceedings against Strafford; BL, Harl. MS 6424 (Bishop Warner's diary), fo. 39. It is noteworthy in this regard that the Countess of Arundel lent her box at Strafford's trial to the wife of Nathaniel Fiennes (Saye's daughter-in-law): Centre for Kentish Studies, Cranfield (Bourchier) MS U269/C267/6: Earl of Bath to his wife, 29 April 1641.

16 Notestein, *D'Ewes Diary*, p. 362.

17 The grant of the four subsidies was obviously both an inducement, which Bedford and the other peers in the Lords' delegation could offer the king, and a form of coercion, in that the king would have been unable to fund his expences, should the subsidy bills have been withheld. But the force of this potential threat against the king should not be exaggerated. Failure to pass the subsidy bills would have affected Parliament no less than Charles, as the two Houses would have found it extremely difficult to raise loans in the City without the subsidies as security; and the Junto's relations with the Scots would have been severely strained, if not broken, should payments to the Scottish army encamped in the North have broken down entirely.

18 W. B. Bidwell and Maija Jansson (eds.), *Proceedings in Parliament 1626*, 4 vols. (New Haven and London, 1991–96), II, 395.

19 For the use of this phrase, ASV, Senato, Dispacci Inghil. 42, fo. 225: Giustinian to the Doge and Senate, 27 February/8 March 1641 (*CSPV 1640–42*, p. 128). Giustinian refers to Bedford and his allies as 'principali Capi delle rivolte dell'anno passato'.

20 ASV, Senato, Dispacci Inghil. 42, fos. 218v–19: Giustinian to the Doge and Senate, 19 February/2 March 1641 (*CSPV 1640–42*, p. 126).

21 Richard Cust, *Charles I: a Political Life* (2005), pp. 16–17.

22 The presence of Hertford within the Lords' delegation – who carried both Tudor and Stuart blood royal, and was a viable

pretender to the throne – may well have helped concentrate the king's mind.

23 ASV, Senato, Dispacci Inghil. 42, fo. 219.

24 Notestein, *D'Ewes Diary*, p. 364.

25 For the king's dress in the 'royal robes', see ASV, Senato, Dispacci Inghil. 42, fos. 219–20; the robes are depicted in van Dyck's 1636 portrait of the king in the Royal Collection, reproduced in *Van Dyck Complete Catalogue*, p. 471.

26 Notestein, *D'Ewes Diary*, pp. 364–5.

27 Ibid., p. 365. A formal delegation from both Houses also attended the king in the Banqueting House, to express the Parliament's thanks for the passing of the Triennial Act; *CJ*, ii, 87.

28 *CJ*, ii, 87.

29 ASV, Senato, Dispacci Inghil. 42, fo. 220: Giustinian to the Doge and Senate, 19 February/1 March 1641 (*CSPV 1640–42*, p. 127).

30 Notestein, *D'Ewes Diary*, p. 263. This contribution was made by Sir Edward Herbert on 19 January, only a matter of days before his promotion to Attorney-General.

31 Thomas de Fougasses (trans. William Shute), *The Generall Historie of the Magnificent State of Venice from the First Foundation thereof vntill this Present. Collected by Thomas de Fougasses, Gentleman of Auignon, out of all Authors, both Ancient and Moderne, that haue written of that Subiect* (1612), pp. 11, 12, 500. This history, one of the majors work on Venice published before the Civil War, was dedicated to one of the eventual promoters of the Triennial Act, the 4th Earl of Pembroke (then styled Earl of Montgomery), and his elder brother, the 3rd Earl.

32 NAS, Hamilton Red Book I, p. 76: Charles I to the Marquess of Hamilton, 25 June 1638; partly printed Gilbert Burnet, *The Memoires of the Lives and Actions of James and William, Dukes of Hamilton* (1677), p. 60.

33 For Argyll's relations with the Junto, see above, Ch. 11.

34 Archibald Campell, 8th Earl of Argyll, *An Honourable Speech made ... by the Earle of Argile (being now Competitor with Earle*

Morton for the Chancellorship) ([Sept.] 1641), pp. 3–4 (BL, E 199/17).

35 ASV, Senato, Dispacci Inghil. 42, fo. 220: Giustinian to the Doge and Senate, 19 February/1 March 1641 (*CSPV 1640–42*, p. 127). All that was left was 'i soli tittoli e le nude apparente di Rè, [e] non sà coprire l'interne passioni che giustamente la cruciano'.

36 BL, Harl. MS 6424 (Bishop Warner's diary), fo. 22.

37 HMC, *Ninth Report*, ii, 499: extracts from Robert Woodford's diary.

38 David Cressy, *Bonfires and Bells: National Memory and the Protestant Calendar in Elizabethan and Stuart England* (1989), p. 77. The London church of St Andrew by the Wardrobe seems to have jumped the gun and rung its bells on 15 February, the evening that the bill was despatched for the royal assent; ibid.

39 Ibid., p. 77.

40 HMC, *Ninth Report*, ii, 499: extracts from Robert Woodford's diary.

41 C. L. Kingsford (ed.), *A Survey of London by John Stow* (Oxford, 1908), pp. 101, 283 (for quotation). I owe my knowledge of this reference to Professor David Cressy.

42 *CJ*, ii, 87.

43 For a subtle study of popular disturbances during this period and the permissive, if not complicit, involvement of the political élites, see John Walter, *Understanding Popular Violence in the English Revolution: the Colchester Plunderers* (Cambridge, 1999).

44 HMC, *Eighth Report*, Appendix (Manchester MSS), ii, 58: Earl of Leicester to [Viscount Mandeville], Paris, 5/15 February 1641.

45 BL, Harl. MS 6424 (Bishop Warner's diary), fo. 20.

46 For O'Neill, see Brian Manning (ed.), *Politics, Religion and the English Civil War* (1973), pp. 58–62; there is an unsatisfactory biography in the *ODNB*.

47 Staffordshire RO, Dartmouth MS D(W)1778/I/i/14: Daniel O'Neill to William Legge, 23 February 1641. O'Neill refers to the 'new Councillors' appointed on the 19th

(with the exceptions of Essex and Mandeville) as having been in favour of the deferral: this means that Bedford was joined by Hertford, Bristol, Saye, and Savile. To O'Neill's surprise, none was more in Strafford's favour than 'your lord', a reference to Legge's superior at the Ordnance Office, the Earl of Newport, Warwick's half-brother. For proceedings in the Lords that day, see also BL, Harl. MS 6424 (Bishop Warner's diary), fos. 22–3.

48 I base this conclusion on Staffordshire RO, Dartmouth MS D(W)1778/I/i/14, which names Essex and Mandeville as having spoken against the deferral, and which refers, very much more obliquely, to Holland and Warwick as having 'lost themselves' by having incurred the king's displeasure, a reference which I take to refer to their opposition to Strafford more generally. For further evidence of their having taken a far more aggressive attitude towards Strafford's impeachment than Bedford, see pp. 206–9, 213.

49 BL, Harl. MS 6424 (Bishop Warner's diary), fo. 23.

50 Notestein, *D'Ewes Diary*, pp. 366n, 374.

51 Ibid., p. 366n.

52 Ibid., p. 374. For the conference on the subject, see *CJ*, II, 88.

53 Notestein, *D'Ewes Diary* p. 301.

54 *PLP*, I, 99, 103.

55 *Clarendon State Papers*, II, 98: Windebank to Charles I, 3 September 1640.

56 *CJ*, II, 83: Clotworthy made the report with Sir Walter Erle, who was to become his chief collaborator in the campaign to disband the Irish army. For the questioning of the Earl of Worcester (and the quotation), see Centre for Kentish Studies, De L'Isle MS U1475/C132/174: William Hawkins to the Earl of Leicester, 11 February 1641 (HMC, *De L'Isle Manuscripts*, VI, 377–8).

57 BL, Harl. MS 164 (D'Ewes diary), fo. 119 (Notestein, *D'Ewes Diary*, p. 366n.).

58 Centre for Kentish Studies, De L'Isle MS U1475/C114/13: Sir John Temple to the Earl of Leicester, 4 March 1641 (HMC, *De L'Isle Manuscripts*, VI, 389).

59 For Warwick acting as the Scots' principal point of contact among the English Treaty Commissioners, see Notestein, *D'Ewes Diary*,

p. 448; NA, SP 16/483, fos. 90v–91r: Earl of Warwick's accounts for the sums received by him for payment to the Scottish Commissioners over the period 28 December 1640–13 August 1641; NA, SP 46/80 (State Papers, supplementary), fo. 175: receipt from the Scottish Commissioners (the signatories include Rothes, Dunfermline, and Loudoun) for £25,000 received between 6 and 20 March 1641; ibid., fo. 178: receipt from the Scottish Commissioners for £30,000, 18, 24, and 31 May 1641; and see above, Ch. 11.

60 Leicester's letter to Viscount Mandeville of 5/15 February 1641, referring to Bristol as 'another notable man of your society', suggests that Bristol was associated with the Junto, and publicly perceived to be so, by early February, if not much earlier. His appointment to the Privy Council seems to have been as part of this 'Junto ticket', rather than purely for his services rendered as one of the Treaty Commissioners; see HMC, *Eighth Report*, Appendix (Manchester MSS), II, 58.

61 HMC, *De L'Isle and Dudley Manuscripts*, VI, 385: William Hawkins to the Earl of Leicester, 25 February 1641; for ambassadorial receptions, see Loomie, *Ceremonies of Charles I*, pp. 297–313.

62 Russell, *Fall of the British Monarchies*, pp. 263, 264.

63 Baillie, *Letters*, I, 305 (for quotation); Centre for Kentish Studies, De L'Isle MS U1475/C114/12: Sir John Temple to the Earl of Leicester, 25 February 1641 (HMC, *De L'Isle Manuscripts*, VI, 387–8).

64 This reading of the Privy Council appointments is based on ASV, Senato, Dispacci Inghil. 42, fo. 225: Giustinian to the Doge and Senate, 27 February/8 March 1641 (*CSPV 1640–42*, p. 128); Staffordshire RO, Dartmouth MS D(W)1778/I/i/14: Daniel O'Neill to William Legge, 23 February 1641; and Centre for Kentish Studies, De L'Isle MS U1475/C114/12: Sir John Temple to the Earl of Leicester, 25 February 1641 (HMC, *De L'Isle Manuscripts*, VI, 387–8).

65 As late as June 1638, Warwick had been receiving payments from the Crown for his work in finishing the fortifications at Languard Point, Suffolk; see NA, T 34/51 (Clerk of the Pells Declared Accounts), fo. 22: £445 13s. 6d. was paid by warrant dated 15 June 1638.

66 Kentish Studies, De L'Isle MS U1475/C114/12: Sir John Temple to the Earl of Leicester, 25 February 1641 (HMC, *De L'Isle Manuscripts*, VI, 387–8).

67 NAS, Hamilton MS, GD 406/1/1419: Earl of Essex to the Marquess of Hamilton, 30 August 1641 (for quotation); for Essex's hostility to Strafford, see Clarendon, *Rebellion*, I, 319–21.

68 Baillie, *Letters and Journals*, I, 305, 309. Charles's efforts to secure leniency towards Strafford, Giustinian believed, had been the prime motive for the latest preferments: ASV, Senato, Dispacci Inghil. 42, fo. 225: Giustinian to the Doge and Senate, 27 February/8 March 1641 (*CSPV 1640–42*, p. 128). Giustinian refers to Bedford and his allies as 'principali Capi delle rivolte dell'anno passato'.

69 NA, SP 16/476, fo. 212; Centre for Kentish Studies, De L'Isle MS U1475/C114/12: Sir John Temple to the Earl of Leicester, 25 February 1641 (HMC, *De L'Isle Manuscripts*, VI, 388): 'It is thought my Lord Digby shall be Secrettary, whereunto my Lord Mandevile also pretendes'.

70 For Jermyn's sense of insecurity at this time, see Centre for Kentish Studies, De L'Isle MS U1475/C114/12: Sir John Temple to the Earl of Leicester, 25 February 1641 (HMC, *De L'Isle Manuscripts*, VI, 387).

71 Centre for Kentish Studies, De L'Isle MS U1475/C114/10: Sir John Temple to the Earl of Leicester, 11 February 1641 (HMC, *De L'Isle Manuscripts*, VI, 379). For Jermyn's portrait, see *Van Dyck Complete Catalogue*, p. 641 (plate IV.A35).

72 Centre for Kentish Studies, De L'Isle MS U1475/C114/10: Sir John Temple to the Earl of Leicester, 11 February 1641 (HMC, *De L'Isle Manuscripts*, VI, 379). Jermyn had made his first visit to Strafford in the Tower shortly after the earl's impeachment; see the list of visitors to Strafford, dated 8 December 1640, in PA, Braye MS 2 (Letters and Papers, 1637–41), fos. 86–7 (HMC, *Manuscripts of the House of Lords*, new ser. XI, 235).

73 Centre for Kentish Studies, De L'Isle MS U1475/C114/8, 9: Sir John Temple to the Earl of Leicester, letters of 27 January and 4 February 1641 (HMC, *De L'Isle Manuscripts*, VI, 368–9, 375–6).

74 HMC, *De L'Isle Manuscripts*., 383: Sir John Temple to the Earl of Leicester, 18 February 1641.

75 Centre for Kentish Studies, De L'Isle MS U1475/C114/12: Sir John Temple to the Earl of Leicester, 25 February 1641 (HMC, *De L'Isle Manuscripts*, VI, 388). Northumberland's sister, the countess of Carlisle, was reported to be 'most zealous ... to endeavour to crosse [the Earl of Holland]' in his ambition. Centre for Kentish Studies, De L'Isle MS U1475/C114/8, 9: Sir John Temple to the Earl of Leicester, letters of 27 January and 4 February 1641 (HMC, *De L'Isle Manuscripts*, VI, 368–9, 375–6).

76 See above, pp. 190-1. Hence, it was the Warwick House peers in the Lords who supported Clotworthy's demands for a speedy trial; see Staffordshire RO, Dartmouth MS D(W)1778/I/i/14: Daniel O'Neill to William Legge, 23 February 1641. This letter makes it clear that Essex and Mandeville spoke against the postponement of Strafford's trial, and suggests strongly that Holland and Warwick were on the same side.

77 For the document's presentation to Parliament, see ASV, Senato, Dispacci Inghil. 42, fos. 226–7: Giustinian to the Doge and Senate, 27 February/8 March 1641 (*CSPV 1640–42*, p. 129).

78 *From the Commissioners of Scotland, 24 February, 1640[/41]* (24 February 1641), single sheet (BL, 669 f. 3/4). On the background see Donald, *Uncounselled King*, pp. 287–8.

79 Richard Cust, 'Charles I and Popularity', in Thomas Cogswell, Richard Cust and Peter Lake (eds.), *Politics, Religion and Popularity in Early Stuart Britain: Essays in Honour of Conrad Russell* (Cambridge, 2002), pp. 235–58.

80 Copies had appeared by 27 February: ASV, Senato, Dispacci Inghil. 42, fos. 226–7.

81 Terence Kilburn and Anthony Milton, 'The Public Context of the Trial and Execution of Strafford', in Julia F. Merritt (ed.), *The Political World of Thomas Wentworth, Earl of Strafford, 1621–41* (Cambridge, 1996), pp. 232–3.

82 ASV, Senato, Dispacci Inghil. 42, fos. 226–7.

83 For 'popularity', see Cust, 'Charles I and Popularity', pp. 235–58.

84 NLS, Wodrow MS Folio 66, fos. 207–8: Archibald Jhonston of Wariston to [?], [February 1641]; quoted in Russell, *Fall of the British Monarchies*, p. 197; Baillie, *Letters*, I, 303–6. See also Stevenson, *The Scottish Revolution, 1637–44*, p. 219; and Donald, *Uncounselled King*, p. 287.

85 NLS, MS Wodrow Folio 66, fo. 207; Russell, *Fall of the British Monarchies*, p. 197.

86 Bristol provided a copy of the declaration to Charles, though it is difficult to determine whether this was an act intended to make trouble for the Scots or merely designed to apply further pressure on the king. Baillie's reaction would suggest the latter, as he was unconcerned that the king had received a copy of the declaration, and, though he regarded Bristol as less friendly towards the Scots than Holland, nevertheless regarded him as being broadly sympathetic to their cause; see Baillie, *Letters*, I, 303–6; and for Bristol as the source of Charles's copy, see BL, Harl. MS 457 (Treaty of London minutes), fo. 71. I am not persuaded by Russell's contention that Bristol was effectively Charles's man among the Treaty Commissioners as early as February 1641, and that his appointment to the Privy Council on 19 February was for 'services rendered' to the king; Russell, *Fall of the British Monarchies*, p. 263. This was not how Baillie and the other Scottish Commissioners read Bristol over the winter of 1640–41, and he appears to have been closely identified with his fellow Petitioner Peers. Bristol does not appear to have become detached from the Junto until after the 4th Earl of Bedford's death in May.

87 *CJ*, II, 76. They were presented to the House of Lords, in their extended form, on 30 January.

88 They were in circulation shortly before 2 March 1641: Kilburn and Anthony Milton, 'The Public Context of the Trial and Execution of Strafford', in Merritt, *Political World of Thomas Wentworth*, pp. 232–3; J. H. Timmis, *Thine is the Kingdom: the Trial for Treason of Thomas Wentworth, Earl of Strafford, First Minister to King Charles I, and Last Hope of the English Crown* (University, AL, 1974), p. 61; D. Freist, 'The Formation of Opinion and the Communication Network in London, 1637–c. 1645' (Unpublished Ph.D. dissertation, University of Cambridge, 1992), pp. 42–3, 121. There was, perhaps, a further motive for the Warwick group's insistence on hastening the trial. Distrustful of Bedford's courtly allies (and in direct competition with them over the succession to the viceroyalty in Ireland), they were necessarily far more reliant on the Scots than their allies at Bedford House. Their predicament was that they could not afford to see the Covenanter army of occupation in the North paid off and returned to Scotland *before* Strafford was convicted and punished, yet they were also aware that the astronomical cost of maintaining that army at the English taxpayer's expense was rapidly turning their once secure military power base into a political liability. Theirs was a race, therefore, to see Strafford condemned and his offices transferred to safe hands (ideally Holland's) before opinion at Westminster turned so decisively against their Scottish 'brethren' that their support was counterproductive.

89 See in particular, [Oliver St John], *The Declaration shewing the Necessity of the Earle of Straffords Suffering* (no named printer; [early April] 1641), BL, E 158/2. The same unidentified printer was responsible for the anonymous *A Discourse shewing in what State the Three Kingdomes are at this Present* (no named printer; [last week of April–first week of May] 1641), BL, E 160/27. This tract is sometimes attributed to John Milton.

90 As early as 22 February, the Bedfordians appear to have been attempting to effect a reconciliation, with Bedford's eldest son, Lord Russell, arranging a conference between the two Houses that would settle their outstanding differences; *CJ*, II, 90; Notestein, *D'Ewes Diary*, pp. 387, 388.

91 *CJ*, II, 90; Notestein, *D'Ewes Diary*, p. 388.

92 Notestain, *D'Ewes Diary*, pp. 394–5, and for the articles, see pp. 396–7.

93 *From the Commissioners of Scotland*, 24 February 1640[/1], single sheet (BL, 669 f. 3/4); National Lib. of Wales, Wynn of Gwydir MS 1677: Maurice Wynn to [?], 9 March 1641. Ironically, it was Charles's disinterest in Laud, his willingness to see him cast to the wolves, that took much of the energy out of

the moves to prosecute him. In the power play between the king and the Junto, Laud had ceased, for the moment, to have any symbolic value. It was to be another three years before there was to be any serious attempt to prosecute his impeachment – and then in very different circumstances where the exigencies of war had invested the unlucky prelate with a new and fatal topicality.

94 BL, Harl. MS 6424 (Bishop Warner's diary), fo. 42v. He was seconded by Lords Brooke (his neighbour and close collaborator), Paget (who was married to his niece), and Andover (who seem to have been uninvolved with the Warwick House group).

95 When some of the London reformists attempted to make loans to Parliament from the City conditional upon 'some finall course' against Strafford, Pym rounded on them suggesting that the Londoners could be *compelled* to loan money: the Parliament, in other words, was not to be blackmailed into hastening the trial – a point on which he appears to have been supported by Strode. Notestein, *D'Ewes Diary*, p. 382.

96 The evidence for the attitudes within Warwick's circle is considered above, pp. 207–9, 212, 213.

97 For the belief that the 'new Councillors' were indulging Strafford in return for royal favour, see *inter alia* Staffordshire RO, Dartmouth MS D(W)1778/I/i/14: Daniel O'Neill to William Legge, 23 February 1641.

98 The best account is to be found in BL, Harl. MS 6424 (Bishop Warner's diary), fos. 26–39.

99 BL, Harl. MS 6424 (Bishop Warner's diary), fo. 39.

100 Ibid., fo. 26: as Strafford appeared as a prisoner at the bar of the House, the king took off his hat, 'graciously'. On the other hand, it is worth noting that Temple reported to Leicester that the king conducted himself with 'greate indifferency': Centre for Kentish Studies, De L'Isle MS U1475/C114/12: Sir John Temple to the Earl of Leicester, 25 February 1641 (HMC, *De L'Isle Manuscripts*, VI, 387).

101 HMC, *De L'Isle Manuscripts*, VI, 376.

102 Centre for Kentish Studies, De L'Isle MS U1475/C114/12: Sir John Temple to the Earl of Leicester, 25 February 1641 (HMC, *De L'Isle Manuscripts*, VI, 387): 'There was such a general division amongst those that heard it', reported Temple, that it was impossible to say whether his defence 'were a good ... or a weake one'.

103 Conrad Russell, 'The Theory of Treason in the Trial of Strafford', *English Historical Review*, 80 (1965), 30–50; and see D. Alan Orr, *Treason and the State: Law, Politics and Ideology in the English Civil War* (Cambridge, 2002).

104 BL, Harl. MS 6424 (Bishop Warner's diary), fo. 26; see also Orr, *Treason and the State*.

105 J. H. Timmis, 'The Basis of the Lords' Decision in the Trial of Strafford: Contravention of the Two-Witness Rule', *Albion*, 8 (1976), 311–19.

106 Centre for Kentish Studies, De L'Isle MS U1475/C114/12: Sir John Temple to the Earl of Leicester, 25 February 1641 (HMC, *De L'Isle Manuscripts*, VI, 387), for both quotations; the day's proceedings are reported in detail in BL, Harl. MS 6424 (Bishop Warner's diary), fos. 35v–36r.

107 BL, Add. MS 72433 (Weckherlin diary), fo. 84. Weckherlin notes that Strafford 'accused divers and amongst them, Mr Treasurer [Vane senior]'.

108 S. E. Lehmberg, 'Parliamentary Attainder in the Reign of Henry VIII', *Historical Journal*, 18 (1975), 675–702; W. R. Stacey, 'Impeachment, Attainder, and the "Revival" of Parliamentary Judicature under the Early Stuarts', *Parliamentary History*, 11 (1992), 40–56.

109 Centre for Kentish Studies, De L'Isle MS U1475/C114/13: Sir John Temple to the Earl of Leicester, 4 March 1641 (HMC, *De L'Isle Manuscripts*, VI, 389).

110 *CJ*, II, 97; Notestein, *D'Ewes Diary*, p. 448 (for quotation).

111 Above, Ch. 2.

112 The opening date for the trial, 22 March, was set a week earlier, on the 15th: BL, Harl. MS 6424 (Bishop Warner's diary), fo. 49v.

113 Calybute Downinge, *A Discoursive Conjecture upon the Reasons that produce a Desired Event of the Present Troubles of*

Great Britain, different from those of Lower Germany ([after March] 1641), quotations at pp. 41 and 1 respectively (BL, E 206/10). For the admission of the king's 'new Councillors' as the *terminus post quem*, see ibid., p. 3: 'It is not to bee denyed but that there is so much similitude betwixt these Brittish troubles and the beginnings of the stirres and storms of the Belgique Provinces (before they settled into a solemne War) that wee had great ground to feare the same cruell Calamities *had not God gratiously supplied his Majesty with these present Counsels'*. For the *terminus ante quem*, the fact that Strafford's trial had not yet begun, see pp. 35, 37–8, where the idea that Strafford should be handed over to Parliament for justice is still merely a 'proposal'.

114 The Netherlands had once formed part of the Roman Province of *Germania Inferior*, or Lower Germany, and the term was used generically in the seventeenth century to describe what, by the 1640s, were the separate states of the Spanish Netherlands and the Dutch Republic.

115 Downinge's discourse is all the more interesting for its exploration of the problems of 'multiple monarchies' more generally. Just as Charles had inherited England, Scotland and Ireland, so Phillip had inherited the Netherlands, as well as Spain and Naples. Britain's 'present troubles' had an obvious historical precursor in the Spanish Netherlands (the 'Lower Germany' of Downinge's title) in the 1560s and 1570, where a noble revolt had been provoked by the religious innovations and bossy clericalism of Cardinal Granvelle (the obvious analogue for Laud) and escalated into a full-scale civil war through Philip II's decision to turn to the tyrannical Duque de Alva (the parallel for Strafford) and to send Alva's Italian army (Strafford's Irish army) to suppress internal dissent. The experience of the noble revolt in the Netherlands provides a means of divining England's likely future should Strafford be allowed to remain unchecked; ibid., p. 24. Referring to Granvelle and Alva, Downinge invites the reader to 'compare them with whom you see cause'; Downinge, *Discoursive Conjecture*, p. 15. Likewise, referring particularly to Alva, he urges the comparison with Strafford: 'see his Majestie's [i.e. Charles I's] carriages towards the like man, of prodigious pride and parts'; ibid., p. 21.

116 Ibid., p. 24.

117 Ibid., p. 22.

118 Ibid., p. 26.

119 Ibid., p. 31.

120 Ibid., p. 33.

121 Ibid., pp. 34–5: 'as full Aristocraticall bodies [such as Parliament] move many times so slowly in solemne waies that their dangers prevent [i.e. overcome] them.'

122 One of the principal reasons for the eventual introduction of the attainder bill on 11 April, claimed the Commons-man, Nathaniel Tomkyns, was that, having discovered that there was no law by which Strafford could be found guilty of treason, the attainder bill was 'to supplie the defect of the lawes therein'; NA, SP 16/479, fo. 56v: Nathaniel Tomkyns to [Sir John Lambe], 12 April 1641. Tomkyns's letters to Lambe are source for the politics of 1641, a well-informed perhaps not least because his wife's nephew, James Kyrle, was a Gentleman of the Chamber to Viscount Saye (he 'waites on his Lordship in his Chamber', Tomkyns observed). It is impossible to prove, but it is at least plausible that Kyrle was the source of much of Tomkyns's information on the inner workings of the Junto; see NA, SP 16/479, fo. 130v: Nathaniel Tomkyns to [Sir John Lambe], 22 April 1641.

123 Downinge, *Discoursive Conjecture*, pp. 41–2.

124 Ibid., pp. 1–2.

125 Ibid., pp. 4–5.

126 Ibid., p. 38.

127 For his use of the phrase 'civil war', see *Archives . . . de la maison d'Orange-Nassau* 2nd ser., III, 445: Earl of Warwick to Prince Willem of Orange-Nassau, May 1641.

128 Russell, *Fall of the British Monarchies*, *passim*; but see, for example, 'The likeliest resolution of the crisis, seen from the beginning of March 1641', it has been suggested, 'was no longer either a settlement or civil war, but the same result Parliaments normally produced: a dissolution, leaving the king in sole possession of the stage, and therefore able to recover from many of the losses he had suffered during the Parliament', ibid., p. 272.

129 How Charles would have paid this must remain conjectural; but if he was to have been funded in 1641 by Worcester on anywhere near the same scale that he funded the king in 1642 – in excess of £100,000 – a single-season campaign would have been financially viable.

130 Russell, *Fall of the British Monarchies*, Ch. 7.

131 George W. Johnson (ed.), *The Fairfax Correspondence: Memoirs of the Reign of Charles I*, 2 vols. (1848), II, 207: William Stockdale to Lord Fairfax, 30 April 1641; Bodl. Lib., MS Tanner 66, fos. 105, 106: officers in the army to the Earl of Holland, [before 22 April 1641]; and see above, Ch. 9.

132 For this possibility, mooted in September 1640, see above, pp. 60–1, 65, 72–3.

133 Centre for Kentish Studies, De L'Isle MS U1475/C114/13: Sir John Temple to the Earl of Leicester, 4 March 1641 (HMC, *De L'Isle Manuscripts*, VI, 389).

134 HMC, *De L'Isle Manuscripts*, VI, 319; *CSPD 1640–41*, pp. 36–7, 208. Percy was captain jointly with his nephew, Viscount Lisle.

135 BL, Harl. MS 163 (D'Ewes diary), fo. 314; Bodl. Lib., MS Rawlinson d. 1099 (Holland diary), fos. 62v–63.

136 PA, MP 20 March 1641, fos. 78–82: officers of the king's army to the Earl of Northumberland, 20 March 1641 (HMC, *Fourth Report*, p. 58, for a summary); see also Gardiner, *History*, IX, 309; Russell, *Fall of the British Monarchies*, p. 292.

137 BL, Harl. MS 163 (D'Ewes diary), fos. 315v, 316v; BL, Harl. MS 478 (Moore diary), fo. 72.

138 BL, Harl. MS 163 (D'Ewes diary), fo. 314. For the dating of Percy's meeting with the king, see Gardiner, *History*, IX, 309n.

139 Centre for Kentish Studies, De L'Isle MS U1475/C114/7: Sir John Temple to the Earl of Leicester, 21 January 1641 (HMC, *De L'Isle Manuscripts*, VI, 367).

140 Centre for Kentish Studies, De L'Isle MS U1475/C114/12: Sir John Temple to the Earl

of Leicester, 25 February 1641 (HMC, *De L'Isle Manuscripts*, VI, 387).

141 BL, Harl. MS 163 (D'Ewes diary), fo. 314: Jermyn and George Goring, another of the plotters, 'weere verie earnest that Suckling should be admitted', but this was opposed by most of the others; see also Gardiner, *History*, IX, 312.

142 BL, Harl. MS 163 (D'Ewes diary), fo. 314. Percy claimed to have disapproved of the proposal to bring the army up to London: BL, Harl. MS 478 (Moore diary), fo. 72. But this is undermined by Wilmot's testimony that 'some things weere darklie spoaken by him touching the bringing upp [to London] of the English armie': BL, Harl. MS 163 (D'Ewes diary), fo. 316v.

143 Centre for Kentish Studies, De L'Isle MS U1475/C114/12: Sir John Temple to the Earl of Leicester, 25 February 1641 (HMC, *De L'Isle Manuscripts*, VI, 388); BL, Harl. MS 163 (D'Ewes diary), fo. 315v; For Newcastle, see *Certaine Instructions given by L. Montrose, L. Nappier, Laerd of Keer and Blackhall* ([late June–July] 1641) p. 7 (BL, 1640/26).

144 BL, Harl. MS 478 (Moore diary), fo. 72; Bh, Harli MS 163 (D'Ewes diary), fo. 315r–v.

145 *Clarendon State Papers*, II, 98: Windebank to Charles I, 3 September 1640.

146 Russell, *Fall of the British Monarchies*, pp. 292–3; Gardiner, *History*, IX, 312–13. Russell suggests that it was not until after 20 March that the Jermyn–Sucking plot began to take shape; but, given the lack of precision in the surviving evidence, Gardiner's estimate of 'somewhere about the middle of March' appears the more realistic dating. See also Hatfield, Salisbury MS 253/6: 'Interrogatories … to Colonel [George] Goring' [before 19 June 1641] (HMC, *Salisbury Manuscripts*, XXII, pp. 356–9). Wilmot appears not to have been privy to the Jermyn–Suckling plot, and claimed not to have 'heard of the English armies bringing upp to London till hee heard it latelie reported' by the parliamentary committee of investigation in June: BL, Harl. MS 163 (D'Ewes diary), fo. 316v.

147 The Commons decided to proceed to a trial on 6 March, when Bulstrode Whitelocke reported to the Lords, on behalf of the trial committee, that the House was ready to make good its charges: *CJ*, II, 98. Much of the next fortnight was spent in making the necessary preparations for the trial, with Whitelocke acting as the principal Commons spokesman in their negotiations with the Lords; *CJ*, II, 101, 103, 104, 105–6.

148 Ibid., p. 100.

149 Hatfield, Salisbury MS 253/6: 'Interrogatories ... to Colonel [George] Goring' [before 19 June 1641] (HMC, *Salisbury Manuscripts*, XXII, 358–9).

150 Above, pp. 258, 265, 293–5.

151 For the Warwick group's hostility to Strafford, see.

152 The evidence for this is presented in Ch. 8.

153 Gardiner, *Constitutional Documents*, p. 136.

154 Centre for Kentish Studies, De L'Isle MS U1475/C114/11: Sir John Temple to the Earl of Leicester, 18 February 1641 (HMC, *De L'Isle Manuscripts*, VI, 384).

155 Downinge, *Discoursive Conjecture*, p. 38.

8. THE THEATRE OF JUDGEMENT

1 Thomas Beard, *The Theatre of Gods Iudgements Revised, and Augmented* (1631), p. 188 (STC 1661.5).

2 [Oliver St John], *A Declaration shewing the Necessity of the Earle of Straffords Suffering* ([April] 1641), sig. A3[v] (BL, E 158/2).

3 Whitelocke, *Memorials*, I, 121 (for the chain); Wenzel Hollar, 'Thomas Wentworth, Earl of Strafford', engraving c. 1641; although it should be noted that there is a line engraving in the National Portrait Gallery by Peeter Huybrechts, after Wenzel Hollar, dating from the early 1640s, which depicts the George as suspended from a ribbon. Line engraving (*c.* 1640).

4 NLW, Wynn of Gwydir MS 1678: Maurice Wynn to Owen Wynn (his brother), 'this Tuesday, as I thinke [the] 22nd March 1640[/1]'. Actually, Tuesday was 23 March; the dating is confirmed by his references to the trial as having opened 'yesterday'; misdated and very briefly calendared in William L. Davies (ed.), *Calendar of the Wynn (of Gwydir) Papers, 1515–1690* (Aberystwyth, 1926), p. 271. For funeral blacks, see College of Arms, Stephen Martin Leake MS 3, pp. 186–193: arrangements for the funeral of the 3rd Earl of Essex, 1646. For Strafford's dressing in black, see also Whitelocke, *Memorials*, I, 121.

5 Ibid.: Maurice Wynn to Owen Wynn, [23] March 1641.

6 *A Briefe and Perfect Relation, of the Answeres and Replies of Thomas Earle of Strafford* (1647), p. 1 (BL, E 417/19). This account of the trial is closely related to the manuscript account 'The proceedings against Thomas Earle of Strrafford', in PA, Braye MS 8, fos. 1–28. Though clearly based on manuscript notes taken at the time, this needs to be treated with some caution because of the late date of its publication and its obvious bias towards the accused. On the other hand, it contains much detail, the accuracy of which can be corroborated, or at least strongly supported, from other sources (as with this detail of Strafford's guard). For another contemporary account of the proceedings, see Staffordshire RO, Dyott MS D661/20/2.

7 NLW, Wynn of Gwydir MS 1678: Maurice Wynn to Owen Wynn, [23] March 1641 (for the timing); *Briefe and Perfect Relation*, p. 1 (for the Trained Bands). The latter source gives 'about' 7 a.m. as the time Strafford 'went ... into the Hall'.

8 Whitelocke, *Memorials*, I, 120.

9 *Briefe and Perfect Relation*, p. 7.

10 For examples of this phrase, see Centre for Kentish Studies, De L'Isle MS U1475/C114/16: Sir John Temple to the Earl of Leicester, 1 April 1641 (HMC, *De L'Isle and Dudley MS*, VI, 396); NLW, Wynn of Gwydir MS 1681: Maurice Wynn to Owen Wynn, 30 March 1641.

11 Whitelocke, *Memorials*, I, 120.

12 Peter Lake and Michael Questier, 'Agency, Appropriation and Rhetoric under the Gallows: Puritans, Romanists and the State in Early Modern England', *Past and Present*, 153 (1996), 64–107; more generally, see V. A. C. Gatrell, *The Hanging Tree: Execution and the English People, 1770–1868* (Oxford, 1994), Ch. 1.

13 Cynthia Herrup, 'Law and Morality in

Seventeenth-Century England', *Past & Present*, 106 (1985), 102–23; eadem, *The Common Peace: Participation and the Criminal Law in Seventeenth-Century England* (Cambridge, 1987); eadem, 'Negotiating Grace', in Cogswell, Cust and Lake (eds.), *Politics, Religion and Popularity in Early Stuart Britain, Essays in Honour of Conrad Russell* (Cambridge, 2002), pp. 124–40.

14 NLW, Wynn of Gwydir MS 1678: Maurice Wynn to Owen Wynn, [23] March 1641.

15 Above, pp. 210–13.

16 Whitelocke, *Memorials*, I, 120.

17 For the Junto's (and others') concerns, see [St John], *Declaration shewing the Necessity of the Earle of Straffords Suffering*, sig. A3[r–v].

18 BL, Harl. MS 6424 (Bishop Warner's diary), fo. 21v: report of Pym's speech at the conference of both Houses, 16 February 1641; for Bedford's view, Clarendon, *Rebellion*, I, p. 319–20.

19 Bodl. Lib., MS Tanner 66, fo. 15: Sir Thomas Wodehouse to [John Potts], Thetford, 23 April 1641. For the footnote quotation, see [St John], *Declaration shewing the Necessity of the Earl of Straffords Suffering*, sig. A3[r–v].

20 For Essex's passionate opposition to any clemency towards Strafford, see Clarendon, *Rebellion*, I, 320–1; for Warwick and Brooke, see above, pp. 95, 101–2, 107–9, 178, 196–5, 199, 203-4.

21 Cust, *Charles I*, p. 21; idem, 'Charles I and Popularity', pp. 237–41.

22 Terence Kilburn and Anthony Milton, 'The Public Context of the Trial and Execution of Strafford', in Julia F. Merritt (ed.), *The Political World of Thomas Wentworth, Earl of Strafford, 1621–41* (Cambridge, 1996), pp. 230–51; Peter Lake, 'Puritans, Popularity and Petitions: Local Politics in National Context, Cheshire, 1641', in Cogswell *Politics, Religion and Popularity*, pp. 259–89.

23 This impression was reinforced by the king's private and public interventions to insist on Strafford's innocence of any treason: see his communication to the Irish Privy

Council of 15 December 1640: NA, SP 63/258/57; and his remarks in the House of Lords when Strafford had presented his written submissions to the charges against him in February 1641: BL, Harl. MS 6424 (Bishop Warner's diary), fo. 39.

24 For the honour culture which formed a central element of the trial's context, see Felicity Heal, 'Reputation and Honour in Court and Country: Lady Elizabeth Russell and Sir Thomas Hoby', *Transactions of the Royal Historical Society*, 6th series, 6 (1996), 161–78; Mervyn James, 'English Politics and the Concept of Honour, 1485–1642', in his *Society, Politics, and Culture: Studies in Early Modern England* (Cambridge, 1986), pp. 308–415; José Antonio Maravall, *Poder, honor, y élites en el siglo XVII* (Madrid, 1979); Kristen B. Neuschel, *Word of Honor: Interpreting Noble Culture in Sixteenth-Century France* (Ithaca and London, 1989); François Billacois, *Le duel dans la société française des XVIe–XVIIe siècles. Essai de psychosociologie historique* (Paris, 1986), esp. pp. 193–219; V. G. Kiernan, *The Duel in European History: Honour and the Reign of Aristocracy* (Oxford, 1988), pp. 92–115.

25 Calybute Downinge, *A Discoursive Conjecture upon the Reasons that produce a Desired Event of the Present Troubles of Great Britain, different from those of Lower Germany* ([after March] 1641), p. 34 (BL, E 206/10).

26 NLW, Wynn of Gwydir MS 1678: Maurice Wynn to Owen Wynn, [23] March 1641.

27 BL, Harl. MS 6424 (Bishop Warner's diary), fo. 53. For the time, see NLW, Wynn of Gwydir MS 1678: Maurice Wynn to Owen Wynn, [23] March 1641, last folio; PLP, III, 4. The trial has an extensive bibliography; see in particular, John H. Timmis, *Thine is the Kingdom: the Trial for Treason of Thomas Wentworth, Earl of Strafford, First Minister to King Charles I, and Last Hope of the English Crown* (University, AL, 1974); Michael Perceval-Maxwell, 'Protestant Faction, the Impeachment of Strafford and the Origins of the Irish Civil War', *Canadian Journal of History*, 17 (1982), 235–55; Patrick Little, 'The Earl of Cork and the Fall of the Earl of Strafford, 1638–41', *Historical Journal*, 39 (1996), 619–35; Kilburn and Milton, 'The Public Context of the Trial and

Execution of Strafford', pp. 230–51; D. Alan Orr, *Treason and the State: Law, Politics and Ideology in the English Civil War* (Cambridge, 2002).

28 W. R. Stacey, 'Impeachment, Attainder, and the "Revival" of Parliamentary Judicature under the Early Stuarts', *Parliamentary History*, 11 (1992), 40–56.

29 *Briefe and Perfect Relation*, p. 1. Given the number of judges threatened with impeachment proceedings themselves, this legal contingent cannot have been large.

30 On the impeachments of the 1620s, see Colin G. C. Tite, *Impeachment and Parliamentary Judicature in Early Stuart England* (1974), pp. 83–217.

31 BL, Harl. 6424 (Bishop Warner's diary), fo. 49v; see also PA, Braye MS 53/6: the 'orders and directions' for the trial, 17–19 March 1641 (*LJ*, IV, 187–90). There had been major 'state trials' in Westminster Hall before (Sir Thomas More's, for example); but these were usually before specially named commissions of oyer and terminer (empowered to try particular offences). As recently as 11 March, it had been agreed that the venue for the trial should be 'the Lords' house': BL, Harl. 6424 (Bishop Warner's diary), fo. 48; for the decision to transfer, see Whitelocke, *Memorials*, I, 119–20.

32 Whitelocke, *Memorials*, I, 121.

33 These details are taken from *Briefe and Perfect Relation*, pp. 1–2, and Wenzel Hollar, *The True Maner of the Sitting of the Lords and Commons of Both Howses of Parliament upon the Tryal of Thomas Earle of Strafford, Lord Lieutenant of Ireland*, engraving, 1641 (BL, 669 f. 4/12).

34 NLW, Wynn of Gwydir MS 1678: Maurice Wynn to Owen Wynn, [23] March 1641.

35 Hollar, *The True Maner of...the Tryal of Thomas Earle of Strafford*, engraving, 1641. For once, the great S. R. Gardiner's account wholly misunderstands the context of the trial. The throne had not been placed there 'for form's sake', but because the House was not properly constituted without it. Arundel acted as the presiding officer not as the 'Lord Steward of the Household' (the court officer responsible for the feeding and government of the royal Household) but as Lord Steward

of England, a completely different post which was one of the medieval 'great offices of state', to which he had been appointed *pro hac vice* for the duration of the trial; see Gardiner, *History*, IX, 302.

36 The Commons' grandstands extended slightly further than the middle of the hall; John Rushworth, *The Tryal of Thomas, Earl of Strafford, Lord Lieutenant of Ireland* (1680), p. 41.

37 One of the best sets of these letters is the minutely detailed series by Maurice Wynn to his brother in Wales, Owen: NLW, Wynn of Gwydir MSS 1678–1685. But there are numerous others.

38 Kilburn and Milton, 'The Public Context of the Trial and Execution of Strafford', pp. 230–51

39 Whitelocke, *Memorials*, I, 120; for the discussion in the Commons of these 'Scaffolds', see Notestein, *D'Ewes Diary*, p. 514.

40 *CJ*, II, 104; Notestein, *D'Ewes Diary*, p. 515. Bulstrode Whitelocke managed the conferences with the Lords which agreed on these arrangements. Essex took a prominent role in the preparatory arrangements on behalf of the Lords; *CJ*, II, 105.

41 BL, Harl. MS 6424 (Bishop Warner's diary), fo. 53.

42 Notestein, *D'Ewes Diary*, p. 514.

43 Whitelocke, *Memorials*, I, 120.

44 Hollar's engraving, which can probably be relied upon in general terms and is corroborated in detail by eyewitness statements, depicts ten rows with approximately twenty to twenty-two places per row in each of the two stands: Hollar, *The True Maner of...the Tryal of Thomas Earle of Strafford*, engraving, 1641. The accuracy of this is borne out by Rushworth who describes the Commons' scaffolds as rising in 'ten Stages of Seats extending farther than the midst of the Hall': Rushworth, *Tryal of Strafford*, p. 41; *Briefe and Perfect Relation*, p. 1.

45 BL, Harl. MS 6424 (Bishop Warner's diary), fo. 52v.

46 For a very different reading, regarding the throne as being there merely 'for form's sake,

... its back against the west wall', see Timmis, *Thine is the Kingdom*, p. 64. The throne actually stood proud of the *south* wall of Westminster Hall.

47 NLW, Wynn of Gwydir MS 1678: Maurice Wynn to Owen Wynn, [23] March 1641.

48 BL, Harl. MS 6424 (Bishop Warner's diary), fo. 52v; John Adamson, 'The *Vindiciae Veritatis* and the Political Creed of Viscount Saye and Sele', *Historical Research*, 60 (1987), 55.

49 It is tempting to conjecture that Saye had been forewarned of the king's intention to attend the trial and to take his place on the throne, and that Saye's intervention on 18 March was a warning shot across the king's bows.

50 NLW, Wynn of Gwydir MS 1678: Maurice Wynn to Owen Wynn, [23] March 1641.

51 Baillie, *Letters*, I, 314. *Briefe and Perfect Relation*, p. 2, states that Charles could not be viewed; but this is contradicted both by Baillie, Wynn and by other sources. Charles had been present on 24 February in the House of Lords, when Strafford had appeared at the bar of the Lords, and had promised never to appear in person again during the debate on the impeachment articles: see BL, Harl. MS 6424 (Bishop Warner's diary), fo. 26; but he later indicated that he would be present at 'the Tryalls for Treason'; ibid., fo. 39.

52 Footnote reference: BL, Harl. MS 163 (D'Ewes diary), fo. 58. For the quotation from Hyde, see Clarendon, *Rebellion*, I, 319.

53 For the performance of these 'usual reverences', see, for example, BL, Harl. MS 163 (D'Ewes diary), fo. 36: entries for 12 April 1641.

54 *A Short and True Relation of the Life and Death of Sir Thomas Wentworth, Knight, Earle of Strafford* (1641), p. 3 (Wing S3557A).

55 Hollar, *The True Maner of the Tryal of Thomas Earle of Strafford,* engraving, 1641. For George Thomason's copy, see BL, 669 f. 12.

56 The refusal to allow Charles to take his place on the throne was all the more striking because, for at least some of the trial proceedings, the ten-year-old Prince of Wales

was allowed to sit in a chair of estate under the canopy, and immediately next to the vacant throne; Hollar, *The True Maner of the Tryal of Thomas Earle of Strafford*, engraving 1641. The statement in Whitelocke, *Memorials*, I, 121, that the Prince of Wales sat in 'a close gallery' seems to be mistaken, or, if the young prince did use the gallery for part of the time, ignores those occasions when he took his place by the throne.

57 The *locus classicus* for this is Ernst Kantorowicz, *The King's Two Bodies: a Study in Medieval Political Theology* (Princeton, NJ, 1957); see also Paul Hammond, 'The King's Two Bodies: Representations of Charles II', in Jeremy Black and Jeremy Gregory (eds.), *Culture, Politics and Society in Britain, 1660–1800* (Manchester, 1991), pp. 13–48; and Jonathan Harris, *Foreign Bodies and the Body Politic: Discourses of Social Pathology in Early Modern England* (Cambridge, 1998).

58 For the quotation, see NAS, Hamilton Red Book I, p. 76: Charles I to the Marquess of Hamilton, 25 June 1638; partly printed Gilbert Burnet, *The Memoires of the Lives and Actions of James and William, Dukes of Hamilton* (1677), p. 60.

59 For Strafford's intentions to accuse the 1640 Conspirators, see above, pp. 100–1.

60 BL, Harl. MS 6424 (Bishop Warner's diary), fos. 13, 39; *LJ*, IV, 150. Lord Paget, one of the later signatories of the Petition of the Twelve, appears to have pursued Strafford with particular animus. It was he, for instance, who argued most forcefully against the request from Lord Goring, made shortly after 11 November 1640, that Strafford might be bailed as a favour to the king and queen: NA. PRO 30/53/9/11, fo. 6r-v (I owe this reference to Conrad Russell); Russell, *Fall of the British Monarchies*, p. 211.

61 Arundel's role is itself an instance of political 'medievalism'. He presided, not (as Gardiner mistakenly thought) as Lord Steward of the Household – an unexceptional post with responsibility for the royal court's overall domestic arrangements – but in his newly appointed and far more powerful capacity as Lord High Steward of England: one of the great medieval officers of state (see Rushworth, *Tryal of Strafford*, p. 101), a figure whose powers were so extensive (*in extremis*, they included the authority to arrest the king), that his commission lasted only for the duration of trial; see *LJ*, IV, 190; Gardiner, *History*, IX, 302. For the significance of the Lord Steward of England, see Gregory King, *The Usual Ceremony Observed by the Lord High Steward and Peers of Great Britain* (1746); John Adamson, 'The Baronial Context of the English Civil War', *Transactions of the Royal Historical Society*, 5th ser. 40 (1990), 96-101. Despite being rumoured to be a closet Roman Catholic, Arundel firmly backed the Junto in their management of the trial, joining with Saye and Brooke to insist that the bishops should withdraw from any role in the consideration of the case, and using his authority in close consultation with the Junto grandees, Bedford, Warwick, and Saye – all men who, like himself, were veterans of the Stuart political world, and had been brought together by their shared hostility to the Duke of Buckingham in the 1620s; BL, Harl. 6424 (Bishop Warner's diary), fo. 39. For the hostility of Arundel and Pembroke to Strafford, see HMC, *Cowper Manuscripts*, II, 281; for the 1620s, see Kevin Sharpe, 'The Earl of Arundel, his Circle and the Opposition to the Duke of Buckingham, 1618-28', in Kevin Sharpe (ed.), *Faction and Parliament: Essays on Early Stuart History* (Oxford, 1978), pp. 209-44; see also J. N. Ball, 'The Impeachment of the Duke of Buckingham in the Parliament of 1626', in *Mélanges Antonio Marongiu: convegno internazionale di studi sulla storia dei parlamenti, Palermo-Agrigento, 1966* (International Commission for the History of Representative and Parliamentary Institutions, 34, Palermo, 1967), pp. 35-48.

62 BL, Harl. MS 6424 (Bishop Warner's diary), fos. 52v-53. Arundel presided as Lord Steward of England *pro hac vice* (see Whitelocke, *Memorials*, I, 120), not as Lord Steward of the Household or Earl Marshal, both offices which he also held; cf. Timmis, *Thine is the Kingdom*, p. 61.

63 Sheffield Central Lib., Elmhirst MS EM 1360 (Sir Robert Pye Papers), fo. 4: Hyde and Glynne shared the office of Custos Brevium in the Court of Common Pleas. For Glynne and Pembroke, see Birmingham Reference Lib., Coventry MS, Grants of Offices, nos. 337, 601 (a reference I owe to Professor Russell); the linkages between Pembroke, Glynne and Hyde are discussed in Russell, *Fall of the*

British Monarchies, p. 215. It is noteworthy that, as the Strafford controversy reached its climax at the end of April, it was Hyde who was the Commons' messenger to the Lords to warn them that Strafford might have an intention to escape, and to request that his guard should be strengthened: *CJ*, II, 130.

64 Whether Maynard's involvement with this group was anywhere as close as Pym's and St John's is difficult to determine from the surviving evidence; but it may be significant that Maynard (a Devon man) and St John (who was not) sat for the same Devon constituency, Totnes, where Bedford had been High Steward since 1632. For Maynard, see Cordelia Ann Stone, 'Devon and Parliament in the Early Stuart Period' (Unpublished Ph.D. dissertation, Bryn Mawr College, 1986), p. 574. For Bedford's role in Totnes, see Devon RO, MS 1579A/7/125 (Totnes borough records) cited in Catherine F. Patterson, *Urban Patronage in Early Modern England: Corporate Boroughs, the Landed Élite, and the Crown, 1580-1640* (Stanford, CA, 1999), pp. 54, 272.

65 For Warwick's electoral influence, see Clive Holmes, *The Eastern Association in the English Civil War* (Cambridge, 1974), pp. 21-2; Jason Peacey, '"Seasonable Treatises": a Godly Project of the 1630s', *English Historical Review*, 113 (1998), 667-79; Keeler, *Long Parliament*, p. 36 (for Clotworthy). I am grateful to Mr Christopher Thompson for a discussion of this point.

66 In addition to what appears to have been a close political affinity, Erle's son was married to Saye's daughter, for the marriage contract, see p. 618, n. 94, below. See also Keeler, *Long Parliament*, p. 167.

67 Rushworth, *Tryal of Strafford*, p. 113.

68 On procedure, see Colin G. C. Tite, *Impeachment and Parliamentary Judicature in Early Stuart England* (1974), pp. 218-19; for the charges, see Russell, *Fall of the British Monarchies*, pp. 281-6; and his 'The Theory of Treason in the Trial of Strafford', *English Historical Review*, 80 (1965), 30-50.

69 Rushworth, *Tryal of Strafford*, p. 155.

70 Nicholas Canny, *Making Ireland British, 1580-1650* (Oxford, 2001), pp. 459-60.

71 *Briefe and Perfect Relation*, p. 8: Glynne argued that 'Lord Strafford was impeached

not with simple, but accumulative, Treason'.

72 NLW, Wynn of Gwydir MS 1678: Maurice Wynn to Owen Wynn, [23] March 1641.

73 The Countess of Carlisle's report of his appearance before the House of Lords in November is characteristic of many: 'the Lieutenant [of Ireland] ded yesterday behave him self in the parlement to the wonder of everie bodie. Indeed, I never hard so great nor so genorale a comendatione of any action.' Centre for Kentish Studies, De L'Isle and Dudley MS U1475/C87/9: Countess of Carlisle to the Earl of Leicester, 26 November 1640 (HMC, De L'Isle Manuscripts, VI, 343). She goes on: 'He continus stiff, verie confident of his overcoming all this[e] acusations, and sartunly that beleefe is absolutly in his hart, for I never saw him one minut discomposd'.

74 BL, Harl. MS 6424 (Bishop Warner's diary), fo. 53; PA, Braye MS 95, fo. 57: copy, in the hand of John Browne (the Clerk of the Parliaments), 13 March 1641 (LJ, IV, 184).

75 Briefe and Perfect Relation, p. 55.

76 Russell, 'Theory of Treason', pp. 43–4; idem, Fall of the British Monarchies, p. 282.

77 Briefe and Perfect Relation, p. 8.

78 Quoted in Anthony Fletcher, The Outbreak of the English Civil War (1981), p. 9. An alternative version of the quotation, part of the speech Strafford delivered on 12 April, is recorded in BL, Harl. MS 163 (D'Ewes diary), fo. 36.

79 The Earle of Strafford Characterized, in a Letter sent to a Friend in the Countrey, 1641 [London? 1641], p. 4 (HL).

80 For Strafford's reputation for eloquence, see also Sir George Radcliffe testimony in Knowler, Strafforde's Letters, II, 435.

81 The accusation was Article 2 in the charges against him; Timmis, Thine is the Kingdom, pp. 73–4.

82 NLW, Wynn of Gwydir MS 1681: Maurice Wynn to Owen Wynn, 30 March 1641.

83 Centre for Kentish Studies, De L'Isle MS U1475/C114/16: Sir John Temple to the Earl of Leicester, 1 April 1641 (HMC, De L'Isle and Dudley MS, VI, 396).

84 Warwickshire RO, OR 1886/CUP.4/21A (John Halford's Accounts, I), unfol., 'Gifts', entry dated 30 March 1641.

85 For Leyton and his local feuds with Strafford, see J. T. Cliffe, The Yorkshire Gentry from the Reformation to the Civil War (1969), pp. 297, 300, 301, 303, 327.

86 Rushworth, Tryal of Strafford, proceedings for 24 March 1641.

87 The adjectives are Whitelocke's, and the more telling for coming from a hostile source; Memorials, I, 121; for Strafford's 'humility', see Rushworth, Tryal, p. 522.

88 Whitelocke, Memorials, I, 121 (for quotation).

89 ASV, Senato, Dispacci Inghil. 42, fo. 247v: Giustinian to the Doge and Senate, 2/12 April 1641 (CSPV 1640–42, p. 138).

90 HMC, Various Manuscripts, II, 261.

91 See also NLS, MS Wodrow Folio 67, fos. 17–18: letter of intelligence [from Jhonston of Warriston] to Lord Balmerino, 2 April [1641]. Timmis refers to this section of the trial as 'the final struggle between Pym and Strafford'; in fact, Pym took a relatively subordinate part in the proceedings in Westminster Hall, undertaking none of the major prosecution speeches between 2 and 10 April, though he did intervene to help out faltering Sir Walter Erle on 8 April.

92 ASV, Senato, Dispacci Inghil. 42, fo. 247v: Giustinian to the Doge and Senate, 2/12 April 1641 (CSPV 1640–42, p. 138).

93 Whitelocke, Diary, pp. 110 (for the Ship Money case), 124 (for quotation). At the time of the Short Parliament in April–May 1640, he claimed he 'held off' from involvement with the dealings of the Scottish Commissioners in London, 'butt divers Lords and gentlemen his friends were deep in with them'; ibid., p. 120. Whitelocke was associated closely with two of the Petitioner Peers, as the retained barrister of one Petitioner Lord (the seventh Earl of Rutland), and brother-in-law to another (Lord Willoughby of Parham, in whose London house he was living at the time). For Whitelocke's slightly awestruck account of his visit to Rutland's Belvoir Castle in the summer of 1635, see his Ruth Spalding (ed.), The Diary of Bulstrode Whitelocke, 1605–75 (British

Academy Records of Social and Economic History, n.s., 13, Oxford, 1990), pp. 101–5; for his business relations with the earl, see ibid., pp. 113, 121 (where Whitelocke describes his revenue 'a little increasing by the buisnes of the Earle of Rutland' in the course of 1640). Whitelocke took up residence in Willoughby's London house at the time of the Short Parliament, and stayed on; see Whitelocke, *Diary*, p. 121. For Willoughby of Parham's signature on some copies of the Petition of the Twelve, see *CSPD, 1640*, p. 641; BL, Add. MS 44848 (State Papers), fos. 283v–84 and Northamptonshire RO, Finch-Hatton MS 2619.

94 Richard Cust, 'Sir Walter Erle', *ODNB*. Erle had been a stalwart supporter of the Junto from the Parliament's opening; unsurprisingly, he was the brother-in-law of William Strode, the introducer of the Triennial Bill; and Erle's son, Thomas, contracted to marry the daughter of his old friend, Viscount Saye, in May 1639; see also Keeler, *Long Parliament*, p. 167.

95 [St John], *Declaration shewing the Necessity of the Earle of Straffords Suffering*, sig. A3. That the relatively inexperienced Whitelocke, aged thirty-five and almost twenty years Pym's junior, was called in to take over at this point is perhaps an admission of the prosecution's ineffectiveness hitherto, and a measure of the Junto's increasing concern.

96 Gardiner, *History*, IX, 318. Whitelocke's account in his *Diary* (pp. 125–6), in which he represents himself as a reluctant participant in Strafford's prosecution, should be treated with some caution. It is hardly likely that he would have been named to the select committee to manage the case against Strafford unless the Junto had been confident at the outset of his support.

97 Rushworth, *Tryal of Strafford*, pp. 543–7; BL, Sloane MS 1467 (Newsletters, 1640–41), fos. 27v–28: letter of intelligence, [April 1641]; 'It is thought Mr Treasurer [of the Household, Vane, senior], by this Testimony of his, is become a lost Courtier'.

98 PA, Braye MS 8, entries for 5 April 1641. The version printed by Rushworth reads 'England', which seems to be a corruption of the text.

99 Rushworth, *Tryal*, p. 559; for Bristol's contribution on this day, see also BL, Harl. MS 164 (D'Ewes diary), fo. 153r–v. (*PLP*, III, 371); and, more hilly, in Lord Robartes's diary, BL, Mam. MS 2233, fo. 243 (*PLP*, III, 396–7).

100 For Clare's trenchant cross-examination of Vane, see Rushworth, *Tryal*, pp. 545–6. A future Parliamentarian, at least during the years 1642–43, the 2nd Earl of Clare was on the fringes of the Petitioner circle, and would have known Essex from the time when his father, John Holles, 1st Earl of Clare, had been Comptroller of the Household of Henry, Prince of Wales from 1610 to 1612. The 2nd Earl had married (in 1626), Elizabeth Vere, the daughter of Lord Vere of Tilbury – the professional soldier with whom Essex served in the Dutch Wars. Saye and the 1st Earl of Clare had been close friends. That said, his motives for his intervention on 5 April 1641 can only be construed extremely tentatively.

101 Rushworth, *Tryal*, p. 545.

102 See Clotworthy's speech of 11 November 1640 (mis-assigned by D'Ewes to Pym) in Notestein, *D'Ewes Diary*, pp. 25–6 (*PLP*, I, 97–8).

103 Rushworth, *Tryal*, p. 545.

104 Rushworth, *Tryal*, pp. 560, 563. For the trial proceedings of 5 April, see PA, Braye MS 8, entries for that day; BL, Harl. MS 164 (D'Ewes diary), fos. 152–5v; continued in BL, Harl. MS 476 (Moore diary), fos. 160–9v.

105 John H. Timmis, 'The Basis of the Lords' Decision in the Trial of Strafford: Contravention of the Two-Witness Rule', *Albion*, 8 (1976), 311–19. For Whitelocke's (possibly retrospective) doubts as to whether the prosecution's evidence would sustain Article 23 against Strafford, see Whitelocke, *Diary*, pp. 125–6.

106 Erle began, but never completed, his legal studies at the Middle Temple, where he was admitted in 1604; Richard Cust, 'Sir Walter Erle', *ODNB*.

107 Whitelocke, *Diary*, pp. 125–6.

108 BL, Harl. MS 164 (D'Ewes diary), fo. 160; BL, Add. MS 14828 (Framlingham Gawdy's notes of the trial), fo. 31v. There is a copy of Northumberland's patent, of 14 February 1640, among the Crawford and Balcarres Papers, and it would be very

interesting to know how it arrived there: see John Rylands Library, University of Manchester, Crawford MS C/14/3/50.

109 Whitelocke, *Diary*, p. 126.

110 The theme of ridicule in early modern English society is discussed in Adam Fox, 'Ballads, Libels and Popular Ridicule in Jacobean England', *Past & Present*, 145 (1994), 47–83; and David Cressy, 'The Downfall of Cheapside Cross: Vandalism, Ridicule, and Iconoclasm', in idem (ed.), *Agnes Bowker's Cat: Travesties and Transgressions in Tudor and Stuart England* (Oxford, 2001), pp. 234–50. See also Claude Le Petit, *Paris ridicule et burlesque au dix-septième siècle* (Paris, 1859).

111 BL, Harl. MS 164 (D'Ewes diary), fo. 160 (*PLP*, III, 460).

112 For the Lords' later orders for the conclusion of the trial, see *LJ*, IV, 210–11; for Glynne and Maynard, BL, Harl. MS 164 (D'Ewes diary), fo. 160.

113 *CJ*, II, 117.

114 The debate is reported in NA, SP 16/479, fo. 55: Nathaniel Tomkyns to [Sir John Lambe], 12 April 1641.

115 *CJ*, II, 118. Tellers for the yeas: Denzell Holles and Sir Edward Hungerford, 167; for the noes, Lord Compton (the eldest son of the Earl of Northampton) and [Thomas] Tomkyns, 128.

116 Keeler, *Long Parliament*, p. 226.

117 BL, Harl. MS 164 (D'Ewes diary), fos. 161, 163v; NA, SP 16/479, fo. 56r–v: Nathaniel Tomkyns to [Sir John Lambe], 12 April 1641.

118 BL, Sloane MS 1467 (Newsletters, 1640–41), fo. 28: letter of intelligence, Tuesday [6 April 1641]; see also *CJ*, II, 116.

119 For the phrase, see NA, SP 16/480/30: William Calley to Richard Harvey, 12 May 1641.

120 Temple reported on 8 April (the day of Erle's débâcle) that the majority of the Lords had concluded that Strafford could not be found guilty of treason: Centre for Kentish Studies, De L'Isle MS U1475/C114/17: Sir John Temple to the Earl of Leicester, 8 April 1641 (HMC, *De L'Isle Manuscripts*, VI, 398). For other evidence of the Lords' disposition to

acquit Strafford of the treason charge, see *Briefe and Perfect Relation*, p. 82.

121 BL, Harl. MS 1601 (Anon. diary), fo. 55v (*PLP*, III, 500), entry for 10 April 1641: 'Mr Pimme beeinge in towne the latter ende of the summer, he went to see Sir Henry Vane [junior] aboute the beginninge of Michelmas terme … [Vane junior] delivered him a paper written with Secretary Vane's hande May the 5th [1640]'.

122 For the notes, see PA, MP 4 February; the notes are printed in HMC, *Third Report*, p. 3, and J. P. Kenyon (ed.), *The Stuart Constitution* (Cambridge, 1966), pp. 481–2. For Bedford's possession of these notes, see BL, Stowe MS 326 (Misc. papers), fos. 75–7, at fo. 77: a memorandum by Sir John Harrison, one of the customs farmers, [post-1649]; for Pym, see NLW, Wynn of Gwydir MS 1683: Maurice Wynn to Owen Wynn, [11 April 1641].

123 See above, pp. 177–8.

124 Footnote source: Centre for Kentish Studies, De L'Isle MS U1475/C114/17: Sir John Temple to the Earl of Leicester, 8 April 1641 (HMC, *De L'Isle Manuscripts*, VI, 398). For other comments on the hostility of the king and queen towards Vane after he revealed these notes, NA, SP 16/479, fo. 56: Nathaniel Tomkyns to [Sir John Lambe], 12 April 1641.

125 That this evidence had been intended for presentation to the court on 10 April is established by Glynne's speech to the Commons later that day, where he 'thought fitt to acquaint the howse what evidence they would have produced too day to the 23 Article': BL, Harl. MS 164 (D'Ewes diary), fo. 162 (*PLP*, III, 496).

126 For Pembroke and Glynne, see Russell, *Fall of the British Monarchies*, p. 215 and n. and above, p. 616, note 63. Interestingly, Pembroke was already cooperating with Hertford (one of the Petitioner Peers) and Holland (who, though not a Petitioner himself, was in close communication with them) over the arrangements for elections in Wiltshire in October 1640: Countess of Holland to Sir James Thynne (her son-in-law), 4 October [1640]: Longleat House, Thynne MS IX (Correspondence, 1639–70), fo. 7. For the proceedings on 10 April, see *LJ*, IV, 212. Hyde states unambiguously that

Pembroke voted for Strafford's execution: Clarendon, *Rebellion*, I, 345; but Pembroke's support of the prosecution can also probably be inferred from his intervention on Monday, 3 May, when he went to pacify the crowd, some 4,000–strong, that came to the Parliament demanding Strafford's death: Bodl. Lib., MS Tanner 66, fo. 83v: Nathaniel Gerrard's newsletter, 6 May 1641.

127 When he was thwarted from presenting before the Lords this 'evidence offered ... for the fuller provinge of the 23rd article' – i.e. Vane's notes – Glynne subsequently presented the evidence to the Commons, later that same day: see *CJ*, II, p. 118; BL, Harl. MS 1601 (Anon. diary), fo. 55. For Pembroke's support for the prosecution, see BL, Add. MS 19398 (Correspondence), fo. 72: letter of intelligence, 3 May 1641; Thomas Herbert [pseudonym?], *Vox Secunda Populi. Or, The Commons Gratitude to the Most Honorable Philip, Earl of Pembroke and Mon[t]gomery* ([June] 1641), p. 5 (BL, E 164/21).

128 NLW, Wynn of Gwydir MS 1683: Maurice Wynn to Owen Wynn, [11 April 1641]; NA, SP 16/479, fos. 55v–56: Nathaniel Tomkyns to [Sir John Lambe], 12 April 1641. Strafford tried to introduce evidence relating to Articles 2, 5, 12, and 15.

129 *CJ*, II, 117.

130 NLW, Wynn of Gwydir MS 1683: Maurice Wynn to Owen Wynn, [11 April 1641], for the identification of Arundel as the figure who gave the Lords' ruling.

131 NA, SP 16/479, fos. 55v–56: Nathaniel Tomkyns to [Sir John Lambe], 12 April 1641.

132 BL, Harl. MS 6424 (Bishop Warner's diary), fo. 54r–v; for the quotation, *CJ*, II, 117.

133 For confirmation that the words 'Withdraw, withdraw!' were directed to the Commons' own counsel, rather than at the Lords, see Minnesota UL, MS 137(Peyton diary), fo. 110; see also NA, SP 16/479, fo. 55v: Nathaniel Tomkyns to [Sir John Lambe], 12 April 1641.

134 NLW, Wynn of Gwydir MS 1683: Maurice Wynn to Owen Wynn, [11 April 1641].

135 NA, SP 16/479, fos. 55v–56: Nathaniel Tomkyns to [Sir John Lambe], 12 April 1641.

136 NLW, Wynn of Gwydir MS 1683.

137 BL, Harl. MS 6424 (Bishop Warner's diary), fo. 54v; NA, SP 16/479, fos. 55v–56: Nathaniel Tomkyns to [Sir John Lambe], 12 April 1641.

138 BL, Harl. MS 163 (D'Ewes diary), fos. 26.

139 BL, Harl. MS 163 (D'Ewes diary), fo. 27.

140 NA, SP 16/479, fo. 56.

141 NA, SP 16/479, fo. 56; the adjournment was *sine die*.

142 NA, SP 16/479, fo. 56.

143 NLW, Wynn of Gwydir MS 1683.

144 NA, SP 16/479, fos. 55v–56: Nathaniel Tomkyns to [Sir John Lambe], 12 April 1641; BL, Harl. MS 163 (D'Ewes diary), fo. 27.

9. STRAFFORD: HUBRIS

1 [Sir John Suckling], *A Coppy of a Letter found in the Privy Lodgeings at White-Hall* (1641), pp. 1–11 (BL, E 163/4), quotation at pp. 1–2. Though the attribution of this letter to Suckling cannot be asserted with absolute confidence, it seems likely that the sentiments attributed to him are substantially his own. For Suckling's subsequent legend, see the verse epistle: [Sir John Mennes], *A Letter sent by Sir John Suckling from France, deploring his Estate* (1641), Wing S6163.

2 *A Short and True Relation of the Life and Death of Sir Thomas Wentworth, Knight, Earle of Strafford* 1641, p. 3 (Wing S3557A).

3 For the phrase, see Rushworth, *Historical Collections*, III, 1, 268.

4 *A Short and True Relation of the Life and Death of Sir Thomas Wentworth*, p. 3.

5 For Essex's stating of these expectations explicitly, see Clarendon, *Rebellion*, I, 320.

6 *CJ*, II, 118.

7 Notestein, *D'Ewes Diary*, p. 45; Pym's contribution, not mentioned by D'Ewes but recorded by Palmer, is ambiguous, with Pym saying, in response to St John's proposal, 'That those Records of Attainder were soe kept because noe body should pry into the Title of the kings Landes which were come to him by Attainder ...'; University of

Minnesota Lib., MS 137 (Peyton diary), pp. 20–1 (*PLP*, I, 191). This can be read either as an attempt by Pym to prevent access to the records (on the grounds that this would pry into the title of the king's lands) or that he was *justifying* access to them (by pointing out that the usual objection to such searches – that they turn up flaws to the king's title to lands – would not apply in this case). Whichever reading is the correct one, neither sustains the claim that 'Pym [who was not named to the Commons' committee to investigate the attainder records] also investigated the possibility of using a bill of attainder against his foe'; J. H. Timmis, *Thine is the Kingdom: the Trial for Treason of Thomas Wentworth, Earl of Strafford, First Minister to King Charles I, and Last Hope of the English Crown* (University, AL, 1974), p. 51; cf. *CJ*, II, 31.

8 *CJ*, II, 31.

9 BL, Harl. MS 457 (Minutes of the Anglo-Scottish Treaty, 1640–41), fo. 33. The English Commissioners replied that this could not be done 'but by Act of Parliament' – i.e. a parliamentary act of attainder.

10 Minnesota UL, MS 137 (Peyton diary), fo. 93 (*PLP*, 568).

11 *CJ*, II, 93; Notestein, *D'Ewes Diary*, p. 411. However, Digby did succeed in having four lawyers added to the current eight-man (Junto-monopolized) committee to prepare the charges – John Selden, Geoffrey Palmer, Bulstrode Whitelocke, and John Maynard – in what seems to have been an effort to improve the effectiveness of the Commons' legal team. It is worth noting that Bedford had no scruples about proceeding by attainder; his later objections, as explained to Edward Hyde, were entirely to do with the practical impossibility of persuading the king to consent to an act of Parliament to which had profound conscientious objections; see Clarendon, *Rebellion*, I, 319.

12 Centre for Kentish Studies, De L'Isle MS U1475/C114/17: Sir John Temple to the Earl of Leicester, 8 April 1641 (HMC, *De L'Isle Manuscripts*, VI, 398).

13 Russell, *Fall of the British Monarchies*, p. 288.

14 NA, SP 16/476, fo. 75: accounts for the payment of Sir John Borough and William Ryley, for research among the records in the Tower, [Feb. 1641]. The payment to Borough for his work is dated 4 January [1641], 'for use in this present Parliament',

15 Even after the attainder bill was passed, the king had to send a warrant under his own sign manual to Chancery for the Lord Keeper to issue two 'writts' under the Great Seal of England, one ordering the Constable of the Tower or his deputy to deliver the prisoner for execution, the other ordering the Sheriff of London to carry out the beheading: NA, C181/5, p. 145.

16 Baillie, *Letters*, I, 350.

17 For the king's conscientious objections to the attainder bill, see Clarendon, *Rebellion*, I, 318–9. Interestingly, Charles conceded to Bedford (as reported in this passage) that he would have accepted a verdict of death on Strafford from the House of Lords (i.e. in the impeachment trial), on the grounds that it would not have required him to be a party to the sentence. But as an impeachment verdict of death would have left the king with far more extensive room to avoid the imposition of this sentence (either by delaying the execution or granting a pardon), it is possible to doubt whether, in making this claim, the king was being entirely ingenuous.

18 BL, Harl. MS 457 (Minutes of the Anglo-Scottish Treaty, 1640–41), fo. 37. As Charles himself had put it, when the option had first been mooted back in December, 'it [would] take away his charitie, especially towards such as had taken his part', a band of loyalists that obviously included his devoted Lord Lieutenant.

19 BL, Harl. MS 457 (Minutes of the Anglo-Scottish Treaty, 1640–41), fo. 37 (for quotation); for Bedford's attitudes towards the attainder, at least as they were by 26 April, see Clarendon, *Rebellion*, I, 319.

20 *CJ*, II, 118; BL, Harl. MS 1601 (Anon. diary), fo. 55: 'Mr Glyn: some evidence offered to day for the fuller provinge of the 23rd article, the former parte of the wordes proved by 2 persons of greate eminency, Sir Harry Vane Junior and Mr Pimme witnesses'. (*PLP*, III, 500).

21 BL, Harl. MS 1601 (Anon. diary), fos. 55v–6 (*PLP*, III, 500–1).

22 For Bedford's possession of these notes,

see BL, Stowe MS 326 (Misc. papers), fos. 75–7, at fo. 77: a memorandum by [the then Sir] John Harrison, one of the customs farmers, [post-1649]; for Pym and Clotworthy, see BL, Harl. MS 1601 (Anon. diary), fo. 55v (*PLP*, III, 500–1).

23 Notestein, *D'Ewes Diary*, p. 28.

24 BL, Harl. MS 1601 (Anon. diary), fos. 55v–6 (*PLP*, III, 500–1).

25 Vane junior occupied the post jointly with Sir William Russell, a kinsman of Bedford's; it is possible to read the shared Russell–Vane Treasurership of the Navy as further evidence of the cooperation between Bedford and Northumberland; BL, Harl. MS 163 (D'Ewes diary), fo. 55.

26 NLW, Wynn of Gwydir MS 1683: Maurice Wynn to Owen Wynn, [11 April 1641].

27 BL, Harl. MS 1601 (Anon. diary), fo. 55v; Harl. MS 164 (D'Ewes diary), fo. 162v (for quotation, emphasis added). This is another instance of the use of the term 'commonwealth' with what appears to be a clearly partisan spin (*PLP*, III, 497).

28 BL, Harl. MS 1601 (Anon. diary), fo. 55v.

29 PA, MP 4/2/1641; the notes are printed in HMC, *Third Report*, p. 3 (my emphasis). I concur with Gardiner's arguments for the authenticity of this document: *History*, IX, pp. 120–1nn.

30 The non-disclosure of Vane's notes until this point is one of the most puzzling aspects of the trial. The desire to protect Vane senior appears to have been one motive; but the non-disclosure also raises the possibility that Pym and his associates were deliberately withholding a potentially lethal piece of evidence in hope that the outcome of the trial would be something less than a capital sentence on Strafford. Whatever the motive for non-disclosure, however, it is hard to avoid the conclusion that, in his attacks on Strafford up to 10 April, Bedford's man was deliberately withholding material that might prove potentially fatal to Strafford. In this regard, it is revealing that there was a moment, later in the trial, also involving the alleged suppression of evidence, where Pym's motives were openly questioned. When the committee managing Strafford's trial lost an important piece of evidence, Lord Digby – who was Bedford's

son-in-law and in a position to know – said archly that it must be 'some unworthy man who had his eye upon place and preferment, wherein he was supposed to allude to Mr Pym himselfe'; NA, SP 16/479/74.

31 *Pace* Russell, the revelation of Sir Henry Vane's notes did not 'technically meet the objection about a second witness'; it merely corroborated Vane's oral testimony, for which he remained the only witness; cf. Russell, *Fall of the British Monarchies*, p. 287. The statute in question was 1 Edward VI, cap. 12; see Clarendon, *Rebellion*, I, 297.

32 So powerful was the effect, indeed, that this disclosure by Glynne and Pym has traditionally been regarded as a deliberately inflammatory curtain-raiser to a new attack on Strafford: a bill of attainder, which was introduced later that same afternoon. The new evidence, it was claimed by C.V. Wedgwood, created an 'atmosphere ... now favourable for the introduction of the bill of attainder' – the far more radical alternative to impeachment and which foreclosed the possibility of a royal reprieve; C. V. Wedgwood, *Thomas Wentworth, First Earl of Strafford, 1593–1641: a Revaluation* (1961), p. 358. Yet this reading seems to be wholly misconceived. In reality, the intentions of Glynne and Pym in disclosing Vane's notes appear to have been diametrically opposite. Both men (like Pembroke and Bedford, their respective backers in the Privy Council) were at this point almost certainly opposed to the attainder. Far from being intended to facilitate the introduction of the attainder bill, the revelation of Vane's notes appears to have been a desperate attempt by the Bedfordians to keep the trial on track: to persuade the Commons that a case could yet be made against Strafford that would persuade the Lords of his guilt. For Pembroke, see HMC, *Cowper Manuscripts*, II, 281. For Pym's initial hostility to the attainder bill, see Anthony Fletcher, *The Outbreak of the English Civil War* (1981), p. 10; and see Paul Christianson, 'The Peers, the People and Parliamentary Management in the First Six Months of the Long Parliament', *Journal of British Studies*, 49 (1971), 594–5.

33 *CJ*, II, 118. BL, Harl. MS 1601 (Anon. diary), fo. 56, records that Vane (senior) initially disowned the notes, claiming that he

'knew it [not] any more than the childe unborne'.

34 On the impact of Vane senior's notes, see Perez Zagorin, *The Court and the Country: the Beginning of the English Revolution* (1969), p. 220.

35 *CJ*, II, 118. One of their concerns was time – a source of anxiety that was doubtless heightened by the precariousness of the current ceasefire with the Scots. Towards the end of the day, the pro-Scots party succeeded in undoing at least part of the damage done the previous day (9 April), when the House had resolved, in a division, to extend the ceasefire by only another fortnight; the pro-Scots party secured a new resolution, this time without a division, extending the ceasefire for a month, from 16 April.

36 David Scott, 'Sir Philip Stapilton', unpublished biography, HPL.

37 BL, Harl. MS 1601 (Anon. diary), fo. 56 (PLP, III, 501).

38 NA, SP 16/479, fo. 56: Nathaniel Tomkyns to [Sir John Lambe], 12 April 1641.

39 Wedgwood, *Thomas Wentworth, First Earl of Strafford*, p. 358; Russell, *Fall of the British Monarchies*, p. 288.

40 Russel, *Fall of the British Monarchives*, p. 288. (for quotation). The attainder bill is not the only initiative to have been ascribed to 'country members'; similarly, it has been argued that 'it was his country stance which led [William] Strode to introduce his bill for annual Parliaments, which later became the Triennial Act'; Fletcher, *The Outbreak of the English Civil War*, p. 39.

41 The evidence for the anti-Straffordianism of Essex, Warwick, and Brooke is considered in the paragraphs which follow.

42 It seems likely that this friendship, which was to become exceptionally close, predated the Parliaments of the 1640s, but, if so, the evidence has eluded this writer and Stapilton's biographer for *The History of Parliament*. One possibility is that Stapilton was drawn into Essex's orbit by the campaign against Strafford. Stapilton was to intervene on 14 April 1641, again in support of the attainder, to prevent the reading of Northumberland's testimony, delivered in the course of the trial, as to Strafford's intentions concerning the

Irish army, knowing full well that this testimony would have contradicted the evidence offered in Vane's notes; see BL, Harl MS 476 (Moore diary), fo. 179v; see also David Scott, 'Sir Philip Stapilton', HPL. Stapilton acted as messenger between the Houses on the matter of Essex's appointment as Lord Lieutenant of Yorkshire in May; see BL, Harl. MS 163 (D'Ewes diary), fo. 202. Among numerous other instances of the closeness between the two, it is noteworthy that Stapilton was bequeathed part of the earl's armour as a keepsake under the terms of Essex's will, written in August 1642: PROB 11/198 qu. 185, fo. 28 (185 Twisse), 1 August 1642.

43 Thomas Cogswell, *Home Divisions: Aristocracy, the State, and Provincial Conflict* (Manchester, 1998), p. 193 (for the quotation in the footnote); and see *Winthrop Papers*, III, 198–9, 209, 233; Keeler, *Long Parliament*, p. 213. David Scott, 'George Fenwick', unpublished biography, HPL; A. P. Newton, *Colonising Activities of the English Puritans* (New Haven, 1914), p. 185.

44 Warwickshire RO, CR 1886/CUP4/21A (Brooke household accounts), unfol., receipts for the quarterly to 20 March 1642. The rent was £48 per annum. On Brooke and Hesilrige, see also Hugh R. Engstrom, Jr., 'Sir Arthur Hesilrige and the Saybrook Colony', *Albion*, 5 (1973), 157–68.

45 There was an obvious reason for the bill's introduction in the Commons, for were Warwick, Essex or Brooke to have done so in the Lords – before the House had come to a formal judgement in the impeachment proceedings – it would almost certainly have been ruled out of order; see Lord Savile's attempt to have the introduction of the Commons' bill declared a breach of privilege because the trial had yet to be concluded: NLS, Wodrow Quarto MS 25, no. 155: [one of the Scottish Commissioners in London] to [unnamed], 27 April 1641.

46 BL, Harl. MS 6424 (House of Lords diary), fo. 58v (for Warwick); Clarendon, *Rebellion*, I, 319 (for Essex); for the support of Paget and Brooke in pressing for the bill's third reading, see BL, Harl. MS 6424 (House of Lords diary), fo. 64v.

47 For Hesilrige's actions in introducing

controversial Junto legislation, see above, pp. 339, 414, 400–1.

48 NA, SP 16/479, fo. 56v: Nathaniel Tomkyns to [Sir John Lambe], 12 April 1641.

49 Ibid.; the original text of Hesilrige's bill seems not to have survived. There is an interesting, but possibly unanswerable question, of when Hesilrige's draft bill was first prepared; the likeliest date would seem to be 9 April, immediately after the disastrous session of the trial devoted to Article 23 on 8 April.

50 See Essex's speech to the conference of both Houses on 15 April 1641, reported to the Commons by Fiennes on the 22nd: BL, Harl. MS 164 (D'Ewes diary), fo. 174 (PLP, IV, 61). For the conference, which, initially, was only partially reported to the Commons, see CJ, II, 121.

51 I am grateful to Professor Malcolm Smuts and Dr David Scott for discussions of this point. Michael Nutkiewicz, 'A Rapporteur of the English Civil War: the Courtly Politics of James Howell (1594?–1666)', Canadian Journal of History, 25 (1990), 21–40.

52 BL, Harl. MS 163 (D'Ewes diary), fo. 42: see Kirton's remarks to the Commons on 14 April (and where his reference to 'Monday' is a mistake for 'Saturday': i.e. 10 April).

53 NA, SP 16/479, fo. 56: Nathaniel Tomkyns to [Sir John Lambe], 12 April 1641.

54 BL, Harl. MS 164 (D'Ewes diary), fo. 167v. Maynard, for instance, did not see an incompatibility in proceeding with the impeachment and with the bill of attainder.

55 CJ, II, 119; BL, Harl. MS 164 (D'Ewes diary), fo. 167v.

56 BL, Harl. MS 164 (D'Ewes diary), fo. 165; CJ, II, 119–20. For Hampden's continuing support for the impeachment process, see BL, Harl. MS 163 (D'Ewes diary), fo. 52: Hampden's contribution on 16 April.

57 CJ, II, 119; BL, Harl. MS 164 (D'Ewes diary), fo. 165.

58 CJ, II, 119; BL, Harl. MS 164 (D'Ewes diary), fo. 167.

59 CJ, II, 120.

60 BL, Harl. MS 163 (D'Ewes diary), fo. 36.

61 BL, Harl. MS 164 (D'Ewes diary), fo. 169.

62 BL, Harl. MS 163 (D'Ewes diary), fos. 36r, 37r, 78; see also John Rushworth, The Tryal of the Earl of Strafford ... upon an Impeachment of High Treason (1680), pp. 557 (for Strafford making this point on 5 April), 638 (for 12 April).

63 BL, Harl. MS 164 (D'Ewes diary), fo. 170; my emphasis (PLP, III, 526).

64 Ibid.

65 Ibid., fo. 170v; Rushworth, Tryal of the Earl of Strafford, p. 661 (for quotation). Wing notes eight printings of this speech, of which the 'authorized version' would appear to be The Declaration of John Pym Esquire, upon the Whole Matter of the Charge of High Treason (1641), BL, 208/8, which is also the version used by Rushworth.

66 BL, Harl. MS 164 (D'Ewes diary), fo. 170r–v (PLP, III, 527).

67 Ibid., fo. 170r (PLP, III, 526).

68 A Briefe and Perfect Relation, of the Answeres and Replies of Thomas Earle of Strafford (1647), p. 67 (BL, E 417/19).

69 Baillie, Letters, I, 348.

70 BL, Harl. MS 163 (D'Ewes diary), fos. 43r, 44r.

71 CJ, II, 120; BL, Harl. MS 163 (D'Ewes diary), fo. 44.

72 BL, Harl. MS 163 (D'Ewes diary), fo. 48; see also St John's contribution on 14 April, trying to avoid a discussion of the law of treason within the House before the attainder bill was passed: BL, Harl. MS 163 (D'Ewes diary), fo. 44. For Maynard's support for the attainder bill see BL, Harl. MS 477 (Moore diary), fo. 1v.

73 BL, Harl. MS 163 (D'Ewes diary), fo. 47. Pym and Strode reiterated the point later in the debate 'verie stronglie'; ibid., fo. 48. There is important additional material in Sir Ralph Verney's account of this day: John Bruce (ed.), Verney Papers: Notes of Proceedings in the Long Parliament temp[ore] Charles I (Camden Society, 1845), pp. 48–9. For the Lords' resolutions this day, see NA, SP 16/479/36. D'Ewes notes that Viscount Mandeville had given the Commons the assurance of the upper House that it was

satisfied with the proofs offered against Strafford: BL, Harl. MS 164 (D'Ewes diary), fo. 176.

74 BL, Harl. MS 163 (D'Ewes diary), fos. 52, 53.

75 BL, Harl. MS 164 (D'Ewes diary), fo. 176; although not noted by the *Commons Journals*, it was Bulstrode Whitelocke, a moderate, close to Pembroke and, it seems, to the Bedfordians, who reported this conference to the House: BL, Harl. MS 476 (Moore diary), fo. 182v; *CJ*, II, 122.

76 *CJ*, II, 122.; BL, Harl. MS 164 (D'Ewes diary), fo. 182.

77 Revealingly, a motion by Sir Henry Anderson, who sat for Newcastle-upon-Tyne, to outlaw Strafford by declaring him *hostis Reipublicae* – an 'enemy to the commonwealth' – failed to find a seconder; BL, Harl. MS 163 (D'Ewes diary), fo. 54: (*PLP*, III, 584). For Anderson's hostility towards Strafford from early in the Parliament, see Roger Howell, *Newcastle-upon-Tyne and the Puritan Revolution* (Oxford, 1967), p. 126 and n.
In what seems to have been a bid to reassert an essentially middle-of-the-road leadership of the House, Pym successfully passed an order for a meeting that afternoon of the Committee on the State of the Kingdom (the so-called Committee of Twenty-Four), a body dominated by anti-attainder reformists, and with Lord Digby as its highest-ranking member. This committee, first appointed on 10 November 1640, was the Commons' most prestigious committee, acting as a revising committee for important items of legislation, including the Root-and-Branch Bill (see above, pp. 176, 184b, a drafting committee for what was to become the Grand Remonstrance (see above, pp. 433·7), and, it also seems, as a body that attempted to exercise moral leadership within the Commons in moments of crisis – hence Pym's proposal that it should meet on 16 April. For Pym's proposal, which was not recorded by the clerk in the *Commons Journal*, see BL, Harl. MS 163 (D'Ewes diary), fo. 51. For the membership of the Committee of Twenty-Four see *CJ*, II, 25; the committee divided on the attainder issue as follows; pro-attainder: Oliver St John, Sir Robert Harley, Sir John Clotworthy, Sir Thomas Barrington, George Perd (who chaired the committee proceedings

on the bill), and possibly Harbottel Grimston; anti-attainder: Lord Digby, Sir Thomas Widdrington, John Selden, John Pym, Sir Walter Erle, Sir John Strangways, Edward Bagshaw, William Pierrepont, John Hampden, Arthur Capell, probably John Crewe, Henry Belasyse, and Sir Benjamin Rudyard; unknown: Sir John Culpepper, Sir Miles Fleetwood, Sir Peter Heyman, Edward Kirton.

78 *CJ*, II, 122 (emphasis added).

79 For the Saturday morning session, see BL, Harl. MS 163 (D'Ewes diary), fo. 58; *CJ*, II, 123. Unhelpfully for the Warwick House group and the pro-attainder lobby, the antiquarian Sir Simonds D'Ewes had discovered that in the case of William de la Pole, Duke of Suffolk, during the reign of Henry VI, the same charge that they had used against Strafford – that he had endeavoured 'to subvert the fundamental lawes of the realme' – had been 'placed amongst the misdemeanors', rather than regarded as a treason; BL, Harl. MS 163 (D'Ewes diary), fo. 64.

80 BL, Harl. MS 164 (D'Ewes diary), fo. 178.

81 BL, Harl. MS 1601 (Anon. diary), fo. 56.

82 BL, Harl. MS 163 (D'Ewes diary), fo. 64.

83 *CJ*, II, 123.

84 Ibid. (emphasis added); BL, Harl. MS 478 (Moore diary), fo. 8.

85 For Holland's involvement in the orders of 17–18 April, see HMC, *Cowper Manuscripts*, II, 280. If Holland himself came under suspicion for these orders (probably unjustly) on this occasion, it was not to be the last time that he was to be suspected of complicity with the king's plans; a letter written by Holland to Essex concerning the disbandment of army's horse in July 1641, was to create (in the event, groundless) fears of another 'Army Plot'.

86 George W. Johnson (ed.), *The Fairfax Correspondence: Memoirs of the Reign of Charles I*, 2 vols. (1848), II, 205–7: William Stockdale to Lord Fairfax, 30 April 1641.

87 Danbie, a generation younger than Strafford, had been brought up in the household of Strafford's closest friend, Sir Christopher Wandesford, whose daughter he

eventually married. During the late 1630s, relations between Danbie and his erstwhile patron (then styled Viscount Wentworth), soured slightly, but they had recovered fully by 1640, when Strafford assigned to Danbie what had been Wandesford's militia regiment. The reason for Danbie's promotion, according to Wandesford, was 'that the world might see he stood right in my lord's [Strafford's] favour and opinion, and that my lord was ready to esteem and regard him as his kinsman ... I procured this to be done for my son ... as a thing which he much desired': North Yorkshire. RO, Swinton Estate MS, ZS, Danby Family Letters and Papers (Microflim 2087), unfol.: Sir Christopher Wandesford to Lady [Katherine] Danbie, 25 May 1640 (I owe this reference to Dr David Scott). For Danbie's career, see David Scott, 'Sir Thomas Danbie', unpublished biography, HPL.

88 Notestein, *D'Ewes Diary*, p. 12 (for quotation); David Scott, 'Sir William Pennyman', unpublished biography, HPL. I am grateful to Dr Scott for alerting me to the strength of Pennyman's and Danbie's connections with Strafford.

89 BL, Harl. MS 6865 (Holles diary), fo. 224v. For the River Tees as a point of confrontation between the Scots and the English, see NLW, Wynn of Gwydir MS 1683: Maurice Wynn to Owen Wynn, 27 April 1641.

90 BL, Harl. MS 163 (D'Ewes diary), fos. 110 and 111; BL, Harl. MS 477 (Moore diary), fo. 23.

91 Above, pp. 324–6.

92 It was a mistake that Warwick was to repeat in 1647, when his treatment of another army's financial demands was to induce a deep strain of anti-parliamentarian sentiment.

93 It was around this time that the Junto leadership received the letter from Sir Thomas Gower reporting the state of the northern army; see CUL, MS Mn. I. 45 (Baker MS); and Bodl. Lib., MS Tanner 66, fos. 105, 106: officers in the army to the Earl of Holland, [before 22 April 1641]. This appears to have been one of the letters that Holland read out at a conference between the two Houses on 22 April 1641; see BL, Harl. MS 165 (D'Ewes diary), fo. 67; BL, Harl. MS 477 (Moore diary), fos. 2–3.

94 *LJ*, IV, 226: for summary of the letter written by the Earl of Holland, as Lord General, to the Berwick garrison, *c.* 24 April 1641.

95 BL, Harl. MS 165 (D'Ewes diary), fo. 67.

96 *LJ*, IV, 226.

97 Footnote references: *Van Dyck Complete Catalogue*, p. 563. For Goring's divulging of the plot to Newport, see Hatfield, Salisbury MS 253/6: 'Interrogatories ... to Colonel [George] Goring' [before 19 June 1641], (HMC, *Salisbury Manuscripts*, XXII, pp. 356–9).

98 It is possible that a number of the Bedfordians – including Pym, Hampden, and Strode – were giving their tacit support for the attainder bill from around this time. As they were aware that Charles was making, at very least, military contingency plans against them, they may well have wanted to use the attainder as a countervailing source of pressure against the king.

99 BL, Add. MS 11045 (Misc. correspondence), fo. 139v, for the dating of the arrival of the news at court to 'Sunday' (i.e. 18 April).

100 *CSPV 1640–42*, p. 145: Giustinian to the Doge and Senate, 30 April/10 May 1641.

101 Jan de Brederode, the senior member the Dutch delegation, denied that the sums were intended to help the king: see his letter to the Prince of Orange, 7 May 1641: Prinsterer, *Archives ... de la maison d'Orange-Nassau*, III, p. 460. For Brederode's status, see Loomie, *Ceremonies of Charles I*, p. 298.

102 BL, Harl. MS 164 (D'Ewes diary), fo. 197; BL, Harl. MS 477 (Moore diary), fo. 31v. The information was provided to the Commons by Matthew Cradock.

103 BL, Harl. MS 477 (Moore diary), fo. 40.

104 See, e.g., BL, Add. 29974 (Pitt corr.), fo. 326: Elizabeth Brandling to Edward Pitt, 20 April 1641: 'tis said that the Prince of Oring will bage [i.e. buy for re-sale] the Earle of Strafford's life'. For 'bage' as the archaic form of the verb 'to badge', see *OED*, s.v. The papal agent, Count Carlo Rossetti, had reported as early as February 1641 that the king's motive for pursuing the Dutch marriage was to procure a mercenary force from the United Provinces, so as to dissolve Parliament

and secure Strafford's release: Hibbard, *Charles I and the Popish Plot,* p. 177.

105 *Briefe and Perfect Relation,* p. 83.

106 David Dalrymple, Lord Hailes, *Memorials and Letters relating to the History of Britain in the Reign of Charles the First* (Glasgow, 1766), pp. 120–1: Jhonston of Wariston to Hepburn of Humbie, [20 April 1641].

107 Johnson (*Fairfax Correspondence*), II, 205–7: Thomas Stockdale to Lord Fairfax, 30 April 1641.

108 *The Declaration shewing the Necessity of the Earle of Strafford's Suffering* ([early April] 1641), sig. B2 [1] (BL, E 158/2).

109 *CJ,* II, 123. It is noteworthy that two future Royalists, Lord Falkland and Sir Ralph Hopton, were both reporters of the conference had with the Lords that day, and in support of the proceedings against Strafford.

110 BL, Harl. MS 163 (D'Ewes diary), fo. 77.

111 In what may well have been a pre-arranged contribution, the distinguished barrister, John Selden, responded to Pym's question by saying it was 'a verie disputable question whether that were Treason or not at common law'. It is tempting to conclude that this was exactly the response Pym had expected to elicit by posing the question. BL, Harl. MS 164 (D'Ewes diary), fo. 178; for Selden's contributions see also, fo. 179v, where he is equally sceptical about whether subversion of the law amounts to treason; see also the report of Selden's remarks in BL, Harl. MS 478 (Moore diary), fo. 8v.

112 Napier, *Montrose and the Covenanters,* I, 365–8: Archibald Jhonston of Wariston to Adam Hepburn of Humbie, 21 April 1641.

113 Napier, *Montrose and the Covenanters,* I, 365–8; Hailes, *Memorials and Letters,* pp. 124–8.

114 Napier, *Montrose and the Covenanters,* I, 356–7.

115 Richard Cust, *Charles I: a Political Life* (2005), pp. 55–9.

116 *CJ,* II, 125.

117 See the following section, p. 253 and n.

118 Napier, *Montrose and the Covenanters,*

I, 356–7: Archibald Jhonston of Wariston to Lord Balmerino, 21 April 1641.

119 The attainder bill was presented to the Lords at 'six o'clocke' that evening, 21 April – *CSPD 1641,* p. 555 – and the City petitions were delivered after the Commons had returned from the Lords and resumed their sitting, which cannot have been much before 7 p.m.; see *CJ,* II, 125.

120 BL, Harl. MS 164 (D'Ewes diary), fo. 183v. For the text of the petition, see Rushworth, *Strafforde's Trial,* p. 57. Two of the captains are named in the Journal: John Venn and John Bradley; *CJ,* II, 125. The date of the presentation of this petition has been confused: the Scottish Commissioners' Day Book gives Monday, 19 April; Maurice Wynn gives the 23rd: both appear to be mistakes for the 21st; see NA, SP 16/480/9; NLW, Wynn of Gwydir MS 1680: Maurice Wynn to Owen Wynn, [23 April 1641] (misdated in the *Calendar of Wynn Papers* to 29 March). The petition was read in the Commons on 24 April – the date which Gardiner erroneously lists as the date of the petition's subscription: Gardiner, *History,* IX, 341; *CJ,* II, 127.

121 For the text of the petition, see BL, Harl. MS 164 (D'Ewes diary), fo. 186v (my emphasis). The king was clearly apprehensive about the London petition, and there is evidence to suggest that he was seeking material to support Strafford's rebuttal of the charge (Article 23) seemingly substantiated by Vane senior's notes of the meeting at Whitehall on 5 May 1640: NA, SP 16/479/25, 37.

122 It is likely that Venn was the principal spokesman of the three 'captains' because he is first-named in the Journal, and because, when he fulfilled a similar role a few days later, he 'spake for the rest': PA, MP 3 May 1641; partly printed in HMC, *Fourth Report,* p. 61. For Venn's appointment as Deputy-President of the Artillery Company, see Matthias Milward, *The Souldiers Triumph and the Preachers Glory. In a Sermon preached to the Captains and Souldiers exercising Arms in the Artillery Garden … the 31. of August, 1641* ([September?] 1641), sig. B2[1] (BL, E 175/7). For Venn's connections with the City's godly community, see [Sir John Berkenhead.], *A Letter from Mercurius Civicus to Mercurius Rusticus, or, Londons Confession* ([Oxford], 25 August.

1643), p. 9 (BL, E 65/32). It is unsurprising to find Lord Brooke's puritan protégé, Thomas Dugard, recording a meeting with Venn about organizing a petition only twelve weeks earlier, in February 1641: BL, Add. MS 23146 (Thomas Dugard diary), fo. 92; for Dugard and Brooke's circle at Warwick Castle, see Ann Hughes, *Politics, Society and Civil War in Warwickshire, 1620-60* (Cambridge, 1987), pp. 71-5.

123 *CJ*, II, 125; the printed *Commons' Journal* confuses the tellers for the yeas with those for the noes; for their correct identification, see BL, Harl. MS 164 (D'Ewes diary), fo. 183; and see also Harl. MS 165 (D'Ewes diary), fo. 85.

124 Emphasis must be placed on the relatively low turnout of commms-men: even in this division, less than half the total membership of the House was actually present, which raises obvious questions about the political outlook of the other half. Was this large-scale absenteeism, as seems likely, a reflection of the non-voters' hostility towards the reformists' dominance of Parliament?

125 *CJ*, II, 125.

126 Ibid.; BL, Harl. MS 164 (D'Ewes diary), fo. 183v (*PLP*, IV, 42).

127 NA, SP 16/479, fo. 130v: Nathaniel Tomkyns to [Sir John Lambe], 22 April 1641.

128 Philip Warwick, *Memoires of the Reign of King Charles I* (1702), p. 160.

129 I owe this point to Professor Fletcher: *Outbreak*, p. 13.

130 Arthur Capel, *Excellent Contemplations, Divine and Moral* (1683), pp. 138-9.

131 *CJ*, II, 125. In the Journal, Barrington and Gerard are mistakenly listed as tellers for the yeas. For Gerard, who was also a close friend and kinsman by marriage of St John (another attainder supporter), see Keeler, *Long Parliament*, p. 186; Searle, *Barrington Letters*, *passim*, and esp. pp. 220-1. The vote is a clear example of how the Strafford question had divided a group that was otherwise closely linked by kinship, religion and ties of friendship: for one example among many, one may note that Viscount Mandeville Oliver St John, and John Pym all served as feoffees for property held in trust for

Barrington's sons; for the settlement, dated 6 March 1639, see Essex RO, D/DC/23/356.

132 *The Lord Digbies Speech in the House of Commons to the Bill of Attainder, of the Earle of Strafford, the 21 of April, 1641* [1641], (Wing B4771A). For the numerous financial connections between Bedford and his son-in-law, see Woburn Abbey, Fourth Earl Addenda 27 (Robert Scawen's inventory, 1635), fos. 4, 6. Bedford's correspondence in BL, Harleian MS 7001 contains numerous attestations to the closeness and affection between the two; see, especially, BL, Harl. MS 7001, fo. 124: Lord Digby to the Earl of Bedford, 21 August 1637.

133 Quoted in Fletcher, *Outbreak*, p. 12.

134 The printed version of Digby's speech should be compared with the summary in BL, Harl. MS 478 (Moore diary), fos. 15v (*PLP*, IV, 45-6).

135 Notestein, *D'Ewes Diary*, pp. 410-11, n. 7.

136 *Lord Digbies Speech*, pp. 8-9; for Bedford's attitudes, see Clarendon, *Rebellion*, I, 319.

137 *Lord Digbies Speech*, pp. 8-9.

138 BL, Harl. MS 478 (Moore diary), fo. 16r-v (*PLP*, IV, 45-6).

139 What is more difficult to explain, however, is why he, in particular, chose to articulate it in such unpromising circumstances, and when others, at least as close to Bedford as himself, seemed to have sided with the attainder lobby or were keeping their heads down until the immediate panic had subsided. Though Digby's motive remains unassayable, one possible explanation is that he was sending a signal to the court that, in spite of all, the Bedfordian compromise still had its advocates, and might survive to be revived at a less volatile time than the present. Revealingly, one of Hertford's servants was later discovered to have 'dispersed' copies of Digby's speech: 'one Moore, belonging to the Earle of Hartford': BL, Harl. MS 163 (D'Ewes diary), fo. 136. For Hertford's support of the Bedfordian compromise, see also above, pp. 198-200.

140 BL, Add. MS 31954 (Edward Nicolas's notes of proceedings), fo. 181v; another copy exists in BL, Add. MS 4180 (Birch transcripts), fo. 181. On other abstentions, see Fletcher, *Outbreak*, pp. 13–14, and Paul Christianson, 'The Peers, the People, and Parliamentary Management in the First Six Months of the Long Parliament', *Journal of British Studies*, 49 (1977), 592–3n.

141 BL, Harl. MS 164 (D'Ewes diary), fo. 400v.

142 For Scawen, see John Adamson, 'Of Armies and Architecture: the Employments of Robert Scawen', in Ian Gentles, John Morrill and Blair Worden (eds.), *Soldiers, Writers and Statesmen of the English Revolution* (Cambridge, 1998), pp. 40–1. This is of a piece with the behaviour of William Hakewill, the barrister and antiquarian who was working extensively for Northumberland during this period (and another future Parliamentarian), who served as one of Strafford's defence counsel during the final stages of the trial. BL, Harl. MS 163 (D'Ewes diary), fo. 58: Hakewill was one of the five counsel who attended Strafford on 17 April. For his service for Northumberland, see Centre for Kentish Studies, De L'Isle MS U1475/A98: Cartwright's acc. (for the Earl of Northumberland) to January 1641; Cumbria RO, D/Lec/107, unfol.: antiquarian notes [after 15 February 1641] on the enfranchisement of Cockermouth, Cumberland.

143 BL, Harl. MS 165 (D'Ewes papers), fo. 85: list of the 'Straffordians' (*PLP*, IV, 51). Kirton was Hertford's steward; see Keeler, *Long Parliament*, 'Edward Kirton', *s.v.*

144 For this process of negotiation, and the Lords' general reluctance to find Strafford guilty on a capital charge, see *A Briefe and Perfect Relation, of the Answeres and Replies of Thomas Earle of Strafford* (1647), p. 82 (BL, E 417/19).

145 On the dating of Pym's 'conversion', see Wedgwood, *Strafford*, pp. 369–70; and Christianson, 'The Peers, the People, and Parliamentary Management', pp. 594–5.

146 Pym was at least named to the committee, even if he did not serve, which had met at 7 a.m. that morning to draft the bill's preamble (with its clear statement 'that Strafford deserves to undergo the pains and forfeitures of high treason'). For the nominations to this committee, see BL, Harl. MS 164 (D'Ewes diary), fo. 181; for its

membership, BL, Harl. MS 478 (Moore diary), fo. 13. Those named were Pym, Hampden, St John, Maynard, and Glynne; but the finished product seems to bear the imprint of St John. For the text of the preamble, see Gardiner, *Constitutional Documents*, pp. 156–7.

147 BL, Harl. MS 164 (D'Ewes diary), fo. 182v. There is a blank in the MS after the words 'as I beleeve', and the words in square brackets are my conjecture; from the context, however, they (or words to the same effect) would seem to be implied by the context.

148 BL, Harl. MS 478 (Moore diary), fo. 17. For the Lords' preferences, see James O. Halliwell (ed.), *The Autobiography and Correspondence of Sir Simonds D'Ewes, Bart, during the Reigns of James I and Charles I*, 2 vols. (1845), II, 263–4.

149 On 22 April, it was agreed that 'Mr Pymme had mistaken the message yesternight at the deliverie of the bill of Attainder and forgotten to tell the Lords that wee would satisfie them by a Committee of both howses': BL, Harl. MS 164 (D'Ewes diary), fo. 183v.

150 *CSPD 1640–41*, p. 158; Keeler, *Long Parliament*, p. 393.

151 *CJ*, II, 126. For Holles's reported efforts to save Strafford's life, see Timmis, *Thine is the Kingdom*, p. 62; Patricia Crawford, *Denzil Holles, 1598–1680: a Study of his Political Career* (1979), pp. 37–8. Only Sir John Hotham, the fifth and final member of the group of conference managers, seems to have been a supporter of a capital sentence.

152 *CJ*, II, 127; BL, Harl. MS 164 (D'Ewes diary), fo. 186v. Lord Russell also carried up the Londoners' petition.

153 It is noteworthy that a number of figures who, later, were close to Northumberland – in particular, Sir John Evelyn of Wiltshire and William Pierrepont – were involved in these manoeuvres: BL, Harl. MS 164 (D'Ewes diary), fo. 184; and while this *might* be an early instance of the working of the 'Northumberland interest' in support of the Bedfordians, the evidence is too fragmentary to pose this explanation as anything more than conjecture.

154 Notestein, *D'Ewes Diary*, pp. 410–11, n. 7.

155 Sir John Coke had written to his father, the former Secretary of State, on 17 April that were the Commons to ask the Lords to pass judgement on Strafford, 'without question they will acquit him, there being no law extant whereupon to condemn him of treason'; HMC, *Cowper Manuscripts*, II, 278.

156 For the unlikelihood of the Lords proceeding to a capital sentence, see above, p. 267, opposing the attainder was that

157 NA, SP 16/480/9 (Scottish Commissioners' Day Book), entry for 24 April 1641. The most revealing intervention, however, came from Viscount Saye, Bedford's closest collaborator in the campaign to save Strafford's life; with Pym now in charge of the deliberations, he was perfectly content to have the attainder considered, apparently confident that the bill's lethal provisions would be excised in the course of its further progress.

158 Rushworth, *Tryal*, pp. 545–6, 559.

159 NLS, Wodrow Quarto MS 25, no. 155: [one of the Scottish commissioners in London] to [unnamed], 27 April 1641.

160 PA, MS Lords Journal, entries (subsequently cancelled) for 27 April; printed in Paul Christianson, 'The "Obliterated" Portions of the House of Lords Journals dealing with the Attainder of Strafford, 1641', *English Historical Review*, 95 (1980), 339–53, at 344.

161 CJ, II, 126.

162 *From the Commissioners of Scotland, 24 February, 1640[–41]* ([Feb.] 1641), single sheet (BL, 669 fo. 3–4).

163 [Oliver St John?], *A Copy of a Letter written to a Private Friend ... touching the Lord Say* ([24 October.] 1643), sig. A2 (BL, E 72/5). The attribution of this tract to St John is suggested by James Farnell, in his 'The Social and Intellectual Basis of London's Role in the English Civil Wars', *Journal of Modern History*, 49 (1977), 653n.

164 *The Declaration shewing the Necessity of the Earle of Straffords Suffering* ([early April] 1641), quotations at sig. A3[2r-v] and sig. A3, respectively (BL, E 158/2).

165 Clarendon, *Rebellion*, I, 319, for the quotations.

166 The passage is a cancelled section of the MS of Clarendon's *History*, I, 318n. But for Hyde's attitudes to Strafford, see also his *The Life of Edward Earl of Clarendon*, 2 vols. (Oxford, 1857), pp. 76–7. Whitelocke's account of this projected agreement closely parallels that of Hyde; see Whitelocke, *Memorials*, I, 120. This is undated, but, from its reference to Cottington's resignation as being part of the overall final settlement, it would date the plan to the period immediately before Tuesday 27 April (the date when Cottington resigned).

167 NA, PRO 31/9/20 (Rossetti transcripts), fos. 115, 136.

168 NA, SP 16/476, fo. 212: the list is an enclosure in Sir John Conyers's letter to Viscount Conway of 29 January 1641, sent from York. For the broader context of Bedford's involvement in these appointments, see above, Ch. 5.

169 BL, Harl. MS 6424 (House of Lords diary), fo. 56; the news was reported to the Commons on 22 April 1641: BL, Harl. MS 164 (D'Ewes diary), fo. 174 (*PLP*, IV, 61). Holland's appointment also marked the end of Robert Scawen's role as Northumberland's military secretary (though not his service in the Percy household), as Holland replaced him with his 'owne secritary': NA, SP 16/479, fo. 138: Sir William Uvedale to Matthew Bradley, 24 April 1641.

170 CSPV, 1640–42, p. 142: Giustinian to the Doge and Senate, 23 April/3 May 1641.

171 BL, Harl. MS 6424 (Bishop Warner diary), fo. 56.

172 LJ, IV, 226. The sums received at Bedford House were, however, relatively small on this occasion: just under £4,400 to be collected by the 'receiver for Barwicke'.

173 Indeed, given Holland's closeness to the two leading attainder-supporters in the Lords (his brother Warwick and cousin Essex), it is not impossible that Charles was hoping to use a grateful Holland to win over Warwick and Essex to the Bedford–Pym strategy of co-operation in return for office.

174 BL, Stowe MS 326 (Misc. papers), fos. 76v–77: Harrison's memorandum; NA, SP 16/479/74: Nathaniel Tomkins to Sir John Lambe, 26 April 1641; *An Exact Collection of all Remonstrances, Declarations, Votes,*

Orders, Ordinances (1643), p. 534 (Wing E1532).

175 HMC, *Eighth Report*, Appendix (Duke of Manchester's Manuscripts), II, 57–8: Earl of Leicester to [Viscount Mandeville], Paris, 5/15 February 1641.

176 BL, Stowe MS 326 (Misc. papers), fo. 76v: Harrison's memorandum. For Harrison's biography, see Keeler, *Long Parliament*, pp. 205–6.

177 BL, Stowe MS 326 (Misc. papers), fo. 76v: Harrison's memorandum; Whitelocke, *Memorials*, I, 120.

178 Whitelocke, *Memorials*, I, 120. For the Chancellorship of the Exchequer, see G. E. Aylmer, *The King's Servants: the Civil Service of Charles I, 1625–40* (1961; rev. edn 1974); Madeleine Gray, 'Exchequer Officials and the Market in Crown Property, 1558–1640', in R. W. Hoyle (ed.), *The Estates of the English Crown, 1558–1640* (Cambridge, 1992), pp. 112–36.

179 Russell, *Fall of the British Monarchies*, pp. 272, 274.

180 BL, Stowe MS 326 (Misc. papers), fo. 326: Harrison memorandum. Bedford told Harrison that Cottington feared a charge 'for some wordes by him spoken in the Councell Chamber that morning when the concultacon was held about dissolving the last p[ar]liament', i.e. the meeting of the Committee of War on 5 May 1640; for the text of the notes, see HMC, *Third Report*, p. 3.

181 Knowler, *Strafforde's Letters*, II, 416: Charles I to the Earl of Strafford, 23 April 1641.

182 NAS, Hamilton MS GD 406/1/1335/1: Earl of Strafford to the Marquess of Hamilton, 24 April 1641.

183 *CJ*, II, 126.

184 *LJ*, V, 226.

185 Clarendon, *Rebellion*, I, 319.

186 Clarendon, *Rebellion*, I, 318–9.

187 For the dating of Warwick's appointment see the endorsement on the letter from Sir John Coke junior to Sir John Coke senior, 26 April 1641: BL, Add. MS 64922 (Coke papers), fo. 24r.

188 I owe this suggestion, and the reference in the preceding note that gives rise to it, to Mr Christopher Thompson.

189 Clarendon, *Rebellion*, I, 320. Hyde dates this promise to the day on which 'the conference had been in the Painted Chamber upon the Court of York' [i.e. the Council of the North] (ibid., p. 318): that is, Monday, 26 April 1641; see *CJ*, II, 128. I am inclined to accept Hyde's dating, notwithstanding that the formal patent did not pass for another five weeks, on 3 June. For Hyde's speech this day see PA, Braye MS 2 (Letters and Papers, 1637–41), fos. 130–5 (Rushworth, *Historical Collections*, Part III, I, 230–3).

190 NA, SP 16/479/74: Nathaniel Tomkins to Sir John Lambe, 26 April 1641. Cottington obtained a warrant for leave of absence from the House of Lords on Saturday 24 April 1641, nominally in regard of his 'indisposicon of body'; NA, SP 16/479, fo. 140. For the campaign against Cottington, see also Clarendon, *Rebellion*, I, 280–1, 305–6, 457.

191 BL, Stowe MS 326 (Misc. papers), fo. 77: Harrison's memorandum (for quotation). For Cottington's resignation, see HMC, *Twelfth Report*, II, 279. Temple also reported that Cottington's resignation might 'preserve him from further question': Centre for Kentish Studies, De L'Isle MS U1475/C114/20: Sir John Temple to the Earl of Leicester, 29 April 1641 (HMC, *De L'Isle Manuscripts*, VI, 402); for the dating of Cottington's resignation, see HMC, *Twelfth Report*, II, 279.

192 This startling development has been explained as stemming from the king himself. It was a device, it has been suggested, 'to tempt Parliamentary leaders with office', and, in the case of the Mastership of the Wards, 'to divide [Saye] from Bedford, whose financial proposals depended on the abolition of the Wards' (Russell, *Fall of the British Monarchies*, p. 289). In fact, the revenues of the Court of Wards were only a minor part of overall Crown income (just over five per cent in 1641), and whether they were kept or abolished had little effect on Bedford's broader financial plans. And no one was doing more than Bedford to ensure that the Mastership of the Wards became available to Saye.

193 Clarendon, *Rebellion*, I, 319.

194 Ibid., pp. 320–1.

195 *The Declaration shewing the Necessity of the Earle of Straffords Suffering* ([April] 1641), sig. A3[r-v] (BL, E 158/2). The dating is based on internal evidence, primarily the pamphlet's recommendation that the 'Lords ... ought as in other Parliaments to give sentence' (sig. B2), which suggests that the trial was approaching its conclusion, but that the attainder bill (of which the pamphlet makes no mention) had not yet been introduced into the Commons.

196 *Declaration shewing the Necessity of the Earl of Straffords Suffering*. sig. A3[v], A3[1], A3[1v].

197 For St John's reference to the Duke of Ireland on 11 November 1640, see Notestein, *D'Ewes Diary*, p. 29.

198 *Declaration shewing the Necessity of the Earl of Straffords Suffering*, sig. A3[1].

199 Ibid., sig. A3[v].

200 Ibid., final page.

201 For Essex's use of this language of 'commonwealth', see, for example, his letter to Hamilton in August 1641, in which he chastises Saye for his neglect of parliamentary affairs, and notes (paraphrasing Hotspur in *Henry IV*, Part I), 'Wee may say well, as Hotspur sayd, ower members love the commonwealt well; but thear owne barns better': NAS, Hamilton MS, GD 406/1/1419: Earl of Essex to the Marquess of Hamilton, 30 August 1641.

202 Clarendon, *Rebellion*, I, 321.

203 For a discussion of the rhetovic of 'the commonsealth', see above, Epilogue.

204 On James I's and Charles I's own aspirations to realize this ideal in the conduct of their governments, see Cust, *Charles I* pp. 19–20.

205 *CSPV 1640–42*, p. 141: Giustinian to the Doge and Senate, 23 April/3 May 1641; Beinecke Lib., MS Osborn Shelves fb 94, Folder 7: Sir Thomas Peyton to Robert Hales, 29 April 1641.

206 *CJ*, II, 130.

207 BL, Harl. MS 163 (D'Ewes diary), fo. 113 (for quotation); for the text of the king's speech, see *CJ*, II, 131. In fact, Charles declared himself to have been 'already upon disbanding' of the Irish army, and was only

prevented from completing the task for lack of funds; however, this seems to have been received as yet another royal pretext for maintaining the army in being.

208 BL, Harl. MS 163 (D'Ewes diary), fo. 113.

209 Centre for Kentish Studies, De L'Isle MS U1475/C114/20: Sir John Temple to the Earl of Leicester, [28] April 1641 (HMC, *De L'Isle Manuscripts*, VI, 402). Temple misdates his letter '29 April', but the reference to St John being about to deliver his argument 'too morrow' establishes the date of the letter as the 28th.

210 *Briefe and Perfect Relation*, p. 82.

211 Gardiner's concluded similarly: 'It was evidently Charles's wisest course to rely on the Lords, and to allow himself to appear before the world, if he must interfere at all on Strafford's behalf, as the guardian of constitutional right'; Gardiner, *History*, IX, 341–2.

212 NA, SP 16/479, fos. 223–5: memorandum on the reform of the Exchequer, [*c*. late April–early May 1641], annotated by the author: 'This was intended for my Lord of Bedford'.

213 Bedford died of smallpox on the morning of 9 May 1641. For the timing of Bedford's death, see Clayton Roberts, 'The Earl of Bedford and the Coming of the English Revolution', *Journal of Modern History*, 77 (49), 611.

214 [Thomas Cademan], *The Earle of Bedfords Passage to the High Court of Parliament* ([May?] 1641), pp. 2–3 (BL, E 158/17). This account of Bedford's final illness and death was published by his physician, Dr Thomas Cademan. With smallpox infections, the feverish symptoms usually appear some three days before the first spots, which then develop (sometimes fatally) over the next ten to fourteen days. Bedford's first spots seem to have appeared on Friday, 30 April (Wedgwood, *Strafford*, p. 371), with death following on the 9th; the onset of his 'feverish disposition' would therefore have been around Wednesday, 28 April or shortly thereafter.

215 For the expectation that Strafford's penalty would 'not ... for the taking away of his life', see Centre for Kentish Studies, De

L'Isle MS U1475/C114/20: Sir John Temple
to the Earl of Leicester, [28] April 1641
(HMC, *De L'Isle Manuscripts*, VI, 402). For
the optimism of Strafford and the king, see
above, p. 269.

216 For the phrase, [Cademan], *The Earle of
Bedfords Passage*, p. 3.

10. STRAFFORD: NEMESIS

1 *A Discourse Shewing in what State the
Three Kingdomes are in at this Present* ([late
April–early May] 1641), sig. A2 (BL, E
160/27). This *Discourse* was published
anonymously, and has been attributed – not
entirely convincingly – to John Milton. It was
also clearly printed by the same unnamed
printer who published, also anonymously, *A
Declaration shewing the Necessity of the Earle
of Straffords Suffering* ([April] 1641), (BL, E
158/2), probably by Oliver St John (whose
argument and distinctive allusions to
Strafford as a wild animal, deployed in his
great nation in Westminster Hall on April).
Both works employ the same large and very
distinctive printer's ornament on their title
pages, and the ornaments to the body of the
text also correspond. Two anonymously
printed anti-Straffordian tracts coming from
the same press may be a coincidence; but they
may also suggest that the printer, whoever he
may have been, had close links, almost
certainly with St John, and possibly with the
anti-Straffordian leadership in Parliament
more generally.

2 BL, Trumbull miscellaneous volume
XLIX/55: Georg Weckherlin to his children, 29
April 1641.

3 BL, Harl. MS 163 (D'Ewes diary), fo. 113v
(*PLP*, IV, 130).

4 BL, Trumbull miscellaneous volume
XLIX/55: Georg Weckherlin to his children, 29
April 1641. The details that follow are derived
from this source, which has not been
published before. See also: BL, Harl. MS 6424
(Bishop Warner's diary), fo. 57r–v: 'Mr St
Johns at a Committee of both Houses in
Westminster Hall endeavoured to prove the
Legality of attainting the L. Strafford by Bill'.

5 For the phrase, NAS, Hamilton MS GD
406/1/1335/1: Earl of Strafford to the
Marquess of Hamilton, 24 April 1641.

6 *CJ*, II, 130.

7 This is my reading of Bedford's summary of
the king's position, as recorded by Hyde:
Clarendon, *Rebellion*, I, 318–9. The king,
Bedford claimed, 'was ready to do all they
could desire if the life of the Earl of Strafford
might be spared'. He would not assent to an
attainder bill that found Strafford guilty of
treason and took away his life. It is possible
to read Hyde's account as implying that the
king would not assent, for reasons of
conscience, to an attainder bill that found
Strafford guilty of any treason, regardless of
the leniency of the punishment; but this would
seem to contradict the king's stated
willingness to do 'all they could desire' if
Strafford's life were spared (i.e. if the attainder
bill did not specify the death penalty).

8 St John had argued in favour of the bill of
attainder in the Commons on 17 and 19 April
(when it had already won the support of the
Bedfordians, Lord Russell and Pym); BL,
Harl. MS 164 (D'Ewes diary), fos. 178, 179v;
and was one of the many Commons-men who
carried the attainder bill up to the Lords on
22 April: Bodl. Lib., MS Tanner 66, fo. 69:
Henry Kinge to Martin Calthorpe, 24 April
1641; see also John Bruce (ed.), *Verney
Papers: Notes of Proceedings in the Long
Parliament temp[ore] Charles I* (Camden
Society, 1845), p. 60.

9 [St John], *Declaration shewing the
Necessity of the Earle of Straffords Suffering*:
the quotations are, respectively, at sigg. A3[v]
(in Latin as 'homo hominibus lupus'), A3[1r],
A3[1v].

10 For the timing of the speech, see BL, Harl.
MS 164 (D'Ewes diary), fos. 191v, 192r-v,
193v; and BL, Harl. MS 163 (D'Ewes diary),
fo. 114; and Centre for Kentish Studies,
Sackville MS (Bourchier Papers),
U269/C267/12: Earl of Bath to his wife, 29
April 1641, from Lincoln's Inn Fields. For the
assistance of Glynne and Maynard, see BL,
Harl. MS 164 (D'Ewes diary), fo. 191v.

11 BL, Harl. MS 163 (D'Ewes diary), fo.
114; the Commons had ordered him 'to sit
... in the middle of the lower rank': *CJ*, II,
130. Glynne and Maynard had been
appointed St John's 'assistants' on 22 April:
ibid., p. 126.

12 St John's speech was subsequently printed,
as a result of a Commons' order of 30 April:
Oliver St John, *An Argument of Law*

concerning the Bill of Attainder of High-Treason of Thomas, Earle of Strafford ([May?] 1641), (BL, E 208/7). Published after the attainder campaign had been won, however, the relationship between the printed text and what had actually been delivered is difficult to determine. I have therefore relied on the contemporary manuscript accounts by eyewitnesses in preference to the printed versions of his speech; in particular those by D'Ewes (for the references, see below) and Moore (BL, Add. MS 477), supplemented by other eyewitness summaries: BL, Trumbull miscellaneous volume XLIX/55: Georg Weckherlin to his children, 29 April 1641; Bodl. Lib. MS Tanner 66, fo. 83: Nathaniel Gerard's newsletter, 6 May 1641; and others (cited below). The printed versions of Pym's speeches on the Strafford question are even more unreliable, as most of them were published only after the attainder had been passed, and Pym had an obvious motive for covering his earlier opposition to the bill and portraying himself as having been on the winning side all along. See also *PLP*, IV, 130–37.

13 BL, Harl. MS 164 (D'Ewes diary), fo. 191v. This passage from St John came immediately after Glynne had read an extract from a statute (apparently, from the subsequent context, one from the reign of Edward III).

14 BL, Harl. MS 164 (D'Ewes diary), fo. 192v; compare BL, Harl. MS 477 (Moore diary), fo. 20r-v.

15 Geoff Baldwin, 'Reason of State and English Parliaments, 1610–42', *History of Political Thought*, 25 (2004), 620–41, quotation at p. 635.

16 BL, Harl. MS 477 (Moore diary), fo. 20r-v.

17 BL, Harl. MS 477 (Moore diary), fo. 20r-v. The contrast St John makes is more effective rhetorically than in law; in order to make it, he has conveniently forgotten that, in the case of the Strafford impeachment, the proceedings in Westminster Hall *were* 'in Parliament', with the peers convened formally as the House of Lords. For the later printed version of St John's text, see St John, *An Argument of Law*, p. 71.

18 Rushworth, *Strafforde's Trial*, p. 703; very similar versions of this phrase appear in the contemporary notes in BL, Harl. MS 477 (Moore diary), fo. 20v; and BL, Harl. MS 164 (D'Ewes diary), fo. 192v. St John developed the point, arguing that the Parliament was like the warrener who 'sets traps for polecats and other vermin for the preservation of the warren'; Rushworth, *Strafforde's Trial*, p. 703. For the impact of this much-reported section of the speech, see, for example, Bodl. Lib, Tanner MS 66, fo. 83: Nathaniel Geraerd newsletter, 6 May 1641.

19 Baldwin, 'Reason of State and English Parliaments', pp. 620–41; and see also *Verney Notes*, p. 65 (I am grateful to Mr Christopher Thompson for this reference).

20 BL, Trumbull miscellaneous volume XLIX/55: Georg Weckherlin to his children, 29 April 1641.

21 Ibid.

22 BL, Harl. MS 164 (D'Ewes diary), fo. 193v.

23 Centre for Kentish Studies, Sackville MS (Bourchier Papers), U269/C267/12: Earl of Bath to his wife, 29 April 1641, from Lincoln's Inn Fields.

24 BL, Harl. MS 164 (D'Ewes diary), fo. 193v.

25 Centre for Kentish Studies, Sackville MS (Bourchier Papers), U269/C267/12: Earl of Bath to his wife, 29 April 1641, from Lincoln's Inn Fields.

26 Bodl. Lib., MS Tanner 66, fo. 77: Henry King to Martin Calthorpe, 1 May 1641. The Bedfordian compromise suffered a corresponding haemorrhaging of support. William Strode, one of the early opponents of the attainder, now declared his backing for St John by urging him to print his speech forthwith, lest it appear in a bowdlerized copy; BL, Harl. MS 163 (D'Ewes diary), fo. 120.

27 BL, Sloane MS 1467 (Newsletters, 1640–41), fo. 130r-v: 'The Protestants' Protestation', [c. May–June 1641].

28 Declaration of Charles I, 12 August 1642; printed in *An Exact Collection of all Remonstrances, Declarations, Votes, Orders, Ordinances* (1643), p. 534 (Wing E1532). The text was written by Hyde, who was in a position to know the accuracy of the claim.

The passage is discussed in Peter Heylyn, *Observations on the Historie of the Reign of King Charles* (1656), pp. 226–7.

29 It is possible that Bedford had had hints of what was coming. St John, after all, had been showing an increasing animus towards Strafford ever since the impeachment trial had collapsed on 10 April. See, for example, Sir Walter Erle's insistence on Monday, 19 April, when St John had failed to appear in the House because he was unwell, that he be fetched from his house: 'the reason why hee was thus sent for', noted D'Ewes, 'was because wee were further to agitate the Bill of Attainder of the Earle of Strafforde': BL, Harl. MS 163 (D'Ewes diary), fo. 69. St John eventually attended, and argued strongly that Strafford's crimes amounted to treason: BL, Harl. MS 164 (D'Ewes diary), fo. 179v.

30 [St John], *A Declaration shewing the Necessity of the Earle of Straffords Suffering*, sig. A3.

31 For Cromwell's relations with St John, see his letter to Mrs St John (possibly St John's second wife), 13 October 1638, printed in W. C. Abbott, *The Writings and Speeches of Oliver Cromwell*, 4 vols. (Oxford, 1988), I, 96–7. An Oliver Cromwell, either the commons-man or a kinsman of the same name, was in St John's service for some time in the late 1630s; see Northamptonshire RO, L(C)854. The two were involved jointly in the arrangements for the settlement of Sir Gilbert Gerard's estates in 1640; see Centre for Buckinghamshire Studies, D–X 1/72. (I am grateful to Mr Christopher Thompson for these two references.) The possibility of Cromwell's connection, through St John, with Warwick's circle is considered in John Morrill, 'The Making of Oliver Cromwell', in John Morrill (ed.), *Oliver Cromwell and the English Revolution* (1990), pp. 34–5, 42–5.

32 Searle, *Barrington Letters*, p. 116: Sir Thomas Barrington to Lady [Joan] Barrington, 29 December 1629.

33 Ibid.

34 Clarendon, *Rebellion*, I, 246; Lindley and Scott, *Journal of Thomas Juxon*, p. 94.

35 For Robert Scawen's unhappy parting with Bedford, see John Adamson, 'Of Armies and Architecture: the Employments of Robert Scawen', in Ian Gentles, John Morrill and Blair Worden (eds.), *Soldiers, Writers, and Statesmen of the English Revolution* (Cambridge, 1998), pp. 39–40.

36 For the earlier relations between Bedford and St John, see above, Ch. 5. It is perhaps suggestive that the Warwick interest had already been made aware of St John's intended tack that Sir John Clotworthy – among the Commons-men closest to Warwick in the early years of the Parliament – should have moved on the previous day that 'Mr Sollicitor may have power to send for what Records [from the Tower, the main archival repository] as hee shall thinke fitt to make use of to morrow against the Earle of Strafford': BL, Harl. MS 164 (D'Ewes diary), fo. 190; *CJ*, II, 130.

37 BL, Harl. MS 164 (D'Ewes diary), fo. 190.

38 Only the day before St John's speech, the Commons had noted the 'contagious sickness, now begun amongst us' – an outbreak of smallpox – as one of 'God's Judgements'; *CJ*, II, 129.

39 [Cademan], *The Earle of Bedfords Passage*, pp. 3–5.

40 Ibid., pp. 2–3.

41 Dr Cademan wrote that 'till Saterday-night [8 May] I am sure hee had no signe of danger'; *The Earle of Bedfords Passage*, p. 5. Wedgwood, *Strafford*, p. 371, gives the evening of Friday, 30 April as the time of the onset of Bedford's illness, though without citing a source. I have not been able to verify this, nor her claim that the king held a discussion with Bedford and Bristol that day. It is characteristic of earlier historians' tendency to father reformist initiatives on Pym almost indiscriminately that the attainder bill, which Hesilrige introduced and Pym opposed, is nevertheless referred to in Wedgwood's account as 'Pym's Bill': ibid., p. 370.

42 Clarendon, *Life*, p. 121. Hyde amplified these points in his *History*, I, 241–2; ii, pp. 547–8. There are hints of this in Essex's snide references to Saye in NAS, Hamilton MS, GD 406/1/1419: Earl of Essex to the Marquess of Hamilton, 30 August 1641.

43 Clarendon, *Rebellion*, I, 335.

44 Gardiner (following a letter printed by Rushworth) gives the names of the two peers who persuaded the king to this intervention on 1 May as Bristol and 'Lord Savile'. Hyde, however, is explicit that the second peer was Saye, a far more likely suggestion, given Saye's close involvement in Bedford's negotiations hitherto; moreover, Hyde was again in a position to know. On Hyde's evidence, Saye's first approach to the king on this topic was made on 30 April, the day after the fateful St John speech; see Gardiner, *History*, IX, 345n; Clarendon, *Rebellion*, I, 335–6.

45 BL, Harl. MS 163 (D'Ewes diary), fo. 122. The Gentleman Usher of the Black Rod came into the Commons with a white stick, rather than the usual black rod, reported D'Ewes, 'that we might perceive hee came not about a dissolution', and was clearly amused that the Commons-men were so on edge.

46 Perhaps the best text of the king's speech is that in BL, Harl. MS 477 (Moore diary), fo. 25 (*PLP*, IV, 164–5); confirmed by BL, Harl. MS 4931, fo. 124; Cambridge UL, MS Kk. VI. 38 (Palmer diary); and see also Bodl. Lib., MS Tanner 66, fo. 75. Seventeenth-century printed versions (including Rushworth) omit the paragraph on the disbandment of the armies.

47 Bodl. Lib., MS Tanner 66, fo. 75r-v; and see MS Tanner 66, fo. 83: letter of intelligence from Nathaniel Gerard, 6 May 1641.

48 The king's opening words referred to how 'it comes to pass that of necessity I must have parte in that Judgment': BL, Harl. MS 477 (Moore diary), fo. 25 (*PLP*, IV, 164). For the theme of Charles's 'conscience', see Kevin Sharpe, 'Private Conscience and Public Duty in the Writings of Charles I', *Historical Journal*, 40 (1997), 645–7; and Cust, *Charles I: a Political Life*, pp. 13–15.

49 HMC, *Tenth Report*, VI, 140.

50 SP 16/480, fo. 1v: the king's speech of 1 May 1641, version copied by Edward Nicholas.

51 BL, Harl. MS 477 (Moore diary), fo. 25 (for quotation); for another text see PA, Braye MS 2 (Letters and Papers, 1637–41), fos. 136–7; printed in substance in Rushworth, *Historical Collections*, III, 1, 239, and the final paragraph, missing from Rushworth, is printed in HMC, *Tenth Report*, Part VI, *Manuscripts of Lord Braye*, p. 140. A variant copy in the fair hand of Edward Nicholas, one

of the Clerks of the Privy Council, survives in NA, SP 16/480, fo.1r-v, and it is tempting to speculate that this was the fair copy of an earlier draft which may well have been Nicholas's handiwork.

52 BL, Harl. MS 477 (Moore diary), fo. 25 (*PLP*, IV, 164).

53 For conscience in the king's speech, see Bodl. Lib., MS Tanner 66, fos. 75–6. On the importance of 'conscience', more generally, in the king's thought see Kevin Sharpe, 'Private Conscience and Public Duty in the Writings of Charles I', *Historical Journal*, 40 (1997), 643–65. For the broader context to the debate on conscience in early modern England, see John Spurr, '"The Strongest Bond of Conscience": Oaths and the Limits of Tolerance in Early Modern England', and Johann P. Sommerville, 'Conscience, Law, and Things Indifferent: Arguments on Toleration from the Vestiarian controversy to Hobbes and Locke', both in Harald Braun and Edward Vallance (eds.), *Contexts of Conscience in Early Modern Europe, 1500–1700* (Basingstoke, 2004), pp. 151–65 and 166–79.

54 James O. Halliwell (ed.), *The Autobiography and Correspondence of Sir Simonds D'Ewes, Bart., during the Reigns of James I and Charles I*, 2 vols. (1845), II, 268.

55 Baillie, *Letters*, I, 350; the Commons' discontent is also reported in NLW, Wynn of Gwydir MS 1684: Maurice Wynn to Owen Wynn, 4 May 1641.

56 The Commons had spent much of the previous day debating how to raise money for the pay of the armies, eventually resolving to levy two subsidies, and to use these as security for an immediate loan (already promised but not yet forthcoming) of £160,000 from the City; BL, Harl. MS 163 (D'Ewes diary), fo. 122.

57 Halliwell, *Autobiography and Correspondence of Sir Simonds D'Ewes*, II, 268. Nor was D'Ewes alone. Sir Edward Dering, shared his pessimism: 'God send [us] good issue,' he wrote on Sunday, 2 May, 'but my despayres begin to go above my fayth in that'; L. B. Larking (ed.), *Proceedings, principally in the County of Kent, in connection with the Parliaments called in 1640* (Camden Society, 80, 1862), p. 46: Sir Edward to Lady Dering, 2 May 1641.

58 Larking, *Proceedings, principally in the County of Kent*, p. 46: Sir Edward to Lady Dering, 2 May 1641.

59 To the earlier provocations was added the news, that same day, that the Commons had passed a bill banning the bishops from secular employments – abolishing, *en passant*, their right to sit in the House of Lords as of 1 August – a measure struck deeply at what the king regarded as one of the central pillars of monarchical power. *CJ*, II, 131; BL, Harl. MS 163 (D'Ewes diary), fo. 121; Harl. MS 164 (D'Ewes diary), fo. 185.

60 The constituents of this plot are discussed later in this chapter; for the plans to bring part or all of the army southwards, see John Rushworth, *The Tryal of Thomas, Earl of Strafford* (1680), pp. 754–5.

61 NA, SP 16/480, fos. 6v-7: Ordnance Office survey, 1 May 1641; endorsed in Edward Nicholas's handwriting on fo. 7v.

62 HMC, *Salisbury Manuscripts*, XXII, 358; Clarendon, *Rebellion*, I, 327; and above, Ch. 9. Mandeville defended Goring, in the summer of 1641, declaring that he was 'an honest Cavillier and addicted to the parliament in all due observance of their comaunds'; BL, Sloane MS 1467 (Newsletters, 1640–41), fo. 39.

63 Above, pp. 101, 103.

64 PA, Braye MS 2 (Letters and Papers, 1637–41), fos. 144–9 (*An Exact Collection*, pp. 215, 223, 224, 227, 232, 234, 236).

65 The claim in the *ODNB* ('Sir John Suckling') that his father had been Secretary of State to James I is without foundation.

66 For the size of his intended force, see BL, Harl. MS 164 (D'Ewes diary), fo. 195; PA, Braye MS 95 (Parliamentary papers), fo. 196: examination of James Wadsworth concerning Sir John Suckling and the troops for Portugal, 4 May 1641; BL, Harl. MS 477 (Moore diary), fo. 27; see also *Times Alteration: a Dialogue betweene my Lord Finch and Secretary Windebancke, ... the Eight of Ian. [1642]* ([March] 1642), single sheet (BL, 669 f. 4/4). This satirical, but well-informed, imaginary conversation refers to 'Sir John [Suckling]' as having intended to go with a troop of horse to serve the Portuguese king against the 'great Don of Spaine [Philip IV]'. The Portuguese ambassador denied any

knowledge of the scheme for raising troops: see *An Exact Collection*, p. 233.

67 *ODNB*, 'Sir John Suckling'; see also, Thomas Clayton and L. A. Beaurline (eds.), *The Works of Sir John Suckling*, 2 vols. (Oxford, 1971), II, 33–119.

68 For the footnote quotation, see *Van Dyck Complete Catalogue*, pp. 603–4; and see also Robert Wilcher, 'John Suckling in the Summer of 1628', *Notes and Queries*, 51 (2004), 21–3.

69 *ODNB*, 'Sir John Suckling'; Mark C. Fissel, *The Bishops' Wars: Charles I's Campaigns against Scotland, 1638-40* (Cambridge, 1994), pp. 28, 57, 78; *Van Dyck Complete Catalogue*, p. 603. An undated letter attributed to Suckling, written during the 1639 campaign, is in Cambridge UL, Add. MS 22 (Misc. corr.), p. 105 (numeration at the bottom right-hand corner); printed in Clayton, *Works of Suckling*, I, 142–4.

70 For Newcastle's alleged involvement in the plot, see Rushworth, *Tryal of Strafford*, p. 755; BL, Sloane MS 1467 (Newsletters, 1640–41), fo. 103: letter of intelligence, [June 1641]. Clayton, *Works of Suckling*, I, 152: Sir John Suckling to the Earl of Newcastle, 8 January [1641]. It has been suggested (ibid., I, p. liii) that this request arose from Suckling's desire to discuss with Newcastle the use of the army against Parliament. This may, in fact, have been so; however, there is nothing in the content of Suckling's letter to Newcastle which, on its own, corroborates this hypothesis. Sir William Pennyman was in London in early May 1641, and was one of the two Commons-men who sought leave to visit Strafford in the Tower on the eve of his execution: *CJ*, II, 142.

71 Clayton, *Works of Suckling*, I, 163–7: Sir John Suckling, 'To Mr Henry German, in the Beginning of Parliament, [December–January] 1640[-41]', see p. 166.

72 'To Mr Henry German', in Clayton, *Works of Suckling*, I, 165.

73 Ibid., p. 164: 'There was not amonge all our Princes a greater Courter of the People than Richard the third, not soe much out of feare, as out of wisedome. And shall the worst of our Kings have striven for that, and shall not the best (it being an Angelicke thinge to gaine Love)?'

74 PA, Braye MS 2 ((Letters and State Papers, 1637–41), fos. 144–59: depositions relating to the Army Plot, 4 May–19 June 1641; HMC, *Cowper Manuscripts*, II, 280–1.

75 BL, Sloane MS 1467 (Misc. papers), fo. 39v: examination of Captain William Billingsley, 13 May 1641. It is worth noting that this was a part of the palace to which, as a Gentleman of the Privy Chamber, Suckling had an automatic right of entrée.

76 Billingsley is described as having been a page to Strafford in Baillie, *Letters*, I, p. 351; see also *CSPD, 1640*, pp. 46, 53. Billingsley is similarly described as 'a captaine ... that had been in neere relation of the Earl of Strafford': BL, Harl. MS 165 (D'Ewes diary), fo. 84v.

77 Hugh Kearney, *Strafford in Ireland, 1633–41: a Study in Absolutism* (Manchester, 1959; new edn, Cambridge, 1989), p. 173. He seems to be one and the same with the William Billingsley who sat in the 1634 Irish Parliament for the constituency of Downpatrick in County Down: *CSPI, 1633–47*, p. 64.

78 BL, Sloane MS 1467 (Misc. papers), fo. 39v: examination of Billingsley, 13 May 1641. See also, BL, Harl. MS 6424 (Bishop Warner's diary), fo. 58 (where Warner mistakenly assumes the attempt to take the Tower took place on Monday, 3 May); BL, Harl. MS 163 (D'Ewes diary), fos. 290, 294; BL, Harl. MS 477 (Moore diary), fos. 34, 40; and Sir William Balfour's deposition before Warwick, Essex, Wharton and Mandeville, [11? May 1641], printed in *An Exact Collection*, pp. 232–3.

79 PA, MS Lords Journal, 3 May 1641; Paul Christianson, 'The Obliterated Portions of the House of Lords Journals dealing with the Attainder of Strafford, 1641', *English Historical* Review, 95 (1980), 347; BL, Harl. MS 165 (D'Ewes diary), fo. 84v.

80 Rushworth, *Historical Collections*, III, 1, 253.

81 The Orange-Nassau marriage provided another unwelcome reminder of how far and how fast his dynasty's prestige had slipped since the Covenanter Revolt. Under more settled circumstances, such a union would never have been contemplated, for in the hierarchical world of princely diplomacy, the house of Orange-Nassau barely rated. Their only claim to sovereign status was their rule of the pocket-sized, French-speaking principality of Orange, a nominally independent outpost in southern France. And although the family enjoyed a primacy of honour within the Dutch Republic, the Orange-Nassaus were emphatically not a royal house. The bridegroom's father, Prince Frederik Hendrik, had been accorded the title 'Highness' (*Hoogheid*) by the Dutch States General only as recently as 1637. The mother of Charles's prospective son-in-law was a commoner who had served in the household of his sister, the exiled Queen Elizabeth of Bohemia. The sense that the Stuarts were marrying beneath them was clearly conveyed at the Dutch prince's first reception at court, on Monday, 26 April, when neither Queen Henriette Marie (a daughter of the King of France) nor even his intended bride would allow him to kiss them, despite it being 'a privilege which is usually granted to princes who marry the daughters of this House'. The arrival of the prince's entourage had been expected from the end of March; see NLW, Wynn of Gwydir MS 1681: Maurice Wynn to Owen Wynn, 30 March 1641. For the young Prince Willem's mother, Countess Amalia von Solms-Braunfels (1603–75), see Jonathan Israel, 'The Courts of the House of Orange, c. 1580–1795', in John Adamson (ed.), *Princely Courts of Europe: Ritual, Politics and Culture under the* Ancien Régime, *1500–1750* (1999), pp. 126, 128. ASV, Giustinian to the Doge and Senate, 3 May 1641 (*CSPV, 1640–42*, p. 142). It was announced that these celebrations had been 'postponed'; but few imagined that these wedding revels would ever now take place; *CSPV, 1640–42*, p. 142); for the king's suspension of wage payments to his household servants, see ASV, Giustinian to the Doge and Senate, 19 April 1641, quoting a confidential conversation with the Earl of Arundel (*CSPV, 1640–42*, p. 139).

82 Loomie, *Ceremonies of Charles I*, p. 310.

83 John Moore, the Commons diarist, was among those who gained access to Whitehall to observe the ceremonies: BL, Harl. MS 477 (Moore diary), fo. 132.

84 BL, Harl. MS 6424 (Bishop Warner's diary), fo. 57v; Bishop Warner of Rochester preached the sermon. For other accounts see,

BL, Harl. MS 477 (Moore diary), fo. 132; John Moore's eyewitness description of the ceremony; and *Archives . . . de la maison d'Orange-Nassau*, 2nd ser., III, 454–63.

85 BL, Harl. MS 477 (Moore diary), fo. 26v.

86 For the ceremonies, see BL, Harl. MS 477 (Moore diary), fo. 132; and for those later in the day, Loomie, *Ceremonies of Charles I*, pp. 311–13.

87 BL, Harl. MS 477 (Moore diary), fo. 132.

88 *An Exact Collection*, p. 234: Lanyon's deposition, 11 May 1641; and BL, Harl. MS 477 (Moore diary), fos. 26v–27. Sir Henry Vane Senior and Commissary Henry Wilmot (who was himself involved in planning another 'army plot' with Henry Percy) attempted to explain away Suckling's activities by stating that he was raising troops for Portuguese service, but this failed to persuade the House of Commons.

89 BL, Harl. MS 477 (Moore diary), fo. 27. Penington seems to have shared the outlook and objectives of the Warwick House group, though whether he was linked to its members in any other way is difficult to determine. It may, however, be significant that when he proposed a bill to 'restrain the increase of buildings in and around' the capital, on 7 May 1641, his co-sponsor of the bill was Harbottell Grimston: *CJ*, II, 138. Gardiner's story that Billingsley's presented himself at the Tower on Sunday morning (2 May) and was refused entrance by Sir William Balfour appears to be without foundation: Gardiner, *History*, IX, 348–9. It has misled numerous subsequent writers; see, e.g., Clayton, *Works of Suckling*, I, p. lv.

90 Clarendon, *Rebellion*, I, 329.

91 See above, p. 284.

92 Prinsterer, *Archives . . . de la maison d'Orange-Nassau*, 2nd ser., III, 445: Earl of Warwick to Prince Willem van Orange-Nassau, 2 May 1641.

93 HMC, *Montagu of Beaulieu Manuscripts*, pp. 129–30: Edward Montagu to Lord Montagu of Boughton, 5 May 1641.

94 Loomie, *Ceremonies of Charles I*, p. 313.

95 HMC, *Montagu of Beaulieu Manuscripts*, pp. 129–30: Edward Montagu to Lord Montagu of Boughton, 5 May 1641.

96 Prinsterer, *Archives . . . de la maison d'Orange-Nassau*, 2nd ser., III, 445: Earl of Warwick to Prince Willen van Orange-Nassau, 2 May 1641.

97 For the first two footnote quotations, see BL, Add. MS 19398 (Misc. letters), fo. 72: William Dillingham, letter of intelligence, 3 May 1641. Other contemporaries agreed: it was a gathering 'citizens of very good account' and 'some of the most substantial citizens' – a point that would have been immediately obvious, not only from their dress, but also because, as gentlemen, they wore swords; NA, SP 16/480/11 and *CSPV 1640–41*, p. 147: Giustinian to the Doge and Senate, 6/16 May 1641. For the Lords' order, see PA, MP 3/5/1641; partly printed in HMC, *Fourth Report*, p. 61.

98 PA, MS Lords Journal, 3 May 1641; Christianson, 'Obliterated Portions', p. 346. Unusually, the petition was presented only to the House of Lords, bypassing the City's four Commons-men.

99 BL, Harl. MS 477 (Moore diary), fo. 27.

100 Both peers were sons of Lady Penelope Devereux, the daughter of the 1st Earl of Essex. Her liaison with the Earl of Devonshire produced, illegitimately, the 1st Earl of Newport; and, legitimately, by her marriage to the third Lord Rich, Robert Rich (later second Earl of Warwick and 4th Lord Rich).

101 PA, MS Lords Journal, 3 May 1641; Christianson, 'Obliterated Portions', p. 347. Charles made a virtue of necessity by issuing a patent of appointment on 6 May 1641: NA, SP 16/480, fo. 27.

102 The other two peers were Lord Strange and Lord Howard of Charlton. There was a quorum fixed at three, so not all the peers named necessarily took part in the delegation. PA, MS Lords Journal, 3 May 1641; Christianson, 'Obliterated Portions', p. 347. The fable that Billingsley's force was actually admitted to the Tower was already current in the 1640s:

103 PA, MS Lords Journal, 3 May 1641; Christianson, 'Obliterated Portions', p. 347. The survey of the gunpowder held in the Tower provided for the king on 1 May may be read as suggesting that the king did not have an entirely innocent interest in these

'municion[s]' during this period; see NA, SP 16/480, fos. 6v–7.

104 *LJ*, IV, 232; PA, MS Lords Journal, 3 May 1641.

105 BL, Add. MS 19398 (Misc. letters), fo. 72: William Dillingham, letter of intelligence, 3 May 1641, estimates the size of the crowd at 10,000; another report of the crowd (apparently as it stood in the afternoon) numbered it at 4,000; though this, too, should be regarded as only the very roughest of estimates; see Bodl. Lib., MS Tanner 66, fos. 83v–4: letter of intelligence, 6 May 1641.

106 *A Briefe and Perfect Relation, of the Answeres and Replies of Thomas Earle of Strafford* (1647), p. 84 (BL, E 417/19).

107 BL, Harl. MS 6424 (Bishop Warner's diary), fo. 58 (for quotation). Another report assigns these words to John Lilburne: HMC, *Braye Manuscripts*, x, 140–1.

108 Julia F. Merritt, *The Social World of Early Modern Westminster: Abbey, Court, and Community, 1525–1640* (Manchester, 2005), p. 82.

109 BL, Add. MS 19398 (Correspondence), fo. 72: letter of intelligence, 3 May 1641; the author thought that Pembroke had told them that the Lords had actually 'signed the bill of Attaynder'.

110 In July 1641, he was to be punished with the deprivation of his office as Lord Chamberlain of the Household: NA, SP 16/482, fo. 178: Thomas Wiseman to Sir John Pennington, 29 July 1641.

111 Thomas Herbert [pseudonym?], *Vox Secunda Populi. Or, the Commons Gratitude to the Most Honorable Philip, Earl of Pembroke and Mongomery [sic]* ([June] 1641), p. 5 (BL, E 164/21).

112 PA, MS Lords Journal, 3 May 1641; Christianson, 'Obliterated Portions', p. 347.

113 Baillie, *Letters*, I, 351.

114 Calybute Downinge, *A Sermon Preached to the Renowned Company of the Artillery, 1 September, 1640, designed to compose the Present Troubles, by discovering the Enemies of the Peace of the Church and State* (1641), p. 32 [recte p. 38] (BL, E 157/4).

115 BL, Harl. MS 477 (Moore diary), fo. 27v.

116 Ibid., fo. 28.

117 BL, Harl. MS 163 (D'Ewes diary), fo. 64.

118 BL, Harl. MS 477 (Moore diary), fo. 27v: the quotation is from Pym's speech of 3 May 1641 (*PLP*, IV, 180).

119 On this theme, see also Peter Lake, 'Antipopery: the Structure of a Prejudice', in Richard Cust and Ann Hughes (eds.), *Conflict in Early Stuart England: Studies in Religion and Politics, 1603–42* (1989), pp. 72–106. On its Elizabethan roots, see Julian Lock, '"How many Tercios has the Pope?": the Spanish War and the Sublimation of Elizabethan Anti-Popery', *History*, 81 (1996), 197–214.

120 The *locus classicus* for this argument is John Morrill, 'The Religious Context of the English Civil War', *Transactions of the Royal Historical Society*, 5th ser., 34 (1984), 155–78; but the argument also suffuses Russell's *Fall of the British Monarchies*, *passim*.

121 [John Oldmixon], *History of England during the Reigns of the Royal House of Stuart* (1730), pp. 141–2: 'Nathaniel Black' [Jhonston of Wariston] to the Earl of Loudoun, 23 June 1640.

122 Centre for Kentish Studies, De L'Isle MS U1475/C114/11: Sir John Temple to the Earl of Leicester, 18 February 1641 (HMC, *De L'Isle Manuscripts*, VI, 384).

123 D'Ewes claimed that Pym and the other members of the drafting committee had 'plotted the whole busines before'; BL, Harl. MS 164 (D'Ewes diary), fo. 196. This adds authority to the claim in the memoirs of the 1640s Commons-man, Sir Dudley North (later 4th Lord North, d. 1677), that the Protestation had been considered 'at a private meeting of the Grandees' on the previous day, 2 May, who decided that it was 'unseasonable' to put it forward at this time. They were effectively bounced into supporting the measure, North claims, by Henry Marten's unilateral action in proposing the measure in the Commons the following morning. Given the late date of North's account, it must be treated with considerable caution. The readiness with which Marten's proposal found supporters among the Junto grandees in the Commons casts doubts on North's suggestion that they had regarded it

as 'unseasonable'; on the other hand, the idea that the 'Grandees' (particularly some of the peers among them) disagreed as to the timing of the measure rings true; it is plausible to imagine Saye, for example, the leader of what remained of the Bedfordian interest, attempting to block a measure that would have been seen as highly provocative by the king and his immediate entourage; see [Dudley North, 4th Baron North], *A Narrative of Some Passages in or Relating to the Long Parliament* (1670), p. 96. For North, see D. B. J. Randall, *Gentle Flame: the Life and Verse of Dudley, Fourth Lord North* (Durham, NC, 1983).

124 BL, Harl. MS 477 (Moore diary), fo. 28; the phrase is George Peard's.

125 The idea of 'an association amongst us' was first mooted by the mercurial figure of Henry Marten, one of the militant anti-Straffordians, whose extremist zeal tended to place him outside either of the major Junto groupings. BL, Harl. MS 477 (Moore diary), fo. 28.

126 Ibid.; for Stapilton's involvement in the attainder, see pp. 242–4, 246, 248; for Barrington and Gerard, see pp. 254–5, 259; for Clotworthy, pp. 226, 241–2.

127 *CJ*, II, 132: the members were John Pym, Sir John Culpeper, Henry Marten, Denzell Holles, William Strode, Sir Philip Stapilton, Sir Thomas Barrington, Sir Robert Harley, Nathaniel Fiennes, John Hampden, John Maynard, and John Glynne. Interestingly, a proposal that St John should be added to the committee was 'distasted by the greater parte of the howse', and therefore failed, though the reason for this opposition is difficult to divine; BL, Harl. MS 164 (D'Ewes diary), fo. 195.

128 *CJ*, II, p. 132. See also, David Cressy, 'Binding the Nation: the Bonds of Association 1584 and 1696', in his *Society and Culture in Early Modern England* (Aldershot and Burlington, VT, 2003), pp. 217–34. The contingency had been first mentioned in the summer of 1640 in a letter of Archibald Jhonston to Lord Loudoun: [Oldmixon], *History*, pp. 141–2.

129 BL, Harl. MS 477 (Moore diary), fo. 28.

130 HMC, *Montagu of Beaulieu Manuscripts*, pp. 129–30: Edward Montagu to Lord Montagu of Boughton, 5 May 1641.

131 Baillie, *Letters*, I, 351.

132 NA, PRO 31/9/20 (Rossetti transcripts): Count Carlo Rossetti to Cardinal Barberini, 7/17 May 1641.

133 BL, Harl. MS 164 (D'Ewes diary), fo. 174 (*PLP*, IV, 61).

134 Ibid.

135 Another possible motive for Essex's desire to keep together a group of experienced officers and commanders may have been his interest in planning another English (or, as the idea later developed, Anglo-Scots) campaign in the Holy Roman Empire to restore the Prince-Elector Palatine to his ancestral territories; for which, see ch. 12, above.

136 The exceptions, in this regard, are Gardiner, who noted the 'shock' which the discovery of the Tower Plot had on both Houses (Gardiner, *History*, IX, 355) and Perez Zagorin, *The Court and the Country: the Beginning of the English Revolution* (1969), p. 22; Keith Lindley, *Popular Politics and Religion in Civil War London* (Aldershot, 1997), p. 22.

137 BL, Harl. MS 6424 (Bishop Warner's diary), fo. 58v.

138 *CJ*, II, 137; BL, Harl. MS 164 (D'Ewes diary), fo. 199; BL, Harl. MS 477 (Moore diary), fo. 39r-v.

139 BL, Harl. MS 6424 (House of Lords diary), fo. 58v. This document is almost certainly that which is now in the Cambridgeshire (Huntington) RO, Manchester MS, which is endorsed in pencil in Warwick's handwriting.

140 BL, Harl. MS 6424 (Bishop Warner's diary), fo. 58v.

141 Ibid., fo. 60.

142 For the phrase, see [St John], *Declaration shewing the Necessity of the Earle of Straffords Suffering*, sig. A3[2].

143 BL, Harl. MS 457 (Minutes of the Anglo-Scottish Treaty, 1640–1), fo. 51v.

144 Staffordshire RO, Dartmouth MS D(W)1778/I/i/14: Daniel O'Neill to William Legge, 23 February 1641.

145 For the witnesses' depositions, signed by Warwick and Essex, see PA, Braye MS 2 (Letters and Papers, 1637–41), fos. 147–8,

149–50, 156–7 (*An Exact Collection*, pp. 220, 223, 232). The bicameral committee to conduct these examinations, which had been appointed on 5 May, comprised ten lords and twenty Commoners: BL, Harl. MS 6424 (Bishop Warner's diary), fo. 62r-v.

146 *CJ*, II, 134–5, 136, 137.

147 Warwick's direct involvement in the payment of the Scottish army is discussed in detail in Ch. 11; for his activities in May 1641, see *LJ*, IV, 246.

148 Anthony Milton, 'Thomas Wentworth and the political thought of the Personal Rule', in Julia F. Merritt (ed.), *The Political World of Thomas Wentworth, Earl of Strafford, 1621–41* (Cambridge, 1996), pp. 133–56.

149 Principally, Essex, Mandeville, Brooke, Wharton, and Howard of Escrick in the Lords; Clotworthy, Harley, Barrington and (via Essex) Stapilton in the Commons.

150 *LJ*, IV, 238. ASV, Senato, Dispacci Inghil. 42, fos. 283–5: Giustinian to the Doge and Senate, 14/24 May 1641 (*CSPV 1640–42*, p. 150); BL, Harl. MS 163 (D'Ewes diary), fo. 142; BL, Harl. MS 477 (Moore diary), fo. 41r-v.

151 *CJ*, II, 139; BL, Harl. MS 164 (D'Ewes diary), fo. 200. Arthur Capell seems to have acted as Warwick's spokesman in the Commons.

152 *LJ*, IV, 239; BL, Harl. MS 164 (D'Ewes diary), fo. 200 (for quotation); BL, Harl. MS 477 (Moore diary), fo. 44.

153 BL, Harl. MS 5047 (Anon. diary), fo. 34v; BL, Harl. MS 164 (D'Ewes diary), fo. 197 (for quotation).

154 Ibid.

155 This objection is made, entirely validly, by in Anthony Fletcher, *The Outbreak of the English Civil War* (1981) p. 56.

156 Here, too, the first move was made by the Junto leaders in the Commons, and after 'much dispute' a resolution was eventually produced that the Lords should 'move his Majesty' that the Earl of Essex should be made Lord Lieutenant of Yorkshire. Once sent to the Lords, however, Warwick assumed sponsorship of the question, just as he had done earlier of the bill of attainder. Here, for the first time, Parliament was presuming to tell the king whom it wanted appointed to a major public office (indeed, an influential military command). BL, Harl. MS 163 (D'Ewes diary), fo. 145. Who proposed Essex as Savile's replacement is not clear from any of the diaries; but the question of the security of Yorkshire had been committed, immediately before the debate on the Lord Lieutenancy, to a committee that included Stapilton, Pym, Holles, Fiennes, Erle, Clotworthy, Hampden, and Strode: BL, Harl. MS 477 (Moore diary), fo. 41v. It is highly likely, therefore, that the proposal emerged from this group.

157 *LJ*, IV, 241. As D'Ewes noted, Savile had not yet been appointed, but in the debate on 7 May many Commons-men spoke 'as if ... Savile weere already made Lorde Leiftenant of that shire': BL, Harl. MS 163 (D'Ewes diary), fo. 145 (*PLP*, IV, 249). The Signet Office warrant for Savile's appointment was actually passed – see NA, SO 3/12 (Signet Office Docket Book), fo. 143v – but it is unclear whether the patent passed the Great Seal.

158 *OED*, 'move', *v.*, 26, (a) and (c).

159 ASV, Senato, Dispacci Inghil. 42, fo. 286: Giustinian to the Doge and Senate, 14/24 May 1641 (*CSPV 1640–42*, p. 152). It is characteristic of the calendaring of these manuscripts, which consistently downplay the role of the Lords, that Essex is referred to in *CSPV 1640–42* as merely '*a* leader of the Puritans'; the Venetian original actually reads 'capo prencipale de[i] Puritani'. Savile, humiliated in his quest for the Lord Lieutenancy of Yorkshire, seems to have nursed a permanent resentment against Essex thereafter.

160 On 7 December, Hesilrige moved to appoint a Lord General and Lord Admiral to command the country's forces, an initiative that led to the creation of the Militia Ordinance, in which Parliament appointed the Lords Lieutenant of every English and Welsh county; Coates, *D'Ewes Diary*, pp. 244–8; Bodl. Lib., MS Rawlinson d. 932 (Sir John Holland's diary), fos. 62v-3. Nor was this the only instance of the crown succumbing to parliamentary pressure. When it came to the next major military appointment, the Constableship of the Tower (vacant since Cottington's resignation in November), the

king had learnt his lesson and avoided a damaging confrontation. His decision, that same week, to appoint Warwick's half-brother, the Earl of Newport, as Constable was merely an attempt to make a virtue of necessity: in fact, Newport was acting, and being treated by others, as if he already occupied that post; BL, Harl. MS 6424 (Bishop Warner's diary), 61v.

161 Russell, *Fall of the British Monarchies*, p. 299. Gardiner noted this point with characteristic acuity: 'The House of Commons is with us [of the 1880s] itself the centre of the national organisation to which the whole country instinctively rallies. In 1641 it was nothing of the kind. All the habits of men led them to look to the King for guidance. Parliaments were but bodies meeting at rare intervals, doing important work and then vanishing away': Gardiner, *History*, IX, 352n.

162 And at a conference with the Commons on 7 May, he explained that Northumberland, as Lord Admiral, had been instructed to see that the navy's ships were in the hands of 'religious officers and commanders' – that is, opponents of any royal coup. *LJ*, IV, 239; BL, Harl. MS 164 (D'Ewes diary), fo. 200, for quotation (*PLP*, IV, 251); BL, Harl. MS 477 (Moore diary), fo. 44.

163 *CJ*, II, 136, 139; BL, Harl. MS 477 (Moore diary), fos. 43, 45v, 47v; and see the discussion in Russell, *Fall of the British Monarchies*, pp. 295–6. There is no clue from D'Ewes, or from the other surviving diarists, as to who introduced this bill; compare BL, Harl. MS 163 (D'Ewes diary), fo. 139.

164 *LJ*, IV, 238, 241; *CJ*, II, 139.

165 NA, PRO 31/9/20 (Rossetti transcripts): Count Carlo Rossetti to Cardinal Barberini, 7/17 May 1641: 'Mercordi ... i Parliamentarii ... di più hanno mincciato il Re di volersi levare la Corona, et incoronare il Principe di Waglia'. Rossetti claimed as his source the 'Lord Viscount' ('Signor Visconte'); Savile, although only a baron in the English peerage, was a viscount in the Irish peerage, and was usually known socially by the higher title.

166 Rushworth, *Strafforde's Trial*, pp. 743–6. Gardiner (*History*, IX, 362) dates this letter to 4 May, a date which appears on the early manuscript copies. However, Radcliffe, in his 'Essay towards the Life of my Lord Strafforde', dates it to 'Friday' – that is, 7

May – testimony that is not lightly to be dismissed. Nevertheless, on balance, the earlier date seems more likely to the correct one; see Knowler, *Strafforde's Letters*, II, 432.

167 Wedgwood, *Strafford*, p. 374.

168 *Camden Miscellany IX*, Part IV, pp. 23–5; printing Sheffield Central Lib., Wentworth Woodhouse Muniments, Strafford MS XL.

169 BL, Harl. MS 163 (D'Ewes diary), fo. 291 (for quotation); Balfour testified that the offer had been made four days before his execution, which was on Wednesday, 12 May; see also Rushworth, *Historical Collections*, Part III, I, 238, 254; HMC, *Portland Manuscripts*, I, 719.

170 *CJ*, II, 132.

171 Clarendon, *Rebellion*, I, 320.

172 Russell, *Fall of the British Monarchies*, p. 296; [St John], *Declaration shewing the Necessity of the Earl of Straffords Suffering*, sig. B2r-v; St John, *Argument*.

173 NA, SP 16/480, fo. 33v: Sir Henry Vane, senior, to [Sir Thomas Rowe?], 7 May 1641. The votes against Strafford are brilliantly analysed in Russell, *Fall of the British Monarchies*, pp. 296–8; see also J. H. Timmis, *Thine is the Kingdom: the Trial for Treason of Thomas Wentworth, Earl of Strafford, First Minister to King Charles I, and Last Hope of the English Crown* (University, AL, 1974), pp. 166–9; Christianson, 'Obliterated Portions', pp. 339–53; PLP, IV, 258–9.

174 *CJ*, II, 140.

175 Warwick had proposed that 'a committee of three or four might be appointed to draw some heads, to secure the land, as well as the sea'; *CJ*, II, 139.

176 *CJ*, II, 135. Stapilton was added on the 7th; *CJ*, II, 138.

177 Ibid., 140.

178 Other preparations for an internal conflict include the order to members of the Commons to scrutinize arms and ammunition in their county arsenals, and consider who currently commanded 'what forts and castles ther are', and report back to the House; BL, Harl. MS 164 (D'Ewes diary), fo. 198.

179 For the time, see ibid., fo. 202v; *CJ*, II, 140; PLP, IV, 276–7.

180 For the circumstances of the meeting between the king and the two Houses, see NA, PRO 31/9/20 (Rossetti transcripts): Count Carlo Rossetti to Cardinal Barberini, 14/21 May 1641; Gardiner, *History*, IX, pp. 363–5.

181 BL, Harl. MS 163 (D'Ewes diary), fo. 154; BL, Harl. MS 477 (Moore diary), fo. 48v.

182 Gardiner, *History*, IX, 364, basing his account on NA, PRO 31/9/18–23 (Rossetti transcripts): Count Carlo Rossetti to Cardinal Barberini, 14/21 May 1641.

183 ASV, Senato, Dispacci Inghil. 42, fos. 280–7: Giustinian to the Doge and Senate, 14/24 May 1641 (*CSPV 1640–42*, pp. 150–2).

184 BN, Paris, MS Français 15995 (Montreuil Dispatches): Montreuil to Cardinal Mazarin, 13/23 May 1641

185 [Thomas Cademan], *The Earle of Bedfords Passage to the High Court of Parliament* ([May?] 1641), title page (for the hour of Bedford's death) and pp. 5–6 (BL, E 158/17).

186 Knowler, *Strafforde's Letters*, II, 432; John Hacket, *Scrinia Reserata: a Memorial Offer'd to the Great Deservings of J[ohn] Williams*, 2 parts (1693), II, 161; NLW, Wynn of Gwydir MS 1685: Maurice Wynn to Owen Wynn, 11 May 1641.

187 Sir William Sanderson, *A Compleat History of the Life and Raigne of King Charles from his Cradle to his Grave* (1658), pp. 414–5. Page references are to the MS pagination to the copy in Yale University Library.

188 VAL, Forster MS 39 (Elector Palatine correspondence) 23/1/10 (Treasury Solicitor Miscellanea): Prince-Elector Charles Louis of the Palatinate to Queen Elizabeth of Bohemia, 18 May 1641. The king, wrote the Prince-Elector, had 'shewed himselfe a good Master and a good Christian and att last a good King'. For the likely attendance at the Council meeting of 9 May, see the detailed discussion in Russell, *Fall of the British Monarchies*, p. 299n.

189 *LJ*, IV, 239; for the state of the Irish army, see Sir Walter Erle's report of 24 April 1641: BL, Harl. MS 164 (D'Ewes diary), fo. 187.

190 Sanderson, *Life and Raigne of King Charles*, p. 414.

191 Ibid.

192 PA, Original Acts, 16 Car. I, cap. 38; Russell, *Fall of the British Monarchies*, p. 300.

193 NA, PRO 31/9/20 (Rossetti transcripts): Count Carlo Rossetti to Cardinal Barberini, 14/21 May 1641.

194 BL, Harl. MS 164 (D'Ewes diary), fo. 207v (11 May 1641); *CJ*, II, 143.

195 BL, Harl. MS 6424 (Bishop Warner's diary), fo. 65v. This entry in Warner needs to be read in conjunction with Edward Montagu's letter of 5 May 1641, cited above.

196 Matthias Milward, *The Souldiers Triumph and the Preachers Glory. In a Sermon preached to the Captains and Souldiers exercising Arms in the Artillery Garden ... 31 of August, 1641* ([September?] 1641), sig. B2[1] (BL, E 175/7).

197 Armoury House, London, Honourable Artillery Company Archives, Quarterage Book 1628–43, unfol., 'John Venn', *s.v.*, entries from 1635. John Venn replaced Matthew Cradock, who died on 27 May 1641, as one of the City's four representatives in the Commons; Valerie Pearl, *London and the Outbreak of the Puritan Revolution: City Government and National Politics, 1625–43* (Oxford, 1961), p. 187.

198 For Venn, and his involvement in the organization of large groups of Londoners in 1641, see above, pp. 300, 471.

199 Peter Heylyn, *Observations on the Historie of the Reign of King Charles* (1656), p. 244.

200 Francis Beaumont and John Fletcher, *A King and No King* (1619); for its later reception, see Zachary Lesser, 'Mixed Government and Mixed Marriage in *A King and No King*: Sir Henry Neville Reads Beaumont and Fletcher', *ELH*, 69 (2002), 947–77.

201 Knowler, *Strafforde's Letters*, II, 432; Gardiner, *History*, IX, 367.

202 Sanderson, *Life and Raigne of King Charles*, p. 418 (my emphasis).

203 Ibid., p. 421. The quotation is from

Psalm 146, verse 3. Sanderson confuses the messenger with his namesake, 'Sir Dudley Carleton, Secretary of State', later 1st Viscount Dorchester, who had died in 1632. Wedgwood accepts the story unquestioningly in her *Strafford*, p. 380. For Carleton, see his letters in BL, Evelyn Collection, Browne Correspondence Box A–C; and Sir Dudley Carleton to Lord Wharton, 14 February 1652: Bodl. Lib., Carte MS 80, fo. 620.

204 Wedgwood, *Strafford*, pp. 376–7.

205 NA, C 181/6, p. 145.

206 PA, MS Lords Journal, 10 May 1641; Christianson, 'Obliterated Portions'.

207 *LJ*, IV, 245.

208 PA, MP 11 May 1641 (*LJ*, IV, 245).

209 Ibid.

210 NA, SP 16/467, fo. 157: Windebank's notes of the Privy Council, 16 September 1640.

211 NA, C 181/6, p. 145: warrants from the king, 11 May 1641. Neither warrant stipulates a time or date for the execution, and both refer to the prisoner by his title as 'Earl of Strafford', rather than as Thomas Wentworth, the style that he had technically resumed, with the forfeiture of his earldom, when the king had given assent to the attainder bill the previous day.

212 Laud, *Works*, III, 442; *CSPD, 1640–41*, p. 540. This would seem to be the 'petition' from Strafford that Warner reports as having been received on 11 May, but 'not read': BL, Harl. MS 6424 (Bishop Warner's diary), fo. 67.

213 *A Briefe and Perfect Relation, of the Answeres and Replies of Thomas Earle of Strafford* (1647), the mispaginated second p. 99 (BL, E 417/19); Strafford's final days are well recounted in Wedgwood, *Strafford*, pp. 380–9.

214 Wenzel Hollar, *The True Maner of the Execution of Thomas Earle of Strafford*, ... *12th of May 1641* (1641); reproduced p. 303.

215 ASV, Senato, Dispacci Inghil. 42, fo. 282v: Giustinian to the Doge and Senate, 14/24 May 1641 (*CSPV 1640–42*, p. 151).

216 BL, Sloane MS 1467 (Newsletters, 1640–41), fo. 37: letter of intelligence, [mid-May 1641].

217 For the timing of the execution, which was between 11 a.m. and noon, see HMC, *Maxwell Stirling Maxwell Manuscripts*, p. 78: Drummond of Riccartoun to Stirling of Kier, 12 May 1641.

218 *Briefe and Perfect Relation*, pp. 99–100. The anecdote, like many others in this partially hagiographic account of Strafford's trial, must be regarded with caution; but it is certainly plausible and entirely in character. The pikemen who probably formed part of the escort are clearly discernible in Hollar's engraving of the execution; see p. 303.

219 *Briefe and Perfect Relation*, p. 104.

220 For the list of the four peers and the mention of the four (unnamed) Commons-men 'apoynted' by Parliament to attend the execution, see NLS, MS Wodrow Quarto 25, fo. 164v: letter of intelligence, 11 May 1641; for the halberdiers and members of Strafford's household, see Hollar, *The True Maner of the Execution of Thomas, Earle of Strafford*.

221 *Briefe and Perfect Relation*, p. 104.

222 NLS, MS Wodrow Quarto 25, fo. 164v: letter of intelligence, 11 May 1641.

223 See Thomas W. Laqueur, 'Crowds, Carnival and the State in English Executions, 1604–1868', in A. L. Beier, David Cannadine and J. M. Rosenheim (eds.), *The First Modern Society: Essays in English History in Honour of Lawrence Stone* (Cambridge, 1989), pp. 305–55.

224 *Briefe and Perfect Relation*, pp. 105–6.

225 The text printed here is the version printed by Rushworth, *Historical Collections*, III, i, 267–8 (emphasis added), which closely resembles that in the *Briefe and Perfect Relation*. Rushworth states that 'the Author took [it] in Characters [i.e. shorthand] from his [Strafford's] Mouth, being then there on the Scaffold'; a claim repeated in his *The Tryal of Thomas, Earl of Strafford* (1680), p. 759.

226 *Briefe and Perfect Relation*, p. 102.

227 Ibid. The presence of a number of noblemen on the scaffold is corroborated by a contemporary manuscript account of the execution, in which Strafford is described as taking 'his everlasting leave from the Lords and others present, as if he had taken but a civill leave for [a journey] to Ireland': BL, Sloane MS 3317, fo. 21r-v. The only 'Lords'

who were part of Strafford's own entourage were the Archbishop of Armagh and the Earl of Cleveland: Rushworth, *Tryal*, p. 759; on the other hand, the fact that Strafford is described as having 'saluted' the noblemen may suggest that they were on an adjacent stand, and therefore unable to be offered his hand; see also BL, Sloane MS 1467 (Newsletters, 1640–41), fo. 37: letter of intelligence, [May 1641].

228 For the collapse of the grandstand near the Beauchamp Tower, see Hollar, *The True Maner of the Execution of Thomas Earle of Strafford*.

229 BL, Harl. MS 477 (Moore diary), fos. 66v–67.

230 *Briefe and Perfect Relation*, p. 98 (*recte* 108); Rushworth, *Historical Collections*, III, 1, 269; F. P. Verney and M. M. Verney, *Memoirs of the Verney Family during the Seventeenth Century*, 2 vols. (1904), I, 206. Strafford's *sangfroid* won critics as well as admirers; one newsletter-writer noted that while some praised his courage, 'Others judg that in all this bravery he still shewed more of the Stoicke then of the pious Christian; much affectation, little sincerity'; BL, Sloane MS 1467 (Newsletters, 1640–41), fo. 37.

11. THE ELEPHANT AND THE DROMEDARY

1 Robert Henryson, *The Morall Fabl[es] of Esope* (Edinburgh, 1621), p. 31 (*STC2* 186). This was the version of Aesop's *Fables* that would have been familiar to the Earl of Montrose and, possibly, to Charles I; see *Certaine Instructions given by the L. Montrose, L. Nappier, Laerd of Keer and Blackhall* ([late June–July] 1641), pp. 3–4 (BL, E 160/26).

2 BL, Harl. MS 163 (D'Ewes diary), fo. 200v.

3 Ibid.

4 This account of the incident is principally based on BL, Harl. MS 163 (D'Ewes diary), fo. 200v, though D'Ewes confuses the names of some of the members with whom he was less familiar. For another account, see BL, Sloane MS 1467 (Newsletters, 1640–41), fo. 74. For Mansell, who was knighted by the 2nd Earl of Essex in 1596, see Andrew Thrush, 'Sir Robert Mansell', *ODNB*.

5 BL, Harl. MS 163 (D'Ewes diary), fo. 200v. Another report, apparently based on hearsay, ascribed the problem to the collapse of part of the ceiling in the gallery; BL, Sloane MS 1467 (Newsletters, 1640–41), fo. 74. The fact that so many of those whom D'Ewes names as being in or near the gallery were West Country men suggests that this was may have been their accustomed seating place within the House. A number of members seem to have had designated seats; D'Ewes's 'constant place', for instance, was at the 'upper end of the howse' – i.e. the end near the Speaker's chair, where the chapel's large east-end window would have provided the best light for note-taking: BL, Harl. MS 163 (D'Ewes diary), fo. 200v.

6 Ibid., fo. 201.

7 [Robert Chestlin], *Persecutio Undecima. The Churches Eleventh Persecution* ([5 November] 1648), p. 7 (BL, E 470/7); for his parish, see *CJ*, II, 853, 865.

8 HMC, *Cowper Manuscripts*, II, 282–3. (I owe this reference to Mr Christopher Thompson.)

9 *CJ*, II, 135.

10 Warwickshire RO, Warwick Castle MS, OR 1886/CUP.4/21A (John Halford's Accounts, I), unfol., 'Forrayne Payments'. The later payments listed here are dated precisely to 15 May 1641; the payments for arms listed immediately before that entry date from the period immediately before that date. The work on gunnery is almost certainly Thomas Smith's *The Art of Gunnery wherein is set forth a Number of Seruiceable Secrets, and Practicall Conclusions* (1600), STC2 22855.5.

11 Ann Hughes, *Politics, Society and Civil War in Warwickshire, 1620–60* (Cambridge, 1987), p. 137, n. 81.

12 Other preparations at Warwick Castle included expenditure on the armoury. There, the local cutler was paid for 'cleanse[ing]' (polishing) the armour and a total of ten metal files were purchased for sharpening swords and halberds; Warwickshire RO, Warwick Castle MS, OR 1886/CUP.4/21A (John Halford's Accounts, I), unfol., 'Forrayne Payments'.

13 For the witnesses' depositions, signed by Warwick and Essex, see PA, Braye MS 2 (Letters and Papers, 1637–41), fos. 147–8,

149–50, 156–7 (*Exact Collection*, pp. 220, 223, 232). The bicameral committee to conduct these examinations, which had been appointed on 5 May, comprised ten Lords and twenty Commoners: BL, Harl. MS 6424 (Bishop Warner's diary), fo. 62r-v. The Lords were the Earls of Bath, Essex, Warwick, March (i.e. the Duke of Lennox), Viscount Saye, and Lords Wharton, Paget, Kimbolton (i.e. Viscount Mandeville), Howard of Charlton and Howard of Escrick: *LJ*, IV, 235. Only failed to sign the Petition of the Twelve Peers; see Appendix.

14 Hence, the (evidentially very dubious) revelation that the bishops had promised to fund the use of the king's army against Parliament, for example, was disclosed in early June to coincide with a new campaign for thoroughgoing ecclesiastical reform, the centrepiece of which was the whole abolition of all English and Welsh bishops; see *Certaine Instructions*, p. 7 (BL, E 160/26), where it is claimed that the bishops were to raise 2,000 horse; see also ASV, Senato, Dispacci Inghil. 42, fo. 308v: Giustinian to the Doge and Senate, 11/21 June 1641 (*CSPV 1640–42*, p. 163). For the role of the Warwick House group in the renewed campaign for the bishops' abolition, see pp. 329–31.

15 For the report to the Commons, see BL, Harl. MS 163 (D'Ewes diary), fos. 313v–317v; ASV, Senato, Dispacci Inghil. 42, fos. 308v–309: Giustinian to the Doge and Senate, 11/21 June 1641 (*CSPV 1640–42*, p. 163); *Certaine Instructions*, pp. 6–7 (BL, E 160/26).

16 ASV, Senato, Dispacci Inghil. 42, fo. 308v: Giustinian to the Doge and Senate, 11/21 June (*CSPV 1640–42*, p. 163).

17 *The Autobiography of Sir John Bramston* (1845), p. 75.

18 Clarendon, *Rebellion*, I, 263n. Hyde also includes Mandeville in this Bedfordian managerial group, though most of the surviving evidence locates him rather closer to Warwick than Bedford in the period up to May 1641, and even closer to Warwick thereafter. See above, p. 226, for Mandeville taking an essentially anti-Bedfordian line over the Strafford impeachment.

19 ASV, Senato, Dispacci Inghil. 43, fos. 2v–3r: Giustinian to the Doge and Senate, 22 July/2 August 1641: 'Le quali di Ré non gli

lasciar altro che il solo titolo, spogliato di credito, e nudo d'ogni auttorità' (cf. *CSPV 1640–42*, p. 187). From Warwick's perspective, the king's actions could not have been better calculated to vindicate the case he had been making, at least since early February: that Strafford was too dangerous to remain alive, and that only by inflicting exemplary punishment on the malefactors of the old régime could the commonwealth be made safe for the future. This insistence that the king should be left with the mere title of king was at one with Argyll's position in Scotland, and became the issue of contention between Argyll and the royalist Plotters. (I am grateful to Professor Allan Macinness for a discussion of this point.)

20 NAS, Hamilton MS, GD 406/1/1419: Earl of Essex to the Marquess of Hamilton, 30 August 1641.

21 Arthur Wilson, *The History of Great Britain being the Life and Reign of King James the First* (1653), p. 162 (Wing W2888).

22 John Adamson, 'The Baronial Context of the English Civil War', *Transactions of the Royal Historical Society*, 5th ser., 40 (1990), 93–120.

23 *CJ*, II, 182.

24 BL, Harl. MS 477 (Moore diary), fo. 27v.

25 At least until the May crisis, both peers appear to have preferred for Strafford to be impeached, and his life spared. In the final votes on the attainder bill, however, Pembroke seems actually to have voted in favour of Strafford's execution; Northumberland appears either to have abstained or voted against the attainder. (The clearest clue to his voting, perhaps, is the decision of his secretary, Robert Scawen, to vote against the attainder in the Commons); see John Adamson, 'Of Armies and Architecture: the Employments of Robert Scawen', in Ian Gentles, John Morrill and Blair Worden (eds.), *Soldiers, Writers, and Statesmen of the English Revolution* (Cambridge, 1998), pp. 36–41.

26 Clarendon, *Rebellion*, I, 354–5; ASV, Senato, Dispacci Inghil. 42, fos. 315–6: Giustinian to the Doge and Senate, 18/28 June 1641 (*CSPV 1640–42*, p. 166).

27 For the usage, see Allan I. Macinnes, *Charles I and the Covenanting Movement,*

1625–41 (Edinburgh, 1991), p. 199.

28 Thomas Herbert [pseudonym?], *Vox Secunda Populi. Or, The Commons Gratitude to the Most Honorable Philip, Earl of Pembroke and Mongomery* [sic], *for the Great Affection which hee alwaies bore unto them* ([June] 1641), p. 4 (BL, E 164/21). For Pembroke's 'punishment' for his 'affection' towards the Junto, see Clarendon, *Rebellion*, I, 345; and NA, SP 16/482, fo. 178: Thomas Wiseman to Sir John Pennington, 29 July 1641.

29 NAS, Hamilton MS GD 406/1/1387: Earl of Holland to Marquess of Hamilton, 16 September 1641; GD 406/1/1405: Earl of Essex to Hamilton, 11 August 1641; GD 406/1/1409: Viscount Mandeville to Hamilton, 18 August 1641; GD 406/1/1410: Earl of Essex to Hamilton, 20 August 1641; GD 406/1/1412: Mandeville to Hamilton, 20 August 1640 [*recte* 1641]; GD 406/1/1424: Essex to Marquess of Hamilton, 7 September 1641. Marchmont Nedham later claimed that Hamilton had been working closely with the king's enemies from the beginning of the Parliament, though the polemical context in which he made these claims requires that they be regarded with caution; see his *Digitus Dei: or God's Justice upon Treachery and Treason* ([9 April] 1649), p. 12 (BL, E 550/6). I am grateful to Dr David Scott for alerting to me to this reference.

30 For the activities of Pembroke, Northumberland, Hamilton, and Holland during the 1630s, the best amount is Sharpe, *The Personal Rule of Charles I.*

31 Clarendon, *Rebellion*, I, 353–4. For a similar point, see Russell, *Causes of the English Civil War*, p. 209; the king's involvement in the Army Plot, argues Russell, 'went a long way towards convincing sober and responsible politicians that Charles was not fit to be trusted with power'.

32 For the controversy caused by Digby's speech and its subsequent publication, see *CJ*, II, 172; BL, Harl. MS 163 (D'Ewes diary), fo. 305v. For Bristol and Digby being reported as implicated in the May plotting, see *CSPV 1640–42*, p. 172. For the decline in Bristol's 'creditt … in both howses' and his consequent efforts to create an alliance with the royalist Duke of Lennox, see NA, SP 16/483, fo. 64r-v: [Thomas Smith, Northumberland's naval

secretary] to the Earl of Northumberland, 10 August 1641.

33 The extent of the Junto's dependency on the Scots' military support was, after all, obvious. Its challenge to royal authority in the summer of 1640, which had brought about the summons of the Parliament in November that year, would have been impossible without it. And, at least until the passing of the act preventing the Parliament's dissolution without its own consent, the Junto leadership had relied on the Scottish army to deter the king from attempting the Parliament's dissolution.

34 Surrey History Centre, Bray MS 52/2/19/8: Edward Nicholas to the king, 18 August 1641.

35 Stevenson, *The Scottish Revolution, 1637–42*, pp. 206–7.

36 David Stevenson, 'Archibald Campbell, 1st Marquess of Argyll', *ODNB*; Allan I. Macinnes, *Clanship, Commerce, and the House of Stuart, 1603–1788* (Edinburgh, 1996), p. 95. I am grateful to Professor Allan Macinnes for advice on the likely date of Argyll's birth.

37 Stevenson, 'Argyll'. From the Pacification of Berwick, the treaty which ended Charles's first war against the Covenanters, in June 1639, Argyll was regarded as *persona non grata* by the king, and was received icily when he attempted, after the conclusion of the treaty, to kiss the king's hands: Broughton Castle, Oxfordshire, Saye and Sele MS III/9b, fo. 1r-v: Sir John Temple to the Earl of Leicester, 20 June 1639 (printed in Collins, *Letters and Memorials* II, 603).

38 Stevenson, 'Argyll'.

39 For similar proposals that Essex might be appointed a temporary dictator in England in 1643, see [Henry Parker], *The Contra-Replicant, his Complaint to His Majestie* [31 January 1643], p. 19 (BL, E 87/5); also discussed in Michael Mendle, *Henry Parker and the English Civil War: the Political Thought of the Public's Privado* (Cambridge, 1995), p. 22.

40 James Gordon, *History of the Scots Affairs from* MDCXXXVII *to* MDCXLI, ed. J. Robertson and G. Grub, 3 vols. (Edinburgh, 1841), III, 182. I owe my knowledge of this source to Professor Stevenson.

41 Stevenson, 'Argyll' (for the quotation).

42 Gordon, *History of the Scots Affairs*, III, 200.

43 This testimony, offered by John Stewart the younger of Ladywell, and the fate of its author are discussed above, p. 347.

44 For the Cumbernauld Band, see Stevenson, *Scottish Revolution*, pp. 206–7; Donald, *Uncounselled King*, pp. 243–4.

45 Henry Guthrie, Bishop of Dunkeld, *Memoirs ... wherein the Conspiracies and Rebellion against King Charles I ... are briefly and faithfully related* (1702), p. 77. MS versions of the memoirs exist in the NLS, Advocates' MS 13. 2. 9; Beinecke Lib., Yale University, MS Osborn b. 169; Houghton Lib., Harvard University, MS Eng. 1078.

46 Stevenson, *Scottish Revolution*, p. 225.

47 Ibid., pp. 224–5.

48 [Lord Napier on sovereign power, *c.* 1641–3]; printed in Mark Napier, *Memorials of Montrose and his Times*, 2 vols. (Edinburgh, 1848), I, 286.

49 BL, Sloane MS 1467 (Newsletters, 1640–41), fo. 102: letter of intelligence, [June 1641] (for Stewart's cousinage with Traquair).

50 Buckminster Park, Lincolnshire, Tollemache MS 3748: summary transcript of the interrogation of Lieutenant-Colonel Walter Stewart before Lord Balmerino, Sir Thomas Hope, and Edward Edgar, 5 June 1641.

51 Ibid. (my emphasis).

52 Broughton Castle, Oxfordshire, Saye and Sele MS III/9b, fo. 1r-v: Sir John Temple to the Earl of Leicester, 20 June 1639 (printed in Collins, *Letters and Memorials*, II, 603).

53 It should be noted, however, that Montrose had probably been in covert communication with Charles from the time of the Pacification of Berwick in the summer of 1639 (a point I owe to Professor Allan Macinnes).

54 Buckminster Park, Lincolnshire, Tollemache MS 3748 (for the 'instructiones'). Professor Russell's claim that 'the king, by 3 March [1641], was negotiating ... with the Covenanters' Scottish enemies' – whom he later discloses as Montrose and Walter Stewart – seems unsustainable. As Montrose himself realized, Charles had an ingrained prejudice against dealing with 'rebels', and, though some approaches were made by Montrose in March, these were not initially addressed to the king. It was probably not until April at the earliest that Charles (and those whom Montrose was relying upon to act as his intermediaries at court) began to take Montrose's offers seriously; compare Russell, *Fall of the British Monarchies*, pp. 272 (for the quotation) and 312. When Lieutenant-Colonel Stewart set out on his first mission to London in early March, 'he carried no letters from the Erle of Montrose, nether did he subscrybe the instructiones, least they s[h]ould be intercepted': Tollemache MS 3748.

55 HMC, *Ninth Report*, Appendix, II, 255: declaration or deposition by Sir Richard Graham [of Netherby], undated [second half of 1641], in the Traquair House MSS.

56 NLS, MS Wodrow Folio 65, fo. 72r-v; printed as *Certaine Instructions given by the L. Montrose, L. Nappier, Laerd of Keer and Blackhall* ([late June–July] 1641), pp. 3–4 (BL, E 160/26). The printing of these *Instructions* was almost certainly at the behest of the English Lords Commissioners for the Treaty or their Commons allies, to whom they were reported in June; BL, Harl. MS 163 (D'Ewes diary), fo. 339v.

57 NA, SO 3/12 (Signet Office Docket Book), fo. 110, for details of Lennox's loans to the king.

58 Buckminster Park, Lincolnshire, Tollemache MS 3748; *Certaine Instructions*, p. 3 (for the text of the instructions); BL, Harl. MS 163 (D'Ewes diary), fo. 339v.

59 *Certaine Instructions*, p. 3 (for quotation). Montrose's own code word in the instructions is 'Genero', one of the many Spanish borrowings (*género* meaning 'kind' or *genus* in Latin) that were fashionable during the period (*junta* or 'junto' being the most obvious); its connection with 'the elephant' seems to come from Henryson's translation of Aesop's *Fables*, in which Aesop lists the various 'kinds' of beast that come before the Lion King: Robert Henryson, *The Morall Fabl[es] of Esope* (Edinburgh, 1621), p. 31 (STC2 186). The elephant and the dromedary were examples of the largest and proudest

beasts, and Montrose and his circle seem to have used them interchangeably for Argyll.

60 NLS, MS Wodrow Folio 65, fo. 72r-v; *Certaine Instructions*, pp. 3–4.

61 Buckminster Park, Lincolnshire, Tollemache MS 3748.

62 These, together with Charles's refusal to ratify the proceedings of the 1639 General Assembly of the Kirk, were outstanding Covenanter grievances from the last Anglo-Scottish treaty, at Berwick in June 1639; see Broughton Castle, Oxfordshire, Saye and Sele MS III/9b, fo. 1r-v: Sir John Temple to the Earl of Leicester, 20 June 1639 (printed in Collins, *Letters and Memorials*, ii, 603).

63 *Certaine Instructions*, p. 3. Russell (*Fall of the British Monarchies*, pp. 312, 313) cites NLS, MS Wodrow Folio 65, fo. 72, to the effect that the instructions say that 'offices [in Scotland] should not be bestowed by the advice of Hamilton, "lest he crush the king"'. What the text actually says is that these offices should not be bestowed 'by advice of the Elephant', and the 'Elephant' cannot refer to Hamilton because, only a few lines later, he is referred to straightforwardly by his title as 'the Marquesse' (a reference which can only be to the Marquess of Hamilton, as at this point Argyll was still an earl, and none of the other peers with the rank of marquess is contextually plausible).

64 For 'L.' (i.e. the Lion), being the code letter for the king, see Buckminster Park, Lincolnshire, Tollemache MS 3748.

65 Henryson, *The Morall Fabl[es] of Esope*, pp. 31, 33 (STC2 186). This was the version of Aesop's *Fables* that would have been familiar to the Earl of Montrose and, possibly, to Charles I; see *Certaine Instructions*, pp. 3–4 (BL, E 160/26).

66 Buckminster Park, Lincolnshire, Tollemache MS 3748; for the charge against Argyll, see above, pp. 314–5, 332–3.

67 Ibid.; for another version of these allegations, see NLS, MS Wodrow Folio 65, fos. 60, 85.

68 Macinnes, *Charles I and the Covenanting Movement*, p. [ii].

69 Buckminster Park, Lincolnshire, Tollemache MS 3748.

70 Ibid.

71 Ibid.

72 On the ideas of the plotters and Lord Napier, their principal 'theorist', see Stevenson, *Scottish Revolution*, pp. 225–6. Napier's 'Letter on Sovereign Power' (often misattributed to Montrose), though possibly written slightly after 1641, seems to provide some indication of the attitudes prevailing in Montrose's circle during the early 1640s; for the surviving copy of the text see NLS, MS Wodrow Quarto 40, no. 2; printed in Mark Napier, *Life and Times of Montrose* (Edinburgh, 1840), p. 157. For the attribution of this text to Lord Napier, see Stevenson, *Scottish Revolution*, pp. 365–6. As Sir John Suckling had put it presciently, early in the conflict, he believed 'the question to be rather a Kinge or noe Kinge there [in Scotland]'; religion was merely being used as a 'visor' (a vizard or mask). Almost wantonly godless himself, Suckling is an unreliable guide to the sincerity of others' religious convictions; as a description of the issues at stake within the Covenanter leadership after its initial military successes of 1639 and 1640, his assessment nevertheless rings true; Beinecke Lib., Yale University, Gordenstoun Family Papers, Box 1 (*c.* 1630–89), unfol.: Sir John Suckling to anon. [undated, *c.* 1640–41].

73 Charles's acceptance of this principle had major implications for the status of bishops within the English Church. For by agreeing to 'Root-and-Branch' reform in Scotland, Charles was implicitly acknowledging that the system of governing the Church through bishops did not exist 'by divine right' – or, in the Latin phrase by which it was known in contemporary debate, *iure divino*: the system of Church government established by Christ himself. By accepting Root-and-Branch in Scotland – at first, presumably privately in his undertakings to Montrose, and then publicly by his ratification of the Covenanter Church reforms in the Scottish Parliament in the autumn of 1641 – Charles profoundly weakened the claims of the English episcopate to exist *iure divino*, as the Laudians and others had claimed.

74 For Warwick's efforts (with Sir Thomas Barrington) to raise the county in 1642, see [Robert Chestlin], *Persecutio Undecima. The Churches Eleventh Persecution* ([5 November] 1648), p. 67 (BL, E 470/7); for the

Artillery Company, see ibid., p. 56, and above, Ch. 2.

75 Walter Stewart's deposition of 5 June 1641 makes it clear that Traquair and Lennox were both, initially, very reluctant to commit themselves to join with Montrose. Both seem to have tried to use the correspondence with Montrose in order to avert any attempts in Scotland to bring down the Earl of Traquair: Buckminster Park, Lincolnshire, Tollemache MS 3748.

76 Ibid. Broxmouth House was the residence of the Earl of Roxburgh, with whom Montrose was evidently staying at the time.

77 Ibid.

78 Ibid.

79 Ibid.

80 Ibid.

81 *CJ*, II, 125.

82 Mark Napier, *Montrose and the Covenanters*, 2 vols. (Edinburgh, 1838), I, 354, 357, 367; VAL, Forster MS 39 (Elector Palatine corr.): Prince Charles Lewis to Queen Elizabeth of Bohemia, 18/28 May 1641.

83 HMC, *Maxwell Stirling Maxwell Manuscripts*, p. 78: William Drummond of Riccarton to Sir George Stirling of Keir, 12 May 1641. For the king's decision, see ASV, Senato, Dispacci Inghil. 42, fo. 291v: Giustinian to the Doge and Senate, 21/31 May 1641 (*CSPV 1640–42*, p. 153); also Edinburgh UL, MS Dc. 4. 16, fo. 107v. Russell's claim that 'the king's journey to Scotland became public knowledge on 21 April' (*Fall of the British Monarchies*, p. 289n) exaggerates slightly, as the initial raising of the subject with the Scottish Commissioners appears to have been far more tentative and speculative than this would suggest.

84 ASV, Senato, Dispacci Inghil. 42, fo. 291v: Giustinian to the Doge and Senate, 21/31 May 1641 (*CSPV 1640–42*, p. 153), where Giustinian conjectured that the visit was 'to set in motion some other design by his presence [in Edinburgh] and to improve his authority'.

85 That said, the Warwick House group almost certainly knew enough about Scottish domestic politics to have regarded Montrose with suspicion. Jhonston of Wariston was already doubtful of his intentions by April, and, mostly likely, shared these reservations with his English friends; see Donald, *Uncounselled King*, p. 296.

86 ASV, Senato, Dispacci Inghil. 42, fo. 291v.

87 Perhaps significantly, this was the day after Bedford's funeral (which was held on the 14th) and three days after Strafford's execution.

88 Warwickshire RO, Warwick Castle MS, OR 1886/CUP.4/21A (John Halford's Accounts, I), unfol., 'Forrayne Payments', purchases made on 15 May 1641. Brooke did not neglect his armoury at Warwick Castle, his country seat; there, the local cutler was paid for 'cleanse[ing]' (polishing) the armour and a total of ten metal files were purchased for sharpening swords and halberds.

89 On 11 May 1641, the Commons belatedly resolved to raise £400,000, a larger sum than had been advanced by any previous Parliament, towards meeting their financial obligations; but this remained merely a 'resolution', and no further steps were taken to turn that resolve into a concrete proposal for the raising of funds; *CJ*, II, 143. The member who moved it was Arthur Goodwin, the father-in-law of the strongly pro-Scottish Junto grandee, Lord Wharton, himself one of the English Treaty Commissioners negotiating with the Scots. It is tempting to see Wharton and his Treaty Commissioner friends behind Goodwin's motion; see BL, Harl. MS 163 (D'Ewes diary), fo. 208 (for Goodwin's motion) and BL, Harl. MS 457 (Minutes of the Anglo-Scottish Treaty, 1640–41), fo. 51v (for Wharton's membership of Warwick's committee of Treaty Commissioners involved in Strafford's trial). For the Scots' pay, see also NA, SP 16/480, fo. 116r-v.

90 Beinecke Lib., Yale, MS Osborn Shelves fb 94, Folder 7: Sir Thomas Peyton to Robert Hales, 29 April 1641.

91 The Scottish Commissioners, meanwhile, were upping their financial demands. A list of grievances, presented to the Commons on 22 May, now claimed payment for their army backdated to June 1640 (the date when they had 'set out'), thereby going back on an earlier agreement that their army should be paid only from October 1640 (the date when the Anglo-Scottish peace talks had begun). 'The

[Scottish] nobilitie', they protested, 'had solde and ingaged ther estates' to pay for the war. BL, Harl. MS 163 (D'Ewes diary), fo. 224 (for the details); the Scottish Commissioners' paper is merely mentioned in *CJ*, II, 155.

92 Stevenson, *Scottish Revolution*, p. 221; Peter Donald, 'New Light on the Anglo-Scottish Contacts of 1640', *Historical Research*, 62 (1989), 221–9;

93 For the text, see 'The desiers of the Scottish Commissioners concerninge Unity of Religion 1640 [i.c. 1641]', 10 March 1641: BL, Add. MS 70003 (Harley Papers), fos. 64–73v; this is Sir Robert Harley's copy. See also Lord Paget's copy of the Scottish Commissioners' response on Church government: Plas Newydd, Anglesey, Muniment Room Box XIV (Papers of the 5th Lord Paget), fos. 59–60.

94 'William Drake's Parliamentary Notebook', in Jansson, *Two Diaries*, p. 49. The passage is noted as 'anonymous' by the editor, but from the context would seem to be an extract from one of the Scottish Commissioners' paper on conformity in religion, first presented to the English Treaty Commissioners on 10 March 1641; compare 'whatsoever peace shall be agreed upon, we cannot see nor conceive the way how our peace shall be firme and durable ... if Episopacie shall be retained in England': [Alexander Henderson?], *Arguments given in by the Commissioners of Scotland unto the Lords of the Treaty, perswading Conformitie of Church Government, as one Principall Meanes of a Continued Peace betweene the Two Nations* ([May] 1641), p. 8 (BL, E 157/2).

95 BL, Add. MS 70003 (Harley Papers), fos. 64–73v. It was probably drafted by Alexander Henderson, Argyll's main protégé among the clergy accompanying the Scottish Commissioners in London, and published, without a named printer, in May as *Arguments given in by the Commissioners of Scotland unto the Lords of the Treaty, perswading Conformitie of Church Government, as one Principall Meanes of a Continued Peace betweene the Two Nations* ([May] 1641), especially pp. 7–9 (BL, E 157/2).

96 Holland (and probably Warwick as well) had offered the Scottish Commissioners a private gesture of solidarity in conniving at the publication of their manifesto of 24 February 1641, with its explicit call for the eradication of bishops; see *From the Commissioners of Scotland, 24 February, 1640[–41]* (24 February 1641), single sheet (BL, 669 f. 3/4). On the background see above, Ch. 7.

97 For Calamy's role in the Remonstrance campaign see Edmund Calamy, *A Just and Necessary Apology* (1646), p. 9 (BL, E 319/25).

98 A. G. Matthews (ed.), *Calamy Revised: being a Revision of Edmund Calamy's* Account *of the Ministers and Others ejected and silenced, 1660–62* (Oxford, 1934), p. l.

99 Yet what was hopeful to Calamy (and therefore presumably to Warwick) was anathema to the Scots. 'Modified episcopacy' was proposed by Ussher and Williams was exactly the reformist halfway house that Loudoun and his fellow Scottish Commissioners had denounced as unacceptable in their representations of early March.

100 This group seems to have included, at very least, Lord Loudoun (Argyll's kinsman); the Earl of Rothes (the son-in-law of the Covenanter commander-in-chief, Alexander Leslie); Archibald Jhonston of Wariston; and Alexander Henderson, the representative of the General Assembly of the Scottish Kirk. The relations between Argyll and the Earl of Dunfermline, the only other peer among the Scottish Treaty Commissioners, are more difficult to assess; but Robert Baillie, one of the Scottish divines accompanying his countrymen, believed that he was thought too favourable towards the king. Dunfermline's omission, in July 1641, from the list of commissioners authorized by the Scottish Parliament to sign the final treaty would suggest that, by this point at least, he was in ill odour with the Argyllian interest in Edinburgh. For the suspicions of Dunfermline, see Baillie, *Letters*, I, 380; for the authorization of the Scottish Commissioners, see *Acts of the Parliament of Scotland*, v, 316–17, 629–30, 641–2; *LJ*, IV, 356–7.

101 Surrey History Centre, Bray MS 52/2/19/8: Edward Nicholas to the king, 18 August 1641.

102 Donald, *Uncounselled King*, p. 300.

103 *CJ*, II, 177–8: Sir John Hotham's report from the Commons' Committee for the King's Army, 17 June 1641.

104 *CJ*, II, 160.

105 For Hotham, see David Scott, '"Hannibal at Our Gates": Loyalists and Fifth-Columnists during the Bishops' Wars – the Case of Yorkshire', *Historical Research*, 70 (1997), 269–93. I am grateful for Dr Scott's advice on Hotham's allegiances.

106 *CJ*, II, 177–8. Warwick's clientele also seems to have taken a major role in the passing of the financial legislation of 1641, on the security of which funds were raised for payment into the treasury at Warwick House; see, for example, Sir Thomas Barrington's carrying of the Tonnage and Poundage bill to the House of Lords on 18 June 1641 – the day after the Commons' report on the sums owed to the Scottish and English armies; *CJ*, II, 178. Another, which passed the Commons on 10 August 1641, allowing collection of Tonnage and Poundage for a further three months, was claimed by Sir Henry Mildmay (another member associated with Warwick's 'interest') to be 'more my worke then any man's in the worlde': NAS, Hamilton MS GD 406/1/1411: Sir Henry Mildmay to the Marquess of Hamilton, 20 August 1641; *CJ*, II, 238–9, 244, 249, 250 (for the bill).

107 *CJ*, II, 178: some £165,000, or around a sixth of the total. One of the incidental consequences of this earmarking of the customs revenues for the payment of the armies was that it prevented the crown from repaying the Earl of Newcastle the loan of £10,000 he had advanced the king in 1640, secured on the 'new impositions on strangers' goods' (the so-called New Customs); NA, SO 3/12 (Signet Office Docket Book), fo. 78v.

108 *CJ*, II, 178.

109 Ibid., pp. 179–80; for Vane's involvement, see Russell, *Fall of the British Monarchies*, p. 336.

110 For the unpopularity of the Scottish levies and the reluctance of Londoners to lend on their security, see Centre for Kentish Studies, De L'Isle MS U1475/C114/22: Sir John Temple to the Earl of Leicester, 29 July 1641 (HMC, *De L'Isle Manuscripts*, VI, 406).

111 Michael J. Braddick, *The Nerves of State: Taxation and the Financing of the English State, 1558–1714* (Manchester, 1996), pp. 12–16; and his, *State Formation in Early Modern England*, c. 1550–1700 (Cambridge, 2000), pp. 213–21.

112 D. H. Pennington, 'The Making of the War, 1640–42', in D. H. Pennington and Keith Thomas (eds.), *Puritans and Revolutionaries: Essays in Seventeenth-Century History presented to Christopher Hill* (Oxford, 1978), pp. 161–85; see p. 172 for

113 NA, SP 16/479, fo. 116: Sir William Uvedale to Matthew Bradley, 20 April 1641.

114 The key development seems to have come at the end of December 1640, when, taking advantage of Bedford's absence through illness, Warwick appears to have set up a seven-man committee, headed by himself, 'to audite the accounts of the moneys' sent for the relief of counties occupied by the Scottish army, and 'to treate with any Comittees of the Commons house as shall be appointed' to deal with these funds. The Treaty Commissioners' audit committee, established on 21 December, comprised the Earls of Warwick and Holland (brothers), Viscount Mandeville (Warwick's son-in-law), Lord Paget (Holland's son-in-law), together with the Earl of Berkshire, and Lords Wharton and Poulett: BL, Harl. MS 457 (Minutes of the Anglo-Scottish Treaty, 1640–41), fo. 36. A month late, the quorum of this committee was conveniently reduced to three, making it possible for a far smaller group – in practice, just Warwick, Holland, and Mandeville – to deal directly with the Commons on the arrangements for the Scottish army's supply; BL, Harl. MS 457 (Minutes of the Anglo-Scottish Treaty, 1640–1), entry for 19 January 1641. As Warwick's accounts reveal, the trio of Holland, Mandeville, and Warwick himself had already been the active quorum even before the order of 19 January; see NA, SP 46/80 (State Papers, supplementary), fo. 171: receipts signed by the Scottish Commissioners for sums received on 28 December 1640 and 9 January 1641 from Warwick, Holland, and Mandeville. Equipped with his fellow Treaty Commissioners' order of 19 January, Warwick was able to exploit his position as a Commissioner to establish lines of communication with the Commons that entirely circumvented the procedures usually governing formal contacts between the two Houses. (I am deeply grateful to Mr

Christopher Thompson for loaning me his transcription of these accounts in SP 46/80.)

115 NA, SP 16/483, fos. 90v-91r: Earl of Warwick's accounts for the sums received by him over the period 28 December 1640-13 August 1641.

116 NA, SP 46/80 (State Papers, supplementary), fo. 171.

117 BL, Harl. MS 163 (D'Ewes diary), fo. 207; CJ, II, 142. There seems to have been almost a competition between the Warwick House group and a 'king's party' (led by Bristol) as to which group could appear to be more solicitous as to the Scots' concerns. Unsurprisingly, Sir Robert Harley (who seems to have voted with the Warwick House interest) took the message to the Lords on 19 May, requesting that they join in a bicameral committee 'for the ascertaining and perfecting [of] the accompts between the Scotts and the northern counties'; CJ, II, 151.

118 NA, SP 46/80 (State Papers, supplementary), fo. 175: receipt from the Scottish Commissioners (the signatories include Rothes, Dunfermline, and Loudoun) for £25,000 received between 6 and 20 March 1641; ibid., fo. 178: receipt from the Scottish Commissioners for £30,000, 18, 24, and 31 May 1641.

119 This was a little more than half the total of £220,750 due to them since 16 October 1640, when the English Treaty Commissioners had first agreed to take responsibility for the Scottish army's pay; NA, SP 16/483, fos. 90v-91r. For the payments from Warwick to the Scottish Commissioners in June and July see NA, SP 46/80 (State Papers, supplementary), fos. 180, 181v, 182, 184r-v.

120 BL, Harl. MS 163 (D'Ewes diary), fo. 323; CJ, II, 177; NA, SP 16/483, fo. 90v-91r.

121 CJ, II, 235; NA, SP 16/483, fos. 90v-91r. This latter account, sworn before William Prynne and Fenton Parsons (members of the Committee for Taking the Accounts of the Kingdom), on 2 March 1647, includes only part of the total, but even this lists instalments totalling £291,361 19s. 4d.

122 This had particular relevance in the case of the Covenanter army in England, where Montrose's fellow Banders commanded a number of the regiments in the army. Guthrie, Memoirs, pp. 77-8.

123 BL, Harl. MS 163 (D'Ewes diary), fo. 322v. Perhaps unsurprisingly, only part of the archive for these disbursements seems to have survived; see NA, SP 46/80 (State Papers, supplementary), fos. 171-92v. Warwick's 1647 discharge from the Committee of Accounts, a Presbyterian-controlled body, dominated by William Prynne, seems to have been highly irregular, as Warwick was granted his discharge merely 'upon Oath', without ever needing to present detailed written accounts as evidence of his receipts and disbursements; NA, SP 16/483, fos. 90v-91r. If one is trying to reconstruct what happened in the administration of these funds, the most likely scenario is that William Jessop – Warwick's secretary and homme d'affaires, and the Providence Island Company's main administrator – dealt with the relevant accounting and bookwork. From December 1640, Jessop (who, on Warwick's orders, had organized the copying and distribution of the Petition of the Twelve Peers in September that year) effectively became a parallel Treasurer-at-War (duplicating for Warwick and the Scots' army what Sir William Uvedale did for the king and the English army). For Jessop's activities at the Providence Island Company, see NA, CO 124/2, fos. 1v, 186; PA, Willcocks MS 2/1/42: William Jessop to Viscount Mandeville, 2 October 1639.

124 In this respect, the developments at Warwick House parallel the way in which the Privy Council was almost entirely superseded during the same period, with its deliberative functions being usurped by the new cadre of Junto grandees, meeting informally, while many of its formal functions – such as its role in dealing with individual petitioners – were taken over by standing committees of the House of Lords; for the Lords and petitions, see James S. Hart, Justice upon Petition: the House of Lords and the Reformation of Justice, 1621-75 (1991), Chs. 2-4; esp. p. 65.

125 BL, Sloane MS 1467 (Newsletters, 1640-41), fo. 76: the Treasury Commissioners were all 'Protestant' members of the Privy Council, who were probably sympathetic towards the Junto's Bedfordian wing: the Lord Keeper (Lord Lyttelton), Lord Privy Seal (the 1st Earl of Manchester), Lord Chief Justice (Sir John Bankes), Lord Newburgh, and Sir Henry Vane, senior. See also, ASV, Senato, Dispacci Inghil. 42, fo. 292v: Giustinian to

the Doge and Senate, 21/31 May 1641 (*CSPV 1640–42*, p. 154).

126 John Morrill, 'Robert Devereux, 3rd Earl of Essex', *ODNB*.

127 Warwick's archive survives only in a fragmented state (e.g. BL, Harl. MS 4712), most of it having been destroyed after the death of the 4th Earl of Warwick's widow in 1678. What must have been extensive financial records relating to the payment of the Scots have been lost. We can only conjecture, therefore, on the nature of the warrants they received for payment. However, if these followed the pattern familiar from other similar warrants, they would have been drawn up by a secretary (probably William Jessop), and signed by the officer or individual authorizing the payment (in this case, Warwick). Similar examples are legion in the series of pay warrants in NA, SP 28.

128 NA, SP 46/80 (State Papers, supplementary), fo. 191: the receipt (signed by Lord Loudoun, Hew Kennedy and John Smyth), is dated 14 August 1641. Of this £80,000 the Scots actually received only £41,111 19s. 4d., the remainder (just over £38,000) being reserved (with Warwick) for the payment for the Scots' debts incurred in the counties of Northumberland, Durham, and the town of Newcastle.

129 BL, Harl. MS 5047 (Anon. diary), fo. 60v.

130 Macinnes, *Charles I and the Covenanting Movement*, p. 203.

131 BL, Harl. MS 163 (D'Ewes diary), fo. 339; *CJ*, II, 182. Warwick's allies in the Commons positioned him to exercise effective control over the commonwealth's future financial dealings with the Scots. When, on 21 June 1641, the Covenanter Commissioners asked to whom they should address themselves when future instalments of the Brotherly Assistance were due, the Commons promptly nominated a commission of eight peers and sixteen Commons-men. Predictably, Warwick was nominated first (even though several of the other earls were owed precedence before him), and of the other peers – all Junto grandees – half were members of his immediate family. The list of sixteen Commons-men was characterized by an equally strong representation of Warwick's friends – beginning, as D'Ewes noted, with

'Sir Thomas Barrington, who sate next [to] mee'. Sir Arthur Hesilrige, perhaps Warwick's most effective ally of all, duly saw that these future instalments of the Brotherly Assistance had the copper-bottomed guarantee of an Act of Parliament. The commission that would oversee the future payments of the Brotherly Assistance to the Scots consisted (in the order listed in the Commons' Journal), of the Earl of Warwick, Viscount Mandeville (his son-in-law), the Earl of Bedford (the fifth Earl, who had succeeded in May 1641), Essex (Warwick's first cousin), Holland (Warwick's brother), and Stamford, and Lords Wharton and Brooke (the latter a friend and neighbour in Holborn). From the Commons were Sir Thomas Barrington, Sir Gilbert Gerard, Sir Henry Mildmay, and John Hampden (all closely associated with Warwick House); Sir Thomas Cheeke (Warwick's brother-in-law); Arthur Capell (a kinsman of Mandeville's and supporter of the Petition of the Twelve), Arthur Goodwin (Wharton's father-in-law), Sir Arthur Ingram (Holland's business partner), Sir Robert Pye (a long-standing Pembroke client), Sir Walter Erle (whose son was married to Saye's daughter), Alderman Isaac Penington (the Junto's principal ally in the City), and five others: Alderman Thomas Soame, Henry Marten, and Sir John Strangways, Sir William Lytton, and Henry Belasyse. For Hesilrige and the bill for securing the Brotherly Assistance on the 'public faith', see *CJ*, II, 248; his relations with Warwick and Brooke are discussed elsewhere in this book, see especially, pp. 242–6.

132 Guthrie, *Memoirs*, p. 83.

133 *CJ*, II, 148: the Commons' resolution on 17 May 1641, on hearing the report of the English Treaty Commissioners, dated 15 March 1641. For the debate, see D'Ewes's diary entries for 17 May. See also *Acts of the Parliament of Scotland*, v, 340 (quoted in Stevenson, *Scottish Revolution*, p. 221); and C. L. Hamilton, 'The Basis for Scottish Efforts to create a Reformed Church in England, 1640–41', *Church History*, 30 (1961), 171–8.

134 *CJ*, II, 148 (for the quotation).

135 BL, Harl. MS 163 (D'Ewes diary), fo. 192.

136 Clarendon, *Rebellion*, I, 263n.

137 BL, Harl. MS 163 (D'Ewes diary), fo. 191. The debate of 17 May resulted only in

the bland resolution (which had no legislative force) that the House approved of the Scots' 'desire of a conformity in Church government between the two nations' and that they would proceed with the mater 'in due time'.

138 BL, Harl. MS 163 (D'Ewes diary), fo. 192. Revealingly, D'Ewes was responding to a proposal from Edward Hyde 'That all wee had now to doe in this first particular [concerning religion] was to vote that wee did allow the answeare which the [English] Lords Commissioners had given to the Scotts proposition', that is, their paper of 15 March 1641. That Hyde could approve a paper drafted and sanctioned by, among others, Warwick and Saye, points up how little practical distance there was between the parties on the question of 'further reformation' during the Parliament's first six months.

139 A pro-episcopal newsletter-writer noted with relief that the Commons' resolution of 17 May 1641 committed the House merely to 'conformity' with Scotland, not 'uniformity', concluding with evident relief: 'So there is another feare over'; BL, Sloane MS 1467 (Newsletters, 1640–41), fo. 38: letter of intelligence, entry for 17 May [1641].

140 Matthews, *Calamy Revised*, p. l.

141 Until May, the Junto group's principal allies in the pulpit – Stephen Marshall, Edmund Calamy, and Cornelius Burges – had shied away from supporting Root-and-Branch, still less any form of Presbyterian settlement on the Scottish model. From the beginning of June, however, Marshall, Calamy, and Burges suddenly adopted a far more aggressively anti-episcopal tone, publishing, that same month, a trenchant *Vindication* of the Calamy-organized Ministers' Remonstrance of February that year. 'Smectymnuus' [Stephen Marshall, Edmund Calamy, *et al.*], *A Vindication of the Answer to the Humble Remonstrance, from the unjust Imputations of Frivolousnesse and Falsehood: wherein the Cause of Liturgy and Episcopacy is further debated* ([June] 1641), BL, E 165/6; Tom Webster, 'Stephen Marshall', *ODNB*. Here, their concern to impress a Scottish audience is not in doubt. No sooner had the Scottish Parliament opened in Edinburgh on 15 July, than Marshall and his confrères addressed themselves directly to the General Assembly

of the Scottish Kirk. Ingratiating themselves to the Covenanter clergy, they now affirmed their desire to see 'the Presbyterian Government [i.e. the Scottish model of ecclesiastical organization]' established in England, on the grounds that this 'hath just and evident Foundation ... in the Word of God'; see Marshall et al. to the General Assembly of the Scottish Kirk, 22 July 1641; quoted in 'Stephen Marshall', *ODNB*; see also BL, Sloane MS 1467 (Notes of parliamentary proceedings), fos. 17, 19v; Anthony Fletcher, *The Outbreak, of the English Civil War* (1981) pp. 102–3.

142 See above, Ch. 6.

143 BL, Harl. MS 163 (D'Ewes diary), fo. 237.

144 Dering's co-operation with the Junto leadership over the introduction of the Root-and-Branch bill was not the first instance of this kind. He had been named on 4 May 1641 to a nine-man Commons committee (which included such Junto loyalists as Sir Thomas Barrington, Sir John Clotworthy, Sir Philip Stapilton, John Hampden, and John Pym) to question Suckling and the other figures involved in the Tower Plot. This role would also have brought him into direct contact with Warwick and Essex, who personally oversaw the interrogations of the leading plotters. *CJ*, II, 134.

145 Sir Edward Dering, *A Collection of Speeches made by Sir Edward Dering Knight and Baronet, in Matter of Religion* (1642), p. 3 (BL, E 197/1).

146 Clarendon, *Rebellion*, I, 314 (for quotation). For his role in introducing the bill, see BL, Harl. MS 163 (D'Ewes diary), fo. 237; and see also Derek Hirst, 'The Defection of Sir Edward Dering, 1640–41', *Historical Journal*, 15 (1972), 193–208; S. P. Salt, 'The Origins of Sir Edward Dering's Attack on the Ecclesiastical Hierarchy c. 1625–40', *Historical Journal*, 30 (1987), 21–52.

147 Dering, *Collection of Speeches*, p. 62. Dering also claims that the bill had been 'brought unto him [Hesilrige]' by 'S[ir] H. V. and O. C.' – almost certainly to be identified as the younger Sir Henry Vane and Oliver Cromwell. Vane junior had of course been closely involved with the Junto, particularly in the Strafford prosecution, since the summer of 1640. Cromwell's involvement in the Root-

and-Branch bill of May 1641 is a culpable omission in John Adamson, 'Oliver Cromwell and the Long Parliament', in John Morrill (ed.), *Oliver Cromwell and the English Revolution* (1990), pp. 49–92.

148 It seems doubtful that the third 'Scoch Lord' in London, the Earl of Dunfermline, would have been on Brooke's guest list; by the spring of 1641 he was already coming to be regarded as too sympathetic to the king's interests, and by August had been removed from the list of Scottish Commissioners authorized to sign the Anglo-Scottish treaty.

149 Warwickshire RO, OR 1886/CUP.4/21A (John Halford's Accounts, I), unfol.

150 BL, Harl. MS 6424 (Bishop Warner's diary), fos. 70–71v; BL, Sloane MS 1467 (Newsletters, 1640–41), fos. 72, 76v–77, 78v; Fletcher, *Outbreak*, p. 101.

151 On 4 June, the reformists were brusquely reminded of the precariousness of their position when part of their answer to the Lords, urging the removal of bishops from the House of Lords, was rejected by the Commons in a division that saw Barrington and Goodwin, with 139 votes, routed by a pro-episcopal majority of 148; *CJ*, II, 157.

152 Ibid., 159.

153 NA, SP 16/481/21: Edward Nicholas to Sir John Penington, 10 June 1641.

154 I am grateful to Professor Allan Macinnes for a discussion of Loudoun's relations with Argyll. For an example of Loudoun acting as Argyll's agent in the preparations for the July 1641 Parliament, see NAS, Hamilton MS GD 406/1/1382: Lord Loudoun to the Earl of Lanark, 13 July 1641.

155 Under the terms of the bishops' abolition bill as it stood at the beginning of August, ecclesiastical affairs in each county were to be administered by nine 'county commissioners', to whom almost all the bishops' powers were to be transferred. The one major exception was to be the power of ordination, which was to be delegated to five clerical deputies. The power over excommunications and capital cases of heresy, however, was reserved to Parliament itself; for the bill, see W. A. Shaw, A History of the English Church during the Civil Wars and *Church under the*

Commonwealth 2 vols. (1900), I, 90–7; Fletcher, *Outbreak*, pp. 102–3.

156 BL, Sloane MS 1467 (Newsletters, 1640–41), fos. 96v. The context of the exchange was a debate on future of bishops' votes in the House of Lords.

157 *CJ*, II, 165,

158 BL, Sloane MS 1467 (Newsletters, 1640–41), fo. 94, entry for Monday 7 June.

159 Ibid., fo. 96; *CJ*, II, 173.

160 BL, Harl. MS 163 (D'Ewes diary), fo. 306v (for the meeting and those present); for Marshall, see 'Stephen Marshall', *ODNB*; and Tom Webster, *Stephen Marshall and Finchingfield* (Chelmsford, 1994); idem, *Godly Clergy in Early Stuart England: the Caroline Puritan Movement, 1620–43* (Cambridge, 1997).

161 BL, Harl. MS 163 (D'Ewes diary), fo. 306v. For Mandeville's admiration for, and evident closeness to, Hampden, see NAS, Hamilton MS GD 406/1/1412: Viscount Mandeville to the Marquess of Hamilton, 20 August '1640' [*recte* 1641]. Sir Robert Harley had also moved the puritan Ministers' Remonstrance – organized by Warwick's protégé Edmund Calamy, and making the case for reformed episcopacy – in the Commons on 23 January 1641 (see Ch. 7); once again, it is highly unlikely that he made this move unprompted.

162 *CJ*, II, 173.

163 For Hyde's chairmanship, see Ibid., pp. 173, 174, 176, 183, 184.

164 BL, Sloane MS 1467 (Newsletters, 1640–41), fo. 98.

165 Ibid., fo. 101: letter of intelligence, entry for [11] June 1641: much was spoken for an against the motion out of 'auncient councells and [Church] fathers'.

166 Webster, 'Stephen Marshall'. This was going even further than most Root-and-Branchers in Parliament, the majority of whom remained hostile to fully fledged Scottish Presbyterianism; see Shaw, *Church under the Commonwealth*, I, 100–2.

167 *CJ*, II, 131; BL, Harl. MS 163 (D'Ewes diary), fo. 121.

168 Ibid., fo. 190.

169 ASV, Senato, Dispacci Inghil. 42, fo. 317v: Giustinian to the Doge and Senate, 18/28 June 1641 (*CSPV 1640–42*, p. 166).

170 Buckminster Park, Lincolnshire, Tollemache MS 3748 (Will Morray Papers): report of the examination of Lieutenant-Colonel Walter Stewart before Lord Balmerino, Sir Thomas Hope, and Edward Edgar, 5 June '1640' [an error for 1641].

171 BL, Harl. MS 292, fo. 142: Charles I to the Earl of Montrose, [June 1641]; and Beinecke Lib., Yale, MS Osborn Shelves Fb 158, fo. 78: a copy of the instructions to Montrose made by John Browne, the Clerk of the Parliaments, [May 1641]. For their discovery in the saddle's pommel, BL, Harl. MS 163 (D'Ewes diary), fo. 339v. Anodyne though this may seem, it nevertheless revealed the extent to which Charles was prepared to accept a tactical retreat during his visit to Edinburgh. Montrose may have been a 'king's-party' Covenanter, but he was a Covenanter and a Presbyterian nevertheless. To do business with him, Charles had to assure him that he was not trying to *undo* the Covenanter revolution in Edinburgh; merely that he intended to ensure that the Covenanter faction which emerged as dominant from the forthcoming Parliament would be favourable to mixed monarchy and opposed to any further military forays into England.

172 The Scottish Commissioners submitted a paper to their English opposite numbers on 9 June, requesting that Traquair, the Scottish 'prelates', and three other 'Incendiaries' should be excluded from the Scottish Act of Oblivion, to be passed in pursuance of the treaty; *CJ*, II, 180.

173 BL, Harl. MS 163 (D'Ewes diary), fo. 339v: D'Ewes's report of Hesilrige's announcement of the interception to the Commons, 22 June 1641. This identifies Traquair as the author of the instructions.

174 *Certaine Instructions*, pp. 4–5 (BL, E 160/26): 'Tablet Propositions for [on behalf of] the King' [from Traquair to Montrose], [May 1641]; but see also the MS versions in Beinecke Lib., Yale University, MS Osborn Shelves fb 158, fo. 78 (a copy in the hand of John Browne, the Clerk of the Parliaments), and in NLS, MS Wodrow Folio 65, fo. 41, no. 12.

175 Stevenson, *Scottish Revolution*, p. 228.

For the circumstances of Argyll's treasonous words, see Russell, *Fall of the British Monarchies*, p. 310; John Leslie, Earl of Rothes, *A Relation of Proceedings concerning the Affairs of the Kirk of Scotland*, ed. David Laing (Bannatyne Club, 37, Edinburgh, 1830), p. 138.

176 Stevenson, *Scottish Revolutio*, p. 225. But note that NAS, Hamilton MS GD 406/1/1361 has Napier attending a Privy Council meeting with Argyll on 17 June 1641; see Russell, *Fall of the British Monarchies*, p. 315.

176 NAS, Hamilton MS GD 406/1/1382: Lord Loudoun to the Earl of Lanark, 13 July 1641. For a similar letter in which Loudoun acts as Argyll's mouthpiece, see NAS, Hamilton MS GD 406/1/1472: Earl of Loudoun to the Marquess of Hamilton, 9 December 1641.

177 There is even a petition to the king, dating from around July 1641, purporting to come from the General Assembly of the Scottish Kirk, requesting the appointment of Will Morray, one of the Grooms of the Bedchamber, to act as the king's man-of-business in the General Assembly. It is unclear, however, whether this was a petition actually presented by the General Assembly, or the text of one that Morray himself had drafted speculatively, in the hope of finding a caucus of support in the General Assembly which was prepared to move it: Buckminster Park, Lincolnshire, Tollemache MS 837: the 'supplication' of the Commissioners of the General Assembly to the king, [July 1641].

178 BL, Harl. MS 163 (D'Ewes diary), fo. 339v (for Hesilrige's presence at the 19 June meeting); Dering, *Collected Speeches*, p. 62 (for the introduction of the Root-and-Branch bill); *CJ*, II, 251 (for Hesilrige's involvement in the impeachment of the bishops, 11 August 1641).

179 Surrey History Centre, Bray MS 52/2/19/8: Edward Nicholas to the king, 18 August 1641.

180 Among the first of the new proposals was one, successfully carried by Barrington and Holles, the effect of which was to make the Duke of Lennox, one of the courtiers who had persuaded the king to become involved in Montrose's plotting, potentially impeachable in England if he took sides against Argyll in

the forthcoming Scottish Parliament. Debated on the same day as Loudoun made his revelations in the Inner Star Chamber, this complex motion hinged on the fact that the Duke of Lennox, though a duke in the Scottish peerage, had been born in England and was therefore an English, not a Scottish, native. The Treaty Commissioners had already agreed a clause declaring that Scottish natives who counselled the king against the Covenanter régime ('incensing' him was the charge) should be extraditable to Scotland to stand trial. After recent developments, the Scottish Commissioners proposed an additional clause that would have made this arrangement 'reciprocal to both Nations': that is, that English natives who 'incensed' – or gave evil counsel – to the king in Scotland should be extraditable from Scotland to England for trial and censure. In effect this meant that the English-born Duke of Lennox could be impeached of treason in England if he took Montrose's part in the forthcoming Scottish Parliament, and it produced an acrimonious Warwick House versus king's party division. The motion was carried, with Barrington and Holles as tellers for the winning side (with 166 votes) against Lord Falkland and Sir John Strangways (with 123). BL, Harl. MS 163 (D'Ewes diary), fo. 334; *CJ*, II, 180–1.

182 Ibid., 182.

183 *CJ*, II, 135. The Committee of Seven is first referred to as a committee on the 'seducing [of] the army', appointed on 5 May; its seventh member, Stapilton, was added on 7 May; *CJ*, II, 138.

184 BL, Harl. MS 163 (D'Ewes diary), fo. 339v.

185 Ibid., fo. 346. Pym had only recently returned to the Commons, having been 'sick of an ague' until around 15 June; see BL, Sloane MS 1467 (Newsletters, 1640–41), fo. 103v. The marginal note in the *Commons Journal* for 24 June, which suggests that Pym was instead reporting from the Commons' Committee on the State of the Kingdom, is misleading; *CJ*, II, 184.

186 Propositions IV, VI, and X; *CJ*, II, 185.

187 Discussed above, pp. 460–1.

188 Proposition VII. There was also to be a 'general pardon' issued by the king

(Proposition VIII), the effect of which would have been to have freed Warwick and the other Petitioner Peers from a future prosecution for treason; *CJ*, II, 185.

189 This term had long done service as the English rendering of the Latin term, *res publica*.

190 ASV, Senato, Dispacci Inghil. 42, fo. 338: Giustinian to the Doge and Senate, 26 June/6 July 1641; the new oath 'obligo à tutti ... prestar giuramento à questa Rep[ubbli]ca' (cf. *CSPV 1640–42*, p. 174).

191 For discussions of the changing usages of the term 'commonwealth', see Clive Holmes, 'Parliament, Liberty, Taxation, and Property', in J. H. Hexter (ed.), *Parliament and Liberty from the Reign of Elizabeth to the English Civil War* (Stanford, CA, 1992), pp. 148–9; Patrick Collinson, '"The State as Monarchical Commonwealth": "Tudor" England', *Journal of Historical Sociology*, 15 (2002), 89–95; and Phil Withington, *The Politics of Commonwealth: Citizens and Freemen in Early Modern England* (Cambridge, 2005).

192 For the quotation of Essex, see [Chestlin], *Persecutio Undecima*, p. 9; the quote is undated, but from the context, probably dates from the first half of 1641. For Essex and Williams's advice on his remarriage, see Morrill, '3rd Earl of Essex'; for the quotation 're[s]publica aeterna', see Lambeth Palace Lib., MS 1030, fo. 62: information presented by Sir J[ohn] M[onson?], 20 October 1635.

193 Propositions III and V; *CJ*, II, 185.

194 *LJ*, IV, 355; That the next monarch – the future Charles II – should be brought up to accept the much diminished role which awaited him, the Ten Propositions demanded that Parliament ensure the education of the Prince of Wales and the other royal children be entrusted to 'persons of publick trust ... especially in matters of religion *and liberty*'. Propositions III and V; *CJ*, II, 185.

195 Gardiner, *History*, IX, 402.

196 *Certaine Instructions*, pp. 6–7.

197 Fyvie Castle, Aberdeenshire, Dunfermline MS 328: for the grant, 25 June 1641; the king's instructions to Dunfermline prior to his departure, dated 30 June 1641, at Whitehall, are Dunfermline MS 1066.

Dunfermline may have been a reluctant convert to the cause of the Covenant; a letter of 9 March 1638 to Hamilton (who was then the King's Commissioner in Scotland) speaks of his reluctance to sign it, despite being put to it by 'the noblemen heir of my freinds', though it is difficult to tell whether this reflects genuine reservations or merely a politique desire to retain Hamilton's (and hence, at this time, the king's) favour: see NAS, Hamilton MS GD 406/1/366: Earl of Dunfermline to the Marquess of Hamilton, 9 March 1638. (I am grateful to Dr John Scally for drawing my attention to this letter.)

198 ASV, Senato, Dispacci Inghil. 42, fo. 344: Giustinian to the Doge and Senate, 2/12 July 1641 (*CSPV 1640–42*, p. 177).

199 For these attempts at dissuasion, see *CJ*, II, 244, 245, 246, 247.

200 *CJ*, II, 235.

201 BL, Harl. MS 6424 (Bishop Warner's diary), fos. 84v, 93; Russell, *Fall of the British Monarchies*, pp. 360–1.

202 *LJ*, IV, 241; BL, Harl. MS 163 (D'Ewes diary), fo. 145; ASV, Senato, Dispacci Inghil. 42, fo. 286: Giustinian to the Doge and Senate, 14/24 May 1641 (*CSPV 1640–42*, p. 152).

203 The diplomatic despatches from London during the summer of 1641 contain numerous references to the king's unpopularity, particularly in the months following the foiling of the Tower Plot.

204 Centre for Kentish Studies, De L'Isle MS U1475/C114/22: Sir John Temple to the Earl of Leicester, 29 July 1641 (HMC, *De L'Isle Manuscripts*, VI, 406).

205 HMC, *De L'Isle Manuscripts*, VI, 555: Leicester's 'Diary of Events, 1636–50'.

206 *CSPV 1640–42*, p. 172: Giustinian to the Doge and Senate of Venice, 23 June/3 July 1641 (for the quotation). For his appointment to the marquessate see, Clarendon, *Rebellion*, I, 320, and BL, Sloane MS 1467 (Newsletters, 1640–41), fo. 71. Hertford's formal patent of appointment came somewhat later, and is dated 10 August 1641: *Complete Peerage*, XII, Part 1, 71.

207 BL, Sloane MS 1467 (Newsletters, 1640–41), fo. 87: letter of intelligence, entry for 19 June [1641], where it is noted 'that the

parliament had an eye upon him [Newcastle] to remove him from the Prince'.

208 *CSPD 1641–43*, pp. 59, 62. The quarrel between Pembroke and Mowbray took place on 27 July; Essex was appointed Lord Chamberlain on 2 August; see also BL, Harl. MS 6424 (Bishop Warner's diary), fos. 82v–83.

209 NA, SP 16/482, fo. 178: Thomas Wiseman to Sir John Pennington, 29 July 1641; for his offence, see Herbert, *Vox secunda populi*, p. 4.

210 ASV, Senato, Dispacci Inghil. 43, fo. 17: Giustinian to the Doge and Senate, 30 July/9 August 1641. As so often in the calendaring of this archive, the English version given in the *Calendar of State Papers, Venetian* is subtly misleading, translating the description of Essex as 'capo principale de[i] Puritani' – 'principal leader of the Puritans' – as merely '*a* leading man *among* the Puritans': *CSPV 1640–42*, p. 195. As additional boon, the king granted Essex the mansion house of the manor of St Mary's-near-the-Walls, York, presumably as an urban base for Essex as Lord Lieutenant of Yorkshire: NA, SO 3/12 (Signet Office Docket Book), fo. 151.

211 For Hyde's reading of the appointment, see Clarendon, *Rebellion*, I, 345.

212 *CJ*, II, 240, 242. For Vane senior's prediction that the Commons would request the appointment of a *Custos Regni* before the king's departure, see NA, SP 81/51/2, fo. 215: Sir Henry Vane senior to Sir Thomas Rowe, 30 July 1641.

213 Russell, *Fall of the British Monarchies*, p. 365; see also BL, Harl. MS 5047 (Anon. diary), fo. 55v.

214 BL, Sloane MS 1467 (Newsletters, 1640–41), fo. 76: letter of intelligence, [undated, *c*. May 1641]. Sir John Bankes (also a close friend of Northumberland's) was regarded as the other candidate for the post voted by 'Comon fame'.

215 BL, Harl. MS 5047 (Anon. diary), fo. 61. Salisbury later protested to Hamilton that this 'was much against my will', but the sincerity of this claim (which Salisbury seems to have expected Hamilton to report to the king) is at very least open to doubt; see NAS, Hamilton MS GD 406/1/1495: Earl of

Salisbury to the Marquess of Hamilton, undated [mid August 1641].

216 BL, Harl. MS 5047 (Anon. diary), fo. 61r-v. Strode and Holles moved that the House might petition the king directly, without consulting the Lords, on the grounds that 'mony moves from us. And then to passe the Tunnage and poundage for a short time'; ibid., fo. 61r.

217 BL, Harl. MS 5047 (Anon. diary), fo. 61v (for Holles); *LJ*, IV, 355. A proposal that the Earl of Berkshire (one of the English Treaty Commissioners, and a peer generally supportive of moderate proposals for reform) should be made Governor of the Prince of Wales was reported to have been mooted in the Commons as early as 15 June 1641: BL, Sloane MS 1467 (Newsletters, 1640–41), fo. 103v: letter of intelligence, [June 1641].

218 Russell, *Fall of the British Monarchies*, p. 366 (for quotations).

219 Compare ibid.

220 BL, Harl. MS 5047 (Anon. diary), fo. 61.

221 While it is true that the formal peace terms offered to the king by Parliament later in the 1640s contain clauses, particularly in relation to the control of the militia, that seem to limit the monarch's control for periods that roughly correspond to the king's presumed life-expectancy, these do not gainsay the fact that the powers of the monarch *vis-à-vis* the Parliament were permanently changed, to the cost of the former, by the statutory reforms of 1641. For a different perspective, see John Morrill, 'Living with Revolution' (Lecture delivered to the University of Oxford, 20 January 2006, forthcoming as the Ford Lectures for 2006).

222 BL, Sloane MS 1467 (Newsletters, 1640–41), fo. 17: letter of intelligence, entry for 28 July 1641; *CJ*, II, 262. The patent of appointment was only delivered to Essex after the king's departure for Scotland; see also *LJ*, IV, 367.

223 BL, Sloane MS 1467 (Newsletters, 1640–41), fo. 17v. Reports current at court during the last days of July suggested that other appointments were likely – Saye as Lord Treasurer, Newburgh as Master of the Wards (in place of Saye), Hampden as Chancellor of the Duchy of Lancaster, Pym as Chancellor of

the Exchequer, and Holles and Mandeville as the two Secretaries of State; however, it is difficult to gauge whether these were ever seriously considered by the king. More questionable is the claim that Charles, shortly before his departure for Scotland, wanted to knight Oliver St John: BL, Sloane MS 1467 (Newsletters, 1640–41), fo. 139: letter of intelligence, 23 August [1641].

224 Further confirmation of this came in early September 1641, when Mildmay was appointed with Pym to join with Warwick 'to take care for distributing the monies ordered to be monthly paid for the supply of the navy'; *CJ*, II, p. 280.

225 NAS, Hamilton MS GD 406/1/1411: Sir Henry Mildmay to the Marquess of Hamilton, 20 August 1641. For Secretary Vane's expectation that he was about to be sacked as Treasurer of the Household, see NA, SP 16/482, fo. 194: Sidney Bere to Sir John Pennington, 30 July 1641.

226 [Sir John Berkenhead], *A Letter from Mercurius Civicus to Mercurius Rusticus, or, Londons Confession* ([Oxford, August] 1643), p. 8 (Wing B6324).

227 BL, Sloane MS 1467 (Newsletters, 1640–41), fo. 14. For Downinge's defence of aristocratic rebellion, see Calybute Downinge, *A Sermon Preached to the Renowned Company of the Artillery, 1 September, 1640, designed to compose the Present Troubles, by discovering the Enemies of the Peace of the Church and State* (1641), p. 32 [*recte* 38] (BL, E 157/4).

228 Clarendon, *Rebellion*, I, 361. (I am grateful to Mr Christopher Thompson for drawing my attention to this passage.) Warwick had been spoken of as a likely successor to the Duke of Buckingham as Lord Warden of the Cinque Ports as early as the late 1620s; Thomas Cogswell, *The Blessed Revolution: English Politics and the Coming of War, 1621–24* (Cambridge, 1989), p. 102. In the event, he did not obtain the Lord Wardenship until the summer of 1643, when the office was conferred by Parliament.

229 ASV, Senato, Dispacci Inghil. 43, fo. 19: Giustinian to the Doge and Senate, 6/16 August 1641 (*CSPV 1640–42*, p. 197). For the background to this 'state audience', see ASV, Senato, Dispacci Inghil. 43, fos. 11v–13: Giustinian to the Doge and Senate, 30 July/9

August 1641 (*CSPV 1640–42*, pp. 192–3).

230 ASV, Senato, Dispacci Inghil. 43, fos. 20v–21r: Giustinian to the Doge and Senate, 6/16 August 1641 (*CSPV 1640–42*, p. 198), where 'Lodon' [*sic*] is reported to have 'arrived in this city on Monday' [i.e. 2 August]. Loudoun reported that the Scottish Parliament 'have viewed and passed all the Treaty, only some few things of explanation altered; some other things there were, wherein they were not fully satisfied in their demands [amongst which, pre-eminently, were their demands concerning the Church], yet [they] have declared this should breed no difference …'; *CJ*, II, 236. For the detail of the Scots' demands on religion, see 'The desiers of the Scottish Commissioners concerninge Unity of Religion 1640 [i.e. 1641]', 10 March 1641: BL, Add. MS 70003 (Harley Papers), fos. 64–73v.

231 NA, SP 16/482, fo. 176v: Sidney Bere to [anon.], 29 July 1641.

232 The first meeting between the English Treaty Commissioners and Loudoun, after the latter's return, was on Tuesday, 3 August (Pym's report of it, made on 4 August, refers to it having taken place 'yesterday'); *CJ*, II, 236.

233 Ibid., 234.

234 For an alternative interpretation, see Fletcher, *Outbreak*, p. 107: 'the principal reason the bill was not discussed after 3 August was probably that the month simply proved too hectic'. In fact, the Commons did briefly return to the question, passing an order on 13 August that they would consider the Root-and-Branch Bill at 9 a.m. on the following Monday morning (16 August). When that day came, however, the House preferred to discuss proposals for a bill to restrain 'the excess of buildings' in London, particularly in Lincoln's Inn Fields; *CJ*, II, 255, 257. It is noteworthy that there was no mention of the Root-and-Branch Bill in the list of legislation prepared by the Commons on 9 August which they hoped would be passed by the *Custos Regni* during the king's absence in Scotland; BL, Harl. MS 5047 (Anon. diary), fos. 60v–61r.

235 Centre for Kentish Studies, De L'Isle MS U1475/C114/24: Sir John Temple to the Earl of Leicester, 11 August 1641 (HMC, *De L'Isle Manuscripts*, VI, 410).

236 *CJ*, II, 906, 914, 937–8; *LJ*, V, 581–3; Shaw, *Church under the Commonwealth*, I, 119–21.

237 The bill was introduced on 9 August 1641 and passed all its parliamentary stages by the following day; *CJ*, II, 247, 249.

238 ASV, Senato, Dispacci Inghil. 43, fos. 2v, 15: Giustinian to the Doge and Senate, despatches of 23 July/2 August and 30 July/9 August 1641 (*CSPV 1640–42*, pp. 187, 193–4).

239 *CJ*, II, 247–8.

240 Ibid., 244–8.

241 Clarendon, *Rebellion*, I, 361 and *Complete Peerage*, '1st Duke of Richmond', *s.v.*

242 NA, SP 16/483, fo. 64r-v: [Thomas Smith, Northumberland's naval secretary] to the Earl of Northumberland, 10 August 1641 (for Bristol's role); Centre for Kentish Studies, De L'Isle MS U1475/C114/24: Sir John Temple to the Earl of Leicester, 11 August 1641 (HMC, *De L'Isle Manuscripts*, VI, 410). For the date of Lennox's creation as Duke of Lennox, see *Complete Peerage*, X, 832.

243 NA, SP 16/483, fo. 64r-v: [Thomas Smith, Northumberland's naval secretary] to the Earl of Northumberland, 10 August 1641.

244 *CJ*, II, 245 (for the Parliament's Sunday sitting on 8 August and its resolution to persuade the king to delay his departure).

245 NA, SP 16/483, fo. 65: [Thomas Smith] to the Earl of Northumberland, 10 August 1641.

246 For the membership of this commission, see NA, SP 17, Case F, no. 2; also listed in Russell, *Fall of the British Monarchies*, pp. 366–7.

247 BL, Evelyn MS, Nicholas Box: Earl of Northumberland to Edward Nicholas, 13 August 1641.

248 NA, SP 16/483, fo. 65: [Thomas Smith] to the Earl of Northumberland, 10 August 1641.

249 *CJ*, II, 249. For the report of the committee established to consider the defence of the kingdom, see *CJ*, II, 257 (14 August).

250 NA, SP 16/483, fo. 175: Earl of Northumberland to Sir Thomas Rowe, 25

August 1641 (my emphasis); for the use of the word 'confusion' to mean civil strife, see also *OED*. Northumberland's health was slowly recovering and he reported that time spent recently at Bath had left him in 'an indifferently good state of health'.

251 NAS, Hamilton MS GD 406/1/1505: Viscount Saye to the Marquess of Hamilton, 18 August 1641. Report of Hamilton's support for Argyle reached Henry Percy, in exile in France, who wrote to Hamilton with the sarcastic commendation: 'I am very glad to heere you have made a frendship with my L[or]d of Arguile [*sic*]. I thinke it a most wise act'; NAS, Hamilton MS GD 406/1/1430: Henry Percy to the Marquess of Hamilton, 20 September 1641. See, too, the letter from Sir Henry Vane senior to Hamilton of 27 October 1641, in which he asks Hamilton to present 'my humblest service to the Earles of Argile and Lanericke [Lanark]': NAS, Hamilton MS GD 406/1/1447.

252 NAS, Hamilton MS GD 406/1/1505: Viscount Saye to the Marquess of Hamilton, 18 August 1641.

12. UNION TRIUMPHANT

1 John Campbell, Lord Loudoun, *The Lord Lowden his Learned and Wise Speech in the Upper House* [sic] *of Parliament in Scotland, September 9, 1641* ([September?], 1641), p. 5 (BL, E 199/13). The title reveals the English printer's ignorance of Scottish political institutions; the Edinburgh Parliament, being unicameral, had no 'upper' House.

2 J. J. Brown, 'The Social, Political and Economic Influences of the Edinburgh Merchant Élite, 1600-38' (Unpublished Ph.D. dissertation, University of Edinburgh, 1985), pp. 2, 10, 14.

3 D. J. T. Englefield, 'The Parliament House, Edinburgh', *Parliamentary Affairs*, 11 (1957-58), 361-6. On the architectural context, more generally, see Deborah Howard, 'Languages and Architecture in Scotland, 1500-1660', Georgia Clarke and Paul Crossley (eds.), *Architecture and Language: Constructing Identity in European Architecture, 1000-1650* (Cambridge, 2001), pp. 162-72; and eadem, 'Scotland's "Three Estates"', in Lucy Gent (ed.), *Albion's Classicism: the Visual Arts in Britain,*

1550-1660 (New Haven and London, 1995), pp. 51-78.

4 NAS, Hamilton MS GD 406/1/1361: Earl of Argyll to the Earl of Lanark, 14 June 1641.

5 Ibid.

6 Guthrie, *Memoirs*, p. 82.

7 Stevenson, *Scottish Revolution*, p. 230. For a more pessimistic contemporary view of the Plotters' likely fate, see NA, SP 16/483/68: Sidney Bere to Sir John Pennington, 18 August 1641.

8 Stevenson, *Scottish Revolution*, pp. 230-1.

9 Ibid., p. 231.

10 Beinecke Lib., Yale, MS Osborn Shelves, Howard of Escrick Box, Sir William Armyne, Sir Philip Stapilton, and John Hampden (Commissioners of the Scottish Parliament) to Speaker Lenthall, 22 August 1641. An identical text was sent by Lord Howard of Escrick, not to the Speaker of the House of Lords, but the Earl of Essex; ibid.

11 The detailed argument supporting this statement is presented in Ch. 11; but for a succinct summary of the king's intentions, see ASV, Senato, Dispacci Inghil. 43, fos. 50-51v: Giovanni Giustinian to the Doge and Senate, 27 August/6 September 1641 (*CSPV 1640-42*, p. 208).

12 For the widespread expectation that the king was planning some form of counter-coup, in order to recover his prerogative rights, see ASV, Senato, Dispacci Inghil. 43, fos. 52, 72, 96: Giovanni Giustinian to the Doge and Senate, despatches of 3/13 September, 10/20 September, and 24 September/4 October 1641 (*CSPV 1640-42*, pp. 212, 215, 223).

13 NA, SP 16/483, fos. 158-9v: Sir Henry Vane senior to Sir Thomas Rowe, Edinburgh, 22 August 1641; SP 16/483/91: Thomas Wiseman to [Sir John Penington], 26 August 1641.

14 NA, SP 16/483, fo. 158: Sir Henry Vane senior to Sir Thomas Rowe, Edinburgh, 22 August 1641.

15 Keith M. Brown, *Kingdom or Province?: Scotland and the Regal Union, 1603-1715* (Basingstoke, 1992); Jenny Wormald, 'The Union of 1603', in Roger A. Mason (ed.), *Scots and Britons: Scottish Political Thought*

and the Union of 1603 (Cambridge, 1994), pp. 17–40.

16 Dougal Shaw, 'St Giles' Church and Charles I's Coronation Visit to Scotland', *Historical Research*, 77 (2004), 481–502.

17 NA, SP 16/483, fo. 158v: Sir Henry Vane senior to Sir Thomas Rowe, Edinburgh, 22 August 1641; *Nicholas Papers*, I, 23–4.

18 NA, SP 16/483, fo. 160: Sidney Bere to Edward Nicholas, 22 August 1641.

19 NLS, Wodrow MS Folio 66, fos. 207–8: Archibald Jhonston of Wariston to [?], [February 1641]; and see also Baillie, *Letters*, I, 303–6.

20 NA, SP 16/483/99: reports of 'diurnal occurrences', 30 August–5 September 1641.

21 Stevenson, *Scottish Revolution*, pp. 234–5.

22 NA, SP 16/483, fo. 160.

23 Sir James Balfour, *Historical Works*, 4 vols. (Edinburgh, 1824–5), III, 45. There is a possibility that the king may even have been induced to propose Balmerino for the position; see *Nicholas Papers*, I, 20. Another striking gesture of reconciliation was the king's invitation to General Alexander Leslie to ride with him in the royal coach through the City of Edinburgh, a sight that was reported to have been greeted with 'loud acclamations'; see ASV, Senato, Dispacci Inghil. 43, fo. 93r-v: Giovanni Giustinian to the Doge and Senate, 17/27 September 1641 (*CSPV 1640–42*, pp. 220–21).

24 NA, SP 16/483/104: Sidney Bere to Sir John Pennington, 30 August 1641.

25 I am grateful to Professor Allan Macinnes for bringing this point to my attention.

26 NA, SP 16/483/104: Sidney Bere to Sir John Pennington, 30 August 1641.

27 Archibald Campbell, 8th Earl of Argyll, *An Honourable Speech made ... by the earle of Argile (being now Competitor with Earle Morton for the Chancellorship)* ([September], 1641), p. 3 (BL, E 199/17).

28 Stevenson, *Scottish Revolution*, pp. 234–5.

29 Balfour, *Historical Works*, III, 51–3; *Acts of the Parliament of Scotland*, v, . 334–45.

30 NA, SP 16/483, fo. 43: summary of the 'The Scotts' Demands' [7 August 1641].

31 Argyll, *An Honourable Speech*, p. 4. On the provisions of the 1640 Scottish Acts of Parliament, see Stevenson, *Scottish Revolution*, pp. 193–4.

32 BL, Sloane MS 1467 (Newsletters, 1640–41), fo. 76: letter of intelligence, [undated, *c.* May 1641]; BL, Harl. MS 5047. (Anon. diary), fo. 61v (for Holles); *LJ*, IV, 355.

33 Stevenson, *Scottish Revolution*, p. 235.

34 NA, SP 16/483/96: Sidney Bere to Sir John Pennington, 28 August 1641.

35 Charles's malleability was an indication, perhaps, of just how much he had been disorientated by the loss of his two principal Covenanter allies. Montrose was a broken reed following his arrest and imprisonment – and the execution of his key witness against Argyll. Another disastrous blow was the death of the Earl of Rothes, who had been one of the most supportive of the Scots Commissioners in London, 'from [whom] his Majestie expected much service in this present conjucture', wrote the courtier, Sidney Bere, on 28 August, 'he having given many assurances thereof'; NA, SP 16/483/96: Sidney Bere to Sir John Pennington, 28 August 1641.

36 Acts of the Parliament of Scotland, v, 354–5; Stevenson, *Scottish Revolution*, pp. 235–6.

37 Ibid., p. 236.

38 Allan I. Macinnes, *Charles I and the Covenanting Movement, 1625–41* (Edinburgh, 1991), pp. 202–3.

39 Charles appears to have been willing to grant him one or the other, but not both; see *Nicholas Papers*, I, 49: Thomas Webb, Secretary to the Duke of Richmond and Lennox, to Edward Nicholas, 21 September 1641.

40 HMC, *Salisbury Manuscripts*, XXII, 365–6: newsletter, 30 September 1641.

41 For the quotation, NAS, Hamilton MS GD 406/1/1434: Sir Henry Vane senior to the Marquess of Hamilton, 7 September 1641 (from Raby Castle, Durham).

42 Stevenson, *Scottish Revolution*, pp. 236–7.

43 Baillie, *Letters*, I, 390; Balfour, *Historical Works*, III, 71.

44 Bodl. Lib., MS Carte 1 (Ormond corr.), fos. 457–60, printed in Carte, *Original Letters*, I, 1, 5: Earl of Wemyss to the Earl of Ormond, 25 September 1641. John Wemyss, 1st Earl of Wemyss (*cr.* 1633), had served as Charles's Commissioner to the General Assembly of the Church of Scotland in July 1641; *Complete Peerage*, XII, Part II, 463.

45 Macinnes, *Charles I and the Covenanting Movement*, p. 203.

46 ASV, Senato, Dispacci Inghil. 43, fo. 107: Giovanni Giustinian to the Doge and Senate, 8/18 October 1641 (*CSPV 1640–42*, p. 225).

47 Bray, *Evelyn Diary and Correspondence*, IV, 74. Edward Nicholas to Charles I, 24 September 1641.

48 *Nicholas Papers*, I, 52: Thomas Webb to Edward Nicholas, 27 September 1641.

49 NA, SP 16/483/91: Thomas Wiseman to [Sir John Pennington], 26 August 1641, for the deaths from plague and other diseases.

50 See ASV, Senato, Dispacci Inghil. 43, fo. 66: Giovanni Giustinian to the Doge and Senate, 3/13 September 1641 (*CSPV 1640–42*, p. 213).

51 *CJ*, II, 273.

52 NAS, Hamilton MS GD 406/1/1417: Viscount Mandeville to the Marquess of Hamilton, 28 August 1641.

53 NAS, Hamilton MS GD 406/1/1424: Earl of Essex to the Marquess of Hamilton, 7 September 1641.

54 *CJ*, II, 281. The Commons' order refers to the sermon being attended by none but 'Parliament-men', a designation that includes the peers. The text of Marshall's sermon makes it clear that he was addressing both the Lords and the Commons, notwithstanding that it was published as a sermon 'preached to the ... Commons'.

55 Stephen Marshall, *A Peace-Offering to God: a Sermon preached to the Honourable House of Commons assembled in Parliament at their Publique Thanksgiving, September 7, 1641* (1641), BL, E 173/31. For Marshall's connections with Warwick, see NA, SP 16/449/48, printed in John Nalson, *An Impartiall Collection of the Great Affairs of State*, 2 vols. (1682), I, 269 (*recte* 279); and Tom Webster, *Stephen Marshall and Finchingfield* (Studies in Essex History, 6, Chelmsford, 1994), p. 17.

56 Jeremiah Burroughes, *Sions Joy. A Sermon preached to the Honourable House of Commons assembled in Parliament, at their Publique Thanksgiving, September 7, 1641, for the Peace concluded between England and Scotland* (1641) BL, E 174/3.

57 It is perhaps an indication of who made the arrangements for Burroughs and Marshall to preach that the Commons-man appointed to thank Marshall (and presumably Burroughes as well) was Sir Thomas Barrington; *CJ*, II, 287. Essex RO, T/B 211/1, no. 39: 'The sum of that Conference which was betwixt one Mr Burroughes, a Minister laitlie suspendit in the Dioces of Norwitch for inconformitie, and John Michaelson, Parson of Chelmesford, the 5 of August last [1638], at Leeghes parva, in the garden of the ... Earle of Warwicke'.

58 Marshall, *A Peace-Offering to God*, p. 5.

59 Burroughes dwelt at length on the connection between constitutional reform and the inauguration of the new godly order. Through the Triennial Act, he argued, 'God indeed opened a doore of hope', but Parliament-men were in fear of 'the shutting of it almost every day'. The latest developments left that constitutional order secure, Burroughes, *Sions Joy*, pp. 25–6.

60 Marshall, *A Peace-Offering to God*, p. 40.

61 Ibid., p. 46.

62 Ibid., p. 17.

63 Burroughes, *Sions Joy*, pp. 25–6.

64 Ibid., p. 24.

65 Jeremiah Burroughs used the pulpit to praise the Scots for setting the example in removing superstitious innovations and to urge the English Parliament to produce a national covenant of its own, clearly based on the Scottish National Covenant of 1638: 'our representative Kingdome [the Parliament], yea, and the body of the Kingdome [the population at large]', Burroughs argued, 'should enter into the Oath and Covenant with the Lord, to defend his truth against Popery and Popish Innovations'; Burroughs, *Sions Joy*, p. 26.

66 *CJ*, II, 246: on Sunday afternoon, 8 August 1641, it was ordered that 'the bill for the abolishing of superstition shall be reported tomorrow morning'; though, perhaps unsurprisingly, come the following morning, nothing was done.

67 For procedure by ordinance at this time, see *CJ*, II, p. 271; and Michael J. Mendle, 'The Great Council of Parliament and the First Ordinances: the Constitutional Theory of the Civil War', *Journal of British Studies*, 31 (1992), 133–62; and Elizabeth Read Foster, 'The House of Lords and Ordinances, 1641–49', *American Journal of Legal History*, 21 (1977), 157–73.

68 For the text of the order, see *CJ*, II, 287.

69 *CJ*, II, 280, 281.

70 The legislation began with a motion from the Speaker on 30 August 1641 that consideration should be had of the taking away of communion rails; BL, Harl. MS 164 (D'Ewes diary), fo. 78v. This resulted in a committee, appointed on 31 August, to consider the placement of communion tables and innovations more generally; this reported on 1 September; see *CJ*, II, 278, 279. The drafting committee consisted of John Pym, Denzell Holles, Oliver St John, Sir Robert Harley, John Selden, Serjeant Wylde, Lord Falkland, Sir John Culpeper, Sir Simonds D'Ewes, John Crewe, Sir Thomas Barrington, Henry Marten, and Sir Henry Mildmay. Perhaps significantly, the Commons leaders chose two days when the Speaker had difficulty starting business, 'for want of the number of 40 members', the quorum; BL, Harl. MS 164 (D'Ewes diary), fos. 78v, 80v.

71 It seems likely that even the Earl of Warwick used the *Book of Common Prayer* in his household chapel during the 1630s. This can be inferred, probably with some confidence, from John Michaelson's 1638 deposition against Jeremiah Burroughes, reporting, *inter alia*, the service in Warwick's household chapel at Leez. Had the *Prayer Book* not been used, Michaelson seems certain to have mentioned the fact, as the purpose of his deposition was to draw attention to irregularities of usage and opinion during Burroughes's period as acting household chaplain; Lambeth Palace Lib., MS 3391 (Bramston papers), fos. 42–3v (copy in Essex RO, T/B 211/1, no. 39).

72 *CJ*, II, p. 279. For Culpeper as an Esquire of the Body Extraordinary, by July 1641, see NA, LC 3/1, fo. 29 (a reference I owe to Dr David Scott). Culpeper's proposal of this measure at this time is all the more surprising in that he also had close relations with the Marquess of Hamilton, and his motives for suggesting the amendment to protect the *Prayer Book* may possibly have been an ill-considered conciliatory gesture towards the measure's opponents in the Commons, rather than an attempt completely to derail the ordinance. Indeed, it is noticeable that, when the ordinance was rejectd in the upper House, Culpeper was one of those who was named to join with Pym to prepare a declaration against the peers' action.

73 BL, Harl. MS 164 (D'Ewes diary), fos. 84r, 83r (in that order); *CJ*, II, 279; for Sir William Masham and Warwick, see Masham's letter to Harbottell Grimston, at Lincoln's Inn, 21 October 1640, written from Warwick's country seat, and informing the recipient of the earl's plans for the forthcoming parliamentary elections (which included placing Sir Thomas Barrington as one of the burgesses for Colchester): Essex RO, D/Y 2/4 (Morant MS), p. 51. Masham and Cromwell also appear to have been close, with one of Cromwell's sons resident in Masham's household in the late 1630s: W. C. Abbott (ed.), *The Writings and Speeches of Oliver Cromwell*, 4 vols. (Oxford, 1988), I, 96–7: Oliver Cromwell to Mrs [Oliver] St John 'at Sir William Masham his House called Oates, in Essex', 13 October 1638.

74 Even so, this pro-Union group found themselves outvoted, mustering only thirty-seven Commons-men against the proposal, against Culpeper's majority of fifty-five; *CJ*, II, 279; BL, Harl. MS 164 (D'Ewes diary), fo. 83. In the division, the two tellers in favour of giving legislative protection to the *Prayer Book* were a future Parliamentarian and client of the Earl of Pembroke, Sir Robert Pye, and Sir Thomas Bowyer; *CJ*, II, 279.

75 Ibid., 283: Commons' proceedings for the afternoon of 8 September; this is the significance of the phrase that the order was passed 'without any addition [i.e. relating to the *Prayer Book*] for the present'. For the final text, without reference to the *Prayer Book*, see *CJ*, II, 287.

76 Ibid., 283.

77 For a different reading, see Russell, *Fall of the British Monarchies*, p. 370. The idea that the Lords' order in favour of the *Prayer Book* was a simple tit for tat reaction against the Commons seems to derive from the account in Edward Nicholas's letter to the king of 10 September 1641; but Nicholas admitted to the king that he was relying only on hearsay, and his account does not stand up to detailed scrutiny; Bray, *Evelyn Diary and Correspondence*, IV, 67-8.

78 BL, Harl. MS 164 (D'Ewes diary), fo. 100; *CJ*, II, 283.

79 Russell, *Fall of the British Monarchies*, p. 370. Russell follows the Earl of Dover's notes (Bodl. Lib., MS Clarendon 21, no. 1603) in suggesting that the Commons published their anti-idolatry measure, provocatively, before they had had their conference of 8 September with the Lords (see Russell, *Fall of the British Monarchies*, p. 369). But Dover's notes are unreliable in numerous points of detail (the earl misdates the debate to 10 August, rather than its actual date, 8 September), and, as Gardiner long ago pointed out, 'Dover was clearly mistaken in saying that the Commons published their order about innovations before the division in the Lords': Gardiner, *History*, x, 16. The provision for printing and publishing the ordinance was one of the actions on which the Commons were clearly seeking for 'their Lordshipps to joine with us, that it might become an ordinance of Parliament': BL, Harl. MS 164 (D'Ewes diary), fo. 100. D'Ewes goes on to add parenthetically of 'the saied order' that it was 'in print', but this merely indicates that the anti-idolatry measure had been printed by the time he wrote up the fair copy of this section of the diary (some time after the events they describe); not that the measure was already in print by the time St John presented it to the Lords at the conference (something that was an impossibility, since the conference took place only a short time after the clause for the ordinance's printing and publishing had been added to the draft text).

80 BL, Harl. MS 164 (D'Ewes diary), fo. 100.

81 *LJ*, IV, 392. The other managers were Viscount Mandeville, the 1st Earl of Manchester (Mandeville's father), Lord Wharton, and the Bishop of Lincoln, John Williams. Only Williams seems to have been out of sympathy with the Warwick House peers at this time; see [John Williams, Bishop of Lincoln], *A Form of Thanksgiving, to be used the Seventh of September, thorowout the Diocese of Lincoln, and in the Jurisdiction of Westminster* ([September] 1641), BL, E 171/12; and the Commons' order against this of 6 September 1641: *CJ*, II, 281.

82 Ibid.; BL, Harl. MS 6424 (Bishop Warner's diary), fo. 95r-v.

83 *LJ*, IV, 392.

84 BL, Harl. MS 6424 (Bishop Warner's diary), fo. 95r-v.

85 *LJ*, IV, 392. Gardiner's paraphrase of the Lords' resolutions on religion is deeply misleading where he states that the peers 'wished that, for the sake of decency, [the communion table] should still be surrounded with rails in its new position'. What the Lords' *Journal* actually says is 'Where there are rails already, they are to be removed with the Communion Tables; but where there are none [i.e. where there the communion table was already without rails], they shall not be inforced upon any [i.e. there should be no further action]'. The meaning of the last clause may be regarded as ambiguous; but, however this text as a whole is read, there is nothing to suggest that the Lords were supporting the railing of the communion table, once moved from the chancel, in its new position; see Gardiner, *History*, x, 15.

86 *LJ*, IV, 392.

87 NAS, Hamilton MS GD 406/1/1418: Edward Nicholas to the Marquess of Hamilton, 28 August 1641, dates Saye's departure for Oxfordshire on 'Thursday last', 26 August.

88 *CJ*, II, 286; *LJ*, IV, 394.

89 For the first phase of iconoclasm, see Eamon Duffy, *The Stripping of the Altars: Traditional Religion in England, c. 1400-c. 1580* (New Haven and London, 1992).

90 NAS, Hamilton MS GD 406/1/1427: Viscount Mandeville to the Marquess of Hamilton, 10 September 1641.

91 *After Debate about the Printing and Publishing of the Order of the 16th of January last* ([September], 1641), single sheet, BL, 669 f. 3/18.

92 For the exodus of the Parliament-men, see ASV, Senato, Dispacci Inghil. 43, fo. 229v: Giovanni Giustinian to the Doge and Senate, 3/13 September 1641 (*CSPV 1640–42*, p. 213). Essex also suggested that he would depart to 'tack[e] a litle fresh aire in the countrie' on 7 September, but was still in London two days later. The virulence of the outbreak of plague currently affecting London and Westminster was an additional inducement to leave the metropolis before the recess adjournment; NAS, Hamilton MS GD 406/1/1418 and 1424: respectively, Edward Nicholas to the Marquess of Hamilton, 28 August 1641; and the Earl of Essex to the Marquess of Hamilton, 7 September 1641. For Essex's continuing presence in London on 9 September, see NA, SP 16/484/19: the Earl of Essex to Sir Thomas Rowe, 9 September 1641 (from the 'Parliament House').

93 An increasingly organized anti-Junto party in the Lords saw their opportunity to scupper the moves towards closer Union with Scotland. Their first attempt, which was unsuccessful, was to reject the Commons' ordinance (replicating an act already passed in the Scottish Parliament) forbidding the recruitment of troops, in either England or Ireland, by foreign powers; *LJ*, IV, 394. The ordinance is recorded as having been passed 'upon the question, by the major part': i.e. there had been a division. Had this anti-Junto party succeeded, the rejection of the ordinance would have inevitably disrupted (as it was doubtless intended to do) the recruitment of troops for the Elector Palatine's new expeditionary force, intended to be mobilized in readiness for the next year's campaigning season; NA, SP 16/483/97: Charles Louis, Prince-Elector of the Palatinate to Sir Thomas Rowe, 29 August 1641.

94 *LJ*, IV, 395; *CJ*, II, 286; for the printed version of the order, *After Debate* (BL, 669 f. 3/18). For the political context of the original order, see Centre for Kentish Studies, De L'Isle MS U1475/C132/171: William Hawkins to the Earl of Leicester, 21 January 1641 (HMC, *De L'Isle Manuscripts*, VI, 366); William Laud, 'Diary', entry for 21 January 1641, in Laud, *Works*, III, 239; and see above, Ch. 5.

95 *LJ*, IV, 395.

96 NAS, Hamilton MS GD 406/1/1427: Viscount Mandeville to the Marquess of Hamilton, 10 September 1641.

97 BL, Harl. MS 164 (D'Ewes diary), fos. 104v, 107v.

98 *After Debate*, BL, 669 f. 3/18; the future Royalists were Lord Dunsmore, the Earl of Dover and the 1st Earl of Denbigh, Viscount Newark (the eldest son of the Earl of Kingston), and Lord Coventry. The final member of the group was the Bishop of Lincoln, who, deprived of any hope of preferment in a Junto government committed to Union with Scotland, was moving into open opposition towards his former allies. He, too, was to side with the king in the Civil War.

99 Ibid.: the 5th Earl of Bedford, the Earl of Clare (Denzell Holles's elder brother), and Lord Hunsdon (eldest son of the Earl of Dover, who was on the opposing side). This printed list is probably a more accurate list of those who protested against the measure than the figure of six given in the Lords' *Journal*; for in some cases, not all those who voiced their protests actually got around to signing the Journal. The figure of eight, rather than six, protesters would seem to be confirmed by Mandeville's statement to Hamilton that 'some eight of us made our protestation against itt'; see NAS, Hamilton MS GD 406/1/1427: Viscount Mandeville to the Marquess of Hamilton, 10 September 1641.

100 The tactics employed by Warwick and his confederates are strikingly similar to the contingency plan first formulated back in February when it looked as though a Lords' majority might find in Strafford's favour: the Lords minority would declare their solidarity with the reformist majority in the Commons and act in defiance of their fellow peers; see Centre for Kentish Studies, De L'Isle MS U1475/C114/11: Sir John Temple to the Earl of Leicester, 18 February 1641 (HMC, *De L'Isle Manuscripts*, VI, 384).

101 For Warwick's prompt action, see BL, Harl. MS 164 (D'Ewes diary), fo. 109 (PLP, VI, 714).

102 Ibid.

103 Ibid.

104 Ibid., fo. 109v (PLP, VI, 715).

105 *CJ*, II, 287. It is extremely difficult to reconcile this statement, approved by the Commons' majority, with Professor Russell's claim that 'the Commons' majority['s] ... real quarrel in the summer of 1641 was with the

Lords as much as with the king'; Russell, *Fall of the British Monarchies*, p. 370.

106 NAS, Hamilton MS GD 406/1/1427: Viscount Mandeville to the Marquess of Hamilton, 10 September 1641.

107 *After Debate* (BL, 669 f. 3/18). This was a single sheet, designed to be pasted up or easily circulated as a handbill. Its partisan quality is evident in the fact that it prints, in full, the formal written dissent entered by eight of the reformist peers (the earls of Manchester, Bedford, Warwick, Newport, Clare, Viscount Mandeville, and Lords Hunsdon and Wharton). The only peer who did not enter a formal dissent, but who otherwise sided with the reformists, was Lord Keeper Lyttelton. Note that the list of dissenters printed in *LJ*, IV, 395, appears to be incomplete.

108 For the impact of the order, see David Cressy, *England on Edge: Crisis and Revolution, 1640–42* (Oxford, 2006), pp. 204–10; Russell, *Fall of the British Monarchies*, pp. 371–2; Anthony Fletcher, *The Outbreak of the English Civil War* (1981), p. 118.

109 For a diametrically opposite view, see Russell, *Fall of the British Monarchies*, p. 370.

110 It is revealing that what became the Commons order of 9 September seemed to have broad support in the Commons, in principle at least. There had been a number of divisions on 6 September which look like party divisions – with Barrington and Arthur Goodwin on one side, and the future Royalists, Sir John Culpeper and Lord Falkland on the other; but these represent disagreements about the finer wording of the ordinance, not an attempt to prevent it passing; see *CJ*, II, 280–1. When it came to the question of publishing the order on 9 September, the declaration justifying the Commons (and the Lords' minority) was drafted by a committee drawn from backers of either side in the previous debates: namely, Pym, Barrington, and St John for the more radical reformists, and Culpeper and Falkland for the more conservative reformists. Too much should not be read into this one instance; but it does suggest, *prima facie*, that the issuing of the Commons' declaration on 9 September was something on which the House was broadly united; indeed, it is

striking that the declaration was accepted by the Commons without a division; see *CJ*, II, 287.

111 BL, Harl. MS 164 (D'Ewes diary), fo. 109v (*PLP*, VI, 715).

112 Hatfield House, Hertfordshire, Salisbury MS 140/241: 'The Protestants Protestation', [9 September 1641], in the handwriting of the 2nd Earl of Salisbury (printed in HMC, *Salisbury Manuscripts*, XXIV, 277).

113 R. F. Young, *Comenius in England* (Oxford, 1932), pp. 38–9, 42–4; H. R. Trevor-Roper, 'Three Foreigners: the Philosophers and the Puritan Revolution', in his *Religion, the Reformation and Social Change, and Other Essays* (1967), p. 266. For Mandeville's involvement in this circle, see what was formerly Manchester MS 453, calendared in HMC, *Eighth Report*, Appendix, II, 54–5: four copies of letters from Comenius to Samuel Hartlib, 16 January to 1 July 1638.

114 C. R. Elrington (ed.), *The Whole Works of . . . James Ussher . . . with a Life of the Author, and an Account of his Writings*, 17 vols. (Dublin, 1847–64), XVI, 52: James Ussher, Archbishop of Armagh, to Samuel Hartlib, Dublin, 12 November 1639. Mandeville also owned at least one manuscript treatise by Durye and one addressed to Durye, both formerly at Kimbolton Castle: Manchester MS 603 and 607: HMC, *Eighth Report*, Appendix, II, 63.

115 John Durye, *A Summary Discourse concerning the Work of Peace Ecclesiastical* (Cambridge, [Aug.] 1641), epistle dedicatory (BL, E 167/3).

116 NA, SP 16/484/19: Earl of Essex to Sir Thomas Rowe, 9 September 1641.

117 The evidence for this statement follows in the rest of this section.

118 *The Lord Lowden his Learned and Wise Speech in the Upper House* [sic], p. 5.

119 Christopher Thompson, 'The Origins of the Politics of the Parliamentary Middle Group, 1625–29', *Transactions of the Royal Historical Society*, 5th ser., 22 (1972), 71–86, at 80–81; and see also Nathaniel Butler's account of a design against Spain's West India fleets in Bodl. Lib., MS Tanner 73/2, fo. 518. See, also, the report of the Earls of Essex and Warwick having dined with Queen Elizabeth

of Bohemia on 23 August 1623: BL, Harl. MS 389, fo. 354 (I owe this reference to Mr Christopher Thompson).

120 Cave filled a vacancy caused by the death of the previous member, Essex's half-brother, Sir Walter Devereux; Keeler, *Long Parliament*, pp. 128–9. Essex held the lease of the manor of Lichfield from 1604, for life, and the Lichfield waits wore his heraldic badge; see *Victoria County History: Staffordshire*, xiv, *Lichfield*, 73–87, at note 139.

121 Of the twenty-five members of the Committee, the following (over half the total) can be listed as Junto supporters: John Pym, Sir Benjamin Rudyard, Samuel Vassall, Sir Robert Harley, Denzell Holles, Sir Richard Cave, Sir Simonds D'Ewes, Sir Thomas Barrington, Robert Scawen (Northumberland's secretary), Sir John Meyrick (Essex's friend and fellow resident of Essex House), Sir Henry Vane junior, [Sir] John Hotham, Francis Rous (Pym's half-brother). For the list of the committee, see *CJ*, ii, 276; for Oliver St John's subsequent addition to it, *CJ*, ii, 278.

122 BL, Harl. MS 164 (D'Ewes diary), fo. 82.

123 Robin J. W. Swales, 'Sir Nathaniel Rich', *ODNB*; he was Warwick's second cousin

124 Thompson, 'The Origins of the Parliamentary Middle Group', pp. 80–81.

125 Archives du Ministère d'Affaires etrangères, Paris, Correspondence politique, Angleterre, 46, fos. 164–5v: Earl of Warwick to Cardinal Richelieu, [c. March 1636] (I am grateful to Professor Malcolm Smuts for providing me with a photocopy of this important MS). For the proposals in 1637, see Correspondence politique, Angleterre, 46, fos. 188, 209, 306; NA, C 115/N8/8800 (a reference I owe to Professor Smuts); and R. Malcolm Smuts, 'The Court and the Emergence of a Royalist Party' (forthcoming). For literary responses to the Palatine cause during this period, see Martin Butler, 'Entertaining the Palatine Prince: Plays on Foreign Affairs, 1635–37', *English Literary Renaissance*, 13 (1983), 319–44.

126 I owe this information to Mr Christopher Thompson.

127 Karen Ordahl Kupperman, *Providence Island, 1630–41: the Other Puritan Colony.*

(Cambridge and New York, 1994), pp. 337–8; eadem, 'Errand to the Indies: Puritan Colonization from Providence Island through the Western Design', *William and Mary Quarterly*, 3rd series, 45 (1988), 70–99; J. H. Elliott, *Empires of the Atlantic World: Britain and Spain in America, 1492–1830* (New Haven and London, 2006), p. 44; and see also Alison F. Games, '"The Sanctuarye of Our Rebell Negroes": the Atlantic Context of Local Resistance on Providence Island, 1630–41', *Slavery and Abolition*, 19 (1998), 1–21.

128 BL, Harl. MS 164 (D'Ewes diary), fo. 82.

129 *CJ*, ii, 280.

130 Ibid.

131 Lord Admiral Northumberland's extended convalescence seems to have provided the occasion for these measures. In mid August, on returning from Bath, he announced that he would be spending the summer at Petworth, his principal house, in Sussex; NA, SP 16/483, fo. 78: Thomas Smith to Sir John Pennington, 13 August 1641. He appears to have made a visit to London in early September; but it was not until late September that Northumberland returned to Syon, his Middlesex residence, in easy reach of London, by that stage appearing 'perfectly recovered and grown full of flesh, and look[ing] healthier than … ever': NA, SP 16/484/44: Edward Nicholas to Sir John Pennington, 28 September 1641.

132 In 1635, before the advent of the Ship Money revenues, it cost some £41,570: NA, SP 16/314/84; and see Andrew Thrush, 'Naval Finance and the Origins and Development of Ship Money', in Mark C. Fissel (ed.), *War and Government in Britain, 1598–1650* (Manchester, 1991), pp. 133–62. For the later period, see J. S. Wheeler, 'Navy Finance, 1649–60', *Historical Journal*, 39 (1996), 457–66.

133 Thomas Cogswell, *The Blessed Revolution: English Politics and the Coming of War, 1621–24* (Cambridge, 1989), pp. 102–3.

134 John Morrill, 'Robert Devereux, 3rd Earl of Essex', *ODNB*. The heroism of Essex's own conduct as a military commander inevitably merged with his father's

posthumous fame as a 'martyr' for the commonwealth, and found various echoes on the London stage during the 1630s; see, for example, Thomas Heywood, *A Challenge for Beauty* (1636), sig. H1, which figures an Essexian hero called 'Ferrers' who is 'The wonder,/And abstract of all vertues'. Ferrers, hardly coincidentally, was the oldest of the Earl of Essex's titles, the barony of Ferrers of Chartley having been conferred on the Devereux in 1461. For the context, see also, Martin Butler, *Theatre and Crisis 1632–42* (Cambridge, 1984), esp. pp. 198–210, 'Elizabethanism in Theatre and Politics'.

135 Ronald G. Asch, 'Charles Lewis [*sic*], Elector Palatine of the Rhine', *ODNB*.

136 BL, Sloane MS 1467 (Newsletters, 1640–41), fo. 14: letter of intelligence, [*c.* 5 August 1641].

137 NA, SP 16/483, fo. 26: Charles Louis, Prince-Elector of the Palatinate, to Sir Thomas Rowe, 6/16 August 1641.

138 NA, SP 16/483/74: Sir Richard Cave to Sir Thomas Rowe, 20 August 1641.

139 NA, SP 16/484/23 and 51: Elizabeth, dowager Queen of Bohemia and Electress of the Palatinate, to Sir Thomas Rowe, 11/23 September and 30 September/10 October 1641.

140 For a contemporary effort to inform public opinion of the state of the Regensburg (or Ratisbon) negotiations, see Calybute Downinge, *A Discoverie of the False Grounds of the Bavarian Party* ([October–November?] 1641), printed for Thomas Bates (BL, E 160/8).

141 Calybute Downinge, *A Discourse upon the Interest of England: Considered in the Case of the Deteinure of the Prince Elector Palatine his Dignities and Dominions* ([September?] 1641), p. 3 (BL, E 160/9). Any thought that the Bavarians could be trusted to act honourably as mediators in the current (and obviously doomed) negotiations at Regensburg was powerfully dispelled in another pro-interventionist treatise by Downinge, composed in the autumn of 1641, and published by Thomas Bates, one of the London stationers evidently closest to the Junto (and who was to be appointed by the Lords to publish the Nineteen Propositions, the Parliament's ultimatum to the king, in

June 1642); see also Calybute Downinge, *A Discoverie of the False Grounds of the Bavarian Party* ([October–November?] 1641), printed for Thomas Bates (BL, 160/8). This tract, which was dedicated to the House of Commons, is declared, on the title page, to have been 'Scene, and Allowed', though, as there is no formal order of approbation from the Commons' Committee for Printing, this would seem to have been an entirely informal approbation. For Bates's printing of the Nineteen Propositions, see *The Oath of the Kings of England taken out of the Parliament Rolle, ... likewise Propositions made by both Houses of Parliament to the Kings Majesty* (4 June 1642), for T[homas] Bates and F. Coules (BL, E 149/23).

142 Downinge, *A Discourse upon the Interest of England*, p. 2.

143 John Durye, *A Summary Discourse concerning the Work of Peace Ecclesiastical* (Cambridge, [August] 1641), pp. 8–9 (BL, E 167/3).

144 NA, SP 16/483/74: Sir Richard Cave to Sir Thomas Rowe, 20 August 1641.

145 NA, SP 16/483/80: Charles Louis, Elector Palatine, to Sir Thomas Rowe, 22 August 1641.

146 For the Scottish background, see John R. Young, 'The Scottish Parliament and European Diplomacy, 1641–47: the Palatinate, the Dutch Republic and Sweden', in Steve Murdoch (ed.), *Scotland and the Thirty Years' War, 1618–48* (Leiden and Boston, MA, 2001), pp. 77–106. Before Young, almost the only consideration of the subject is C. V. Wedgwood, 'The Elector Palatine and the Civil War', *History Today*, 4 (1954), 3–10.

147 *Newes from Scotland. His Maiesties Manifest touching the Palatine Cause* (Edinburgh and London, [September] 1641), p. 4 (BL, E 171/17).

148 Ibid., p. 7.

149 *LJ*, IV, 390–1, for Essex, with Manchester and Wharton, drawing the Commons' attention to the Spanish ambassadors' enlisting of men in London.

150 *CJ*, II, 285; *CSPV 1640–42*, pp. 213–4.

151 The Elector Palatine had written to Sir Thomas Rowe as early as 29 August stating

that the king 'and the two Parliaments' would not allow any men to leave 'these dominions, until I know whether I may have use of them': NA, SP 16/483/97.

152 [James Howell], *The True Informer, who in the Following Discours or Colloquy, discovereth unto the World the Chiefe Causes of the Sad Distempers in Great Brittany and Ireland* ([12 April] 1643), p. 23 (BL, E 96/10).

153 BL, Harl. MS 164 (D'Ewes diary), fos. 94v–5r (*PLP*, VI, 680–1).

154 Ibid., fos. 95, 105v (*PLP*, VI, 680–1).

155 For the phrase, Ibid., fo. 102v.

156 Ibid, fo. 98.

157 NA, SP 16/483/94: Earl of Bristol to [Sir Thomas Rowe], 28 August 1641.

158 *The Lord Lowden his Learned and Wise Speech in the Upper House*, p. 3.

159 Ibid., p. 4.

160 John Campbell, Lord Loudoun, *A Second Speech made by the Lord Lowden in the Parliament of Scotland, the 24 of Septemb[er] 1641* ([October], 1641), p. 3 (BL, E 199/14).

161 NA, SP 16/484/19: Earl of Essex to Sir Thomas Rowe, 9 September 1641, from the Parliament House. The latter detail is revealing, as it suggests that Essex was at the Palace of Westminster on the day of the royalist ambush which prevented the passing of ordinance against religious 'innovations'.

162 NAS, Hamilton MS GD 406/1/1427: Viscount Mandeville to the Marquess of Hamilton, 10 September 1641.

163 The Commons Committee met on Tuesdays and Saturdays during the recess: *The Diurnall Occurrences, or Dayly Proceedings of Both Houses* (1641), p. 364 (BL, E 523/1); though Nicholas records meetings taking place on a Sunday, the usual Privy Council meeting-day; see Bray, *Evelyn Diary and Correspondence*, IV, 66, 78, 83. The implications of the campaign to implement the Commons' order of 8 September are discussed in the following chapter.

164 ASV, Senato, Dispacci Inghil. 43, fos. 89–94v: Giovanni Giustinian to the Doge and Senate, 17/27 September 1641. Most of these

dispatches seems to have been drafted by Giustinian's clever, English-speaking secretary, Gieronimo Agostini (for whose ability to speak English, see *CSPV 1640–42*, p. 249). The Recess Committees did turn out to contain the seed of a dangerous new development; it was the first of a series of major bicameral committees, which, over the following decade, took over an ever-expanding portfolio of executive powers from the Parliament: from the Committee of Safety of 1642–44, to the Committee of Both Kingdoms of 1644–46, and the Derby House Committee of 1646–48; see John Adamson, 'The Triumph of Oligarchy: The Munagement of War and the Committee of Both Kingdoms', in Chris R. Kyle and Jason Peacey (eds.), *Parliament at Work: Parliamentary Committees, Political Power and Public Access in Early Modern England* (Woodbridge, 2002), pp. 101–27.

165 For the first payment of this 'Brotherly Assistance', see NA, SP 46/80 (State Papers, supplementary), fo. 191: the receipt (signed by Lord Loudoun, Hew Kennedy and John Smyth), is dated 14 August 1641; see also BL, Harl. MS 163 (D'Ewes diary), fo. 339; *CJ*, II, p. 182. The extent of Warwick's influence in these arrangements is considered, above, Ch. 11, note 131.

166 ASV, Senato, Dispacci Inghil. 43, fo. 72: Giovanni Giustinian to the Doge and Senate, 10/20 September 1641 (*CSPV 1640–42*, p. 215). The section is in code in the original manuscript. For Northumberland's return from Bath, see NA, SP 16/483, fo. 78: Thomas Smith to Sir John Pennington, 13 August 1641, where Smith notes that Northumberland intended to go to Petworth, Sussex, 'next Monday'. Northumberland was at Petworth by 25 August, where he declared himself much recovered and intending to go to London shortly; see NA, SP 16/483, fo. 175: Earl of Northumberland to Sir Thomas Rowe, 25 August 1641.

167 ASV, Senato, Dispacci Inghil. 43, fo. 72: Giovanni Giustinian to the Doge and Senate, 10/20 September 1641. *CSPV 1640–42*, p. 215, misreads the manuscript 'diritti' (rights) for 'denti', rendering this passage, in consequence, as 'the point that just [*sic*] offends the *teeth* of his prerogative'.

168 These appointments are listed in detail, above, Ch. 11; for the quotation, ASV, Senato, Dispacci Inghil. 43, fo. 72: Giovanni

Giustinian to the Doge and Senate, 10/20 September 1641 (*CSPV 1640–42*, p. 215).

169 Bray, *Evelyn Diary and Correspondence*, IV, 76: Edward Nicholas to Charles I, 27 September 1641.

170 Surrey History Centre, Bray MS 52/2/19/16: Edward Nicholas to Thomas Webb, 5 October 1641. The reference to 'ordinances' is worthy of note, as Parliament had yet to pass any such legal instruments (which were tantamount to statutes, though issued on the authority of the Lords and Commons alone, without requiring the royal assent). Nicholas's mention of them at this point may suggest that their introduction (as a means of legislating without the king) was already being discussed by 5 October.

171 Bray, *Evelyn Diary and Correspondence*, IV, 74, 80, 81–2: Edward Nicholas to Charles I, letters of 27 September, 3 October, 5 October 1641.

172 Inveraray Castle, Argyllshire, Argyll Muniments Bundle 61: ante-nuptial contract, dated 10 January and 22 April 1642 (I owe this reference to Dr John Scally); NAS, Hamilton MS GD 406/1/1459 and 1472: Earl of Loudoun to Marquess of Hamilton, 22 November 1641 and 9 December 1641. Both parties to the planned marriage were under age at the time of the ante-nuptial contract; see also John Scally, 'Counsel in Crisis: James, 3rd Marquis of Hamilton and the Bishops' Wars, 1638–40', in John R. Young (ed.), *Celtic Dimensions of the British Civil Wars: Proceedings of the Second Conference of the Research Centre in Scottish History, University of Strathclyde* (Edinburgh, 1997), pp. 18–34.

173 NAS, Hamilton MS GD 406/1/1427: Viscount Mandeville to the Marquess of Hamilton, 10 September 1641. There is a similarly revealing moment in Mandeville's letter to Hamilton of 20 August 1641, sent via Lord Howard of Escrick, in which he assures Hamilton that 'The Chamberlaine [the Earl of Essex] will write to you', adding: 'return him, I pray, some kindnes'; NAS, Hamilton MS GD 406/1/1412. See also: 'My Lord', wrote Mandeville to Hamilton on 20 August, 'yff you have any Commands for mee heare, honnor mee with them and afford mee the honnor and tytle off your Lordship's most humble servant'; NAS, Hamilton MS GD

406/1/1412: Viscount Mandeville to the Marquess of Hamilton, 20 August [1641] (Mandeville has wrongly written the year as '1640'). Hamilton's seventeenth-century (and highly exculpatory) biographer, Gilbert Burnet, claimed that Hamilton was in communication with Essex, Mandeville, and, in particular, with Lord Saye; and that this was merely 'to prepare them to a better Correspondence with the King'. This is at best a naive, at worst a deliberately misleading, account of Hamilton's role in the autumn of 1641; see Gilbert Burnet, *The Memoires of the Lives and Actions of James and William, Dukes of Hamilton and Castleherald* (1677), p. 188. Revealingly, it was to Mandeville that the former Scottish Commissioners to London, Lord Loudoun and the Earl of Dunfermline, also directed their correspondence; see BL, Harl. MS 164 (D'Ewes diary), fo. 100, referring to a letter from Lord Maitland (later 2nd Earl of Lauderdale) to Viscount Mandeville, dated at York, 3 September 1641, and enclosing a further letter from Loudoun and Dunfermline.

174 The commission was composed of two peers and four Commons-men. From the Lords came the 5th Earl of Bedford and Lord Howard of Escrick, both of whom had been involved in promoting the Petition of the Twelve Peers, as had Nathaniel Fiennes and John Hampden, from the Commons. The two other Commons-men were Sir Philip Stapilton, who had first moved that a bill of attainder might be used against Strafford; and Sir William Armyne, the only member of the group that does not seem to have a history of prior involvement with the Junto leadership.

175 NA, SP 16/483, fo. 74: notes of advice prepared by Nicholas 'Au R[oi]' [For the king], 13 August 1641.

176 'You may saffely communicate any thinge unto Mr Hamden', Mandeville assured Hamilton, 'and confide in him [and] I beseech you to putt respects upon my Lord Howard [of Escrick] and doe whatt you may to oblige him, for hee is noble and honest and your servant': NAS, Hamilton MS GD 406/1/1412: Viscount Mandeville to the Marquess of Hamilton, 20 August [1641].

177 Beinecke Lib., Yale, MS Osborn Shelves, Howard of Escrick Correspondence, Folder 3.23: Howard of Escrick and the other

parliamentary commissioners in Edinburgh to Viscount Mandeville, 28 September 1641. A number of their letters (including this just quoted) read as though they were written in the expectation that they would be intercepted and potentially used as evidence against them. This letter is also discussed in Russell, *Fall of the British Monarchies*, p. 322.

178 The Scots proposed the sending of a further group of commissioners to London to negotiate those items, including matters of trade, which had not been dealt with under the provisions of the Anglo-Scottish Treaty ratified in August 1641.

179 NA, SP 16/484/51: Elizabeth, titular Queen of Bohemia to Sir Thomas Rowe, 30 September/10 October 1641 (emphasis added).

180 NA, SP 16/484/60: Earl of Bristol to Sir Thomas Rowe, 2 October 1641.

181 For the phrase, see *The Lord Lowden his Learned and Wise Speech in the Upper House*, p. 3.

182 NA, SP 16/484/2: Edward Nicholas to [Sir John Pennington], 1 September 1641.

183 HMC, *Ormonde Manuscripts*, new ser., 1, 46: Thomas Salvin to the Earl of Ormond, 5 October 1641.

184 For the Elector Palatine's popularity, see ASV, Senato, Dispacci Inghil. 42, fo. 229v: Giovanni Giustinian to the Doge and Senate, 5/15 March 1641 (*CSPV 1640–42*, p. 130).

13. COUNTER-REVOLUTION AND REVOLT

1 Carte, *Life of Ormond*, v, 285: Lord Gormanston to the Earl of Clanricard, Gormanstown, 21 January 1642 (a reference I owe to the kindness of Dr David Scott).

2 Trinity College Lib., Dublin, MS 816 (Rebellion Depositions), fo. 90: deposition of Thomas Ashe, reporting the claims of one of the Catholic rebels of October 1641; quoted in Nicholas Canny, 'What Really Happened in Ireland in 1641?', in Jane Ohlmeyer (ed.), *Ireland from Independence to Occupation, 1641–60* (Cambridge, 1995), p. 29. The most important recent studies of the origins of the Irish insurrection of 1641 (in part, adumbrated this earlier essay of 1995) is to be found in Nicholas Canny, *Making Ireland*

British, 1580–1650 (Oxford, 2001), pp. 461–550. For the insurrection itself, see Michael Perceval-Maxwell, *Outbreak of the Irish Rebellion of 1641* (Dublin, 1994); and, stressing the economic dimension to the uprising, Raymond Gillespie, 'The End of an Era: Ulster and the Outbreak of the 1641 Rising', in Ciaran Brady and Raymond Gillespie (eds.), *Natives and Newcomers: the Making of Irish Colonial Society, 1534–1641* (Dublin, 1986), pp. 191–214; and his 'Harvest Crises in Early Seventeenth-Century Ireland', *Irish Economic and Social History*, 11 (1984), 5–18.

3 ASV, Senato, Dispacci Inghil. 43, fo. 27r-v: Giovanni Giustinian to the Doge and Senate, 13/23 August 1641 (*CSPV 1640–42*, p. 200).

4 For Irish reactions to events in England and Scotland during 1641, one of the best accounts remains Aidan Clarke, *The Old English in Ireland, 1625–42* (1966), Chs. 8 and 9, and pp. 220–9; and Perceval-Maxwell, *Outbreak of the Irish Rebellion*.

5 NA, SP 16/482, fo. 196: Robert Reade to Thomas Windebank, 30 July/9 August 1641, from Paris (emphasis added). It is possible to associate the vehemently anti-Catholic pamphlet, which appeared around September 1641, with these pro-Catholic initiatives reported by Reade; see *To the Honourable the Knights, Citizens, and Burgesses of the Commons House in Parliament ... in Answer to the Humble Petition of the Lay-Catholikes of England* ([Sept.] 1641), BL, E 169/11.

6 Evidence of the Junto leaders efforts to distance themselves from the charge of radical Puritanism can be found in [Henry Parker], *A Discourse concerning Puritans. A Vindication of those, who uniustly suffer by the Mistake, Abuse, and Misapplication of that Name* (1641), BL, E 204/3, a work which exonerates Saye and Brooke from the charge, and which was almost certainly written with Saye's approval, and probably at his behest.

7 On the sporadic enforcement of the measures against Catholic clergy, see Caroline M. Hibbard, *Charles I and the Popish Plot* (Chapel Hill, NC, 1983), pp. 218–9.

8 *To the Honourable the Knights, Citizens, and Burgesses of the Commons House in Parliament ... in Answer to the Humble Petition of the Lay-Catholikes of England*, p. 6.

9 'A. B. C.', *A True Coppy of a Bold and Most Peremptory Letter, Sent to the Honourable Earle of Salisbury* ([late] 1641) p. 2 (BL, E 172/12).

10 For the controversy within the Irish Parliament over its relationship with the English Parliament, see Perceval-Maxwell, *Outbreak of the Irish Rebellion*, p. 173.

11 James S. Hart, *Justice upon Petition: the House of Lords and the Reformation of Justice, 1621–75* (1991), p. 65; and above, Ch. 4.

12 Minnesota UL, MS 137 (Peyton diary), fo. 133; Culpeper was speaking on 21 June 1641 (*PLP*, v, 257). (I am grateful to Dr David Scott for this reference.)

13 Perceval-Maxwell, *The Outbreak of the Irish Rebellion*, p. 173; and see his Ch. 7, more generally, for the controversies over constitutional arrangements affecting England and Ireland.

14 *CJ*, II, 60, 281–2; *LJ*, IV, 395, 401. Two involved *causes célèbres* carried over from Strafford's reign: those of Adam Loftus, 1st Viscount Loftus of Ely, who had served as Chancellor of Ireland from 1619 to 1638; and Francis Annesley, 1st Lord Mountnorris (and from 1642 2nd Viscount Valentia), who had been Treasurer at Wars for Ireland in the 1630s. Ironically, the three other litigants – William Brabazon, 1st Earl of Meath; Thomas Dillon, 4th Viscount Dillon; was a Royalist in the 1640s; and Nicholas Netterville, 1st Viscount Netterville of Dowth – were all to be Royalists in the 1640s. The only non-noble litigant was 'Edward Fay, gentleman'.

15 This was the more ironical as Leicester appears to have believed that Ireland was dependent on the king, rather than the English Parliament; Perceval-Maxwell, *The Outbreak of the Irish Rebellion*, p. 177.

16 *CJ*, II, 285.

17 Bristol, acting it seems on behalf of the king, had raised the matter in Parliament, and reported the activities of the Spanish ambassador on 6 August: BL, Harl. MS 163 (D'Ewes diary), fo. 425. The Lords had requested a conference with the Commons on whether 3,000 or 4,000 should be the maximum number of troops allowed the Spanish; but the matter was not discussed at a conference before the king's departure and no parliamentary consent was given. Charles nevertheless gave his consent to the raising of 4,000 men on 9 August, without parliamentary approval; *LJ*, IV, 345; Clarke, *Old English in Ireland*, p. 155. For the interests of Spain, France and the Holy See in Ireland, see Tadhg Ó hAnnracháin, 'The Strategic Involvement of Continental Powers in Ireland 1596–1691', in Pádraig Lenihan (ed.), *Conquest and Resistance: War in Seventeenth-Century Ireland* (Leiden, 2001), pp. 25–52, at pp. 36–8.

18 See, in particular, the contribution of Sir Richard Cave (probably speaking on behalf of the Elector Palatine and Essex) in the Commons: BL, Harl. MS 164 (D'Ewes diary), fo. 72v; and Perceval-Maxwell, *Outbreak of the Irish Rebellion*, p. 189. There are few clearer examples of the Law of Unintended Consequences. By preventing the export of these levies, the English Parliament also overruled the Irish Lords Justices (the two governors who acted as joint-viceroys in the absence of the Lord Lieutenant), who wanted Ireland rid of these men 'unapt ... to labour', and played into the hands of the Catholic lobby in the Dublin Parliament which was anxious to retain the soldiers in Ireland, lest developments in England and Scotland should make these forces useful to the king's interest in the future; for the background, see Clarke, *Old English in Ireland*, p. 155. How many were involved in the Ulster insurrection of October 1641 is impossible to estimate.

19 The complex politics of the Irish army are exhaustively discussed in Perceval-Maxwell, *Outbreak of the Irish Rebellion*, pp. 184–91. *Pace* Professor Perceval-Maxwell, the English House of Lords did not 'agree' to allow the Spanish to transport troops in August; they agreed on the terms of a conference with the Commons on the subject, but as that conference was never brought to a conclusion, the matter fell into abeyance. For evidence that the levies recruited for Spain ended up fighting with the Confederates, see Ulick Bourke, *The Memoirs and Letters of Ulick, Marquiss of Clanricarde* (1757), pp. 17, 30.

20 *CJ*, II, 285, for the text of the ordinance of 9 September 1641 against the transporting of levies from England and Ireland.

21 Longleat House, Wiltshire, Devereux

Papers I, fo. 371: Nicholas Whyte to Sir
Walter Devereux at Essex House, 22 March
1639; Sir Christopher Wandesforde to Sir
Walter Devereux, 28 March 1639: Devereux
Papers I, fo. 373. In 1639, the capital value
of Essex's lands in Ireland was put at over
£20,000: Devereux Papers I, fo. 351:
Nicholas Whyte to the Earl of Essex, 28
January 1639.

22 Owen Connolly, Clotworthy servant, was
one of the first to give an account of the
insurrection plot to the Lord Justice, Sir
William Parsons, on 22 October 1641;
however one reason why Clotworthy may not
have received information from Connolly is
that the latter was possibly 'more deeply
involved [in the plot] than he cared to admit'.
For his account, see HMC, *Ormond
Manuscripts*, new ser., II, 1–3; Clarke, *Old
English in Ireland*, p. 161n (for endnote
quotation).

23 Clarke, *Old English in Ireland*, pp.
154–61, is one of the best explications of their
course.

24 As Clarke put it, 'the disbandment and
subsequent re-enlistment of the soldiers of
[Strafford's] new army were an essential part
of the context within which a rebellious
conspiracy secretly matured'; ibid., p. 156.
For Catholic fears of the English Parliament,
and the willingness of Ireland's Catholic
communities to recognize the 'the authority
of the king', while denying 'the authority of
the English Parliament in Ireland', see
Perceval-Maxwell, *Outbreak of the Irish
Rebellion*, p. 201.

25 Carte, *Life of Ormond*, v, 280: Lords of
the Pale to the nobility and gentry of County
Galway, 29 December 1641.

26 Perceval-Maxwell, *The Outbreak of the
Irish Rebellion*, pp. 206–8.

27 Ibid., p. 206 (for quotation); for the
relations between the various O'Neills, see
Jerrold Casway, *Owen Roe O'Neill and the
Struggle for Catholic Ireland* (Philadelphia,
PA, 1984), Appendix I, p. 273.

28 Ibid., Appendix II, p. 274.

29 This reading of the Irish plots follows
closely the account in Perceval-Maxwell,
Outbreak of the Irish Rebellion, pp. 205–6.

30 For Daniel's understanding of

Westminster politics, see, for example,
Staffordshire RO, Dartmouth MS
D(W)1778/I/i/14: Daniel O'Neill to William
Legge, 23 February 1641. The king's
annoyance at the Commons' Recess
Committee's imprisonment of the two Army
Plotters, Sir John Berkeley and Daniel
O'Neill, in September 1641 ('I hope some day
they may repent there severitie') is also
noteworthy; see Bray, *Evelyn Diary and
Correspondence*, IV, 78.

31 The Earl of Leicester – from May 1641,
the new Lord-Lieutenant of Ireland – was the
grandson of the Elizabethan viceroy of
Ireland, Sir Henry Sidney, who had led an
earlier campaign to suppress the power of the
O'Neills (in the 1560s and 1570s). The Earl
of Essex was the son of the Lord Lieutenant
of Ireland who had campaigned against the
O'Neills unsuccessfully in the 1590s. And the
Earl of Newport was the son of the viceroy
who had finally vanquished O'Neill power,
Lord Mountjoy, the author of a scorched-
earth policy in Ulster that had earned him the
lasting hatred of the Irish.

32 'Relation of Lord Maguire', in Mary
Hickson, *Ireland in the Seventeenth Century,
or the Irish Massacres of 1641–42*, 2 vols.
(1884), II, 341–54, quotation at p. 344.

33 Essex had been mentioned as a possible
Lord Lieutenant of Ireland in the course of
the Bedford negotiations on office in early
1641; the idea was still current in the late
autumn, for which see John Cragge, *A
Prophecy concerning the Earle of Essex that
now is* ([October–November], 1641), sig. A2v
(BL, E 181/8).

34 Perceval-Maxwell, *Outbreak of the Irish
Rebellion*, pp. 206–8. The three colonels,
were Sir James Dillon, Richard Plunkett and
Hugh Byrne (who had formerly served in John
O'Neill's regiment in Spain).

35 Quoted in Clarke, *Old English in Ireland*,
p. 228.

36 For the colonels' plot, see Perceval-
Maxwell, *The Outbreak of the Irish
Rebellion*, pp. 207–11.

37 Clarke, *Old English in Ireland*, pp. 157,
228; Perceval-Maxwell, *Outbreak of the Irish
Rebellion*, pp. 209–12; *CSPI, 1633–47*, p.
342.

38 'Lord Maguire's relation', in Hickson,

Ireland in the Seventeenth Century, II, 341-54; Clarke, *Old English in Ireland*, p. 160.

39 Ibid.

40 Though their plight was doubtless exacerbated, in 1641, by the presence of 8,000 further underemployed young men in the form of the Irish army; see Canny, *Making Ireland British*, pp. 473-5.

41 Trinity College depositions, quoted in Canny, *Making Ireland British*, p. 493.

42 Tadhg Ó hAnnracháin, 'Disrupted and Disruptive: Continental Influence on the Confederate Catholics of Ireland', in Allan Macinnes and Jane Ohlmeyer (eds.), *The Stuart Kingdoms in the Seventeenth Century: Awkward Neighbours* (Dublin, 2002), pp. 135-50; and Declan Downey, 'Augustinians and Scotists: the Irish Contribution to Counter-Reformation Theology in Continental Europe', in Brendan Bradshaw and Dáire Keogh (eds.), *Christianity in Ireland: Revisiting the Story* (Dublin, 2002), pp. 96-108.

43 Canny, *Making Ireland British*, p. 490.

44 'In explaining why the rebellion had occurred most accounts centred on events outside Ireland. The most common reason given was that the English Parliament had passed legislation requiring Catholics to attend the Protestant service or, according to other versions of the rumour, lose their land or be executed. For this legislation they blamed the Scots who had recently defeated the king in the second Bishops' War. Some claimed that the London Puritans had already seized the Catholic queen, Henrietta Maria, and intended to execute her. The king, it was said in Tyrone, was already dead, executed by the Scots': Raymond Gillespie, 'Destabilizing Ulster, 1641-42', in Brian Mac Cuarta (ed.), *Ulster 1641: Aspects of the Rising* (Belfast, 1997), p. 114.

45 Trinity College depositions, quoted in Canny, *Making Ireland British*, p. 492.

46 Trinity College Lib., Dublin, MS 829, fos. 302-5: deposition of Peter Mainsell; quoted in Canny, *Making Ireland British*, p. 529.

47 Trinity College Lib., Dublin, MS 809, fos. 5-12; quoted in Canny, *Making Ireland British*, p. 489.

48 Trinity College Lib., Dublin, MS 836, fo. 82; quoted in Canny, 'What Really Happened in 1641?', p. 30 (my emphasis). Here, too, Irish fears were not wholly fanciful. A number of the leading Junto peers were keen advocates of establishing new Protestant plantations in Ireland; the Marquess of Hamilton, for example – by the autumn of 1641, 'the most considdarable subject in these twoe [British] Kingedomes' – had been an enthusiast for the policy in the 1630s; and almost all the major Junto grandees, including the new Lord Lieutenant, the Earl of Leicester (the grandson of Sir Henry Sidney, the architect of an earlier policy of Anglicization in Ireland), were widely known as 'Puritans'. Two of them – Essex and Newport – were the sons of fathers hated in Catholic Ireland for their part in the suppression of Tyrone's Rebellion of the 1590s. NAS, Hamilton MS GD 406/1/1451: Sir Henry Mildmay to the Marquess of Hamilton, 13 November 1641 (for the Hamilton quotation); Jane Ohlmeyer, 'Strafford, the "Londonderry Business" and the "New British History"', in Julia Merritt (ed.), *The Political World of Thomas Wentworth, Earl of Strafford, 1621-41* (Cambridge, 1996), pp. 209-29 (for Hamilton's interests in Irish plantation). See also Wallace T. MacCaffrey, 'Sir Henry Sidney', *ODNB*; for Leicester, see Ian Atherton, 'Robert Sidney, second Earl of Leicester', *ODNB*.

49 Canny, *Making Ireland British*, p. 516.

50 In one gruesome tale, Henriette Marie's own confessor was reported to have been 'executed and quartered in the queen's presence' – a story which had a least some foundation in fact: there had been an execution and quartering of a priest at Tyburn in late July; but not in the queen's presence and not the queen's confessor. Indeed, there is some evidence that the queen's Household was actively feeding stories of the persecution of English Catholics in order to inflame opinion in Ireland; see Canny, *Making Ireland British*, pp. 516-7.

51 Carte, *Life of Ormond*, v, 285: Lord Gormanston to the Earl of Clanricard, Gormanstown, 21 January 1642.

52 Professor Canny, who rightly points to the long-term causes of the Irish insurrection of 1641, nevertheless endorses the 'high-political' explanation of the revolt to the

extent that the 'recent political events in Scotland and England can be said to have provided the occasion for a rising in Ireland'; Canny, *Making Ireland British*, p. 550.

53 Ibid., p. 490.

54 ASV, Senato, Dispacci Inghil. 43, fo. 59: Giovanni Giustinian to the Doge and Senate, 27 August/6 September 1641 (*CSPV 1640–42*, p. 210). Giustinian estimated (probably exaggeratedly) that 200,000 people had evacuated London, including all the ambassadors.

55 ASV, Senato, Dispacci Inghil. 43, fo. 96v: Giustinian to the Doge and Senate, 24 September/4 October 1641; 'le redine [*sic*] del Governo' (cf. *CSPV 1640–42*, p. 222).

56 For the Junto's dependency on popularity, see Bray, *Evelyn Diary and Correspondence*, IV, 76: Edward Nicholas to Charles I, 27 September 1641.

57 BL, Harl. MS 164 (D'Ewes diary), fo. 109v (*PLP*, VI, 715). No such declaration was, in fact, issued, despite what D'Ewes claims to have been a favourable response to the proposal in the Commons.

58 Above, Ch. 12.

59 *After Debate about the Printing and Publishing of the Order of the 16th of January last* ([September], 1641), single sheet, BL, 669 f. 3/18.

60 Bray, *Evelyn Diary and Correspondence*, IV, 79: Edward Nicholas to Charles I, 29 September 1641.

61 No minute books have survived for either of the Recess Committees, though something of the Commons business can be reconstructed from D'Ewes's notes of the meetings of 12, 16 and 19 October 1641: Coates, *D'Ewes Diary*, pp. 1–11; and from *Diurnall Occurrences*, sigg. Bbb–Ccc3. Summary minutes of the meetings of 12 and 16 October also comprise the bulk of the pamphlet misleadingly entitled *Heads of Severall Petitions and Complaints made against Sir Iohn Conyers* ([Oct.] 1641), pp. 1–4 (BL, E 173/14).

62 *CJ*, II, 282, 284.

63 *Die Mercurii 8[Octav]o Septemb[ris] 1641* ([Sept.] 1641), single sheet (BL, 669 f. 3/14).

64 *CJ*, II, 287 (my emphasis).

65 *Diurnall Occurrences*, p. 368. [Commons' Recess Committee], *Die Martis 28 Septemb[ris] 1641. At the Committee appointed by the Commons House of Parliament to sit during the Recesse* ([Sept.] 1641), single sheet (Society of Antiquaries, London; Wing 2nd edn. E2529). On 28 September, the Commons Recess Committee discovered that while the Lords' order enjoying the use of the *Prayer Book* had been read in Churches, their own order had been widely ignored. On the implementation, see Julie Spraggon, *Puritan Iconoclasm during the English Civil War: the Attack on Religious Imagery by Parliament and its Soldiers* (Woodbridge, 2003), pp. 67–8.

66 Bray, *Evelyn Diary and Correspondence*, IV, 79: Edward Nicholas to Charles I, 29 September 1641.

67 Coates, *D'Ewes Diary*, p. 6.

68 *Heads of Severall Petitions and Complaints*, p. 2 (emphasis added).

69 Coates, *D'Ewes Diary*, p. 6. They were harmless, thought D'Ewes, and should be left as a 'monument to the miserable ignorance of those times'. The petition from the parishioners presented on 12 October appears to have been a counter-petition to one earlier presented by the churchwarden, Master Herringe, who had evidently first raised the question with the committee because the parishioners refused to pay for the cost of his having removed the offending inscriptions. Although the St Mary Woolchurch case first appears in the surviving 'minutes' of the Recess Committee's activities on 12 October (see *Heads of Severall Petitions and Complaints*, p. 2), his 'indiscreet' iconoclasm seems to have been perpetrated without reference to the printed Commons Order. A 'Mr Herringe', almost certainly the churchwarden (as he is the only person of that name in the parish), is listed among the inhabitants of St Mary Woolchurch in 1638, with rents of £50, a detail that places him among the half dozen wealthiest members of the parish; T. C. Dale (ed.), *The Inhabitants of London in 1638* (1931), pp. 121–22.

70 Jacqueline Eales, *Puritans and Roundheads: the Harleys of Brampton Bryan and the Outbreak of the English Civil War* (Cambridge, 1990), p. 115 (for quotation);

HMC, *Eleventh Report*, Appendix, VII, 147; also discussed in David Cressy, *England on Edge: Crisis and Revolution, 1640–42* (Oxford, 2006), p. 205.

71 *CJ*, II, 287 (for the text of the Commons' Order). Professor Cressy notes that at Wigmore, Sir Robert Harley 'implemented the Commons order with a vengeance', though, in fact, Harley's actions had no authority from the Commons; and see Cressy, *England on Edge*, p. 205.

72 HMC, *Buccleuch and Queensbury Manuscripts*, III, 415–6; quoted in Cressy, *England on Edge*, p. 205.

73 [Commons' Recess Committee], *Die Martis 28 Septemb[ris] 1641*, single sheet (Society of Antiquaries, London; Wing 2nd edn. E2529). This order accompanied the printed edition of the Commons' Declaration of 9 September, a declaration which was a more extended document than the Order of 8 September (from which it should be distinguished). After printing the text of the order (*Declaration*, pp. 1–4), it recounted the fact that the Lords' (rival) order concerning divine service of 16 January 1641 had only been passed by eleven peers, with nine other lords dissenting (*Declaration*, pp. 4–5); see *A Declaration of the Commons in Parliament: made September the 9th, 1641* ([28–29 Sept.] 1641), pp. 1–5 (BL, E 171/13).

74 *CJ*, II, 287. The closest the order approached to a sanction was that instances of non-compliance could be brought to the attention of Justices of the Peace, who were to investigate the claims and report them to Parliament before 30 October 1641. As Dr Spraggon has pointed out, the 8 September Order effectively bypassed the higher clergy, making it possible, for the first time, for parish clergy and churchwardens to destroy images without seeking prior approval from the local ordinary. At one level this was 'radical', in that it bypassed the episcopate; but on the other hand, by removing any central administrative oversight from the process of local reformation, it also provided *carte blanche* for non-compliance by parishes clergy and congregations who were opposed to the measures proposed; see Spraggon, *Puritan Iconoclasm during the English Civil War*, p. 65.

75 On the few occasions when the Recess Committee did intervene to order the removal of superstitious objects – as when it summoned the minister of St Giles in the Fields, Westminster, for refusing to destroy 'some scandalous pictures' – it was invariably in response to petitions or complaints from parishioners, not as part of any campaign to enforce the Commons' Order of its own; see Coates, *D'Ewes Diary*, p. 5: D'Ewes' notes of the Commons Recess Committee for 12 October 1641.

76 *Diurnall Occurrences*, p. 371 (sig. Ccc).

77 Coates, *D'Ewes Diary*, pp. 6–7.

78 Compare Charles I, *By the King a Further Proclamation prohibiting the Exportation of Corne and Graine* (1631), STC2 8974; and idem, *By the King. A Proclamation and Declaration to inform our Loving Subjects of our Kingdom of England of the Seditious Practices of Some in Scotland* (1639), STC 1984:24.

79 [Commons' Recess Committee], *Die Mercurii 8[Octav]o Septemb[ris] 1641. Wheras Divers Innovations in or about the Worship of God* ([c. 1 Oct.] 1641), single sheet (BL, 669 f. 3/14).

80 [Commons' Recess Committee], *Die Martis 28 Septemb[ris] 1641*, single sheet; [Commons' Recess Committee], *Declaration of the Commons in Parliament: made September the 9th, 1641*.

81 Surrey History Centre, Bray MS 85/5/2/9: Edward Nicholas to Charles I, 6 October 1641. This is fully a month before the earliest instance of the usage 'King Pym' found by Gardiner: on, or shortly after, 8 November. The Recess Committee's order read out in churches on 3 October appears to have been the origin of the soubriquet. For the parliamentarian general, Lord Fairfax, equally satirically, as 'King Tom', see *Mercurius Psitacus*, no. [1] (14–21 June 1648), p. 3 (BL, E 449/8).

82 I. W., *Certaine Affirmations in Defence of the Pulling Down of Communion Rails* ([Sept.] 1641), sig. A2 (BL, E 171/1).

83 For suggestive anecdotal evidence, see Cressy, *England on Edge*; Spraggon, *Puritan Iconoclasm during the English Civil War*, pp. 138–44; and Russell, *Fall of the British Monarchies*, pp. 402–4.

84 For an example, see the attempts by a godly minority in St Giles Cripplegate, London, to establish an afternoon lecture (one of the 'godly' practices approved of by the 8 September Order), to meet on Thursdays, but which were obstructed by the Laudian incumbent, Dr William Fuller (the Dean of Ely), and his curate, Timothy Hutton; see *The Petition and Articles exhibited in Parliament against Dr Fuller, Deane of Ely* ([Oct.] 1641), sig. A3[1] (BL, E 175/1). It is noteworthy that the first attempt to establish this afternoon lecture was not made until 8 October, an entire month after the order had been passed. It further suggests that it was not until the Declaration of 9 September appeared in print (in the first week of October) that parishioners realized the full implications of the order's terms. Interestingly, it was not until the beginning of October 1641 that Nehemiah Wallington's parish of St Leonard Eastcheap got round to demolishing its 'superstitious pictures in the glass': Nehemiah Wallington, *Historical Notices of Events occurring chiefly in the Reign of Charles I*, ed. R. Webb, 2 vols. (1869), I, 259.

85 Spraggon, *Puritan Iconoclasm during the English Civil War*, Chs 3 and 4.

86 *CJ*, II, 287.

87 BL, Evelyn Collection, Nicholas Box: Lord Cottington to Edward Nicholas, Fonthill, Wiltshire, 16 September 1641.

88 Cressy, *England on Edge*, p. 196 (for quotation).

89 *A Discovery of 29 Sects here in London, all of which, except the First, are Most Divelish and Damnable* ([Sept.], 1641), pp. 2, 4, 7 (BL, E 168/7).

90 ASV, Senato, Dispacci Inghil. 43, fo. 96: Giovanni Giustinian to the Doge and Senate, 24 September/4 October 1641 (*CSPV 1640–42*, p. 222).

91 Spraggon, *Puritan Iconoclasm in the English Civil War*, pp. 133, 143–4.

92 NA, SP 16/484/68; quoted in Russell, *Fall of the British Monarchies*, p. 403. For examples, see Cressy, *England on Edge*, pp. 197–8.

93 Bray, *Evelyn Diary and Correspondence*, IV, 82: Edward Nicholas to Charles I, 5 October 1641.

94 I owe this observation to Conrad Russell.

95 NA, SP 16/484/63: 'P. W.' to Sir Henry Vane, 5 October 1641. Conrad Russell plausibly suggests Philip Warwick or Sir Peter Wyche, the new Comptroller of the [King's] Household, as the possible author; Russell, *Fall of the British Monarchies*, p. 404n.

96 Valerie Pearl, *London and the Outbreak of the Puritan Revolution: City Government and National Politics, 1625–41* (Oxford, 1964), pp. 302–3. Gurney was knighted on the king's return: *Ovatio Carolina* ([Nov.] 1641), p. 13 (BL, E 238/4).

97 Pearl, *London and the Outbreak of the Puritan Revolution*, p. 124.

98 ASV, Senato, Dispacci Inghil. 43, fo. 72v: Giovanni Giustinian to the Doge and Senate, 10/20 September 1641 (*CSPV 1640–42*, p. 215). For the unpopularity of the poll tax, see also M. J. Braddick, *Parliamentary Taxation in Seventeeth-Century England: Local Administration and Response* (Woodbridge, 1994), p. 235.

99 ASV, Senato, Dispacci Inghil. 43, fos. 72v, 90, 97, 207v: Giustinian to the Doge and Senate, 10/20, 17/27 September, and 24 September/4 October, 8/18 October 1641 (*CSPV 1640–42*, pp. 215, 220, 222, 225). Giustinian's despatch of 8/18 October notes the appearance of bills attacking the parliamentary leaders as 'traitors to the king, the kingdom and the nobility, and of having conspired with the Scots to injure the people [of England]' (ibid., fo. 107v).

100 *The Sisters of the Scabards Holiday: or, a Dialogue between Two Reverent and Very Vertuous Matrons, Mrs. Bloomesbury, and Mrs. Long-Acre* ([Oct.], 1641), pp. 1–6 (BL, E 168/8).

101 *Diurnall Occurrences*, p. 371. For the printed order, also issued by the king's printer, Robert Barker, see [Lords' and Commons' Recess Committees], *Die Martis 5 Octobris. 1641. It is this Day Ordered* ([Oct.] 1641), single sheet (BL, 669 f. 3/19).

102 *Heads of Severall Petitions and Complaints*, p. 1. When complaints were raised to the Commons Recess Committee about Essex's conduct of the disbandment, Pym's response (as 'chiefe committee') was to defend Essex and declare that as general was a member of the 'higher House', the Commons

Committee had no power to call him to account. *The Heads of Severall Petitions Delivered by many of the Troopers against the Lord General* ([Oct.] 1641), pp. 2–3 (BL, E 172/14); *Diurnall Occurrences*, p. 369.

103 Bray, *Evelyn Diary and Correspondence*, IV, 85: Edward Nicholas to Charles I, 9 October 1641; *Diurnall Occurrences*, p. 371 (sig. Ccc): 5 October. For a further case, a week later, involving the troopers under the command of Colonel Henry Wilmot, the Army Plotter, see Coates, *D'Ewes Diary*, p. 3 (notes of the Commons' Recess Committee for 12 October). Enough of the 'Principall Commanders in the late Northern Expedition' were still in London at the end of November to form the tail of the king's entry procession into the capital on the 25th; *Ovatio Carolina* ([Nov.] 1641), p. 16 (BL, E 238/4).

104 BL, Harl. MS 5047 (Anon. diary), fo. 61r-v.

105 ASV, Senato, Dispacci Inghil. 43, fo. 107v: Giustinian to the Doge and Senate, 8/18 October 1641 (*CSPV 1640–42*, p. 225); emphasis added.

106 *Diurnall Occurrences*, p. 376.

107 ASV, Senato, Dispacci Inghil. 43, fo. 145v: Giustinian to the Doge and Senate, 29 October/8 November 1641 (*CSPV 1640–42*, p. 236); the reference is to 'Nuovi Cartelli . . .'.

108 *The Puritanes Impuritie, or, the Anatomie of a Puritane* ([Oct.] 1641), pp. 1–6 (BL, E 173/8).

109 This theme is developed at length in Russell, *Causes*, Ch. 6.

110 Bray, *Evelyn Diary and Correspondence*, IV, 76: Edward Nicholas to Charles I, 27 September 1641.

111 Ibid.: apostil by the king to Nicholas's letter of 27 September 1641. Charles's comments were made on the date he received the letter, 2 October. For the connection between the Junto leaders and the queen's circle, see R. Malcolm Smuts, 'The Puritan Followers of Henrietta Maria in the 1630s', *English Historical Review*, 93 (1978), 26–45.

112 Nicholas was appointed a clerk extraordinary to the Council on 20 May 1627 (*Acts of the Privy Council, 1627*, p. 287); he was promoted as a clerk in ordinary on 9

October 1635; and paid through to 29 September 1641; NA, PC 2/45 (Privy Council Registers), p. 141; E 403/1754, 3 January 1642).

113 Bray, *Evelyn Diary and Correspondence*, IV, 80: Edward Nicholas to Charles I, 3 October 1641.

114 Surrey History Centre, Bray MS 85/5/2/11: Edward Nicholas to the Earls of Bath, Newcastle, Huntingdon, Devonshire, Cumberland, Bristol, Northampton, and Lords Coventry, Paulet, Cottington, and Seymour, 8 October 1641. For Devonshire's reply, see BL, Evelyn Collection, Nicholas Box: Earl of Devonshire to Edward Nicholas, Hardwick, Derbyshire, 18 October 1641.

115 Far more used to such management were the bishops, all of whom depended on the Crown for their appointments – and, not least, for any hopes of further preferment. Giustinian exaggerated when he said that 'being beneficed by the king', the bishops 'have always been accustomed to support his designs in Parliament' – but only slightly. ASV, Senato, Dispacci Inghil. 42, fos. 125v-6: Giustinian to the Doge and Senate, 18/28 September 1640.

116 On Juxon's appointment, the Venetian ambassador heard several 'complain fiercely that the most conspicuous offices and the greatest authority in the royal council are falling by degrees into the hands of ecclesiastics, to the prejudice of the [lay] nobility': *CSPV 1632–36*, p. 531. (I owe this reference to Professor Kevin Sharpe.) For the anticlericalism provoked by Juxon's appointment in 1636, see Kevin Sharpe, *The Personal Rule of Charles I* (New Haven and London, 1992), pp. 400–01.

117 It is revealing, in this regard, that he spent six days staying with Lord Cottington in early September, at Cottington's house, Fonthill, Wilshire, on his way back to London from Bath: see BL, Evelyn Collection, Nicholas Box: Lord Cottington to Edward Nicholas, Fonthill, Wiltshire, 16 September 1641.

118 Surrey History Centre, Bray MS 85/5/2/11: memorandum by Edward Nicholas, noted on his circular letter to royalist peers, 8 October 1641; Bray, *Evelyn Diary and Correspondence*, IV, 94: Edward Nicholas to Charles I, 21 October 1641.

119 Bray, *Evelyn Diary and Correspondence*, IV, 72. The list was Ralph Brownrigg; Richard Holdsworth; Henry King; John Prideaux, Regius Professor of Divinity at Oxford; and Thomas Winiffe, the Dean of St Paul's.

120 Russell, *Fall of the British Monarchies*, p. 412.

121 Surrey History Centre, Bray MS 52/2/19/18: Edward Nicholas to Sir Henry Vane, 9 October 1641. It is worthy of note that Nicholas writes of 'his Majesties *dominions*' – the plural possibly suggesting a co-ordinated strike against Charles's enemies in both England and Scotland.

122 This important (and hitherto overlooked) piece of evidence as to Charles's plans survives in Giustinian's despatch of 15/25 October 1641. In it he states that a courier had arrived from the queen on 13/23 October (from which it can be deduced it left Edinburgh around 5/15 October, as Nicholas's correspondence makes clear that most messages to and from Edinburgh at this time took eight days). It announced the king's intention to 'be in this kingdom' by 29 October, old style (which Giustinian, using the Julian [new style] calendar for his Venetian audience, renders as 'the 8th of next month [new style]'): ASV, Senato, Dispacci Inghil. 43, fo. 123r-v: Giustinian to the Doge and Senate, 15/25 October 1641. Giustinian saw the queen regularly and was frequently taken into her confidence, so his testimony in this regard can probably be taken as highly reliable. As evidence of the queen's regard for the ambassador, see, for example, Henriette Marie's offer to act as godmother to his newly-born son; ibid., fo. 126.

123 Bray, *Evelyn Diary and Correspondence*, IV, 79: Edward Nicholas to Charles I, 29 September 1641, and the king's annotations, by return, of 5 October.

124 Above, Ch. 11; and see *Certaine Instructions given by the L. Montrose, L. Nappier, Laerd of Keer and Blackhall* ([late June–July] 1641), pp. 3–4 (BL, E 160/26).

125 For Roxburgh as Lord Privy Seal, see Stevenson, *Scottish Revolution*, p. 54;

126 Buckminster Park, Lincolnshire, Tollemache MS 3748.

127 Balfour, *Historical Works*, III, 36. Lord Ker – the eldest son of Robert Ker, 1st Earl of Roxburgh – had been at Eton in the early 1630s: Logan Pearsall Smith, *The Life and Letters of Sir Henry Wotton* (Oxford, 1907), II, 408.

128 HMC, *Fourth Report*, I, 167: Will Morray's deposition, 25, 27 October 1641.

129 Morray's role in the developing plot is well attested in the depositions printed in HMC, *Fourth Report*, I, 166, 167.

130 Above, Ch. 11.

131 R. Malcolm Smuts, 'William Murray [*sic*], first Earl of Dysart', *ODNB*.

132 For 'representation through intimacy', see David Starkey, 'Intimacy and Innovation: the Rise of the Privy Chamber, 1485–1547', in idem (ed.), *The English Court: from the Wars of the Roses to the Civil War* (1987), pp. 82–3.

133 Stevenson, *Scottish Revolution*, p. 238, suggests plausibly that Charles 'seems at least to have known that some sort of intrigue for helping him by violent action was afoot, and weakly to have done nothing either to stop it or to help ensure that it succeeded'. I would demur only on the last point, because in allowing Morray to become involved so deeply in the conspiracy, the king was *ipso facto* lending the venture his credit and, in so doing, greatly enhancing its likelihood of success.

134 HMC, *Fourth Report*, I, 164: Lieutenant-Colonel Robert Home's deposition, 12 October 1641.

135 HMC, *Fourth Report*, I, 166–7: depositions of Colonel John Cochrane and Will Morray. Morray's attempts to represent this initial meeting as being at Cochrane's instigation should, perhaps, be treated with considerable scepticism. For his regiment, see Stevenson, *Scottish Revolution*, p. 238.

136 HMC, *Fourth Report*, I, 166: Cochrane's deposition.

137 Ibid., p. 167: Morray's deposition.

138 Ibid.: Morray's deposition. Morray also admitted to discussing Hamilton and Argyll with Colonel Cochrane.

139 *Acts of the Parliament of Scotland*, V, pp. 354–5; David Stevenson, *The Scottish Revolution, 1637–42* (Newton Abbot, 1973), pp. 235–6.

140 Russell, *Fall of the British Monarchies*, p. 320. None felt the threat more keenly than the Earl of Roxburgh, who stood to be debarred from office thereby, and he publicly declared his resentment before an ever more imperious Argyll. Ludovic Lindsay, 16th Earl of Crawford, had been in Spanish service in the 1630s and appears to have commanded a Scottish unit on Charles I's side during the Bishops' Wars of 1639–40: David Stevenson, 'Ludovic Crawford, 16th Earl of Crawford', *ODNB*.

141 Stevenson, *Scottish Revolution*, p. 236.

142 As Russell has observed, 'The king's involvement, though not finally proved by the depositions, is so overwhelmingly probable that only the most hardened of defence lawyers would think it open to reasonable doubt. Will Murray, both because of his nearness to the king and because of his menial status, was not the man to start a plot independently'; Russell, *Fall of the British Monarchies*, p. 327.

143 *The Truth of the Proceedings in Scotland*, p. 2.

144 Baillie, *Letters*, I, 391.

145 *The Truth of the Proceedings in Scotland*, p. 2.

146 A form of words was agreed on and accepted by Ker, who publicly acknowledged his claims to be 'groundlesse', while the Parliament passed a resolution vindicating Hamilton as 'a Loyall Subject to his Majesty and a faithfull Patriot to his Countrey'; *The Truth of the Proceedings in Scotland*, pp. 3–4.

147 Carte, *Original Letters*, I, 6–7; Balfour, *Historical Works*, III, 94–7; see also Stevenson, *Scottish Revolution*, p. 237.

148 For the countermeasures which the presence of these noble retinues provoked, see *The Kings Most Excellent Majesties Proclamation and the Estates of Parliament in Scotland ... concerning the Unnecessary Confluence of His Liege-People to Edinburgh [14 October]* (20 Oct. 1641), pp. 4–5 (BL, E 177/4).

149 For its decline in England, see Lawrence Stone, *The Crisis of the Aristocracy, 1558–1641* (Oxford, 1964); see also, Stephen I. Boardman, 'Politics and the Feud in Late Mediaeval Scotland' (unpublished Ph. D.

dissertation, University of St Andrews, 1989).

150 HMC, *Fourth Report*, I, 164: deposition of Colonel Alexander Stewart, 22 October 1641.

151 *Nicholas Papers*, I, 49–51: Thomas Webb to Edward Nicholas, Edinburgh, 21 September 1641.

152 Beinecke Lib., Yale, MS Osborn Shelves, Howard of Escrick Correspondence, Folder 3.23: Howard of Escrick and the other parliamentary commissioners in Edinburgh to Viscount Mandeville, 28 September 1641.

153 *The Truth of the Proceedings in Scotland*, p. 1.

154 Baillie, *Letters*, I, 390–91 (my emphasis).

155 Charles had nominated Loudoun as Chancellor (and had him accepted) on 30 September, after his earlier nominee, the Earl of Morton, a king's-party man, had been rejected by the Parliament; see *Complete Peerage*, VIII, 159; *Nicholas Papers*, I, 49–53.

156 *The Truth of the Proceedings in Scotland*, p. 4: the places went to Lord Chancellor Loudoun; the Earl of Argyll; John Kennedy Earl of Cassillis; William Cunningham, 9th Earl of Glencairn; Lord Balmerino (President of the Parliament); and John Lindsay, 10th Lord (and later 1st Earl of) Lindsay. All but Glencain, a king's-party man, appear to have been disposed to support Argyll's faction. For Cassillis and Lindsay 'plott[ing]' together with Loudoun, Argyll, and Hamilton 'before fyve in the morning' during the course of 'the Incident', see HMC, *Fourth Report*, I, 168.

157 For the phrase, see *The Truth of the Proceedings in Scotland*, p. 4 (for quotation), pp. 5–6.

158 *Nicholas Papers*, I, 49–51: Thomas Webb to Edward Nicholas, Edinburgh, 21 September 1641.

159 Baillie, *Letters*, I, 390–1; his patent of creation is dated 6 October 1641: *Complete Peerage*, II, 488.

160 *The Truth of the Proceedings in Scotland*, p. 4. Parliament had appointed a committee (headed by Lord Chancellor Loudoun and the Earl of Argyll) consisting of six representatives each from the nobility, barons (lairds), and burgesses (the representatives of the major towns) to effect 'a faire

accomodation in all things'. It appears to have been in his capacity as the senior member of this committee that Loudoun was to have received his instructions from the king.

161 Buckminster Park, Lincolnshire, Tollemache MS 4110. In the archive, it immediately follows a series of notes (Tollemache MS 4109) on the Scottish argument presented on 6 and 7 October, partially in a secretary's hand, which Charles seems to have had to hand in compiling his 'Notes for my L. Chancelors memorie'. I communicated this discovery to Professor Russell, who first published extracts from these manuscripts in 1991 in his *Fall of the British Monarchies*, pp. 323–4, where he takes a rather more optimistic view than I do of the possibility of a genuine compromise settlement in the first week of October.

162 Buckminster Park, Tollemache MS 4110 (emphasis added). For the quotation from Hyde, see *Complete Peerage*, VIII, 159n.

163 Buckminster Park, Tollemache MS 4110.

164 Ibid.: Edinburgh, Stirling and Dumbarton ('Dumbartaine' in the MS) were the castles in question.

165 Ibid. (for the quotation in the main text); Bray, *Evelyn Diary and Correspondence*, IV, 80 (for the footnote quotation). Professor Russell read this clause as being a proposal to revive the 'Anglo-Scottish Bedchamber' of James VI and I; but as Charles I's Bedchamber already contained a considerable number of Scots, and hence was already an 'Anglo-Scottish Bedchamber', it would seem that this request was intended to have a wider application, permitting Scottish appointments to all offices at court, including the Privy Council – as Nicholas's letter of 3 October also assumed. On political role of the Bedchamber, see Neil Cuddy, 'The Revival of the Entourage: the Bedchamber of James I, 1603–25', in Starkey, *The English Court*, pp. 173–225; and John Adamson, 'The Tudor and Stuart Courts, 1503–1714', in idem (ed.), *The Princely Courts of Europe: Ritual, Politics, and Religion under the Ancien Régime, 1500–1750* (1999), pp. 110–12.

166 For a rather different interpretation of these annotations, see Russell, *Fall of the British Monarchies*, pp. 323–25.

167 I deduce this from the fact that the king's

'Notes' survive among Will Morray's papers at Buckminster Park, Lincolnshire.

168 The phrase is Endymion Porter's: see Russell, *Fall of the British Monarchies*, p. 326.

169 The following account is based on the depositions of the leading actors in the plot, taken before the Scottish Parliament, copies of which were sent to London in October 1641: HMC, *Fourth Report*, I, 163–70; together with NAS, Hamilton MS GD 406/1/1440, 1441; *Hardwicke State Papers*, II, 299; Baillie, *Letters*, I, 392; Balfour, *Historical Works*, III, 94. For the detailed, and largely accurate, report of the plot offered to English audiences, see *The Truth of the Proceedings in Scotland*, pp. 6–10.

170 HMC, *Fourth Report*, I, 164: deposition of Lieutenant-Colonel Robert Hume, 12 October 1641.

171 Ibid., p. 165: deposition of the Earl of Crawford, 23 October 1641.

172 For their residence at 'the King's Court', see Coates, *D'Ewes Diary*, p. 9.

173 HMC, *Fourth Report*, I, 163, 164: depositions of Captain William Stewart, 12 and 21 October 1641, and Colonel Alexander Stewart, 22 October 1641.

174 Ibid.: depositions of Captain William Stewart, 12 October 1641, and Colonel Alexander Stewart, 22 October 1641.

175 Russell, *Fall of the British Monarchies*, pp. 326–7.

176 *The Truth of the Proceedings in Scotland*, p. 7.

177 For the depositions, see HMC, *Fourth Report*, I, 163–9.

178 Carte, *Original Letters*, I, 3; Stevenson, *Scottish Revolution*, p. 239.

179 The appointments are discussed in detail in Stevenson, *Scottish Revolution*, pp. 240–41.

180 BL, Evelyn Collection, Nicholas Box: Endymion Porter to Edward Nicholas, Edinburgh, 19 October 1641.

181 Coates, *D'Ewes Diary*, p. 8; John Hampden, Sir William Armyne et al., *The Discovery of a Late and Bloody Conspiracie*

at Edenburg, in Scotland ([Oct.] 1641), pp. 1–3 (BL, E 173/13).

14. ENGINES OF WAR

1 John Bond, *Englands Reioycing for the Parliaments Returne. Declaring the Kingdomes Happinesse in their Councells, and their Iustice in their Consultations against Papists, Arminianisme, and Popish Superstition* ([Oct.] 1641), p. 6 (BL, E 173/9).

2 Surrey History Centre, Bray MS 52/2/19/21: Edward Nicholas to Thomas Webb, 11 October 1641.

3 ASV, Senato, Dispacci Inghil. 43, fos. 66, 68v-9: Giovanni Giustinian to the Doge and Senate, 3–13 September 1641 (*CSPV 1640–42*, pp. 213, 214). For the plague's, see Dispacci Inghil. 43, fo. 102: Giovanni Giustinian to the Doge and Senate, 24 September/4 October 1641 (*CSPV 1640–42*, p. 223); and see also Surrey History Centre, Bray MS 85/5/2/14: Edward Nicholas to Thomas Webb, secretary to the Duke of Richmond and Lennox, 15 October 1641.

4 BL, Harl. MS 6424 (Bishop Warner's diary), fo. 97.

5 Surrey History Centre, Bray MS 52/2/19/22: Edward Nicholas to Thomas Webb, 12 October 1641 (for quotation); Bray, *Evelyn Diary and Correspondence*, IV, 90: Edward Nicholas to Charles I, 15 October 1641.

6 Surrey History Centre, Bray MS 85/5/2/15: Edward Nicholas to the Duke of Richmond and Lennox, 15 October 1641. The parliamentary record would suggest that the Junto was right in assessing the deterrent effect of the plague; a division recorded on 22 October reveals that there were 129 members present in the Commons – roughly a quarter of its total membership: see Coates, *D'Ewes Diary*, p. 25.

7 A revealing vignette of attendances at meetings of these 'prime governors' is provided by the Lord keeper's report, in December 1641, relating a conference among the Junto leaders in 'the summer' (probably in July and August, as Nathaniel Fiennes is mentioned as present, and he was later to depart, in September, as one of the English Commissioners to Scotland). Newport mentioned that those present included the

Earl of Essex, Newport himself, Viscount Saye and Mandeville, Lords Savile and Wharton, and (from the Commons), Viscount Dungarvan (the eldest son of the 1st Earl of Cork), John Pym, Nathaniel Fiennes, and Sir John Clotworthy; Coates, *D'Ewes Diary*, p. 353. Perhaps the only anomalous figure here is Lord Savile, who seems to have been at least partially estranged from the Junto leadership after Strafford's execution.

8 Surrey History Centre, Bray MS 52/2/19/22: Edward Nicholas to Thomas Webb, 12 October 1641. Nicholas noted that a friend had heard Mandeville doing precisely this, though his informant was more impressed by the libels' cogency than by their satire: 'though ther bee a little foolery in it, yet there is much trueth mixt with it'. For examples of contemporary satire see *A Discovery of 29 Sects here in London, all of which, except the First, are Most Divelish and Damnable* ([Sept.], 1641), pp. 2, 4, 7 (BL, E 168/7); most of the libels, however, would have been either printed single sheets or manuscript squibs, and few seem to have survived.

9 Surrey History Centre, Bray MS 52/2/19/16: Edward Nicholas to Thomas Webb, 5 October 1641.

10 For these items at its previous meeting, see Coates, *D'Ewes Diary*, pp. 6–8.

11 The letters from the Parliamentary Commissioners in Edinburgh had been sent on 14 October: see Coates, *D'Ewes Diary*, p. 9; and HMC, *Fourth Report*, I, 102: Nathaniel Fiennes, Sir William Armyne, Sir Philip Stapilton, and John Hampden to John Pym and the members of the Commons Recess Committee, 14 October 1641.

12 Nathaniel Fiennes et al., *The Discovery of a Late and Bloody Conspiracie at Edenburg, in Scotland* ([Oct.] 1641), pp. 1–2 (BL, E 173/13); printing PA, MP 14 October 1641 (calendared in HMC, *Fourth Report*, I, 102).

13 Fiennes, *Discovery of a Conspiracie*, pp. 2–3.

14 For Frost as a servant of the Parliamentary Commissioners in Edinburgh, see *CJ*, II, 322. He returned to Edinburgh in November, commended by the Commissioners as 'a very discreet man, and one fit to be trusted'. For

Frost's earlier activities for Lord Brooke, see above, pp. 38/543 n.136.

15 D'Ewes, who was present at Pym's presentation of the news to the Recess Committee on 19 October, describes these as 'certaine intelligence come out of Scotland besides this Letter [from the parliamentary commissioners]': Coates, *D'Ewes Diary*, p. 9.

16 Coates, *D'Ewes Diary*, p. 9.

17 This point received strong corroboration once the depositions of witnesses, examined in relation to the Incident, were forwarded to London later in the month. These are now in the PA, and printed in HMC, *Fourth Report* (Appendix: House of Lords), pp. 163–70. For other accounts, see *Hardwicke State Papers*, II, 299–303; Balfour, *Historical Works*, III, 94–135.

18 The printed version of Hampden's letter from Edinburgh listed the noblemen who were to be 'cut off' (that is, murdered), extending the list to include (besides Hamilton, Argyll, and Lanark), the Earls of Loudoun and Lindsay, Lord Balmerino, and General Alexander Leslie. John Hampden *et al.*, *The Discovery of a Late and Bloody Conspiracie at Edenburg, in Scotland* ([Oct.] 1641), p. 4 (BL, E 173/13).

19 Coates, *D'Ewes Diary*, pp. 8–9.

20 NAS, Hamilton MS GD 406/1/1544: Copy of a letter to Lord Lindsay, 16 October 1641. Although the letter is dated 16 October, the references to 'Monday next' appear in the context of a quotation (or paraphrase) of Lord Almond's order to his vassals, which was clearly issued considerably earlier. Thus, 'Monday next' would seem to refer to 11 October, the day the first part of conspiracy was intended to have been sprung, rather than to 18 October, the 'next' Monday after the date of the letter.

21 Surrey History Centre, Bray MS 85/5/2/3: the king's answer to the Scottish Parliament concerning the appointment of officers of state, [16 September 1641].

22 NAS, Hamilton MS GD 406/1/1562: the Earl of Lauderdale to the Marquess of Hamilton, 'Monday' [i.e. 1 November 1641]; Russell, *Fall of the British Monarchies*, pp. 327–8.

23 Bray, *Evelyn Diary and Correspondence*, IV, 80: Edward Nicholas to Charles I, 3 October 1641.

24 Perhaps the key text is J. S., *The Truth of the Proceedings in Scotland. Containing the Discovery of the Late Conspiracie. With Divers Other Remarkable Passages* ([Nov.] 1641), BL, E 173/29, issued without the identification of either printer or publisher. However, the printer can be identified from the distinctive ornament on p. 1 as Bernard Alsop; for the re-use of this ornament in an acknowledged publication by Alsop, see *The Kings Most Excellent Majesties Proclamation and the Estates of Parliament in Scotland* ([Nov.] 1641), sig. A2 (BL, E 177/4). Alsop was employed as a printer by the Recess Committee of September–October 1641 (see Wing E2640; BL, E 171/8); was the London printer of Argyll's speeches in the Scottish Parliament (see BL, E 199/15), and a tradesman who seems to have had close connections with the London godly (he printed works, *inter alia*, by Thomas Hooker and Henry Burton). Alsop frequently worked at this time for the publisher, Thomas Bates, another figure with close associations with the reformist parliamentary leadership, and the future publisher of speeches by Lord Brooke and the younger Sir Henry Vane.

25 *The Discovery of a Late and Bloody Conspiracie at Edenburg, in Scotland* ([Oct.] 1641), p. 4 (BL, E 173/13), for the conspirators' hit list. It is noteworthy that the printer of this letter, John Thomas, was also supplied (possibly by Mandeville) with the texts of other Scottish material: see *The Duke of Lenox his Honourable and Worthy Speech in the High Court of Parliament in Scotland, Octob[er] 28. 1641* ([Nov.] 1641), BL, E 199/20. And in November he was to be provided – again, probably by the Junto leadership – with the text of another 'horrible and bloody … conspiracie', this time the reported plot by the Earl of Worcester to raise Catholics in Wales: see *A Discovery of a Horrible and Bloody Treason and Conspiracie* ([Nov.] 1641), BL, E 176/12, which was issued together with the verbatim text of an order by the Lords for the apprehending of 'Priests and Jesuites'.

26 See especially, J. S., *The Truth of the Proceedings in Scotland. Containing the Discovery of the Late Conspiracie* ([Oct.] 1641), BL, E 173/29, printed by Bernard

Alsop (though issued anonymously).

27 BL, Sloane MS 1467 (Newsletters, 1640–41), fo. 152v: letter of intelligence [from Edward Rossingham?], 28 October 1641.

28 Clarendon, *Rebellion*, I, 391n.

29 Ibid.

30 Ibid.

31 Something of the intimacy between Feilding and Warwick is suggested by the ceremony for the introduction of Warwick's eldest son, Lord Rich, who received a summons to the House of Lords, *in vita patris*, and was introduced on 27 January 1641; his two supporters were Lord Newnham Paddox (i.e. Lord Feilding) and Lord Robartes (one of Warwick's sons-in-law); *LJ*, IV, 145.

32 NAS, Hamilton MS GD 406/1/1442: Lord Feilding to the Marquess of Hamilton, 22 October 1641 (emphasis added).

33 That the king was believed to be implicated from the first (even before the extent of Will Morray's involvement in the plot became known) is evident from the Venetian ambassador's remark that the court 'tries to have it believed that the king has no share in these transactions'; *CSPV 1640–42*, p. 232: Giustinian to the Doge and Senate, 22 October/November 1641.

34 Such a scenario was all the more plausible because of the number of soldiers in and around London. In the Edinburgh plot, anti-reformist elements in the army were to have played a key role in capturing the capital and neutralizing opposition. In London, where the demobilized soldiers from the northern army were already a nuisance, it was easy to imagine that these troops had a more sinister motive for their presence than simply the quest for their arrears of pay. For the problems with these reformadoes, see *The Heads of Severall Petitions delivered by Many of the Troopers against the Lord General and Some Other Officers of the Army* ([Oct.] 1641), BL, E 172/14.

35 Clarendon, *Rebellion*, I, 391n.

36 John Bond, *Englands Reioycing for the Parliaments Returne. Declaring the Kingdomes Happinesse in their Councells, and their Iustice in their Consultations against Papists, Arminianisme, and Popish*

Superstition ([Oct.] 1641), p. 6 (BL, E 173/9).

37 Ibid., p. 5. It was not his only bid for powerful patrons; his pen was moved, with apparently similar careerist motives, to celebrate the king's return in November 1641: *King Charles his Welcome Home, or a Congratulation of All his Loving Subiects in Thankefulnesse to God for his Maiesties Safe and Happie Returne from Scotland, 1641* ([Nov.] 1641), BL, E 177/18.

38 *CJ*, II, 287.

39 NAS, Hamilton MS GD 406/1/1427: Viscount Mandeville to the Marquess of Hamilton, 10 September 1641.

40 BL, Harl. MS 164 (D'Ewes diary), fo. 109v.

41 Coates, *D'Ewes Diary*, p. 20.

42 Bray, *Evelyn Diary and Correspondence*, IV, 95: Edward Nicholas to Charles I, 21 October 1641.

43 An order was made on Monday, 25 October 1641 for the question to be considered on 'Wednesday come sevennight' – i.e. Wednesday, 3 November. But when 3 November came round, nothing further was done; *CJ*, II, pp. 294, 303–5. Another order was made on Tuesday, 9 November for 'contemnors of the Order of 9 Sept.' to be considered on 'Saturday morning'; but, again, the Saturday came and went without any discussion of the 9 September Order; *CJ*, II, 309, 314–5.

44 Coates, *D'Ewes Diary*, p. 79; there is no mention of this debate in the *Commons Journal*, presumably because it failed to reach any form of resolution.

45 Coates, *D'Ewes Diary*, p. 150 (emphasis added).

46 Ibid. Against this reading, however, can be cited Nicholas's claim that Grimston had been estranged from the parliamentary leadership since the spring of 1641, when (Nicholas later alleged) he had been suspected, with Lord Digby, of trying to conceal evidence against Strafford: see BL, Add. MS 31954 (Nicholas's Notes of the Long Parliament), fo. 184v. Nicholas's observations are worthy of respect; however, his information was at best second hand, as he was not himself a member of the Commons, and this claim is difficult to square with what else is known of Grimston's

parliamentary behaviour, which suggests ongoing sympathy with, and loyalty to, the objectives of the Warwick House circle and the Junto leadership more generally.

47 *CJ*, II, 290.

48 *LJ*, IV, 398.

49 BL, Add. MS 34485 (Diurnal Occurrences), fos. 79v-80 (emphasis added).

50 *CJ*, II, 290. Pym reported the 'heads' for the conference with the Lords later that same day; Coates, *D'Ewes Diary*, p. 15.

51 *LJ*, IV, p. 399. The peers nominated were Manchester (Lord Privy Seal), Northumberland (Lord Admiral), Holland (Lord General), Saye (Master of the Wards), and Paget (Holland's son-in-law). The odd man out in this company was the mercurial Earl of Bristol, who was by this stage working closely with the king. Indeed, Charles's response to Nicholas's letter of 21 October contained an instruction for Bristol to 'renew that dispute betwixt the two Houses concerning the Parliament Protestation [of May 1641]'; see Bray, *Evelyn Diary and Correspondence*, IV, 95: Edward Nicholas to Charles I, 21 October 1641. The Commons contingent that worked with the six peers was comprised of Pym, Gerard, Lewes, Rudyard, St John, Selden, Erle, Holles, Vane junior and the Royalists, Falkland, Strangways, and Edmund Waller; *CJ*, II, 290–1.

52 *LJ*, IV, 401.

53 *CJ*, II, 291. The formal text of the resolution reads: 'that if there be any tumult to oppose the acts confirmed by both kingdoms [i.e. the Treaty of Union and attendant legislation], and that his Majesty will command any assistance to suppress them, that both Houses will be ready to maintain his Majesty, in his greatness, and to suppress those that are disturbers of the peace'. This is the resolution referred to by D'Ewes as having been proposed by Pym; see Coates, *D'Ewes Diary*, p. 21. How firmly this resolution actually committed the English Parliament (at least as regarded by the Junto leadership) to waiting for a request from the king before it acted to suppress 'tumults' must be open to doubt.

54 BL, Harl. MS 164 (D'Ewes diary), fo. 197: entry for 4 May 1641 (*PLP*, IV, 193). A variant of the proposal had surfaced in June

as one of the Ten Propositions, the Commons' list of desiderata for further reform (Gardiner, *Constitutional Documents*, p. 164); and again in August, when the two Houses had dared to nominate the Earls of Pembroke and Salisbury to the Lord Stewardship of the Household and the Lord Treasurership.

55 The phrase is Conrad Russell's; Russell, *Fall of the British Monarchies*, p. 412.

56 D'Ewes, for example, regarded parliamentary approval of the great officers (a proposal for which was contained in Article VI of the Parliament's draft Instructions to its Commissioners in Scotland) as a matter 'of verie dangerous consequence', and an encroachment on the historic and lawful prerogatives of the Crown; see Coates, *D'Ewes Diary*, p. 105 (for the quotation), and his diary entries for November 1641 more generally.

57 No one imagined that Charles had nominated Lord Loudoun (one of the architects of the Covenanter revolt) as Lord Chancellor of Scotland except under extreme political duress.

58 Coates, *D'Ewes Diary*, p. 101.

59 BL, Hargrave MS 98 (Heraldic papers), fos. 68v–73v: Pym's 'Certain Select Observations'. This is a later fair copy of what purports to be an original composition by Pym. The format of the document would suggest that the original was drawn up for practical use, possibly as a work of reference for his own use or, more likely, for one or more of the Junto's patrician grandees.

60 Ibid., fo. 69: Pym's 'Certain Select Observations' (emphasis added in quotation). 'When Kings were first Ordained in this Realm', Pym noted, the kingdom was divided into forty 'portions', each committed to an earl – a principle that was shortly to form the basis of an ordinance for a wholesale reorganization of the militia, with peers (almost invariably earls) nominated as Lord-Lieutenants by Parliament to administer their 'portion'.

61 Ibid.: Pym's 'Certain Select Observations', fo. 71r-v. It is worth noting that Pym used an almost identical argument in the debate on the great officers on 8 November. Responding to Orlando Bridgeman (a future Royalist, who had distinguished the precedent of 15 Edward

III), Pym argued that his proposal was 'a petition and nott an Act which would bee sayd to bee in derogation off the prerogative;' Bodl. Lib., MS Rawlinson d. 932 (Sir John Holland's diary), fo. 16r-v.

62 BL, Hargrave MS 98 (Heraldic papers): Pym's 'Certain Select Observations', fos. 69–73v.

63 Ibid., fo. 69.

64 BL, Add. MS 34485 (Diurnal Occurrences), fos. 79v-80.

65 For its origins, see above, Ch. 13; its composition and future development is considered in the Epilogue.

66 CJ, II, 131; BL, Harl. MS 163 (D'Ewes diary), fo. 121 (for quotation) (PLP, IV, 160).

67 Coates, D'Ewes Diary, p. 21.

68 BL, Harl. MS 6424 (Bishop Warner's diary), fo. 97 (where it is suggested, erroneously, that the bill had its third reading on Friday, 22 October); CJ, II, 291, 292, 293. There was evidently a debate on the second reading, on Friday, 22 October, where there was a division during the committee proceedings (and therefore not recorded in the Commons' Journals), which revealed the presence of 129 Commons-men; Coates, D'Ewes Diary, p. 25. For the problems the Commons had at this time with ensuring that their house was even quorate, see the entry in D'Ewes's diary for 23 October, where he records that the Serjeant-at-Arms was ordered to go into Westminster Hall to round up Commons-men who were 'walking ther'; ibid., p. 30.

69 Coates, D'Ewes Diary, p. 25 and n. 10, p. 27.

70 CJ, II, 292; Coates, D'Ewes Diary, p. 24.

71 BL, Harl. MS 6424 (Bishop Warner's diary), fo. 97.

72 Ibid., fo. 98v.

73 Surrey History Centre, Bray MS 85/5/2/11: Nicholas's draft letter to Bath, Bristol, and others, 8 October 1641; BL, Harl. MS 6424 (Bishop Warner's diary), fo. 97.

74 Coates, D'Ewes Diary, p. 24n. For the wider significance of the issue of bishops' votes, see John Adamson, 'Parliamentary Management, Men-of-Business, and the

House of Lords, 1640–49', in Clyve Jones (ed.), A Pillar of the Constitution: The House of Lords in British Politics 1640–1784 (1989), pp. 21–50.

75 Coates, D'Ewes Diary, p. 40 (debate of Tuesday, 26 October 1641).

76 Before the Lords, St John made the case, with Pym, for the removal of the thirteen bishops: see Ibid., p. 43; LJ, IV, 407–8.

77 Robert Goodwyn was to be an active Parliamentarian during the Civil War; for his speech, see Coates, D'Ewes Diary, pp. 44–5.

78 Ibid., p. 44.

79 Ibid., p. 45; D'Ewes added 'I thinke most [of what] hee saied was premeditated'.

80 Bray, Evelyn Diary and Correspondence, IV, 101: Edward Nicholas to Charles I, 29 October 1641. Nicholas's account of the debate includes a number of important details that are omitted by D'Ewes, not least the names of the speakers (other than Hyde) who argued in defence of the king's rights.

81 CJ, II, 131; BL, Harl. MS 163 (D'Ewes diary), fo. 121 (for quotation).

82 Coates, D'Ewes Diary, p. 45.

83 Bray, Evelyn Diary and Correspondence, IV, 101: Edward Nicholas to Charles I, 29 October 1641.

84 This is the major contention in Russell, Fall of the British Monarchies.

85 The key elements which appeared to have been abandoned by the Junto by October 1641 included any further attempt to abolish bishops 'Root and Branch' and any thought of abolishing the Book of Common Prayer.

86 Bray, Evelyn Diary and Correspondence, IV, 101. Nicholas himself, however, doubted whether the last had been heard of the matter.

87 CJ, II, 297. It is perhaps a measure of how innocuous this 'petition' was expected to be that the Royalists, Hyde, Waller, and Belasyse (as well as D'Ewes, who was also a defender of the king's prerogative) all agreed to serve on the committee, alongside the likes of Pym, Barrington, and Hesilrige.

88 Bray, Evelyn Diary and Correspondence, IV, 107: Edward Nicholas to Charles I, 1 November 1641.

89 Coates, *D'Ewes Diary*, p. 45.

90 Bray, *Evelyn Diary and Correspondence*, IV, 107: Charles received Nicholas's letter of 1 November on Saturday, 6 November, and at that point predicted (in the event accurately) that it would be another fortnight before he would be back in England. The date he gave for his arrival was 20 November 1641.

91 For the importance of O'Connolly's role in the management of news relating to the Irish insurrection, see Michael Perceval-Maxwell, *The Outbreak of the Irish Rebellion of 1641* (Montreal and Kingston, 1994), pp. 240, 270.

92 For Leicester House, see L. W. Cowie, 'Leicester House', *History Today*, 23/1 (1973), 30–7.

93 Coates, *D'Ewes Diary*, pp. 61–3; *LJ*, IV, 412–16; Nalson, *Impartial Collection*, II, 514–22; HMC, *Ormonde Manuscripts*, n.s., II, 1–6.

94 Coates, *D'Ewes Diary*, p. 61.

95 Perceval-Maxwell, *Outbreak of the Irish Rebellion*, p. 270 (for quotation); Coates, *D'Ewes Diary*, pp. 61–2 (for the reading of O'Connolly's evidence to the Commons).

96 BL, Sloane MS 1467, fo.153: newsletter, 21 October 1641: 'The Lords of the Counsel sate all last Weeke about the Irish affaires. The Papists are said to fly thither with incredible numbers and all their substance [wealth]'. This would suggest that Leicester's immediate circle of friends on the Council – Northumberland, Essex, Holland, Warwick, and Mandeville – may have had some hint of the threat well before the final confirmation of the rebellion came on 31 October. They would also have been acutely aware that, in the event of a military campaign being necessary in Ireland, the king still retained the power of appointment to all army commands; and that, within the Privy Council itself, Junto peers still constituted a minority of the Board as a whole. In the event of any military campaign, the Junto had confidence in Leicester, but knew full well that Leicester's continuance in office was entirely at Charles's whim, and that the power to determine policy lay with a Privy Council they did not control. Under these circumstances, the 'premeditated' revival on 28 October of the Junto's earlier demand for parliamentary control of appointments to major offices and the Privy Council looks suspiciously like an attempt to try to remedy these two weaknesses in advance of what, by that date, was an already expected military crisis in Ireland.

97 Indeed, Northumberland – with what seems discreet parliamentary pressure – had forced Leicester's appointment as Lord Lieutenant on an otherwise 'colde' Charles I, back in May. Barely four weeks into the session, Northumberland had marked out either Windebank's Secretaryship or the Lord Lieutenancy of Ireland for his brother-in-law, Leicester, though he found the king averse to the proposal. Early in the Parliament, Northumberland had assured Leicester that he was 'resolved to trye what [I] can do by *Parlement*, if [I] see a likelynesse of fayleing the other way, and by one of these I do confidently believe that *Leicester* shall be either *Secretary* or *go into Ireland*'; Centre for Kentish Studies, De L'Isle MS U1500/C2/45: Earl of Northumberland to the Earl of Leicester, 10 December 1640 (not calendared by the HMC; italicized words are in code in the original manuscript). Only at the beginning of October 1641, however, did Leicester relinquish his role as ambassador in Paris, and in the weeks following his return he found himself thoroughly integrated into the counsels of the Junto. For an alleged plot to assassinate Leicester and three of his military cousins eight weeks later, see *A Happy Deliverance, or, a Wonderfull Preservation of Foure Worthy and Honourable Peeres of this Kingdome and Some Others* ([Jan.] 1641/[2]), BL, E 132/16.

98 For their appearance in the Commons, see Coates, *D'Ewes Diary*, p. 61. The oldest of the Councillors present, Charles Wilmot, first Viscount Wilmot (in the Irish Peerage), had been born in 1571 and named to the English Privy Council in 1628; *Complete Peerage*, XII, Part 2, 719–20.

99 *CJ*, II, 300.

100 Whitelocke, *Memorials*, I, 138.

101 Coates, *D'Ewes Diary*, p. 67; the Commons were asked to join this delegation with a proportionable number. The same day, 2 November, the Commons named a new Standing Committee for Irish Affairs, the first-named of which were, inevitably, Sir John Clotworthy and John Pym; *CJ*, II, 302.

102 Coates, *D'Ewes Diary*, p. 72; *CJ*, II, 303. I am grateful to Mr Christopher Thompson for his advice on Sir William Masham's connections.

103 Coates, *D'Ewes Diary*, pp. 78, 82; *CJ*, II, p. 304 (for quotation).

104 *CJ*, II, 302; Coates, *D'Ewes Diary*, pp. 68–9 (for Strode's role in proposing the bill); agreed by the Lords on 9 November: *LJ*, IV, 429.

105 *CJ*, II, 300, 303; Coates, *D'Ewes Diary*, p. 70.

106 Coates, *D'Ewes Diary*, p. 74.

107 Ibid., p. 87; *CJ*, II, p. 306 (for their reading on 5 November).

108 It is noteworthy that on 5 November, when the depositions were eventually read in full, Morray's were the first to be presented to the House; Coates, *D'Ewes Diary*, p. 87; see also J. S., *The Truth of the Proceedings in Scotland. Containing the Discovery of the Late Conspiracie. With Divers Other Remarkable Passages* ([Nov.] 1641), p. 2 (BL, E 173/29).

109 Bray, *Evelyn Diary and Correspondence*, IV, 101.

110 For the importance of this date in the political calendar, see David Cressy, *Bonfires and Bells: National Memory and the Protestant Calendar in Elizabethan and Stuart England* (1989), Ch. 9, 'Remembering the Fifth of November'.

111 Coates, *D'Ewes Diary*, p. 55.

112 Ibid., p. 81.

113 Cornelius Burges, *Another Sermon preached to the Honorable House of Commons now assembled in Parliament, November the Fifth, 1641 ... wherein, among Other Things, are shewed a List of some of the Popish Traytors in England* (1641), Wing B5668. 'Every one that departeth from iniquity [namely, 'the Godly' – as a printed marginal note to the text makes clear], maketh himself a prey', Burges argued. 'And so it was with David: witnesse Architophel, a Privie Councellor, and Absolem, that came forth out of his owne bowels'; ibid., p. 10.

114 Burges, *Another Sermon*, p. 25.

115 Ibid., p. 42. The quotations are from the

Mémoires sur les règnes de Louis XI et de Charles VIII (first published in Paris, 1524), by the French royal counsellor, Philippe de Comines (*c.* 1447–*c.* 1511). The final third of the printed version of Burges's sermon includes an exhortation to the Commons to press ahead with the reform of the Church by calling a national synod of divines Burges, *Another Sermon*, (pp. 63–4). It may be significant that Burges did not actually deliver this section in St Margaret's Church, on the grounds that the Commons were pressed for time (see his Epistle Dedicatory). An alternate explanation is that his patrons – Pym and the Junto leaders in the Commons – deemed this an inopportune moment to raise the question of 'further reformation'.

116 R. Malcolm Smuts, 'William Murray [*sic*]', *ODNB*.

117 Coates, *D'Ewes Diary*, p. 87.

118 For Charles I as a king 'smitten in this wits', a theme that was to become a leitmotiv in Pym's own attempts to explain Charles's behaviour, see John Adamson, 'Pym as draftsman: an Unpublished Declaration of March 1643', *Parliamentary History*, 6 (1987), 133–40.

119 Given that Morray was about to be unmasked by Pym later that morning as the leading conspirator in the plot to murder Hamilton and Argyll, it is not unreasonable to suspect collusion between Burges and Pym: the two men were old friends and had served together as members of the Bedford household since the 1620s. *Pace* Professor Wilson, however, it was Arthur Goodwin, rather than Pym, who nominated Burges as the Gunpowder Day preacher; see J. F. Wilson, *Pulpit in Parliament: Puritanism during the English Civil Wars, 1640–48* (Princeton, 1969), p. 106.

120 Coates, *D'Ewes Diary*, pp. 87–9; Bodl. Lib., MS Rawlinson d. 932 (Sir John Holland's diary), fos. 5v-6.

121 For the depositions, now in PA, see HMC, *Fourth Report* (House of Lords MSS), pp. 167–70.

122 Coates, *D'Ewes Diary*, p. 90.

123 *CJ*, II, 306; Coates, *D'Ewes Diary*, p. 90 (for Pym's role, and the ordinances' drafting).

124 *CJ*, II, 304, 306.

125 *CJ*, II, 306; Coates, *D'Ewes Diary*, pp. 90–1. In fact, Newport was authorized to supply 8,000 foot and 1,000 horse, together with 'munition and necessaries', suggesting that the eventual strength of Leicester's army was expected to be roughly double its size during its first phase of recruitment.

126 Bodl. Lib., MS Rawlinson d. 932 (Sir John Holland's diary), fo. 12v – as reported by Holland on 6 November; compare D'Ewes account of 5 November: Coates, *D'Ewes Diary*, pp. 94–5.

127 Coates, *D'Ewes Diary*, p. 95.

128 Bray, *Evelyn Diary and Correspondence*, IV, 114: Edward Nicholas to Charles I, 6 November 1641.

129 Bodl. Lib., MS Rawlinson d. 932 (Sir John Holland's diary), fos. 12v–13v.

130 Culpeper clearly recognized this implication and argued obliquely against Pym's clause, on the grounds that 'hee thought Ireland to be a parte of England and [therefore] that *wee* ought to defend it'; Coates, *D'Ewes Diary*, p. 99 (emphasis added).

131 *CJ*, II, 307.

132 *LJ*, IV, 431.

133 Sir John Northcote's notes of proceedings record Cromwell as having moved the second reading of the bill for annual Parliaments (which eventually metamorphosed into the Triennial Act); Strode and possibly William Pierrepont, were its proposers. *Northcote Notes*, p. 112; Notestein, *D'Ewes Diary*, p. 188–9.

134 Coates, *D'Ewes Diary*, pp. 97–8; *CJ*, II, 306.

135 *CJ*, II, 306.

136 Coates, *D'Ewes Diary*, pp. 244–5.

137 ASV, Senato, Dispacci Inghil. 43, fo. 161: Giustinian to the Doge and Senate, 5/15 November 1641 (*CSPV 1640–42*, p. 242).

138 *CJ*, II, 307b; Coates, *D'Ewes Diary*, p. 186.

139 NA, SP 16/485/76: the Earl of Northumberland to Sir Thomas Rowe, 12 November 1641.

140 BL, Sloane MS 1467 (Newsletters,

1640–41), fo. 146: letter of intelligence, [November 1641].

141 Coates, *D'Ewes Diary*, p. 45.

142 The political nature of the prosecution did not prevent the Junto leadership from seeking the assistance of a number of prominent king's-party lawyers, among them Orlando Bridgeman, Edmund Bagshaw, and Robert Holborne; *CJ*, II, 314. Sir John Culpeper also appears to have spoken against the impeached bishops; see Bodl. Lib., MS Rawlinson d. 932 (Sir John Holland's diary), fos. 29v–30v.

143 *CJ*, II, 314; Coates, *D'Ewes Diary*, pp. 133–5.

144 *LJ*, IV, 437: of the sixteen peers on this committee, ten were to be future Parliamentarians: Essex, Pembroke, Warwick, Bristol, Holland, North, Kimbolton (Viscount Mandeville), Brooke, Grey of Wark, and Robartes.

145 *A Discovery of a Horrible and Bloody Treason and Conspiracie against the Protestants of this Kingdome in General, but especially against Divers of the Nobility and Many of the Honourable House of Commons* ([Nov.] 1641), BL, E 176/12.

146 Bray, *Evelyn Diary and Correspondence*, IV, 127: Edward Nicholas to Charles I, 18 November 1641.

147 *CJ*, II, 315. For Pym's and Hampden's involvement in the preparation of these 'heads' for a conference with the Lords; Coates, *D'Ewes Diary*, pp. 138–9.

148 Coates, *D'Ewes Diary*, p. 147; *CJ*, II, 316. For Cromwell, see Coates, *D'Ewes Diary*, pp. 97–8; *CJ*, II, p. 306.

149 Bray, *Evelyn Diary and Correspondence*, IV, 116: Charles I's apostil of 13 November, written on Edward Nicholas's letter to him of 8 November 1641.

150 *LJ*, IV, 438. When debated in the Lords on 13 November, the sixth article of the Instructions (which contained the ultimatum on the great offices) was merely 'read', without the Lords coming to any decision.

151 See *LJ*, IV, 443 for the call of the House of Lords on 17 November.

152 NA, SP 16/485/76: Earl of Northumberland to Sir Thomas Rowe, 12

November 1641 (emphasis added).

153 'The Earl of Pembrokes Speech' [19 December 1642], in *Two Speeches made in the House of Peers* (1642/[3]), pp. 3–4 (BL, E 84/35). The authorship of this speech is questionable, but the views ascribed to Pembroke nevertheless seem to have been authentic enough.

154 Coates, *D'Ewes Diary*, p. 149. The matter had come up as a potential clause in the Remonstrance of the kingdom's ills, in preparation during November.

155 *CJ*, II, 316. The ordinance was completed and passed the Commons on 15 November, though its title, as recorded in the Commons' Journal, is slightly misleading, as it simply described as an ordinance 'for putting the Trained Bands into a posture of defence'. For the appointment of Essex, see Coates, *D'Ewes Diary*, p. 147.

156 *CJ*, II, 25, for the naming of the Junto-dominated committee that was appointed to draw this 'declaration', on 10 November 1640.

157 Bray, *Evelyn Diary and Correspondence*, IV, 117: Edward Nicholas to Charles I, 8 November 1641.

158 Ibid.

159 Ibid., 127: Edward Nicholas to Charles I, 18 November 1641.

160 *CJ*, II, 317; Coates, *D'Ewes Diary*, p. 150.

161 *CJ*, II, 317.

162 Ibid.; Coates, *D'Ewes Diary*, pp. 150–1 and Bodl. Lib., MS Rawlinson d. 932 (Sir John Holland's diary), fo. 35v, for the debate. Only in relation to the question of whether some of the bishops had introduced 'idolatry' (a matter which had implications for the still pending impeachment of Archbishop Laud) is there evidence of the Junto's allies (in this case Warwick's neighbour, Sir Thomas Barrington) insisting on a division, which he had Sir Martin Lumley won by 124 votes to 99; *CJ*, II, 317. For the footnote quotation from Rudyard, see Bodl. Lib., MS Rawlinson d. 932 (Sir John Holland's diary), fos. 47–8.

163 Bodl. Lib., MS Rawlinson d. 932 (Sir John Holland's diary), fo. 35v. The quoted text is edited for clarity; the original text reads

'Whyle any thinge is in establishing is wisdome to preserve the respect off what is established'. In the same debate Harbottell Grimston, an advocate of reforming the episcopate, argued *against* the Order of 8 September; Coates, *D'Ewes Diary*, p. 150.

164 Ibid., p. 185.

165 Bodl. Lib., MS Rawlinson d. 932 (Sir John Holland's diary), fo. 49 (Coates, *D'Ewes Diary*, p. 184n); spelling in quotation partly modernized.

166 Bray, *Evelyn Diary and Correspondence*, IV, 133: Edward Nicholas to Charles I, 22 November 1641; Coates, *D'Ewes Diary*, p. 186 (for Hyde and Culpeper).

167 Bray, *Evelyn Diary and Correspondence*, IV, 117: Edward Nicholas to Charles I, 8 November, and the king's apostil to it of 13 November. The annotated letter would have been returned to Nicholas around 19 or 20 November: in good time for the major debate on the Remonstrance on 22 November.

168 Bodl. Lib., MS Rawlinson d. 932 (Sir John Holland's diary), fos. 48–9. For Culpeper's hostility to the printing of the Remonstrance, see Coates, *D'Ewes Diary*, p. 186.

169 For Dering, one of the most complex and paradoxical figures in the Parliament, see Derek Hirst, 'The Defection of Sir Edward Dering, 1640–41', *Historical Journal*, 15 (1972), 193–208; S. P. Salt, 'The Origins of Sir Edward Dering's Attack on the Ecclesiastical Hierarchy, c. 1625–40', *Historical Journal*, 30 (1987), 21–52; Jason Peacey, 'Tactical Organization in a Contested Election: Sir Edward Dering and the Spring Election at Kent, 1640', in Chris R. Kyle, (ed.), *Parliament, Politics, and Elections, 1604–48* (2001), pp. 237–72.

170 Rushworth, *Historical Collections*, Part III, I, 425; I owe this reference to Conrad Russell. For Dering's role as a teller against the Remonstrance, see *CJ*, II, 322.

171 Figures taken from the divisions listed in *CJ*, II, 322.

172 The votes on either side then were 151 (for the Junto), and 110 against; *CJ*, II, 307b; Coates, *D'Ewes Diary*, p. 105 (for the vote of 8 November).

173 This is the implication of the text of *CJ*,

II, 322: 'The question [was] propounded whether the word "published" should stand in the order for the not printing of the declaration [i.e., the Remonstrance]'; this presupposed the existence of an order prohibiting printing *and* publishing, the point being that non-print publication (i.e. manuscript copies) were to be permitted under the terms of the revised resolution. And it was this latter alternative that the Commons, in a division decided by 124 votes to 101, finally adopted.

174 *CJ*, II, 322.

175 D'Ewes account of the later stages of the Remonstrance debate is compromised by the fact that he was not present after 4 p.m.; Coates, *D'Ewes Diary*, pp. 186–7.

176 *CJ*, II, 322. The vote whether the word 'published' should stand in the resolution against having the Remonstrance 'printed and published' was decided by 124 votes to 101. The formal resolution not to print the Remonstrance without the particular leave of the Commons was then so certain to succeed that it was passed without a division.

177 As Conrad Russell has observed, the document itself was influenced by 'consultation' between the Junto's supporters in both Lords and Commons. The decision to go ahead with the Remonstrance, 'was probably taken with the approval of the minority faction in the House of Lords [the Junto peers], and was probably designed by them, as much as by the Commons, to put pressure on their recalcitrant colleagues'; Russell, *Fall of the British Monarchies*, p. 424.

178 BL, Add. MS 31954 (Nicholas's History of the Parliament), fo. 185v; compare BL, Add. MS 4180, fo. 174. For the time of night, see Coates, *D'Ewes Diary*, p. 187.

179 Bray, *Evelyn Diary and Correspondence*, IV, 131; also printed in M. A. E. Green (ed.), *Letters of Queen Henrietta Maria* (1857), p. 46: Queen Henriette Marie to Edward Nicholas, [received] 20 November 1641. (I owe this reference to Dr David Scott.)

180 *CJ*, II, 325.

15. THE RETURN OF THE KING

1 *King Charles his Entertainment and*

Londons Loyaltie ([Nov.] 1641), pp. 5–6 [*recte* pp. 7–8] (BL, E 177/13).

2 Ibid., pp. 5–6; for the size of the escort see *Ovatio Carolina* ([Nov.] 1641), p. 13 (BL, E 238/4).

3 LMA, Common Council Journal 39, fos. 245v, 246v, 252v. The church bells are noticed as having been rung during the second part of the entry procession, the stage from Guildhall to Whitehall, though this does not preclude their having been rung earlier; Lawrence Price, *Great Britaines Time of Triumph. Or, the Solid Subiects Observation* ([Nov.] 1641), sig. A3 (BL, E 177/17).

4 For Charles's failure to use the royal entry before 1641, see R. Macolm Smuts, 'Public Ceremony and Royal Charisma: the English Royal Entry in London, 1485–1642', in A. L. Beier, David Cannadine, and J. M. Rosenheim (eds.), *The First Modern Society: Essays in English History in Honour of Lawrence Stone* (Cambridge, 1989), pp. 65–93.

5 Bray, *Evelyn Diary and Correspondence*, IV, 113: Edward Nicholas to Charles I, 6 November 1641. It is noteworthy that Charles made no comment on the proposal in his reply to Nicholas; see ibid.

6 For the roles of Gurney and Nicholas, see Valerie Pearl, *London and the Outbreak of the Puritan Revolution: City Government and National Politics, 1625–43* (Oxford, 1964), pp. 125–6, 302–3.

7 Even the marriage of his daughter, Mary, to the Prince of Orange, had passed without public celebrations, nominally on the grounds that the wedding had taken place in Lent, but in practice because the king was unable to fund their expected cost.

8 Indeed, Charles's initial insistence, in his instructions to the Lord Chamberlain, that he would only spend a night at Whitehall before retiring to Hampton Court may well have been partly connected with his desire to live more thriftily, and not in Whitehall, where the economies forced on him by the reluctance of the Parliament to grant him Tonnage and Poundage were daily on show. For the instructions, see Bray, *Evelyn Diary and Correspondence*, IV, 131: Queen Henriette Marie to Edward Nicholas, [received] 20 November 1641.

9 For Nicholas's concern that Charles should

be seen to be courting the people, see Bray, *Evelyn Diary and Correspondence*, IV, 127: Edward Nicholas to Charles I, 18 November 1641.

10 HMC, *Twelfth Report* (Coke Manuscripts), II, 295.

11 LMA, Repertories 50, fo. 227; for the preparations, see Common Council Journal 39, fos. 245v, 246v, 252v; and Common Council Journal 40, fo. 8.

12 Bray, *Evelyn Diary and Correspondence*, IV, 132; Edward Nicholas to Charles I, 22 November 1641.

13 *Ovatio Carolina* ([Nov.] 1641), p. [ref. to the gift] (BL, E 238/4 Price, *Great Britaines Time of Triumph*, sig. A3.

14 David Gurney, *The Record of the House of Gournay* (1848), p. 534.

15 Bray, *Evelyn Diary and Correspondence*, IV, 132: Edward Nicholas to Charles I, 22 November 1641.

16 Gardiner, *History*, X, 83–5, notes the significance of the event as marking the beginning of a new period in the relations between the king and the 'parliamentary opposition'; but does not deal in detail with the royal entry. Part of the arrangements for the entry are described in Anthony Fletcher, *The Outbreak of the English Civil War* (1981), pp. 161–2; and, very briefly, in Russell, *Fall of the British Monarchies*, pp. 429–30.

17 The king's-party men who were removed were Huntly, Airth, Linlithgow, Home, Tullibardine, Galloway, Dumfries and Carnwath; the only major royalist allies who remained on the list were the Duke of Richmond and Lennox (who resided at the English court anyway), and the Earls of Morton, Perth, and Roxburgh (the last perhaps the most surprising of the inclusions); for these appointments see David Stevenson, *The Scottish Revolution: the Triumph of the Covenanters* (Newton Abbot, 1973), pp. 229–40.

18 *Acts of the Parliament of Scotland*, V, 404–5.

19 Lords Loudoun and Lindsay had, in fact, been granted earldoms in 1633, but the grants had been suspended by the king on account of the two peers' opposition to his policies, revealed in the Scottish Parliament of that

same year; Stevenson, *Scottish Revolution*, p. 241.

20 *Five Most Noble Speeches Spoken to his Majestie returning out of Scotland into England* ([Nov.] 1641), sig. A3[v] (BL, E 199/32); this tract was printed for John Greensmith, who printed a number of pro-king's-party works at this time.

21 Ibid., sigg. A3[v]-A3[1].

22 *Ovatio Carolina*, pp. 11–12. This promise to maintain the pristine Elizabethan state of the English Church became a recurrent theme in royal apologetic, culminating in a solemn oath-taking by the king, before Archbishop Ussher, in July 1643; *The Kingdomes Weekly Intelligencer*, no. 28 (25 July–1 Aug. 1643), pp. 217–18 (BL, E 63/1).

23 *Ovatio Carolina*, pp. 11–12.

24 Price, *Great Britaines Time of Triumph*, sig. A3. The element of uncertainty registered in the text to which this footnote relates arises from the fact that there was more than one Artillery Company in London. By far the most important, however, was the City Artillery Company, and this is therefore the likeliest source of the 'Artillery men' mentioned in Lawrence Price's tract.

25 [Sir John Berkenhead], *A Letter from Mercurius Civicus to Mercurius Rusticus, or, Londons Confession* ([Oxford, 25 August] 1643), p. 4 (BL, E 65/32).

26 *Five Most Noble Speeches*, sig. A3[1].

27 Arundel had returned from his embassy to the Dutch Republic shortly before 15 October; see Surrey History Centre, Bray MS 52/2/19/26: Edward Nicholas to Lord Cottington, 21 October 1641; ASV, Senato, Dispacci Inghil. 43, fo. 125v: Giustinian to the Doge and Senate, 15/25 October 1641 (CSPV 1640-42, p. 230).

28 For the significance of the Sword of State and its place in court processions, see John Adamson, 'The Tudor and Stuart Courts, 1509–1714', in John Adamson (ed.), *The Princely Courts of Europe: Ritual, Politics, and Religion under the Ancien Régime, 1500–1750* (1999), pp. 94–117, esp. pp. 102–3.

29 *Ovatio Carolina*, pp. 14–15.

30 Ibid., lists the Earl Marshal, the Earl of

Arundel, as one of the participants in the procession, the one officer in the king's entourage whose Protestant credentials were questionable. Arundel was probably a crypto-Papist, but was sufficiently discreet for this not to have been publicly known, and this did not stop him from backing both the prosecution of Strafford and the passing of the Triennial Act. He was regarded as sufficiently pro-parliamentarian during the Civil War for his name to continue to appear on the roll of the Westminster House of Lords until his death in 1646.

31 *King Charles his Entertainment and Londons Loyaltie*, p. 5. For the numbers, see Price, *Great Britaines Time of Triumph*, sig. A2v: there were forty mounted liverymen from each of the twelve City companies.

32 Hamilton was also a member of the English House of Lords by virtue of his peerage as Earl of Cambridge.

33 *Ovatio Carolina*, pp. 14–16.

34 Among this group, only the 1st Earl of Lindsey, perhaps, was to be unambiguously royalist in the war ahead. He fought, and was mortally wounded, at the battle of Edgehill in October 1642. How he would have reacted politically had he lived beyond the autumn of 1642 must remain an open question.

35 *Ovatio Carolina*, p. 14.

36 Ibid., pp. 16–17.

37 Ibid., p. 17.

38 Ibid., p. 18.

39 Ibid., p. 19.

40 By implication, those noblemen who were demanding still further reform were nothing more than an unreasonable and unrepresentative clique. This, of course, had been the charge which the king had attempted to prove just over twelve months earlier, when, confronted with the revolt by the Petitioner Peers, he had summoned the entire English nobility to the Great Council of Peers at York in an attempt to prove that he still commanded the loyalty of most peers. That attempt had failed because the majority of the peerage had sided with the Petitioner Lords.

41 *CJ*, II, 324.

42 *Ovatio Carolina*, pp. 14–16, lists nineteen members of the English House of Lords

actually taking part in the procession.

43 Price, *Great Britaines Time of Triumph*, title page.

44 Ibid.; for the quotation, see *King Charles his Entertainment and Londons Loyaltie* ([Nov.] 1641), p. 4 [*recte* p. 6] (BL, E 177/13).

45 Price, *Great Britaines Time of Triumph*, sig. A2[v].

46 *Ovatio Carolina*, p. 15.

47 Ibid., p. 16; *Diurnall Occurrences*, p. 371 (sig. Ccc).

48 Particularly disconcerting for the Junto was the appearance of 'the warlike Artillery [Company] men in the glittering armour,' who gave the king 'a Martiall-like welcome,' probably as the procession passed their training ground on its approach to Moorgate. Price, *Great Britaines Time of Triumph*, title page. For a map showing the streets used in the processional route and the site of the Artillery Ground, see Ralph Hyde (ed.), *The A to Z of Georgian London* (1981), pp. 10–11.

49 *Ovatio Carolina*, p. 21.

50 Ibid.; for the bonfires, see Price, *Great Britaines Time of Triumph*, sig. A3v.

51 Ibid..

52 Clarendon, *Rebellion*, I, 456, for the connection between the entry of 25 November and the origins of the term 'Cavalier'.

53 The earliest usage in the title of a book printed in England seems to have been in one of the works by the Gentleman Extraordinary of the Privy Chamber, Sir Francesco Biondi, in his *Eromena, or, Love and Revenge. Written originally in the Thoscan [sic] Tongue, by Cavalier Gio. Francesco Biondi* (1632), STC2 3075. D'Ewes was using the term six weeks later, meaning specifically the demobilized soldiers who had sided with the king: Coates, *D'Ewes Diary*, p. 398 (entries for 10 Jan. 1642).

54 *The Sucklington Faction: or (Sucklings) Roaring Boyes* (no printer, [Dec.?] 1641), single sheet (BL, 669 f. 4/17); reproduced in the Colour Plates.

55 Clarendon, *Rebellion*, I, 456.

56 It was a gesture that must have won favour

among the disbanded troopers who had been petitioning against Essex and Holland since early October; see, *The Heads of Severall Petitions Delivered by many of the Troopers against the Lord General* ([Oct.] 1641), pp. 2–3 (BL, E 172/14); *Diurnall Occurrences*, p. 369.

57 Essex reported this to the House of Lords on 26 November: *LJ*, IV, 452–3, 455; *CJ*, II, 325.

58 *LJ*, IV, 452–3.

59 Coates, *D'Ewes Diary*, p. 45; D'Ewes added 'I thinke most [of what] hee saied was premeditated'.

60 *LJ*, IV, 452–3.

61 Nicholas was appointed to the junior of the two Secretaryships, the one vacated by Windebanke's flight. *Pace* Professor Russell, it was Vane's post as one of the two Secretaries of State, not Windebank's, which remained for the moment unfilled; cf. Russell, *Fall of the British Monarchies*, p. 436. Vane's office was left vacant until the appointment of Viscount Falkland in January 1642.

62 ASV, Senato, Dispacci Inghil. 43, fos. 236v–237: Giovanni Giustinian to the Doge and Senate, 10/20 December 1641 (*CSPV 1640–42*, p. 261 and n.).

63 HMC, *Buccleuch Manuscripts*, I, 286.

64 Violet Rowe, *Sir Henry Vane the Younger: a Study in Political and Administrative History* (1970), p. 120; BL, Add. MS 31116 (Laurence Whitaker's diary), p. 440.

65 Archives du Ministère des Affaires étrangères, Paris, Correspondence politique, Angleterre, 48: Imbault, marquis de la Ferté to [Mazarin?], 7/17 December 1641. NA SP 16/486/36: Thomas Smith to Sir John Pennington, 10 December 1641.

66 *CSPV 1640–42*, p. 272: Giustinian to the Doge and Senate, 31 December 1641/10 January 1642. Newport was granted keys to give him access to Whitehall on 30 December by the Lord Chamberlain's department, leading Professor Russell to conclude that the king did not distrust him at this date; Russell, *Fall of the British Monarchies*, p. 440n, citing NA, LC 5/135, unfol., entry for 30 December 1641. However, as Newport remained as a Privy Councillor, this seems to have been routine; moreover, as Newport's first-cousin,

Essex, was still Lord Chamberlain at the time, the grant of keys may have owed more to his favour than the king's. For the identification of the venue for Newport's remarks, Holland House in Kensington, see Coates, *D'Ewes Diary*, p. 362.

67 ASV, Senato, Dispacci Inghil. 43, fo. 237r-v: Giustinian to the Doge and Senate, 10/20 December 1641 (*CSPV 1640–42*, p. 262).

68 HMC, *Buccleuch Manuscripts*, I, 286, 288.

69 Coates, *D'Ewes Diary*, pp. 189, 196–7.

70 *CJ*, II, 326; Coates, *D'Ewes Diary*, pp. 207–8, 216.

71 The proposal reported to have been approved by the Lords (see NA, SP 16/486/15), though no reference is made in either the completed Journal or in the Manuscript Minutes. I owe this observation to Conrad Russell.

72 *Privy Council Registers*, XII, 200–201. For the extent of the king's landed revenue, see R. W. Hoyle, 'Introduction: Aspects of the Crown's Estate, *c.* 1558–1640', in idem (ed.), *The Estates of the English Crown 1558–1640* (Cambridge, 1994) pp. 1–57.

73 Clarendon, *Rebellion*, II, 539–40.

74 BL, Evelyn Collection, Nicholas Box, unfol.: Earl of Pembroke to Edward Nicholas, 29 November 1641.

75 BL, Evelyn Collection, Nicholas Box, unfol.: Edward Nicholas to the Earl of Pembroke, summary, [around 30 November 1641]; my emphasis.

76 Whether Nicholas was right in this assumption is another matter. The proposal, which had been made first in August, was revived in November by the Sussex Commons-man, Harbert Morley of the Glynde. But I have as yet found no formal connection, still less 'dependency,' between Pembroke and Harbert Morley. Morley, however, certainly belonged to the Commons' 'godly', and was to be one of the most zealous Sussex Parliamentarians during the Civil War; Jason Peacey, 'Harbert Morley', draft biography, HPL.

77 *CJ*, II, 326; Coates, *D'Ewes Diary*, pp. 208 (for the Commons' proposal of 29 November), 239; BL, Evelyn Collection,

Nicholas Box, unfol.: Earl of Pembroke to Edward Nicholas, 29 November 1641. St John, the Junto's principal lawyer (and Glynne's colleague in Lincoln's Inn), was probably the next most active Commons-man involved in the bishops' impeachment. Other Junto-men actively supported it: see, e.g., Hesilrige (Coates, *D'Ewes Diary*, p. 217), and Wylde (ibid., p. 237). For the quotation cited in the footnote, see Laud *Works*, IV, 418–9.

78 For their defensiveness at this time, see ASV, Senato, Dispacci Inghil. 43, fo. 237r-v: Giustinian to the Doge and Senate, 10/20 December 1641 (*CSPV 1640–42*, p. 262).

79 Clarendon, *Rebellion*, II, 540.

80 HMC, *Buccleuch Manuscripts*, I, 286, 288.

16. TREASON AVENGED

1 Coates, *D'Ewes Diary*, p. 347.

2 James Salmon, *Bloudy Newes from Ireland, or the Barbarous Crueltie by the Papists used in that Kingdome* ([Dec.] 1641), title page (BL, E 179/9).

3 Salmon, *Bloudy Newes from Ireland*, title page. For another examples of this genre, see John Venn [attrib.], *A True Relation of th Most Wise and Worthy Speech made by Captain Ven…with a Description of the Estate of Ireland* ([Jan.?] 1641[/2]), p. 5 (BL, E 181/21).

4 Salmon, *Bloudy Newes from Ireland*, sig. A3[v].

5 Claus Uhlig, 'Spensers Irische Barbaren: zur Argumentation von *A View of the Present State of Ireland*', in August Buck and Tibor Khniczay (eds.), *Das Ende der Renaissance: Europaische Kultur um 1600* (Wiesbaden, 1987), pp. 135–54; Lisa Jardine, 'Mastering the Uncouth: Gabriel Harvey, Edmund Spenser and the English Experience in Ireland', in John Henry and Sarah Hutton (eds.), *New Perspectives on Renaissance Thought: Essays in the History of Science, Education and Philosophy in Memory of Charles B. Schmitt* (1990), pp. 68–82; Blair Worden, *The Sound of Virtue: Philip Sidney's Arcadia and Elizabethan Politics* (New Haven and London, 1996).

6 Sir John Temple, *The Irish Rebellion: or, an History* (1646), pp. 2–4.

7 For an example of the numerous expressions of this sentiment, see Edmund Calamy, *England's Looking-Glasse, presented in a Sermon preached before the Honorable House of Commons, at their Late Solemn Fast, December 22. 1641* (1641[/2]), pp. 9, 34 (BL, E 131/29).

8 For this coinage, see Patrick Collinson, 'The Monarchical Republic of Queen Elizabeth I', *Bulletin of the John Rylands University Library of Manchester*, 69 (1987), 394–424.

9 For a striking contemporaneous reference to the 'representative' function of the Parliament, advanced by a leading member of Warwick's circle, see Calamy, *Englands Looking-Glasse, presented in a Sermon*, p. 45 (BL, E 131/29). The sermon was preached at the fast held on 22 December 1641.

10 Clarendon, *Rebellion*, I, 481.

11 Coates, *D'Ewes Diary*, p. 72; CJ, II, 303; and see above, p. 423.

12 Analysis of the committee lists produces a minimum number of Junto supporters of forty-eight (a minimum of ten from the Lords and thirty-eight from the Commons) out of a total membership of seventy-two; LJ, IV, 417, 417; CJ, II, 302.

13 CJ, II, 302; for the Committee for Irish Affairs' role in the formulation of policy and the preparation of 'instructions' to officers, see, for example, CJ, II, 311, 313, 362. From 12 November, the lower House ordered that all its resolutions concerning Ireland were to be 'proposed' (i.e. referred) by the Commons' contingent on the Committee for Irish Affairs to their upper-House colleagues as a matter of course; CJ, II, 313. For the later role of bicameral standing committees as organs of government, see John Adamson, 'The Triumph of Oligarchy: the Committee of Both Kingdoms and the Management of War', in Chris R. Kyle and Jason Peacey (eds.), *Parliament at Work: Parliamentary Committees, Political Power and Public Access in Early Modern England* (Woodbridge, 2002), pp. 101–27.

14 Leicester's regiment, it was reaffirmed on 16 December, was to consist of 1,500 men; Coates, *D'Ewes Diary*, p. 301. The other two regiments were to be of 1,000 each.

15 The Lord Lieutenant's rights of appointment were in theory respected; in

practice, however, the Committee for Irish Affairs drew up the list of 'recommendations' for these posts, and the dithering Leicester had little alternative but to give them his rubber-stamp; see, for example, Sir John Hotham's report of 11 November 1641: Coates, *D'Ewes Diary*, pp. 121–2.

16 Coates, *D'Ewes Diary*, p. 127. Dungarvan's sister, Lady Mary Boyle, had married Charles Rich (Warwick's son) on 21 July 1641. Dungarvan was the eldest son and heir of the 1st Earl of Cork.

17 Coates, *D'Ewes Diary*, p. 129; note, also, the order of the Commons on 30 December 1641, in which Mildmay and Barrington were ordered to prepare an ordinance as security for a loan of £30,000 from the Merchant Adventurers. For Pembroke's relations with Pye, which went back into the early 1630s, see Sheffield City Lib., Elmhirst MS 1351: Sir Robert Pye to the Earl of Pembroke, 10 September 1631; for his later relations, see Elmhirst MS 1352/10: the Earl of Pembroke to Sir Robert Pye, Sir Benjamin Rudyard and Sir William Lewes, 6 October 1645.

18 *CJ*, II, 362; for Venn, see above, pp. 66, 79; and for his alleged influence over the London apprentices, John Venn [attrib.], *A True Relation of th Most Wise and Worthy Speech made by Captain Ven...with a Description of the Estate of Ireland* ([Jan.?] 1641[/2]), pp. 1–3 (BL, E 181/21); *LJ*, IV, 429; for the connections between Skippon, Essex and the Artillery Company, see above, pp. 66–7.

19 *CJ*, II, 361; *LJ*, IV, 494.

20 *CJ*, II, 340. Jessop's name is misspelled in the Journal as 'Mr Jesson'.

21 *CJ*, II, 312. I am grateful to Professor Allan Macinnes for a discussion of Argyll's ambitions in Ulster.

22 Shipping was also one of Warwick's concerns. Using his network of contacts in the maritime trade, he monitored shipments of arms from foreign ports (Dunkirk in particular) that were suspected of being destined for the Irish rebels. And towards the end of December, he devised yet another scheme, helpfully conveyed to the House of Commons by Pym, whereby Warwick would provide two of his own ships to transport the advance party of the new army to Ireland; *CJ*, II, 361; *LJ*, IV, 492, 494.

23 For the conduit of war as a means of bonding the two British nations, see above, pp. 367–70.

24 The idea, ubiquitous in twentieth-century writing on the period, that this complex series of connections — of ideology, patronage, domestic service, and kin — somehow converged in the person of John Pym would doubtless have been greeted by seventeenth-century Parliament-men with considerable puzzlement and amusement.

25 The evidence upon which these claims are based is set out later in this chapter; see above, pp. 480–1.

26 *The Kings Maiesties Speech the 2nd Day of December, 1641. To the Honourable House of Parliament* ([Dec.] 1641), sig. A2[v] (BL, E 199/30).

27 For Digby's role in opposing the king's policies of confrontation, see above, pp. 485–90, 492–5.

28 For Roxburgh's role in the planned October coup, see above, pp. 408–9; for the meeting at Roxburgh's house, Buckminster Park, Lincolnshire, Tollemache MS 3748; for his early career, see *Complete Peerage*, XI, 215. For his letter on the Incident, see BL, Evelyn Collection, Nicholas Box: Earl of Roxburgh to Edward Nicholas, Edinburgh, 13 October 1641.

29 NA, PRO 31/3/73 (Baschet's Paris transcripts), fo. 10r-v; Gardiner, *History*, X, 138; Russell, *Fall of the British Monarchies*, p. 449.

30 It was also evident, from the moment of Charles's return, in the reaction to his decision, on 25 November, to withdraw the military guard which Essex had placed on Parliament for its defence. Predictably, perhaps, Warwick was one of the two peers chosen by Parliament to protest at the guard's removal. However, it is a measure of the alarm created within the king's own constituency by the new 'Cavaliers' that it was Lord Digby — so often caricatured as an impetuous warmonger — who accompanied Warwick on his mission to court; *CJ*, II, 326. For Digby after 1642, see Ian Roy, 'George Digby, Royalist Intrigue and the Collapse of the Cause', in Ian Gentles, John Morrill, and Blair

Worden (eds.), *Soldiers, Writers and Statesmen of the English Revolution* (Cambridge, 1998), pp. 68–90. A major new study of the king's party of 1640–42 and of the Civil-War Royalists, by Dr David Scott, is currently in progress.

31 The evidence for these taxonomies will be found, I hope to the reader's satisfaction, in what follows in this chapter.

32 Centre for Kentish Studies, De L'Isle MS U1475/C114/11: Sir John Temple to the Earl of Leicester, 18 February 1641 (HMC, *De L'Isle Manuscripts*, VI, 384).

33 *CJ*, II, 330.

34 The ultimatum was to be presented by a committee — a third of whose members were either the sons or close kinsmen of peers — who were to demand that the Lords either pass the bills they were currently obstructing or face the consequences; *CJ*, II, 330. The twelve-man committee was almost a roll-call of the Junto leadership in the lower House; its members were Pym, Nathaniel Fiennes (son of Viscount Saye), Sir Philip Stapilton, William Strode, Sir Arthur Hesilrige (brother-in-law of Lord Brooke), Denzell Holles (the brother of the 2nd Earl of Clare), Sir Samuel Rolle, John Hampden, Sir John Hotham, Sir Walter Erle (whose son was married to Saye's daughter), Henry Marten, and — the only future Royalist in the group — Sir John Culpeper.

35 *CJ*, II, 330; Coates, *D'Ewes Diary*, p. 228.

36 Coates, *D'Ewes Diary*, p. 373: 'it was first ordered [on 31 December] that the select Committee of Irish affaires, because it consisted of some members of the Lords howse as well as of ours, should have libertie to adiourne themselves to what place they would. . .and all that would come weere to have voices' — i.e. it was open to any member of the Commons to attend and debate at the committee meeting.

37 Nor was the military dimension of this threat left as merely implicit, for at the same moment as they approved this ultimatum to the king's-party Lords, the Commons simultaneously ordered Pym and his allies to come up with a unilateral plan for 'the guarding of the towns of Hull and Newcastle': Hull, the second-largest arsenal in the kingdom (after the Tower); and Newcastle,

the strategically vital seaport (as it had been in the 1640 revolt), controlling the coal supply to London. *CJ*, II, 330.

38 However much traditional ideas of deference may have been weakening in England by the early 1640s, they remained a powerful social force, both at Westminster and in the world beyond. On this theme more generally, see Andy Wood, '"Poore Men Woll Speke One Daye": Plebeian Languages of Deference and Defiance in England, *c.* 1520–1640', in Tim Harris (ed.), *The Politics of the Excluded, c. 1500–1850* (Basingstoke and New York, 2001), pp. 67–98; and J. G. A. Pocock, 'The Classical Theory of Deference', *American Historical Review*, 81 (1976), 516–23.

39 Coates, *D'Ewes Diary*, p. 244. It is worthy of note that this bill (like the bill of attainder against the Earl of Strafford), was one of the several items of major reformist legislation to emerge from Sir Arthur Hesilrige's capacious pockets. Like that earlier bill, it was probably the product of consultation between Hesilrige and his brother-in-law (and landlord), Lord Brooke.

40 Named speakers who supported the bill include Strode and St John (who argued for the necessity of 'a plenitude off power [being] intrusted in some persons, in case off danger off invasion, whether it be foreign or Intestine'), and the bill was supported at a subsequent division by Denzell Holles and Sir William Armyne; see Coates, *D'Ewes Diary*, p. 245n; *CJ*, II, 334. Sir Thomas Barrington's reaction to the bill is, at first sight, puzzling, as he moved that it might be rejected and 'another bill to the same purpose' substituted in its place. Barrington clearly supported the *principle* of parliamentary appointment of these 'great officers'; and one possible explanation of his intervention is that he may have been protecting the interests of his friend and ally, Warwick. Did he hope to have Warwick nominated as Lord Admiral rather than Northumberland; or did he know that there was already another bill in preparation.?

41 *CJ*, II, 349.

42 Coates, *D'Ewes Diary*, p. 327; Clarendon, *Rebellion*, I, 446–7 (for St John's authorship).

43 Coates, *D'Ewes Diary*, p. 245 (emphasis added).

44 Gardiner, *History*, x, 95.

45 One of the rare exceptions to this rule is the Commons' resolution of 6 December which merely 'recommended' to the Earl of Leicester, as Lord Lieutenant of Ireland, that if 'any gentleman of quality [in Ireland], fit for that service' offered to raise specialist cavalry (dragoons or 'carabines') to serve against the rebels, he should regard himself at liberty to accept the offer, since these cavalrymen might be raised 'at easier rates' (i.e. less expensively) in Ireland 'than here'; see *CJ*, II, 333.

46 For the king's insistence that the army for Ireland should be composed of volunteers, see his reply to the Parliament, presented to the Commons on 29 December, in which he agreed merely that an army of 10,000 men should be raised, 'by commissions which *he* [not Leicester] shall grant', to consist of 'ten thousand volunteers'; impressment was implicitly ruled out; see *CJ*, II, 361; *LJ*, IV, 494.

47 *LJ*, IV, 463; for Saye's support for the bill, see Bodl. Lib., MS Clarendon 21, no. 1603 (Earl of Dover's diary), entries for 6 December 1641; for its history in the Commons, see *CJ*, II, 326, 330.

48 *CJ*, II, 330, where the bill is referred to as one 'for the better raising and levying of soldiers for the defence of England and Ireland'.

49 *LJ*, IV, 463; and for the contents of the bill, see Gardiner, *History*, x, 95. The bill would nevertheless have allowed the king to raise volunteer forces against internal insurrection.

50 *CJ*, II, 341, for John Wylde's report of the state of the amendments, 13 December 1641.

51 *LJ*, IV, 463. The king's party began its delaying tactics with a request to the Commons to provide reasons why the clause denying the king's power to impress troops under the prerogative had been included in the bill.

52 *LJ*, IV, 494; Prinsterer, *Archives...de la maison d'Orange-Nassau*, 2nd ser., III, 498: Jan van der Kerckhove, Baron of Heenvliet, to the Prince of Orange, 7/17 January 1642. For attempts by the Commons Junto-men to press the Lords to accept the Scots Commissioners' offer to raise ten thousand men, see Stapilton's messages of 13, 15 and

21 December, *CJ*, II, 342, 343–4, 351–2.

53 *CJ*, II, 291; ASV, Senato, Dispacci Inghil. 43, fo. 144v: Giovanni Giustinian to the Doge and Senate, 29 October/8 November 1641 (*CSPV 1640–42*, p. 236).

54 Charles I, *By the King. A Proclamation for the Attendance of the Members in Both Houses in Parliament* ([12 December] 1641), Wing (2nd edn) C2600.

55 ASV, Senato, Dispacci Inghil. 43, fos. 243 and 248 (the latter contains the decodings): Giovanni Giustinian to the Doge and Senate, 17/27 December 1641 (*CSPV 1640–42*, p. 263).

56 Archives du Ministère d'Affaires etrangères, Paris, Correspondence politique, Angleterre, 48: marquis de la Ferté-Imbault, despatch from London, 16/26 December 1641. This dating is consistent with the evidence presented by a member of the French ambassador's circle, Hercules Langres, to the Commons (sitting as a committee in Grocers' Hall) on 7 January 1642. Explaining what he knew in advance of the attempt to arrest the six members, he explained that 'some 3 weekes since' — that is on or around 15 December — he had heard from a 'Monsieur Fleurie', a French officer who had joined the ranks of the Cavaliers at Whitehall, that 'ther would bee troubles shortelie here in England'. Of itself, this phrase is too imprecise to prove that Fleurie already knew of a plan to arrest any Parliament-men at this time; but it is at least interesting that this is how his interlocutor, Langres, appears to have read it: hence his decision to draw it to the attention of the Commons.

57 Charles I, *By the King. A Proclamation for Obedience to the Lawes ordained for Establishing of the True Religion in this Kingdom of England* ([10 December] 1642), BL, 669 f. 3/24.

58 Charles I, *Proclamation for the Attendance of the Members in Both Houses.*

59 For Charles's plans to look to Culpeper and Hyde as royal servants in the Commons, see below, pp. 486–8. The king's decision to offer office to Pym, as late as January 1642, would also seem to be incompatible with his having decided to seek capital sentences against those who were to be impeached.

60 See below, pp. 485–7.

61 Cottington's sedulous efforts to avoid having to appear in the House of Lords to support the king's party in the autumn of 1641, and his general invisibility from the spring of that year, is a case in point; see Bray, *Evelyn Diary and Correspondence*, IV, 124–5: Queen Henriette Marie to Edward Nicholas, 12 November 1641.

62 Clarendon, *Rebellion*, I, 447n (printing a cancelled portion of Clarendon's *Life*).

63 S. R. Gardiner, '[The] Plan of Charles I for the Deliverance of Strafford' *English Historical Review*, 12 (1897), 114–6, pp. 114–6.

64 *The Kings Maiesties Speech the 2nd Day of December, 1641. To the Honourable House of Parliament* ([Dec.] 1641), sig. A2[v] (BL, E 199/30).

65 In overall outline, the key elements of these plans seem not to have changed substantially since they had first been mooted in November 1640: winning control of the Tower of London and using it, if necessary, to intimidate the City; and then using loyal elements in the (now disbanded) army to dissolve Parliament by force and to arrest the Junto leaders. These had been the key elements of the Tower Plot in May 1641 to rescue Strafford and bring the impeachment trial to an end; and, on the evidence of Count Carlo Rossetti, the king continued to be attracted to the idea throughout 1641; see Gardiner, '[The] Plan of Charles I for the Deliverance of Strafford', 114–6, printing Archivio Segreto Vaticano, Nunziatura di Colonia 22: Carlo Rossetti, despatch of 30 January/9 February 1642 (I am grateful to Mr Christopher Thompson for drawing my attention to this article); the quotation is from Gardiner, ibid., p. 114. For the Cologne archives, see Michael F. Feldkamp, *Studien und Texte zur Geschichte der Kölner Nuntiatur*, III, *Inventar des Fonds Archivio della Nunziatura di Colonia im Vatikanischen Archiv* (Vatican City, 1995).

66 ASV, Senato, Dispacci Inghil. 43, fo. 249: coded section of the despatch from Giovanni Giustinian to the Doge and Senate, 17/27 December 1641 (*CSPV 1640–42*, p. 264).

67 For the sending of the summons, see ASV, Senato, Dispacci Inghil. 43, fo. 243: coded section of the despatch from Giovanni Giustinian to the Doge and Senate, 17/27 December 1641 (*CSPV 1640–42*, p. 263).

68 Clarendon, *Rebellion*, I, 454.

69 Coates, *D'Ewes Diary*, p. 226.

70 BL, Sloane MS 1467 (Newsletters, 1640–41), fo. 146: letter of intelligence, [November 1641]; Coates, *D'Ewes Diary*, p. 226 (for D'Ewes's speech and the passage quoted).

71 CJ, II, 340–41; Bodl. Lib., MS Rawlinson d. 932 (Sir John Holland's diary), fo. 75v.

72 Coates, *D'Ewes Diary*, p. 271; CJ, II, 339.

73 CJ, II, 339.

74 For the efforts to suppress the petition, see CJ, II, 342, 350; Bodl. Lib., MS Rawlinson d. 932 (Sir John Holland's diary), fo. 71*.

75 CJ, II, 350: report by George Perd, 20 December 1641.

76 Coates, *D'Ewes Diary*, p. 295.

77 CJ, II, 344; Coates, *D'Ewes Diary*, p. 295; for the text, see [House of Commons], *A Remonstrance of the State of the Kingdom* ([Dec.] 1641), title page (BL, E 181/2).

78 CJ, II, 344: in favour of the Remonstrance's printing, Denzell Holles and Sir Walter Erle, 135 votes; against, Sir John Culpeper and [John] Ashburnham, 83.

79 *Remonstrance of the State of the Kingdom*, pp. 47–8.

80 Calamy, *England's Looking-Glasse, presented in a Sermon*, p. 34.

81 CJ, II, 353, for an example of the Commons' growing exasperation at the Lords' continued blocking of the impressment bill.

82 CJ, II, 352.

83 The ensuing conference, following the delivery of Holles's message, was arranged by Sir Thomas Barrington, and managed by Holles, Pym, Stapilton, Vane junior, Fiennes, and Hampden; CJ, II, 353.

84 For the best general study, see Keith Lindley, *Popular Politics and Religion in Civil War London* (Aldershot, 1997).

85 Coates, *D'Ewes Diary*, p. 216n.

86 Clarendon, *Rebellion*, I, 484.

87 *Articles of High Treason, and Other High*

Misdemeanors ([Jan.] 1641[/2]), sig. A3[r-v] (BL, E 131/2); *LJ*, IV, 501.

88 Coates, *D'Ewes Diary*, p. 271; *CJ*, II, 339.

89 *His Maiesties Speciall Command under the Great Seale of England to the Lord Major of the Honourable City of London* ([mid-Dec.], 1641), sig. A2 (BL, E 179/19).

90 *His Maiesties Speciall Command*, sigg. A2r-v. The author of this pamphlet wrote 'Friday, Decemb. 4'; but the Friday was 3 December, not the 4th

91 NA, SP 16/486/14; SP 16/488/30: both quoted in Pearl, *London*, p. 130.

92 Clarendon, *Rebellion*, I, 448.

93 Coates, *D'Ewes Diary*, p. 330. These were reported to the Commons by Sir Walter Erle on 21 December; but the decision appears to have been taken not later than Monday the 20th.

94 Coates, *D'Ewes Diary*, p. 330; *CSPD 1641–43*, pp. 210, 211.

95 Precisely how extensive were the reformists' gains in the Common Council elections of 1641 is a matter of some debate. Most contemporary commentators were agreed, however, that a large proportion of the existing leadership of the Common Council (on whose members Gurney was depending for the suppression of the tumults) was ousted in favour of new men, actively supportive of the reformist cause. For the implications of the Common Council elections, see Valerie Pearl, *London and the Outbreak of the Puritan Revolution: City Government and National Politics, 1625–43* (Oxford, 1961), pp. 132–9.

96 Nehemiah Wallington, *Historical Notices of Events occurring chiefly in the Reign of Charles I*, ed. Rosamond Webb, 2 vols. (1869), I, 274.

97 *His Maiesties Speciall Command*, sig. A2.

98 Clarendon, *Rebellion*, I, 448.

99 For the suggestion that Balfour's resignation was forced, see Edward M. Furgol, 'Sir William Balfour', *ODNB*.

100 Basil Morgan, 'Sir Thomas Lunsford', *ODNB*.

101 At the behest of the king, the Speaker of the Commons presented a petition from the 'Reformadoes' on 23 December 1641; but, in the wake of the Lunsford affair, it was read and immediately ignored; Coates, *D'Ewes Diary*, p. 341.

102 *His Maiesties Speciall Command*, sig. A3v.

103 Stephen Marshall, *Reformation and Desolation: or a Sermon tending to the Discovery of the Symptomes of a People to whom God will by No Meanes be reconciled* [22 December 1641] ([March] 1642), p. 43 (BL, E 131/30).

104 Marshall, *Reformation and Desolation*, pp. 47–8.

105 *CJ*, II, 354, 355.

106 *LJ*, IV, 488.

107 *CJ*, II, 357.

108 *LJ*, IV, 489. This declaration was presented to the House of Lords by Holles.

109 *LJ*, IV, 489. S. R. Gardiner interpreted this delay more charitably, regarding it as intended, by the likes of Bristol, 'to give Charles an opportunity of withdrawing from his false position', i.e. of having appointed so disreputable a figure as Lunsford as Lieutenant of the Tower. Such a speculation is possible, and not necessarily incompatible (at least as an interpretation of some peers' hopes) with the reading which I have suggested above. But given that the king's party in the Lords had consistently used deferral as a form of *de facto* rejection, it seems more likely that the majority of the king's-party peers may well have supported Charles's decision to have a loyalist like Lunsford in command at the Tower. D'Ewes was probably not alone in regarding the Lords' earlier refusal to join with the Commons in calling for Lunsford's dismissal as a 'positive and categoricall deniall'; Coates, *D'Ewes Diary*, p. 344. For Gardiner's alternative view, see *History*, X, 111.

110 Coates, *D'Ewes Diary*, p. 347. The use of the past perfect tense suggests that this passage may possibly have been a later gloss by D'Ewes.

111 *CJ*, II, 357.

112 *CJ*, II, 357.

113 The possible identities of these 'men of violence' are considered above, p. 481.

114 *The Scots Loyaltie to the Protestants of England and Ireland, by proffering to Both Houses of Parliament Speedie Ayd* ([Dec.] 1641), sig. A2 (BL, E 181/16). Clarendon, *Rebellion*, I, 454–5.

115 Clarendon, *Rebellion*, I, 456.

116 PA, House of Lords MS Minutes, 27 December 1641.

117 *The Scots Loyaltie*, sig. A2[r-v].

118 For the origins of this misrule see, Chris Humphrey, *The Politics of Carnival: Festive Misrule in Medieval England* (Manchester, 2001); and on the problems of order within the capital, see Keith Lindley, 'Riot Prevention and Control in Early Stuart London', *Transactions of the Royal Historical Society*, 5th ser., 33 (1983), 109–26; and idem, *Popular Politics and Religion in Civil War London*.

119 For the assaults on bishops in their coaches, see Clarendon, *Rebellion*, I, 454.

120 For Williams, see above, pp. 128–9, 170–1; for the celebrations attending his release from the Tower in November 1640, see Dorothy Gardiner (ed.), *The Oxinden Letters, 1607–42* (1933), p. 187: James Oxinden to his brother, Henry, 27 November 1640; HMC, *De L'Isle Manuscripts*, VI, 342: William Hawkins to the Earl of Leicester, 19 November 1640.

121 Williams was offered the post in November though not formally appointed until early December 1641; see Bray, *Evelyn Diary and Correspondence*, IV, 82, 116: Edward Nicholas to Charles I, 5 October and 8 November 1641; and see also Charles Knighton, 'The Lord of Jerusalem: John Williams as Dean of Westminster', in idem and Richard Mortimer (eds.), *Westminster Abbey Reformed, 1540–1640* (Aldershot and Burlington, VT, 2003), pp. 232–59. For Williams's subsequent military activities see N. R. F. Tucker, *Prelate-at-Arms: an Account of Archbishop John Williams at Conway during the Great Rebellion, 1642–50* (Llandudno, [1938]).

122 Devon RO, Drake of Colyton MS 1700 M/CP 20; NA, SP 16/486/110: Robert Slingsby to Sir John Penington, 30 December 1641. Hyde states that Williams's robes were 'torn from his back'; Clarendon, *Rebellion*, I, 471. The incident is also discussed in

Gardiner, *History*, X, 117, and Russell, *Fall of the British Monarchies*, p. 442.

123 PA, House of Lords MS Minutes, 28 December 1641. For Pierce's time as Bishop of Bath and Wells, see Kevin Sharpe, *The Personal Rule of Charles I* (New Haven and London, 1992), pp. 335–6.

124 *LJ*, IV, 493.

125 For these sermons, the *locus classicus* is H. R. Trevor-Roper, 'The Fast Sermons of the Long Parliament', in idem (ed.), *Essays in British History presented to Sir Keith Feiling* (London and New York, 1964), pp. 85–138; and see also the more systematic study, John F. Wilson, *Pulpit in Parliament: Puritanism during the English Civil Wars, 1640–48* (Princeton, NJ, 1969).

126 Coates, *D'Ewes Diary*, p. 354. The quotation is from a letter from the Earl of Cork to the Earl of Holland, dated from Wigmore on 17 December, and sent down to the Commons on 28 December.

127 *LJ*, IV, 493.

128 *LJ*, IV, 493. In fact, Charles's accusation against Newport — that he had suggested using the queen and royal children as hostages in the event of further serious problems with the king — impugned the loyalty of a series of the Junto leaders who had been present when the alleged words were spoken. In vindicating Newport, therefore, the petition to the king went into a degree of detail unusual in such a public document in recounting the setting, and listing the witnesses present by name. The supposedly seditious words were alleged to have been spoken by Newport 'at a meeting in Kensington [probably at Mandeville's house], where the Earl of Essex, the Earl of Newport, the Lord Viscount Saye and Sele, the Lord Mandeville, the Lord Wharton, [all] members of the Lords' House, [and] the Lord Dungarvon [the Earl of Cork's eldest son], Mr Nathaniel Fiennes, Sir John Clotworthy, and Mr John Pym, members of the House of Commons, were all present, when [the party was in] a discourse of some plots that should be done in this kingdom or in Scotland...' The two Houses' petition to the king of 28 December was thus far more than simply the vindication of a sacked royal servant. It sent a clear message to the Whitehall court that the 'cabinet council' glimpsed here had returned to being the dominant interest at

Westminster, and once again commanded the support of majorities in both Houses.

129 Hyde stated clearly that the fear 'that the House of Peers would have made that use of the bishops being kept from the House that they would, in that time, have passed the bill itself for taking away their votes' was the prime reason why the bishops issued their Protest tabled in the Lords on 30 December; and that the king 'had the same imagination'. Hyde himself believed that the Lords would not have made use of the bishops' absence in this way, though this judgement is (at least) questionable, and, after the numerous instances of the Junto leaders' use of sharp practice in matters of procedure, the king was perhaps justified in his more sceptical attitude towards the likely actions of the Lords; see Clarendon, *Rebellion*, I, 473. In point of fact, the Junto leaders in the Commons appear to have substantiated the king's fears: on 31 December, Perd was ordered to go to the Lords to remind them of the 'bill sent up from this House for the taking away [of] the bishops' votes'; *CJ*, II, 364.

130 Keeler, *Members of Parliament*, pp. 256–7.

131 Thus, at least, my interpretation of Coates, *D'Ewes Diary*, pp. 352–3; Gardiner came to a similar conclusion: Gardiner, *History*, x, 116.

132 *CJ*, II, 358. For their findings, see Coates, *D'Ewes Diary*, p. 357.

133 Coates, *D'Ewes Diary*, p. 357.

134 BL, Add. MS 64807 (Thomas Standish diary), fos. 20r-v. This diary, compiled by Thomas Standish of Duxbury Hall, near Chorley, Lancashire, provides an important supplement to the fuller accounts of D'Ewes and others. He sat for the Lancashire constituency of Preston-in-Amounderness, and died in the autumn of 1642. (I am grateful to Dr David Scott for drawing my attention to this diary.)

135 Coates, *D'Ewes Diary*, p. 357; BL, Add. MS 64807 (Standish diary), fo. 20v (emphasis added).

136 Because no resolution was taken, there is no reference to this debate in the Commons' Journal, though it is extensively reported in both D'Ewes's and Standish's diaries; for its

resumption on Wednesday 29 December, see *CJ*, II, 361.

137 For the expectation that the summons might yield results, see ASV, Senato, Dispacci Inghil. 43, fos. 243 and 248 (the latter contains the decodings): Giovanni Giustinian to the Doge and Senate, 17/27 December 1641 (*CSPV 1640–42*, p. 263).

138 NA, LC 5/135 (Lord Chamberlain's Warrant Books), unfol., entries for 28 December; SO 3/12 (Signet Office Docket Book), fo. 181v; and see Russell, *Fall of the British Monarchies*, p. 441.

139 *Diurnall Occurrences in Parliament from the Second of January to the Tenth, 1641[/2]* ([Jan. 1642]), p. 1 (BL, E 201/6). The Commons complained on 3 January that 'there is a guard, in a warlike manner, placed at Whitehall'; *CJ*, II, 366.

140 Sir William Fleming was the grandson of Lilias, *née* Graham (who married the 1st Earl of Wigtown); she, in turn, was Montrose's aunt.

141 For Sir William Fleming see J. G. Fotheringham (ed.), *The Diplomatic Correspondence of Jean de Montereul and the Brothers de Bellièvre, French Ambassadors in England and Scotland*, 2 vols. (Edinburgh, 1898–99), I, 172n; for Sir William's father, see, *Complete Peerage*, 'John Fleming, 2nd Earl of Wigtown'.

142 See above, ch. 11. It is noteworthy that early in 1641, Montrose actually stayed with Roxburgh at the latter's seat, Broxmouth House: Buckminster Park, Lincolnshire, Tollemache MS 3748. For Roxburgh's involvement in the Incident, see HMC, *Fourth Report*, I, 163, 164: depositions of Captain William Stewart, 12 and 21 October 1641, and Colonel Alexander Stewart, 22 October 1641.

143 *CJ*, II, 361; *LJ*, IV, 494.

144 *CJ*, II, 361.

145 Whether the two ships in question were actually owned by Warwick or merely leased by him is unclear from the Journal entries. However, the fact that the ship-owner and Commons-man, Samuel Vassall (with whom Warwick was an occasional co-investor), owned a vessel that matches closely the tonnage of the ship mentioned by Warwick —

the *Mayflower of London*, a ship of 405 tons, armed with 29 guns — suggests that the larger of the two vessels may possibly have been his. A ship of 400 tons (though not as large as the biggest of the king's ships) would compare with the largest and most heavily armed of the merchantmen employed in the parliamentarian fleet of the 1640s; see R. McCaughey, 'The English Navy: Politics and Administration, 1640–49' (Unpublished D.Phil. dissertation, New University of Ulster, 1983), pp. 254–5, 280. Samuel Vassall held lands in Eastwood in Essex, a manor owned by the 2nd Earl of Warwick (*ex informatione* Mr Christopher Thompson); and see also Philip Benton, *The History of Rochford Hundred*, 2 vols. (Rochford, Essex, 1867, consecutively paginated), pp.747–9. Samuel's son, Stephen, was the incumbent of the Rich living of Rayleigh, Essex; see also Alnwick Castle, Northumberland, MS XII. 7, Box 1 (for Warwick's 1633 rental) and Box 2 C (for Warwick's 1645 rental), both *sub* 'Eastwood Manor'. (I owe these references to the Vassall brothers to the kindness of Mr Christopher Thompson).

146 *LJ*, IV, 495; PA, House of Lords MS Minutes, 28 December 1641.

147 For contemporary evidence that Digby's proposal was read as invalidating the act against the Parliament's dissolution without its own consent, see the Commons 'speech' falsely attributed to Pym, *A Worthy Speech made by Master Pym, to the Lords on Fryday the Thirty One of December concerning and Information against the Lord Digby* ([Jan.?] 1641[/2]), p. 2 (BL, E 199/49). No speech by Pym to the Lords that day is reported in any of the diaries or Journals of either House.

148 PA, House of Lords MS Minutes, 28 December 1641. For the 'tumults among them' on 28 December, see *CJ*, II, 359.

149 *CJ*, II, 361; BL, Add. MS 64807 (Standish diary), fo. 21. It should be noted that a page seems to have been torn out of Standish's diary at this point, with a consequential loss of what must have been part of his entry for 29 December 1641.

150 For the suggestion that Digby was the most likely source of this proposal, see Gardiner, *History*, X, 122–3.

151 *To the Kings Most Excellent Majesty, and the Lords and Peeres now assembled in*

Parliament. The Humble Petition and Protestation of all the Bishops* (1642), [29 December 1641] (BL, 669 f. 3/27). Another recension of the Protest made its purpose still plainer: this included a clause invalidating any laws 'as shall *hereafter* passe' until such time as the king could guarantee that the bishops could attend in safety. For the text of the Bishops' Protest, see *LJ*, IV, 496–7; but compare the slightly fuller text cited above (BL, 669 f. 3/27, whence comes the quotation), which is also the version printed in Clarendon, *Rebellion*, I, 472–3. The relation between the two versions requires further study. Among the possible explanations are that the *LJ* text is the 'authentic' version, and the differences in the BL text represent later interpolations; alternatively, it is equally possible that the BL text is the 'correct' one and that the omission of the 'hereafter' clause is simple secretarial error. In support of this second reading, it may be noted that the BL text purports to be a 'vera copia', attested by John Browne, the Clerk of the Parliaments.

152 Prinsterer, *Archives. . .de la maison d'Orange-Nassau*, 2nd ser., III, 498: Jan van der Kerckhove, Baron of Heenvliet, to the Prince of Orange, 7/17 January 1642; and Clarendon, *Rebellion*, I, 471–2, for a rather confused chronology of the presentation of the Protest. Clarendon claims that the Protest was presented to the king 'two hours' before it was presented to the Lords. As the Lords met at 9 a.m. on 30 December, this would suggest that Williams was at Whitehall around 7 a.m. This is a possible hour for the king to receive Privy Councillors, but not a likely one; it would seem more plausible that the audience with the king took place on Wednesday the 29th.

153 Clarendon, *Rebellion*, I, 474. The reaction was similar in the Commons after the conference, on 30 December, at which the Lords conveyed the news of the bishops' Protest: spirits were buoyant, with 'most men expressing a great deal of alacrity of spirit for this indiscreet and unadvized Act of the Bishopps'; Coates, *D'Ewes Diary*, p. 365.

154 *LJ*, IV, 497. For Bankes's promotion in February 1641, see above, p. 157.

155 *CJ*, II, 363; Coates, *D'Ewes Diary*, pp. 367–8; *LJ*, IV, 497–8. The two sent to Black Rod were the solidly Calvinist Thomas

Morton of Durham and the elderly Robert Wright of Coventry and Lichfield, who had craved the peers' 'best constructions, for he did it not [i.e. sign the petition] with any traitorous intention'; *LJ*, IV, 499.

156 *CJ*, II, 363.

157 *CJ*, II, 362; Coates, *D'Ewes Diary*, p. 366.

158 Coates, *D'Ewes Diary*, p. 366.

159 Russell, *Fall of the British Monarchies*, p. 444. It might equally have indicated that the proposers felt that Westminster was becoming too disorderly for business to be conducted safely. The motion does not necessarily imply that its proposer believed they faced an 'armed attack' by the king.

160 *CJ*, II, 364.

161 *LJ*, IV, 496, 498; indeed, it is hard to account for this vote in the Lords unless some of the peers who usually supported the Junto opposed this motion.

162 NA, SO 3/12 (Signet Office Docket Book), fo. 179 (for the warrant). Payments were made on this warrant in instalments, at least one of them on 5 May 1642: NA, E 403/2814 (Auditors' Order Books, 1641–42), fo. 23v.

163 Coates, *D'Ewes Diary*, p. 357.

164 BL, Add. MS 64807 (Standish diary), fo. 21.

165 NA, LC 5/135 (Lord Chamberlain's Order Book), p. 5. *Pace* Russell, far from this being evidence 'of hardening resolution' on the king's part, it seems to be part of a deliberate policy of bridge-building towards the former reformists, particularly those who had tried to save Strafford from the scaffold (a group that includes Saye, Bristol, Southampton, Hertford, Digby, Hyde — and even Pym, to whom the king was reported to have offered the Chancellorship of the Exchequer on 1 July); compare Russell, *Fall of the British Monarchies*, p. 447.

166 L. B. Larking (ed.), *Proceedings, principally in the County of Kent, in Connection with the Parliaments called in 1640, and especially with the Committee of Religion appointed in that Year* (Camden Society, 80, 1862), p. 68.

167 For the timing, see Larking, *Proceedings in Kent*, p. 68. Culpeper was sworn of the Privy Council that same day, Saturday 1 January: *Privy Council Registers*, XII, 207. This entry confirms Gardiner's conjecture that 'Culpepper [*sic*] may very well have been informed of his appointment on the 1st'; Gardiner, *History*, X, 127. For the best survey of Culpeper's career, see David Scott, 'Sir John Culpeper', draft biography, HPL.

168 Hyde argues that the motive for these promotions was that the king had 'found the inconvenience and mischief to himself of having no servant of interest and reputation...in the House of Commons', though this does not appear to have been the whole story; Clarendon, *Rebellion*, I, 492–3.

169 *The Life of Edward Hyde, Earl of Clarendon*, 3 vols. (Oxford, 1828), I, 100–1; Clarendon, *Rebellion*, I, 460–1.

170 Clarendon, *Rebellion*, I, 460–1.

171 Gardiner, '[The] Plan of Charles I for the Deliverance of Strafford', pp. 114–6: Carlo Rossetti, despatch of 30 January/9 February 1642.

172 *CJ*, II, 365–6; [William Fiennes, Viscount Saye and Sele], *Vindiciae Veritatis* (1654), p. 33 (BL, E 811/2).

173 *PJ, January–March 1642*, p. 23, for the phrase quoted (D'Ewes diary).

174 What Digby expected to happen next is a matter for conjecture, but there seem to have been three viable options: one was for Charles to use the recent coercion of the Parliament as a pretext for its dissolution, though this would, potentially, have created more problems than it solved; the second, in theory, was for the king to adjourn the Parliament to another town (in the autumn, Cambridge had been mooted as an alternative venue that would have been free from the menace of the London crowds), though, as this would have required the consent of the two Houses, that consent was highly unlikely to have been forthcoming. The third, and arguably likeliest, option would have been that of a temporary suspension, perhaps until 12 January, by which time Charles expected to have the support of a majority of the returning absentees. Any suggestion as to the implications of this third scenario must be highly conjectural, but there are reasons for believing that, if the king and Digby had

prevented any further reformist legislation being passed in the interim, then the changed circumstances after 12 January would have substantially strengthened the king's overall position — at least to the point where it could have resisted further encroachments on the prerogative.

175 Hyde was almost certainly correct, as we have seen, in attributing these initiatives to Digby (of whose 'volatile and unquiet spirit' he was critical). The substance of Hyde's charge against Digby was that the king would have been better off by 'doing nothing' and waiting for the return of 'the members who were absent from both Houses...so that the angry party...would have been compelled to have given over all their designs for the alteration of the government both in Church and State'. As a view of the king's position after mid-January, by which time the absent members were supposed to have returned, this is highly plausible. Hyde, however, does less than justice to Digby's position (and the rationality of the king's following it) by ignoring the near two-week period between 1 and 12 January when the 'angry party' — the Junto supporters — would have been masters of *both* Houses.

176 Clarendon, *Rebellion*, 1, 484. The suggestion that Charles consulted only narrowly over the impeachments would tend to be confirmed by the participation of Culpeper, the newly appointed Chancellor of the Exchequer, and Falkland, the newly appointed Secretary of State, in presenting the king with the Commons' protest against his course of action, on 3 January: *CJ*, 11, 367.

177 For the peers' scepticism about even the legality of the king's mode of procedure from the moment the general impeachment articles were delivered on 3 January 1641, see *LJ*, IV, 501. They questioned 'whether any person ought to be committed to custody upon a general accusation from the king...before it be reduced into particulars'. For those, like the Attorney-General, charged with bringing the prosecutions, this hardly betokened a co-operative House of Lords.

178 For a different view of the impeachments from the one advanced here, see Russell, *Fall of the British Monarchies*, p. 448.

179 Ibid.

180 *LJ*, IV, 500.

181 *PJ, January-March 1642*, p. 4 (D'Ewes). D'Ewes makes it clear that the attempt to seize the Commons-men's papers had been made before the accusation was presented to the House that afternoon; see also *CJ*, 11, 366.

182 *CJ*, 11, 367. Fleming's connections with Montrose are discussed earlier in this chapter.

183 *CJ*, 11, 367.

184 *Articles of High Treason, and other High Misdemeanors* ([3–4 Jan.] 1641[/2]), title page (BL, E 131/2).

185 *LJ*, IV, 503. The *Articles of High Treason* were in circulation by 4 January 1642.

186 *LJ*, IV, 501; *Articles of High Treason, and Other High Misdemeanors* ([Jan.] 1641[/2]), sig. A2[r-v], for quotation (BL, E 131/2); emphasis added. This is the edition published by the king's printer, Robert Barker, in what seems to have been a deliberate bid by Charles to influence public opinion. It is noteworthy that Russell, in his discussion of the charges against the five members, makes no mention of the clause to 'deprive the King of his Regall Power' and suggests that the key instance of exercising a tyrannical power that was likely to be cited against them (inevitably, in Russell's view, a matter involving religion) would have been the Commons' Order of 8 September against 'innovations'. It is perhaps worth noting that had this actually been the prosecution case, Holles, Hesilrige and the others accused could have promptly retorted that they were no more guilty of this charge than were Falkland and Culpeper – the king's recent appointees as Secretary of State and Chancellor the Exchequer – both of whom had worked closely with Pym in the promulgation of the 8 September Order. Inept as Charles may occasionally have been, it seems highly unlikely that he would have made this his preferred line of attack; compare Russell, *Fall of the British Monarchies*, p. 448.

187 *Articles of High Treason*, sig. A3.

188 *Articles of High Treason*, sig. A3[v].

189 BL, Egerton MS 2546 (Political papers), fo. 20: the king's instructions to Sir Edward Herbert, [2 January 1642].

190 It is perhaps no coincidence that this list is both a catalogue of the hardline advocates of Strafford's death in the spring of 1641 and, in a wider British context, of the leading

members of the Argyll-Hamilton interest in Scotland.

191 BL, Egerton MS 2546 (Political papers), fo. 20: the king's instructions to Sir Edward Herbert, [2 January 1642] (*Nichalas Papers*, I, 67).

192 See above, ch. 7, Section II; and ch. 10.

193 Clarendon, *Rebellion*, I, 505–6.

194 BL, Egerton MS 2546 (Political papers), fo. 20. With his usual fastidiousness, he personally crossed out Mandeville's name from the list of witnesses and amended the number of Parliament-men being accused from 'five' to 'six'.

195 Clarendon, *Rebellion*, I, 484.

196 BL, Add. MS 64807 (Standish diary), fo. 21.

197 *LJ*, IV, 501.

198 *PJ, January-March 1642*, p. 5.

199 *CJ*, II, 367.

200 *LJ*, IV, 502. In their submission to a conference with the Lords, the Commons' representatives complained that the accused members 'have [had] their persons assaulted, and laid in wait for, and the chambers, studies, and trunks have been ransacked and sealed'. This may be read to suggest that some form of physical altercation had taken place in the course of the sealing of the studies; on the other hand, it is scarcely credible that the Commons-men would have escaped arrest had there been any serious attempt to apprehend them by force.

201 *CJ*, II, 367.

202 *CJ*, II, 367.

203 *LJ*, IV, 502. This was almost universally expected to be the Earl of Essex; he, with the Duke of Richmond, were appointed to be the bearers of the two Houses' message.

204 For Hyde's optimistic expectations of the likely effects of the return of the absent members of both Houses, see Clarendon, *Rebellion*, I, 477.

205 *LJ*, IV, 501; *CJ*, II, 366. For Strode's deep personal antipathy towards the queen, see BL, Add. MS 64807 (Standish diary), fo. 28.

206 On the fate of the Somerset House Capuchins, see Caroline Hibbard, *Charles I*

and the Popish Plot (Chapel Hill, 1983), pp. 218–9.

207 *CJ*, II, 366.

208 *PJ, January-March 1642*, p. 8 (D'Ewes diary).

209 Wallington, *Historical Notices of Events*, I, 280.

210 *LJ*, IV, 502.

211 *PJ, January-March 1642*, p. 8 (D'Ewes diary).

212 This uncertainty is admirably described by Gardiner, *History*, X, 136.

213 *PJ, January-March 1642*, p. 8 (D'Ewes diary). Isaac Penington, the radical alderman and Commons-man, was also despatched with the message.

214 *PJ, January-March 1642*, p. 11 (D'Ewes).

215 *LJ*, IV, 503.

216 *PJ, January-March 1642*, p. 9 (D'Ewes diary).

217 *PJ, January-March 1642*, p. 9 (D'Ewes diary); *CJ*, II, 367, for the identification of Fleming's role on 3 January.

218 ASV, Senato, Dispacci Inghil. 43: Giovanni Giustinian to the Doge and Senate, 7/17 January 1642 (*CSPV 1640–42*, p. 276).

219 For Roxburgh's presence, see Russell, *Fall of the British Monarchies*, p. 449; for the Elector Palatine, *PJ, January-March 1642*, p. 9 (D'Ewes).

220 ASV, Senato, Dispacci Inghil. 43: Giovanni Giustinian to the Doge and Senate, 7/17 January 1642 (*CSPV 1640–42*, p. 276); *LJ*, IV, 502; *CJ*, II, 367.

221 Hibbard, *Charles I and the Popish Plot*, pp. 218–9.

222 The story is reported by Gardiner, *History*, X, 136 and appears plausible in substance, if perhaps questionable as to phraseology.

223 *PJ, January-March 1642*, pp. 11, 25; NA, PRO 31/3/73 (Baschet's Paris transcripts), fo. 10r-v.

224 *PJ, January-March 1642*, p. 23 (D'Ewes), for Hyde; Gardiner, *History*, X, 138 (for Roxburgh).

225 *CJ*, II, 368.

226 Ibid.

227 Ibid.

228 Ibid.

229 Coates, *D'Ewes Diary*, p. 393, for an example of Sir Robert Harley reporting a motion 'sent to us from the Select Committee for Irish affaires of 26 Lords and 52 Commoners who sate alsoe at Grocers' hall'.

230 *CJ*, II, 369.

231 LMA, Guildhall, Common Council Journal 40, fo. 15.

EPILOGUE

1 James Howell, *The True Informer, who...discovereth unto the World the Chiefe Causes of the Sad Distempers in Great Brittany and Ireland* (Oxford, [March] 1643), p. 35 (*recte* 41) (BL, E 96/10).

2 NA, SP 16/488, fo. 52v: Sidney Bere to Sir John Penington, 6 January 1642. Bere was secretary to the diplomat, *virtuoso* and architect, Sir Balthazar Gerbier.

3 *CJ*, II, 372.

4 *PJ, January-March 1642*, p. 24.

5 *A Great Conspiracy of the Papists, against Worthy Members of Both Houses of Parliament* ([January] 1642), sigg. A2[v]-A3, printing 'R. E.' to 'Mr Anderton', [*c.* 3 January 1642] (BL, E 131/14). For its reading to the Commons-men on 11 January, see *PJ, January-March 1642*, pp. 32-4.

6 *A Great Conspiracy of the Papists*, sig. A2[v].

7 *CJ*, II, 406 (reprinted in *PJ, January-March 1642*, p. 551); *LJ*, IV, 625-7, for the final version of 5 March 1642 (*PJ, January-March 1642*, pp. 552-5).

8 The phrase is Howell's, *The True Informer*, title page.

9 Russell, *Causes*, p. 14.

10 Russell, *Causes*, p. 213.

11 Ibid., pp. 335-6, quotation at p. 336.

12 Russell, *Causes*, Ch. 1, quotation at p. 10.

13 Russell, *Causes*, p. 17.

14 Russell, *Causes*, p. 213.

15 See, for example, Russell, *Causes*, p. 211: '[Charles] did not create the British problem, though he failed to handle it with the care that was needed. He did not create religious division, though he exploited and exacerbated it with all the strength at his command...' Likewise, Russell's interpretation of the Nineteen Propositions of June 1642 emphasises their intention 'to exclude the king from the process of government' in the way that Henry VI had been excluded while insane; but with the implication that a restoration of the normal regal powers would have followed the accession of a new king; Russell, *Fall of the British Monarchies*, p. 515.

16 Russell, *Causes*, p. 11.

17 Russell, *Causes*, p. 7.

18 Russell, *Causes*, p. 160 (for extended quotation); for his views on the Nineteen Propositions, see ibid., p. 159, and his *Fall of the British Monarchies*, pp. 515-6.

19 Russell, *Causes*, p. 7.

20 Notestein, *D'Ewes Diary*, pp. 364-5 (*PLP*, II, 463).

21 ASV, Senato, Dispacci Inghil. 42, fo. 117v: Giustinian to the Doge and Senate, 5/15 September 1640.

22 NA, SP 16/467, fo. 157: Windebank's notes of the Privy Council, 16 September 1640.

23 Notestein, *D'Ewes Diary*, p. 263; and see above, p. 193.

24 Discussed above, p. 168.

25 See above, Ch. 5. Even if a lifetime gift of the customs revenues were to have been granted to the king (as Charles was clearly hoping there would), this was subject to review by future Parliaments at three-yearly intervals and could have been rendered inoperable, if not revoked, in the event of malfeasance by the Crown.

26 PA, MP 30 March 1641, fos. 78-82, at 79-80: petition of the officers of the king's army in the North to the Earl of Northumberland, York, 20 March 1641. (I am grateful to Dr David Scott for alerting me to the importance of this passage.)

27 *CJ*, II, 280.

28 BL, Harl. MS 164 (D'Ewes diary), fo. 174 (*PLP*, v, 61); discussed above, p. 291.

29 Above, pp. 286-7.

30 *LJ*, IV, 241; NA, SO 3/12 (Signet Office Docket Book), fo. 143v; and above, pp. 294-5.

31 ASV, Senato, Dispacci Inghil. 42, fo. 286: Giustinian to the Doge and Senate, 14/24 May 1641 (*CSPV 1640-42*, p. 152).

32 Coates, *D'Ewes Diary*, p. 45; D'Ewes added 'I thinke most [of what] hee saied was premeditated'.

33 Clarendon, *Rebellion*, I, 321.

34 Essex RO, T/B 211/1, no. 39: 'The sum of that Conference which was betwixt one Mr Burroughes, ... and John Michaelson, Parson of Chelmesford, the 5 of August last [1638]'.

35 Jeremiah Burroughs, *Sions Joy. A Sermon preached to the Honourable House of Commons assembled in Parliament, at their Publique Thanksgiving, September 7, 1641, for the Peace concluded between England and Scotland* (1641) pp. 25-6 (BL, E 174/3).

36 For the first payment of this 'Brotherly Assistance', see NA, SP 46/80 (State Papers, supplementary), fo. 191: the receipt (signed by Lord Loudoun, Hew Kennedy and John Smyth), is dated 14 August 1641; see also BL, Harl. MS 163 (D'Ewes diary), fo. 339; *CJ*, II, 182. The extent of Warwick's influence in these arrangements is considered, above, Ch. 11, note 131.

37 The relevance of the Dutch Revolt to their own predicament was not lost on the Covenanters and the English Commonwealthsmen. Hence, we find Jhonston of Wariston reading Emanuel van Meteren's *Historie des Pays-Bas*, one of the most widely circulated of all histories of the Dutch Revolt, as he drafted the National Covenant in 1638, and Robert Baillie 'coming round to the principle of resistance' after studying Grotius; see Hugh Dunthorne, 'Resisting Monarchy: the Netherlands as Britain's School of Revolution in the late Sixteenth and Seventeenth Centuries', in Robert Oresko, G. C. Gibbs, and H. M. Scott (eds.), *Royal and Republican Sovereignty in Early Modern Europe: Essays in Memory of Ragnhild Hatton* (Cambridge, 1997), p. 139.

38 Calybute Downinge, *A Discoursive Conjecture upon the Reasons that produce a Desired Event of the Present Troubles of Great Britain, different from those of Lower Germany* ([after March] 1641), p. 3 (BL, E 206/10).

39 ASV, Senato, Dispacci Inghil. 43, fos. 89-94v: Giustinian to the Doge and Senate, 17/27 September 1641.

40 ASV, Senato, Dispacci Inghil. 43, fos. 89-94v: Giovanni Giustinian to the Doge and Senate, 17/27 September 1641.

41 ASV, Senato, Dispacci Inghil. 42, fo. 220: Giustinian to the Doge and Senate, 19 February/1 March 1641 (*CSPV 1640-42*, p. 127).

42 *A Great Conspiracy of the Papists*, sig. A2[v].

43 For the connections with 1640, see above, Ch. 1, and esp. pp. 46-51.

44 *LJ*, IV, 501; *Articles of High Treason, and Other High Misdemeanors* ([Jan.] 1641[/2]), sig. A2[r-v], for quotation (BL, E 131/2).

45 Burroughes, *Sions Joy*, pp. 25-6.

46 For the phrase, [Thomas Cademan], *The Earle of Bedfords Passage to the High Court of Parliament* ([May?] 1641), p. 3 (BL, E 158/17).

47 Russell, *Causes*, p. 14.

48 Sir John Wray, *Eight Occasionall Speeches, made in the House of Commons this Parliament* ([mid-]1641), p. 1 (BL, E 196/10).

49 Downinge, *Discoursive Conjecture*, pp. 1-2.

50 Stephen Marshall, *A Peace-Offering to God: a Sermon preached to the Honourable House of Commons assembled in Parliament at their Publique Thanksgiving, September 7, 1641* (1641), p. 40 (BL, E 173/31).

51 PA, MP 30 March 1641, fos. 80-1.

52 I am grateful to Dr David Scott for a discussion of this point.

53 On balance, however, it does suggest that the plans to use military force against the Parliament were not only real, but also sanctioned by the king and potentially capable of success. These plans are discussed above, Ch. 10.

54 BL, Harl. MS 6424 (Bishop Warner's diary), fo. 58v.

55 NA, LC 5/134 (Lord Chamberlain's order book), p. 418.

56 This theme in English political discourse has not yet received the scholarly attention that it deserves; for a stimulating exception, however, see Quentin Skinner, 'John Milton and the Politics of Slavery', *Prose Studies*, 23 (2000), 1-22; and idem, 'Classical Liberty, Renaissance Translation, and the English Civil War', in his *Visions of Politics*, II, *Renaissance Virtues* (Cambridge, 2002), pp. 320-2.

57 NA, SP 16/503, fo. 153: deposition by Sir Arthur Hesilrige, 6 December 1644.

58 [William Fiennes, Viscount Saye and Sele], *Vindiciae Veritatis. Or an Ansvver to a Discourse intituled, Truth it's Manifest* (1654), p. 6 (BL, E 811/2).

59 *A Declaration and Resolution of the Lords and Commons. . .concerning His Majesties late Proclamation for the Suppressing of the Present Rebellion, under the Command of Robert earl of Essex* (15 Aug. 1642), p. 7 (BL, E 112/6).

60 Carte, *Life of Ormond*, V, 285: Lord Gormanston to the Earl of Clanricard, Gormanstown, 21 January 1642.

61 Russell, *Fall of the British Monarchies*, pp. 303-4.

62 Russell, *Fall of the British Monarchies*, pp. 304, 329, 373; and see the critique by John Morrill, 'The Causes of Britain's Civil Wars', in his *The Nature of the English Revolution*, p. 259.

63 Russell, *Fall of the British Monarchies*, p. 329.

64 Russell, *Fall of the British Monarchies*, p. 304; for Vane's letter, see Surrey History Centre, Bray MS 52/2/19/8.

65 VAL, Forster MS 39 (Elector Palatine corr.), no. 20: Prince-Elector Charles Louis to Queen Elizabeth of Bohemia, Edinburgh, 29 August 1641.

66 HMC, *Ormonde Manuscripts*, new ser., I, 46: Thomas Salvin to the Earl of Ormond, 5 October 1641.

67 VAL, Forster MS 39 (Elector Palatine corr.), no. 20: Prince-Elector Charles Louis to Queen Elizabeth of Bohemia, Edinburgh, 29 August 1641. No sooner had General Leslie returned home to Edinburgh, than he was undertaking to 'moove this Parlament [of Scotland] to make some proposition to that of England' for the restoration of the Elector Palatine.

68 John Durye, *A Summary Discourse concerning the Work of Peace Ecclesiastical* (Cambridge, [Aug.] 1641), pp. 9-10 (BL, E 167/3).

69 John Campbell, Lord Loudoun, *The Lord Lowden his Learned and Wise Speech in the Upper House* [sic] *of Parliament in Scotland, September 9, 1641* ([September?], 1641), p. 3 (BL, E 199/13).

70 Above, pp. 365-8.

71 Russell, *Fall of the British Monarchies*, p. 398. Russell argued that 'the decision to call on Scottish help for the reconquest of Ireland meant more Scottish commissioners in London, and therefore held out the hope of the renewal of the axis between the Parliament and the Scots which had been Pym's [sic] standby at the beginning of the Parliament'. Those Scottish commissioners would have come to London irrespective of the 'Irish Rebellion'; indeed, in most respects, the Junto's planning of the Irish reconquest, from the outset, as an Anglo-Scottish campaign flowed naturally from the discussions which had been taking place since the early summer on future joint military operations by the two 'commonwealths'. All that had changed was the intended theatre of war.

72 Henry Parker, *The Generall Junto or The Councell of Union* (1642), pp. 29-31 (BL, 669 f. 18/1). According to Thomason, who annotated his copy, this tract was printed at the expense of the Commons-man, Sir John Danvers, in a run of fifty copies. The Marquess of Hamilton was among those presented with Parker's work. Parker's proposal (possibly at Danvers's prompting) advocated the inclusion of Irish representatives in this General Junto, something that is unlikely to have found favour with either Warwick or Argyll. In due course, an Anglo-Scottish executive did come into being, early in 1644, with the creation of the Committee of Both Kingdoms, though the extent to which it functioned as a 'council of

union' was, in practice, very limited.

73 Above, pp. 362-3.

74 Russell, *Causes*, p. 213 (for the quotation in the footnote), and see also pp. 16-7, 187; and idem, *Fall of the British Monarchies*, pp. 398, 406-7; see, too, his remarks on the 'stability of English society' in 1641, ibid., p. 302.

75 Russell, *Causes*, p. 213.

76 Here, it has been suggested, the catalyst for the revolt was the king's refusal, under pressure from the English Parliament, to confirm the Irish 'Graces', a series of concessions by the Crown intended, *inter alia*, to give Catholics some security as to land-tenure and freedom from the obligation to take certain oaths; Russell, *Fall of the British Monarchies*, p. 393.

77 On the French diplomacy at this period, see Anja Victorine Hartmann, *Von Regensburg nach Hamburg: die diplomatischen Beziehungen zwischen dem französischen König und dem Kaiser vom Regensburger Vertrag (13 Oktober 1630) bis zum Hamburger Präliminarfrieden (25 Dezember 1641)* (Münster, 1998).

78 BL, Harl. MS 164 (D'Ewes diary), fo. 95 (*PLP*, VI, 681).

79 Above, pp. 367-8, 371.

80 Michael Mendle, 'The Great Council of Parliament and the First Ordinances: the Constitutional Theory of the Civil War', *Journal of British Studies*, 31 (1992), 133-162, especially 147-50.

81 *CJ*, II, 285; *CSPV 1640-42*, pp. 213-4; for the Spanish ambassador, see Russell, *Fall of the British Monarchies*, pp. 395-6 and [James Howell], *The True Informer, who in the Following Discours or Colloquy, discovereth unto the World the Chiefe Causes of the Sad Distempers in Great Brittany and Ireland* ([12 April] 1643), pp. 22-3 (BL, E 96/10).

82 Above, pp. 454-7, 482-3.

83 [Thomas Morton, Bishop of Durham], *The Necessity of Christian Subjection. Demonstrated, and proved by the Doctrine of Christ* ([March] 1643), p. 6 (BL, E 93/11).

84 For a succinct and perceptive summary of the general trends in writing on English republicanism, see Blair Worden,

'Republicanism, Regicide and Republic: the English Experience', in Martin van Gelderen and Quentin Skinner (eds.), *Republicanism: a Shared European Heritage*, 2 vols. (Cambridge, 2002), I, 315-27.

85 [Peter Heylyn], *Augustus. Or, an Essay of those Meanes and Counsels whereby the Commonwealth of Rome was altered, and reduced, unto a Monarchy* (for Henry Seile, 1632), pp. 2-3 (*STC2* 13268).

86 [Thomas Morton, Bishop of Durham], *The Necessity of Christian Subjection. Demonstrated, and proved by the Doctrine of Christ* ([March] 1643), p. 7 (BL, E 93/11).

87 Sir Edward Walker, *Historical Discourses* (1705), p. 304.

88 Gilbert Burnet, *The Memoires of the Lives and Actions of James and William, Dukes of Hamilton* (1677), p. 60. See also Donald, *Uncounselled King*, pp. 83-4.

89 Prinsterer, *Archives...de la maison d'Orange-Nassau*, 2nd series, IV, 2: Jan van der Kerckhove, Lord of Heenvliet, to the Prince of Orange, relating his audience with the queen of 18/28 January 1642.

90 Gasparo Contarini, *The Common-Wealth and Government of Venice*, trans. Lewes Lewkenor (1611), p. 18 (*STC2* 5642)

91 John Durye, *A Summary Discourse concerning the Work of Peace Ecclesiastical* (Cambridge, [Aug.] 1641), p. 9 (BL, E 167/3).

92 Stephen Marshall, *Reformation and Desolation: or, a Sermon tending to the Discovery of the Symptomes of a People to whom God will by no Meanes be Reconciled* ([early] 1642), pp. 40 (for the quoted phrase), 43-4, 51 (BL, E 131/30).

93 Edmund Calamy, *Englands Looking-Glasse, presented in a Sermon, preached before the Honorable House of Commons,...December 22. 1641* ([early] 1642), p. 45 (BL, E 131/29).

94 John Corbet, *An Historicall Relation of the Military Government of Gloucester, from the Beginning of the Civill Warre betweene King and Parliament, to the Removall of Colonell Massie from that Government* (1645), sig. A2[v] (BL, E 306/8).

APPENDIX

1 This list of the original Twelve is also given in the letter from the royal chaplain, Dr John Pocklington to Sir John Lambe, 14 September 1640: NA, SP 16/467, fo. 127r-v; other versions are: BL, Add. MS 1710 (Miscellaneous historical papers), fo. 118v.

2 Bulstrode Whitelocke, *Memorials of the English Affairs*, 4 vols (Oxford, 1853), I, p. 105. The Hertfordshire Petition was delivered to the king at York by Arthur Capel of Hadham (1604–49), who also seems to have been on the fringes of the Warwick–Mandeville circle. He was born and brought up in Essex (his father was Sir Henry Capel of Raines Hall), and his mother, Theodosia Montagu (the daughter of the 1st Lord Montagu of Boughton and niece of the 1st Earl of Manchester), was Mandeville's first cousin; and he was a 'kinsman and friend' of Sir Thomas Barrington, one of the central figures in Warwick's social network; for Capell, see Keeler, *Members of Parliament*, s. v.

3 Hertford's name is listed twice in this copy of the petition, once as an earl, and the second time as 'Lord Hartford'. The error may be one of simple duplication, or alternatively the copyist has mistranscribed the name of another peer whose name began with Her- or Har-. Lord Herbert of Cherbury, a future Parliamentarian, might be a possibility; but in the absence of corroboration from another MS, this must remain speculative in the extreme.

4 BL, Add. MS 38847 (Hodgkin Papers), fo. 24, gives 'Mogumrie' [Montgomery?], but this would seem to be a simple misreading of 'Mulgrave'; the earldom of Montgomery was held by the Earl of Pembroke in 1640 (who is listed lower down among the signatories on this copy).

5 Eldest son of the Earl of Berkshire, and in 1641 consistently identified with the reformist group in Parliament; see, e.g., his membership of the committee to investigate the army plots of May 1641: *LJ*, IV, 235.

6 The signature of 'Lord Sandys' appears uniquely (and puzzlingly) in this copy of the Petition. This must have been an error on the part of the copyist as the barony had been in abeyance following the death of the 4th Baron Sandys in 1629; the correct reading would seem to have been 'Savile'.

INDEX